FOR REFERENCE

Do Not Take From This Room

Nineteenth-Century Literature Criticism

Guide to Gale Literary Criticism Series

For criticism on	Consult these Gale series
Authors now living or who died after December 31, 1959	*CONTEMPORARY LITERARY CRITICISM (CLC)*
Authors who died between 1900 and 1959	*TWENTIETH-CENTURY LITERARY CRITICISM (TCLC)*
Authors who died between 1800 and 1899	*NINETEENTH-CENTURY LITERATURE CRITICISM (NCLC)*
Authors who died between 1400 and 1799	*LITERATURE CRITICISM FROM 1400 TO 1800 (LC)* *SHAKESPEAREAN CRITICISM (SC)*
Authors who died before 1400	*CLASSICAL AND MEDIEVAL LITERATURE CRITICISM (CMLC)*
Authors of books for children and young adults	*CHILDREN'S LITERATURE REVIEW (CLR)*
Dramatists	*DRAMA CRITICISM (DC)*
Poets	*POETRY CRITICISM (PC)*
Short story writers	*SHORT STORY CRITICISM (SSC)*
Black writers of the past two hundred years	*BLACK LITERATURE CRITICISM (BLC)*
Hispanic writers of the late nineteenth and twentieth centuries	*HISPANIC LITERATURE CRITICISM (HLC)*
Native North American writers and orators of the eighteenth, nineteenth, and twentieth centuries	*NATIVE NORTH AMERICAN LITERATURE (NNAL)*
Major authors from the Renaissance to the present	*WORLD LITERATURE CRITICISM, 1500 TO THE PRESENT (WLC)*

ISSN 0732-1864

R

Volume 71

Nineteenth-Century Literature Criticism

*Excerpts from Criticism of the
Works of Novelists, Poets, Playwrights,
Short Story Writers, Philosophers, and Other
Creative Writers Who Died between 1800
and 1899, from the First Published Critical
Appraisals to Current Evaluations*

Janet Witalec
Editor

GALE

DETROIT · LONDON

STAFF

Janet Witalec, *Editor*

Denise Evans, Daniel G. Marowski, *Contributing Editors*
Suzanne Dewsbury, Ira Mark Milne, *Associate Editors*
Craig Hutchison, *Assistant Editor*
Aarti D. Stephens, *Managing Editor*

Susan M. Trosky, *Permissions Manager*
Kimberly F. Smilay, *Permissions Specialist*
Steve Cusack, Kelly A. Quin, *Permissions Associates*
Sandra K. Gore, *Permissions Assistant*

Victoria B. Cariappa, *Research Manager*
Tracie A. Richardson, Cheryl Warnock, *Research Associates*
Phyllis Blackman, *Research Assistant*

Mary Beth Trimper, *Production Director*
Deborah L. Milliken, *Production Assistant*

Christine O'Bryan, *Desktop Publisher*
Randy Bassett, *Image Database Supervisor*
Robert Duncan, Michael Logusz, *Imaging Specialists*
Pamela A. Reed, *Imaging Coordinator*

Library of Congress Catalog Card Number 84-643008
ISBN 0-7876-1246-4
ISSN 0732-1864
Printed in the United States of America

10 9 8 7 6 5 4 3 2 1

Contents

Preface vii

Acknowledgments xi

Preface

Since its inception in 1981, *Nineteenth-Century Literature Criticism* has been a valuable resource for students and librarians seeking critical commentary on writers of this transitional period in world history. Designated an "Outstanding Reference Source" by the American Library Association with the publication of its first volume, *NCLC* has since been purchased by over 6,000 school, public, and university libraries. The series has covered more than 300 authors representing 29 nationalities and over 17,000 titles. No other reference source has surveyed the critical reaction to nineteenth-century authors and literature as thoroughly as *NCLC*.

Scope of the Series

NCLC is designed to introduce students and advanced readers to the authors of the nineteenth century, and to the most significant interpretations of these authors' works. The great poets, novelists, short story writers, playwrights, and philosophers of this period are frequently studied in high school and college literature courses. By organizing and reprinting commentary written on these authors, *NCLC* helps students develop valuable insight into literary history, promotes a better understanding of the texts, and sparks ideas for papers and assignments. Each entry in *NCLC* presents a comprehensive survey of an author's career or an individual work of literature and provides the user with a multiplicity of interpretations and assessments. Such variety allows students to pursue their own interests; furthermore, it fosters an awareness that literature is dynamic and responsive to many different opinions.

Every fourth volume of *NCLC* is devoted to literary topics that cannot be covered under the author approach used in the rest of the series. Such topics include literary movements, prominent themes in nineteenth-century literature, literary reaction to political and historical events, significant eras in literary history, prominent literary anniversaries, and the literatures of cultures that are often overlooked by English-speaking readers.

NCLC continues the survey of criticism of world literature begun by Gale's *Contemporary Literary Criticism (CLC)* and *Twentieth-Century Literary Criticism (TCLC),* both of which excerpt and reprint commentary on authors of the twentieth century. For additional information about *TCLC, CLC,* and Gale's other criticism series, users should consult the Guide to Gale Literary Criticism Series preceding the title page in this volume.

Coverage

Each volume of *NCLC* is carefully compiled to present:

- criticism of authors, or literary topics, representing a variety of genres and nationalities
- both major and lesser-known writers and literary works of the period
- 4-8 authors or 4-6 topics per volume
- individual entries that survey critical response to an author's work or a topic in literary history, including early criticism to reflect initial reactions, later criticism to represent any rise or decline in reputation, and current retrospective analyses.

Organization

An author entry consists of the following elements: author heading, biographical and critical introduction, list of principal works, excerpts of criticism (each preceded by a bibliographic citation and an annotation), and a bibliography of further reading.

- The **Author Heading** consists of the name under which the author most commonly wrote, followed by birth and death dates. If an author wrote consistently under a pseudonym, the pseudonym will be listed in the author heading and the real name given in parentheses on the first line of the biographical and critical introduction. Also located at the beginning of the introduction to the author entry are any name variations under which an author wrote, including transliterated forms for an author whose language uses a nonroman alphabet.

- The **Biographical and Critical Introduction** outlines the author's life and career, as well as the critical issues surrounding his or her work. References are provided to past volumes of *NCLC* in which further information about the author may be found.

- Most *NCLC* entries include a **Portrait** of the author. Many entries also contain reproductions of materials pertinent to an author's career, including manuscript pages, title pages, dust jackets, letters, and drawings, as well as photographs of important people, places, and events in an author's life.

- The list of **Principal Works** is chronological by date of first publication and identifies the genre of each work. In the case of foreign authors with both foreign-language publications and English translations, the English-language version is given in brackets. Unless otherwise indicated, dramas are dated by first performance, not first publication.

- **Criticism** in each author entry is arranged chronologically to provide a perspective on changes in critical evaluation over the years. All titles of works by the author featured in the entry are printed in boldface type to enable the user to easily locate discussion of particular works. Also for purposes of easier identification, the critic's name and the publication date of the essay are given at the beginning of each piece of criticism. Unsigned criticism is preceded by the title of the journal in which it appeared. Publication information (such as publisher names and book prices) and some parenthetical numerical references (such as page and line references to specific editions of works) have been deleted at the editors' discretion to provide smoother reading of the text. Footnotes that appear with previously published pieces of criticism are reprinted at the end of each essay or excerpt. In the case of excerpted criticism, only those footnotes that pertain to the excerpted text are included.

- A complete **Bibliographic Citation** provides original publication information for each piece of criticism.

- Critical excerpts are prefaced by **Annotations** providing the reader with a summary of the critical intent of the piece. Also included, when appropriate, is information about the critic's reputation, individual approach to literary criticism, and particular expertise in an author's works, as well as information about the relative importance of the critical excerpt. In some cases, the annotations cross-reference excerpts by critics who discuss each other's commentary.

- An annotated list of **Further Reading** appearing at the end of each entry suggests secondary sources on the author. In some cases it includes essays for which the editors could not obtain reprint rights.

Cumulative Indexes

- Each volume of *NCLC* contains a cumulative **Author Index** listing all authors who have appeared in Gale's Literary Criticism Series, along with cross-references to such biographical series as *Contemporary Authors* and *Dictionary of Literary Biography.* Useful for locating authors within the various series, this index is particularly valuable for those authors who are identified with a certain period but who, because of their death dates, are placed in another, or for those authors whose careers span two periods. For example, Fyodor Dostoevsky is found in *NCLC,* yet Leo Tolstoy, another major nineteenth-century Russian novelist, is found in *TCLC* because he died after 1899.

- Each *NCLC* volume includes a cumulative **Nationality Index** which lists all authors who have appeared in *NCLC*, arranged alphabetically under their respective nationalities.

- Each new volume in Gale's Literary Criticism Series includes a cumulative **Topic Index**, which lists all literary topics treated in *NCLC, TCLC, LC 1400-1800*, and the *CLC* Yearbook.

- Each new volume of *NCLC*, with the exception of the Topics volumes, contains a **Title Index** listing the titles of all literary works discussed in the volume. In response to numerous suggestions from librarians, Gale has also produced a **Special Paperbound Edition** of the *NCLC* title index. This annual cumulation lists all titles discussed in the series since its inception. Additional copies of the index are available on request. Librarians and patrons have welcomed this separate index: it saves shelf space, is easy to use, and is recyclable upon receipt of the following year's cumulation. Titles discussed in the Topics volume entries are not included in the *NCLC* cumulative index.

Citing *Nineteenth-Century Literature Criticism*

When writing papers, students who quote directly from any volume in Gale's Literary Criticism Series may use the following general forms to footnote reprinted criticism. The first example pertains to material drawn from periodicals, the second to material reprinted from books:

[1]T.S. Eliot, "John Donne," *The Nation and Athenaeum*, 33 (9 June 1923), 321-32; excerpted and reprinted in *Literature Criticism from 1400-1800,* Vol. 10, ed. James E. Person, Jr. (Detroit: Gale Research, 1989), pp. 28-9.

[2]Clara G. Stillman, *Samuel Butler: A Mid-Victorian Modern* (Viking Press, 1932); excerpted and reprinted in *Twentieth-Century Literary Criticism,* Vol. 33, ed. Paula Kepos (Detroit: Gale Research, 1989), pp. 43-5.

Suggestions Are Welcome

In response to suggestions, several features have been added to *NCLC* since the series began, including annotations to excerpted criticism, a cumulative index to authors in all Gale literary criticism series, entries devoted to criticism on a single work by a major author, more illustrations, and a title index listing all literary works discussed in the series.

Readers who wish to suggest authors, single works, or topics to appear in future volumes, or who have other suggestions, are cordially invited to write: The Editors, *Nineteenth-Century Literature Criticism,* The Gale Group, 27500 Drake Rd., Farmington Hills, MI 48331-3535; call toll-free at 1-800-347-GALE.

Acknowledgments

The editors wish to thank the copyright holders of the excerpted criticism included in this volume and the permissions managers of many book and magazine publishing companies for assisting us in securing reproduction rights. We are also grateful to the staffs of the Detroit Public Library, the Library of Congress, the University of Detroit Mercy Library, Wayne State University Purdy/Kresge Library Complex, and the University of Michigan Libraries for making their resources available to us. Following is a list of the copyright holders who have granted us permission to reproduce material in this volume of *NCLC*. Every effort has been made to trace copyright, but if omissions have been made, please let us know.

COPYRIGHTED EXCERPTS IN *NCLC,* VOLUME 71, WERE REPRODUCED FROM THE FOLLOWING PERIODICALS:

Bronte Society Transactions, v. 13, 1965; v. 16, 1971; v. 19, 1987. All reproduced by courtesy of the Brontë Society.—*Bulletin of the John Rylands University Library of Manchester*, v. 66, Autumn, 1983. Reproduced by permission of the Director and University Librarian, the John Rylands University Library of Manchester.—*English Studies in Africa*, v. 31, 1983 for "Metastasis: Or Dumas, Joyce and the Dark Avenger" by Don MacLennan. © Witwatersrand University Press 1983. Reproduced by permission of the publisher and the author.—*Essays in Theatre/Études Théâtrales*, v. 14, May, 1996 for "Paris Was Always Burning: (Drag) Queens and Kings in Two Early Plays by Alexandre Dumas, pére" by Adrian Kiernander. Reproduced by permission of the author.—*The French Review*, v. 40, 1967; v. 58, May, 1985. Copyright © 1967,1985 by the American Association of Teachers of French. Both reproduced by permission.—*Mosaic*, v. IX, Spring, 1976. © Mosaic 1976. Acknowledgment of previous publication is herewith made.—*The National and English Review*, July, 1952 for "The Neglected Side of Dumas" in A. Craig Bell. Reproduced by permission of the author.—*The New Criterion*, v. 9, May, 1991 for "Alexandre Dumas, Fact and Fiction" by Renée Winegarten. Reproduced by permission of Georges Borchardt, Inc. for the author.—*PMLA*, v. 109, March, 1994. Copyright 1994 by PMLA. Reproduced by permission of the Modern Language Association of America.—*Revue Des Langues Vivantes Tijdschrift Voor Levende Talen*, v. XXXIX, 1973 for "The Vampire Theme: Dumas Pére and the English Stage" by A. Owen Aldridge. Reproduced by permission of the author.—*Romance Quarterly*, v. 34, February, 1987. Copyright © 1987 Helen Dwight Reid Educational Foundation. Reproduced with permission of the Helen Dwight Reid Educational Foundation, published by Heldref Publications, 1319 18th Street, NW, Washington, DC 20036-1802.—*Stanford French Review*, v. XI, Fall, 1987 for "Militancy in the Making: The Example of 'Le Bachelier'" by Gretchen Van Slyke. Reproduced by permission of the publisher and the author.—*Studies in Romanticism*, v 33, Winter, 1994. Copyright © 1994 by the Trustees of Boston University. Reproduced by permission.—*The Wordsworth Circle*, v. XIII, Winter, 1982; v. XXIII, Spring, 1992. © 1982, 1992 Marilyn Gaull. Both reproduced by permission of the editor.

COPYRIGHTED EXCERPTS IN *NCLC,* VOLUME 71, WERE REPRODUCED FROM THE FOLLOWING BOOKS:

Bell, A. Craig. From a foreword to *Fernande: The Story of a Courtesan by Alexandre Dumas*. Translated by A. Craig Bell. Robert Hale, 1988. © English translation A. Craig Bell 1988. Reproduced by permission.—Bell, A. Craig. *From The Novels of Anne Brontë: A Study and*

From *Anne Brontë: A New Critical Assessment*. Vision Press Limited and Barnes & Noble, 1983. © 1983 by P. J. M. Scott. All rights reserved. Reproduced by permission of Rowman and Littlefield.—Shaw, Barnett. From in an introduction to *Alexandre Dumas, Pére: The Great Lover and Other Plays*. Frederick Ungar Publishing Co., 1969. Copyright © 1969, 1977, 1979 by Barnett Shaw. All rights reserved. Reproduced by permission.—Stivale, Charles J. From "'Le Plissement' and 'la fêlure: The Paris Commune in Vallès 'L'Insurgè' and Zola's 'La Dèbâcle'" in *Moderninity and Revolution in Late Nineteenth-Century France*. Edited by Barbara T. Cooper and Mary Donaldson-Evans. University of Delaware Press, 1992. Copyright © 1992 by Associated University Presses, Inc. All rights reserved. Reproduced by permission.—Trench-Bonett, Dorothy. From an introduction to *Charles VII at the Home of His Great Vassals*. Translated by Dorothy Trench-Bonett. The Noble Press, Inc., 1991. Copyright © 1991 by Dorothy Trench-Bonett. All rights reserved. Reproduced by permission.—Winnifrith, Tom. From *The Brontë's and their Background: Romance and Reality*. Macmillan, 1973. © Tom Winnifrith 1973. All rights reserved. Reproduced by permission of Macmillan, London and Basingstoke.—Wolfson, Susan J. From "'Domestic Affections' and 'the spear of Minerva': Felicia Hemans and the Dilemma of Gender" in *Re-Visioning Romanticism: British Women Writers, 1776-1837*. Edited by Carol Shiner Wilson and Joel Haefner. University of Pennsylvania Press, 1994. Copyright © 1994 by the University of Pennsylvania Press. All rights reserved. Reproduced by permission of the publisher.—Wordsworth, Jonathan. From an introduction to *Revolution and Romanticism, 1789-1834*. Woodstock Books, 1994. Reproduced by permission.

PHOTOGRAPHS AND ILLUSTRATIONS APPEARING IN *NCLC*, VOLUME 71, WERE RECEIVED FROM THE FOLLOWING SOURCES:

A title page for "A Series of Plays: In Which It Is Attempted to Delineate The Stronger Passions of the Mind: Each Passion Being the Subject of A Tragedy and A Comedy" by Joanna Baillie, 1798 London edition, photograph. The Department of Rare Books and Special Collections, The University of Michigan Library. Reproduced by permission.—A title page for "Agnes Grey" by Anne Bronte, 1924 Edinburgh edition, photograph. The Department of Rare Books and Special Collections, The University of Michigan Library. Reproduced by permission.—A title page for "Jacques Vingtras L'Bachelier" by Jules Valles, 1924 Paris edition, photograph. The Department of Rare Books and Special Collections, The University of Michigan Library. Reproduced by permission.—A title page for "Jacques Vingtras L'Enfant" by Jules Valles, 1927 Paris edition, photograph. The Department of Rare Books and Special Collections, The University of Michigan Library. Reproduced by permission.—A title page for "Jacques Vingtras L'Insurgé - 1871-" by Jules Valles, 1826 Paris edition, photograph. The Department of Rare Books and Special Collections, The University of Michigan Library. Reproduced by permission.—A title page for "Le Comte de Monte-Cristo" by M. Alexandre Dumas, Paris edition, photograph. The Department of Rare Books and Special Collections, The University of Michigan Library. Reproduced by permission.—A title page for "Records of Woman: With Other Poems" by Felicia Hemans, 1828 second edition, photograph. The Department of Rare Books and Special Collections, The University of Michigan Library. Reproduced by permission.—Anne Bronte, from a drawing by Charlotte Bronte in the possession of the Rev. A. B. Nicholls, 1859, photograph. Corbis-Bettmann. Reproduced by permission.—Anne, Emily and Charlotte Bronte by Patrick Branwell Bronte, located at the National Portrait Gallery, 1939, photograph. Corbis-Bettmann. Reproduced by permission.—Baillie, Joanna, photograph. Archive Photos, Inc. Reproduced by permission.—Hemans, Felicia Dorothea Browne, photograph. Archive Photos, Inc. Reproduced by permission.

Joanna Baillie

1762-1851

Scottish poet, dramatist, and drama critic.

For additional information on Baillie's life and works, see *NCLC*, Volume 2.

INTRODUCTION

Although Baillie was well recognized and respected among the literati during her lifetime, her works fell into neglect soon after her death and have only re-surfaced in literary scholarship within the last several decades. She is now recognized for her significant influence on such contemporary writers as William Wordsworth, Lord Byron, and Percy Bysshe Shelley, and is considered by many critics to have served as a model for later women writers. Long overlooked, Baillie's works, which include twenty-six plays and several volumes of poetry, provide insight into the history of dramatic theory and criticism as well as into the history of women's roles in theatre.

Biographical Information

Baillie was born in 1762 in Bothwell, Lanarkshire, Scotland to James Baillie, a clergyman, and his wife Dorothea Hunter. Baillie was born a premature twin; her unnamed sister died within hours of delivery. Her parents already had two children, Agnes and Matthew. In the late 1760s, Baillie's father was promoted to a higher position at the collegiate church at Hamilton, a country setting that allowed Baillie the opportunity to enjoy outdoor activities. Though her brother attended school, Baillie did not, relying instead on her father for her education. James Baillie, as was typical for the time, stressed to his daughter the importance of developing her moral faculties over her intellectual skills and emphasized that one should not give into one's emotions. Baillie was not fond of her studies and did not learn to read until, as she stated, she was nine years old (her sister Agnes recalled Baillie learning to read at age eleven). In the early 1770s, both Baillie sisters were sent to a Glasgow boarding school, and it was there that Joanna first developed an interest in books, writing and adapting stories to entertain her classmates. Baillie also became interested and quite proficient in the study of mathematics, abstract theorizing, problem solving, and philosophy. In 1778, when James Baillie died, the family became dependent on Dorothea's brother, William Hunter, a well-known anatomist, who provided them with financial security as well as residence at his estate in Long Calderwood. Upon Hunter's death in 1783, Matthew inherited his

uncle's medical school and London home, and the Baillie family moved to London to manage the new household. In 1790, while living in this London home, Baillie published, anonymously, *Poems; Wherein It Is Attempted to Describe Certain Views of Nature and of Rustic Manners*. The small volume did not receive sufficient notice or circulation to satisfy Baillie, and she reprinted much of it, along with other poems written while she was in her seventies, in an expanded version entitled *Fugitive Verses*, in 1840. Upon Matthew's marriage, the Baillie women moved to Hampstead, where they remained for the rest of their lives. In 1798, Baillie published, again anonymously, the first of what would eventually be three volumes of plays. These volumes were entitled *A Series of Plays: In Which It Is Attempted to Delineate the Stronger Passions of the Mind, Each Passion Being the Subject of a Tragedy and a Comedy,* but were more commonly known as *Plays on the Passions*. The first volume contained, among others, *Basil*, a tragedy on love; *The Tryal*, a comedy on love; and possibly Baillie's most famous play, *De Monfort*, a tragedy on hatred. Baillie died in 1851.

Major Works

Baillie's first publication, *Poems; Wherein It Is Attempted to Describe Certain Views of Nature and of Rustic Manners,* received little attention until after she had established a literary career. The first volume of *A Series of Plays,* however, which Baillie published anonymously, quickly became the focus for discussion in literary circles, making this her first critically acclaimed work. Previously, success on the stage had been a prerequisite for the publication of a drama, but Baillie had combined an assortment of plays that had never been performed, and the daringness of such a presentation piqued the interest of many readers. In the preface, Baillie revealed her intent to trace the passions "in their rise and progress in the heart." She stated further that "a complete exhibition of passion, with its varieties and progress in the breast of man, has, I believe, scarcely ever been attempted in Comedy." Critics enjoyed speculating about the identity of the author, which nearly everyone assumed was a man. But, once it was pointed out that there were heroines in the dramas more often than heroes, speculation began that the writer might be a woman. Baillie's authorship of the work was not revealed until 1800, when the third edition was published with her name on the title page. Sir Walter Scott, suspected by some as being the author, became friends with Baillie and encouraged her to write more dramas. The second volume of *A Series of Plays,* published in 1802, was well received by the public. Another collection entitled *Miscellaneous Plays* (1804) contains *Rayner* and *Constantine Paleologus* (two tragedies that were less radical than her previous plays) as well as the comedy *Country Inn.* Baillie produced her play *The Family Legend* in 1810, and it became an unqualified success that was performed again in 1815 and in 1821. In 1812, Baillie's last volume of *A Series of Plays* was published, and it seemed to represent a departure from her earlier theories. Baillie noted that the second and last volume of the series had not received as much praise as the first had, and she retired from active publishing for a number of years. Travels in Scotland were the inspiration for *Metrical Legends of Exalted Characters* (1821). Then Baillie served as editor for Scott and other poets for *A Collection of Poems, Chiefly Manuscript, and from Living Authors* (1823). In *Lines to Agnes Baillie on Her Birthday* (1849), one of Baillie's final works, she wrote about the childhood years of the two Baillie sisters.

Critical Reception

Baillie was extraordinarily respected in her lifetime. Sir Walter Scott frequently mentioned her in the same breath as Shakespeare. He claimed: "If you want to speak of a real poet, Joanna Baillie is now the highest genius in the country." Lord Byron said, "Women, except Joanna Baillie, cannot write tragedy." Nevertheless, many critics of her time found serious problems with her plays. What seemed commendable in print was quickly determined to be totally impractical for the stage. The chief complaints were that the plays contained too much dialogue and not enough action, and that they were too intellectual, too long, and essentially not performable as proper theater. The case of the play *De Monfort* illustrates the degree of the problem. Although *De Monfort* had been selected as one of Baillie's easier works to produce and is often considered one of her finest dramas, it closed after only several performances. Baillie admitted to some of the problems, defended others, and agreed to cuts and revisions, but ultimately to little avail. After Baillie's death, her works were gradually forgotten, and it was not until recently that Baillie's writings have gathered new interest, particularly by drama historians and women readers who realize the historical importance of Baillie's search for answers to problems involving relationships between the sexes. Scholar Catherine B. Burroughs (1994) finds that the study of Baillie and other women writers of her era "will reveal that traditional conceptions of theatre theory must undergo reevaluation if one is to appreciate the wealth of theoretical discourse that survives from this period."

PRINCIPAL WORKS

*Poems; Wherein It Is Attempted to Describe Certain Views of Nature and of Rustic Manners (poetry) 1790

**A Series of Plays: In Which It Is Attempted to Delineate the Stronger Passions of the Mind, Each Passion Being the Subject of a Tragedy and a Comedy. 3 vols. (drama) 1798, 1802, and 1812

Miscellaneous Plays (drama) 1804

The Family Legend (drama) 1810

Metrical Legends of Exalted Characters (poetry) 1821

A Collection of Poems, Chiefly Manuscript, and from Living Authors [editor] (poetry) 1823

A View of the General Tenor of the New Testament Regarding the Nature and Dignity of Jesus Christ; Including a Collection of the Various Passages in the Gospels, Acts of the Apostles, and the Epistles Which Relate to That Subject (poetry) 1831

Dramas. 3 vols. (drama) 1836

Fugitive Verses (poetry) 1840

Ahalya Baee (poetry) 1849

Lines to Agnes Baillie on Her Birthday (poetry) 1849

*Much of this work is reprinted in *Fugitive Verses.*

**This series is often referred to as *Plays on the Passions.*

CRITICISM

Margaret S. Carhart (essay date 1923)

SOURCE: "Joanna Baillie's Place in Literature," in *The Life and Work of Joanna Baillie (Yale Studies in English* LXIV), Yale University Press, 1923, pp. 190-206.

[*Below, Carhart contends that Baillie's insistence that her plays present moral instruction and that individuals represent particular emotions was at the expense of believable characters. Carhart also traces the development of Baillie's works as they moved from emphasizing the intellectual to emphasizing the emotional.*]

North: James, who is the best female poet on the age?

Shepherd: Female what?

Tickler: Poet.

Shepherd: Mrs. John Biley. In her *Plays on the Passions* she has a' the vigor o' a man, and a' the delicacy o' a woman. And Oh, Sire, but her lyrics are gems, and she wears them gracefully, like diamond-drops danglin' frae the ears o' Melpomene. The very worst play she ever wrote is better than the best o' ony ithcr body's that hasna kickt the bucket.[1]

No woman, according to Jeffrey, was capable of understanding human passions, or of depicting the soul of a man swayed by the baser emotions. Yet Joanna Baillie attempted this very task, and, in large degree, succeeded. Her life was sheltered from all harsh contact with the world; she herself was never shaken by any of the passions that stir the soul of a man to the depths. And yet she devoted the best years of her life to delineating these emotions which were personally unknown to her, and produced characters whose chief fault is that they show too plainly the power of emotion. The age was interested in the analysis of the passions. Pope arranged the groups in much the same order that Joanna Baillie adopted:

Love, hope, and joy, fair pleasure's smiling
    train,
Hate, fear, and grief, the family of pain,

These mixed with art, and to due bounds
    confined,
Make and maintain the balance of the mind.[2]

Freed from the bonds of reason, they become the masters of life. In this latter guise, Joanna Baillie chose to show them in tragedy. The idea did not originate with her, for in 1781 at the Haymarket Theatre had appeared *The School of Shakespeare, or Humours and Passions.* The performance consisted of five acts:

Act   I.   Vanity, Henry IV, 1st part.
Act II.   Parental Tenderness, Henry IV, 2d
part.
Act III.   Cruelty, Merchant of Venice.
Act IV.   Filial Piety, Closet-scene in Hamlet.
Act   V.   Ambition, Henry VIII.[3]

The same title was kept in a performance at Drury Lane in 1808, but the acts were changed:

Act   I.   Ambition, Macbeth.
Act II.   Vanity, Henry IV.
Act III.   Revenge, Merchant of Venice.
Act IV.   Cowardice, Twelfth Night.
Act   V.   Slander, Much Ado about Nothing.[4]

Imagination must have been the dominant characteristic of Joanna Baillie's mind, because she was able to follow the emotion she depicted into the heart of the character, and to identify herself with it. This imaginative ability led her to make her most serious dramatic mistake. She was curious about the effect of an emotion upon an unusual person under unusual circumstances, and she thought that all the drama-reading and theatre-going world was equally curious. If a drama portrayed an emotion embodied in a human being, she was satisfied. As a result, she produced thirteen dramas, the chief characters in which wcre, as a rule, personifications of definite elements of human nature rather than genuine human beings. In her ***Plays of the Passions,*** that is to say, Miss Baillie was interested not in the characters, but in the emotions. She did not try to show the emotional person under a variety of conditions which would arouse varying feelings. She tried to represent a normal or a superior person who was controlled by one emotion, and who became to her, consequently, a type.

A comparison of ***Romiero*** and *Othello* will illustrate her use of jealousy. Romiero has no more ground for suspicion of his wife than has Othello; he has, moreover, less temptation to doubt. Romiero returns from an absence, finds Zorada, his wife, out of the castle, sees her return from the garden with Maurice, and is jealous. There is no Iago to suggest evil, and to fan the blaze of emotion whenever it shows signs of dying out. When Romiero is left alone, he rails against 'the heart of woman.' After a talk with Maurice, in whom he fails absolutely to detect signs of guilt, Romiero says:

> The very eye and visage, light and
>   thoughtless;
> A woman's varying blushes with the tint
> Of sun-burnt hunter mix'd; the very form,
> Slight as a stripling, statured as a man,
> Which has—detested spell! so oft beguiled
> The female fancy, prizing worthless show.

The only evidence of an attempt to conquer this emotion occurs in the lines which immediately follow:

> Can it be so? O no! it cannot be;
> I but distract myself. I'll crush within me
> All thoughts which this way tend, as
>   pois'nous asps
> That sting the soul and turn its bliss to bane.

His determination, however, is short-lived, for in the same speech he determines to watch his wife and Maurice closely that night. Zorada is harboring her father, whom Romiero has sworn to deliver to justice whenever he is caught, and her mind is confused, so that her behavior is not natural. Everything Romiero construes as guilt:

> Is virtue thus demure, restrain'd, mysterious?
> She, too, who was as cheerful as the light,
> Courting the notice of my looks! no, no!
> Some blasting change is here.

With this conviction firmly settled in his mind, Romiero takes but a step to belief in her impurity, and the tragedy follows. Miss Baillie partially redeems Romiero by making the murder of Zorada an accident, when she tries to protect her father from her husband's dagger. In this drama is no question from first to last as to Romiero's motive; it is jealousy, practically unchecked by any other passion. Othello, on the other hand, kills Desdemona as the result of a combination of motives, among which jealousy is perhaps not the greatest. Romiero is an example of jealousy; Othello is an example of a human being, struggling with conflicting emotions, of which jealousy is one. Romiero is a fiction of the imagination; Othello is a representation of nature.

Joanna Baillie's aim is clearly expressed in the Introductory Discourse, when she says that the passions should be shown in drama, not merely at a critical moment, but through their entire course. Each tragedy was to be the biography of a passion; its birth, its life, and its ultimate conclusion, were to be shown. So in *Basil,* the tragedy on love, the hero is a victim of love at first sight; he forgets his duty to his country as a military leader of importance, and his obligations to

his soldiers and his friend; he ultimately takes his own life in despair over the wrong he has done. The emotions in the comedies were more difficult to handle; as, for example, in the case of love, the passion must be left to continue indefinitely if the marriage was to be a happy one.

The early dramas on the Passions are built on this theory of the importance of an individual emotion, shown in its entirety; and hence are artificial. Real life is not so simple a matter emotionally as these dramas suggest. *Basil* and *De Monfort* fail to hold our deepest attention mainly because they are not genuine representations of nature. By the time Miss Baillie reached ambition, she realized the impossibility of the program she had laid out for herself, and modified it. In *Ethwald* ambition is developed in ten acts. This fact in itself makes the drama more vivid, as we are freed from the restrictions of five acts, and see the dramatic growth of ambition through years. *Ethwald* also strikes another new note: the hero suffers from more than one emotion in his rise towards absolute power. As a young man, love of a maid plays its part; fear threatens to overcome him when he stops to consider the crime he has committed; there is even a suggestion of remorse for infidelity to his friend. As all these feelings are present, from time to time a struggle occurs in his heart, in spite of the fact that ambition always wins. Ethwald is a human being.

The high-water mark of the *Plays of the Passions* is reached in the last, *Henriquez.* Remorse is the avowed subject of the drama, but it is not isolated. It runs its course from the hour of the murder to the time when the hero is led away to his death. But remorse does not stand alone; from time to time it is associated with many other emotions. Henriquez loves his wife devotedly; he murders his friend because of the conquest of jealousy over the good traits of his character; remorse comes when the cause of his jealousy is removed, and he finds that his wife is true to him; he hopes for pardon for his deed as the result of his reparation, and firm in that hope he dies. Fear and hatred alone are lacking. Henriquez is a truly dramatic character. He is individual, a man endowed with unusual ability, fighting the varied conflicts of life, and moved by different emotions, against which reason does not always prevail.

The only emotion which Miss Baillie found it impossible to pigeonhole is love. That passion runs through all the dramas, showing itself in so many different situations that it is, in fact, the one passion fully described from first to last. Basil dies for love of Victoria; De Monfort exhibits a selfish love for his sister; Aurora bases her hope of happiness entirely on her love for Ermingard; Zorada dies for love of her father; Leonora risks life and reputation because of her love for Osterloo; Countess Valdemere pretends to love

Baron Baurchel in order to secure great gifts from him; and so on through the long list of Joanna Baillie's characters.

Before the tale of her plays dealing with the emotions was finished, Miss Baillie began writing independent plays. In these, thirteen in number, she threw aside all theory, and wrote freely. The two dramas that have had the longest runs on the stage, ***The Family Legend*** and ***Constantine Paleologus,*** belong to this group. It is noteworthy that the plots of these two plays are the only ones that are not entirely original with her; ***The Family Legend*** was based upon a Scottish legend, and ***Constantine Paleologus*** upon history. Even in the latter case, however, the most interesting character, Valeria, is created entirely by her imagination in order to explain and emphasize the bravery and patriotism of the last emperor of the Greeks in Constantinople.

If Joanna Baillie's theory of drama were entirely wrong, we should find her greatest successes among the plays of her later life, after she had completed her difficult task. As a matter of fact, however, most of her best work is found in the late ***Plays on the Passions.*** By that time she had freed herself from the shackles of her early theory, retaining only what was best. Her conception of the dramatic world was entirely theoretical and intellectual. To those who demand intellectual profit from the drama, her accomplishment seems remarkable. But the public demands from a play more than mental stimulus; in the degree in which Joanna Baillie added emotional to intellectual appeal, she was successful.

Joanna Baillie went 'simply, naturally, strongly to the very heart of the mystery of man's strongest passions and most solemn sacrifices.'[5] In occasional passages she shows an uncanny knowledge of the human heart, and of the ways in which intense emotion affects character. It is hard to believe that her most successful heroes were conceived by a woman, and an unmarried Scotch woman at that. In ***Henriquez*** her grasp on her subject is almost masculine. Tytler and Watson emphasize especially this combination of masculine and feminine qualities: 'She had a great man's grand guilelessness rather than a woman's minute and subtle powers of sympathy; a man's shy but unstinted kindness and forbearance rather than a woman's eager but measured cordiality and softness; a man's modesty in full combination with a woman's delicacy; and, as if to prove her sex beyond mistake, she had, after all, more than the usual share of a woman's tenacity and headstrongness when the fit was upon her.'

Her greatest success, however, if we except Henriquez, is in the women whom she has created. The early heroines are rather shadowy and conventional. Victoria is more of a *casus belli* than a living woman; and Agnes Withrington is typical of the busy comedy that

Miss Baillie criticized so sweepingly. With Jane De Monfort, a model woman, Miss Baillie begins her pictures of noble womanhood. Gracious, dignified, clever, and affectionate, Jane De Monfort has enough virtues to make her an ideal, and enough faults to keep her human. The fact that this great heroine was past her first flowery youth helped to convince the reading world that the author was a woman. The satire on women expressed by Countess Valdemere in ***The Siege*** remains in the reader's memory long after the braggart Count is forgotten. The outspoken frankness of the Scotch woman hated the flattery and cajolery of English society so keenly as to give an edge to her caricature in Countess Valdemere. Orra is another character who haunts the reader's mind, this time arousing neither admiration nor scorn, but pity. The lonely girl, whose instinctive fear of the supernatural is worked upon by a group of the most heartless villains in all drama, is indeed a coward. Her physical fear, however, is in no way repulsive; the moral cowardice of her only guardian, Catharine, is much more objectionable. And so we come to Aurora, the beautiful girl, who typifies fidelity more fully than hope, and to Helen of Argyle, the shadowy Scotch girl, who is the centre of ***The Family Legend,*** although she seldom appears on the scene.

Joanna Baillie's women are, with few exceptions, virtuous. Nina and Catharine are the victims of evil men, both of whom have deserted women who had loved them. The chief punishment meted out to Valdemere is that he shall marry Nina, and that punishment consists only in the fact that she is of lower social rank than he, and cannot furnish her lord with a convenient fortune. Catharine is the most pitiful character in all these dramas, a woman ruled by the fear of shame. Rudigere holds her as his slave because, in spite of her lofty character, she left the path of virtue for him. Fear of exposure is stronger in her than honor, and through it she is made a party in the torture of Orra. Rudigere's death satisfies our sense of justice, more because of the freedom it brings to her than as a punishment for his ill-treatment of Orra. In ***Rayner*** occurs the one truly evil character, a courtesan who deserts her lover, when he is sick and in danger, for a man with more money. Mira has no redeeming quality, an estimate we should expect from the author's narrow experience of life.

Granted that an unusual theory limited the dramatic freedom of Joanna Baillie, and that she broke away from strict adherence to it in order to represent life as she saw it, in what form did she express her ideas? Again she establishes a high ideal for herself in the Introductory Discourse. If one emotion is to be shown completely, its contours must not be blurred by the passions of minor characters. This demand for clearness of impression necessitated a simplicity of plot-construction seldom found in drama, and led her to abandon all sub-plots. The result is interesting to the student of the dramas: upon a reader the effect is, in most cases, pleasing; upon the spectator it proved to be less satisfactory.

A plot which develops one emotion in one set of characters, without any interruption from minor threads of narrative, makes a strong impression upon the reader. Such simplicity of outline in drama, as in other forms of art, is restful and satisfying. We read within a comparatively brief time the story of the downfall of Henriquez, and of his final attainment of real sublimity of character through suffering. The catharsis is actual, even with our modern light opinion of the sanctity of life; pity and fear are unadulterated by any less noble feelings. *Henriquez* on the stage, however, would be overpowering. The cumulative effect of the hero's remorse, as portrayed by a great actor, would be too heavy a burden for any normal audience.

In *Orra* the same consistent effect is produced. With Aurora in *The Beacon,* we watch the fire in constant expectation. The minor characters who enter and depart serve the purpose of the brave Aurora; none is intent upon his own affairs. Expectation is the keynote, more definitely than hope. When Ermingard arrives, we feel a temporary satisfaction of our emotional demand, but the feeling is short-lived. Hope is still necessary, hope for the reunion of two noble lovers, unjustly separated. With some justification of the hope of a happy outcome, the story closes. Such simplicity is noble in every respect; it is an ideal towards which serious dramatists strive. It is, however, not the characteristic which secures a favorable report from the box-office.

This simplification of plot is intentional. In *De Monfort,* Miss Baillie included originally the rudiments of a second thread of action. Before the opening of the present third act, occurred a brief conversation in which Countess Freberg betrayed active jealousy of Jane De Monfort. In the fourth edition, and in the collected works, this scene is entirely omitted. As a result, the emotion that Countess Freberg shows in talking with her husband is not effective, as it leads to nothing. If this motive had been developed, the tension of the audience would have been relieved, and the events leading to the final catastrophe could have been more fully motivated. Another example of this repression occurs in *The Trial.* We are told at the very beginning that Mariane has become engaged to Withrington's favorite nephew without the uncle's consent. A partial reconciliation between Mariane and Withrington occurs in Act I; no further attention is paid to this plot until the very end of Act V, when Withrington pompously announces that Mariane is 'engaged to a very worthy young man, who will receive with her a fortune by no means contemptible.' Such an opportunity for complication Shakespeare would never have ne-

glected. It would be possible to pile up similar instances, where dramatic effectiveness has been allowed to suffer for the sake of one definite emotional appeal.

In the *Miscellaneous Plays* there are several examples of a sub-plot used to good effect. In *The Match,* the love-affair of the nephew and niece of the protagonists furnishes an invaluable foil to the indecision and complication of Latitia's mental processes. Without the sub-plot, the play would be uninteresting and monotonous.

Life is mercifully lightened by patches of sunshine when everything seems dark. Work, or friendship, or providence, provides an outlet for pent-up emotion. Should not the same relief be provided for a long-continued strain of powerful dramatic representation? The failure of Joanna Baillie to break the tension in the plots is serious. Again we may attribute the weakness to her theory, rather than to ignorance of life. The single emotion controlled her—the type, and not the living being. Her eyes were fixed on the lesson to be derived from the portrayal of the loss of reason and of the rule by passion; they were not fixed on life.

None of the dramas which have been professionally produced has any complication of plot, or dramatic relief. Each moves steadily and evenly toward a goal that is evident from the first, unrelieved by any decided change of feeling. The audiences of Joanna Baillie's day were accustomed to startling sensations, and rapid change of emotion. As a result, they yawned over the growing hatred of *De Monfort,* and applauded *The Family Legend* only when they themselves were complimented by a patriotic note.

She realized fully the danger she ran of losing the attention of her audience, and tried to compensate for this lack of plot-intricacy by pomp and display. She believed that a splendid procession, a ceremonial banquet, or a battle, would 'afford to a person of the best understanding a pleasure in kind, though not in degree, with that which a child would receive from it; but when it is past he thinks no more of it.' The first act of *Basil* furnishes an example of this use of military parade. As soon as the procession passes, the emotional note of the tragedy is struck. In *Ethwald* a battle is used in the same way; a comic battle figures in *The Siege.* A similar effect is produced by the introduction of a banquet or masquerade. *De Monfort* affords the best opportunity for brilliant display, but in this case the action of the drama is advanced during the masquerade. In production, this scene was intensified so as to increase the relief from the tragic tone. *Basil, The Siege, Henriquez, Rayner, The Family Legend, The Phantom, Enthusiasm,* and *The Bride,* all contain group-celebrations of some sort, that serve this definite purpose.

The ignorance of psychology that caused this entire absence of emotional relief accounts for many other technical weaknesses. Her stage was too often left vacant, scenes changed with puzzling and unnecessary frequency, interest was often lost by a too early certainty as to the outcome, and scenes and acts were often allowed to close with an anticlimax. All these defects were due to her failure to appreciate the importance of technique, and not to lack of ability. An example of skilful use of suspense occurs in Act II of *De Monfort.* Jane has finally broken down her brother's reserve, and succeeded in rousing him to a desire for manhood.

What a most noble creature wouldst thou be!

she exclaims; he replies:

Ay, if I could: Alas! Alas! I cannot.

Jane's answer is so genuine that it arouses hope in the spectator:

Thou canst, thou mayst, thou wilt.
We shall not part till I have turn'd thy soul.

They go to her closet with his final promise,

Do as thou wilt, I will not grieve thee more.

The fact that the following act ends with much the same hopeful tone may account in part for the degree of stage-success which was accorded this drama.

The Stripling is the most successful of all the dramas in the use of suspense. When Young Arden declares that he has thought of a plan to save his father's life, we have no clue to his purpose. His excitement over the sudden idea suggests a trick upon Robinair, by means of which he will save his mother's honor. The discovery that he plans to murder the man who holds the only evidence against his father, comes as almost too great a surprise, and his apprehension and death are not anticipated.

One of the best examples of action which ends with a complication of emotion, so that we are eager for the next scene, is Act IV of *De Monfort.* Rezenvelt crosses the stage; an owl hoots in evil omen; he hears the convent bell,

That, to a fearful superstitious mind,
In such a scene, would like a death-knell
    come.

He passes into the forest, where we know De Monfort and death are waiting for him, and the curtain falls. One powerful ending, such as this, proves the ability that Joanna Baillie possessed.

Suggestion has been made in several places that Joanna Baillie emphasized the passions even at the sacrifice of effectiveness, for the sake of a moral purpose. She firmly believed that ancient drama had been made to serve evil ends, and criticized the most popular modern comedy on the same ground. A drama was to her an opportunity to teach a strong moral lesson to a mass of middle-class people. Her aim amounted to a Greek catharsis, for she hoped, by representing the tempest that is aroused by unbridled emotion, to show the 'rising signs' of its coming, and the 'situations that will most expose us to its rage.' As a result of this sincere purpose, she has shown us a great variety of middle-class people who are threatened by the predominance of an evil passion, or who are ennobled by their fidelity to one that is good. She was wise enough, not to preach outright, with the exception of a few soliloquies that express genuine emotion. Instead of antagonizing in that way those whom she hoped to reach, she gave to all her characters reward for nobility, or punishment for vice. To secure such wholesale justice was difficult in the case of so evil a group of men as the conspirators in *Orra,* but she made their own evil-doing recoil upon themselves. Her ignorance of life is more apparent here than anywhere else. Her idea of crime seems to be confined to the sixth commandment. Murder runs through the dramas like a crimson thread. It seems to be her sole means of producing plot-complication: of punishing a criminal, freeing from punishment one who is innocent in spirit, but guilty in action, of securing revenge.

None of her heroes is sacrilegious or profane; adultery is almost unknown; dishonor of parents is rare; and one's neighbor's goods are secure. Most of the characters speak as Joanna Baillie herself would speak in their situations; in this respect also they are projections of her imagination.

Middle-class people speaking middle-class language in unusual circumstances require expert treatment if they are to be interesting. Her characters think and talk too much, and act too little, to interest the ordinary people of her day—or, we may say, of any day. True to Greek ideals, she omitted the act, and presented the meditation before and after it. This may be illustrated by De Monfort's murder of Rezenvelt. He went to the forest determined to do the deed, but the murder occurred after the curtain falls on Act IV. All of Act V is spent in comments on the murder, and in the emotional reaction in De Monfort that results—again off the scene—in his death.

The moral purpose of these dramas by Joanna Baillie was a sufficient warrant for her attempts at depicting the more terrible emotions. The criticism we must make is directed not towards the purpose, but towards the means by which she tried to secure it. Here, again, is not the explanation to be found in her ignorance of the character of the mass of people? She judged people by those whom she knew, and the fact that her own world approved so enthusiastically both her aim and her accomplishment shows that she read it aright. What she did not understand was the mind of the man of lower intellectual level than her own, who formed the mass of the English people, and who judged a man according to his actions, not his contemplations.

The importance of dialogue was much magnified in Miss Baillie's eyes. However much we may miss the clever business of Shakespeare, or even the devices of the circumstantial comedy that she so deeply scorns, we are seldom disappointed in her dialogue. There are in her tragedies speeches of as great beauty as those of any dramatist since Shakespeare. If all Joanna Baillie's poetry were on the level of her highest verse, she would rank with our great poets. The dialogue of the tragedies is as superior to that of the comedies as are the tragic to the comic heroes. In them the emotion shakes the hero to the depths of his nature, and when his reserve is gone, he utters his emotion freely, too often in long monologues and soliloquies. These speeches, again, beautiful as they are in themselves, help to destroy the reality of the scene. The reader inevitably feels that Miss Baillie is here trying to follow closely in the footsteps of Shakespeare, and failing because her dramatic instinct is less fine than his.

But Joanna Baillie is more than a dramatic moralist, she is an ambitious poet as well. In the Introductory Discourse of 1798 she enunciated clearly a theory of poetry definitely agreeing with the aims of the Lake poets. It is no wonder that Wordsworth admired her. She strove in her *Plays on the Passions* for that genuine representation of nature which was the basis of all his poetry. Wordsworth and Coleridge received greater ridicule from the reviewers than did Joanna Baillie; yet they persevered. Joanna Baillie failed on the stage, but succeeeded in the closet. In her dramas she used the language of the middle-class Englishmen about middle-class characters, but did not produce even a middle-class result on the stage. Her many dramas, however, long continued popular with the reading public, as a glance at the list of editions of her dramas will show. Young and old were influenced by the simplicity and the 'unsophisticated expression' of truthful thought and feeling in her stories. The very simplicity of the plots helped, as she intended, to call attention to the natural language which she used. As a result, many Englishmen who never troubled to read the preface to the *Lyrical Ballads,* and who scorned Wordsworth's poems as lacking elevation of tone, were won over unconsciously to the new theory.

Joanna Baillie wrote at a time when the poetic literature of England was breaking away from the formal manner of the preceding generation. Life was throbbing in the new poetry, in essay, and in novel. The drama alone seemed to lack the new stimulus; there were no English or Scotch dramatic writers of note. Into this dead calm came suddenly the *Plays on the Passions,* with a theory of truth to life as it really is in language, and to emotion as it appeared to the author. Their effect upon dramatic production was decided. The consistent simplicity of plot, the unfaltering determination to raise the moral tone of theatrical representations, and the insistence that the 'wages of sin is death,' all forced themselves into the literary consciousness of the English people.

With a theory of so high an æsthetic value, a purpose of so noble a moral tone, and an imagination of so vivid a character, is it any wonder that Joanna Baillie's contemporaries placed her above all women poets, except Sappho? Since the middle of the nineteenth century several English women have surpassed her in accomplishment; none has surpassed her in tenacity to a noble purpose or in literary influence. In spite of Home's success with his one popular drama, *Douglas,* Joanna Baillie stands to-day as the greatest Scotch dramatist.

Notes

[1] Wilson, *Noctes Ambrosianae* 3. 227.

[2] Pope, *Essay on Man* 2. 117-120.

[3] Genest 6. 202.

[4] *Ibid.* 8. 73.

[5] *Athenœum,* Jan. 11, 1851, p. 41.

Works Cited

Genest, John. *Some Account of the English Stage from the Restoration in 1660 to 1830.* Bath, 1832.

Tytler, S. and Watson, T. L. *Songstresses of Scotland.* London, 1871.

Wilson, J. *Noctes Ambrosianae.* London, 1829.

Joseph W. Donohue, Jr. (essay date 1970)

SOURCE: "Romantic Heroism and Its Milieu," in *Dramatic Character in the English Romantic Age,* Princeton University Press, 1970, pp. 70-94.

[*In the following excerpt, Donohue contends that the public failure of* De Montfort *was due largely to Baillie's unpopular but important innovation of internalizing conflict within the play's characters.*]

A decade and a half after *The Carmelite,* there appeared on the enlarged stage of the Drury Lane (rebuilt in 1794) a play that fully synthesizes Cumberland's exploitation of mental distress with the pictorial atmospherics evident since *Douglas*. But the synthetic qualities of Joanna Baillie's *De Monfort,* important though they are, are secondary to its innovations. The issues raised by this uncommonly ambitious tragedy reflect at once the imminently crucial dilemma of the patent houses and the complex problems of dramaturgy implicit in the rise of the Romantic hero. "The scenery was magnificent," observed the theatrical composer Michael Kelly of the production at Drury Lane in April of 1800, and "the cathedral scene, painted by Capon, was a *chef d'oeuvre. . . .*"[10] Despite such magnificence, Kelly recalled, the play "would not suit the public taste" and was withdrawn, a demonstrable failure, after eight poorly attended performances.[11] It is possible to speculate why, and in doing so to explore some of the characteristics that even then were "stigmatizing" the legitimate drama, from which, as if to spite itself, the closet drama was splitting off and beginning its own anemic growth. Without taking a vindictive attitude toward playwrights who write from theory instead of from first-hand experience, one may see in *De Monfort* the inordinate influence of psychology on a playwright concerned perhaps as much as any other living writer with the forces that drive men to act.

Man has a natural desire to see his fellow human beings tested for "the fortitude of the soul," Joanna Baillie asserted in her lengthy **"Introductory Discourse"** in the first volume of her *Plays on the Passions,* as they are familiarly called.[12] The idea is based on a predilection that informs all of her writing. It is not so much with culmination that Joanna Baillie is concerned, but with process. The trouble with the common tragic hero of the day, she claims, is that he is introduced at the very apex of his fury; similarly, the fault of contemporary theatrical production is that it concentrates too much on events (pp. 38-39). In effect, she points out, these qualities are gross distortions of the true purpose of tragedy, which is "to unveil to us the human mind under the dominion of those strong and fixed passions, which, seemingly unprovoked by outward circumstances, will from small beginnings brood within the breast, till all the better dispositions, all the fair gifts of nature are borne down before them . . ." (pp. 30-31).

From dissatisfaction with the superficial display of current drama, both serious and comic, grew Joanna Baillie's plan for reform. In a series of plays she would "delineate the progress of the higher passions in the human breast," each passion forming the subject of a tragedy and a companion comedy (pp. 41, 56). Certainly few more ambitious projects had fired the lofty minds of her age. The "scientific" comprehensiveness of the idea rivals Sir Joshua Reynolds' design to set forth the history of western art in a series of carefully inclusive lectures. Yet, while it vividly reflects con-

temporary intellectual and cultural tendencies, just as Reynolds' *Discourses* do, the fruits of her plan bear only minimally on the practice of playwrights who succeeded in mounting their products on early nineteenth-century stages. Minimally, that is, except in one major area where the resemblance is crucial: in the concept of dramatic character.

The relationship of her concept to that evident on the boards of London theaters and in contemporary criticism appears both in *De Monfort* itself and in the brief description of the tragedy included in the **"Introductory Discourse."** Expectedly, she defines the passion that forms the subject of the play. Hate, she affirms, is "that rooted and settled aversion, which from opposition of character, aided by circumstances of little importance, grows at last into such antipathy and personal disgust as makes him who entertains it, feel, in the presence of him who is the object of it, a degree of torment and restlessness which is insufferable" (p. 64). The play will be devoted to depicting this insupportable agony, and the character who manifests the passion in all its subtlety will be one with whom we wholly sympathize. Hate itself is vicious, without question. But, under Joanna Baillie's direction, "it is the passion and not the man which is held up to our execration" (p. 65). This statement of a fundamental divorce of character from the emotion that consumes him places her theory and the play which endeavors to support it in the mainstream of developing notions apparent in the drama, acting, and criticism of this new age. The date of the production of *De Monfort* at Drury Lane just at the turn of the century conveniently sets it at a point of transition from influential eighteenth-century tradition to the innovations that swiftly followed.

The first three acts, comprising some eight scenes dominated almost completely by the chief character, establish the inveterate hatred for Rezenfelt which De Monfort has for many years harbored in his heart. Not until the second scene of Act III do we discover, from Rezenfelt himself, that from their youth De Monfort had allowed this fixed hatred for him to feed almost unaccountably on boyish rivalries. Rezenfelt's unsympathetic description of De Monfort's proud youthful vying for "pre-eminence" (p. 362) can do little at this late point to displace the sympathy for him already established over the space of two and one half acts. This "retrospective" structure (p. 64) allows room both for the attention the playwright gives to the present circumstances of her troubled hero and for her unorthodox way of relating him to other characters. From his first entrance in Act I, De Monfort appears possessed by a melancholy which, try though he may, he cannot shake. Having returned to the house of his former landlord, he must greet the local gentry and so confronts his dread enemy, now a wealthy landowner and suitor for the hand of his sister Jane. In the first two acts the dramatist openly departs from several well-established Gothic patterns. The mutual discovery and reunion of brother and sister take place, not in Act V, but in Act II. More important, the conventional evil genius who predictably torments hero and heroine for almost the whole play has here been transformed into the discreetly polite and friendly Rezenfelt. De Monfort considers him a consummate hypocrite, but Rezenfelt's behavior contradicts this judgment. The most he can be accused of is an understandable impatience with De Monfort's monomania.

The meaning of these dramaturgical innovations, slight as they may seem, is of great importance for understanding the concept of dramatic character developed in this tragedy. Heavily indebted to notions of man's essential goodness, late eighteenth-century drama and criticism had contrived to remove the source of evil from man himself and place it outside him in the form of gratuitous chance, usually labeled *fate* or *destiny.* Joanna Baillie has gone one step further: she returns the source of evil to the breast of man; but in doing so she does not compromise the sentimental premise under whose weight her pen moves. The relegation of evil to this interior position creates a character who manifests a fundamental division between virtuous nature and vicious passion. The Fletcherian disjunction of character and event has been redefined as an ethical disjunction of human virtue from human acts. Gothic drama, beginning with Home's *Douglas,* placed special emphasis on an event that took place years before and continues to exert its effects thereafter. *De Monfort* internalizes this convention by redefining it as a psychological process in which an evil passion inexplicably takes root in the fallow soul of man and slowly chokes away his life force. Since the operation of fate has now been relegated to the human soul, the dramatist has no reason to base her play on a series of impassioned encounters with forces in the outside world, least of all anything so pettily obvious as the machinations of a villain or the fifth-act discovery of a sister. She has informed the reader in her introductory treatise that she eschews the sensationalism of performed drama. What she does not say is that she has single-handedly (and perhaps unwittingly as well) effected on the stage a transformation in the nature of dramatic character whose repetition in the closet drama of subsequent years appears unmistakably evident. The reader's comparison of *De Monfort* with *Manfred* will go far toward illuminating the unexplained sickness of soul which drives Byron's melancholy hero to attempt suicide by hurling himself from a precipice in the Alps.

A reason may now be suggested for the failure of *De Monfort* on the stage. To call the play undramatic is to cloud the issue. Its failure more probably lies in the simple fact that it was too revolutionary in concept for an audience so accustomed to convention. Strictures may justly be applied to many dramas of this period

for merely exploiting sensationalism. But the author who wrote such dramas to order was nevertheless able to catch up his audience in an intriguing series of predictably "unpredictable" events to which characters respond with passion and often with utter bewilderment. Reactions of this kind may bear only superficial fidelity to the psychological processes explored by Locke, Hume, and others; they nevertheless demonstrate a *theatrical* correlation of events and mental responses missing from *De Monfort* and from the closet drama that enshrines the tendencies it manifests. "Some sprite accurst within thy bosom mates To work thy ruin," Jane De Monfort laments to her brother early in the play (II.ii, p. 339). This force, and not that of exterior happenings, brings about his unspeakable death, by a kind of spiritual internal bleeding. The events especially of the fourth and fifth acts serve only as inconsistent and distorted reflections of what is essentially interior and formless.

To be sure, the play has a share of qualities eminently realizable on the Drury Lane stage. The wood in which De Monfort murders Rezenfelt in Act IV is genuine horrific Gothic, a perfect environment for a man wandering the trackless forest of his own mind where, De Monfort mutters to himself,

> As in the wild confusion of a dream,
> Things horrid, bloody, terrible, do pass,
> As tho' they pass'd not; nor impress the mind
> With the fix'd clearness of reality.
> (IV.i, p. 377)

Similarly, the pencil of William Capon, a master of atmospheric and antique scenery, contributed great effectiveness to the closing scenes, including the celebrated "cathedral" scene, laid in the halls and chambers of a convent isolated in the wood.[14] But no amount of scenery and lighting, even when complemented by the musical *savoir faire* of Kelly and the acting virtuosity of Kemble as De Monfort and Mrs. Siddons as the noble Jane, could apparently compensate for the lack of theatricality implicit in the fact that the essential conflict of the play is severed from objective reality and entombed within the mind and heart of its chief character.

Notes

[10] *Reminiscences of Michael Kelly,* 2 vols. (1826), II, 177.

[11] Of the last few performances Thomas Dutton wryly observed, "The crowded houses, and unbounded applause, with which *De Montfort* [sic] continues to be received, are unhappily confined to the *Play-bills*"— *The Dramatic Censor; or, Weekly Theatrical Report,* II (1800), 134.

[12] *A Series of Plays: In Which it is Attempted to Delineate the Stronger Passions of the Mind. Each Passion*

Being the Subject of A Tragedy And A Comedy, p. 7. Published in London in 1798, it was augmented by a second and yet a third series over succeeding years; for full citations see Allardyce Nicoll's handlist in his *History,* 2nd edn., IV (Cambridge, Eng., 1960), 257-258. . . .

[14] See Sybil Rosenfeld and Edward Croft-Murray, "A Checklist of Scene Painters Working in Great Britain and Ireland in the 18th Century," *TN,* XIX (1964), 13-15; and Rosenfeld, "Scene Designs of William Capon," *TN,* X (1956), 118-122 and plates.

Bibiliographical Note

Two recent articles . . . maybe mentioned here: M. M. Kelsall, "The Meaning of Addison's *Cato*," *RES,* XVII (1966), 149-162, and C. F. Burgess, "Lillo Sans Barnwell, or The Playwright Revisited," *MP,* LXVI (1968), 5-29, a badly needed re-assessment of Lillo's dramaturgy.

Om Prakash Mathur (essay date 1978)

SOURCE: "Joanna Baillie," in *The Closet Drama of the Romantic Revival* (*Poetic Drama and Poetic Theory* 35), edited by James Hogg, Universität Salzburg, 1978, pp. 308-19.

[*Below, Mathur argues that Baillie's plays are, for the most part, dramatically unsound but acknowledges Baillie's strength as a poet.*]

The dramatic works of the major poets of the Romantic Revival show the varied manifestations of the phenomenon of the closet drama and its distinguishing characteristics. But there were quite a few other writers also who, by choice or necessity, pursued the same path and made their own contribution to the form. It will be interesting to see what this contribution was and how it stands in relation to that of the major poets.

The earliest and, historically, the most important of these writers was Joanna Baillie who received perhaps a little more than her due of praise from a number of her illustrious contemporaries. Sir Walter Scott often mentioned her with Shakespeare,[1] for he thought that she was showing "the means of regaining the true and manly tone of national tragedy."[2] In all she wrote twenty-six plays published at various times between 1798 and 1836.

Miss Baillie was a dramatist with a purpose and a plan. Believing that "the theatre is a school in which much good or evil may be learned",[3] she wanted to create a drama which "improves" us by giving us "knowledge" "of our own minds" through "the thoughts" and "behaviour of others".[4] In order to realise this moral object she decided to create a gallery of Passions to warn and to guide her fellowmen. She planned "to write a series of tragedies of simpler construction, less embellished with poetical decorations, less constrained by that lofty seriousness which has so generally been considered as necessary for the support of tragic dignity, and in which the chief object should be to delineate the progress of higher passions in the human breast, each play exhibiting a particular passion".[5] She projected a similar series for comedy, "in which bustle of plot, brilliancy of dialogue, and even the bold and striking in character, should, to the best of the author's judgment, be kept in due subordination of nature".[6] In these comedies and tragedies the "chief antagonists" were not to be outward circumstances and events, but "the other passions and propensities of the heart"[7] portrayed with "those minute and delicate traits which distinguish them in an infant, growing and repressed state".[8]

But Miss Baillie often broke away from her own plan, and wrote from time to time "an unconnected or (may I so call it?) a free, independent play"[9] not bound down to the portrayal of a particular passion. She hoped that such a play "might have a chance of pleasing upon a stage",[10] though she continued to believe that plays written according to her plan were "capable of being made upon the stage more interesting than any other species of drama".[11]

Miss Baillie had obviously no love for 'closet' drama,[12] though she fully realised the limitations of the large-sized contemporary theatres,[13] in which mere spectacle—"splendid pantomime, or pieces whose chief object is to produce striking scenic effect"—was preferred to "well-written and well acted Plays".[14] After the comparative failure of **De Montfort** at the Drury Lane theatre, her dislike of the monopoly theatres grew greater, for a few years later she reacted sharply when Sir John Sinclair asked her to write a play on Darius for either of the London playhouses. She declared that she would not "suffer" her plays "to be offered to either of those theatres through any medium whatever", though she was prepared to write a tragedy upon some interesting, but more private and domestic story than that of Darius, . . . to be offered to the Edinburgh theatre, or any other theatre in the United Kingdom he may think proper, those of London excepted."[15] But her disapproval of the London theatres did not make her recoil from acted drama. While publishing the first volume of her plays, she clearly repudiated the supposition that she had written them for the closet rather than the stage".[16] A few years later, she re-asserted that her "strongest desire" was "to add a few pieces to the stock of what may be called our national or permanently acting plays",[17] so as to leave behind her in the world "a few plays, some of which might have a chance of continuing to be acted even in our canvass theatres and barns".[18] She even withheld a number of her plays from publication, so that they might be offered, through her executor, to "some of the smaller London theatres".[19]

Yet only seven of her dramas were professionally produced,[20] and in spite of the support they received from the fame of the authoress, good acting, spectacle and music, they were only rarely successful outside Scotland,[21] though their closet-perusal made her one of the foremost dramatists of her times.[22]

This paradox is inherent in her equipment and her objective as a dramatist. She had little practical experience of the stage, and her 'plan' followed in the majority of her plays, detracted from their overall effectiveness as dramas. This, while true of all her plays, is seen more particularly in the more prominent ones: in *Basil: A Tragedy, De Montfort, The Election, Orra* and *The Dream* from the 'Passion-group'; and in *Rayner, Constantine Paleologus* and *The Family Legend* from the 'miscellaneous group'.

Basil: A Tragedy seeks to depict the disastrous consequences of the passion of Love, through the story of the youthful and gallant general, Basil, who loses all his fame and commits suicide, only because his newfound love for Victoria has detained him in Mantua for a day. The passion of Hatred is the subject of *De Montfort,* in which the hero's deep and persistent hatred for Rezenvelt defeats all attempts at reconciliation, and culminates in his murdering Rezenvelt, resulting, finally, in his arrest and death. *The Election* is a comedy on hatred, which shows how Baltimore's hatred for Freeman ends only when they are revealed to be half brothers. *Orra* and *The Dream* are both tragedies on the Fear of Death. In *Orra,* the fear is that of the supernatural, for the young heroine, not willing to marry according to the choice of her guardian, Hughobert, is sent to a lovely castle on the borders of the Black Forest, where she goes mad for fear. *The Dream* portrays the Fear of Death as being present in the heart of even the bravest. General Osterloo is detained at a wayside monastery and condemned by the Prior to death for a past crime. An attempt to save him fails, and as the blow of the executioner is about to descend, he dies of shock.

The *Plays on the Passions* are by themselves the best illustration of the academic and dramatic unsoundness of Miss Baillie's plan. In it logic takes the place of observation. Passions are not compartmentalised in life, nor can they be in literature. And in these plays themselves they often mingle. Love, for instance, is found in most plays. The passion of fame weighs more with Count Basil than that of love:[23] he kills himself on the loss of the former without caring to enjoy the latter. Even consciously, the dramatist was forced to mix the Passions, as in *The Siege* (a comedy on Fear), the hero of which is "a mixed character" whose "leading traits"

are "conceit and selfishness" and not cowardice and fear.[24] The dramatist's ambitious designs gave way in another respect too: not all the passions can be portrayed from their inception to their consummation. She needed ten Acts to portray ambition in *Ethwald,* and the roots of hatred in *De Montfort* and *The Election* were present long before the beginning of the plays. From the dramatic point of view, even more serious objections to her plan can be advanced, for an unsound dramatic core vitiates the parts. The interest of the play becomes internal: action is sacrificed to thought, and events to manifestations of passion. The movement of the plot resembles the circling currents of a whirlpool more than the swift onward flow of a stream. This downgrading of the importance of action leads to much irresponsibility in the conduct of the plot which sheds its natural verderous garment of events and puts on the sombre robes of meditation. On a comparison with Shakespeare's tragedies after which some of Miss Baillie's plays are clearly modelled, we find the plots too bare and the action too insubstantial. Sometimes too fundamental a role is assigned to coincidence. The root cause of the tragedy of Basil is the coincidence of the battle and his love for Victoria. In *De Montfort,* the sudden appearance of Conrad, and his disappearance after the crisis has been precipitated, can only be put down to a careless handling of the plot. Another insignificant character who is made to play an undeservedly important role is Hereulf at whose unworthy hands the brave Ethwald is made to die. Such arrangements do not impress either the reader or the spectator. For the latter the authoress has tried to sugar-coat the bitter passion-pill by providing spectacle and Gothic motifs. But at least one of these is overdone—the device of murder, which is pressed into service as a convenient mode of rounding off a situation. What is natural in Shakespeare appears stereotyped in Joanna Baillie.

Joanna Baillie could, however, introduce some beautiful and effective scenes. Her crowd scenes are generally well-conceived and well-executed. *Basil: A Tragedy* alone contains two such scenes—the opening scene and the scene of mutiny. *The Election* also has well-managed crowd-scenes. Here, again, Shakespeare seems to have been her model. But the provision of such occasional and isolated scenes or the employment of other tawdry devices cannot compensate for the deeper dramatic deficiencies.

Miss Baillie seems to have realised the possible harmful effects of her plan in the realm of characterisation, for she avowedly "endeavoured fully to delineate the character of the chief person of drama, independently of his being the subject of a particular passion".[25] She "endeavoured also distinctly to discriminate the inferior characters."[26] But her success in both these respects has been, to say the least, limited. She tends to forget the man in her passion, and so even within the limited range of passions she attempted to portray, the main characters seem to be in line with case-histories reported in medical bulletins rather than human beings with whom we come in contact every day. De Montfort is rightly called a "strange man" (IV.ii), and Baltimore a "madman" (V.iii). The difference between the case-history of a Passion and a complete human being will be apparent if we compare Basil with Antony, De Montfort with Othello, or Ethwald with Macbeth. The dramatist's success with her minor characters has also been partial, for while she has undoubtedly been able to give them distinctive traits, there is a superficiality about them which no amount of variety can cure. They hardly appear as living. Geoffrey, Mirando, Jerome, Glottenbal and the many servants—all, no doubt, strut their hour or two upon the stage but then are wiped clean off the state of memory.

The plays of the miscellaneous group are twelve in number. Though less interesting in the closet as psychological studies of certain passions, they are on the whole better theatre. *Rayner* portrays a weak hero, who is mistakenly sentenced to death for a murder committed by another, but is saved from the gallows when the real murderer confesses his crime. *Constantine Paleologus* is one of Miss Baillie's best plays. It shows the Greek Emperor Constantine and his small band of devoted followers bravely but unsuccessfully resisting the Turkish siege. The play is full of striking contrasts in theme and character. In *The Family Legend,* Miss Baillie was more at home, for its theme is characteristically Scottish—a feud between two families. To end the quarrel, Helen of Argyll is married to Maclean, but, with the full knowledge and implicit approval of her husband, an unsuccessful attempt is made on her life, and she somehow reaches her father's house. The Macleans believe she is dead, and go unsuspecting to a banquet given by her father. After the banquet, Helen discloses herself, and the dazed Maclean is challenged to a duel by her brother outside the castle, and is fatally stabbed.

The miscellaneous plays, though less characteristic of the dramatist, are more traditional in nature and reveal a firmer grasp on the material. Their plots, with just a few exceptions like *The Country Inn,* contain more action and dramatic events than the *Plays on the Passions* do. She rightly claims for *Rayner* a variety of tone, a "varied conduct . . . , sometimes gay and even ludicrous, sometimes tender or even distressing", and also that she has endeavoured to make all these varied incidents "arise naturally from the circumstances of the story".[27] But her works, as she admits, suffer from another serious drawback. They do not possess "that strength and compactness of plot, that close connection of events producing one another . . . , which is a great perfection in every dramatic work".[28] Even the

plot of *Constantine Paleologus,* one of her best plays, lacks an inner motivation: the events just happen. *The Family Legend* is much more successful from this point of view, though the element of chance, in the timely rescue of Helen of Argyll, is the hub of the story. Like the plot, the characterisation of these plays is also more varied, comprehensive and on the whole, more effective than that of the plays of the 'Passion-group'. The weak and human Rayner, struggling with temptation; the noble but luxurious Constantine awaking himself, like Byron's Sardanapalus, into magnificent action; the loving but timid Maclean—are all life-like creations. None of the heroes of the *Plays on the Passions,* not even the brooding Montfort, can equal the straightforward and uninhibited characterisation found in these plays.

Joanna Baillie's strongest point in her plays is her poetic power. Of the *Plays on the Passions* a critic wrote, "These dramas are noticeable for the sustained vigour of their style and for the beautiful lyrics with which they are interspersed, but they have neither passion, interest, nor character."[29] The same is more or less true of the style of the other plays. As dramas they are long forgotten, but their poetry pleases still. Here is an example portraying the beginning of love in Count Basil's heart:

> 'Farewell, my lord.' O! what delightful
>   sweetness!
> The music of that voice dwells on the ear!
> 'Farewell, my lord!'—Ay, and then look'd she
>   so—
> The slightest glance of her bewitching eye,
> Those dark blue eyes, commands the inmost
>   soul.
> Well, there is yet one day of life before me,
> And whatso'er betide, I will enjoy it.
> Though but a partial sunshine in my lot,
> I will converse with her, gaze on her still,
> If all behind were pain and misery.
> Pain! Were it not the easing of all pain,
> E'en in the dismal gloom of after years,
> Such dear remembrance on the mind to wear
> Like silv'ry moon-beams on the 'nighted deep,
> When heaven's blest sun is gone?
>
>   (*Basil: A Tragedy,* II, ii)

She uses prose too with equal effect. She re-wrote certain parts of *Rayner,* particularly the comic ones, in "plain prose", for the original blank verse appeared to her "sufficiently rugged and hobbling".[30] She later proceeded to experiment with prose even in a tragedy. *The Dream* is written wholly in prose, so that "the expression of the agitated person might be plain though strong, and kept as closely as possible to the simplicity of nature".[31] But even in her prose Miss Baillie does not cease to be a poet. A passage like the following has all the force of poetry, for it portrays a subdued but powerful feeling:

"*Jerome. (to Osterloo.)* Did you hear my son,
what the Prior has been saying to you?

Osterloo. I heard words through a multitude
of sounds.

Jer. It was the Prior desiring to know if
you have any wishes to fulfil, regarding
worldly affairs left behind you unsettled.—
Perhaps to your soldiers you may.

*Ost. (interrupting him eagerly, and looking
wildly round.)*
My soldiers! are they here?

Jer. Ah, no! they are not here; they are
housed for the night in their distant
quarters: they will not be here till the
setting of tomorrow's sun.

Ost. (groaning deeply) To-morrow's sun!

Jer. Is there any wish you would have
conveyed to them?
Are there any of your officers to whom
you would send a message or token of
remembrance?

Ost. Ye speak again imperfectly, through
many ringing sounds, *(Jer. repeats the
question in a slow, distinct voice.)*

Ost. Aye, there is: these,—
*(Endeavouring to tear off his cincture
and some military ornaments from his
dress.)* I cannot hit upon these fastenings.

Jer. We'll assist you my son. *(Undoing his
cincture or girdle etc.)*

Ost. (Still endeavouring to do it himself.)
My sword too, and my daggers.—My last
remembrance to them both.

Jer. To whom, my lord?

Ost. Both—all of them.

                        (**The Dream**, III.iii)

Joanna Baillie was not a closet dramatist by intention:
her desire rather was to breathe a new life into the
theatre. But not being, nor caring to be, familiar with
the stage, she could not make her plays stage-worthy.
The romantic and Gothic nature of the incidents is
neutralised by a heavy moral tone, and the occasional
sublimity and dignity of her poetry by a pervading
"wooden and wordy"[32] style. She probably wrote for a
stage of her own conception. G. Wilson Knight calls
her plays "stage-worthy".[33] But they can be produced
on the popular stage only after substantial cuts and
alterations. Things, however, being what they are, she
must take her place not in the playhouse but in the
closet. The following lines of her own may well be
allowed to sum up, in essence, the impression left by
her dramas:

> The speech, indeed, with which he welcomed
> us,
> Too wordy and too artificial seem'd
> To be the native growth of what he felt.
>   (**The Family Legend**, V.ii)

Notes

[1] For instance, Scott's commendatory lines printed at
the beginning of *The Complete Works of Joanna Baillie*
(Philadelphia, 1832).

[2] *Essay on the Drama*, in *The Prose Works of Sir Walter
Scott*, [vol. VI] (London, 1834), p. 387.

[3] "Introductory Discourse", in *Complete Works*, p. 22.

[4] *Ibid.*, p. 17.

[5] "Introductory Discourse", in *Complete Works*, p. 18.

[6] *Ibid.*, p. 22.

[7] *Ibid.*, p. 23.

[8] *Ibid.*, p. 22.

[9] "To the Reader", in *Complete Works*, p. 238.

[10] *Ibid.*, p. 238.

[11] *Complete Works*, p. 238, footnote.

[12] She had no taste for mere reading, and preferred
dramatic narration to it. In *The Election: A Comedy*,
Charles says that "no story read can ever be like a
story told by a pair of moving lips, and their two
lively assistants the eyes, looking it to you all the
while, and supplying every deficiency of words."
(III. i).

[13] *Complete Works*, pp. 336-339.

[14] *Ibid.*, p. 336.

[15] M. S. Carhart, *The Life and Work of Joanna Baillie*
(New Haven, 1923), p. 25.

[16] "Introductory Discourse", in *Complete Works*, p.
24.

[17] "To the Reader", in *Complete Works*, p. 238.

[18] *Ibid.*, p. 238. A number of her plays were written
with definite actresses in view. Her various introductory notes bear ample testimony to the fact that stage-
production was constantly in her mind. In *De Montfort*,
she even went to the extent of indicating in a footnote
(in Act V, Sc. iv) where the curtain should drop in a
theatrical production, for "what comes after, prolongs
the piece too much when our interest for the fate of De
Montfort is at an end."

[19] Carhart, p. 53. They were published in 1836,
when, because of the theatrical conditions in En-

gland, she relinquished "all hope of their production on the London stage." (*Ibid.*)

[20] Miss Carhart has given the details of the productions in England, Scotland and elsewhere. (*The Life and Work of Joanna Baillie,* pp. 109-165).

[21] Among the important successful productions of Joanna Baillie's plays may be mentioned the Edinburgh production (1810) of *De Montfort,* the Edinburgh production (1810) of *The Family Legend,* and the Edinburgh production (1820) of *Constantine Paleologus.* As regards the other important productions, the following comment on the world premiere of *De Montfort* (the first play of Miss Baillie to be performed) may be taken as more or less representative, "The audience yawned in spite of themselves, in spite of the exquisite poetry, the vigorous passion, and the transcendent acting of John Kemble and Mrs. Siddons." (Carhart, *The Life and Work of Joanna Baillie,* p. 18).

[22] Miss Carhart, for instance, calls her "the greatest Scotch dramatist" (*The Life and Work of Joanna Baillie,* p. 206). Among her own contemporaries, Byron hailed her as "our only dramatist since Otway" (*Letters and Journals of Lord Byron,* ed. R. E. Prothero, [rev. ed.] Vol. III, 1922, p. 399). Scott's praise of her has already been noticed.

[23] Rosinberg says about him:

> One fault he has; I know but only one;
> His too great love of military fame
> Absorbs his thoughts, and makes him oft appear
> Unsocial and severe.
>
> (*Basil: A Tragedy,* I.i)

[24] *Complete Works,* p. 335.

[25] *Complete Works,* p. 238.

[26] *Ibid.*

[27] *Complete Works,* p. 240.

[28] *Complete Works,* p. 241.

[29] Mary F. Robinson, Introduction to Joanna Baillie in Ward's *English Poets,* Vol. IV.

[30] *Complete Works,* p. 240.

[31] *Ibid.,* p. 335.

[32] Hesketh Pearson, *Walter Scott: His Life and Personality* (London, 1954), p. 70.

[33] G. Wilson Knight, *The Golden Labyrinth* (London, 1962), p. 210.

P. M. Zall (essay date 1982)

SOURCE: "The Cool World of Samuel Taylor Coleridge: The Question of Joanna Baillie," in *The Wordsworth Circle,* Vol. XIII, No. 1, Winter, 1982, pp. 17-20.

[*In the following essay, Zall provides an overview of Baillie's literary career and explores the drawbacks of Baillie's high reputation.*]

Wordsworth pictured Joanna Baillie as the very model of "an English gentlewoman,"[1] but she was in fact Scots born and bred, descended from Wallace himself on her father's side. Born in 1762, she spent her first twenty-one years in Scotland developing an accent that remained a part of her charm until her death in 1851. In her English years, devoted to writing plays aimed at reforming middle class morals, it was not her nationality that impeded her message so much as her being a gentlewoman unfamiliar with her medium, one whose knowledge of plays came from the page rather than the stage. And yet such accomplished professionals as Scott and Byron celebrated Joanna Baillie as the nation's leading dramatist. Reading her plays today leaves one wondering why: "One can account for the contemporary reputation," says W. C. Renwick, only by "acceptance of what a modern reader refuses."[2]

She was not a ready reader herself, spending her first seven years in rural splendor of Lanarkshire where, with older siblings Agnes and Matthew, she reveled in rough country sports, a regular tomboy who could compose songs but could not read. "I could not read," she told a friend, "till nine years old." "O Joanna," protested sister Agnes, "not till eleven!" (p. 6).[3] The idyll had a dark underside as well, for her parents allowed no show of feelings, and one of her deepest recollections was yearning for her parents' caresses that never came. One day, impulsively clasping her mother's knees, she was brushed back. "But," she recalled, "I knew she liked it" (p. 6). Her next seven years in boarding school at Hamilton were no more promising, except that besides doing well in drawing, music and sports, she began making up plays. She would clamber to the roof and secretly try out scenes which she would later have her classmates perform— to what effect we know not.

As she turned fourteen, her father was named Professor of Divinity at Glasgow, and the family followed him into the intellectual ferment there. It was not long before Miss Joanna was turning her brother's Latin lessons into English verse. But after merely two years of Glasgow, the death of her father split the family, with brother Matthew going to Oxford for medical training and the rest of the family returning to bucolic Lanarkshire. In 1783, however, their uncle Dr. John Hunter, the celebrated London surgeon, died, leaving his practice and home to Matthew who at once sent for his mother and sisters to come and keep house for him. For the next sixty-eight years, then, Joanna Baillie lived in and around the heart of London's intellectual life, only occasionally visiting Scotland as any national celebrity would.

After seven years in London, Miss Baillie published her first book, a volume of verses that had no sale. Then, one fateful afternoon as she plied her needle by her mother's side, the inspiration came to apply her verses to plays. Her first play, **"Arnold,"** was so inept she destroyed it. When her brother's marriage dispatched the Baillie ladies to a cottage of their own in Hampstead, she was inspirited again by the intellectual ferment there and began composing plays of high seriousness aimed at ameliorating the moral condition of the middling classes of society. In 1798 came the first of an eventual three volumes descriptively entitled, *A Series of Plays: in which it is attempted to delineate the stronger passions of the mind, each passion being the subject of a tragedy and a comedy.* Though this first volume was anonymous, a second edition the following year had her name attached and brought her critical acclaim between 1800-1804 and affectionate fame the rest of her life.

This first volume contained a tragedy and a comedy on the passion of Love, along with a tragedy on Hate, **"De Monfort,"** her masterpiece, the only one, except for **"Basil"** to be produced on the stage. Yet her reputation soared remarkably. Scott called her the "best dramatic writer since the days of Shakespeare and Massinger"; Byron echoed that she was "our only dramatist since Otway"; and even Jeffrey, while joking that as a subject the passions were "almost as unpoetical as that of the bard who began the tale of the Trojan war from the age of Leda," conceded that Miss Baillie's talents were "superior to those of any of her contemporaries among the English writers of tragedy."[4] One must assume that such praise referred to the plays on the page not on the stage, for today they seem unplayable.

Aside from occasional passages in charmingly simple blank verse, the tragedies particularly appear sometimes ludicrous, as when the hero of **"The Dream"** (in prose) cheats the executioner's axe by dying of fright on the chopping block (*Works* [1851], p. 275). **"De Monfort,"** the masterpiece, is less ludicrous than most. We meet DeMonfort in Augsburg, whence he has fled from Vienna to escape the very sight of the man he hates, Rezenvelt, who also turns up in Augsburg. Mutual friends, Count and Countess Freberg, bring them together at a lavish dinner party, where Lady Jane DeMonfort comes seeking her vanished brother. Slowly she draws from him the secret of his deepseated loathing: from childhood, Rezenvelt, though of inferior birth, has excelled him in every endeavor and, worst of all, having bested DeMonfort in a duel, refused to take his life.

Lady Jane reconciles her brother to Rezenvelt but a false rumor, initiated by Countess Freberg from jealousy of Lady Jane's charms, reaches DeMonfort that his sister has followed to Augsburg because she is Rezenvelt's mistress. Infuriated, he attacks Rezenvelt with a dagger. Rezenvelt disarms him and, having promised Lady Jane to be friends, refuses to retaliate and instead promises to return the dagger in the morning. This magnanimity drives DeMonfort mad. He tracks Rezenvelt through the forest in the black of night and stabs him in the back. Captured by neighborhood monks, he is carried with Rezenvelt's corpse to their monastery where Lady Jane appears, clasps DeMonfort in her arms as he expires from a broken heart, and delivers a fulsome eulogy of his goodness that has no grounds in the play.

The play was first performed at Drury Lane, April 29, 1800, with Kemble and his sister, Mrs. Siddons, in the starring roles and with elaborate staging: "A church of the fourteenth century, with its nave, choir, and side aisles, magnificently decorated," about fifty-six feet wide, thirty-seven feet high, and fifty-two feet deep. Against such a gigantic set the actor playing Rezenvelt had to read such meditative lines as these upon hearing an owl's cry in the dark forest:

> Oft when a boy, at the still twilight hour,
> I've leant my back against some knotted oak,
> And loudly mimick'd him, till to my call
> He answer would return, and, through the
>   gloom,
> We friendly converse held.
>
> (*Works,* p. 95.)

"The excitement was great," recalled one first-nighter, "and the disappointment commensurate. . . . The audience yawned in spite of themselves and in spite of the exquisite poetry, the vigorous passion, and the transcendent acting" (pp. 17-18).

Practicing reviewers were likewise disappointed, their expectations having been aroused by Miss Baillie's reputation. Thomas Dutton of the weekly *Dramatic Censor* could not find a copy of her text before seeing the performance of May 2, and thus did not know whom to blame, Miss Baillie or her adaptor, Kemble: "We never saw a Tragedy so woefully deficient, more culpably ill-conducted" (2:129). A week later, he had found a copy and could accuse her for such structural faults as failing to provide a foil for DeMonfort's unrelieved villainy and—horrible from Miss Baillie's point of view—superimposing an immoral conclusion: "Instead of incurring the punishment of his crime, and being made an example to society, he is relieved from ignominy, dies of a broken heart, and is pompously lamented, instead of being execrated and despised. So much," added Dutton, "for the *morality* of the Drama" (2:130).

Miss Baillie, conceding Dutton's point about the conclusion having no justification in the previous action, added a note to subsequent editions of her text: "The last three lines of the last speech are not intended to give the reader a true character of DeMonfort, whom I have endeavoured to represent throughout the play as, notwithstanding his other good qualities, proud, suspicious, and susceptible of envy, but only to express the partial sentiments of an affectionate sister, naturally more inclined to praise him from the misfortune into which he had fallen" (**Works,** p. 104). And to the fourth edition (1802) she prefixed a lengthy explanation of her over-riding moral purpose: to delineate the way the "mind moves under the dominion of . . . strong and fixed passions . . . to enable us to recognize them in ourselves" (**Works,** pp. 29, 42). Her plots were kept simple, she said, and her language kept close to that of the middling and lower classes where expressions of powerful passions were yet unaffected by the artificial embellishment of modern tragedy, for her aim was to appeal primarily to the middleclass and through them to the lower classes.

It is unlikely that many of the middleclass saw the play, for the consensus of observers is that on the first nights, the *bon ton* packed the house and that succeeding performances drew fewer and fewer spectators till, on the eighth night, the play closed. This failure, however, was no doubt attributable less to its morals than to the many cuts inflicted in trying to fit it to the stage. We can see some of them in three different manuscript versions of the play now at the Huntington Library: (1) the copy submitted for licensing, April 3, 1800, by Kemble; (2) a copy by Thomas Campbell, the poet, deriving from Kemble's copy but with some passages more faithful to Miss Baillie's text; and (3) revisions to Campbell's copy made by Mrs. Siddons, March 29, 1802, apparently for some unrecorded performance, perhaps in a provincial theater or a private reading. All three reflect the frustration of trying to bring **"DeMonfort"** out of the closet.

For instance, Thomas Dutton had complained about the play's lacking a foil for the villain. In two of the manuscript versions this flaw is magnified because they delete the scene in which Rezenvelt refuses a second time to take DeMonfort's life with a magnanimity contrasting to DeMonfort's pusillanimity. Campbell's copy retains the scene and so do subsequent editions of Miss Baillie's plays. She did, however, profit from Dutton's criticism and revised a scene to heighten the parallels in pusillanimity of DeMonfort and the Countess. Where the Countess had merely been innocently teased about Lady Jane's charm by her page and her maid, in the fourth edition she is given a violent quarrel with the Count who, besides blaming her for overdressing like "a May-day queen," now berates her for speaking ill of Lady Jane—leaving the Countess in a state fit to spread false rumors no matter how fatal. Both the Kemble and Campbell copies show other

changes that undermine Miss Baillie's already tenuous structure. The role of the person who carries the false rumor, for example, was cut from two scenes to a few lines, making him a mere *diabolos ex machina*. This was nothing compared to Mrs. Siddon's butchering—trimming at least 425 lines from the Campbell copy, including those that gave the Countess any motivation at all. She cut 225 lines from the final act alone, including many assigned to her own role as Lady Jane. And in the process, she fortuitously reduced the objectionable eulogy at the end down to four lines. In one of the few instances of rewriting Miss Baillie's verse, she revised these lines in the original:

> And now I have a sad request to make,
> Nor will these holy sisters scorn my boon;
> That I, within these sacred cloister walls,
> May raise a humble, nameless tomb to him,
> Who, but for one dark passion, one dire deed,
> Had claim'd a record of as noble worth,
> As e'er enrich'd the sculptur'd pedestal.
> (*Works,* p. 104.)

Mrs. Siddons makes the passage less declamatory, more dramatic:

> And for his sake who to the wretched is
> Most piteous suffer me holy sisters
> To raise within these sacred cloister walls
> An humble, nameless, tomb to him. . . .
> (HM32693, p. 119.)[5]

Such changes reflect Mrs. Siddons frustration in trying to make **"DeMonfort"** playable, for she truly admired it. Taking leave of Mrs. Baillie on their first visit, she asked: "Make me some more Jane DeMonforts" (**Works,** p. xi).

The play was resurrected in November, 1821, but despite the auspices of Byron and the valiant efforts of Edmund Kean, even the eager cooperation of Miss Baillie in revising it for them herself (p. 123), **"DeMonfort"** played only five nights. As a man of the theater, Kean knew it could not succeed; "it would never be an acting play" (p. 127) no matter how admirable its poetry. Similarly, Elizabeth Inchbald, prefacing **"DeMonfort"** in her *British Theatre* (1808), despaired of its success because "the smaller, more curious, and new created passions . . . will be too delicate for the observation of those who hear and see in a mixed, and, sometimes riotous, company" (p. 3). She lamented that "the authoress has studied theatrical productions as a reader more than as a spectator" (p. 5). In celebrating Mrs. Siddons' performance as Lady Jane, Thomas Campbell concurred: "If Joanna Baillie had known the stage practically," he said, "she would never have attached the importance which she does to the development of single passions in single tragedies," substituting for the sense of fatality essential in tragedy "the wilful natures of beings themselves."[6]

Even her own modern biographer, Margaret Carhart, concurs that Miss Baillie's knowledge of the theater was thin and adds that so was her knowledge of theater-goers: "She used the language of the middle-class Englishman about middle-class characters, but did not produce a middle-class result on the stage" because she judged their minds according to the minds of her acquaintances, while "the mass of the English people . . . judged a man according to his actions, not his contemplations" (p. 204).

Her legion of acquaintances did her future reputation disservice in another respect. Despite her failure as a playwright, their adulation encouraged her to persevere as a dramatist. By 1812, the plays on passions reached three volumes and she had branched out to "serious musicals" (**"The Beacon"**), domestic drama (**"The Family Legend"**) and, her first love, volumes of verse—all eagerly received by a widening circle of admirers, especially those who paid pilgrimage to the cottage at Hampstead, now center of personality cult: "To those who knew her well," wrote Lucy Aikin, "the value of all she writes is incalculably increased by its affording so perfect an image of her own pure, benignant and ingenuous spirit. Her character, more, I think, than any I have ever known, deserves to be called a heavenly one."[7]

Visiting in 1818, lively Maria Edgeworth reported the typical conversation there: "Both Joanna Baillie and her sister have a great deal of agreeable and *new* conversation—not old trumpery literature over and over again and reviews, &c but new anecdotes of people, and circumstances worth telling apropos to every subject . . . and frank free observations on character without either ill nature or fear of committing themselves— Quite *safe* companions—no blue-stocking tittle-tattle or habits of worshipping or being worshipped—" And, in 1830, she reported: "I saw various comers and goers, morning, dinner and evening visitors. . . . Whole gangs of mighty rich well drassed remarkably well drassed . . . most of them nauseously affected"—even Wordsworth, his wife, and daughter ("terribly tiresome").[8] Henry Crabb Robinson with a more sophisticated eye saw the same placidity in the midst of this stream: "Nothing more unimportant and insignificant than her conversation . . . yet no *ennui*. I recollect nothing that was said by any one, and only that I passed an agreeable evening."[9] Calm of mind, all passion spent.

Notes

[1] Edith J. Morley, ed., *Henry Crabb Robinson on Books and Their Writers,* 3 vols. (1938), 2:547.

[2] *English Literature, 1789-1815* (1967), p. 231.

[3] Unless otherwise noted, references in parentheses are to Margaret S. Carhart, *The Life and Work of Joanna Baillie* (1923).

[4] Carhart surveys her contemporary reputation, pp. 31-52.

[5] Reproduced by permission of the Librarian, Huntington Library.

[6] *Memoir of Mrs. Siddons* (1834), pp. 208-209.

[7] A. L. LeBreton, ed., *Correspondence of William Ellery Channing and Lucy Aikin* (1874), pp. 260-261.

[8] Christiana Colvin, ed., *Letters from England, 1813-44* (1971), pp. 116, 455.

[9] Morley, ed., 2:547.

Daniel P. Watkins (essay date 1992)

SOURCE: "Class, Gender, and Social Motion in Joanna Baillie's *DeMonfort*," in *The Wordsworth Circle,* Vol. XXIII, No. 2, Spring, 1992, pp. 109-17.

[*In the following essay, Watkins stresses the historical value of* De Monfort'*s depictions of social conditions and class conflicts.*]

Recent scholarly work on Romanticism and feminism has begun to bring Joanna Baillie back from the dead in literary history. For instance, as Stuart Curran states, "two years before Wordsworth's celebrated preface, [Joanna Baillie] had published her own seventy-two-page argument for naturalness of language and situation across all the literary genres," and, in her capacity as dramatist, she was often compared to Shakespeare.[1] Despite the efforts of Curran and a few other notable scholars, however, the hard labor of reviving and critically investigating Baillie's literary accomplishment, particularly her dramas, has barely begun. While the reason for this may be attributed to the masculine biases that continue to influence Romantic scholarship and criticism, Baillie herself has contributed to the difficulty of the critical task by writing plays that were failures on stage in her own day and that continue to baffle (and bore) many readers. Her plots are often embarrassingly simple, her characterizations subordinated to a fixed idea, her handling of emotion compromised by her commitment to cold logic. Such matters overwhelm critical efforts to place her alongside, say, Coleridge and Wordsworth as one of the great Romantic writers.[2]

These weaknesses notwithstanding, Joanna Baillie is one of the important writers of the Romantic period. For one thing, she displays what Curran, in "The I Altered" calls an "alienated sensibility" (203), which gives her critical imagination leverage in treating the social structures of value and belief. For example, while her major drmatic effort is suggested in the title of her *Series of Plays: in which it is attempted to delineate the stronger passions of the mind,* she does not treat human passion in the abstract. Rather she situated it among social and historical pressures of immense complexity: specific details and material situations disclose the inner workings of social life during the Romantic period. Further, despite her awareness of the limitations of theater in her day, she chooses drama to reveal, in ways that lyric poetry cannot, the ideological conflicts disturbing and shaping the passions that constitute her primary thematic and psychological interest. As a genre in decline, drama in the Romantic age is at once weighted with nostalgia and desire for the once-powerful and stable social world that had brought it to prominence, and, at the same time, pressured by the confidence, individualism, and sheer defiance of the social energies struggling to assert (like Keats's Apollo) their newfound power and authority. Baillie's imagination intervenes powerfully in this social, historical, *and* formal generic crisis, tracking the complex intersections of psychological, social, and imaginative motion at an intense moment of historical—specifically class and gender—anxiety, when one structure of authority and belief is on the verge of displacement by another.

DeMonfort (1798) provides an excellent introduction to the social and historical richness of Baillie's work, for it depicts in detail many of the social problems—ranging from class and domestic life to gender and law—caught in the crossfire of this certain and radical transformation of society. Written as a psychological drama about the workings of the passion of hatred, it is much more than this, as its psychological interests draw upon deeper and broader social, historical, and cultural realities that determine the specific contours of individual psychological turmoil. In Baillie's hands, hatred is more than a psychological, private, self-generating, or autonomous passion; it is an *effect* of large, if submerged, social forces and conditions. Nor is it a sign of the essential character of DeMonfort, the protagonist, but rather a symptom of a radically splintered self—a self that presumes social privilege and autonomy while suffering from claustrophobic social transformations that overwhelm, and are unresponsive to, that presumed privilege and autonomy. Thus even as DeMonfort *claims* to be the personal measure of human value in the world of the drama he experiences displacement of his personal and psychological authority. In exploring the deep turmoil between these two extremes, the drama discloses the contingent nature of hatred, illuminating its dependence upon antecedent material conditions (set down in the text of the drama itself) that constitute the ontological ground upon which psychological issues—however powerful, or expressive—must be situated.

The following pages investigate some of the social conditions that undergird the psychological interests of DeMonfort's character. While the logical and historical connections between these conditions are not fully elaborated in my argument, they are shown to be part of a common social reality within which characterization and dramatic action are situated, and from which these take their life and draw their credibility. After sketching these concerns, I shall return to a consideration of the psychological characterization of DeMonfort in an effort to socialize his isolation, alienation, and violence, and to show thereby that his troubles are not his alone, but those of his class.

The most severe crisis described in the drama, the one within which all other issues must be situated, is the transition from an aristocratic to a bourgeois society. The primary spokespersons for these worlds in conflict are (respectively) DeMonfort and Rezenvelt, and in them can be seen, on the one hand, the anxieties and despair resulting from the loss of aristocratic social authority and, on the other, the energy and defiance arising from the acquisition of bourgeois social position. DeMonfort himself recognizes this social dimension of his personal affliction, as he describes for his sister how mere contempt for one of a lower social order transmogrifies over time into obsessive hatred when the lowly begin to advance socially:

> . . . As we [DeMonfort and Rezenvelt]
>   onward pass'd
> From youth to man's estate, his narrow art,
> And envious gibing malice, poorly veil'd
> In the affected carelessness of mirth,
> Still more detestable and odious grew.
> There is no living being on this earth
> Who can conceive the malice of his soul,
> With all his gay and damned merriment,
> To those, by fortune, or by merit plac'd
> Above his paltry self. When, low in fortune,
> He look'd upon the state of prosp'rous men,
> As nightly birds, rous'd from their murky
>   holes,
> Do scowl and chatter at the light of day,
> I could endure it: even as we bear
> Th' impotent bite of some half-trodden worm,
> I could endure it. But when honours came,
> And wealth, and new not titles, fed his pride;
> Whilst flatt'ring knaves did trumpte forth his
>   praise,
> And grov'ling idiots grinn'd applauses on
>   him;
> Oh! then I could no longer suffer it!
> It drove me frantic—What, what would I give!
> What would I give to crush the bloated toad,
> So rankly do I loath him!
>
>   (2.2)

Later in the drama, this same story is related from the opposite perspective by Rezenvelt, who explains to Count Freberg that

. . . Though poor in fortune
I still would smile at vain-assuming wealth:
But when unlook'd for fate on me bestow'd
Riches and splendour equal to his own,
Thou I, in truth, despise such poor distinction,
Feeling inclin'd to be at peace with him,
And with all men beside, I curb'd my spirit,
And sought to sooth him.

(3.2)

The tension evident in these descriptions twice erupts in physical confrontation between the two men, with Rezenvelt each time disarming DeMonfort and sparing his life, a fact which both personally humiliates DeMonfort and reverses the social order of privilege, as DeMonfort comes to owe his life to Rezenvelt.

This purely personal dimension of the transformation of social life is given social significance by developing public responses to individual life, as is seen, for instance, in the fact that it is Rezenvelt, rather than DeMonfort, who is respected and lauded for social benevolence. While even DeMonfort's own servant, Manuel, is unhappy with his increasingly unpredictable master—" . . . for many times is he / So difficult, capricious, and distrustful, / He galls my nature" [1.1])—and while DeMonfort's peers, and even his sister, scold him for his personal conduct, the social elite commend the character, virtue, and generosity of Rezenvelt. As Count Freberg remarks to DeMonfort:

This knight is near a kin to Rezenvelt,
To whom an old relation, short while dead.
Beqeath'd a good estate, some leagues distant.
But Rezenvelt, now rich in fortune's store.
Disdain'd the sordid love of further gain.
And, gen'rously the rich bequest resign'd
To this young man, blood of the same degree
To the deceas'd, and low in fortune's gifts.
Who is from hence to take possession of it.

(2.2)

Such generosity inspires public celebration and respect among the aristocracy itself (excepting DeMonfort)— "For, on my honest, faith," Count Freburg says, "of living men / I know not one, for talents, honour, worth, / That I should rank superior to Rezenvelt" (2.2)— creating a social space of privilege and authority for an individual who was once on the margins of society. As this social space enlarges, DeMonfort knows, aristocracy weakens.

The class conflict exemplified in the tension between DeMonfort and Rezenvelt provides the structural center of the play. It is a conflict, as I have suggested, that depicts the inevitable demise of aristocracy and probable triumph (despite Rezenvelt's eventual death by murder) of the bourgeoisie. As such, it is a conflict that is constitutive of the social reality depicted in the drama, embracing and conditioning every characterization, thematic issue, episode, action, and expression of belief or value used to construct the dramatic action.

The pervasive rumblings in the social world of the drama can be glimpsed, initially, in two seemingly minor matters relating to the tone of the drama: anxiety and claustrophobia. Despite their immediate plot-level function as tonal details that deepen the psychological interest of DeMonfort's character, they connect to the class issues just sketched as signals of the social threat under which DeMonfort's character is drawn. For DeMonfort the world is unstable, broadening outward even to a small town in Germany, where he has sought escape; it no longer possesses a proper center. At the same time the world is closing in on him, denying him even air to breathe, as friends and foes alike pressure him conduct himself according to their expectations.

The most visible means by which anxiety functions in the plot of the drama is through knocking—real or imagined—on doors to rooms inhabited by DeMonfort, destroying his peace of mind, and on doors behind which are the spiritually pure. This is seen almost immediately in Act 1, after DeMonfort has arrived at old Jerome's apartments. At a serious moment, when DeMonfort is commiserating with his host, whose wife has died two years before, a loud knocking on the door so unsettles DeMonfort that he loses all composure: "What fool comes here, at such untimely hours, / to make this cursed noise?" (1.1). In the following scene, after a servant has announced that Rezenvelt has been seen nearby, Demontfort, enraged, denouncing his arch enemy, (calling him such names as "cursed reptile" [1.2]), hears a knocking at his door, jolting him from his frenzy. Later, after he has murdered Rezenvelt and the action of the drama has shifted to a convent, nuns and monks are interrupted twice from their prayers and conversation by loud knocking, knocking which brings news of Rezenvelt's murder.

Such knocking is complemented at various moments by DeMonfort's intense listening for activities just beyond his actual notice, or for events that he believes are about to occur. For instance, at one of the soireés he attends, in the middle of a lighthearted conversation, he stops abruptly, distracted by a noise the others do not hear:

Lady Freberg: Praise us not rashly, 'tis not
    always so.
DeMonfort: He does not rashly praise, who
    praises you;
            For he were dull indeed—
        [*Stopping short, as if he heard
    something.*
Lady Freberg: How dull. indeed?

DeMonfort: I should have said—It has
escap'd me now.—
            [*Listening again, as if he heard
something.*
Jane: What, hear you aught?
DeMonfort [*Hastily*]: 'Tis nothing.

(2.2)

What he hears—or imagines that he hears—of course, is the approach of Rezenvelt. The anxiety of this scene is repeated in a pathological manner later, just before the murder. Alone after dark on the barren path where Rezenvelt will soon pass, DeMonfort is described in a stage direction as "looking behind him, and bending his Ear to the Ground, as if he listened to something" (4.1). When Rezenvelt comes on stage, he too is described by the stage direction as wary, anxiety-ridden, listening: "Enter REZENVELT, and continues his way slowly across the Stage, but just as he is going off, the Owl screams, he stops and listens, and the Owl screams again" (4.1).

These details are meant to create suspense, or tension, on stage, though it is arguable that Baillie does not handle them as well as she might for this purpose. But whatever their success as devices of suspenseful theater, they effectively signal social-psychological instability. In the various exchanges just described we are reminded that retreat from one's community assures no protection from the troublesome crosscurrents of daily life; that the home itself is not safe from those crosscurrents; that public and festive exchange is burdened by external pressures; that nature is alive with the energies of human struggle and violence; that religious seclusion cannot keep the world at bay. In short, the personal anxiety seen on the surface of these details is saturated in the institutions and conduct of society itself, constituting a troubled stream that runs through a world that wants to be—and assumes that it can be—secure in its values, beliefs, and daily practices.

If the details of anxiety course through the many settings of the drama in a way that suggests the largeness of the world and the severity of its troubles, images of claustrophobia pull the opposite direction, suggesting that the world is not large enough to allow even a single individual free and comfortable breathing space. For example, near the beginning of the play, after learning of Rezenvelt's presence in the community, DeMonfort remarks to Freberg, "Come, let us move: / This chamber is confin'd and airless grown" (1.2). One act later, after agreeing to confess the source of his mental anguish to his sister Jane, DeMontford comments:

I'll tell thee all—but oh! thou wilt despise me,
For in my breast, a raging passion burns,

To which thy soul no sympathy will own.
A passion, which hath made my nightly couch
A place of torment; and the light of day,
With the gay intercourse of social man,
Feel like th' oppressive airless pestilence.

(2.2)

Still later, he responds to Freberg's story of Rezenvelt's enormous generosity with the comment. "This morning is oppressive, warm, and heavy: / There hangs a foggy closeness in the air; / Dost thou not feel it?" (2.2). Finally, upon being informed by Grimald that Rezenvelt is in love with Jane, DeMonfort responds: "'Tis false! 'tis basely false / What wretch could drop from his envenom'd tongue / A tale so damn'd?—It chokes my breath" (3.3). These statements are accompanied by less direct remarks that nonetheless suggest the stifling nature of DeMonfort's social environment. He tells Jane that Rezenvelt "presses me" (2.2); in describing his hatred for Rezenvelt, he likens himself to a plant "whose closing leaves do shrink / At hostile touch" (2.2); in promising to maintain a noble countenance in Rezenvelt's presence, he tells his sister: "The crooked curving lip, by instinct taught, / In imitation of disgustful things, / To pout and swell, I strictly will repress" (2.2).

The social and psychological point here of course is that because Rezenvelt is everywhere in society—from DeMonfort's home town to Amberg, where he has sought refuge, from DeMonfort's apartments to public gatherings, from the garden outside DeMonfort's window to the barren areas outside Amberg—there is literally nowhere for DeMonfort to situate himself that is free from his enemy's presence. The two, finally, are even laid side by side in death, a grimly ironic reminder of the extent to which Rezenvelt presses upon, and helps to define, every aspect of DeMonfort's existence. DeMonfort's claustrophobia is a psychological response, to be sure, but it reflects at the same time the literally shrinking world of the aristocracy, at least as that class is represented in its presumed superiority and autonomy by DeMonfort. As DeMonfort's world grows smaller, Rezenvelt's grows larger: Rezenvelt is literally everywhere that DeMonfort turns, a fact that ultimately produces a crisis subject to resolution only by passing through the tragic territories (DeMonfort believes) of violence and death.

If anxiety and claustrophobia are signs of tense psychological pressure produced by antagonistic class relations, the festivities described through much of the early part of the drama suggest one way that the aristocracy deals with that tension. These decadent pastimes constitute, moreover, an arena of social exchange in which both the downward negotiation of aristocratic social life and the upward motion of bourgeois respect and authority become visible.

In the opening scene, shortly after DeMonfort has arrived at Jerome's, Count and Lady Freberg enter unannounced, and at an extremely late hour, to welcome him to town. The Frebergs, DeMonfort is told, are on their return "from a midnight mask" (1.1). During their conversation, Count Freberg, sensing DeMonfort's melancholy humor, promises to "re-establish" his friend by making available to him the highest pleasure in life, partying: "Little time so spent, / Doth far outvalue all our life beside. / This is indeed our life, our waking life. / The rest dull breathing sleep" (1.1). Before the Frebergs leave, they make good their promise, inviting the morose DeMonfort to a party already set for the very next evening that they themselves will host. The anticipated pleasure of the evening is expressed confidently by Lady Freberg: "To-morrow night I open wide my doors / To all the fair and gay; beneath my roof / Music, and dance, and revelry shall reign" (1.1). Still later in the drama, shortly after the Freberg party, DeMonfort is invited to yet another festivity by Count Freberg, this one to be hosted by Old Count Waterlan in honor of Rezenvelt (see 2.2).

The repeated extravagant parties, and planning of future parties, define the public activity of the world of the drama, and thus they are a key to its values and direction of social meaning. Two social realities are fundamentally connected to the valorization of decadence. First, in the conduct of the Frebergs is seen the predictable last fling of a social class that has lost its central and authoritative role in society. If DeMonfort's extreme sullenness represents the dark, reactive personal side of class erosion, the Frebergs' party fever represents its cynically indulgent side. While Count Freberg's hedonistic commitments are in no way cold or malicious, neither are they attuned to social realities outside the scope of his personal pleasure. For him, a party, at its most serious and his personal sphere of experience, as is evidenced by his good-hearted yet dismally failed efforts to bring Rezenvelt and DeMonfort (who, in his view, possess "two minds so much refin'd" [3.2]) together in friendship. At its most common level of occurrence, the parties and festivities that seem to constitute the central portion of Freberg's life are a public display of obscene wealth and conspicuous consumption, an ugly gesture refusing all claims of the world beyond aristocratic self-gratification.

Second, the endless parties and plans for more parties provide interesting insight into the actual social and political compromises that necessarily accompany social transformation. The difficulty and complexity of these compromises are glimpsed most readily in the fact that one major difference between DeMonfort and Count Freberg is that the latter has accepted the rising Rezenvelt as an equal, and perhaps even as a superior, while the former detests Rezenvelt literally more than death itself. While the aristocratic DeMonfort denies completely the social position that has been accorded to Rezenvelt, thus assuring his increasing alienation from society, the aristocratic Freberg embraces it enthusiastically and publicly, displaying his acceptance of a new social arrangement in the many parties and social gatherings around which he has organized his life.

But Freberg's regard for Rezenvelt signals more than acceptance; it signals a far-reaching social compromise with presumed social payoffs for both the aristocracy and the inchoate bourgeoisie. The environment of the party is socially significant in this regard because in it the newly rich Rezenvelt finds public support and applause from a social class whose historical position has been characterized by cultural credibility and political authority; he finds himself, that is, meeting the approval not merely of individuals but of a long tradition of social and cultural privilege, as his leisure is their leisure, his pleasure their pleasure. The expensively clad and ostentatiously privileged aristocracy, on the other hand, welcome Rezenvelt into their company both because of what they perceive as his individual merit and because of his newly-acquired wealth, the latter of which, according Count Freberg, he possesses with all proper decorum. (see 3.1). The fact is, of course, that in honoring Rezenvelt, Count Freberg and his fellow aristocratic party-goers attach themselves to, and gain renewed social identity from, one whose privilege and recognition have surpassed their own. As Count Freberg says bluntly to DeMonfort: "I know not one, for talents, honour, worth, / That I should rank superior to Rezenvelt" (3.1).

The tensions, compromises, and negotiations caught up in radical transformation are seen at other levels of social life as well. One site upon which they receive their most interesting and compelling depiction is the female body. The social significance attached to women, and specifically to their physical features, appear in the comments of Lady Freberg's page about Lady Jane, who has just arrived at the Freberg residence, but who has not yet been introduced or identified. In this young man's eyes, the woman who turns out to be Lady Jane is a veritable goddess, one who is "So queenly, so commanding, and so noble, / I shrunk at first, in awe" (2.1). Such descriptions continue from the page's mouth with no sign of abating until Lady Freberg at last, in exasperation, interrupts him to say, "Thine eyes deceive thee, boy, / It is an apparition thou has seen" (2.1). When Count Freberg interjects that perhaps the page has not seen an apparition but rather Lady Jane. Lady Freberg coldly responds, "No; such description surely suits not her" (2.1). Lady Freberg's unease with Jane's presence is seen again moments later in Count Freberg's admiring comments about Lady Jane after she has left the room, which prompt Lady Freberg's cold response that what Count Freberg admires in Jane is in fact "pride" (2.1).

This small, lightly-humorous scene discloses competition between women for the attention and admiration of men. But the competition is by no means socially inno-cent. While Jane is "no doting mistress," and "No fond, distracted wife" (2.1.) of DeMonfort, she is nonetheless a competitor for his attention and affection, and for the attention and affection of other men. As such she threat-ens Lady Freberg's (ostensibly) secure position as pre-ferred object of masculine admiration, a fact that raises the issue of the cultural value attached to the female body. Unlike the social position of men, determined largely by class (as in the conflict between Rezenvelt and DeMonfort), that of women is determined by patri-archy, irrespective of class. This means that both bour-geois and aristocratic men stand in positions of power with respect to women, and thus women in the world of the drama, as is most clearly seen in the various actions and comments of Lady Freberg, self-consciously trans-form themselves so that they might be objects of choice and thereby attach themselves to some sort of social authority, be it bourgeois or aristocratic. One sign of the ongoing and shaping power of patriarchy in the midst of class struggle can be found in Rezenvelt's lengthy, self-satisfied survey of the women at the Freberg's party:

> . . . [M]en of ev'ry mind
> May in that moving crowd some fair one find,
> To suit their taste, though whimsical and
>   strange,
> As ever fancy own'd.
> Beauty of every cast and shade is there,
> From the perfection of a faultless form,
> Down to the common, brown, unnoted maid,
> Who looks but pretty in her Sunday gown.
>
>   . . . . .
>
> And if the liberality of nature,
> Suffices not, there's store of grafted charms,
> Blending in one, the sweets of many plants,
> So obstinately, strangely opposite,
> As would have well defy'd all other art
> But female cultivation. Aged youth,
> With borrow'd locks in rosy chaplets bound,
> Clothes her dim eye, parch'd lip, and skinny
>   cheek
> In most unlovely softness.
> And youthful age, with fat, round, trackless face.
> The downcast look of contemplation deep.
> Most pensively assumes.
> Is it not even so? The native prude,
> With forced laugh, and merriment uncouth.
> Plays off the wild coquet's successful charms
> With most unskilful pains; and the coquet.
> In temporary crust of cold reserve,
> Fixes her studied looks upon the ground
> Forbiddingly demure.
>
>   . . . . .
>
> I'faith, the very dwarfs attempt to charm,
> With lofty airs of puny majesty,
> Whilst potent damselfs, of a portly make,

> Totter like nurslings, and demand the aid
> Of gentle sympathy.
> From all those diverse modes of dire assault,
> He owns a heart of hardest adamant,
> Who shall escape to-night.
>
>   (2.1)

According to this cynical view, women are objects to be plucked by desiring men, and their value as objects is not in the least class specific, but rather form spe-cific. From native prudes to coquets to damsels of a portly make, the women of whom Rezenvelt here speaks are varieties of Lady Freberg—women who seek to insert themselves into the arena of social value, and to hold their place in that arena, through the use of their bodies. In such a world, friendship and trust between women are impossible—as it is impossible between Lady Freberg and Lady Jane—as every woman is a threat to every other woman.

The most illuminating insight into the social and cul-tural significance of the female body, and into the workings of patriarchy, can be found in the scene describing Lady Jane's appearance in disguise at the Freberg party. In denying view of her face, the dis-guise both focuses attention on her physical form and inspires masculine fantasy to create a dream face for that form. As Rezenvelt comments: " . . . this way lies attraction" (2.1). Refused access to her face, he quickly, as does DeMonfort, imagines her as far superior to other women in her presence: "We bid you welcome, and our beauties here, / Will welcome you the more for such concealment" (2.1).

Beyond the obvious masculine erotic fantasies about the faceless (dehumanized) female body, however, is another, more delicate, matter of sexual politics, one still related to the cultural value of the female body but charged with a combined class and erotic interest—incest. The conver-sation between DeMonfort and his disguised sister ap-proaches sexual longing, as Jane, protected by the veil that she wears, speaks freely of one "who has, alas! for-saken me" (2.1), of one who shared his life with her entirely: "Within our op'ning minds, with riper years / The love of praise, and gen'rous virtue sprung: / Through varied life our pride, our joys, were one" (2.1). DeMonfort, for his part, responds in kind, remarking first upon his sister's "virtuous worth," and then celebrating her un-usual beauty, which, he says, is at least as great as that which he imagines lies behind the veil of his unknown companion: "And though behind those sable folds were hid / As fair a face as ever woman own'd, / Still would I say she is as fair as thee" (2.1). Furthermore, he re-marks with considerable pride that his sister, in her younger years, declined the offers of many suitors, pre-ferring to remain devoted to her brother (2.1).

Their relationship, as it is manifested in this exchange, is distinguished by DeMonfort's admiration for her beauty and virtue; by his recognition of her undying love for him; by Jane's view of the couple (at least in earlier days) as soul-mates with a single identity; and by their mutual sense of an absolute faithfulness to one another that overwhelms all other potential love interests.[3] The details of this relationship develop within a complicated web of psychological and historical interest that charges incest with social significance. Perhaps most important to an understanding of the larger and determining contexts of the relationship is the fact that DeMonfort and Jane were left orphaned very early in life, compelling Jane not only towards close companionship with her brother, but also toward a role as mother to him. As DeMonfort puts it:

> [W]ithin her house,
> The virgin mother of an orphan race
> Her dying parents left, this noble woman
> Did, like a Roman matron, proudly sit,
> Despising all the blandishments of love
>
> (2.1)

In purely psychological terms, the relationship may thus be seen as reflecting Oedipal and pre-Oedipal desires that were interrupted by the death of the parents and then transferred to the sister, where they were allowed to flourish, as the law of the father had been effectively removed. This view is enforced by the descriptions of guilt that DeMonfort experiences—"My heart upbraids me with a crime like his" [2.1]—even as his love for Jane expands.

But their love is also socially formed, as the death of the parents is also, in the larger context of the drama, the death of the parent class. DeMonfort and Jane are an "orphan race," marginalized from the main flow of social life, as is evidenced in Demontfort's extreme alienation and in Jane's disguise. Their love is a kind of mutual support, a desperate defense against a changing world that has begun to displace their parents' authority, and even to isolate the orphaned children from one another. This movement toward isolation is suggested near the end of the disguise scene when Rezenvelt steps between Jane and DeMonfort as he moves to unveil her. It is emphatically depicted in subsequent scenes where rumours abound that Rezenvelt and Jane are planning to marry, which of course would sever the Jane-DeMonfort relationship. In these ways, the psychological explanations of the mutual affection between Jane and DeMonfort become mediated by historical and social considerations; the ostensibly self-generating and local Oedipal conflict modulates from an example of private psychological phenomena into an *effect* of public turmoil and pressure: the determinants of personal life, on this view, are to be found not only in the individual psyche but also in social and historical reality.

It should be clear from the cast of this argument that even at this level of personal and social life the female body, or at least the female person, is the site upon which the drama of masculine need, desire, and demand gets played out. Even as the relationship between Jane and DeMonfort is characterized by mutual affection, it is Jane's body and person—as ideal beauty and as mother—that are the repository of DeMonfort's desire. Her role as "Other" to a masculine "Subject" is consistent throughout the drama. Whether she appears disguised (as in this scene), or plainly dressed (as in the scene, described above, involving Lady Freberg's page), or troubled by deep grief (as in the final scenes following DeMonfort's death), she is made to bear the weight of masculine circumstance, to be formed at the pleasure of both aristocratic and bourgeois patriarchy. Even in the final scene, when she appears to display greatest nobility of character, she fulfills the role of "Roman matron" described earlier by DeMonfort; virtually all of the principal male characters gather around her (along with the Abbess and nuns), one supporting her, one embracing her knees, one holding her robe—her body is literally the focal point for the expression of collective emotion.

Two additional issues that are raised only briefly, religion and law, help to illuminate the social anxiety and historical crisis at the center of the dramatic action. Both of these issues appear only very late in the action, after the murder of Rezenvelt, and, in the context of that murder, they function emphatically as markers of the direction of social meaning, pointing up the social and ideological transformations symbolized by DeMonfort's tragic deeds.

Immediately after the murder of Rezenvelt, in Act 4, the scene shifts inside a convent chapel, providing the first clear glimpse of religion in the world of the drama. And, as will be the case nearly twenty years later, in Charles Robert Maturin's *Bertram,* the world of the monks and nuns is initially portrayed as suffering from the severe shock of a storm that "howls along the cloisters" (4.2). Amidst the seething and tumultuous energies of nature, the nuns and monks attempt to preserve the integrity of their religious practice, carrying out a solemn ritual for someone recently deceased. The ritual, however, is interrupted, first by a hysterical lay sister, who has heard a piercing human cry above the storm blast, and then by frantic knocking on the chapel door by a monk who has seen the murdered corpse of Rezenvelt just beyond the chapel. These disturbances are further compounded by the arrival of yet another shocked monk, who has seen the greatest horror of all: the person of DeMonfort, who, following his murderous deed, has come to resemble the living dead.

On one level, these frantic developments in the plot, shifted as they are onto the territory of institutional religion, suggest the threat under which traditional faith operates in a world marked increasingly by alienation, decadence, severe class conflict, and tragic violence. The anxiety that is felt by the religious themselves is pointed up in the fact that one nun sees revenge as the only proper response to the murder: "The good Saint Francis will direct their search: / The blood so near his holy convent shed, / For threefold vengeance calls" (4.3). This anxiety gradually modulates through the final scenes of the play into a morbid fascination with death and dying, as various nuns and monks gather outside DeMonfort's holding room in the convent, listening as the life of the despair-ridden murderer slowly slips away. Indeed, the sound of death echoes with growing resonance through the entire convent, disturbing the inhabitants with its nightmarish rumblings. Unable to sleep and wandering the halls of the convent, one lay sister remarks to the monk Bernard and several nuns, just outside DeMonfort's room:

> I cannot rest. I hear such dismal sounds,
> Such wailings in the air, such shrilly shrieks,
> As though the cry of murder rose again
> From the deep gloom of night. I cannot rest:
> I pray you let me stay with you, good sisters.
>
> (5.4)

The literal storm that so disturbed the nuns and monks when they were first introduced into the dramatic action has modulated into a psychological storm that disturbs their rest and threatens their very faith.

The unrest facing the institution of religion is set against the confident authority of the institution of law, which also appears in the final portions of the story. Though only briefly present, the officers of the law serve a clear and important function: they provide a stabilizing presence at a moment of growing instability, asserting firm control of a situation that is but confusingly handled by an uncertain and anxiety-riddled religion. Their power, as they themselves describe it, is absolute, a secular equivalent of—and replacement for—the Divine Law that, as we have seen, is under siege. As one officer states, in the very first pronouncement by a representative of law, "we are servants of the law, / And bear with us a power, which doth constrain / To bind with fetters this our prisoner" (5.2). The power he speaks of is never identified in practical social terms, except insofar as it is said to be bolstered by sacred custom, and yet this power is real, and an unmistakable sign that the world has changed; it is a sign of a world in which the aristocracy has been overthrown and its religion paralyzed, both replaced by a firmer and more vibrant authority.

That DeMonfort, at least on some level, recognizes the change signalled by the presence of a secular authority representing civil life is grimly and sarcastically shown in his submission to his accusers:

> Here, officers of law, bind on those shackles,
> And, if they are too light, bring heavier
>   chains.
> Add iron to iron, load, crush me to the
>   ground;
> Nay, heap ten thousand weight upon my
>   breast,
> For that were best of all.
>
> (5.2)

DeMonfort's last best resistance, he knows, is a Manfred-like assertion of will and integrity followed shortly by death. Whatever triumph he might be said to enjoy over the ascendant bourgeoisie and its representatives of social authority must be understood within this purely negative context. When the officers of the law return in the final scene of the drama to bear DeMonfort away to punishment, they are told that he has died, and this news leaves them powerless and looking foolish: "I am an officer on duty call'd, / And have authority to say, how died?" (5.4). DeMonfort's death in the convent marks a personal victory and at the same time points to the much larger social defeat of the aristocracy and the institution of religion that once represented its highest values and strongest authority.

Before turning to a final set of comments about the social significance of DeMonfort's character, I want to touch once more upon the important role of Lady Jane, this time considering her character in terms of class as well as of patriarchy. It would seem, with the death of Rezenvelt and the ensuing despair of DeMonfort, that the bourgeois elements in the drama are successfully contained, and that aristocratic values, despite the actions of DeMonfort, come to be valorized, presented nostalgically in DeMonfort's final anguishing days as signs of the highest personal and social integrity. The descriptions of DeMonfort's death, however, are followed by an interesting portrayal of Jane suggesting that her character has changed through the course of the drama in ways that keep a bourgeois sensibility alive. Indeed, after Rezenvelt's murder and DeMonfort's death, Jane's character gradually begins to represent, in idealized form, an individualism and subjectivity over against aristocratic and religious structures of value—to display, that is, bourgeois sensibilities shorn of the ugliness associated with Rezenvelt's character. Rezenvelt, as one of the newly rich rubbing shoulders with the landed aristocracy through much of the play, must of course be seen as the public example of the *embourgeoisment* of society. But Jane comes to embody its personal integrity, its intensity of personal commitment, and its impeccable personal values. Rather than Count Freberg, or the Abbess, Jane becomes the focal point of social life—Count Freberg, the monks and nuns, and even the servants Jerome and Manuel defer to her. She is one whose "simple word" (5.4) carries the weight of truth, and whose simple conduct expresses respect for the long history of aristocratic hegemony, acceptance of a changed world, and recognition of the course that individual conduct must now take.

It is fitting that Jane becomes an example of bourgeois value, because, as I have argued, in the drama women are one primary locus of masculine power and desire, and hence of social meaning. If in the earlier scenes women were shown to be malleable, transformed in ways that reflected the direction of an essentially masculine reality, in the final scenes Jane is transformed once again, this time moving to the foreground of the dramatic action, not as a primary agent of social change, but rather as an idealized projection of change that has already occurred, symbolized in the ugly and physical struggles between Rezenvelt and DeMonfort. On such a view, the integrity evident in her final speeches is certainly her own, but the meaning of her comments and actions belongs to social currents that, historically, have positioned and valued women in quite specific ways.

I want now, finally, to consider briefly Baillie's portrayal of DeMonfort, and to propose that the deep psychological passions seen in his character are best understood against the trajectory of social transformation that has been sketched thus far. The psychological confusion and the passion of hatred seen in DeMonfort are, in the context of the dramatic action, signs of a radically divided subject. From the beginning, DeMonfort unyieldingly—and desperately—asserts the authority of an autonomous, stable subject, and he seeks a reflection of that stability and autonomy in the world around him. At both the biological and social levels, however, stability has been denied, as his parents' early death has left him orphaned, and as an emergent bourgeoisie has left him socially marginalized. Unable to discover the stability he desires, either in social life or in the personal world inhabited by himself and his sister (he fears that she plans to marry Rezenvelt), he is cast loose upon a stream of ever-changing personal and social events within which he, as subject, is repeatedly displaced and reconstituted—as generous master, as cold tyrant, as dignified aristocrat, as old friend, as arch-enemy, as caring brother, as betraying brother, as superior nobility, as murderer. The chain of this movement is suggested in DeMonfort's many literal changes of scene: upon arriving in Amberg, he is seen at various times in the meager apartments of old Jerome; in the ostentatious surroundings of the Freberg estate; in the barren wilderness outside Amberg; in the convent. With each new location his character modulates, changing according to the demands and possibilities of the world within which he moves.

Amidst these fluctuations of personal and social life, DeMonfort's character never approaches wholeness, or autonomy, despite his repeated claims that his life is under his command. One of the bleakest, and clearest, examples of the contradictions tearing at his character appears in the final scene, in which he gives himself over, as if by choice, to be placed in chains by the officers of the law. Even at this moment of absolute physical defeat he speaks from a position of apparent superiority, explicitly revealing what has been the case from the beginning: personal desire and need notwithstanding, his is a character entirely subject to social forces—Rezenvelt's money, the rumored pending marriage of Rezenvelt and Jane, Count Freberg's regard for Rezenvelt—that he has all along attempted to repress, but which always return to haunt him, and with increasing severity until, finally, he believes that the only way to free himself is through an act of extreme violence.

As this brief explanation makes clear, DeMonfort's troubles are involved with matters of passion and psychology. But passion and psychology are socially mediated. What might appear to be pure Oedipal and pre-Oedipal confusion is connected vitally to DeMonfort's overwhelming sense of alienation from the specific social configuration of the world around him; what we might prefer to see only as one man's personal quarrel with another derives fundamentally from the changing direction of wealth in society; what might be described, in pathological terms, as one lunatic's violent ambush of an innocent individual occurs necessarily alongside the demise of an entire social class. Thus DeMonfort's movements are never his alone; his is "the gait disturb'd of wealthy, honour'd men" (1.2.) generally in his world. While his specific actions are unique to his character, the passion of hatred that energizes those actions is fired in the oven of rapidly-increasing social change whose flames are felt not only by DeMonfort, but by everyone—from Count Freberg to Rezenvelt to Lady Jane to the nuns and monks in the convent.

That *DeMonfort* has been all but forgotten by literary history is no doubt partly attributable to shortcomings in the play itself—it is long, melodramatic, ill-suited for the popular stage. But the fate of the drama, and of Baillie's work generally, is also attributable to the inability—or unwillingness—of scholarship to probe the deeper structures of a work whose significance is barely glimpsed on its surface. Like many of Byron's dramas, which have hardly fared much better, *DeMonfort* works not so much through action and dialogue as through ideological disclosure, which Baillie achieves by focusing on social relations rather than individual events. This focus necessarily slows the pace of dramatic action—and thus damages stageability—but the payoff is a comprehensive and profound picture of personal life drenched in the many currents of social circumstance.

More than forty years ago, Bertrand Evans called for a complete revaluation of Joanna Baillie's works (200). When that revaluation comes—and the present discussion is meant to encourage it—it will best serve Baillie by recognizing and emphasizing that the strength of her dramatic imagination lies not so much in her probings of individual psychology, or in any narrowly-defined poetic beauties that she may have achieved, but rather in her wide and deep historical vision. Only through an exploration of the historical dimensions of her imagination can the considerable achievement of her dramatic works be recovered.

Notes

[1] Stuart Curran, "The I Altered," in Anne K. Mellor, *Romanticism and Feminism* (1988), 185-86.

[2] For the typical critical attitude toward Baillie's work, see, for example, Om Prakash Mathur's remark that "She tends to forget the man in her passion, and so even within the limited range of passions she attempted to portray, the main characters seem to be in line with case-histories reported in medical bulletins rather than human beings with whom we come in contact every day." *The Closet Drama of the Romantic Revival* (1978), 315; or W. L. Renwick's dismissive comment that "No real dramatist would deliberately sit down to write a whole series of *Plays on the Passions: English Literature 1789-1815* (1963), 232. For a more favorable assessment, see Bertram Evans, *Gothic Drama from Walpole to Shelley* (1947), 200-15.

[3] In these respects, the relationship between Jane and DeMonfort looks forward to the semi-incestuous relationships depicted in Byron's poetry, for example the Selim-Zuelika affair in *The Bride of Abydos,* or the Hugo-Parisina affair in *Parisina*. For a discussion of the social dimension of incest in these works, see Daniel P. Watkins, *Social Relations in Byron's Eastern Tales* (1987), 51-52 and 134-35.

Anne K. Mellor (essay date 1994)

SOURCE: "Joanna Baillie and the Counter-Public Sphere," in *Studies in Romanticism,* Vol. 33, No. 4, Winter, 1994, pp. 559-67.

[*In the essay below, Mellor argues that Baillie's works offered alternative, feminist views to contemporary readers in place of the commonly extolled views of white middle-class males.*]

Joanna Baillie was the leading playwright of the romantic era; she was hailed by her peers as the most original and successful of all contemporary dramatists. Sir Walter Scott claimed that Baillie was "certainly the best dramatic writer whom Britain has produced since the days of Shakespeare and Massinger."[1] Her competitor, Byron, commented crudely but with admiration, "When Voltaire was asked why no woman has ever written even a tolerable tragedy? 'Ah (said the Patriarch) the composition of a tragedy requires *tes-

ticles'.*—If this be true," Byron continued, "Lord knows what Joanna Baillie does—I suppose she borrows them."[2] Byron further declared Joanna Baillie to be "our only dramatist since Otway & Southerne" (*Letters* 3: 109) and urged the Drury Lane Theater in Covent Garden to remount a production of *De Montfort* with Edward Kean, a production that took place in 1821. The opening and equally famous production of Baillie's *De Montfort* was staged in 1800 at Drury Lane with Sarah Siddons as Jane de Montfort and John Philip Kemble as de Montfort.

What did her contemporaries see in Baillie's now almost entirely neglected work that we have overlooked? Current feminist interrogations of Habermas' concept of the public sphere can illuminate the social and political significance of Baillie's drama. In *The Structural Transformation of the Public Sphere,* Habermas defined the eighteenth-century bourgeois or classic public sphere as a discursive community distinct from state interests, one whose commitment to rationality potentially guaranteed access to all citizens regardless of class, gender or race. Although Habermas implicitly equated participation in the political public sphere with the ownership of property, and defined "public opinion" as rational debate among property-owning men, he did allow for the participation of women (together with apprentices and servants) as *readers* in the "literary public sphere."[3] In her *Beyond Feminist Aesthetics,* Rita Felski argues that, despite the blindness of this bourgeois public sphere to its own material basis in the privileges of the middle-class white male, a commitment to rationality as such represented an emancipatory moment in human history which cannot be reduced to false consciousness. She then complicates Habermas' model of a bourgeois public sphere by suggesting that we can theoretically and historically locate a "counter" public sphere to that constructed by a masculine bourgeois Enlightenment ideology, a public sphere in which the values and concerns of women predominate.[4]

If we identify this counter-public sphere in large part with the "literary public sphere" acknowledged by Habermas, we can track the emergence in the late eighteenth-century in England of a feminist public sphere, a sphere controlled by women. In the mid 1770s, a few enterprising booksellers began the practice of "lending" their books to readers for a nominal fee; by the end of the century, booksellers had discovered that they could make as much money from the lending as from the sales of their books. The popularity and rapid growth of these commercial lending libraries in England, to which users subscribed for an annual fee, meant that books became widely accessible for the first time to a new and ever-growing readership, a readership composed in large part of upper- and middle-class women who had the leisure time to read. Since reading was thought to be a particularly genteel occupation for such women, and since women's only access to a serious education was through reading good books, the majority of the reading public, for all genres, was female. We must remember that for women in the early nineteenth century in England the very act of reading was potentially a feminist act: it implicitly asserted the rights of women to gain access to knowledge and to exercise their rational faculties on a par with men.

The emergence of a female reading audience produced a demand for female authorship, since women preferred to read literature, especially novels, written by women. Of the dozen best-selling authors in England between 1780 and 1820, ten were female. Their writings, taken together, constructed a literary or "counter" public sphere, one specifically designed to educate female public opinion. Here I have time to discuss only one writer from this group, the leading dramatist of the period. I have chosen to focus on a dramatist because, as Julie Carlson argues in her recently published *In the Theatre of Romanticism: Coleridge, Nationalism, Women* (Cambridge UP, 1994), in the eyes of the male romantic poets and critics, the theater as a whole was culturally gendered as "feminine," as both the object of the male specular gaze and the arena of vulgar spectacle or display. Moreover, in this period, the actual stage was dominated by women: the most famous and successful player by far was the actress Sarah Siddons (her portrait by Joshua Reynolds, "Sarah Siddons as the Tragic Muse," now hangs in the Huntington Art Gallery). Employing this concept of a counter-public sphere, I wish to suggest that Joanna Baillie consciously used the theater to re-stage and revise the social construction of gender. In both her **"Introductory Discourse"** to *A Series of Plays on the Passions* (London, 1798) and in the first tragedy in that series, **Count Basil,** Baillie challenged hagemonic constructions both of "human nature" and of gender and offered an alternative account of the "emancipatory" potential within social practices.

Baillie begins her **"Discourse"** with a definition of human nature's primary motivation or "great master propensity" as "sympathetic curiosity" (4), a definition that contests the assertions of Hobbes, Locke, Burke and a host of other philosophers, including modern "rational choice" social scientists, that human beings are primarily motivated by self-interest. Baillie claims that all human beings desire knowledge of others and experience a sense of identification with others. She assumes that the subject or self can be constructed only in relation to other selves, and that knowledge is produced, not from "objective" or detached observation, but rather from empathetic identification, an identification that is then articulated through the stories we tell of what and whom we meet, what she calls "tattling." Her epistemology conforms to what modern feminist philosophers have defined as "women's ways of knowing" or "stand-point theory." In Sandra Harding's classic formulation of this epistemological position, a

"strong" (as opposed to a "weak") objectivity can be achieved, not by positing a universal subject removed from local circumstances (as assumed by Habermas and by contemporary scientists), but only by acknowledging that all knowledge-producers are historically and culturally located, and by attempting to correct for the inherent biases or limited standpoints of a given set of experimenters or observers.[5]

Baillie's **"Introductory Discourse"** is specifically to *A Series of Plays in which it is attempted to delineate The Stronger Passions of the Mind;* she further claims that the development of the individual is governed most powerfully by feelings and desires, passions which must be held in check by reason if they are not to become self-destructive. Asserting that human character is organic and developmental, growing not from Locke's "white paper" or blank slate but from an inherent "propensity" or seed, she both anticipates William Wordsworth's influential assertion that "fair seed-time had my soul" and also argues that this growing seed takes its final shape from its interactions with its environment. Each of her tragedies studies the growth of a single passion that, unchecked by the rational advice of others, destroys the hero; her comedies hold that obsessive passion up to the derision of others, laughing its possessor back into a more moderated feeling.

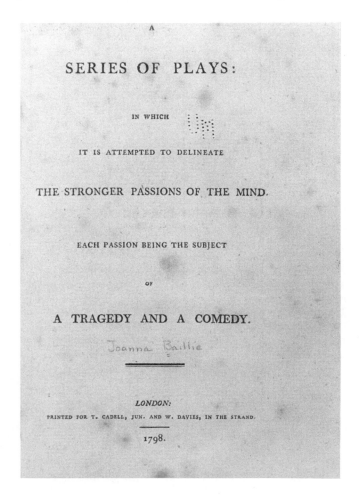

Significantly, in Baillie's plays, it is the male characters who are prey to unregulated passion, while the female characters are the voices of rational moderation. She thus denies the traditional gender definition of the female sex as irrational, impulsive, and uncontrollable. At the same time she insists that there is no significant psychological or mental sex-difference between males and females. As she claims in her **"Introductory Discourse,"** "I believe that there is no man that ever lived, who has behaved in a certain manner, on a certain occasion, who has not had amongst women some corresponding spirit, who on the like occasion, and every way similarly circumstanced, would have behaved in the like manner" (36).

The function of drama, Baillie asserts, is to arouse the sympathetic curiosity of the viewer so that the audience will both identify with her characters and learn from their errors. "The theater is a school" (58), she claims, and like the other female literary critics of her day, she wished to use literature to educate her audience to a more responsible morality. In order to do this, she recognized, drama must be probable or "natural"—it must show "the plain order of things in this every-day world" (21), including the way that the passions develop and change over time, in their "infant, growing, and repressed state" (59). Despite her claims for the universality of the growth of the human passions, we must recognize that there is a potentially limiting class bias in Baillie's concept of human nature. For Baillie, what is "natural" is what is "middling and lower" class, English, and domestic—she rejects both the "artifice" of the aristocracy and the potentially disruptive "ballad-reading" of the "lowest classes of the labouring people, who are the broad foundation of society, which," she claims, "can never be generally moved without endangering every thing that is constructed upon it" (57-58).

To achieve a "natural" or probable revelation of the human passions, Baillie devised several specific dramatic techniques: the frequent use of the soliloquy; a focus on but one passion and one plot (with no distracting subplots or unrelated incidents); the staging of processions, balls, banquets and other social rituals or ceremonies in place of subplots in order to arouse audience attention but avoid distraction; and the confinement of the action to a small, intimate, often domestic space (a house, a town-square). Eschewing what she considered to be bad comedy—the rhetorical excesses of satirical comedy, the amorality of witty comedy, the hypocrisies of sentimental comedy, and the contrivances (or "ambushed bush-fighting") of "busy" comedy or farce—Baillie wrote what she called "Characteristick Comedy," a comedy devoted to the representation of the "motley world of men and women in which we live" (49), using ordinary language and focusing on the damage done by emotional excesses.

We must recognize the large cultural authority to which Baillie laid claim. Echoing Andrew Fletcher of Saltoun, she suggests that "if I have the writing of its [Drama], let who will make the laws of a nation" (57). Baillie thus positions herself as the unacknowledged legislator of the British nation, superior to the historian, philosopher and poet. In her view, the dramatist alone can combine an abstract moral lesson with a concrete appeal to our "sympathetic curiosity," an appeal that will—in this first articulation of what we now call "reader-response" theory—produce political action, cultural ideology and meaning itself. Although Baillie employs a conventional modesty topoi, craving the "forbearance of my reader" (69), she at the same time firmly asserts both the originality and the pedagogical value of her dramatic project: she is the first to attempt to reveal the growth of individual passions, from love and hatred to remorse and sexual jealousy, by writing *paired* plays, a tragedy and a comedy on each passion. By moving the realm of private, psychological feelings from the domestic "closet" to the public stage, Baillie implicitly asserts that a hitherto culturally marginalized "women's realm," the realm of feelings, sympathy, and curiosity, is in fact the basis of all human culture, and especially of political culture. Good domestic management thus becomes her model for good politics; a rational control of passion that produces harmonious and loving family relationships becomes the model for peaceful national and international relations.

Turning now to what I consider to be Baillie's finest play, **Count Basil** (1798), I would like to discuss it briefly as an example of some of the claims made above. **Count Basil** is Baillie's examination in the genre of tragedy of the passion of love, her response to Shakespeare's interrogation of the conflicting claims of honor and love in *Antony and Cleopatra* and to John Dryden's rehearsal of those same issues in his *All for Love*. Equally important, this play is about the control of the public sphere, a debate between two opposing methods of government.

Count Basil begins by publically staging the meeting of two opposing processions, two genders, two value-systems. From one side, accompanied by martial music, comes the military procession of Count Basil and his soldiers, who are hailed for their discipline and military success; from the opposite side, accompanied by "soft music," comes the Princess Victoria and her women, who are hailed for their beauty and their public display of filial devotion and religious duty. Two bodies are here presented for the specular desire of both the audience and of Count Basil: the wounded body of the old soldier Geoffrey and the "splendid" body of Victoria. Overtly, this display stages the tension between military honor and erotic love, between masculine heroism and feminine graciousness. But Baillie is not simply rewriting *Antony and Cleopatra*. Instead, she insists in this opening scene on what is *absent:* Geoffrey's arm ("this arm . . . Which now thou seest is no arm of mine" [76]) and Victoria's mother ("She is fair, But not so fair as her good mother was" [79]).

This absence at the center of the public sphere is further identified, as the play proceeds, with the amoral, machiavellian policies of Victoria's father, the Duke of Mantua, who schemes to keep Basil in his court long enough for his secret ally, the King of France, to defeat Basil's Austro-Hungarian Emperor. Pretending hospitality, the Duke employs his daughter as a pawn in his policy. Unknowingly, Victoria graciously urges Basil to stay with her, and Basil, infatuated with her beauty, acquiesces.

Basil stays in Mantua one day, two days, three days, despite the urgent demands of his cousin, fellow officer, and chief advisor, Count Rosinberg, that he continue on his march at once. Rosinberg's motives are called into question, however, both by his misogyny (the only woman he knows whose love will never change is his "own good mother" [88]) and by his infatuation with his younger cousin. His "foolish admiration" claims that "when Basil fights he wields a thousand swords" (80-81), and he embraces Basil with the ardor of a jealous lover ("my friend! / I love thee now more than I ever lov'd thee" [161]) when Basil agrees to leave Victoria (Act IV, Scene 3). As we come to recognize, in **Count Basil** the hero's struggle is not between erotic passion and military duty but rather between three kinds of passion: heterosexual love, homosocial love, and self-love. Basil's heterosexual infatuation with Victoria might well be reciprocated, we are led to believe, as Victoria begins to recognize the difference between Basil's mature devotion and the hypocritical attentions of her previous lovers, and to respond judiciously to Basil's passion for her. But Basil already has another love, as he confesses: "From early youth, war has my mistress been, / And tho' a rugged one, I'll constant prove, / And not forsake her now" (86). As the play unfolds, we see this prior love unveiled as a powerful homosocial bonding of Basil with his men, and especially with Rosinberg, who is passionately devoted to Basil and hostile to any woman who might interrupt that bond. Two bodies are here displayed for Basil's specular desire: the "divine" body of the beautiful Victoria and the scarred body of the old soldier Geoffrey. Weeping with his men over the body of Geoffrey, Basil manifests his deeper emotional bond, with his men. When Basil betrays that bond, when his men mutiny, Basil's self begins to split apart. The "wounded soldier" whose mask Basil wears at the ball is not only the rejected lover of Victoria, as he claims, but also the rejecting lover of his own wounded men.

But the wounded love which drives Basil to suicide is finally neither heterosexual nor homosocial. It is, as Basil admits, "his great love of military fame" (81): the wound to his own "glorious name." His failure to fight at Pavia did no harm to his own men or to his Emperor's cause, since the French King was soundly defeated by another general. Nor did it, as Old Geoffrey tells him, do any lasting damage to Basil's own military career, since his previous victories remain untouched and his "soldier's fame is far too surely raised / To be o'erthrown with one unhappy chance" (179). Only Basil's self-love is fatally wounded, and it is that unregulated self-love that causes his self-destruction. Thus Baillie uncovers the dominating passion of the masculine public sphere: an egotistic self-love that seeks only its personal aggrandizement, whether through machiavellian policy or military success. Both the Duke's policy, the profit-and-loss calculations of a "petty tradesman" (107), and Basil's desire for military glory finally overwhelm their possessors: the Duke is betrayed by his own followers, especially Gauriceio, while Basil is betrayed by his own love of fame. Basil's self-love can thus be seen as the ghostly, absent arm of Old Geoffrey: what men seek and most admire is that heroic arm which is but an empty sleeve.

Opposed to this masculine public sphere in Baillie's play is another sphere of action and value, what we might think of as a feminist or counter-public sphere, the space assigned to the absent mother. This space is filled by the Countess Albini, who "stands in" for Victoria's mother, as Victoria acknowledges: "Still call me child, and chide me as thou wilt. / O! would that I were such as thou couldst love! / Couldst dearly love! as thou didst love my mother" (111). The Countess Albini is Baillie's homage to Mary Wollstonecraft, to the ideal woman Wollstonecraft envisioned in *A Vindication of the Rights of Woman* published six years before Baillie wrote this play. She is the embodiment of rational judgment, the one who sees Victoria's faults, the one who unmasks at the ball, the one who can advise all the characters honestly and judiciously, the one who urges Rosinberg to persuade Basil to leave before permanent harm is done (131). She engages in the same revisioning of gender roles as did Wollstonecraft, advocating not the "poor ideal [ie. "most unreal"] tyranny" of feminine beauty but rather the domestic "duties of an useful state" (109) and a love grounded in "sincerity and truth" (130). In effect, she argues for what I described in my *Romanticism and Gender* as a family politics: the model of the well-managed home and an egalitarian family joined by the domestic affections as the paradigm for successful political government. As even the misogynist Rosinberg acknowledges, of all women, only the "brave Albini" can "so wisely rule, / Their subjects never from the yoke escape" (163).

But the Countess Albini "disdains" (163) to rule a masculine public sphere founded on self-interest; her reign is over a counter-public sphere, in this play associated with the interior or "closeted" spaces of the bedroom where she advises Victoria and the ballroom where she rightly warns Rosinberg. Her rule of reason and the "fettered" control of the emotions does not yet extend to the public spaces of the ramparts where Basil meets his mutinous soldiers or the forest where Basil declares his passionate love for Victoria. Significantly, it is in these "wild" or open spaces (of the town street, of the forest) that uncontrolled emotions reign. Basil brings his rebellious men to tears by threatening to shoot himself, while his own heart, as he leads Victoria aside during the hunt, is "bursting" (169) as he "walks up and down with hurried step, tossing about his arms in transport" (stage direction, 171). And it is outdoors, during a dark night, first in a graveyard and then in a hidden cave, that Basil, having learned that General Piscaro has alone defeated the King of France at Pavia, flings aside the sensible arguments of Old Geoffrey and rushes off in a frenzy of wounded self-love to kill himself.

The ending of the play is ambiguous. Basil dies, as his men weep beside him and Rosinberg passionately declares his love for him. Excessive masculine emotion is thus explicitly identified with death, as all who admired Basil "love him fall'n" (192)—love him who has fallen, but also, these concluding words imply, love him because he has fallen, because those who inhabit the masculine public sphere can love only themselves or that which is finally not there, the empty sleeve of Geoffrey's arm.

Victoria vows to spend her days grieving in a "dark, shaded cloister" (190), both assuming responsibility and doing penance for Basil's unregulated passion: "I've wrecked a brave man's honour" (175); "I have murder'd thee!" (189). But since we know Victoria to be innocent of any conscious effort to deceive Basil—and even suspect that she might well have returned his love sincerely in time, we cannot endorse her self-blame. While Victoria defines her coming life in a convent as "sad and lonely" and "cheerless" (190), might we not also see it as a possible return to a countersphere, a space where women reign? At the very least, her cloistered life endorses Albini's view that the female pursuit of the "worthless praise" and "silly adoration" of a male lover does "degrade a noble mind" (167). Finally, I would argue, Baillie suggests that it is men who destroy themselves through an excess of emotion and women who have the ability to free themselves from the follies and prejudices of their youth, to take up all standpoints, and to see a larger truth. As in **De Montfort** and many other plays by Joanna Baillie, it is finally the wise woman who combines rational prudence with sympathetic understanding and thus acts best for the nation.

Notes

All citations of Joanna Baillie are from *A Series of Plays: in which it is attempted to delineate the Stron-*

ger Passions of the Mind. Each Passion being the Subject of a Tragedy and a Comedy (London: T. Cadell, 1798). This volume is available in a facsimile reprint from Woodstock Books (Oxford and New York, 1990).

[1] Sir Walter Scott, letter to Miss Smith, March 4, 1808, in *Familiar Letters of Sir Walter Scott* (Boston: Houghton Mifflin & Co., 1894) 1: 99.

[2] Lord Byron, *Letters and Journals,* ed. Leslie Marchand (Cambridge: Harvard UP, 1976) 5: 203.

[3] Jürgen Habermas, *The Structural Transformation of the Public Sphere: An Inquiry into a Category of Bourgeois Society,* trans. Thomas Burger, with the assistance of Frederick Lawrence (Cambridge, MA: MIT Press, 1989) 56.

[4] Felski, *Beyond Feminist Aesthetics: Feminist Literature and Social Change* (Cambridge, MA: Harvard UP, 1989).

[5] Sandra Harding, "Rethinking Standpoint Epistemology: What is 'Strong Objectivity'?" in *Feminist Epistemologies,* ed. Linda Alcoff and Elizabeth Potter (New York: Routledge, 1992) 49-82.

Marjean D. Purinton (essay date 1994)

SOURCE: "Joanna Baillie's *Count Basil* and *De Monfort:* The Unveiling of Gender Issues," in *Romantic Ideology Unmasked: The Mentally Constructed Tyrannies in Dramas of William Wordsworth, Lord Byron, Percy Shelley, and Joanna Baillie,* University of Delaware Press and Associated University Presses, 1994, pp. 125-62.

[*In the following essay, Purinton places Baillie within the context of other women writers of her time and examines the overlap of political and gender issues in* Count Basil *and* De Monfort.]

Many of the feminist polemics in the 1790s expose a desire to unveil the fictions that have held women in bondage. "Custom," "habit," and "prejudice" are frequently shown to have enslaved women; oppression of women was thus known to take mental forms as well as economic and physical forms. In the **"Introductory Discourse"** to her **Series of Plays** (1798), Baillie emphasizes the mental forms inherent in her work: "The Drama improves us by the knowledge we acquire of our own minds, from the natural desire we have to look into the thoughts, and observe the behaviour of others."[1] While criticism of Baillie's dramas (and there has been but little) has centered on her depiction of human passions in psychological, dramaturgical, and aesthetic terms, I propose that her plays suggest ideological issues.[2]

Baillie's plays emanate from a period of polemical discourse focused upon gender relations and women's rights. The revolution in women's manners excited by writers like Mary Wollstonecraft, Mary Hays, Maria Edgeworth, Clara Reeve, and Hannah More parallels the political upheavals of the French Revolution and its aftermath. Gender issues are conflated with the historical events of the period and so too become politicized. This conflation of politics with the passions explicitly appears in Baillie's **"Introductory Discourse"**: "Those strong passions that, with small assistance from outward circumstances, work their way in the heart, till they become the tyrannical masters of it, carry on a similar operation in the breast of the Monarch, and the man of low degree" (42). Baillie here indicates that external social and political circumstances determine and often dictate internal emotions. She describes this relationship, existing in humankind at all stations, as a tyrannical master/slave dichotomy. Passions are engaged with the external conditions, and her language politicizes those external conditions.

The master/slave dichotomy is recapitulated, in both social and domestic dimensions, by the hegemony of monarch over subjects and by the hegemony of men over women. The passions to which Baillie alludes in her prefatory prose and that she dramatically depicts in her plays cannot be simply private, individualized psychological manifestations. The challenge to an ideology demanding an oppressed/oppressor dichotomy in political configurations appears as submerged content in Baillie's handling of gender issues. **Count Basil** and **De Monfort** dramatically question a mental structuration that accepts as absolute and fixed truth a gender relationship based on opposition. The geographical and historical displacements of both dramas actually mask the contemporary issues of gender relations embedded in each play; the plays are not about the past but the present, not about individual characters but about polemics and ideology. It is useful to examine first a social and intellectual discourse, and then subsequently to analyze Baillie's plays within that context.

An interest in collective passions and their ideological roots appears repeatedly in the prose polemics of the late eighteenth century. In the preface to *Maria; or, The Wrongs of Woman* (1798), Mary Wollstonecraft claims that her aim in this novel is to portray passions. She indicates that her history of Maria ought to be considered as that of woman in general rather than that of an individual character. According to Wollstonecraft, the main object of the novel is "the desire of exhibiting the misery and oppression, peculiar to women, that arise out of the partial laws and customs of society."[3] Critical of novels perpetuating the double standard by depicting heroines who are born immaculate and who act like goddesses, Wollstonecraft seeks to present the wrongs of woman, "matrimonial despotism of heart and conduct" (22), that degrade the mind.

Using different genres, Wollstonecraft and Baillie use human passions to explore an ideology that enslaves women. Imprisoned physically at the beginning of the novel, Maria comments that the "world [is] a vast prison, and women born slaves" (27). The narrative of Maria's escape from the edifice which imprisons her parallels the liberation of woman from a collective mentality dictated and maintained by man to keep her subservient.[4] Similarly, Baillie's plays present dramatically the mental and physical prisons in which Victoria and Jane De Monfort are held captive. The interiorization of the cave at the end of *Basil* and the convent at the end of *De Monfort,* like the prison in *Maria,* paradoxically reveal externalities of collectively derived oppressions. The passions that concern Wollstonecraft and Baillie are not solely individualized, psychological manifestations; they derive from custom, prejudice, and collective fictions. The passions reflect outward circumstances engendered by an ideology that keeps women subservient to men.[5]

Like Baillie's **"Introductory Discourse,"** Maria's narrative conflates political oppression with sexual oppression. Blaming men for the fictionalities and institutions which enslave women, Maria alleges that women are reduced to property controlled by fathers and husbands. Marriage is a powerfully oppressive prison. At the end of the novel, the judge expresses wariness about innovation and new-fangled notions that encroach upon the good old rules of male-directed conduct. He claims that English society does not want French principles in public and private life. Linking the French Revolution of politics with the feminist revolution of manners, the judge reminds woman of her duty (a male contrivance) to love and to obey the man chosen by her parents and relations. A victim of these prejudices, woman escapes one prison (patriarchal home) to be caged in another (male-dominated marriage). In *Letters Written during a Short Residence in Sweden, Norway and Denmark* (1796), Wollstonecraft politicizes gender issues in terms familiarly associated with the French Revolution. "Men," Wollstonecraft writes, "are domestic tyrants, considering them as fathers, brothers, or husbands; but there is a kind of interregnum between the reign of the father and husband, which is the only period of freedom and pleasure that the women enjoy.[6] Totally oppressed by men, women are free only during the short absence of direct masculine management.

Mary Hays also writes of the passions in her *Appeal to the Men of Great Britain in Behalf of Women* (1798). Dispelling judgment and condemnation usually associated with change, Hays argues that women must take charge of their own passions and then effect reform.[7] Concern for the passions surfaces in Hannah More's *Thoughts on the Importance of the Manners of the Great to General Society* (1788). Emphasizing the motives and principles of a woman, More contends that correcting mere surface-level behaviors "is only attacking symptoms, and neglecting the moral disease."[8] More argues that passion can be a freedom-denying tyranny; this tyranny appears dramatically in Baillie's plays in the configurations of gender issues.

Wollstonecraft's 1787 prose narrative *Mary, A Fiction* centralizes passions, and the misery and oppression created by laws and customs of a society defined and controlled by men. Like all women, Mary falls victim to an education that indelibly inculcates the triadic oath of love, honor, and obedience—the duty of submission to the benevolently powerful male. Given the opportunity of expanding her mind beyond the proper domestic and social graces through conversations with male philosophers during her trip to Lisbon, Mary discovers a new world. She grows excited from viewing new modes of thought. Examining new opinions, she reads voraciously and questions her prejudices. According to the narrator, Mary sees "that apparently good and solid arguments might take their rise from different points of view."[9] The impetus of the feminist revolution involves expanding the female mind individually and reconstituting social mentality collectively. In Letter IV of *Letters Written during a Short Residence in Sweden, Norway and Denmark,* Wollstonecraft remarks: "As the mind is cultivated, and taste gains ground, the passions become stronger, and rest on something more stable than casual sympathies of the moment" (35). The passions are inextricably connected with a collective mentality, and that collective mentality is inherently political. The passions on which Baillie's plays focus suggest submerged meanings when we consider them in the context of the feminist issues of the 1790s. The plays, the novel, and the feminist polemics all project the mentally contrived tyranny from which women must seek to liberate themselves.

Many feminist polemics of the late-eighteenth century question an ideology which posits men in a superior position over women and which keeps women in subjection by false notions about femininity. In *A Vindication of the Rights of Woman with Strictures on Political and Moral Subjects* (1792), Wollstonecraft blames that state of womanhood on a false system of education which reifies a separate sphere and inferior position for women. Wrongly believing that this maintains cultural order and happiness, women inculcate it upon their daughters from generation to generation. The education of female youth perpetuates an enslaving cycle of subordination and dependency. The treatise indicts the educational system codified by men who,

> considering females rather as women than human creatures, have been more anxious to make them alluring mistresses than affectionate wives and rational mothers; and the understanding of the sex has been so bubbled by this specious homage, that the civilized women of the present century, with a

few exceptions, are only anxious to inspire love, when they ought to cherish a nobler ambition, and by their abilities and virtues exact respect.[10]

Wollstonecraft advocates equality between the sexes so that women can achieve a realization of "self" which the present system denies them. Men, however, resist any attempts to destroy a gender hegemony they believe is divinely created and biologically endowed. Counterattacking any plans to change gender relations, men strive to keep woman in her place, and, unfortunately, she often complies. Wollstonecraft claims: "Men endeavour to sink us still lower, merely to render us alluring objects for a moment; and women, intoxicated by the adoration which men, under the influence of their senses, pay them, do . . . seek" to liberate themselves from this bondage (8). Gender relations constitute a social and political construct that humankind has created, deified, made absolute and fixed, and to which it has become enslaved.[11]

Hays argues that from the cradle, hypocrisy and disguise are inculcated upon women. As youth, women are not allowed to tell lies; yet they paradoxically receive encouragement in falsehood (*Appeal to the Men of Great Britain in Behalf of Women,* 205-6). Wollstonecraft explains: "Women are told from their infancy, and taught by the example of their mothers, that a little knowledge of human weakness, justly termed cunning, softness of temper, outward obedience, and a scrupulous attention to a puerile kind of propriety, will obtain for them the protection of man" (*A Vindication of the Rights of Woman,* 19). These lessons of propriety and social custom render woman dependent on man, subject to his control, and subordinate to his status. Hays and Wollstonecraft imply that on the stage of life, women must live the fictional roles prescribed by male directors and written by male playwrights. Baillie's dramatic women struggle against the culturally defined roles that real and fictional women were expected to play.

Wollstonecraft questions this deification of man that renders him lord and master over woman. Conflating gender subservience with political subjection, Wollstonecraft uses political argument to question the truth that maintains that women are inferior to men: "Till it is proved that the courtier, who servilely resigns the birthright of a man, is not a moral agent, it cannot be demonstrated that woman is essentially inferior to man because she has always been subjugated" (*A Vindication of the Rights of Woman,* 37). The mind, Wollstonecraft argues, has no inherent sexual distinction. Gender is imposed on mentality by those who seek to use it as a tool of tyranny and oppression. Female mental limitations are mere fictionalities accepted by women as a result of their conditioning (*A Vindication of the Rights of Woman,* 42). Wollstonecraft observes: "Taught from their infancy that beauty is woman's sceptre, the mind shapes itself to the body, and, roaming round its gilt cage, only seeks to adorn its prison" (44). *A Vindication of the Rights of Woman* advocates an emancipation of the minds of women from the slavery to which men, like the dominion of tyrants, have subjected them. Sexual difference is itself a fiction. As Wollstonecraft argues, "The sexual distinction which men have so warmly insisted upon, is arbitrary" (193).

Similarly, Hays maintains that "mind, as has been finely said, is of no sex" (104); therefore, "it is not in the power of education or art to unsex it" (187). Hays argues that education, particularly in those areas generally relegated to the masculine sphere of knowledge, can offer no threat to the so-called feminine mind. The concept of a feminine mind is a male-constructed fiction. In *Strictures on the Modern System of Female Education with a View of the Principles and Conduct Prevalent among Women of Rank and Fortune* (1799), Hannah More argues that the Creator had created differences between male and female minds; she nonetheless concedes that of "the *degree* of that native difference a just estimate can never be formed till the understandings of women are made the most of . . . [till] their minds shall be allowed to reach to that measure of perfection . . . which their Maker intended they should attain."[12] Noting Christianity as the equalizer and leveler of sexual differences, More points out that in Christ Jesus, "there is neither 'rich nor poor,' 'bond nor free,' so there is neither 'male nor female'" (2:30).

A Vindication of the Rights of Woman encourages women to effect a revolution in female manners. By reforming themselves, women will reform the world. Wollstonecraft maintains that "the most salutary effects tending to improve mankind might be expected from a Revolution in female manners" (192). Hays similarly equates political and domestic revolution: "It is astonishing however, that principles of private and domestic justice, do not at least keep pace in the minds of men, with those of a public and political nature" (288). Echoes of the French Revolution can be found in Hays's reminder that there is no husband who may not frequently pull the reins of authority too tight, perhaps so tight as to crack the whole domestic machine (see 289). Just as political tyrants have been toppled when they have yanked too tightly their reins of authority, and just as the political authorities of monarchical government were beheaded in France, so domestic tyrants and a male-determined social machinery can be overthrown.

In *Letters for Literary Ladies: To Which Is Added, "An Essay on the Noble Science of Self-Justification"* (1795), Maria Edgeworth also advocates a gradual revolution in female manners: "It must take a length of time to alter associations and opinions, which, if not *just,* are at least *common* in our sex."[13] Edgeworth emphasizes a total change of manners of society (for both men and women), and the revolution about which she writes is mental. She reminds readers that "in the mind as well as in the body, the highest pitch of disease is often attended with an unconsciousness of its existence" (Letter 5: Caroline to Lady V———," 60). For women, an awareness of the powerful ideology that held them in bondage constituted an important first step toward their freedom.

Clara Reeve's *Plans of Education: With Remarks on the systems of Other Writers: In a Series of Letters Between Mrs. Darnford and Her Friends* (1792) is often considered an acceptance of the prejudices against which Hays, Wollstonecraft, and other feminists wrote, yet even here Reeve advocates a reform for women. In the preface to her *Plans,* Reeve claims: "I rejoice to see that there is a spirit of reformation arisen among us, and hope it will proceed, and be effectual to the whole body of the common people of this land."[14] Although she fears radical revolution and although her methods of reform differ from those of the feminists, Reeve nonetheless agrees that change must uncover the root of educational deficiencies. She maintains that, "when the fountain is poisoned, the streams are polluted, and all who drank [*sic*] of them are distempered and infected" (29). Specific references to the French Revolution reveal Reeve's fear of revolution as a corrective for social and political ills. Still, she sees the French Revolution as a warning to kings, both political and domestic, against impoverishing and oppressing their people: "It warns them to reform the errors and corruptions of their governments, and to prevent the necessity of a revolution" (214). Feminists such as Wollstonecraft and Hays would allege that the warning might be justly and aptly applied to the heads of households as well as to the heads of governments.

More advocates a conservative reformation in female manners, education, and imagination. Although she describes the present educational program in England as "a defective system of society" (*Strictures on the Modern System of Female Education,* 2:29), she cautiously urges only a gradual reformation of that system rather than its elimination (see 1:22-23). In *Thoughts on the Importance of the Manners of the Great to General Society* (1788), More argues that reformation must begin with the great, for their example will change the habits and actions of the poor. As More contends, this top-down method of reform permeates the social foundations on which customs rest (see 99-102). Reform that merely exchanges one restrictive doctrine for another provides a superficial remedy. In her own way, More advocates ideological reform.

All these writers urge a reformation that challenges the unquestioned acceptance of oppressor/oppressed gender relations. Both Hays and Wollstonecraft beg readers to resist the prevailing opinions and customs deeply rooted in their culture. Wollstonecraft argues that readers resist "being the modest slaves of opinion" (*A Vindication of the Rights of Woman,* 51). In the advertisement of her treatise, Hays recommends a gentle emancipation from error "deeply rooted" and "fondly cherished" by all humanity. Hays claims, "The gradual emancipation of women, shackled and enslaved by a thousand absurd prejudices,—would in this enlightened age, produce the most salutary effects" (277). Edgeworth writes that "those who depend merely on the force of habit and of prejudice alone, expose themselves to perpetual danger" ("Answer to . . . ," *Letters for Literary Ladies,* 60-61). Habit and prejudice enslave women continually. Reeve claims: "The false sentiments, false refinements, and false systems of modern times, have counteracted the laws of nature and reason, and condemned a great number of women to a life of perpetual celibacy" (120). It comes as no surprise to see Baillie's major female characters, Victoria and Jane De Monfort, commit themselves to lifetime celibacy in religious hermitages.

Hays, like Wollstonecraft, challenges the culture's acceptance of a woman's subjection to the power and authority of her husband. She argues that the unreasonable power which posits male as superior to female is a fabrication of man, codified by tyrannical, unjust, and vexatious clauses against poor, defenseless women (see 12-13). She demonstrates that God created men and women equal in rank and utility, an equality that no human laws can supersede (see 21). Equating political and sexual tyranny, Hays claims that men, like barbarous tyrants, try to fashion women to suit their own passions and prejudices (see 31-32). Like Wollstonecraft, Hays maintains that women are held in perpetual bondage by the system of education that ensures the survival and transmission of male-created fictions. Women are, she says, enveloped by an artificial cloud that prevents their minds from receiving an enlightened education. She writes: "Of all the systems,—if indeed a bundle of contradictions and absurdities may be called a system,—which human nature in its moments of intoxication has produced; that which men have contrived with a view to forming the minds, and regulating the conduct of women, is perhaps the most completely absurd" (47). Men construct arbitrary authority to perpetuate a double standard of morality and behavior. To please her husband is a woman's duty. Such a fiction, writes Hays, "is perhaps as unfortunate a system of politics in morals, as ever was introduced for degrading the human species" (56). This male-determined system reduces virtue to "a mere political engine in the hands of the most powerful" (60). In "An Essay on the Noble Science of Self-Justification" (1795), Edgeworth questions the arbitrary authority constituted in linguistic structures. She writes: "Right and wrong, if we go to the foundation of things, are, as casuists tell us, really words of very dubious signification, perpetually varying with custom and fashion."[15] Edgeworth states that opinion alters the signification of words like right and wrong.

Men brandish such labels as though they were externally derived, absolute values so that they may keep women dependent on them.

The new systems of education advocated by feminists like Hays and Wollstonecraft offer women knowledge—a direct challenge to male superiority. Hays points out the male aversion to the feminine acquisition of knowledge. She challenges women to act against the erroneous principle upon which men construct their whole system: "That men are superior beings, when compared with women; and that consequently, nature and reason, invest them with authority over the weaker sex" (95). This so-called truth, she argues, constituted in the language of prejudice, remains to be proven; it survives as an unexamined opinion. Men perpetuate this fiction and the systems that encode it because they fear that women, once their eyes are opened to their natural equality and its consequences, would not so tamely submit to the cruel injustice with which they are treated. Unwilling to share their power, men keep it to themselves and codify it as their own separate sphere (see 96-99). Under the present social configuration, women are chained and blindfolded with respect to their own rights and capabilities (see 100-104). Education can help rend asunder the "mysterious veil formed by law, by prejudice, and by precedent" (100). Edgeworth notes that although they are not inherently inferior to men, women are forced to see things always through a veil, "or cease to be women" ("Letter From a Gentleman to His Friend Upon the Birth of a Daughter," *Letters for Literary Ladies,* 7). In "Essay on Education and Manners," a section of *Plans of Education,* Reeve acknowledges that education and experience have the capacity for drawing "back the veil that blinded them [young female students], and shews them the defects of all those things they once admired" (24). The feminist polemics of the 1790s recurrently express a desire to unveil the fictions disguised as truths that have held them in bondage. Baillie's dramas likewise unveil these historical issues; the feminist polemics of the 1790s are inscribed within **Count Basil** and **De Monfort.**

Feminist writers of the 1790s hope to redefine the female role and function. As helpmates for men, women should be companions and equals to their masculine counterparts—not inferiors or slaves. To achieve this repositioning, Hays and Wollstonecraft recognize that custom and prejudice are powerful sovereigns and that when they are "stamped upon the human mind, leave traces never to be entirely effaced, however differently modified" (*Appeal to the Men of Great Britain in Behalf of Women,* 128). Hays argues that women must bear responsibility for accepting these customs as assumed authority. Women are driven to acquiesce from prudence and necessity and not out of inferiority, she reminds readers. Men's claims of superiority and authority are founded on a presumption of pride, a love of unrestrained dominion and pleasure (see 138-39). Subjection is not necessary for the happiness of either sex. Edgeworth demonstrates similarly how custom has restricted women from achieving the fullest possible development of their mental capabilities (see *Letters for Literary Ladies,* 5-10). Women think they are happy because custom dictates subjugation as happiness. Feminist writers of the 1790s advocate ideological changes rather than superficial modifications. As a first step toward ideological revolution, Hays suggests that society must reform its habits and expel its prejudices. The double standard which relegates women to one of two positions—drudges or ornaments—cannot continue. Hays points out that men are guided by the "complexion of the times" (187) in their ideas about women. Hays exclaims:

> But when men try to stamp a marked inferiority on the whole sex,—when they insinuate that they are made of baser materials, or mixed with more alloy,—it is time, perhaps, to endeavour at least, to stop the progress of a species of folly, which has already taken too deep root among mankind; much to the injury of the best interests of society. (203-4)

As Hays argues, the ideological foundation of a double standard is so thoroughly embedded within all cultural customs that only revolution at the ideological level will render gender relations cooperative rather than oppositional. *Count Basil* and *De Monfort* represent and mediate these cultural customs.

As we have seen, *The Borderers* dramatically presents ideas expressed in the political polemics of the 1790s. The prose tracts and Wordsworth's tragedy challenge an ideology generating a futile cycle of revolution/restoration, tyranny/rebellion, oppressed/oppressor. The feminist polemics of the 1790s attack the same bifurcated ideology. Gender issues presented in the prose, including double standards, separate spheres, and sexual subjugation, appear as latent content in *Count Basil* and *De Monfort.* Both the plays and the polemics demonstrate the mental forms of oppression to which women were subjected.

Count Basil is set in Mantua during the sixteenth century, a time and place that seem far removed from British politics of the 1790s. The purported focus of the play is the detaining of Basil's forces from participation in the battle of Pavia, a concern that seems to bear no import to gender issues. The contemporaneousness of the play's ideological concerns is submerged as latent content, and the historical relevance to English politics is dramatically displaced. The play opens with a pageant led by Princess Victoria to Saint Francis's shrine. Even before the first lines are spoken, Victoria is associated with religious ceremony, a dominion often ascribed to the feminine sphere of activities. Described as

"the fairest of the fair,"[16] the beautiful princess is making a generous contribution to the shrine in thanks for the recent restoration of her father's health. The dutiful daughter is paying homage on behalf of Mantua's political patriarch and her familial patriarch.

Led by Count Basil, a general rumored to be a cold and demanding martinet, a military procession interrupts and usurps the religious parade. The military (masculine) train pauses and pays obeisance to the female, religious one as the two cross. The polarities are vividly depicted: masculine activity, public power, and force are juxtaposed to feminine passivity, private utility, and obedience. The female procession represents submissiveness in the form of worship. The male procession represents dominion in the form of might. In this opening scene, separate spheres encoded in gender-specific activities and reified by the political system are vividly depicted before either Victoria or Basil utter a word. The descriptions that observers of both processions reinforce these bifurcations: Victoria is a fair, beautiful princess; Basil is a tough, commanding general. As heads of their respective sexes, each symbolizes an aggregate entrapped by a mental structuration that engenders the bifurcations they represent and enact.

The opening scene depicts a cultural mentality in which the sexes function in separate and unequal spheres. The idea of dissolving gender dichotomies was a dangerous concept. In *Strictures on the Modern System of Female Education,* More adamantly opposes gender relations based on anything different from what the intersection of the two processions in *Count Basil* reify:

> Each sex has its proper excellencies, which would be lost were they melted down into the common character by the fusion of the new philosophy. Why should we do away distinctions which increase the mutual benefits and satisfactions of life? Whence, but by carefully preserving the original marks of difference stamped by the hand of the Creator, would be derived the superior advantage of mixed society? (2:21)

Wollstonecraft would chuckle at the symbolism represented in the two processions, each marked by its gender and its gender-specific activities. The men pay honor and obeisance to the women; this action simply reifies the women's subservient position. Wollstonecraft could be referring to the attention Victoria receives from Basil's troops when she maintains, "I lament that women are systematically degraded by receiving the trivial, attentions, which men think it manly to pay to the sex, when, in fact, they are insultingly supporting their own superiority" (*A Vindication of the Rights of Woman,* 57). Emphasizing the inequality of this culturally defined existence and its utter fictionality, Hays argues that sexual equality is a subject that "necessarily involves many public and political, as well as private and domestic concerns" (100). The political issue of sexual equality in England during the 1790s marches before the reader's eyes in the opening processional scene of ***Count Basil.***

One of Basil's officers, Valtomer, comments on the striking beauty of Princess Victoria, and he claims that she deserves to be privileged even among princesses. Since "she is too noble for a petty court" (83), she deserves the honor of the emperor's throne. Enthusiastically, Valtomer exclaims: "She should be queen of revelry and show" (83). Another officer, Frederick describes Victoria as "the goddess of delight" (83) and protests that "it is treason but to call her woman; / She's a divinity, and should be worshipp'd" (83). Laughing at the officers' desires to have the living beauty of the female procession they have just observed captured by a painter, Basil's friend Rosinberg reminds them that "ev'ry woman hath some 'witching charm, / If that she be not proud, or captious" (84).

The masculine conversation reveals the degradation women suffer under the protection of an ideology based on bifurcations. Woman is simultaneously divine—an object of worship—and bewitching—an object of derision. Her beauty and her charm are her prized possessions, and both may be used as powerful female weapons. In defense of women, Hays addresses this allegation:

> And if indeed, women do avail themselves of the only weapons they are permitted to wield, can they be blamed? Undoubtedly not; since they are compelled to it by the injustice and impolicy of men. Petty treacheries—mean subterfuge—whining and flattery—feigned submission—and all the dirty little attendants, which compose the endless train of low cunning; if not commendable, cannot with justice be very severely censured, when practiced by women. Since alas!—The weak have no other arms against the strong! Since alas!—Necessity acknowledges no law, but her own! (91).

Hays argues that women are taught to cultivate and to exercise such artful snares. Their position demands this code of behavior. The officers' conversation confirms this expectation. Men, as well as women, play their artificial roles according to the scripts of the cultural mentality. Wollstonecraft confirms what Baillie's play depicts: "Women likewise acquire, from a supposed necessity, an equally artificial mode of behaviour" (*A Vindication of the Rights of Woman*, 131).

Basil pretends not to be moved by Victoria's beauty. His interest is revealed, however, by his seemingly idle comment about the fretted gold olive branch which she bore in her hand. In a quiet voice, Basil asks:

> Mark'd you her hand?
> I did not see her hand,
> And yet she wav'd it twice.
>
>   (83)

When Rosinberg inquires about his friend's pensiveness, Basil further admires Victoria, "her form, her face, her motion, ev'rything" (84). He vividly recalls first seeing her enchanting smile.

Disturbed at Basil's infatuation with the princess, Rosinberg confesses that the general's praise displeases him. For a man like Basil, Rosinberg explains, love will prove "no easy guest" (86). Basil scoffs at his friend's concern. Can he not admire feminine beauty and perfection without falling in love? "From early youth," Basil assures his friend, "war has my mistress been" (86), and he has no intention of forsaking her now. The joys of love were not made for him. Basil substitutes "hasty flashes of contending steel" for the "glances from my love," and he exchanges "the cannon's roar" for "soft breathing sighs" (86). Masculine work (war) is separated from and even substituted for domestic activity (love). For Basil, the two spheres operate exclusive of one another. He privileges war above love and metaphorically transfigures war into love. He privileges public duty above private desire. In doing so, Basil represses female sexuality as an otherness and a baseness to which his lofty and great position is immune.

Rosinberg is also concerned that Basil has not yet given orders for the troops to march. They are expected to meet allied forces and together to battle against forces representing Francis I. He longs to leave Mantua and its delightful temptations. What is this new and powerful charm, Rosinberg asks, that affects Basil's mind? Why in the midst of war does he "let [his] mind be haunted by a woman" (87)? Were Basil to die in battle, Rosinberg protests, a woman would not care. Basil would represent to her a mere battle statistic. For Rosinberg, the only constant woman is his mother—actually his aunt. In his relationship with this woman, Rosinberg experiences no sexual oppositions: "Rivals we are not, though our love is one" (88). Rosinberg too represses female sexuality by relegating all private, emotive, nurturing functions to a mother figure, a woman to whom he returns after war and public duty have been fulfilled. This woman is not his equal. She functions as a housekeeper and a tranquilizer, and as an unconditionally bonding parent whose sphere revolves in a separate rotation from Rosinberg's political activity. While Basil transfigures love into war, Rosinberg conflates conjugal love with parental love as though they were equal and synonymous. It is his way of retaining patriarchal control over a potential rival, an independent female will.

Rosinberg guards against any rivals in his friendship with Basil, and he resists any intrusion of the independent female will. Suppressing Basil's interest in Victoria, Rosinberg reminds his young friend of their earlier experience during a public festivity in Vienna, a city whose reputation for prostitution in the sixteenth century made it infamous. On that occasion, Basil cautioned Rosinberg against being caught "with some gay dame, / To laugh and ogle, and befool thyself" (89). Such undignified activity, Basil says, "suits not with a man of thy endowments" (89). Both Rosinberg and Basil have cast themselves as "unsexed" men whose "divine" and lofty natures do not require common carnal and sensual activity with women. As males, Rosinberg and Basil are privileged over females; as males of high military rank and "higher parts" (82), they privilege themselves over other men. Reifying their superior positions, Rosinberg's language also veils the homoerotic potential in their relationship.[17]

Gender issues are explored in the interplay between two sets of rivals and a brother/sister relationship in *De Monfort.* These seemingly individual conflicts function as a paradigm for the battle of the sexes on a cultural level. Without informing his sister Jane, the haughty De Monfort travels by a secret route to his quarters in Amberg, Germany. De Monfort remains enigmatic about his motive for this sudden visit, but he confesses that he seeks freedom. A malcontent, De Monfort is a man of enormous pride and cynical suspicion. Like Manfred, Werner, Cenci, and Oswald, he harbors within himself some secret sin, some source of guilt and remorse. Shunning associations with friends, servants, and his sister, De Monfort prefers isolation. He is greatly annoyed at the merry intrusion of his friends, the Count and Countess Freberg, shortly after his arrival in Amberg. His melancholic temperament makes him see life dualistically. Reality is either life-embracing or life-denying, giving or taking. He immediately sees the worst side of human nature and assumes diabolical schemes are personally inflicted on him. His actions betray a constantly wary and distrustful mental orientation.

When De Monfort learns that the Marquis Rezenvelt, a lifelong rival whom he detests and envies, is also in Amberg, he is violently distressed. He claims that this "cursed reptile" haunts him and seeks his demise.[18] De Monfort is even more anxious when he discovers that Freberg has befriended Rezenvelt. Without disclosing the cause for this long-term hatred, De Monfort alleges that Rezenvelt's presence makes him "mad" (323). As with Beatrice's protestation of "mad" in *The Cenci,* the meaning of "mad" is problematic. For some unrevealed reason, De Monfort is obviously angry. The heightened mystery surrounding this rivalry, which Rezenvelt seems not to acknowledge, prompts readers to question De Monfort's psychological stability and the cultural pressures that help characterize his mentality. His soliloquy in act 1 indicates that Rezenvelt plays the part of the friend only to mask his deceit and his hatred:

> Malignant villain!
> The venom of thy mind is rank and devilish,
> And thin the film that hides it.
>
> (323)

Using serpent imagery, De Monfort maintains that Rezenvelt's mask of friendship covers a fiend-like mind. The fact that De Monfort's characterization of Rezenvelt's mind may be aptly applied to his own prompts readers to consider the possibility of a hidden cultural poison affecting a collective mentality and that this is the latent content presented in the early scenes of the play. A poisoned collective mentality pervades the court in *Count Basil* as well. The Duke of Mantua, Victoria's father, is secretly allied with the forces of Francis I who oppose Basil and his troops. It is in the Duke's interest, therefore, to detain the love-stricken Basil in Mantua and thus prevent his forces from joining those on the battlefield. The Duke encourages Victoria and her ladies to use their persuasive powers in convincing Basil to remain in Mantua longer. Significantly, Victoria's first spoken words in the play constitute an apology for her lengthy procession and any delay it may have caused Basil's soldiers. She betrays an ideology that places her in a subservient role to that of the men; it also puts the female, religious ceremony in a secondary position to that of the masculine, military march. Rosinberg quickly asserts that they must not linger, for they face

> a thousand masked foes
> Some under show of rich luxurious feasts,
> Gay, sprightly pastime, and high-zested
>   game;—
> Nay, some, my gentle ladies, true it is,
> The very worst and fellest of the crew,
> In fair alluring shape of beauteous dames,
> Do such a barrier form t'oppose their way,
> As few men may o'ercome.
>
> (93)

The masked, disguised, wicked foe to which Rosinberg refers is woman, and the game posing as the barrier to masculine activities of war is love.

Isabella, Victoria's attendant, asks whether Rosinberg has suffered much from this wicked foe. Indignant, Victoria spouts:

> If love a tyrant be,
> How dare his humble chained votaries,
> To tell such rude and wicked tales of him
>
> (94)

Friend and governess to Victoria, the Countess of Albini is convinced that Rosinberg has never truly loved, despite Rosinberg's protestations that he has experienced love's bondage. Importantly, the characters' banter about love is expressed in political terms: love is tyranny and holds its victims in bondage. The tyranny, however, is mental. Responding to Victoria's assertion that to call love bondage constitutes pedantry, Basil adds: "These are the fetters that enchain the mind, / But such as must not, cannot be unloos'd" (94). Victoria replies: "No, not unloos'd, but yet one day relax'd, / To grant a lady's suit, unus'd to sue" (94). Someday, perhaps, the mental fetters binding men and women to prescribed gender roles defined by separate and unequal spheres may be relaxed so that ideological change may occur. Both sexes are presently constrained. Love is a figure representing the configuration of gender relations based on a politically oppressive ideology.

Escorting Basil to the Duke's picture gallery, Victoria seizes the opportunity to encourage Basil to remain in Mantua another day. Basil protests that she asks the very thing "a soldier may not give" (97), the "lifeblood from [his] heart" (96). Eventually, however, Victoria persuades him. Using her feminine, artful snares, she convinces Basil that his refusing her suit constitutes an offense. "By heav'n I'll grant it," Basil says, resignedly, "I'll do anything, / Say but thou art no more offended with me" (97). His promise, Victoria claims, is his pardon. Wollstonecraft cites this kind of manipulation as a source of power women fail to perceive in themselves: "Women . . . sometimes boast of their weakness, cunningly obtaining power by playing on the weakness of men; and they may well glory in their illicit sway, for, like Turkish bashaws, they have more real power than their masters" (*A Vindication of the Rights of Woman,* 40). Gender relations are like military operations in which words and looks are used as the weapons of destruction and imprisonment. In this war, as Rosinberg feared, Victoria wins the first battle.

In soliloquy, Basil convinces himself that the divine Victoria must be beyond human, sensual love: "No man on earth is worthy of her love— / Ah! if she could, how blest a man were he" (98). He elevates Victoria to the level of a goddess, untouchable and unreachable by human hands. Confronted by Rosinberg, Basil confesses how impossible it is for him not to yield to Victoria's invitation to linger another day in Mantua. Disgusted, Rosinberg pronounces Basil "weaker than a child" (100). Dismissing the insult, Basil cries:

> By heav'n! I feel a new-born pow'r within me
> Shall make me twenty-fold the man I've been
> Before this fated day
>
> (100)

Victoria essentially releases from Basil a repressed sexuality, a masculinity that his friendship with Rosinberg or his dedication to the military cannot satisfy. Ironically, the repressed masculinity betrays characteristics relegated to the feminine sphere: emotional rather than intellectual, nurturing rather than confrontational, passive rather than active. Baillie's play dramatically depicts the dissolving and blurring of gender dichotomies that writers of the 1790s feared might occur as a result of the revolution in feminine manners.

Rosinberg notes how this ill-fated day makes Basil "other than thy former self" (100). Assuredly, Basil is absorbing the formerly alienated otherness. Rosinberg hopes that Basil's flirtation and infatuation will not substantially alter his commitment to the masculine sphere: "It cannot change thee / To ought I shall not love" (100). Exchanging vows with Rosinberg, Basil pledges to be worthy of his friend's noble heart: "I would not be the man thou couldst not love / For an Imperial Crown" (100). Fostered by an ideology based on double standards, these homoerotic inclinations have created strong and inflexible mental shackles, even though Victoria's brief presence has offered the enslaved Basil a sense of their becoming loosened bindings. As the Duke and his minister Gauriceio discuss their clandestine plan of detaining Basil in Mantua, both agree to use Victoria to further their political ploy. She is unaware of her exploitation. Revealing an ideology that privileges men above women, the Duke says of Victoria:

> She is a woman;
> Her mind, as suits the sex, too weak and
>   narrow
> To relish deep-laid schemes of policy.
>
> (101)

Victoria, as the Duke reports, would hold such schemes in "high derision" (101). He claims that she "will not serve us but with bandag'd eyes" (101). Like many women who are objects of masculine machinations, Victoria is blind to her function and role. The Duke characterizes women as objects, mindless forms to be molded by men to shapes and schemes that complement their masculine political activity. In the Duke's scheme, the political and domestic worlds collide, and Victoria is subservient in both. Even when she accepts a separate sphere of activity, woman is not allowed to exert leadership within "her" sphere. Hays notes the arbitrainess of these public and private spheres: "And though it is often alleged, that the public influence of the men, is balanced by the private influence of the women . . . it is in the private and domestic scenes of life, above all others, where women are supposed to be obliged to act with the greatest humility and circumspection" (89).

The mentality represented by the Duke recapitulates the ideology which More wants to see left intact, despite surface level modifications:

> Of the different powers of the sexes, one may
> venture, perhaps, to assert, that women have equal

parts, but are inferior in wholeness of mind in the integral understanding: that though a superior woman may possess single faculties in equal perfection, yet there is commonly a juster proportion in the mind of a superior man. (*Strictures on the Modern System of Female Education,* 2:26)

The Duke similarly privileges the male as mentally superior to the female. Women's minds are machinery to be deployed by the "master-spirits in the world" (101). They are "but as tools his secret ends to work,/ Who hath the skill to use them" (101).

Victoria easily falls into her father's schemes, for she has already been victimized by an education that preaches obedience to masculine authority-figures—fathers and husbands. Wollstonecraft points out the dangerous tyranny parents exercise over their children. Arguing that unconditional obedience is the catchword of tyrants of every description, Wollstonecraft claims that parental affection "is but a pretext to tyrannize where it can be done with impunity" (*A Vindication of the Rights of Woman,* 150-51). Parents demand blind obedience, and females, in particular, remain too much under the dominion of their parents. Wollstonecraft concludes: "A slavish bondage to parents cramps every faculty of the mind" (155). Woman's mental limitations are held intact by an ideology which refuses to allow her to acquire knowledge of her own enslavement. Her vision is continually impaired by the metaphorical veil she wears. Hays argues that women, awakened to a sense of their injuries, "would behold with astonishment and indignation, the arts which had been employed, to keep them in a state of perpetual babyism" (97). It is in the Duke's political and domestic interests to keep Victoria blindfolded about her compliance with the scheme to detain Basil and to affect the upcoming battle. He cannot afford rebellious soldiers or a rebellious daughter.

The Duke storms at Gauriecio's warning about potential resistance, uprisings, and even civil war among the northern states. Indignant, the Duke asks if this is how "ungrateful miscreants thus return / The many favours of [his] princely grace" (104). Speaking as though his rebellious states were his children, the Duke rages:

> 'Tis ever thus indulgence spoils the base,
> Raising up pride, and lawless turbulence,
> Like noxious vapours from the fulsome marsh
> When morning shines upon it—
> Did I not lately, with parental care,
> When dire invaders their destruction
>   threaten'd,
> Provide them all with means of their defence?
> Did I not, as a mark of gracious trust,
> A body of their vagrant youth select
> To guard my sacred person? Till that day
> An honour never yet allow'd their race.

> Did I not suffer them upon their suit
> T'establish manufactures in their towns?
> And after all some chosen soldiers spare
> To guard the blessings of interiour peace?
>   (104-5)

On the surface level, the Duke's tirade refers to the rebellious northern subjects who seek independence from the Duke's domination. Submerged, however, we see operating the same ideology that holds women enslaved to the patriarchal hierarchy. With the controlling image of the generous but abused parent, the Duke's arguments might have been directed toward rebellious women as well as those northern political agitators. Much like these subjects, women had been held in bondage sugarcoated to make them feel beholden and indebted to their captors. Consider the antifeminist arguments that enumerate the money, gifts, blessings, and advantages men provide women—much like those the Duke cites as favors he has bestowed on the ungrateful northern upstarts. Such indulgences only provide masters with the means of yanking the chains binding their servants, for gratitude is a strong shackle. The tyrant/slave dichotomy of rulers and subjects in political situations recapitulates and parallels the tyrant/slave dichotomy created by culturally prescribed gender roles. Sexual oppression is political oppression, and the same ideology dictates both.

Like insurgents, women seek a release of their independent will. Masculine and princely gifts or favors demand submission in return. Both women and the patriots wish to be independent of any bondage or gimmicks inducing submission to others. The Duke responds by reifying the "chain of being" notion that men and rulers, women and subjects, each have a station to occupy:

> But they beyond their proper sphere would
>   rise;
> Let them their lot fulfil as we do ours;
> Society of various parts is form'd;
> They are its grounds, its mud, its sediment,
> And we the mantling top which crowns the
>   whole.
> Calm, steady labour is their greatest bliss,
> To aim at higher things beseems them not.
>   (105-6)

The Duke's rationalization betrays the status quo response to political and gender rebellion: stay in your place; attempts to move beyond your clearly defined sphere or to rise above your permanently designated position wreak havoc and chaos. Do not tamper with divine order.[19] The Duke hopes to squelch such aspirations by reinforcing the routine of labor and by keeping potential troublemakers in ignorance. Calling such an existence "bliss," the Duke hopes to control their actions by regulating their minds. He bids Gauriecio to give the traitors a promise of relief which he has no intention to keep. Like the political patriots, women are deceived by false words and masked intentions that they perceive as genuine.

At the same time that the Duke maneuvers subjects of his kingdom like pawns in a chess game, Victoria orders away the actual chess game she and Isabella have been playing. She turns from maneuvering chess pieces to maneuvering rhetoric in a banter with Isabella about men and love. Seeking a verbal checkmate, Victoria promises: "May men no more look foolish in my presence" (108). Victoria confesses her abhorrence for the alluring and powerful beauty of women who use it playfully and deceitfully to conquer men. Victoria claims she would rather be "a plain, good, simple, fireside dame" (109) than one whose

> flatt'ring words and tuneful praise,
> Sighs, tender glances, and obsequious service,
> Attend her presence.
>
> (109)

Albini sarcastically quips:

> And is, indeed, a plain domestick dame,
> Who fills the duties of an useful state,
> A being of less dignity, than she
> Who vainly on her transient beauty builds
> A little poor ideal tyranny?
>
> (109)

Endorsing genuineness and usefulness as characteristics more desirable in women than artificiality and ornamentation, Albini reminds Victoria that she who finds her self-esteem only in others' admiration "is the very servant of her slaves" (109). At times, Albini continues, she may deceive herself and "o'er men she may a childish pow'r exert, / Which not ennobles but degrades her state" (109). Victoria chides Albini for her severity and asks whether human passions were created only to be "curb'd, subdu'd, pluck'd by the roots" (109). Albini tries to show Victoria that her behavior, so consistent with what is expected from women, serves only to confirm and to perpetuate the mentality that enslaves women. Just as Albini says to Victoria, Wollstonecraft reminds women to take the lead in polishing their manners everywhere, for "that being the only way to better their condition" (*Letters Written during a Short Residence in Sweden, Norway and Denmark,* 181).

Albini admonishes Victoria for her cruel and careless behavior toward Basil. For the pleasure of a little power, Victoria causes unremitting pain. Edgeworth reminds readers: "*Power* over the minds of others will not, therefore, in domestic, any more than in public life, be an object of ambition to women of enlarged understandings" ("Answer to . . . ," *Letters for Literary*

Ladies, 55). In behaving like the coy woman of artful snares, Victoria tightens the shackles that bind her sex to its subservient position. Albini asks her:

> Was it not ungen'rous
> To fetter Basil with a foolish tie,
> Against his will, perhaps against his duty?
>
> (110)

In using her power to inflict pain, Victoria emulates the masculine model of oppression. Like Beatrice of Shelley's *Cenci,* Victoria becomes the very tyrant her sex opposes.

Victoria admits to Isabella that she deserves the governess's stern and severe reproofs. Deeming Albini worthy of the highest respect, Victoria says, "her nobler mind / procures to her the privilege of man" (112). There must be something man-like about women whose minds reflect intellectual activities ascribed to the masculine sphere.[20] Victoria's comment reveals her commitment to an ideology demanding separate spheres for men and women. The characters subscribe to that rigidly defined and fixed notion, and they account for deviations—Basil's becoming soft and emotional and Albini's insightful reasoning prowess—as anomalies or aberrations. It somehow never occurs to them, as it does to the reader of the play, that there is nothing atypical about these behaviors; rather, it is their notion of separatedness—what distinguishes masculine and feminine—that reflects error.

The playful exchange between Victoria and Mirando, an orphan boy whom Victoria favors, also betrays latent sexual content. Mirando wants to "scramble up her robe, / As naughty boys do when they climb for apples" (112). He wishes he were "tall enough to reach Victoria's lips" (112), and he vows his love to Victoria "because she's pretty" (113). At an young age, Mirando reflects the inculcations of separations marking gender-role identity. A woman is a beautiful plaything, a toy, a source of sexual pleasure. Wollstonecraft observes how this fiction has become accepted as truth: "She was created to be the toy of man, his rattle, and it must jingle in his ears whenever, dismissing reason, he chooses to be amused" (*A Vindication of the Rights of Woman,* 34). Mirando emulates older male models, including the count of Maldo and the marquis of Carlatzi, whom he claims love Victoria and were, at one time, her suitors. Mirando offers to show them how Count Wolvar escorted Isabella from court. He contorts his body into an exaggerated bowing posture, he whispers softly, and he ogles affectedly. He explains that Isabella responded to the Count by casting her eyes downward and smiling. This mockery of court manners and sexual decorum illustrates how the acceptance of a cultural mentality passes from generation to generation with little doubt as to its validity. What Mirando, whose name suggests mirror, enacts as childish imitation now, he will, in a few years, pursue earnestly as the proper and prescribed behavior for his sex.

Like Isabella, Jane De Monfort is a beautiful and grace-ful woman much admired. When Freberg reveals his unabashed admiration for Jane, Lady Freberg checks her husband's praise: "Such lofty mien, and high as-sumed gait I've seen ere now, and men have call'd it pride" (328). This significant comment associates male characteristics with the lovely Jane. The feminist tracts of the 1790s debate the liberation of the independent female and its potential usurpation of male hegemony. In several passages of her *Appeal to the Men of Great Britain in Behalf of Women,* Hays disputes this notion: "Women may be truly masculine in their conduct and demeanor, without wounding the delicacy of the men" (180). Hays argues that when we speak of a masculine woman, we mean it in a pejorative and reproachful way: "We allow ourselves to be run away with by a vague idea,—an undefined term,—of which we do not take the trouble to know the precise meaning, or the exact bounds" (173).

While some of Jane's actions, characterized as "mascu-line," challenge the existing mentality, Lady Freberg's actions reify the prevailing ideology. A woman occu-pied solely with domestic concerns and trifles, Lady Freberg tells her page: "My little spaniels are unkempt; / My cards unwritten, and my china broke" (345). Try-ing on a newly fashioned robe, she complains to Theresa, her servant, "that sleeve is all awry" (345). As a tyrant of her domestic realm, Lady Freberg reveals her jeal-ousy of Jane and her suspicions that her servants and husband may be more loyal to the graceful and elegant Jane than to her. She quips: "All do not think me like a May-day queen, / Which peasants deck in sport" (346). Denying that her husband loves her, Lady Freberg claims:

> He takes no pride in me.
> Elsewhere his praise and admiration go,
> And Jane De Monfort is not mortal woman.
>
> (346)

For the second time, the Countess tries to dismiss her supposed rival by casting her in feminine-denying terms. It is hard to do battle with a "saint" who has sacrificed for her younger sisters and who has traversed through the tough winter storm to comfort her unhappy brother. It is much easier to hate a "whore" who has come "through wintry storms to seek a lover" (347). The rivalry between Jane and Lady Freberg recapitu-lates the one between De Monfort and Rezenvelt, and like the masculine battle, this feminine struggle re-plays a collective and cultural battle of social relations based on bifurcations.

The dialogue between Lady Freberg and Jane is seem-ingly confined to the woman's domestic sphere, but that arena is itself bifurcated into two oppositional and distinct categories of roles. These women seem to reify within their own already segregated sphere of identity the exact ideology that divorced them from the mascu-line by seeing two opposite roles and functions for the feminine. The integration of passions ascribed to these two roles, madonna or whore, is, like the integration of masculine and feminine passions, never considered. Exploiting this ideological fiction masked as truth, Lady Freberg declares that she can exact her vengeance by spreading a rumor that Jane has come to Amberg

> Under pretence of finding out De Monfort,
> To meet with Rezenvelt. When Freberg hears
> it
> 'Twill help, I ween, to break this magick
> charm.
>
> (347)

The rumor, hopes Lady Freberg, will reduce Jane's saintly position to that of a common and scheming lover.

At the end of the play, the requiem and funeral for the departed sister at the Gothic convent chapel foreshadow the death of another sister, Jane, and by extension, the death of the independent female will. Jane rushes to the convent to save De Monfort from some desperate and hideous deed, but she arrives after he has slain Rezenvelt. As a social outcast like Basil, Werner, Manfred, and Marmaduke, who suffer fragmentation and alienation when oppositions are pushed to their limits, De Monfort denies Jane access to himself. He cries:

> I now am nothing.
> I am a man, of holy claims bereft;
> Out from the pale of social kindred cast;
> Nameless and horrible.
>
> (394)

Jane ignores his protests and offers her embrace, her comfort, and her love. Fearing that Jane's name and reputation will be soiled by his deed, De Monfort tries to disassociate himself from family ties and from the identity signified by a name. But Jane vows she will never forsake him. Impressed with her steadfast loy-alty and courage, De Monfort determines to rouse up his "manhood" for her sake and to meet his fate bravely. Yet, his noble strength dissipates when the strong, "masculine" Jane leaves his side. Defending the ex-pression of so-called masculine traits in women, Hays asserts: "Women in general possess even fortitude, that first of masculine virtues, in a much greater degree, and of a much superior kind, to that possessed by the men" (175). Under extremely stressful conditions, Jane exemplifies the "masculine" fortitude which Hays so highly applauds.

De Monfort speaks with sadness about his final sepa-ration from his sister. It is Jane who responds to his emotional tremors with strong, masculine vigor. He depends on Jane's religious assurances, and he hopes her words will constitute a fiction of heaven stronger than his mentally constructed hell. Empowered by language, Jane can speak her prayer; De Monfort cannot articulate his supplication.[21] It is Jane who complains to the officers about the use of chains on De Monfort. She argues that her brother has no power to escape because "distress hath bound him with a heavy chain" (399). This scene inverts the figure which the feminist polemics of the 1790s reflect—woman held captive by mental chains. Much like the men depicted in the feminist tracts, the officers protest that they must perform their duty prescribed by sacred law in binding De Monfort. He complains, however, that he suffers more from witnessing his sister's servile supplications on his behalf than from the confining fetters. Like many women struggling for emancipation, De Monfort rationalizes that although he is physically confined, he is mentally free. But the physical trappings of confinement, prisons, chains, and guards are all figures for the mentality enslaved that must be liberated. Mary Hays makes a similar argument in "On the Influence of Authority and Custom on the Female Mind and Manners": "absurd despotism which has hitherto enslaved the female mind . . . the understandings of women have been chained down."[22] De Monfort is temporarily proud of the mental victory he believes he has achieved. Like Prometheus, he has learned to reclaim the curse that makes him a mental prisoner, enslaved to a tyranny of his own creation. His struggle is that of the feminists of the 1790s who seek a social and cultural reclamation of the curse that holds gender relations to separate spheres.

De Monfort's heroic courage and "manly spirit" (402) are short-lived, and he becomes increasingly depressed. His mental toughness coincides with the physical presence of Jane, an implication that gender integration rather than separation offers stability. Rushing to De Monfort's side, Jane, "like a heaven inspir'd angel" (403), tries to comfort her dying brother. Freberg exalts Jane as a goddess. The prevailing cultural mental structuration cannot accept her strength in masculine terms, but it can deify her beyond human proportions. Commenting on this cultural phenomenon, Hays writes:

> If therefore we are to understand by a masculine woman, one who emulates those virtues and accomplishments, which as common to human nature, are common to both sexes; the attempt is natural, amiable, and highly honorable to that woman, under whatever name her conduct may be disguised or censured. For even virtue and truth, may be misnamed, disguised, and censured; but they cannot change their natures, in compliance with the tyranny of fashion and prejudice. (173-74)

Depicted dramatically in her response to the crisis in her brother's life, Jane's brief challenge of the ideol-ogy governing gender roles and functions offers readers an alternative to the disguise and censorship women were compelled to endure.

Important scenes in both plays depict the literal disguises of costume parties. In *Count Basil*, the Duke of Mantua hosts a masque at his grand apartments. Disguised as a poet, Rosinberg pleads with a guest that he is but "a poor abandon'd lover out of place" (127) and so is ready to engage with any mistress who will have him. Playing the melancholic lover to any lady's delight, he knows the ploys of courtly love, including the invention of "proper pretty little quarrels" (127). Rosinberg assures the shepherdess with whom he banters that for the lady's fame, he shall carve her name on every tree, write madrigals, odes and sonnets in praise of her lovely face, and make love-posies for her thimble's edge. He promises another, costumed as a nun, that if she were to ascend the convent's walls, he would meet her on the open plain and aid her every step to freedom. He brags to another guest disguised as a sultana that he can bear every "burst of female passion" (128) and ill treatment "like a lamb" (129). The dames taunt Rosinberg with verbal and physical blows. He is rescued by a gracious mistress who promises to soothe him with winning smiles and to bind his soul with flattery's charms. She further pledges that when he bestows homage to her that she will lay aside her "studied woman's wiles" (130) and become a "simple maid" (130).

This banter reifies prescribed gender roles. At this masque, we witness a recapitulation of an ideology demanding male and female spheres of activity. Visual gimmicks and verbal puns undermine genuine and sincere communications in which the sexes participate on an equal basis. Both genders play the parts dictated by an ideological script.

Disguised as a wounded soldier, Basil wanders about and searches for Victoria. Unable to recognize Victoria, he laments: "What veil conceals thee?" (132). A figure disguised as a female conjurer enters and tries to inspect Basil's fictitious wound. Failing to recognize the conjurer as Victoria, Basil explains to the costumed form that the woman-inflicted wound from which he suffers cannot be redressed. His retaliatory arrow could never reach the height that she enjoys; only a prince could dare aspire to the station of the lady who has wounded his heart with her scorn and spite. Unveiling, Victoria denies Basil's charges. As she leaves, Basil curses his "unmanly fears" (134). When human behaviors and responses are restricted within certain parameters, emotions are repressed. Those who try to conform to the social prescriptions suffer anguish and conflict. Basil feels he is less of a "man" because he is perplexed with ambivalent feelings for Victoria.

When Victoria and Basil confront one another, unmasked and embarrassed, Basil confesses that he can think about nothing but love. Victoria warns him that he has presumed too much

> On those unguarded words, which were in
>   truth
> Utter'd at unawares, with little heed,
> And urge their meaning far beyond the night.
>
>   (135)

Basil is not only blind to the disguises and fictions surrounding him, but he also makes language mean what he desires. Words assume the role created by the one writing the script.[23] He reads into Victoria's words meanings of his own creation. Desperately pressed to make an exit before her father sees them conversing, Victoria finally admits that she cannot hate Basil. He infuses implications of love into her hasty words.

A song culminates the masque. The performers sing: "Who in thy simple mien would trace / The tyrant of the human race?" (138). As the song protests, love is potentially deceptive. Defined in oppositional terms— weal and woe, bliss and bane—love enslaves those who wear its chains. Love is a condition of despotism. Observing that tyranny gives force to the man's passion, Wollstonecraft remarks that "most men treat their mistresses as kings do their favourites: *ergo* is not man then the tyrant of the creation?" (*Letters Written during a Short Residence in Sweden, Norway, and Denmark,* 160). Wollstonecraft implies a response to the question posed by the lyrics of the song: man is tyrant, and love is his powerful tool of oppression.

Disguises at the masque operate simultaneously at several different levels. As I have indicated above, a similar metadramatic use of disguise appears in *Werner.* There is the obvious and literal level of costumed and concealed identities intended as delight and recreation. The seemingly playful banter among Rosinberg and the variously disguised ladies reveals how language, even cloaked as sport, reifies gender relations defined by separate identities. While the dialogue echoes conceptual paradigms of courtly love from the Middle Ages and lovesickness associated with the Renaissance, it also recapitulates ideologically based prescriptions which dictate behavior. The fact that these women are disguised as a shepherdess, a nun, a sultana, a maid, and a conjurer visually emphasizes the roles a collective and cultural ideology allows them to play, both in real life and at the make-believe masque. They enact more of what they are than they may realize.

Hosted by the Frebergs in *De Monfort,* a party offers a dramatic convention in which masking and veiling can operate at several levels. Complimenting the nobly simple decorations for the party, Freberg tells his wife:

> And here, my love,
> The gay profusion of a woman's fancy
> Is well display'd.
>
>   (324)

Freberg's comment betrays an ideology which divorces the domain of female fancy from a logical masculine mentality. Appearing early in the play, the party depicts two important but submerged concerns: the poisoned mentality pervasive in this culture, and the operation of an ideology which bifurcates gender relations. At first, Jane eschews the Frebergs' invitation to their party because she fears that her presence will only further agitate De Monfort. She must play her part, not as a "doting mistress" (327), not as a "fond distracted wife" (327), but as De Monfort's sister who must patiently wait to greet him at a time when she will not "dash his mirth with tears" (328). As a foil to the masculine, egocentric, self-serving De Monfort, Jane is the feminine, nurturing, selfless other. At Freberg's suggestion, she agrees to attend the party. Although the evening's gala is not a masque, she can conceal herself "behind the double foldings of a veil" (328). Jane, too, is afflicted with a cultural malady that casts her in this role. In *Maria; or, The Wrongs of Woman,* Maria articulates the cultural disease that poisons its collective mentality: "A false morality is even established which makes all the virtue of women consist in chastity, submission, and the forgiveness of injuries" (147).

The party itself is a battle field for gender confrontations. Freberg teases a group of gallants: "Are there no beauties in that moving crowd / To fix your fancy?" (329). Rezenvelt attests to the varieties of beautiful women available:

> Men of ev'ry mind
> May in that moving croud some fair one find,
> To suit their taste, tho' whimsical and strange,
> As ever fancy own'd.
>
>   (329-30)

As Rezenvelt describes them, women are objects or commodities to be selected as at a market or auction block. He compares the myriad of feminine attributes to a unique hybrid garden:

> There's store of grafted charms
> Blending in one the sweets of many plants
> So obstinately, strangely opposite,
> As would have well defy'd all other art
> But female cultivation.
>
>   (330)

He ridicules the strange and unattractive mixtures of the aged youth and the youthful aged, the prude and the coquette—all feminine stereotypes engendered by an ideology of bifurcated gender roles. Arguing with

Freberg that his disdain for women is not at all severe, Rezenvelt protests that it is the male who is victimized by female charms:

> From all those diverse modes of dire assault,
> He owns a heart of hardest adamant,
> Who shall escape to-night.
>
> (331)

The battle of the sexes implies that there must be an oppressor and an oppressed, a dominant gender. Rezenvelt further suggests that the means by which females entrap and control males involves deception and trickery—like Victoria's "artful snares" (163).

De Monfort himself assumes that the mysterious, alluring masked woman has been jilted by a lover or husband and that the pain she claims she wishes to conceal behind the sable veil derives from some romantic fiasco. For what other cause could make a woman so distressed? De Monfort's assumptions disclose a mental structuration generating separate spheres of activities for men and women. Jane arouses his guilt when she explains that she has been forsaken by her brother. Recalling his own sister, De Monfort praises her "noble virtuous worth" (334) and her beauty. He describes her unselfish and saintly generosity to her dying parents, her family loyalty and responsibility, even at the expense of her own happiness and courtship. De Monfort's testimony reveals a reverence for his sister which transforms her into a personified deity.[24] Her perfection counters his foibles. Her unselfishness opposes his self-indulgence. She gives, and he takes. She loves, and he hates.

The mystery of De Monfort's source of depression deepens with his refusal to reveal his "secret troubles" (335) to Jane. Trying to gain her brother's confidence, Jane recalls how as young orphans, they stood side by side

> Like two young trees, whose boughs, in early
>   strength,
> Screen the weak saplings of the rising grove,
> And brave the storm together—
> I have so long, as if by nature's right,
> Thy bosom's inmate and adviser been,
> I thought thro' life I should have so remain'd,
> Nor ever known a change.
>
> (336)

Jane resigns herself to a humbler station than her former role of comforter and confidante. Assuming her subservient position, she vows to remain De Monfort's close attendant and the soother of griefs she must not know. She assumes the role of martyr—a role, unlike that of a "masculine woman," considered dignified and proper for women to accept in relation to the needs of man. She is willing to make personal sacrifices to appease the male ego. On bended knee at De Monfort's feet, Jane promises that she will never hate him—no matter what raging passion burns and torments him. She will seek to nurture and to transform his soul.

These culturally and ideologically defined gender roles become the tool by which political deceptions are effected in *Count Basil*. Masking their loyalty, the Duke and Gauriecio use Victoria's femininity—her feminine wiles disguised as love—to arrest Basil's military march and the deployment of his troops. While this dramatic action echoes Restoration motifs of heroic love, the conflict between loyalty to domestic, private feminine life and political, public, masculine duties further exposes bifurcated roles and functions based on sex. The ideology that engenders the deceptions and separations between men and women also generates the political and military confrontations.

All of these submerged and parallel ideological conflicts are further complicated by the dramatic presentation. They are depicted and played out within the context of a masque, an overt "theatre" of disguise. The masque is, in turn, embedded within the structure of a drama, another conventional and obvious form of role-playing. With its questioning of the culturally contrived roles assigned to men and to women, the feminist polemics of the 1790's inform the conflicts staged as a play. Like the other romantic dramas, *Count Basil* and *De Monfort* are ultimately about the mentality which motivates the characters and which dictates the conflicts. As the other dramas do, they achieve this by opening upon several layers of meaning operating simultaneously within the dramatic structures. Their metadramatic layerings paradoxically conceal and reveal ideological content.

Social unrest appears in *Count Basil* figured as political mutiny. Angered at the discovery of munity among his troops, Basil calls their actions "ungen'rous," prompted by "unmanly thought" (141). He asks whether anyone attempted to reason with the soldiers about this folly, and he describes the troops' emotional gullibility about fantastic lies as a feminine reaction, an "unmanly thought" (141). The mutiny symbolizes discord with a brotherhood of loyalties and alliances. Defined by public, physical activity, this separate sphere is disbanding—partly because Basil himself has broken ranks to associate with the softer sphere and partly because emotional rumor, often personified as female, has infiltrated the camp. The collision of previously separated masculine and feminine activities at the camp creates, momentarily at least, chaos and confusion. This crisis directs, on the surface level, the dramatic action, but it also challenges ideological codifications on which a culture operates. It is, of course, advantageous to Rosinberg and Basil to retain the separate spheres presently directing sexual activities, for it is from that mental structuration that they derive their rank and power. Gender roles and hierarchical positions are jeopardized by mutiny. As in political revolution (*The Borderers* and *Prometheus Unbound*) and in familial rebellion (*The Cenci, Werner,* and *Manfred*), the master/slave dichotomy is threatened with inversion: slaves becoming masters and masters becoming slaves. Tyranny is merely transferred to the newly empowered group.

Basil regains control of his soldiers and orders them to fight for their cause "manfully" (146). Defeating feminine rumor with masculine action and logic, Basil cleverly challenges the manly courage of his troops and begs them not to "earn with savage mutiny" (148) their own destruction. The soldiers pledge obedience to Basil and renew their allegiance to fight at Pavia. Basil then manipulates the soldiers with the pièce de résistance. In claiming to have rejected a promotion so he could remain with his gallant troops, Basil makes the soldiers indebted to him. True to their word, the soldiers obey Basil's order; silent, dejected, and humiliated, they exit. Basil has successfully used his own arsenal of artful snares to subjugate his troops. Hays reminds her readers that this passion to excel and to lead others is, in man, termed ambition, but "when applied to woman it commonly receives the denomination of vanity, or at best of pride" (77). Because Basil dupes his soldiers into unconditional obedience and worship, his actions are termed logical. Victoria's verbal manipulations are considered "artful snares and feminine wiles."

Similarly, De Monfort struggles with the torment of being an effeminate male. Moved by Jane's deprecation, De Monfort finally reveals that his hatred for Rezenvelt causes his suffering. De Monfort and Rezenvelt had learned over the years to mask their rivalry as friendship, but beneath, his facade, the hatred grew. De Monfort explains:

> As we onward pass'd
> From youth to man's estate, his narrow art,
> And envious gibing malice, poorly veil'd
> In the affected carelessness of mirth,
> Still more detestable and odious grew.
>
> (340)

De Monfort describes his rival's deceptive arts in effeminate terms. Much like Jane's veiled face, his concealed motives and actions are not "masculine." They belong to the affected, emotional, deceptive repertoire of womanly wiles. The bifurcations that distinguish the rivals are given semantic signification that marks an oppositional gender orientation: the masculine and his other. De Monfort reflects special sensitivity to the mobility and advantages Rezenvelt's deceptions achieved for him within the rigidly hierarchical German class structure. Unlike De Monfort, Rezenvelt was not born into nobility. Incensed at Rezenvelt's ability to play to the upper class, De Monfort resents the unearned accolades he has won

by trickery from the gullible gentry. Rezenvelt functions like a woman who has overreached her proper station in life.

Ironically, De Monfort's hatred springs from Rezenvelt's earlier generosity in refusing to spear the swordless De Monfort during a duel. Rezenvelt's offer to return the forfeited sword during the battle becomes, in De Monfort's poisoned mind, an insult and a curse. As in Beatrice's reaction to rape in *The Cenci,* De Monfort's perception of the act, rather than the act itself, makes the action and its agent odious to him. De Monfort interprets Rezenvelt's generosity and human decency as enslavement, a way for Rezenvelt to inflict continual torture and shame. The oppositional rivalry and veiled hatred existing between De Monfort and Rezenvelt depict the mental structuration that lies behind the sexual rivalry emanating from gender relations based on an ideology of bifurcations. While we may smile at De Monfort's false sense of honor or Rezenvelt's clever tactics of harassment, we must remember what Hays, Wollstonecraft, and others cite as the male methods to keep woman in a state of "perpetual babyism." In Wollstonecraft's letter of 13 September 1787 to the bookseller and publisher Joseph Johnson, she cries: "I long for a little peace and independence! Every obligation we receive from our fellow-creatures is a new shackle, takes from our native freedom, and debases the mind, makes us mere earthworms."[25] De Monfort explains to Jane that when Rezenvelt was in his proper place, when he was "some half-trodden worm" (340), he could endure him better than he can now that he has joined the circle of the privileged. The conflict between the sexes is here recapitulated as a conflict between social and economic classes; the ideological paradigm that is common to both forms of the conflict is thus disclosed.

Although Jane attempts to arrange a meeting of reconciliation between her brother and Rezenvelt, the confrontation only deepens the rivalry. Rezenvelt spurns De Monfort's cold and respectful handshake of friendship. He desires an emotional, affectionate reconciliation. He finds De Monfort's extension of masculine respect unacceptable. Their rivalry continues to be characterized by attributes emanating from separated gender roles. As distinct masculine and feminine expectations and reactions, these two forces will be oppositional, and reconciliation will be impossible. Their differences are, in fact, becoming larger.

De Monfort is trapped into believing Grimbaldi's false rumor concerning an impending marriage between Rezenvelt and Jane. He reifies the lie in his interpretation of Jane's words and actions. Like Beatrice Cenci, he feels encircled by "stinging scorpions" (370). Convinced that Jane has come to Amberg to seek Rezenvelt's love rather than for sisterly attention to him, De Monfort curses the couple of unseemly opposites: fair and loathsome, excellent and base, heaven and hell. Moved by his belief that Rezenvelt will have Jane, De Monfort vows revenge. He will allow no violation of his saintly sister by his enemy, the personification of his alter ego. The ensuing sword battle reenacts the earlier duel, with Rezenvelt disarming De Monfort but refusing to inflict the final and deadly thrust. This confrontation serves as a paradigm for rivalries on a cultural level, including conflicts of class and gender.

While De Monfort blindly believes the rumor generated by Grimbaldi (male), Basil dismisses the warning issued by Albini (female) as false. When Rosinberg shares with Basil the warning that Albini had whispered to him during the masque, Basil dismisses its validity because of its source—a woman. Basil laughs and says, "She is a woman, who avoids all share / In secret politicks" (155). Basil argues that Albini cannot possibly be concerned with military and political affairs, for these constitute the masculine and public arena. He situates Albini in the feminine sphere to which the Duke had earlier resigned Victoria. Albini's concern, private and feminine, centers upon Victoria—an exclusively domestic arena. Rosinberg detests Victoria and curses "the fatal beauty of that woman, / Which has bewitch'd" (156) Basil into forsaking his military duty. He confesses he is vexed to see Basil "so enthralled by a woman" (156). Rosinberg reifies binary gender roles in urging his friend to play the lover's part another time; now, he insists, is the time to play the soldier's part. To save Basil from "the yawning gulph, / To which blind passion guides [his] heedless steps" (158), Rosinberg appeals to his friend's identity as a soldier:

> If thou prizest honour,
> A soldier's fair repute, a hero's fame,
> What noble spirits love; and well I know
> Full dearly dost thou prize them, leave this
>   place,
> And give thy soldiers orders for the march.
>
> (159)

Honor, fame, and heroism are themselves mental constructs. Rosinberg implies, however, that they are fixed standards which Basil's actions now threaten to undermine. Edgeworth demonstrates the mental origin of the abstractions that Rosinberg holds so dear: "Fame and praise are mental *luxuries* which become, from habit, absolutely necessary to our existence; and in purchasing them we must pay the price set upon them by society" ("Letter 4," *Letters for Literary Ladies,* 54). The price society exacts is sexual oppression: gender roles based on separate spheres. The entire argument between Basil and Rosinberg reifies incongruous gender roles, for according to the mental paradigm upon which the argument rests, Basil cannot be both lover and soldier.

Ironically, it is Victoria's "artful snares" (163) that win out against Rosinberg's logical debate. Basil agrees to meet with Victoria one more time during the court's hunting expedition. Defeated, Rosinberg spitefully tells Isabella that the rule of women is "a short liv'd tyranny / That ends at last in hatred and contempt" (163). Isabella refutes Rosinberg's narrow view of feminine statesmanship: "Nay, but some women do so wisely rule, / Their subjects never from the yoke escape" (163). Successful rule is characterized by a male-defined, master/subject dichotomy. According to Rosinberg, to be successful rulers, women must adopt the paradigms established by men. Isabella's comment reinforces this idea. The revolution of manners which Hays and Wollstonecraft encourage, however, offers an alternative to this acceptance of masculine-determined structures of authority. As the feminist polemics of the 1790s argue and as *Count Basil* dramatically depicts, women must restructure the mental paradigm from which notions and codes for successful leadership emanate.

Basil's brief encounter with Victoria at a grove near the forest is interrupted by a messenger bringing news that the imperial army under Piscaro has defeated the enemy near Pavia's walls. The battle over, the French king has been taken prisoner and thousands of the enemy slain. Seeing Basil's utter dismay and depression at the news, Victoria assumes the blame for Basil's detainment in Mantua and therefore his tardiness to the battlefield. Fearing Basil may do something desperate, Victoria cries: "I've fool'd a noble heart—/ I've wreck'd a brave man's honour" (175). Basil runs to the forest, enters a cave, and shoots himself with a pistol.

Believing he has become effeminate in turning away from the masculine duty of military confrontation and in turning to the feminine allurement of domestic pleasure, Basil is convinced he has forsaken his sexual role. Summoned by Victoria, Rosinberg enters the cave and finds his friend mortally wounded. Basil explains his action: "Shame knows no kindred; I am fall'n, disgrac'd; / My fame is gone, I cannot look upon thee" (183). In his last breaths, Basil gasps: "It was delusion, all delusion, Rosinberg" (184). The delusion is the divided-gender fiction that an ideology produces and that results in such tragic consequences. Although the soldiers gathered around Basil weep, they attempt to conceal their "feminine" outbursts of emotion. Standing over Basil's body, Rosinberg blames "cursed passion" (187) for his friend's destruction. Constrained and repressed within culturally prescribed limits, such passion eventually destroys individuals caught in such enslavement.

Entering the cave and seeing Basil's body, Victoria claims responsibility for Basil's death: "Is this the sad reward of all thy love? / O! I have murder'd thee" (189). Rosinberg quips that "woman's grief is like a summer storm, / Short as it violent is" (189). Victoria vows that from this time she will not enjoy giddy days of frivolity; instead,

To the dark, shaded cloister wilt thou
    [Rosinberg] go,
Where sad and lonely, thro' the dismal grate
Thou'lt spy my wasted form, and then upbraid
    me.

                                        (190)

She will spend her remaining days in a convent and near Basil's lone tomb. Her earthly bed shall be as cold, dark, and cheerless as his grave. She has accepted a metaphorical death to parallel Basil's physical death—separate spheres to the very end.

While the denouement is dramatically deficient and aesthetically unsatisfying, the suicide and the mournful gathering in the cave impel readers to work beyond a neat settlement in the end and to consider the ideological extensions and ramifications of a culture defined by binary gender roles. Only in the cave do the seemingly oppositional forces of human love and military power briefly converge and dissipate. Careful reading discloses that even the respective suicides selected by Basil and Victoria are determined by culturally defined gender roles. Having missed the opportunity to be a great military hero, Basil ironically fires a pistol into his heart. Having missed the opportunity to experience passionate and conjugal love, Victoria commits herself to a lifetime of celibacy, the dreary passionless life of a cloistered nun. How thoroughly masculine for Basil, and how thoroughly feminine for Victoria. Like the feminist polemics of the 1790s, *Count Basil* demonstrates that a mental revolution must occur before political oppositions, including gender relations, can be reformed.

Like Basil and Victoria, De Monfort fails to move beyond the rivalry and oppositions that a separated sphere ideology infuses into all human interactions. He dies from mental enslavement, mental torture, and mental wounds. He acts upon the fictions he constructs, believing them to be externally derived, absolute truths. He enacts the victim of an ideology unchallenged and life-denying. But Jane, too, falls victim to that ideology she questions but cannot, individually, change. Like Victoria, she announces her own consignment to the convent and her commitment to the holy order. Opposing the practice of feminine escape to retreats, hermitages, and cloisters, More writes: "Action is the life of virtue, and the world is the noblest theatre of action. Perhaps some of the most perfect patterns of human conduct may be found in the most public stations, and among the busiest orders of mankind" (*Thoughts on the Importance of the Manners of the Great,* 78). Women cannot keep retreating from the battle for liberation. Jane essentially entombs herself as she enshrines her brother—the ultimate sacrifice. In accepting "holy orders," she reifies an ideology of separated gender functions, and she closets herself from further sexual relationships or feminist activities. No longer a

familial and physical sister to De Monfort, she accepts the role of a spiritual and metaphysical sister of God. Her role can be defined only in relation to another dominant and masculine one. Her identity is determined by and dependent upon a contrast with the masculine identity. Jane remains always a "sister"—a female counterpart to a male figure.

Count Basil and *De Monfort* offer no solutions to the largest sorts of conflict which they present. The denouements of the plays are unsettling because they are not tightly resolved, and thus they point to the irresolute nature of the passions the plays present. If the characters seem underdeveloped, it is because they represent mental structurations of cultural collectivity. If the plots seem simple and shallow, it is because they move vertically onto latent ideological meanings as they advance in a linear direction. The dramatic conflicts are themselves representations of social configurations. Like the feminist polemics of the 1790s, Baillie's plays politicize gender not as a biological function but as a cultural practice. Unlike Victoria and Jane, who closet themselves from social interaction. Baillie vigorously and actively participates in a political revolution that seeks to unveil the customs, habits, and prejudices that enslave women.

Notes

[1] Joanna Baillie, "Introductory Discourse," in *A Series of Plays: In Which It Is Attempted to Delineate The Stronger Passions of the Mind: Each Passion Being the Subject of A Tragedy and A Comedy,* 3 vols. (1798; New York: Garland, 1977), 1:37. Future citations are to this edition and volume.

[2] See the review of *A Series of Plays,* by Joanna Baillie, in *Edinburgh Review, or Critical Journal* 19 (Feb. 1812): 261-90; William Hazlitt, *Lectures on English Poets,* 3d ed. (1841; New York: Russell & Russell, 1968), 284-86; George W. Bethune, *British Female Poets with Biographical and Critical Notices* (1858; Freeport, N.Y: Books for Libraries, 1972), 159-60; Frederic Rowton, *Female Poets of Great Britain with Copious Selections and Critical Remarks* (Philadelphia: Carey and Hart, 1949), 287-97; M. Norton, "The Plays of Joanna Baillie," *Review of English Studies* 23 (1947): 134-43; Bertrand Evans, *Gothic Drama from Walpole to Shelley* (Berkeley: University of California Press, 1947), 200-207; Margaret S. Carhart, *The Life and Works of Joanna Baillie* (1923; New York: Archon, 1970), 71-102, 191-204.

It is significant that even in recent studies of romantic drama, Baillie's plays have received limited, if any, critical attention. See, for example, Marilyn Gaull, *English Romanticism: The Human Context* (New York: Norton, 1988), 101-3; Jeffrey N. Cox, *In the Shadows of Romance: Romantic Tragic Drama in Germany,*

England, and France (Athens: Ohio University Press, 1987), 44, 118-21; Richard Courtney, *Outline History of British Drama* (Totowa, N.J.: Littlefield and Adams, 1982), 150; Om Prakash Mathus, *The Closet Drama of the Romantic Revival* (Salzburg: Institut für Englische Sprache und Literatur, 1978), 308-19; Stuart Curran, *Shelley's "Cenci": Scorpions Ringed with Fire* (Princeton: Princeton University Press, 1970), 173-75.

[3] Mary Wollstonecraft, *Maria; or, The Wrongs of Woman* (1798; New York: Norton, 1975), 21.

[4] Tilottama Rajan claims that *The Wrongs of Woman* is structured as a series of attempts by people who are literally or metaphorically imprisoned to communicate to others who are outside the prison-house of the social text. See "Wollstonecraft and Godwin: Reading the Secrets of the Political Novel," *Studies in Romanticism* 27 (1988): 223-36.

[5] In "Class, Gender, and Social Motion in Joanna Baillie's *De Monfort*," *Wordsworth Circle* 23:2 (1992): 109-17, Daniel P. Watkins discusses historically determined class and gender anxiety inscribed in *De Monfort*. Watkins argues that Baillie does not treat human passion in the abstract. The drama draws upon deeper and broader social, historical, and cultural realities that determine the individual psychological passion of hatred. According to Watkins, "In Baillie's hands, hatred is more than a psychological, private, self-generating, or autonomous passion; it is an effect of large, if submerged, social forces and conditions" (109).

[6] Mary Wollstonecraft, *Letters Written during a Short Residence in Sweden, Norway, and Denmark,* ed. Carol H. Poston (1796; Lincoln: University of Nebraska Press, 1976), 160.

[7] Mary Hays, *Appeal to the Men of Great Britain in Behalf of Women* (1798; New York: Garland, 1974), 224.

[8] Hannah More, *Thoughts on the Importance of the Manners of the Great to General Society* (London: T. Cadell, 1788), 16.

[9] Mary Wollstonecraft, *Mary, A Fiction, and The Wrongs of Woman,* ed. Gary Kelly (London: Oxford University Press, 1976), 23.

[10] Mary Wollstonecraft, *A Vindication of the Rights of Woman with Strictures on Political and Moral Subjects,* 2d ed., ed. Carol H. Poston (1975; New York: Norton, 1988), 7.

[11] See Julia Kristeva, *About Chinese Women,* trans. Anita Barrows (1974; London: Marion Boyars, 1977). Kristeva alleges that the abyss between the two sexes is marked by their different relationships to the law (religious and political), which is, paradoxically, the very condition of their alliance; see 17-19.

[12] Hannah More, *Strictures on the Modern System of Female Education with a View of the Principles and Conduct Prevalent among Women of Rank and Fortune* (1799; New York: Garland, 1974), 2:29.

[13] Maria Edgeworth, "Letter From a Gentleman to His Friend Upon the Birth of a Daughter," in *Letters for Literary Ladies: To Which Is Added, "An Essay on the Noble Science of Self-Justification"* (1795; New York: Garland, 1974), 42.

[14] Clara Reeve, *Plans of Education: With Remarks on the Systems of Other Writers: In a Series of Letters Between Mrs. Darnford and Her Friends* (1792; New York: Garland, 1974), vii.

[15] Maria Edgeworth, "An Essay on the Noble Science of Self-Justification," in *Letters for Literary Ladies* (1795; New York: Garland, 1974), 4.

[16] Joanna Baillie, *Count Basil: A Tragedy,* in *A Series of Plays* (1798; New York: Garland, 1977), 1:75. Future citations are from this edition and volume, and are indicated by page number.

[17] H. I. Marrou, in *A History of Education in Antiquity,* trans. George Lamb (1956; Madison: University of Wisconsin Press, 1982), says: "Love between men is a recurring feature of military societies, in which men tend to be shut in upon themselves. The exclusion— the utter absence—of women inevitably means an increase in masculine love" (27). See chapter 3, "Pederasty in Classical Education," 26-35.

[18] Joanna Baillie, *De Monfort: A Tragedy* in *A Series of Plays* (1798; New York: Garland, 1977), 1:316. Future citations are from this edition and volume and are indicated by page number.

[19] Kristeva suggests that this symbolic paternal order defined by Christianity creates an endless battle for women between her sexual body and tradition; see her *About Chinese Women,* 26-27.

[20] H. E. Haworth, "Romantic Female Writers and the Critics," *Texas Studies in Literature and Language* 17 (1976), interestingly notes that when the first volume of Baillie's plays appeared anonymously in 1798, they were considered so powerful that they were thought to be written by a man; see 728. Edmund Kean's review of the revival of *De Monfort* in *New Monthly Magazine* and *Literary Journal* 8 (1822), claims that the female mind rarely has complete command over the sterner emotions that belong to tragedy, but that Baillie's tragic theory defends woman on this point; see 9. See also Carhart, *The Life and Works of Joanna Baillie,* 14-16;

Mary McKerrow, "Joanna Baillie and Mary Brunton: Women of the Manse," in *Living By the Pen: Early British Women Writers,* ed. Dale Spender (New York: Macmillan, 1991), 160-61.

[21] In the "Introductory Discourse" to the plays, Baillie claims that she prefers to have the dramas staged rather than read, but that she had no channel of public introduction to effect their production. Unlike Jane's, Baillie's words could not be spoken. She believed that they were silenced by a social configuration that denied her sex public access in visible and vocal forums; see 1:66. It is also interesting to compare this scene with act 2 of *Prometheus Unbound.* Asia's gift of speech to Prometheus enables him to revoke his curse.

[22] Mary Hays, "On the Influence of Authority and Custom on the Female Mind and Manners," in *Letters and Essays, Moral and Miscellaneous* (London: T. Knott, 1793), 19-20.

[23] The motifs of conjurer and disguise are also important in Samuel Taylor Coleridge's *Osorio* and are strikingly similar in their dramatic usage to the disguises in Baillie's play.

[24] According to Watkins, the conversation between De Monfort and his disguised sister approaches sexual longing. He identifies their love with a historical interest that links both incest and orphans to social significance. See "Class, Gender, and Social Motion in Joanna Baillie's *De Monfort,*" 113-14.

[25] Mary Wollstonecraft, "Letters to Mr. Johnson, Bookseller, in St. Paul's Church-Yard," in *Posthumous Works of the Author of "A Vindication of the Rights of Woman"* (1798; Clifton, N.J.: Augustus M. Kelley, 1972), 2:65.

Works Cited

Baillie, Joanna. *Count Basil: A Tragedy.* In vol. 1 of *A Series of Plays: In Which It Is Attempted to Delineate The Stronger Passions of the Mind: Each Passion Being the Subject of A Tragedy and A Comedy.* 1798. New York: Garland, 1977.

———. *De Monfort: A Tragedy.* In vol. 1 of *A Series of Plays: In Which It Is Attempted to Delineate The Stronger Passions of the Mind: Each Passion Being the Subject of A Tragedy and A Comedy.* 1798. New York: Garland, 1977.

———. "Introductory Discourse." In vol. 1 of *A Series of Plays: In Which It Is Attempted to Delineate The Stronger Passions of the Mind: Each Passion Being the Subject of A Tragedy and A Comedy.* 1798. New York: Garland, 1977.

[Byron, George Gordon, Lord.] *Manfred: A Dramatic Poem.* In vol. 4 of *The Complete Poetical Works,* edited by Jerome J. McGann. Oxford: Clarendon, 1986.

———. *Werner, or, The Inheritance.* In *Byron: Poetical Works,* edited by Frederick Page. 1970. New edition with corrections edited by John D. Jump. Oxford: Oxford University Press, 1986.

Edgeworth, Maria. "An Essay on the Noble Science of Self-Justification." In *Letters for Literary Ladies: To Which Is Added. "An Essay on the Noble Science of Self-Justification."* 1795. New York: Garland, 1974.

———. *Letters for Literary Ladies: To Which Is Added "An Essay on the Noble Science of Self-Justification."* 1795. New York: Garland, 1974.

Hays, Mary. *Appeal to the Men of Great Britain in Behalf of Women.* 1798. New York: Garland, 1974.

———. "On the Influence of Authority and Custom on the Female Mind and Manners." In *Letters and Essays, Moral and Miscellaneous.* London: T. Knott, 1793.

More, Hannah. *Strictures on the Modern System of Female Education with a View of the Principles and Conduct Prevalent among Women of Rank and Fortune.* 1799. 2 vols. New York: Garland, 1974.

———. *Thoughts on the Importance of the Manners of the Great to General Society.* London: T. Cadell, 1788.

Reeve, Clara. *Plans of Education: With Remarks on the Systems of Other Writers: In a Series of Letters Between Mrs. Darnford and Her Friends.* 1792. New York: Garland, 1974.

[Shelley, Percy Bysshe] *The Cenci: A Tragedy, in Five Acts.* In *Shelley's Poetry and Prose,* edited by Donald H. Reiman and Sharon B. Powers. New York: Norton, 1977.

———. *Prometheus Unbound: A Lyrical Drama in Four Acts.* In *Shelley's Poetry and Prose,* edited by Donald H. Reiman and Sharon B. Powers. New York: Norton, 1977.

[Wollstonecraft, Mary.] *Letters Written during a Short Residence in Sweden, Norway, and Denmark.* 1796. Edited by Carol H. Poston. Lincoln: University of Nebraska Press, 1976.

———. *Maria; or, The Wrongs of Woman.* 1798. New York: Norton, 1975.

———. *Mary, A Fiction and The Wrongs of Woman.*

1798. Edited by Gary Kelly. London: Oxford University Press, 1976.

————. *A Vindication of the Rights of Woman with Strictures on Political and Moral Subjects.* 2d ed. 1792. Edited by Carol H. Poston. New York: Norton, 1988.

Wordsworth, William. *The Borderers: A Tragedy.* Edited by Robert Osborn. Ithaca, N.Y.: Cornell University Press, 1982.

Jonathan Wordsworth (essay date 1994)

SOURCE: Introduction to *Revolution and Romanticism, 1789-1834,* Woodstock Books, 1994, np.

[*Below, Wordsworth praises Baillie's poetry and explores its strong influence on William Wordsworth's lyrical ballads.*]

Among the many volumes of the period amiably titled *Poems on various subjects, Poems on several occasions,* Joanna Baillie's 1790 collection has a curmudgeonly air: POEMS; *wherein it is attempted to describe* CERTAIN VIEWS OF NATURE *and of* RUSTIC MANNERS; *and also, to point out, in some instances, the different influence which the same circumstances produce on different characters.* All these instructions on one octavo titlepage. We are being buttonholed—told how to read and what to look for—by an author who doesn't even put her name to the book. It was to be the same with Baillie's second publication eight years later: A SERIES OF PLAYS: *in which it is attempted to delineate* THE STRONGER PASSIONS OF THE MIND, *each passion being the subject of* A TRAGEDY AND A COMEDY.

In both cases we are dealing with poetry written to support a theory. *A series of plays* makes clear the (still anonymous) author's intentions in a 72-page Introductory Discourse. In 1790, though her ways of thinking seem largely established, Baillie has yet to become a dramatist, and yet to formulate her views in detail. After the titlepage instructions we are permitted to start straight in:

> The cock, warm roosting 'midst his feather'd
>   dames,
> Now lifts his beak and snuffs the morning air,
> Stretches his neck and claps his heavy wings,
> Gives three short crows, and glad his task is
>   done,
> Low, chuckling, turns himself upon the roost,
> Then nestles down again amongst his mates.
> The lab'ring hind, who on his bed of straw,
> Beneath his home-made coverings, coarse, but
>   warm,
> Lock'd in the kindly arms of her who spun
>   them,

> Dreams of the gain that next year's crop
>   should bring . . .
> Now wakes from sleep at the unwelcome call,
> And finds himself but just the same poor man
> As when he went to rest . . .
> He rubs his eyes, and stretches out his arms;
> Heigh ho! heigh ho! he drawls with gaping
>   mouth,
> Then most unwillingly creeps out of bed,
> And without looking-glass puts on his clothes.

>   (pp. 1-2)

The writer it seems has a sense of humour. The first 'character' introduced after the weighty claims of her titlepage is a cock. Responding to the 'circumstance' of morning, he crows perfunctorily, and nestles back amongst his mates. No less comfortable with his single wife, the human labourer stretches, yawns, and creeps unwillingly into the day. There can be no doubt that we have witnessed a scene of 'rustic manners', and one in which the same circumstance has produced on different characters a different influence. At the same time, Baillie's poetry has offered a charming and unusual mixture of observation and improbability. No cock before or since has 'snuffed' the air, or crowed to rule, yet the arms of the labourer's wife, and the coarse blankets she has woven, touch us with their tender actuality.

Baillie takes her theorizing seriously, but fortunately does not push it at us all the time. Half way through the 1790 volume she offers a series of four lovers, with four different temperaments (melancholy, cheerful, proud, and sound-hearted), each of whom says farewell to his mistress (variously Phillis and Phill.) in three-and-a-half not very inspiring pages. Later she presents 'Addresses to the Night' from, a fearful mind, a discontented mind, a sorrowful mind, and a joyful mind. It is all a bit mechanical, and doesn't bring out her best poetry. As playwright Baillie will claim that her drama is based on dominant passions—love in *Count Basil* and *The tryal,* hate in *De Monfort*—but the plays work, when they work at all, despite the theory. Consuming passion cuts against character and idiosyncracy; it is difficult to show in its beginnings, and once established tends to be monotonous. The 1790 studies are an attempt to portray mood, without personality—temperament, with no narrative implication. They have the potential to become dramatic monologues, but the voices are thin. Sameness of style masks intended difference of attitude. Even when the writing itself is good, it is not easy to tell the moods apart. Despite the violence of the third line, and the langour of the fourth, the cloud-study of *Address to the night* (4)—

> Athwart the sky in scatter'd bands they range
> From shape to shape, transform'd in endless
>   change;

Then piece-meal torn, in ragged portions stray,
Or thinly spreading, slowly melt away.

(p. 137)

—is the product, allegedly, of a joyful mind.

It is the underlying assumptions that give interest to Baillie's attempts to portray mood and temperament. 'Into whatever scenes the novelist may conduct us', she writes in the Introductory Discourse of 1798,

> still is our attention most sensibly awake to every touch faithful to nature; still are we upon the watch for every thing that speaks to us of ourselves.

> The fair field of what is properly called poetry, is enriched with so many beauties, that in it we are often tempted to forget what we really are, and what kind of beings we belong to. Who, in the enchanted regions of simile, metaphor, allegory and description, can remember the plain order of things in this every-day world? From heroes whose majestick forms rise like a lofty tower, whose eyes are lightening, whose arms are irresistible, whose course is like the storms of heaven, bold and exalted sentiments we will readily receive . . . I will venture, however, to say, that amidst all this decoration and ornament, all this loftiness and refinement, let one simple trait of the human heart, one expression of passion genuine and true to nature, be introduced, and it will stand forth alone in the boldness of reality, whilst the false and unnatural around it, fades away on every side, like the rising exhalations of the morning. (**Series of plays,** 20-1)

In an impeccably natural image, the mists of artificiality are purged, burnt off, by the presence of the genuine. It is clear that Baillie's thinking in the Introductory Address was known to Coleridge and Wordsworth as they worked on *Lyrical ballads,* and influenced the wording of the Advertisement. By this date, however, there was a trend towards naturalness and simplicity that had been less obvious in 1790.

Baillie of course was Scottish. She and her mother and sister moved to London in 1784, but she had been educated in Glasgow, where her father was for a time Professor of Divinity. She would have known Blair's primitivist *Dissertation on Ossian* (1765) and *Lectures on rhetoric and belles lettres* (1783). And she knew Burns (Kilmarnock 1786, London 1787), who made the link between ancient poetry of the heart—spurious in the case of Ossian—and its modern rural equivalent. Where both Susannah Blamire (*Stoklewath,* c. 1772) and Wordsworth (*Evening walk,* 1793) base their poems of the countryside on Goldsmith's elegant *Deserted village,* Baillie's **Winter day** and its companion-piece have the uncondescending ordinariness of the *Cotter's Saturday night:*

The toil-worn Cotter frae his labor goes—
  This night his weekly moil is at an end—

[drudgery]
Collects his spades, his mattocks, and his hoes,
  Hoping the morn in ease and rest to spend,
And weary, o'er the moor, his course does hameward bend.

At length his lonely Cot appears in view,
  Beneath the shelter of an aged tree;
Th'expectant wee-things, toddlan, stacher through [stagger]
  To meet their Dad, wi' flichterin' noise and glee.
His wee bit ingle, blinkan bonilie, [little fire]
  His clean hearth-stane, his thrifty wifie's smile,
The lisping infant, prattling on his knee,
  Does a' his weary kiaugh and care beguile, [anxiety]
And makes him quite forget his labor and his toil.

(Kilmarnock, 125-6)

Burns is not at his best, but the idiom he creates, for an English public and with English sources in mind, could be assimilated without the pastiche implied in copying the broader Scottish poems. Writing a free blank verse, willing to use both the shortened line and the extra syllable, Baillie creates a poetry that moves more easily than Burns's spenserians, and has the same power of tender observation:

On goes the seething pot with morning cheer,
For which some little wishful hearts await,
Who, peeping from the bed-clothes, spy, well pleas'd,
The cheery light that blazes on the wall,
And bawl for leave to rise.—
Their busy mother knows not where to turn,
Her morning work comes now so thick upon her.
One she must help to tye his little coat,
Unpin his cap, and seek another's shoe.
When all is o'er, out to the door they run,
With new comb'd sleeky hair, and glist'ning cheeks,
Each with some little project in his head.
One on the ice must try his new sol'd shoes:
To view his well-set trap another hies,
In hopes to find some poor unwary bird
(No worthless prize) entangled in his snare;
Whilst one, less active, with round rosy face,
Spreads out his purple fingers to the fire,
And peeps, most wishfully, into the pot.

(pp. 3-4)

Looking back, Baillie recalled just one review of **Poems** 1790. It was a significant one, however, written by the Reverend William Enfield, later to publish an essay (*Is verse essential to poetry?*) that played its part in the genealogy of *Lyrical ballads*. In the *Monthly review* for November 1791, Enfield recommended Baillie's poetry: to 'those readers whose taste is not too refined, or too fastidious, to be pleased with true and lively pictures of nature, sketched with a careless hand'—readers, 'who are capable of discerning and admiring the fair form of simplicity, though negligently clad in a rustic garb'. He is anxious, but he is judicious too. In important ways the anonymous publication in front of him was unusual. The poems

> can, individually, boast no wild fictions to seize the fancy; and they have little of that richness of melody which, in many of our modern poets, so sweetly captivates the ear: but they contain minute and circumstantial descriptions of natural objects, scenes, and characters; and they express, in easy though peculiar language, the feelings of undisguised and uncorrupted nature.

On every point Enfield is right. Neither here, nor in the plays, does Baillie have 'wild fictions' to seize the imagination. Even in her fluent stanzaic poems, she is far from being one of the 'sweet singers' of the '80s, captivating the ear with melody. With its admixture of Scottish ('red and grumly', 'black and grumly'), her language is truly 'easy though peculiar'. Above all, at this turning-point in literature, she does indeed show the 'feelings of undisguised and uncorrupted nature'. There is no artifice about the child who 'Spreads out his purple fingers to the fire, / And peeps, most wishfully, into the pot'. Burns would have been proud to own him—and Wordsworth too.

Baillie has a voice of her own, and it is genuinely new. She should be valued in her own right, not for what may seem anticipations of later, greater verse. But no reader of the *Ruined cottage* could fail, as they come upon the *Lamentation,* to think of Margaret, linked in death to the image of the 'rank speargrass', 'By mist and silent raindrops silvered o'er':

> The fallen leaves light rustling o'er thee pass,
> And o'er thee waves the rank and dewy grass
> (p. 68)

And no reader of the *Prelude* could fail to hear in Baillie's poem the vocabulary and associative thinking of Wordsworth's 'spot of time' ('when storm / And rain beat on my roof at midnight . . . The workings of my spirit thence are brought'):

> At ev'ry wailing of the midnight wind
> Thy lowly dwelling comes into my mind.
> When rain beats on my roof, wild storms
>   abroad,
> I think upon thy bare and beaten sod . . .
> (pp. 69-70)

That Wordsworth did borrow from Baillie, we know. Two to three months before the *Prelude* 'spots of time' were composed, he had based *There was a boy* on a speech in **De Monfort.** Could he perhaps in 1798-9 have had access to **Poems** 1790 as well as the **Series of plays**? It is a curious thought that if he did, he might well not have known that the volumes were by the same writer. Baillie's anonymity was carefully preserved.

Among the pairings characteristic of Baillie's **Poems** (and of her way of thinking) is the *Story of other times, somewhat in imitation of the poems of Ossian* and the *Storm-beat maid, somewhat after the style of our old English ballads.* Blair had described MacPherson's 'translation' of the Celtic poet, Ossian, as having 'The two great characteristics of . . . tenderness and sublimity':

> His poetry, more perhaps than that of any other writer, deserves to be styled, *The Poetry of the heart.* It is a heart penetrated with noble sentiments, and with sublime and tender passions; a heart that glows, and kindles the fancy; a heart that is full, and pours itself forth.

> (*Works of Ossian,* 2 vols 1765, ii 384-5)

By 1790 most readers accepted that *Fingal* (1762) and *Temora* (1763) were fakes. But Ossian had a special appeal. Those wishing for the genuine, the pure, the primitive (Goethe among them) were provided by Macpherson with a sort of meaningful plangency, half-told stories endlessly evocative of lives and passions purer than their own. Baillie catches the tones, without (any more than anyone else) being able to move the poetry on beyond romantic nostalgia:

> Matchless in the days of their love were
>   Lochallen and the daughter of Lorma.
> But their beauty has ceas'd on Arthula; and
>   the place of their rest is unknown.
> (p. 151)

Ballads were a different matter. Not only was the past they belonged to genuine, the form allowed for innovation. Baillie's **Storm-beat maid** is an important poem:

> All shrouded in the winter snow,
>   The maiden held her way;
> Nor chilly winds that roughly blow,
>   Nor dark night could her stay.

> O'er hill and dale, through bush and briar,
>   She on her journey kept . . .
> (p. 97)

Sad, beautiful, living in an other-worldly realm of the mind that is all her own, the Storm-beat Maid travels through a winter landscape of which she takes no heed.

Though ghostly, she is alive. Her presence, though, is such that it can best be described in terms of the natural world:

> Her face is like an early morn,
>   Dimm'd with the nightly dew;
> Her skin is like the sheeted torn, [*Read* thorn?
>   Like a thornbush, 'sheeted' with blossom]
> Her eyes are wat'ry blue.
>
> And tall and slender is her form,
>   Like willow o'er the brook;
> But on her brow there broods a storm,
>   And restless is her look.
>
>   (pp. 102-3)

Travelling on, insensible of all around her, the Maid comes to a castle where a wedding-feast is taking place. As we suspect, it is her lover who is to be married; what we do not expect is his reaction to her coming:

>   cursed be the woman's art,
>   That lur'd me to her snare!
> And cursed be the faithless heart
>   That left thee to despair!
>
> Yet now I'll hold thee to my side,
>   Tho' worthless I have been,
> Nor friends, nor wealth, nor dizen'd bride,
>   [bedecked]
>   Shall ever stand between.
>
> When thou art weary and depress'd,
>   I'll lull thee to thy sleep;
> And when dark fancies vex thy breast,
>   I'll sit by thee and weep.
>
> I'll tend thee like a restless child
>   Where'er thy rovings be;
> Nor gesture keen, nor eye-ball wild,
>   Shall turn my love from thee.

Baillie has written in 1790 what is by any standards a lyrical ballad. The flimsy plot has no significance; everything in the ***Storm-beat maid*** depends on states of mind. In terms of Wordsworth's 1800 Preface, 'the feeling therein developed gives importance to the action and situation, and not the action and situation to the feeling'.

In fact it might seem that Baillie has not merely invented the Wordsworthian lyrical ballad, she has combined in one poem its two major different aspects. The lover's response in the final lines anticipates the Alfoxden poetry of relationship and tenderness (see also *Mother to her waking infant,* pp. 170-3), and with it the interest in abnormal states of mind. Baillie, however, is writing in the ballad-metre used in four out of five of the Goslar Lucy Poems. The metre is a com-

mon one (occurring, for instance, in the *Ancient mariner* and *We are seven*), but the coincidence of rhythm heightens our sense that the Storm-beat Maid and Lucy belong to the same uncanny world of imagination. The Maid, of course, is mad; but her madness is never exemplified in act or speech. It is felt as a powerful strangeness. To use the terms that Wordsworth applied to Lucy, her character is 'spiritualized'.

With the *Lamentation* it looks as though resemblances of mood and situation may have brought Baillie's phrasing to mind as Wordsworth worked on the *Ruined cottage* and *Prelude* 'spots of time'. With the ***Storm-beat maid*** it is easy to imagine his being impressed by the poem, and at some later stage writing *Lucy Gray* (first of the Lucy Poems, and nearest to ballad narrative) in the same metre and something of the same idiom. In the case of *Address to the muses* we see Baillie at her cheekiest, and Wordsworth at his closest to direct borrowing. 'I to the muses have been bound', he writes, as the final scene of the *Idiot boy* is about to begin,

> These fourteen years, by strong indentures;
> Oh gentle muses! let me tell
> But half of what to him befel,
> For sure he met with strange adventures.
>
> Oh gentle muses, is this kind?
> Why will ye thus my suit repel?
> Why of your further aid bereave me?
>   (*Lyrical ballads,* 172)

Using the same tones exactly, and the same repetition, Baillie had written in consecutive stanzas of ***Address to the muses,***

> O lovely sisters! is it true,
> That they are all inspired by you? . . .
>
> O lovely sisters! well it shews
> How wide and far your bounty flows:
> Then why from me withhold your beams?
>   (pp. 76-7)

Engaged two weeks later on *Peter Bell,* Wordsworth invokes, not the muses, but 'spirits of the mind', wonderful half-comic presences who similarly do, and do not, represent the human imagination:

> Your presence I have often felt
> In darkness and the stormy night;
> And well I know, if need there be,
> Ye can put forth your agency
> When earth is calm, and heaven is bright.
>
> Then, coming from the wayward world,
> That powerful world in which ye dwell,
> Come, Spirits of the Mind! and try,

Tonight, beneath the moonlight sky,
What may be done with Peter Bell!

(*Peter Bell,* 59)

Baillie in *Address to the muses* had written:

Ye are the spirits who preside
In earth, and air, and ocean wide;
In hissing flood, and crackling fire;
In horror dread, and tumult dire;
In stilly calm, and stormy wind,
And rule the answ'ring changes in the human
    mind.

High on the tempest-beaten hill,
Your misty shapes ye shift at will;
The wild fantastic clouds ye form;
Your voice is in the midnight storm . . .

(p. 78)

Baillie, like the Wordsworth of *Lyrical ballads,* is funny, sad, tender, affectionate, capable of many moods of 'passion genuine and true to nature'. As a playwright she achieved a very high reputation among her contemporaries. Looking back, though, it seems a pity that such a good writer should have turned to drama in a period when no one quite pulled it off. She had it in her to be a poet of real stature.

Catherine B. Burroughs (essay date 1997)

SOURCE: "Private Theatricals and Baillie's *The Tryal,*" in *Closet Stages: Joanna Baillie and the Theater Theory of British Romantic Women Writers,* University of Pennsylvania Press, 1997, pp. 143-68.

[*In the following essay, Burroughs explores "closet plays"—plays performed for private audiences—and their usefulness to women authors in advancing feminist perspectives. Burroughs also discusses domestic relations in* The Tryal, *as well as Baillie's theory of comedy, which emphasized the importance of presenting realistic, everyday situations.*]

No pay, we play, so gay, all day—
Curse the expense, chase care away!
    —Richard Brinsley Peake, *Amateurs and
        Actors: A Musical Farce in Two Acts*

If here our feeble powers
Have lightly wing'd for you some wintry
    hours;
Should these remember'd scenes in fancy
    live,
And to some future minutes pleasure give,
To right good end we've worn our mumming
    guise,

And we're repaid and happy—ay, and wise.[1]
    —Joanna Baillie, "Epilogue to the
Theatrical Representation at Strawberry Hill"[2]

As the epigraphs above suggest, one of the primary aims of putting on plays in the upper-class British home was to amuse those who had enough money to buy off boredom. Private theatricals were often unabashedly elitist projects, not only in the sense that many took place in exclusive domestic environments, but because they required, in addition to time, a great deal of money to arrange. Sybil Rosenfeld writes that Lord Barrymore's expenses for cake alone at the opening night reception of his private theater at Wargrave in 1789 were "rumoured" to have been £20, small change after the £60,000 that was spent on building the theater itself (18-19). To overcome the luxury of boredom was the impetus behind the staging of Elizabeth Inchbald's 1798 adaptation of August von Kotzebue's *Lovers' Vows* (1791) in Jane Austen's *Mansfield Park* (1814), perhaps the best-known work of literature that features the late-eighteenth-century phenomenon of amateur acting. The eagerness with which most of Mansfield's youthful residents embrace John Yates's proposal to put on a play is not only indicative of "a love of the theatre," which the narrative labels "so general" (147); Yates has arrived onto an already indolent scene embodied by the frequently supine Lady Bertram, and his proposal to mount a private theatrical follows on a painfully aimless visit to Mr. Rushworth's country house, during which each person's "spirits were in general exhausted" (133).

From the perspective of a feminist theater historian, however, the exclusivity of those private theatricals which took place in aristocratic and upper-middle-class domestic environments was important for providing certain women (and sometimes their servants) with a forum for experimenting with the theater arts.[3] It would be misleading to suggest that British private theatricals constituted some sort of avant-garde movement at the height of their vogue (1780-1810).[4] Even though new works were performed on private stages, they often derived from the canonical plays that dominated eighteenth-century patent theaters and also constituted the bulk of private theatrical offerings.[5] But because private entertainments were often produced in isolated settings, making theatrical activity accessible to a group of people who were not necessarily theatergoers, they inevitably deviated from London productions in spirit; they were certainly more conducive to spontaneity. Often rehearsed in the context of a house party that could go on for several weeks, and in small spaces that rendered more permeable the customary barriers between spectator and actor, the private theatrical could offer its participants a deeply personal and imaginative experience, not only allowing for a great deal of playfulness and delight in the act of improvisation, but also encouraging a serious self-consciousness about the performative features of social acting. As Gillian Russell (1995) has observed, in the context of her discussion of the military's amateur theatricals in Georgian Britain, the "phenomenon of amateur theatricals was . . . part of a broader struggle for the definition and control of various kinds of sociability in late eighteenth-century Britain" (128).

Because scholars have been preoccupied with debating the degree to which the turn to the closet in the period's canonized theater criticism does—or does not—express an "antitheatrical prejudice," the actual theater that was produced in the closeted spaces of the private sphere during the Romantic period has often been overlooked. This theater of the closet, though not exclusive to women, was particularly friendly to women's creative endeavors, and it is this theatrical context that Joanna Baillie's earliest comedy, *The Tryal* (1798), explores. Written during the British private theater movement and considered for a private theatrical production at Bentley Priory in 1803, *The Tryal* probes some of the tensions created by the trend among certain aristocratic and upper-middle-class women to write and direct improvisational performances in domestic spaces. Through the character of Agnes Withrington, an heiress who directs two women in a plot designed to determine the motives of the men who would marry her, *The Tryal* looks closely at those "ordinary" and "familiar" circumstances that comprised "Characteristic Comedy," Baillie's term for plays like her own that featured emotional trials on domestic stages.

Although Baillie did not identify herself with the English feminist movement of the 1790s, her theoretical discourse suggests that the domestic sphere, rather than being merely a place to retreat from the problematic stage practices of London theaters, could offer women interested in theater and drama a space for creative development. Baillie's theory encourages us to look at Romantic theater and drama in ways that highlight women's contributions to the period. Her language privileges the closet of "the great man," but she also advocates the performance of those dramas forged in private space to suggest that closets are not only sites of reading—of unperformability, disembodiment, and masculine intellection—but that they also contain a rich performance history in which women have actively participated before, during, and since the Romantic period. In this way, Baillie can be seen as contributing to the eighteenth-century trend to focus on domestic space in order to celebrate women's cultural worth.

Women and the Private Theatrical

Defined as "performance wholly or mainly by amateurs [presented] to selected or invited audiences, as opposed to the general public" (Rosenfeld, *Temples of Thespis* 9), private theatricals are usually distinguished in narratives of theater history from those plays that were acted privately by professionals.[6] Therefore, as

Sybil Rosenfeld notes, the first amateur actors in England may be considered the priests and guild members who performed church-sponsored mystery and morality plays (ibid. 8-9). By contrast, because the performers of early Tudor "household revels" were on retainer as specialists of acting, they corresponded to what we would today call "professionals."[7] As Keith Sturgess has written, by 1620 the word "private" in reference to theater meant that a play was to be performed "indoors" (3), and these private theaters—conceived along the lines of "a club, an academy, and an art-house" (4)—were attended largely by aristocratic audiences attempting to distance themselves from the rowdier playgoers of outdoor stages. The associations of aristocracy with theater in an exclusive domestic setting were reinforced by seventeenth-century masques and "aristocratic entertainments" such as John Milton's *Arcades* performed at Harefield in the early 1630s. Yet the rage for private theaters in England did not ignite until the eighteenth century, when this mostly aristocratic pastime was encouraged by developments in France, which had more than sixty private theaters by 1750 in Paris alone (Marvin Carlson 51), and during the last quarter of the century boasted variations on the private theatrical, such as the pornographic dramas often featured in "clandestine theatres."[8]

These "clandestine theatres" require a brief mention here, since the fact that French women "assumed great importance in the development of this theatre culture" (Toepfer 66) points to some parallels in Great Britain. Neither England, Scotland, Ireland, nor Wales produced a figure quite like France's Duchess de Villeroi, who—in a move presaging certain aspects of feminist theater in the 1980s[9]—sometimes excluded men from the audience for the purpose of featuring "plays glorifying lesbian love and setting the scene for huge sapphic orgies involving women from the opera and the Comedie Française" (66). But just as the private theater scene in mid-eighteenth-century France had its Marie Antoinette and Marie-Madeleine Guimard, and the German court theater its Charlotte von Stein in the 1770s,[10] so the British private theatrical community enjoyed the passionate commitment to private entertainment of many (primarily aristocratic and upper-middle-class) women.

By organizing, sponsoring, writing, and performing in private theatricals, eighteenth-century women were following the example set in earlier eras by English aristocrats such as Alice Spenser, Dowager Countess of Derby, who acted in Jacobean masques and attended country-house entertainments (Brown 15), Queen Henrietta Maria, who in the early seventeenth century took the then unusual step of appearing in two court pastorals (Sturgess 57), and the Princesses Mary and Anne, who performed in Crowne's *Calisto* in 1675. By the dawn of the next century it was not unusual to find wealthy women directing their children, grandchildren, or friends in an evening of theater of which they were the primary organizers, or writing plays for them, as in the case of the Countess of Hardwicke, whose *Court of Oberon* blended together a French piece with her original composition in order to "render it more suitable to her juvenile performers, the youngest of whom was but two years old."[11] An anonymous letter to the editor of the *European Magazine* written in 1788 indicates how firmly the private theater movement had taken hold by century's end:

> The practice of people of distinction and fortune to erect theatres, and commence actors to perform in them, *en famille,* is now so general, and is indeed, under certain restrictions, so very praise-worthy and innocent, that a sort of general account of all the play-houses and players of *ton,* to be continued occasionally, would perhaps be a pleasant, not to say profitable, companion or vade-mecum to those places of resort: and it might, appositely enough, be called The Fashionable Rosciad. (66)

Among the amateur playwrights and actresses in Great Britain were Elizabeth Cobbold, whose memoirist wrote that not only was she "a very frequent attendant on the theatre," but she "herself also possessed much taste and skill in dramatic composition, and wrote several pieces of great merit" (Jermyn 16). Though it was not the case, as the character of Bombast says in Archibald Maclaren's play, *The Private Theatre* (1809), that "little theatres furnish actors for the great, as little rivers furnish salmon for the sea" (I.ii.12), nevertheless amateur performer Charlotte Twistleton received acting training on the private stage at Adlestrop House sufficient to launch a professional career. Between 1780 and 1805 Elizabeth Berkeley Craven either composed, translated, adapted, or altered nineteen plays.[12] As Lady Craven she organized and appeared in private performances in Warwickshire, and upon relocating with her second husband from Germany to England, as the Margravine of Anspach she supervised the building and operation of a private theater in the 1790s at Brandenburgh House in Hammersmith. Here she alternately performed the functions of actress, playwright, producer, translator, musician, and singer. "My taste for music and poetry, and my style of imagination in writing, chastened by experience, were great sources of delight to me," she wrote in her memoirs in 1826:[13]

> I wrote *The Princess of Georgia,* and the *Twins of Smyrna,* for the Margrave's theatre, besides *Nourjad* and several other pieces; and for these I composed various airs in music. I invented *fetes* to amuse the Margrave, which afforded me a charming contrast to accounts, bills, and the changes of domestics and chamberlains, and many other things quite odious to me. (2:106)

Craven's reference to the domestic context in which her comedies, pantomimes, and musical dramas were

forged reminds us to pay particular attention to private settings in constructing women's theater history. For it is often in domestic spaces, far away from the traditional stage, that much of women's drama and theatrical art has actually been produced. For instance, Kirsten Gram Holmstrom's study of monodrama, "attitudes," and *tableaux vivants* devotes a large portion of the text to an analysis of a trend among upper-class European women to create "mimoplastic art" in the public spaces of their homes between 1770 and 1815 (128). Whether striking neoclassical poses and manipulating costume pieces, as in the case of Lady Emma Hamilton (whose stark gestures framed by special lighting effects anticipated photographers' models in the twentieth century), or miming scenes to music as did Ida Brun, or creating "art-historical etudes" (216) as did Henriette Hendel-Schutz (in which academic audiences could discuss with her the intellectual and artistic choices she had made), it is clear that the domestic setting was essential to these women for developing "a new genre on the borderline between pictorial art and theatre" (139).

Conceived and rehearsed on the home front and attended by a group of acquaintances, friends, and relatives theoretically inclined to tolerate women's ventures into acting and playwrighting, the British private theatrical gave those who would otherwise have had no theatrical experience a mode for exploring the theater arts. In the case of professional female actors, private performances also afforded opportunities for participating in theater in ways often unavailable to them on the public stage. Professional actress Harriot Mellon complained that "'there never was such a stupid task as drilling fine people!,'" but an evening of private theater at Strawberry Hill was nevertheless an occasion for her to manage the stage, in addition to occupying the position of "privy-councillor in all matters relative to costume and other little etceteras known only to the initiated in Thespian mysteries" (Baron-Wilson 1:280). Elizabeth Farren, another well-known actress of the period, frequently undertook the task of directing the amateur actors at Richmond House's private theatricals in 1787-88, "the most fashionable and exclusive . . . of their time" (Rosenfeld, *Temples of Thespis* 34).[14]

Private settings also helped some women inadvertently theorize acting. By focusing on the problem for the actress of being in the public eye while trying to adhere to cultural expectations for the proper performance of femininity, a number of women writers produced discourse that not only theorizes this problem as an indicator of the actress's heightened sensitivity to gender performances but also employs a mode of theorizing in which "onstage" and "offstage" documents at times intersect. Private playwright Elizabeth Craven, for instance, tells an anecdote in her *Memoirs* (1826) in which she focuses on the body of the amateur actor in a domestic setting to produce acting theory for a public audience. Craven recalls the following incident from her early teens when she was in Paris watching a performance that featured the famous actress Hyppolite Clairon:

> I remember, when I was thirteen years old, I was taken to the *Theatre François* at Paris, to see the performance of *Semiramis*. This character so much excited my laughter, that my mother ordered me to be taken home to the Hotel Beaufreau before the piece was finished, because my noise offended the *parterre*. I did not know that it was Mademoiselle Clairon who performed the part of *Semiramis*; but twenty years afterwards, when I was playing the part of the Sultan in *Almenorade*, my foolish memory recalled to mind *Semiramis*, and I imitated that declamation, which I then recollected. There were only twenty-five persons who composed the audience, all friends of the Margrave, who burst out into exclamations of my performance; and after, the play was over, they declared that I must have seen Mademoiselle Clairon, whom, they said, I had so closely imitated. I protested that, to the best of my recollection, I had never seen her. They insisted that it was herself, and that I must have seen her repeatedly to have followed her manner so exactly. Declamation on the French stage was quite in fashion, and I had been so particularly struck with this kind of acting, that it had lain dormant in my mind till the occasion brought it forth. (1:217-19)

Late-twentieth-century performance theorist and actor Hollis Huston has recently (1992) observed that "only the actor's smart body can stand across the gap between theory and performance" (10), and in Craven's anecdote we see how the uncontrollable laughter of a teenage girl who witnesses a professional production sows the seeds for the adult amateur's subsequent performance in a private setting. Only when Craven goes to write about this private performance in a memoir aimed at a public audience, however, does she produce what can be described as a theory of performance, one that draws on the memory of girlish giggles to suggest her imitation of Clairon embodies Craven's critique of the French declamatory style.

Gender and Space

Feminist geographers and anthropologists have been especially interested in how the spatial features of women's lives structure their creative responses. Shirley Ardener's statement that *"behaviour and space are mutually dependent"* (2) informs Daphne Spain's thesis "that initial status differences between women and men create certain types of gendered spaces and that institutionalized spatial segregation then reinforces prevailing male advantages" (6). One way of segregating the sexes is through architecture, and a number of critics in a variety of fields have represented the eighteenth century as the period when the concept of using "architecture to reinforce prevailing patterns of privilege and to assert power" (Spain 7) began to have a significant impact.

Peter Brooks argues that eighteenth-century domestic architecture took its cue from the "new and intense concern for privacy in the Enlightenment" (49): the "well-demarcated private apartments, boudoirs, 'closets,' and alcoves of eighteenth-century upper- and middle-class housing . . . supported the realization of new values attached to the individual and to the intimacy required for an individual's commerce with family, friends, and self" (28). Philippa Tristram reaches a similar conclusion—that the eighteenth-century house "made generous provision for those who wished to make their journeys privately, within the mind"—even though it was "essentially public with its absence of corridors and its interconnecting rooms" (3). This "new emphasis on the family and home as a refuge—as a personal world that afforded protection from the anonymity of industrial society" (Wekerle, Peterson, and Morley 9)—expressed a growing belief in the individual's right to govern private life. But the problem with any idealization of inwardness, of course, lies in the fact that, for women, there is often no individuality outside of their functioning relationship to domestic space, the "place" to which, since the industrial age, they have been consigned. As Doreen Massey has observed in relation to the concept of a public/private dichotomy, any attempt in the past to "confine women to the domestic sphere was both a specifically spatial control, and through that, a social control on identity" (179).

Although women who participated in private theatricals did not own their domestic dwellings or necessarily receive credit for their contributions to private entertainment, their role as organizers of domestic space gave them at least a measure of control over some of the ways in which their social identity was configured and represented. Reginald Brimsley Johnson has noted, for example, how the English bluestocking circle arranged domestic space in specific ways—from Elizabeth Montagu's semicircle to Elizabeth Vesey's zigzags to Mrs. Ord's "chairs round a table in the centre of the room" (10-11)—in order to create different conversational modes.

In addition to providing nonactors with a theatrical playground, the private theatrical also encouraged audiences to appreciate domestic space for the fact that it allowed them to "indulge in delicacies and subtleties that would be thrown away at Drury Lane or Covent Garden" (Rosenfeld, *Temples of Thespis* 168), a fact that could make social issues more vivid. Anthropologist Victor Turner (1982) has written at length about the idea that "theatre is the most forceful, *active* . . . genre of cultural performance, . . . a play society acts about itself" (104). It is "this proximity of theatre to life," in Turner's view, that "makes of it the form best fitted to comment or 'meta-comment' on conflict" (105). "When we act in everyday life, we do not merely re-act to indicative stimuli, we act in frames we have wrested from the genres of cultural performance." It therefore follows, Turner writes, that stage acting should concentrate on "bring[ing] into the symbolic or ficti-tious world the urgent problems of our reality" (122).

Those who made theater in their homes between 1770 and 1810 confronted the performative aspects of their actual experience through the process of self-con-sciously adopting roles for the private stage. For women especially, whose performance of femininity was tested perhaps most stringently in the semipublic spaces of the domestic sphere, the private theatrical provided often unlooked-for opportunities to analyze how social identities are constructed and represented.[15] As Bruce Wilshire has observed, in *Role Playing and Identity: The Limits of Theatrical Metaphor* (1982), "theatre is an aesthetic detachment from daily living that reveals the ways we are involved in daily living—particularly our empathetic and imitative involvements" (ix). But it was just this potential to disturb domestic harmony by revealing "the ways we are involved in daily living" that made the private theatrical particu-larly problematic where women were concerned.[16]

In an essay called "Remarks upon the Present Taste for Acting Private Plays" (1788), playwright Richard Cumberland expressed his anxiety about amateurism by referring specifically to female actors in private theaters: the "Andromache of the Stage may have an infant Hector at home, whom she more tenderly feels for than the Hector of the scene; he may be sick, he may be supperless; there may be none to nurse him, when his mother is out of sight, and the maternal inter-est in the divided heart of the actress may preponderate over the Heroine's" (116). Disturbed by a trend in which the act of playwrighting appears to him demystified, is "thoroughly bottomed and laid open," and is "now done by so many people without any difficulty at all" (115), Cumberland warned that this fashion "should be nar-rowly confined to certain ranks, ages, and conditions in the community at large," and that "young women of humble rank and small pretensions should be particu-larly cautious how a vain ambition of being noticed by their superiors betrays them into an attempt at display-ing their unprotected persons on a stage, however dig-nified and respectable." If they "have both acting tal-ents and charms," Cumberland continues, "I tremble for their danger" (118). Professional actress Ann Catherine Holbrook sounded an equally pessimistic note about amateur acting in her memoirs published in the early nineteenth century: "The Metropolis, particularly, teems with this evil [private theatricals], which is of much greater magnitude than is generally supposed, as it tends to discourage industry in youth, and fill them with hopes, as shallow in foundation, as a fairy vision;—castle-building here is at its summit" (52).

The Tryal: Amateur Acting and Female Liberation

Joanna Baillie's associations with such "castle-build-ing" extended back to her childhood, a reminder of the pervasiveness of amateur theatricals in late-eighteenth-century culture.[17] Sarah Tytler and J. L. Watson noted that at school Baillie became "the chief figure in some-thing like private theatricals" (2:193)—school plays figuring as amateur performances. In the *Dictionary of National Biography,* George Barnett Smith wrote that Baillie—like her heroine in **The Tryal,** Agnes Withrington—"was early distinguished for her skill in acting and composition, being especially facile in the improvisation of dialogue in character" (1:886). Catherine Jane Hamilton made a similar observation: "at school, by her sister's report, she was principally distinguished in being the ringleader of all pranks and follies, and used to entertain her companions with an endless string of stories of her own invention. She was also addicted to clambering on the roof of the house to act over her scenes alone and in secret" (1:114). Perhaps owing to these personal associations, Baillie centered her earliest comedy, **The Tryal,** around improvisational acting as the means by which certain women struggle to assert themselves, even if only tem-porarily, over the plot that shapes their domestic lives.

It is interesting to contemplate the fact that Baillie's first comedy was almost performed for the first time on a private stage by amateur actors, since this mode of representation might have caused its participants to view **The Tryal** metatheatrically, to appreciate some of the ways in which this play investigates amateurism and private entertainment in relation to gender and space. Hanna Scolnicov has recently written, in *Woman's The-atrical Space* (1994), that "the very shape a play gives its theatrical space is indicative of its views on the na-ture of the relationship between the sexes and on the position of women in society" (6-7). Such is certainly the case with Baillie's comedy, which depicts a woman caught between what she calls "a reasonable woman's desire" (196) to direct her own future and cultural imperatives that require her to marry.[18] Nevertheless, for the first part of the play Agnes Withrington at-tempts to take charge of her destiny by creating, per-forming in, and directing an improvisational theatrical in the privacy of her uncle's home: the social and clos-eted spaces of a fashionable English house in Bath become the setting for amateur acting. Wanting to be certain that the man she marries is "sensible" (I.i.204), for much of **The Tryal** the "sun-burnt" Agnes (III.i.238) resembles the merrily assertive Beatrice of Shakespeare's comedy *Much Ado About Nothing.* Like her cousin, Mariane—who has become engaged without her uncle's consent—Agnes is portrayed as independent and strong-willed, qualities that both amuse and unsettle her uncle Anthony Withrington. Mariane observes to Agnes that, before she arrived on the scene, Mariane thought her uncle "severe and unreasonable, with his fiddle faddle fancies about delicacy and decorum; but since you came amongst us, Agnes, you have so coaxed him, and laughed at him, and played with him, that he has become almost as frolicksome as ourselves" (I.i.202).

The frequency and ease with which the two young women touch their uncle's body indicate the relaxed atmosphere over which Withrington presides, and show how the dynamic of this domestic space encourages the women to use their imaginations. Introduced by the stage directions as "hanging upon [Withrington's] arms, coaxing him in a playful manner as they advance towards the front of the Stage" (I.i.195), Agnes and Mariane are subsequently described as "clapping his shoulder" (I.i.196), "stroaking his hand gently" (I.i.199), resting an "arm on his shoulder" (I.i.200), "leaping round his neck" (I.i.201), and taking "him by the hands and begin[ning] to play with him" (I.i.238). For a time female laughter reigns as Agnes, using winks and gestures to control the movement of bodies in domestic space, directs her cousin Mariane and her maid, Betty, in an improvisation designed to expose the greed of Agnes's suitors and determine the true character of Harwood, the man whom Agnes wants to marry.

Given this jocular familiarity between uncle and nieces, one might expect that Agnes and Mariane could persuade Withrington temporarily to become an actor in their plot. But he will not participate, foreshadowing Fanny Price's staunch refusal in *Mansfield Park* to perform in a private production given by her cousins. The language with which Withrington refuses suggests that the nexus of amateurism, women, and private performance is central to the dramaturgy of **The Tryal:** "It would be very pleasant, truly," he says teasingly, "to see an old fellow, with a wig upon his bald pate, making one in a holy-day mummery with a couple of madcaps" (I.i.195). This comparison between Agnes and Mariane's proposed improvisation and "holy-day mummery" recalls that the origins of English amateur acting were in the Christian church, once the locus of theatrical activity in spite of its anxiety about theater's potential to lure audiences into identifying with and imitating characters represented on stage. Christianity's historical ambivalence toward English theater is embodied in Uncle Withrington's ambivalence toward his nieces' amateur acting. As **The Tryal** progresses, Withrington's seeming approval of amateurism gives way to his attempt to regain control of his domicile, which he fears is becoming, under Agnes's direction, the scene of what we might call "street theater." In act 3, Withrington says that his house seems foreign to him—like "a cabin in Kamschatka,[19] and common to a whole tribe"—because it has been infiltrated by entertainers, animals, and indigent children:

> In every corner of it I find some visitor, or showman, or milliner's apprentice, loitering about: my best books are cast upon footstools and window-seats, and my library is littered over with work-bags; dogs, cats, and kittens, take possession of every chair, and refuse to be disturbed: and the very beggar children go hopping before my door with their half-eaten scraps in their hands, as if it were an entry to a workhouse. (III.i.60)

Alarmed at the means by which Agnes and Mariane reveal the absurdity of their suitors' performed postures, Withrington expresses his anxiety about the security of his nieces' gender and class position by saying that "all this playing, and laughing, and hoydening about, is not gentlewomanlike; nay, I might say, is not maidenly. . . . A high-bred elegant woman is a creature which man approaches with awe and respect; but nobody would think of accosting you with such impressions, any more than if you were a couple of young *female tinkers*" (III.i.240; my emphasis). Indeed, although he is extremely fond of his nieces and seems at times to enjoy the exuberance of their high-spirited acting, Withrington continually criticizes their jolly improvisations by equating theatricality with foolery, witchery, and madness. It is therefore no surprise when he comes to complain that he "can't approve of every farce you please to play off in my family, nor to have my relations affronted, and driven from my house for your entertainment" (III.i.239), or when he declares, a few lines later, "I am tired of this" (240).

The "this" is Agnes's plot, which requires that Mariane pretend to be Agnes in order to "get the men to bow to us, and tremble" (240-41) and that Agnes and her servant Betty produce a feminist variation of *The Taming of the Shrew*.[20] By acting peevishly and staging several tantrums for the sole purpose of discerning how well Harwood can tolerate a woman who expresses herself passionately, Agnes investigates why female anger is so upsetting to many men. She senses that the veneer of tolerance worn by her suitors during the courtship ritual masks their disgruntledness at having to affect such a pose, that such seeming delight in the woman wooed will give way to a desire to control her person. Therefore, much of the fun for Agnes in staging this improvisation rests with exposing the real motives of her suitors, such as Sir Loftus Prettyman who, when treated to a dose of Mariane's affected indifference, vows, in a series of asides: "when she is once secured, I'll be revenged! I'll vex her! I'll drive the spirit out of her. . . . I'll tame her!" (IV.iii.271). Exposing the avaricious motives of her suitors is Agnes's ultimate aim.

Harwood has no difficulty passing Agnes's test. But the play does not allow the lovers to come together so easily, and it is this complication that raises some of the problems faced by women who would do theater in the privacy of their homes. A monologue in act 5 marks the turning point of the play, for it is at this juncture that Agnes abandons the trajectory of her original improvisation in order to devise another plot responsive to her uncle's concerns. Here is Withrington's speech:

> To be the disinterested choice of a worthy man is what every woman, who means to marry at all, would be ambitious of; and a point in regard to her marriage, which a woman of fortune would be unwilling to leave doubtful. But there are men whose passions are of such a violent, overbearing nature, that love in them may be considered as a disease of the mind; and the object of it claims no more perfection or pre-eminence among women, than chalk, lime, or oatmeal do amongst dainties, because some diseased stomachs do prefer them to all things. Such men as these we sometimes see attach themselves even to ugliness and infamy, in defiance of honour and decency. With such men as these, women of sense and refinement can never be happy; nay, to be willingly the object of their love is not respectable. (Pauses). But you don't care for all this, I suppose? It does well enough for an old uncle to perplex himself with these niceties: it is you yourself the dear man happens to love, and none of these naughty women I have been talking of, so all is very right. (V.ii.276-77)

On the one hand, this monologue reads as the expression of Withrington's concern for Agnes's welfare; but on the other it seems designed to make her incredulous that any man could actually desire her as his wife. He "withers" Agnes's spirits by insinuating that Harwood's apparent devotion to her may be something to shun rather than to admire, since "there are men whose passions are of such a violent, overbearing nature, that love in them may be considered as a disease of the mind." If Harwood is indeed the indiscriminately passionate man that Withrington implies, then the object of his love can be discounted. For such a man—in claiming from women "no more perfection or pre-eminence . . . than chalk, lime, or oatmeal may do amongst dainties"—can be assessed as having a "diseased stomach." This diseased appetite might cause a man to "attach" himself "even to ugliness and infamy," a choice of words that Agnes in all probability interprets as a reference to herself, accustomed as she is to having her physicality criticized. Although her uncle implies that Agnes is a woman of "sense and refinement," he goes on to say that if one "willingly" allows herself to be the object of such a diseased person, then she is "naughty." This is a statement the harshness of which Withrington apparently recognizes when he disingenuously trivializes his judgments as "niceties." You are still "respectable," he tries to convey to Agnes, after having implied just the opposite.

Agnes is stunned. The young woman who has earlier described herself as "light as an air-ball!" (III.i.238), in reference to the fun she derives from her private theater, now becomes quite somber and quiet, telling Withrington that she has "ventured farther than I ought"

(V.i.278). She apologizes for her direction of the first plot, through which she has already achieved her goal of proving Harwood genuinely attracted to her character. Mariane, who enters the stage after Withrington's speech to find Agnes looking glum, immediately asserts that she is "very sure the plot is of [Withrington's] hatching, then, for I never saw Agnes with any thing of this kind in her head, wear such a spiritless face" (V.i.279). From this point on in the play Agnes "seems thoughtful" and speaks with "a grave and more dignified air" (V.i.277). By contrast—as if to symbolize his regaining control of the domestic space—her uncle borrows a gesture that we have come to associate with Agnes and Mariane when they were at their most confident: he "claps" Agnes on "her shoulder affectionately" (V.i.278).

At the beginning of *The Tryal,* in answer to Withrington's question about "who will fall in love with a little ordinary girl like thee," Agnes pointedly reminded him that "an old hunks of a father" once prevented his marrying the beautiful rich lady who was in love with him (I.i.197). Withrington comes dangerously close to exerting this kind of patriarchal control when he suggests the insufficiency of Agnes's first plot to determine Harwood's suitability. Indeed, in an apparent gesture toward Rousseau's *La Nouvelle Heloise* (1761)—in which Wolmar, the reigning patriarch at novel's end, devises a two-tiered trial to test the virtue of his wife, Julie, and her former lover, Saint-Preux—Withrington urges a second test that will determine whether Harwood elevates desire for virtue over his desire for Agnes's person. Agnes's original plot had been constructed, not to discover whether Harwood would choose virtue over the flawed woman in a quest after some feminine ideal, but rather to see how he would deal with imperfections, idiosyncrasies, and mood swings. In the scenes that follow, Agnes designs a new plot, but her contributions as an actor and director are curtailed. Instead, her cousin Royston takes centerstage, performing in an improvisation to which Agnes is but a silent witness, sequestered behind a screen. (In fact, at several points during this scene, Agnes chafes at her passive position, complaining about Royston's inability to understand what good acting is and his compulsion to explain to others what is intended as stage illusion.)

That it is a serious risk for Agnes to undertake this second plot is confirmed when the scene is later performed. Presented with a letter written by Agnes, Harwood is so undone by the implications of Agnes's impropriety that "his hand trembles" and he has trouble holding it. Subsequently "staggering back," "[he] throws himself into a chair . . . and covers his upper face with his hand" (V.ii.289-90). "See how his lips quiver," Royston exclaims, "and his bosom heaves! Let us unbutton him: I fear he is going into a fit." As Harwood starts to rise to leave the room, "he falls back again in a faint" (V.ii.290). The potential danger to Harwood's health casts a skeptical light on the merit of what in retrospect can be seen as Withrington's unnecessary interference in Agnes's private theatrical, even though Harwood proves himself to be vitally concerned that Agnes not behave immorally, thus passing the test and satisfying Withrington's concerns.

I want to suggest that Withrington's misgivings about Harwood do not derive simply from the former's uneasiness over the dramaturgy of Agnes's plot, which reveals the potential of private theatricals to destabilize domesticity. Withrington's doubt about Harwood's virtue may also mask his unease about the way in which Harwood "does" his gender. Described as wearing "a plain brownish coat" (I.i.204)—Baillie's sartorial signal that Harwood is destined for the physically plain Agnes (whom he nevertheless recognizes as "the most beautiful native character in the world" [I.ii.210])—Harwood the future lawyer is characterized in direct opposition to "your men of fashion" (I.ii.211), the pretentious Sir Loftus and his sidekick, Jack Opal. Harwood's idealism about his profession, his scholarliness, and his open enthusiasm pair him with Agnes as the "heartwood" of the play. Both are genuinely interested in extending themselves to help others, as Agnes's private staging suggests when she opens up Withrington's fashionable home to poverty-stricken children. Likewise, Harwood is praised for conceiving of the practice of law as more than "a dry treasuring up of facts in the memory," as (additionally) the profession of one "who pleads the cause of man before fellow-men," and who must therefore "know what is in the heart of man as well as what is in the book of records" (II.ii.228). When Agnes thanks Harwood for promising to marry her at play's end, she predicts that he "shall . . . exert your powers in the profession you have chosen: you shall be the weak one's stay, the poor man's advocate; you shall gain fair fame in recompense, and that will be our nobility" (V.ii.299). Throughout the play Harwood claims that he is looking for a real partner rather than an idealized paragon: "insipid constitutional good nature is a tiresome thing" (IV.i.253), he says to himself; "we ought not to expect a faultless woman" (IV.i.258), he confesses to his friend Colonel Hardy; "I can't bear your insipid passionless women: I would as soon live upon sweet curd all my life, as attach myself to one of them" (V.ii.288), he exclaims to Royston.

Yet though clearly the hero destined for Baillie's heroine, Harwood is also characterized as a man who often assumes an exaggeratedly expressive gesture and speech typically associated with femininity: he runs breathlessly onto the stage; he hangs around Agnes without apology; he blurts out his feelings. Furthermore, in act 4, Harwood offers to thread Agnes's needle, albeit "awkwardly" (IV.ii.66); and in the final act of the play, like many of the heroines in English Romantic drama

who, when confronted with surprising news, sink to the ground, Harwood does something quite unusual for a male character in a play from this period: he swoons. Given Withrington's concerns about Agnes's femininity in the context of her original improvisation, Harwood's characterization seems to require that Uncle Withrington assert his role as patriarch of a fashionable home and propose a further test for the young lawyer, one designed to answer some of the questions that Withrington has about the degree to which Harwood's masculine identity can be regarded as secure, and one that requires Agnes to restrict her involvement in private theater.

The Private Theatrical in Fiction

With its focus on women and amateur acting, Joanna Baillie's *The Tryal* may be compared to several other works of fiction from this period that feature the private theatrical movement in order to debate its effect upon domestic stability. Because women powerfully influenced the dynamics of domestic space, fictional works from the British Romantic period that treated the private theatrical often focused their anxiety on women characters. The issue of women acting on any stage (whether public or private) has been throughout British history a source of deep concern for certain segments of the population, and the idea that closet spaces were becoming formally theatricalized during the late eighteenth century often aroused strong responses.

For instance, Richard Brinsley Peake's *Amateurs and Actors* (1818) links private theatricals to disorder and impropriety through a plot in which the two main female characters run amok. It is the lot of a retired manufacturer named Elderberry—"simple in wit and manners, and utterly unacquainted with Theatricals" (10)—to try to retrieve his ward, Mary Hardacre, from an elopement that uses a private performance as a strategy to override parental consent. Mary's lover, David Dulcet, has arranged to announce their marriage to his relatives immediately after he and Mary have participated in a private production of *Romeo and Juliet,* which will be attended by Dulcet's family. The plot also contains the conflict between a poor country actor, Wing, and his estranged wife, Mary Goneril, a "Strolling Tragedy Actress" (10), who has run off with a manager but finds herself hired to act Juliet on the same private stage with her former husband.

As the person who perceives Dulcet's house as "a receptacle for lunatics" (30), Elderberry is presented as a ridiculous figure for his ignorance about amateur acting. But amateur performances are also satirized with equal force, especially in the exchanges between O. P. Bustle, the manager of a provincial theater hired to supervise this private production, and Wing. "[W]e who know something of the matter," says Bustle, "must laugh at private performers. As Garrick observed, one easily sees, when the Amateurs are acting, that there is not an *Actor* among them" (17). This is a theme anticipated by Archibald Maclaren's musical drama, *The Private Theatre* (1809), which ties together private entertainment, domestic disorder, and moral corruption. Modewart chastises his brother for writing private plays by saying: "Let us have no more of your Pantomimical Funerals. Convert your private theatre into a public school, or useful work-shop. Mind your own business, and leave the trade of acting to those who make it their profession" (II.i.24).

But although private theaters made many uneasy because they brought acting into the home, the idea that amateurism could provide a corrective to professional stage practices was a theme also consistently sounded during this period. In the same essay cited above (1788), Richard Cumberland admitted that the aristocracy was usually better suited than the professional actor to perform a variety of theatrical roles, because in "all scenes of high life they are at home; noble sentiments are natural to them; low-parts they can play by instinct; and as for all the crafts of rakes, gamesters, and fine gentlemen, they can fill them to the life" (116). That the amateur can narrow the gap between actor and character in the service of greater realism and less artificiality ironically plays into the hands of anti-theatrical commentators, who worry precisely about this merging of actor with role. But this conflation is also one of the reasons amateurism (or "informalism") continued to be championed throughout the nineteenth century and into the twentieth, from the time of its institutional origin with the founding of the Pic Nic in 1802, "the first amateur dramatic society in high life" (Rosenfeld, "Jane Austen" 43). In 1917, for example, American pastor John Talbot Smith described what he identified as "the parish theatre" movement in language that celebrated amateur drama's radical simplicity. An amateur play is "the parent of the professional drama" because it "acts towards its offspring as country grandmothers often do, taking the worn-out creature back to the simplicity of the farm, lecturing it on its origin, reminding it of the simplicity which should be at the root of the healthy variety, and otherwise steadying its mind and its nerves" (7). Less colorfully, Bonamy Dobrée wrote in 1947 that he was "very anxious that the amateur stage should play its full part in the development of the drama" (26), for the "amateur very often beats the professional—not at his own game, but in doing something different" (27): "By this I mean that the amateur approaches any play he is going to take part in as something to be related to life; . . . the amateur is not bound by tradition; he has no grooves to get out of" (28). Late-twentieth-century theorists who look to performers unaffiliated with either academic or commercial programs for supposedly "purer" and simpler acting styles share with advocates of amateurism like Dobrée an admiration for theater forged in the workshops of daily life. Hollis Huston, for example,

celebrates the street performer for creating "the simple stage" (1)—that is, a space in which "one performs according to a rule that is ours, that answers our agenda rather than someone else's" (7).

Eleven years before **The Tryal** was published, James Powell's farce about the rage for amateur acting, *Private Theatricals* (1787), also featured a plot in which the head of a household tries to control his family's and servants' enthusiasm for putting on private plays. But, unlike Baillie, Powell reserved for his leading female character a subversive moment at play's end. The actress playing Lady Grubb is allowed to advance "to the front of the Stage," where she asserts her love of private theater: "But if my audience do but approve, I shall bless the day when I first commenc'd my PRIVATE THEATRICALS" (II.viii.37).[21]

The manager of a private production of *Romeo and Juliet,* Lady Grubb is shown to appreciate theater so intensely that her enthusiasm wars against the domestic orderliness her husband has come to value. Nothing is as it should be, Alderman Grubb worries at play's start: all "the fine leaden gods on my lawn she [Lady Grubb] has thrown down to make room for her own whim":

> instead of my Jupiter and Juno, here we have tragedy on one side, and comedy on the other, for all the world like an April day; look one way it is all clouds and tears, look the other it is all sun-shine and laughter. Then there was my grotto at the head of my canal, where I had placed my beautiful figure of a river god with a great tub under his arm, with the water spouting out of it, she has thrown down too; and a marble Shakspeare placed at top, and a Ben Jonson at the bottom. My hermitage likewise she has pulled to pieces and rebuilt, and now called Prospero's cave. (I.ii.6)

From Grubb's perspective, his wife's passion for theater has destroyed his authority. Even his servants, like Betty the maid in **The Tryal** and the "five . . . under-servants" in *Mansfield Park* (described as "idle and dissatisfied" [206] for having been introduced to theater), elude his control. The kitchen servants have recently seemed to create a scene from "Bedlam": in "one corner," Grubb recounts in a monologue, "stood a captive Zara rattling a jack chain":

> In another a Juliet making her quietus, not with a bare bodkin; but a bare rolling pin. In another an Alexander brandishing a spit, and a pot lid, and in the middle stood the fat scullion holding a brass candlestick in one hand and rubbing her greasy fist with the other! Exclaiming, "yet here's a spot! out damn'd spot! out I say, not all the water in the sea would cleanse this little hand." And d-m-e! if I believe it would. Presently out burst from the closet a great lusty fellow with "Die all! die nobly! die like demi gods!" and kicks over a tea table with a

set of your lady-ship's best Dresden china, which came to the ground with a hideous crash. (I.ii.11-12)

This cacophony strikes Lady Grubb differently, for she is passionately involved in acting and playwrighting, in decorating and managing her private theater. For her, domestic chaos is "such divine confusion" (II.ii.25).

The struggle for control of domestic space culminates in Grubb's determination to "stick up for the 'Rights of Man' once in my life." Citing Blackstone's maxim "every man's house is his castle" (II.iii.28), Grubb brings the rehearsals to an end when he surprises his wife in an amorous scene with a professional actor named Buskin and catches their daughter about to elope with Villars, an amateur performer. It is left to Villars the amateur to condemn the "present rage for theatrical performances, [which] has grown to a ridiculous pitch," because this trend is "productive of much mischief to the morals of society, by admitting the loose and profligate (who are a scandal to the age) into the houses of virtue, whose reputation and honor they generally endanger" (II.vii.35). But then the dramaturgy undercuts his moralizing when Lady Grubb steps forward and addresses the audience directly about how "blessed" was the day when she first became involved in private theater.

This kind of moment is missing from *The Tryal,* which charts the process by which the owner of a fashionable home reasserts his control over domestic space, in his view rendered chaotic by amateur performance. As we have seen, Anthony Withrington resembles several other characters in the fiction of the private theatrical movement who function to suggest that amateur acting on private stages is potentially disruptive. Although not a consistently antitheatrical force like Austen's Sir Thomas Bertram in *Mansfield Park,* who is so upset by his children's experiment with private theater that he burns "every unbound copy of 'Lovers' Vows' in the house" (206) when he returns from the West Indies, still Withrington closes *The Tryal* with words that evoke Austen's description of how Sir Thomas "reinstates himself" upon his arrival at Mansfield Park: one of the tasks that Sir Thomas performs before he can resume "his seat as master of the house at dinner" is to oversee the dismantling of the little theater in the billiard room (206). Similarly reestablishing himself as the benevolent host of an orderly domicile, Withrington says to the company gathered onstage at the end of *The Tryal:* "Now, let us take our leave of plots and story-telling, if you please, and all go to my house to supper" (V.ii.299).

Baillie's Theory of Comedy

Read in the context of the amateur entertainment vogue, Baillie's first comedy emerges as an exploration of

how some women sought to theatricalize domestic space in order to respond to "a reasonable woman's desire" to control the representation of women's social reality. Indeed, Baillie's eight comedies richly reward students of late-eighteenth- and early-nineteenth-century culture by attending to some of the more pressing social issues of the period. *The Election* (1802), which resembles Maria Edgeworth's novel *Castle Rackrent* (1800), focuses on the dilemma of the landed gentry (some of whom had titles but little money) in order to explore the struggle between Lord Baltimore and Charles Freeman to see who will be elected to represent the borough. This plot also debates the dilemma of how to educate young women, by weighing the importance of "refinement" against the acquisition of a variety of artistic and linguistic "skills."[22] In *The Second Marriage* (1802) Baillie confronts anxious responses to class struggle and social mobility[23] by showing how the persecution of a second wife by the family that has recently lost its beloved mother and mistress expresses an ideology of domestic insularity. The Seabrights' triumphant casting off of their new stepmother, Lady Sarah (a comic Lady Macbeth), raises questions about why this woman—whose most serious fault is her penchant for economizing—must be banished at play's end, when she has actually shown herself a virtuous wife by working earnestly to help her ambitious husband fulfill his dream of a baronet's title. *The Alienated Manor* (1836) brings together an estate improver, a German philosopher, and a black servant named Sancho to discuss jealousy through a plot that centers on women's boredom in marriage. The bluestockings' salon-like gatherings and the alarmed responses to their intellectualism are gently mocked in *The Match* (1836), when Latitia Vane's lady-in-waiting, Flounce, tells the butler she hopes that her mistress will "remain as she is, with her lovers, and her confidants, and her flatterers, and her concerts, and her parties, and all proper suitable things that a rich lady ought to have. . . . but if she takes it into her head that a lady of thirty should give up gay dressing, and apply to her learning, and become a book-fancier, and a blue-stocking virtuoso, what's to become of my perquisites? It would make your hair stand on end, to hear all the nonsense I have heard about them there books" (700).

Perhaps because Baillie's comedies address topics that would have interested some early-nineteenth-century playgoers through a subtle exploration of her characters' emotional trials, critics have generally had difficulty appreciating them. Baillie alluded to the unpopularity of her comic plays in her preface to the second edition of *Miscellaneous Plays* (1805) when she wrote that the comedy *The Country Inn* (1804) "has been generally disliked" (386). Seven years after publishing *The Tryal,* Baillie had come to realize that, to "those who are chiefly accustomed, in works of this kind, to admire quick turns of thought, pointed expression, witty repartée, and the ludicrous display of the transient passing follies and fashions of the world, this play will have but few attractions" (389).

Time has proved her thus far prophetic. In 1930 Allardyce Nicoll wrote that every one of Baillie's comedies "is stilted. Not a laugh rises from a single scene" (I:209). More recently, in 1974, Terence Tobin overlooked Agnes's dilemma to focus on the sub-plot—Mariane Withrington's secret engagement—and concluded that a lack of "complications" dooms *The Tryal,* a critique that echoes Margaret Carhart's over fifty years earlier (*Plays by Scots* 199-200). Tobin asserted that the "exclusion of all other elements but the dominant feeling is more suited to tragedy than comedy, which thrives on complications. These are absent in *The Tryal.* . . . This comedy is over-simplified and never achieves the portrayal of the desired emotion. The couple's love resembles that of arranged marriages which abound in novels of the period" (195-96).

As Tobin failed to notice, *The Tryal*'s complications arise from Baillie's characterization of Agnes, whom Alice Meynell summarized in 1922 as "hard to capture" (61). Yet Meynell is almost alone in appreciating Baillie for making "such pretty eighteenth-century sport of her theme (her hero keeping the fine sensibilities, expressed with impassioned elegance, of Steele's *Conscious Lovers*) that it is not easy to realize that she passed the middle of the nineteenth century, albeit in extreme old age. . . . It is the exceeding sweetness of the two good girls bent upon their frolic (which is also a romp) that makes the charm of this happy play. They exchange names upon the wildest impulse consistent with their Georgia manners" (59). But Thomas Lawrence, who proposed *The Tryal* for a private theatrical in 1803, is thus far the only reader of the play I have found to praise it for those very features that Baillie herself advocated in her theory of comedy. In a letter to his sister, Lawrence wrote that he was "for Miss Bailey's Comedy, *'The Trial,'* one slightly spoken of by the world, but which I am sure, Mr. Homer would like for *its truly natural dialogue and character*" (cited in Rosenfeld, *Temples of Thespis* 154; my emphasis).[24]

Baillie articulated her theory of comedy at length in her **"Introductory Discourse,"** the essay she attached to the volume of plays in which *The Tryal* appeared in 1798 and which—as I discussed in Chapter 3—suggests that domestic spaces are fruitful sources of theater and drama. Baillie's belief that it is comedy's "task to exhibit" people "engaged in the busy turmoil of ordinary life, . . . and engaged with those smaller *trials* of the mind by which men are most apt to be overcome" (11; my emphasis) caused her to prefer realistic situations that she could have encountered in her own life. In contrast to the "satirical, witty, sentimental, and, above all, busy or circumstantial Comedy," Baillie

advocated what she called "Characteristic Comedy," a genre that represents "this motley world of men and women . . . under those circumstances of ordinary and familiar life most favorable to the discovery of the human heart" (12). This kind of play

> stands but little in need of busy plot, extraordinary incidents, witty repartée, or studied sentiments. It naturally produces for itself all that it requires. Characters, who are to speak for themselves, who are to be known by their own words and actions, not by the accounts that are given of them by others, cannot well be developed without considerable variety of judicious incident; a smile that is raised by some trait of undisguised nature, and a laugh that is provoked by some ludicrous effect of passion, or clashing of opposite characters, will be more pleasing to the generality of men than either the one or the other when occasioned by a play upon words, or a whimsical combination of ideas; and to behold the operation and effects of the different propensities and weaknesses of men, will naturally call up in the mind of the spectator moral reflections more applicable, and more impressive than all the high-sounding sentiments with which the graver scenes of Satirical and Sentimental Comedy are so frequently interlarded. (13)

Eschewing contrivance, artificiality, and self-conscious wit, Baillie's theory argues that the "most interesting and instructive class of Comedy" (12) derives from what we might today be inclined to call "situational" writing in which "even the bold and striking in character, should, to the best of the author's judgment, be kept in due subordination to nature" (14). Such dramas amuse and teach us in proportion to the degree that they present credible or "probable" events.[25]

But even as Baillie argued for a more subtle kind of dramatic writing—one focused on "the harmonious shades" of character—she wanted to avoid dwelling on "senseless minuteness" (13). Her entire dramatic project was shaped by her desire to exhibit the passions, to trace an emotion's "varieties and progress in the breast of man" (14). Nevertheless, Baillie criticized eccentric characterizations: "Above all, it is to be regretted that those adventitious distinctions among men, of age, fortune, rank, profession, and country, are so often brought forward in preference to the great original distinctions of nature" (15), because such an approach has "tempted our less skillful dramatists to exaggerate, and step, in further quest of the ludicrous, so much beyond the bounds of nature, that the very effect they are so anxious to produce is thereby destroyed, and all useful application of it entirely cut off, for we never apply to ourselves a false representation of nature" (14). It is in "ordinary life," Baillie emphasized throughout her theater theory, that "strong passions will foster themselves within the breast; and what are all the evils which vanity, folly, prejudice, or peculiarity of temper lead to, compared with those which such unquiet inmates produce?" (14). By seeking to justify a focus on "unquiet inmates" in domestic settings, Baillie's theory of comedy suggests that we should pay close attention to the drama and theater produced in closet spaces, a theatricality largely controlled by women confined to the private sphere.

Thirty-six years old when she published her first plays—which, in addition to *The Tryal,* included *Count Basil* and *De Monfort* (discussed in Chapter 4)—Baillie argued the need for a *mature* comedy, one that featured characters in "the middle stages of life; when they are too old for lovers or the confidents of lovers, and too young to be the fathers, uncles, and guardians, who are contrasted with them; but when they are still in full vigour of mind, eagerly engaged with the world, joining the activity of youth to the providence of age, and offer to our attention objects sufficiently interesting and instructive" (13). Because the character of Agnes Withrington is young, she may at first strike readers as the opposite of "reserved." But in fact, it is Agnes's very openness and impetuosity in the first part of *The Tryal* that fire this piece with energy. Baillie's biographer, Margaret Carhart, finds the characterization of Agnes "typical of the busy comedy that Miss Baillie criticized so sweepingly" (196). Yet Agnes is also nothing if not "thoughtful," and the complexity of her struggle to determine whether her beloved Harwood is morally the best match for her is at the heart of the play's plot. Although her uncle eventually succeeds in restraining Agnes's theatrical experiments, Baillie gives us a play in which the struggle of her heroine to control the rituals of courtship centers on her attempt to theatricalize domestic space according to her own design.

Though not generally regarded as a women's movement, the British private theatrical is significant for those scholars who are trying to fill in the picture of women's history in theater. In addition to affording a certain class of women increased opportunities for theatrical endeavor, the private theatrical movement anticipated subsequent developments that highlight the achievement of women in theater. For example, Madame Vestris's management of the Olympic theater in the 1830s—conceived as an alternative to the London patent stages—is a logical outgrowth of an eighteenth-century phenomenon in which a number of women had the experience of managing small theaters for the first time.[26] In praising Vestris's direction of the theater in the dedication letter he attached to *The Two Figaros* (1836), playwright James Robinson Planché wrote that "the model is not less instructive because it is made on so small a scale and preserved in the cabinet of a lady" (cited in Griffinhoof, 1830). Likewise, Frances Maria Kelly's "Little Theatre in Dean Street," which was built in the 1830s "as an extension to her private house" (Francis 156), resembles the private theaters of the previous era, in that Kelly planned to feature those fledgling performers whom she trained in the acting school, which she also moved to her house from the Strand.[27] Biographer Basil Francis describes Kelly's idea of this little theater as follows:

> she felt she needed a *model* theatre, one which would incorporate all the alterations and improvements she had in mind. The majority of the theatres in which she played were ill-designed, both before and behind the curtain; for years she had suffered from backstage arrangements that were grossly inadequate, and had been obliged to pick her way to the stage across piles of properties and scenery through tangles of ropes and counterweights and antique stage-machinery. What she had in mind was a "modern" Little Theatre, well-appointed, both from the view of the player and playgoer, with "modern" machinery, ample entrances and exits, comfortable dressing-rooms and above all a stage that would incorporate every new improvement that the mind of man could devise. (155)

Though Kelly's dream went unrealized (as the result of stage machinery so noisy that the actors could not be heard), her desire to create a space for actor training and performance within the bounds of her home reminds us once again to pay closer attention to the theatrical experiments originating within domestic settings, and in the closeted spaces in which many lived a large portion of their lives, for it is in these locations that fascinating theatrical experiments have been conceived and launched.

Even in the late twentieth century, when an astonishing array of theatrical venues is now available to women who work on commercial and academic stages, some of the more interesting theatrical experiments performed by women have paid homage to this domestic tradition. Hanna Scolnicov observes that "it is the new feminist playwrights [Maureen Duffy, Pam Gems, Caryl Churchill, Charlotte Keayley] who go back to the recognizable, mimetic spaces, to what for them is still the unresolved question of the home" (155). Performance artists have also brought renewed attention to those domestic environments in which so much of women's theatrical art has been produced and enacted. For example, Leslie Labowitz performed *Sproutime* (1980) in her home in Venice, California, for an audience "who were also her friends, [and who] entered her dark garage to discover racks of germinating seeds from floor to ceiling and Labowitz, nude, watering her plants" (Case, *Feminism and Theatre* 58). Judy Chicago's famous art exhibit, *Dinner Party,* which featured place settings in the form of clitorises alluding to the achievements of specific women in history, in certain ways recalls the noted private entertainment hosted by Madame Vigée-Lebrun in late-eighteenth-century France, at which friends arrived for a dinner party to discover the entire dining room decked out with the accoutrements of Grecian culture and the hostess and her daughters classically dressed.

Because the private theatrical movement celebrated those very spaces in which women had for centuries been making theater, a study of this late-eighteenth-century trend focuses our attention on several facts important to British women's theater history. It reminds us that a particular class of women have had a long history of theatricalizing closet space, which associations of the Romantic closet with antitheatricality, or the act of simply reading plays, fail to reveal. A focus on the private theatrical also helps us more readily appreciate the degree to which some plays from the Romantic period confront the issue of how women have sought to control domestic spaces, for both theatrical and nontheatrical purposes. Moreover, the act of opening up British Romantic closets in order to expose the variety of theatrical activities that actually took place there can deepen our understanding of how private spaces and domestic settings influenced public stages. In addition, studying a play like Baillie's **The Tryal** can motivate us to focus anew on the dramaturgy of other women playwrights from the Romantic period in order to learn more about how fictional writings complement and interrogate nonfictional discourse; to expand the contexts for discussing women's theories of the stage; and to revise conceptions of early-nineteenth-century British theater as a culture of exciting theatricality in which a wide array of spaces were explored for their dramatic and theatrical potential.

Notes

[1] This quotation is from the facsimile edition (Georg Olms Verlag, 1976) of Baillie's 1851 collected works. All further references to Baillie's poetry, prose, and dramas—with the exception of *The Tryal* (see note 19 below)—are from this edition. In the case of the dramas, I cite them by act, scene, and page number.

[2] Baillie composed this verse for Mary Berry's private play *The Fashionable Friends* (1800, private theatrical; 1802, published), which, although conceived as a private theatrical, also received a public showing against Berry's wishes. According to the editor of Berry's letters and journals, Lady Theresa Lewis, a "month after Miss Berry returned from France, she had the mortification of finding that the play which had been acted in private with such flattering success the preceding year at Strawberry Hill, did not receive the sanction of the public voice. It was brought out at Drury Lane with a cast of parts, comprising names which must have greatly conduced to its success, and the cause of its failure cannot be attributed to a want of ability on the part of the performers" (cited in *Extracts of the Journals and Correspondence of Miss Berry* 2:194).

[3] A partial list of those women who participated in late-eighteenth-century private theatricals (through a combination of acting, writing, and organizing) includes: Joanna Baillie, Mary Berry, Frances Burney, Marianne Chambers, Elizabeth Knipe Cobbold, Elizabeth Berkeley Craven (the Margravine of Anspach), Mary Champion Crespigny, Elizabeth Farren, Catherine Galindo, Elizabeth Inchbald, Frances Anne Kemble, Harriot Mellon, Eliza O'Neill, Amelia Opie, Sarah Siddons, Mariana Starke, and Peg Woffington.

The introduction by Gwenn Davis and Beverly A. Joyce to *Drama by Women to 1900* (1992) observes that private theatricals, "like closet drama, had aristocratic origins, but became a general pursuit" (xii). Davis and Joyce's list of women who created private theatricals between the seventeenth and nineteenth centuries includes: Queen Henrietta Maria, Elizabeth Craven, Lady Georgiana (Russell) Peel, Lady Victoria Russell, Lady Bell, Lady Cadogan, Gabrielle De Nottbeck, Florence Gailey, Jean Ingraham, Frances Peard, and Winnie Rover (xii).

[4] Marvin Carlson notes that as late as 1833 in England a private theater was erected at the castle of Chatsworth (56).

[5] These canonical works included plays by women writers, among them Susanna Centlivre, Hannah Cowley, and Elizabeth Inchbald. For a list of the most popular plays performed on the eighteenth-century private stage, see Sybil Rosenfeld, *Temples of Thespis* (1978), 169-70.

[6] My information for this history is collected from the following sources: Charles Kendal Bushe's *The Private Theatre of Kilkenny* (1825), composed mostly of the information on playbills, along with the prologue and epilogue spoken to each play and reviews of performances; Tom Moore's review of that volume in the *Edinburgh Review* (1827), which after stating "There is no subject that we would sooner recommend to a male or female author, in distress for a topic, than a History of the Private Theatres of Europe" (368) situates British private theatricals in the context of private theaters in ancient Greece, Renaissance Italy, and modern Russia and France; Sybil Rosenfeld's *Temples of Thespis: Some Private Theatres and Theatricals in England and Wales, 1700-1820* (1978), which includes two helpful appendices drawn from her survey of records pertaining to "120 places in which private theatricals were held" (7): one listing the performance of private theatricals by year and the other identifying those English plays "first performed at private theatricals" (180); and Marvin Carlson's chapter called "The Jewel in the Casket," in *Places of Performance* (1989). Nina Auerbach's *Private Theatricals: The Lives of the Victorians* (1990), while promisingly titled, focuses not on the private theatrical phenomenon but rather uses the term to discuss "the

source of Victorian fears of performance," which she argues "lay in the histrionic artifice of ordinary life" (114).

[7] Further information about these players is provided by Suzanne R. Westfall's *Patrons and Performance* (1990).

[8] See Karl Toepfer's fascinating account of this phenomenon, including erotic marionette theater, in chapter 2 of his *Theatre, Aristocracy, and Pornocracy: The Orgy Calculus* (1991).

[9] See Case's chapter 4 of *Feminism and Theatre* (1988) for a discussion of this trend, led by theater groups such as Lavendar Cellar Theatre, Medusa's Revenge, and Red Dyke Theatre.

[10] For more information on von Stein and her theatrical activities, see Katherine R. Goodman, "The Sign Speaks" (1992).

[11] This quotation is from the preface to the Countess of Hardwicke's play, *The Court of Oberon, or The Three Wishes,* in which the writer explains why it took so long for the play to "see the light." (The play was written in the late seventeenth century.) On the occasion of Princess Victoria's intent to patronize "a Bazaar, for the succour of the distressed Irish," it was "suggested that among the contributions made by Ladies of their Fancy works for the profit of the Bazaar, this [play] might also find a place.—Yet it could scarcely have been ventured upon without the condescending permission of Her Royal Highness the Duchess of Kent, to dedicate this little work to Her Royal Highness the Princess Victoria."

[12] Elizabeth Berkeley Craven's original dramas are listed in Broadley and Melville's Introduction to her memoirs (1826), republished under the title *The Beautiful Lady Craven* (1914).

[13] The French edition of Craven's memoirs (1828) was republished in 1991 by Mercure de France in an edition annotated by Jean-Pierre Guicciardi (with an introduction).

[14] Although it is common to find professional actors participating in private theatricals, they often express a combination of amusement and frustration about the experience. Elizabeth Inchbald wrote in a letter that to "my extreme sorrow I am at present under the dread of being a party in a private theatrical myself."

> I was surprised into a promise, and now go every morning to attend rehearsals; still I foresee many impediments, which I will as far as in my power increase. One is, the drama on which they have fixed has a supper in it, and I have represented that the hurry of clearing away the table, which is a part

of the comic incidents of the piece, will probably break the wine bottles and throw the hot dishes against the beautiful hangings and furniture of the room. This observation gave Mr. Monk Lewis, M.P., (who is one of the performers,) an opportunity of saying an excellent thing to the lady of the house, who, alarmed at my remark, immediately cried out she would not have a *real* supper, but that every thing should be *counterfeit*. On which she rang for her butler, and ordered him to go and bespeak a couple of wooden fowls, a wooden tongue, wooden jellies, and so forth. "Nay," cried Monk Lewis, "if your ladyship gives a wooden supper, the audience will say all your actors are STICKS." (cited in Boaden, *Memoirs* 2:56)

In 1831, Frances Anne Kemble discussed her participation in Francis Leveson's adaptation of Victor Hugo's *Hernani* at Bridgewater House as follows: "I have consented to this, not knowing well how to refuse, yet for one or two reasons I almost think I had better not have done so. I expect to be excessively amused by it, but it will take up a terrible deal of my time, for I am sure they will need rehearsals without end" (*Records of a Girlhood* 365).

[15] Observing that the "amateur theatricals at Barbone in effect initiated Frances Burney into the performance of womanhood," Gillian Russell writes that "the amateur theatricals of the minor gentry . . . not only enacted and defined family relationships but also educated the younger generation in the gendered roles which they would perform as adults" (131).

[16] For further discussion of women, theatrical contamination, and private life, see Joseph Litvak's first chapter, "The Infection of Acting: Theatricals and Theatricality in *Mansfield Park*," in *Caught in the Act: Theatricality in the Nineteenth-Century English Novel* (1992). His discussion of the commentaries on theater by Thomas Gisborne, Hannah More, Elizabeth Inchbald, and William Hazlitt is especially relevant to my argument here.

[17] This pervasiveness is recognized by Sybil Rosenfeld in "Jane Austen and Private Theatricals" (1962), who writes: "there were apprentices' theatricals, military and naval theatricals, children's and school theatricals and small theatres in which amateurs could try out their histrionic abilities for a modest fee" (42).

[18] My text for *The Tryal* is the 1990 reprint of Baillie's 1798 *Series of Plays* published by Woodstock Books. (N.B.: the 1851 edition of this play spells *The Tryal* as *The Trial*.)

[19] Kamchatka is a peninsula of northeast Russia between the Bering Sea and the Sea of Okhotsk (Stamp 224).

[20] Margaret Carhart has observed that "Harwood's rail-

ing against Agnes is an echo of the tone of Petruchio in *The Taming of the Shrew,* and Agnes' description of her suitors recalls the similar scene in *The Merchant of Venice*" (73).

[21] For a brief discussion of this play, see Smith and Lawhon, *Plays about the Theatre in England, 1737-1800* (1979), 135-37.

[22] See also Mrs. Overall's letter in Baillie's *The Match,* at which Emma smiles but which the indecisive Latitia defends: "Education of every kind has, till lately, proceeded upon a wrong principle. Every body taught the same things, without regard to talent or capacity. Should not a boy's instruction be adapted to his genius?" (I.ii.688).

[23] See Daniel P. Watkins's discussion of class issues in Baillie's *De Monfort,* in *A Materialist Critique of English Romantic Drama* (1993).

[24] Rosenfeld also cites a letter written by Harriet Cavendish concerning the same private theater, which indicates that another Baillie play, *Count Basil,* was also under consideration. Like *The Tryal,* however, it went unperformed (158).

[25] For a discussion of this emphasis on the "probable" or "credible" by Romantic women writers, see Anne K. Mellor, "A Criticism of Their Own" (1995).

[26] See, for example, chapter 5 of Sandra Richards's *The Rise of the English Actress* (1993), in which she writes of Madame Vestris:

> Her greatest contribution to the status of actors was the introduction of salaries paid in advance, a practice wholly against the grain of what was considered thrifty management. The move was instrumental in generating a reconsideration of professional rights among all players. It culminated in the British Actors' Association and its present system of insisting that two weeks' salary per company member be held by Equity as insurance against managerial breaches. (104)

[27] For more information about Kelly's acting career, her theater, and her acting school, see Holman (1935) and Francis (1950).

Works Cited

[Anonymous]. "To the Editor of the *European Magazine.* Plan for a Fashionable Rosciad; and some account of Mr. Fector's Private Theatre at Dover." *The European Magazine, and London Review* 14 (1788): 66-67.

Ardener, Shirley. "Ground Rules and Social Maps for Women: An Introduction." In *Women and Space: Ground Rules and Social Maps,* ed. Shirley Ardener, 1-30. London: Croom Helm; New York: St. Martin's Press, 1981.

Austen, Jane. *Mansfield Park.* Ed. Tony Tanner. London: Penguin Books, 1985 (orig. 1814).

Baillie, Joanna. *The Dramatic and Poetical Works (1851).* Hildesheim and New York: Georg Olms Verlag, 1976. Facsimile edition.

————. *A Series of Plays.* Oxford: Woodstock Books, 1990.

————. *Series of Plays (1798-1812).* Ed. D. H. Reiman. New York: Garland Press, 1977. Facsimile edition.

————. *The Tryal. A Series of Plays,* 195-299. Oxford: Woodstock Books, 1990.

————. *A View of the General Tenour of the New Testament Regarding the Nature and Dignity of Jesus Christ.* London, 1831.

Baron-Wilson, Mrs. [Margaret] Cornwell. *Memoirs of Harriot, Duchess of St. Albans.* 2 vols. London: Henry Colburn, 1839.

Brooks, Peter. *Body Work: Objects of Desire in Modern Narrative.* Cambridge and London: Harvard University Press, 1993.

Brown, Janet. *Taking Center Stage: Feminism in Contemporary U.S. Drama,* Methuen, N.J., and London: The Scarecrow Press, 1991.

Carhart, Margaret. *The Life and Work of Joanna Baillie.* New Haven: Yale University Press, 1923.

Carlson, Marvin. *Places of Performance: The Semiotics of Theatre Architecture.* Ithaca and London: Cornell University Press, 1989.

————. *Theories of the Theatre: A Historical and Critical Survey, from the Greeks to the Present.* Ithaca and London: Cornell University Press, 1984; rpt. 1993.

Case, Sue-Ellen. *Feminism and Theatre.* New York: Methuen, 1988.

Craven, Elizabeth Berkeley. *The Beautiful Lady Craven: The Original Memoirs of Elizabeth Baronness Craven afterwards Margravine of Anspach and Bayreuth and Princess Berkeley of the Holy Roman Empire (1750-1828).* 2 vols. London: John Lane The Bodley Head, 1914 (orig. 1826).

————. "Dedication" to *The Fashionable Day.* London: G. Kearsley, 1780.

————. *Memoires.* Edition presentée and annotée par Jean-Pierre Guicciardi. Paris: Mercure de France, 1991.

————. Vol. 1 of *Memoirs of the Margravine of Anspach, Written By Herself.* 2 vols. London: Henry Colburn, 1826.

Cumberland, Richard. "Remarks upon the Present Taste for Acting Private Plays." *The European Magazine, and London Review* 14 (1788): 115-18.

Dobrée, Bonamy. *The Amateur and the Theatre.* London: The Hogarth Press, 1947.

Francis, Basil. *Fanny Kelly of Drury Lane.* London: Rockliff Publishing Corporation, 1950.

Griffinhoof, Arthur (pseud). *Memoirs of the Life of Madame Vestris.* Privately printed, 1830.

Hamilton, Catherine Jane. "Joanna Baillie." Vol. 1 of *Women Writers: Their Works and Ways,* 110-31. 2 vols. London and New York: Ward, Lock, Bowden, and Co., 1892-93.

Holbrook, Ann Catherine. *The Dramatist; or, Memoirs of the Stage. With the Life of the Authoress, Prefixed, and Interspersed with, A Variety of Anecdotes, Humorous and Pathetic.* Birmingham, Eng.: Martin and Hunter, 1809.

Holmstrom, Kirsten Gram. *Monodrama, Attitudes, Tableaux Vivants: Studies on Some Trends in Theatrical Fashion, 1770-1815.* Uppsala: Almquist and Wiksells Boktryckeri, 1967.

Huston, Hollis. *The Actor's Instrument: Body, Theory, Stage.* Ann Arbor: University of Michigan Press, 1992.

Inchbald, Elizabeth. *Remarks for the British Theatre (1806-09). By Elizabeth Inchbald.* Introduced by Cecilia Macheski. Delmar, N.Y.: Scholars' Facsimiles and Reprints, 1990.

Jermyn, Laetitia. "A Memoir of Mrs. Elizabeth [Knipe] Cobbold." *Poems by Mrs. Elizabeth Cobbold. With a Memoir of the Author.* Ipswich: J. Row, 1825.

Johnson, Reginald Brimley. "Introduction." *Bluestocking Letters,* 1-18. London: John Lane The Bodley Head, 1926.

Maclaren, Archibald. *The Private Theatre: or, the Highland Funeral.* London: A. Macpherson, 1809.

Massey, Doreen. *Space, Place, and Gender.* Minneapolis: University of Minnesota Press, 1994.

Nicoll, Allardyce. *A History of Late Eighteenth-Century Drama, 1750-1800.* Cambridge: Cambridge University Press, 1927.

————. Vol. 1 of *A History of Early Nineteenth-Century Drama.* 2 vols. Cambridge: Cambridge University Press, 1930.

Peake, Richard Brinsley. *Amateurs and Actors: A Musical Farce in Two Acts.* London: John Cumberland, 1827 (orig. 1818).

Powell, James. *Private Theatricals: A Farce. In Two Acts.* 1787.

Rosenfeld, Sybil. "Jane Austen and Private Theatricals." *Essays and Studies* 15 (1962): 40-51.

————. *Temples of Thespis: Some Private Theatres and Theatricals in England and Wales, 1700-1820.* London: Society for Theatre Research, 1978.

Rousseau, Jean-Jacques. *La Nouvelle Héloise.* Translated and abridged by Judith H. McDowell. University Park: Pennsylvania State University Press, 1968.

Russell, Gillian. *The Theatres of War: Performance, Politics, and Society 1793-1815.* Oxford: Clarendon Press, 1995.

Scolnicov, Hanna. *Woman's Theatrical Space.* Cambridge: Cambridge University Press, 1994.

Smith, George Barnett. "Joanna Baillie." *The Dictionary of National Biography,* 1:885-89. 22 vols. Oxford: Oxford University Press, 1921.

Smith, John Talbot. *The Parish Theatre: A Brief Account of Its Rise, Its Present Condition, and Its Prospects.* Longmans, Green, and Co., 1917.

Spain, Daphne. *Gendered Spaces.* Chapel Hill and London: University of North Carolina Press, 1992.

Sturgess, Keith. *Jacobean Private Theatre.* London and New York: Routledge and Kegan Paul, 1987.

Tobin, Terence. *Plays by Scots.* Iowa City: University of Iowa Press, 1974.

Tristram, Philippa. *Living Space in Fact and Fiction.* London and New York: Routledge, 1989.

Turner, Victor. *Ritual to Theatre: The Human Seriousness of Play.* New York: Performing Arts Journal Publications, 1982.

Tytler, Sarah, and J. L. Watson. Vol. 2 of *The Songstresses of Scotland.* 2 vols. London: Strahan and Co. Publishers, 1871.

Wekerle, Gerda R., Rebecca Peterson, and David Morley. "Introduction." In *New Space for Women,* ed. Gerda R. Wekerle, Rebecca Peterson, and David Morley, 1-34. Boulder, Colo.: Westview Press, 1980.

Wilshire, Bruce. *Role Playing and Identity: The Limits of Theatre as Metaphor.* Bloomington: Indiana University Press, 1982.

FURTHER READING

Biography

Carswell, Donald. "Joanna Baillie." In his *Sir Walter: A Four-Part Study in Biography*, pp. 262-86. London: John Murray, 1930.

Biography of Baillie emphasizing the high regard Sir Walter Scott held for her personally and professionally.

Criticism

Brewer, William D. "Joanna Baillie and Lord Byron." *Keats-Shelley Journal: Keats, Shelley, Byron, Hunt, and Their Circle* 44 (1995): 165-81.

Examines Baillie and Lord Byron's literary relationship, including their influences on each other's works.

Burroughs, Catherine B. "English Romantic Women Writers and Theatre Theory: Joanna Baillie's Prefaces to the *Plays on the Passions*." In *Re-Visioning Romanticism: British Women Writers, 1776-1837*, edited by Carol Shiner Wilson and Joel Haefner, pp. 274-96. Philadelphia: University of Pennsylvania Press, 1994.

Study of Baillie's strongly theoretical theater criticism in the prefaces to her plays.

———. "'Out of the Pale of Social Kindred Cast': Conflicted Performance Styles in Joanna Baillie's *De Monfort*." In *Romantic Women Writers: Voices and Countervoices*, edited by Paula R. Feldman and Theresa M. Kelley, pp. 223-35. Hanover, N.H.: University Press of New England, 1995.

Summarizes *De Monfort* and discusses its importance, particularly in terms of "the relationship between 'the closet' and public staging," a topic that interested Baillie throughout her career.

———. "'A Reasonable Woman's Desire': The Private Theatrical and Joanna Baillie's *The Tryal*." *Texas Studies in Literature and Language* 38, Nos. 3/4 (Fall/Winter 1996): 265-84.

Considers *The Tryal* within the context of private theatrical performances. A substantial reworking of this essay is included in the entry above.

Cox, Jeffrey N. "Joanna Baillie: Gothic Women." In *Seven Gothic Dramas, 1789-1825*, edited by Jeffrey N. Cox, pp. 50-7. Athens: Ohio University Press, 1992.

Examines Baillie's use of Gothic conventions to explore women's roles in society.

Evans, Bertrand. "Joanna Baillie and Gothic Drama." In his *Gothic Drama from Walpole to Shelley*, pp. 200-15. Berkeley and Los Angeles: University of California Press, 1947.

Describes the chief Gothic characteristics of Baillie's plays.

Insch, A. G. "Joanna Baillie's *De Monfort* in Relation to Her Theory of Tragedy." *The Durham University Journal* n.s. XXIII, No. 3 (June 1962): 114-20.

Argues that *De Monfort* is Baillie's best tragedy precisely because it does not completely follow Baillie's dramatic theory.

Norton, M. "The Plays of Joanna Baillie." *The Review of English Studies* 23, No. 90 (April 1947): 131-43.

Discusses Baillie's plot constructions and her comments on the performances of her plays.

Plarr, Victor G. "Walter Scott and Joanna Baillie." *The Edinburgh Review* 216 and 217 (October 1912 and January 1913): 355-71 and 170-81.

Examines previously unpublished letters of Sir Walter Scott to Baillie, which include commentary on several of her plays.

Additional coverage of Baillie's life and career is contained in the following source published by Gale Research: *Dictionary of Literary Biography,* Vol. 93.

Agnes Grey

Anne Brontë

The following entry presents criticism of Brontë's novel *Agnes Grey* (1847). For a discussion of Brontë's complete career, see *NCLC*, Volume 4.

INTRODUCTION

Brontë's first novel, *Agnes Grey,* was originally published under her pseudonym Acton Bell in 1847 and details the life of a governess in mid-Victorian England. Many critics take its main subject and title character to be a literary projection of Brontë herself, citing numerous parallels between Brontë's life and that of her fictional creation. Scholars are careful, however, to acknowledge that *Agnes Grey* is a work of imaginative fiction that addresses social concerns, including the at times degrading treatment of governesses, the consequences of the Victorian cult of domesticity, and Brontë's critique of burgeoning materialism and declining morality in mid-nineteenth-century Britain. To a large degree overshadowed by her sister Charlotte's *Jane Eyre*—a similar work that was published before Anne's novel, but composed after it—*Agnes Grey* has been considered somewhat artistically inferior to, and has certainly enjoyed a great deal less popularity than, Charlotte's novel. Nevertheless, twentieth-century critics have deemed *Agnes Grey* an important work of Victorian realism that demonstrates Brontë's humor, perceptive eye for detail, talent for storytelling, and unmistakable taste for the unconventional.

Plot and Major Characters

The younger of two daughters of an Anglican clergyman, Agnes Grey spends her early years living modestly but comfortably in the north of mid-nineteenth- century England. When Agnes is still a young adult, however, her somewhat imprudent father, Richard Grey—seeking to strengthen the family finances through speculative investment—loses his capital following a maritime disaster that sinks his friend's merchants ships. Eager to assist the newly impoverished household in whatever way she can, Agnes determines to become a governess, despite the initial disapproval of her parents. Naively optimistic, she takes a position in the household of the upper-class Bloomfields. Hired by the discompassionate Mrs. Bloomfield, Agnes is charged with the care and instruction of her four children, whom she soon discovers are ill-mannered, undisciplined, even cruel. Unable to control or educate the Bloomfield brood—on one

occasion she finds it necessary to kill a nest of birds to prevent the youngest boy, Tom, from torturing them—Agnes is shortly given notice. She soon locates a new governess position, gaining employment with the Murray family of Horton Lodge. Treated with little respect by her aristocratic employers, Agnes discovers that her new pupils—Charles, John, Matilda, and Rosalie, who range in age from nine to sixteen—are only a slight improvement over their unprincipled predecessors. Confronted with these troubles, Agnes encounters Edward Weston, the new curate in Horton, and swiftly falls in love with the simple, sincere, and unassuming young cleric. Meanwhile, the Murray boys depart for school, leaving her in charge of only Matilda and Rosalie. Time passes and the materialistic and flirtatious Rosalie, now eighteen, leaves Agnes's care. Several months later, Rosalie marries Sir Thomas Ashby, a wealthy and influential man whom she does not love. Meanwhile, Agnes's father dies and her mother decides to establish a school in the seaside town of A——. From this moment, Agnes spends only six more weeks in Horton, then bids farewell to Mr. Weston and joins her mother in A——.

Approximately one year later, she receives a letter from her former student Rosalie inviting her to Ashby Park. When she arrives, Agnes greets a cynical Lady Ashby, now a mother and clearly struggling in a bad marriage. Several days after her return to A——, Agnes encounters Edward Weston walking along the beach. He has secured a position as vicar in a nearby parish. Soon after, the two marry and have children of their own.

Major Themes

One of several "governess novels" written and published in the mid-1800s, *Agnes Grey* falls into the tradition of the female bildungsroman, or novel of development, and thus dramatizes the theme of innocence and youthfulness passing into experience. Unlike many such works of the same era, however, *Agnes Grey* is thought by critics to treat certain subjects absent from, or only vaguely sketched, in the woman's bildungsroman. Various scholars observe in the novel a critique of mid-Victorian social attitudes, especially as they relate to morality, childrearing, the treatment of women, the surging tide of materialism, and the hypocritical cult of domesticity. Agnes's numerous confrontations with the recalcitrant children she is hired to educate are said to condemn the domestic deficiencies of the British upper classes—personified in the idle, cold, materialistic, and largely disinterested parents of the Murray and Bloomfield children. Commentators have also seen in *Agnes Grey* a clever depiction of the feminine struggle to acquire independence and a voice in the affairs of a society that relegates women to domestic functions.

Critical Reception

Many scholars believe the novel that was to become *Agnes Grey* was originally entitled *Passages in the Life of an Individual* (a work in progress referred to by Brontë in her correspondence), and it has been assumed since the time of its publication to be autobiographical in character. Although the novel was significantly drawn from material in Brontë's own life and is marred to a degree by moral didacticism, *Agnes Grey* has earned the respect of literary critics as an important work of fiction, but none have quite equaled George Moore's 1924 assessment of the novel as "the most perfect narrative in English literature." Later critics of *Agnes Grey* have done much to undo the influence of Brontë's elder sister, Charlotte, whose condescending and apologetic attitude toward Anne's literary talent set a precedent for much subsequent criticism. Thus, in the contemporary era, commentators have lauded *Agnes Grey* for the simple brilliance of its narrative technique as well as for its

unadorned style, psychological clarity, and insightful observations on the nature of Victorian society.

CRITICISM

George Moore (essay date 1924)

SOURCE: "Chapter XVII," in *Conversations in Ebury Street,* Chatto & Windus, 1969, pp. 211-23.

[*In the following excerpt of a literary conversation originally published in 1924, Moore calls* Agnes Grey *"the most perfect prose narrative in English literature" and goes on to describe the story.*]

MOORE. . . . If Anne had written nothing but *The Tenant of Wildfell Hall* I should not have been able to predict the high place she would have taken in English letters. All I should have been able to say is: An inspiration that comes and goes like a dream. But, her first story, *Agnes Grey,* is the most perfect prose narrative in English literature.

GOSSE. The most perfect prose narrative in English literature, and overlooked for fifty-old years!

MOORE. The blindness of criticism should not surprise one as well acquainted with the history of literature as you are. You have noticed, no doubt, that I avoid whenever I can the word fiction, for the word has become degraded by association with circulating libraries and has come to mean novels that sell for six months and are never heard of afterwards. *Agnes Grey* is a prose narrative simple and beautiful as a muslin dress. I need not remind you, Gosse, that, it's more difficult to write a simple story than a complicated one. The arrival of Agnes at the house of her employer (she is the new governess) opens the story, and the first sentences, the eating of a beefsteak is among the first, convince us that we are with a quick, witty mind, capable of appreciating all she hears and sees; and when Agnes begins to tell us of her charges and their vulgar parents, we know that we are reading a masterpiece. Nothing short of genius could have set them before us so plainly and yet with restraint—even the incident of the little boy who tears a bird's nest out of some bushes and fixes fish hooks into the beaks of the young birds so that he may drag them about the stable-yard. Agnes's reprimands, too, are low in tone, yet sufficient to bring her into conflict with the little boy's mother, who thinks that her son's amusement should not be interfered with. The story was written, probably, when Anne Brontë was but two or three and twenty, and it is the one story in English literature in which style, characters and subject are in perfect keeping. In writing it Anne's eyes were always upon the story itself and not upon her readers; a thought does not seem to have come into her mind that a reader would like a little more drama, a little more comedy, that a picnic or a ball would provide entertainment. Whilst writing about Agnes Grey's first set of pupils she had in mind Agnes's second set, and was careful that the first situation should lead up to the second. Agnes is not dismissed, nor does she even, as well as I remember, leave for any definite reason. The house had become disagreeable to her and she leaves, rests for a while at home, and hearing of a situation in which she would have the charge of two growing girls, she accepts it, and the reader is relieved to find Agnes, whom he has begun to appreciate, among less harsh surroundings. One of her pupils is about to pass out of the schoolroom into the world; the other is a sort of tomboy who likes kittens and puppies, and the society of the stable-yard and harness-room better than that of the drawing-room, her hour not having yet come. At the end of the first term, a term of six months or a year, Agnes Grey goes home, and after a short holiday she returns to her pupils, very tired, for the journey has been a long one. But whilst Agnes has been resting at home Miss Murray has been to her first ball, and Agnes must really come to the schoolroom at once to hear all about it. And so absorbed is Miss Murray in herself, in her dress, in her partners, in the flowers that were given to her, in the words that were spoken to her during the dances and the sitting-out in quiet corners, that she fails to perceive how inappropriate the occasion is for the telling of her successes. Agnes Grey gives all the attention she can give to her pupil, but is too tired to respond, and Miss Murray, feeling, no doubt, that Agnes thinks she is exaggerating her successes, insists still further: As for *me,* Miss Grey—I'm so *sorry* you didn't see me! I was *charming*—wasn't I, Matilda? And the younger sister, who has not been to the ball, answers:

Middling.

The word lights up the narrative like a ray of light cast by Ruysdael into the middle of a landscape.

GOSSE. I am afraid you writers of prose narratives appreciate other people's narratives only when you find your own qualities in them.

MOORE. What you say is most unjust. You have read a great deal of poetry, but your appreciations of poetry are not limited to the exact qualities you possess yourself. Why, therefore, should you think that I cannot appreciate anything that is not part of my own possession?

GOSSE. I don't think it's quite the same thing. . . . But tell me what becomes of the governess.

MOORE. She makes the acquaintance of a curate and visits the alms-houses with him, and here Anne rises to

greater heights in patter than Jane Austen, for Jane's patter is drawing-room patter, whilst Anne's patter is in Yorkshire jargon. I don't know if you will acquiesce in my belief that the language of the fields is more beautiful than that of the town, and that the cottage supplies better stuff for art than the drawing-room.

GOSSE. Not better than the palace. Shakespeare—

MOORE. Wouldn't it be just as well to leave Shakespeare out of this argument?

GOSSE. You haven't told me yet what becomes of Agnes Grey?

MOORE. She leaves her situation and goes, I think, to recover her health by the sea, and meeting on the esplanade the parson with whom she visited the alms-houses—he has gone there for his vacation—

GOSSE. The end of the walk is an engagement!

MOORE. And why shouldn't it be? The simple is never commonplace.

GOSSE. The commonplace is yesterday's artifices, and I will admit that I have often wondered why criticism should have raised up thrones for Charlotte and Emily, leaving Anne in the kitchen.

MOORE. A sort of literary Cinderella.

GOSSE. A blindness of fifty years of which you have no cause to complain, since it has called you to fulfil the part of the fairy godmother.

MOORE. Critics follow a scent like hounds, and I am not certain that it wasn't Charlotte who first started them on their depreciation of Anne. I cannot give chapter and verse here, but in one of her introductions she certainly apologises for **The Tenant of Wildfell Hall,** pleading extenuating circumstances: Anne's youth, her sickness, her inexperience of life. Three phthisis-stricken sisters living on a Yorkshire moor, and all three writing novels, were first-rate copy, and Charlotte's little depreciations of the dead were a great help, for three sisters of equal genius might strain the credulity of the readers of the evening newspapers. Such insight as would enable the journalist to pick out the right one would be asking too much of journalism.

GOSSE. Could you have picked out the right?

MOORE. Not at the time of the publication of Anne's books, but fifty years is a long while to wait. My case against Charlotte does not end with an implicit defamation of her sister, for in her novel *Villette* she is guilty of the most bare-faced plagiarism. We may rob the dead, but not the just departed, and of all the poor dead sister hardly yet cold in her coffin. Like her sisters, Charlotte wrote well, but she did not write out of the imaginations of her mind, and, the first volume of *Villette* being almost an autobiography, her talent rises all the while; but the story needed in the second volume a girl representative of her sex, something more than a tracing of Charlotte's own youth, and so it came to pass that Charlotte found herself constrained to lay hands on Miss Murray, which she could do easily, a mere change of name being enough to hide the theft, for nobody had read *Agnes Grey.*

GOSSE. Love is said to be blind, but if all that you say is true, criticism is even blinder, for though many charges have been brought against Charlotte, plagiarism is not one of them.

MOORE. The critics of the Brontës were interested more in Charlotte's flirtation with the schoolmaster in Belgium, which, if it were true, mattered very little, and if it were not, didn't matter at all. But you, Gosse, should not have allowed Charlotte to climb the wall by means of somebody else's ladder and then to kick it away.

GOSSE. As I have not read *Agnes Grey* I must take your remarks on trust, but I will read the story.

MOORE. I wish you would, and write an article about Anne, for then the truth would become known.

GOSSE. Why not write it yourself? The story is true to you, and to me it is only a partial truth.

MOORE. Were I to write it, it would be looked upon as one of my paradoxes, or a desire to tread upon somebody's corns. But as soon as you begin to read, the story will possess you and you will long to reveal the true Charlotte and her patrons, the dinner at the publishers, and the dinner at Thackeray's, a dozen pompous men standing before the fire, their coat-tails lifted, their eyes fixed on the timid girl who had discovered bigamy and written it out all by herself. The nostrils of the twentieth century like not the smell of these broken victuals, and yet—

GOSSE. And yet the lake darkens and the loiterers along the waterside have disappeared; probably gone home to supper, every one. I'll let you out at the farther gate.

Will T. Hale (essay date 1929)

SOURCE: "Anne Brontë: Her Life and Writings," in *Indiana University Studies,* Vol. XVI, No. 83, March, 1929, pp. 3-44.

[*In the following excerpt, Hale suggests that* Agnes Grey *is primarily an autobiographical work and that it is of interest to the scholar of the mid-Victorian novel and for the insights it provides into the mind of Brontë herself.*]

Agnes Grey is the barest sort of story, without color and without humor. Unlighted by the least play of fancy, it presents a bald, literal chronicle of events as drab as life itself. It has no improbabilities, no flights of the imagination, no romance. It is realism in the literal sense of the word, life as it actually is, without exaggeration and without adornment. It is just the sort of realism that William Dean Howells asserted that he wrote when he called Dickens' novels romances. Produced at the same time (1846) as *The Professor,* it seems to have been inspired by the same theory of the novel as Charlotte had in conceiving her first work, which was rejected by six publishers in succession because it lacked thrilling excitement and startling incident. That the young sister should have been influenced by the older seems only natural when one recalls the habit of the Brontë girls to discuss the composition of their stories every night before going to bed as they paced up and down the floor together.

Like Charlotte's other novel, *Jane Eyre,* it is a domestic novel of humanitarian purpose, and sets forth the ills and humiliations of a governess' life. Both sisters had suffered grievously while serving as governesses, and these works of theirs show how bitterly the remembrances rankled in their breasts. *Agnes Grey* almost literally describes Anne's own experiences at Mrs. Ingham's and the Robinsons', evidently with the purpose of informing the public as to the treatment accorded young women who had to make their living by going out to teach. Aside from this didactic purpose and the author's declared aim to instruct the reader,[108] the book contains none of the usual paraphernalia of the novel of instruction: it never preaches, and proclaims no doctrines.

Autobiographical in the main, beyond a doubt, it is, as Charlotte has declared, "the mirror of the mind of the writer."[109] Agnes is Anne in every respect. One sees the strict seclusion in which Anne was brought up, the way the older members of the family dominated her, her going forth, young and inexperienced, into a harsh world, her grief at leaving home and her homesickness while away, the vulgarity and rudeness to which she was exposed, the meanness and hardness of her life as governess, and the terrible agony of a young heart deprived of youth's young dream of love. Only on the last page Agnes does find the love that Anne was never to know; but in the fruition of Agnes' hopes, one can see the terrible frustration of poor Anne. Almost without reserve she exposes her baffled heart, fulfilling more truly than she realized her promise in the first chapter to "candidly lay before the public what I would not disclose to the most intimate friend."[110] No more pathetic document can be found than this chronicle of the wild hunger of a blighted human heart robbed of its natural destiny.

Telling for the most part Anne's own story, the novel naturally has no real plot. Agnes goes out as governess in an ill-bred family of impossible children, changes her position after a short time, falls in love with Edward Weston, the curate, and, after some slight difficulties, marries him in the end and has three children, Edward, Agnes, and little Mary. This is all that happens. The characterization, too, is but slight. Described in a sort of catalog method upon their introduction, the different characters make but a dim impression upon the mind and live only while one is reading the novel. It is impossible to visualize them. The dialog, also, adds nothing to the verisimilitude. Unnatural and stilted, it is as lifeless and colorless as the rest of the story. No children ever talked as the youngsters do in this book.[111] The earmarks of the governess are over it all.

The narrative is permeated, also, with Anne's mid-Victorian evangelical religious conceptions. Since her father's sympathies were with what at that time was known as the Evangelical group in the English Church, it was only natural that her ideas should have been of the same cast.[112] This group, which was closest in points of doctrine to the dissenters, was essentially "Low Church" in its attitude towards the ceremonies and symbols of the Church, and in theology was decidedly Calvinistic. Thruout the story Agnes Grey's thinking is dominated by such conceptions, and her whole attitude of mind is colored by them.[113] When the unhappy girl, for example, is enjoying the prospect of going to church, where she will have the pleasure of seeing her lover preach, at once she is disturbed by "the secret reproaches of my conscience, which would too often whisper that I was deceiving my own self, and mocking God with the service of a heart more bent upon the creature than the Creator."[114] Again, when she thinks of her future life without her lover and is naturally distressed over the prospect, she takes herself to task thus: "It was wrong to be so joyless, so desponding; I should have made God my friend, and to do His will the pleasure and business of my life; but faith was weak, and passion was too strong."[115] Then, when she feels that she would rather die than live without her lover, she checks herself thus: "Should I shrink from work that God has set before me, because it was not fitted to my taste? Did not He know best what I should do, and where I ought to labour? and should I long to quit His service before I had finished my task, and expect to enter into His rest without having laboured to earn it? 'No; by His help I will arise and address myself to my appointed duty. If happiness in this world is not for me, I will endeavour to promote the welfare of those around me, and my reward shall be hereafter.'"[116] And when at last she has got her lover, and certainly ought to be satisfied, she declares that her purpose is to "keep in mind the glorious heaven beyond, where both may meet again, and sin and sorrow are unknown . . . and . . . endeavour to live to the glory of Him who has scattered so many blessings in our path."[117]

Hand in hand with this mid-Victorian evangelicalism goes the mid-century's fondness for tears. These flow copiously from page to page upon the slightest provocation; indeed, they were the only luxury the poor governess had. Abundant as they are, they always seem to be voluntary, however, and strictly under her control, to be called forth when she wanted them. For instance, when she thought of leaving her sister to go away to be a governess, she buried her face in her hands, "and they were presently bathed in tears."[118] And as she drove away, she drew her veil over her face, "and then, but not till then, burst into a flood of tears."[119] Years later, when she feared that Rosalie Murray was going to take her lover from her, she wanted to cry, but had to postpone her tears until after dinner: "Right glad was I to get into the house, and find myself alone once more in my own room. My first impulse was to sink into the chair beside the bed; and laying my head on the pillow, to seek relief in a passionate burst of tears; there was an imperative craving for such an indulgence; but alas! I must restrain and swallow back my feelings still," for the dinner bell was ringing.[120] And some time afterward, when she thought that she was hearing her lover preach for the last time, she confesses to the reader, "I was often on the point of melting into tears during the sermon—the last I was to hear from him"; and when it was over, she continues, "I longed to seek the retirement of my own room, or some sequestered nook in the grounds, that I might deliver myself up to my feelings—to weep my last farewell, and lament my false hopes and vain delusions." But when he suddenly addressed her, she boasts, "I was very much startled; and had I been hysterically inclined, I certainly should have committed myself in some way then. Thank God, I was not."[121] After all that he has been thru, the reader, too, says, "Thank God," from the bottom of his heart.

With such characteristics as have been pointed out, this novel has what value today? Very little except for the scholar who is studying the period or tracing the development of the mid-Victorian novel. For him, however, it has much that is interesting and valuable. In the first place, as a type of the mid-Victorian novel written by a woman, it reveals certain distinctive qualities. It follows the trend of the age in its emphasis upon the emotions, its humanitarian purpose, and its interest in the lower classes.[122] Based largely upon the quiet, prosaic experiences of a governess, it lacks excitement of any kind, and what interest it has lies in the revelations of the heroine's personality and her mild adventures of the heart. For herself she has revealed with a good deal of verisimilitude. Everywhere in the book her gentle, charming personality makes itself felt. Transcribing the minute details of a governess' life, however, with literal exactitude and no imagination, the narrative approximates reporting rather than an artistic presentation of life. And yet it does seem real. It has all the actuality of a transcript from Anne's own life. The most probable passages are those that the author drew from her own experience; the least probable are those she manufactured, such as the love scenes. But the whole story includes only the smallest segment of human affairs, shows no knowledge of the developments of the time in scientific achievement or appliances, gives no hint of the material progress of the outside world, and presents no philosophy of life.

In the second place, the scholar of the period will be interested in the picture it paints of the manners and morals in the mid-Victorian English village. It furnishes a vivid insight into the life of a governess at this time and a true, tho circumscribed, view of a woman of the middle class living the inhibited life so common to the female members of the mid-Victorian household.

Lastly, its greatest value, perhaps, will lie in the light it throws upon the mind and character of the author. For it unmistakably reveals much of her inner self: her hatred of the life of a governess, her fondness for children,[123] her evangelical ideas, her lack of a sense of humor, her tenderness of heart, and her suppressed, frustrated life. Twenty-seven tho she was when she published this novel, and a woman so far in the twenties in this era was long on her way toward spinsterhood, so little had she seen of the actual world and so much had she lived her life within her own self, she seems like an unsophisticated child revealing things about herself she should not tell. What could be more charming and more child-like than Agnes' agreement with herself not to think so much about her lover?—"So said I in my heart; and from that hour I only permitted my thoughts to wander to Edward Weston—or at least to dwell upon him now and then—as a treat for rare occasions."[124] What could be more touching than her confessions to the reader of her love for him?—"He had not breathed a word of love, or dropped one hint of tenderness or affection, and yet I had been supremely happy. To be near him, to hear him talk as he did talk; and to feel that he thought me worthy to be so spoken to—capable of understanding and duly appreciating such discourse—was enough."[125] What could be more womanly and more mid-Victorian?

Notes

[108] Cf. *Agnes Grey* (The World's Classics), p. 1: "All true histories contain instruction; though, in some, the treasure may be hard to find, and when found, so trivial in quantity, that the dry, shrivelled kernel scarcely compensates for the trouble of cracking the nut. Whether this be the case with my history or not, I am hardly competent to judge."

[109] [Clement K. Shorter, *Charlotte Brontë and Her Circle,* 1896,] p. 162.

[110] P. 1. Cf. p. 113: "I began this book with the intention of concealing nothing; that those who liked might have the benefit of perusing a fellow-creature's heart: but we have *some* thoughts that all the angels in heaven are welcome to behold, but not our brother men—not even the best and kindest among them."

[111] Cf. pp. 19-20, 46.

[112] Charlotte's and Emily's pro-Protestant and anti-Catholic bias was strongly evident during their stay in Belgium. Cf. [Mrs. Elizabeth Cleghorn Gaskell, *Life of Charlotte Brontë,* edited by Clement K. Shorter (New York: Harper and Brothers, 1901),] pp. 243-4.

[113] Cf. *Agnes Grey,* pp. 83-4.

[114] *Ibid.,* p. 139.

[115] *Ibid.,* p. 153.

[116] *Agnes Grey,* p. 177.

[117] *Ibid.,* p. 207.

[118] *Ibid.,* p. 12.

[119] *Ibid.,* p. 12.

[120] *Ibid.,* p. 138.

[121] *Agnes Grey,* pp. 172-3.

[122] Cf. pp. 86-107, etc.

[123] *Agnes Grey,* p. 9.

[124] *Ibid.,* pp. 177-8.

[125] *Ibid.,* pp. 171-2.

Susan Brooke (essay date 1965)

SOURCE: "Anne Brontë at Blake Hall: An Episode of Courage and Insight," in *Brontë Society Transactions,* Vol. 13, No. 3, 1965, pp. 239-50.

[*In the following essay, Brooke describes Brontë's experiences as a governess at Blake Hall and the influence they may have had on* Agnes Grey.]

Blake Hall was my grandmother's old home, so that memories of the house go back to the earliest days of my childhood. For us children it was a place where wonderful Christmas parties were presided over by a genial great uncle and aunt and, like all houses which have been inhabited by the same family for several generations, it was also exciting because of the past associations which clung around its fabric.

There were stories which took one back to the Napoleonic wars, the Luddite risings and other strange happenings of the nineteenth century, but perhaps what interested us most was the fact that Anne Brontë had been governess to our grandmother's eldest sister and brother. When some of the Brontë novels were read to us they seemed to reveal further glimpses of a background that was already partly familiar, and even the characters in *Wuthering Heights, Shirley,* and *Jane Eyre,* appeared in some peculiar way to belong to the world of Blake Hall, so that it was often rather difficult to remember whether a story came from one of the novels or from reminiscences we had overheard. Later on, however, when we read books about the Brontës, we were surprised to learn that some writers assumed this background to be almost, if not entirely, imaginary, while people like Mr. Bloomfield (not to mention Heathcliff and Rochester) were supposed to have no parallels in the world of ordinary life.

In reality, of course, the Brontës were acute observers of the West Riding scene, and their descriptions of people are alive with local colour. They all knew the Mirfield neighbourhood where Blake Hall was situated, and, although the provincial society which they delineated has vanished without leaving many records, it is important to emphasise that it once had a perfectly objective existence, incredible though this may seem to people brought up in different traditions.

In fact it seems as if the only social phenomenon which eluded the analysis of the Brontë sisters was the contemporary class system, with its ever-changing economic background. At this period ladies were not supposed to know anything about business affairs—indeed they were trained to turn a blind eye to most masculine activities. This attitude might not have had any significant effect on novels dealing with drawing-room life in the more old-fashioned parts of England, but the Brontës happened to live among people whose absorbing passion was the acquisition of wealth, and who were subject to all kinds of violent tensions caused by the success or failure of their speculations. It is possible that the impression of fantasy which surrounds some of their male characters is connected with the mystery of their working life. These men seem to drift into their homes from some unknown hinterland to which we hold no clues, whereas their prototypes were all deeply involved in financial schemes of one kind or another and often came back suffering from nervous irritation after hours of exhausting work, trying out new machinery or initiating some risky trading project. What must have seemed irrational or peculiar in their behaviour becomes more understandable now when we realise that the chief concerns of their life were never discussed or even mentioned in front of women.

As children we were supplied with a rich background of local knowledge, so that we could make our own interpretations where guidance was lacking, and against this vivid tapestry of historical fact the Brontë novels appeared more real than they would have done without it. Thus our acquaintance with Blake Hall and its former occupants enabled us to appreciate the strange character of Mr. Bloomfield in *Agnes Grey.* In fact, in some curious way we seemed to know more about him than the governess, so that on certain occasions we felt like giving her a desperate warning: "Look out—don't you see how he'll catch you out next time."

These governess heroines appealed to us intensely, but we could imagine the fury that their naive behaviour would arouse in their employers; for they were innocent lambs who not only lived among tigers, but dared to criticise the tigers' standards of morality, so that at every moment they appeared to be inviting their own destruction.

Like her sisters, Anne Brontë was meticulously exact in her observations, although they tended to be restricted to a narrower range of experience. The problems of family life and the bringing up of children were particularly interesting to her, and in *Agnes Grey* she showed what happened when a governess's views on these matters clashed with those of the parents. For anyone who knew the background there could be no doubt that her experiences at Blake Hall were woven into this book, but since this fact has never been clearly acknowledged it seems worth while recapitulating some of the evidence on this point.

Anne went to Blake Hall in April, 1839. She was then aged nineteen, and this was her first situation as a governess. Charlotte described her departure in a letter to Ellen Nussey written on April 15th:

> Poor child! She left us last Monday; no one went with her: it was her own wish that she might be allowed to go alone, as she thought she could manage better and summon more courage if thrown entirely upon her own resources. We have had one letter from her since she went. She expresses herself very well satisfied and says that Mrs. Ingham is extremely kind; the two eldest children alone are under her care, the rest are confined to the nursery, with which and its occupants she has nothing to do.

It is noticeable that nothing was said about the master of the house, either in this letter or in later ones. The reasons for reticence on this point become understandable in the light of further knowledge. The family at Blake Hall was eventually to become a large one, but at this period only five of the thirteen children had been born. Their names in order of precedence were: Cunliffe (b. 1832), Mary (b. 1834), Martha (b. 1836), Emily (b. 1837), and the baby Harriet (b. 1838) who only survived a year.

The lack of parental discipline which Anne found such a disturbing feature of the children's upbringing was characteristic of many Yorkshire households at this period, for among the newly-enriched families of the West Riding there had been a certain reaction against the stricter code of an earlier generation; and those who aspired to any position in the countryside were particularly anxious to avoid the stigma of middle class manners. Boys were frequently over-indulged by their parents and if they teased or bullied their sisters it was merely considered a sign of manliness.

On the other hand girls were usually brought up to feel that they were of little value compared with their brothers, and had no claim to equal treatment. Female rebellions could be quelled more easily when the girls were young, but among intelligent children there was often a lingering feeling of revolt against what seemed an inexplicable injustice. It is significant that the first observations made by Agnes Grey were connected with this point. The two elder children in the story had just received their new governess when the following conversation took place:

> "Oh Tom, what a darling you are!" exclaimed his mother. "Come and kiss dear mamma; and then won't you show Miss Grey your schoolroom and your nice new books?"

> "I won't kiss you mamma; but I will show Miss Grey my schoolroom and my new books."

> "And my schoolroom, and my books, Tom," said Mary Anne. "They're mine too."

> "They're mine," replied he decisively. "Come along Miss Grey, I'll escort you."

Similar conversations recur throughout the whole of Miss Grey's narrative, and it is clear that Tom was being brought up to be a little bully who considered himself far more important than his sisters, while Mary Anne was reacting with violent resentment against an attitude which she already felt to be intolerably unfair.

For anyone who knew the family at Blake Hall it must have been obvious that there was a close resemblance between the young Inghams and the Bloomfields in **Agnes Grey.** Their ages corresponded exactly and their psychological tendencies seem to have been precisely similar. In fact there can be little doubt that **Agnes Grey** contains an accurate description of Anne's first experience as a governess. In order to perceive the affinity between the fictional children and the real ones, it is only necessary to compare the salient features of the household portrayed in the novel with the known characteristics of family life at Blake Hall, as described in the Brontë correspondence and in the reminiscences of the family.

Perhaps one of the most significant incidents in the novel is the account of the bird trap which was justified on the grounds that the birds were doing harm in the garden. Nothing brings out more clearly the difference between Anne Brontë and her employers. When the boy Tom had exhibited his trap to the governess, the following conversation took place:

> "Why do you catch them?"

> "Papa says they do harm."

> "And what do you do with them when you catch them?"

> "Different things. Sometimes I give them to the cat; sometimes I cut them in pieces with my penknife; but the next I mean to roast alive."

The boy then went on to defend his activities on the grounds that they had been sanctioned by his father:

> "Last summer he gave me a nest of young sparrows and saw me pulling off their legs and wings and heads, and never said anything except that they were nasty things, and I must not let them soil my trousers: Uncle Robson was there too, and he laughed and said I was a fine boy."

The next time that Uncle Robson came on a visit he found fresh opportunity of teasing the governess, and at last she was faced with the choice between ignoring what was happening or displeasing the adults and their favourite child. Needless to say, there was no hesitation on the part of Anne Brontë's heroine, and on perceiving that some young birds were about to be tortured by her pupil, she dropped a stone on the intended victims, crushing them dead beneath it.

For acting in this independent manner the governess received a chilly reprimand from her mistress:

> "I am sorry Miss Grey, you should think it necessary to interfere with Master Bloomfield's amusements; he was much distressed about you destroying the birds."

Soon after this incident the governess was told that her services would not be required after midsummer. Mrs. Bloomfield assured her that her character and general conduct were unexceptionable, but the children had made so little progress that Mr. Bloomfield and she "felt it their duty to seek some other mode of instruction." This notice was given at a time when Agnes had begun to congratulate herself that at last she had instilled something into her pupils' heads. "I wished to say something in my own justification," she wrote afterwards, "but in attempting to speak I felt my voice falter; and rather than testify any emotion or suffer the tears to overflow that were already gathering in my eyes, I chose to keep silence and bear all like a self-convicted criminal."

It was obvious that the new governess with her passionate idealism and hatred of cruelty had aroused intense resentment both in the head of the family and in his friend Uncle Robson. A governess was expected to be intellectually subservient; to express opinions of any kind was a breach of etiquette, and to utter sentiments which ran counter to those of her employers was an unpardonable offence.

There can be little doubt that the feelings experienced by Agnes Grey were those of Anne Brontë when she left Blake Hall after a sojourn of only two terms. But fortunately there was no lack of sympathy in the family at Haworth. After Anne lost her post Charlotte wrote to Ellen Nussey on January 24, 1840:

> You could never live in an unruly violent family of modern children such for instance as those at Blake Hall. Anne is not to return. Mrs. Ingham is a placid mild woman; but as for the children it was one struggle of life-wearing exertion to keep them in anything like decent order. I am miserable when I dwell on the necessity of spending my life as a governess. The chief requisite for that station seems to be the power of taking things easily as they come, and of making oneself comfortable and at home wherever one may chance to be—qualities in which all our family are singularly deficient.

Undoubtedly Charlotte was correct in her diagnosis. Having the temperaments of artists, the Brontës were highly critical and perfectionist, but these qualities were the reverse of those required for managing small children or finding pleasure in their company. Morever it is obvious from *Agnes Grey* that Anne had little affection for children of this type and no sympathy whatever for the ideas of their parents. Like her sisters she saw the darker side of domestic life in greater detail than the brighter aspects, and was able to sense the psychological undercurrents which have a more decisive influence over the fate of individuals than their conscious thoughts.

Although there can be no doubt that the description of Wellwood House contains many memories of Blake Hall, there seems to have been a certain reluctance to recognise this fact. For instance in one edition of *Agnes Grey* there is a photograph of Blake Hall with the words "Horton Lodge" below it. It can be stated quite definitely that there is no reason to accept this identification. The Murrays of Horton Lodge, who figure in the second half of the book, had no resemblance to the Inghams in their appearances, ages, or ideas, and from the descriptive passages it is evident that their home was situated in a more rural part of Yorksire, probably nearer Knaresborough.

No one could have differed more from the jovial blustering Mr. Murray "with scarlet cheeks and crimson nose," than the serious long-faced owner of Blake Hall, who seems to have been rather thinly disguised as Mr. Bloomfield. It would probably be fair to say that Joshua Ingham had some, if not all, of Mr. Bloomfield's peculiarities, the chief difference being that he was more of a gentleman—in the conventional sense—than Anne Brontë's character would suggest. A keen churchman and a zealous magistrate, he was respected by men of his own type, and in appearance he was a fine featured man, although not strikingly handsome like his younger brother Sir James. Many of his character traits appear to have been faithfully observed, including his irritable temper and curious wish to inflict punishments. In this connection it is significant that one of his daughters, Frances, used to tell how she had been terrified of her father as a child. One day at a time when she thought no one was about she was admiring her corkscrew ringlets in a mirror when her father caught sight of her through an open door and striding into the bedroom cut off all her hair "as a punishment for vanity." On another occasion the same daughter was so frightened to see her father standing motionless at the top of a dark flight of stairs, that she fell and injured her back. Similarly the children in *Agnes Grey* were said to live in "habitual fear of their father's peevish temper." Often the governess saw him watching her pupils from his window, or stealthily following them through the grounds and coming upon them when they least suspected he was around.

In this type of household the father was sometimes deliberately frightening to women as well as to children, for among certain West Riding families a harsh repression of all tenderness had left behind it a contempt for what were considered feminine values and a tendency to jeer at any woman who attempted to raise herself above the coarse standards of sporting society. Such treatment was not confined to the governess—although she was apt to embody something that was particularly disliked. The squire of Blake Hall had an aunt called Hannah Taylor, who remembered all her life the occasion on which she had asked her brother-in-law (the father of Joshua) to move some of his recumbent dogs away from the fire so that she could get herself warm. Without more ado she was hoisted off her feet and deposited behind the open fireplace, where she was told she could stay until she learnt to mind her own business.

The background which produced this type of behaviour was one in which social life revolved around masculine sports and amusements. There was no equivalent of the feminine society described by Jane Austen, and women had to adapt themselves to a life that was often lonely and crude. Families which had been fanatically puritan in the seventeenth century continued to produce shrewd but narrow-minded and close-fisted men who expected women to have a high standard of household management without any leanings towards independence of culture.

The Brontës became so familiar with the tyrant-bully type of Yorkshireman that they reproduced some of his features in nearly all their male characters, and in the case of Charlotte there seems to have been a kind of half-grudging admiration for this type of hero. Perhaps this fixation was one of the reasons why the Brontë novels received so much criticism from people who were ignorant of the West Riding and its social history. The exact description of sadistic behaviour inside the family circle was to many readers so unpalatable that it was taken to imply a morbid imagination, whereas in reality the novels were based on the keenest observation. Anne Brontë's account of conversations and situations is so true to type that it could only have been made possible by careful notes written in odd moments.

People who take the view that Anne relied on her imagination for the scenes in *Agnes Grey* appear to forget that we have other sources of information about the families she described. For instance the prosaic journals of Miss Weeton contain similar accounts of family life in the north of England during the earlier half of the nineteenth century.

Ernest Raymond writes that he finds it hard to accept *Agnes Grey* as a true picture of life at Blake Hall, because the children are too bad for belief and the parents too cruel. He points out that Anne referred to the kindness she received at Blake Hall, but does not appear to notice that Anne simply mentioned the kindness of Mrs. Ingham in her letters. She said nothing whatever about Mr. Ingham, and this is comprehensible in the light of what we know from other sources. There is no reason to suppose that Anne thought them both alike in their characters and in fact the reverse seems to have been the case.

In order to understand the people described it is necessary to know something about their historical background. The Ingham forebears had lived in the Calder valley between Halifax and Wakefield for hundreds of years, and all their links were with puritan families of the same type, many of them having traditions of fighting for the Parliamentary side in the Civil War. The records of Oliver Heywood show that some members of the family were ardent Nonconformists, the Blake Hall branch being descended from an Ossett family which was connected with Heywood's religious circle in the seventeenth and eighteenth centuries. Certain

individuals in the family continued in the Nonconformist tradition, but those who prospered became orthodox members of the Anglican church and forgot their puritan origins.

As merchants, bankers and coal-owners some of the Inghams accumulated fortunes in the eighteenth and nineteenth centuries, but unlike many families of a similar type they had little ambition to move up the social ladder. For neighbours they preferred the sporting squirearchy, although something prevented them from ever really belonging to it. Occasionally the family produced men of outstanding talent, their ability being usually expressed in such subjects as finance, law and commerce.

Before going to Blake Hall, Anne Brontë had not been entirely ignorant about the family history. Benjamin Ingham, the friend of Charles Wesley, had been a frequent visitor to Haworth in the eighteenth century, and the memory of his long preaching journeys throughout the Pennines still lingered there, while among educated evangelicals the name was inseparably connected with those of Count Zinzendorf, Lady Huntingdon, Henry Venn, and other leaders of the eighteenth century revival. Perhaps these hallowed associations had some influence on the Rev. Patrick Brontë when he decided to let his daughter take up the post at Blake Hall. If so, he must have been sadly disillusioned by her experience.

Mrs. Ingham was described by Charlotte Brontë as "a placid mild woman," and it seems likely that she was unable to assert herself when it came to preventing cruelty or keeping order among her children. It is also possible that at this particular time she was worried about the baby Harriet who died in 1839. In any case she had probably resigned herself to seeing many things which she did not like, realising that it was unwise to oppose the ideas of sporting countrymen. Her own family, the Cunliffes, also had their roots in the wild Pennine region of the Lancashire-Yorkshire borderland, and like the Inghams they had moved down into the more rewarding parts of the West Riding. Her father, Ellis Cunliffe (later Cunliffe-Lister) was M.P. for Bradford and one of her brothers was the eccentric mechanical genius who became the first Lord Masham. She had several other brothers and it is possible that one of these had some of Uncle Robson's characteristics.

Among the minor characters in *Agnes Grey,* the kind but fussy grandmother might be an impression of Joshua Ingham's mother. A miniature at Blake Hall showed this lady as a handsome old woman in a lace mantilla. She came of a family long established at Batley, the Taylors of Purlwell Hall—another dynasty of puritanical origin. Her husband's mania for hunting and gambling had caused her considerable anxiety. She wanted her sons to be successful in their careers, but realised that there was an unpredictable element in her husband's family—a wild uncontrollable streak that might come out in the future as it had in the past. It was during her lifetime that a beautiful dinner service decorated with hunting scenes was put out of sight. Her younger son became an eminent judge, but was unsympathetic towards his nephews. One of these, William Ingham, who later won fame as an explorer in New Guinea, asked his uncle to use his influence with the Colonial Office on his behalf, but Sir James did not think it worth helping one who had failed in his Oxford examinations. The bitterness of this fact was strongly felt after the young man's death at the hands of cannibals. [See note 2.]

It seems clear that the wild behaviour of the Blake Hall children was not in any way exaggerated, since stories told by members of the family resembled those recounted by the governess in **Agnes Grey.** Although it may seem incredible that a couple of children aged seven and five could reduce a girl of nineteen to tears, it was related that the young Inghams were able to do this on more than one occasion. No doubt Anne was partly to blame for what happened, but any young woman who had to conform to the conditions described in **Agnes Grey** might have found it difficult to keep order among her charges.

My grandmother used to tell how one morning a parcel of native cloaks arrived at Blake Hall from South America, whereupon the children donned these flapping scarlet garments and dashed out into the park, screaming that they were devils and would not return to do their lessons. Having no means of exerting any influence over her pupils, Anne went off in tears to Mrs. Ingham. This incident was probably one of a series of similar happenings, and reminds us of the scene in **Agnes Grey** when the children ran out into the snow-covered grounds in their slippers, and pranced about in front of the drawing room windows. Needless to say, in both cases the mother's sympathy was all on the side of her offspring, the governess being regarded as both ineffectual and over-severe. In her old age Mrs. Ingham told one of her grandchildren that she had once employed a very unsuitable governess called Miss Brontë who had actually tied the two children to a table leg in order to get on with her own writing. On entering the schoolroom the mother had been met by this horrifying sight and, of course, the governess had been suitably reprimanded.

No doubt the trials of the environment were made worse by Anne's inexperience and loneliness. Be that as it may, where she saw cruelty and discrimination others remembered a sporting family with a particular interest in animals of every kind—both wild and domestic. The place was so full of birds and beasts that people said it was like a "regular Noah's Ark." Many stories were told about the domestic pets; for instance it was re-

corded that one of the parrots developed a kind of second sight during the Crimean War, and suddenly swinging on its perch cried out "poor Cunliffe" over and over again. Subsequent inquiry showed that the eldest son was in special danger at that particular moment.

After Joshua Ingham's death his widow went to live at Torquay with her two elder daughters who remained unmarried. The younger girls, who were more adaptable than their sisters, all obtained more or less suitable mates, although in my grandmother's case it was said that she had married beneath her, for her husband was a West Riding manufacturer, and mid-Victorian snobbery drew a particularly heavy line between those who owned coal mines and those who manufactured cloth, the latter being regarded as totally unacceptable even in the outer fringes of country society. After her marriage several of her relations never spoke to her again, but fortunately this was not felt to be a great deprivation.

Mary, who had been Anne Brontë's pupil, lived longer than her brothers and sisters, and died in 1922. As a girl she had been the family beauty, having inherited the swarthy good looks of some of her ancestors, but it was rumoured that her chance of marriage had been ruined by another member of the family who had mislaid a letter in which she had accepted an important proposal. She remained a rather eccentric spinster with unorthodox views on several subjects, and annoyed her relations by calling herself Miss Ingham-Cunliffe. She was never mentioned to us as children and we knew nothing of her existence. It was a pity that she was unable to join the new forces of emancipation which were opening up opportunities for women, but it is tempting to imagine that some seeds of revolt had been sown by Anne Brontë in those far away days of the nineteenth century.

Although the Ingham children were extremely brave and adventurous, their footsteps were often dogged by some tragic fatality, which may not have been wholly disconnected with the way they were brought up. In their home life there could have been no greater contrast than that between the Brontë children and those of Blake Hall. In the former case there was great hardship and tragedy, but the world of imagination flourished and the light of genius transformed the humble circumstances of parsonage life. At Blake Hall, on the other hand, action was considered far more important than thought. There was little admiration for talent and ambition was stifled unless it expressed itself in conventional forms. The tone of provincial society in Yorkshire was taken from various distinguished old families, without much judgment. As a result there existed a widespread and vulgar type of snobbery in which individuals lost their personality and initiative. No Brontë could dream of preparing children to enter this type of world, yet it was what most parents wanted above everything else.

When thinking of the old days in the house which no longer exists, one cannot help feeling that Anne Brontë was one of the few people who saw that all was not well with the children's upbringing. She had the courage to warn the parents without fearing for her own position, whereas many governesses would have taken the easier way described by Charlotte of saying nothing and making themselves as comfortable as possible. Far from being over-imaginative, she had the perception and foresight that might have helped to avert more than one tragedy, and could have prepared a happier pattern for the future. The main things she lacked were encouragement, support, and experience. These were denied her by the nature of the environment, mainly because she refused to compromise with what she considered cruelty and injustice.

Bibliography: Ingham Family

Robert S. Whittaker: *The Whitakers of Hesley and Palermo.*

This book is privately printed, but obtainable in the British Museum and some other libraries. It contains the only detailed pedigrees of the Inghams and related families. Although it is mainly concerned with the elder branch (Leeds and Palermo) it has many references to the Yorkshire background in general.

Irene D. Neu: "An English Businessman in Sicily, 1806-1861," *Business History Review of America,* Vol. XXI, Number 4: Winter, 1957.

This article has detailed references to Yorkshire sources for the history of the family. For other economic activities see local histories of West Riding towns.

Religion: For Presbyterian background see Heywood's *Diaries.* For religious activities of B. Ingham and others, see *Christianity in Yorkshire,* edited Popham; Wesley's *Journal; Dictionary of National Biography,* and other sources.

Notes

[1] The Blake Hall Upbringing:

In some respects the general atmosphere resembled that of certain Irish houses of the same period, but, of course, the sense of humour was absent. Joshua Ingham would not allow any of his daughters to enter a shop, but a draper drove out from Huddersfield occasionally, with certain frugal necessities. A dancing master with a fiddle also called and the girls used to dance for nearly a whole day at a time. Later they drove over to the York balls. Aunt Hannah Taylor, who was an evangelical

with an old feud against her High Church nephew Joshua, used to express her disapproval of this worldliness by leaving religious tracts at Blake Hall, which the daughters were forbidden to read. There were very few new clothes, but the daughters had to brush their hair for nearly an hour every day (without, however, taking any interest in the result). They were not expected to lace their own boots, but neither were they allowed female luxuries like hand mirrors or perfume. In an establishment where the vital interests were horse-breeding and similar affairs, none of the inmates had much interest in the industrial life growing up outside their gates.

[2] W. B. Ingham, 1850-1878:

William Ingham (one of the younger sons of Joshua and Mary) exhibited some of the best characteristics of the Blake Hall upbringing. A long article in *The Times* for August 24th, 1929, describing some of his adventures in New Guinea, including a famous fight with a 13-ft. alligator, was followed by many letters of appreciation. Stewart Cox of the Royal Geographical Society wrote: "We had been together in the same house at Malvern College from 1865 to 1869 and as his fag I worshipped him. He made the alligator pay for killing his servant just as he gave a big bully who damaged his fag all he deserved. . . ." After his death, a town in Queensland was named "Ingham."

[3] Blake Hall as a home:

Despite its somewhat austere exterior, Blake Hall was a home with its own type of Yorkshire hospitality. In structure the house was high and narrow, the front part being dated 1774, and the older parts going back to the seventeenth century. Everything was very well looked after; the furniture, brass and silver work gleamed in the cosy interior, where there were old oak chests, crimson carpets and lovely pieces of blue china. The ground floor sitting room had oak bookcases filled with brown leather volumes and figures of Chelsea china. There was also a cupboard where special toys were kept, including a peacock which wound up and spread its tail. A small door with an embroidered velvet curtain over it led into the garden. The chairs were covered with plain red cretonne.

The dining room had a simplicity and charm that reminded one of a Caldicott illustration. There were no curtains—only oak shutters—and the china cupboard was filled with a dessert service decorated with hunting scenes. There were old portraits on the walls, and a stormy landscape near the window. A parrot meditated by the fireplace or addressed a few words to the rosy-cheeked manservant who had known the house for nearly fifty years. At the foot of the stairs was a study called "the magistrate's room," lined with black carved oak dating back to the seventeenth century.

Upstairs there was a drawing room with Dresden china candle brackets and miniatures on a small table. Here there was a huge fireplace with blue tiles, curtains of gold brocade and chairs covered with the finest "petit point" embroidery. At the back of the house beyond the stables and laundry there was a large tithe barn and a charming black and white building called "the old Rectory" which had a flagged garden. Here Joshua Ingham's mother lived for some time after her husband's death.

(Note 3 is based on reminiscences by Mrs. B. Gundreda Brooke.)

Inga-Stina Ewbank (essay date 1966)

SOURCE: "Anne Brontë: The Woman Writer as Moralist," in *Their Proper Sphere: A Study of the Brontë Sisters as Early-Victorian Female Novelists,* Harvard University Press, 1966, pp. 49-85.

[*In the following excerpt, Ewbank comments on the unadorned style of* Agnes Grey *then contrasts the work with several other "governess novels" of the same period in order to discover the uniqueness of its theme.*]

'All true histories contain instruction.' Thus the first sentence of *Agnes Grey,* and here we have the link between the intention of the novel and the technique Anne Brontë used in writing it. There is no attempt to make the sugar hide the pill: in the first paragraph we are told that the book 'might prove useful to some, and entertaining to others'. A few chapters later, the purpose is whetted, as we are reminded that 'my design, in writing the last few pages, was not to amuse, but to benefit those whom it might concern'. Those concerned are further defined:

> if a parent has, therefrom, gathered any useful hint, or an unfortunate governess received thereby the slightest benefit, I am well rewarded for my pains.

From these statements of what would seem to be a narrowly didactic, even pedagogic intention, *Agnes Grey* would appear to belong in that tradition of instructive fiction which includes books like Miss Edgeworth's *Parent's Assistant* or Mrs. Hofland's *Ellen, The Teacher.* It does certainly owe something to that tradition, but very far from everything. To Anne Brontë, being a governess had been, in Keats's phrase, a kind of soul-making; and so the 'instruction' in *Agnes Grey* goes much further than merely telling parents how to manage their children and governesses how to handle their pupils and make the best of their lot. The 'instruction' lies in the 'true history' of *Agnes Grey* as a whole.

There is no reason to suspect that Anne shared Miss Stodart's suspicion of fiction *qua* fiction. We know

that she contributed to the Gondal legends and that she found pleasure in reading novels. Yet, for the purposes of instruction, truth is more impressive than fiction—hence her insistence on *Agnes Grey* being a genuine autobiography. As a 'true' fictitious autobiography her novel is formally a straight descendant of *Robinson Crusoe* and *Moll Flanders* (absurd as the comparison with the latter might seem); but in its essential subject—the growth and development of a woman's mind—it is more deeply related to the Romantic tradition of autobiography. Autobiographical form had re-entered the novel via the *Bildungsroman;* in Bulwer Lytton's *Pelham,* for example, it provides some kind of unity and meaning in what would otherwise be merely a set of episodes. But, to my knowledge, no novel of the period is as emphatic as *Agnes Grey* in stressing the 'truth' of its fiction. So anxious is Anne Brontë for her reader to suspend his disbelief that she makes her characters refer to the actual novel form: 'Had I seen it depicted in a novel', says Agnes Grey about some particularly shameful conduct of one of her pupils, 'I should have thought it unnatural.'

It is, I think, this desire for 'true fiction' which has determined the narrative technique and style of *Agnes Grey.* Both are utterly plain and simple—with the strength as well as the weaknesses of those attributes. The narrative structure follows a simple chronological pattern: Agnes Grey, to help the family finances, takes first one position as a governess and then, having been unjustly discharged for incompetence after less than a year, another, which she keeps for a couple of years. While in her second situation, she falls in love with the curate of the parish, Edward Weston. Before she is sure of his feelings, she loses her father, and she and her mother set up a small school in a seaside town called A——. Mr. Weston, who now has his own parish not far from A——, seeks her out, woos and—obviously without any difficulty—wins her. This is told, as by Agnes some years after her marriage, in a consistent first-person narrative, with no recourse to letters or diaries, and—chiefly—in short, simple sentences.

The weakness in this method lies in Anne's occasional failure to perceive how very thin is the borderline between plainness and dullness. In her anxiety to picture life that is drab, she sometimes produces art that is dull. The story drags with repetitiveness as Agnes moves from the miseries of the Bloomfield school-room to those of the Murrays', and the dispassionateness of the style at times verges on boredom. We see, however, that the author herself is aware of the dangers of uncompromising verisimilitude:

> As I cannot, like Dogberry, find it in my heart to bestow *all* my tediousness upon the reader, I will

not go on to bore him with a minute detail of all the discoveries and proceedings of this and the following day. (Chapter VII)

The strength of her technique lies above all in its being functional—that is, in the directness of effect. There is nothing to intervene between the reader and the concerns of the novel, no glamorising (this extends to the heroine herself, who is plain and unassuming in appearance), no striving for spectacular effects, no spurious excitement. There is not even a pathetic death-bed, though with the death of Agnes's father the opportunity was there, and few mid-nineteenth-century novelists would have let it pass.[1] There is nothing, in fact, to detract from the reader's growing understanding of how relentlessly drab is a governess's existence.

Practically no use is made of setting and natural scenery. Again, this must have been deliberate, for some of her poems—notably the **'Lines Composed in a Wood on a Windy Day'**—show that she was responsive to nature and enjoyed describing its various aspects. But a snowy landscape to a governess is only something which she should try to prevent the children from rolling about in; and parks—however beautiful—are places in which she takes instructive walks with her reluctant pupils. When descriptions of nature do occur in *Agnes Grey,* it is for particular purposes. There is a moving account at the end of the first chapter, of Agnes looking back on her home as she leaves it for the first time:

> We crossed the valley, and began to ascend the opposite hill. As we were toiling up, I looked back again: there was the village spire, and the old grey parsonage beyond it, basking in a slanting beam of sunshine—it was but a sickly ray, but the village and surrounding hills were all in sombre shade, and I hailed the wandering beam as a propitious omen to my home. With clasped hands, I fervently implored a blessing on its inhabitants, and hastily turned away; for I saw the sunshine was departing; and I carefully avoided another glance, lest I should see it in gloomy shadow like the rest of the landscape.

The landscape here is used only for its obvious symbolical meaning to Agnes. The much more extended descriptions of sea and beach in the final chapters serve a similar function. The reunion with Mr. Weston on the beach at sunrise, and his sunset proposal, mean an end not only to the 'drab-coloured' governess-existence but also to the darkness and despair of a lonely and hopeless-seeming pilgrimage:

> I shall never forget that glorious Summer evening, and always remember with delight that steep hill, and the edge of the precipice where we stood together watching the splendid sun-set mirrored

in the restless world of waters at our feet—with hearts filled with gratitude to Heaven, and happiness, and love—almost too full for speech.

External nature and internal emotion meet and fuse into one experience for Agnes Grey, much as they do for Wordsworth on the top of Snowdon in *The Prelude.*

The plainness of the style involves a great restraint in the use of metaphorical language. Feelings are generally conveyed directly, by a single adjective—'happy', or 'sad', or 'exasperated'—or not at all. Mostly she just relates the bare facts of an episode and lets the emotions remain implicit. The exceptions to this tend to be somewhat self-conscious, as when she wants to describe Agnes's sense of up-rootedness on arriving in a new family:

> I awoke the next morning feeling like one whirled away by enchantment, and suddenly dropped from the clouds into a remote and unknown land . . . ; or like a thistle-seed borne on the wind to some strange nook of uncongenial soil, where it must lie long enough before it can take root and germinate, extracting nourishment from what appears so alien to its nature, if, indeed, it ever can.

She finds, in fact, that she has been led into a parable of Agnes's situation rather than an analysis of feeling; and so she breaks off: 'But this gives no proper idea of my feelings at all.'

A similar kind of restraint is exercised when it comes to passing comments on the attitudes, actions or behaviour of people other than Agnes. One of the sources of strength in the novel is the author's ability to bring out, and evaluate, people's character without any button-holing or superfluous comments. Agnes communicates the news of her sister's impending marriage to her pupil, Miss Murray, like this:

> 'Who is she to be married to?'
>
> 'To Mr. Richardson, the Vicar of a neighbouring parish.'
>
> 'Is he rich?'
>
> 'No—only comfortable.'
>
> 'Is he handsome?'
>
> 'No—only decent.'
>
> 'Young?'
>
> 'No—only middling.'

'O Mercy! what a wretch! What sort of a house is it?'

'A quiet little vicarage, with an ivy-clad porch, an old-fashioned garden, and—'

'O stop!—you'll make me sick. How *can* she bear it?'

'I expect she'll not only be able to bear it, but to be very happy. You did not ask me if Mr. Richardson were a good, wise or amiable man; I could have answered yes to all these questions. . . .'

. . . . .

'And will she go about in a plain shawl, and a large straw bonnet, carrying tracts and bone soup to her husband's poor parishioners?'

'I'm not so clear about that, but I dare say she will do her best to make them comfortable in body and mind, in accordance with our mother's example.'

With great economy of means and a perfect selection of details, she achieves a genuine effect of two people talking and of two diametrically opposed standards of value up against each other. It is the craft of the realistic novelist and the Morality play writer in one.

Descriptions of outward appearance are generally kept down to a thumb-nail sketch. It is conduct that counts, observed in realistic *minutiae*. In our first meeting with Mr. Bloomfield we get both appearance and revealingly selected details of behaviour:

> He had a large mouth, pale, dingy complexion, milky blue eyes, and hair the colour of a hempen cord. There was a roast leg of mutton before him: he helped Mrs Bloomfield, the children, and me [we notice the order of precedence!], desiring me to cut up the children's meat; then, after twisting about the mutton in various directions, and eyeing it from different points, he pronounced it not fit to be eaten and called for the cold beef.

The realism is spiced with a sardonic kind of humour here, just as her tongue is in her cheek in the dialogue between Agnes and Miss Murray. One imagines what Dickens would have made out of lunch with the Bloomfields. Anne Brontë's technique, unlike Dickens's, is that of understatement: after Mr. Bloomfield has, volubly, found fault with the beef, too, and with the arrangements made for that evening's dinner, she only allows herself to say that Agnes is

> very glad to get out of the room with my pupils; for I never felt so ashamed and uncomfortable in my life, for anything that was not my own fault.

The same dry realism, and absence of emotional commentary, can be seen in the description of the Bloomfield children's behaviour. Instead of the conventional miniature adults of much early Victorian fiction, we have here children that would not be out of place in a modern Child Guidance Clinic, kicking and spitting and defying authority in all possible ways.

Because of the prevailing reticence, the rare outburst and the rare metaphor get a peculiarly stinging power, as for example in Agnes's disgust at Rosalie Murray's conduct during her engagement. The young lady is having her last fling, desperately flirting with any available man, and making malicious attempts at stealing Mr. Weston. This provokes Agnes to the point of saying:

> I could only conclude that . . . dogs are not the only creatures which, when gorged to the throat, will yet gloat over what they cannot devour, and grudge the smallest morsel to a starving brother;

—an image which suggests that Anne could 'write up' a feeling if she wanted to, but that—in the cause of 'true fiction'—she was deliberately writing down.

Sentimentality, then, is completely absent from *Agnes Grey*. There are fewer tears in this novel than in any other mid-nineteenth-century novel that I have read. Exaggerated sentiment, so the author seems to have reasoned, would only set up a smoke-screen between the reader and the novel; it would falsify the human condition that the novel is about. It is to that human condition that we must now turn our attention.

Agnes Grey is a novel by a governess about a governess. To understand the way that the governess theme is handled here, it is, I think, helpful to compare it with some other novelists' handling of the same theme.[2] Apart from *Jane Eyre* . . . at least four novels in the decade or so before *Agnes Grey* had dealt at some length with the governess problem: Mrs. Sherwood's *Caroline Mordaunt* (1835);[3] Lady Blessington's *The Governess* (1839)—its heroine, somewhat confusingly in this context, named Clara Mordaunt; Harriet Martineau's *Deerbrook* (1839); and Elizabeth Missing Sewell's *Amy Herbert* (1844). With the governesses in all these novels Agnes Grey shares certain basic features. They are all young ladies in straitened circumstances, used to better things, but forced to earn their living among people who are often socially, and nearly always morally and intellectually, inferior to themselves. The course of events which forces Lady Blessington's Clara Mordaunt to become a governess is typical:

> Clara Mordaunt was the only child and orphan of a merchant, whose unsuccessful speculations had led to bankruptcy and—suicide. Brought up in affluence,

AGNES GREY

By Anne Brontë

WITH A MEMOIR OF HER SISTERS BY CHARLOTTE BRONTË

ILLUSTRATED

EDINBURGH: JOHN GRANT
31 GEORGE IV. BRIDGE
1924

large sums had been expended in her education, and being gifted with great natural abilities, her proficiency satisfied, not only her doting father, but surprised the professors who instructed her.

The father of Miss Martineau's governess, Maria Young, died and she herself became a semi-invalid in an accident; Miss Sewell's Emily Morton 'lost her father and mother both in one month'; and Mrs. Sherwood's Caroline Mordaunt was deprived of father and mother 'whilst yet in my tender infancy'. Agnes Grey differs from these young ladies in having, at least for the best part of the novel, both her parents alive. But her father is a poor clergyman who has lost his small private fortune in a shipwreck (the only melodramatic touch in the novel), and her mother is the daughter of a country squire who cut her off without a penny when she insisted on marrying Mr. Grey—thus providing Agnes with the requisite background of poverty and gentility combined. This background is not only effective for novel purposes: it also reflects an actual social condition of the period.[4] That condition was acutely, but cruelly, set out by Miss Rigby in reviewing *Jane Eyre* and *Vanity Fair* together with the *Governesses' Benevolent Institution Report for 1847:*

We need the imprudencies, extravagancies, mistakes, or crimes of a certain number of fathers, to sow that seed from which we reap the harvest of governesses.[5]

The 'there but for the grace of God' attitude which Miss Rigby's comment suggests is perceptible behind all the four governess novels mentioned. One difference in the work of Anne Brontë, writing her novel when finally back at the parsonage after years of homesickness and humiliation, is the feeling that there, despite the grace of God, had she been.

The real definition of a governess, in the English sense, is a being who is our equal in birth, manners, and education, but our inferior in worldly wealth,

Miss Rigby goes on to say. As an almost inevitable consequence of the social position of the governess, the theme of social humiliation pervades all these novels. Clara Mordaunt is told by one of her pupils that 'Mamma [who is herself hardly a lady] said that governesses were *never ladies,* but merely useful to teach young people how to behave as ladies'.

Emily Morton is first introduced to us in an embarrassing scene where—despite the 'delicate features and sweet expression of the peculiarly lady-like young girl'—she undergoes the indignity of being confused with the lady's maid; and the author seems to take a masochistic pleasure in letting her suffer constant slights, consciously and unconsciously given, in a house of noble young ladies, in comparison with whom the Ingram ladies in *Jane Eyre* are models of tact and consideration. Agnes Grey is very much in this tradition, when on her arrival in a new family she has to wait to see her employer:

I did not see her till eleven o'clock on the morning after my arrival, when she honoured me with a visit, just as my mother might step into the kitchen to see a new servant girl—yet not so, either, for my mother would have seen her immediately after her arrival, and not waited till the next day; and, moreover, she would have addressed her in a more kind and friendly manner.

The implications of the comparison with her mother's treatment of a servant need hardly be commented on. Even her pupils never forget that she is 'a hireling and a poor curate's daughter'; no visitor to the family ever condescends to speak to her; no one gives her her due as a lady. Agnes Grey tries hard, despite constant insults and innuendoes, to 'subdue every resentful impulse, suppress every sensitive shrinking, and go on perseveringly doing my best'. Yet, there is more rebelliousness in her than in the conventional novelist's governess, as appears, for example, when she has to walk back from church with her pupils and their friends:

It was disagreeable, too, to walk behind, and thus appear to acknowledge my own inferiority; for, in truth, I considered myself pretty nearly as good as the best of them, and wished them to know that I did so, and not to imagine that I looked upon myself as a mere domestic.

Here the similarities between **Agnes Grey** and at least three of the other four novels end. For, while the social position and the indignities of these governesses are very similar, the uses made of that position and those indignities for the purposes of the novel are very different. In both *Deerbrook* and *Amy Herbert,* the governesses are slightly out of the focus of the plot. They serve more as catalysts than as active agents. Maria Young, in a novel where the interest is already dispersed between two heroines and two heroes, is passive as far as plot goes, and shows no trace of character development. Referred to in adjectives like 'wise', 'sensible', 'learned', and—most eulogistic of all—'philosophical,' she sets up a standard of moral and intellectual womanhood in the novel, facing the miseries of her solitary life with stoical fortitude. *Amy Herbert* is a novel with little structure and less psychological insight. Its interest is sentimental-moral, and Emily Morton, governess in the house of the title-character's aunt and uncle, is only one of two moral examples in the book (the other is Amy Herbert's saintly mother). To her the governess-ship is a blessed trial or martyrdom: it gives her the chance, which she never misses, to exercise Christian patience and humility.

> She had no mother, no friends; her daily life was one of wearying mortification and self-denial; and yet Emily Morton had never been heard to utter a single murmur. She had never been known to compare her lot with others, or to wonder why she was deprived of the comforts enjoyed by them; and her heart was a perpetual well-spring of quiet gratitude, which made the heaviest trials of her life sources of improvement to herself, and of blessing to those around her.

Significantly, neither of these paragons ends up in marriage. Maria Young, at the end of *Deerbrook,* looks forward with masochistic bravery to going to the wedding between her best friend and the man she herself loves (and who courted her before she became lame and poor and an orphan). Emily's haven is reached when she gets a better position where, instead of 'ridicule or contempt', she is treated with 'the truest esteem and regard'.[6] Both these novels, then, insert studies of the ideal governess—not so much *qua* governess as *qua* Christian stoic—into novel structures where they are not essential. Both, while gaining in general and social interest, lose considerably in concentration.

With both Lady Blessington's *Governess* and Mrs. Sherwood's *Caroline Mordaunt* the case is different. In both, as in **Agnes Grey,** the novel centres on its heroine-governess, and its structural pattern, too, simply consists in following the central character from one position to another. But here the three part company. The real interest in Lady Blessington's novel does not lie in the governess *per se;*[7] it lies in the various social milieus that Clara passes through by virtue of being a governess. Clara is a convenient vehicle in a picaresque tour of various strata of English society: the parvenu Williamson family, the cranky poetess Mrs. Vincent Robinson, the high society of the Lord and Lady Axminster establishment, and the gourmand Manwarrings. Much of the treatment of the different social circles is satirical, and most heavily under fire is the vulgarity—'the solecisms in good breeding and still more in grammar'—of the Williamsons. Clara's own high breeding seems to have fitted her not so much for teaching their children as for ridiculing the bourgeois manner of these parvenus, their conversations (they continually misuse and misunderstand French), their taste in clothes (Mrs. Williamson looks like a radish, in pink and green), and so on. The literary circles of would-be poets and poetesses get their share of the satire, too.

Clara does suffer the customary humiliations, but her solution is not to fight it out: it is to be restored, by money and marriage (in that order), to her proper niche in society. Rich heiress becomes poor governess, but the poor governess eventually (thanks to the timely death of a rich uncle) becomes rich heiress again and marries lord. This pattern of success story is common enough in the 'fashionable' novels of Lady Blessington; and the fact that Clara spends her time of ill-fortune as a governess has nothing to do with her ultimate good fortune.

Caroline Mordaunt is, in most ways, an antithesis to Lady Blessington's novel.[8] Caroline's course, through one governess's position after another, is not a picaresque satire but a domesticated Pilgrim's Progress; her various humiliations do not lead to the arms of a lord but to those of The Lord. True, she marries at the end, but the bridegroom is a clergyman (who wants, not romance but 'a housekeeper') of humble means. Mrs. Sherwood's intention is to show how Caroline, who starts as an irreligious and self-opinionated young woman, is brought by degrees to mortification and the Church. Her story, if we are to label it, is as much a Low Church religious novel as a governess tale. It ends by stating its two morals explicitly and emphatically. The first is that the heroine becomes a good Christian by realising 'how my various misadventures had been calculated to humble me, and bring me to a knowledge of myself'; the second is an admonition to mothers to educate their daughters for the task of being 'a respectable wife in a humbler station' rather than governesses of intellectual and social pretensions. Needless to say, this novel has rather less artistic merit than that which treats of the more worldly Miss Mordaunt.

In *Agnes Grey,* as in *The Governess,* there is social contrast between the employing families. The Bloomfields live in 'a manufacturing district, where the people had nothing to do but make money'; they are definitely underbred; and Agnes's mother refers to them as 'those purse-proud tradespeople and arrogant upstarts'. The Murrays belong to the squirearchy and live in a country-house; they even move in the circles (and have the vices) of the society of the 'fashionable' novels. But social observation of this kind occupies a very subordinate place in the novel.

This, however, does not mean that Anne Brontë is not interested in social issues: on the contrary, *Agnes Grey* is a work much concerned with the nature of human relationships, both in the larger unit of society as a whole and in the smaller unit of the family—husband and wife, parents and children. Underlying the chronological pattern of the autobiography, there is a pattern of what we may call 'social' themes. These themes are developed by simple contrasts, as clear-cut as those in a Morality play. The vicar, Mr. Hatfield, and the curate, Mr. Weston, are as antithetical as the Bad Angel and the Good; and throughout the best part of the novel, episodes are arranged so as to provide testing ground for them. We first meet them in church, where the vicar's exhibitionism is ruthlessly observed:

> He [Mr. Hatfield] would come sailing up the aisle, or rather sweeping along like a whirlwind, with his rich silk gown flying behind him . . . , mount the pulpit like a conqueror ascending his triumphal car; then sinking on the velvet cushion in an attitude of studied grace, remain in silent prostration for a certain time; then, mutter over a Collect, and gabble through the Lord's Prayer, rise, draw off one bright lavender glove to give the congregation the benefit of his sparkling rings, lightly pass his fingers through his well-curled hair, flourish a cambric handkerchief, recite a very short passage, or, perhaps a mere phrase of scripture . . .

Contempt, as usual, brings out Anne Brontë's power of metaphor. Mr. Hatfield's sermons are only concerned with outward observance, 'church discipline, rites and ceremonies, apostolical succession, the duty of reverence and obedience to the clergy'; or else he will take sadistic pleasure in delivering a hell-fire oration, not being ashamed to be seen after the service 'laughing [with the gentry] at his own sermon, and hoping that he had given the rascally people something to think about'. The curate, on the other hand, is characterised by the 'evangelical truth of his doctrine, as well as the earnest simplicity of his manner, and the clearness and force of his style'. What may look at first like a rather specialised ecclesiastical conflict between a Ritualist and an Evangelical churchman, soon proves to be a much more fundamental moral issue. Several chapters take us to the cottages of the poor, whom the vicar despises—one of his favourite topics being 'the necessity of deferential obedience from the poor to the rich';

while the curate sends them coal out of his small stipend, consoles their troubled minds, and goes to any trouble to carry out his pastoral duties. The relationship with the family from the Hall, and with their governess, is another touchstone: the vicar bows and scrapes to the Murrays and ignores Agnes; the curate sees the true worth of people and treats them accordingly. Thus Agnes and Mr. Weston are very clearly lined up against the Murray-Hatfield group; here again the cottagers perform an important thematic function, as the Murrays' condescending, thoughtless and even insulting treatment of them, like the vicar's, is contrasted with Agnes's, and the curate's, true charity. What is at stake in these antithetical attitudes is symbolically expressed in an episode which takes place while Agnes is at the Bloomfields'. A great deal is made of the children's cruelty to animals and the way this is condoned, or encouraged, by their elders. One day Agnes finds the boy with a nest of fledgling birds, gloating at the prospect of slowly tormenting each of them to death. Agnes, in an outburst of revulsion, drops a stone on the intended victims, and is afterwards severely rebuked by Mrs. Bloomfield for interfering with Master Bloomfield's amusements:

> 'You seemed to have forgotten', said she calmly, 'that the creatures were all created for our convenience.'

This, of course, is also the attitude of the family (and of the Murrays and their likes) to their inferiors, be they governesses or cottagers. Mrs. Gaskell tells us how she and Charlotte once discussed this particular passage in *Agnes Grey,* and how it provoked Charlotte to say that

> none but those who had been in the position of a governess could ever realize the dark side of 'respectable' human nature; under no great temptation to crime, but daily giving way to selfishness and ill-temper, till its conduct towards those dependent on it sometimes amounts to a tyranny of which one would rather be the victim than the inflicter.[9]

Agnes Grey is not a social problem novel in the sense that *Mary Barton,* or even *Shirley,* is; but in the comments implied, rather than stated, in its thematic structure, it cries out against *using* your fellow beings.

Relationships within the family unit, and above all on the question of marriage, are also starkly contrasted, in black and white. Here, again, the two clergymen set up an antithesis: the rector's undignified courtship of Miss Murray is developed at length, until it culminates in an ungraciously rejected proposal, in deliberate and pointed contrast to the restrained and slowly-growing affection between Agnes and Mr. Weston. Via the Murray family Agnes gets in touch with the world of high society, where mothers match-make and daughters marry pounds and titles. 'I *must* have Ashby Park, whoever shares it with me', Rosalie Murray proclaims. Anne Brontë is here obviously drawing on the kind of material that the novelists of manners used so profusely; but in comparison with the detachedly amused view of the marriage game in such a novel as Mrs. Gore's *Mothers and Daughters,* Anne's use of the theme is a firmly moralistic one. Thus Rosalie, on a woman's attitude to marriage:

> 'To think that I could be such a fool as to fall in love! It is quite beneath the dignity of a woman to do such a thing.'

But, it is implied, it is not beneath the dignity of a woman to sell herself on the slave-market. This speech is particularly effective, as it is directed to Agnes who has just begun to experience love. The contrasts in attitudes, understandings and moral imagination are all the greater for being implied rather than spoken. But Rosalie is not allowed to get away with it. Just before her reunion with Mr. Weston, Agnes is made to visit her former pupil, now in possession of her coveted Ashby Park, so that we may learn what Rosalie's marriage, after one year, has come to,

> 'I detest that man', whispered Lady Ashby with bitter emphasis, as he [a horseman] slowly trotted by.

> 'Who is it?' I asked, unwilling to suppose that she should so speak of her husband.

> 'Sir Thomas Ashby', she replied with dreary composure.

Rosalie's account of her husband's mode of life is a clear *exemplum horrendum;* it points forward to the more extended use of this kind of material in ***The Tenant of Wildfell Hall.***

It is worth noticing how Agnes's own family background is used in this context. Her mother's rejection of the life of an heiress for true love and a worth-while life is another contrast to the Murray way of thinking, and the issue is not just one of the past; it is brought up again when the mother spurns her father's offer of reconciliation at the cost of repentance.

Thus—to return to *The Governess* after this detour— while Lady Blessington is engaged in detached and satirical observation of society through the eyes of her governess, Anne Brontë is deeply 'committed' in the matter of social morality—that is, her novel deals with social situations in so far as they involve moral issues. What a modern reader may find most difficult to take in ***Agnes Grey*** are the suggestions of self-righteousness which pervade Agnes's attitude to her pupils and their parents, and which are crystallised in occasional comments—as, for example, when the Murray girls are maliciously intervening between Agnes and Mr. Weston and she consoles herself by thinking: 'though he knew

it not, I was more worthy of his love than Rosalie Murray'. If we find this quality in the novel intolerable, then we are debarred from enjoying all those works of fiction (of which *Mansfield Park* is as clear an example as ***Agnes Grey***) in which the author assumes that he or she shares with the reader an attitude, and the only possible attitude, to moral absolutes. In a novel so sure of what is right and what is wrong, so wholly occupied with mapping its world into black and white areas, as is ***Agnes Grey,*** being holier than thou becomes a matter of calm *a priori* classification rather than of personal pride. Yet ***Agnes Grey*** does not, like Mrs. Sherwood's *Caroline Mordaunt,* use the governess theme as a simple moral tract.

The most important distinction between ***Agnes Grey*** and any earlier governess novel is Anne Brontë's concentration on the task of governess-ship as such and, further, on what happens to the individual mind in situations such as those which Agnes Grey goes through. It is what happens inside Agnes, not around her, that matters. Throughout the first section of the novel—with the Bloomfields—there is transmitted a very clear image of a young girl, full of idealistic educational theories, exhilarated at the thought of making her own way in the world, coming up against the hard reality of spoilt children and unsympathetic employers. Her theories prove of no avail, her own childhood experiences do not apply to this brood, the work wears her out. But still she perseveres: 'They may crush, but they shall not subdue me!' Her pupils in her second position are older, but her efforts at making any kind of impression on them are as unavailing. It is here that we get to the deep hurt at the heart of the book, the insight into a human situation which none of the other governess novels even approaches. The real degradation, to Agnes Grey, is not that of social humiliation, slight and neglect; it is one of absolute human isolation and of emotional and spiritual starvation:

> Never, from month to month, from year to year, except during my brief intervals of rest at home, did I see one creature to whom I could open my heart, or freely speak my thoughts with any hope of sympathy, or even comprehension. . . . Never a new idea or a stirring thought came to me from without; and such as rose within me were, for the most part, miserably crushed at once, or doomed to sicken and fade away, because they could not see the light.

There is a rhetorical force in the language here which suggests that we are approaching the central experience in the novel. Agnes fears that this kind of life is actually contaminating her:

> Already, I seemed to feel my intellect deteriorating, my heart petrifying, my soul contracting, and I trembled lest my very moral perceptions should

become deadened, my distinctions of right and wrong confounded, and all my better faculties be sunk at last, beneath the baneful influence of such a mode of life.

Thus it is that the focus widens, from the governess, to any mind deprived of sympathy, isolated from its likes, and exposed to nothing but coarsening influence. The imagery used, and the notion behind it, cannot but recall Wordsworth's *Immortality Ode*: 'The gross vapours of earth were gathering round me, and closing in upon my inward heaven.' The initial enthusiastic Innocence of Agnes Grey is becoming the Experience of moral darkness. On the background of this, her feelings for Mr. Weston are seen as something other than a poor governess's infatuation with an eligible curate:

Mr. Weston rose, at length, upon me, appearing, like the morning star in my horizon, to save me from the fear of utter darkness.

The pathos of Agnes's need for any ideal outside the moral murkiness and sterility of her position is such as to justify the exalted imagery, with its definite religious undertones. In Anne's portrayal of Agnes's love, there is none of the passion that we find in the novels of her sisters, but there is another kind of intensity: the sense of love as an epiphany, as Grace. The same sense inspired her poem, **'The Power of Love'**, written after *Agnes Grey* was completed:

'Tis not my own strength has saved me;
    Health, and hope, and fortitude,
But for love, had long since failed me;
    Heart and soul had sunk subdued.

In her poems of spiritual struggle, divine intervention is expressed by the same kind of imagery as is first used for Agnes's love for Weston, and as reappears when her love is reciprocated in the last two chapters. The pattern of wavering between 'despair' (or, as in the passage just quoted, 'utter darkness') and hope is, perhaps, most evident in the poem called **'Fluctuations'**, where the 'cold and gloomy night', the 'gloomy darkness', are contrasted with the brightness of the sun and the 'silvery gleam' of the moon. In itself the imagery is commonplace enough; but in its context it suggests that the pattern of the spiritual and the emotional experience (for they are one and the same thing) in *Agnes Grey* is the same as that in Anne Brontë's most central poems. The denouement of *Agnes Grey*, then, is not just a conventional happy ending, but a victory for Hope against Despair.

To those who know something about the life of Anne Brontë, the ending of *Agnes Grey* may seem like a piece of wish-fulfilment, like the opposite of the poem where she dreams that her 'life of solitude is past', but wakes up to a reality of deprivation:

But then to wake and find it flown,
    The dream of happiness destroyed;
To find myself unloved, alone,
    What tongue can speak the dreary void!

A heart whence warm affections flow,
    Creator, Thou hast given to me;
And am I only thus to know
    How sweet the joys of love would be?
                              (**'Dreams'**)

Maybe it is, and maybe the prototype of Mr. Weston was Willie Weightman, Mr. Brontë's curate, who died in 1842 and whom Anne loved, according to most of her biographers.[10] The cliffs on which Agnes's hope is fulfilled are obviously those of Scarborough which Anne Brontë loved, and where—in one of the most pathetic chapters of the Brontë saga—she was taken to die, within three years of completing *Agnes Grey*. The sunrise epiphany seems to represent a conjunction of images which had long been in her mind: in the Parsonage Museum there is a drawing by Anne of a girl on a cliff facing the rising sun. It is called 'Sunrise over the Sea' and belongs to the Weightman period; its date (November 13, 1839) suggests that she might have had in mind the approaching end to her governess-ship with the Ingrams of Blake Hall. But it is wrong to let the pathos of any autobiographical aspect blind us to the wider meaning of the ending in the 'true' autobiography of *Agnes Grey*. 'All true histories contain instruction.' To have left Agnes with nothing but a 'rayless arch of sombre grey' (**'Self-Communion'**) would have been closer to the actuality of Anne's own life; but it would have been what Professor Pascal in his book on *Design and Truth in Autobiography* calls a 'wrong' truth.[11] By postulating a reciprocated love, fulfilled in marriage, Anne must have felt that she was creating a 'right truth': she made her novel more morally impressive, more generally instructive. This, obviously, does not mean to say that she is 'instructing' by holding out, like a carrot to a donkey, a happy marriage to every persevering governess. It means that *Agnes Grey* is an attempt to hand on to the novel-reading public her own belief, expressed in so many of her poems, that Hope and Joy will eventually come to those who live 'upright and firm, through good and ill' (**'Vanitas Vanitatum'**).

Notes

[1] Compare the protracted death of one of the pupils which is the highlight of Miss Sewell's governess novel, *Amy Herbert*.

[2] There is a useful survey of the governess in literature in Chapter II of Patricia Thomson, *The Victorian Heroine: A Changing Ideal, 1837-1873* (1956), but I disagree with the author's opinions on the social attitudes expressed in *Agnes Grey* and on the literary merits of

this novel. An illuminating study of the social position of the governess is to be found in Wanda F. Neff, *Victorian Working Women: An Historical and Literary Study of Women in British Industries and Professions, 1832-1850* (1929), Chapter V, 'The Governess'.

[3] The date of Mrs. Sherwood's novel is given by *C.B.E.L.*, conjecturally, as 1845, but the *English Catalogue* shows it to be 1835. Strictly speaking, *Caroline Mordaunt* is not a novel but a tale for the young. But . . . the borderline between didactic, even juvenile, fiction and the novel proper is very thin; and *Caroline Mordaunt* could easily be classed as a religious novel, with a strongly Evangelical tone and a moralistic intention. Similar to Lady Blessington's *The Governess* in structure, it is diametrically opposed in tone and attitude. A comparison of the two, however, invites itself, if only because of the similarity in titles—*Caroline Mordaunt* is subtitled 'The Governess'—and in heroines' names—the heroine of *The Governess* is called Clara Mordaunt. Mrs. Sherwood was known as the author of exceedingly pious works, not least through the many editions of her 'improved' version of Sarah Fielding's *The Governess* (initially published in 1749; Mrs. Sherwood's *The Governess; or, the Little Female Academy* first appeared in 1820), in which she replaced fairy-tales with 'such appropriate relations as seemed more likely to conduce to juvenile edification' (her Preface, iv). Charlotte M. Yonge, who includes Sarah Fielding's work, in its original form, in her collection of children's classics, *A Storehouse of Stories* (1870), I, 89-222, speaks (p. vii) of 'Mrs. Sherwood's adaptation to her own Evangelical style'.

[4] Cf. Chapter I, [esp. p. 27, of *Their Proper Sphere: A Study of the Brontë Sisters as Early-Victorian Female Novelists,* by Inga-Stina Ewbank, Harvard University Press, 1966].

[5] *Quarterly Review,* LXXXIV (December 1848), 176. These are, of course, some of the lines which Charlotte Brontë quotes in *Shirley.* . . .

[6] This, too, is the pattern of the *Belle Assemblée* story, 'The Young Governess', . . . in which the heroine advances from a job as 'daily governess' with some very unpleasant people to one as 'in-door governess' in a good and kind family. It was probably the least revolutionary version of the success theme in the governess novel.

[7] That this was due to the pressure of her reading public rather than to her own inclination, is indicated by her letter about *The Governess,* quoted in Michael Sadleir's study of her life and work, *Blessington-D'Orsay: A Masquerade* (1933), 275: 'It was my anxious wish to point attention and excite sympathy towards a class from which [more is] expected and to whom less is

accorded, than to any other. . . . I felt this so much that I wished to make my book a much more grave one; but the publisher, thinking only of the sale, bargained for its being interspersed with lively sketches, which in my opinion interfere sadly with the original intention.' Clearly her 'original intention' was one which, if fulfilled, would have anticipated the governess-novel-with-a-purpose of the 1840s; instead she had to live up to her reputation as a fashionable woman and a novelist of fashionable life and write a typical 'she-novel' (this is how the *Fraser* reviewer described her novel *The Two Friends* (1835)—see Sadleir, 250).

[8] See note [3].

[9] *Life,* 154-5. In the same context Mrs. Gaskell relates an occurrence which epitomises the reasons why the Brontës, and particularly Charlotte, so hated the life of a governess. In one of her situations Charlotte had managed, after many difficulties, to gain the respect and affection of her charges—so much so that one small boy, 'in a little demonstrative gush', put his hand in hers and said, 'I love 'ou, Miss Brontë'. But cold water was immediately poured on this display of unseemly feelings, by the children's mother exclaiming, before all the children, 'Love the *governess,* my dear!'

[10] See, e.g., Winifred Gérin, *Anne Brontë,* and Ada Harrison and Derek Stanford, *Anne Brontë: Her Life and Work* (1959).

[11] Roy Pascal, *Design and Truth in Autobiography* (1960).

W. A. Craik (essay date 1968)

SOURCE: "*Agnes Grey,*" in *The Brontë Novels,* Methuen, 1968, pp. 202-27.

[*In the following essay, Craik offers an overview of* Agnes Grey, *surveying its characterization, theme, narrative technique, and style. In addition, Craik compares the work with those of Brontë's sisters Emily and Charlotte, suggesting that it bears stronger affinities with the eighteenth-century novel than it does with their writings.*]

No one could call Anne Brontë's two novels masterpieces; but she deserves neither to be ignored, nor to be regarded only as a pale copy of her sisters. She is absorbing on at least three, though not equal, counts: as the first novel writer of the family, using material later used by Emily and Charlotte; as a norm from which to judge the powers of her sisters in using such material; and as a novelist in her own right with a mode and flavour of her own—worthy of attention, original and good. She resembles Charlotte in having similar experiences to draw upon, and in feeling in her second novel a moral duty to write of an uncongenial topic; she resembles both her sisters in finding man's inhumanity to man a fitting element in a love story; and in being startlingly unconventional, unsophisticated, and candid. She uses some of the methods of both in organizing her material. But her own personality, her way of considering the experiences she puts before her heroines, and the idiom in which her heroines present them, are not so much akin to her sisters as to the eighteenth century. If the reader goes to Anne Brontë for what either Charlotte or Emily offers, he is disappointed. If he takes pleasure in Fanny Burney or Maria Edgeworth—or, to name a greater, Jane Austen—he will find her manner congenial and her writing attractive. While I propose to relate her novels to those of Charlotte or Emily where the connection is useful to either sister, I intend also to assess them on their own terms, for what they attempt and achieve.

Anne Brontë has suffered like her sisters from the Brontë legend. She has also suffered from the sisters themselves. One thing that is best forgotten is the image of the 'gentle Anne', as she is termed by Charlotte and Arthur Nicholls, since without the legend and the comment one would not see much 'gentleness' in her, even in *Agnes Grey.* One thing well remembered however is that *Agnes Grey* is probably the first prose for publication written at Haworth Parsonage, and would be read and absorbed by her sisters before *Wuthering Heights, The Professor,* and the story it most resembles, *Jane Eyre,* were written. If any credit for conception is to be claimed it must be by Anne. The attempt must therefore be made to think of her with a mind reasonably uncoloured by *Jane Eyre* and *Wuthering Heights,* while not yet forgetting the juvenile fantasies that themselves colour all three.

Agnes Grey is an unpretentious work about an unpretentious heroine. It is probably a recasting of the work mentioned in the 'Birthday Note' of 1845, where she remarks: 'I have begun the third volume of *Passages in the life of an Individual':* a title more apt to what is now *Agnes Grey* than the one it possesses, which, like the story, is unassuming, and does not adequately suggest what is actually offered. One would summarize the main story as one in which a clergyman's younger daughter, compelled by her father's fallen fortunes to earn her living as a governess in two middle-class country families, and later, at his death, to help her mother run a small school, meets, while in her second place of employment, a worthy young clergyman whom she later marries. The other plot concerns the young and beautiful pupil, a coquette, who marries a degenerate young landowner for his money and position. Few plots could be less sensational; even *The Professor,* by contrast, seems a heady brew. Of the few exciting moments Anne Brontë offers herself, she makes very little, reducing them by covering them briefly—as

Agnes' father's death, which is comprised in a few words at the end of Chapter 18—or by a calm literal manner of telling—like her meeting with Mr Weston on the sands (Chapter 24)—or by a dash of astringent or sardonic humour—as when she suppresses her reply to Mrs Bloomfield:

> 'You seem to have forgotten,' said she calmly, 'that the creatures were all created for our convenience.'

> I thought that the doctrine admitted some doubt.

> (Chapter 5)

Clearly her aim is not excitement or sensation, and, as will later be examined, is not indicated properly by such a summary, which is actually misleading. One does not, in fact, read *Agnes Grey* for the story, and its importance does not lie in the story, a matter which immediately sets Anne Brontë apart from her sisters. Like Jane Austen, Anne Brontë, working her way through it without excitement or sensationalism, produces some unique incident, pungent characters, and, above all, a serious, penetrating and new exposure of society.

Also like Jane Austen, she keeps to what she knows. The material is plainly drawn from her own life. Anne Brontë herself is a clergyman's daughter, the youngest of the family, compelled to teach to earn her living, employed in the families of the gentry, while Agnes Grey's eventual modest though happy marriage is what Anne Brontë could without impropriety envisage for herself. Like Charlotte, she draws on more than herself. The loathsome Bloomfield children in her first post are the Inghams of Anne's first post at Blake Hall; the Murray household resembles closely that of the Robinsons, with whom she stayed some years, as Agnes stays with the Murrays.[1] Some of the most telling incident also is from life, notably the one that most readers remember best, in which Agnes destroys the nest of young birds to prevent a brutal child from torturing them.

It is as tempting therefore with Anne Brontë as with Charlotte to identify the narrator with the author, to consider that what is revealed of Agnes must also be true of Anne. It is not necessarily any more true of Agnes Grey than of Jane Eyre. While the narrative stance adopted in *Agnes Grey* is very much more simple than that of *Jane Eyre,* it is no mere autobiographical fantasy. Considerable degrees of detachment may be seen between the 'I' at different points in the narrative, and the 'I' who comments on them. Quite clearly the childish eighteen-year-old girl of the opening chapters is greatly below the narrator and also the reader, not only in quietly accepting that she is fit only to 'go and practise [her] music, or play with the kitten' (Chapter 1), but in thinking that the clear remembrance of my own thoughts in early childhood would [in training children] be a surer guide than the instructions of the most mature adviser.

(Chapter 1)

As Agnes grows up the gap narrows, as it does as Jane Eyre grows up. But it never closes. Quite clearly the Agnes of the closing section is not only older but wiser than the young self narrating the events; yet at twenty-three, she still asks her mother's permission before accepting Mr Weston's invitation to a walk (Chapter 25). There is no suggestion, despite the moral and instructive tone of parts of the narrative, that this is the proper, or accepted, way to act for a woman of twenty-three (only a year younger than Lucy Snowe), as there is for instance in the works of Charlotte M. Yonge. Anne Brontë always represents Agnes as someone younger and less experienced than herself or the reader, who is much less often on terms of wholehearted sympathy with her than with Jane Eyre. As a narrator, she has more in common with Esther Summerson in *Bleak House.*

She has in common with Esther that she also is not the absolute centre of interest. She is what makes the action cohere, but she is not necessarily the protagonist. She is the means by which the novel progresses, the author's purpose in it is achieved, and the events and characters are connected. But unlike *Jane Eyre's,* the important events concern others, notably Rosalie Murray, as much as herself, and the personalities she delineates are almost as clearly seen, and as interesting, as her own. One remembers Rosalie's flirtation with the rector Mr Hatfield better than Agnes's meetings with the curate Mr Weston, remembers the Bloomfield children's revolting habits more than the horror they inspire in Agnes; one sees the horse-loving Matilda or her mother 'who required neither rouge nor padding to add to her charms' (Chapter 7) quite as clearly as the quiet, plain, little heroine. Anne Brontë, while clearly showing, and expecting to elicit, sympathy for the hard-pressed Agnes, is not primarily concerned with her responses. Agnes does not actually create the reader's reaction to those with whom she comes into contact, nor do Anne Brontë and the reader judge them by how they treat her, as one judges those who come into contact with Jane Eyre. The whole of Rosalie's flirtation with Mr Hatfield proceeds without Agnes being moved by it at all, except to detached moral disapproval. Yet it is fully as significant and absorbing as Rosalie's next attempt, to flirt with Mr Weston, from which Agnes suffers considerable pain. What makes the second flirtation a graver matter than the first is what it reveals about Rosalie, that she is so taken up with coquetterie that she must descend from the willing and socially acceptable vicar to the unmoved and socially impossible curate. Agnes's feelings have very little to do with the artistic purpose here.

Agnes indeed as a personality can be effaced for quite long stretches. There are several points at which a secondary narrator supersedes her: as in Chapter 11, where the cottager Nancy retails the contrasting visits and behaviour to her of the two clergymen, or in Chapter 14, where Rosalie tells her own story. These, and scenes in which the story is told to Agnes, who merely comments, bear a resemblance to the method of *Wuthering Heights.* There are also many points at which the scene proceeds by way of dialogue in which Agnes takes no part and passes no comment. If so neutral a narrator has a precedent, it is found in Scott's *Redgauntlet,* which opens with the letters to and fro of Alan Fairford and his friend Darsie Latimer, the bulk of the narrative being that of Fairford, who is no more the all-absorbing hero than is Agnes. Scott has soon to abandon the method; Anne Brontë can continue in it. It is clear that her purpose in using her material, and adopting the first-person narrator, is an original and largely self-taught one; it is not a tentative movement towards either Charlotte Brontë's or Emily's. She is attempting an examination of a section of society, which, seen from the unusual view that a governess enjoys, exposes itself, its standards, its follies, and its failings for the reader's assessment, not necessarily so that an unusual judgement may be passed, but so that long-held opinions may be rescrutinized, refreshed, and confirmed.

Such a purpose affects the relationship between author, narrator and reader. Anne Brontë never forgets either herself, her creation, or her reader. Identification with Agnes is impossible, because of the childishness already noted, nor can one ever lose oneself in the action, since it is usually either comic or reprehensible. Emotional response is called up for a purpose, so that understanding and appreciation shall, as with Jane Austen, lead to moral judgement, the way to which is pointed by a whole variety of means, all befitting Agnes, but all making the detachment between herself and the reader very clear. Anne Brontë assumes a reader as rational and reasonable as Agnes's most mature self. Sometimes her tone is of serious straightforward utterance of dicta known to both, and given because they summarize what has gone, or prepare what is to follow:

> Habitual associates are known to exercise a great influence over each other's minds and manners. Those whose actions are for ever before our eyes, whose words are ever in our ears, will naturally lead us, albeit, against our will—slowly—gradually—imperceptibly, perhaps, to act and speak as they do.

(Chapter 11)

It is with such well-grounded fears of her own deterioration in bad company that Agnes welcomes Mr Weston. Frequently she is much more oblique, as in her closing reply to Rosalie's wish 'to enjoy myself thoroughly, and coquet with all the world, till I am on the verge of being called an old maid; and then, to escape the infamy of that, after having made ten thousand conquests, to break all their hearts save one, by marrying some high-born, rich, indulgent husband, whom, on the other hand, fifty ladies were dying to have.'

'Well, as long as you entertain these views, keep single by all means, and never marry at all, not even to escape the infamy of old-maidenhood.'

(Chapter 9)

The story begins

All true histories contain instruction; though, in some, the treasure may be hard to find, and, when found, so trivial in quantity that the dry, shrivelled kernel scarcely compensates for the trouble of cracking the nut. Whether this be the case with my history or not, I am hardly competent to judge; I sometimes think it might prove useful to some, and entertaining to others, but the world may judge for itself: shielded by my own obscurity, and by the lapse of years, and a few fictitious names, I do not fear to venture, and will candidly lay before the public what I would not disclose to the most intimate friend.

(Chapter 1)

It never loses sight of its opening. The purpose revealed—to establish moral standards, whether those of Agnes or others, to measure their conduct against them, and thus establish the worth of both the conduct and of the standards on which it is based—is plainly Anne Brontë's own, not her character's, since Agnes modestly disclaims what her whole history is designed to reveal—the possession of the 'treasure' of instruction. Agnes is plainly rather a mask behind which her author may retire, than a means by which, in Agnes's words, Anne Brontë herself can 'candidly lay before the public what I would not disclose to the most intimate friend'. She is showing herself ironically and wittily aware of the illusions of the fictional memoir which involves so improbable a laying before the public, and so establishes the terms on which she uses it. Anne Brontë, intending to be moral, avoids, again like Jane Austen, ever alienating her reader by instructing him in person. Agnes is her mouthpiece, a creation whose judgement the reader can always trust, but who is yet sufficiently his inferior in years and experience to make an appealing guide. The form of the candid, unsophisticated, unprofessional memoir is one very suited both to such a purpose and such a narrator. It makes the direct addresses to the reader acceptable and even desirable. They are frequent:

As I cannot, like Dogberry, find it in my heart to bestow *all* my tediousness on the reader, I will not

go on to bore him with a minute detail of all the discoveries and proceedings of this and the following day.

(Chapter 7)

A few more observations about Horton Lodge and its on goings, and I have done with dry description for the present.

(Chapter 7)

As I am in the way of confessions, I may as well acknowledge that, about this time, I paid more attention to dress than ever I had done before.

(Chapter 17)

The diffidence that provokes these remarks makes Agnes an engaging guide, and prevents her from being a pontifical or priggish one. While one may suspect that the author also is diffident, she is proved to have chosen her form well, since it turns what could have been a defect to good use.

The narrative method and the form are, indeed, more cunning than they seem. The story is basically in two main sections, one comprising Agnes's experiences with the appalling Bloomfield family at Wellwood (Chapters 2-5), the other her several years' stay with the Murrays at Horton Lodge (Chapters 7-20). The sections are preluded by an account of her home life and the circumstances leading to her becoming a governess (Chapter 1); they are interrupted by several returns home for holidays (Chapter 3), for her sister's wedding (Chapter 8), and for her father's death (Chapter 18); and they are concluded by the brief account of her stay in her mother's school at A—— (Chapters 21, 24, 25), and by her visit to the married Rosalie, Lady Ashby (Chapters 22, 23). The proportions of the material indicate clearly enough that this is not merely the chronicle of Agnes's life in these years. A minority of it is devoted to matters most touching her in her home life; her sister's marriage is passed over in a brief conversation with Rosalie:

'Who is she to be married to?'

'To Mr Richardson, the vicar of a neighbouring parish.'

'Is he rich?'

'No—only comfortable.'

'Is he handsome?'

'No—only decent.'

'Young?'

'No—only middling.'

'O mercy! what a wretch!'

(Chapter 8)

An exchange whose prime purpose is to display Rosalie's views on marriage, and reveals nothing of the relationship between Agnes and her sister. Similarly Agnes's father's death is dwelt on less than the callous behaviour of Mrs Murray, who

> concluded with saying I might have the phaeton to take me to O——.

> 'And instead of *repining, Miss Grey, be thankful for the *privileges* you enjoy. There's many a poor clergyman whose family would be plunged into ruin by his death; but *you,* you see, have influential friends ready to continue their patronage, and to show you every consideration.'

(Chapter 18)

Anne Brontë's business in the novel is with the society and attitudes she can examine through Agnes, rather than with Agnes herself. The examination becomes more subtle and complex (though one would never call it deep), as the novel goes on. The moral weight clearly regulates the shape not only of the whole but of its parts. Agnes's troubles with the Bloomfields occupy three chapters only; her stay with the Murrays, thirteen. What looks like disproportion results in balance, and shows the modest discretion of the author, as well as the purpose guiding her. Anne Brontë begins with the straightforwardly preposterous standards of the Bloomfields, who see no wrong in allowing a frustrated child to 'spit in the faces of those who incurred her displeasure' (Chapter 3); in encouraging a seven-year-old boy to kick not only the dog, but his governess; and who consider tormenting animals a child's legitimate amusement. Even with the Bloomfields, however, the rendering of character is convincing:

> 'Damme, but the lad has some spunk in him too! Curse me, if ever I saw a nobler little scoundrel than that! He's beyond petticoat government already:—by G—— he defies mother, granny, governess, and all!'

(Chapter 5)

and the reasoning perversely ingenious:

> 'I think,' said she, 'a child's amusement is scarcely to be weighed against the welfare of a soulless brute.'

> 'But, for the child's own sake, it ought not to be encouraged to such amusements,' answered I, as

meekly as I could, to make up for such unusual pertinacity. 'Blessed are the merciful, for they shall obtain mercy.'

'Oh, of course! but that refers to our conduct towards each other.'

'The merciful man shows mercy to his beast,' I ventured to add.

'I think *you* have not shown much mercy,' replied she, with a short, bitter laugh; 'killing the poor birds by wholesale, in that shocking manner, and putting the dear boy to such misery, for a mere whim!'

(Chapter 5)

The events at the Bloomfields' are so startling, and often shocking, that three chapters spent on them are enough; to continue or elaborate them would be to repeat, and to dull the effect. Once Anne Brontë has supplied an instance of the selfish and stupid father

> 'remember that, in future, when a decent dish leaves this table, they shall not *touch* it in the kitchen. Remember *that,* Mrs Bloomfield!'

(Chapter 3)

and of the consequences in a selfish and stupid son; and once she has made her point about the suffering that can be inflicted by both upon the helpless and the dependent, their use is over. Anne Brontë recognizes also that the grotesque is incapable of growth, and so moves her heroine away forthwith from a household of grotesques.

The transition to Horton is both smooth and artistic. Mood and themes are carried over. When Agnes first arrives at Horton, she is in charge of a family whose two youngest members are barbarians of a larger growth; John is 'rough as a young bear, boisterous, unruly, unprincipled, untaught, unteachable' and Charles 'only active in doing mischief, and only clever in inventing falsehoods' (Chapter 7). Though Anne Brontë wisely wastes no time on Agnes's tussles with them, which must repeat her tussles with the Bloomfields, their unpleasing presence connects Horton with the earlier section, while their speedy departure prepares for something new.[2]

The Murray girls are more mature and consequently more complex. Through them the novel moves on to consider not only the effects of negligent upbringing on behaviour, but the young person's own application of the deficient principles he has been given. The young boys having gone to school, the story concentrates on Rosalie, the most brilliant of the family, and the greatest disaster. The truths she exemplifies require a series of events, not mere isolated anecdotes, hence the greater length devoted to the telling. The story follows her 'coming-out' into society, her successes, her admirers, her betrothal to Sir Thomas Ashby, her encouragement and rejection of the clergyman Mr Hatfield, her attempt to captivate the curate Mr Weston, her wedding, and finally her married life. Anne Brontë firmly follows her on her career even after it has effectively ceased to be Agnes's, and drives home her message dramatically when Agnes visits Rosalie a year after her marriage (Chapter 22), to see the frustration and boredom to which her ambitions have led her. With this episode the social wheel has come full circle, Agnes Grey's function as narrator has been fulfilled, and the novel has completed its course. Rosalie has now become the parent, in her own household ruined by false values, with an unwanted child about to grow up to become, inevitably, another victim of its circumstances, as its mother has been. The situation is now seen from the mother's view:

> 'What pleasure can I have in seeing a girl grow up to eclipse me, and enjoy those pleasures I am forever debarred from? But supposing I could be so generous as to take delight in this, still it is *only* a child; and I can't centre all my hopes in a child; that is only one degree better than devoting oneself to a dog. And as for all the goodness and wisdom you have been trying to instil into me—that is all very right and proper, I dare say; and if I were some twenty years older, I might fructify by it; but people must enjoy themselves when they're young—and if others won't let them—why, they must hate them for it!'

> (Chapter 23)

The final episode, which settles Agnes in the situation she merits, drives home by contrast the points made at Ashby Park, and gains its power as much from this function, as for the happiness it brings to Agnes.

By contrast with her sisters', Anne Brontë's characters seem unsubtle. Though remarkably vigorous and memorable (considering how concisely they make their effects), they undoubtedly lack the strong flavour of Charlotte's, or the sublimity of Emily's. They are much closer to common life than either, and, equally, much further from any easily identifiable literary influence. They all have the rather simple force and the conviction of the documentary, the kind of personality that emerges from the sociological survey rather than the literary imagination. Excluding Mr Weston, they are of two separate kinds: those who form Agnes's family, and those whom she encounters away from home. The differences are of attitude as well as function and treatment, and indicate once more where Anne Brontë's interests lie. She wastes little time on the Grey family, large though it must figure in Agnes's mind. Clearly

she could, without destroying the balance of the book, delineate the elder sister Mary more clearly, or spend more time on the mother, but to do so would alter the tone, since these characters are conceived in a different spirit from the rest. Their purpose also is different. They are the first on whom the candid Agnes exercises her judgement for the reader's benefit, thereby gaining the reader's confidence in her. Since we recognize how justly and acutely she assesses those who are virtuous in themselves, in circumstances we can readily enter into, whom we can readily recognize for ourselves, we are prepared to trust her summings-up of strangers, whose actions might well seem close to incredible. Agnes's family are not so much the stuff of nineteenth-century fiction, as of the eighteenth-century essay:

> my father was completely overwhelmed by the calamity—health, strength, and spirits sunk beneath the blow; and he never wholly recovered them. In vain my mother strove to cheer him by appealing to his piety, to his courage, to his affection for herself and us. That very affection was his greatest torment: it was for our sakes he had so ardently longed to increase his fortune—it was our interest that had lent such brightness to his hopes, and that imparted such bitterness to his present distress.

> (Chapter 1)

The eighteenth-century note is no disadvantage: Agnes analysing her father is as reliable as Fielding analysing Squire Allworthy, or Dr Johnson summarizing Rasselas. The note persists when the analysis is more acute and verges on the humorous:

> My mother like most active, managing women, was not gifted with very active daughters; for this reason—that being so clever and diligent herself, she was never tempted to trust her affairs to a deputy, but on the contrary, was willing to act and think for others as well as for number one.

> (Chapter 1)

Like the essayists, she reveals no more of the character than is perceptible to the intelligent observer, and has no occasion to go deeper. Her father's sufferings, even though they hasten his death, receive no more analysis than the above. Anne Brontë is happy, however, to allow dialogue to suggest relationships and underlying characteristics, and can do so economically and pleasantly, though she has no intention of using it, like Emily Brontë, for characters' deliberate self-revelation. The suggestion of cross-purposes, and modes of thought, is neatly done when Mrs Grey suggests that Mary should try to sell some of her drawings, while Agnes is preoccupied with her own plan to become a governess:

'I wish *I* could do something,' said I.

'You, Agnes! well, who knows? You draw pretty well too; if you choose some simple piece for your subject, I dare say you will be able to produce something we shall be proud to exhibit.'

(Chapter 1)

The atmosphere at home is admirably created, providing the settled existence behind Agnes which makes her resilient in the face of her astonishing experiences, so much more realistic than those in *Jane Eyre* or *Villette,* whose heroines Charlotte Brontë deliberately deprives of the refuge of a safe home. Economically, Anne Brontë continues to epitomize Agnes's home in her mother. She is the main speaker in the opening chapters, and the one who remains at the end, when, elder sister married, Agnes resigns her post to help her now widowed mother run her school. She represents a norm of good sense and right feeling, little emphasized but impressive, which prevents the disproportion of a world full of vice and folly, which would result from dwelling wholly on the families who employ Agnes.

Edward Weston, curate of Horton, on the other hand, is possibly the shadowiest hero ever invented by a woman novelist. If Agnes were the all-absorbing heroine, this would be a very serious charge. In fact, though he cannot rouse much interest in the reader, or demand long consideration, he does adequately what he is called upon to do. He is primarily the doer of good deeds in a naughty world, the only well-principled person of her own class, other than her family, whom Agnes meets. He functions always as a moral force. He is the immediate contrast to the worldly and careless clergyman Mr Hatfield, and, even as the man Agnes loves, what are stressed are his moral qualities:

I could think of him day and night; and I could feel that he was worthy to be thought of. Nobody knew him as I did; nobody could appreciate him as I did.

(Chapter 17)

Lack of information is a dramatic asset when he is marked down by Rosalie as her last victim. The reader, like Agnes, knows his virtue, but has no way of knowing his emotional temperament, or how he will respond to Rosalie's advances. While the end of the story is certain—by the convention of the novel he will marry Agnes—there is no way of telling whether he will succumb to Rosalie and then, disillusioned, recover, or whether he will be acute enough to resist her.[3] A modest originality of Mr Weston's is to be an early instance of the unhandsome hero. The man 'a little, a very little, above the middle size' with 'his face too square for beauty', eyebrows 'too projecting' and eyes 'brown in colour, not large, and somewhat deepset, but strikingly

brilliant' (Chapter 11) is the counterpart of a heroine with 'marked features, pale hollow cheek, and ordinary dark brown hair', just as Mr Rochester is the counterpart of Jane.[4] Anne Brontë does here, calmly, without any sense in the writing that she is being novel, what Charlotte Brontë afterwards does with panache— a man who has no charms save in the eye of the narrator.

All the other characters are knaves or fools in some degree, even the children. Their failings are what justify their literary existence. Such a statement suggests that **Agnes Grey** must be either a satire, or a work of very limited interest. The nature of Agnes herself prevents it being the first, while the functions of the other characters prevent its being the second. Like the Grey family, the rest are seen only from outside, by the intelligent observer Agnes, whose author never allows her to guess at or speculate on the variety of impulses and motives which produce the behaviour she observes. Anne Brontë never causes the reader to worry what there can have been in common between Mr and Mrs Murray, for example, to cause them to marry, nor suggests how they may behave to each other in situations where Agnes herself could not observe them. She does not resolve the difficulty of how a selfish woman can endure the company of her own intolerable children. But she chronicles with such precision that the immediate incident rings so true as not to invite such speculation. Anne, like Emily, observes personalities, and allows them to expose themselves; she does not analyse or dissect; a feature which reveals that she is closer to Emily in this matter than to Charlotte, who is as much concerned with interior causes as with effects. The purpose of Anne Brontë's characterization is not psychological, but social. Actions and attributes are selected to lead the reader to consider their social and personal consequences, not their causes.

It is therefore wise of her to begin with the inhabitants of Wellwood. The reader's natural tendency with a child is to consider it as a being with a potential, but no past, who is very much the direct consequences of the influences it feels. The distasteful Bloomfield brood—Tom, Mary Ann, and Fanny—are presented firmly as the results of irresponsible overindulgence, to be judged themselves for conscious vices, and to cause judgement to be made both on their parents, and, by extension, on the grossly deficient moral and social standards by which the parents live. Good care is taken that they shall not be pitied as victims, either of the system or each other: Tom Bloomfield, enjoying brutality and torment, is his uncle Robson in miniature; Mary Ann, whom he bullies, is deliberately, systematically and inflexibly perverse, and the bad habits of both, and of the even younger Fanny, are such as to rouse more revulsion in the reader than in the narrator. Agnes herself and the nursery-maid Betty (who puts in a brief appearance in Chapter 3) prevent the reader from supposing that the children suffer from lack of affection, since it is offered and rejected. Anne Brontë clearly believes in original sin, as well as natural good, and in training as the very necessary force that will turn a child into a good man. The Bloomfield children's purpose, since they occupy only four hair-raising chapters, is to prepare the way for the Murrays, a more subtle and exhaustive study of the corruption of the individual, and the effects of wrong training on a faulty nature. Agnes, brooding on her charges, remarks:

> the children would, in time, become more humanized: every month would contribute to make them some little wiser, and, consequently, more manageable; for a child of nine or ten, as frantic and ungovernable as these at six and seven would be a maniac.

(Chapter 3)

The Murrays, in their early teens, bear her out, and the reader, when he meets them, is prepared to regard them in the same way as the Bloomfields, looking only to the consequences they bring about, not to what caused them to become what they are.

The parents of these unhappy offspring are revealed with the same documentary precision, though, because they impinge less on Agnes, and are less to the purpose, more briefly. Again the eighteenth-century note is heard, and the characters of Mr and Mrs Bloomfield, the Grandmother, and Uncle Robson seem true to type without ever seeming trite. They are revealed through the individual, small, significant encounter, and usually through dialogue. Mr Bloomfield suddenly and arbitrarily interrupts the narrative, just as he suddenly and arbitrarily descends on Agnes and his children, to abuse them and her and depart; Uncle Robson, a more positive evil though a temporary one, makes his devastating comment on his nephew, Tom, raging over the loss of his birds' nest, and departs likewise:

> 'Curse me, if ever I saw a nobler little scoundrel than that! He's beyond petticoat government already!— By G— he defies mother, granny, governess, and all! Ha, ha, ha! Never mind, Tom, I'll get you another brood tomorrow.'

(Chapter 5)

Mrs Bloomfield on the other hand makes an impressive first appearance doing nothing; all the while Agnes wrestles with tough, cold, meat, with her hands numb from five hours' exposure to the bitter wind, what is being sensed is the tough, cold, numb Mrs Bloomfield silently watching her.

The handling of the convincingly unreasonable characters here leads forward to Horton, where the characters are to be unreasonable in ways more elaborate, and seemingly more like what usually appear in a novel. In the background are the neglecting father, and the worldly mother, seeing only what is to her daughter's social and financial advantage, bending all her efforts to an early and profitable marriage; in the foreground the two contrasting young women, the hoyden and the coquette; and attending on Rosalie an assortment of suitors, amongst whom the brutish and successful landowner contrasts, in his turn, with the aspiring social climber, the rector. Here also Anne Brontë successfully imposes her own tone, and, while using the stuff of convention, sees it not at all in the conventional way, contriving never to slip into the merely grotesque on the one hand, or on the other to allow herself or the reader to be seduced by the charm of what is inescapably reprehensible. The personality and position of Agnes herself imposes proportion, since what looms largest to her is also what matters most to the story and them. The method is economical in itself, and performed with natural economy. The characterization here has the same verve as at Wellwood, but is far more varied in its methods. The least significant personalities are suggested with splendid precision. The setting, the kind of character, the cool justice which is accorded them, the humane partly-involved narrator, the mingling of humour with instruction, all suggest, not another of the Brontës, but Trollope. While it is clear that his handling of elaborate ecclesiastical politics and the edges of high society is beyond her, so are her just proportioning of means to her end, her impulse to understate rather than elaborate her points, beyond Trollope. Mr Murray for instance is only of concern as the father figure for an unsatisfactory family in general, and as the one who authorizes and condones Matilda in her hunting and swearing. Agnes never see him 'to speak to' (Chapter 12) as she says, but 'the figure of a tall stout gentleman with scarlet cheeks and crimson nose' (Chapter 7), precisely noted at the beginning of her account of the family, remains firmly fixed in the reader's mind. Mrs Murray, more important since her influence is upon the more important daughter Rosalie, is permitted to impress herself by speech, by quietly devastating self-exposure:

> 'I have hitherto found all the governesses, even the very best of them, faulty in this particular. They wanted that meek and quiet spirit which St Matthew, or some of them, says is better than the putting on of apparel—you will know the passage to which I allude, for you are a clergyman's daughter.'

(Chapter 7)

Her moral values, her self-satisfaction, her relationship to her governess need no more explanation. On the rare occasions when it is necessary to suggest her motives, the method is equally laconic:

having notwithstanding the disadvantages of a country life so satisfactorily disposed of her elder daughter, the pride of her heart, [she] had begun seriously to turn her attention to the younger.

(Chapter 18)

'satisfactorily' suggests her own opinion, 'disposed' suggests Agnes's; while the conventional phrase 'pride of her heart' takes on a new richness applied to a relationship which has displayed all too much 'pride' and a total lack of 'heart'.

The younger daughter Matilda contrasts with her sister (her main function in the novel), demonstrating that, while to be sophisticated like Rosalie is unadmirable, to lack the quality may be, not admirable, but merely uncouth; to be deceitful like Rosalie is wrong, but merely to be frank in admitting is but little better:

> 'I pretended to want to save it, [a leveret killed by her dog] as it was so glaringly out of season; but I was better pleased to see it killed.'

(Chapter 18)

Anne Brontë's art shows in Matilda, as so often elsewhere, in her discretion and restraint. Though Matilda is reportedly foul-mouthed, the reader hears very little of her, since to do so would make her too uncouth to be an impressive opposite to Rosalie. Her stable language is heard no more once its comic point has been made:

> 'I'll never say a wicked word again, if you'll only listen to me, and tell Rosalie to hold her confounded tongue.'

(Chapter 9)

Rosalie is almost as much the heart of the novel as Agnes herself. She embodies the most serious moral preoccupations, she is the most closely-observed, her career is the most complete, she is the most self-exposing, and she is the object of the most serious and complete concern not only of the narrator but of the author. Whereas Agnes understates her own affairs of the heart (out of diffidence and modesty), Anne Brontë allows no such consideration to prevent the reader from observing Rosalie at all the most memorable points in her career. This career extends from the childhood period, when she is the product of her environment and education, through that when, as a young woman, she chooses her course for herself, to her married life when she experiences the consequences of her conduct. The account of a governess is the ideal one for mapping such a course. Agnes is intimate enough for her pupil to confide in her, but not enough respected either to influence or repress her. Hence Rosalie explains her-

self as does no other character, laying bare her opinions (she has very few feelings) on what she has already done, and her plans for what she proposes to do. Frequently these opinions and plans loom larger than the events connected with them: for instance, the reader has Rosalie's account of her coming-out ball (Chapter 9), not the ball itself; her words immediately after being married (Chapter 18), but not the wedding. The disproportion between the events and the importance they assume in her career (the coming-out ball takes more space than the wedding), allows the moral point to make itself, with very little help from Agnes as commentator. Equally pertinent is the disproportion between characters, revealed through how Rosalie regards them. Her husband, Sir Thomas Ashby, is mentioned no more than is essential for the reader's benefit—he is 'the greatest scamp in Christendom' and 'any woman of common decency' is 'a world too good for him' (Chapter 14)—but the rector Mr Hatfield looms large in the narrative, both in her conversation and account of her thoughts, and in events in which they both take part. Rosalie is indeed the main reason why events and characters appear, even when she is not present.[5]

The ways in which Rosalie is presented show considerable assurance and unobtrusive skill. Since Anne Brontë's purposes do not include psychological development and interpretation, an opening description which fixes permanently the main features of a personality serves her well. Rosalie receives the most comprehensive and significant one in the novel. Her looks, the obvious beginning of a description, are a significant one here, revealing that this young lady's face is her fortune. Though such a character is not unusual, the account is far from conventional, and has the astringent edge of truth, which renders vivid both the subject and the speaker:

> on a further acquaintance, she gradually laid aside her airs, and in time, became as deeply attached to me as it was possible for *her* to be to one of my character and position: for she seldom lost sight, for above half-an-hour at a time, of the fact of my being a hireling, and a poor curate's daughter.

(Chapter 7)

Once she is thus established, she makes most of her effects by speech, of which she has more than any other single person (excluding Agnes herself and the other temporary narrator, Nancy Brown). Like so many of Anne Brontë's effects, her speech is successful in context, being completely appropriate and exactly serving its purpose; but it contains much less that is immediately striking in extract. Self-exposure, by a frankness that ironically reveals more to Agnes and the reader than she intends, is its most frequent feature:

> 'Brown said that she was sure no gentleman could set eyes on me without falling in love that minute;

and so I may be allowed to be a little vain. I know you think me a shocking, conceited, frivolous girl, but then you know, I don't attribute it *all* to my personal attractions: I give some praise to the hairdresser, and some to my exquisitely lovely dress—you must see it tomorrow—white gauze over pink satin . . . and so *sweetly* made! and a necklace and bracelet of beautiful, large pearls!'

'I have no doubt you looked very charming; but should that delight you so very much?'

'Oh, no! . . . not that alone: but then, I was so much admired; and I made so *many* conquests in that one night—you'd be astonished to hear—'

'But what good will they do you?'

'What good! Think of any woman asking that!'

'Well, I should think one conquest would be enough, and too much, unless the subjugation were mutual.'

(Chapter 9)

The hints here of the maid Brown's idiom which opens the speech, the limited wit in Rosalie which acknowledges the hairdresser's and costumier's help, but entertainingly misunderstands Agnes's question 'should that delight you?', and cannot save her from the vulgarism of 'conquests' (emphasized by Agnes's literal and polysyllabic periphrasis, 'subjugation'—recalling Charlotte Brontë's humour); all these are neatly and unobtrusively suggested without either idiosyncratic diction or unnatural idiom.[6]

The method which serves the Rosalie of the early chapters works just as well for the dissatisfied married woman as for the pleasure-loving girl. Absence of proper feeling shows itself in her letter to Agnes (Chapter 21), where she speaks in the same offhand tone of her child, her dog, and her pictures:

'I forget whether you like babies; if you do, you may have the pleasure of seeing mine . . . the most charming child in the world, no doubt . . . and you shall see my poodle too, a splendid little charmer imported from Paris, and two fine Italian paintings of great value . . . I forget the artist.'

(Chapter 21)

Her acute, though faulty, reasoning is obvious again in her confidences, where this time Agnes's comment is an unspoken one:

'as soon as he heard we were there, he came up under pretence of visiting his brother, and either

followed me, like a shadow, wherever I went, or met me, like a reflection, at every turn. You needn't look so shocked, Miss Grey; I was very discreet, I assure you; but, you know, one can't help being admired.'

(Chapter 22)

Though static, the character is by no means elementary. Anne Brontë, having established the deficiencies, allows the considerable charm of youth and high spirits, and gives Rosalie all the assets deriving from doing what the reader longs to have done—putting the pretentious Mr Hatfield in his place. Similarly she can let Rosalie infuse some transitory excitement into the story by attempting to charm Mr Weston: her charm and intelligence have been just enough to make Agnes's anxiety seem justified, and the chance that Mr Weston may succumb seem one worth considering.

Mr Hatfield himself is a small but throughly adequate piece of work. His purposes as the foppish, ambitious clergyman, with no sense of his calling, are easily fulfilled by lively details of his behaviour:

[Mr Hatfield] would come sailing up the aisle, or rather sweeping along like a whirlwind, with his rich silk gown flying behind him, and rustling against the pew doors, mount the pulpit like a conqueror ascending his triumphal car; then sinking on the velvet cushion in an attitude of studied grace, remain in silent prostration for a certain time.

(Chapter 10)

But such details as this, and kicking Nancy Brown's cat out of his way, do not suggest the power and originality of the scene, reported verbatim by Rosalie (Chapter 14), of his astonishing proposal to her, which proceeds by way of conventional protestation, through astonishment and chagrin, to repressed rage and a direct *tu quoque* and threat of blackmail to protect wounded pride.

The principles of economy and the strong sense of means to an end that dictate the personality and role of the narrator, the shape of the whole, and the handling of characters, determine also the selection and manipulation of material within the individual scenes, and the style. It is even more plain here that Anne Brontë is an author whose effects are made by accumulation and interrelation of simple details, very simply expressed, whose power is largely lost when they are seen in isolation. Her greatest single asset, apart from the handling of Agnes herself, is, as has already been examined, her use of dialogue. As well as revealing personality and exposing standards and lapses, speech is often used as an economical and dramatic means to other ends. There are occasional intrusions of transitory characters like Mr Smith 'the draper, grocer and tea-dealer of the village' (Chapter 1) whose gig takes Agnes to her first post. His comment:

> 'It's a coldish mornin' for you, Miss Agnes, and a darksome un too; but we's, happen, get to yon' spot afore there comes much rain to signify.'

and the laconic little dialogue that follows, create an accurate and atmospheric vignette without holding up the narrative, and create variety between the author's account of her home, and that of the Bloomfields which is to follow. Nancy Brown's long account of her spiritual troubles in Chapter 11 is another instance of speech whose end is structural. It again forms a welcome break in Agnes's story, and provides information it is not in her power to give, in a novel, compact, and racy way. While so long an account is not naturalistic, Anne Brontë balances most professionally the demands of easy reading with keeping up a convincing dialect, wisely relying more on idiom than on phonetic reproduction:

> 'After he was gone, Hannah Rogers, one o' th' neighbours came in and wanted me to help her to wash. I told her I couldn't just then, for I hadn't set on th' potaties for th' dinner, nor washed up th' breakfast stuff yet. So then she began a calling me for my nasty, idle ways. I was a little bit vexed at first; but I never said nothing wrong to her: I only told her, like all in a quiet way, 'a I'd had th' new parson to see me; but I'd get done as quick as ever I could, an' then come an' help her. So then she softened down.'

(Chapter 11)

One hears Yorkshire speech as effectively here as in the much less decipherable Joseph of *Wuthering Heights.*

Scenery, setting, and the weather are plainly elements of situation as important to Anne Brontë as to her sisters. Like them she feels a whole scene through its central emotion, without ever suggesting sentimentality or the pathetic fallacy. Frequent and delicate notice of details of setting, of the weather, the seasons, or the passage of time, all vivify both the action and the subdued personality of Agnes herself. Here Anne Brontë rightly feels confident that mere allusion will evoke a response, without relying on description. She can be vivid and oddly moving with the most commonplace materials, precisely because what she uses is so familiar that she can depend upon the reader's response. Agnes, arriving exhausted at Horton Lodge after a winter day's travelling, where she gets no proper welcome, goes up to her room:

> Then, having broken my long fast on a cup of tea, and a little thin bread and butter, I sat down

beside the small, smouldering fire, and amused myself with a hearty fit of crying.

(Chapter 7)

Anne Brontë always thus underplays rather than overplays her hand, marking the story's most moving moments by bringing some small detail into sharp focus, as in this brief account of Agnes's first journey from home:

> We crossed the valley, and began to ascend the opposite hill. As we were toiling up, I looked back again: there was the village spire, and the old grey parsonage beyond it, basking in a slanting beam of sunshine—it was but a sickly ray, but the village and surrounding hills were all in sombre shade, and I hailed the wandering beam as a propitious omen to my home. With clasped hands, I fervently implored a blessing on its inhabitants, and hastily turned away; for I saw the sunshine was departing; and I carefully avoided another glance, lest I should see it in gloomy shadow like the rest of the landscape.

(Chapter 1)

There is a deliberate rejection here of the significant or symbolic, for the sunshine moves naturally with the clouds; the significance is only what Agnes imagines, while what she describes has all the charm of reality. Like her sisters, Anne Brontë has also a strong sense of time passing. Each event in the story is precisely placed in its season, usually by its month.[7] In a story where the most significant happenings will almost certainly take place on Sundays—when going to church involves meeting the clergyman—such care might be imposed rather than voluntary. But Anne Brontë can delineate time passing like a prose Tennyson; the passage where Agnes at Ashby Park waits and muses in her sitting-room is almost her *Mariana:*

> I sat musing on Lady Ashby's past and present condition; and on what little information I had obtained respecting Mr Weston, and the small chance there was of ever seeing or hearing anything more of him throughout my quiet, drab-colour life, which, henceforth, seemed to offer no alternative between positive rainy days and days of dull, grey clouds without downfall.
>
> At length, however, I began to weary of my thoughts, and to wish I knew where to find the library my hostess had spoken of, and to wonder whether I was to remain there, doing nothing till bedtime.
>
> As I was not rich enough to possess a watch, I could not tell how time was passing, except by observing the slowly lengthening shadows from the window, which presented a side view, including a

corner of the park, a clump of trees, whose topmost branches had been colonized by an innumerable company of noisy rooks, and a high wall with a massive wooden gate, no doubt communicating with the stable yard, as a broad carriage-road swept up to it from the park. The shadow of this wall soon took possession of the whole of this ground as far as I could see, forcing the golden sunlight to retreat inch by inch, and at last take refuge in the very tops of the trees. At last, even they were left in shadow—the shadow of the distant hills, or of the earth itself; and, in sympathy for the busy citizens of the rookery, I regretted to see their habitation, so lately bathed in glorious light, reduced to the sombre, work-a-day hue of the lower world, or of my own world within. For a moment, such birds as soared above the rest might still receive the lustre on their wings, which imparted to their sable plumage the hue and brilliance of deep red gold; at last, that too departed. Twilight came stealing on—the rooks became more quiet—I became more weary, and wished I were going home tomorrow.

(Chapter 22)

As this passage and the previous ones reveal, expression is wholly ruled by what she has to say. The demands of sound, rhythm, or the well-wrought period do not concern her. She does not reject the oddly-used word 'basking', in the second passage; nor does she acknowledge, in the third, that the rhythm of the third sentence concludes at the words 'wooden gate': completeness demands the rather awkwardly attached dependent phrase and clause beginning at 'no doubt communicating . . . ', and completeness justifies its presence and its form. These sensitive and even lyrical descriptions all belong to Agnes, and bear on her role in the narrative. She is passive and sensitive, a central perception more fine than any other, and so a most accurate measurement of the other characters, though she is not at all the most absorbing interest for the reader.

On its small scale Agnes Grey has much in common with *Mansfield Park,* and Agnes herself with Fanny Price, who is in a similar position, has a rather similar nature, and performs the same functions. Anne Brontë resembles her sisters only where material is concerned (only occasionally do her methods suggest Emily), and resembles the eighteenth century in the type of characterization and the firm morality; the Victorians she suggests are those very different from the Brontës, Mrs Gaskell and Trollope; while a remarkable affinity exists between her and that other modest writer, of deep personal religion, pervadingly humble subjects, and a deceptively simple, literal style—Mark Rutherford.

Notes

[1] Mrs Robinson is better known as the object of Branwell Brontë's ill-founded passion than as the

original of Anne's portrait, which is considerably more cooly damning than anything in Branwell's history, though that also indicates a true mother of the daughter figured forth in Rosalie.

[2] The two girls also are mere schoolgirls at first, Matilda only thirteen, and Rosalie, at sixteen, still 'something of a romp' (Chapter 7), who has yet to grow up into the accomplished coquette.

[3] Any treatment of Weston such as that of Mr Rochester and Blanche Ingram would, though possibly creating more absorbing personalities, be to no useful end, since the movement at this point cannot turn away from Rosalie herself (the 'Blanche Ingram' of the episode) who is being swept on to uncongenial wedlock.

[4] He and Mr Rochester may well have a similar source, sharing as well as looks a fine voice, while at one point Mr Weston even uses a Rochester image

'The human heart is like india-rubber; a little swells it, but a great deal will not burst it.

(Chapter 12)

anticipating Mr Rochester's declaring himself as 'hard and tough as an India-rubber ball: pervious, though, through a chink or two still, and with one sentient point in the middle of the lump.' (*Jane Eyre*, Chapter 14.)

[5] A striking instance is in Agnes's visit to the old blind woman Nancy Brown, where Nancy's long account of her religious doubts dwells as much on Mr Hatfield's deficiencies as on Mr Weston's excellences; the former need to be known in order to gauge the falseness of his sentiment to Rosalie, the latter to create anxiety about her attempts, as she herself says, to 'fix' him (Chapter 15), though it also obviously reveals him as a fitting husband for Agnes.

[6] Such success with plain language is one outside the power of either Charlotte or Emily Brontë, and places Anne rather with Mrs Gaskell or Trollope.

[7] Rosalie's 'coming-out' ball takes place on 3 January, Agnes visits Nancy in the third week in February, Mr Weston gives her primroses at the end of March, Mr Hatfield's courtship, refusal, and Rosalie's change to Mr Weston proceed day by day, and she is married on 1 June.

Guy Schofield (essay date 1971)

SOURCE: "The Gentle Anne," in *Brontë Society Transactions,* Vol. 16, No. 1, 1971, pp. 1-10.

[*In the following excerpt, Schofield examines the gentle humor of* Agnes Grey *and the novel's sources in Brontë's own life.*]

May Sinclair has written: "There is in the smallest of the Brontës an immense, a terrifying, audacity. Charlotte was bold and Emily was bolder; but this audacity of Anne's was greater . . . because it was willed, it was deliberate, open-eyed. Anne took her courage in both her hands when she sat down to write **The Tenant of Wildfell Hall.**"[1] She did, and she never flinched from the consequences flung at her by her critics.

All the same, **Agnes Grey** is an infinitely better book because it falls within the natural range of Anne's literary capacity. It is her own story, unadorned, direct, beautifully told, perfectly visualised—the classic "documentary" as we might say of a Victorian governess. George Moore said it was "the most perfect prose narrative in English letters . . . a narrative simple and beautiful as a muslin dress." That celebrated judgment has provoked not a little misgiving, and it is hard to justify, yet when I re-read **Agnes Grey** in preparing this talk I found new rich veins of reflection and characterisation in it, and specimens of word-handling that delighted me. There is something shimmeringly *complete* about **Agnes Grey.** You feel it is a task attempted and done with loving precision. The author herself seems to realise this in the eight words that end her tale: "And now I think I have said sufficient." There is an endearing charm in the humility of that quiet curtain.

Agnes Grey, of course, idealises the unfulfilled love that influenced Anne's short life; but before turning to this I would draw attention to one of her qualities that, had she lived and written more, might have given us another kind of Brontë altogether. I mean her sense of fun. In the glimpses she offers we see it as more robust, more true, more alive to the ludicrous, than anything revealed by her sisters. One feels that this capacity for fun was there all the time, ready to ripple forth whenever the clouds were not too thick about her. Look at this account of Mr. Bloomfield at luncheon, in **Agnes Grey:**

> He had a large mouth, pale dingy complexion, milky blue eyes, and hair the colour of hempen cord. There was a roast leg of mutton before him: he helped Mrs. Bloomfield, the children and me, desiring me to cut up the children's meat; then, after twisting the mutton in various directions and eyeing it from different points, he pronounced it not fit to be eaten, and called for the cold beef.
>
> 'What is the matter with the mutton, my dear?' asked his mate.
>
> 'It is quite overdone. Don't you taste, Mrs. Bloomfield, that all the goodness is roasted out of it? And

can't you see that all that nice red gravy is completely dried away?'

> 'Well, I think the *beef* will suit you.'
>
> The beef was set before him and he began to carve, but with the most rueful expressions of discontent.
>
> 'What is the matter with the *beef*, Mr. Bloomfield? I'm sure I thought it was very nice.'
>
> 'And so it *was* very nice. A nicer joint could not be; but it is *quite* spoiled', he replied dolefully.
>
> 'How so?'
>
> 'How so? Why, don't you see how it is cut? Dear, dear!—it is quite shocking.'
>
> 'They must have cut it wrong in the kitchen, then, for I'm sure I carved it quite properly here yesterday.'
>
> 'No doubt they cut it wrong in the kitchen—the savages! Dear, dear! Did ever anyone see such a fine piece of beef so completely ruined? But remember that in future when a decent dish leaves this table they shall not *touch* it in the kitchen. Remember *that*, Mrs. Bloomfield!'

Notwithstanding the ruinous state of the beef, the gentleman managed to cut himself some delicate slices, part of which he ate in silence. When he next spoke it was, in a less querulous tone, to ask what there was for dinner.

> 'Turkey and grouse', was the concise reply.
>
> 'And what besides?'
>
> 'Fish.'
>
> 'What kind of fish?'
>
> 'I don't know.'
>
> *"You don't know?"* cried he, looking solemnly up from his plate, and suspending his knife and fork in astonishment.
>
> 'No: I told the cook to get some fish—I did not particularise what.'
>
> 'Well, that beats everything! A lady professes to keep house and doesn't even know what fish is for dinner! Professes to order fish and doesn't specify what!'

The silly ass was told by his wife to order dinner for himself in future. Agnes Grey, we read, was ashamed and uncomfortable to have witnessed such a scene, but I wager that in writing it Anne Brontë was laughing.

Her satire was gentle, like Anne herself, but it was percipient. See how she pinions the rector, Mr. Hatfield:

> Mr. Hatfield would come sailing up the aisle, or rather sweeping along like a whirlwind, with his rich silk gown flying behind him and rustling against the pew doors, mount the pulpit like a conqueror ascending his triumphal car; then sinking on the velvet cushion in an attitude of studied grace, remain in silent prostration for a certain time, then mutter over a Collect and gabble through the Lord's Prayer, rise, draw off one bright lavender glove to give the congregation the benefit of his sparkling rings, lightly pass his fingers through his well-curled hair, flourish a cambric handkerchief, recite a very short passage, or perhaps a mere phrase of Scripture, as a headpiece to his discourse and finally deliver—a composition.

Sometimes Mr. Hatfield would deliver a "sunless and severe" sermon and on coming out of church would laugh at the recollection of it, "hoping that he had given the rascally people something to think about; perchance exulting in the thought that old Betty Holmes would now lay aside the sinful indulgence of her pipe, which had been her daily solace for upward of thirty years; that George Higgins would be frightened out of his Sabbath evening walks, and Thomas Jackson would be sorely troubled in his conscience, and shaken in his sure and certain hope of a joyful resurrection at the last day."

For Yorkshire folk it is pleasant also to spot those little idiomatic touches that stamp Anne Brontë in another sense as "one of us". In *Wildfell Hall* there is talk of preparing tea "against they come in". There is advice concerning a lady to "let her down easy". Agnes Grey says "I proceeded to *clomp down* the two flights of stairs" and elsewhere she "demolishes some spice cake." Anne Brontë knew very well that you can't nibble Yorkshire spice cake; it requires to be demolished.

All that is engagingly homespun, but the core of the novel is of a different substance.

Anne had allowed a year or two to elapse after the death of the man she loved before re-creating and re-endowing him as Mr. Weston in *Agnes Grey.* We identify the real purpose to which she had set her pen in that re-creation. The very first paragraph of the book declares the author's intention of laying before her readers "what I would not disclose to the most intimate friend."

The story of her love for the young curate of Haworth, William Weightman, has been told and re-told, and you know it well. You know how he blew in upon the close atmosphere of the parsonage like a breeze of Spring,

bringing to life all sorts of little jollities, taking the girls for walks, manipulating an adventure to Keighley, slipping them preposterous Valentines when their father wasn't looking. They called him Celia Amelia because of his curly-haired good looks; he didn't mind. He made them happy—and he made Anne happy in a way, and to a degree, she had never known before. But as at every turning in her history, hope was to be snuffed out before it could burgeon into fulfilment.

In 1842, when she was away at Thorp Green, near York, living the dismal existence of a governess, William Weightman died, a victim of cholera at the age of 28.

He appears to have caught the disease when visiting the sick in Haworth. "Unclerical, fickle, light-hearted" were some of the words Charlotte used in describing him: they were true but only partially so. He was diligent in his pastoral duties, generous, and always kind. There was much more to him than Charlotte perceived, and Anne knew this and loved him for it though that love had to remain indeterminate, unavowed, idealised. She never forgot him. He was in her waking mind and vividly in her dreams. Just as the love story in *Agnes Grey* was wrapped around his memory, so he inspired the best of her poetry.

Here I come to something I would like very much to emphasise. Anne Brontë's poems are not by any stretch of imagination important. Compared with Emily's magnificent verse they are fragile little things. Some are juvenile fantasies, some are pious efforts in the manner of Cowper—one must never forget that Anne's religion was a constant, and sometimes a haunting, reality—but in my judgment those that were inspired by the memory of William Weightman contain a few stanzas that are among the most moving of their kind in our language.

They have been disregarded; they have been deemed to be but superficial expressions of sorrow and innocent dismay. They are not profound. They do not seek to unravel Freudian mysteries. They are quite out of line with contemporary attitudes—simple indeed, elementary in structure. But I will argue with anybody that, at their fleeting best, they merit a deal more regard than the world has conceded to them. For they are not contrived; they spring from a suffering heart and a fine intelligence and cannot be dismissed by the unprejudiced critic.

It is easy to be deceived by their simplicity, but in the examples I am going to read I ask you to note the lines that lift themselves high above any reproach of being commonplace.

Here are some, written in 1844, two years after Weightman's death:

> Yes, thou art gone! and never more
> Thy sunny smile shall gladden me;

But I may pass the old church door
And pace the floor that covers thee.

May stand upon the cold damp stone
And think that, frozen, lies below
The lightest heart that I have known,
The kindest I shall ever know.

A year later she wrote a poem called **"Night"**:

I love the silent hour of night,
For blissful dreams may then arise,
Revealing to my charmed sight
What may not bless my waking eyes.

And then a voice may meet my ear
That death has silenced long ago;
And hope and rapture may appear
Instead of solitude and woe.

Cold in the grave for years has lain
The form it was my bliss to see;
And only dreams can bring again
The darling of my heart to me.

Again, two years later, a poem called **"Severed and Gone"** contains these verses:

Ah no! thy spirit lingers still
Where'er thy sunny smile was seen;
There's less of darkness, less of chill
On earth than if thou had'st not been.

Thou breathest in my bosom yet,
And dwellest in my beating heart;
And while I cannot quite forget,
Thou, darling, can'st not quite depart.

Life seems more sweet that thou did'st live,
And men more true that thou wert one;
Nothing is lost that thou did'st give,
Nothing destroyed that thou hast done.

"Nothing is lost that thou did'st give"—the implications of that line tell us the little that sufficed to help Anne Brontë on her way. What had Willey Weightman given her? A brief acquaintance with genuine human kindness and consideration, some merriment, a handclasp of honest regard, probably a few secret moments of tenderness and delight. These were the crumbs for which she was so grateful. It was by these that her naturally loving heart was stirred to its depth. We realise how frozen must have been the climate to which it was accustomed. Whatever William Weightman's youthful carefreeness may have been, he deserves to be remembered thankfully for what he did to charm and sustain that lonely girl. When we put a flower on her grave we should put one also on his.

Another ray of light, another small reward, came Anne Brontë's way. In one of those little birthday notes which she and Emily exchanged are these words:

> This is Emily's birthday. She has completed her 23rd year and is, I believe, at home. Charlotte is a governess in the family of Mr. White. Branwell is a clerk in the railroad station at Luddenden Foot and I am a governess in the family of Mr. Robinson. I dislike the situation and wish to change it for another. I am now at Scarborough . . . Four years ago I was at school. Since then I have been a governess at Blake Hall, left it, come to Thorp Green, and seen the sea and York Minster . . .

In our modern world where travel and change of scene are prime objects of existence it is not easy for us to realise how circumscribed life was in those days, even for people more sophisticated than the Brontës. To have seen the sea and York Minster may seem laughingly modest accomplishments. For Anne, however, they were more than journeys made and wonders contemplated. They were profound experiences. In the stone vastness of the Minster, and the turbulent vastness of the sea, she found a sense of dimension that enthralled her, and in the dashing of the waves on a windy day an exuberant joy.

It was in 1841 that she first went to Scarborough with her employers, the Robinsons. From that moment Scarborough became for her a sort of earthly paradise. She loved the view from St. Nicholas Cliff where they lodged—the spot where the Grand Hotel now stands—and she loved to walk along the sands, buffeted by the wind and slapped by the spray. Round Castle Hill her imagination wove the final love scene of *Agnes Grey.* Here was her heart's harbourage. As Winifred Gérin has written, Scarborough burst open her whole being with "an onrush of inexpressible emotion . . . whatever she saw, she saw with the eyes of the spirit."[2] Haworth may have remained home for Anne Brontë but she found elsewhere a place of deeper spiritual satisfaction. The sea drew her more powerfully than the moors, and it is eloquently just that her body should have been laid to rest on Castle Hill, within sound of the great breakers.

I will not dwell overlong on the closing scenes except to draw from them the heroic stature of this "least of the Brontës" as she has been untruly called. In December 1848 her beloved Emily died. Within a month a lung specialist from Leeds pronounced the inevitability of early death for Anne. All that could be done, he said, was to alleviate suffering. Two days later, knowing this, she wrote her last poem.

I hoped amid the brave and strong
My portioned task might lie,

To toil amid the labouring throng
  With purpose keen and high;
But Thou hast fixed another part,
  And Thou hast fixed it well . . .

As soon as spring arrived it was decided that she should be taken where she longed to go—to Scarborough. In a letter dated April 5th, 1849, she wrote to Ellen Nussey: "I wish it would please God to spare me, not only for Papa's and Charlotte's sakes but because I long to do some good work in the world before I leave it. I have many schemes in my head for future practice—humble and limited indeed—but still I should not like them to come to nothing and myself to have lived to so little purpose. But God's will be done."

Accompanied by Charlotte and Ellen Nussey she went to Scarborough in May. The journey, part by road and part by rail, was via Keighley, Leeds and York. The dying girl had to be carried by porters. At York she was taken in a bath chair to see the Minster once more. The weather was warm and sunny.

On May 25th they arrived at their lodgings on the south cliff. Anne was delighted to gaze down at the sea again. They hired a donkey carriage for her to drive along the sands. One evening, despite a fall from exhaustion, she willed herself to walk a little way on to the Spa bridge in order to watch a fine sunset pouring its last rays on Castle Hill. She must have recalled her own words about Castle Hill in *Agnes Grey:* "I shall never forget that glorious summer evening and always remember with delight that steep hill on the edge of the precipice where we stood together watching the splendid sunset mirrored on the restless world of waters at our feet."

Two days later she died on the couch in their sitting room. Her last words to the weeping Charlotte were "Courage, Charlotte, courage!"

She was 29 years old.

May Sinclair has written: "Of these tragic Brontës the most tragic, the most pitiful, the most mercilessly abused by destiny, was Anne." Those words are true.

Emily was a mystic, dwelling very largely in a world beyond the fluctuating pressures of this "bourne of time and place." Because of this we can accept Maurice Maeterlinck's judgment that "her heart was radiant with silent gladness. Of her happiness none can doubt." Charlotte lived to find much fulfilment and satisfaction in literary fame and marriage to a kind, if uninspiring, husband.

But to Anne, who asked so little, less than little was granted. Her ambition was not lofty—just to live on to do something useful—and her desires were those of most normal people, a home, a loving partner, a family fireside. All were denied. She endured at the very heart

of the whole Brontë tragedy. Upon her the burden and the pain fell most acutely because she was more compact of ordinary human sensibility. Even the collapse of Branwell imposed itself more intimately on her than on the others.

Yet May Sinclair was wrong when she went on to say, "This delicate thing was broken on the wheel of life." She was not. Her spirit was never broken. She went her way of deprivation—occasionally, it is true, with a tear—but never with moan or bitterness. We call her "the gentle Anne", and so she was, but within the vesture of physical frailty there was a spirit immeasurably strong. In Charlotte's own words, written at a time when Anne was battling with repeated bouts of illness, she had an extraordinary heroism of endurance. "I admire but I certainly could not imitate her", said Charlotte.

When from our distance of time we look back on those astonishing women of Haworth, we are conscious, I think, that our admiration falls into two categories. We honour them for their imperishable contribution to English literature, and we honour them for the brave lives they lived in the face of adversity. It is within this second category that we see the real geatness of Anne.

All very well for George Saintsbury to call her "but a pale reflection of her elders"; all very well for others to call her the smallest, the least, of the Brontës. Those are detached literary verdicts. How *can* she be deemed the least who, at her departing, had to give strength to the brokenhearted author of *Jane Eyre*—"Courage, Charlotte, courage!"

Notes

[1] *The Three Brontes* (1912).

[2] *Anne Brontë* (1959).

Tom Winnifrith (essay date 1973)

SOURCE: "The Brontës and Their Betters," in *The Brontës and Their Background: Romance and Reality,* Macmillan, 1973, pp. 160-94.

[*In the following excerpt, Winnifrith discusses Brontë's harsh portrayal of Victorian aristocracy in* Agnes Grey *and* The Tenant of Wildfell Hall.]

We do not know a great deal about the life of Anne, and it is perhaps too easy to represent *Agnes Grey* as straight autobiography with the Inghams of Blake Hall portrayed by the Bloomfields of Wellwood House and the Murrays of Horton Lodge standing for the Robinsons of Thorp Green. Anne's experiences with the children of the two households may be accurately mirrored in her account of the fiendish young Bloomfields and frivolous young Murrays. But the Inghams, coming from a well-established Yorkshire family, were unlike Mr Birdwood, a retired tradesman who had realised a considerable fortune; Blake Hall was not a new house, surrounded by mushroom poplars, and one of the Ingham girls in later life was scorned for marrying beneath her into trade.[87] If we are looking for models for the Bloomfields, Charlotte's employers, the Whites of Upperwood House, seem a much more likely prospect.[88] The Robinsons of Thorp Green were an aristocratic family, being related to the Marquess of Ripon, but Mr Robinson was a clergyman with Evangelical sympathies.[89] Since Anne Brontë three times in the novel draws a pointed distinction between a bad worldly match and a good marriage to a poor man, and in each case the poor man is a clergyman, we must regard Mr Robinson's profession as in some sense detracting from his worldliness. There is a fourth clergyman who is himself worldly, Mr Hatfield, whose seven hundred a year, though not enough for Miss Murray, was three and a half times Mr Brontë's salary; unlike Agnes Grey's father or her brother-in-law, Mr Richardson, or Mr Weston, he is not a good man, and may possibly be modelled on Mr Robinson. At all events Anne cannot resist making even him an example of the danger of putting wealth before virtue, since Miss Murray in marrying Sir Thomas Ashby obviously suffers far more than if she had become Mrs Hatfield.[90] There is no parallel here with the fate of Lydia Robinson who eloped with an actor called Henry Roxby, and was cut off without a penny.[91]

Nor can there be any biographical parallel between the marriage of Agnes Grey's parents and that of Anne Brontë's parents in spite of the theory to this effect of W.P.P. Mr Grey is a clergyman, and when he marries has some private means as well which he loses through rash investment. Unlike St John Rivers and even Mr Helstone, who have no private means but are considered quite eligible, Mr Grey is not considered good enough by his wife's family who refuse to give them any part of their fortune, and only reappear in the story to send a hard-hearted letter on the occasion of Mr Grey's death.

Unlike the very similar story of Jane Eyre's parents which at least serves to explain Jane's orphaned state, the story of Agnes Grey's parents serves no useful purpose unless it be to give Agnes a vaguely aristocratic lineage while at the same time providing material for a little anti-aristocratic propaganda. There is thus the same ambiguity as we found in Charlotte's works, and this impression is strengthened in a significant passage where Agnes Grey's mother compares the treatment suffered by Agnes at the hands of the vulgar Bloomfields with the treatment to be expected from a more aristocratic family.

> This time, you shall try your fortune in a somewhat higher family—in that of some genuine thorough-

bred gentleman, for such are far more likely to treat you with proper respect and consideration than those purse-proud tradespeople and arrogant upstarts. I have known several among the higher ranks who treated their governesses quite as one of the family; though some, I allow, are as insolent and exacting as anyone else can be: for there are bad and good in all classes.[92]

But though there are bad and good in all classes we do not see much good in the aristocrats of *Agnes Grey,* although the aristocratic Murrays are slightly better than the upstart Bloomfields.

The satire against the Bloomfields is crude and obvious. The children behave badly, Mr Bloomfield is rude to his wife about the food, and Uncle Robson is not a gentleman. The mushroom poplar groves of Wellwood House, an appropriate name for a mansion of a would-be gentleman, symbolise the *nouveau riche* atmosphere of the Bloomfield household.[93] By contrast the wide park, stocked with deer, and beautiful old trees of Horton Lodge, shows that the Murrays are proper gentlefolk, although their behaviour both in general and towards their governess still leaves much to be desired.

The trouble with the Murrays is that though themselves well up on the aristocratic ladder they are anxious to climb still further, by a more aristocratic match. As a result Rosalie Murray spurns her more attractive suitors in order to become Lady Ashley, although she would have much preferred to have become a Peeress.[94] Her delight in her title is reminiscent of Ginevra Fanshawe, but is even more short-lived. Also reminiscent of Ginevra Fanshawe is Rosalie's contempt for the humble nature of Agnes's sister's marriage to Mr Richardson, who is neither handsome nor young, but only good.[95] Mr Richardson is of course but a pale shadow of the novel's hero, Mr Weston, whose origins are not touched upon, although he is eventually wealthy enough to marry Agnes. Mr Weston's condescending kindness to the poor, in notable contrast to the *brusquerie* of the socially ambitious Mr Hatfield, gives the novel a democratic air, and it is unfortunate that this impression is spoilt by clumsy pieces of snobbery. Agnes Grey's family are proud of their aristocratic origins, although her maternal grandfather, described vaguely as a squire, behaves worse than the Murrays. Cast off by this squire's family 'our only intercourse with the world consisted in a stately tea party, now and then, with the principal farmers and tradespeople of the vicinity (just to avoid being stigmatised as too proud to consort with our neighbours)'.[96] And yet Agnes is curiously ignorant of aristocratic ways. Was Mr Grey with a snug little property of his own as well as a small incumbency really such a bad match for a squire's daughter?[97] Why was he so much inferior to the rich nabob who married Agnes's aunt and who inherited Agnes's mother's portion? In the same way it is not clear why Mr Hatfield should be so unsuitable a husband for Rosalie Murray. Rosalie's enthusiasm for titles and determination to have one herself is frankly vulgar, and the distinction between the Bloomfields and the Murrays, like the similar distinction between Ginevra Fanshawe and the Watsons, becomes blurred. Finally the authentic note of rancour from the unnoticed governess comes out without any concealment in the following passage:

> Nota-bene—Mr Hatfield never spoke to me, neither did Sir Hugh or Lady Meltham, nor Mr Harry or Miss Meltham, nor Mr Green or his sisters, nor any other lady or gentleman who frequented that church: nor, in fact, any one that visited at Horton Lodge.[98]

The obvious contrast between the humble and virtuous Mr Weston and Agnes Grey, and the richer and more vicious world of the Bloomfields and Murrays, is repeated in **The Tenant of Wildfell Hall.** In the part of the novel that centres around Wildfell Hall we see a humble but on the whole happy society, whereas Helen Huntingdon's narrative reveals the corrupt dissipation which ruined the more elevated society of Grassdale Manor. Whereas **Agnes Grey** had been too slight a work to attract critical attention, **The Tenant of Wildfell Hall,** deriving notoriety from *Jane Eyre,* was attacked for its bold social doctrines. The reviewer in *Fraser's*[99] had no objection to the exposure of the ugly hypocritical visage of Society, but thought it both improbable and wrong that Gilbert Markham should marry Helen Huntingdon. Against the straightforward snobbery of comments such as the remark that Gilbert 'is no doubt highly attractive to young ladies of his own calibre' it is difficult to argue, but the gap between Helen Huntingdon and Gilbert Markham is smaller than the reviewer in *Fraser's* thinks. There is a curious mystery about Helen's origins. She only sees her father once, and he does not leave her much money. Her brother is the squire of the Wildfell Hall neighbourhood, but not too grand to contemplate marriage with Jane Wilson and to converse on easy terms with Gilbert Markham. Gilbert, who introduces himself as the son of a sort of gentleman farmer, and is described with a trace of sarcasm by Helen as 'the fine gentleman and beau of the parish',[100] is not deterred by thoughts of his presumption in aspiring to marry above his station until he arrives at Staningley. By this time Helen's husband and uncle have both died, and it is Helen's wealth which causes Markham's neighbour in the coach to suggest that 'she'll marry none but a nobleman' and Markham himself, as deferential as *Fraser's* to 'the fitness of things', to ask himself:

> And could I bear that she should think me capable of such a thing?—of presuming upon the acquaintance—the love, if you will—accidentally contracted, or

rather forced upon her against her will, when she was an unknown fugitive, toiling for her own support, apparently without fortune, family or connections; to come upon her now, when she was reinstated in her proper sphere, and claim a share in her prosperity, which, had it never failed her, would most certainly have kept her unknown to me for ever.[101]

Helen does think Gilbert capable of such presumption, and he marries her, apparently without meeting either the anticipated slights and censures of the world, or the sorrow and displeasures of those she loved. Indeed both Helen and her aunt seem enthusiastic that the marriage should take place, and it is perhaps this enthusiasm which raised the hackles of the reviewer in *Fraser's.* But we can easily understand the readiness of Helen and her aunt to accept Gilbert, since the whole book is aimed at showing how much better his world is than the society from which Helen had chosen her previous husband. Anne Brontë is less blatant than in **Agnes Grey** in drawing the contrast between the two worlds. In **Agnes Grey** we are actually told that Mr Richardson is good and Sir Thomas Ashby bad, but in **The Tenant of Wildfell Hall,** we are left to judge for ourselves the difference between the healthy society described in the first part of the book and the evil atmosphere surrounding Grassdale Manor. Nor does Anne Brontë make the mistake of painting the humbler society in too rosy colours. Unlike Mr Weston and the Grey family who are almost too good to be true, the Markham family and their friends are not without faults. Fergus and even Gilbert are boorish, although their antics are but pale shadows of the dissipation of Huntingdon and his friends, and the Markhams do work for their living. Mrs Markham and Rose interfere too much in the affair between Gilbert and Mrs Graham, although this slight excess of over-protectiveness is much better than the complete failure of Helen Huntingdon's family to prevent her from making a foolish match. Eliza Millward and Jane Wilson indulge in scandalous gossip about Mrs Graham and Lawrence, but this gossip, although unpleasant and rewarded by Jane and Eliza losing the respect of Gilbert and Lawrence, is a more venial fault than the real adultery of Annabella and Huntingdon, a sin which might have been nipped in the bud with a little more frank speaking. Finally, Jane Wilson, the least attractive figure among Markham's acquaintances, is the worst type of snob, aspiring to marry Lawrence and, when she fails, retiring into the country town to avoid living with her rough brother Robert. Here she lives.

> in a kind of close-fisted, cold, uncomfortable gentility, doing no good to others, and but little to herself; spending her days in fancy work and scandal; referring frequently to her 'brother the vicar', and her 'sister, the vicar's lady', but never to her brother the farmer and her sister, the farmer's wife; seeing as much company as she can without too much expense,

but loving no one and beloved by none—a cold-hearted, supercilious, keenly, insidiously censorious old maid.[102]

But this brutal portrait is more than balanced by that of the hard, pretentious, worldly minded Mrs Hargrave earlier in the book,[103] whose anxiety to make good matches for her daughters is partly the result and partly the cause of her determination that her son should be enabled to hold up his head with the highest gentleman in the land. Whereas Jane Wilson merely does no good to anyone, Mrs Hargrave does positive harm to the character of her son Walter, and her wish to gain a rich man as a son-in-law almost ruins the lives of both her daughters.

Jane Wilson and Mrs Hargrave are minor characters, and it is perhaps unfair to compare the narrative of Gilbert Markham with the diary of Helen Huntingdon by taking these two characters from the two sections of the novel. But the passage decribing the eventual fate of Jane Wilson, although it occurs in a rather clumsy disposal of minor characters,[104] does reveal that Anne Brontë, whose knowledge of English families outside her own was greater than that of Emily and Charlotte,[105] did have something of an ear for some of the delicate gradations of social snobbery. Jane Wilson's willingness to speak about one brother and reluctance to mention the other is a touch worthy of *Middlemarch,* and we sometimes regret that Anne Brontë abandoned her portrait of middle-class provincial life for her account of the aristocracy, of which she knew so little. There are several features of life at Grassdale Manor which would strike a hostile critic like Miss Rigby as unconvincing. In the first place we may note the narrow canvas on which Anne chooses to paint her unflattering portrait. With the exception of the unimportant Mr Boarham and Mr Grimsby all the characters in Helen Huntingdon's narrative are related to each other. Huntingdon has two friends apart from Grimsby, namely Hattersley and Lord Lowborough, and they marry Helen's two chief acquaintances, Milicent Hargrave and Annabella Wilmot, who are both nieces of Helen's first admirer. Milicent's sister marries Helen's brother, and the novels ends by announcing a marriage between Helen Hattersley and the young Arthur Huntingdon. Now it would be possible to find parallels for this closely knit circle of acquaintances both in other novels of this period and in families known to the Brontës.[106] But to limit the characters in this way, while it may be suitable for a novel of provincial life, is not suitable to a portrait of the aristocracy. It is inherently improbable that Huntingdon, who whatever his faults is an eminently sociable man, should limit his acquaintances to two or three boon companions, especially when he spends half the year in London. It is also improbable that two of these boon companions should choose a wife out of the very small circle of Helen Huntingdon's female acquaintances.

Anne Brontë's ignorance of the aristocracy is hard to distinguish from her inability as a novelist to develop a wide range of characters, but if *The Tenant of Wildfell Hall* is meant to show us the superiority of the honest yeomanry over the dissolute squirearchy then it is certainly a failing that life at Grassdale Manor seems very like the life of a yeoman, apart from some incidental and not very convincing idleness and dissipation. *Wuthering Heights* has a similar stark economy of characters but we do not accuse Emily Brontë of being either a bad novelist or an undiscriminating observer of the social scene for this reason. We do sometimes wonder why Edgar Linton became so withdrawn from his neighbours after his wife's death, although Emily gives some explanation in drawing some attention to his melancholy and making Lockwood comment on the remoteness of the locality. In general, however, *Wuthering Heights* succeeds, where *The Tenant of Wildfell Hall* fails, in painting a realistic contrast between two ways of life, the rough hard farming life of Wuthering Heights, and the more comfortable squire's life of Thrushcross Grange.

Notes

[87] [*Brontë Society Transactions*] 68 (1958), p. 242.

[88] See J. Malham Dembleby, *The Confessions of Charlotte Brontë* (Bradford, 1954), pp. 198-217, for resemblances between the Whites and the Birdwoods. Mrs White's maiden name was Robson.

[89] Winifred Gerin, *Branwell Brontë,* [London, 1961] pp. 216-26. But see Chapter 3 [of *The Brontës and Their Background: Romance and Reality,* by Tom Winnifrith, Macmillan, 1973] for differences between Thorp Green and Horton Lodge.

[90] Mr Hatfield appropriately marries a rich but elderly spinster (*Agnes Grey,* [in *The Life and Works of Charlotte Brontë and Her Sisters,* edited by H. Ward and C. K. Shorter, Haworth ed., 7 vols. (London, 1889-1890),] p. 536).

[91] *Branwell Brontë,* p. 252.

[92] *Agnes Grey,* p. 408.

[93] Ibid., pp. 368, 423.

[94] Ibid., p. 432.

[95] Ibid., p. 429.

[96] Ibid., pp. 356-7.

[97] Ibid., p. 356. We may compare the very different attitude shown by Mr Oliver to St John Rivers, although Mr Oliver is not a squire, but a self-made manufacturer.

[98] Ibid., p. 436.

[99] See the reviews in *Sharpe's London Magazine and Fraser's Magazine*, cited in Chapter 7 [of *The Brontës and Their Background: Romance and Reality*, by Tom Winnifrith, Macmillan, 1973].

[100] *The Tenant of Wildfell Hall*, [in *The Life and Works of Charlotte Brontë and Her Sisters*, edited by H. Ward and C. K. Shorter, Haworth ed., 7 vols. (London, 1889-1890),] pp. 1, 401.

[101] Ibid., p. 485-7.

[102] Ibid., p. 448.

[103] Ibid., p. 235.

[104] Anne seems almost relieved to get rid of her characters, and this is one more indication that she was a reluctant novelist.

[105] Her four years at Thorp Green as a sociable and fairly amiable family are in marked contrast to Charlotte's short career as a governess. Charlotte did of course spend time away from home, but only in the unworldly atmosphere of Miss Wooler's school and M. Heger's Pensionnat.

[106] See Chapter 8 [of *The Brontës and Their Background: Romance and Reality*, by Tom Winnifrith, Macmillan, 1973] for the way in which Ellen Nussey's friends are also her relations.

Winifred Gérin (essay date 1976)

SOURCE: "Acton Bell," in *Anne Brontë*, revised ed., Allen Lane, 1976, pp. 209-34.

[*In the following excerpt, originally published in 1959, Gérin summarizes the facts of Brontë's composition of* Agnes Grey *and the early critical reception of the novel.*]

Anne Brontë's own copy of *Agnes Grey* (it was a compact volume of 363 pages), which is preserved in Princeton University Library, is full of the author's corrections of . . . numerous errors.[1] One can imagine her sitting, with bowed head, the light of the lamp falling on her pretty hair, absorbed in her task. *Agnes Grey* was published in one volume; it had not the breadth to take up two like Emily's *Wuthering Heights*, far less three, like Charlotte's *Jane Eyre*. Yet it held in its modest dimensions a perfection of its own.

"*Agnes Grey*," wrote Charlotte a week after the book had come out, "is the mirror of the mind of the writer." She could not have more exactly defined its worth.

Though *Agnes Grey* may have fallen into relative obscurity nowadays it must not be forgotten that in George Moore's opinion it was "the most perfect prose narrative in English literature. . . . As simple and beautiful as a muslin dress . . . the one story in English literature in which style, characters and subject are in perfect keeping."[2]

These are high claims indeed and worth recalling in any attempt to assess the book's lasting worth.

Agnes Grey, as its original title shows, had been begun as an autobiography. Its value today is still permanently enhanced by the fact that it relates, with startling adherence to truth, the circumstances of Anne's two experiences as governess.

For good or for ill, Anne did not leave it there. The artist within her took charge and the book, begun with one intention, had very soon far exceeded it and become a full-scale work of fiction.

Not full-scale in the sense of bulk; one of *Agnes Grey*'s chief merits is its exquisite proportions. It is well proportioned as a French interior is well proportioned, with each article of furniture on so small yet perfect a scale that no object appears crowded or overwhelmed by its fellows.

Yet it was inevitable that the dual purpose of the book should emerge; that those portions which were derived from fact should be more vividly realised and that the purely fictitious incidents should be slurred over, as inappropriate, as it were, to the fuller treatment. Thus the happy ending to which, as fiction, Anne had not the heart to deny her heroine, is written in so low and subdued a key that it saddens rather than elates the reader. Judged from the standpoint of art this is a mistake; the story of *Agnes Grey* begun in such buoyant style, with so much wit and sparkle, should not modulate into a minor key and close in solemnity since, in spite of some tribulations, the heroine's happiness is assured.

So the author, at least, would have us believe. But the sadness of Anne's own experience in love broods over the tale and makes us rather doubt the ordering of the facts at the story's close. They are so very lightly sketched in, with none of the bite and incision of outline in which the exposition and middle of the book are etched, that one sees them as through a mist, only partially discernible.

That does not diminish their charm. There is, indeed, an elegiac charm pervading the whole of the latter half of the book, from Chapter 13 to the end, which fully makes up for the loss of the vivacity and humour of the opening. But the difference is there. *Agnes Grey* is a book that falls in two, not only because it is part-autobiographical and part-fictional, but because, written over a period of probably at least three years, it reflects the tragic change in Anne's circumstances.

It seems likely that she began writing *Passages in the Life of an Individual* in her second year at Thorp Green, in 1842. She may even have begun it much earlier, during the interregnum at home following her dismissal from the Inghams. Whenever it was, she could still view her experiences at Blake Hall with enough humour to derive an artistic satisfaction from their narration. The opening chapters of the book, all those relating to Blake Hall indeed, are instinct with satirical observation and, what is rarer far, with a sense of humour as regards her own failures and distresses. The style is elastic and reveals a cheerful mind "full of bright hopes and ardent expectations".

It is this section of the book, the first six chapters in particular, in which Anne showed herself, to quote George Moore again, to have not only all Jane Austen's qualities but some others as well. (Her true literary progenitors, one is tempted to suggest, were Goldsmith and Maria Edgeworth; for she probably never read Jane Austen any more than Charlotte had done.)

Her time for writing would be very limited once she was fully engaged in teaching at Thorp Green. With the tragic autumn of 1842 and the death of Willy Weightman, a burden so great was added to her already flagging spirits that the zest and animation went out of her writing, however much she needed writing of some sort to absorb her. But all the delight was gone. There is observation as sharp of the Murray family as of the Bloomfields, but bitterness has replaced the good humour, and disappointment effectually dimmed the youthful ardour. The opening chapters of *Agnes Grey* are the work of a young person, still full of sanguine hopes; the latter half betrays the effort of a stricken heart.[3]

An identical circumstance attended the composition of *Shirley* and left similar indelible traces of the conflicting states of mind in which it was written, but Charlotte, unlike Anne, had by the time she was writing her third novel achieved a greater mastery of her medium. Time which militated in favour of Charlotte was to be so cruelly lacking for the development of Anne. There is tantalising promise in both her books of the masterpiece that should have come thereafter.

Agnes Grey is as different from *Wildfell Hall* as two books by one and the same author can well be, yet unmistakably they are from the same pen: an uncompromising honesty invests both tales.

This quality it is which gives *Agnes Grey* its distinctive value. It is the honesty of the author which insists upon that self-analysis of the heroine's feelings and motives which constitutes not only the book's original-

ity but its truth. Character described from *without* is one thing—and Anne was to show herself a mistress at tersely satirical portraiture—but that which is revealed to us, by growing degrees, from *within,* is far more rare and nearer the movement of life. Though the plot of *Agnes Grey* is too static to arouse keen excitement in the reader, there is nothing static in the characters. The flux of feeling, the uncertainty of temper, the deteriorating effect of time, it is *these* considerations that hold our attention and make us wonder right to the very end *how* the characters will finally resolve their problems.

The literary qualities of the book are best judged by their *appropriateness;* the style suits the matter, and though Anne always excelled in purely descriptive passages—her loving eye for all aspects of the natural scene being perfectly matched by her fastidious choice of language—there is no writing for the sake of writing.

The book is rich in such observation of character as the following:

"Mr Bloomfield," she writes of her first employer, "was a retired tradesman who had realised a very comfortable fortune, but could not be prevailed upon to give a greater salary than £25 to the instructress of his children."

Here is the grandmother of the Bloomfield family— "Hitherto, though I saw the old lady had her defects (of which one was a proneness to proclaim her perfections) I had always been wishful to excuse them, and to give her credit for all the virtues she professed, and even imagine others yet untold."

For a parson's daughter the following sketch of a worldly cleric is full of savour. "Mr Hatfield would come sailing up the aisle, or rather sweeping along like a whirlwind, with his rich silk gown flying behind him and rustling against the pew doors, mount the pulpit like a conqueror ascending his triumphal car; then, sinking on the velvet cushion in an attitude of studied grace, remain in silent prostration for a certain time. . . "

So much of the psychological interest of *Agnes Grey* derives from the personal experience of the author that the tendency is to consider it rather in its autobiographical than in its literary connection. It is part of Anne's quality, however, that though she told nothing but the truth, by the force of imagination she seemed to be inventing, and it is Agnes Grey with whom readers are concerned, not Anne Brontë.

Its essential truthfulness no competent critic has ever doubted. Charlotte Brontë, stung by Lewes's accusations of extravagance and improbability in her own

Jane Eyre, wrote of *Agnes Grey* to her publishers: "*Agnes Grey* should please such critics as Mr Lewes for it is 'true' and 'unexaggerated' enough."[4] As the reviewer in *Douglas Jerrolds' Weekly* wrote: "The author, if not a governess, must have bribed some governess very largely, either with love or money, to reveal to him the secrets of her prison house . . . ," so convincingly did Acton Bell set forth "the minute torments and incessant tediums" of her situation.[5]

In this respect one near-contemporary reader's views are peculiarly worth recording. Lady Amberley noted in her diary for 1868: "read *Agnes Grey,* one of the Brontës, and should like to give it to every family with a governess and shall read it through again when I have a governess to remind me to be human."[6]

In due course the professional reviews arrived at the parsonage, regularly forwarded to the authors by Mr Newby. The discerning critic on *Douglas Jerrolds' Weekly* was of opinion that *Agnes Grey* was a tale "well worth the writing and the reading"; that on *Britannia* (who had a mind to discern sublimity in *Wuthering Heights*) found nothing to call for special notice in *Agnes Grey,* but conceded that "some characters and scenes" were nicely sketched in.

It was the writer on *The Atlas* who gave Emily's and Anne's novels the most exhaustive review. As was inevitable, he compared the two productions. *Agnes Grey* he found "more level and more sunny. Perhaps", he added, "we should best describe it as a somewhat coarse imitation of Miss Austin's [*sic*] charming stories". It did not offend "by any startling improbabilities", and he found the incidents relating to the governess's life "such as might happen to anyone in that situation of life and, doubtless, have happened to many. The story, though lacking the power and originality of *Wuthering Heights,* is infinitely more agreeable. It leaves no painful impression on the mind—some may think it leaves no impression at all. *We are not quite sure that the next novel will not efface it.*"

In the last line Anne may have read a challenge which strangely accorded with her then intentions, for, by the time she was reading the *Atlas* critic's review, she was already engaged on writing her second novel.

Abbreviations

AB   Anne Brontë

AG   *Agnes Grey*

CB   Charlotte Brontë

WSW   W. S. Williams

BST   Brontë Society Transactions

SLL   *The Brontës, Life and Letters* by C. K. Shorter

In quoting from Anne Brontë's novels, *Agnes Grey* and *The Tenant of Wildfell Hall,* the text of [*The Brontë Novels,* 6 vols., London, in] Smith, Elder and Co's edition of 1900 has been used throughout, but the page references, for the greater convenience of modern readers, apply to the current reprints in the *Nelson Classics.*

Notes

[1] AB's copy of AG: see Dr Charles A. Huguenin's article on Brontë MSS in Princeton University Library, BST 1955.

[2] George Moore on AG: see *Conversations in Ebury Street,* [London, 1930] 214-23.

[3] Observation of character: AG, chap. I, 11; chap. IV, 36; chap. X, 79.

[4] CB to WSW, 14th December 1847, SLL I, 375.

[5] *Douglas Jerrolds' Weekly:* for the texts of the reviews of *Wuthering Heights* and *Agnes Grey,* see E. M. Weir's "Contemporary Reviews of the First Brontë Novels", BST 1947.

[6] Lady Amberley: quoted from the text in Patricia Thomson's *The Victorian Heroine,* [Oxford, 1956] 53.

P. J. M. Scott (essay date 1983)

SOURCE: "*Agnes Grey:* Accommodating Reality," in *Anne Brontë: A New Critical Assessment,* Vision Press Limited, 1983, pp. 9-44.

[*In the following essay, Scott evaluates the realism, theme, style, and contemporary relevance of* Agnes Grey, *acknowledging the work's simplicity and brevity but seeing these as among its strengths.*]

Agnes Grey has three principal purposes: a paedogogic one; a protest against tyranny; and an attempt to reconcile the passionate yearning heart with life's realities, with its actual possibilities.

We underrate the novel if its brevity and simplicity of construction cause us to think the handling of these themes is slight.

As a story it is simple enough. The eponymous young heroine, who narrates the whole, grows up in a good-natured loving North of England family, the daughter of a clergyman, who loses on a business speculation even the 'snug little property of his own' which has amplified hitherto their modest circumstances. As well as making drastic retrenchments the family now considers ways and means of supplementing his meagre stipend. Mrs. Grey suggests to the older of her two surviving children Mary the drawing of pictures for sale. Agnes herself volunteers to become a governess and after much opposition from the other members of the household carries her point.

> At last, to my great joy, it was decreed that I should take charge of the young family of a certain Mrs. Bloomfield; whom my kind, prim aunt Grey had known in her youth, and asserted to be a very nice woman. Her husband was a retired tradesman, who had realised a very comfortable fortune; but could not be prevailed upon to give a greater salary than twenty-five pounds to the instructress of his children. I, however, was glad to accept this, rather than refuse the situation—which my parents were inclined to think the better plan.

After a long cold journey in the middle of the succeeding September, she arrives at the Bloomfields' mansion Wellwood only to discover chilly hospitality from the mistress of the house and that its children are undisciplined cruel egotists. Tom (aged 7), Mary Ann (almost 6) and Fanny (almost 4 on their new preceptress's coming) are her charges and heavy work they make for her. The parents expect Agnes Grey to keep these artful savages in order, having themselves indulged them all along and continuing to impose no settled course of restraints and encouragements of their own.

Tom indeed has the most barbarous instincts towards animals, and retails 'a list of torments' he intends to inflict upon 'a brood of little callow nestlings' which he has just filched from a neighbouring plantation, but

> while he was busied in the relation, I dropped the stone upon his intended victims and crushed them flat beneath it. Loud were the outcries, terrible the execrations, consequent upon this daring outrage. . . .

> But soon my trials in this quarter came to a close—sooner than I either expected or desired; for one sweet evening towards the close of May, as I was rejoicing in the near approach of the holidays, and congratulating myself upon having made some progress with my pupils (as far as their learning went at least, for I *had* instilled *something* into their heads, and I had at length brought them to be a little—a very little—more rational about getting their lessons done in time to leave some space for recreation, instead of tormenting themselves and me all day long to no purpose), Mrs. Bloomfield sent for me, and calmly told me that after Midsummer my services would be no longer required. She assured me that my character and general conduct were unexceptionable; but the children had made so little improvement since my arrival, that Mr. Bloomfield and she felt it their duty to seek some other mode of instruction. Though superior to most children of their years in abilities, they were decidedly behind them

> in attainments: their manners were uncultivated, and their tempers unruly. And this she attributed to a want of sufficient firmness, and diligent, persevering care on my part. (Ch. 5)

This failure Agnes actually finds disappointing, but with fresh hope she sets out on another governess-employment, gained by placing an advertisement of her qualifications in the newspapers. It takes her (at £50 a year) to

> the family of Mr. Murray, of Horton Lodge, near O——, about seventy miles from our village: a formidable distance to me, as I had never been above twenty miles from home in all the course of my twenty years' sojourn on earth; and as, moreover, every individual in that family and in the neighbourhood was utterly unknown to myself and all my acquaintances. But this rendered it only the more piquant to me.

It turns out, however, that Horton Lodge is far from being a sanctuary of sweetness and light. Here again her employers have a very limited sense of her identity and needs as a human being. Mr. Murray is largely absent from her purview, a blusterous red-faced portly country gent. His wife is a giddy social butterfly, chiefly concerned, in the later phases of the story, about making 'good' matches for her two daughters—at whatever such trifling cost as matrimonial misery.

These girls and their brothers also, like the Bloomfields, have been 'outrageously spoiled', so that 'Master Charles . . . his mother's peculiar darling . . . was . . . only active in doing mischief, and only clever in inventing falsehoods: not simply to hide his faults, but, in mere malicious wantonness, to bring odium upon others.' However, of both boys' instruction and management the new governess is delivered twelve months after her arrival by the dispatch of the younger to follow his brother at a boarding school.

At all times and seasons the youngsters torment Miss Grey with their selfish irrational conduct, and by all the family her convenience or comfort is never consulted. Likewise the local squirearchy never speaks to her or takes any notice of her existence and in Mr. Hatfield, the vicar of the parish, Anne Brontë satirizes much that she despised and hated in the Established Church of her days—among other things, the alternation between sermons 'sunless and severe' and ingratiation of wealthy parishioners. Yet Agnes is comforted to note how the new curate, Mr. Edward Weston, nowise resembles him.

Meanwhile she receives a blow-by-blow account from day to day of the intrigues in cynical flirtation, and for heartless marriage, on the part of her elder charge

Rosalie Murray, who aims at rich wedlock to a baronet while teasing both the parson and Harry Meltham, a younger son of the local hall.

Visiting one Nancy Brown, an elderly pauper of the village, who, as well as by physical disablement has been 'somewhat afflicted with religious melancholy' (Ch. 11), Agnes has learned of Mr. Weston's good offices as a comforting pastor in this household of hidden suffering. And indeed she finds that the new young curate, not specially winsome in his ways or of his person as he is, has done like offices in other poor homes, including material help:

> 'Just for all the world!' exclaimed his [a poor consumptive labourer's] wife; 'an about a three wik sin', when he seed how poor Jem shivered wi' cold, an' what pitiful fires we kept, he axed if wer stock of coals was nearly done. I telled him it was, an' we was ill set to get more: but you know, mum, I didn't think o' him helping us; but howsever, he sent us a sack o' coals next day; an' we've had good fires ever sin: an' a great blessing it is, this winter time. But that's his way, Miss Grey: when he comes into a poor body's house a seein' sick folk, he like notices what they most stand i'need on; an' if he thinks they can't readily get it therseln, he never says nowt about it, but just gets it for 'em. An' it isn't everybody 'at 'ud do that, 'at has as little as he has: for you know, mum, he's now't at all to live on but what he gets fra' th' rector, an' that's little enough, they say.'

It comes as all the harder to bear for the plain governess (as she deems herself) when Rosalie Murray with her very real beauty and charm exercises the idle prenuptial time of her espousal to Sir Thomas Ashby in attempting to engage the curate's affections as well; since by then Agnes has thoroughly fallen in love with Mr. Weston and highly esteems his quiet virtue, strength of character, courage and independence of spirit.

This last quality appears uppermost, for all that Weston has occasionally taken the opportunity of walking with, talking to Miss Grey and plucking flowers for her, when he bears very calmly the news of her departure from Horton following the death of her father back at home and the resolution there taken by mother and daughter to hire and conduct a ladies' seminary in a coastal resort at the other side of the country. (Her sister Mary is by now married to a poor person of her own.)

As the weeks pass with no further word coming from him, Agnes abandons the faint hope raised by his last question ("'It is possible we may meet again,' said he; "will it be of any consequence to you whether we do or not?"'); and she accepts the erewhile Rosalie Murray's invitation to stay at Ashby Park. There she observes the beginning of a life of married unhappiness which exhibits a new pathos in the bride's fate, even as or though that young woman herself is bored with her infant child.

Back at the watering-place which is now scene of both home and work to her, Agnes goes one summer morning early for 'a solitary ramble on the sands while half the world was in bed'. Here she encounters Weston again and it turns out he 'never could discover' her address, that he has lately been installed in a living only two miles distant. He visits her and her mother from now on regularly, and one evening taking her for a walk towards a cliff with a magnificent sea-view, he proposes.

With their marriage and a restrospective summary of their happiness over subsequent years, as co-workers in the church and as parents of three children no less than as partners, the tale concludes.

Stated like that the story is bald and bare to the point of banality; and indeed the anticlimactic mood or effect of its closing phase is something which deserves attention. But two things give the whole a solidity and value quite out of the run-of-the-mill. First, the substantiality of its heroine's nature, which is mediated to us by the quality of her language as narrator. And second, deriving from this, the amount of ground the book covers in its brief compass.

Ars est celare artem. A wholly perspicuous literary style is one of the highest attainments, whether conscious or 'given', of a writer. To create a complete picture of a living world 'out there' in front of your readers by linguistic means of which they are unaware or rendered unobservant—well, the power to do that inheres only in a few classics, let alone lesser works. Some great authors are justly valued for the idiosyncrasy of their style: a chief value in reading them is contact with the highly individual voice which their pages offer—say those of Sir Thomas Browne or Jeremy Taylor, Marcel Proust or the later Henry James. But the other, the 'quiet thing', is much more difficult of achievement.

Anne Brontë's narrative manner operates like a transparent pane of glass. We stare straight through it at the subjects under consideration.

> All true histories contain instruction; though, in some, the treasure may be hard to find, and when found, so trivial in quantity, that the dry, shrivelled kernel scarcely compensates for the trouble of cracking the nut. Whether this be the case with my history or not, I am hardly competent to judge. I sometimes think that it might prove useful to some, and entertaining to others; but the world may judge for itself. Shielded by my own obscurity, and by the lapse of years, and a few fictitious names, I do not fear to venture; and will candidly lay before the public what I would not disclose to the most intimate friend.

Thus the very opening of the novel.

This is not hemming and hawing, a proemial warming-up which, for all the good it does, could just as well be cut. We need to be supplied with a motive for what follows—for why is Agnes Grey telling her story? Yet we don't want a prologomenon which testifies to nothing so much as its author's self-importance with either blatant arrogance or coy pseudo-apology; and neither type of effusion is here traceable.

The narrative is confessedly offered as having a didactic drift and potential moralistic value, but in a direct quiet manner which is self-conscious in all the right ways and none of the wrong ones. To this the absence of any turgid lumbering in the style testifies; indeed negatives will characterize the best terms of our praise for this side of Anne Brontë's accomplishment, and just because it is so thoroughly accomplished. Those first four sentences are paced so as to move with a light various rhythm; but not to draw attention to themselves as so doing. Though their declared focus is the historian herself we have already become unconscious, by the end of that short paragraph, of a mind behind it manipulating a rhetoric.

> As we drove along, my spirits revived again, and I turned, with pleasure, to the contemplation of the new life upon which I was entering. But though it was not far past the middle of September, the heavy clouds and strong north-easterly wind combined to render the day extremely cold and dreary; and the journey seemed a very long one, for, as Smith observed, the roads were 'very heavy'; and certainly, his horse was very heavy too: it crawled up the hills, and crept down them, and only condescended to shake its sides in a trot where the road was at a dead level or a very gentle slope, which was rarely the case in those rugged regions; so that it was nearly one o'clock before we reached the place of our destination. Yet, after all, when we entered the lofty iron gateway, when we drove softly up the smooth, well-rolled carriage road, with the green lawn on each side, studded with young trees, and approached the new but stately mansion of Wellwood, rising above its mushroom poplar-groves, my heart failed me, and I wished it were a mile or two farther off. For the first time in my life, I must stand alone: there was no retreating now. I must enter that house, and introduce myself among its strange inhabitants. But how was it to be done? True, I was near nineteen; but, thanks to my retired life and the protecting care of my mother and sister, I well knew that many a girl of fifteen, or under, was gifted with a more womanly address, and greater ease and self-possession, than I was. Yet, if Mrs. Bloomfield were a kind, motherly woman, I might do very well, after all; and the children, of course, I should soon be at ease with them—and Mr. Bloomfield, I hoped, I should have but little to do with. (The opening of Ch. 2)

The balance here of narrative, description, commentary and self-revelation is very finely judged. We move without effort from the young appointee's inward musings to the exterior scene, first in its totality and then particulars—as her new place of work swings into view; then back again to the interior ponderings which have now (at the crisis of the journey as it were) become self-examination. Look how different the devices are which make actual to us the horse's gait, the pace of the journey, on the one hand, and on the other the effect of the whole new Wellwood topography upon its present recruit's eye and spirit. 'Condescended to shake its sides in a trot' is a lovely mimesis, full of close observation and gentle irony where the paratactic sentence with a very simple structure of clauses also conveys the laboured progress the travellers enjoy. Which is immediately followed by the rather breathless rhythm of the prose at the entrance to the grounds of Agnes's new abode:

(1) Yet, (after all) . . .
(2) when we entered . . .
  (2a) when we drove . . .
  (2a/i) with the green lawn . . .
  (2a/iA) studded with young trees,
(3) and approached
  (3a) rising above . . .

The dependency of these numerous clauses one upon another, the accumulation of them before the wave of the sentence breaks at 'my heart failed me' (its main verb), well conveys the rising apprehension, even to panic, of the new arrival.

We move at once into quick *erlebte Rede:*

> For the first time in my life, I must stand alone: there was no retreating now. I must enter that house, and introduce myself among its strange inhabitants. But how was it to be done?

At the remove of only one tense this is her self-address of the actual historical moment; provoking in its turn a reflection on her general situation, her identity as a social being altogether, in the more relaxed amplitude of which we are given two points of view: the young woman's, little more than a girl, to whom all this happened at the original time, and that of the more experienced judicious narrator of after years who is telling her tale. ('True, I was near nineteen, etc. . . . .')

This very fluency of representational competence all but matches Dickens's art on like occasions in his first-person-told *Bildungsromane, David Copperfield* and *Great Expectations;* so that there seeps into our subconscious the conviction that a narrator, who has speech and therefore life itself so much under her hand and is such a true reflector of the world, possesses in herself a human value which makes important the novel's trajectory of its old theme, innocence passing through experience.

The duality of vision—the older Agnes mediates to us the experiences of her younger self—is in the main handled with secure success. There are, at least for me, only a couple of instances where uncertainty obtrudes. Is there a cringing kittenishness in the heroine's speech and attitude during the second half of Chapter 1? Is it that, recording the same, the novelist is using the quietly ironic eye she deploys upon other human weakness in her pages? Or is it simply truthful psychological portraiture; is this exactly how her heroine would speak and move, in consequence of a life spent hitherto in greatly sheltered innocence? We may be the more wary of censuring this first of such 'lapses', if that is what they be, given the truly virile range and variety of tone—the moral insight and control—in the paragraphs preceding it.

Likewise with a certain moment in Chapter 11:

> One bright day in the last week of February, I was walking in the park, enjoying the threefold luxury of solitude, a book, and pleasant weather; for Miss Matilda had set out on her daily ride, and Miss Murray was gone in the carriage with her mamma to pay some morning calls. But it struck me that I ought to leave these selfish pleasures, and the park with its glorious canopy of bright blue sky, the west wind sounding through its yet leafless branches, the snow-wreaths still lingering in its hollows, but melting fast beneath the sun, and the graceful deer browsing on its moist herbage already assuming the freshness and verdure of spring— and go to the cottage of one Nancy Brown, a widow, whose son was at work all day in the fields, and who was afflicted with an inflammation in the eyes. . . .

The governess here strikes me as being somewhat— and the least bit disagreeably—'pi'. Such pleasures as appreciating Nature's glories are not 'selfish' but of themselves wholesome; at least, in a life not given up to indulgence and sloth, which anyway has few enjoyments or releases in it. There is arguably a kind of embarrassment on the narrator's part herself communicated to us in the way the sentence that conveys the new resolution to visit the cottager is worked up with a lengthy subordination of clauses, to end so (as it were) consciously in bathos (indicated no less with the hyphenation which introduces the closing cadences). Perhaps this is again simple psychological fidelity on Anne Brontë's part: at a time when her personality is under assault from various angles, Agnes Grey is attempting to shore it up and find refuge in deliberate self-conscious rectitude. Her problem at Horton Lodge is that everything there constitutes a continual raid on her self-esteem. We may be offered here, archly from the narrator's view, a glimpse of her method for compensation. But we are not sure. The tale as a whole is not told in a mode, like Jane Austen's, which alerts us *all the time* to the smallest nuances of tone as likely to be critical of the heroine's motivations, in however fugitive, slight and complex a fashion.

Complex but assured in its disposition of tones is the episode of the primroses, the symbolic moment in which Edward Weston indicates his concern for Miss Grey and even a particular interest in her.

> Whether I walked with the young ladies or rode with their parents [to church of a Sunday], depended upon their own capricious will: if they chose to 'take' me, I went; if, for reasons best known to themselves, they chose to go alone, I took my seat in the carriage. I liked walking better, but a sense of reluctance to obtrude my presence on any one who did not desire it, always kept me passive on these and similar occasions; and I never inquired into the causes of their varying whims. Indeed, this was the best policy—for to submit and oblige was the governess's part, to consult their own pleasure was that of the pupils. But when I did walk, the first half of the journey was generally a great nuisance to me. As none of the before-mentioned ladies and gentlemen ever noticed me, it was disagreeable to walk beside them, as if listening to what they said, or wishing to be thought one of them, while they talked over me, or across; and if their eyes, in speaking, chanced to fall on me, it seemed as if they looked on vacancy—as if they either did not see me, or were very desirous to make it appear so. It was disagreeable, too, to walk behind, and thus appear to acknowledge my own inferiority; for, in truth, I considered myself pretty nearly as good as the best of them, and wished them to know that I did so, and not to imagine that I looked upon myself as a mere domestic, who knew her own place too well to walk beside such fine ladies and gentlemen as they were—though her young ladies might choose to have her with them, and even condescend to converse with her when no better company were at hand. Thus—I am almost ashamed to confess it—but indeed I gave myself no little trouble in my endeavours (if I did keep up with them) to appear perfectly unconscious or regardless of their presence, as if I were wholly absorbed in my own reflections, or the contemplation of surrounding objects; or, if I lingered behind, it was some bird or insect, some tree or flower, that attracted my attention, and having duly examined that, I would pursue my walk alone, at a leisurely pace, until my pupils had bidden adieu to their companions, and turned off into the quiet, private road.

> One such occasion I particularly well remember: it was a lovely afternoon about the close of March; Mr. Green and his sisters had sent their carriage back empty, in order to enjoy the bright sunshine and balmy air in a sociable walk home along with their visitors, Captain Somebody and Lieutenant Somebody else (a couple of military fops), and the Misses Murray, who, of course, contrived to join them. Such a party was highly agreeable to Rosalie; but not finding it equally suitable to my taste, I presently fell back, and began to botanise and entomologise along the green banks and budding hedges, till the company was considerably in advance of me, and I could hear the sweet song of the happy lark; then my spirit of misanthropy began to melt away beneath the soft, pure air and genial sunshine: but sad thoughts of early childhood, and yearnings for

departed joys, or for a brighter future lot, arose instead. As my eyes wandered over the steep banks covered with young grass and green-leaved plants, and surmounted by budding hedges, I longed intensely for some familiar flower that might recall the woody dales or green hillsides of home: the brown moorlands, of course, were out of the question. Such a discovery would make my eyes gush out with water, no doubt; but that was one of my greatest enjoyments now. At length I descried, high up between the twisted roots of an oak, three lovely primroses, peeping so sweetly from their hiding-place that the tears already started at the sight; but they grew so high above me that I tried in vain to gather one or two, to dream over and to carry with me: I could not reach them unless I climbed the bank, which I was deterred from doing by hearing a footstep at that moment behind me, and was, therefore, about to turn away, when I was startled by the words, 'Allow me to gather them for you, Miss Grey,' spoken in the grave low tones of a well-known voice. Immediately the flowers were gathered, and in my hand. It was Mr. Weston, of course—who else would trouble himself to do so much for *me?* (Ch. 13)

We are shown several of the concomitants when a human being is treated as a convenience, not as a full independent entity with a valued life. As her companions look through or talk over her, Agnes has no socially recognized means of reacting which repudiates her loss of status and yet which does not itself denigrate her. Even *feeling* resentment is demeaning, because it acknowledges a hurt and that means living at the standards and level of this third-rate company itself. Yet not to feel it, nor to attempt showing it in any way, would seem a loss of caste as a human identity; perhaps cowardly also, possibly too quietist in attitude.

It is a poisoning air Agnes Grey breathes at Horton, bringing decay into all aspects of her own nature, which cannot wholly be separated off (this is Anne Brontë's point) as something intrinsically distinct from her environment and *its* morality. It may well put us in mind of Fanny Price's dilemma at Mansfield Park, the predicament that is her entire role there—or of any good Austen character faced with delinquency in a constricted unalterable and inescapable social group. She is imprisoned and the impossibility of dealing wholly healthfully with the pressures upon her is illustrated for us in several features of this 'sequence'.

First of all there is the backbiting cattiness that mars her account of her young charges' visiting swains: 'Captain Somebody and Lieutenant Somebody else (a couple of military fops)'. This governess has a score of big just grievances against the Misses Murray, but we see resentment turning to general misanthropy in parlance so dismissive of those identities. And she who was once like a saint from Olympus in comparison with the mentality of her pupils begins, oppressed by their injustice, to sound like a cantankerous gossip of

no elevated mind at all: 'for, in truth, I considered myself pretty nearly as good as the best of them, and wished them to know that I did so, and not to imagine that I looked upon myself as a mere domestic, who knew her own place too well to walk beside such fine ladies and gentlemen as they were—'.

That is not so very far off the internal chatter of Mrs. Petito, the lady's maid in Maria Edgeworth's *The Absentee* (published 1812, a novel which almost certainly Anne Brontë had read in her formative years):

'It will do very well, never mind,' repeated Petito, muttering to herself as she looked after the ladies whilst they ran downstairs, 'I can't abide to dress any young lady who says never mind, and it will do very well. That, and her never talking to one confidentially, or trusting one with the least bit of her secrets, is the thing I can't put up with from Miss Nigent; and Miss Broadhurst holding the pins to me, as much as to say, do your business, Petito, and don't talk. Now, that's so impertinent, as if one wasn't the same flesh and blood, and had not as good a right to talk of everything, and hear of everything, as themselves. And Mrs. Broadhurst, too, cabinet councilling with my lady, and pursing up her city mouth, when I come in, and turning off the discourse to snuff, forsooth, as if I was an ignoramus, to think they closeted themselves to talk of snuff. Now, I think a lady of quality's woman has as good a right to be trusted with her lady's secrets as with her jewels; and if my Lady Clonbrony was a real lady of quality, she'd know that, and consider the one as much my paraphernalia as the other. So I shall tell my lady tonight, as I always do when she vexes me, that I never lived in an Irish family before, and don't know the ways of it. Then she'll tell me she was born in Hoxfordshire; then I shall say, with my saucy look, "Oh, was you, my lady? I always forget that you was an Englishwoman." Then maybe she'll say "Forget! you forget yourself strangely, Petito." Then I shall say, with a great deal of dignity, "If your ladyship thinks so, my lady, I'd better go." And I'd desire no better than that she would take me at my word, for my Lady Dashfort's is a much better place, I'm told, and she's dying to have me, I know.'

Mrs. Petito is much more amusing and less justified in her situation than Agnes Grey in hers, yet a similar note is discernible in the musings of the latter heroine upon her wrongs, a kind of bleat-bleat-bleat of, itself, no very elevated mind.

In *Reflections on the Psalms* C. S. Lewis referred to what is centrally in question here:

It seemed to me that, seeing in them [the cursings in the Psalms] hatred undisguised, I saw also the natural result of injuring a human being. The word *natural* is here important. This result can be obliterated by grace, suppressed by prudence or social convention, and (which is dangerous) wholly disguised by self-deception. But just as the natural result of throwing a lighted match into a pile of shavings is to produce a fire—though damp or the intervention of some more sensible person may prevent it—so the natural result of cheating a man, or 'keeping him down' or neglecting him, is to arouse resentment; that is, to impose upon him the temptation of becoming what the Psalmists were when they wrote the vindictive passages. He may succeed in resisting the temptation; or he may not. If he fails, if he dies spiritually because of his hatred for me, how do I, who provoked that hatred, stand? For in addition to the original injury I have done him a far worse one. I have introduced into his inner life, at best a new temptation, at worst a new besetting sin. If that sin utterly corrupts him, I have in a sense debauched or seduced him. I was the tempter.[1]

Agnes Grey is not utterly corrupted by her experiences first at Wellwood and then Horton; but we are shown they do set fair to wreck her life. In a girl who started out guileless, ingenuous and open-minded, they have induced a sense of human incompetence and insufficiency that all but precludes marriage for her.

The author may here be writing very much from the heart. Of the three surviving Brontë sisters the various contemporary testimony has concurred with the view that Anne was the pretty one; she was personable and appealing as Charlotte, all self-consciously, was not. But if you are convinced you are unattractive—and in ways not only bodily—if you deem yourself unnoticeable and unmarriageable, unmarried is how you will tend to stay. It is really the function not of a look in a mirror which reveals actual deformity and repulsiveness: rather, a social and psychological disablement. And it is self-fulfilling. All compliment, all awakening interest in another party will appear mere vapour to you, will receive no appropriate response; indeed it will be repressed, stillborn, even in its very conception (within other people's awareness of you) by your habitual deportment, and paralysing self-estimate.

We the readers can see that Edward Weston is doing something not certainly but potentially 'speaking', in plucking those flowers for Miss Grey, but the latent significance of that gesture (not yet articulate for either of them, no doubt) the object of his attention misses: and the full text of her self-denigration we get in Chapter 17, concluding with this:

> They that have beauty, let them be thankful for it, and make a good use of it, like any other talent; they that have it not, let them console themselves, and do the best they can without it: certainly, though liable to be over-estimated, it is a gift of God, and not to be despised. Many will feel this who have felt that they could love, and whose hearts tell them

that they are worthy to be loved again; while yet they are debarred by the lack of this or some such seeming trifle, from giving and receiving that happiness they seem almost made to feel and to impart.

The primroses episode is as subtly handled as it needs to be. We should not respect Agnes if she were the sort of woman who saw flirtation in every male smile and a marriage proposal round every corner: that itself would betoken psychological disablement of a less attractive kind. And indeed the little scene *is* variously interpretable. Weston may simply help her pick her flowers out of politeness, or speak with her motivated by charity towards someone he recognizes as humanly very cut off and lonely; any sort of amorous implication is not—and should not be—explicit between them. For such a thing to be raised to the level of consciousness at all in either breast would signalize a crudity of response each to the other which would make them lesser people than they are.

What Anne Brontë is delineating with beautiful delicacy is one of those moments when someone may or may not be feeling his/her way toward you (in the sense of a more special relationship than good neighbourliness) and with a feeling the character of which they themselves have by no means analytically grasped; which the well-integrated person, when mutually disposed, will accept—i.e. *leave*—at that, to ride upon the air with its own vibration.

Locked by the behaviour of her successive households of employment, however, into a steep fall of self-confidence, Agnes Grey responds to Edward Weston's every word and gesture in a manner that would choke off interest in all but the most tenacious of suitors. On her side she keeps hoping for his attachment but has lost, because she has been discouraged from ever gaining, the social aplomb (i.e. through self-confidence) to ripen another's attention into regard and regard into courtship—which entails permitting, not hastening nor retarding, a process of self-confidence in the other party. All this is implicit in the inadequacy of her account of the business: 'It was Mr. Weston, of course—who else would trouble himself to do so much for *me?*'

Most of the time she is gauche in his company, we see, and speaks so much at cross-purposes as even to fail of giving her admirer knowledge of her new address in the coastal town where she and her mother are to set up their school when she leaves Horton.

All this is the more satisfactorily handled, in an artistic point of view, for not being explicit between author and reader—throughout. It is quietly intimated to us, but totally adumbrated, how this young couple come near to missing their best fulfilment in life on account of the sheer quantity of discouragement which, unawares, the heroine places in the hero's track: a misdirection itself born of *her* discouragement. And that that is to be laid at the door of the people with whom she has worked is illustrated most flagrantly when the Murray girls keep their instructress indoors and, in their meetings with Weston, allege she stays there by choice:

'And he asked after you again,' said Matilda, in spite of her sister's silent but imperative intimation that she should hold her tongue. 'He wondered why you were never with us, and thought you must have delicate health, as you came out so seldom.'

'He didn't, Matilda—what nonsense you're talking!'

'Oh, Rosalie, what a lie! He did, you know; and you said—Don't, Rosalie—hang it!—I won't be pinched so! And, Miss Grey, Rosalie told him you were quite well, but you were always so buried in your books that you had no pleasure in anything else!' (Ch. 17)

Rosalie Murray, not being emotionally inhibited, obviously *is* aware of the curate's potential devotion to her teacher and, wanting to engross all worthy male compliments in the district to herself, feigns lack of interest on the part of the one toward the other. It is very cruel and wrong, and *Agnes Grey*'s further substantiality as a portrait of life lies in anatomizing for us where such callousness derives.

In successive phases the two engagements its heroine takes on illustrate the origin and process of bad upbringing. The youngsters Agnes goes to are monsters of self-conceit and uncharitableness because they have been, and continue to be, parentally neglected. Basically their fathers and mothers do not care about them (as individuals); which is why they do not discipline them.

Chapter 3 demolishes all the modern cant about children being sacrosanct from bodily inflictions. Was there ever a gentler spirit than Anne Brontë's or her heroine's? Yet as Agnes is moved to protest:

Master Tom, not content with refusing to be ruled, must needs set up as a ruler, and manifested a determination to keep, not only his sisters, but his governess in order, by violent manual and pedal applications; and, as he was a tall, strong boy of his years, this occasioned no trifling inconvenience. A few sound boxes in the ear, on such occasions, might have settled the matter easily enough: but as, in that case, he might make up some story to his mother, which she would be sure to believe, as she had such unshaken faith in his veracity—though I had already discovered it to be by no means unimpeachable—I determined to refrain from striking him, even in self-defence; and, in his most violent moods, my only resource was to throw him on his back, and hold his hands and feet till the frenzy was somewhat

abated. To the difficulty of preventing him from doing what he ought not, was added that of forcing him to do what he ought. Often he would positively refuse to learn, or to repeat his lessons, or even to look at his book. Here, again, a good birch rod might have been serviceable; but, as my powers were so limited, I must make the best use of what I had.

For when all else fails the only thing which will speak to a morally deaf child is physical pain. Reasoning, civilized offered responses are unavailing because an alien language; and this in turn owing to the child's essential previous neglect.

Agnes Grey could not be more urgently relevant to our own society now: an age (as it seems to me) where perhaps most parents in all classes are in essentials just like the besotted Bloomfield and Murray adults. In too many cases nowadays folk appear to get married and have children, not for the love of those undertakings in themselves but as some sort of venture into additional human status, a further inward-looking *self*-endorsement. Mrs. Bloomfield is not interested in her offspring except as very tangential extensions of her own self-esteem and social aura: the hard work of a mother's love interests her not at all. That would involve effort, toil, care of a merely boring kind, because she is not in the first place bothered about having a *relationship* with her children. She wants them, but as items which can go in and out of some sort of cupboard in her life marked 'Progeny', and shut up there with a surrogate, the governess, who is officially employed to turn them into rational well-conducted creatures but who has hardly any real chance of doing so.

For the children, like all children, know when essentially they are minor tangentialities in their parents' values—always a ripe source of delinquency; and like all the cruelly indifferent, father and mother substitute a phoney humanitarianism in the place of true upbringing, as a sop to Cerberus and makeshift for the lapse on their part of the one thing needful, their attention.

Given that a majority of marriages and child-rearings are like this in the U.K. today (to judge by the theft endemic among 'middle' and 'upper'-class children, the pink and green hairstyles of the punk rockers—for what are these things but desperate cries for attention?) *Agnes Grey* can hardly be set aside as no tract for the times—our times.

The parents of 1983 are like the silly couples at Wellwood and Horton: they are wishful of anything for their children except to give them, consistently, out of a true devotion, their time, their interest, their selves: to bother with them. And then we wring our hands in adult colloquy about the rising crime wave of an affluent society and wonder how on earth atrocity can increase where social conditions are improved, historically, almost out of recognition. But children do not live by bread alone; they cope with life according as they are loved; which means being bothered with, related to, continually, by their progenitors and home-makers.

In the two youths who some months ago actually broke into the house of an old woman of 96 and raped her, we see the breakdown of even the most (one would have thought) fundamental taboos of creaturely life; and without question they must have been subhuman to be able to do that. Yet what was even their act but a revenge upon the bad parenthood generally prevalent in our society? And a function of the rottenness of that state, that primary tie, in our day is the general refusal, codified by the intelligentsia into a dogma, to have real discipline around, including corporal punishment, whether at home or at school. For as the devil Screwtape points out to his minion Wormwood:

> The use of Fashions in thought is to distract the attention of men from their real dangers. We direct the fashionable outcry of each generation against those vices of which it is least in danger and fix its approval on the virtue nearest to that vice which we are trying to make endemic. The game is to have them all running about with fire extinguishers whenever there is a flood, and all crowding to that side of the boat which is already nearly gunwale under. Thus we make it fashionable to expose the dangers of enthusiasm at the very moment when they are all really becoming worldly and lukewarm; a century later, when we are really making them all Byronic and drunk with emotion, the fashionable outcry is directed against the dangers of the mere 'understanding'. Cruel ages are put on their guard against Sentimentality, feckless and idle ones against Respectability, lecherous ones against Puritanism; and whenever all men are really hastening to be slaves or tyrants we make Liberalism the prime bogey.[2]

Exactly. In our epoch, when children's great predicament is that they are undisciplined (because ignored and unloved), the spectre which raises so very many teachers' and parents' hands in horror is the mere idea of corporal—indeed of any real—punishment.

Thus it is that both sets of parents can be so little aware of their offspring's true characters, can demand of Miss Grey that she turn them out as superior in behaviour to the hoydenism which at best, for instance, the girls display; and yet be affornted at any suggestion of bit or curb in a coherent process of character-training (*viz.* Mrs. Murray's reproaches in Ch. 18).

Hence it is that Tom Bloomfield can be so hideously cruel to animals, and his siblings with him (Chs. 2 and 5), in scenes which have provoked disbelief. Much that we pride our humanity upon are virtues and reci-

procities acquired, by no means guaranteed as birth-right for the species; and *homo sapiens* tends to love and care for living things only as he knows love and care experientially himself. When children are brought into the world by begetters who are not interested in them—when they are denied the primary experience of love so completely as *that*—how will they have 'natural' feelings towards plants, the animal kingdom or their own kind?

Anne Brontë, in Chapters 21 and 22, sends her heroine to stay with the young married Rosalie Murray within a year of her becoming a lady of the manor at Ashby Park, not simply to fill out her story, nor to exhibit supernatural piety in forgiveness and charitable feeling on the observant governess's part towards a former tormentor; but to trace into a new generation yet again the consequences of this sort of denial which was prevalent amongst the higher classes in her day and which—perhaps with so much relative prosperity materially—has now spread through our society as a whole.

What Agnes discovers in that brief cheerless visit is not merely, as expected, that Rosalie does not care for her husband, is already at enmity with his family and something of a prisoner in the round of her rural wedded condition—*because* there is so little real affection and respect on both sides of a marriage made from paltry motives. The new mother cannot even love her child, and has just the same disparaging dismissive feelings about the baby to whom she herself has given birth that were all she really inspired in her own parent:

> 'But I can't devote myself entirely to a child,' said she: 'it may die—which is not at all improbable.'

> 'But, with care, many a delicate infant has become a strong man or woman.'

> 'But it may grow so intolerably like its father that I shall hate it.'

> 'That is not likely; it is a little girl, and strongly resembles its mother.'

> 'No matter; I should like it better if it were a boy—only that its father will leave it no inheritance that he can possibly squander away. What pleasure can I have in seeing a girl grow up to eclipse me, and enjoy those pleasures that I am for ever debarred from? But supposing I could be so generous as to take delight in this, still it is *only* a child; and I can't centre all my hopes in a child: that is only one degree better than devoting oneself to a dog. And as for all the wisdom and goodness you have been trying to instil into me—that is all very right and proper I dare say, and if I were some twenty years older, I might fructify by it: but people must enjoy themselves when they are young; and if others won't let them—why, they must hate them for it!'

Egotism in its turn will no doubt be the psychological portion of a child so raised; and that self-conceit disables others who are not even guilty of being blood-kindred is what the previous chapters of the novel have shown, with the assault on the governess's capacity for happiness made by her ordeal in both her situations of employment. Her experience of the outer world, after a sheltered childhood, proves to be of an arena where people look over or through her and withhold all sense of her having a human value; so she all but becomes unmarriageable. Philip Larkin has put it memorably:

> Man hands on misery to man.
> It deepens like a coastal shelf.[3]

and Anne Brontë is here tracing the process in its origins.

Agnes Grey, then, is about the way all of us tend to mutilate one another's lives—radically—in affording our fellow creatures less than full respect as equal beings having an independent importance like to our own: which is as much as to say, the manner to some degree most of us treat each other most of the time.

The novel is also about coping, however; about making something workable out of the human mess. Its heroine achieves this in virtue of her moral education in a loving environment, her training and religious piety from a background of fine sensibility—and the randomness of life itself.

She starts with supplemental advantages that may by no means be underived. Her imagination and the sly humour which animates a considerable portion of her narrative themselves constitute a resilience under the pressures all around. Take the following, for example, concerning the senior Mrs. Bloomfield:

> Hitherto, though I saw the old lady had her defects (of which one was a proneness to proclaim her perfections), I had always been wishful to excuse them, and to give her credit for all the virtues she professed, and even imagine others yet untold. (Ch. 4)

It is the subtlety of the final nuance there which invigorates—as it is indeed the function of a vigour in the writer. That sentence is a straightforward, obvious enough piece of satire until its last clause briefly makes us skid. There the hyperbole of feeling is shown in the context to have several constituents. The young woman is desperately lonely and clutching at straws:

> Kindness, which had been the food of my life through so many years, had lately been so entirely denied me, that I welcomed with grateful joy the slightest semblance of it.

She is also setting up as a judicious judge, self-consciously slightly witty, though we cannot forget she is

only 19. The tone is of a self-possession and social ease which are not really secure, and yet which is the honest property of a genuinely discriminative mind.

It is the ability to transmit trace-elements of this sort of light weight yet significance which made me before think of Jane Austen and Professor George Whalley's words on that novelist's 'delight in effortless virtuosity, in catching by an impossible fraction of a hair's-breadth the savour of a nuance of implication'.[4]

This is not the leading hallmark of Agnes Grey's mind and rhetoric; Anne Brontë's themes are different. Yet the capacity to mock the old lady, mock herself and make several serious points with the necessary fugitiveness that characteristically we find here, itself represents a human value which is also a defence—however much that is to be seen as more securely acquired in retrospect than at the time.

Or we can turn to Chapter 19. Here a less qualified kind of irony operates which signifies a very amiable robustness in the moral nature of the bereaved family that the surviving Grey womenfolk have now become:

> 'Your grandpapa has been so kind as to write to me. He says he has no doubt I have long repented of my "unfortunate marriage," and if I will only acknowledge this, and confess I was wrong in neglecting his advice, and that I have justly suffered for it, he will make a lady of me once again—if that be possible after my long degradation—and remember my girls in his will.'

But Mrs. Grey intends to answer with defiance and specifies the various heads of her reasoning why, concluding

> 'Will this do, children?—or shall I say we are all very sorry for what has happened during the last thirty years, and my daughters wish they had never been born; but since they have had that misfortune, they will be thankful for any trifle their grandpapa will be kind enough to bestow?'

> Of course, we both applauded our mother's resolution; Mary cleared away the breakfast things; I brought the desk; the letter was quickly written and despatched; and, from that day, we heard no more of our grandfather, till we saw his death announced in the newspaper a considerable time after—all his worldly possessions, of course, being left to our wealthy, unknown cousins.

A word *en passant* here. Does not *Agnes Grey* very considerably more than any other Brontë novel stick to the sort of realism which Charlotte Brontë sought to infuse into the nineteenth century's fiction at the commencement of *her* public foray?[5]

Finally, in proof of our heroine's vitality as a centre of discriminations we have her ear for dialogue. Anyone who can reproduce as faithfully as she does very different styles of speech, sometimes in proximity together, and even the variations of an individual's modes of discourse, has by definition an extrovert awareness of others and life's variety which itself confers hope upon her fate as well as facilitating an active conscience.

> 'I have another place to go to,' said he, 'and I see' (glancing at the book on the table) 'some one else has been reading to you.'

> 'Yes, sir; Miss Grey has been as kind as to read me a chapter; an' now she's helping me with a shirt for our Bill but I'm feared she'll be cold there. Won't you come to th'fire, miss?' . . .

> 'Miss Grey,' said he half-jestingly, as if he felt it necessary to change the present subject, whether he had anything particular to say or not, 'I wish you would make my peace with the squire, when you see him. He was by when I rescued Nancy's cat, and did not quite approve of the deed. I told him I thought he might better spare all his rabbits than she her cat, for which audacious assertion he treated me to some rather ungentlemanly language; and I fear I retorted a trifle too warmly.'

> 'Oh, lawful sir! I hope you didn't fall out wi' th' maister for sake o' my cat! he cannot bide answering again—can th' maister.'

> 'Oh, it's no matter, Nancy: I don't care about it, really; I said nothing *very* uncivil; and I suppose Mr. Murray is accustomed to use rather strong language when he's heated.' (Ch. 12)

The slight orotund pomposity of language, the relatively elaborate grammatical organization in the longest sentence there quoted contrasts with the other remarks Mr. Weston makes to his two parishioners. He is embarrassed both at the context and content of what he finds to say at that juncture and his diction subtly alters, accordingly.

The use and aid of such equipment for an ethical being has already been shown in the way Agnes reports her tearful self-pity and maudlin self-contempt during the primroses episode: 'Such a discovery would make my eyes gush out with water, no doubt; but that was one of my greatest enjoyments now.' The self-indulgence is there contained and disciplined by a conscience, we realize, habituated to exercise and examination.

Starch of a more nutritive kind is supplied by her religion. Ultimately she has not been brought up to expect, i.e. demand, of this world a nice time. (Osip Mandelstam's words to his wife, before dying for his brave outspokenness, put the matter at its most bleakly direct: 'Why do you think you ought to be happy?')

Indeed the more I study Anne Brontë's work the more it seems to me she is first and foremost a Christian writer; and this creates problems in connection with a late-twentieth-century readership at least analogous to the question of the validity, for our society now, of Europe's medieval poetry, shot through as most of that is with a religious interpretation of existence. The issue is so large I choose to try and take the bull by the horns in a separate section later. Suffice it to say here it is significant that Anne Brontë, as was remarked before, accomplishes the most 'realistic' story of any fiction the Haworth sisters chose to publish. *Agnes Grey* has no unanswered questions like the method of Heathcliff's making his fortune before he returns to Wuthering Heights, or *Jane Eyre* with its magnificent psychology yet preposterous plot.

It rides beautifully between the Scylla and Charybdis of any social realist in the form. On the one side, it does not yield to softness: in E. M. Forster's words, 'the temptation's overwhelming to grant to one's creations a happiness actual life does not supply.'[6] On the other hand, it does not flog its characters with a grim Hardyesque determinism of misery, something no less fantastic, at least in its artistic effect. The Brontës' actual life-history reads fully as unfortunate as *Jude the Obscure*'s, but were it hawked in a fiction we should probably withhold credence. The trouble with Hardy for me is that, like real life sometimes (as Forster has elsewhere also remarked), he 'gets things wrong',[7] and the awful trajectories of his heroes' courses all but overwhelm the other, wonderful features of his prose writing because they create the impression of an universe deliberately malign without 'arguing the case', imaginatively speaking, for such a view; sufficiently at least to carry conviction during the space of the reading. 'Yet *why* are these people so remarkably stupid and dogged by such unusual quantities of stupendous ill-luck?' is my repeated moan as I trace the agonies of Jude and his fellow-sufferers. 'If "It", as Goldsworthy Lowes Dickinson called the First Cause, were so implacably cruel, surely the first amoeba would never have managed to crawl out of the slime.'

I *think* the complaint has little to do with the portion of tragedies in one's own life. Different authors can penetrate us with the sense, at least for the nonce, that 'not to be born is best' or, in C. S. Lewis's words immediately after the death of his wife, trying out the voice of *advocatus diaboli* 'Fate (or whatever it is) delights to produce a great capacity and then frustrate it. Beethoven went deaf. By our standards a mean joke; the monkey trick of a spiteful imbecile.'[8] But they do so, these other writers, by means more solidly based and inwardly structured.

Agnes Grey suffers enough and various afflictions to become representative of ordinary humanity—equally in the lower-to-middle middle classes of her day, and at large. Her home life is happy at first, but her father loses his money and by the standards of their caste their means become almost desperately straitened; and the psychological as well as material costs of this débâcle are registered. She sets out to earn her own living and add something to the common funds besides, by teaching; and finds the task not only unpleasant but degrading—not once but twice over. Her sister marries, modestly. Her mother becomes a widow, and when they set up a school together they have to work hard to make ends meet with no provision in view should either of them be stricken ill, except that of falling hard upon her brother-in-law and *his* thin means. Agnes loves, but her affection seems unrequited and she has to reconcile herself to the nearly certain prospect of a future as a hapless old maid.

This constitutes a sufficient series of possibilities followed up by frustrations. More would look like authorial obtuseness. We should say in that case, 'Well if life is really tougher still than this—more painful, of its own intrinsic logic, *inevitably*—it is hardly worth caring about in the first place. With the words of Ernest Hemingway's heroine at the end of *A Farewell to Arms,* "It's just a dirty trick" (Ch. 41), our most appropriate response would be to turn our faces thankfully to the wall whenever we could and like her expire with an expression of contempt upon them.' On the other hand, if Agnes Grey's career were pleasanter we should be tempted to retort, 'Very nice, but where have all the bereavements and economic hardships gone, the frustrations intellectual and emotional? There seem to be plenty more of such things in the world outside than between the covers of this book. It's just a novelette of female wish-fulfilment.'

In short, it appears to me Anne Brontë pitches the matter just right. The duplication of unsatisfactory households in which her heroine works makes a social criticism even as it builds the picture of a whole social world. The upper classes in her time have too much power, too much freedom to be bad. That they use these liberties ill is thoroughly exemplified, not only by the characters of the Bloomfields and the Murrays and their on the whole repulsive children, but by the local squirearchies in each case surrounding them and their various relations and friends.

This is the book's Tyranny-theme in its political aspect: that in such a society as early Victorian Britain, certain individuals can disregard too many aspects of the Golden Rule just because they have lots of money. It is all-significant that more than one type of gentry abuses equally their freedoms of cash and time: Mr. Bloomfield the self-made tradesman, Mr. Murray of the 'genuine thoroughbred gentry' (Ch. 6) and the lower aristocracy with whom he associates. The implication of this is evident for us, though never worked out or

otherwise than implicit in the text: the need so to restructure society's economics that one group does not exist in a state of nearly complete possession and others in almost total dependence. And indeed upon the same theme the British nation has exercised itself more impressively than most other communities, historically considered, during the past century and a half.

Terry Eagleton, writing from a Marxist point of view, offers generous appreciation of certain features of Anne Brontë in general and the present work in particular. E.g.,

> Whereas Lucy Snowe's chiding of Polly Home and Ginevra Fanshawe betrays less reputable motives than mere moral disinterestedness, Agnes Grey admonishes her obnoxious charges with a remarkable freedom from personal malice—the more remarkable because we have in this work a more direct and detailed account of the social violence to which the governess is subjected than anything we find elsewhere in the Brontës.[9]

Noting that 'Her fraught relation to her pupils . . . provides a painfully lucid image of "genteel" poverty's unwilling alliance with morally irresponsible wealth',[10] he accurately indicates *why* 'Agnes's responses are cooler, more equable than those we find in a Charlotte protagonist's truck with the gentry'; it is because here the heroine's 'own *amour-propre* is not fundamentally at stake'.

He declares also that she and the book avoid smugness. He confesses its lucidity:

> Its final line—'And now I think I have said sufficient'— neatly captures the laconic modesty of the whole, the sense of a work attractively reserved in feeling without any loss of candid revelation.[11]

Yet ultimately, he argues, 'the orthodox critical judgement that Anne Brontë's work is slighter than her sisters' is just',[12] because there is only 'one brief moment in **Agnes Grey** when Agnes, dispirited by her fruitless efforts to instil moral principle into the Murrays' spoilt brats, wonders whether her own standards of rectitude might not be insidiously eroded by daily contact with such dissoluteness.'[13] Always in her work there is a 'partial unhinging of the "moral" from a nurturing social context.'[14]

But such a complaint is more about the novel's subject-matter than its treatment thereof. For the predicament, how to be a relatively responsible moral agent and cope with inhabiting a delinquent social world, when life itself also offers plenty of frustrations, is one in which every decent reader of the book must be interested. Anne Brontë does not (*pace* Dr. Eagleton) oppose the 'social' and the 'moral': that primroses episode alone, to which I keep referring simply as a type of the whole, showed us the governess's feelings on being not recognized by society as a full human entity not only being analysed by her; they were presented (by the author which notionally she has become) as more complex, fraught and vulnerable—the tone does this, the juxtaposition of events in the passage quoted— than she herself recognized at the time. She is more pained and compromised than she admits. That is what we are made and given to see, exemplified as it is by the way a certain literariness will rub shoulders uneasily with more direct colloquial narrative: 'I presently fell back, and began to botanise and entomologise . . . '. We realize that she does not entirely know any longer how to manage her self-awareness while yet being conscious that it is perilously near to sentimental self-pity.

Her religious convictions and training preserve her however, we can see, from progressive mere self-endorsement and ultimately cranky isolation. They save her from a collapse of the self, in giving an exterior standard— the Gospels' hopes and commands—by which to keep measuring her conduct and attitudes. Faced with the lapse, pretty well, of her hope of marriage and doomed, as it appears, to a future of worthiness but boredom, she articulates this:

> Should I shrink from the work that God had set before me, because it was not fitted to my taste? Did not He know best what I should do, and where I ought to labour? and should I long to quit His service before I had finished my task, and expect to enter His rest without having laboured to earn it? (Ch. 21)

Nor is it that she strikes us, on such occasions, as some haloed goody-goody, in her commitment to the 'strait gate and narrow way': she can show the refreshing fierceness of the truly, likeably virtuous from time to time, when appropriately provoked. Writing of Mr. Robson's encouragement of his nephew Tom Bloomfield's 'propensity to persecute the lower creation, both by precept and example', we have the following:

> As he frequently came to course or shoot over his brother-in-law's grounds, he would bring his favourite dogs with him; and he treated them so brutally that, poor as I was, I would have given a sovereign any day to see one of them bite him, provided the animal could have done it with impunity. (Ch. 5)

Significantly it is when she has resigned herself, *actively,* to her lot—a worthy one as an instructress in the seminary of her own making but a fate without joy—that the break comes. *Agnes Grey* illustrates thus the Christian gloss upon Elizabeth Bowen's great dictum, 'We are constructed for full living. Occasion rarely

offers'; and E. M. Forster's apt comment in *A Passage to India,* 'Adventures do occur, but not punctually.'

'Unless the grain dies. . . .' Only when the heart has resigned its earthly hopes (especially its very dearest ones) in favour of obedience to its supreme marriagebond, its role as Bride of the Lamb, can God afford to make this-worldly happiness available to those He loves as children who *can* be saved. Until then, awarding us the felicities we ache, the reliefs we gasp for, as the central fulfilments in our lives, He is just encouraging us to dance off down a mirage-track to ultimate death beside the transitory water-holes of our own imaging.

After plenty of happy upbringing, followed by oppression and suppression, Agnes has to lose her last great hope this side of the grave—beyond that of doing her duty as a Christian—and she has to live on quite a while with that lost hope rendered seemingly permanent as lost; before its realization arrives after all.

When it does so, Prince Charming hardly sweeps her off in a glass coach at one bound, nor with brightly caparisoned chargers. Edward Weston's situation and character are perfect for the book's purposes. He is sturdy and real enough to be reassuring: no mere cardboard cut-out of a perfect cleric with extremely modest means. Yet he is intrinsically un-exciting enough to figure in the reader's lay-mind as not—like marriage to Mr. Darcy for Elizabeth Bennet in *Pride and Prejudice*—a brilliant upshot for the heroine's career, both socially and emotionally. After their re-encounter by happy chance (here Life's own helpful randomness comes in) on the sands of Agnes's new home town, it takes some time before he proposes marriage, some weeks indeed—and then the romance is very quiet. Winifred Gérin has censured the close of the novel as exposing interests uncombined, not unified, on the author's part:

> Yet it was inevitable that the dual purpose of the book should emerge; that those portions which were derived from fact should be more vividly realised and that the purely fictitious incidents should be slurred over, as inappropriate, as it were, to the fuller treatment. Thus the happy ending to which, as fiction, Anne had not the heart to deny her heroine, is written in so low and subdued a key that it saddens rather than elates the reader. Judged from the standpoint of art this is a mistake; the story of *Agnes Grey* begun in such buoyant style, with so much wit and sparkle, should not modulate into a minor key and close in solemnity since, in spite of some tribulations, the heroine's happiness is assured.[15]

But that misses the various points of which the accomplishment is here achieved. (1) The book is about the business of reconciling oneself to possible modes of happiness, not extremely unlikely ones—as well as to actual species of suffering. Were the hero handsome, witty, rich and charming, we should ignore the whole as a day-dream: for how often could portionless young governesses, gauche of manner and no brilliant beauties withal, get proposals from such as they—then or now? (2) It helps solve the aesthetic problem for most novels with a happy ending—the suggestion, artistically constituted by the very *procédé* of the plot, that life has now stopped, albeit on a plateau of fulfilments. We cannot imagine Elizabeth and Darcy living through their first married quarrel or the death of a child; rightly—we do not want to and there would be no value in the exercise. It would be a 'How many children had Lady Macbeth?' sort of question. But here it is of the essence of the piece, our well knowing that trials face the couple of the concluding scene—several of these in his pastoral life and her parish-work at Horton we have beheld already. Life carries on at the close of **Agnes Grey** and it is the real life where *'il faut cultiver son jardin'*. If the young pair do not attempt to penetrate the aristocracy nor hold themselves entirely aloof from it but keep fairly distant from certain classes' routines and blandishments with no sense of loss, it is in order to stay 'unspotted from the World' in the sense that we associate that term with 'the Flesh and the Devil'. This is no question of retreat or escapism, quite the reverse. We see two committed social workers taking up their task in the broad blaze of historical day and the middle of public highways at the end of Anne Brontë's first novel. Miss Grey's fate, far from being a sort of transcendent one, untied to the earth, like the brides' at the ends of most comedy, means happiness; but happiness in the world outside the covers of a human celebration, and amidst that world's problems.

What could be set down for a flaw is the book's failure to convey the lovers' feelings for each other, or at least its heroine's for its hero, from the inside in their full 'romantic' aspect. This is a *manque* writ larger in **The Tenant of Wildfell Hall.** In both works we know that the characters have powerful amorous inclinations towards each other: but as a Briton and an Australian are well aware that their respective countries exist on opposite shores of the globe without appreciating those terrains in their reality until they have paid a visit the one to the other. When not only Helen Graham's response to Arthur Huntingdon, in the early time of their acquaintance, is mediated to us *sans* its full alleged erotic colouring and necessary emotional intensity, but also Huntingdon's later for Annabella Lowborough and, here, Agnes Grey's for Edward Weston, we are likely to suspect that some sort of psychological inhibition was operative in this author—perhaps an excess of delicacy. But we must also appreciate that conveying passion is no facile undertaking, artistically considered. Henry James was surely a born novelist if ever there has been one, and his pages throb with the sexual interest woken by men and women in each other: *The Awkward Age* seems to me white hot, like poor Nanda Brookenham's face there, with the passion of her feel-

ing for Vanderbank. But it is not till as late in his career as *The Golden Bowl* (1905) that James can make his characters convincingly embrace, and had he died at the same early age as Anne Brontë (he would have been 29 years and 4 months old in August 1872) what would he have left to show of *his* excellent craftsmanship, his true novelistic gift and inspiration? Well, one novel *Watch and Ward* (1869); nineteen tales, up to 'Guest's Confession'; and some substantial travel and critical writings—but no such masterwork as *A Portrait of a Lady.*

While this is a flaw in **The Tenant** and a serious one, we may even vindicate it in **Agnes Grey,** the unsubstantiated *inner* life of the lovers' feelings for each other; since throughout the whole, Weston is seen, necessarily for the novel's effect, *ab exteriori* (being registered through the anxious uncertain eyes of the governess), and the tale concludes with the relief of her emotions in his proposal, a rescue and fulfilment about which it would be tasteless in her to brag.

That their religious commitment has its own dangers Anne Brontë is also concerned to illustrate. In the case of old Nancy Brown (Ch. 11, 'The Cottagers') she shows the religious melancholy infused into nineteenth-century life in consequence of the Evangelical Movement and its reanimation of a living Church in her society. This elderly widow is harrowed by the very creed which ought to comfort her:

> ' . . . th' prayer-book only served to show me how wicked I was, that I could read such good words an' never be no better for it, and oftens feel it a sore labour an' a heavy task beside, instead of a blessing and a privilege as all good Christians does. It seemed like as all were barren an' dark to me. And then, them dreadful words, "Many shall seek to enter in, and shall not be able." They like as they fair dried up my sperrit.'

With this instance Anne Brontë is not only working out a major quarrel with herself—there is little evidence to contradict the view of both her sister Charlotte and her biographer that it was in battling against religious melancholy that most of her own brief life was spent—she is 'being fair' as a creative spirit and implying, with exemplary equity, how the very philosophy she commends to society carries, like any doctrine which is a reading of History and an ethos, its own pitfalls too:

> ' . . . I tried to do my duty as aforetime: but I like got no peace. An' I even took the sacrament; but I felt as though I were eating and drinking to my own damnation all th' time. So I went home, sorely troubled.'

As well as the moral strengthening and psychic power, for the individual and the community, deriving from Christian conviction, there will be casualties who need aid.

Aid may come in the form of direct sensible and perceptive pastoral counsel. Mr Weston the new curate points out that we love by practice; in acting out a pretence of the Saviour's commands, our habits become reality, the Beast behind the beautiful mask becomes a Beauty.

> 'But if you cannot feel positive affection for those who do not care for you, you can at least try to do to them as you would they should do unto you: you can endeavour to pity their failings and excuse their offences, and to do all the good you can to those about you. And if you accustom yourself to this, Nancy, the very effort itself will make you love them in some degree—to say nothing of the goodwill your kindness would beget in them, though they might have little else that is good about them. . . .' (Ch. 11)

Divine counsel will also be available, advice not made with hands or uttered by human voices—in the grandeur, the elevating loveliness of Nature. A kind of *basso ostinato* runs through this book as through all of Anne Brontë's work, a first-hand experience of Nature as restorative, invigorating, a spiritual sanctuary and very present help in trouble. Again and again the heroine is struck by some prospect or deliberately goes to feed upon some part of the physical environment which encompasses mere men, finding there new strength and fresh comfort.

> And then, the unspeakable purity and freshness of the air! there was just enough heat to enhance the value of the breeze, and just enough wind to keep the whole sea in motion, to make the waves come bounding to the shore, foaming and sparkling, as if wild with glee. Nothing else was stirring—no living creature was visible besides myself. My footsteps were the first to press the firm, unbroken sands;—nothing before had trampled them since last night's flowing tide had obliterated the deepest marks of yesterday, and left it fair and even, except where the subsiding water had left behind it the traces of dimpled pools, and little running streams. (Ch. 24)

Hence the appositeness of her meeting Weston again, after thinking perpetually to have lost him, upon these sands of 'A-'. She has come to drink once more at the only fount where such perceptions and thirsts as (say) Wordsworth's could be slaked; and in doing so for its own sake has had everything else she cares for added unto her.

Which makes another point. Good Chance also exists. That too is part of God's Creation, the reality with which we humans have to come to terms. Weston may well be suspected of having accepted a living near 'A-' in the hope of one day running into his heart's best find. He

has helped, if we will, give Luck a nudge, even a hearty one. But now he and his bride-to-be have been assisted by the randomness of things as well as hindered, in the past, by their cruelty: here it has expressed itself in his being offered such a living as 'F-', 'a village about two miles distant', in the first place; and in the second, their re-encountering as they do.

Nevertheless there *is* an aspect in which the story is consummated with a sense of anti-climax. Miss Gérin has the right idea by the wrong end. Similarly to Colonel Brandon in *Sense and Sensibility,* though with rather more individualized character, Agnes Grey's lover constitutes no thrilling human presence; and we wish wistfully that he did.

But then by what right should he? Like most of us, the governess herself, considered whether physically or morally, socially or intellectually, is not the catch of catches. Yet she has a passionate yearning heart and the instinctual wisdom to fix upon what it can elevate to absolute value *by its very devotion.* Thus much we deduce, I think, across the trajectory of her rhetoric. For as Metropolitan Anthony Bloom once pointed out,[16] it is the character of Love to make significant what is even of itself trivial. And Weston is far more than that.

It is questionable all the same whether Agnes could so elevate a man like Mr. Hatfield, Horton's worldly vicar, or some member of Rosalie Murray's set of squirearchical-aristocratic admirers, even if she were noticed by them. They lack a dimension of conscience and feeling necessary to give those responses which can make Love a prosperous horticulturist. Her marriage with the former curate however can *become* something great (we again intuit), though he is not the most exciting individual since Sir Philip Sidney. She has herself planted half the garden her devotion will raise in the soil of this man's worthiness, somewhat stolid as it is. But that won't make its fruits and blooms any less real or precious than they already promise to be.

All this shows as mattering the more in the context of a novel which has illustrated only too vividly through most of its course what people are like when morally untutored by either precept of suffering.

The subject-matter and style of this book are of the first importance—in their very quietness. In a sense Anne Brontë's relegation is the final proof of her success. Her compact but richly realized fable about what life is like and how to live works so totally, it is eclipsed by fierier rockets of illumination that throw a more fitful glare upon the scene. *Agnes Grey* is full of the way in which people have to make ends meet—financially, psychologically—in the real world; and Life's own creative play there as well.

Notes

[1] Op. cit., Fontana edition (London, 1967), p. 26.

[2] *The Screwtape Letters* (London, 1942), pp. 128-29.

[3] *High Windows* (London, 1974), p. 30.

[4] In *Jane Austen's Achievement,* ed. Juliet McMaster (London, 1976), pp. 121-22.

[5] 'By the time she wrote [*The Professor*] her taste and judgment had revolted against the exaggerated idealisms of her early girlhood, and she went to the extreme of reality, closely depicting characters as they had shown themselves to her in actual life: if there they were strong even to coarseness—as was the case with some that she had met with in flesh-and-blood existence—she "wrote them down an ass;" if the scenery of such life as she saw was for the most part wild and grotesque, instead of pleasant or picturesque, she described it line for line. The grace of the one or two scenes and characters which are drawn rather from her own imagination than from absolute fact, stand out in exquisite relief from the deep shadows and wayward lines of others, which call to mind some of the portraits of Rembrandt.'—Mrs. Gaskell's *Life* (ed. Ward & Shorter), p. 313.

[6] E. M. Forster, *Maurice* (London, 1971): quoted in P. N. Furbank's Introduction, letter to G. L. Dickinson of 13 December 1914.

[7] *Abinger Harvest* (pocket edn., London 1940), from 1932 review of Jane Austen's Letters, p. 158.

[8] *A Grief Observed* (London, 1961), section II, para. 1.

[9] Terry Eagleton, *Myths of Power: A Marxist Study of the Brontës* (London, 1975), p. 123.

[10] Ibid., p. 124. The quote immediately following in my text is from this page also.

[11] Ibid., p. 126.

[12] Ibid., p. 134.

[13] Ibid., p. 123.

[14] Ibid., p. 132.

[15] W. Gérin, *Anne Brontë* (London [1959]; rev. edn., 1976), p. 230.

[16] At a religious meeting-and-discussion session in York University, *circa* 1978.

Priscilla H. Costello (essay date 1987)

SOURCE: "A New Reading of Anne Brontë's *Agnes Grey,*" in *Brontë Society Transactions,* Vol. 19, No. 3, 1987, pp. 113-8.

[*In the following essay, Costello recounts the plot of* Agnes Grey *and examines the novel as one that "criticizes the corruption of moral and ethical values" in Victorian society.*]

Anne Brontë's first novel, **Agnes Grey,** published in 1847, is ordinarily either ignored by literary critics or treated summarily as a charming though not too serious endeavour. It is an apparently simple story of a parson's daughter who endures the trials of a governess, and eventually marries the young minister she loves. Underneath this simplicity, however, is not only a realistic and unmelodramatic account of the life of a governess, but also a study of Victorian values. Through a portrayal of five different families, Anne Brontë gives us a microcosm of Victorian society, with five class levels. Through her analysis of these families, she criticizes the corruption of moral and ethical values in a society that is becoming increasingly materialistic.

Brontë's heroine, Agnes Grey, follows a particular pattern of development: she moves from the security of her family through an increasing sense of alienation as governess to a resolution in her attachment to Mr Weston and the establishment of a family of her own. We meet her first at home, a parsonage in the north of England. The description of her family life is typical of that of the country parsonage. A close and loving family, they lead a fairly insular life. Although the Reverend Richard Grey, the minister of the village and moorland parish, "was deservedly respected by all who knew him',[1] they kept much to themselves. As Agnes writes:

> Our only intercourse with the world consisted in a stately tea-party, now and then, with the principal farmers and tradespeople of the vicinity (just to avoid being stigmatised as too proud to consort with our neighbours), and an annual visit to our paternal grandfather's (p. 394).

Financial necessity, however, forces both daughters to earn a living: Mary, the elder, paints and sells her pictures; Agnes decides to go out as a governess. Despite the family's protests, voiced in Mary's plea, "What would you do in a house full of strangers?" (p. 399), Agnes leaves for a post in a wealthy tradesman's house. Her feelings upon leaving her home and village are movingly portrayed.

As the story follows Agnes through two different posts as governess, and then as a visitor in the home of one of her former charges, we see her growing alienation from real inclusion in family life. As a governess she of course occupies an ambiguous position, regarded as neither servant nor family member, so although living in a home with a family, Anne is an outsider, within it.

Naïvely thinking that her first employer, Mrs Bloomfield, will be "a kind, motherly woman" (p. 403), she is met by the cold, distant and formal mistress of Wellwood House. At least here Agnes is greeted by her employer, who shows her to her room, gives her lunch, and introduces her to the children she will be in charge of. In her next post she does not meet Mrs Murray until the second day; when she first arrives, she is casually led to the schoolroom by the butler, and then up to her room with only tea and bread as her solitary meal. Here she feels even more lonely and desolate than at Wellwood House.

The Bloomfield children are little horrors, and Agnes is trapped in the impossible position characteristic of her post, being responsible for their education and behaviour, but forbidden to discipline them. She is, in fact, at the mercy of the children whom she had dreamed of tenderly guiding and nurturing when she was at home in the parsonage.

At Wellwood, Agnes is an integral part of the family's routine, if not the recipient of their affection and regard. The Bloomfield family and the governess eat their midday meal together. Agnes is constantly with the children, even sharing a bedroom with the little girl, Mary Ann, and various adults periodically visit the schoolroom. Yet she has the esteem of none: the children scorn and tease her, the adults disdainfully discuss her behind her back.

Dismissed from her post (ironically for not being sufficiently firm with the children), Agnes leaves Wellwood for the parsonage, thinking that what she has learned from this experience is "to love and value my home" (p. 431). At the personage, however, she realizes that the necessity of earning her own living is even greater because of her father's ill health and his anxiety for his daughters' futures.

At her second post at Horton Lodge, not only is her entrance or welcome into the Murray family less formal or planned, but here she is less frequently included in family routines. She has all her meals in the schoolroom with her pupils. She sees Mrs Murray only occasionally, and Mr Murray more rarely and then only if they accidentally meet in the hall, or in the grounds of the estate. Although she is supposed to teach all four children, the boys soon go away to school, while the girls spend little time over their studies, deciding on their daily activities without consulting their governess. Agnes' duties are therefore even less essential than at the Bloomfields, and she becomes little more than a companion or chaperone. Here, too, she is held in little

esteem by parents, children and servants alike, although the elder girl, Rosalie, begins to like her as time goes on.

Agnes leaves Horton Lodge, not because she is dismissed, but because her home and family has broken up. Her sister Mary has married and her father has died, and now Agnes and her mother plan to start a school together. This, however, necessitates leaving the parsonage, home to Agnes all her life, which grieves her; she must also say goodbye to the Reverend Edward Weston, with whom she has fallen in love.

Now the novel's plot begins to turn in a more positive direction as Agnes rejoins her mother in their new "abode"; but before its final resolution, she again experiences being an outsider within a strange family: she is invited by her former pupil, Rosalie Murray, to visit Ashby Park where she stays as a guest for several days. Despite the friendly greeting from Rosalie, who professes affection and friendship, Agnes not only has no role to fulfil as she did as a governess, but spends most of the day completely alone and completely removed from such little family activity as goes on among Lord and Lady Ashby, their baby, and old Lady Ashby. She leaves for home: "finding I could render myself so little serviceable, my residence at Ashby Park became doubly painful" (p. 538).

At this point she is reunited with Edward Weston and becomes his wife. Her mother, Mrs Alice Grey, insists on continuing to live on her own to run the school, but she will spend her vacations alternately with each daughter, thus becoming the one who unites the two families.

Agnes Grey's story not only illustrates a pattern of movement from alienation to attachment, but it provides a framework for Anne Brontë's more serious criticism of society.

Each family Agnes stays with is both increasingly materialistic and less a family, in Brontë's sense of the word. Each progressively demonstrates the corruption of moral and ethical values, and of the family virtues of love, harmony and cohesiveness. As Agnes moves from the parsonage, to Wellwood House (the "new but stately mansion" of the Bloomfields), to Horton Lodge (the large house and estate of Squire Murray), to Ashby Hall (the elegant mansion and park of Lord Ashby), each marriage becomes more socially prominent and "approved", but at the same time more false and unhappy. Agnes' marriage to the Reverend Edward Weston at the end of the novel reaffirms the moral and family values established initially in the picture of the Grey family.

Life at the parsonage demonstrates the importance of family and moral values over materialistic ones. All work together closely, in harmony, and the Grey marriage is a happy one based on love. Mrs Grey, a squire's daughter, had given up her luxurious life and inheritance to marry a poor country parson, but Agnes says "she would rather live in a cottage with Richard Grey than in a palace with any other man in the world" (p. 393). However, even here the growing materialism of Victorian society leaves its mark: Richard Grey has difficulty accepting the fact that his wife is truly happy in the simple parsonage, and wants to supplement the income from his incumbency and small property. A failed business venture undermines both his finances and his self-confidence, and his mental depression leads to physical illness. Anne Brontë, with acute psychological insight, writes that "the cheerfulness with which she [Alice Grey] bore her reverses, and the kindness which withheld her from imputing the smallest blame to him, were all perverted by this ingenious self-tormenter into further aggravations of his sufferings" (p. 397). The minister's illness and his retreat into depression forces the women in the family to think of various ways to survive, and Mrs Grey proves to be the stronger partner in this marriage through her ability to grapple with reality and through her skill in financial and household management.

When Agnes takes her place as governess in the Bloomfield family, she is going a step up in the social scale, for Mr Bloomfield is "a retired tradesman who had realized a very comfortable fortune" (p. 401). However, he offers Agnes only a meagre salary, and his general attitude toward her and toward his servants is one of rude contempt, characteristic of the *nouveau riche* whose ill treatment of their social inferiors seems necessary to bolster their own self-esteem.

Certainly the Bloomfield family as a whole, and each of its members, is despicable. Despite the appearance of the newly built but stately mansion with its formal gardens, the family life within is discordant and corrupt. The marriage, though formally correct, seems quite loveless; at one point Agnes is an embarrassed witness to a sarcastic argument they have over the dinner menu. The children are unruly and untaught; adored by their mother, who views them as angels, they are actually ill-tempered, deceitful, and nasty. Furthermore, they are encouraged in their cruel treatment of helpless animals, particularly by their father and uncle, both whom are pictured as coarse, vulgar and arrogant men who drink to excess. Uncle Robson is also encouraging of the worst sexist extremes, teaching Mary Ann to value personal appearance and flattery, and young Tom to drink and swear.

Agnes despairs of being able to teach these children anything because they lack any moral sense: "They knew no shame; they scorned authority which had no terrors to back it; and as for kindness and affection,

either they had no hearts, or such as they had were so strongly guarded, and so well concealed, that I, with all my efforts, had not yet discovered how to reach them" (p. 430). Agnes leaves Wellwood House hoping "that all parents were not like Mr and Mrs Bloomfield" and "certain all children were not like theirs. The next family must be different . . ." (p. 431).

The next family is another step up: Mr Murray of Horton Lodge is a country squire. Mrs Grey believes this higher social position will prove more suitable for her daughter, for she affirms, "Such are far more likely to treat you with proper respect and consideration than those purse proud trandespeople and arrogant upstarts" (p. 434).

The Murrays, however, live very un-family-centered lives: Mr Murray spends much of his time fox hunting and riding, while his wife goes to parties and dresses in fashion. They seem to care little for Agnes' teaching qualifications in "Music, singing, drawing, French, Latin and German" (p. 434). The boys are soon sent off to school, while the girls are to be prepared simply to take their prescribed place in upper class society.

The real corruption of values in this family is most evident in the fostering of the marriage of the eldest daughter, Rosalie, to Sir Thomas Ashby. Rosalie has been taught to value in marriage not love, respect and honesty, but status and money. Even though Sir Thomas is known to be dissipated and corrupt, his wife will become Lady Ashby of Ashby Park, and that is the prime goal of Rosalie and her mother. Mrs Murray is willing to sacrifice her daughter's happiness for status.

This materialism motivates all of their behaviour, and Rosalie's efforts are geared toward captivating potential suitors and eclipsing all others with her beauty and elegant appearance. The whole family goes to church every Sunday, the girls often twice, not for spiritual edification, but to be seen and admired. Even the few charitable acts by Rosalie and Matilda were performed largely for the "flattering homage" (p. 459) they received, or to appear to others to be concerned and charitable.

A steady contrast to both the Bloomfields and Murrays is the figure of Agnes Grey; she tries unsuccessfully to replace her charges' materialistic values with the values she had been taught at home, those of truthfulness, piety and compassion. These values lead her to two poor families, both cottagers near Horton Lodge, where, since affluence is not even within the realm of imagined possibility, the virtues of piety and simplicity have flourished. Agnes visits the family of Mark Wood (who is dying of consumption), and also the widow Nancy Brown, who keeps house for her fieldworker son. While reading the Bible to Nancy, Agnes comes to know the curate, Edward Weston better: his kindness, "strong sense . . . and ardent piety" (p. 471) reaffirms her faith in human goodness and strikes a common chord in her own heart.

It is when Agnes Grey visits the most socially prestigious home, Ashby Park, that she finds the most unhappy marriage and most disrupted family life. There are four family members under the one roof (Sir Thomas and Lady Ashby [Rosalie Murray], their infant daughter, and old Lady Ashby), each of whom lives an existence separate from the others, meeting only occasionally for formal, strained meals. Rosalie's marriage progresses beyond indifference or lovelessness to actual hatred; she tells Agnes when they see Sir Thomas riding through the estate, "I detest that man!" (p. 536). Rosalie has discovered that being Lady Ashby does not compensate for marriage to a gambler, drunkard and womanizer. Furthermore, she hates her mother-in-law who, she says, is "a tyrant, an incubus, a spy" (p. 533), and cannot bring herself to love even her baby, whom Sir Thomas had already rejected because it is a girl. Rosalie complains, "what pleasure can I have in seeing a girl grow up to eclipse me . . ." (p. 537) and adds, "I can't centre all my hopes in a child: that is only one degree better than devoting oneself to a dog" (p. 538). Rosalie's values have been so corrupted that Agnes fears she will not be able to find any comfort or happiness in life. Ashby Park, such a primary marriage goal for Rosalie and her mother, has become for its mistress a desolate prison.

The distinction that Anne Brontë makes between a house and a home is clarified in a conversation between Edward Weston and Agnes. They affirm that a home is not merely a place one lives in, but a repository of affection and domestic enjoyment. Edward and Agnes share not only this definition, but the moral and ethical values that bring them together.

It is obviously relevant and interesting that the type of family in this novel that epitomizes the ideal character of family life is that of the country parson, the type in which Anne Brontë herself lived in Haworth. In the novel it is illustrated in the home of the Reverend Richard and Alice Grey, in that of Mary and the Reverend Mr Richardson (whose forthcoming marriage Agnes describes to her pupil, Rosalie), and, finally, in that of Edward and Agnes. These are all marriages based on love whose family values derive from moral ones. Agnes recalls the moment when she and Edward pledged their troth:

> I shall never forget that glorious summer evening, and always remember with delight that steep hill, and the edge of the precipice where we stood together, watching the splendid sunset mirrored in the restless world of waters at our feet—with hearts filled with gratitude to Heaven, and happiness, and love—" (p. 547).

My analysis of *Agnes Grey* is derived from a larger study I have done of the Brontës which reveals that the family was the dominant social structure and emotional force in their lives and that family is the thematic and structural core in all seven of the sisters' novels[2]. Though varied in subject and approach, each novel posits a similar pattern of development for its protagonist. Agnes Grey is characteristic of the heroine/hero whose family connection is already disrupted or fragmented at the outset, or soon becomes so; a heroine/hero who grows increasingly alienated from society/life, an alienation expressed through lack of inclusion within a family; who gradually rejoins society through attachment to another or others, culminating in full participation in a family of her/his own.

Agnes' movement toward love-attachment is handled largely within the Victorian social norm, but even within this conservatism emerges the Brontës' didactic use of the family to reform society: in *Agnes Grey,* as in the six other Brontë novels, family is used to identify the deterioration of society's values. The corruption of moral values by a growing materialism is seen in the distortion of family values and affection.

Therefore, viewing *Agnes Grey* within this larger framework, Anne Brontë's early novel assumes a new significance as both a social statement and as a deliberately structured work of art.

Notes

[1] *Agnes Grey* (1847; reprint in *The Tenant of Wildfell Hall* and *Agnes Grey,* London: J. M. Dent, New York: E. P. Dutton, 1922), p. 393. All page references in parentheses within the text refer to this 1922 edition.

[2] For a full discussion of the importance of family to the Brontës, consult my PhD dissertation, *The Parson's Daughters: The Family Worlds of Charlotte, Emily and Anne Brontë,* 1983, The Union for Experimenting Colleges and Universities, USA.

Elizabeth Langland (essay date 1989)

SOURCE: "*Agnes Grey:* 'all true histories contain instruction,'" in *Anne Brontë: The Other One,* Macmillan, 1989, pp. 96-117.

[*In the following essay, Langland characterizes* Anges Grey *as a novel of female development "that both draws from a tradition of other such novels and departs significantly from it."*]

Agnes Grey tells a story of female development. What makes it distinctive from previous novels by women with female protagonists is that Agnes more closely follows a male pattern of development. The classic starting point for the male *Bildungsroman,* or novel of development, is the protagonist's dissatisfaction with home and a corollary desire to gain experience in the larger world. While Agnes cannot simply take to the open road like a male hero, she nonetheless longs 'to see a little more of the world' (*AG* [*Agnes Grey,* Everyman's Library (London and Melbourne, Dent, 1958)] 4). She resists being kept the '*child* and the pet of the family . . . too helpless and dependent—too unfit for buffeting with the cares and turmoils of life' (*AG* 4). She wants 'To go out into the world; to enter upon a new life; to act for myself; to exercise my unused faculties; to try my unknown powers; to earn my own maintenance . . .' (*AG* 10). Anne's sounding of these aims heralds the arrival of a heroine new to fiction, one to whom, as we have seen, Charlotte owes a major debt. Jane Eyre's famous call for general equality has some of Agnes Grey in it: 'Women are supposed to be very calm generally: but women feel just as men feel; they need exercise for their faculites and a field for their efforts as much as their brothers do'.[1] But where Jane Eyre quickly finds her restlessness appeased by the arrival of Rochester, Agnes actually seeks that field for her efforts and exercise for her faculites.

The novel apparently had its origins in Anne Brontë's own experiences as governess first with the Inghams of Blake Hall and then with the Robinsons of Thorp Green. When Anne returned to Thorp Green in the new year of 1842, she began a story called 'Passages in the Life of an Individual'.[2] This work details her own experiences in her two posts and may or may not be a source for her first novel. But even if Anne mined her personal experiences for *Agnes Grey,* we should not confuse Agnes with Anne or neglect to appreciate the high level of artistic shaping present in the published novel. Three years and increasing literary sophistication wrought their effects. Too often, *Agnes Grey* has been read primarily to learn about Anne. Our goal here is to read it as the exquisite novel that George Moore praised in *Conversations in Ebury Street.*

I

Agnes Grey is foremost a novel dealing with education; it is a novel *of* education (Agnes's) and *about* education (her attempts as governess to educate her charges) whose goal is to bring about an education in the reader. Thus, Brontë opens her novel with the claim: 'All true histories contain instruction' (*AG* 3). There is, as a result, a constantly informing reciprocity of subject and form. For even as Agnes makes only slight gains with her recalcitrant students, she is continually taking home the lessons to herself, learning from the experience, and emerging more fully and forcibly as a self-determining individual. And in the process of displaying her own education, she brings the reader new knowledge.

Because Agnes is a female protagonist seeking to become educated and knowledgeable about the world, she is distinctive in the nineteenth-century novel. Although Anne Brontë seems to have been largely oblivious of any feminist or ideological agenda, her commitment to women's activity and influence in the world and her suspicion of men as providers led her to promulgate a feminist thesis: that women must look to their self-provision. Indeed, if *Agnes Grey* takes any stance, it is that the novel should both entertain and instruct, combine the *dulce* with the *utile.* This attitude, as we have seen, she learned from the eighteenth-century masters. Yet even as Anne Brontë intends that her novel should instruct, she rigorously insists that the only valid instruction comes from an unswerving commitment to the representation of 'truth'. Because all meaning derives from her representing reality as she saw it, her work remains strongly novelistic and does not become didactic. Anne Brontë focuses, then, on representing as fully as possible the quotidian details of Agnes Grey's employment as governess, and she lets any instruction emerge from that representation.

Agnes's progression from the Bloomfields' to the Murrays', from young charges between the ages of four and seven, to charges between the ages of fourteen and seventeen, marks her own self-progress and shapes the reader's developing understanding. When she arrives at the Bloomfields', Agnes is but a child herself, as she admits, having been spoiled and pampered by her family. But Agnes is naive only in experience; in principles and understanding she is mature. This maturity makes even more dramatic the disparity between the 'pampered' and 'indulged' Agnes and the pampered and indulged Bloomfields. Basically, Agnes has been indulged only in being overly protected. In contrast, the Bloomfield children are fairly sophisticated in the ways of the world and have even learned to manipulate their world quite cleverly. The indulgence they have been allowed in the unbridled exercise of their passions, has resulted in an early corruption of their principles.

It is immediately clear to the reader that, in this contest between governess and pupils, the pupils will quickly gain the upper hand precisely because they have neither internal nor external bridles while Agnes knows both the self-restraint taught her by her principles and the external restraints imposed on her as the Bloomfields' 'servant'. Let us address the latter point first. Agnes is clearly instructed that she is not to punish the children. She recognises immediately that 'I had no rewards to offer; and as for punishments, I was given to understand, the parents reserved that privilege themselves; and yet they expected me to keep my pupils in order. Other children might be guided by the fear of anger, and the desire of approbation; but neither the one nor the other had any effect upon these' (*AG* 22). In an eloquent passage, Agnes sets out the plight of the governess:

> I returned, however, with unabated vigour to my work—a more arduous task than any one can imagine, who has not felt something like the misery of being charged with the care and direction of a set of mischievous turbulent rebels, whom his utmost exertions cannot bind to their duty; while, at the same time, he is responsible for their conduct to a higher power, who exacts from him what cannot be achieved without the aid of the superior's more potent authority: which, either from indolence, or the fear of becoming unpopular with the said rebellious gang, the latter refuses to give. I can conceive few situations more harassing than that wherein, however you may long for success, however you may labour to fulfil your duty, your efforts are baffled and set at nought by those beneath you, and unjustly censured and misjudged by those above. (*AG* 29)

Through Agnes Grey, Anne Brontë has pinpointed what makes the situation of the governess intolerable: entire responsibility for those she cannot bend to her will.

This situation becomes the condition for Agnes's achievement and our evaluation of that achievement. Agnes will serve in two posts, the first of which will challenge her physically, the other spiritually. In both posts, huge demands will be made on her energies, yet she will be given little authority to fulfill those demands. Her success will be measured by her imaginative and flexible adjustment to the limitations imposed on her.

A schoolmistress, in contrast to a governess, has remarkable freedoms. When Agnes joins her mother to open a school, she remarks the difference between the life of a schoolmistress and the life of a governess:

> I set myself with befitting energy to discharge the duties of this new mode of life. I call it *new,* for there was, indeed a considerable difference between working with my mother in a school of our own, and working as a hireling among strangers, despised and trampled upon by old and young. (*AG* 134)

It is interesting to compare Anne's representations of the governess's life with Charlotte's. Charlotte never succeeded in her posts as governess in a private home, yet, surprisingly, her novels fail to represent the difficulties and humiliations in that position. In *Jane Eyre,* the eponymous heroine finds herself in charge of a docile, if vain, child and in the presence of a motherly housekeeper. The task of teaching her charge scarcely consumes her time, and she has huge tracts

of leisure for dalliance with Rochester. It is a highly romanticised portrait of the governess's life.

Agnes Grey, in contrast, finds her job as governess endless and exhausting. She rarely sees her employer, Mr Bloomfield, and he speaks to her only when exasperated with her failure to control the children. She must do continual battle with recalcitrant and tyrannical pupils. The young master of the family, Tom, amuses himself by 'pulling off [the] legs and wings, and heads of young sparrows' (*AG* 18). To prevent another such episode of torture, Agnes herself drops a heavy stone and crushes a nest of fledglings that Tom has secured. When thwarted in his pleasures, he becomes violent and frenzied and Agnes's 'only resource was to throw him on his back, and hold his hands and feet till the frenzy was somewhat abated' (*AG* 22). Mary Ann, the oldest daughter, alternates between rolling on the floor in passive obstinacy or emitting 'shrill, piercing screams, that went through [Agnes's] head like a knife' (*AG* 25). When the younger Fanny joins her siblings, Agnes finds herself now with a creature of 'falsehood and deception, young as she was, and alarmingly fond of exercising her two favourite weapons of offence and defence; that of spitting in the faces of those who incurred her displeasure, and bellowing like a bull when her unreasonable desires were not gratified' (*AG* 27).

Despite her early recognition that her situation is untenable, Agnes has no choice but to behave as if she is dealing with students as susceptible as herself. As a result she is continually forced to confess her own failure: 'With me, at her age, or under, neglect and disgrace were the most dreadful of punishments; but on her they made no impression' (*AG* 25). Her early admission to Mrs Bloomfield that 'I am sorry to say, they [the pupils] have quite deteriorated of late' (*AG* 27) sets the stage for her dismissal after only six months, a dismissal which her mistress attributes to a 'want of sufficient firmness, and diligent, persevering care on [Agnes's] part' (*AG* 41).

Her second position, with the Murrays at Horton Lodge, secures her older pupils, less physically demanding but more intellectually demanding. Agnes never loses this position, but the threat of an arbitrary dismissal always hangs over her. Mrs Murray seems to echo Mrs Bloomfield in chastising Agnes: 'I have no desire to part with you, as I am sure you would do very well if you will only think of these things and try to exert yourself a *little* more: then, I am convinced, you would *soon* acquire that delicate tact which alone is wanting to give you a proper influence over the mind of your pupil' (*AG* 122). We have moved from 'sufficient firmness . . . and persevering care' to 'delicate tact'.

On one level, nothing has changed: Agnes is still expected to compensate for the parents' unacknowledged deficiencies in childrearing. On another level, there are substantial changes: something much more subtle is now demanded of Agnes.

If the Bloomfields initiate her education, acquaintance with the Murrays refines it. She begins with four pupils, but the two boys are quickly dispatched to school. Rosalie, sixteen years, and Matilda, fourteen years, remain, and to these, Agnes is sufficiently close in age that she might seem a sister rather than a governess. Nevertheless, there is never any confusion on that score, because of both rank and character. Agnes's inferiority in the former and her superiority in the latter keep her from intimacy with the Murray sisters. Yet it is important to note that Agnes's superiority of character helps breach the social distance. Agnes remarks of Rosalie, 'And yet, upon the whole, I believe she respected me more than she herself was aware of; because I was the only person in the house who steadily professed good principles, habitually spoke the truth, and generally endeavoured to make inclination bow to duty . . .' (*AG* 52). Rosalie is possessed of a good temper, 'but from constant indulgence and habitual scorn of reason, she was often testy and capricious; her mind had never been cultivated' (*AG* 52). Matilda has high animal spirits—'full of life, vigour, and activity'—but 'as an intelligent being, she was barbarously ignorant, indocile, careless, and irrational' (*AG* 54).

As at the Bloomfields, Agnes is severely limited in her authority. She is immediately instructed by Mrs Murray that 'when any of the young people do anything improper, if persuasion and gentle remonstrance will not do, let one of the others come and tell me; for I can speak to them more plainly than it would be proper for you to do' (*AG* 51).

Whereas the Bloomfields needed simple discipline before instruction could begin, the Murrays are sufficiently mature to have acquired some outward restraint and a concern for social reputation. Thus, Agnes can focus on much more subtle points of principle. She observes the sisters' want of discretion, of discrimination, of judgment, of compassion, of generosity. She delineates with precision their rage for attention that leads them to appropriate and use other people for their own amusement. Rosalie and Matilda condescend to the cottagers, treating them as 'stupid and brutish', yet expect the people to 'adore them as angels of light, condescending to minister to their necessities, and enlighten their humble dwellings' (*AG* 70). Rosalie encourages Mr Hatfield in a flirtation to entertain herself and to have the pleasure of disappointing him. Although engaged to Thomas Ashby, she seeks to snare Mr Weston in her nets before the engagement is publicly announced. Rosalie knows of Ashby's reputation as a reprobate, yet lacks the understanding to have concern for her own future with him. Throughout all, Agnes is anticipating, discrimi-

nating, and judging, learning the value of sound principles, individual integrity, and personal independence.

Although Agnes does not confront active and intentional evil at the Murrays, she finds herself grappling with a more insidious because more subtle and pervasive evil stemming from a confusion of right and wrong. Work at the Bloomfields was physically strenuous; work at the Murrays is morally strenuous. Agnes reveals to the reader that:

> Already I seemed to feel my intellect deteriorating, my heart petrifying, my soul contracting; and I trembled lest my very moral perceptions should become deadened, my distinctions of right and wrong confounded, and all my better faculties be sunk, at last, beneath the baneful influence of such a mode of life. (*AG* 80)

This corruption of innocence by the 'baneful influence of such a mode of life' will become a central theme in *The Tenant of Wildfell Hall.* Here, the fear is sounded only at the moment that it is removed: 'Mr Weston rose at length upon me, appearing like the morning-star in my horizon, to save me from the fear of utter darkness' (*AG* 80). In addition, Agnes does not fall prey to the corruption because she imprints her character on the Murray sisters more than they influence her. She recognises at one point that they 'became a little less insolent, and began to show some symptoms of esteem' (*AG* 58).

Agnes herself gives us the full measure of her achievement by parroting her pupils' own evaluation of her. Because Brontë filters the Murray sisters' changes of opinion through Agnes's more generous and discriminating sensibility, we are able to appreciate two key things: (1) the respect Agnes has genuinely earned; and (2) Agnes's subtle and ironic understanding of the limits of that respect. Agnes summarises her influence in this way:

> Miss Grey was a queer creature: she never flattered, and did not praise them half enough; but whenever she did speak favourably of them, or anything belonging to them, they could be quite sure her approbation was sincere. She was very obliging, quiet, and peaceable in the main, but there were some things that put her out of temper: they did not much care for that, to be sure, but still it was better to keep her in tune; as when she was in a good humour she would talk to them, and be very agreeable and amusing sometimes, in her way; which was quite different to mamma's, but still very well for a change. She had her own opinions on every subject, and kept steadily to them—very tiresome opinions they often were; as she was always thinking of what was right and what was wrong, and had a strange reverence for matters connected with religion, and an unaccountable liking for good people. (*AG* 58-59)

It is a measure of Agnes's own successful education that she has succeeded to the degree she has, especially in view of the limitations put on her powers.

If Agnes is often severely crippled in her efforts to teach her students by the restraints imposed by the Bloomfields and Murrays, she is, in key ways, enabled in these situations by her own self-restraints. She does not complain or lament or indulge in self-pity. She can see beyond the particular situation to her larger goals, and she 'longed to show my friends that, even now, I was competent to undertake the charge and able to acquit myself honourably to the end' (*AG* 28). Although we may find aspects of Agnes's self-suppression excessive—she says, for example, 'I judged it my wisest plan to subdue every resentful impulse, suppress every sensitive shrinking' (*AG* 28-29) or 'I sometimes felt myself degraded by the life I led, and ashamed of submitting to so many indignities' (*AG* 58)—the episodes culminate in self-affirmation rather than self-negation. She is both enabled and emboldened. She may adopt a policy of compliance to her employers, but the fact that it is a policy suggests the measure of control she preserves. She always has the choice of returning to her home; thus, she assesses her situation on the basis of the autonomy she has achieved rather than on the difficulties she encounters. Consequently, although Agnes is like many nineteenth-century heroines in having to turn inward to cultivate her spiritual resources, she differs from those heroines because this mode culminates in increasing mastery of the secular world. Although dismissed from her first post, Agnes chooses to depart from her second to open a school with her mother. The result is a female *Bildungsroman,* or novel of development, that both draws from a tradition of other such novels and departs significantly from it. Cultivation of the spiritual life, leading to mastery of the passions, seems to ensure a greater degree of self-determination for Agnes rather than an increase in self-abnegation typical of the protagonist of the female *Bildungsroman.* All of Agnes's pupils have been tossed about by their passions and, even with maturity, they remain unable to curb their indulgence in whims and their rage for attention. Agnes can see the evils to which they are vulnerable in maturity and, learning to conquer potential weaknesses in her own character, establishes herself as an independent woman.

Brontë's Agnes cannot replicate exactly the pattern of a male protagonist in a *Bildungsroman.* For example, the hero's two love affairs, one sexual and one spiritual, would culminate in social expulsion for a female protagonist. Nonetheless, Brontë uses the physical stresses suffered under the Bloomfields and the spiritual stresses endured under the Murrays as analogues for those other definitive developmental experiences en route to maturity. So Agnes, like the male protagonist, concludes her journey in her achievement of individual autonomy and social authority.

Through teaching, Agnes has plumbed her own strengths and honed her own understanding. She has completed her own education. Anne Brontë has carefully structured the novel to emphasise this completion. We have acknowledged that the novel was, perhaps, autobiographical in its inception, but Brontë shaped her materials towards novelistic ends. Agnes, as narrator, focuses on those episodes in which her education is being forwarded. She passes over her returns to home during the holidays. Her longing for such holidays is strongly represented to ensure our appreciation of her stoicism, but Brontë does not represent the holidays themselves because they are not germane to the novel's subject. Brontë opens Chapter four with Agnes's words, 'I spare my readers the account of my delight on coming home . . . I returned, however, with unabated vigour to my work . . .' (*AG* 29). Later, Agnes comments, 'for I *was* lonely. Never, from month to month, from year to year, except during my brief intervals of rest at home, did I see one creature to whom I could open my heart, or freely speak thoughts with any hope of sympathy, or even comprehension' (*AG* 79). But those precious, brief intervals do not make their way into the plot. Agnes concludes her tenure with the Bloomfields remarking, 'vexed, harassed, disappointed as I had been, and greatly as I had learned to love and value my home, I was not yet weary of adventure, nor willing to relax my efforts' (*AG* 41). Her several months at home are related in three pages and primarily establish two central points: Agnes must succeed in the world, and a woman need not marry to succeed. Agnes's mother counsels the father, 'But it's no matter whether [our daughters] get married or not: we can devise a thousand honest ways of making a livelihood' (*AG* 42).

II

Distinctively, the novel is neither male—nor marriage—oriented. Although it will conclude with wedding bells, that traditional bourne of eighteenth- and nineteenth-century novels, the reader is not led to expect marriage as Agnes's fulfilment. We may contrast what Anne Brontë does with what Jane Austen does. Both writers are concerned with the education of their protagonists. We may say that Austen yokes the heroine's movement toward marriage with her education; that is, an Austen protagonist must learn to discern the true from the false, the flashy from the substantial, the truly amiable man from the merely agreeable one. This is particularly true for Elizabeth Bennet and Emma Woodhouse. Their lessons in discernment culminate in their choice of suitable partners. Agnes's lessons, in contrast, all culminate in her independency. Perhaps this emphasis signals Anne Brontë's very different experiences. The Brontës were much poorer and of a lower class than the Austens; thus

Anne had to think constantly about profitable employment while Austen never worked. More important, Anne could never rely on her brother for support as Austen could on hers. As a result, Brontë's feminism ultimately takes on a different character.

Anne Brontë has structured her narrative to emphasise the acquisition of independence. Her heroine meets a suitable man, a clergyman Mr Weston, relatively late in the novel. She first recognises his excellence and then discovers in herself symptoms of a growing attraction. When she leaves him to open a school with her mother, she has made this choice to depart. She has been encouraged to believe he might seek her hand, and, at first she pines for this resolution like a typical heroine. She reveals that:

> I knew my strength was declining, my appetite had failed, and I was grown listless and desponding;— and if, indeed, he could never care for me, and I could never see him more—if I was forbidden to minister to his happiness—forbidden, for ever, to taste the joys of love, to bless and to be blessed— then, life must be a burden, and if my Heavenly Father would call me away, I should be glad to rest. (*AG* 136)

But no sooner has Agnes reached this pitch than she resolves, "'No, by His help I will arise and address myself diligently to my appointed duty'" (*AG* 137). The consequence is a rapid restoration of tranquillity of mind and 'bodily health and vigour'.

At this point we may note that there exists many another heroine of spunk who recovers her spirits without a proposal. We may recall Elizabeth Bennet's thoughts when doubtful that Darcy will propose again: 'If he is satisfied with only regretting me, when he might have obtained my affections and hand, I shall soon cease to regret him at all'.[3] But, while Darcy immediately makes his appearance in Austen's novel, Brontë's narrative seems deliberately to shift to another scene and to a new focus: Rosalie's marriage. Agnes is invited by her former pupil to visit her in her splendour as Lady Ashby. What she finds is a woman in misery, yet another reminder that marriage does not necessarily culminate in fulfilment for a woman and, indeed, may mark her further imprisonment. When Agnes returns home, full of a sense of her own riches, she is rejuvenated: 'Refreshed, delighted, invigorated, I walked along, forgetting all my cares, feeling as if I had wings to my feet, and could go at least forty miles without fatigue, and experiencing a sense of exhilaration to which I had been an entire stranger since the days of early youth' (*AG* 150).

It is only at this point of physical health, mental equanimity, and the personal fulfilment of financial and emotional independence that Mr Weston arrives to propose. The marriage simply stands as a coda to Agnes's journey toward autonomy.

The novel not only proposes that marriage *per se* does not constitute fulfilment, but also, as we have seen in the example of Rosalie, that marriage to the wrong partner might condemn one to a life of unhappiness. I suggested earlier that the novel was neither marriage- nor male-oriented and the two are obviously related. The entire novel presents only one admirable man: Mr Weston. Although he is a good man, he is not at all romanticised. In contrast to Charlotte's heroes and Emily's Heathcliff, he is not stern, commanding, and forceful. He is strong mainly in his commitment to principle and duty. He is somewhat phlegmatic and unemotional, deliberate and precise. Anne seems to avoid any romantic idealisation of men, particularly of men with power and money. In them, she finds large scope for abuse.

The men who employ her, Mr Bloomfield and Mr Murray, are contemptible. Neither man does her the courtesy of introducing himself. She infers their identities from their behaviour. Neither is prepossessing. Mr Bloomfield is a 'man of ordinary stature—rather below than above—and rather thin than stout, apparently between thirty and forty years of age: he had a large mouth, pale, dingy complexion, milky blue eyes, and hair the colour of a hempen cord' (*AG* 20). Mr Murray is a 'tall, stout gentleman, with scarlet cheeks and crimson nose' whom Agnes often hears 'swearing and blaspheming against the footmen, groom, coachman, or some other hapless dependent' (*AG* 50). Neither exercises any proper authority over his children. Their deficiencies reveal themselves in the defects of their children.

The most pernicious effect of these careless fathers is the automatic assumption of authority, importance and careless disdain for so-called lesser creatures they bequeath their sons. We will recall that Tom Bloomfield, Agnes's first charge, likes to torture fledglings which his papa says is 'just what *he* used to do when *he* was a boy. Last summer he gave me a nest full of young sparrows, and he saw me pulling off their legs and wings, and heads, and never said anything . . .' (*AG* 18). But not only birds suffer under this masculine dictatorship. Women do as well. When Agnes protests, 'Surely, Tom, you would not strike your sister! I hope I shall *never* see you do that', he replies, "'You will sometimes: I am obliged to do it now and then to keep her in order'" (*AG* 16). And this general attitude is fostered in young boys by the men who surround them. Mr Robson, Mrs Bloomfield's brother, 'encouraged Tom's propensity to persecute the lower creation, both by precept and example' (*AG* 37). He chortles when Tom heaps opprobrious epithets upon Agnes—'Curse me, if ever I saw a nobler little scoundrel than that.

He's beyond petticoat government already . . .' (*AG* 39)—recalling Walpole's characterisation of Mary Wollstonecraft as a 'hyena in petticoats'. Anne Brontë will explore and expose more fully this masculine arrogance toward women in *The Tenant of Wildfell Hall,* but it is evident even here that the subject concerns her greatly. Here, too, she links, as she will in *The Tenant,* male drinking, masculinity, and male tyranny. Mr Robson encourages his nephew 'to believe that the more wine and spirits he could take, and the better he liked them, the more he manifested his bold and manly spirit, and rose superior to his sisters' (*AG* 37).

In linking women with the 'lower creatures', Anne Brontë also suggests in this novel that a woman may take the measure of the man from his treatment of animals. Mr Hatfield, the vain and arrogant rector in the Murray's parish, consumed by his flirtation with Rosalie Murray, kicks a poor lady's cat 'right across th' floor, an' went after [the Murray girls] as gay as a lark' (*AG* 74). And he harasses the poor woman's spirit much as he harasses her cat's body. Mr Weston, in contrast, 'spake so civil like—and when th' cat, poor thing, jumped on to his knee, he only stroked her, and gave a bit of a smile: so I thought that was a good sign; for once, when she did so to th' Rector, he knocked her off, like as it might be in scorn and anger . . .' (*AG* 75-76). Agnes has formed an affection for a little terrier at the Murrays' and is heart-broken when he is taken away and 'delivered over to the tender mercies of the village rat-catcher, a man notorious for his brutal treatment of his canine slaves' (*AG* 118). Mr Weston heralds his arrival to propose to Agnes with this little canine messenger, whom he has rescued from the rat-catcher. Agnes's satisfaction that Snap, the terrier, now 'has a good master' anticipates her own acceptance of Mr Weston.

It seems that Charlotte may have drawn this mode of characterisation from her sister. In *Shirley,* the eponymous character argues that to know if a man is truly good, 'we watch him, and see him kind to animals, to little children, to poor people'.[4] In praising Robert Moore, Caroline Helstone replies, 'I know somebody to whose knee that black cat loves to climb; against whose shoulder and cheek it likes to purr. The old dog always comes out of his kennel and wags his tail, and whines affectionately when somebody passes'. Charlotte intensifies her similarity to Anne's description in a succeeding passage: 'He quietly strokes the cat, and lets her sit while he conveniently can, and when he must disturb her by rising, he puts her softly down, and never flings her from him roughly'.[5] Louis Moore, too, has his excellence measured by his sympathy with animals. And Shirley's cousin, Henry, is distinguished from the usual school-boy by his behaviour with animals. Shirley reveals, 'Generally, I don't like school-boys: I have a great horror of them. They seem to me

little ruffians, who take an unnatural delight in killing and tormenting birds, and insects, and kittens, and whatever is weaker than themselves . . .'[6] Finally, as if recalling *Agnes Grey,* Martin Yorke is reminded at one point 'of what he had once felt when he had heard a blackbird lamenting for her nestlings, which Matthew had crushed with a stone'.[7] Charlotte has learned from Anne a very powerful mode for realistically delineating male tyranny.

Anne deserves recognition for the clarity with which she details men's contempt for women in Victorian society and for the corollary recognition that, given this contempt and the power men hold in marriage, women are likely to suffer in that relationship. In her first position, Agnes witnesses a scene in which Mr Bloomfield berates his wife for her presumed negligence of duties. Agnes relates that, 'I never felt so ashamed and uncomfortable in my life for anything that was not my own fault' (*AG* 21). When Rosalie Murray marries the reprobate Lord Ashby—described as 'disagreeably red about the eyelids', with 'a general appearance of langour and flatness, relieved by a sinister expression in the mouth and the dull, soulless eyes'—she anticipates that because he adores her, he will 'let [her] have her own way' (*AG* 146). But she discovers to her chagrin and pain that '*he will* do as he pleases, and I must be a prisoner and a slave'. Rosalie cries out, 'Oh, I would give ten thousand worlds to be Miss Murray again! It is *too* bad to feel life, health, and beauty wasting away, unfelt and unenjoyed, for such a brute as that!' (*AG* 147). Ironically, Rosalie has earlier glimpsed her impending prison and confided to Agnes, 'But if I could be always young, I would be always single' (*AG* 64). Less vain than Rosalie and independent of male approval, Agnes is more suspicious of marriage as woman's fulfilment.

Even her parents' own example has given Agnes cause to proceed cautiously and to ensure her own autonomy before committing herself to another. Although Anne Brontë represents Mrs Grey's decision to marry a 'poor parson' as a positive one, one for which Agnes's mother is wholly admirable, Mr Grey is painted less sympathetically. Agnes confides that 'saving was not my father's forte. He would not run in debt (at least, my mother took good care he should not), but while he had money he must spend it' (*AG* 5). Ultimately Richard Grey decides to speculate with his small capital and loses it. Agnes, her sister, and her mother all survive the shock, but Mr Grey 'was completely overwhelmed by the calamity' (*AG* 6). Not only does he plunge them into poverty, but, incapable of rising to the challenge himself, he becomes an additional burden on his struggling family. His weakness leaves them vulnerable and ultimately increases their responsibility. In contrast, Mrs Grey is resourceful, energetic, strong, and determined. She ultimately heads a little community of women that provides a much more positive image of relationship than that of heterosexual marriage.

Anne Brontë, however, does not allow this female community to resolve her novel. As I've pointed out above, Agnes ultimately marries. But she does so only after we have been made to feel she has the option of self-support and of a nurturing female community. These are unusual options to find represented in a novel set in Victorian England. And, lest we feel that, after all, Agnes, like many another heroine before her, has succumbed to marriage as the only viable option, we have the positive portrait of successful Mrs Grey, who refuses to live with her daughters, 'saying she could now afford to employ an assistant, and would continue the school till she could purchase an annuity sufficient to maintain her in comfortable lodgings . . .' (*AG* 157). This might yet be Agnes's fate, and not a bad one, we feel, in a world that encourages male strength to take the form of tyranny and that indulges male weakness.

III

I've suggested above that the novel's strength lies in its quiet realism. Here, it is well to note what cannot be too often emphasised: Anne Brontë's talent for painting her milieu. She gives us, more accurately than most of her contemporaries, a sense of what Victorian female leisured life was like. She communicates the lassitude, the emptiness, the boredom. She makes us experience the significance of social rank: the disdain in which Agnes is held by the neighbouring gentlemen, the rudeness with which servants—taking a cue from their masters—treat her. We share the frustration of being a servant, subject to the whims of one's masters, whether these whims take the form of either demanding that she finish the tedious parts of pictures and of fancywork or encouraging her to appear unobtrusive when unwanted and infinitely accommodating when needed.

No one has communicated better than Anne Brontë the sheer physical demands of the period. I have already detailed her exhausting struggles with her pupils. Travel, too, is particularly demanding. When Agnes first arrives at the Bloomfields, she has only a minute to try to put herself in order and is dismayed at her appearance: 'The cold wind has swelled and reddened my hands, uncurled and entangled my hair, and dyed my face of a pale purple; add to this my collar was horridly crumpled, my frock splashed with mud, my feet clad in stout new boots' (*AG* 14). Her second journey is even more difficult. Agnes leaves on a dark winter morning and relates that 'the heavy snow had thrown such impediments in the way of both horses and steam-engines, that it was dark some hours before I reached my journey's end, and that a most bewildering storm

came on at last . . . I sat resigned, with the cold, sharp snow drifting through my veil and filling my lap, seeing nothing . . .' (*AG* 47). Brontë captures, too, Agnes's nausea from being stuffed into a carriage and riding backward, and her humiliation at being forced to dawdle behind a walking party because she is regarded as a 'mere domestic, who knew her own place too well to walk beside such fine ladies and gentlemen . . .' (*AG* 85).

Because *Agnes Grey* is dedicated to portraying a truth about Victorian life, Brontë eschews dramatic scenes. Many readers will find the 'plot' turgid, so little happens. But that is, as I have argued, because the novel is about education. It intends to keep the reader focused on the life of a mind.

Certain classic themes are generated out of these formal ends. First, the family is the primary focus of education. All subsequent influence cannot wholly eradicate the deficiencies produced by early indulgence and insufficient guidance. But if the understanding has been trained and the passions reigned in, then a great flowering is possible.

A corollary theme suggests that money and a monied, class society lie at the base of this pernicious indulgence. Having been encouraged by their wealth and social position to think well of themselves, the upper classes fail to ground their pride properly in their understanding, judgment, and discrimination. Anne Brontë makes it evident that in moving to the Murrays' Horton Lodge, Agnes has enjoyed an accession of social prestige: 'The house was a very respectable one; superior to Mr Bloomfield's, both in age, size, and magnificence' (*AG,* 56). Mrs Grey has distinguished the Bloomfields from the Murrays terming the former 'purse-proud tradespeople and arrogant upstarts' while the latter are characterised as 'genuine thorough-bred gentry' (*AG* 44, 46). However, although the Murray's outrank the Bloomfields, they share their coarseness and crudity. There is more superficial polish but no increase in real elegance. And when Agnes finally visits that star in the social firmament—Rosalie Murray, now Lady Ashby—she remarks on departing:

> It was with a heavy heart that I bade adieu to poor Lady Ashby, and left her in her princely home. It was no slight additional proof of her unhappiness that she should so cling to the consolation of my presence, and earnestly desire the company of one whose general tastes and ideas were so little congenial to her own. (*AG* 148).

We feel that Agnes, who cannot possibly envy Rosalie Murray nor desire *her* company, possesses a life both richer and more meaningful.

Growing out of Brontë's perception that money and power corrupt, is her recognition that the only real source of happiness lies in cultivating the spiritual life and pursuing the dictates of religion. Agnes tells Rosalie, by way of farewell: 'The best way to enjoy yourself is to do what is right and hate nobody. The end of Religion is not to teach us how to die, but how to live; and the earlier you become wise and good, the more of happiness you secure' (*AG* 148). We discover, then, that the religious theme is linked to the educational theme that controls the novel; religion helps teach us how to live the good life. It provides the foundation for moral principle, and it stands as a bulwark against despair. By thoroughly integrating the religious theme with the educational one, Brontë precludes the intrusion of any awkward or disruptive moral didacticism into her tale. When we finish the novel, we must feel that Brontë has accomplished her end of furthering our instruction through her protagonist's. But, perhaps more important, we feel that the process has gone on unobtrusively while we were fully engaged with the quiet story of an unassuming young woman.

And, once more, we are reminded of Brontë's triumph: her ability to take materials superficially so unengaging, so devoid of dramatic incident, and to involve us so deeply in them. Finally, Anne Brontë's achievement in *Agnes Grey* must be measured by her success in transforming a radical theme of women's education and independence into a subject matter so wholly reasonable. Brontë's next novel, to be her last, will demonstrate the as-yet-unexplored reach of her talent and suggest what might have been had she lived.

Notes

[1] Charlotte Brontë, [*Jane Eyre,* New York, W. W. Norton., 1971], p. 96.

[2] Winifred Gérin, *Anne Brontë,* [London, Allen Lane, 1959; 1976], p. 176.

[3] Jane Austen, *Pride and Prejudice* (Harmondsworth, Penguin, 1972), p. 370.

[4] Charlotte Brontë, *Shirley* (Harmondsworth, Penguin, 1974), p. 224.

[5] Ibid., p. 225.

[6] Ibid., p. 436.

[7] Ibid., p. 531.

Robert Liddell (essay date 1990)

SOURCE: *"Agnes Grey,"* in *Twin Spirits: The Novels of Emily and Anne Brontë,* Peter Owen, 1990, pp. 79-91.

[*In the following essay, Liddell compares Brontë's development with that of her fictional counterpart, Agnes Grey.*]

In Emily [Brontë's] birthday paper of 1845 (written a day late, on 31 July) Anne wrote: 'I have begun the third volume of *Passages from the Life of an Individual.* I wish I had finished it.' This is reasonably conjectured to have been her novel *Agnes Grey,* which was sent to the publisher a year later, or an earlier draft of it.

Anne is profoundly depressed: 'I for my part cannot well be flatter or older in mind than I am now.' She has recently returned to Haworth, thankful to have left her position as governess with the Robinson family at Thorp Green, but deeply distressed by Branwell's dismissal from the position of tutor in the same house, only a fortnight before. She is also unhappy for other reasons that she has not revealed. We do not know how deeply she had cared for her father's curate, William Weightman (d. 1842), but for long she had mourned his loss, and he would not be there to enliven life at Haworth:

The lightest heart that I have known,
The kindest I shall ever know.

For Anne there seems to have been no more escape into the romantic fictions of Gondal—'The Gondals are not in first-rate playing condition'—although the same day Emily could write: 'The Gondals flourish bright as ever. . . . We intend sticking by the rascals as long as they delight us, which I am glad to say they do at present.'

Anne was to spend the winter at Haworth, with the drugged and drunken Branwell as another inmate of the parsonage. 'Ever since her experiences at Thorp Green she exhibited in all she wrote a view of life, much more realistic and more socially orientated.'[1] In this view: 'All true histories contain instruction'—and *Agnes Grey* certainly does, though it is not literally true as autobiography.

It is the story of a young girl who goes out as a governess in the hope of helping her clerical family, ruined by financial loss. Anne had gone out as a governess six years before, in April 1839.

It will be well, in each of her situations, to isolate Anne's own experience (so far as it is known) from the experience of Agnes in the novel, sometimes too readily identified with it. This will be important in the case of her time at Thorp Green, a period so critical to herself and her brother.

Anne first went to Blake Hall, Mirfield, to the Inghams, a well-established Yorkshire family. They had young and undisciplined children, and Charlotte wrote that her life there was 'one struggle of life-wearing exertion to keep the children in anything like decent order.' There, though 'harassed and exiled', she kept up her own courage; it is related that she was once found writing at a table, with two small Inghams tied to two of the legs. She remained there for about a year, and her dismissal was disguised as a separation by mutual consent; thereafter she was remembered in the family as 'ungrateful', a typical employer's word.

Agnes Grey's first situation was at Wellwood with the Bloomfield family; it is strange that Anne should have given them so aristocratic a name, for she has otherwise revenged herself on her first employers, by making Mr Bloomfield a 'retired tradesman', a vulgar and violent person of whom even his wife was in terror. Mrs Bloomfield was 'cold, grave and forbidding'; but the children, Tom and Mary Ann, whom Agnes was expected to call 'Master' and 'Miss' Bloomfield were very lively, not to say unruly. We do not know if all Tom Bloomfield's hideous cruelty to birds is fact or fiction. Anne, with the love of animals that characterized all three sisters, might almost automatically attribute such conduct to a child that she was holding up to execration. She was even over-successful, for she inspired George Moore to invent a further atrocity[2]: 'the incident [not in the book] of the little boy, who tears a bird's nest out of some bushes, and fixes hooks into the beaks of the young birds so that he may drag them about the stableyard.'

Agnes Grey was (like her creator and all the Brontës) without the virtue that Jane Austen called 'candour': the gift of seeing the better side of other people's words or actions. Overhearing the grandmother asking Mrs Bloomfield if Agnes were a 'proper person' to have charge of the children—a reasonable grandmotherly enquiry— she was 'satisfied' that the old lady's evident sympathy for her had been 'hypocritical and insincere', and scorned to make herself agreeable by the small attentions and enquiries that were appropriate in their respective situations, as 'flattery' was against her principles.

Agnes's miserable life at Wellwood (we may hope) is now the lot of few people, though an analogous and very disagreeable experience must be endured by many a teacher in charge of large and haphazardly assembled classes:

> . . . the misery of being charged with the care and direction of a set of mischievous turbulent rebels, whom his utmost exertions cannot bind to their duty; while, at the same time, he is responsible for their conduct to a higher power, who exacts from him what cannot be achieved without the aid of the superior's more potent authority; which, either from indolence, or the fear of becoming unpopular with the said rebellious gang, the latter refuses to give. (Chapter 4)

Those who administer what the Gondals might call 'Palaces of Instruction', may still treat their teachers (who are sometimes better educated than themselves) with no more consideration than governesses habitually received from their employers. Teachers, however, generally live outside; and even within school they may be helped and comforted by the loyalty of their colleagues. Nevertheless I have been told of classes in a *lycée* who were literally the death of their instructors; and there is no sign that discipline among the young is improving. Agnes's history still contains 'instruction'.

A governess, seldom required to produce proof of being well educated (not so easy to do in a time before degrees), might owe her appointment entirely to her recommendation as 'the daughter of a gentleman'. It was therefore necessary for her to insist on her 'gentry', as it was her one qualification. Those who would not have hired her without it were seldom prepared, once she was in their employ, to treat her as a lady, and as part of the family. Jane Austen's 'poor Miss Taylor' was deservedly respected, but her good fortune was exceptional. Nor need we think, complacently, that the almost proverbial experiences of the governess were 'old, unhappy, faroff things'. In the inter-war years I knew a household where the mistress had a new governess almost every year; her husband, a most amiable, retired military man, said to me, about the governesses' awkward position: 'they're like fellers risen from the ranks.'

Women in their walk of life were particularly exposed to snubs. An employer needed to be scrupulously polite, with the attention that Fénelon recommends almost as a further refinement of charity: 'que notre charité soit toujours attentive pour ne pas blesser le prochain. Sans cette attention la charité, qui est si fragile en cette vie, se perd bientôt. Un mot dit avec hauteur, un air sec ou dédaigneux peut altérer les esprits foibles. . . .' Charlotte and Anne were 'esprits foibles' in this sense, if anyone were, and only too prone to take "attention' for condescension. Anne never applied her talents as a satirist to herself.

It appears that Anne probably went to her second situation in May 1840. She went to Thorp Green Hall, near York, to be governess to the three Misses Robinson, Lydia, Elizabeth and Mary, and to coach the boy Edmund in Latin. The Revd Edmund Robinson did not exercise his holy orders. At the time of Anne's arrival he was an enthusiastic member of the local hunt; but his health declined, and he was an invalid at the time of her departure. When after four months Anne wished to change her situation, she was induced to stay on; and when it was desired to provide a tutor for Edmund early in 1843, she arranged for Branwell to fill that post. She had a month's holiday at Christmas, and another in June, and after it accompanied the Robinsons on their yearly summer holiday to Scarborough. It is impossible to form a reliable portrait of Mrs Robinson, confused as we must be by the lyricism of Branwell and the recklessness of Mrs Gaskell. It is probable that there was (or appeared to be) a guilty relationship between her and Branwell from the beginning of 1845, and that Anne was greatly upset by it. She noted later that she had had some 'very unpleasant and undreamt of experiences of human nature', but did not reveal what they were.

On 17 July Edmund was brought by a servant to join his parents at Scarborough. The same day Mr Robinson wrote a letter to Branwell, who had returned to Haworth, sternly dismissing him, and threatening him with exposure. We do not know with what proceedings, 'bad beyond expression', Mr Robinson meant to charge Branwell, but these can hardly have included misconduct with his wife. It looks as though Mrs Robinson were acting with her husband in the dismissal of Branwell[3] (who may have been becoming a nuisance, even a threat), though she did later send him money. It was a convenient moment to get rid of him, and the letter may have been mere bluster; Branwell would have crumpled up under any accusation, and was in no position to defend himself.

Anne's friendly relations with her pupils were maintained by a recommenced correspondence; the effect of this was to give her matter for thought on 'love, marriage, sin and its results and man's ultimate destiny',[4] which bore fruit in her novel *The Tenant of Wildfell Hall.*

After some months at home, Agnes set out for a second situation. She was to be governess in the family of Mr and Mrs Murray at Horton Lodge, where there were no nursery children, and many of the horrors of Wellwood were absent. The Murrays do not throw much light on Anne's employers at Thorp Green, and perhaps she had reason to avoid saying much about them. Mr Murray was 'a blustering, roistering country squire', usually on horseback, as Mr Robinson may have been at first. Mrs Murray was 'a handsome dashing lady of forty'. All she seemed to require from the governess was showy accomplishment for the girls, and as much Latin grammar as possible for the boys to prepare them for school—all to be acquired with the minimum of exertion on the part of the children.

Agnes, as she herself tells us, was 'the only person in the house who steadily professed good principles, habitually spoke the truth, and generally endeavoured to make inclination bow to duty.' Rosalie, the elder daughter,

> . . . had never been perfectly taught the distinction between right and wrong; she had, like her brothers and sisters, been suffered, from infancy, to tyrannize over nurses, governesses, and servants; she had not

From left to right: Anne, Emily, and Charlotte Brontë as painted by their brother, Patrick, about 1835.

> been taught to moderate her desires, to control her temper, or bridle her will, or to sacrifice her own pleasure for the good of others. Her temper being naturally good, she was never violent or morose . . . (Chapter 7)

Indeed she came to have some esteem and even affection for Agnes.

As for the younger girl:

> As an animal, Matilda was all right, full of life, vigour and activity; as an intelligent being, she was barbarously ignorant, indocile, careless and irrational; and, consequently, very distressing to one who had the task of cultivating her understanding. . . . As a moral agent, Matilda was reckless, headstrong, violent, and unamenable to reason.

She swore like a trooper, but she was truthful, whereas Rosalie was capable of artfulness.

The elder boy, John, was almost eleven when Agnes came to Horton Lodge: 'frank and good-natured in the main', but 'unruly, unprincipled, untaught, unteachable'. He was sent to school after a year. Charles, the second boy, was spoilt by his mother: 'a pettish, cowardly, capricious, selfish little fellow', impossible to teach under his mother's eye, and Agnes's worst trial. He followed John to school a year later.

This was a world tolerable, if compared with Wellwood, and Agnes remained for more than four years. Her pupils were insolent, unmannerly and inconsiderate; they cared nothing for order or regularity, had meals or lessons when it pleased them, and obliged Agnes to submit to their lack of programme. But they were too old for the violence of the young Bloomfields.

Agnes was maturer than she had been at Blake Hall; her life had taught her to submit with more humility to its various indignities, and she can report with humour Mrs Murray's little sermon on 'the meek and quiet spirit, which St Matthew, or one of them says is better than the putting on of apparel.'

If she is to be judged as she judges others, the verdict on Agnes will be just but severe. She was aware that some of her sufferings were her own fault:

> I frequently caught cold by sitting on the damp grass, or from exposure to the evening dew, or some insidious draught, which seemed to have no injurious effect on them [her pupils]. . . . But I must not blame them for what was, perhaps, my own fault; for I never made any particular objections to sitting where they pleased; foolishly choosing to risk the consequences rather than trouble them for my convenience. (Chapter 7)

Agnes seems to have been something of a hypochondriac, for her uncomfortable position in the family carriage, 'crushed into the corner farthest from the open window', and with her back to the horses, during a drive of only two miles to church on Sundays, might make her sick, and must be followed by a depressing headache.

She was unwilling to give her pupils credit for the better motives which in part influenced their behaviour. When the Misses Murray would 'amuse themselves with visiting the poor cottagers on their father's estate, to receive their flattering homage', it is conceded that their object might also be 'perhaps to enjoy the purer pleasure of making the poor people happy with their cheering presence and their occasional gifts, so easily bestowed, so thankfully received'. But without meaning to offend, the girls behaved very rudely on many such occasions.

Agnes's chief unhappiness came from living with 'unprincipled' people and she had a longing for persons of her own sort. (As we, worse corrupted by 'evil communications' may sometimes have a nostalgia for 'good' people—if we have ever known any.) Presently she was to be gratified. The rector, Mr Hatfield, however, was not likely to be of any comfort to her with his 'high and dry' sermons about such matters as church discipline and the apostolic succession.

It must be admitted that Agnes (rightly unashamed of her 'principles') wore them a little too ostentatiously, was too quick to reproach conduct that was no business of hers, and had not been offered for her approval. At a grand ball, Rosalie had danced with 'Lord F.', who obviously admired her: 'I had the pleasure of seeing his nasty cross wife ready to perish with spite and vexation.' Agnes, from whom only a civil smile was required, cried, 'Oh, Miss Murray! you don't mean to say that such a thing could really give you pleasure. . . .' Rosalie answered good-humouredly: 'Well, I know it's very wrong; but never mind! I mean to be good some time—only don't preach now, there's a good creature.'

A new curate, Edward Weston, arrived; he preached evangelical sermons and read the service with reverence. Agnes soon met him, for sometimes when she was free she went to read to a cottager, Nancy Brown, whose sight was failing. One day Mr Weston appeared with Nancy's cat in his arms, having rescued it from the gamekeeper. At last Agnes had found a congenial spirit, and very soon he occupied much of her thought, though it would seem that he was not a recreation of William Weightman, from whom he is not only differentiated by his evangelicalism, but also by his seriousness and his physical characteristics.

Rosalie, of course, began to imagine a flirtation between the curate and the governess, of which there was none, though Agnes's heart had been touched. Rosalie herself, who was quite heartless, was half engaged to Sir Thomas Ashby, the most eligibile *parti* thereabouts, a debauchee, but a baronet, and the owner of a fine house and park. Meanwhile she amused herself by captivating poor Mr Hatfield the rector, a gallant and personable man, but without the means and the social position that Miss Murray thought her due. Agnes was sometimes posted as a watchdog by Mrs Murray, but Rosalie could always find ways of avoiding her and carrying on a flirtation. Unfortunately the rector was so much encouraged that he 'presumed' to make an offer of marriage, and had to be sent about his business.

Rosalie missed his attentions; she was now without an admirer, and decided to 'fix' Mr Weston. The unhappy Agnes took this with immense seriousness. '"Oh God, avert it!" I cried internally—"for his sake, not for mine."' Anne Brontë's next heroine, Helen Graham, will be too sophisticated to offer half-sincere explanations to the Almighty—and will have more knowledge of herself and others, and more sense of humour.

Rosalie became a frequent visitor to the cottage, where she hoped to meet the curate. She stole Agnes's seat in church, which commanded a view of the pulpit, to which Agnes must now turn her back; and chance meetings were arranged from which the governess was excluded.

There was as yet no reason to suppose that Mr Weston's happiness at all depended on Rosalie Murray or on Agnes Grey, but the latter's thought was full of him.

> Besides my hope in God, my only consolation was in thinking that, though he knew it not, I was more worthy of his love than Rosalie Murray, charming and engaging as she was; for I could appreciate his excellence, which she could not: I would devote my life to the promotion of his happiness; she would destroy his happiness for the momentary gratification of her own vanity. (Chapter 17)

She also found it natural to 'seek relief in poetry', whether in 'the effusions of others, which seem to harmonize with our existing case or in attempts to give utterance to these thoughts and feelings. . . .' She quotes one specimen: 'cold and languid as the lines may seem, it was almost a passion of grief to which they owed their being.'

> Oh, they have robbed me of the hope
> My spirit held so dear;
> They will not let me hear that voice
> My soul delights to hear.

This undateable poem[5] raises several problems. It would appear to have been written before Weightman's death (September 1842), and 'the question of the identity of the "they" is not easily soluble.'[6] It has been suggested[7] that the occasion of these lines was the return of Anne to her situation at Thorp Green early in 1842. She had again intended to relinquish it, and may have hoped to remain at Haworth to keep house during her sisters' absence at school in Brussels (and perhaps to enjoy the society of Weightman). 'They' will then be her employers, who had entreated her to return, and perhaps her father.

The poem fits perfectly into its present position; 'they' are Rosalie Murray and her sister, who prevent Agnes from meeting Edward Weston. Though probably written for Weightman, it is now used for an imaginary character—thus, like other novelists, Anne can make use of the past.

Rosalie married, and travelled abroad with Sir Thomas Ashby. Agnes consequently was more thrown with Matilda, whom her mother was trying to have groomed into young ladyhood; unfortunately the governess's precepts and prohibitions went no way with the girl. Agnes had to endure some reprimands from Mrs Murray:

> The young lady's proficiency and elegance is of more consequence to the governess than her own, as

well as to the world. If she wishes to prosper in her vocation she must devote all her energies . . . to the accomplishment of that one object. . . . The *judicious* governess knows this: she knows that, while she lives in obscurity herself, her pupil's virtues and defects will be open to every eye; and that, unless she loses sight of herself in their cultivation, she need not hope for success. (Chapter 18)

Matilda, however, yielded in some degree to her mother's authority. It was the circumstances of her own life that made Agnes offer her resignation. She was called home by her father's illness, but got back too late to see him alive. She and her mother then formed the project of opening a school, with 'a few young ladies to board and educate', and as many day pupils as they could get. Agnes was to return to Horton Lodge after a short vacation to give notice of her final departure. During her last weeks there she had to say goodbye to Mr Weston, who also was leaving the place; she built fancies on his few and correct words. For some time afterwards she suffered from poor health, and low spirits, although she had achieved half of what would be a Brontë happy ending: a small independent school in partnership with a member of her own family, and in 'A -, the fashionable watering-place', that is in Scarborough particularly dear to Anne.

Her former pupil Rosalie, now Lady Ashby, invited her to stay at Ashby Park, where her unhappiness and boredom in the married state, despite her splendid surroundings, sent Agnes back with more satisfaction to her own house and duties. During the summer Mr Weston, now vicar of a neighbouring parish, appeared on the sands—and not long afterwards a final happy ending was achieved in his marriage with Agnes Grey.

The time at Thorp Green, so important in Anne's development, is very insufficiently documented. We can see at once that 'Agnes Grey' could not have written *The Tenant of Wildfell Hall.* 'Those', says one writer, 'who insist that life with the Murrays of Horton Lodge is an accurate picture of life with the Robinsons of Thorp Green must follow the story through to its conclusion, and find the model for Henry Weston (*sic*). . . .'[8] Why should they not stop before he comes in? And in any case he was 'Edward' not 'Henry'. Another writer, Winifred Gérin, who does identify the experiences of Agnes closely with those of Anne Brontë is at least obliged to mention the difference in composition between the Robinson and the Murray families. But she says, astonishingly: 'To read *Wildfell Hall* in the light of Anne's and Branwell's experiences at Thorp Green is the only way to realise the book's true purpose and inspiration—which was not the story of Branwell's downfall, but of the world that made such a downfall possible.'[9] We knew Branwell well enough before he went there in 1843 to imagine that no place could make his downfall improbable.

We know very little about life at Thorp Green. Until the last year Anne seems to have been ready (if not always contented) to withdraw from time to time her attempts at leaving. It was the first time she had had to share her life with people of a different sort; at Blake Hall she had been little more than a nursery governess, and further excluded from family life. Here she had to adjust herself to life with persons who had not her 'principles', to live in what (compared with Haworth) must have been a more 'permissive' society. If we judge not only from the book, but from her later friendship with her two younger pupils, we can feel that she had won a certain admiration by her steadiness; she must have been rather impressive.

The Revd Edmund Robinson did not exercise his holy orders; nevertheless he was locally respected, and must have been enough of a clergyman to have an orderly house. Anne, some two years after her employment there, arranged for Branwell to be engaged as tutor for the boy Edmund, and a year after his appointment Charlotte could write: 'Anne and Branwell are *both* wondrously valued in their situations.' Life at Thorp Green does not appear to have been at all like that at Grassdale Manor, the home of the profligate Arthur Huntingdon in **The Tenant.** It is elsewhere that Branwell had learned to drink.

We do not know much more if we try to identify Mrs Robinson with Mrs Murray in **Agnes Grey,** though she is called 'a handsome, dashing lady of forty'; Arabella Lowborough, the adulteress in **Wildfell Hall** went 'dashing on for a season' after her abandonment—I do not know if we may associate the two characters. If the children (as we are told) threatened their mother 'to tell papa about Mr Brontë' there must have been at least some indiscretion; and it is not certain that Mr Robinson was perfectly faithful to his wife. Something must have gone wrong in 1845, when Anne had those 'unpleasant experiences'.

Anne had the precious support of organized religion, without which her 'principles' might not have availed. It was the religion to which, no doubt, the Robinsons paid some sort of allegiance, of which Mr Robinson was a minister, and to whose charities Mrs Robinson contributed. In her own strong position Anne could live as an innocent in a rather unedifying world, and become felt as a moral influence. Her own evangelical position was becoming more assured, and she was to have a reformative purpose in writing her second novel, which was not yet developed in **Agnes Grey.**

Notes

[1] Chitham and Winnifrith, *Facts and Problems,* p. 92

[2] Cit. Ada Harrison and Derek Stanford, *Anne Brontë: Her Life and Work,* 1959, pp. 227-8

[3] Winifred Gérin, *Branwell Brontë,* 1961, pp. 240ff

[4] Edward Chitham, *The Poems of Anne Brontë,* 1979, p. 14

[5] Ibid., no. 12

[6] Ibid., p. 171

[7] Harrison and Stanford, *Anne Brontë,* pp. 78f

[8] Daphne du Maurier, *The Infernal World of Branwell Brontë,* 1972, p. 148

[9] Gérin, *Branwell Brontë,* p. 317.

A. Craig Bell (essay date 1992)

SOURCE: *"Agnes Grey,"* in The Novels of Anne Brontë: A Study and Reappraisal, Merlin Books Ltd., 1992, pp. 1-30.

[*In the following essay, Bell studies the sources, structure, style, and characters of Brontë's "quiet, controlled, realistic"* Agnes Grey.]

Like not a few novelists the Brontës began their career in the belief that they were first and foremost poets; and in fact their first work to be printed was their collective *Poems, by Currer, Ellis and Acton Bell* published by Aylott & Jones in May, 1846. It was the complete failure of this little volume to make any impression on the literary world that drove them to try their fortunes yet again with novels. In Charlotte's words in her Biographical Notice of Ellis and Acton Bell:

> Ill-success failed to crush us: the mere effort to succeed had given a wonderful zest to existence; it must be pursued. We each set to work on a prose tale: Ellis Bell produced "Wuthering Heights", Acton Bell **"Agnes Grey"**, and Currer Bell also wrote a narrative in one volume[1]. These MSS. were perseveringly obtruded upon various publishers for the space of a year and a half; usually their fate was an ignominious and abrupt dismissal.

> At last "Wuthering Heights" and **"Agnes Grey"** were accepted on terms somewhat improverishing to the two authors; Currer Bell's book found acceptance nowhere, nor any acknowledgement of merit, so that something like a chill of despair began to invade his heart . . .

> I was just then completing "Jane Eyre", at which I had been working. . . . in three weeks I sent it off; friendly and skilful hands took it in. This was in the commencement of September, 1847; it came out

before the close of October following, while *Wuthering Heights* and *Agnes Grey,* my sisters' works, which had already been in the press for months, still lingered under a different management. . . .

Wuthering Heights and *Agnes Grey* were finally brought out in one volume by Newby in the December of 1847—viz. two months after the publication by Smith and Elder of *Jane Eyre.*

The contrast between the two novels could not have been more startling: *Wuthering Heights* a blaze of febrile imagination, genius at white heat; *Agnes Grey* quiet, restrained, soberly realistic. And it was perhaps unfortunate for Anne that her tentative first essay as novelist should have been juxtaposed with one of the outstanding masterworks of fiction. Comparisons, generally odious, were made then and have gone on being made ever since. Yet, immature though *Agnes Grey* is, the novel has had, and still has, its admirers, notably George Moore, who in his *Conversations in Ebury Street* goes as far as to declare: ' . . . her first story, *Agnes Grey,* is the most perfect prose narrative in English literature. . . . It is the one story in English Literature in which style, characters and subject are in perfect keeping.' The critical reader and writer of today will no doubt shrug off such an assessment as adulatory, and only to be explained by Moore's saturation in French fiction and his passion for style and form—two aspects in which English novelists have always been indifferent. Be that as it may, so sensitive a critic, and a novelist, was not likely to throw bouquets where none was merited, and there can be no doubt that he would have been horrified by the treatment meted out to Anne Brontë at the hands of posterity. But before exploring the novel itself it may be as well to begin by querying an assumption which has generally been accepted as fact, namely, that the mysterious never-discovered *Passages in the Life of an Individual* to which Anne refers in her diary note of July 31st, 1845[2], is the original if cumbersome title of, and the same novel as, *Agnes Grey.* This may well be so; but if we go carefully into dates and references we shall find that there is no absolute and incontestable proof of the supposition, nor for assuming that Anne began on the work in 1842[3]. All we know for certain of the *Passages* is that Anne had begun the third volume of it in July, 1845. Nothing else about it is known, and several queries remain unresolved.

In the first place, to assume the work to be identical with *Agnes Grey* implies that the 'Individual' of the title must necessarily be a feminine one. But it is already an arbitrary assumption in the light of Emily's statement in her diary paper dated the same as Anne's. She writes:

The Gondals still flourish as bright as ever. I am at present writing a work on the First Wars. Anne has been writing some articles on this, and a book by Henry Sophona. We intend sticking firm by the rascals as long as they delight us, which I am glad to say they do at present.

There is no reason why the imaginary writer Henry Sophona should not be the principle character of a narrative in much the same way that Charlotte had made Charles Wellesley both writer and character[4]: and though we have no certain ground for supposing that the 'book by Henry Sophona' was the *Passages,* we have no proof that it was not either. Furthermore, it should not be forgotten that in her Birthday note of July 30th, 1841, Anne had written: 'I am now engaged in writing the forth volume of *Solara Vernon's Life.'* What was this work? Again, might it have some connection with the *Passages?* Like the Henry Sophona book it has disappeared into the limbo of the lost, and the Brontë student can only figuratively tear his hair in frustration when he considers on the one hand the wealth of material he might have had and on the other the little he actually has.

As regards the uncertain date of the composition of *Agnes Grey* then, we must renounce the *Passages* as giving us any firm clue; but taking all references into account, and particularly Charlotte's letter dated 6 April, 1846, to Aylott & Jones in which she states that 'C., E., and A. Bell are now preparing for the press a work of fiction consisting of three distinct and unconnected tales', the last months of 1845 and the first of 1846 would seen the most likely.

Whether or not *Agnes Grey* was the same novel as the *Passages,* after having been turned down by several publishers during the space of some eighteen months (according to Charlotte), it was accepted along with *Wuthering Heights* by Newby in the summer of 1847, and the two novels were published together by him in the December of that year as a three volume tome, Emily's novel taking up the first two volumes, Anne's the third volume.

Let us now turn to the novel itself which I propose to examine under three headings: (1) sources of inspiration (2) style and structure (3) characterisation.

I—Sources of Inspiration

Ever since the book's appearance it has always been assumed that it was strictly autobiographical, and Anne's own words and those of Elizabeth Gaskell tend to confirm the general belief. In her Preface to the second edition of *The Tenant of Wildfell Hall* Anne Brontë writes: 'As the story of *Agnes Grey* was accused of extravagant over-colouring in those very parts that were copied from the life, with a most scrupulous avoidance of all exaggeration, so . . .'; and in her *Life* Elizabeth Gaskell remarks: *'Agnes Grey'*—the novel in which . . . Anne pretty literally describes her own life as a governess . . .' Nevertheless, too much weight can be given to this aspect of the story. For every writer, especially one of genius, however realistically he may transcribe a background and certain events which he knows from experience to be true, will inevitably bring to bear some touches to enhance and even distort plain fact. And that is why, as regards *Agnes Grey,* wherein fact goes hand in hand with fiction, we should be wary of trying to separate the two or to search for it in aspects of the author which would otherwise lie outside our knowledge of him or her.

Of course, this is not to deny that there is a strong autobiographical element in the novel. Like that of her creator, the childhood of *Agnes Grey* is spent in a vicarage in the North of England, and the walks taken with her sister Mary are among scenery reminiscent of the Haworth moors. A governess, too, like Anne, *Agnes Grey* also has two short successive posts, the one comparatively near her home, the other much further away: and like Anne, she is nineteen when she first leaves home. As for the Bloomfields and the Murrays, if we are to credit the general run of critics, Anne had no need of creative imagination to bring them to life— only her recollection of them as she found them. Again, this may be in part true, but only in part; for to take only one instance: we know for a fact that, quoting Anne, Charlotte in a letter to Ellen Nussey refers to Mrs. Ingham as being 'extremely kind', and in another as 'placid and kind', whereas in the novel Agnes describes Mrs. Bloomfield as 'cold, grave and forbidding'. Clearly Anne was simply taking novelist's licence here for the purpose of emphasising the lack of sympathy and understanding shown by the Bloomfields for her heroine. What was to prevent her from doing the same with the characters of the children in small or large degree in order to heighten the overall dramatic effect? This is even more apparent in her treatment of the Robinsons under the name of Murray. Had they been as inhumane as the latter are described in the novel, would Anne have risked, or even considered, suggesting her own brother, the impressionable Branwell, to them as tutor to their son? And even if—as we know she did—she left Thorp Green in disgust of her own accord, let it not be forgotten that in 1842 the Robinsons begged Anne to return to them, and that in fact she did go back for three more years. And finally we know for fact that in 1847, two years after Anne had left them, the two Robinson girls (one of them now married) began writing to her and making her their confidante, and in the December of 1848 even went so far as to go to Haworth to see their one-time governess—neither of which events suggests mutual abhorrence, to say the least.

Then too on the question of the clerics of the novel various theories have been put forward from time to time. Some have seen in Edward Weston, with whom Agnes falls in love and finally marries, a replica of Willie Weightman, even though there exists no positive proof that Anne did love him. But J. M. Dembleby[5] and others have seen Weightman as being more nearly portrayed in Mr. Hatfield, pointing to the latter's ardour in courting Rosalie Murray, to his dandyism and to his High Church leanings as being known characteristics of Weightman. So there is room for doubt and speculation on this aspect too.

The influences referred to above may be considered as those of association. But others have also to be taken into account—literary influences above all. Like many young, inexperienced authors, for her first original published story Anne Brontë betrays in style, matter and form the influence of writers she admired and had taken to heart. Three works above all others can be singled out. These are Goldsmith's *The Vicar of Wakefield,* her father's *Maid of Killarney* and her sister Charlotte's *The Professor.* Let us consider each in turn.

The first had become an accepted 'classic' by the early 19th century, and we would have no reason to doubt the Brontës' knowledge of it even if Charlotte had not selected it in *The Professor* as the book used by M. Pelet's seminary 'because it is supposed to contain prime examples of conversational English'. The influence of Goldsmith's story on *Agnes Grey* is apparent both in the style and the matter. Take for example the opening passage:

> All true histories contain instruction; though, in some, the treasure may be hard to find, and when found, so trivial in quantity, that the dry, shrivelled kernel scarcely compensates for the trouble of cracking the nut. Whether this be the case with my history or not, I am hardly competent to judge. I sometimes think it might prove useful to some, and entertaining to others; but the world may judge for itself. Shielded by my own obscurity, and by the lapse of years, and a few fictitious names, I do not fear to venture; and will candidly lay before the public what I would not disclose to my most intimate friend.

> My father was a clergyman of the North of England, who was deservedly respected by all who knew him; and, in his younger days, lived pretty comfortably on the joint income of a small incumbency and a snug little property of his own. My mother, who married him against the wishes of her friends, was a squire's daughter and a woman of spirit. In vain it was represented to her, that if she became the poor parson's wife, she must relinquish her carriage and her lady's maid, and all the luxuries and elegances of affluence; which to her were little less than the necessaries of life. A carriage and a lady's maid were great conveniences; but, thank Heaven, she had feet to carry her, and hands to minister her own necessities. An elegant house and spacious grounds were not to be despised; but she would rather live in a cottage with Richard Grey than in a palace with any other man in the world.

Finding arguments to no avail, her father, at length, told the lovers that they might marry if they pleased; but, in so doing, his daughter would forfeit every fraction of her fortune.

This is pure 18th century, with echoes of Goldsmith and Maria Edgeworth. It was only to be expected, of course, that first chapters should be the most uncharacteristic, those in which the young author would lean most heavily on her antecedents. But as she progresses, as she warms to her task and grows in confidence, a more natural, more contemporary style becomes apparent. One has only to contrast the above passage with—to take a random example—the account of Agnes's visit to the demesne of Lady Ashby, alias her one-time pupil, Rosalie Murray.

As we were strolling in the park, talking of what my companion had seen and heard during her travelling experience, a gentleman on horseback rode up and passed us. As he turned, in passing, and stared me full in the face, I had a good opportunity of seeing what he was like. He was tall, thin, and wasted, with a slight stoop in the shoulders, a pale face, but somewhat blotchy, and disagreeably red about the eyelids, plain features, and a general appearance of languor and flatness, relieved by a sinister expression in the mouth and the dull soulless eyes.

"I detest that man!" whispered Lady Ashby, with bitter emphasis, as he slowly trotted by.

"Who is it?" I asked, unwilling to suppose that she would speak so of her husband.

"Sir Thomas Ashby," she replied, with dreary composure.

"And do you *detest* him, Miss Murray?" said I, for I was too shocked to remember her name for the moment.

"Yes I do, Miss Grey, and despise him, too; and if you knew him you would not blame me."

"But you knew what he was before you married him."

"No, I only thought so; I did not half know him really. I know you warned me against it, and I wish I had listened to you; but it's too late to regret that now. And besides, mamma ought to have known better than either of us, and she never said anything against it—quite the contrary. And then I thought he adored me, and would let me have my own way; he did pretend to do so at first, but now he does not care a bit about me. Yet I should not care for that; he might do as he pleased if I might only be free to amuse myself and to stay in London, or have a few friends down here; but *he will* do as he pleases, and I must be a prisoner and a slave. The moment he

saw I could enjoy myself without him, and that others knew my value better than himself, the selfish wretch began to accuse me of coquetry and extravagance; and to abuse Harry Meltham, whose shoes he was not worthy to clean. And then, he must needs have me down in the country, to lead the life of a nun, lest I should dishonour him or bring him to ruin; as if he had not been ten times worse in every way, with his betting-book, and his gaming-table, and his opera-girls, and his Lady This and Mrs. That—yes, and his bottle of wine, and glasses of brandy and water too! Oh, I would give ten thousand worlds to be Miss Murray again! It is *too* bad to feel life, health and beauty wasting away, unfelt and unenjoyed, for such a brute as that!" exclaimed she, fairly bursting into tears in the bitterness of her vexation.

This is different stuff altogether, and anticipates *The Tenant of Wildfell Hall*.

Nor is the influence of *The Vicar of Wakefield* confined only to style. Events, even, are copied with naive variation. Like Dr. Primrose, Agnes's father, in a despairing endeavour to enrich himself for the benefit of his family, entrusts all he can spare to a mercantile friend, the only difference being that in Goldsmith's novel the vicar loses his money through the dishonesty of the merchant, whereas in Anne Brontë's her father loses his because of the wreckage of the merchant's ships. Following which both families make heroic efforts in domestic retrenchment, the former by selling their two ponies, the latter parting with their 'useful phaeton . . . together with the stout well-fed pony' and making other domestic sacrifices.

From her father's modest little tale it is difficult not to believe that Anne took a hint from both the behaviours of Agnes and one of her clerics. The visits paid by Agnes to the poor widow Nancy Brown are strongly reminiscent of those of Flora Loughlean in *The Maid of Killarney* to the old and widowed Nancy. The similarity is underlined by the comparable circumstances of the two widows. Nanny, Irish and theoretically a Catholic, prizes the visits and Bible readings of Flora just as Nancy Brown does those of Agnes. Moreover Nancy, like Nanny, believes that the core of the Christian message is to be found in the Scriptures; but nevertheless hides her Bible under her pillow when the priest visits her. Like the priest, the High Church Hatfield does not approve of the hours devoted by Nancy to her Bible, and informs her that her time would be better spent attending church where she would hear the Christian truths expounded by those best fitted to interpret them.

Finally, *The Professor*. Study of these first novels of the two sisters can only strengthen belief that to begin with at least a strong mutual influence was engendered. We know from Elizabeth Gaskell's *Life* how 'The sisters . . . at this time . . . talked over the stories they were engaged upon, and described their plots. Once or twice a week, each read to the others what she had written, and heard what they had to say about it.' This being so, it is surely not far-fetched to believe that their communal ideas rubbed off, as it were, on one another, consciously or unconsciously. And if we analyse the two novels in question we shall find them analogous to two streams which run parallel to each other, now coming close but never merging, now diverging again, but always alike in direction. In both the common initial inspiration is to narrate the story of an ordinary human being who has to earn his living and for whom existence, largely for this reason, is an obscure, patient and courageous struggle. Added to which, even at this initial stage, there is the fact that the two 'subjects', or themes, were deliberately chosen by their authors because of their human veracity and moral force. In her Preface to *The Professor,* which remained unpublished until after her death, Charlotte declares that her 'hero' (William Crimsworth) would be an average working man and the story 'plain and homely'. In fact everything she has to say about Crimsworth and her novel can, with the mere substitution of the feminine for the masculine, be applied to the story of Agnes Grey. And it may be noted that both Crimsworth and Agnes are made to earn their living by the same profession—that of teaching. Not only so, but their love-life too follows similar paths, Agnes with Weston, Crimsworth with Frances Henri. In each of the novels circumstances separate the couples before they can declare their love—circumstances which change in the approved Victorian manner to allow the closing scenes to ring with harmonious wedding bells.

Other details too are mutually reminiscent. In the very first chapters Crimsworth and Agnes find themselves driven to seek work for comparable family reasons. Agnes's mother, daughter of an affluent squire, marries the poor clergyman Richard Grey against the wishes of her father, who disinherits her. Hard-pushed to live in reasonable comfort on Grey's stipend, they are brought face to face with poverty when most of his little capital disappears with the wreck of his business friend's ships. It is now that Agnes, though unfitted for the task, determines to earn her keep by becoming a governess. Similarly, when Crimsworth's father dies, a bankrupt, his widow can expect no help from her 'aristocratic brothers' who have never forgiven her for her mésalliance.

In chapter 13 of *Agnes Grey,* Mr. Weston picks flowers for Agnes; and in the next chapter deigns to give Mr. Hatfield the sprig of myrtle which he has begged for with such insistence. In chapter 12 of *The Professor,* Crimsworth persuades Zoraide Reuter to pick him a branch of lilac. In chapter 17 of *Agnes Grey* Rosalie and Matilda Murray plan to prevent Agnes from seeing Mr. Weston. In chapter 18 of *The Professor,* Mlle Reuter dismisses Frances Henri so that Crimsworth shall not see her again.

Some quite surprising parallels are to be noted too in the construction of the two novels. Both run to 25 chapters, similarly portioned out as regards the story of Crimsworth on the one hand and Agnes on the other. As already noted, the two characters begin their careers in similar circumstances. Chapters 2 to 5 of both novels narrate a check, a false beginning in the two characters' respective careers: Agnes failing to give satisfaction to the Bloomfields, who dismiss her; Crimsworth quarrelling with his brother after working for him for three months and leaving him. In chapter 6 Crimsworth and Agnes draw the lesson of their lack of success and prepare themselves for new experiences. In chapter 7 the scenes are set for different surroundings: Horton for Agnes, for Crimsworth Belgium and Brussels. In chapter 20 both leave their employers. The last five chapters see each in more secure and happier circumstances and fulfilled in their love-life.

All these parallels are too striking, too persistent, to be dismissed as coincidences. There must have been some degree of communication, even collaboration, between the two sisters. And this being so we are provided with further evidence that *Agnes Grey* is not just autobiography but in much greater degree than is generally reckoned a work of fiction, shaped to the demands of literary art rather than slavishly following a series of autobiographical events.

II—Style and Structure

The best way to substantiate the claim in the concluding paragraph made above, namely, that the novel is a work of fiction as much as an autobiography, is to give the reader a résumé of the story. Those who are already familiar with it may find new seed of thought for their assessment of the work; those who do not know it may perhaps be stimulated into reading it.

Agnes Grey is the younger of the two daughters of an Anglican clergyman, Richard Grey. She and her sister Mary enjoy a happy and protected childhood and adolescence. But this happiness and sense of security are shattered when her father loses all his invested capital by the wreck of his merchant friend's ships. In order to avoid being a drag on the family and to pull her own weight, Agnes, against the wishes of her family who have always 'babied' her and considered her unfit to cope with such a job, decides to become a governess—one of the few means in those days by which an intelligent woman could hope to earn a living. She anticipates with naive optimism the mental rewards of helping to train children in the paths of 'Virtue, Instruction and Religion'. In the home of the Bloomfields, her first employers, she is quickly disillusioned. The Bloomfields and their kin are ignorant, vulgar and pretentious, their children idle, coarse, undisciplined and vicious. After eight months of struggle with them Agnes is unable to improve their minds or their conduct, and Mr. and Mrs. Bloomfield, considering her inefficient, give her notice.

Refusing to accede to defeat Agnes eventually finds a second post with a Mr. and Mrs. Murray of Horton Lodge. But there she soon discovers that she is regarded as little better than a servant and her pupils scarcely less tractable than the Bloomfields. There are four of them—two girls and two boys: Rosalie, Matilda, John and Charles, aged sixteen, fourteen, eleven and nine respectively. Like the earlier pupils at Wellwood, they resent their governess and are determined to make life as difficult and frustrating as they possibly can for her. A point worth observing is that while Anne's description of Mrs. Murray as 'a handsome, dashing lady of forty, who certainly required neither rouge nor padding to add to her charms,' may lay claim to being a likeness of Mrs. Robinson, that of Mr. Murray as 'a blustering, roistering country squire' devoted to fox-hunting, farming and drinking, can hardly portray her husband, the Rev. Edmund Robinson, 'soon to become a premature, valetudinarian and to die at the age of forty-six[6]'. In this one detail alone we see the mingling of fact with imagination on the part of Anne Brontë.

A new circumstance, however, enables Agnes to bear up against the trials and tribulations of her position. A young clergyman, Edward Weston, has lately become the curate of the parish of Horton. His quiet seriousness appeals to Agnes, and her growing secret love for him brings her unguessed happiness.

The weeks and months pass. Now eighteen, Rosalie 'comes out' and Agnes only has Matilda to educate. For her part, Rosalie has only one thought—to attract and flirt with men. Mr. Hatfield becomes one of her most ardent admirers, and she leads him on to such a degree that, believing she cares for him, he proposes to her: upon which she leaves him flat, then, out of boredom, proceeds, in front of Agnes, to make herself fascinating to Mr. Weston, leaving the poor governess in a state of dread lest she should succeed in taking him from her.

But some six months later Rosalie becomes Lady Ashby. She does not love Sir Thomas in the least, and marries him merely for his rank and fortune. Soon after this event Agnes learns that her father is dangerously ill. She leaves Horton at once only to arrive home too late and find that her father has died. Her mother, refusing to be dependant on anyone, decides to open a school at A——, a fashionable seaside place, and after a final six weeks at Horton, where she bids farewell to Edward Weston, she joins her mother at A——.

There, just under a year later, she receives an invitation from Rosalie, now mother of a baby girl, to visit her at Ashby Park. She finds her former pupil hard and cynical, with her marriage already in ruins.

Agnes returns to A——, and three days later, in the course of an early morning walk along the sands, she comes face to face with Edward Weston.

From him she learns that he left Horton and got the living of a parish bordering A——, and had been trying to locate her ever since his arrival. There is no obstacle now to prevent their happy union, and Agnes soon becomes Mrs. Weston. When she comes to recount her story she is the happy mother of three children.

We have already commented on the construction of the novel, and to our own comments may be added the interesting analysis of W. A. Craik[7]. Craik contends that the novel is more complex and subtle than may appear at first reading and stresses the fact of its being the story of not simply one character, but of two, namely Agnes Grey and Rosalie Murray; that as regards the former, the two episodes narrating her governess posts first at Wellwood and then at Horton are aligned not simply by chronological succession as a superficial reading might suppose; and finally that to no small degree the first episode is made to serve as a deliberate prelude to the longer and more important second. Hence the apparent imbalance between the four chapters devoted to the Bloomfields and the fourteen chapters given to the Murrays. The characters of the respective families vindicate Anne Brontë's intention here. The Bloomfields, whether exaggerated or not, are 'grotesques', their vulgarity, stupidity and sheer egoistic cruelty make them scarcely human, and certainly beyond the softening influence of any governess; and Anne Brontë perceived clearly that to devote an equal length of time and as many chapters to them as to the Murrays would serve only to surfeit the reader[8]. She therefore hastily passes on to the still unpleasant but more human Murrays. From then onwards Rosalie Murray becomes just as important to the story as the titular heroine, and in fact may be said to steal the limelight. Moreover, even when Agnes has left Horton more than a year, Rosalie, now Lady Ashby, invites her to come and visit her. Anne Brontë needed Rosalie Murray to drive home to her readers the dangers of lax parental authority and to show to what tragic results they could lead. This is underlined, without any preaching, by letting the reader see the contrast in the marriages of the two principle characters: that of Rosalie made through vanity and self-interest and ending in impasse; that of Agnes made through genuine affection and respect and blessed by children and a happy fireside home.

The simplicity of the structure and the directness of its style are in part responsible for the general under-rating of the novel and for certain criticisms which I believe to be mistaken. A typical example is that of Melvin R. Watson. In the chapter 'Form and Substance in the Brontë Novels' which occurs in his *From Jane Austen to Joseph Conrad*[9] he criticises **Agnes Grey** for . . . "its false start in chapters II-V, its lack of pointing and emphasis, its failure to achieve the climax which should have occurred in chapter XVIII, and the coincidences which crowd the last chapters . . .". The second of his criticisms alone is justified: the rest are very dubious. I have already replied to the first by stating my conviction that the so-called 'false-start' was a deliberate plan on the part of Anne Brontë to make it a sort of prelude to the main body of the narrative. In my opinion there is nothing 'false' about it.

The 'climax' in chapter XVIII to which this critic refers is evidently the death of Agnes's father. On receiving her mother's letter telling her of his serious illness, she leaves Horton at once and makes all speed for home.

> My mother and sister both met me in the passage— sad—silent—pale.
>
> I was so much shocked and terror-stricken that I could not speak. . . . .
>
> "Agnes!" said my mother, struggling to repress some strong emotion.
>
> "Oh, Agnes!" cried Mary, and burst into tears.
>
> "How is he?" I asked, gasping for the answer.
>
> "Dead!"
>
> It was the reply I had anticipated: but the shock seemed none the less tremendous.

And that is the sole account we have of the death of Richard Grey. Now in the sum total of the narrative Agnes's father plays a merely indirect and minor role. Why then, we ask, should his death be made 'the climax' of the novel? On the contrary, should not Anne Brontë be lauded for dealing with the event so tersely and for avoiding the dreadful deathbed so beloved of so many Victorian novelists? In addition to which we demand also by what authority, what literary dogma, must a novel, in order to be considered well constructed, follow a curve of ascent and descent—a curve Melville Watson criticises **Agnes Grey** for not following?

As for the 'coincidences' which, according to him, 'crowd the last chapters', they are at the most two. The first is the nomination of Weston as vicar to a parish neighbouring A—— a little less than a year after he and Agnes had parted at Horton. The second is the accidental meeting on the beach at A——. But can the two events really be accounted pure coincidence? By his words to Agnes on their meeting he makes it clear that he has been searching for and making enquiries about her in a determination to find her; and far from their accidental meeting being a stretch of coincidence, anyone with any experience of the contrariness of life must have been made aware that where directed, organised effort to achieve a thing has failed, chance frequently brings about the passionately desired end[10]. Anne Brontë, I think, had come to know this, and had the strength of her conviction. The means, surely, justify the end. And in any case, to reject Anne Brontë and accept Hardy on the score of coincidence is to strain at gnats and swallow camels.

III—The Characters

The characters in the novel play no small part in eliciting the lavish praise bestowed on it by George Moore. Passing over Agnes herself for the moment, they may be divided into three groups: her family, the Bloomfields and the Murrays. Edward Weston has a special niche to himself in view of the role he plays in Agnes's life.

As regards the first group—the family—it will be observed that Anne Brontë devotes comparably few pages to them. But it will be observed too that while Agnes's sister, Mary, remains a mere shadow in the background, her parents leave on the reader's mind a sense of complexity, particularly her father. Esteemed and beloved both by his parishioners and his family, generous to the needy, constantly occupied in carrying out his religious duties and doing good, there is nevertheless something in his character which Agnes, scrupulous in her veracity, sees as a vague imperfection. She notes a certain sombreness in his nature, an impulsiveness, an instability even, causing him to veer inexplicably at times from optimistic cheerfulness to obsessive sadness. He is impractical and imprudent, confounds reality with chimeras, contracts debts, risks his capital on the word of a friend. She even refers to 'his morbid imagination;' and his egoism allows him, when he is ruined and stringent economy becomes the watchword of the family, to be pampered with his favourite dishes and warmed by a fire they can ill afford.

His wife is in direct contrast, strong where he is weak. She had no hesitation in sacrificing rank and fortune in order to marry the man she loved. Richard and she were made for each other, she used to say after his death. The instinctive desire to protect a more delicate being, one who had need of her, must surely have played a strong part in her decision. To her two daughters Mrs. Grey was always a thoughtful mother, clever, active and strong. Agnes, indeed, did not hide from herself a wish that she had been less generously endowed with some of these qualities and had left more initiative to her daughters, both mental and physical, rather than treating them like children—she, Agnes, in particular, being the baby of the family and never allowed to forget it. So, on hearing Agnes's intention to earn her keep and become a governess, her mother can scarcely believe her ears, and she and her husband and Mary try to laugh the idea out of the girl's head, though she is eighteen at the time.

The Bloomfields of Wellwood are the first 'outsiders' Agnes has to live with, and the shock of discovering that such people exist at all comes as a shattering blow to her ignorance of human nature. The family consists of the two parents and four children—Tom, Mary Anne, Fanny and Harriet aged seven, six, four and two respectively. To consider the parents first.

Anne Brontë has made Mr. Bloomfield violently antipathetic and seemingly without a single likable trait. He is bad-tempered and boorish, and given to drinking. The children are afraid of him and cringe from his verbal explosions and sometimes, even, blows. He is a tyrant to his wife as the scene at the dinner table in which he criticises her cooking and her management shows. A successful retired business man, money and a climb up the social scale have served only to accentuate the fundamental meanness of his nature. In front of Agnes he speaks of Tom and Mary Anne as Master Bloomfield and Miss Bloomfield, treats her as a servant and clearly regards her as being of inferior rank, even blaming her before the children for failure to cope with her duties.

His wife is equally antipathetic, though in a different way. Seen through Agnes's eyes her salient characteristic is a marble-like coldness, at least towards her governess. This does not prevent her from being full of solicitude for the welfare of her children; but this solicitude is blind and makes her completely ignorant of their true nature. While confessing to Agnes that they are "not very advanced in their attainments," she labours under the delusion that "they are clever children, and very apt to learn"—an opinion that time shows to be utterly purblind, as the poor governess was to find to her cost. In fact from the very first day Agnes realised she could count on neither help nor understanding from the mother.

Many readers of the novel, especially those of our own time, have felt the Bloomfield brood to be crudely overdrawn. But as we have already seen[11], Anne Brontë resented such criticism strongly and went out of her way to deny its truth. Monstrous though they are, there is no reason why her word should be doubted. Those who have had to do with children in the mass, even children from normal homes, know only too well the thoughtlessness and cruelty they can show towards one another. Given a background such as the Bloomfield parents, with no sense of moral or mental discipline, the most vicious conduct should occasion no surprise. From her first introduction to them Agnes is brought to realise that both Tom and Mary Anne, the two who are

to be her pupils, are not only ignorant scholastically, but ignorant of the first elements of social behaviour, and idle and vicious into the bargain. Dissimulation, hypocrisy and lying are their normal means of escaping punishment and for getting the blame for their delinquencies placed on their governess. Mary Anne is stupid and lazy and, like the worst type of girl, affected and a born coquette. Tom is even more revolting. A male chauvinist, egoist and sadist in embryo, he considers himself the 'boss' of the classroom, and that everything and everyone belongs to him by right of sex and age. He is vain and sets out to monopolise all Agnes's attention at the expense of his sisters. A natural tyrant, he expects not only his sisters but Agnes as well to pander to his caprices, and when thwarted does not hesitate to hit and kick them. Worst of all is his repulsive sadism. Unreproved by his parents, who consider it manly to be cruel, he sets traps for moles, weasels and birds and takes a vicious delight in torturing them. He swears and even drinks, encouraged by Uncle Robson, a fatuous would-be dandy who idles his life away in drink and pleasure, regards women with contempt as inferior beings and helps to corrupt his nephew by declaring he is going the right way to show the world he is a real man.

The family picture is completed by the presence of a grandmother, Mr. Bloomfield's mother. At first, deceived, Agnes takes her for a dear old lady, but soon discovers that the old woman's apparent goodwill is only a hypocritical cover for a furtively nasty nature. When by a colder attitude Agnes lets her see she has fathomed what she really is, the old woman never forgives her; and it is not a little due to her snide remarks criticising Agnes that the Bloomfields decide to give their governess her notice.

Telling herself philosophically that no position could be worse than hers had been with the Bloomfields, Agnes, determined as ever to do her share in easing the family financial burden, in answer to her advertisement finds herself taken on as governess by the Murrays of Horton Lodge.

The milieu here provides Anne Brontë with characters and scene very different from those of Wellwood. The Murrays belong to the "gentry" class, and this allows her not only to describe the family itself but quite a few personages who gravitate round the Murrays. These can be divided into two groups: on the one hand the poorer working people like old Nancy Brown and the farm hand Mark Wood; on the other the relations and social acquaintances.

To take the family first. As might be expected, Mr Murray's role in the narrative and his personal contact with the governess or his family are slight. A typical husband in this, he leaves all the household organising to his wife. He is, besides, far too busy devoting himself to the serious pursuits of fox-hunting, racing and drinking to give any time and thought to such a triviality as the education of his children. That is a woman's business. The only time Agnes sees anything of him is on Sundays when they go to church. But unlike Mr. Bloomfield he does not criticise her, and even condescends to nod at her on the rare occasions he passes by and give her a short "Morning, Miss Grey".

His wife, too, is physically and mentally an equal contrast to Mrs. Bloomfield. Vivacious and attractive, she lives in a world of social rivalries, her 'chief enjoyments [being] in giving or frequenting parties, and in dressing at the very top of the fashion'. Yet under her gay exterior Agnes soon discovers an equal indifference and hardness to that of Mrs. Bloomfield along with similar delusions as to the true nature and capabilities of her children. These, Agnes finds very early, if not as vicious as the Bloomfields, are bad enough to make her job anything but a sinecure. Charles, the youngest, was his mother's 'peculiar darling,' and by far the worst of the four, being sly, sullen and utterly spoilt. John she found unruly, unprincipled and unteachable—at least by a governess and under his mother's eye. Only when the two boys were sent away to school could Agnes's job be described as anything less than an almost unbearable daily misery.

With only the two girls left on her hands her task became more endurable, though only slightly so, for neither is a willing or dutiful pupil. Their different natures are drawn with broad strokes: Rosalie, the eldest, at seventeen, obsessed by 'the ruling passion . . . the all-absorbing ambition to attract and dazzle the other sex'; Matilda, approaching fifteen, 'a veritable hoyden . . . as an animal . . . all right, full of life, vigour and activity; as an intelligent being she was barbarously ignorant, indocile, careless and irrational'. Taking her cue from her father and the stable men she swore like a trooper, and was only happy when riding her pony or romping with her brothers and her dogs[12].

Rosalie's career runs its inevitable course. After flirting shamelessly with married and unmarried men alike, her vanity and social ambition lead her finally to marry Sir Thomas Ashby with his coveted rank, wealth and estate, though she does not love him in the least. A year after their marriage she is brought to the point of hating her husband and having no natural maternal affection for her baby girl. Her disillusionment is so vividly, so almost brutally conveyed[13], that the reader cannot be other than moved by it to pitying the already cynical and disenchanted young woman, realising as he must that her behaviour, cynicism and marital failure spring as much from false principles inculcated in childhood by blindly egotistical and unprincipled parents as from her own defects. Moreover, she wins our sympathy to some point by one likeable trait, namely, her esteem and, as far as her warped nature allows, her

affection for her governess, proved as we have already intimated, by her invitation to Agnes to visit her after her marriage[14]. From all this it ensues that Rosalie is the most important character in the novel after Agnes herself. Outside the Murrays the most important protagonists are the two clerics—Mr. Hatfield, the rector, and Edward Weston, his curate—and in them Anne Brontë has delineated two very opposite and antagonistic characters, the former a ladies' man, gallant and debonair, the latter simple and sincere and devoted to his calling. Hatfield falls into Rosalie's tantalising snare, but it is his pride rather than his heart that is hurt when she snubs him and throws him callously over. Agnes reads him as shallow and 'confident in his own graces,' but finds herself more and more attracted by the less prepossessing but more unaffected and intellectual Weston, who besides, far from regarding her as beneath his notice as does Hatfield, goes out of his way to be friendly and to talk to her. His kindness, not only for her but for his poorer and less fortunate parishioners, turns her high regard for him slowly into a stronger feeling. When the time comes for her to leave the Murrays in order to help her mother with the school she has started in A—— she knows she is deeply in love with him, and the parting from him on her last Sunday at Horton outside the church wrings her heart. But how does he feel about her?

> . . . a low voice beside me said: "I suppose you are going this week, Miss Grey?"
>
> "Yes," I replied . . .
>
> "Well," said Mr. Weston, "I want to bid you good-bye—it is not likely I shall see you again before you go."
>
> "Good-bye, Mr. Weston," I said. Oh, how I struggled to say it calmly! I gave him my hand. He retained it a few seconds in his.
>
> "It is possible we may meet again," said he; "Will it be any consequence to you whether we do or not?"
>
> "Yes, I should be very glad to see you again."
>
> I *could* say no less. He kindly pressed my hand, and went.

And that is the sum of their parting. Clearly we are made to feel that Weston is already in love with Agnes; yet that is all he can say and do about it. The reader may well feel that he scarcely deserves to be given the reward of meeting her again. The circumstances deserve comment.

It was almost certainly the deliberate intention of Anne Brontë to make her heroine's lover as far removed from the romantic fictional type as possible—even anti-romantic. This tallies with her sister Charlotte's portrayal of Crimsworth and Frances Henri in *The Professor*—incidently yet another similitude—and with their mutual determination to have no truck with cheap sentimentalism, vapid alluring heroines and heroes too gallant and too romantic to be true. The reasons for Charlotte's bias is of course obvious. Plain, insignificant-looking and with no feminine figure and charm herself, she envied in her secret heart women who possess physical charm, and yet at the same time forced herself to despise them and the men who ran after them while ignoring women like herself who had what such insipid beauties lacked—intellect and moral strength. So, avenging herself on actuality, she created through the medium of her novels the fulfilment of her hidden desires. Her heroes and heroines, though triumphant in the end, are never handsome or romantic. In the Brontë code you could never have your cake and eat it: you can't be vivacious, handsome and attractive and still make a happy marriage. There must be a fatal flaw somewhere, some moral balancing of the unfair odds. So Rochester must pay for his sexual delinquencies: first by the madness of the dazzling, stimulating Bertha Mason, his Creole wife, then, as if that were not enough, by disfigurement and mutilation later. When Crimsworth discovers Zoraide Reuter's treachery, he finds solace in the love of the plainer but more sincere and literary Frances Henri and is happy; she has to fall back on the middle-aged man-of-the-world Peret with dubious prospects of married bliss. Similarly in *Agnes Grey.* The attractive, unprincipled Rosalie Murray must be made to pay for her promiscuous flirtations and conquests by a marriage of selfish social ambition and a ruined life.

But, decree the Brontës, true worth wins in the end; and so Crimsworth gets his Frances and Weston his Agnes, and they are blessed with contented homes and happy children while the more superficially exciting 'baddies' get their desserts. If this cuts no ice with us, it certainly appealed to the Victorian moral code for which the virtuous had always to be rewarded and the unprincipled punished.

A final comment on the novel. If the reader feels a certain lack of impact and sense of drama, let him reflect that this is due in part to the want of experience in the young author, but is at the same time deliberate. He must keep in the forefront of his mind the fact that she purposely set herself to pen (as did Charlotte with *The Professor*) a plain, unvarnished, realistic tale relating simply the life of ordinary everyday persons without exaggeration, without the invention of romantic scenes, sensational events or melodramatic sentiment. As far as it is possible for a writer to bring off such a story convincingly, Anne Brontë has succeeded in her aim; and her novel links itself as co-equal with that other similarly conceived novel *The Vicar of Wakefield*

for its quiet restraint achieved by a simple, factual, disciplined style which is all of a piece with her narrative. This is what George Moore had in mind when he asserted it to be 'the most perfect narrative in English literature . . . the one story . . . in which style, characters and subject are in perfect keeping.' As already admitted, this will probably strike the modern reader as excessively adulatory bearing Jane Austen in mind (to say nothing of Elizabeth Gaskell's *Cousin Phyllis* and *Cranford*); but the last words of his encomium at least are undeniably true. It is a style wonderfully attuned to subject and mood. Like certain actors, Anne Brontë is a master of the throw-away line, the deliberately under-played role. A perfect example is the little duologue (chapter 8) in which Agnes tells Rosalie her sister is going to be married.

"Is she—when?"

"Not till next month . . ."

"Why didn't you tell me before?"

"I've only got the news in this letter, which you stigmatise as dull and stupid, and won't let me read."

"To whom is she to be married?"

"To Mr. Richardson, the vicar of a neighbouring parish."

"Is he rich?"

"No, only comfortable."

"Is he handsome?"

"No, only decent."

"Young?"

"No, only middling."

"Oh mercy! What a wretch! What sort of house is it?"

"A quiet little vicarage, with an ivy-clad porch, an old-fashioned garden, and——"

"Oh stop!——you'll make me sick. How *can* she bear it?"

"I expect she'll not only be able to bear it, but to be very happy. You did not ask if Mr. Richardson were a good, wise or amiable man; I could have answered Yes to all these questions." . . .

That passage may be said to telescope Anne Brontë's attributes as a novelist—at least at this comparatively early apprenticeship period. (With *The Tenant of Wildfell Hall* she was to extend her range enormously.) Of course, those readers who prefer the more full-blooded melodrama of *Jane Eyre* will probably find her tongue-in-cheek sense of humour and quiet irony unsatisfying. Certainly it has to be admitted that, like some of the novels of Willa Cather[15], arguably the greatest American novelist after Henry James, *Agnes Grey* is a flat landscape and lacking dramatic conflict. Yet as George Moore observed, it has its own restrained beauty nonetheless. And if Edward Weston's manner of making his love known appears formal and cold, one may be forgiven for preferring it to the factitious passion of the Rochester-by-moonlight wooing[16].

In conclusion. Perhaps the most perceptive comments on *Agnes Grey* are the indirect and direct dicta respectively of Nathaniel Hawthorne and Charlotte Brontë. Discussing Trollope's novels the former enthused: 'They . . . are just as real as if some giant had hewn a great lump out of the earth and put it under a glass case, with all the inhabitants going about their daily business, and not suspecting that they were being made a show of.' While no balanced judgement can place *Agnes Grey* on a par with Trollope's best novels, Hawthorne's evaluation, down-scaled, fits it well enough. Charlotte's description of her sister's novel as being 'the mirror of the mind of the writer' too, though vague, is acceptable. That mind is a quiet, controlled, realistic, detached one, but searching nonetheless. *Agnes Grey* shows us that mind in its burgeoning. It had to await the cruel passage of time and the inspiration of *The Tenant of Wildfell Hall* before it could come into full flowering.

Notes

[1] Viz. *The Professor.*

[2] See [*The Novels of Anne Brontë: A Study and Reappraisal,* by A. Craig Bell, Merlin Books, Ltd., 1992, p. xi].

[3] See Winifred Gérin's *Anne Brontë,* p. 176

[4] See her *Albion and Marina* and *My Angria.*

[5] See Dembleby, *The Confession of Charlotte Brontë;* as to the letter written by Charlotte to Ellen Nussey the 7th April, 1840.

[6] Gérin: *Anne Brontë.*

[7] W. A. Craik, *The Brontë Novels.*

[8] George Moore was the first to point out this structural aspect of the novel. (See his *Conversations in Ebury Street.*)

[9] Published by the University of Minnesota Press, 1958

[10] A further resemblance here to *The Professor.* After searching all the likely places for Frances Henri, Crimsworth comes across her by pure chance in the Protestant cemetery.

[11] See [*"I—Sources of Inspiration"*].

[12] In passing one is unable to resist quoting a passage which Anne Brontë gives as an specimen of Matilda's coarseness of expression. This occurs in chapter 9 where we find this piece of dialogue between the mincing Rosalie and her hoyden of a sister:

> "Well, now get along," replied Miss Murray; "and do, dear Matilda, try to be a little more lady-like. Miss Grey, I wish you would tell her not to use such shocking words; she *will* call her horse a mare, it is so inconceivably shocking! And then she uses such dreadful expressions in describing it; she must have learned it from the grooms . . ."

This is obviously almost direct reportage, and must take all the prizes as a specimen of Victorian prudery and hypocrisy.

[13] See [*"I—Sources of Inspiration"*].

[14] See [*"I—Sources of Inspiration"*].

[15] E.g. *Death comes for the Archbishop, Shadows on the Rock, The Professor's House, One of Ours.*

[16] *Jane Eyre,* chapter XXIII.

Elizabeth Hollis Berry (essay date 1994)

SOURCE: "*Agnes Grey:* 'Pillars of Witness' in 'The Vale of Life,'" in *Anne Brontë's Radical Vision: Structures of Consciousness,* English Literary Studies, 1994, pp. 39-70.

[*In the following essay, Berry surveys the imagery of* Agnes Grey, *evaluating its thematic significance and artistry.*]

"All true histories contain instruction," reads the opening sentence of *Agnes Grey.*[1] This pointed assertion, linking truth with history and instruction, suggests a didacticism which, as Anne Brontë is careful to demonstrate at the outset, is tempered with an "entertaining" (3) or witty analysis of social structures. She addresses the reader directly in the opening paragraph, referring to the "kernel" of truth contained in the "nut" of her "history": a history which she thinks "might prove useful to some, and entertaining to others" (3). In this way Anne Brontë sets up the authentic base for her story and indicates a cogently defined balance between art and moral utility.

The cryptic suggestiveness of the opening "nut" image works well in securing the reader's attention, and it immediately becomes clear that the self-styled honesty or directness of her writing is not to be mistaken for simplistic moralizing or lack of conceptual depth. There is more to *Agnes Grey* than a simple moral tale. After illustrating Anne Brontë's controlled style and intellectual purpose in the reference to the "instruction" contained in "true histories," the first sentence continues: "though, in some, the treasure may be hard to find, and when found, so trivial in quantity that the dry, shrivelled kernel scarcely compensates for the trouble of cracking the nut" (3). The mock self-deprecation of the nut image suggests that the metaphorical "treasure" in *Agnes Grey* will be anything but "dry" or "shrivelled." Evidently, Anne Brontë's images are meant to convey symbolic truths, and her social and moral observations are to be found inside their shells.

Within the image patterns of her narrative are subtly intertwined motifs which operate cumulatively to create progressively deeper shades of meaning. The poetic aspect of Anne Brontë's writing lies in her imagery, and here her work shares certain similarities with that of Emily Brontë. But *Agnes Grey* and *The Tenant of Wildfell Hall* differ from *Wuthering Heights* in their detailing of a spiritual passage towards a *moral* end.[2] Anne Brontë is painstakingly careful to point out in the first lines of *Agnes Grey* that her illustrations of this particular pilgrim's progress have an instructional purpose. Yet, at the same time that she presents fiction as an instructional tool, she clearly exploits the complex allusiveness of image-filled poetic language and its embodiment of feeling. The combined expressive and structural function of her imagery simultaneously gives her fiction moral and poetical qualities.

Reflected in the analytical and confessional aspects of her lyric poems, Anne Brontë's recognition of poetry as a philosophical and therapeutic record of experience is echoed in the narrative of *Agnes Grey.* At a crucial point in Agnes Grey's spiritual development, she emphasizes the mediational value of poetry when "long oppressed by any powerful feelings which we must keep to ourselves . . . and which, yet, we cannot, or will not wholly crush" (153). In the chapter appropriately entitled "Confessions" Agnes describes poetry as both "penetrating and sympathetic" and explains how she uses it as experiential analysis, to recognize and cope with life's changing patterns:

> Before this time, at Wellwood House and here [at Horton Lodge], when suffering from home-sick melancholy, I had sought relief twice or thrice at this secret source of consolation; and now I flew to it again, with greater avidity than ever, because I seemed to need it more. I still preserve those relics of past sufferings and experience, like pillars of witness set up, in travelling through the vale of life, to mark particular occurrences. (154)

The "vale of life" through which Agnes travels on her journey to self-discovery is described by the images of different houses and the spaces between them. These images of enclosed or open spaces are the metaphorical "pillars of witness" which are "set up" to mark her progress as she moves from the "old grey parsonage" (15) of home to the grander establishments of Wellwood House and Horton Lodge, and, finally, a "respectable looking house" (196) by the sea. Comparable to the settings that mark Jane Eyre's progress from Gateshead to Ferndean, the landscapes and elements which form the open spaces between the houses create the emotional atmosphere of Agnes's passage and mark the psychological and spiritual significance of each step along the way.

As Anne Brontë maps out the particular "vale of life" through which Agnes travels, the metaphorical "pillars of witness" which are used to chart her progress give greater insight into the character's consciousness than was commonly found in other works of the governess type.[3] Unlike other protagonists from governess novels of the period, Agnes Grey is not a stereotype: she expresses an egalitarian individualism which is, like the landscape of her native hills and "woody dales" (112), roundly defined. In discriminating between Agnes's vigorous enthusiasm for the freedom of the seashore and her fear of "petrifying" (103) in the dark recesses of her employers' great houses, Anne Brontë refers to natural topography and seasonal change to illustrate a major thematic concern with the boundaries and limits imposed on the captive spirit by social structures of ownership within a repressive hierarchy. Lamenting the captive spirit's plight, Anne Brontë identifies herself as a "captive dove" in the poem of the same name, and her two fictional heroines are equally represented as captives whose awareness of what lies outside their confines adds to the "despair" of imprisonment until they escape from the drudgery of a soulless existence.[4]

Characters and relationships are repeatedly given definition, then, by reference to features of external setting. The choice of weather imagery for this purpose is one which Anne Brontë shares with her sisters, particularly Emily, and, as in *Wuthering Heights,* weather patterns are carefully schematized throughout *Agnes Grey* and *The Tenant.* Chitham, after noting some of the obvious similarities between *Wuthering Heights* and *The Tenant,* remarks that these similarities "stem from common Brontë preoccupations."[5] One such preoccupation was undoubtedly the weather, which appears as a major force in the letters of both Charlotte and Anne. Anne's poignant, cross-written letter (to Ellen Nussey) shortly before her death in 1849 makes particular mention of weather patterns. Here, as in her novels, she refers suggestively to the impact of weather on the inner landscape of the psyche when she agrees that May "is a trying month," for the "earlier part is often cold enough"; but with characteristic equanimity, she asserts that experience supports her belief in a natural pattern of mitigating warmth later: "we are almost certain of some fine warm days in the latter half when the laburnums and lilacs are in bloom."[6]

Agnes Grey's relationship with her employers and with Edward Weston can be charted through clearly linked weather images. Upon Agnes's arrival at the Murrays' house, the weather assures her of an oppressively limiting, ice-bound experience. She is shown rising "with some difficulty from under the super-incumbent snow-drift," which has been deposited on her by a "most bewildering storm" (60). Suggesting the kind of perilous, snow-covered pitfalls encountered by Lockwood in the third chapter of *Wuthering Heights,* the heavy load of this snow points to the bewildering and heavily-taxing experiences which await Agnes at Horton Lodge. Agnes is trapped by her social inferiority in the Murray household, just as she is restricted in her movements by the freezing snow.

The varying intensity of Agnes's relationship with Weston is also indicated by the weather. From the "bright sunshine and balmy air" (111) which sets the mood for their happy encounter over the primroses, the weather changes to "one of the gloomiest of April days, a day of thick, dark clouds, and heavy showers" (141) when Rosalie Murray determines to "fix that man" (139), and seems to be securing Weston's interest. Again, towards the close of the novel, weather imagery emphasizes the mounting apprehension and emotional "heat" which Agnes feels when she and Weston rediscover each other, feelings which are significantly displayed in the chapter's initial focus on "the heat of the weather" (203). The emotional tension of their reunion is then effectively released when both the weather and Weston's silence break. Weston's explanatory statement, "it was not my way to flatter and talk soft nonsense" (207), and his confession of love for Agnes both take place on a day when a "thunder-shower had certainly had a most beneficial effect upon the weather" (206). Agnes's growing inner sense of calm resolution is also correlated with the change in the weather: "a heavy and protracted thunder-shower during the afternoon had almost destroyed my hopes of seeing him that day; but now the storm was over, and the sun was shining brightly" (205). In this concluding chapter, where Anne Brontë recreates a sunny inner calm after the outer storm, the mild, sunny weather acts as a metaphor for the serenity of an integrated consciousness that balances life's problems with faith. Mirroring this preoccupation with spiritual reconciliation, a comparable concern with the weather's emotional import occurs in Emily Brontë's representation of a soft wind blowing peace over the sleeping spirits at the end of *Wuthering Heights.*

Anne Brontë also uses wind imagery in **Agnes Grey** for the delineation of character. Certain figures are characterized by images of winds blowing both hot and cold, the effects of hot and cold air also defining an imbalance in particular characters and metaphorically representing forms of communication. The unseasonably cold and windy weather upon Agnes's arrival at the Bloomfield residence in September implies that winter has begun early, signifying a wintry mood which, in emotional terms, accords with Agnes's new experience. Although Agnes's spirits are high with positive expectations, Anne Brontë stresses (through the meteorological specificity of a "north-easterly wind") that the miserable weather makes the journey noticeably longer and harder to bear: "the heavy clouds, and strong northeasterly wind combined to render the day extremely cold and dreary, and the journey seemed a very long one" (16). The cold, biting wind provides emphatic metaphorical support to Agnes's experience of Mrs. Bloomfield's bitterly unwelcoming reception and also emphasizes her vulnerability as the young governess in the hands of a new employer. Mrs. Bloomfield's way of speaking to Agnes evokes an emotional winter: she is "chilly in her manner" (17), and to her newly-arrived employee she directs "a succession of commonplace remarks, expressed with frigid formality" (17).

Anne Brontë's choice of wind imagery here combines with the physical description of Agnes to show her blighted both by the actual physical cold without and the emotional cold within. Her exposure to the "bitter wind" has left her hands "almost palsied" (18) by the numbing cold, in an enactment of the psychological chill that freezes her faculty of speech and reduces her to an inarticulate nonentity. Agnes later recalls that the few words she is able to speak are "spoken in the tone of one half-dead, or half-asleep" (17). Echoing the expression of those forlorn, imprisoned Gondal figures in Anne Brontë's poetry, Agnes's description of her impaired voice emphasizes the silencing and numbing effect of her passage to this alien place. Agnes's distress is marked by feebly self-deprecating humor: "'My hands are so benumbed with the cold that I can scarcely handle my knife and fork,'" apologizes Agnes, "with a feeble attempt at a laugh" (18). Mrs. Bloomfield's words maintain the icy imagery in an answer meant to silence the underling: "'I dare say you would find it cold,' replied she with a cool, immutable gravity that did not serve to reassure me" (18). In this metaphorical embodiment of social barriers, Agnes is emotionally left out in the cold.

Yet, moving beyond the limited emotional scope of the Gondal poems, this part of the narrative reveals Anne Brontë's wry humor. In an acutely rendered psychological representation of shame, she creates a scene where Agnes's childlike discomfort is countered by an ironic, detached perspective of the adult. She achieves this through her choice of diction: Agnes is "sensible that the awful lady was a spectator to the whole transaction" of her inept attempt to cut the tough meat (18).

The elevated formality of the language that presents a powerful authority figure set against the absurdity of the situation indicates two disparate levels of experience which recreate a psychological paradox. On one level, Agnes recognizes herself as a dependent child, sitting with a fork in her fists, "like a child of two years old," grappling with her dinner; on another level, she recalls the daunting impression of authoritarian pomposity in the "awful lady" growing proportionately more grandiose as she witnesses the absurd "transaction" (18).

Anne Brontë uses this dramatization of discomfort in combination with the winter imagery to indicate Agnes's alienation from her employers, her laconic self-representation firmly contained within the context of oppression. Agnes's "palsied" hands (18) and her inability to converse refer metaphorically to the recurring theme of freedom versus restraint. Through these details, Anne Brontë demonstrates how the power of self-expression is taken away from Agnes, and her active self is held in check, prevented from any freedom of expressive action by the deadening bonds of social tyranny.

Throughout *Agnes Grey*, Anne Brontë's use of weather imagery provides an analogous commentary on characters and their methods of communication. The way in which certain characters blow hot or cold like the wind suggests their inherent distance from, or proximity to, a golden mean of spiritual balance. In her method of signifying, one feels that Brontë grasped a notion comparable to that of the redefining semiotic force within language,[7] for radical redefinitions emerge from her acute representation of the ways in which different characters communicate. Encoded in the way her characters speak or maintain silence is a wealth of information about role, power, gender and intellect. While Mr. Murray, a florid "hearty bon-vivant" (63), puffs away stoutly in his own milieu, he is almost devoid of expression when faced with a lowly female minion such as Agnes. Hatfield, too, is all expressive energy when he comes "flying from the pulpit in such eager haste to shake hands with the squire" (84), or "sweeping along like a whirlwind, with his rich silk gown flying behind him, and rustling against the pew doors" (85), but he can find barely a murmur of comfort for the impoverished family of "poor Jem" (his dying parishioner) or for a sadly troubled Nancy Brown (100-101).

What emerges from Mr. Murray's failure to communicate (other than by extremes) is a demonstration of hierarchical boundaries. Both his limits as a man and his powerful position at the head of the squirearchy are encoded in the scant greeting reserved for Agnes. This barely acknowledges her existence and offers a form of silent dismissal for that female sub-species, the governess. His "'Morning Miss Grey,' or some such brief salutation," is delivered with an "unceremonious

nod" (63); whereas his "blustering" personality is known to Agnes from other sources and from the sound of his raucous laughter in the distance or his frequently voluble blaspheming against the hapless male servants. In Agnes's significant remark that she never sees him "except on Sundays," when he joins other highly-respected but similarly unsympathetic members of the community in church, Brontë points to the hypocrisy of a fixed social order.

Like Arthur Huntingdon in *The Tenant,* Mr. Murray is a representation of what Juliet McMaster calls "the masculine ethos of the Regency";[8] by setting off his meagre dialogue with the earnest governess against the rough profusion of his speech with the male servants, Brontë's rendering of this ethos is instructive. Her analysis of social structures indicates that it is not simply a question of Agnes's being culturally unworthy of his conversation: what Brontë implies is, rather, a psycho-social dysfunction on the part of Mr. Murray which prevents either rational or affective dialogue. This inability to speak the same language as their young employee places both Mr. and Mrs. Murray firmly in the old order, whereas the enlightened governess, with her concepts of equality and moral integrity, heralds a new era which is altogether foreign to the Murrays and their unquestioning ilk. Thus the only sounds to penetrate Agnes's isolated world echo an intemperate roughness which violates the gentle humanitarian values she holds dear. In *Agnes Grey,* then, the lack of meaningful dialogue between master and servant, mistress and governess, demonstrates the supposed insignificance of the "hireling" (69): in these scenes, Anne Brontë's images re-enact the voicelessness of those who do not signify within an unbalanced social structure.

This concern with the influence of social structures on forms of expression and types of character emerges again in Anne Brontë's use of facial imagery. Pointing to the thematic emphasis on balance according to a divinely ordained natural order, Brontë also delineates her characters' emotional states through her depiction of facial coloring. The ability to hide feelings with practised ease, as Rosalie Murray does, is countered in the narrative by a moral lesson on the price to be paid for artifice of any kind. When Hatfield's hot and misguided pursuit of Rosalie ends in her rejection of him, the first indication of his pain is shown in his loss of color, which implies a loss of face. In contrast, the coquette's controlled dissimulation enables her to keep her "countenance so well that he could not imagine that I [Rosalie] was saying anything more than the actual truth" (127). The effect is given further emphasis when it is reported through Rosalie's callous recollection: "You should have *seen* how his countenance fell! He went perfectly white in the face" (127).

Although such facial images are used by other novelists (such as Jane Austen and Maria Edgeworth—whose work she well knew), Anne Brontë indicates a keenly observed awareness of the blush as psychological marker. Giving a slight twist to the symbolic link between warm coloring and healthy vitality, Brontë shows some characters with heightened color as they exert an unnatural or excessive control over others. The extremely violent passions and "insensate stubbornness" of Mary Anne Bloomfield are marked by the "high colour in her cheeks" (32,19); and Rosalie's news of her dishonest conquest is conveyed "with buoyant step, flushed cheek, and radiant smiles showing that she, too, was happy, in her own way" (126). Resonating with the moral implications suggested by earlier narrative depictions of guilty pleasure, this image of the blushing check recalls the unhealthy flush of "distemper" which signals Eve's downfall after she has eaten the fruit in *Paradise Lost*.[9]

In the case of Rosalie, this changing facial imagery embodies the destructive tendencies of her character and indicates how she sufers through her misuse of power. A similar embodiment of destructive energy is presented in the grim portrait of Rosalie's ill-chosen husband, whose face, "pale, but somewhat blotchy, and disagreeably red about the eye-lids," is a physiognomical map of debauchery (192). Brontë furthers the impression of their marriage's devastating impact on Rosalie through images that recollect the former vitality of the young bride:

> a space of little more than twelve months had had the effect that might be expected from as many years, in reducing the plumpness of her form, the freshness of her complexion, the vivacity of her movements, and the exuberance of her spirits. (184)

This list of Rosalie's former glories, preceded by the verbal "reducing," has the effect of a flashback which demonstrates through the syntactic shape of the sentence a measurable reduction of her vital self. Although the character of Rosalie is ultimately treated in a relatively sympathetic light, these metaphorical pointers to her physical and moral flaws unobtrusively imply the value of a thinking woman (Agnes), set against the dubious worth of one who is frivolous and unprincipled. Brontë makes this implicit comparison between the two by showing Rosalie's thoughtless actions focalized in Agnes's pained but caring reactions to her former pupil. Thus when Agnes counsels Rosalie to be a dutiful wife and a loving mother, to find "genuine affection" (194) at least from caring for her unwanted daughter, "the unfortuate young lady" (195) recognizes the "wisdom and goodness" (194) in Agnes's views but refuses to acknowledge their relevance in a life she feels is "wasting away" for want of youthful passion (193). Although clearly self-made, the thoughtless Rosalie's plight is subtly emphasized by Agnes's shrewdly ironic perspective, combined with her "heavy heart" at the young woman's

tearful clinging and "intreaties," as "poor Lady Ashby" desperately begs for "consolation" from the governess

> whose general tastes and ideas were so little congenial to her own, whom she had completely forgotten in her hours of prosperity, and whose presence would be rather a nuisance than a pleasure, if she could but have half her heart's desire. (195)

Equally effective in its subtle emphasis, Brontë's use of heat imagery suggests the moral gulf between two spiritually antithetical male characters: Murray and Weston. Revealing a social paradox in her representation of these two figures, Brontë portrays Weston as the ideal of manhood, whose character emphasizes, in Winifred Gérin's words, "the silent worth of a deeply charitable nature,"[10] and exemplifies the thematic interest in spiritual balance. Weston's fiery defence of Nancy Brown's lost cat in the face of the angry Squire Murray and his gamekeeper offers an ironic comment on different kinds of emotional heat.

Supposing that Murray is "accustomed to use rather strong language when he's heated" (108), Weston explains his confrontation with the greedy landowner in words which imply that his own warmth is of a softer genus than that of the hot-tempered Murray:

> "Miss Grey," said he . . . "I wish you would make my peace with the squire, when you see him. He was by when I rescued Nancy's cat, and did not quite approve of the deed. I told him I thought he might better spare all his rabbits than she her cat, for which audacious assertion, he treated me to some rather ungentlemanly language, and I fear, I retorted a trifle too warmly." (107-108)

Placed in this context, the heat image becomes more than an indication of temperament and takes on more widely reaching social and moral implications. Clearly, Murray's heat has nothing to do with a burning concern for fellow beings, the kind of heartfelt warmth evinced by the three characters who sit discussing the incident in the gentle glow of Nancy's cottage fire. In his egalitarian attempt to redress the social balance, Weston's warmly indignant retort contrasts the "ungentlemanly" response of Squire Murray who is hotly defending his territorial rights as landowner. Murray's is the unbalanced heat of a choleric and irrational tyrant, a sign of his excess in contrast to the warm indignance of one who would challenge social inequities. Unlike the Murray family, whose unjust use of wealth and position cannot be excused, Weston represents the kind of warm character who is blameless and needs no apology. Weston's egalitarian mentality will allow the possibility of conciliation, but the squire's extreme nature and position will not. With wry significance, Anne Brontë gives Weston the final comment: "then with a peculiar half-smile, he added,

'But never mind; I imagine the squire has more to apologise for than I.' And left the cottage" (108).

Central to the middle chapter (12) in which these scenes take place is the archetypal symbol of the hearth or fireplace, the source of other kinds of "warmth." Signaled by its obviously pivotal situation in the narrative, the health is a key image in *Agnes Grey,* just as it is in *The Tenant.* The hearth not only recurrently defines the importance of family within Anne Brontë's scheme, but it also offers a focus for her ethical inquiry into the contradictions of a society that houses the frigid, over-indulged "superiors" in far better circumstances than those of the caring, disenfranchised workers.

Early in the novel, the warmth of loving devotion which fuels Agnes Grey's exemplary family is suggested in the reference to her parents' bond: "if she [Agnes's mother] would but consent to embellish his humble hearth, he [Agnes's father] should be happy to take her on any terms" (4). The mutual respect expressed in Agnes's parents' marriage is of primary importance in enabling them to deal with the financial misfortunes that leave their hearth humbled to the point of emptiness. Agnes recalls the family's united response to a period of ill-fortune when her father's mercantile investments are literally sunk in a shipwreck:

> then we sat with our feet on the fender, scraping the perishing embers together from time to time, and occasionally adding a slight scattering of the dust and fragments of coal, just to keep them alive. (8)

Although short of physical heat, Agnes's family is rich in emotional warmth, and the close family ties are actually heightened by their scant rations. In the Grey family the valued commodity of warmth is "carefully husbanded" (8), and because they look after the fire (as they look after each other) the "perishing embers" of family life are kept alive.

The warm farewells of these loving people she has left at home emphasize the bleakness of Agnes's reception at Wellwood. Her "bright hopes, and ardent expectations" (13) are abruptly shattered by her discovery that Mrs. Bloomfield is not the "kind, motherly woman" (16) she hoped would meet her. Her employer is as cold and dreary as the autumn weather. Again, arriving at Horton Lodge in a snow storm that mirrors the emotional climate, Agnes discovers icy desolation, as the "kind and hospitable reception" which she naively anticipated is coolly withheld (60). The imagery stresses that this pilgrim endures a cold and "formidable passage" (59) from place to place, and her movements are not eased by any nurturing warmth from the hierarchical establishment.

The governess's enforced isolation and lowly status are immediately brought home to Agnes by the distant situation of her allotted living quarters. The bleak space reserved for her is placed away from the warm core of the house: "up the back stairs, a long, steep, double flight, and through a long narrow passage" (61). Even more suggestive of her removal from human warmth is the "small, smouldering fire" (61) whose paucity of flame offers a poignant comment on the lack of a great blaze of warm comfort to greet the solitary traveller. What awaits her is a visibly deadening, disturbingly blank "wide, white, wilderness" of the "alien" unknown (62). This inhospitable landscape suggests a winter of the soul, where her imprisoning servitude is metaphorically reinforced by the cold, cramped room, in which Agnes's spirit must smoulder like the fire until it is released and given the freedom to burn brightly.

Mrs. Murray's attitude and stance implicitly exclude Agnes from any warm acceptance. She is pictured standing by the fire, while commenting tersely on the weather and the "rather rough" (64) journey of the previous day. Brontë gives us the spatial impression of the mistress standing between the fireplace and her new governess, effectively blocking any warmth from Agnes who ruefully compares herself to a "new servant girl" accorded scant consideration (64). Agnes points out that this treatment differs markedly from the comfort or welcome offered to a newcomer by her own mother (also a "lady"), who, in contrast to Mrs. Murray, "would have seen her immediately after her arrival . . . and given her some words of comfort" (64). Within the compass of Anne Brontë's tale, however, the comfort never comes from the rich: the gentlefolk avoid gentle acts of kindness when a poor family needs help, leaving an impoverished curate to provide the consumptive laborer "poor Jem" with the life-sustaining warmth of a good fire. The worldly cleric, Hatfield, offers no help other than "some harsh rebuke to the afflicted wife," or a "heartless observation," but Weston reacts with thoughtful generosity, as Nancy Brown reports: "when he seed how poor Jem shivered wi' cold an' what pitiful fires we kept . . . he sent us a sack of coals next day; an' we've had good fires ever sin'" (101).

From Brontë's differentiation between the cottages' honest warmth and the frigidly "proper" (39) households of the ill-bred rich, emerges a trenchant dialectic that runs beneath the surface of her apparently quiet narrative. Within the "shells" of these images of the hearth and fireplace is a discussion about innate divisions in the mainstream Victorian sensibility. Contemporary belief systems incorporated a strong sense of moral endeavor within an apparently incompatible stress on material gain. The fireplace stood at the core of the Victorian home, and became a popular symbol for the sort of solid virtues and lofty idealism which are noticeable by their absence from the rich houses of *Agnes Grey.* The sustaining warmth and hearty strength associated with the hearth are more likely to be found in the humble cottages of characters such as Nancy Brown, than in the "great" houses of the Murrays or the Bloomfields. These carefully placed images reveal the radically charged perception that whereas the cottage fireside is closed to nobody, only a privileged inner circle is invited to share the manorial hearth.

Implicit in Anne Brontë's variations on the hearth motif is an indictment of society's hypocritical endorsement of two such mutually exclusive notions—that of loving one's neighbors, and that of boldly exploiting them either for personal gain or in the name of maintaining the established order. The Evangelical emphasis on duty, which was so stringent a part of Anne Brontë's consciousness, led to an awareness of the need to conform socially. Yet, a mind and heart attuned to the egalitarian doctrines of non-conformist theology could not avoid the troubling conclusion that the existing structure was dangerously riven. The hearth, as the functional heart of family life, is an effective focus for her examination of social and spiritual divisions.

After years at Horton Lodge with the Murrays, denied the nurturing warmth of the family hearth, of acceptance as an equal, of "real social intercourse" (102), or even of companionship, Agnes understandably (perhaps even inevitably) experiences an inner death. Identifying as "a serious evil" (102) the savage influence exercised on her moral consciousness by such "ignorant" (102), restrictive employers, she begins to fear for her soul:

> Already, I seemed to feel my intellect deteriorating, my heart petrifying, my soul contracting, and I trembled lest my very moral perceptions should become deadened, my distinctions of right and wrong confounded, and all my better faculties be sunk, at last beneath the baneful influence of such a mode of life. (103)

The terms "petrifying," "contracting," and "deteriorating" suggest the sort of forensic observations which might be used for scientific purposes to record the inexorable destruction of life by the "baneful influence" of blind external forces. The statement is not simply that growth is inhibited in the absence of warmth or light: what makes the imagery memorable is that these objectively distancing terms are applied to something as intensely subjective as the internal anguish of a soul in torment.

Anne Brontë does, however, make it clear that relief and sustenance can be found for the "contracting" soul (103) in the living glow of Nancy Brown's kitchen fire, where "there's room for all" (106). This openly shared fire offers a comforting respite from the artificial restraints of Agnes's almost "deadened" (103) existence in the frigid environment of the mansion house. By juxtaposition, Brontë demonstrates how

Agnes's cry from the very heart she fears is "petrifying" is immediately answered in the spiritual and moral reassurance of the scene where Nancy's cat is restored to its fireside place by Mr. Weston. Both Agnes's and Weston's commitment to a truly benevolent ideal of service takes them to the heart of Nancy's predicament and to a fireside which welcomes all—regardless of rank or fortune. The conviction that all are entitled to share the fire is borne out in a series of concerned protestations, from Nancy's "Won't you come to th' fire, miss?" to Weston's "But it strikes me I'm keeping your visitor away from the fire" (107). Their love of and concern to share the fireside (specifically mentioned in Thackeray's definition of a "gentleman")[11] identify the happy trio seated by Nancy's humble fire as nobler souls. Regardless of rank, these three are clearly closer to the lofty ideals of well-bred gentility than anything evinced by the ironically styled "angles of light" (90) up at the manor.

This spatially differentiated detailing of the natural nobility to be found in the cottage as distinct from the Lodge is ironically reinforced in the narrative by references to misplaced acts of charity. Agnes specifies the ways in which the "grand ladies" misconstrue the very meaning of nobility in the shabby condescension of their pretence at charitable actions. Focusing on Rosalie Murray's hunger for a noble title, Brontë comments scathingly on the ignoble practices of those like Rosalie, who would wish to be ennobled without any true understanding of the social implications or moral responsibilities associated with privilege. Brontë's sharp recognition of the gulf between inner and outer enrichment shows the largesse distributed by the grand ladies to be entirely devoid of Agnes's genuine benevolence. The controlled outrage in Agnes's double-edged comments reveals the ladies' charity as cold indeed:

> I could see that the people were often hurt and annoyed by such conduct, though their fear of the "grand ladies" prevented them from testifying any resentment; but *they* never perceived it. They thought that, as these cottagers were poor and untaught, they must be stupid and brutish; and as long as they, their superiors, condescended to talk to them and to give them shillings and half-crowns, or articles of clothing, they had a right to amuse themselves, even at their expense; and the people must adore them as angels of light, condescending to minister to their necessities, and enlighten their humble dwellings. (90)

Adroitly emphasizing the glaring absence of fine qualities in these ladies and gentlemen, Brontë's technique of ironic signifying dwells on light images here in order to stress the darker side of privilege. The irony gains its bite from the realization that behind the conventional light imagery linking angels—or spirituality—and enlightenment lies the truth that blind hypocrisy's damaging reality is neither angelic nor enlightening.

Here Anne Brontë's language figures forth the ideal of enlightened humility rewritten in scenes emblematic of humiliation. For these ladies and gentlemen, as the narrative unfolds, the hearth is manifestly lacking in heart; the fireside is not the hub of solidly virtuous, Christian family life. Instead, we see it in Anne Brontë's terms, as a focal point for the realization that behind the condescending mask of virtue lurks a material, self-serving beast.

Referring at certain points in the narrative to the beastly or brutal aspects of the aspiring gentlefolks' ways, Anne Brontë (not surprisingly) uses animal imagery. Her interpretation of the word "animal" has, however, two aspects: she shows human brutality as animal-like, belonging to a lower order of beings, yet at the same time she also allows for the acceptance of all animals as God's "creatures" (86). In one system (the natural order) all are worthy; in the other (the social order) only the powerful or the beautiful signify. From the debased value system of a class which prizes external appearance above all else comes a catalogue of worth such as young Master Bloomfield's classification of species with its inherent endorsement of cruelty: "it's a pity to kill the pretty singing birds, but the naughty sparrows and mice and rats I may do what I like with," he chillingly recounts (22). Brontë thus divides her animal imagery to illustrate two separate elements in her thinking: the general admission that all God's creatures are worthwhile, set against the inhuman beastliness of some human behavior. Agnes makes this distinction in her comments on Matilda Murray: "As an animal, Matilda was all right . . . as an intelligent human being she was barbarously ignorant, indocile, careless and irrational" (68).

The roots of a punitive social structure are suggested in the picture of ruthlessly destructive behavior which Anne Brontë presents through her references to animals. Little Fanny Bloomfield is so hopelessly overindulged that she spits in the faces of those who cross her and bellows "like a bull" (34) when she is not humored. John Murray is "as rough as a young bear" (69) to the extent that he proves to be "unteachable—at least for a governess under his mother's eye" (69). That last, almost parenthetical, comment says everything about the problems Agnes encounters with her charges. The parents pass on their debased values to their children, who, in turn, pass them on to all they meet. Tom Bloomfield's father plays an instructive role in his son's brutal treatment of the young sparrows. When young Bloomfield pulls off "their legs and wings and heads," to which savagery his father's only comment is that "they were nasty things, and I must not let them soil my trousers," the elder Bloomfield confirms sick disequilibrium in a harshly materialistic social order (22).

These implications in the animal imagery move towards a culminating sense that such unprincipled materialists as the Bloomfields are really more the embodiment of predatory animals than civilized beings. Presenting the reader with images of feral opportunism, Brontë's language demonstrates that the scene at the Bloomfield house is oddly redolent of a den of wolves: when visitors arrive, the children clamber over them like a litter of hungry cubs. As Agnes observes, "they would indecently and clamourously interrupt the conversation of their elders, roughly collar the gentlemen, climb their knees uninvited, hang about their shoulders, or rifle their pockets, pull the ladies' gowns, disorder their hair, tumble their collars and importunately beg for their trinkets" (51). Agnes's allusion to her pupils' wild antics offers a precise reference to the untamed world they embody when she sees them, in animal terminology, "quarreling over their victuals like a set of tiger's cubs" (42). Similarly, although the figure of Uncle Robson has a comic touch with his "foppery of stays," Brontë suggests that something sinister and bestial lurks about his "little grey eyes, frequently half-closed" (46). In the manner of a predator, he brings his bird-nesting "spoils" to the children, who in turn run hungrily "to beg each a bird for themselves" (47).

With some irony, in view of her own status as brood mare to a noble sire, it falls to Rosalie Murray (one of the "ignorant wrong-headed girls" [102]) to demonstrate the contrasting usage of the words "beast" and "creature," when, in the insensate prattle of a grasping coquette she crudely assesses the comparative worth of the men present at the "odious" Sir Thomas Ashby's ball. In the space of two sentences she refers to Agnes as a "good creature" and to Sir Thomas as "young, rich, and gay, but an ugly beast nevertheless" (81), a distinction which proves to have moral as well as physical implications. For Rosalie herself Brontë reserves the most unpleasant animal metaphor to express the mindless rapacity of her determination to "fix" Weston, once Agnes's devotion to him is clear, largely to prove her superior force in a crass sexual power game. Agnes falls victim to a society which keeps her powerless, while Rosalie—indulging in "excessive vanity"—relishes the freedom to enact her cruel urge to snare and enslave. Through the eyes of painful frustration Agnes sees Rosalie take on the vicious animal shape of Tennyson's "Nature, red in tooth and claw."[12] Agnes's bitter observations place Rosalie at the level of a greedy, gloating dog:

> I could only conclude that excessive vanity, like drunkenness, hardens the heart, enslaves the faculties, and perverts the feelings, and that dogs are not the only creatures which, when gorged to the throat, will yet gloat over what they cannot devour, and grudge the smallest morsel to a starving brother. (149-50)

Similarly revealing, the careful juxtaposition of Rosalie's urge for a noble title with her sister's allusion to horse breeding allows Brontë to illustrate the dehumanizing effects of the marriage market. She shows that Rosalie's fascination with pedigree has more to do with the breeding animal conjured up in Matilda's reportedly "shocking" reference to her "fine blood mare" (78) than it does with vigorously independent womanhood. Although Rosalie insists that her sister's use of the word "mare" is "so *inconceivably* shocking!" (79), in the same instant she launches into an inventory of the noble pedigrees present at her ball: "two noblemen, three baronets and five titled ladies!" (79). Anne Brontë's positioning of these images of "breeding and pedigree" (79) implies that Rosalie's chosen role is ultimately debasing: that of a brood mare, mated with the most prestigious sire.

Equally informative is the way people treat their animals. In complete contrast to the harsh treatment meted out to the family pets of the Bloomfield and Murray families, the cherishing care given by Nancy Brown to her cat is an exemplar of domestic harmony and affection. In an expression of mindless barbarity, Uncle Robson's favorite dogs are dealt with "brutally" (47), and Miss Matilda inflicts upon her erstwhile pet Snap "many a harsh word and many a spiteful kick and pinch" (118) before he is taken away from Agnes (who loves her "warm-hearted companion") and "delivered over to the tender mercies of the village ratcatcher, a man notorious for his brutal treatment of his canine slaves" (155). As an enactment of the brutality meted out to all lesser beings (human or animal), Rector Hatfield's treatment of the hapless terrier is a deplorably cruel reflection of the hierarchy: "Mr. Hatfield, with his cane, administered a resounding thwack on the animal's skull, and sent it yelping back to me, with a clamorous outcry that afforded the reverend gentleman great amusement" (121). The irony in "reverend gentleman" is obvious to the reader, who is by now fully aware that his conduct throughout is neither gentlemanly nor worthy of reverence.

Nancy's cat, by contrast, is her "gentle friend" (91), and the affectionate bond between them serves to confirm the gap in awareness which separates the poor cottager from her supposed moral and spiritual superiors. The cat, which is pictured lovingly "with her long tail half encircling her velvet paws, and her half-closed eyes dreamily gazing on the low, crooked fender" (91), appears in a far more sympathetic light than the man of the cloth who unceremoniously knocks her off his knee, "like as it may be in scorn and anger" according to Nancy (97). Brontë infuses with irony Nancy's comment, "you can't expect a cat to know manners like a Christian, you know, Miss Grey" (97), since the cat appears at this moment more one of God's creatures than the clergyman.

The social tensions and inequities within the "shells" of Brontë's animal images are also outlined in two distinct images of enclosed space which are established as opposing structures of consciousness at the beginning of *Agnes Grey*. A significant source of antithetical imagery in the novel, the contrast between the material confines of the large houses and the spiritual freedom to be found in humbler dwellings reinfores the novel's psycho-social commentary. This symbolic use of setting was briefly touched upon in an unsigned review from the *Christian Remembrancer* of 1857: the kitchens of Anne and Emily Brontë are, it says, "low, and tell a tale."[13] Although clearly pejorative in purpose, this little remark comes unintentionally close to defining Anne Brontë's method of fusing the outer setting with the inner world of her characters in order to advance the psychological process and, as the anonymous reviewer suspected, "tell a tale," or, as Brontë herself intended, a "true" history (3). Early on in her tale she shows that Agnes's mother is pulled toward the "elegant house," but the humble "cottage" (4) draws her in the opposite direction and wins: "An elegant house and spacious grounds were not to be despised: but she would rather live in a cottage with Richard Grey than in a palace with any other man in the world" (3-4). Although focalized in the character of Agnes's mother, this emphatic comment anticipates Agnes's own character, revealing her pragmatic but passionate consciousness linked to that of her sensible, loving mother.

From its placement at the beginning of the novel, this glimpse of a "good" woman who knows the value of a "good" man presents in miniature a set of images that figure prominently later in the narrative. The picture of contrasting spaces and the figurative meanings attached to them gives an indication of the novel's themes, and, in this way the spatial and architectural images (common metaphors for consciousness) suggest a human need to be attuned to spiritual as well as material levels of being in order to achieve inner growth or balance. The superficial splendor promised for Rosalie's coming-out ball, for example, is immediately countered by an image of a small house, a "quiet little vicarage, with an ivy-clad porch" (77), which, unlike the rich estate of her intended husband, offers Rosalie more likelihood of real fulfillment. From her instructive use of these contrasting images, Anne Brontë makes it clear that the woman who develops as a whole person does so only on the basis of self-reliance. Agnes says of her mother: "A carriage and a lady's maid were great conveniences; but thank Heaven, she had feet to carry her, and hands to minister to her own necessities" (3). Her mother's autonomy prefigures Agnes's own journey towards independence and selfhood. Emerging from the expository spatial imagery in the early part of the novel is a suggestively configured picture that indicates ongoing thematic concerns. The last glimpse Agnes has of her home as she leaves for her new life is one which shows the solid "old grey parsonage" and the "village spire" together, illuminated by a "slanting beam of sunshine" (15). This image, which shows earthly structures linked to heaven by a beam of light, indicates the spiritual pathway ahead.

Throughout *Agnes Grey* interiors are not described in detail, but their contained inner spaces delineate boundaries or limits on the corporeal if not the spiritual freedom of those who live within. The restraint on Agnes is manifestly powerful when she reveals how she has been kept effectively a prisoner in the school-room. Although it is delivered with characteristic understatement, her comment on the deliberate curtailment of her free time betrays an abusive situation which amounts to covert enslavement, couched in the language of powerlessness: "my kind pupil took care I should spend it neither there [with Nancy Brown] nor anywhere else beyond the limits of the school-room" (147). The irony of the words "kind" and "care" indicates Agnes's bitterness without laboring the point about being held captive, for it becomes clear that there is no space for any expansion of the self in a world where she has no choice.

Yet, by careful juxtaposition, Anne Brontë also points out the illusory nature of the Murray sisters' physical liberty which they flaunt at every opportunity for self-display, while Agnes is kept indoors, her person judged to be insignificant, unworthy of public space or approbation. Closely following the picture of Agnes's confinement to the school-room is a penetrating summary of what Rosalie expects from her "inauspicious match" (147) with Sir Thomas Ashby. Beneath Rosalie's catalogue of social and material advantages is Brontë's unspoken belief that inner freedom counts for far more than the feigned liberty of profligate materialism. Brontë's representation of the marriage market's psychological crux here is acute. Although Rosalie is prepared to trade marital happiness for material gain, she fears the "inauspicious" coupling with a lugubrious character whose conjugal ownership of her will be irrevocable. No amount of positive effusions about power and property can hide the underlying suspicion that she is herself property, trapped in a position of powerlessness. Beneath Rosalie's fluttering anticipation that the marriage will broaden her social horizons is the quiet dread of its restrictive finality. Brontë reveals Rosalie's ambivalence in a paragraph that opens with her looking forward to an expansion of her world:

> Rosalie was pleased with the thoughts of becoming mistress of Ashby Park; she was elated with the prospect of the bridal ceremony and its attendant splendour and eclat, the honeymoon spent abroad, and the subsequent gaieties she expected to enjoy in London and elsewhere. (147)

Later in the same paragraph, Brontë implies that despite the triumphant expectations of the bride-to-be, her world, like her courage, actually appears to be shrinking. These expressions of wealth and freedom are rapidly undercut by the negative observations that "she seemed to shrink from the idea of being so soon united" and "it seemed a horrible thing to hurry on the inauspicious match" (147). That such words as "horrified," "warnings," and "evil" follow the reference to Rosalie's pleasurable "thoughts" and "prospects" shows the disparity between any sort of spiritual "union" and the dismal actuality of the marriage market (147). In combination with the spatial and architectural imagery, this passage re-frames the double-edged maxim that walls do not a prison make. Anne Brontë's judicious use of irony suggests that the Murrays are locked into a system of self-seeking materialism which can only stifle any nascent spirituality and must ultimately prove destructive to the soul.

Through recurring imagery of roads, lanes, walls, and windows, Anne Brontë introduces the realization that, counter to any outward appearance, the Murrays' world is actually severely limited. Within that socially delimited space, various forms of emotional control heartlessly restrict the growth of its occupants in a way repugnant to Anne Brontë's egalitarian consciousness. "But why can't she read it in the park or garden?" asks an anxious Mrs. Murray, when her nubile daughter seems to be escaping the set bounds of her genteel existence by taking her book to the field, "like some poor neglected girl that has no park to walk in, and no friends to take care of her" (119-20). Here the idea of the park where the friends ironically "take care of her" suggests a curtailment of true freedom, for, unlike Agnes who is free to cross social barriers when she is allowed to go out, the Murray daughters are entirely trapped in the limiting prejudices of the landowning class. Subsequently, the contradictions in Mrs. Murray's peculiar brand of caring are fully revealed. That the maternal interest smacks more of property management than love, is attested by Agnes's reaction to the coldly commercial exchange of this ill-fated marriage. When considering Rosalie's "inauspicious match" with the ugly Sir Thomas Ashby, Agnes confesses, "I was amazed and horrified at Mrs. Murray's heartlessness, or want of thought for the real good of her child" (147). Agnes's dismay emphasizes a maze-like confusion in social structures where human values are mixed up with property, and caring is confused with acquisition or control.

Rosalie's flirtation with Hatfield and her persistent ramblings "in the fields and lanes that lay in the nearest proximity to the road" (124) implicitly represent a flirtation with potential freedom and real life. Since she rejects Hatfield, whom Agnes believes would be far better than the sinister Sir Thomas, it only remains for her ramblings to be curtailed within the confines of yet another, grander, park—the funereal sounding Ashby Park—and an unhappy but "princely" home (195). "I'm bound hand and foot" (122), says Rosalie before her marriage, lamenting the cessation of her flirtatious activities now that Sir Thomas is on the scene, and her remark is actually prophetic. Her seigneurial aspirations, however, plainly override any rational consideration of the dreadful consequences: "I *must* have Ashby Park, whoever shares it with me" (123). With these petulant words, Anne Brontë demonstrates a fundamental absurdity in the language of acquisition, for Rosalie is evidently marrying the space rather than the man, a pathetic misprision which reveals the bride's blindness about who is actually acquiring what or whom. The desperate tone of this statement suggests that in society's upper echelons the real passion is reserved not for human feeling, but for property. Altogether the most trenchant irony is that this foolish young woman will be the possessed, rather than the possessor of all this wealth.

The difference between Rosalie or Matilda's life and that of their governess is not just the difference between riches and poverty or between advantage and disadvantage. It is, rather, the difference between mindless superficiality and a spiritually profound, intelligent consciousness. In her characterization of Agnes, Brontë offers her reader a subtle definition of individual initiative: Agnes takes charge of her own life and seizes her opportunity with gusto "to go out into the world; to enter upon a new life; to act for myself; to exercise my unused faculties; to try my unknown powers; to earn my own maintenance" (12). As with Helen Huntingdon in **The Tenant,** Agnes's road to self-realization has its "snares and pitfalls."[14] She can be kept in the schoolroom by her demanding pupils or "crushed" into the corner of the carriage where she is continually reminded of her inferior place in life, since even personal spaces are defined for her by the often thoughtless, sometimes hostile actions of her employers. "Such a nasty, horrid place, Miss Grey; I wonder how you can bear it," says Rosalie of Agnes's place in the carriage (72), and one understands that the "place" described in such terms of disgust gestures beyond the particular corner to a generally undesirable situation in society.

However, the restraints placed on the governess are (by dint of her moral and spiritual integrity) less far-reaching than those placed on her pupils. Despite her boisterous ways—she is "full of life, vigour, and activity" (68)—Miss Matilda's world is ultimately as narrow as her elder sister's, contained as it is within the boundaries of the park and the marriage market. Agnes observes that as soon as Rosalie is married off, the next hapless daughter to fall victim to her mother's matrimonial schemes is an unwilling Matilda:

> Now also she was denied the solace which the companionship of the coachman, groom, horses, greyhounds and pointers might have afforded; for her mother, having notwithstanding the disadvantages of a country life so satisfactorily disposed of her

elder daughter, the pride of her heart, had begun seriously to turn her attention to the younger. (158)

Again, through the double meanings implied by the words "denied," "solace," "disadvantages," "satisfactorily," "heart," and "attention," the language in this sentence details the underlying corruption of human relations in an acquisitive society. Inherent in the subjection of women, whose role as chattels is actually upheld by mothers such as Mrs. Murray, is the sad fact that this conniving, material heart denies maternal solace to her daughters and refuses them the healthy attention they need.

In this limited, closed world, it is, then, hardly surprising that the window represents some form of release. Mary Wollstonecraft had pointed to the promise of freedom evoked by an open window in chapter 11 of *The Wrongs of Woman* in 1798, and Charlotte Brontë also gave the window a powerful place in the imagery of *Jane Eyre,* where it functions not only as an aid to looking out but also to let strong, supernatural influences into Jane's world. Similarly, in *Wuthering Heights,* Emily Brontë shows the window as a place where the boundaries between this world and the afterlife can be crossed, a place where searing truth comes into the containing structures of social intercourse and souls can depart; it is also a place where, in Virginia Woolf's comment about Emily's novel, the reader experiences a "suggestion of power underlying the apparitions of human nature."[15]

When Agnes first arrives at Horton Lodge, she views the alien scene through a window that reveals the "unknown world—a wide, white wilderness," symbolizing the *tabula rasa* of her new existence upon which the marks of her future life are yet to be inscribed (62). After her disastrous marriage, Rosalie's increasing awareness of her self-made shackles gains pointed emphasis, as she looks "listlessly towards the window" (133). By means of the window image, Anne Brontë demonstrates that in scorning her chance of a relatively fulfilled marriage only to lose herself in material bondage, Rosalie feels a loss she cannot confront. The promise of an unfettered life that beckons beyond the window is bound to confirm the dreariness of her days within: "There's no inducement to go out now; and nothing to look forward to" (133), she laments. The finality in her tone suggests that while she refuses to perceive the full import of what lies beyond the window, her complaint about the lack of future prospects contains more than a grain of truth.

Again, later in the narrative, when Agnes visits Rosalie—now Lady Ashby—freshly ensconced in her stately mansion, Agnes's seat by a "wide, open window" (186) puts her within sight of light and liberty as she looks out from a darkening and enclosed world: "I sat for a moment in silence, enjoying the still, pure air and the delightful prospect of the park, that lay before me, rich in verdure and foliage, and basking in yellow sunshine . . ." (186). Unencumbered by worldly possessions or concerns, Agnes is manifestly more at liberty to enjoy the spiritually rich prospects of an enlightened existence because she can truly see what life sets before her through the window of the soul.

Agnes's imaginative response implies that whatever is seen through the window has much to do with the heart and soul of the viewer. Thus Agnes's description of the "prospect" is suffused with a glow of inner vitality, as opposed to the "languor and flatness" and "dull, soulless eyes" (192) of Sir Thomas Ashby or the "dreary composure" (193) of his bride who openly detests him. By contrast, Agnes is a thriving, soulful character who has gained vision and meaning from her experiences. This descriptive passage, like the longer one that follows, confirms the impression that with the inner depth of loving faith (an enlightened consciousness), the life and light beyond the walls are never quite extinguished:

> The shadow of this wall soon took possession of the whole of the ground as far as I could see, forcing the golden sunlight to retreat inch by inch, and at last take refuge in the very tops of the trees. (189)

As Agnes sits by the window, looking out from Rosalie Ashby's "elegant mansion" (or prison) at the inspirational "golden sunlight" significantly retreating to the treetops, two major image clusters reveal the difference between Agnes's broadly balanced outlook and Rosalie's severely limited consciousness. These two prominent sets of images both emphasize the salutory effects of the outdoors: one is light imagery (which is paramount and which I shall examine later), and the other is nature imagery.

The curative influence of nature and the restorative effects of being outdoors resound throughout Anne Brontë's writings. In the poems examined earlier, flowers, in particular, provide a focal point for several instances of self-evaluation and healing. Floral images in different poems and passages in the novels show a sound Victorian awareness of the language of flowers and, at the same time, they are a generic representation of divine benevolence—a God-given source of strength and beauty. The poem **"In Memory of a Happy Day in February"** echoes this confirmation of a divine continuum which Anne Brontë identifies in nature as a whole. More specifically, in her poem **"The Bluebell"** she points to flowers as individual reflections of personality: "A fine and subtle spirit dwells / In every little flower," each one breathing "its own sweet feeling" that reflects the onlooker's perception "With more or less of power" (*Poems* 73). Here the bluebell offers a "silent eloquence" which speaks of Anne Brontë's own recollections of childhood freedom: "Those sunny days of merriment / When heart and soul were free" (*Poems* 74). Similarly, in *Agnes Grey* the paradoxically "silent eloquence" of flower and nature images speaks volumes about characters and their emotional states. Agnes might compare herself with a "thistle seed borne on the wind to some strange nook of uncongenial soil" (62), but what actually forms her character has more to do with the "rugged regions" (16) where she was born. Brontë explores this concept of a rugged individualism, set against the "depressingly flat" (71) preserves of the conventional establishment, in her comparison of the landscapes surrounding the great houses where Agnes, though superior in spirit, serves as a social inferior. While the Bloomfields' grounds are distinguished by a parvenu plot with a "smooth-shaven lawn" and a "grove of upstart poplars," the Murrays' park is less nouveau riche, but still "depressingly flat to one born and nurtured among the rugged hills" (71) of "the north of England" (3).

Anne Brontë pointedly structures this grand but uncongenial setting to demonstrate how Agnes experiences the unnerving effects of social imbalance, enacted through elitist attitudes in the "tyranny and injustice" (73) of her young charges and the social isolation imposed on her by their unfeeling snobbery. Their refusal to acknowledge her presence is an attempt to dehumanize her, to reduce her to a "vacancy" (111). But Agnes resolutely refuses to accept her invisible status and finds confirmation of her own individual worth (and emotional warmth) in the beauties of the hedgerows. She escapes from her enforced position of servitude by concentrating on the flowers: "along the green banks and budding hedges . . . my spirit of misanthropy began to melt away beneath the soft, pure air and genial sunshine" (112).

Agnes's longing for some familiar visual link with her childhood—"some familiar flower that might recall the woody dales or green hill-sides of home" (112)—is gratified by the sight of the primroses: "At length I descried, high up between the twisted roots of an oak, three lovely primroses, peeping so sweetly from their hiding place that the tears already started at the sight" (112). This poignant response is a silent recognition of her own vitality and "sweetness" which she is forced to suppress in her lonely drudgery. It is also a tearful acknowledgment that the cheerful spring flower, like the primrose in **"Verses by Lady Geralda"** or the flowers in **"Lines Written at Thorp Green,"** recalls a certain confidence and youthful promise which Agnes now feels is blighted. Mr. Weston's role in reaching up to gather the primroses is also deeply symbolic because in one gesture he is restoring to Agnes both the freedom of her lost youthful self and her hope for the future.

According to Victorian flower lore, these dual symbols of Agnes's past and future—the oak and the primrose—represent strength, youth, and love's doubts and fears. Traditionally, the primrose image has an ambiguous meaning. In her book *Flower Lore* (1879), a Miss Carruthers of Inverness (*sic*) wrote that the primrose is associated with "modest unaffected pride" (201).[16] But one of several meanings is also "early youth," given in Kate Greenaway's *The Illuminated Language of Flowers* (1884), offering another interpretation of the primrose image with which Anne Brontë would have been familiar.[17] As far as **Agnes Grey** is concerned, the choice of image is particularly appropriate. The floral allusion to youth parallels Agnes's own yearning for the open spaces of a happy, unfettered childhood, and the reference to a flower which conveys both pride and modesty accords with the tenacity which attends the primrose's (and Agnes's) ability to survive the more inhospitable reaches of icy health and moorland.

This association with tenacity, rugged isolation, and sweetness, signified by the wildflowers preferred by both Agnes and Mr. Weston, indicates shared characteristics of tenderness and independence. That the flowers are guides to character is borne out in flower language when Mr. Weston questions Agnes about violets—which mean "steadfastness" according to Miss Carruthers (204) or "modesty," "faithfulness" and "watchfulness" according to Greenaway (56). Agnes, surprisingly, denies having any connection with violets: "I have no particular associations connected with them, for there are no sweet violets among the hills and valleys round my home" (113). Her favorite flowers are "Primroses, blue-bells, and heath-blossoms," which signify early youth, constancy, and solitude (Greenaway, 48, 22, 34). Agnes's curious dissociation from the "sweet violets" indicates something of her rugged background and suggests that Brontë's heroine is no shrinking violet; nor is she modestly, faithfully, watchful (which implies dependency): once her painful obsession with Edward Weston is overcome, Agnes turns away from watchful dependence towards a solitary path, where she strives for autonomy and self-sufficiency.

Unlike her pupils, Agnes exhibits a plain, simple honesty (suggested by her love of wild flowers) which counters the manipulative dishonesty indulged in by Rosalie Murray in the course of her amorous adventures. When Rosalie is playing her calculated game of dalliance with Mr. Hatfield, she is shown holding a sprig of myrtle—traditionally carried as a symbol of love by a bride in her wedding bouquet. However, Anne Brontë uses this floral emblem with an ironic twist to reveal Rosalie's superficiality, for she is clearly unaware that there is any meaning attached to it other than an entirely frivolous one: "a graceful sprig of myrtle, which served her as a very pretty plaything" (120). The image of the brideflower as plaything indicates that love—in the sense of mutual respect and caring—has no serious place in the life of someone like Rosalie: nubile sweetness is just another piece in a power game which allows her vanity to be gratified at the expense of others. An even more overt demonstration of her foolishness is presented in Rosalie's final reaction to her abject suitor, Hatfield: she impatiently gives the myrtle away with a toss of her head, metaphorically tossing away the opportunity for loving reciprocity in a marriage of equals. Even though she recognizes Hatfield's worth as superior to the "ugly" rake Sir Thomas Ashby, she is adamant that "poor Mr. Hatfield" (122) could never be a serious contender for her acquisitive "preference" because his income barely amounts to seven hundred a year: "I never should forget my rank and station for the most delightful man that ever breathed. . . . Love! I detest the word! as applied to one of our sex, I think it a perfect insult" (122). Rosalie's misunderstanding of the word "love" demonstrates figuratively the blind materialism that confuses superficialities with true meaning and restructures lives according to the empty reckonings of commercial exchange.

In contrast to the mindlessness of Rosalie—who presents a perfect foil to the character of Agnes—the profoundly sensitive, Christian consciousness of Agnes is conveyed through images of light and shade. A conventional metaphor for consciousness, light here conveys the brightly transcendent potential of a love that reflects the divine presence, showing Agnes linked to the higher ideal. As the representation of a caring, spiritual person linked to the ideal of receiving God's love and the responsibility of dispensing that love to those she meets in life, Agnes takes the idea of love (both in its sacred and profane senses) very seriously. The confirmation of a "divine truth" identified by Anne Brontë in light generally is echoed in the poem **"In Memory of a Happy Day in February"**:

> It was a glimpse of truths divine
>   Unto my spirit given
> Illumined by a ray of light
>   That shone direct from Heaven!
>   (***Poems*** 82)

Light also as a symbol for love and hope is a poetic staple, but Brontë's psychologically probing language, as she examines Agnes's developing consciousness, imparts a compelling spiritual inquiry to the interplay of light and shade.

As Agnes Grey struggles to reconcile her anguish at the lack of human love in her life with her spiritual beliefs, her mind is so numbed by loneliness that she can no longer see the heavenly light. Her wearisome isolation causes her to become unbalanced and fearful that the light of spiritual inspiration is virtually clouded out: "the gross vapours of earth were gathering around me, and closing in upon my inward heaven" (103). In her troubled state Agnes is earthbound, and Brontë shows that Agnes's preoccupation with her earthly love for Mr. Weston forces her (like the stifling Earth spirit in "The Three Guides") to lean dangerously in the direction of an obsession: "And thus it was that Mr. Weston rose at length upon me, appearing like the morning star in my horizon, to save me from the fear of utter darkness" (103).

Towards the end of the novel, when faced with the loss of her love, Agnes finds it hard to relinquish the spiritual sustenance she has derived from him. Weston has become the only "bright object" on a gloomy horizon: "How dreary to turn my eyes from the contemplation of that bright object, and force them to dwell on the dull, grey, desolate prospect around, the joyless, hopeless, solitary path that lay before me" (155). Central to this embodiment of depression, however, is Anne Brontë's point that Agnes has sufficient intelligence to recognize how her desperate need—"a painful troubled pleasure, too near akin to anguish"—is unhealthy enough to be "evil," for it hinders true development and effectively keeps her in "fetters" (155). She is also given the foresight to comprehend that she cannot progress until this "troubled pleasure" is relinquished, allowing the total experience of a solitary life. Like Jane Eyre, who also determines to follow a solitary path after wrenching herself away from Rochester, Agnes experiences a profound insight, seeing the fullness of wisdom intervene and guide her away from spiritual destruction: "It was," Agnes perceives pragmatically, "an indulgence that a person of more wisdom or more experience would doubtless have denied herself" (155). Agnes learns to walk the "solitary path" (155) with joy and hope before she is finally enabled to join Mr. Weston.

Part of this learning process puts Agnes into the deeply contemplative state we see when she sits at Rosalie Ashby's window. The dismal lethargy into which she has sunk calls forth one of the more purple passages in the novel, and Brontë's writing here carries an air of spiritual hiatus which is emotionally fitting at this point in her heroine's development. Again, the light and shade images are crucial:

> The shadow of this wall soon took possession of the whole of the ground as far as I could see, forcing the golden sunlight to retreat inch by inch, and at last take refuge in the very tops of the trees. At last, even they were left in shadow—the shadow of the distant hills, or of the earth itself; and, in sympathy for the busy citizens of the rookery, I regretted to see their habitation, so lately bathed in glorious light, reduced to the sombre, worky-day hue of the lower world, or of my own world within. For a moment, such birds as soared above the rest might still receive the lustre on their wings, which imparted to their sable plumage the hue and brilliance of deep red gold; at last that too departed. (189)

What stands out in this passage, apart from the rather florid prose, is that the shadows of structures (such as walls and buildings) are shown to have taken "possession" of the open spaces and to have obliterated the sunlight. Agnes is "observing the slowly lengthening shadows from the window," in such a way as to suggest that her vision of social constrictions is gaining clarity. As the imagery here implies, she must move away from earthly entrapments and the danger of being "possessed" by the shadows of earth, towards a higher, more enlightened spiritual plane.

The use of dramatic coloring or *chiaroscuro* in this verbal picture succeeds in evoking Agnes's spiritual dilemma. Anne Brontë highlights the darker brush strokes (suggesting both Agnes's and Rosalie's blighted dreams) with lustrous touches which imply a stubborn spark of hope gleaming only in the eye of the believer. The elongated vowel sounds recall arcs of flight (Agnes's flights of fancy) and the encroaching shadows correspond with Agnes's increasing awareness that her dream of a life with Mr. Weston must be allowed to fade in the realism of "the sombre, worky-day hue of the lower world."

Yet at this climactic moment, she still retains a glimpse of something "so lately bathed in glorious light" that promises a glimmer of hope for the future. As Brontë shifts her focus from the contemplative person within to the busy scene without, she develops a tension between movement and inaction, introversion and extroversion, thought and deed. We are left with the suspicion that, unlike Rosalie Ashby whose active self has been obscured by the shades of materialism, Agnes will not opt for a passive role: she will resolve her dilemma by actively stepping out of a "quiet, drab-colour life" (189), and reaching for the higher ideal, she will be liberated like one of the birds that soars above the rest to catch the closing brilliance of the day.

An interpretation such as this accords with Anne Brontë's own beliefs, and within the context of her religious philosophy it is perhaps predictable that Agnes must make peace with her Maker before she can progress much further. Yet, the description of Agnes's epiphany is not simply given in limited religious or moral terms. Deeply religious though she was, Anne Brontë gives us an inspirational view of more than the god-head revealed in nature. She also shows us selfhood discovered in a way that echoes the radical affirmation of feminine selfhood proposed by Mary Wollstonecraft fifty years earlier: Agnes is presented primarily as a complex person who is finally put in touch with all aspects of herself.

As in *The Tenant,* the image of the sea reflects this limitless personal potential. The sea represents an agent of liberation for Agnes, who finds release in its ceaseless, unrestrained activity: "it was delightful to me at all times and seasons, but especially in the wild commotion of a rough sea breeze" (196). Agnes's expansive world, with its sea breezes and freedom beyond time or season, is an instructive contrast to the incarceration of Lady Rosalie Ashby in her elegant mansion where the lifeless, material images speak of passing time and death.

Compared with the "delightful" dynamism and freedom of the seashore (shaped by "foaming and sparkling" waves, "dimpled pools, and little running streams" [197]) where Agnes is liberated, Rosalie's surroundings are dully limited, joylessly defined by static objects and oppressive walls. Within the "splendid house and grounds" for which Rosalie has bargained away her life, having coveted it "whatever price was to be paid for the title of mistress" (181), she is surrounded by conspicuous materialism with "many elegant curiosities" (185) but is altogether lacking in love. She cynically estimates her baby girl's place in all this as "only one degree better than devoting oneself to a dog" (194). Confirming the inherent imbalance of this position, the young mother's "melancholy sigh" signifies the fruitlessness of her acquisitive existence, "as if in consideration of the insufficiency of all such baubles to the happiness of the human heart, and their woeful inability to supply its insatiate demands" (186). This blind obeisance to things—"baubles," as Agnes comments in the reductive language that shows Anne Brontë's own snort of disapproval (186)—again shows Rosalie to be less the possessor than the possessed; she is clearly owned by her own vapid materialism. The marble busts that surround her are metaphors for truncated, captive selves, captured in cold, white stone, while the little timepiece and "little jewelled watch" (186), which Rosalie ironically shows Agnes with unknowing "animation," mark the empty passage of her wasted life.

This sterile, soulless world presents the antithesis to Agnes's now sunny, purposeful life. Juxtaposed against these interior scenes of Rosalie's suffocating union with a man she detests are Agnes's seaside escapades, in which her healthy delight in autonomous action identifies her as a woman free from the bondage of dependency. Unlike Rosalie Ashby, Agnes no longer needs a man to validate her existence; she becomes fully self-actualized. Signalling the transformation from a "drab-colour life" (189) which oppresses Agnes at Ashby Park, the imagery in the later seascape radiates light and color. "No language can describe," writes Anne Brontë, although she succeeds in doing so admirably,

the effect of the deep, clear azure of the sky and ocean, the bright morning sunshine on the semicircular barrier of craggy cliffs surmounted by green swelling hills, and on the smooth, wide sands, and the low rocks out at sea—looking, with their clothing

of weeds and moss, like little grass-grown islands—and above all, on the brilliant, sparkling waves. (196-97)

These images of light bouncing from the different tactile surfaces of sea to shore and back again recreate the electrifying vitality of a divinely empowered life force. Seen through Agnes's eyes, the scene on the sands is sparkling with sunlight and bursting with energy, its expansive vigor indicating her own expanding sense of self. This liberating energy creates a peculiarly balanced environment: "Just enough heat to enhance the value of the breeze, and just enough wind to keep the whole sea in motion, to make the waves come bounding to the shore, foaming and sparkling as if wild with glee" (197). Through the repeatedly modified images of heat and wind, with the boundless action of the living waves below—reflecting "brilliant" light—Brontë's imagery allows the reader to experience a divinely balanced still point at the center of motion, a Miltonic echo of creation's "bright essence."[18] Both Agnes and the personified waves embody the effervescent "glee" of a being who has finally broken free from shackles; Agnes has become an empowered entity, a vital person in her own right.

Appropriately, this transcendent state occurs in solitude, when "nothing else was stirring—no living creature was visible besides myself" (197). As well as the suggestive Miltonic echoes of creation in these images, Agnes's psychic rebirth is also likened to the birth of Aphrodite from the waves. The sense that the sea becomes a source of spiritual renewal is reinforced also by the early morning setting, with the pristine beauty of a freshly renewed landscape: "My footsteps were the first to press the firm, unbroken sands:—nothing before had trampled them since last night's flowing tide had obliterated the deepest marks of yesterday, and left it fair and even" (197). At this point Agnes is not only physically refreshed but spiritually transfigured, feeling as though she had wings on her feet and "could go at least forty miles without fatigue" (197). The euphoria of her self-discovery gives her courage to venture out onto the slippery rocks where she is poised on a "little mossy promontory" (197), surrounded by a sea of living water. Similarly, when Edward Weston proposes to her, they are symbolically poised on the edge of a precipice, from which they watch "the splendid sun-set mirrored on the restless world of waters" at their feet (208). Their union, unlike that of the ill-matched Ashbys, is demonstrably blessed when it is defined by all these profoundly resonant images of power and creation.

In these contrasting scenes, language evokes seasonal change, and image perfectly mirrors the psychological development of character. The correspondence between the outer landscape and the inner life of Brontë's characters is of paramount importance in her writing. Throughout

Agnes Grey imagery of nature and open spaces reflects the successive stages through which Agnes passes as she moves from the rugged hills of her childhood, through the "depressingly flat" spaces of her governess years, to the personal high point on that sea-cliff which affords a prospect of creative union in the fulfilment of marriage to her equal. Countering the images of buildings and their lifeless contents, images which relate to nature and open spaces add a spiritual dimension to the narrative; together, they act as "pillars of witness," testifying to the actualization of Agnes's escape from social degradation and the "indignities" (74) which limit her existence in the socially structured establishments where she serves.

Admittedly, *Agnes Grey* is restricted in focus, concerned as it is with the psychological development of one main character within the scope of Brontë's original title for the novel—*Passages in the Life of an Individual,* mentioned in her birthday note of 31 July 1845. Yet it has a textual richness which could be identified as a peculiarly feminine grasp of "the intricacies of personal relationships" (as Ian Watt says in his analysis of the supremacy enjoyed by the woman novelist). Such psychological acuity combined with moral vision places Anne Brontë firmly within the literary heritage of other great women writers such as Mary Wollstonecraft, Ann Radcliffe, Maria Edgeworth, Frances Burney, and Jane Austen.[19] Anne Brontë's bold analysis of realistic relationships through interconnected poetic images exemplifies an elaborately structured and affectively subtle technique which reveals her as a writer who was ahead of her time. Robert Barnard's comparison of her writing with that of her sisters contains the lucid observation that her work "looks forward," and he places her at a literary crossroads that leads towards psychological and social realism.[20]

In *Agnes Grey* Anne Brontë's technical achievement lies in the creation of a closely-woven textual fabric, the apparent simplicity of which is deceptive. With this first novel, she does not explore the more complex turns of plot or dramatic enigmas that shape her sisters' works and that are to give the dimension of instructive parody to *The Tenant.*[21] The "instruction" promised at the beginning of *Agnes Grey* is present in both novels, but the narrative development of *Agnes Grey* shows a straightforward approach which accords openly with its plainly stated moral purpose. But, while the "quietness" and "realism" of this direct method are important,[22] Anne Brontë's achievement in *Agnes Grey* goes beyond a simple representation of scenes from a life; her keenly rendered psychological enquiry is powerful in its quiet intensity. From the cryptic thoughtfulness of the opening nut metaphor to the succinct finality of its closing statement, "And now I think I have said sufficient" (208), *Agnes Grey* combines an intentionally straightforward style with iterative images that both entertain and instruct. In addition to setting the

novel's boundaries of restraint, the two framing statements indicate the formal structure of the text and provide an ideal vehicle for exploring major themes of balance and imbalance, oppression and liberty, restraint and growth. Terry Eagleton's perception accurately characterizes the final line of *Agnes Grey* which, in his words, "neatly captures the laconic modesty of the whole, the sense of a work attractively reserved in feeling without any loss of candid revelation."[23]

This reserve is both a stylistic and thematic feature of Anne Brontë's work. The apparent stillness of her writing, compared with that of her sisters, is not, however the stillness of creative timidity or inarticulation. One image from late in the novel effectively answers the plethora of critical suggestions that her writing lacks power. Her reserved but poetic style bears comparison with the calm but not inactive surface of the sea, above which Agnes stands on her "mossy promontory" (197), exulting in the contained power and unseen depths of the tidal water:

> and then I turned again to delight myself with the sight and sound of the sea dashing against my promontory—with no prodigious force, for the swell was broken by the tangled sea-weed and the unseen rocks beneath; otherwise I should have been deluged with spray. (198)

Life imitating art in this instance, the experience of the reader parallels the experience of the heroine who turns again to delight herself with the sensory impressions of the scene. The reader does not emerge from the sight and sound of Anne Brontë's narration "deluged with spray," but one is left with an abiding sense of its assiduous swell—of intertwined image patterns embedded beneath and controlling its surface movement.

Yet, Brontë's method is an entirely self-conscious one, as can be seen from carefully placed authorial statements referring to form and content. These have, moreover, a dual function. First, the self-reflexive comment mid-way through the narrative, "Had I seen it in a novel, I should have thought it unnatural" (149), together with repeated references to the "benefit" (36) or "patience" (36, 63) of the "reader" (63, 146) and the "prolixity" (36), "prosing" (146), "reflections" (146), "design" (36) or "arguments" (146) of the writer, combine to undermine the separation between narrator and story, drawing the reader into the fictional world. This effectively questions the borderline between reality and fiction, giving the impression of lived personal experience which supports the novel's didactic, moral purpose. But such comments also testify to an awareness of the writer's rhetorical method and the careful underpinning of theme with image, a deliberate artistry which conjoins poetry with moral instruction and is the structural base of her style. In Anne Brontë's ordering of thematic motifs within the interlocking image patterns of structural imagery one finds every sign of the unobtrusively crafted textual fabric which George Moore saw as "simple and beautiful as a muslin dress."

Notes

[1] Ed. Hilda Marsden and Robert Inglesfield (Oxford: The Clarendon Press, 1988), 3.

[2] Although I would question Inga-Stina Ewbank's assertion that Anne Brontë is a "moralist first and a woman second," it is clear from the prefatory statements in both *Agnes Grey* (at the beginning of Chapter 1) and *The Tenant* (in the preface to the second edition) that her purpose was to make moral sense of social problems. In response to suggestions that *Wuthering Heights* does not have a sense of good and evil, Ewbank emphasizes that it is an exploration of the "human condition" and its characters are "in various ways, presented as moral beings." I believe that an equally strong case can be made for reading Anne Brontë's fiction as an exploration of the "human condition" which, no less than the work of her sister, requires an unbiased and thorough approach. See Ewbank, *Their Proper Sphere* (Cambridge, Massachusetts: Harvard University Press, 1966), 85, 96.

[3] One thing the other governess novels share is an emphasis on social inferiority. The governesses in Harriet Martineau's *Deerbrook* (1839) and Mrs. Sherwood's *Caroline Mordaunt* (1835) are stereotypes of angelic self-sacrifice. See Ewbank's survey of the governess novels, *Their Proper Sphere*, 59-60.

[4] The dove in the poem is, like Agnes, confined within a prison-like structure, and its view of the world beyond emphasizes the "despair" of its imprisonment:

> In vain! In vain! Thou canst not rise—
> Thy prison roof confines thee there;
> Its slender wires delude thine eyes,
> And quench thy longing with despair.

"The Captive Dove," 31 October 1843, in Edward Chitham, ed., *The Poems of Anne Brontë* (London: Macmillan, 1979), 93.

[5] See Edward Chitham and Tom Winnifrith, *Brontë Facts and Brontë Problems* (London: Macmillan, 1983), 99.

[6] From a facsimile copied at The Brontë Parsonage Museum, Haworth. See also T. J. Wise and J. A. Symington, eds., *The Brontës: Their Lives, Friendships and Correspondence,* 2 vols. (Oxford: The Shakespeare Head Press, 1980), I:321.

[7] I refer here to Julia Kristeva's idea that the radical linguistic force of the semiotic inside language redefines meanings through silence and contradiction. See, for example, "Stabat Mater," trans. Arthur Goldhammer, in *The Female Body in Western Culture,* ed. Susan Rubin Suleiman (Cambridge, Massachusetts: Harvard University Press, 1985), 109.

[8] "'Imbecile Laughter' and 'Desperate Earnest' in *The Tenant of Wildfell Hall,*" *Modern Language Quarterly,* 43 (1982): 354.

[9] John Milton, *Paradise Lost,* in *Complete Poems and Major Prose,* ed. Merritt Y. Hughes (Indianapolis: Odyssey, 1981), IX:887, 1036.

[10] Winifred Gérin, *Anne Brontë: A Biography* (London: Penguin, 1976), 145.

[11] William Makepeace Thackeray, *The Four Georges,* ed. Hannaford Bennett (London: John Long, 1923), 149.

[12] Tennyson, *In Memoriam,* in *Poems of Tennyson,* ed. Herbert Warren (Oxford: Oxford University Press, 1921), 349.

[13] Unsigned review, *Christian Remembrancer,* 97 (July 1857): 87-105; in *The Brontës: The Critical Heritage,* ed. Miriam Allott (London: Routledge & Kegan Paul, 1974), 369.

[14] In the Preface to the second edition of *The Tenant of Wildfell Hall,* ed. Herbert Rosengarten (Oxford: Clarendon, 1992), Anne Brontë asks her critics, "Is it better to reveal the snares and pitfalls of life to the young and thoughtless traveller, or to cover them with branches and flowers?" (xxxviii).

[15] Virginia Woolf discusses both Charlotte and Emily Brontë in this essay on *Jane Eyre* and *Wuthering Heights. Collected Essays,* 4 vols. (London: The Hogarth Press, 1966), I:189.

[16] *Flower Lore* (1879; rpt. Detroit: Singing Tree Press, 1972), 197, 201.

[17] Jean Marsh indicates that many early nineteenth-century dictionaries of the language of flowers gave confusingly mixed meanings. But the confusion of entries in the dictionary part of Kate Greenaway's *The Illuminated Language of Flowers,* published in 1884, is sorted out by Marsh's cross-indexed entries in the modern reprint (London: Macdonald and Jane's Publishers, 1978), 17, 48, 56.

[18] *Paradise Lost,* III:6. Milton's invocation of God's "holy Light" was clearly in Anne Brontë's mind as she wrote *Agnes Grey,* for she also refers (twice: 63, 208) to the dark and deep "world of waters" (III:11) invested by that Light; see Hilda Marsden's and Robert Inglesfield's notes to the Clarendon edition.

[19] See Ian Watt, *The Rise of the Novel* (Berkeley: University of California Press, 1957), 337-40. On the woman as moralist, see also Janet Todd, *The Sign of Angellica: Women, Writing and Fiction, 1660-1800* (New York: Columbia University Press, 1989), 228.

[20] Robert Barnard, "Anne Brontë: The Unknown Sister," *Edda* 78 (1978): 33-38.

[21] For elements of parody in *The Tenant,* see Edward Chitham and Tom Winnifrith, *Brontë Facts and Brontë Problems* (London: Macmillan, 1983), 104.

[22] P. J. M. Scott, "*Agnes Grey:* Accommodating Reality," chapter 1 in his study *Anne Brontë: A New Critical Assessment* (London: Vision Press, 1983), 31, 43.

[23] Terry Eagleton, *Myths of Power: A Marxist Study of the Brontës* (London: Macmillan, 1975), 126.

Maria H. Frawley (essay date 1996)

SOURCE: "'An Alien among Strangers': The Governess as Narrator in *Agnes Grey,*" in *Anne Brontë,* Twayne Publishers, 1996, pp. 82-116.

[*In the following excerpt, Frawley probes the narrative technique and themes of social isolation and alienation and of female voicelessness in* Agnes Grey.]

Agnes Grey *and the Family Plot*

The domestic ideology to which Brontë responded in her novel represented the nuclear family as a panacea for most social ills. In many ways, the married woman and mother stood at the center of this idealized family, for she was keeper of the home and selfless beholder of the moral virtues associated with family life. In its evocation of Agnes's family life, *Agnes Grey* participates in an important cultural moment in the history of the family, one that complicates this sentimental picture of the traditional Victorian family. Through the structure of the novel itself, as well as in the selection of materials she attributed to Agnes, Brontë ensured that her heroine's experiences as a governess would be read as related to—even an outgrowth of—her experiences within her family.

First and foremost among these is her experience as a daughter. After the opening paragraph that invokes the novel's claim to "true history," Agnes situates her self in relation to her parents. Significantly, she begins with her father, subtly linking his moral character with his economic position: "My father was a clergyman of the north of England, who was deservedly respected by all who knew him; and, in his younger days, lived pretty

comfortably on the joint income of a small incumbency and a snug little property of his own" (*AG,* 1). Of her mother, Agnes writes:

> My mother, who married him against the wishes of her friends, was a squire's daughter, and a woman of spirit. In vain it was represented to her that, if she became the poor parson's wife, she must relinquish her carriage and her lady's-maid and all the luxuries and elegances of affluence; which to her were little less than the necessaries of life. (*AG,* 1)

The way in which Agnes positions her parents enables Brontë to demarcate several class boundaries. Her father clearly belongs to the middle class, although at its lower end; he is a respected person by the standards of his own neighborhood, if a poor parson by the standards of those above him on the social scale. Whereas Agnes characterizes her father by the dual standards of his morality and his economic position, her mother's class is modified by a characterization of her personality. Twice in her opening narrative she refers to her mother's "high spirit," representing it as that which, in combination with her aversion to the attraction of riches, accounts for her otherwise unthinkable decision to "bury herself" in a "homely village" (*AG,* 2). Agnes's narrative of her parents' marriage tells an ambiguous story of social slippage. She proclaims that "you might search all England through and fail to find a happier couple" (*AG,* 2), evidently wanting her readers to respect the standards by which her mother chose to live. Yet, at the same time, she documents the process by which her family and especially her father were tempted to speculate away their little wealth in hopes of improving their economic standards, and describes the "bitterness" and "distress" that ensue (*AG,* 5).

Emphasizing self-sacrifice, Brontë uses Agnes's narrative to show the ways that she defines herself as submissive. She relates this submissiveness to Agnes's sense of daughterly duty. Agnes carefully documents the family's lowered living conditions and the sacrifices made as a result of her father's mistakes:

> The useful pony phaeton was sold, together with the stout well-fed pony—the old favourite that we had fully determined should end its days in peace, and never pass from our hands; . . . Our clothes were mended, turned, and darned to the utmost verge of decency; our food, always plain, was now simplified to an unprecedented degree—except my father's favourite dishes; our coals and candles were painfully economized—the pair of candles reduced to one, and that most sparingly used; the coals carefully husbanded in the half-empty grate: especially when my father was out on his parish duties, or confined to bed through illness. . . . As for our carpets, they in time were worn threadbare, and patched and darned even to a greater extent than our garments. (*AG,* 5-6)

Agnes's catalog of sufferings stands out from other episodes recounted in her narrative both in its precision and in its breadth; on few other occasions does she pay so much attention to supplying her readers with so many specific instances of the point she wants to make. Noteworthy in her account is the attention she pays to the sacrifices her family makes in order that her father's pride not be further damaged. Significantly, their sacrifices involve more than simply relinquishing material goods; their morality itself is compromised, Agnes implies, in several ways. Giving up plans to save a horse from overwork or early death is, in Agnes's mind, comparable to a spiritual sacrifice, as later passages detailing her intense feelings about cruelty to animals reveal; wearing clothes that hover near the "verge of decency" places her family in a precarious moral status as well.

Brontë paves the way for Agnes's account of life as a governess via this story of her parents and her life at home during her formative years. Just as Agnes's mother survives her journey down the social ladder through a combination of middle-class resourcefulness and evangelical morality, so too does Agnes illustrate her own ability to withstand economic and social hardships by enacting the very same virtues her mother represented.[8] This opening portion of the novel further enables Brontë to introduce a theme of social isolation. Although Agnes carefully accounts for the temptations that led to her father's unfortunate financial mistakes, the focus of her narrative of family history is on their social isolation, first that endured by her mother after she had agreed to marry a "poor parson," and later by the entire family as they deliberately alienated maternal relations by refusing offers of financial help that were contingent on an admission that the marriage was ill-founded. In both instances, the social isolation is imposed on them by outsiders but is willingly accepted as well. Just as Brontë's poetic personas found that situations of exile facilitated an exploration of self, so too does Agnes Grey eventually discover reasons to embrace the isolation she experiences as a governess.

Brontë suggests that Agnes is able to accept the social isolation of governessing because it is part of her heritage. One of the features of her family life that Agnes selects for emphasis is her rural heritage, which Brontë presents through the familiar rhetoric of solitude and isolation. Agnes presents her rural heritage as a function of her father's position—and hence, indirectly, her family's social isolation—but also as a more essential part of her identity. As the narrative progresses, Brontë implies that Agnes's rural heritage helps to account for her naivete and lack of preparation for the world that awaits her as a governess. Indeed, at first they threaten to prevent her access to that world: awaiting a response to her inquiries regarding governess work, she writes, "But so long and so entire had been my parents' seclusion from the world, that many weeks elapsed before

a suitable situation could be procured" (*AG,* 9). Her sense of an experientially impoverished background continues to haunt her once she leaves. As she explains to herself upon arrival at the Bloomfield residence, "True, I was near nineteen; but, thanks to my retired life and the protecting care of my mother and sister, I well knew that many a girl of fifteen, or under, was gifted with a more womanly address, and greater ease and self-possession" (*AG,* 12). These concerns are reiterated in her account of life with the Murray family, where she writes, "But this gives no proper idea of my feelings at all; and no one that has not lived such a retired, stationary life as mine can possibly imagine what they were: hardly even if he has known what it is to awake some morning and find himself in Port Nelson, in New Zealand, with a world of waters between himself and all that knew him" (*AG,* 49).[9]

Significantly, Brontë locates Agnes's experience with social isolation not just with her parents but with her rendering of childhood itself. Agnes's sense of her secluded childhood leads her to long for its metonymic equivalent in nature—the "woody dales or green hillsides" or "brown moorlands" that she reminisces about (*AG,* 88). More often, though, she refers obliquely to the social isolation that characterized her own upbringing. As she explains early in the novel:

> Mary and I were brought up in the strictest seclusion. My mother . . . took the whole charge of our education on herself, with the exception of Latin—which my father undertook to teach us—so that we never even went to school; and, as there was no society in the neighbourhood, our only intercourse with the world consisted in a stately tea-party, now and then, with the principal farmers and tradespeople of the vicinity (just to avoid being stigmatized as too proud to consort with our neighbours), and an annual visit to our paternal grandfather's; where himself, our kind grandmamma, a maiden aunt, and two or three elderly ladies and gentlemen, were the only persons we ever saw. (*AG,* 2)

As Brontë has Agnes explain it, the social isolation endured by the family is partly chosen and shapes Agnes's experiences as a child in several ways. Although her account of family heritage had earlier emphasized her mother's disregard for the social hierarchy of which she was a part, this anecdote, by distinguishing between "neighbours" and "society," reveals just the opposite. Agnes implies that her family's encounters with local farmers and tradespeople were artificial, designed to hide the social pride that they really felt.

Most important, Brontë links the social isolation of Agnes's family not only to Agnes's developing class-consciousness but also to her own sense of a private life. Although Agnes hints at regret at not attending school as other children in the neighborhood do, her account reveals a more tangible level of discomfort with her background:

> Sometimes our mother would amuse us with stories and anecdotes of her younger days, which, while they entertained us amazingly, frequently awoke— in *me*, at least—a secret wish to see a little more of the world. (*AG*, 2)

Agnes admits here to a latent attribute of her identity, a desire for experience beyond that provided within the confines of her home. She ensures that this desire is unknown to those closest to her. Brontë's use of italic to emphasize Agnes's sense of separation from her sister ("in *me*, at least,") is also noteworthy, underscoring as it does divisions within the seemingly homogeneous unit of the family. Agnes's sense of her self as separate from her family parallels as well certain moments in the text when she reveals her discomfort with the kind of attention her family gives her.

Throughout the opening portion of the novel, Brontë uses rhetoric to reveal that Agnes commands little respect as an individual within her family. Agnes occupies—in her own mind, at least—an almost invisible place in the family. Early on in her narrative, Agnes explains that being the youngest child, and only one of two from an original group of six to survive "the perils of infancy and early childhood," she "was always regarded as the *child,* and the pet of the family," a designation that resulted in making her "too helpless and dependent—too unfit for buffeting with the cares and turmoils of life" (*AG*, 2). When the financial woes brought on by her father's speculations begin, opportunities for her sister Mary to help out by painting are encouraged, but Agnes is passed over without a word, told only to "Go and practise [her] music, or play with the kitten" (*AG*, 6). As Agnes explains, "though a woman in my own estimation, I was still a child in theirs" (*AG*, 6).

The Grey family's reaction to her suggestion, revealing the extent to which her lack of status has become deeply inculcated in their thinking, is a key feature of Brontë's critique of the family, which shows the extent to which Agnes's sense of self is at stake in the debate about whether she should work as a governess. When Agnes initially announces her presence by saying, "I wish *I* could do something," her family reacts negatively both to the idea of working as a governess and, significantly, to the idea of Agnes's working at all. As Agnes writes, "My mother uttered an exclamation of surprise, and laughed. My sister dropped her work in astonishment, exclaiming, '*You* a governess, Agnes! What *can* you be dreaming of!'" (*AG*, 7). Further countering her suggestion, her mother says, "'But, my love, you have not learned to take care of *yourself* yet: and young children require more judgment and experience

to manage than elder ones'" (*AG*, 7). Recollecting her father's reaction, Agnes writes: "'What, my little Agnes a governess!' cried he, and, in spite of his dejection, he laughed at the idea" (*AG*, 8). In the first two of these instances, Mary's emphasis on *you* and Mrs. Grey's emphasis on *yourself* call into question Agnes's status as an autonomous individual with her own independent identity, which she had put forward with her own emphasis on *I*. Although attuned to the implications of her family's behavior (at least in retrospect), Agnes absorbs some of their patterns of thought—patterns that deny her an independence and maturity comparable to her age, and result in her seeing herself as somehow less than fully developed and able to act on her own.

The family plot that opens the novel introduces other themes as well, among them Agnes's affinities with the natural world and especially with animals. Clearly the most important theme, in terms of setting the stage for her subsequent experiences, has to do with the sense of self that Agnes develops within her family and with how it determines the effect her work experiences will have on her. In many ways, the novel's emphasis on Agnes's subsequent psychological development once she has left home becomes a commentary on the home life she left. In doing so, Brontë deepens the interpretive interest of Agnes's subsequent governess experience by linking it to a broader critique of the domestic ideal and of related ideologies of gender and class that sentimentalized the family and that restricted societal understandings of a woman's capacity for self-determination.

"A Stranger in a Strange Land": The Governess Story

The phrase "a stranger in a strange land" would seem at home in almost any episode in **Agnes Grey** devoted to the heroine's life as a governess. It comes in fact from the correspondence of Brontë's father. In response to a letter he had received from a fellow clergyman expressing sympathy on the death of his wife, Maria Branwell Brontë, Patrick Brontë wrote, "Had I been at D[ewsbury] I should not have wanted kind friends; had I been at H[artshead] I should have seen them and others occasionally; or had I been at T[hornton] a family there who were ever truly kind would have soothed my sorrows; but I was at H[aworth], a stranger in a strange land" (*BLFC*, I, 58). The phrase captures his sense of exile as an Irishman living in Yorkshire as well as the overwhelming emotional alienation of losing his wife, an alienation only partially mitigated, his later comments imply, by his religious faith.

It is this combined sense of geographic exile and emotional or psychological alienation that plague Agnes Grey as she struggles to survive in a world that she feels is radically unfamiliar to her. Perhaps no other theme so preoccupied Brontë. As the title implies, **The**

Tenant of Wildfell Hall would bring exile and alienation to the foreground: Helen Huntingdon is both physically banished from her home and alienated, by virtue of her alias as the widow Mrs. Graham, from her self. Just as Brontë in her poetry created characters who were exiled from their home and family to explore the process of self-examination that inevitably ensued, so too in *Agnes Grey* she uses Agnes's sense of alienation as a springboard for self-scrutiny. Indeed, Agnes describes the "strange feeling of desolation" with which she greeted her first morning in the Murray home as follows:

> I awoke . . . feeling like one whirled away by enchantment, and suddenly dropped from the clouds into a remote and unknown land, widely and completely isolated from all he had ever seen or known before; or like a thistle-seed borne on the wind to some strange nook of uncongenial soil, where it must lie long enough before it can take root and germinate, extracting nourishment from what appears so alien to its nature: if, indeed, it ever can. (*AG,* 49)

Although Brontë has Agnes reveal a cynicism born out of her difficult experiences with the Bloomfield family, the young woman who commences a career as a governess is not yet disillusioned. The young woman who leaves her home to begin work as a governess is not simply one who has not been provided with sufficient opportunities to establish an autonomous identity. Brontë represents Agnes's condition in almost pathological terms; she is passive—at least on the outside—to an extreme degree. Although she expresses her inward determination to persevere in her plans for work despite the obstacles presented at home, she manages to act on that determination only indirectly, pressuring her mother to approve her plans and obtain her father's consent. Significantly, when the plans finally come to fruition, Brontë uses the passive voice; Agnes says, "At last, to my great joy, it was decreed that I should take charge of the young family of a certain Mrs. Bloomfield" (*AG,* 9). Most often, Brontë establishes Agnes's passivity by calling attention to her voice—or, more precisely, to her lack of voice. Upon hearing her family's arguments against her desire to work, she writes, "I was silenced for that day, and for many succeeding ones" (*AG,* 8). Perhaps more pointedly, Agnes's sister asks her "Only think . . . what would you do in a house full of strangers, without me or mamma to speak and act for you— . . . ?" (*AG,* 8).

Such comments help the reader to understand that because Agnes's background is so empty of opportunities for autonomous action, or self-government, she is especially unprepared for governess work—for work that will, literally, require her to govern others. Brontë ironically suggests that her awareness of what she lacks ultimately drives her to governessing. Imagining herself as a governess, Agnes writes:

> How delightful it would be to be a governess! To go out into the world; to enter upon a new life; to act for myself; to exercise my unused faculties; to try my unknown powers; to earn my own maintenance, and something to comfort and help my father, mother, and sister, beside exonerating them from the provision of my food and clothing; to show papa what his little Agnes could do; to convince mamma and Mary that I was not quite the helpless, thoughtless being they supposed. (*AG,* 8)

The dire economic circumstances of her family and her potential role in alleviating their stress function within this passage as little more than an afterthought. Her primary incentive, Brontë implies, is self-oriented; she wants to establish independence and to prove that her identity is not that which her family has accorded her.

Adding to the reader's sense of Agnes's unrealistic optimism are the naiveté and idealism that Brontë reveals in her anticipation of her actual duties as a governess:

> And then, how charming to be entrusted with the care and education of children! Whatever others said, I felt I was fully competent to the task: The clear remembrance of my own thoughts in early childhood would be a surer guide than the instructions of the most mature adviser. I had but to turn from my little pupils to myself at their age, and I should know, at once, how to win their confidence and affections: how to waken the contrition of the erring; how to embolden the timid, and console the afflicted; how to make Virtue practicable, Instruction desirable, and Religion lovely and comprehensible. (*AG,* 8-9)

Undercutting the domestic ideology that revealed itself in 19th-century conduct books and works of instruction for women, Brontë ensures that Agnes uses the same idealistic rhetoric to approach the task of governessing.[10] According to Agnes's internal logic, the skills she already possesses as a woman will be exactly the skills that she will need in her work. In this passage Brontë foreshadows as well the impact that Agnes's negative experience as a governess will have on her self-esteem; anticipating only success, she draws here on her "own thoughts," likens her future pupils to herself, and fantasizes about proving others wrong. The narrative that follows is at least partly predictable: Agnes discovers that her own childhood has little prepared her to understand the childhood experiences of others, still less to impart her own values to those children. But just as Agnes's anticipation of life as a governess revolves at least as much around her own potential growth as around issues of work, so too does the narrative of her experience turn inward. In the process, Brontë reveals the ways in which Agnes's expectations about self-development are both achieved and disappointed.

While Agnes delineates her goals for governessing along two distinct lines—one having to do with her success as a teacher, the other involving more personal goals—Brontë shows that the important thing was that the strands are interwoven. On one level, for instance, Agnes evidences a strong desire for children of her own, which reveals itself early in her encounter with the Bloomfield family when she meets the children: "The remaining one was Harriet, a little broad, fat, merry, playful thing of scarcely two, that I coveted more than all the rest—but with her I had nothing to do" (*AG,* 14). Her desire for a child of her own turns more bitterly ironic late in the novel when she is confronted with Lady Ashby's indifference to her own infant girl. Since Agnes is unaware during these episodes that she will in fact one day have children of her own, she is reduced first through her role as a governess and later as a teacher to accepting a very limited role in relation to children.

Another way that Brontë relates Agnes's personal and career goals for self-development is through the concept of reform. Brontë stresses the extent to which Agnes approaches governessing as an opportunity for self-reform, a chance to develop those attributes she feels confident that she has but has yet to develop and perfect. While she recognizes that the children for whom she will be responsible pose serious challenges, she is—at least for a time—confident that she will be able to alter their personalities and to reform their characters. The language and behavior of the Bloomfield children shock her, but, she writes, "I hoped in time to be able to work a reformation" (*AG,* 15). Later, of "Master" Bloomfield she writes, "in time, I might be able to show him the error of his ways" (*AG,* 17). Despite continued failure to achieve her goals, she persists in her belief that reformation of character is possible: "irksome as my situation was," she writes, "I earnestly wished to retain it. I thought, if I could struggle on with unremitting firmness and integrity, the children would in time become more humanized" (*AG,* 27).

Agnes's efforts at reform enable Brontë to analyze the expectations that domestic ideology placed on the middle-class woman by virtue of her role as moral educator. Brontë shows that Agnes is most frustrated by her sense that what reformation she does achieve is fragile at best; bad examples from a father or uncle are all it takes to negate the progress she thought she had achieved. Although Agnes gradually relinquishes her belief in her own powers to effect fundamental change, Brontë shows the impact of her subsequent sense of failure. The attraction that Agnes eventually develops for the curate Edward Weston may be related to his own desire to reform his parishioners and his relative success at it; at the conclusion of her narrative, for instance, Agnes reports with pride that "Edward, by his strenuous exertions, has worked surprising reforms in his parish" (*AG,* 164). Her sometimes excessive admiration of her mother may also relate to her sense that her mother manages others more effectively than she herself is able to do. The possibilities and problems of reform—of self, of the children one supervises and instructs, or of the parishoners one oversees—manifest another way in which Brontë used her writing to question the stability of selfhood over time. In *Agnes Grey,* Brontë shows that failure to change—literally to re-form and to better one's self—can have disastrous consequences.

Agnes's relative failure to achieve the reforms she had so desired in her students is not surprising. Brontë provides so much evidence of the horrific behavior of Agnes's charges and the physical hardships she endures that the reader cannot doubt that she was faced with an impossible task. Although Agnes hints at her own lack of confidence, Brontë ensures that Agnes's readers will not doubt her. The children she tends pull her hair, threaten to destroy her personal belongings (including her cherished writing desk), affront her conscience and sensibilities with their abhorrent conduct toward the natural world (e.g., maliciously whipping horses, beating dogs, and torturing young birds), and ignore her warnings and threats. Throughout these episodes, Brontë draws the reader's attention not to the children themselves (who seem larger than life in their faults) but to Agnes as she reacts to her experiences and develops as a result.

Brontë signals the emotional implications of Agnes's experiences through her physical changes, which her family notices when she returns home on vacation and, at the end of the novel, after permanently resigning from her position. Brontë prepares readers to anticipate that Agnes will be "a good deal paler and thinner than when [she] first left home" (*AG,* 44), through a series of references to her hunger. Agnes's stint at the Bloomfield residence is marked by many occasions during which she fails to eat: when she arrives for the first time after an arduous journey she is presented with "beefsteaks and half-cold potatoes," which she finds inedible (*AG,* 13); later in her stay she notes the "frugal supper of cold meat and bread" she is invited to partake of (*AG,* 18); on still another occasion, after struggling to get the children dressed and prepared for breakfast, she finds the breakfast food cold on the table. In these and other instances, the cold food that Agnes fails to eat parallels the frigid demeanor of her employers, and particularly of Mrs. Bloomfield, whom she describes as "cold, grave, and forbidding—the very opposite of the kind, warm-hearted matron my hopes had depicted her to be" (*AG,* 18). Her subsequent stay at Horton Lodge, the Murray family residence, is little better. Of her first meal there, Agnes writes: "Having broken my long fast on a cup of tea and a little thin bread and butter, I sat down beside the small, smouldering fire, and amused myself with a hearty fit of crying" (*AG,* 48).

In these instances, Brontë invokes a trope of nourishment common in women's writing of the 19th century. Agnes herself recognizes that the nourishment she needs is emotional, writing at one point in her stay with the Bloomfields: "Kindness, which had been the food of my life through so many years, had lately been so entirely denied me, that I welcomed with grateful joy the slightest semblance of it" (*AG,* 31). Later, she describes a short stay at home as "quiet enjoyment of liberty and rest, and genuine friendship, from all of which I had fasted so long" (*AG,* 41). The references in *Agnes Grey* to nourishment, both physical and emotional, are legion and help Brontë to show the impact of Agnes's diminished social status as a governess. Indeed, the process by which Agnes literally becomes thinner parallels the process by which the reader becomes increasingly aware of her social invisibility.

Throughout the novel, Brontë marks Agnes's social invisibility in two important and interrelated ways, both of which reveal the dissonance of class status for the governess. Agnes's sense of her status manifests itself through her preoccupation with her visible presence or lack of it. She discovers as a governess that her presence in a variety of public settings is necessary to make manifest the social status of her employers, but that her presence must also be unacknowledged. The situation that Brontë depicted in *Agnes Grey* was, in fact, fairly realistic; explaining the dilemmas of social status introduced by the figure of the governess, one historian has written, "So excruciating was the problem to all concerned that many employers and their friends adopted the cowardly, though effective, tactic of simply pretending not to 'notice' the governess on those occasions when she was obliged to be in their company" (Hughes 1993, 99-100). Brontë presents similar situations, using them to reveal the emotional anguish that they engender in her heroine. For example, describing Mr. Robson—Mrs. Bloomfield's brother—Agnes writes, "He seldom deigned to notice me; and, when he did, it was with a certain supercilious insolence of tone and manner that convinced me he was no gentleman: though it was intended to have a contrary effect" (*AG,* 36). Although Agnes seems on the surface to recognize and disparage the pretensions of Mr. Robson and others like him, the very frequency with which she notes encounters like this point to an unresolved bitterness as well.

Another strategy that Brontë uses to manifest Agnes's social invisibility is emphasizing her lack of an effective voice. Agnes's awareness of her own sense of "voicelessness," for which she accepts partial responsibility, becomes a major subject of the narrative itself and ultimately enables Brontë to explore through her representation of Agnes, situated as she was in the private sphere, the unempowered position of middle-class women. The related issues of social invisibility and voicelessness so dominate Agnes's narrative that

they—rather than, for example, the physical conditions of her life as a governess—become the actual subject of the novel.

Brontë's preoccupation with Agnes's developing sense of presence and voice reveals itself early on in her account of governessing—in fact, in the same episode in which she is first presented with a meal that she is unable to eat. While she attempts out of politeness to eat her meal, she becomes self-conscious about the conversation with Mrs. Bloomfield, noting both that lady's "succession of commonplace remarks, expressed with frigid formality" as well as her own failure to respond: "I really *could* not converse," she writes (*AG,* 13)—a statement that she would echo at several other points in her narrative. Introducing a situation that would recur in other portions of the narrative, Brontë exacerbates Agnes's sense of self-consciousness by making her the object of another's gaze. Adding to her sense of discomfort at this point is an awareness that Mrs. Bloomfield is watching her eat: "sensible that the awful lady was spectator to the whole transaction, I at last desperately grasped the knife and fork in my fists, like a child of two years old" (*AG,* 13). In her own estimation, Agnes is reduced to a child—just the thing she had hoped to disprove through her venture into governessing in the first place. She accounts for her behavior in several ways: she is physically cold from her journey and her hands are literally "benumbed" from the long drive (*AG,* 13). At the same time, she is nervous about what her new life will be like and already disheartened by her encounters with Mrs. Bloomfield. Most obviously, though, she begins to become conscious of her self as powerless.

Agnes's self-consciousness escalates as the weeks go on. Her difficulties with the unruly Bloomfield children are made worse by her worry about what their parents will think, or—to be more precise—see. Struggling to keep up with Tom and Mary Ann on a walk outside, she thinks: "But there was no remedy; either I must follow them, or keep entirely apart from them, and thus appear neglectful of my charge. . . . I was in constant fear that their mother would see them from the window, and blame me. . . . If *she* did not see them, some one else did" (*AG,* 19). Agnes's fears seem justified: her actions and behaviors are closely monitored. Brontë repeatedly represents the Bloomfield estate or rooms within the estate as panoptic; no matter what her position, Agnes is subject to the constant surveillance of her employers. Just as Mrs. Bloomfield watched her in the dining room, Mr. Bloomfield watches from the window as the children play outdoors and is "continually looking in to see if the schoolroom [is] in order" (*AG,* 34). Even visitors to the home scrutinize Agnes's actions; she spitefully characterizes the senior Mrs. Bloomfield as "a spy upon my words and deeds" (*AG,* 31).

Brontë counterbalances in several ways Agnes's painful sense that she is being watched. Although Agnes doesn't directly acknowledge the irony of it, her work policing her charges entails a good deal of espionage as well. She at one point characterizes her job as one of "instruction and surveillance," implying that the two were equally weighted. Some of this is, in fact, commanded of her, as when Mrs. Murray directs her to follow Rosalie in the park to ensure that she doesn't have an "unsightly" encounter with the Reverend Hatfield. Yet from her ostensibly invisible position Agnes also monitors the behavior of those around her and records it, often in minute detail.

The emphasis that Brontë narrative places on Agnes's sense of presence, of watching and being watched, shifts slightly in the second half of the novel, when the character Edward Weston is introduced. Some of Agnes's self-consciousness about her lack of presence persists, as for example when she records Hatfield's failure to notice her while handing the Murray girls into their carriage after the church service. In characteristic fashion, Agnes accepts some of the blame for her situation, attributing it in part to her personality and in part to her role as a governess: "I liked walking better, but a sense of reluctance to obtrude my presence on any one who did not desire it always kept me passive on these and similar occasions," she writes. "Indeed, this was the best policy—for to submit and oblige was the governess's part, to consult their own pleasure was that of the pupils" (*AG,* 87).

Nonetheless, Agnes wants her readers to blame others; describing the "great nuisance" of walking home from church with others, she notes:

> As none of the before-mentioned ladies and gentlemen ever noticed me, it was disagreeable to walk beside them, as if listening to what they said, or wishing to be thought one of them, while they talked over me, or across; and if their eyes, in speaking, chanced to fall on me, it seemed as if they looked on vacancy— as if they either did not see me, or were very desirous to make it appear so. (*AG,* 87)

The passage clearly reveals Agnes's self-consciousness about her lack of social visibility, but it also suggests that she, too, is driven by pride. Rather than simply walk at the pace that would occur naturally, she refuses to do anything that would allow others to think she cared what they said. As she continues:

> It was disagreeable, too, to walk behind, and thus appear to acknowledge my own inferiority; for, in truth, I considered myself pretty nearly as good as the best of them, and wished them to know that I did so, and not to imagine that I looked upon myself as a mere domestic, who knew her own place too well to walk beside such fine ladies and gentlemen as they were. (*AG,* 88)

At this point in her narrative, Agnes "shamefully" acknowledges that she worked hard "to appear perfectly unconscious or regardless of their presence" (*AG,* 88)— an ironic confession, given her bitterness about similar treatment on their part.

Part of the role that Weston serves is to allow Brontë to curb what Agnes at one point refers to as her "spirit of misanthropy" (*AG,* 88). Significantly, he does so by noticing Agnes, thus enabling Brontë to symbolically subvert the class-consciousness that would make her, as a governess, unworthy of public attention. Not surprisingly, Agnes registers his notice immediately. She describes their accidental encounter at the cottage of Nancy Brown, for example, as follows:

> "I've done you a piece of good service, Nancy," he began: then seeing me, he acknowledged my presence by a slight bow. I should have been invisible to Hatfield, or any other gentleman of those parts. (*AG,* 84).

Brontë stresses Agnes's level of self-esteem by having her insist on remaining hidden from view, refusing to accept a chair by the fire with Weston and Nancy Brown and continuing to sew silently by a window in the corner of the cottage. But it is significant that she gradually takes measures to make her presence known. In chapter 17, "Confessions," she writes, "I may as well acknowledge that, about this time, I paid more attention to dress than ever I had done before" (*AG,* 114). Her success in doing so is established in the narrative when the Murray sisters effectively bar her from going with them to church, ensuring that she won't be seen by Weston and that all of his attention will thus be reserved for them. When Agnes finally does meet him again after this point, she writes, "it was something to find my unimportant saying so well remembered: it was something that he had noticed so accurately the time I had ceased to be visible" (*AG,* 129).

Although throughout the narrative Brontë shows Agnes struggling with an inability to make her presence felt, this passage suggests that her sense of presence is tied to a sense of voice. Both are intimately connected to a sense of self that, at this point in the narrative, is beleaguered at best. From the very beginning of Agnes's account of life as a governess, Brontë emphasizes viocelessness as the distinguishing feature of her work. Remembering some warnings from her mother, she vows to "keep silence" on the faults of her charges (*AG,* 18), a decision reinforced early on by Mrs. Bloomfield's directive in regard to handling problems with the children. She effectively censors Agnes by saying, "If persuasion and gentle remonstrance will not do, let one of the others come and tell me; for I can speak to them more plainly than it would be proper for you to do" (*AG,* 52). Brontë reintroduces the theme of censorship with Mrs. Murray. As Agnes writes, "Having said what she wished, it was no part of her plan to wait my answer: it was my business to hear, and not to speak" (*AG,* 127). Although Agnes is "roused to speak" in her own defense on more than one occasion with both the Bloomfield and the Murray families, she consistently decides to "subdue" and "suppress" her impulses (*AG,* 27). What makes governessing difficult, she implies, is less the physical hardships or the embarrassment of lowered social status than the stress of having to continually restrain herself.

The emphasis on repression that is at the heart of Brontë's account of Agnes's experiences as a governess is central to the novel's romance plot as well. Like other Victorian writers, Brontë understood the power of sexuality and of sexual impulses to determine behavior and yet at the same time appreciated its "fugitive nature," its "resistan[ce] to definition, examination, and regulation."[11] Brontë showed further how the challenges of understanding and regulating erotic impulses were especially formidable for a woman like Agnes Grey, whose gender and status as a governess combined to render her passive. The challenge of exercising restraint in the presence of her charges and superiors becomes exacerbated for Agnes by the necessity of repressing her feelings for Weston. Listening to Rosalie chatter about her conversation with Weston during one of the Sundays in which she had been prevented from attending church, Agnes thinks:

> I was accustomed, now, to keeping silence when things distasteful to my ear were uttered; and now, too, I was used to wearing a placid smiling countenance when my heart was bitter within me. . . . Other things I heard, which I felt or feared were indeed too true: but I must still conceal my anxiety respecting him, in indignation against them, beneath a careless aspect; others, again, mere hints of something said or done, which I longed to hear more of, but could not venture to inquire. So passed the weary time. (*AG,* 120)

Although Agnes's situation is clearly painful, Brontë heightens the reader's appreciation of the intensity of Agnes's desire by focusing on the extent to which she controls that desire, choosing to keep her thoughts and feelings to herself rather than risking an open confession. Agnes's repression becomes a mechanism of self-control and a means of self-identification. In another important passage, she admits that not even her mother or her sister could be privy to her thoughts:

> I fear, by this time, the reader is well-nigh disgusted with the folly and weakness I have so freely laid before him. I never disclosed it then, and would not have done so had my own sister or my mother been with me in the house. I was a close and resolute

dissembler—in this one case at least. My prayers, my tears, my wishes, fears, and lamentations, were witnessed by myself and Heaven alone. (*AG,* 121)

Curiously, Agnes does not explore why she felt so strongly about keeping her emotions to herself. Providing a small source of consolation is her religious faith, which enables her to feel that even in this silence she is not alone.

Brontë shows that, although silence is partially imposed upon Agnes, it is also a position that she adopts in self-defense. The politics of speaking out or choosing not to speak enter Brontë's narrative in other ways as well, as for example in the story of Rosalie's flirtation with Hatfield. When the flirtation comes to its end, Hatfield requests that Rosalie "keep silent" about his proposal of marriage, threatening her by remarking that "if you add to [my injury] by giving publicity to this unfortunate affair, or naming it *at all,* you will find that I too can speak" (*AG,* 101). The self-deprecating Agnes cannot, of course, wield power through speech in the same way as Rosalie. When she is dismissed from the services of the Bloomfield family, for instance, she writes:

> I wished to say something in my own justification: but in attempting to speak, I felt my voice falter; and rather than testify any emotion, or suffer the tears to overflow that were already gathering in my eyes, I chose to keep silence, and bear all like a self-convicted culprit. (*AG,* 41)

Brontë advances her study of the social and psychological implications of Agnes's silence in several ways. On many occasions throughout the narrative, Agnes admits that she cannot hold others entirely responsible for her silence. Of Mrs. Bloomfield's failure to allow her more than two weeks' vacation time during her first earned holiday, she notes:

> Yet she was not to blame in this; I had never told her my feelings, and she could not be expected to divine them; I had not been with her a full term, and she was justified in not allowing me a full vacation. (*AG,* 28)

Such self-critical gestures recur throughout Agnes's narrative and enable Brontë to bring to the foreground the issue of Agnes's reliability as a narrator and enhance the reader's understanding of the extent to which the nature of subjectivity itself is under scrutiny in the novel. Of the Murray children's desire to take lessons in the open air and on damp grass, which frequently made Agnes catch a cold, she writes, "But I must not blame them for what was, perhaps, my own fault; for I never made any particular objections to sitting where they pleased; foolishly choosing to risk the consequences, rather than trouble them for my convenience" (*AG,* 58-59). Here as elsewhere Agnes conveys an attitude of both martyrdom and self-deprecation.

Weston's role is again crucial to Brontë's exploration of Agnes's self-deprecating nature, for he openly expresses that which Agnes only partially accepts about her own role in representing herself as beleaguered. On one of the occasions when the two walk home together after church, he introduces the topic of social disposition and when she complains that her position denies her opportunities to make friends, he responds, "The fault is partly in society, and partly, I should think, in your immediate neighbours: and partly, too, in yourself; for many ladies, in your position, would make themselves be noticed and accounted of" (*AG,* 108). Although Weston is not saying here anything that Agnes has not already thought to herself, it is significant that he voices her thoughts, that he feels open enough with her to do so, and that he is unencumbered by social decorum, a trait she appreciates. As she subsequently thinks, "such single-minded straightforwardness could not possibly offend me" (*AG,* 109).

Nonetheless, it is precisely the fact that Weston is *not* what he initially seems that makes him attractive to Agnes. Although she is immediately drawn to him as a clergyman, approving his style of delivering a sermon and revering his "strong sense, firm faith, and ardent piety" (*AG,* 83), it is not until she hears of his attentions to the poor cottager Nancy Brown that he becomes "like the morning-star in [her] horizon" and a "subject for contemplation" (*AG,* 82). As Agnes explains it, "when I found that to his other good qualities was added that of true benevolence and gentle, considerate kindness, the discovery, perhaps, delighted me the more, as I had not been prepared to expect it" (*AG,* 83). Shortly after this admission, Agnes recollects her encounter with Weston at Nancy Brown's cottage and reminds her readers that he—unlike others—openly acknowledges her presence and speaks to her. Here, as elsewhere in the novel, Brontë stresses the importance of such attention in encouraging Agnes to distinguish Weston from others. As she had earlier emphasized, "Mr Hatfield never spoke to me, neither did Sir Hugh or Lady Meltham, nor Mr Harry or Miss Meltham, nor Mr Green or his sisters, nor any other lady or gentleman who frequented that church: nor, in fact, any one that visited Horton Lodge" (*AG,* 67).

The story of Agnes's visits to Nancy's cottage and to other homes of poor laborers also enables Brontë to explore how Agnes represents herself to others when divested of the governess role. Just as her family's fall into poverty had seemed to Agnes to be an opportunity to better herself, so too does her friendship with Nancy Brown allow her to improve herself. Even before the arrival of Weston, Agnes recognizes that Nancy Brown is the one person that she is open with, the one to whom she could "freely speak [her] thoughts" (*AG,* 81). Importantly, Agnes sees her relationship with Nancy as mutually beneficial; she seeks to help her, but she also realizes that Nancy's "conversation was calculated to render me better, wiser, or happier than before" (*AG,* 81). Like Helen Huntingdon in *The Tenant of Wildfell Hall,* Agnes worries that her association with people unworthy of her respect will inevitably exert an adverse influence on her, that the alliance with the Bloomfields and Murrays "[will] gradually bring [her] feelings, habits, capacities, to the level of their own" (*AG,* 82). Here again Agnes's expression of self-doubts exemplifies the ways that Brontë used her writing to question the stability of selfhood. Whereas earlier in the narrative Agnes had felt dismayed at her failure to reform her charges, here her frustration with governessing concerns the malleability of her self. Nancy Brown unwittingly enables Agnes to believe in its stability.

Brontë fulfills a variety of additional functions through the character of Nancy Brown. Nancy's story enables Brontë to invert the commonly held association of poverty with immorality by suggesting that Agnes's sense of morality is better served in the company of the impoverished. She also facilitates Agnes's growing recognition of what it means to speak "freely," as she apparently does with Nancy Brown, and as Weston eventually does with her. The story of Nancy Brown thus indirectly reintroduces the thematic of voice and voicelessness that runs throughout *Agnes Grey,* and indeed throughout all of Brontë's writing. Although Agnes does not realize it, her readers have become increasingly aware that while governessing has censored Agnes's public voice, it has also facilitated the emergence of an important internal voice. Agnes does speak "freely" with someone other than Nancy Brown, in other words; as her narrative progresses, she develops an ongoing conversation with her self.

Notes

[8] The connection between Agnes and her mother and their description of kindred willingness to approach their reduced conditions with enthusiasm are interesting in light of Anne Brontë's own connection to poverty via her mother. Maria Branwell Brontë wrote an essay titled "The Advantages of Poverty in Religious Concerns" that sought to disavow the association of poverty with moral evil and to advocate "the instruction and conversion of the poor" (27). Although this essay was never published in the Brontë's lifetime, it is printed in *BLFC,* I, 24-27.

[9] Agnes's reference to New Zealand here may reflect Anne Brontë's family's affiliation with Mary Taylor, a schoolmate and friend of Charlotte's who traveled to New Zealand to find work. For more on this connection, as well as on the influence of Robert Southey's

works on Brontë's use of New Zealand, see Jane Stafford's "Anne Brontë, *Agnes Grey* and New Zealand," *Brontë Society Transactions* 20, 2 (1990), 97-99.

[10] For a thorough discussion of the ideological work performed by conduct and advice manuals in Victorian England, see Nancy Armstrong's *Desire and Domestic Fiction* (1987).

[11] For an excellent overview of Victorian attitudes toward sexuality, see "Victorian Sexualities," a special issue of *Victorian Studies* edited by Andrew H. Miller. The quoted passages come from Miller's brief introduction to major aspects of the topic, entitled "Editor's Introduction," *Victorian Studies* 63, 3 (Spring 1993), 269-72.

[12] The term "private speech" is drawn from literature on Bakhtin's Vygotskian psycholinguistics and has correlates in Bakhtin's theories of narrative and voice. For a good discussion that bridges Vygotskian psycholinguistics and literary theories, see James Wertsch's *Voices of the Mind* (Cambridge, Mass.: Harvard University Press, 1992).

Works Cited

Brontë, Anne. *Agnes Grey*. 1st ed., 3d of 3 vols. In Emily Brontë and Anne Brontë. *Wuthering Heights and Agnes Grey*. London: T. C. Newby, 1847. In-text citations appear as *AG*.

Hughes, Kathryn. *The Victorian Governess*. London: Hambledon Press, 1993.

T. J. Wise and J. A. Symington, eds. *The Brontës: Their Lives, Friendships and Correspondence,* 4 vols. Oxford: The Shakespeare Head Press, 1932. Reprint,

Philadelphia: Porcupine Press, 1980.

FURTHER READING

Criticism

Bentley, Phyllis. *The Brontë Sisters*. Harlow, Essex: Longman Group Ltd., 1971 (Reprint), 42p.
> Mentions *Agnes Grey*'s "quiet piety" and "cool eye for domestic hypocrisy."

Eagleton, Terry. "Anne Brontë." In *Myths of Power: A Marxist Study of the Brontës*, pp. 122-38. London: Macmillan, 1988.
> Offers a Marxist analysis of *Agnes Grey* and *The Tenant of Wildfell Hall*. Eagleton contends that both novels "pivot on a simple binary opposition between immoral gentry and righteous protagonist."

Edgerley, C. Mabel. "Anne Brontë." *Transactions and Other Publications of the Brontë Society* IX (1965): 173-80.
> Biographical sketch that describes some of the details of the writing of *Agnes Grey*.

Harrison, Ada, and Derek Stanford. "Anne Brontë as Novelist." In *Anne Brontë: Her Life and Work*, pp. 221-46. London: Methuen, 1959.
> Briefly assesses the style of Brontë's *Agnes Grey*, particularly in relation to *The Tenant of Wildfell Hall*.

Prentis, Barbara. "The Self and the World." In *The Brontë Sisters and George Eliot: A Unity of Difference*, pp. 67-86. London: Macmillan, 1988.
> Observes that in *Agnes Grey* Brontë moves beyond autobiography to social criticism.

Additional coverage of Brontë's life and career is contained in the following source published by Gale Research: *Dictionary of Literary Biography*, Vol. 21.

Alexandre Dumas (*père*)

1802-1870

(Full name Alexandre Dumas Davy de la Pailleterie) French novelist, dramatist, memoirist, historian, essayist, and short story and travel sketch writer.

For further information on Dumas's life and works, see *NCLC,* Volume 11.

INTRODUCTION

Popular in his own time, Dumas *père* has remained a favorite storyteller among generations of readers throughout the world. His best-known works are the novels *Les trois mousquetaires* (1844; *The Three Musketeers; or, The Feats and Fortunes of a Gascon Adventurer*) and *Le comte de Monte-Cristo* (1845; *The Count of Monte Cristo*), adventure stories that abound with swordfights, lavish costumes, beautiful women, and narrow escapes. But these represent a minute portion of writings produced by this enormously prolific author, whose published novels, plays, stories, essays, and other works number in the hundreds. Due to his prolific output and the high entertainment value of his fiction—not to mention questions concerning his collaboration with other writers—critics have often judged Dumas harshly. Nonetheless, his work as a dramatist, which include the plays *Henri III et sa cour* (1829; *Henry III and His Court*) and *Antony* (1831), helped to usher in the Romantic era on the French stage.

Biographical Information

Dumas's father, Thomas-Alexandre Dumas, was the son of a marquis and a Haitian slave, and he took his family name from his African mother. After Thomas's death in 1806, Dumas was raised by his mother, an innkeeper's daughter named Marie-Louise-Elisabeth Labouret, in the town of Villers-Cotterêts, near Paris. He attended the local parochial school, and when he was older worked as a clerk but moved to Paris at the age of twenty, lured by the theater. Influenced by the dramatic works of Shakespeare, the poetry of Lord Byron, and the historical romances of Sir Walter Scott, Dumas collaborated with two others in writing a one-act play, *La chasse et l'amour* (1825). The young playwright used the pseudonym Davy, taken from the name of his paternal grandfather; but soon he was writing under his own name and began producing a series of important dramas that included *Henri III and His Court, Antony,* and *Christine; ou Stockholm, Fountainebleau, et Rome* (1830).

During the Revolution of 1830, Dumas became interested in republican politics, and with the return of monarchy under King Louise Philippe, he decided to leave France in 1832. There followed several years of travel in Switzerland, Russia, Italy, and other parts of Europe, adventures Dumas began recording in *Impressions de voyage* (1833-37; *The Glacier Land*) and numerous other books of travel essays. In the 1840s, having returned to France, he embarked on the most fruitful decade of his life, years which saw the serial publication of *The Three Musketeers, The Count of Monte Cristo,* and dozens of other novels. He was so prolific, in fact, that critics began to raise questions concerning his use of collaborators such as Auguste Maquet. In 1845, French journalist Eugène de Mirecourt charged publicly that Dumas ran a "literary factory" in which he exploited the efforts of slave-like scribes. The slander case against Mirecourt, which Dumas won, was not the only harbinger of bad tidings as the 1840s came to a close. During those years of prosperity, Dumas spent money lavishly, and built a mansion dubbed the "Château de Monte-Cristo," which housed his many lovers, pets, and hangers-on. By 1850 he was bankrupt, and was forced to sell his home. Also in that year the Théâtre Historique, which he had founded in 1847 to stage his own dramas, went bankrupt. Dumas fled to Brussels to avoid his creditors, and continued to write at a feverish pace, this time without the help of Maquet or other collaborators.

By 1853 his finances were back in order, and he returned to Paris, where his memoirs had been published to great success. He also founded and began writing for several journals with titles based on his most acclaimed novels, including *Le mousquetaire* and *Le Monte-Cristo.* As passionate in his personal life as he was in his work, Dumas had enjoyed a number of lovers and fathered several illegitimate children, including the future writer Alexandre Dumas *fils* in 1824. He was married briefly in the 1840s to actress Ida Ferrier and engaged in a celebrated affair with the American actress Adah Isaacs Menken in the late 1860s. His voluminous literary output continued, though slackened somewhat from its zenith in the 1840s, and he continued to travel widely. But his fortunes steadily declined, and when he died in his son's home at the age of sixty-eight, little remained of the riches Dumas had accumulated in his highly successful career.

Major Works

Like his contemporary and rival Honoré de Balzac, Dumas set out to produce a vast body of fiction that would depict the width and breadth of a society, specifically France from the Middle Ages to his own time. In so doing, he produced his two best-known works, *The Three Musketeers* and *The Count of Monte Cristo,* as well as dozens—even scores—of other novels. (English-speaking readers may be disappointed to scan his list of published writings in vain for *The Man in the Iron Mask:* the book is actually a compilation taken from several of his works and did not exist as such during Dumas's lifetime.) In writing these "historical romances," as they were called, Dumas pioneered the genre of historical fiction, bringing together actual events and people with characters and incidents of his own creation. *The Three Musketeers,* for instance, is drawn from the quasi-historical memoirs of a figure called M. d'Artagnan; Dumas, for his part, drew the characters of D'Artagnan, as well as Athos, Porthos, and Aramis, out of those memoirs. He built their adventures around events involving King Louis XIII, Cardinal Richelieu, and other prominent personages of seventeenth-century France. Likewise *The Count of Monte Cristo,* a tale of unjust imprisonment and revenge, has its roots in an account from the Napoleonic era. Less well-known at the time, but more significant to modern critics because it offers insights into Dumas's views on his African heritage is *Georges* (1843; *George; or the Planter of the Isle of France*). Like *Monte Cristo,* it is a tale of revenge, with the important difference that it is Dumas's only story—and one of the few works of Western literature prior to the twentieth century—in which the hero is a mulatto. Another work little-known in his time, but more noted in the twentieth century, is his examination of a courtesan's career in "respectable" society, *Fernande* (1844; *Fernande; or, The Fallen Angel*). But such topical novels are the exception rather than the rule in an *oeuvre* that includes far more works depicting the French past of Medieval times and the Renaissance.

In his later years, Dumas produced an obscure novel destined to attract more attention after his lifetime: *La terreur prussiene* (1866; *The Prussian Terror*) sounded an alarmist warning regarding a militaristic Germany, which by the time of his death had invaded France. Interestingly, the work was first translated into English in 1915, when Britain was engaged in war with Germany on the battlegrounds of Dumas's homeland. Principal among Dumas's dramatic works is *Antony,* a tale of seduction, intrigue, and murder that shocked Paris audiences because it was set not in the classical past, but in contemporary France. Similarly, *La tour de Nesle* (1832; *The Tower of Nesle*) presents a scandalous plot involving sex and betrayal, this time set in medieval France. Also notable are several plays depicting lives and events surrounding monarchs, including *Henry III and His Court,* which vies with Hugo's *Cromwell* for the title of first play of the Romantic era; *Christine,* about Queen Christina of Sweden; and *Charles VII chez ses grands vassaux* (1831; *Charles VII at the Homes of His Great Vassals*). Dorothy

Trench-Bonett, who produced the first English translation of the latter 160 years after its writing, referred to it as one of the first pieces of Western literature that offered a protest against the slave trade. Other than his novels and plays, the third significant component of Dumas's *oeuvre* is comprised of his travel writings and other essays, including his celebrated autobiography *Mes mémoires* (1852-54; *My Memoirs*), which did not appear in English until 1907.

Critical Reception

Of all his works, Dumas's historical romances are best known in the English-speaking world, where he has enjoyed at least as great a following as he has among French readers. In France, he is most noted for his dramatic writings, which critics have long recognized as groundbreaking works. Not only was *Antony* innovative in its use of a contemporary setting for a classic tale of erotic intrigue, the staging of *Henry III and His Court* in February of 1829 made it the first Romantic play, although Hugo's *Cromwell* was actually written earlier. In spite of his contributions to French and world literature, however, in his own day Dumas often found himself the butt of harsh criticism. His work was routinely dismissed as mere entertainment of the lightest sort—hardly more substantial than *The Wandering Jew* and other works of his largely forgotten contemporary, Eugène Sue. Certainly Dumas ranked low in comparison to the more critically celebrated (though sometimes almost equally prolific) writers of his time such as George Sand, Balzac, and even Victor Hugo. In addition, the sheer volume of his works—not to mention his habit of padding his writing with excessive quotations and dialogue—made him appear more like a human writing machine than an artist. His astounding output, in fact, left him open to questions regarding the authorship of works produced under the name "Alexandre Dumas." But he proved in his later work that collaboration was not an absolute requirement for production on his part, and observers have pointed out that no joint authorship has ever been claimed for *My Memoirs* and any number of his widely praised non-fiction works.

The sheer endurance of his historical romances, which have seen countless film interpretations, seems in itself a sign of Dumas's singular power as a creative talent, and his reputation has steadily increased over time. Though his work has enjoyed scant critical attention in proportion to its sheer bulk, he remains a figure of interest. In the late twentieth century, critics have continued to investigate his lesser-known writings for their contemporary relevance. Of greatest interest, perhaps, has been the fact of his African ancestry and its influence on *George* and other works. This racial theme, along with various sexual aspects of Dumas's work, including androgyny (*Christine*), promises to provide decades' worth of fruitful critical inquiry.

PRINCIPAL WORKS

La chasse et l'amour [As Davy] (drama) 1825

Henri III et sa cour [translated as *Catherine of Cleves*; also published as *Henry III and His Court*] (drama) 1829

Christine; ou Stockholm, Fountainebleau, et Rome (drama) 1830

Antony [*Antony*] (drama) 1831

Charles VII chez ses grands vassaux [*Charles VII at the Homes of His Great Vassals*] (drama) 1831

Napoléon Bonaparte; ou, Trente ans de l'histoire de France (drama) 1831

Richard Darlington (drama) 1831

Térésa (drama) 1832

La tour de Nesle [*The Tower of Nesle*] (drama) 1832

Gaule et France [*The Progress of Democracy*] (history) 1833

Impressions de voyage. 5 vols. [*The Glacier Land*; also published as *Travels in Switzerland*] (travel essays) 1833-37

Don Juan de Marana; ou, La chute d'un ange [*Don Juan de Marana*] (drama) 1836

Kean, ou Désordre et génie [*Edmund Kean, or The Genius and the Libertine*] (drama) 1836

Caligula (drama) 1837

**Crimes célèbres.* 8 vols. [*Celebrated Crimes*] (essays) 1839-40

Une année à Florence (travel essays) 1841

Excursions sur les bords du Rhin (travel essays) 1841

Nouvelles impressions de voyage: Midi de la France [*Pictures of Travel in the South of France*] (travel essays) 1841

Le capitaine Aréna (travel essays) 1842

Le chevalier d'Harmental (novel) 1842

Le speronare [partially translated as *Journeys with Dumas: The Speronara*] (travel essays) 1842

Le corricolo [*Sketches of Naples*] (travel essays) 1843

Georges [*George; or The Planter of the Isle of France*] (novel) 1843

La villa Palmieri (travel essays) 1843

Fernande [*Fernande; or, The Fallen Angel: A Story of Life in Paris*] (novel) 1844

Les trois mousquetaires. 8 vols. [*The Three Musketeers; or, The Feats and Fortunes of a Gascon Adventurer*] (novel) 1844

Louis XIV et son siècle. 2 vols. (history) 1844-45

Le comte de Monte-Cristo. 8 vols. [*The Count of Monte Cristo*] (novel) 1845

Une fille du Régent [*The Regent's Daughter*] (novel) 1845

Les Frères corses [*The Corsican Brothers*] (novel) 1845

La Reine Margot [*Marguerite de Valois*] (novel) 1845

Vingt ans après [*Twenty Years After; or, The Further Feats and Fortunes of a Gascon Adventurer*] (novel) 1845

Le chevalier de Maison-Rouge. 6 vols. [*Marie Antoinette: or, The Chevalier of the Red House: A Tale of the French Revolution*] (novel) 1845-46

La dame de Monsoreau [*Chicot the Jester; or, The Lady of Monsoreau*; also published as *Diana of Meridor; or, The Lady of Monsoreau*] (novel) 1846

Le Bâtard de Mauléon [*The Half Brothers; or, The Head and the Hand*; also published as *The Bastard of Mauléon*] (novel) 1846-47

Mémoires d'un médecin: Joseph Balsamo [*The Memoirs of a Physician*] (novel) 1846-48

Les quarante-cinq [*The Forty-Five Guardsmen*] (novel) 1847

Impressions de voyage: De Paris à Cadix [*From Paris to Cadiz*] (travel essays) 1847-48

Le vicomte de Bragelonne; ou, Dix ans plus tard [*The Vicomte de Bragelonne; or, Ten Years Later*] (novel) 1848-50

Le véloce; ou, Tanger, Alger et Tunis [*Tales of Algeria; or, Life Among the Arabs*] (travel essays) 1848-51

Oeuvres complètes. 286 vols. (novels, short stories, travel essays, memoirs, histories, and essays) 1848-1900

Le collier de la reine [*The Queen's Necklace*] (novel) 1849-50

La tulipe noire [*Rosa; or, The Black Tulip*] (novel) 1850

Ange Pitou [*Taking the Bastille; or, Six Years Later*] (novel) 1851

Le Vampire (drama) 1851

Pietro Tasca (drama) 1852

Mes mémoires [*My Memoirs*] (memoirs) 1852-54

La Comtesse de Charny [*The Countess de Charny; or, The Fall of the French Monarchy*] (novel) 1852-55

Isaac Laquedem (novel) 1853

Catherine Blum (novel) 1854

Souvenirs de 1830 à 1842. 8 vols. (memoirs) 1854-55

Les Mohicans de Paris [*The Mohicans of Paris*] (novel) 1854-58

Samson (drama) 1856

Black [*Black, The Story of a Dog*] (novel) 1858

De Paris à Astrakan (travel essays) 1858-59

Le Caucase: Voyage d'Alexandre Dumas [*Adventures in the Caucasus*] (travel essays) 1859

Les Louves de Machecoul [translated in two parts as *The Royalist Daughters* and *The Castle of Souday*] (novel) 1859

Les Garibaldiens, révolution de Sicile et de Naples [*The Garibaldians in Sicily*] (history) 1861

Théâtre complet d'Alexandre Dumas. 15 vols. (dramas) 1863-74

Le Comte de Moret [*The Count of Moret; or, Richelieu and His Rivals*] (novel) 1866

La terreur prussiene [*The Prussian Terror*] (novel) 1866

Histoire de mes bêtes [*My Pets*] (essays) 1867

Les blancs et les bleus [*The First Republic; or, The Whites and the Blues*] (novel) 1867-68

Souvenirs dramatiques (essays) 1868

The Romances of Alexandre Dumas. 60 vols. (novels) 1893-97

Oeuvres d'Alexandre Dumas père. 38 vols. (novels) 1962-67

*Most of Dumas's prose works were originally published serially in periodicals. In addition, due to the controversy surrounding the authorship of many of his works, Dumas's collaborators are not identified here.

**This work also includes essays written by Auguste Jean François Arnould, Narcisse Fournier, Pier Angelo Fiorentino, and Jean Pierre Félicien Mallefille.

CRITICISM

Gamaliel Bradford (essay date 1926)

SOURCE: "Alexandre Dumas," in *A Naturalist of Souls: Studies in Psychography,* Houghton Mifflin Company, 1926, pp. 179-205.

[*In the following essay, Bradford provides an overview of Dumas's career and works and defends him against critics who appraise his writing as mere entertainment.*]

Mr. Davidson, whose excellent volume on Dumas must be the foundation of any careful study of the subject, dismisses his author with the remark: 'Except for increasing the already ample means of relaxation, he did nothing to benefit humanity at large.' Is not this a rather grudging epitaph for the creator of '**Monte Cristo**'? Are the means of relaxation so ample that we can afford to treat '**La Tour de Nesle**' and '**La Reine Margot**' as alms for oblivion? Would Stevenson have read '**Le Vicomte de Bragelonne**' six times, would you or I have read '**Les Trois Mousquetaires**' more times than we can count, if other relaxation of an equally delightful order were indeed so easily obtainable? In spite of the flood of historical novels and all other kinds of novels that overwhelmed the nineteenth century, story-tellers like Dumas are not born every day, nor yet every other day.

For he was a story-teller by nature, one who could make a story of anything, one who did make a story of everything, for the joy of his own child-like imagination. 'I am not like other people. Everything interests me.' The round oath of a man, the smile of a woman, a dog asleep in the sun, a bird singing in a bush, even a feather floating in the breeze, was enough. Fancy seized it and wove an airy, sunbright web about it, glittering with wit, touched with just a hint of pathos; and as we read, we forget the slightness of the substance in the grace and delicacy of the texture.

It is an odd thing, this national French gift of story-telling, of seeking by instinct the group-effect, as it were, of a set of characters, their composite relations to one another and the development of these relations in dramatic climax. English writers, from Chaucer down, dwell by preference on the individual character, force it only with labor and difficulty into the general framework, from which it constantly escapes in delightful but wholly undramatic human eccentricity. To the French habit of mind, such individuality is excrescent and distasteful. Let the characters develop as fully and freely as the action requires, no more. They are there for the action, not the action for them. Hence, as the English defect is dull diffusion and a chaos of disorder, so the French is loss of human truth in a mad eagerness for forcible situations, that is to say, melodrama.

Even in Hugo, in Balzac, in Flaubert, in Zola, one has an uneasy feeling that melodrama is not too far away. In Dumas it is frankly present always. The situation—something that shall tear the nerves, make the heart leap and the breath stop—for Dumas there lies the true art of dramatist and novelist. And what situations! No one ever had more than he the two great dramatic gifts, which perhaps are only one, the gift of preparation and the gift of climax. 'Of all *dénouements,* past, present, and I will say even to come,' writes Sarcey, 'that of "**Antony**" is the most brilliant, the most startling, the most logical, the most rapid; a stroke of genius.' '**Henri III,**' '**Richard Darlington,**' '**La Tour de Nesle**' are full of effects scarcely inferior. If one thinks first of the plays, it is only because in them the action is more concentrated than in the novels. But in novel after novel also, there is the same sure instinct of arrangement, the same masterly hand, masterly for obtaining the sort of effect which the author has chiefly in view.

And perhaps the melodrama is not quite all. The creatures are not always mere puppets, wire-pulled, stirring the pulse when they clash together, then forgotten. We hate them sometimes, sometimes love them, sometimes even remember them. Marguerite and Buridan are not wholly unreal in their wild passion. The scene of reconciliation between the Musketeers in the Place Royale has something deeper than mere effect. And these are only two among many. Under all his gift of technique, his love of startling and amazing, the man was not without an eye, a grip on life, above all, a heart that beat widely, with many sorrows and many joys.

Then the style is the style of melodrama, but it is also far more. No one knew better how and when to let loose sharp, stinging, burning shafts of phrase like the final speech of Antony, *'Elle m'a résisté; je l'ai assassinée,'*—shafts which flew over the footlights straight to the heart of every auditor. But these effects would be nothing without the varied movement of narration, the ease, the lightness, the grace—above all, the perpetual wit, the play of delicate irony, which saves sentiment from being sentimental and erudition from being dull.

Dumas's style has been much abused, and in some ways deserves it. Mr. Saintsbury considers that the plays have 'but little value as literature properly so-called,' and that 'the style of the novels is not more remarkable as such than that of the dramas.' But how far more discerning and sympathetic is Stevenson's characterization of it: 'Light as a whipped trifle, strong as silk; wordy like a village tale; pat like a general's despatch; with every fault, yet never tedious; with no merit, yet inimitably right.' As for dialogue—that subtlest test of the novelist's genius—which neither Balzac, nor Flaubert, nor Zola could manage with flexibility or ease, Dumas may have used it to excess, but who has ever carried it to greater perfection? In M. Lemaître's excellent, if somewhat cynical, phrase, Dumas's dialogue has 'the wonderful quality of stringing out the narrative to the crack of doom and at the same time making it appear to move with headlong rapidity.' But let it string out, so it moves. And surely Dumas's conversations do move, as no others ever have.

In the hurry of modern reading, few people have time to get at Dumas in any but his best-known works. Yet to form a complete idea of his powers, one must take a much wider survey. All periods, all nations, all regions of the earth, came at one time or another under his pen. Of course this means an inevitable superficiality and inaccuracy. But one overlooks these defects, is hardly aware of them, in the ease, the spirit, the unfailing humanness of the narrative. Take a minor story like **'L'Isle de Feu,'** dealing with the Dutch in Java and with the habits and superstitions of the natives, snake-charming, spirit-haunting, etc. Everywhere there is movement, life, character, the wit of the **'Impressions de Voyage,'** the passion of **'La Reine Margot.'** And if Dumas does not quite anticipate the seductive melancholy of Loti's tropics, he gives hints of it which are really wonderful for a man who had never been south of latitude thirty.

Perhaps, outside of the historical novels, we may select four very different books as most typical of Dumas's great variety of production. First, in **'Conscience l'Innocent,'** we have a simple idyllic subject, recalling George Sand's country stories: peasant life, rural scenes, sweet pictures of Dumas's own village home at Villers-Cotterets, which he introduced into so many of his writings. Second, in the immense canvas of **'Salvator,'** too little appreciated, we have a picture of contemporary conditions, the Paris of Sue and Hugo, treated with a vividness far beyond Sue and a dramatic power which Hugo never could command. Third, comes the incomplete **'Isaac Laquedem,'** the vast Odyssey of the Wandering Jew, in which the author planned to develop epically the whole history of the world, though the censorship allowed him to get no further than the

small Biblical portion of it. Few of Dumas's books illustrate better the really soaring sweep of his imagination, and not many have a larger share of his *esprit*. Lastly, there is **'Monte Cristo,'** which, on the whole, remains, doubtless, the best example of what Dumas could do without history to support him. 'Pure melodrama,' some will say; in a sense, truly. Yet, as compared with the melodrama of, for instance, **'Armadale'** and **'The Woman in White,'** there is a certain largeness, a somber grandeur, about the vengeance of Dantès which goes almost far enough to lift the book out of the realm of melodrama, and into that of tragedy. And then there is the wit!

But it is on historical romance, whether in drama or fiction, that Dumas's popularity must chiefly rest. He himself felt it would be so, hoped it would be so; and his numerous references to the matter, if amusing, are also extremely interesting. He speaks of his series of historical novels as 'immense pictures we have undertaken to unroll before the eyes of our readers, in which, if our genius equalled our good will, we would introduce all classes of men from the beggar to the king, from Caliban to Ariel.' And again: 'Balzac has written a great work entitled "The Human Comedy." Our work, begun at the same time, may be entitled "The Drama of France." ' He hopes that his labors will be profitable as well as amusing: 'We intentionally say "instruct" first, for amusement with us is only a mask for instruction. . . . Concerning the last five centuries and a half we have taught France more history than any historian.' And when some one gently insinuates that from a purely historical point of view his work cannot stand with the highest, he replies with his usual charming humor, 'It is the unreadable histories that make a stir; they are like dinners you can't digest; digestible dinners give you no cause to think about them on the next day.'

After all, humor apart, we must recognize the justice of Dumas's claim; and the enduring life and perpetual revival of the historical novel go far to support it. Mankind in general do love to hear about Henry IV, Richelieu, and the Stuarts, about Washington and Lincoln and Napoleon, and in hearing they do learn, even against their will. Pedants shake their heads. This birthdate is incorrect. That victory was not a victory at all. When Dr. Dryasdust has given the slow labor of a lifetime to disentangling fact from fiction, how wicked to mislead the ignorant by wantonly developing fiction out of fact! As if Dr. Dryasdust really knew fact from fiction! As if the higher spiritual facts were not altogether beyond his ken and his researches! As if any two pedants agreed! Take the central fact of history, the point from which everything of importance and interest emanates—human character, the human soul. What pedant can reach it, can analyse it with his finest microscope? Napoleon was born on such a day, died on such a day, this he did, that he did. But was he in any sense patriotic, an idealist, a lover of France? Was he a suspicious, jealous, lascivious tyrant? Was he sometimes one, sometimes the other? State documents and gossiping memoirs give no final answer to these questions, only hints and cloudy indications bearing upon them, from which the genius of the historian must sketch a figure for itself. Therefore, as many historians, so many Napoleons, and in the end my Napoleon, your Napoleon. If so, why not Alexandre Dumas's Napoleon, said Dumas, having perhaps as much faculty of imaginative divination as you or I, or even as several historians whom we will not mention.

In fact, Dumas has undoubtedly taught the history of France to thousands who would otherwise have had little concern with it. And his characters live. Catherine de' Medici and her sons, Louis XIV, Mazarin, the Duc de Richelieu, Marie Antoinette—we know them as we know people whom we meet every day: in one sense, perhaps not at all; but in another sense, intimately. Great actions call for a large background, which should be handled with the wide sweep of the scene-painter, not with the curious minuteness of the artist in miniatures. The very abundance of these characters, the vastness of the canvas, help the reality, and in this matter of amplitude Dumas and Scott show their genius, and triumph over the petty concentration of later imitators. Nor are the characters wholly or mainly of Dumas's own invention less vivid than those historical; for Dumas learned from Scott the cardinal secret of historical romance, which Shakespeare did not grasp, that the action of the story should turn, not on real personages, but on fictitious heroes and heroines, whose fortunes can be moulded freely for a dramatic purpose. Dumas himself says somewhere that people complain of the length of his novels, yet that the longest have been the most popular and the most successful. It is so. We can wander for days in the vast galleries of the **'Reine Margot'** series, charmed with the gallantry of La Mole, the vivacity of Coconnas, the bravado of Bussy, above all, the inimitable wit and shrewdness of Chicot, who surely comes next to d'Artagnan among all Dumas's literary children. And d'Artagnan—what a broad country he inhabits! How lovely to lose one's self there in long winter evenings, meeting at every turn a saucy face or a gay gesture or a keen flash of sword that makes one forget the passage of time. 'I never had a care that a half-hour's reading would not dissipate,' said Montesquieu. Fortunate man! How few of us resemble him! But if a half-hour's reading of anything would work such a miracle, surely a novel of Dumas would do it.

As for the man himself, he happily created such characters as d'Artagnan and Chicot because he resembled them, and was in his own person as picturesque a figure as any that talks passion in his plays, or wit in the endless pages of his novels. I do not know that he had ever read Milton's oracular saying that he who would

be a great poet should make his life a true poem; but, in any case, he pointed it aptly by showing that the best way to write romantic novels is to make a romantic novel of your own career. Born in 1802, in the most stirring period of French history, one quarter African by blood, he worked his way upward from bitter poverty and insignificance to sudden glory and considerable wealth. Ambitious for political as well as literary success he took a more or less active part in the various commotions of the second quarter of the century, so that he was able to say of himself with some truth and immense satisfaction, 'I have touched the left hand of princes, the right hand of artists and literary celebrities, and have come in contact with all phases of life.'

A great traveler, a great hunter, he had innumerable adventures by flood and field. Quick in emotion and quicker in speech, he made friends everywhere and some enemies. Peculiarly sensitive to the charms and caresses of women, he had no end of love-affairs, all more or less discreditable. Thoughtless, careless, full of wit, full of laughter, he traveled the primrose way, plucking kisses like spring blossoms, wrapping his cloak more tightly round him when he ran into winter storms of envy, jealousy, and mocking. What wealth he had he squandered, what glory, he frittered away. And as he was born in a whirlwind of French triumph, so he died, in 1870, in a wilder whirlwind of French ruin and despair.

The man's life was, indeed, a novel; and in writing his **'Memoirs'** he dressed it out as such, heightening, coloring, enriching the golden web of memory, as only he knew how to do; so that I am almost ready to call these same memoirs the best of his works, even with **'Les Trois Mousquetaires'** and **'La Tour de Nesle'** in fresh remembrance. Such variety and vivacity of anecdote, such vivid, shifting portraiture of characters, such quick reality of incident, such wit always. But the best of it, unquestionably, is not Talma, nor Dorval, nor Hugo, nor the Duke of Orleans, but just Alexandre Dumas. It is said that once, when a friend asked him how he had enjoyed a party, Dumas replied, 'I should have been horribly bored, if it hadn't been for myself.' Readers of the **'Memoirs'** will easily understand how other society might have seemed dull in comparison.

From all the tangled mass of anecdote and laughter let us try to gather one or two definite lines of portraiture for the better understanding of this singular personage, 'one of the forces of nature,' as Michelet called him in a phrase which Dumas loved to repeat.

And to begin with the beginning. Did the creator of Buridan and Chicot have a religion, did he trouble himself with abstract ideas? You smile; and certainly he did not trouble his readers very much with these things. Yet in his own opinion he was a thinker, and a rather deep one. Read, in the preface to '**Caligula**,' how the public received with awe 'this rushing torrent of thought, which appeared to it perhaps new and daring, but solemn and chaste; and then withdrew, with bowed head, like a man who has at last found the solution of a problem which has vexed him during many sleepless nights.'

In his turbulent youth the author of '**Antony**' was a disbeliever, as became a brother of Byron and Musset; 'there are moments when I would give thee up my soul, if I believed I had one.' But in later years he settled down to the soberer view which appears in the dedication of '**La Conscience**' to Hugo: 'in testimony of a friendship which has survived exile and will, I hope, survive death. I believe in the immortality of the soul.' And again and again he testified to the power of his early religious training, which 'left upon all my beliefs, upon all my opinions, so profound an impression that even today I cannot enter a church without taking the holy water, cannot pass a crucifix without making the sign of the cross.' Nor do these emotions spring from mere religiosity, but from an astonishingly, not to say crudely, definite form of belief: 'I know not what my merit has been, whether in this world or in the other worlds I may have inhabited before; but God has shown me especial favors and in all the critical situations in which I have found myself, he has come visibly to my assistance. Therefore, O God, I confess thy name openly and humbly before all skeptics and before all believers.' What revivalist of to-day could speak with more fervor? If only one did not suspect a bit of the irony that shows more clearly in the conversation with his old teacher, whose prayers Dumas had requested. 'My prayers?' said the abbé. 'You don't believe in them.'-'No, I don't always believe in them. That is very true; but don't worry: when I need them I will believe in them.' On the strength of that remark we might almost call Dumas the inventor of Pragmatism before Professor James.

And the irony is rooted in a truth of character. Dumas was a man of this world. He might dream of the other at odd moments, in vague curiosity; but by temperament he was a frank pagan, an eater, a laugher, a lover, a fighter, gorgeously in words, not wholly ineffectively in deeds, even after we have made the necessary discount from his own version of his exploits. He had inherited something of his father's magnificent physique and something of his father's courage. When he tells us that 'since I arrived at manhood, whenever danger has presented itself, by night or by day, I have always walked straight up to danger,' we believe him—with the discount aforesaid; and we believe him all the more, because like every brave man, he does not hesitate to confess fear. 'It was the first time I had heard the noise of grapeshot, and I say frankly that I will not believe any one who tells me that he heard that noise for the first time without perturbation.'

In truth, the religion, the courage, the fear—all, and everything else in the man, were a matter of impulse, of immediate emotion. He was quite aware of this himself. When he proposed his Vendée mission to Lafayette, the latter said to him, 'Have you reflected on what this means?'—'As much as I am capable of reflecting about anything: I am a man of instinct, not of reflection.' The extraordinary vanity of which he was justly accused, of which he accuses himself—'everybody knows the vain side of my character'—was only one phase of this natural impulsiveness. He spoke out what others think—and keep to themselves. Mr. Davidson has admirably noted that in Dumas's case vanity was perfectly compatible with humility. He had no absurdly exaggerated idea of his own powers. But he liked to talk about himself, to be conspicuous, to be the central figure on every stage. The African blood, of which he was not ashamed—'I am a mulatto,' he says repeatedly—told in him; the negro childlikeness. He was a child always, above all childlike in this matter of vanity. Readers of 'Tom Sawyer' will remember that that delightful youth, on hearing the beatific vision of Isaiah, which pictures such a varied menagerie dwelling in harmony, with a little child to lead them, had one absorbing wish: that he might be that child. Dumas was precisely like Tom Sawyer; witness this delightful prayer of his youth: 'Make me great and glorious, O Lord, that I may come nearer unto thee. And the more glorious thou makest me, the more humbly will I confess thy name, thy majesty, thy splendor.'

The same childlike temper, the fresh, animal instincts of a great boy, explain, if they do not excuse, the disorders of Dumas's life.

In this connection it is hardly necessary to do more than to point out his hopeless aberration from all Anglo-Saxon standards of propriety and decency. It would be easy to lash such aberration, but it is perhaps better to consider it in connection with the man's character as a whole, and to remember that his life was as far as possible from being a generally idle or dissipated one. He never smoked, cherishing, in fact, a grudge against tobacco, which he regarded as an enemy to true sociability. He was moderate in eating and drinking. Above all, he was an enormous worker. No man essentially vicious, no man who had not a large fund of temperance and self-control, could have produced a tithe of Dumas's legacy to posterity. But what is most interesting of all in this matter of morals is Dumas's entire satisfaction with himself. I doubt if any other human being would deliberately have ventured on a statement so remarkable as the following: 'When the hand of the Lord closes the two horizons of my life, letting fall the veil of his love between the nothingness that precedes and the nothingness that follows the life of man, he may examine the intermediate space with his most rigorous scrutiny, he will not find there one single evil thought or one action for which I feel that I should reproach myself.' Comment on this would only dim its splendor. Yet people say that the '**Memoirs**' of Dumas lack interest as human documents! He was an atrocious hypocrite, then, you think? Not the least in the world. Simply a child, always a child.

A child in money matters also. No one could accuse him of deliberate financial dishonesty; but to beg and borrow and never to pay was the normal condition of things. To promise right and left when cash was needed, then to find one's self entirely unable to fulfil one's promises—still childlike. Only, persons of that childlike temper, who have not genius, are apt to end badly. And then, after all, to write in cold blood that one has never had a single action to reproach one's self with! I trust the reader appreciates that passage as I do.

And if the child lacked a sense of money property, how should he be likely to have a sense of property in literature? Shakespeare, Schiller, dozens of others, had had ideas which were useful. Why not use them? A few persons had previously written on the history of France. Distinguished historical characters had left memoirs describing their own achievements. It would have been almost disrespectful to neglect the valuable material thus afforded. Let us quote the histories and borrow from the memoirs. As for mentioning any little indebtedness, life is not long enough for that. We make bold to think that what we invent is quite as good as what we take from others. So it is—far better. A careful comparison of '**Les Trois Mousquetaires**' with the original d'Artagnan '**Memoirs**' increases rather than diminishes one's admiration for the author of the novel.

But it will be said, even after borrowing his material, Dumas could not write this same novel without the assistance of a certain Maquet. Again the same childlike looseness in the sense of property. Could a genius be expected to write three hundred[1] volumes without helpers for the rough work? He must have hodmen to fetch bricks and mortar. And perhaps the builder, hurried and overdriven, may set the hodmen to lay a bit of wall here and there, may come to leave altogether too much to hodmen so that the work suffers for it. What matter? Had ever any Maquet or Gaillardet or Meurice, writing by himself, the Dumas touch? As Mr. Lang justly points out, no collaborator has been suggested for the '**Memoirs**' and I have already said that the '**Memoirs**' belong, in many respects, to Dumas's best, most characteristic work.

Then, a child is as ready to give as to take. So was Dumas. In money matters it goes without saying. He was always ready to give, to give to everybody everything he had, and even everything he had not and some one else had. 'Nature had already put in my heart,' he says of his childhood, 'that fountain of general kindliness through which flows away and will flow away,

everything I had, everything I have, and everything I ever shall have.' But it was not only money, it was time and thought, labor and many steps. This same fountain of general kindliness was always at the service even of strangers. For instance, Dumas himself tells us that, happening once to be in a sea-port town, he found a young couple just sailing for the islands and very desolate. He set himself to cheer them up, and his efforts were so well received that he could not find it in his heart to leave them, though pressing business called him away. He went on board ship with them, and only returned on the pilot boat, in the midst of a gale and at the peril of his life, so says the story. Even in the matter of literary collaboration, Mr. Davidson justly points out that Dumas gave as well as took, and that the list of his debtors is longer than that of his creditors.

And in the highest generosity, that of sympathy and appreciation for fellow workers, the absence of envy and meanness in rivalry, Dumas is nobly abundant. He tells us so himself, not having the habit of concealing his virtues: 'Having arrived at the summit which every man finds in the middle of life's journey, I ask nothing, I desire nothing, I envy nothing, I have many friendships and not one single hatred.' More reliable evidence lies in the general tone of enthusiasm and admiration with which he speaks of all his contemporaries. Musset avoided him, Balzac insulted him; yet he refers to both with hearty praise very different from the damning commendations of the envious Sainte-Beuve. Lamartine and Hugo he eulogizes with lavish freedom, not only in the often-quoted remark, 'Hugo is a thinker, Lamartine a dreamer, and I am a popularizer'—a remark more generous than discriminating—but in innumerable passages which leave no possible doubt of his humility and sincerity. 'Style was what I lacked above everything else. If you had asked me for ten years of my life, promising in exchange that one day I should attain the expression of Hugo's 'Marion Delorme,' I should not have hesitated, I should have given them instantly.'

These things make Dumas attractive, lovable even, as few French writers are lovable. With all his faults he has something of the personal charm of Scott. Only something, however; for Scott, no whit less generous, less kindly, had the sanity, the stability, the moral character, why avoid the word? which Dumas had not. And in comparing their works—a comparison which suggests itself almost inevitably; 'Scott, the grandfather of us all,' said Dumas himself—this difference of morals strikes us even more than the important differences of style and handling of character. It is the immortal merit of Scott that he wrote novels of love and adventure as manly, as virile, as heart can wish, yet absolutely pure.

Now, Dumas has the grave disadvantage of not knowing what morals—sexual morals—are. Listen to him:

'Of the six hundred volumes (1848) that I have written, there are not four which the hand of the most scrupulous mother need conceal from her daughter.' The reader who knows Dumas only in **'Les Trois Mousquetaires'** will wonder by what fortunate chance he has happened on two volumes out of those 'not four.' But he may reassure himself. There are others of the six hundred which, to use the modern French perversion, more effective untranslated, the daughter will not recommend to her mother. The truth is, Dumas's innocence is worse than, say, Maupassant's sophistication. To the author of **'La Reine Margot'** love, so called, is all, the excuse, the justification, for everything. Marriage—*ça n'existe pas;* Dumas knew all about it. He was married himself for a few months—at the king's urgent suggestion. Then he recommended the lady to the ambassador at Florence with a most polite note, and she disappeared from his too flowery career. Therefore, Dumas begins his love-stories where Scott's end, and the delicate refinement, the pure womanly freedom of Jeannie Deans and Diana Vernon, is missing in the Frenchman's young ladies, who all either wish to be in a nunnery or ought to be.

The comparison with Scott suggests another with a greater than Scott; and like Scott, Dumas did not object to being compared with Shakespeare, who, by the way, has never been more nobly praised in a brief sentence than in Dumas's saying that 'he was the greatest of all creators after God.' There are striking resemblances between the two writers. Shakespeare began in poverty, lived among theatrical people, made a fortune by the theater. Only, being a thrifty English *bourgeois,* he put the fortune into his own pocket instead of into others'. Shakespeare made a continuous show of English history and bade the world attend it. Shakespeare begged, borrowed, and stole from dead and living, so that his contemporaries spoke of his

   'Tiger's heart wrapped in a player's hide.'

Doubtless Maquet and Gaillardet would have been willing to apply the phrase to their celebrated collaborator. Thus far the comparison works well enough. But Shakespeare had a style which was beyond even that of **'Marion Delorme.'** And then, Shakespeare felt and thought as a man, not as a child; his brain and his heart carried the weight of the world.

What will be the future of Dumas? Will his work pass, as other novels of romantic adventure have passed? Three hundred years ago idle women—and men—read 'Amadis de Gaul' and the like, with passion. Says the waiting-woman in Massinger's 'Guardian':

> 'In all the books of *Amadis de Gaul*
> The *Palmerins* and that true Spanish story,
> *The Mirror of Knighthood,* which I have read
>   often,
> Read feelingly, nay, more, I do believe in't,
> My lady has no parallel.'

Where are *Amadis* and the *Palmerins* now? Two hundred years ago the same persons read with the same passion the novels of Scudéry and La Calprenède. 'At noon home,' says Mr. Pepys, 'where I find my wife troubled still at my checking her last night in the coach in her long stories out of 'Grand Cyrus,' which she would tell, though nothing to the purpose, nor in any good manner.' And hear Madame de Sévigné on 'Cléopatre': 'The style of La Calprenède is abominable in a thousand places: long sentences in the full-blown, romantic fashion, ill-chosen words—I am perfectly aware of it. Yet it holds me like glue. The beauty of the sentiments, the violent passions, the great scale on which everything takes place and the miraculous success of the hero's redoubtable sword—it carries me away, as if I were a young girl.' *Le succès miraculeux de leur redoutable épée;* if one tried a thousand times, could one express more precisely and concisely one's feelings about **'Les Trois Mousquetaires'**? Yet 'Grand Cyrus' is dead, and 'Cléopatre' utterly forgotten. No bright-eyed girl asks for them in any circulating library any more.

Shall d'Artagnan, 'dear d'Artagnan,' as Stevenson justly calls him—'I do not say that there is no character so well drawn in Shakespeare; I do say that there is none I love so wholly'—d'Artagnan, whose *redoutable épée* makes such delightful havoc among the nameless *canaille,* whose more redoubtable wit sets kings and queens and dukes and cardinals at odds and brings them to peace again—shall d'Artagnan, too, die and be forgotten? The thought is enough to make one close **'Le Vicomte de Bragelonne'** in the middle and fall a-dreaming on the flight of time and the changes of the world. And one says to one's self that one would like to live two or three centuries for many reasons, but not least, to read stories so absorbing that they will make one indifferent to the adventures of d'Artagnan.

Notes

[1] Perhaps it would be well to explain the different numerical estimates of Dumas's works. As now published in the Lévy collection they fill about three hundred volumes, but in their original form they ran to twelve hundred, more or less.

Jared Wenger (essay date 1940)

SOURCE: "Violence as a Technique in the Dramas and Dramatizations of Dumas *père*," in *The Romanic Review,* Vol. XXXI, No. 3, October, 1940, pp. 265-79.

[*In the following essay, Wenger analyzes the violent scenes in Dumas's dramatic works according to a tripartite model involving "Play," "Show," and "Struggle."*]

Alexandre Dumas the elder has an appeal for popular and scholarly reader alike. The present study of his dramas springs from this appeal, is undertaken because of his fame as a novelist, and is inspired by an interest in the problems of fiction. This is no paradox. Dumas is remembered today largely for his romances; yet he began his career with a drama, and, like Voltaire, he was fascinated by the stage throughout his life. Once more it is true: scratch a novelist and you find a playwright.[1] The dramatic works of a man like Dumas present an interesting aspect of the general problem of the relations of fiction and the theatre. Because of this, and because scenes of violence, with which we are particularly concerned here, often find their most effective form upon the stage; and finally because every study demands a certain simplification, it seems preferable to *approach* Dumas rather as dramatist than novelist.

A critic may perhaps object that Dumas' dramas are justly buried in oblivion, or at least are fittingly disposed of by Gustave Lanson: "Surtout Dumas a le sens de l'action. . . . Il a inventé, ou exploité plus qu'on n'avait fait avant lui un certain genre de pathétique: celui qui naît d'une angoisse physique, devant la souffrance physique."[2] One can only answer, first, that no talent is deservedly forgotten, and, second, that the problems of tempo, action, and the technique of violence[3] are important enough to justify the present study: that is—a qualitative review of the violent scenes in Dumas' sixty-six collected plays.[4]

Before launching into our analysis, let us adopt for novel and drama a convenient tripartite arrangement of their many and various elements. Let us attempt further a classification that will include, however roughly, both the psychological and logical phases of these two art forms—that will comprehend, in other words, the point of view of both reader and writer of fiction, both spectator and performer of drama. On this basis, we may say that the three fundamentals of the novel are: the attitude of the tale-teller and his listeners, the raw material of the narrative, and the author's critical depiction and judgment of life. Similarly, drama has its tripartite basis in the Play (or Illusion), the Show (or Spectacle), and the Struggle; and in this analysis we have preferred Anglo-Saxon terms, not necessarily because "the voice of the people uttereth only truth," but because the frequent occurrence of these terms in popular speech indicates how clearly even the uncritical realize the elements and properties of dramatic art.

Play is a word much misused in the vernacular, yet in its connotation of "Illusion" it represents doubtless the most fundamental element of drama—the child-like "let's pretend" of actor and watcher which corresponds to the "tell me a story" attitude in fiction. *Show* is (in the Elizabethan sense of the term) that which is shown and seen, the raw material of drama—so necessary an attribute that it is often vulgarly mistaken for the whole scope of dramatic art, ranging as it does from pure spectacle at one extreme to the careful depiction of emotion, character, and background. *Struggle* is the element of drama which has been, since the Greeks at

least, its most thorough means of interest and suspense, related to the savage joy in physical conflict and the civilized devotion to sport, and elevated by critics since Aristotle into the noblest fundamental of dramatic art. In other words, drama is based on the play instinct, is made evident by show, and makes its appeal largely through struggle. Let us use these three elements in evaluating the violent scenes of Alexandre Dumas *père*.

PLAY. The illusion of vitality is characteristic of the dramas of Dumas. The dramatist—an exemplar of bodily prowess and animal appetite, one of these nineteenth-century Rabelaisians, like Balzac and Gautier and Hugo—revelled in his own physical exuberance, and revealed this very personal trait in his dramas,[5] especially in two characters which are himself in very thin disguise: Porthos and D'Artagnan. Porthos, as we know, was addicted to feats of strength and food-consumption—traits which he shares with his creator. The Porthos ideal inspires such scenes as the following: the actor Kean blackening a prize-fighter's eye; a Scottish laird drubbing a whole troop of varlets; Catilina hurling a gigantic discus into the river Tiber; Gorenflot, a Renaissance monk, consuming great quantities of food.[6] Such scenes are never very deceptive: they are consistently on the level of "let's pretend." The spectator of course realizes the exaggeration of these incidents and characters, but rejoices in the pretence, the illusion, the "fun."

Where Porthos makes a muscular appeal to the play instinct, D'Artagnan appeals because of his quicker wit and nimbler grace. He is a subtler character, but none the less reminiscent of his creator. The D'Artagnan type is revealed by a mannerism or trick of speech. Thus Buridan strides vaingloriously into **La Tour de Nesle:** "J'ai fait vingt ans de guerre; j'ai fait vingt ans d'amour." A gambler cries: "Je jouerais la peste que je voudrais la gagner." Another, accused of trickery, laughs: "C'est peut-être vrai, mais je n'aime pas qu'on me le dise," and throws the dice in his adversary's face. The effect is not glaringly original: its relations with the tricks of the popular dramatist are obvious; yet these terse speeches are sufficiently characteristic and frequent to merit some title: they might be referred to as D'Artagnanesque language. Similar bravura passages occur in many plays; indeed, there are two D'Artagnanesque characters in **La Reine Margot,** and the Gascon makes a last triumphant bow as the jester Chicot of **La Dame de Monsoreau.**[7] D'Artagnan always delights by his impertinence: he, like Porthos, represents drama at the level of "play." Thus, D'Artagnan and Porthos, despite superficial differences, are brothers under the skin and children of Dumas: brawn and brains, they are united by their kinetic appeal.

The appeal to the play instinct is likewise evident when the author depicts—as he obviously enjoys doing—turbulent election scenes, whether in modern England or

Republican Rome. Similarly, we feel he takes a playful pleasure in confronting his characters with the apparatus of the torture chamber. And in his comedies he usually finds a physical or playful basis for mirth: the change of a youth's voice, or two Scotsmen who turn London street-corners until they become giddy. An element of very physical "pretence" is also discoverable in the description of the debilities of Catilina in the play of that name; and in **La Dame de Monsoreau** Dumas makes the reader and spectator actually feel the shivering of the cold-blooded "mignons": this is his way of emphasizing their effeminacy.[8] However, it must be added that episodes like these represent a transition from the "illusory" to the spectacular or picturesque phase of dramatic action.

SHOW. This second type of violence is achieved in Dumas' plays largely by devices of make-up, costume, stage-decoration, local color, and gesture. As for make-up, it would be tedious to list the examples of blood and bruises: a severed human head is brought forth from a cask (reminiscent of a similar trick in Shakespeare's *Richard III*); or Cassandra is shown with an axe in her skull.[9] As a device of stage-decoration, the simulation of dizzy height by means of precipices, gulfs, high windows, vertiginous ruins, is just as frequent: the most gory episode is that of the Vampire who is hurled to his death at the foot of a precipice.[10] This is stage-decoration with a kinetic appeal.

Such violent and spectacular effects as these come mostly from the bag of tricks of actor, stage-carpenter, and artificer of melodrama. "Show" of a higher level is the local color by which the Romantic School set great store. Dumas is an obedient Romantic in this respect; yet, in addition, he betrays—as one will note by listing the settings and periods of his plays—a remarkable search for the violent phases of period and locale. Thus, beginning with his *exotic* settings:

Classical: Caligula hurling his consul to a murderous mob; punishment by strangling, burial alive, or artery-severing; slaves thrown to man-eating lamprey-eels; turbulent crowds.

British: noisy elections; prize-fighting and fisticuffs in general; acrobatics; Scotch claymores.

German: consumptives (who spit blood); cruel doctors; sadistic sons; and characteristic (*Sturm und Drang*) misunderstandings between father and son, or uncle and nephew.

Italian: use of poignards; the Corsican vendetta.

Spanish and Oriental: truculence between brothers or between father and son; duelling; patricide, or mortal insult offered to a father.[11]

And, continuing with the French *period* settings:

Medieval: towers and dungeons; rough mobs; thieving gypsies (in the fashion of Hugo's *Notre Dame de Paris*); the madness of Charles VI (very much after Shakespeare's manner).

Renaissance: religious wars; blood feuds; the poisons of Catherine de Medicis and her astrologer; sword-play in profusion.

Louis XIII period: musketeers; duels; religious wars.

Louis XIV: elegance; Fronde; civil war and religious persecution.

Regency: musketeer characters still; the secret police of Cardinal Dubois.

Louis XV: elegant and cynical immorality; duelling.

Revolution and Empire: the howling mob as in Republican Rome or Democratic Britain; saber-to-chest attitude and challenge: "Au nom de la République!"[12]

This catalogue discloses that, except for such obviously "elegant" periods as that of Louis XIV, Dumas emphasizes the violent shades of exotic and historical color; further, that he seems to have studied each period and locale sufficiently well to find material for at least three plays apiece.

Dumas' "modern" plays have certainly a more restricted setting; yet they too have their violent color: the Byronic hero, the dying consumptive, rape, abduction, clandestine *accouchements,* and the duel.[13] Even so, the colorful exuberance of all these plays—exotic, historical, and modern—cannot conceal the fact that Dumas has achieved here little that is altogether original. He has merely emphasized in a rather athletic way the spectacular effects of the Romantic School in general and of melodrama in particular.

STRUGGLE. We pass by very slight gradations to a third element of drama, an element revealed largely in gesture, speech, and situation. Each of these has also a higher and lower degree of poignancy. Gesture, for example, presents on the lower level of this scale many muscular and, at the same time, spectacular effects, which are half struggle, half show. Let us list some of the most effective of these moments: an impetuous lover stills his ardor by tearing at his breast; an emprisoned Spaniard bites the iron bars of his cell; the actor Kean relieves his rage by breaking a chair; Milady de Winter grinds her teeth and "twists her body" in wrath; a German hero beats his brow moist with the sweat of mental anguish; a medieval nobleman assuages his grief by throwing himself to the floor and rolling about.[14]

But there is also a higher type of gesture. It is exemplified at its best when the Duchess of Guise puts her arm, already bruised by her husband's iron glove (she shows the marks), through the rings of a door bolt. Similarly: Antony tears off his bandages that he may have the "happiness" of bleeding to death in his mistress's home; a Bedouin seizes his treacherous lady-love by the hair; a murderous husband hurls his wife roughly to the floor; a lover marks wicked Queen Marguerite's face with a pin from her head-dress; an infernal spirit pricks with an iron pen the arm of a guilty nun; Milady is branded on the shoulder; and a villainous stepmother is mauled and killed by a vicious dog. In all these instances of violent gesture, a sadistic quality is uppermost; and, what is more, the cruelty is usually directed against women. It is true that mistreatment of women, common in the earlier plays, declines with the years, until Dumas allows only his most despicable characters (Milady and Orsola) to be so used.[15] Even so, feminine suffering, revealed in gesture, remains one of the most memorable violent effects of Dumas' plays.

Like gesture, dialogue has a higher and lower grade of violence. Of the latter type, Dumas' act-endings have been much admired. The curtain falls as the Duke of Guise orders: "Qu'on me cherche les mêmes hommes qui ont assassiné Dugast!" Christina of Sweden is similarly brutal and brief: "Qu'on l'achève!" Henry VIII warns Catherine Howard: "Préparez-vous à répondre aux juges qui ont condamné Anne Boleyn!" These curtain-lines would be incomplete without mention of Monte-Cristo's famous cry: "The world is mine!"—a cry more familiar in English than in the original French ("A moi le monde!"), as it was heard literally around the world in the performances of countless melodrama troupes. However, it is with Dumas an old formula, first used in *L'Alchimiste* (1839): "Ce trésor est à moi!"[16]

For all their effectiveness, these act-endings are merely happy *trouvailles* of the melodramatist's art—of which the ordinary style is shown at its worst in this ungrammatical sample from *Les Mohicans de Paris* (1860): "Je veille sur toi, et, fusses-tu dans les griffes de Satan, par le Dieu vivant, je t'en tirerai!" On a higher level are bits of pseudo-historical dialogue: the dreadful cry of Charles IX during the Massacre, "Il faut que je tue quelqu'un!" or Cromwell's characterization of a particularly violent Puritan, "Mordaunt, vous êtes un terrible serviteur!" Related to such speeches are various neat, D'Artagnanesque phrases ("Madame, où mettez-vous le poison dont vous vous servez d'habitude?—Cette femme a dû passer par ici, car voilà un cadavre").[17] Despite their "smartness," these speeches do not represent our author's highest effects in the realm of dialogue; rather his best-remembered phrases are those of women: "Vous me faites mal, Henri! Vous me faites horriblement mal!" Or: "Qu'elle est froide cette lettre! qu'elle est cruellement froide!"[18] Here again we catch the sadistic note, and the note of feminine suffering. The suffering of women indicates struggle of a more poignant type, and represents, as we shall see later, one

of Dumas' most original contributions to the violence of gesture and dialogue.

As with dialogue, so with situation—there is a higher and lower degree of violence. Dumas' subjects are typical of Romanticism: scenes of terror, hypnotism, convulsive love, gambling, duels, brutal cynicism. There is the prolonged and violent death of Tomson in *Richard Darlington,* a scene in which he clings to a moving carriage-wheel; but this depends partly upon stage-setting for its effect. Violence of a higher degree is probably best represented by *Le 24 février,* a one-act play, which, though it was performed at a theater called *Gaieté,* dealt with a gruesome infanticide, fratricide, and a hint of patricide; but this play was adapted from the German.[19] Thus, Dumas' stage-crimes cannot be called more abhorrent than those of his colleagues: unnatural murder, rape, incest and threat of incest, intense physical torture, furtive births and criminal infanticide are no different in his plays than in those of other Romantics.[20] These gruesome incidents are quite pronounced as late as 1850 (*Urbain Grandier*), although they gradually become rarer with the years.

Dumas' originality lies rather in another direction: his drama excels not so much in crime as in punishment, which is personified in the character of the *bourreau* or headsman, surely the most pervasive and long-lived of all his violent devices. This figure first stalks darkly into *Richard Darlington,* appears in fifteen plays, and makes a farewell appearance only in the last of the Dumas dramas, *Les Blancs et les bleus* (1870). Certainly it would be hard to find a more recurrent character;[21] yet it is precisely in the excessive use of the hangman that Dumas' violent situations reach their climax, over-reach it, and tend—as a natural result—to the absurd. The *bourreau* is make-believe, "play" again: the cycle is complete.

Thus, we may sum up finally our tripartite catalogue. In its Play elements, Dumas' action is rich, befitting his own rich physical nature. In its Show elements, his work presents little variety from the devices of Romanticism, though his local color is often quite athletic. Finally, in its Struggle elements, his action becomes at moments distinctly original.

The debts of these plays are many and obvious. There is something at once earnest, pathetic, and engaging in the humility of Dumas toward his School and toward his betters. He invariably acknowledges his borrowings in the most flattering manner possible—by clever imitation. Thus we easily catch overtones of all his principal sources.

For example: Antony is asked how many times he has loved: "Demandez à un cadavre combien de fois il a vécu." Yaqoub the Saracen says to his new master:

"Vous payez cher un cadavre." A headsman to his son: "Malheureux, tu ne sais pas que je suis né pour punir." Richard Darlington to his wife (with unintentional pun): "Jenny, vous êtes mon mauvais génie."[22] We are tempted to write after all such expressions: "Schiller." Without meaning thereby to cite chapter and verse as literal sources for these lines, one can at the same time feel in them to what extent the spirit of Schiller—that is, the youthful Schiller—had permeated the writers of Dumas' generation and been absorbed by them. Likewise we can be reasonably sure that cruel sons and brutal German doctors in Dumas' plays come also from Schiller (*Die Räuber* especially). Similarly, one catches a Byronic note (or, at any rate, the continental translation of Byron) in such a phrase as the following: "Vous avez une intention que je ne puis comprendre; vous marchez vers un but que je ne connais pas."[23] Also Byronic are various sadistic young men (Antony, Alfred d'Alvimar, the Duc de Richelieu), heroes of early Dumas plays. When Bertuccio exclaims: "Je ne suis pas fou: je suis Corse!" one is reminded of Victor Hugo.[24] Likewise, when we encounter laboratory scenes, medicine or pseudo-science, and the Mephistophelian character,[25] we may be sure that Goethe is the ultimate inspiration. Scenes of English democracy, Scottish honor, the tortured wife (Jenny Darlington) usually suggest Scott (particularly *Kenilworth* and *The Surgeon's Daughter*). Spanish scenes draw heavily from a variety of sources—Hugo (Castillian honor, angel-and-demon antithesis, Charles V's election), the Spanish drama and in particular the Duke of Rivas (monastery scenes and blood-feuds between hidalgos), even old Corneille (the mortal insult of a blow). The figures of the huntsman and the human bloodhound come from Fenimore Cooper. Kotzebue provides his figure of the "Stranger." Even the Wandering Jew is present.[26] There is, finally, a very extensive debt to the *Arabian Nights*, reminiscent of Dumas' youthful reading: Monte-Cristo's treasure-trove was surely inspired by Ali Baba's Sesame, and in a late and unimportant little play we find a horse named Bab-Ali.[27]

Thus we see, however briefly and incompletely, Dumas' debt not only to Romantic literature in general, but to a variety of sources. Still, making every allowance for conventionalities and for collaborators,[28] there is a residue which cannot be explained away: the Janus-faced portrait of the author (D'Artagnan and Porthos); a trick of speech which may be called D'Artagnanesque; a fondness for scenic effects of height—precipices and so forth; a tendency to make local color emphasize the athletic genius of a people or an age (though here he is in debt to Scott); neat curtain-lines; the abiding figure of the *bourreau;* and the suffering of women portrayed in gesture and speech. These elements—though they vary in their originality—are frequent enough, and fundamental enough, to be considered *Dumas' own.*

It is perhaps fitting at this point and in the light of these themes to review Dumas' dramatic career chronologically. Below are listed certain of the most characteristic moments of that career, the titles being plays to which reference has already been made in most cases, and the names in parenthesis being the heroes or villains in each case.

1829: ***Henri III et sa cour*** (Duc de Guise)

1830: ***Christine*** (Monaldeschi)

1831: ***Napoléon Bonaparte*** (character of the Spy)

1831: ***Antony***

1831: ***Richard Darlington*** (Tomson)

1832: ***La Tour de Nesle*** (Buridan)

1833: ***Angèle*** (Alfred d'Alvimar)

1839: ***Mlle de Belle-Isle*** (Duc de Richelieu)

1839: ***L'Alchimiste*** (Fasio)

1847: ***La Reine Margot*** (La Môle, Coconnas)

1847: ***Le Chevalier de Maison-Rouge***

1848: ***Monte-Cristo,*** Parts I and II

1849: ***Le Comte Hermann*** (Fritz Sturler)

1850: ***Urbain Grandier***

1856: ***La Tour Saint-Jacques*** (Raoul de la Tremblaye)

1858: ***Les Forestiers*** (Bernard Guillaume)

1860: ***La Dame de Monsoreau*** (Chicot, Bussy d'Amboise)

1864: ***Les Mohicans de Paris*** (Salvator)

As can be seen, Dumas' dramatic career covered five decades. The first (1820's) saw his school-boy efforts, his acquisition of dramatic technique and verse form in an adaptation of Schiller's *Fiesco,* and his début in ***Henri III.*** The second decade (1830's—seventeen plays of the collected work) introduced most of his favorite themes: Shakespearian murder scenes, a long line of Byronic heroes and Mephistophelian villains, the type of D'Artagnan, the consumptive hero, the Walter Scott types of intrigue, and the theme of buried treasure. The third decade (1840's—twenty plays) marked a relapse from the earlier Romantic frenzy into the production of well-made plays for the Théâtre-Français;[29] but in the second half of the period there was a rebirth of the old-time somber violence in the dramatizations which now for the first time made their appearance.[30] The fourth decade (1850's—eighteen plays) began with one of the least original works,[31] but in *La Tour Saint-Jacques* marked the climax of Dumas' great medieval reconstructions and dramatizations for his Théâtre Historique, and with *Les Forestiers* sounded momentarily a new and refreshingly realistic note. During the last decade (1860's), Dumas' dramatic talent wore itself out; for, with the exception of the two famous dramatizations noted above, the plays were all inferior.[32]

This chronology helps to make clear an essential antithesis: the difference between Dumas the *dramatist* and Dumas the *dramatizer*. The chief dramas, as we have seen, make their most sensational appearance in the thirties; the dramatizations, taken from his popular romances and arranged for the stage by himself or with collaborators, begin in the forties. Some of them, it is true, are mere pot-boilers: *Madame de Chamblay, Gabriel Lambert, Le Gentilhomme de la montagne, Le Chevalier d'Harmental* and *Le Chevalier de Maison-Rouge* (both almost incomprehensible in their dramatic guise), and *Urbain Grandier.* These are often hampered by too much plot, too many characters, too many settings.[33] However, a few other dramatizations rival the earlier dramas in violence: the Musketeer series, the Monte-Cristo tetralogy (though not all equally), *Les Mohicans de Paris,* and a last masterly effort, *La Dame de Monsoreau.* And these works, complicated and lengthy as they were (one of them ran to nine hours in performance), were almost uniformly successful. We need only recall the figures of Milady, Mordaunt, La Carconte, the Villefort family, Chicot, to understand their success. For these dramatizations provide the last and most characteristic aspect of Dumas' violence, an aspect which serves more than any other to link him to the later nineteenth century. They support and contribute to that atmosphere which we are forced, for want of a better term, to call "Clinical Suspense"—a sentiment which springs, in the case of novel-reader and drama-seer, from an excessive and disgusting cumulation of physical strain and tension.

For illustration: two examples of this type of suffering, certainly two which come readily to mind, are Milady de Winter and M. de Villefort. Here are people beset with all manner of cruel problems, cumulating in rapid succession. They are confronted with prison, banishment, branding, burning, disgrace, sudden death, madness—a succession of grim horrors—until at last our hatred of the criminal turns to vague sympathy, then surfeit becomes open disgust, which leads to a kind of impersonal aloofness. The characters themselves have ceased long since to have any personal function, have become mere puppets in the force of cumulative suffering. In other words, the hurricane has become important in itself.

Yet we must not believe that because the character has lost his identity in the process, he has lost every valid literary function. An example is the horrid death of La Carconte in the second Monte-Cristo play. It is not enough that this woman must plan and execute a violent murder and herself endure an even more violent death: she must also be suffering from fever at the time! The very chattering of her teeth adds to the aura of physical suffering which surrounds and finally obscures her.[34]

For the source of this technique we can go back to Dumas' first great play, *Henri III et sa cour.* Here indignity and suffering crowd upon the Duchess of Guise until we cease to think of *her,* and think only of her bruised and broken arm subjected to hurt and agony. It is safe to say that not the Duchess of Guise, but the Duchess of Guise's arm is the heroine of the tragedy.

Mme de Guise, however, pales a trifle when compared with her successors. The three greatest pathological characters in Dumas' plays—Villefort, La Carconte, Milady—made their first appearance in serial stories; and even on the stage they reflect the lengthy serial story in their long-drawn agonies. Here is, indeed, a case where novel has added to the power of drama. These dramatizations even make possible a comparison between Dumas and the Greeks. In plays like these we feel something of the same shameless and dreadful crowding of woe and grief (though seen in their most physical aspects) that we encounter in the myths set on the stage by the great Greek dramatists. There are distinctions, to be sure: where the Classic audience saw behind the suffering, Destiny; where the Neo-Classicists saw Character; Dumas saw only Suffering itself.[35] Now, though this element of "clinical" suffering existed more or less from the first in Dumas' plays, one must also remember that it occurred after 1840 most strikingly in the dramatizations. Therefore we may say that Dumas' most original effect of violence owes part of its originality to fictional technique; and furthermore that the dramatizations of Dumas scarcely deserve the neglect to which scholars have often consigned them.

The final antithesis which will best serve to evaluate Dumas' technique, and will likewise help to set him in his period, is a distinction between GESTURE and POSTURE. This difference can be stated in the following terms: gesture aims always at some significance, some symbolism; whereas posture aims merely toward an arrangement effectively picturesque to the *spectator.* Gesture is un-self-conscious, active, and individual; posture is aloof, and consciously conceives of itself in relation to a whole composition. A historical example: Cromwell's smearing with ink the faces of his fellow regicides is good gesture; the attitudinizing of the Girondins at the foot of the guillotine is mere posture.[36] Though posture is indispensable to the drama of Dumas—he would scarcely be a Romantic or an heir to the spirit of 1789 without it—still he manages, contrary to Hugo, to subordinate posture to gesture; and this he accomplishes chiefly through his "clinical" technique, which itself owes much to his dramatizations.

In other words, we are prepared to say that Romanticism, in all its forms and personalities, existed on several different levels, the self-conscious and the conscious, the unconscious and the subconscious. It was at its worst (or is least agreeably tolerated today) in its self-conscious and conscious manifestations; it is most significant, powerful, and inexorable in its unconscious and subconscious manifestations; and it was here that Alexandre Dumas *père* played his most effective part. For it was this latter aspect of Romanticism which contributed most to the following period. Dumas, and others of his kind, help to complete the unity of the nineteenth century by forming a connecting link with the Symbolists and *fin-de-siècle* decadents.[37] As dramatist and dramatizer, he represents not only the cross-fertilization of the arts in the Romantic period but also the break-down of the hierarchy of letters during the whole century. Debtors of Dumas' school of literature were such aristocrats or esoterics as Barbey d'Aurevilly, Villiers de l'Isle-Adam, Rimbaud. Even the greatest of the *raffinés*, Proust, had a taste for the vulgar—proved by such terms as his *meilhachalévisme*, or such phrases as "aimant *opéracomiquement* les femmes." Havelock Ellis goes so far as to say, in a penetrating passage, that Proust—like most of us—burlesques and scorns what he most loved.[38] This does not mean that a later generation of Frenchmen turned consciously to Dumas, though in the democratic, paradoxical nineteenth century extremes rubbed elbows; but the young men of 1870 and 1890 were open to the unconscious influences of Romanticism, even when they most scorned its topmost flights—which were, as a consequence, its most transitory. The type of violence purveyed by Dumas became an element, even a stock-in-trade, in the work of Baudelaire, Verlaine, Wilde. As Mario Praz has indicated,[39] there are some elements which even the humblest men of letters share with the greatest; and in the presentment of physical suffering and anguish the serial writers and melodramatists of the mid-nineteenth century paved the way for the Bohemian, anti-popular authors of the Decadence.

Though Dumas may be denied the title of first-rank artist, he is certainly a first-rate artisan—*kraftgenialisch,* as the Germans call their muscular authors; and, as a preparation for the spirit of the late nineteenth century, his Clinical Technique is certainly a force to be reckoned with.

Notes

[1] Cf. Arthur W. Pinero, *Robert Louis Stevenson as a Dramatist,* Papers on Playmaking, IV, of the Dramatic Museum of Columbia University, 1914; W. S. Hastings, *The Dramas of Honoré de Balzac,* Baltimore, 1917; Ramon Fernandez, "Le Message de Meredith," *Messages,* Paris, Gallimard, 1926; F. B. Van Amerongen, *The Actor in Dickens,* New York, Appleton, 1927; etc., etc.

[2] G. Lanson, *Histoire de la littérature française,* 21ᵉ éd., pp. 977-978.

[3] Cf. the present writer's "Speed as a Technique in the Novels of Balzac," *PMLA,* March 1940.

[4] Calmann-Lévy, 25 vols., 1889-1899.

[5] Invaluable and indispensable is the work of F. W. Reed, *A Bibliography of Alexander Dumas Père,* London, Neuhuys, 1933; much material is also to be found in H. Parigot, *Le Drame d'Alexandre Dumas,* Paris, Calmann-Lévy, 1899. Both are especially good for biographical elements in Dumas' plays. There is a pleasant description of the "playful" fantasy of Dumas in Léon Daudet, *La Tragique Existence de Victor Hugo,* Paris, Michel, 1937, pp. 168-172, etc.

[6] Porthos: *Kean,* III, 4; *Le Laird de Dumbiky,* I, 1; *Le Comte Hermann,* I, 1; *Catilina,* II, 7; *Les Mousquetaires,* VI, 4. Eating: *La Tour Saint-Jacques,* III, 3; *La Dame de Monsoreau,* v, 5.—References are by act and scene, the Roman numeral marking the tableau (if the play is so divided) or the act.

[7] D'Artagnan: *La Tour de Nesle,* I, 3; *Un Mariage sous Louis XV,* I, 8; *Halifax,* Pr. 5; *La Jeunesse des Mousquetaires,* II, 3; v, 3; *Les Mousquetaires,* x, 2; *La Reine Margot,* II, 9; *La Dame de Monsoreau,* x, 5.

[8] "Play" elements: *Richard Darlington,* II; *Catilina,* V; *La Reine Margot,* XI, 9; *La Guerre des femmes,* VI, 1; *Le Chevalier d'Harmental,* VI, 2. Comedy: *L'Invitation à la valse,* Scs. II, 12; *L'Envers d'une conspiration,* II, 6. Medical and physical: *Catilina,* III; *La Dame de Monsoreau,* II, 1.

[9] Blood: *Charles VII chez ses grands vassaux,* IV, 3; *La Tour de Nesle,* IX, 4; *Caligula,* Pr. 9; *Le Chevalier de Maison-Rouge,* X, 1; *Catilina,* I, 10; II, 8; VI, 9; *Les Blancs et les Bleus,* VI, 6; *Les Mohicans de Paris,* I, 19; *L'Orestie,* I, 12.

[10] Precipices, etc.: *Le Vampire,* VIII; *La Noce et l'Enterrement,* III (burial alive); *Henri III et sa cour,* V; *Christine,* Pr.; *Richard Darlington,* IV; VIII, 3; *Don Juan de Marana,* I, 5; VI, 3; *Le Roman d'Elvire,* II, 13, 17. Also: *La Tour de Nesle, Kean, Caligula, Paul Jones, Lorenzino, Les Demoiselles de Saint-Cyr, Le Laird de Dumbiky, La Reine Margot, Monte-Cristo* (1), *Villefort, La Jeunesse des mousquetaires, La Guerre des femmes, La Tour Saint-Jacques, La Dame de Monsoreau.*

[11] Exotic color. Classical: *Caligula; Catilina; L'Orestie;* British: *Richard Darlington; Kean; Le Laird de Dumbiky; Les Mousquetaires; L'Honneur est satisfait; L'Envers d'une conspiration;* German: character of Henri Muller, *Angèle; Le Comte Hermann; Le 24 février; La Conscience;* Italian: *Christine; Lorenzino; Monte-Cristo* (first and second Parts); *Teresa;* Spanish and Oriental: *Don*

Juan de Marana; Le Gentilhomme de la montagne; Charles VII chez ses grands vassaux; Le Vampire.

[12] Historical color. Medieval: *Charles VII chez ses grands vassaux; La Tour de Nesle; La Tour Saint-Jacques;* Renaissance: *Henri III et sa cour; La Reine Margot; La Dame de Monsoreau;* Louis XIII: *La Jeunesse des Mousquetaires; Les Mousquetaires; Urbain Grandier;* Louis XIV: *La Guerre des femmes; Les Demoiselles de Saint-Cyr; La Jeunesse de Louis XIV;* Regency: *Une Fille du régent; Le Chevalier d'Harmental;* Louis XV: *Paul Jones; Mlle de Belle-Isle; Un Mariage sous Louis XV; Louise Bernard; Le Verrou de la reine;* Revolution and Empire: *Napoléon Bonaparte; Le Chevalier de Maison-Rouge; La Barrière de Clichy; Les Blancs et les Bleus.*

[13] Modern: *Antony,* I, 2; III, 7; *Teresa; Angèle,* I, 8; III, 8; V, 4; *Le Comte de Morcerf,* I, 4; *Le Marbrier,* II, 15; *Les Mohicans de Paris; Gabriel Lambert; Madame de Chamblay.*

[14] Colorful gestures: *Henri III et sa cour,* V, 2: *Kean,* IV, 8; *La Jeunesse des mousquetaires,* IX, 3; *La Conscience,* II, 7, 10; *La Tour de Nesle,* III, 3; also *Don Juan de Marana, Le Comte Hermann, L'Envers d'une conspiration, Les Forestiers, Intrigue et Amour.*

[15] Sadistic gestures: *Henri III et sa cour,* III, 5; V, 2; *Antony,* I, 6; *Charles VII chez ses grands vassaux,* V, 5; *Richard Darlington,* IV, 3; *La Tour de Nesle,* II, 4, 5; *Don Juan de Marana,* VIII, 2; *Intrigue et Amour,* VI, 3; *Le Chevalier de Maison-Rouge,* VIII, 7; *La Jeunesse des mousquetaires,* Pr. 8; *Les Mohicans de Paris,* I, 19, 26.

[16] Act-endings: *Henry III et sa cour,* I, V; *Christine,* V; *Catherine Howard,* VI; *Les Mohicans de Paris,* VIII; *L'Alchimiste,* II; *Monte-Cristo* (2e Partie), I; also *Angèle,* IV; *Antony,* I.—Compare as a combination of act-ending and gesture the last two instances, particularly where Angèle throws herself headforemost to the floor—something of a feat for a woman just out of childbed.

[17] Pseudo-historical dialogue: *La Reine Margot,* III, 3; *Les Mousquetaires,* V, 8; also II, 6; X, 2. "Smart" dialogue: *Villefort,* IX, 5; *La Jeunesse des mousquetaires,* XII, 7; cf. a particularly effective scene in action, *Le Chevalier d'Harmental,* IX, 4.

[18] *Henri III et sa cour,* III, 5; *Antony,* II, I.—Note how the rhythm of the sentences reinforces the anguish. A study of the use of repetition for stage-effect would not be wasted: for example, it is little used in *Le Bourgeois Gentilhomme,* but grows in frequency throughout the eighteenth century: cf. *Turcaret, Le Philosophe sans le savoir.* The relations of eighteenth-century comedy with melodrama should be noted.—Note also the rhythm of D'Artagnanesque speech: "C'était une croix et pas autre chose; c'était au bras gauche et pas autre part" (*La Tour de Nesle,* VIII, 4).

[19] Violent situations: (fear) *Christine,* V, 1; (love) *Catherine Howard,* II, 3; IV, 3; (gambling) *Mlle de Belle-Isle;* (duels) *Angèle, Halifax, L'Envers d'une conspiration, La Dame de Monsoreau;* (hypnotism) *Urbain Grandier;* (death) *Richard Darlington,* VII, 2; (patricide) *Le 24 février,* esp. Scs. 3, 7.

[20] Abhorrent crimes: *Antony,* II, 7; *Teresa,* III, 12; *La Tour de Nesle; Angèle,* III; *Caligula,* II, 5; *Paul Jones,* V, 6; *Halifax,* III, 9, 10; *La Reine Margot,* X, XIII; *Catilina,* I, 7, 9; IV, 5; *Urbain Grandier,* II, 1; XI, 4; *Le Marbrier,* II, 15; III, 6; *L'Orestie,* I, 12; II, 11; *Le Gentilhomme de la montagne,* V, 6. Clandestine: *Richard Darlington,* Pr. 7; *La Tour de Nesle,* IV; *Angèle,* III, 8; *Paul Jones,* II, 3; *Monte-Cristo* (Ire Partie), IX; *Catilina,* II, 1.

[21] Headsman and hangman: *Richard Darlington, Catherine Howard, L'Alchimiste, Lorenzino, La Reine Margot, Villefort, La Jeunesse des mousquetaires, Les Mousquetaires, Catilina, Le Chevalier d'Harmental, La Guerre des femmes, Le Comte Hermann, Urbain Grandier, L'Envers d'une conspiration, Le Gentilhomme de la montagne, Les Blancs et les bleus.*—The device is all the more pathetic in its last manifestation because it is not at all germane to the plot: the headsman is obviously present only to please the author.—Cf. the *bourreau* character in Balzac's *Épisode sous la Terreur* and in Joseph de Maistre's *Soirées de Saint-Pétersbourg.*

[22] Schillerian tone: *Antony,* II, 4; *Charles VII chez ses grands vassaux,* II, 5; *Richard Darlington,* V, 7; cf. *Intrigue et Amour,* IV, 3.—Dumas' debts to Schiller are very thoroughly treated by Edmond Eggli, *Schiller et le romantisme français,* Paris, Gamber, 1927, II, 300-380, *passim.*

[23] Byronic tone: *Monte-Cristo* (2e Partie), IV, 3.

[24] Hugoesque tone: *Monte-Cristo* (Ire Partie), VIII, 9.

[25] Buridan, of *La Tour de Nesle,* should be noted as a character who starts out as D'Artagnan, and changes, in mid-career, to Mephistopheles. Here the character changes his function; but Schiller's play, *Don Karlos,* actually changes its hero after the third act. The Romantics easily swept aside questions of consistency which would have bothered the Neo-Classics.

[26] The various influences are treated clearly but not exhaustively by Parigot, *op. cit.* Reed, *op. cit.,* contains valuable information of Dumas' youthful adaptations: Schiller's *Fiesco* and Scott's *Ivanhoe* (now lost). *Kabale und Liebe* was also adapted; but Schiller is also present in *Le Comte Hermann, Christine, Le 24 février* (adapted from Werner), *La Conscience.* Goethe in *Henri III, La Tour de Nesle, Catherine Howard, Don Juan de Marana, Le Comte Hermann.* Byronic hero in *Napoléon Bonaparte* (the Spy), *Antony, Charles VII, Teresa, Angèle,*

Kean, Mlle de Belle-Isle (the Duc de Richelieu), *Paul Jones* (final appearance, and here with democratic overtones, "the rights of man"). Scott's influence dominant in *Richard Darlington, Le Laird de Dumbiky, L'Envers d'une conspiration.* Shakespeare adapted in *Hamlet* (considerably toned down!), and there was a youthful translation of *Romeo and Juliet,* from which he was able to use bits in *Kean* and *Les Mohicans de Paris* (balcony scene and Queen Mab speech). Hugo especially in *Lorenzino* and *Le Gentilhomme de la montagne.* Corneille in the latter play. Rivas and the Spanish tradition in *Don Juan de Marana* and *Le Gentilhomme de la montagne* (Dumas' least original play). Cooper in *Le Comte Hermann; Les Forestiers,* v, II; *Les Mohicans de Paris,* v, 7; judgment of him in *Le Marbrier,* II, 6. Kotzebue in *Louise Bernard.* Wandering Jew theme in the latter play and *Morcerf.*

[27] Arabian Nights: *La Noce et l'Enterrement* (burial alive, as of Sinbad the Sailor); *Villefort,* I, 3; *Les Mousquetaires,* XI, 2; *La Chasse au chastre,* I, 2; *La Tour Saint-Jacques,* IV, 10; *Le Roman d'Elvire,* III, 3; *Le Gentilhomme de la montagne,* II, 10; III, 3.

[28] There are divided opinions on the subject of Dumas' collaborations: G. Simon, *Histoire d'une collaboration,* Paris, Crès, 1919, tends to exaggerate them; Reed, *op. cit.,* takes the opposite stand, with more evidence.

[29] *Un Mariage sous Louis XV, Les Demoiselles de Saint-Cyr, Halifax, Louise Bernard, Mlle de Belle-Isle.*— The relationship of the *pièce bien faite* with the melodrama, and their antecedents, need further elucidation, though there is much of value in Parigot, *op. cit.,* pp. 159 ff. and ch. xi.

[30] *Le Comte Hermann* marks the summit of Goethian and Schillerian influence, and introduces the Cooper woodsman-character.

[31] *Urbain Grandier* even goes back to Scribe's operatic *Robert le diable* for its demoniacal settings.

[32] *L'Envers d'une conspiration* resembles the earlier well-made plays with British settings; but *Le Gentilhomme de la montagne* is a hodge-podge; *Gabriel Lambert* is confused; and *Les Blancs et les bleus* is only a military melodrama. *Madame de Chamblay* contains a last faint echo of *l'homme fatal* of 1830; and we find therein a rather pathetic attempt to introduce peasant themes and sociological discussion after the manner of Balzac and the new school of Realism (II, 9; IV, 5).—There is also an attempt in all these later pieces to tone down the old violence: in *Les Mohicans,* Madame Orsola is killed off stage.

[33] It would be interesting to note the number of changes of scene necessary to most of Dumas' dramatizations (not counting the spectacular plays); also the number of double, triple, and even quadruple sets he and his collaborators find indispensable to the action: *Le Chevalier d'Harmental* sins notably in this respect.—These, and other problems that confront the dramatizer, are very well discussed in the essays of a contemporary, Sidney Howard: cf. his prefaces to dramatizations of Sinclair Lewis's *Dodsworth,* New York, Harcourt, Brace, 1933, and Humphrey Cobb's *Paths of Glory,* New York, French 1935.

[34] Dumas' debts cannot hide his originality: obviously La Carconte is suggested by Lady Macbeth; but it is in the heaping up of physical suffering that Dumas is original.

[35] The comparison is complicated by the whole Greek concept of Fate and Destiny, is further confused by the fact that long acquaintance with the legends robs them of much of their brutality, and is finally obscured by the awe with which we tend to approach the Classics.

[36] Similarly, the ending of Hugo's *Quatre-Vingt-Treize* is posture; whereas his *Travailleurs de la mer* ends in a magnificent gesture.—Note also Egon Friedell's curious comparison of the French Revolutionary heroes to Schillerian characters, *A Cultural History of the Modern Age,* New York, Knopf, 1931-1932, II, 396-397.

[37] There is no need to discuss here his gift to later melodrama and historical drama. Sardou doubtless learned much from Dumas: for instance, the trick, apparently originated in the expatriate Scotch heroes of Scott, of injecting a Frenchman as commentator into his historical scenes (in *Patrie,* for example, or against the Byzantine background of *Théodora*). This trick Dumas had introduced in the Gaul Acquila, of *Caligula,* with the additional virtue of relating him to the plot.

[38] Havelock Ellis, *From Rousseau to Proust,* Boston and New York, Houghton, Mifflin, 1935, p. 374.

[39] Mario Praz, *The Romantic Agony,* London, Oxford, 1933, pp. 197 ff., 378 ff., finds for example in Eugène Sue's *Mystères de Paris* similar elements to those employed by Verlaine and Pierre Louÿs.—We might add that Dumas' *Caligula,* in its presentation of the abstract brutality of the Ancient World, is also a preparation for Louÿs' *Aphrodite.*

Richard Parker (essay date 1944)

SOURCE: "Some Additional Sources of Dumas's *Les trois mousquetaires,*" in *Modern Philology,* Vol. XLII, No. 1, August, 1944, pp. 34-40.

[In the following essay, Parker discusses a number of works that influenced Les trois mousquetaires, *most notably the memoirs of the Comte de Brienne.]*

From the time of the publication of *Les trois mousquetaires* in 1844, when the author in his preface tried to throw his readers off the trail by his reference to the nonexistent folio manuscript No. 4772 or 4773 (he was uncertain which!), there has been a merry chase in tracking down the sources of Dumas's masterpiece. With the feigned naïveté of the ingenious literary plunderer that he was, he slyly admits having used the *Mémoires de M. d'Artagnan*.[1] And, indeed, out of the first volume of this work, the only one of the three that he seems to have consulted, Dumas[2] derived the account of D'Artagnan's departure from Gascony on his famous nag; his encounter with Rochefort ("Rosnay" in the *Mémoires*); his arrival in Paris and meeting with Porthos, Athos, and Aramis; the story of the gold-embroidered belt with the false back; the affair with the innkeeper's wife, i.e., the beautiful Mme Bonacieux; the intrigue with the perfidious Milady (whose role is vastly developed by Dumas); the almost incredible tale of D'Artagnan's masquerading as the Comte de Wardes; the rivalry between the King's Musketeers and the Cardinal's Guards, etc. In short, most of the picturesque background and many of the characteristic incidents were taken by Dumas from this early example of the realistic novel with historical setting.[3] It must be observed, however, that Dumas's handling of the material lends a movement, a sharpness of character, a verisimilitude, a dramatic element—in fine, an interest—which the memoirs of the contemporary Courtilz fail to attain.[4]

Though whole books have been written on the origins of D'Artagnan,[5] most writers give as Dumas's sole source the *Mémoires* of Courtilz.[6] Woodbridge,[7] however, points to Dumas's use of the *Mémoires de M. L. C. D. R.* (Comte de Rochefort) for the dramatic incident of the discovery of the *fleur de lys* branded on Milady's shoulder. For the famous story of the diamond pendants[8] given by Anne of Austria to Buckingham, a number of commentators have categorically asserted that Dumas alone is responsible. Samaran, judged by many to have done the most reliable work on D'Artagnan, writes:

> Les lecteurs des *Trois Mousquetaires* . . . s'étonneront peut-être de ne pas trouver dans les pages qui vont suivre les renseignements qu'ils attendent sur le beau Buckingham, les amours d'Anne d'Autriche. . . . Il faut donc . . . les prévenir qu'Alexandre Dumas a un peu abusé de leur complaisance quand il leur a montré le jeune d'Artagnan se taillant sa part—et quelle part!—dans ces subtiles intrigues et ces mirifiques exploits.[9]

Lloyd Sanders, though he is acquainted with the La Rochefoucauld source (which I shall consider later), is provoked that we should know nothing "about the ball at which Anne of Austria confounded the Cardinal by appearing with the diamonds on her. That is

pure Dumas."[10] Likewise, Charles Sellier declares that the diamond-necklace incident "is due entirely to the imagination of the romancer."[11]

On the other hand, Lenotre[12] claims as the source for this story Roederer's comedy *Les Aiguillettes d'Anne d'Autriche*.[13] Roederer, basing his plot on seventeenth-century memoirs, has further complicated the story by having Buckingham and a valet in the service of the Duchess of Carlisle ("Mme de Winter" in Dumas) each cut off two pendants from the Queen's string of twelve. This duplication of the theft, I take it, was rendered necessary by the playwright's adherence to the unities of time and place; for by this device he saved the time needed for manufacturing the stolen pendants and also eliminated a trip to England. Moreover, one of the three acts of the play is devoted to the efforts of the Queen to induce the Cardinal, ridiculously garbed, to perform a dance before her. These modifications change the story so fundamentally that I am inclined to believe that, at the most, the play could have served only to call Dumas's attention to the dramatic possibilities of the tale.

The primary sources for the story of Buckingham's infatuation for Anne of Austria are, in reality, to be found in the memoirs of La Porte,[14] La Rochefoucauld,[15] Mme de Motteville,[16] and the Comte de Brienne.[17] The first three of these relate the opening incident of the intrigue, when the Duke of Buckingham, in the garden at Amiens, overstepping the bounds of convention, attempted to seize the Queen in his arms so ardently that she was forced to call her retinue. He later turned back from his homeward trip and appeared unexpectedly at Anne's very bedside, from which he had fairly to be driven.

A comparison of these three accounts will serve to show Dumas's indebtedness to each. The point of view of the memorialists is quite different. La Porte, the *valet de chambre* of the Queen and later of Louis XIV, apparently not in the close confidence of any of the principals, saw events almost as an outsider. Though he played a role as messenger between Mme de Chevreuse and Anne of Austria, he seems to have been unaware of what was going on, and he paid for his obtuseness with his dismissal by the jealous Louis XIII.[18] In Dumas's novel he is depicted as having much more astuteness, and he enjoys the complete confidence of the Queen. Moreover, he is closely woven into the story by being the godfather of Mme de Bonacieux. Mme de Motteville, who was really much more intimate with the Queen and had the story directly from her, though at a later date, is intent only upon preserving the reputation of her mistress and proving her guileless innocence. According to Mme de Motteville, it is to the evil influence and machinations of Mme de Chevreuse that the whole unfortunate incident is due. Dumas pays little attention to this apologia of Mme de Motteville and pictures the Queen as being swept along by the ardor of the gallant Englishman. La Rochefoucauld, who may very well have heard the story from the originator of the intrigue, Mme de Chevreuse, with whom he was long infatuated, tells the anecdote like a sophisticated and skeptical man of the world, making the Queen and Buckingham equally culpable.[19]

Dumas makes use of this tale rather by indirection when he has the Duke of Buckingham, pleading his love in a passionate secret interview with Anne, recall to her his daring declaration in the garden at Amiens.[20] The incident, as related by Dumas, follows La Porte and La Rochefoucauld in that it takes place at night, whereas Mme de Motteville does not mention the time. He follows Mme de Motteville and La Porte in laying the scene outdoors, while La Rochefoucauld has it take place in a private room of the Queen. The Duke's unexpected return to see the Queen is related by all three authors as taking place on the next day and in Amiens; but Dumas places the second meeting a week later and in Paris, thus bringing the historical personages in contact with his own characters. The result of this affair, according to Dumas, was the dismissal of Mme de Vernet and Putange, the Queen's squire, and the fall from favor of Mme de Chevreuse. La Rochefoucauld makes no mention of these repercussions, but Mme de Motteville includes La Porte himself among those dismissed. Since Dumas was reserving an important role for the Queen's confidential valet, he ignores this detail. La Rochefoucauld, however, is the only one to mention the ambitious and romanesque scheme of the Duchess of Chevreuse and the Comte de Hollande to duplicate their own love affair by bringing Anne of Austria and the Duke of Buckingham together in the same relation. Dumas has the Duke support his suit by the example of this lesser love. Although Dumas is indebted to all three of these memoirs, he follows much more closely the spirit of La Rochefoucauld's account.

An interesting borrowing of Dumas from Mme de Motteville is Buckingham's explanation of his purpose in seeking war in order to further his love suit. Here is her analysis of the Duke's motives:

> Cet homme [Buckingham] brouilla les deux couronnes pour revenir en France, par la nécessité d'un traité de paix, lorsque, selon ses intentions, il aurait fait éclater sa réputation par les victoires qu'il prétendoit remporter sur notre nation.[21]

Dumas has Buckingham say:

> Quel but pensez-vous qu'aient eu cette expédition de Ré et cette ligue avec les protestants de La Rochelle que je projette? Le plaisir de vous voir! . . . Cette guerre pourra amener une paix, cette paix nécessitera un négociateur, ce négociateur ce sera moi.[22]

What is particularly interesting here is that this nicely illustrates the chief principle of Dumas's philosophy of history, namely, that little causes bring about important events.

The second incident in this plot is the affair of the diamond pendants, first given by Louis XIII to his spouse and then presented by her to the fascinating Englishman. For private or official reasons, Mme de Motteville and La Porte did not see fit to record this part of the intrigue that so compromises the Queen. However, it is related with some gusto by La Rochefoucauld,[23] and with more verve and greater detail by the Comte de Brienne.[24] The tenor of the story is the same in Dumas and the two sources. Anne of Austria presents a string of twelve diamond pendants to the Duke of Buckingham as a token of her affection. An agent of the Cardinal succeeds in cutting off two of these pendants, whereupon Buckingham closes the ports of England to all departures of ships, has two identical stones cut, and sends the present back to the Queen of France in time to foil Richelieu's plot to dishonor her in the eyes of the King. For the sake of comparison and better comprehension I will enumerate the principal details of the intrigue as they are recorded in Dumas and the Comte de Brienne.

1. *Dumas:* Anne herself presents the pendants to Buckingham.

Brienne: Gift of pendants conveyed by Mme de Chevreuse.

2. *Dumas:* Mme Lannoy learns of the present.

Brienne: As in Dumas, but without lengthy questioning.

3. *Dumas:* Letter of Richelieu to Milady bidding her steal two pendants.

Brienne: Richelieu sends letter to Countess of Clarik.[25]

4. *Dumas:* Richelieu suggests that the King give a ball.

Brienne: As in Dumas.

5. *Dumas:* Milady writes to Richelieu that she has the diamonds.

Brienne: No answer to Cardinal's letter.

6. *Dumas:* Queen sends D'Artagnan to England for the jewels.

Brienne: The Duke divines the Queen's danger on discovering his loss.

7. *Dumas:* Buckingham discovers his loss on arrival of D'Artagnan.

Brienne: His valets inform Buckingham of theft on return from ball.

8. *Dumas:* Buckingham places an embargo on all ships leaving England.

Brienne: The same.

9. *Dumas:* This will be interpreted by the French as an act of war.

Brienne: It is so interpreted.

It will be seen that in most of the essential details there is agreement between Dumas and the Comte de Brienne. I have not added the account of La Rochefoucauld, for in no case is there agreement with him when the incident is not mentioned by the Comte de Brienne. Moreover, the only changes made by Dumas in Brienne's account are obviously to give a place for his own character D'Artagnan. I conclude, therefore, that the *Mémoires* of the Comte de Brienne served Dumas for the construction of this part of his plot and that he had no need of recourse to the scanty narrative of La Rochefoucauld.

The denouement of the whole intrigue occurs at the King's ball, when the Queen confounds the Cardinal by appearing dressed in all twelve pendants, which have arrived just in time through the heroic efforts of D'Artagnan and his comrades.[26] Though the idea of having this highly dramatic scene take place at a spectacular ball is due to the genius of Dumas, he is indebted exclusively to the *Mémoires* of Brienne for the description of the setting.[27] For this Dumas went to the *Eclaircissemens* of the same volume he had been using, where he found, ready at hand, the full account of a fete given at the Hôtel de Ville on February 24, 1626, for the King and Queen. In some places Dumas has followed this description to the letter.

Preparations for this event had been going on for two weeks (not one, as Dumas's time shrinkage requires him to state). The city authorities had erected stages for the seats of the ladies, procured hundreds of wax tapers, ordered a large quantity of food, and invited the bourgeois of Paris to attend. Dumas follows closely these details, adding a comment here and there and mentioning the hiring of musicians at double the ordinary wage. Then he falls back upon almost a word-for-word description out of the Comte de Brienne:

> *Brienne:* Et le mardi 24 dudit mois, jour de caresme prenant, sur les dix heures du matin, seroit venu audit Hostel-de-Ville le sieur Delacoste, enseigne des gardes-du-corps du Roy, suivi de deux exempts et de nombre d'archers du corps, qui ont demandé audit sieur Clément toutes les clefs des portes, chambres et bureaux dudit Hostel-de-Ville, qu'il leur a à l'instant baillées avec un billet attaché à chacune clef pour la reconnoître; et se sont, lesdits gardes, saisis de toutes lesdites portes et avenues dudit Hostel-de-Ville.[28]

> *Dumas:* A dix heures du matin, le sieur de La Coste, enseigne des gardes du roi, suivi de deux exempts

et de plusieurs archers du corps, vint demander au greffier de la Ville nommé Clément, toutes les clés des portes, des chambres et bureaux de l'hôtel. Ces clés lui furent remises à l'instant même; chacune d'elles portait un billet qui devait servir à la faire reconnaître, et à partir de ce moment le sieur de La Coste fut chargé de la garde de toutes les portes et de toutes les avenues.[29]

Various later arrivals are then enumerated by Dumas almost as they actually occurred, except that the novelist makes the "bon nombre d'archers" into the specific "cinquante" and omits references to the town officials and their dinner. Then he continues his reproduction of Brienne, this time interpolating the reference to M. des Essarts, who is the commanding officer of D'Artagnan:

> *Brienne:* Sur les trois heures de relevée sont venues deux compagnies des gardes dans la Grève, l'une françoise, l'autre suisse, le tambour sonnant.[30]

> *Dumas:* A trois heures, arrivèrent deux compagnies des gardes, l'une française, l'autre suisse. La compagnie des gardes-françaises était composée moitié des hommes de M. Duhallier, moitié des hommes de M. des Essarts.[31]

Dumas here neatly adds his own character to M. Duhallier, whose arrival had already been mentioned by Brienne.

Other unimportant guests are described by Brienne but are dismissed in a sentence by Dumas. Now the romancer begins to cut down on the time elapsed. Note also his explanatory details:

> *Brienne:* Sur les onze heures du soir y est venue madame la première présidente, qui a esté reçue par mesdits sieurs de la ville, et placée à la première place.

> Sur la [*sic*] minuit, l'on a dressé la collation des confitures pour le Roy, dans la petite salle du costé de l'église Saint-Jean, où a esté aussi dressé le buffet d'argent de la ville, gardé par quatre archers. . . . [32]

> *Dumas:* A neuf heures arriva madame la première présidente. Comme c'était, après la reine, la personne la plus considérable de la fête, elle fut reçue par Messieurs de la Ville et placée dans la loge en face de celle que devait occuper la reine.

> A dix heures on dressa la collation des confitures pour le roi, dans la petite salle du côté de l'église Saint-Jean, et cela en face du buffet d'argent de la ville, qui était gardé par quatre archers.[33]

Dumas passes over the description of the three tables full of fried fish. And the lateness of the hour seems to have startled the modern writer, for he forbears mentioning the fact that the musicians played all night for the crowd of bourgeois until the arrival of the royal party at four o'clock. In Dumas the King arrives at midnight but excuses himself, even as in the real account, for his tardiness. Dumas alters the excuse nicely to suit his needs:

> *Brienne:* Laquelle Majesté s'est excusée de ce qu'elle venoit si tard, que ce n'étoit pas sa faute, ains des ouvriers qui n'avoient pas achevé assez tost les préparatifs.[34]

> *Dumas:* Sa Majesté répondit en s'excusant d'être venue si tard, mais en rejetant la faute sur M. le cardinal, lequel l'avait retenu jusqu'à onze heures pour parler des affaires de l'Etat.[35]

The King and Queen and their suite immediately upon their arrival repair to their dressing-rooms to don their costumes for the ballet.[36] The names of all twelve participants in the ballet are listed by Dumas exactly as they are found in the Comte de Brienne. The King's role, which in the actual ballet was that of a "gentilhomme persan lettré" in Part II and a Spanish guitar-player in Part III, is changed to that of a hunter—a change be it noted, that is entirely in conformity with Louis's real character. From this point on, Dumas goes quickly into the denouement, narrating the opportune return of the jewels by D'Artagnan and the discomfiture of the Cardinal. This part of the plot is wholly Dumas's. It is perhaps surprising that Dumas did not use the riotous scene that followed, when the crowd, as in a President Jackson reception, overturned the tables in their eagerness to devour as much food as possible. The comedy element, however, would not have suited the high seriousness of the revenge motif.

In reproducing Brienne's account, Dumas has shortened the narrative considerably; made the details more specific; modernized the spelling and language; advanced the time to fit into his story; interpolated references to his own fictional characters; introduced an extensive account of the Queen; and brought in the Cardinal, who was actually not present. Though we see that Dumas lifted whole paragraphs from the *Mémoires* of Brienne, we must observe that the narrative—vivid, fast-moving, and dramatic—is wholly his; and the borrowed descriptions have become an integral part of the picture of the past that is, as has been frequently pointed out, more realistic than his very sources. And it is this extraordinary facility of Alexandre Dumas for turning dry-as-dust memoirs into living, thrilling tales that has caused ***The three musketeers*** to be read as avidly now as when it was first published one hundred years ago.

Notes

[1] Gatien de Courtilz de Sandras, *Mémoires de Mr. d'Artagnan, capitaine lieutenant de la première compagnie des mousquetaires du roi, contenant*

quantité de choses particulières et secrettes qui se sont passées sous le regne de Louis le Grand (3 vols.; Cologne: Pierre Marteau, 1700). Later editions appeared at Amsterdam in 1704 and 1715.

[2] I shall not enter into the complicated question of the real authorship of the works signed by Dumas—a question which three court cases and a prison sentence for Mirecourt (Jacquot), compiler of the notorious *Fabrique de romans: maison d'Alexandre Dumas et compagnie,* only partially settled. Although August Maquet, to whom Dumas himself sent a copy of *Les trois mousquetaires* with the dedication "Cui pars magna fuit," had an important role as historical investigator and preparer of the first drafts of various chapters, neither he nor any of the other employees of "Dumas and Company" ever published alone anything of merit. Consequently, it is perfectly just to speak, as I shall do, of the work as by Dumas. For able presentations of both sides of this question, cf. articles by Gustave Simon in *Revue de Paris,* May-June, 1919, pp. 98-112, and by G. Lenotre in *Revue des deux mondes,* XLIX (1919), 862-88.

[3] B. M. Woodbridge, *Gatien de Courtilz, sieur du Verger: étude sur un précurseur du roman réaliste en France* (Baltimore: Johns Hopkins Press, 1925). He gives an analysis of the *Mémoires,* including a brief comparison with *Les trois mousquetaires,* and classifies the work as a realistic novel rather than a bona fide memoir.

[4] Cf. H. Parigot, *Alexandre Dumas, père* (Paris: Hachette, 1902), p. 122. The author declares of Dumas: "Nul n'a mieux restitué la manière et le sentiment de ce 17ᵉ siècle."

[5] Eugène d'Auriac, *D'Artagnan, capitaine-lieutenant des mousquetaires* (Paris: Baudry, 1846); Jean de Jourgain, *Troisvilles, D'Artagnan et les trois mousquetaires: études biographiques et héraldiques* (Paris: Champion, 1910); Charles Samaran, *D'Artagnan, capitaine des mousquetaires du roi: histoire véridique d'un héros de roman* (Paris: Calmann-Lévy, 1912). Other less-informed writers have written more popular articles in the literary magazines. These latter and the recent general biographies in English by A. F. Davidson, P. H. Fitzgerald, H. S. Gorman, F. H. Gribble, G. Pearce, and H. A. Spurr offer nothing new in the way of sources of *Les trois mousquetaires.*

[6] E.g., J.-M. Quérard, *Les Supercheries littéraires dévoilées* (Paris: Paul Daffis, 1869-70), I, 387. He devotes considerable space to a rather malevolent *enquête* on Dumas's works, affirming that "il est aujour-d'hui bien prouvé que l'auteur des *Trois mousquetaires* en a puisé la pensée dans le premier volume de *Mémoires de d'Artagnan*"; see likewise I, 1106. So also C. Glinel (*Alexandre Dumas et son œuvre* [Rheims: F. Michaud, 1884], p. 386) declares: "L'idée de ce roman a été puisée dans les *Mémoires de M. d'Artagnan.*"

7 P. 49.

8 I.e., the *ferrets* or *aiguillettes de diamants* (cf. *Les trois mousquetaires,* Vol. I, chaps. viii-xxii *passim*).

9 Pp. 83-84.

10 "D'Artagnan and Milady," *Cornhill magazine,* XLIX, 224.

11 "The real d'Artagnan," *Harper's,* CV, 278-81.

12 *Revue des deux mondes,* XLIX, 869.

13 In Antoine-Marie Roederer, *Intrigues politiques et galantes de la cour de France sous Charles IX, Louis XIII, Louis XIV, le Régent et Louis XV, mises en comédies* (Paris: Charles Gosselin, 1832).

14 *Mémoires de P. de La Porte, premier valet de chambre de Louis XIV, contenant plusieurs particularités des règnes de Louis XIII et de Louis XIV* ("Collection des mémoires relatifs à l'histoire de France," ed. A. Petitot and Monmerqué, Ser. II, Vol. LIX [Paris: Foucault, 1827]), pp. 297-99.

15 *Œuvres de La Rochefoucauld,* nouvelle edition . . . par M. D. L. Gilbert et J. Gourdault (Paris: Hachette, 1874), I, 7-13.

16 *Mémoires de Madame de Motteville* ("Collection des mémoires relatifs à l'histoire de France," ed. Petitot [Paris: Foucault, 1824], Vol. XXXVI), pp. 342-49. This source, unmentioned by any commentator, should have been the most obvious, for Dumas cites Mme de Motteville's *Mémoires* directly to testify to her impecuniousness (*Les trois mousquetaires* [Paris: Calmann-Lévy, n.d.], I, 205).

17 *Mémoires inédits de Louis-Henri de Loménie, Comte de Brienne, secrétaire d'état sous Louis XIV* (Paris: Ponthieu, 1828), I, 331-45.

18 La Porte, p. 298.

19 Cardinal Richelieu, who could certainly have added some piquant details to this intrigue, dismisses the subject in a few noncommittal sentences describing the official acts of Buckingham's embassy (cf. *Mémoires du cardinal de Richelieu, publiés d'après les manuscrits originaux pour la Société de l'Histoire de France* [Paris; 1921], V, 98-99). Retz merely mentions, in passing, the Duke's love of the Queen and her favorable response (cf. *Mémoires du cardinal de Retz . . .* [Paris: Ledoux, 1820], II, 496).

20 Dumas, I, 152-54.

21 Mme de Motteville, I, 248.

22 I, 154.

23 I, 11-13.

24 I, 331-36.

25 Milady bears the name of the Countess of Clarik in Brienne and the Countess of Carlille in La Rochefoucauld. The lack of certainty in the name of this agent of the Cardinal gives an excellent opening for Dumas to take possession of the role for his infamous Countess de Winter (Milady).

26 Dumas, Vol. I, chap. xxii.

27 I, 336-45.

28 I, 339.

29 I, 257.

30 I, 339.

31 I, 257.

32 I, 340.

33 I, 257.

34 I, 341.

35 I, 258.

36 This ballet, which Dumas called the *Ballet de la Merlaison,* was really entitled *Grand bal de la douairière de Billebahaut,* and the descriptive verse to accompany the various *entrées* was published by Mathurin Hénault in 1626.

A. Craig Bell (essay date 1952)

SOURCE: "The Neglected Side of Dumas," in *The National and English Review,* July, 1952, pp. 32-60

[*In the following essay, Bell briefly examines more than a dozen of Dumas's lesser-known novels and other works.*]

On July 24 this year the Mayor of Villers-Cotterets is unveiling a new statue[1] to mark the 150th anniversary of the birth of the little town's most illustrious citizen—Alexandre Dumas. The ceremony will be attended by admirers from all over the world; for despite austere critics and academic historians of literature, Dumas continues to hold the attention of posterity.

Anniversaries of the births and deaths of great writers have in reality little significance; if their works survive at all they are timeless, and if they do not live in the affection and esteem of posterity no amount of eulogy, however erudite, will give them new life. Nevertheless they provide occasion and material for the pointing of a moral or the adorning of a tale, and for the making of comparisons which are not always odious. I will begin by stating that precisely a hundred years ago, when Dumas' celebrity was just past its peak, and until about the time of his death, the name of a contemporary was frequently linked with his merely on account of the equal popularity of a couple of works; and I leave it to the French Academy and such-like highly respectable literary institutions to enlighten us as to why there is unlikely ever to be a statue erected to Eugène Sue, and why the *Mystères de Paris* and *The Wandering Jew* have long ago dropped out of circulation while **Monte-Cristo** and ***Twenty Years After*** live on.

"Genius is always prolific." The dictum, attributed both to Haydn and to Beethoven, is true enough. One might even add to it and say: "Genius is always too prolific," recalling the colossal output of nineteenth-century French writers. (The complete works of Balzac, Hugo, Georges Sand and Dumas would form a reasonable library.) Like all such writers Dumas has had to pay the price of an almost incredible fertility, namely, that of having a mere handful of his works perpetuated, and the rest consigned (in many instances unjustly) to oblivion.

But it is useless for the critic to shake his head over this "squandering of genius," as it has been termed, and to call to mind the meticulous (dare one say over-meticulous?) Flaubert. No amount of revision and polish would have been any use to such as Balzac and Dumas, consumed by the dæmon of creation. They wrote their best when they wrote at their fastest. Balzac wrote *La Cousine Bette* in six weeks and Dumas the first four volumes (roughly a quarter) of **Monte-Cristo** in sixteen days. With them speed and inspiration were indivisible.

To try to assess in the brief space of one article the achievement of a man who wrote nearly sixty novels, without counting a host of plays, books of travel, memoirs, *causeries,* poetry, history and even cookery, is virtually impossible. One can only make a general survey. But even this may be useful if, during the course of it, we endeavour to throw light on dark corners and to break down traditional barriers of prejudice and caution.

To the average reader and critic Dumas is first, foremost and all the time, a writer of historical romances rather than a novelist. This view is imposed by blind tradition, merely because the historical romances from the outset achieved such popularity as to overshadow the rest of his works out of all proportion to merit or justice. And it is all but forgotten, at least in this country, that Dumas began his literary career as a dramatist and that for more than a decade (1830-43) he was known in France chiefly as a playwright. He was, in fact, one of the very few writers who have achieved success both as dramatist and novelist. It was Walter Scott, that predominant influence on French Romanticism, together with Froissart, Barente and Thierry, who turned him to history. The death of the "Wizard of the North" in 1832 spurred on his ambition to "do for France what Scott had done for Britain." He began, not by writing historical romance, but a serious historical study—*Gaule et France.* In the course of his career Dumas wrote something like a dozen works in this vein. The fact that they were not successful and have been utterly forgotten does not alter the fact that his attitude towards history was always one of respect, even reverence. He never regarded history as a mere picturesque background for bloody intrigues, or as an escape from contemporary realities, as so many third-rate writers of historical romance have since done. This is worth remembering and should be set against his oft-quoted dictum: "It is permissible to violate history provided you have a child by her." And it is worth while recording that **The Three Musketeers,** perhaps the most famous historical romance ever written, only came into being fortuitously. For it was while making researches for a history of the reign of Louis XIV that he chanced to come across the *Mémoires de d'Artagnan* of Gatien de Courtilz.

It was not, in fact, until 1838, when he was thirty-six, that Dumas produced his first historical romance. This was **Acté,** set in the reign of Nero. It was neither a failure nor a success. Read to-day, it comes apparent that Dumas had not yet found himself. It was not until three years later, with **Le Chevalier d'Harmental** (known in English as *The Conspirators*), that it became apparent that the successor to the author of *Quentin Durward* had been found. The first of Dumas' great historical romances, it still remains one of the best.

The next three—**Sylvandire, Ascanio** and **Cécile**—bear too obvious traces of Maquet's hand, and fall short. Then with **The Three Musketeers** and **Monte-Cristo** in 1844, the spate begins. I shall say nothing of the historical romances produced thereafter. Posterity has decreed that they shall be the Dumas who is for Everyman. That achievement received its full measure of reward in its own time and has never ceased to receive it. Instead, I should prefer to draw attention to an achievement which, while it is quite as great, has been unjustly overlooked by all except the few who are adventurous enough to stray off the well-beaten track and to explore for themselves: I mean the achievement of Dumas the novelist as distinct from Dumas the historical romancer.

That this is an achievement may be gathered from the fact that Dumas wrote over twenty novels of contemporary life, of which some seven or eight are to be counted among his best works—an assertion which will doubtless be hotly disputed, especially by those who have never read them. All the same, it is a fact little known, even to Dumas enthusiasts, that Dumas began his career as a writer of fiction in 1836 with two novels of contemporary society—*Pauline* and *Pascal Bruno.* Both must be accounted indifferent. Then, following hard on *Acté* (already mentioned) came *La Chasse au Chastre* and *Le Capitaine Pamphile,* and with them Dumas can be said to have found himself. They are indeed two bottles of the brightest Dumas vintage, sparkling with a humour and a fantasy which Dumas alone brought to French literature.

Between the appearance of *Le Chevalier d'Harmental* in 1842 and *The Three Musketeers* in 1844, no less than seven novels were written. Of these three are historical romances, and are negligible; the others, novels of modern society, are of far greater power and interest. They comprise: *Georges,* a tale of racial antagonism in the Isle de France; *Amaury,* a study of paternal love and jealousy; *Fernande,* the story of a courtesan; and *Gabriel Lambert,* the story of a galley slave Dumas purported to have met at Toulon. The two latter stand out from the others. In some ways, indeed, they are among the most remarkable of all Dumas' novels. Had they appeared among the vast *Comédie Humaine* of Balzac they would not have been out of place.

The fallen woman has always been a theme of attraction for French writers, from Prévost to modern times. Manon Lescaut, Marion de Lorme, Bernerette, Marguerite Gautier, Nana, are all famous courtesans of fiction. Fernande is Dumas' one and only contribution to the gallery. As was to be expected he takes the sentimental Romantic view, selecting the exceptional, educated girl, an officer's daughter who has been seduced by her guardian, and who only awaits some real deep love to shed all grossness. This Romantic attitude had been adopted by Hugo with *Marion de Lorme,* and was to achieve its apogee later by Dumas' son in *La Dame aux Camélias.* There is nothing here of the realistic brutality of Balzac's Valérie Marneffe (in *La Cousine Bette*) or Zola's Nana, or the icy, ruthless objectivity of Prévost's Manon. Nevertheless it would be wrong to condemn Dumas' novel on that count merely. The exceptional can be as convincing and true as the average; it all depends on how it is done. Within its limits *Fernande* is a first-rate novel, one of the outstanding examples of nineteenth-century Romantic fiction.

Having touched the magical spring of historical romance, Dumas wrote little in a different vein for the seven years following the appearance of *The Three Musketeers* in 1844. But with the Revolution of 1848 and the *coup d'état* of 1851, a change came over the political and literary scene. Romanticism became gradually outmoded, and the Romanticists themselves were exiled, self-exiled, dispersed or finished. Dumas himself, his greatest days over, his magnificent château "Monte-Cristo" stripped and sold to pay his debts, his theatre, the "Historique," bankrupt, fled to Brussels to work in peace. There, free from pestering creditors and would-be collaborators, his thoughts swung backwards to the place of his birth and the days of his youth, and laying aside his colossal autobiography, *Mes Mémoires* (one of his greatest works) he dashed off that trilogy of pastoral novels—*Conscience l'Innocent, Catherine Blum* and *Le Meneur de Loups*—three of the most delightful and perfect novels that came from his pen, redolent of country life and with ordinary country folk as the characters.

Returning to Paris in 1854, he brought out his own journal *Le Mousquetaire,* for which he wrote among other things those charming sketches of the animal life at his former palatial mansion of "Monte-Cristo," under the title of *Histoire de mes Bêtes,* and continued *Mes Mémoires.* He also wrote several historical romances, but none of them came up to the standard of those written in the greatest days.

Then in 1857 came the great Naturalistic novel of Flaubert—*Madame Bovary.* Dumas read it and disliked it, but it influenced him nevertheless. The growing posthumous influence of Balzac, although he had no sympathy with the latter's work, made itself felt too, as also the later work of Georges Sand. He saw clearly that the endless *feuilleton* was finished, the historical romance out of favour and Romanticism itself a spent force. So, just as the spirit of the age had urged him to write *Antony* and the Romantic dramas of the 1830's, and the historical romances of the 1840's, now he returned to the *genre* of his earlier *Fernande* and *Gabriel Lambert,* and produced between 1857 and 1860 seven novels of contemporary life, of which *Black, Le Chasseur de Sauvagine, Le Fils du Forçat* and *Le Père la Ruine* are outstanding.

These novels are unique among Dumas' output, and reveal an even greater transformation in technique and style than do the later novels of Dickens from his earlier ones. With their concentration on the smaller, domestic issues, their attention to detail, their careful building up of background and deliberate unfolding of the story, above all, in the *milieu* and the ordinary, unromantic nature of the characters, they are almost Naturalistic. *Le Père la Ruine,* indeed, is sheer tragedy, grim and stark in its relentless impetus.

It is one of the injustices of posterity, and the price of an excessive popularity, that these great novels have never received their due share of recognition. If he had not written historical romances and left only the novels to his name, Dumas would still have been one of the outstanding novelists of the nineteenth century. Only a public unconscious of real values, only critics who are content to remain ignorant of hidden worth, could allow publishers to go on printing and reprinting the same handful of romances, leaving these novels unread.

But fiction and drama were only two facets of Dumas' genius. Poetry, history, short story, biography, travel, journalism—he was to attempt them all. Space forbids discussion of each here. It is enough to say that, poetry and history excepted, he left something of enduring worth in each *genre*. He was not a short story writer like Mérimée, Daudet or Maupassant; but *Un Bal Masqué, Le Cocher de Cabriolet* and *Marianna* can hold their own in any representative anthology of the *conte. Mes Mémoires,* already mentioned, in spite of its inordinate length, inequalities and *longueurs,* is a remarkable work. And no survey of his achievement would be complete without reference to his books of travel, which contain some of his best writing and were among his most popular works in France. *En Suisse,* describing his travels in Switzerland in 1832, and *De Paris à Cadix,* recounting his trip to Spain in 1847, are particularly fine, as also is the unclassifiable *Les Garibaldiens*—translated by R. S. Garnett (Benn, 1929) as *On Board "The Emma"*—which, vividly narrating Dumas' own part in Garibaldi's Sicilian campaign, and published serially in *La Presse,* gives him the claim of having been the first accredited war correspondent, and remains the outstanding production from his pen in the last decade of his life.

Even so hurried and cursory a glance over Dumas' gargantuan output must, surely, give an impression of astounding vitality, fecundity and diversity. Not even Scott, or Dickens, created more hugely and intensely. Very superior critics, who see no further than Flaubert, Henry James, Proust and James Joyce, may sneer and belittle: but the greatest intellects such as Hugo, Lamartine, Heine, Georges Sand and Bernard Shaw have paid their tributes to Dumas. He was a "force of nature," as Michelet apostrophized him in wonderment and admiration, and has reserved for himself a deep and lasting place in the affection of posterity.

Notes

[1] The former bronze statue, by Carrier-Belleuse, erected on the centenary of Dumas birth, was removed and melted down for war purposes by the Nazis during their occupation of France.

Marcel Girard (essay date 1968)

SOURCE: Introduction to *The Forty-Five,* by Alexandre Dumas, J. M. Dent and Sons Ltd., 1968, pp. v-xiii.

[In the following essay, Girard outlines the historical setting of The Forty-Five.*]*

The Forty-five is a sequel to *Marguerite de Valois* and *Chicot the Jester,* especially to the latter, and it is dif-

ficult to follow the plot or to understand the characters without bearing in mind the earlier episodes. The three novels together form a huge chronicle of the reigns of Charles IX and Henri III, from 1572 to 1585, that is to say from the Massacre of St Bartholomew to the death of the Duc d'Anjou; a terrible epoch, well suited to inspire a novelist.

Why did Alexandre Dumas break off at that date? Surely the assassination of Henri III, last of the Valois, in 1589 would have made a much better ending to a period of history. Those four years of struggle between the king and the League, tragically terminated by the murder of both protagonists, offered material for no less exciting a tale. Moreover, some of the secondary intrigues covered by *The Forty-five* are not concluded, and we remain a little hungry. Internal evidence suggests that Dumas had not had time to finish; and in fact the Revolution of 1848 called him to other activities—politics and journalism—which led him ultimately to ruin and exile. We shall therefore never learn from his pen what became of Chicot, or whether the beautiful Duchesse de Montpensier yielded to the advances of young Ernauton de Carmainges. Never mind! The curious reader can always refer to the usual history books.

For history—need we say it once again?—is the raw material of the novel, and provides Dumas with his brilliant title: *The Forty-five.* Nothing so intrigues and excites a reader as those numbers which skilful authors use as titles for their works. Balzac had led the way with his *Story of the Thirteen.* Forty-five can equally pass as a cabbalistic number. The Duc d'Epernon himself explains to the king why he has chosen just forty-five noblemen to protect him against murder and conspiracy. Notice that grouping, at once magical and tactical:

'I will explain, Sire. The number three is primordial and divine; furthermore, it is convenient. For instance, when a cavalier has three horses, he is never reduced to going on foot. When the first is weary, the second is at hand; and the third replaces the second in case of wounds or disease. You will always have, then, three times fifteen gentlemen—fifteen in active employment, thirty resting. Each day's service will last twelve hours, and during those twelve hours you will always have five on the right hand, five on the left, two before and three behind. Let any one attack you with such a guard as that!'

Those forty-five Gascon nobles, who present themselves at the gates of Paris on the day of Salcède's execution in October 1585, are a strange collection. Badly dressed, empty purses, mouths full of astonishing Gascon oaths (*mordieu! parfandious! cap de Bious! Ventre saint-gris!*), mounted on old farm-horses, they are a fair embodiment of those age-old types of young provincials who 'go up' to the capital in search of fame, love and money. They are so many copies of the most famous of all Gascons, d'Artagnan, as we see him arriving in Paris at the beginning of *The Three Musketeers;* or, again, of La Mole and Coconnas who make their entry in the first pages of *Marguerite de Valois.* Indeed those sensational arrivals illustrate a theme of the nineteenth rather than of the sixteenth century. Here too Balzac, with his Rastignac, has shown the way. The pity is that Dumas has not given his Forty-five more prominence, more unity, more *esprit de corps.* A few members of the group we come to know fairly well: Loignac their captain, Sainte-Maline, Chalabre and one or two others—above all Ernauton de Carmainges, so handsome and so gentle. But the group *as a group* we hardly know at all; we seldom see it living and acting as a collective reality. The real interest of the Romantic Age centred upon individuals only: the hour of Unanimism had not yet struck! Despite the title, Dumas makes us share much more in the thoughts and feelings of Henri de Bouchage, for example, and above all of Chicot, who is here, as in the earlier volumes, his spokesman and, so to speak, his other self.

The historical situation is the outcome of a ten-year struggle for power between four political forces; a hypocritical contest, stealthy, delivering its blows with velvet-gloved hands, making more use of poison and calumny than of the sword. It is none the less a fight to death.

First we have the king, Henri III—'Henriquet', as the common people nicknamed him from contempt. Aged only thirty-four, but prematurely old, effeminate and tortuous, he has bequeathed to history a sorry reputation. Modern historians, however, tend to rehabilitate him, and even Dumas presents him here in a more favourable light than in the previous volumes. Despite caricature and shady jokes, he embodies the reason of State against faction, political intelligence in the service of national unity. Delicacy, fairness—yes, and a measure of courage—appear in his conduct, and I find him possessed of a certain charm, owing perhaps to his dark character of fallen angel condemned without a hearing Like Chicot, I would be tempted to follow and serve him—even while loading him with blame—because he represents in Paris the only valid force that can prevent the realm from disintegration.

The Guise party, forming what is called the League, is an assembly of all the 'factious' who, under pretext of serving the Catholic faith and opposing the Reformation, seek to win for themselves titles and lucrative employments. At the head of the League, the three princes of Lorraine and their sister (the Guise) mean to supplant the Valois on the throne of France. They rely on the most fanatical elements of the clergy, those 'leaguer-monks' such as Frère Borromée, who handle a sword more readily than a rosary and wear coats of mail under their habits. Behind them looms the sombre figure of His Most Catholic Majesty, Philip II, King of Spain, who would like to use, or at least to neutralize, France in order to wage his war against England. None of these conspirators will stop at anything. Mademoiselle de Montpensier, a madly romantic young woman who has fiendishly allowed Salcède to be executed on the Place de Grève, goes so far as to organize the king's removal by employing in turn the methods of seduction, of force, of lies, of a disordered and vain imagination. History will show the Leaguers successful for a moment in obtaining control of Paris—the famous *Journée des Barricades;* but Henri III will arrange for the assassination at Blois, by his Forty-five, of the Duc de Guise and the latter's brother the Cardinal de Lorraine. Thus he will recover his authority, but not for long: Jacques Clément, a young monk who appears for a moment here, will in turn avenge the League by killing the king with a knife-thrust to the belly. Finally, this long rivalry will profit Henri de Navarre: the Bourbon dynasty, not that of Guise, will succeed to the House of Valois.

The king has another and equally dangerous rival in the person of his own brother François, formerly Duc d'Alençon and now Duc d'Anjou. Just as Henri III succeeded his brother Charles IX, so the ties of blood do not prevent him from plotting under the tacitly condoning eyes of the Queen Dowager, their mother Catherine de Médicis. We recall Anjou's cowardly assassination of Bussy d'Amboise and his pursuit of Diane de Méridor with his sadistic attentions. Politically he is even more fatal and more odious. That little ill-famed man, the very embodiment of evil as Dumas presents him, had extravagant ambitions. First he solicited the hand of Elizabeth of England, despite their difference in age; but Elizabeth, who in 1579 had had the contract drawn up for political reasons, refused at the last minute to proceed, notwithstanding two journeys to London by her suitor. In default of England, he sought to become sovereign of the Low Countries, and had himself proclaimed Duke of Brabant and Count of Flanders with the apparent consent of William the Silent. The Flemings, however, were against him and he had to undertake a campaign against Antwerp which is a model of ignominy. After causing the death of thousands of French noblemen, he will fly like a coward but lose none of his big-headedness. History tells us that he actually died at Château-Thierry, as in the novel, but on 10th June 1584 according to l'Estoile's *Diary,* not in the following year. Likewise, the date of the disastrous siege of Antwerp is 17th January 1583, and history says nothing on this occasion about dikes being breached and consequent floods. Dumas, in order to heighten the effect of his story, has antedated an event that took place during the wars of Louis XIV. Finally, and above all, there is no evidence that the Duc d'Anjou was poisoned, let alone by Diane de Méridor! According to her biographers Diane was at that time living quietly at the Château de Montsoreau, near Saumur, where she had rejoined her husband after the death of her lover.

Here we have a good illustration of Dumas' attitude towards history. For him, as for most romantic authors, 'artistic truth' takes precedence of 'factual truth'. There is an accepted principle that the novel must not be a mere re-presentation of events: what must appear above all else is *the idea*. Now, factual detail is often the fruit of chance; it does not enable us to sort out the real play of cause and effect, the mutual operation of characters and of circumstances. History has been transmitted to us in a state of disorder. The role of fiction, therefore, is to re-establish the true order of things, the true order of the mind. It is possible, for example, that the Duc d'Anjou died, in l'Estoile's words, 'of a serious haemorrhage, accompanied by a slow fever which had gradually weakened him and reduced him to skin and bone'. But of what importance is that? So far as Dumas is concerned, what matters is that Anjou, at the age of thirty-four, paid the penalty of unbelievable crimes of which he had been guilty no less in his private life than in his political activity. Whatever may have been the instruments employed by fate—sickness or poison— Anjou's death accords with the logic of his character and with that of his period. The hand of Diane appears as the hand of vengeance, of an almost abstract justice, which transcends the accidental circumstances of the event.

Lastly, there is the fourth, though somewhat belated, political force: the party of Henri de Navarre, king of that famous little province on the Pyrenean frontier, leader of the Protestants, the future Henri IV. It is undoubtedly with him that Dumas' sympathy lies. That intelligent Gascon, brave and libertine, the 'Vert-Galant', the 'good king' of popular song, was a political brain of exceptional quality. He was the creator of France's prosperity at the beginning of the seventeenth century, the champion of tolerance and apostle of national unity. Like Chicot, Dumas cannot but yield to the charm of that attractive and brilliant personality.

However, the hour of Henri IV has not yet come. The future hero has taken refuge in his province, which he enlarges slightly by seizing the city of Cahors; he uses rather like a hostage his own wife, sister of Henri III, the celebrated Queen Margot, whom he deceives with La Fosseuse, but who cuckolds him in return with Turenne, neither of which facts will prevent them from making common cause; in a word, he moves his pawns so that they may be in a position of strength at the right moment. In ***The Forty-five,*** the reader does not witness the last phase (1588-94) of that climb to power. If he wishes to know more about those events and their attendant circumstances, he will be able to consult, among other works, Michelet's *History of France* ('The Sixteenth Century', Book II, Part 3, chapters 10-15), in which the romantic historian takes over from the historical novelist, although the views of the world taken by those two writers present fundamental differences.

The world of Alexandre Dumas, as we see it at the end of this long chronicle of the reign of Henri III, has all the characteristics of a poetical world: it is created 'from the head', conjured up 'from within'. There is nothing intellectual about the mental processes of our author; they are diametrically opposed to the objective methods of a scientific mind, such as the true historian must possess. If we have several times caught him in the act of flaunting history, the fact is that his inner vision is so strong that his pen cannot submit to reality. No, reality must bow to his vision.

How did Dumas see the world? He saw it as a theatre. In the episodes provided for him by ancient sources, he does not look, in the manner of an historian, for social, religious, economic or strictly political causes: as on the stage, he sees only the confrontation of personalities. The historical actors play their parts, good or evil, with their personal ideas and passions.

This kind of 'psychomachy' is wholly within the romantic tradition, which conceives society as a juxtaposition of individuals. Men and women speak, move, lay plans, succeed or fail, as in the theatre; history is made by and through them. A naïve and popular concept, but one that will always please the majority of readers more than will today's habit of reconstructing history in the light of ideologies.

The psychological level of this theatre is not very high. André Gide went so far as to describe its performers as mere 'puppets'. That is rather unfair: Dumas' puppets, after all, are endowed with minds and hearts, though it must be admitted that their motives are over-simplified. The truth is that everything happens as if each scene were based upon a picture; and indeed at that period *genre* painting was highly favoured in all countries. Dumas' text might serve as a commentary upon the great compositions of, say, Paul Delaroche, his contemporary, whose 'Princes in the Tower' or 'Assassination of the Duc de Guise' are contemplated with a shudder by visitors to the Louvre or the Musée de Chantilly. When you read Dumas' account of the death of the Duc d'Anjou, you receive the impression that he is describing the attitudes of the persons concerned as they might have appeared on canvas. 'Henri was sitting beside the head of the couch whereon his brother was extended. Catherine was standing in the recess in which the bed was placed, holding her dying son's hand in hers. The Bishop of Château-Thierry and the Cardinal de Joyeuse repeated the prayers for the dying, which were joined in by all who were present, kneeling, and with clasped hands.' In this way the story unfolds like a succession of 'historical scenes', which, as I have elsewhere remarked, correspond to the several numbers of a serial novel.

Such a design from another pen would give a completely static effect. Fortunately, Dumas' nature is so strong that it animates all he touches. His concept is saved from 'woodenness' by what we may call his prodigious instinct for life. That vigour which, in the last resort, is the master quality of Alexandre Dumas, grips the reader, convinces him and compels his willing and confident assent. Consider, for example, that unlikely pursuit across Flanders and northern France, where we see Diane de Méridor and her faithful Rémy, amid fearful perils, trying to overtake the Duc d'Anjou and wreak revenge. How can the modern reader, who is generally sceptical, consent to walk in the footsteps of those two determined shadows? Because Dumas leads him firmly by the hand, obliging him to follow; and such is the constraint that never for a moment can he decide to close the book and leave his heroes, who through war and flood have become his friends, until he reaches that forest, where of course Rémy will cut Aurilly's throat, and until he comes to the palace of Château-Thierry, where of course Diane will poison the infamous duke. The movement of the story is like that of destiny—it sweeps us along: we cannot escape.

That inevitability, however, does not weigh heavy and oppress the reader as it does in most novels of the romantic era. All is saved by the liveliness of the story. Oddly enough, Dumas is a gay author—which certainly does not mean a comic author. He is a happy author and makes us happy because he has a sense of humour. This humour enables us to accept situations that would otherwise be intolerable. It is he, for instance, who lightens the dreadful scene in the 'Corne d'Abondance', that cheap lodging-house from which we know that one of the two adversaries, Chicot or Borromée, will not come out alive. True, we are present at a scene of veritable butchery; but through the narrative, among the wine bottles and the repartee, there moves a breeze of refreshing gaiety which lessens its horror. That humour is like the air that sustains life. Dumas does not take himself too seriously, and there perhaps lies the reason for his remarkable success.

There is only one human activity about which he never jests: love. Love indeed plays an important part in *The Forty-five,* no less important than that of politics and war. It is in fact the driving force, for it will determine the inner motives of the actors. Even those who have no share in it, either because they do not love or because they are not loved, will use the love of others to achieve their ends, to set their snares, to organize conspiracy and to forge the links of alliance. The crazy love of Henri de Bouchage for Diane de Méridor; the unclean love of the Duc d'Anjou for the same Diane; the loving friendship of Rémy le Haudoin for Diane again, which we guess to be very strong; the desperate love of Ernauton de Carmainges for the beautiful but Machiavellian Duchesse de Montpensier; the ironic and frivolous love of Henri de Bourbon for La Fosseuse; the scandalous loves of Marguerite de Navarre; and lastly the mournful love, reaching beyond the grave, of Diane

for her murdered lover—all those happy and unhappy passions sustain the interest of the historical narrative, breathe into it their warmth and emotion, endow it with more humanity.

Humanity: here at last is the key-word that alone can explain the enduring popularity of Dumas' novels after more than a hundred years. The word must be understood not according to its psychological but according to its moral content. His concept of man proceeds not from observation but from a sort of wager: men are good or they are evil—sheer Manichaeism! What are we to think of it? One might embark on a long and fruitless discussion of human nature. Is it simple or complex; given or acquired; responsible or irresponsible? Dumas believes that there are men naturally good and others purposely evil. Chicot, Diane, Rémy, du Bouchage, Henri de Bourbon are among the good. The Duc d'Anjou, Aurilly, the Duc de Mayenne, the Duchesse de Montpensier, Borromée are among the evil. The subject of *The Forty-five,* as of the earlier volumes, is the struggle between good and evil. The heroes are redressers of wrong: they pursue a cause or a sacred vengeance. The moral point of view may irritate twentieth-century readers; it is in fact the weakness of the novels of Dumas, as of those by Victor Hugo and other romantic authors. From the artistic and aesthetic standpoint their method is too heavy-handed. But the public at large does not feed upon art and aesthetics alone; it needs consolation, reassurance. In the eternal 'combat of day and night' the ordinary man takes sides and gets excited.

'The false and the marvellous are more human than the true man,' wrote Paul Valéry. Alexandre Dumas verifies that saying, for there is no writer at once more false and more human. The false, however, is relative and open to dispute. The human is absolute and imposes itself as a sensible reality of the heart. That was understood by his great contemporaries, his peers, all of whom were his friends. 'You are a force of nature,' Michelet wrote to him. 'He is an Enceladus, a Prometheus, a Titan,' declared Lamartine. And his work was hymned in verse by Victor Hugo as 'glittering, numberless, dazzling, happy, in which daylight shines'. Times have changed, but the huge romantic massif of Dumas has scarcely been affected by erosion. Despite the new means of escapism and the universal triumph of the television screen, his books are read everywhere. None will refuse assent to this judgment of Apollinaire, which sums up all the esteem and all the friendship which this great man deserves: *The wonderful Dumas.*

Barnett Shaw (essay date 1969)

SOURCE: Introduction to *Alexandre Dumas, Père: The Great Lover and Other Plays*, adapted by Barnett Shaw, Frederick Ungar Publishing Co., 1969, pp. 1-4.

[In the following essay, Shaw offers a condensed overview of Dumas's life and works.]

Alexandre Dumas was the son of a mulatto general, Thomas-Alexandre Dumas, who served under Napoleon. His grandfather was the Marquis Davy de la Pailleterie, who had married a native named Marie-Cessette Dumas while running a plantation on the island of Haiti. Both Dumas and his father ignored the title to which they had a right, preferring to use the name Dumas.

Dumas was born in Villers-Cotterets, forty miles from Paris, on July 24, 1802. After finishing his schooling he went to Paris and obtained a position as clerk for the Duke of Orleans. It was not long before he had a mistress, and in 1824, a son. The son, Alexandre Dumas fils, was destined to become a writer like his father and even for a time to surpass him in popularity as a dramatist. For Dumas père, still in his twenties, a farce written with a friend had a modest success and started young Alexandre on a serious career as a dramatist.

Dumas swept through nineteenth-century Paris like a whirlwind. He was the uncrowned "King of Paris" who—according to a contemporary—could have filled every theatre if all other dramatists had stopped writing. Victorien Sardou called Dumas the best man of the theatre of his century. His influence in the field of drama has been enormous, although often overlooked by writers of theatre history. His *Henri III et sa cour* (1829) was the first great triumph of the Romantic movement. His *Antony* (1831) was the first romantic drama in modern dress, attacking the accepted idea of marriage and proclaiming the rights of love. The play created a sensation in Paris, and it became the inspiration for hundreds of "triangle" plays that persist to this day.

The intense passion and power of *Antony* were again put to work in *Kean* (1836), a play whose hero was ostensibly the English actor Edmund Kean, but in reality Dumas himself. The play has never left the stage in France, and a movie version was made many years ago.

Dumas created the historical drama, the play of "cape and sword," first in the most popular melodrama of all time, *La tour de Nesle* (1832), and later in the dramatizations of his *Les trois mousquetaires, Le Chevalier de Maison Rouge,* and other novels. Dumas, who became as popular a novelist as he was dramatist, put most of his novels on the stage, and even built his own *Théâtre Historique* where they were presented. It was also in this theatre that Dumas first produced his verse translation of *Hamlet,* to be the standard version of that Shakespeare play in France until 1916, racking up 207 performances at the Comédie-Française. One of the big events in Paris during February, 1848, was the performance of *Monte Cristo,* a play so long that it had to be produced on two successive eve-

nings. To critics who said the play was too long, Dumas replied: "There are neither long nor short plays, only amusing plays and dull ones."

Dumas also tried his hand at comedy, and was very successful. Three of his comedies, *Les demoiselles de Saint-Cyr, Un mariage sous Louis XV,* and *Mademoiselle de Belle-Isle,* played in repertory at the Comédie-Francaise for many years.

The playwright's travelogues were as widely popular as his novels and plays. His accounts of his trips to Switzerland, Russia, and Algeria are like no other travel books ever written. English editions of these travel books appeared in the United States in the 1960s.

Dumas monopolized Parisian society as he did the theatre and the novel. When he entered a room, women sighed and men grew envious. When he spoke, the most eloquent held their breath to listen. Not the most modest of men, he was quite aware of his magnetism and charm. Once, when asked if he had enjoyed a certain gathering, he replied: "I should have been quite bored if I hadn't been there."

With unbounded enthusiasm Dumas could draw an astounding number of facts from the depth of a phenomenal memory. He usually wrote fourteen hours a day, in a perfect hand, seldom making a correction, and without groping for a word. Very often he had a novel or play complete in his head before he sat down to write. He wrote the first volume of *Le Chevalier de Maison Rouge* in sixty-six hours on a bet.

But in 1845 Dumas met with ill luck; he was attacked as a plagiarist by a disgruntled writer named Mirecourt. The accuser was sentenced to two weeks in prison for libel, but much damage was done to Dumas's reputation. For many years in France, Dumas was belittled as an improvisor. Writers were jealous of this giant of a man who dominated every field of literature. Today, the true genius of Alexandre Dumas is recognized more than ever; new editions of his works appear constantly in France, and as translations in other lands.

Fiorentino, with whom Dumas collaborated on some works dealing with Italy, said: "Dumas is not a dramatic writer, he is the drama incarnate. And how many believed themselves to be his collaborators who were only his confidants! In his books, but above all in his plays, his collaborators had only the slightest share. He remodeled the scenarios, changed the characters, added or cut down scenes, and wrote all in his own hand."

George Bernard Shaw, in his *Dramatic Criticism,* said: "Dumas père was what Gounod called Mozart, a summit of art. Nobody ever could, or did, or will improve on Mozart's operas, and nobody ever could, or did, or will improve on Dumas's romances and plays."

It was the revolution of 1848 that hastened the decline of Dumas. Shortly after the *coup d'état* of 1851 with which Louis-Napoleon declared himself emperor, Dumas fled to voluntary exile in Brussels. His theatre went into bankruptcy, and creditors seized his cherished chateau of Monte Cristo at Port-Marly, a mansion into which he had poured vast sums.

A few years later he returned to Paris in an attempt to recoup his fortune. He tried his hand at the editorship of several newspapers, and he continued to write at a furious pace. He had plays on the boards every year until 1869, the year before he died. But the quality of his work declined under the intense pressure. Plays on the level of *Antony, Kean,* and *Mademoiselle de Belle-Isle* did not come again from his pen. The two exceptions were a one-act gem called *Romulus,* which he wrote for the Comédie-Française, and a full-length historical comedy-drama called *La jeunesse de Louis XIV.* This play, which in many ways surpasses *Les trois mousquetaires,* was accepted by the Comédie-Française, but was stopped by the censors. It had a successful run in Brussels, however, and played in Paris after the death of Dumas, well into the twentieth century.

Dumas died in December, 1870, at the home of his son near Dieppe, as Bismarck's troops were invading France. Four years earlier, in his novel titled *La terreur prussienne,* he had warned of the danger of Prussian imperialism. The writer was buried in the cemetery of Villers-Cotterets, beside his mother and father.

Both Dumas, father and son, were dramatists. The father became a novelist, but never stopped writing plays. The son started as a novelist but eventually devoted himself to the theatre. His chief claim to fame today resides in one play, *La dame aux camélias,* called *Camille* in English-language versions, which was also the basis for Verdi's opera *La traviata.* Neither as novelist nor dramatist was the son capable of creating heroic characters like those that dominate the father's work: d'Artagnan, Edmond Dantes, Chicot the jester, Bussy d'Amboise, Porthos, Athos, Aramis, Annibal de Coconnas, and Cagliostro. All of those men except Edmond Dantes had actually lived, but they had been long forgotten until Dumas père immortalized them. Dumas put himself into his heroes.

In 1883 a statue of Dumas père, designed by Gustave Doré, was unveiled in Paris, on the Place Malesherbes. Dumas is seated at the summit; on one side a group of people is reading one of the romances that have been printed and reprinted in every language, and on the other side is a bronze of D'Artagnan with drawn rapier. At the statue's inauguration, one speaker said that if every person who had been thrilled by *The Three Musketeers* or *The Count of Monte Cristo* had contributed a penny to the memory of Dumas, the statue could have been cast in solid gold.

Published posthumously, with the help of Anatole France, was Dumas's *Grand dictionnaire de cuisine.* Culinary art was just another interest in the life of the irrepressible Alexandre Dumas. Far from being a dull collection of recipes, his cookbook is an amazing series of anecdotes, with interesting treatises on food, dining, wine, and even mustard.

The fabulous chateau of Monte Cristo, about which Dumas wrote in only one book, his charming *Histoire de mes bêtes,* has been declared a national monument by the French government, and an organization called *L'association des amis d'Alexandre Dumas,* founded by the popular French writer Alain Decaux, is engaged in restoring the chateau and the spacious gardens to their former splendor.

Meanwhile the name of Alexandre Dumas père survives—on the printed page, on the stage, and in more than three hundred films based on his plays and novels, in France, England, the United States, and even in Japan, where thirty movies have been made from his works.

His future remains unlimited.

A. Owen Aldridge (essay date 1972)

SOURCE: "The Vampire Theme: Dumas Pere and the English Stage," in *Revue des Langues Vivantes,* Vol. XXXIX, No. 4, 1973, pp. 312-24.

[*In the following essay, originally presented as a paper in 1972, Aldridge discusses the sources of Dumas's little-known drama* Le Vampire *(1851).*]

One of the least known of all the works of Alexandre Dumas, père, is his drama *Le Vampire,* 1851. It is so obscure that it has not even been honored by a separate printing, but is merely available in the collected edition of the author's dramatic works.[1] The play is important, however, in the biography of Dumas and in the history of comparative literature in the nineteenth century. It not only figures in the development of the vampire theme, but also reveals literary relations between France and England in a precise source-influence perspective. Dumas derived the central character and atmosphere of his drama from a famous English shocker story, *The Vampire,* 1818, attributed to Byron, but actually written by the latter's physician Dr. John William Polidori. Then Dumas' drama was adopted by two British dramatists, Dion Boucicault and Augustus G. Harris. Boucicault used Dumas' play as the basis of the first act of a "sensation drama" *The Vampire,* 1852, and Harris appropriated Dumas' work wholesale and produced it under the title *Ruthven,* 1859. The resemblances between the original and Harris' copy are so close, that one might almost say that the English drama is a translation of the French or at the least a paraphrase in Dryden's sense, "where the author is kept in view by the translator, so as never to be lost." Since Harris makes no reference of any kind to a French original, his *Ruthven* must be considered an arrant plagiarism.

Studies of Dumas, whether biographical or critical, do not for the most part even mention his play **Le Vampire,** but many of them treat his reactions to the performance of another play also named *Le Vampire* by Charles Nodier in 1823. Nodier's play had originally been produced at the Théâtre Porte Saint-Martin in 1820 and was revived in 1823 in the same theatre with the same artists in the leading roles.[2] Dumas spreads into five chapters of his **Mémoires** his reminiscence of a performance of the play and his conversation with the author during an intermission.[3] At the time Dumas was young and naive and had never heard of vampires. During the intermission chat, Nodier told the impressionable youth of his personal contact with a vampire a few years previously on a trip to Illyria, the region bordering Transylvania. In the house where he lodged at Spalatra an old man had died and returned from the dead three days after being buried. He asked his son for food and after nourishing himself retired. The son informed Nodier and predicted a return of the spectre. Nodier kept watch at his window and two days later saw the old man appear at the door at midnight. The son later reported that the old man had eaten and drunk as before, and had said in parting that he expected the son to visit him at the same time on the next evening. On the morning of the second day following, the son was found dead in bed. The authorities opened the grave of the old man and found his body perfectly preserved and breathing. They drove a stake through his heart; he cried out loudly and emitted blood through his mouth. Nodier even tried to give a scientific aura to the notion of vampires by describing an experiment he had carried on with a microscopic animal, which he called a "rotifer." This animal died, but was preserved for three years on a grain of sand. Each time Nodier wet it with a rain drop, it came back to life.

The performance of Nodier's play *Le Vampire* together with the author's conversation provided Dumas with the inspiration not only for his own play of the same name, but also for a play on the Don Juan theme, which obtained a certain fame. He recalls in his **Mémoires:** "Cette intervention d'êtres immatériels et supérieurs, dont la destinée même fait le côté fantastique plaisait à mon imagination et peut-être est-ce cette soirée qui sema dans mon esprit le germe de **Don Juan de Márana,** éclos onze ans après seulement."[4]

The theme for Nodier's drama came from a sensational short story by Lord Byron's physician Dr. John William Polidori, which was based on an idea of Byron himself. Byron never completed his vampire story, which

was first published in 1819 under the title "A Fragment-Translation from the Armenian."[5] In this tale, the narrator sets out on travels accompanied by a friend Augustus Darvel, a figure of great mystery. At Smyrna in the Turkish cemetery, Darvel dies after giving extensive instructions concerning the manner of his burial. He asks to be interred at the exact spot where a stork is seen, and gives the narrator a ring which is to be flung into salt springs precisely at noon on the ninth day of the ninth month. Finally, he exacts a solemn pledge from the narrator to conceal the fact of his death from every human being. The two major themes introduced in this fragment are the pledge to conceal death (so that the vampire may later reappear in society) and the combination of attraction and repulsion in the personality of the vampire.

In Polidori's tale, practically a continuation of Byron's, an English gentleman Aubrey embarks on a tour of the continent with a fascinating man of mystery, Lord Ruthven.[6] After discovering that Ruthven possesses vicious habits of gambling and seduction, Aubrey makes his way alone to Greece. Here he meets an innocent, young and beautiful girl, Ianthe, who accompanies him on expeditions in quest of archeological remains and acquaints him of the existence and nature of vampires. One stormy night he discovers that she has been attacked and killed by one of them. Aubrey is so affected by this tragedy that he falls desperately ill and remains in a coma for many days. When he recovers consciousness, he discovers that Ruthven has been nursing him. They resume their travels and are attacked by robbers, Ruthven receiving a fatal wound. Before dying he makes Aubrey swear that he will not reveal his fate until a year and a day have passed. Aubrey later discovers that the robbers had exposed Ruthven's body to the moonlight. When Aubrey returns to England he finds Ruthven already on the scene and wooing his sister. He again becomes gravely ill and recovers consciousness only on the last day of his promised year of silence when he learns that Ruthven is to marry Miss Aubrey on the morrow. By the time he is able to reveal the truth about Ruthven, his sister is already dead, having "glutted the thirst of a vampire." It is important to notice that in this narrative, Ruthven merely disappears, presumably to take advantage of more victims. In all later versions, he is overcome by the forces of good.

Polidori's tale was published in the *New Monthly Magazine* in April 1819. In the next year it was translated by Charles Nodier and published in two editions under the title *Lord Ruthven, ou Les Vampires.*[7] Nodier also adapted it to the stage in a three act melodrama which was produced for the first time at the Théâtre Porte Saint-Martin on 13 June 1820 under the title *Le Vampire.* This was only fourteen months after the appearance of Polidori's tale.

Without question, Nodier's play should be interpreted as an early manifestation of French romanticism, a precursor of *Hernani*.[8] It opens with an introductory vision based on a setting from Ossian, the grotto of Staffa, and incorporating other characters from Scottish legend, Ithuriel and the bard Oscar. Another name from Ossian is applied to Aubrey's sister—Malvina—who had been merely Miss Aubrey in Polidori's original. In the prologue, Nodier establishes that his play is to deal with "certains âmes funestes, dévouées à des tourments que leurs crimes se sont attirés sur la terre, jouissent de ce droit épouvantable, qu'elles exercent de préférence sur la couche virginale et sur le berceau." The reference to the cradle is not borne out by any other vampire literature.

The first act follows Polidori closely. Sir Aubrey had met Ruthven in Athens and together they had resolved that Ruthven should marry Aubrey's sister Malvina. Attacked by brigands, Ruthven had been slain and his body placed in the moonlight. Aubrey on returning to Scotland had arranged that Malvina would marry Count Marsden, the brother of Ruthven. Marsden, by the way, is another name introduced by Nodier. When Marsden appears, he is not a brother, but Ruthven himself. He provides a plausible explanation and wins the hand of Malvina. In the second act, two new characters, Edgar and Lovette are united in marriage, and the bard Oscar sings a song warning her against Ruthven. The latter succeeds in isolating her and is about to take her honor when Edgar appears and kills him. Ruthven exacts from Aubrey the promise not to tell Malvina of his death until twelve hours have passed, and he is left alone in the moonlight. In the third act, the revived Ruthven claims the hand of Malvina. Aubrey kept by his promise from denouncing him, falls into a physical decline and is carried off by domestics. As the wedding hour approaches, Aubrey escapes from his captors and is stabbed by Ruthven. In the final moments, Malvina faints, the exterminating angel appears in a cloud, and Ruthven is swallowed in the shadows.

Less than two months after the initial French performance, a "free translation" of Nodier's drama by J. R. Planché was presented at the Theatre Royal English Opera House under the title *The Vampire; or, The Bride of the Isles*.[9] Oddly enough, Planché in the printed version apologized "to the Public for the liberty which has been taken with a Levantine Superstition, by transplanting it to the Scottish Isles." This suggests that he was personally responsible for the Scottish setting, whereas of course it already existed in Nodier's version. Furthermore since Byron was himself half Scottish, Nodier could certainly be excused for assuming that the characters he had created also belonged to that nationality. Vampirism, moreover, was already associated with the North of England, if not with Scotland. In 1816, John Stagg had published a ballad-like poem entitled "The Vampyre" in a collection entitled *The Minstrel of the North*. Planché in his autobiography observed that he tried in vain to persuade the theatre manager to allow him to change the setting "to some

place in the east of Europe," but the impresario "had set his heart on Scotch music and dresses," and the latter were moreover already in stock.[10]

In his "Introductory Vision," Planché substituted the spirits Unda and Ariel from Rosicrucian lore for Nodier's Ossianic characters, probably in order to diminish the Scottish atmosphere. Unda and Ariel explain that a vampire needs to marry a fair and virtuous maiden from whom he may drain her blood supply, but they do not say, as some legends do, that the vampire obtains a release from his condition by this means. His "race of terror" will merely come to an end unless he obtains some "virgin prey."

Further information concerning vampires is conveyed during the first act by M'Swill, a comic character, described as a henchman of Ronald, Baron of the Isles, the counterpart of Sir Aubrey. The only name which Planché adopts from his predecessors, however, is Ruthven, Earl of Marden. It is Ronald's son who had died in Greece, cared for by Ruthven. Ronald was present at his son's death, and later he and Ruthven were attacked by bandits. Ruthven was killed and his body placed in the moonlight. Ruthven's brother is expected in Scotland to claim the hand of Ronald's daughter, Margaret, but he turns out to be the original Ruthven, who explains that he had recovered from his wounds. In a soliloquy Ruthven reveals that he feels contrition for his misdeeds and pity for his victims. "Daemon as I am, that walk the earth to slaughter and devour, the little that remains of heart within the wizard frame—sustained alone by human blood, shrinks from the appalling act of planting misery in the bosom of this veteran chieftan. . . . Margaret! unhappy maid! thou art my destined prey! thy blood must feed a Vampire's life, and prove the food of his disgusting banquet." On the eve of a wedding between Robert and Effie, Ruthven forces himself on the young girl and is shot by Robert. Ruthven dies in the arms of Ronald, first making the latter promise to keep silent about his death until the next morning and to throw a ring into Fingal's cave. The business of the ring goes back to Byron's original fragment and is not found in Polidori.

When Ronald goes to the cave in the second act to throw the ring, he finds Robert hiding and hears a voice commanding, "Remember your Oath." Robert and Ronald fight inconclusively. Margaret despite earlier misgivings now feels a strong attachment to Ruthven and is anxious for the marriage to take place. Since Ronald cannot expose Ruthven because of his oath, his confusion gives the appearance of madness. He frees himself in time to confront Ruthven in the chapel just before the wedding. Ruthven seizes Margaret and attacks Ronald, but Robert intervenes. The moon sets and Ruthven vanishes into the ground.

Planché also had the ingenious notion of combining the Don Juan theme with the vampire theme. Although many points of resemblance and some of actual contact may be perceived in the two literary traditions, the only work wich actually brings them together is Planché's "operatic burlesque burletta" entitled *Giovanni the Vampire, or, How Shall We Get Rid of Him?* presented at the Adelphi Theatre, 15 January 1821. Unfortunately the printed text is limited to an "Introductory Vision" and to the words of the songs in the rest of the production.[11] The characters include Giovanni the Vampire; Leporello, his valet; the Ghost of the Commandant; and Donna Anna, Daughter of the Commandant. The author's purpose was to bring about through burlesque the "total annihilation" of the composite character of the vampire seducer. The author in his address to the public after referring to the "Levantic superstition concerning Vampires," comments on "the wonderful resemblance which exists between the notorious Don Giovanni, and the supernatural beings aforesaid; not only in their insatiable thirst for blood, and *penchant* for the fair sex, but in the innumerable resuscitations which both have, and still continue to experience." There is considerable truth based upon shrewd observation in this parallel even though it may have been intended primarily for satirical effect.

Needless to say, Planché's burlesque failed to drive either Don Juan or Ruthven out of circulation. Two separate German operas were based on Nodier's play: *Der Vampir* by W. A. Wohlbrück with music by H. Marschner, produced in Lepizig, 28 March 1928, and *Der Vampyr* by C. M. Heigel with music by P. J. von Lindpainter, produced in Stuttgart, August 1928.[12] The Wohlbrück-Marschner version follows Nodier very closely although the cast of characters is increased.[13] Ruthven is still the vampire, but the lord of the manor is the father, not the brother of Malvina. The latter is engaged to Aubrey, who has sworn not to reveal that Ruthven is a vampire. Malvina's father wants her to marry Ruthven in order to unite the two families. There are two other young girls, Ianthe and Emmy, who are irresistibly attracted to Ruthven, and who glut his thirst. In the end, Aubrey finally reveals the secret of Ruthven and is rewarded with the hand of Malvina and the blessing of her father.

The von Lindpainter-Heigel version departs rather drastically from its source.[14] The action takes place in France. Ruthven does not appear, but Graf Aubri is the vampire. Isolde, daughter of Port d'Amour, is to be married to Count Hippolyte, when Graf Aubri appears, as from the dead, and wins the favor of both Isolde and her father. In the meantime he appeals to supernatural forces for aid in the conquest of Lorette on the eve of her wedding.[15] Hippolyte kills Aubri, who exacts a pledge from Port d'Amour not to reveal his fate until midnight. Hippolyte predicts his triumph over Isolde, but she appeals to God, and good defeats evil in a happy ending.

In the summer of 1829, Planché was given the opportunity of adapting the Wohlbrük-Marschner opera to the English stage. Leaving the music untouched, he revised the libretto, laying the scene of action in Hungary, which he considered more appropriate for the vampire theme, and substituting a Wallachian Boyard for the Scottish chieftain.[16]

We know that Dumas' drama **Le Vampire** was directly inspired by Nodier since we have the author's own account of the circumstances of inspiration, but comparison of Dumas' drama with Nodier's reveals few similarities. The principal link between the two plays is the name of Dumas' vampire, Lord Ruthven. Dumas' play was written with the collaboration of Auguste Maquet and produced at the Ambigu-Comique, 20 December 1851.

Dumas' first sign of originality is placing the action in Spain. Up to this time the only other vampire literature associated with the Iberian peninsula was a very obscure collection of stories, *Manuscrit trouré à Saragosse,* written in French by a Polish Count, Jean Potocki, and published in Russia in 1804-1805.[17] Dumas' opening scene represents the courtyard of an inn where preparations for a wedding are in progress. The inn-keeper dismisses Lazare, who has been accused of flirting with the bride. Lazare is a comic character with resemblances to Beaumarchais' Figaro and da Ponte's Leporello. A group of French travelers enter, led by the romantic hero Gilbert, who finds himself strangely attracted to a Moorish girl, who had arrived the preceding day and had attracted attention by the paucity of her diet, composed entirely of a few grains of rice eaten with sticks of ivory. This circumstance reveals that she is a ghoul. Bringing a ghoul and a vampire together in the same play was a *tour de force* comparable to the achievement of Grabbe who united Faust and Don Juan in a tragedy produced in 1829. In twentieth century terms, it perhaps could be considered comparable to a motion picture entitled *Dr. Erotica Meets the Daughter of Fanny Hill.* Dumas' source was the story in the *Arabian Nights,* of Sidi Nouman, a beautiful bride who eats nothing but rice, which she nibbles grain by grain, and eventually is perceived in the cemetery devouring a corpse which had been buried the same day.[18] Since there is no room at the inn, the travelers decide to continue their journey toward the Chateau de Tornemar, a forbidding structure in the neighboring mountains which all the inhabitants of the area are afraid to approach. They are joined by a girl of noble demeanor, Juana, who has fled from a convent in order to keep a rendezvous at the chateau with her fiancé. In the second act, the travelers arrive at Tornemar and discuss supernatural beings while dining. Gilbert announces that he is a descendant of La Feé Mélusine and expresses belief in the existence of supernatural beings. The legend of Mélusine, written down in the fifteenth century by Jean d'Arras, concerns a beautiful maiden who is partly transformed into a serpent on every Saturday. In vampire lore the legend resembles that of the *lamia* in

Greek literature, the beautiful woman who also turns into a serpent. In Greek tradition, the serpent woman is usually a force of evil; whereas Mélusine in Dumas' play represents goodness and benevolence.[19] Gilbert describes some of the fairy lore depicted in medieval tapestries, and another traveler turns the subject to ghouls who take the form of beautiful women, specifically referring to the story in the *Arabian Nights* on which the character of the Moorish Girl is based. After another traveler comments on the pleasure derived from telling stories of apparitions and vampires while seated in a group around a warm fire, the conversation turns to vampires in Peru, who appear at the stroke of midnight. Nodier had mentioned Peru in one of the stories in his collection *Infernalia,* 1822, but otherwise there were no connections between this part of the world and the vampire tradition.[20] Just as the speaker refers to midnight, the hour of twelve sounds and Ruthven appears in the castle, followed by Lazare who has been engaged as his valet. Lazare tells the story of the castle: it had formerly been inhabited by the youngest of three brothers who invited the others to visit him and then murdered them on the way; as a result every time people pass the night there, several are found dead on the succeeding morning. Shortly after Lazare reveals that the last heir of the castle is Juana's fiancé, the latter's dead body is found in an antechamber, and it is later revealed that he has fallen prey to the ghoul. Almost at the same moment a cry comes from Juana's room, she is also found dead, and Ruthven emerges through her door. Gilbert strikes him mortally, but Ruthven before dying offers a plausible explanation for his presence and exacts a promise from Gilbert to expose his body to the moonlight on the mountain.

The third act takes place in a chateau in Brittany. Gilbert's sister, Hélène, announces his imminent arrival. He is preceded, however, by Lazare who has been engaged as Gilbert's valet; he reports that he had encountered a masked man en route. When Gilbert appears, he tells of narrowly escaping a bullet shot on the road because of the intervention of a mysterious woman. As he reveals that he is engaged to a beautiful Dalmatian lass, Antonia, Hélène announces that she is to be married on the very next day to a Scotsman, George. The latter, who appears almost immediately, turns out to be no other than Ruthven; he offers the explanation that he had not been really killed in Spain, but merely wounded. The Ghoul disguised as a peasant girl exhorts Gilbert to sleep that night in the hall of the castle which is hung with tapestries. She is the one who had already saved Gilbert on the road as well as the Moorish girl of the first act. While Gilbert sleeps, the fairy Mélusine appears in a vision. She reveals that the same forces of evil which had killed Juana are about to descend upon Hélène and that Ruthven is a vampire.

The fourth act begins with a comic scene featuring the pusillanimous Lazare who has reentered the service of Ruthven. Gilbert accuses Ruthven of requiring the sacrifice of two virgins every year, and as a result everyone assumes that Gilbert is suffering mentally. Ruthven in solitude calls on his supernatural enemy to appear—this turns out to be the Ghoul, who is pitted against Ruthven because she wants Gilbert for herself. In their confrontation it is made clear that if either denounces the other, that one will become mortal again and that Ruthven has only twelve hours to live unless he can obtain a virgin. Lazare reveals to Hélène the truth about Ruthven. The vampire kills Hélène offstage just as midnight strikes. Gilbert rushes to her door, and engaging Ruthven in a death struggle, throws him out of a window to the foot of a precipice.

The scene shifts in the fifth act to a Circassian palace, where Lazare has brought Antonia with the aid of the Ghoul, now known as Ziska. Gilbert appears, lamenting his sister's death, and recognizes Ziska from her previous appearances. Ziska reveals her deep love for him and offers to use all her supernatural powers in his behalf, but he rejects her. A tempest blows up, and a shipwreck takes place off shore. Lazare throws out a rope hoping to rescue some hapless sailors, and as he pulls, Ruthven emerges from the sea. Gilbert, realizing that the fiend is still at large, offers himself to Ziska provided that she save Antonia from Ruthven. Ziska gives him a poison with which he and Antonia may join themselves forever in death, but before they are able to take it she makes a supreme sacrifice, giving him a sword which has been blessed and which will annihilate the vampire and his powers forever. As soon as Ziska provides this explanation she dies, having paid the penalty for betraying one of her own race. Gilbert thereupon deals Ruthven the final blow. The play ends with a heavenly tableau in which Juana and Hélène as angels raise Ziska from the earth and give their blessing to Gilbert and Antonia.

The final tableau has a strong resemblance to the ending of another play by Dumas produced fifteen years previously. This play, ***Don Juan de Maraña, ou, la Chute d'un ange,*** 1836, is more famous, but not necessarily better than ***Le Vampire.*** In the concluding scene, the spirit of one of the protagonist's victims who has become an angel offers her forgiveness, and thereby leads him to repent.[21] In this connection it is significant to recall Dumas' assertion in his ***Mémoires*** that the earliest inspiration for his ***Don Juan de Maraña*** came from Nodier's *Le Vampire.*[22]

A scant six months after the Paris production of Dumas' play, an adaptation incorporating the essential elements of its first two acts appeared on the London stage under the title, *The Vampire.* Written by an Irish-born dramatist, Dion Boucicault, who performed in many of his own works, the play incorporates the ingenious device of tracing the career of a vampire during the course of three separate centuries, a device possibly borrowed from the Gothic novel *Melmoth.* The first act concerns the seventeenth; the second, the eighteenth; and the third, the contemporary nineteenth. The names of the characters are different from those in Dumas' play, but the plot is the same. Boucicault compressed into one act the essential ingredients of the first two acts of Dumas' play, but he was forced to leave out the characters of Mélusine and the Ghoul. Boucicault made his debut as an actor in the title rôle at the first London performance, 14 June 1852. "Charles Kean deemed 'vampires' beneath his tragic dignity; so Boucicault himself appeared as the supernatural creature. . . . Oddly enough, Boucicault's Irish brogue, which always came out strong except in French dialect parts, did not seem anachronistic."[23] *The Vampire* belonged to a genre which Boucicault labelled "sensation drama." "Sensation is what the public wants," he said to William Winter, "and you cannot give them too much of it."[24] Despite the strong dose of sensation combined with Boucicault's effective acting, the play was not a great success, and the author brought out a revised version in only two acts entitled *The Phantom.*

In this version, the first scene represents a Welsh inn during the time of Cromwell. The innkeeper, Davy, has just taken a bride and is about to celebrate his nuptials, when Lucy Peveryl appears on the way to meet her fiancé at sundown in the ruins of nearby Raby Castle. She is followed by Lord Clavering and a large party who decide to escort her to the castle. Davy is superstitious and a coward, but, nevertheless, consents to act as guide. As they settle down at the castle, Lord Clavering recounts a story of a Bohemian vampire "who had died some fifty years before but who had made a compact with the fiend to revive him after death." At the end of the story a newcomer arrives and is made welcome. He is Alan Raby, who pretends to be a poor gentleman, but he is recognized by Davy as the former Puritan lord of the castle who had been slain ten years previously. Davy is cowed, however, into keeping silent. He retires to an adjoining room and discovers the slain body of Lucy's fiancé. Almost immediately Lucy runs screaming from another room and dies in the arms of Lord Clavering. Soon after Raby emerges from the same room and is shot by Clavering. Before dying, Raby convinces Clavering that he had not been the killer of Lucy and agrees to forgive Clavering for shooting him if the latter will carry his body to the mountain peaks and expose it to the first rays of the moon. Clavering does so, and in the final scene of the act, Raby, his body bathed in light, addresses the moon as "Fountain of my life."[25]

Boucicault's play, despite its resemblance to Dumas' *Le Vampire,* may be considered an original work. It draws upon Dumas only in the first act and follows an independent path in the later scenes. The setting is completely changed as are the names of the characters. The dialogue, moreover, is not directly translated from Dumas, but is newly written. Practically no element of originality whatsoever, however, may be found in another play on the theme seven years later, *Ruthven* by Augustus Glossop Harris, produced at the Royal Grecian Theatre, 25 April 1859.[26] It is almost a word for word translation of Dumas' *Le Vampire,* incorporating a few plot changes, primarily in the direction of simplification. Harris leaves out the character of Mélusine and the French chamber of tapestry. All the other major characters are the same, and they even bear the same names. Harris compresses the five acts of his source into four acts by merging the first two of Dumas and greatly shortening the third. Whenever he makes changes in dialogue, his version is usually more explicit. Dumas, for example, has the ghoul remark concerning Juana: "Il te faut deux heures pour aller retrouver ton beau fiancé. . . . Je l'aurai joint dans trois minutes!" Harris has her say, "It will take thee two hours, Juana, before you can be in the arms of your affianced husband—he shall be in mine long ere that." Similarly, the ghoul in Dumas remarks in the succeeding scene: "Il était jeune! il était beau! . . . Me voilà redevenue jeune et belle! . . . A l'an prochain, Gilbert!" Harris has her say: "He was young and handsome—no matter, I have once more a new lease of existence! Gilbert, it is thou that art next doomed."

It is hardly necessary to give a plot summary of *Ruthven* since it would be almost identical to that of *Le Vampire.* The only differences are minor, and for the most part they appear at the end of the play. Dumas has Gilbert kill Ruthven with a sword; Harris has him do it with a pistol. Dumas has Gilbert learn from Mélusine that Ruthven is a vampire; Harris substitutes a dream vision. The last act in Dumas takes place on the Black Sea; in Harris, on the Bay of Naples. In Dumas, Ziska offers Gilbert the poison which will enable him to be united forever with Antonia; in Harris, Gilbert has carried it with him for years. Harris' only major innovation concerns an amulet in the form of a cross which Gilbert gives to his sister and which disappears on the night of her death in a mysterious way. When Gilbert is about to take poison, Ziska offers him the amulet, explaining that she had taken it from Hélène's body, thinking that it could someday be used to "save an innocent virgin, and exterminate Ruthven." Ruthven hires two ruffians to bring Antonia to him in a churchyard, but he is repelled by the amulet. Gilbert knocks him to the ground and commands him to repent as the clock begins to strike. At the stroke of midnight, the vampire disappears in smoke.

Even though greater tolerance has traditionally been extended to dramatists than to poets and novelists in the matter of borrowing from other writers, Harris' drama is so close to the original that it cannot possibly be explained euphemistically as an adaptation. In a sense, Harris was paying a great compliment to

Dumas by appropriating his work wholesale, but at the same time he was perpetrating a fraud on his audiences by his arrant plagiarism.

Twelve years later a farce joining the vampire theme with literary plagiarism was produced at the Royal Strand Theatre: *The Vampire, a Bit of Moonshine,* written by R. Reece. The main character is a vampire who makes a living by writing horror stories stolen from other authors. According to the author, the play is based upon "a German legend, Lord Byron's story, and a Boucicaultian drama." Literary justice would have best been served if Harris were the main target, but apparently this dubious honor was accorded to Boucicault since the protagonist of the farce was an Irishman speaking in an exaggerated brogue.

Many other vampire dramas and vampire films have followed Harris' play, but none of them have portrayed the character of Darvel-Ruthven, the joint creation of Byron, Polidori and Dumas.

Notes

[1] *Théatre complet de Alexandre Dumas* (Paris, 1865), II, 399-535.

[2] Jean Larat, *La Tradition et l'exotisme dans l'œuvre de Charles Nodier (1780-1844),* (Paris, 1923), p. 128.

[3] *Mes Mémoires,* LXXIV-LXXVIII. (Paris, Colmann-Lévy s.d.), III, 148-209.

[4] Like his drama on the vampire theme, Dumas' *Don Juan* was also imitated in an English play, to be precise, in Arnold Bennett's *Don Juan de Marana.*

[5] Roland Prothero, ed., *Works of Lord Byron* (London, 1899), III, 446-454.

[6] "The Vampyre: A Tale by Lord Byron," in *New Monthly Magazine,* XI (April 1, 1819), 193-206.

[7] Larat, op. cit., p. 127.

[8] It is so presented by Henri Peyre in *Qu'est-ce que le romantisme?* (Paris, 1971), p. 78.

[9] 6 August 1820, according to Planché's *Recollections and Reflections* (London, 1901), p. 27; 9 August, according to printed edition of *The Vampire* (London: Printed for John Lowndes, 1820).

[10] *Recollections and Reflections* (London, 1901), p. 27.

[11] Printed for John Lowndes (London, 1821).

[12] These dates are taken from Hugo Riemann, *Opera-Handbuch* (Leipzig, 1887).

[13] *Der Vampir, Romantische Oper in vier Aufzügen* (München, 1883).

[14] *Der Vampyr, Romantische Oper in drei Akten* (München, 1828).

[15] Hippolyte is a name probably derived from a character in E. T. A. Hoffmann's vampire story *Cyprians Erzählung,* 1821, but otherwise there is no connection between the two works. Hoffman's Hippolit is a count who discovers that his new bride is a ghoul.

[16] *Recollections,* p. 104.

[17] Roger Caillois, ed., *Manuscrit trouvé à Saragosse* (Paris, 1958).

[18] "Histoire de Sidi Nouman," *Les Mille et une nuits . . . traduit par Galland* (Paris, 1839), III, 222-226. This is also the source of Hoffman's *Cyprians Erzählung,* mentioned above.

[19] Dumas' play was produced in the year preceding the publication of Gerard de Nerval's sonnet *El Desdichado,* which also incorporates elements from the Mélusine legend.

[20] (Paris, 1822), p. 80.

[21] In an earlier version of the same scene, three allegorical angels contend for his fate; one calls for vengeance; another for mercy; and the last for justice. Leo Weinstein, *The Metamorphoses of Don Juan* (Stanford, 1959), p. 111.

[22] It is important to notice also that the most popular Don Juan play in Spain, Zorrilla's *Don Juan Tenorio,* 1844, was produced eight years after Dumas' *Don Juan de Maraña.* Although critical opinion is divided concerning the degree of resemblance between the two works, it seems most unlikely that the Spanish dramatists would not have known and used the work of his eminent French contemporary.

[23] Townshend Walsh, *The Career of Dion Boucicault* (New York, 1915), p. 45. Neither Walsh nor R.G. Hogan, author of *Dion Boucicault* (New York, 1969) realized that *The Vampire* was related to Dumas. The astute vampirian, Montague Summers, however, made the connection, *The Vampire His Kith and Kin* (London, 1928), p. 315. Another of Boucicault's plays produced earlier in the same year, *The Corsican Brothers,* also derived from Dumas. A devastating review of Boucicault's *The Vampire* appears in Henry Morley's *Journal of a London Playgoer* (1851-1866), (London, 1891), pp. 45-46. According to Morley, "Spectral Melodrama" in the piece had "reached the extreme point of inanity."

[24] Winter, *Other Days* (New York, 1908), p. 130.

[25] In the New York, 1856 edition of The Phantom, described as *Bourcicault's Dramatic Works, No. 3,* the dramatist's name in consistently spelled with an *R* even though a printed signature leaves it out. The reason for this, according to William Winter, is that about 1859-60 "he made the interesting discovery that his ancestry was French, ancient, noble, and aristocratic" and that his name should be spelled in the French style. *Other Days* (New York, 1908), p. 130.

[26] *Ruthven: A Drama in Four Acts* (London, Thomas Hailes Lacy, n.d.).

Douglas Munro (essay date 1983)

SOURCE: "Two 'Missing' Works of Alexandre Dumas, Père," in *Bulletin of the John Rylands University Library of Manchester,* Vol. 66, No. 1, Autumn, 1983, pp. 198-212.

[*In the following essay, Munro examines the publishing histories of two little-known works by Dumas, the historical romance* Le comte de Moret *and the drama* Pietro Tasca.]

This article is primarily concerned with the "missing" manuscripts of two works by Alexandre Dumas, père, **Le comte de Moret** and **Pietro Tasca.** But these, it should be noted, are not alone among his works in being "missing", for various other manuscripts of his, all plays, may also, for a variety of reasons, be counted as lost. First, I may instance the manuscript of **Les Gracques.** This was one of his early attempts at writing a tragic drama, in verse, and in **Comment je devins auteur dramatique**[1] he states "Je composai d'abord une tragédie des 'Gracques', de laquelle je fis justice, en la brûlant aussitôt sa naissance"—that would be in 1827. L.-Henry Lecomte repeats this statement,[2] as does Quérard[3] who goes on to refer to Dumas' **Fiesque de Lavagna,** which was another drama in verse, adapted from Schiller, the manuscript of which, according to him, went the same way as that of **Les Gracques.** It may well be that Dumas did burn the manuscripts, but could it be possible that some sheets escaped the flames or that there were earlier drafts?

There was next, possibly written more or less at the same time as **Les Gracques,** a prose drama entitled **Les puritaines d'Écosse,** which was drawn from Scott's *Old Mortality.* Dumas, in collaboration with Frédéric Soulié, had planned the outline of the play and had indeed started writing it, but, again according to Lecomte,[4] it was never finished. Dumas confirmed this in his **Mes mémoires**[5] where he wrote: "[Scott] avait deux caractères qui séduisaient invinciblement Soulié, c'étaient John Balfour de Burley et Bothwell. Le sujet choisi, nous nous mîmes avec ardeur à l'œuvre; mais nous avions beau nous réunir, le plan n'avançait pas". Presumably, whatever was written has vanished for ever.

The influence of Scott on Dumas was quite extraordinary. Several years earlier than the attempt at writing **Les puritaines d'Écosse,** he had written a "Mélodrame en 3 actes et à grand spectacle" entitled **Ivanhoe.** Fortunately, this is one manuscript which has not been lost; it is now held by the Bibliothèque de Dieppe (Cat. MS. 81 / AS 15), having been given to that library by Dumas, fils, in or about 1886. It comprises thirty-four white, numbered leaves, written on both recto and verso, with, on the first leaf, *Ivanhoe* in Dumas' hand. The play was performed at the Dieppe Casino in May 1966 by the 'Compagnie Jehan-Ango', and in the announcement of the performance it was stated that this "spectacular melodrama" was written in 1819. Dumas was then only seventeen years old.

About 1835 Dumas wrote a play of five acts and six tableaux, with an epilogue, to which he chose to give the title **L'Écossais.** This was based on *Quentin Durward* and apparently closely followed the original. It was never performed or published. Charles Glinel in his article "Le théâtre inconnu d'Alexandre Dumas père",[6] wrote: "Le manuscrit original, composé vers 1835 ou 1836, retrouvé par Frédérick Lemaître en 1871, donné par lui au libraire Laplace, fut remis par ce dernier le 7 juin 1877 à Alexandre Dumas fils. Nous avons acquis après la mort de Laplace une copie de "L'Écossais" qu'il fait exécuter soigneusement par Mlle. Augustine Métayer, et qui est élégamment reliée avec un curieux récit du sort du manuscrit original et avec les pièces justificatives". What happened to the original is now not known.

Then there is the five-act play **Gulliver** which, again, was neither performed nor published. The curious thing here is that Dumas' publishers Calmann-Lévy, in their *Catalogue raisonné des œuvres de Alexandre Dumas,* issued in 1902, the centenary of the year of his birth, reproduced on page (17) a "page autographe d'Alexandre Dumas' 'Gulliver', féerie inédite". Lecomte[7] wrote: "Sont entièrement perdus: 'Jane Eyre', drame en 5 actes; 'Les âmes vaillantes', drame en 5 actes, destiné à L'Ambigu; 'Gulliver', féerie en 5 actes, pour laquelle Dumas traita en 1850 avec la Porte-Saint-Martin, sans que cette convention eût des suites; et 'Samson', opéra fait avec Edouard Duprez, et dont quelques fragments furent exécutés à l'école spéciale de chant, en 1856". The manuscript must be presumed to be lost. In so far as **Samson** is concerned, there was published in 1856 *Première séance de l'année 1856. Exécution de fragments de l'opéra* (inédit) *de 'Samson', poème de MM. Alex. Dumas et Ed. Duprez.* Vaugirard, Impr. Choisnet, 8vo., pp. 8. I shall refer to **Les âmes vaillantes** later in this article, but, as regards **Jane Eyre,** which obviously was based on the Charlotte Brontë novel, Dumas referred to it at some length in his 'causerie' "Comment j'ai fait jouer à Marseille le drame des 'Forestiers'", published in *Bric-à-brac,*[8] and Charles Glinel simply mentions it, entitling it **Jeanne [sic] Eyre,** along with **Les âmes vaillantes,** in his article 'Le theatre inconnu d'Alexandre Dumas père'[9] as "ne se retrouvent pas".

There is a further original manuscript of a Dumas drama which is most certainly irretrievably lost, nor was it ever published. It is of a comic opera in two acts entitled *La Bacchante (Thaïs),* written in collaboration with Adolphe de Leuven and Amédée de Beauplan, with music by Eugène Gauthier, and first performed at the Opéra-Comique on 4 November 1858. Glinel, in the article "Le théatre inconnu d'Alexandre Dumas père", wrote:[10] "Dumas avait eu l'idée avec de Leuven et Amédée de Beauplan un opéra-comique sur un sujet antique, intitulé 'Thaïs', sorte de pendant de 'Galathée'. Il avait même écrit, et nous en avons le manuscrit, les trois premières scènes du livret. Tous trois convinrent de déplacer l'action et d'en changer l'époque. La scène se passa dès lors dans une villa de Florence, en 1550, et la pièce dont il s'agit devint 'La Bacchante'. Elle était écrite surtout pour Marie Cabel. Une indisposition du ténor Jourdan interrompit les représentations après la troisième soirée et Meyerbeer dont on répétait 'Le Pardon de Ploërmel', écrit aussi pour Mme Cabel, fit si bien que 'La Bacchante' ne fut pas reprise". Unfortunately, the libretto and score were both destroyed in a fire in the Salle Favart. Glinel went on to write, in a further instalment of *Le théatre inconnu,*[11] "Heureusement M. de Spoelberch de Louvenjoul avait obtenu des auteurs une copie du livret et d'Eugène Gautier [*sic*] une réduction au piano de l'œuvre musicale. 'La Bacchante' n'est donc pas perdue pour tout le monde et nous devons à l'obligeance inépuisable du savant bibliophile et dilettante bruxellois la copie intégrale du livret".

Finally, there was a translated version of Shakespeare's *Romeo and Juliet* which was again neither performed nor published and which, apparently, was made in collaboration with Paul Meurice. *Romeo et Juliette* consisted of five acts and eleven tableaux, and, according to Glinel,[12] the entire manuscript was in the hand of Meurice. Although this may have been so, I am inclined to the belief that Dumas, in fact, did the translating, dictating it to his friend. Charles Chincholle[13] stated that the play was in alexandrines, and Benjamin Pifteau[14] told of Dumas reading it to his friends in his chambers in the Rue de Richelieu somewhere about 1864. What happened to the original manuscript is unknown, but it seems at one stage to have been passed by Meurice to Dumas, fils, who allowed Glinel to make a copy of it. Thereafter it disappeared. Extracts from it may be found in several of Dumas' works, most notably in his *Souvenirs d'une favorite* and *La fille du marquis* and, oddly enough, in his *Grand dictionnaire de cuisine,* where he quotes forty-one lines from the play in his article dealing with the preparing and cooking of larks.

I. *Le comte de Moret: The Vicissitutes of a 'Vanished' Romance*

Between 17 October 1865 and 23 March 1866, with only occasional lapses, Dumas contributed as a 'feuilleton' to a Paris daily literary paper, *Les Nouvelles,* an historical romance entitled *Le comte de Moret. Les Nouvelles,* a short-lived and seemingly not very successful venture, was founded by one Jules Noriac. It was first published on 20 September 1865, ran into difficulties in the Spring of 1866, and was taken over by Dumas on his own account and renamed, on 18 November 1866, *Le Mousquetaire,* after that earlier and most famous of his journals, the original series of which had ceased publication on 7 February 1857.

Copies of *Les Nouvelles* were lodged with the Bibliothèque Nationale, but the 'run' is now incomplete and lacks those numbers published on 18 and 21 October, 1, 2, 3 and 27 November 1865, and 1 March 1866, in all of which parts of *Le comte de Moret* appeared.

The romance hinges on the war in Piedmont and the imaginary career of Antoine, comte de Moret, the illegitimate son of Henri IV, who was believed to have been killed during the battle of Castelnaudary in 1632, although his body was never found. A legend persisted that, seriously wounded, he had escaped finally to die as an aged hermit in Anjou during the reign of Louis XIV.

Dumas' story opened on 5 December 1628 and ended in 1630. It really covers a brief period following the conclusion of *The Three Musketeers* with the return of Louis XIII and Cardinal Richelieu from the siege of La Rochelle. Other historical personages in the romance are the two queens, Anne of Austria and Marie de Medici, the duchesse de Chevreuse, and Montmorency. And Dumas introduces a new soldier of fortune—Etienne Latil—who has many of the attractive characteristics of d'Artagnan.

In 1850 Dumas had already written what was, in effect, the sequel to *Le comte de Moret,* a story entitled *La Colombe,* related in the form of letters and dealing with the imagined fate of that remarkable man. The period covered by *La Colombe,* according to the dating of the letters, was 5 May 1637 to 10 September 1638, although their contents covered events both at, as well as after, the battle of Castelnaudary. The writing of a story in the form of letters is a most unusual one for Dumas, but it worked successfully.

La Colombe never appeared in serial form and was first published in Belgium as: *La colombe,* / par / Alexandre Dumas. / Bruxelles, / Librairie du Panthéon / 1850. The format is 15 x 9½ cm. and the number of pages 128. It appeared in the publishers' series *La Nouveauté Littéraire* with yellow paper wrappers. One other edition, in a slightly larger format and of 112 pages, was published in Brussels in the same year by Alphonse Lebègue.

Both these editions preceded the book's first publication in France under the title of *Histoire d'une colombe,* by Alexandre Cadot (1851, 8vo., 2 volumes, pp. 305 and 319), the second volume including Dumas' *Chateaubriand*

and *Le roi Pépin.* The *Semaine Littéraire du Courrier des Etats-Unis. Receuil Choisi de romans, feuilletons, ouvrages historiques et dramatiques, en prose et en vers des auteurs modernes les plus renommés* (New-York, F. Gaillardet), published the work in 1853 under the title of *La colombe,* volume 5, part 4, pp. (1)-34 in double columns.

The first appearance of the work in English was in the *London Journal* in 1857, and it was again published by Methuen in Alfred Allinson's translation in 1906. It was never published as a translation in the United States.

Copies of *Les Nouvelles* must have found their way to the United States, and a first, emasculated translation of *Le comte de Moret* appeared and was, as stated on the verso of the title, "entered according to Act of Congress in the year 1867 by Henry L. Williams". The title-page reads as follows: "*The / count of Moret: / or, / Richelieu and his rivals.* / By Alexandre Dumas, / Author of *Monte-Christo, The three guardsmen,* etc., etc. / Translated from the French / By Henry L. Williams, Jr. / New York; / Published by Henry L. Williams, / 119 Nassau Street". The book is in-octavo and consists of pages (3)-160 printed in double columns; there are fifty-five chapters and an epilogue. The translator has omitted pages from the conclusion of Dumas' original and substituted material of his own, giving, moreover, no indication that he has done so. There is, indeed, another gap in one run of ten chapters. Williams must have had no knowledge of the logical sequence of the story which had been written earlier as *La Colombe,* otherwise he would surely never have had the ineptitude to rewrite the conclusion as he did.

In the following year the book was published again. It appeared as: *The count of Moret; / or, / Richelieu and his rivals.* / by / Alexander Dumas. / Author of *The count of Monte Cristo, The chevalier,* etc., etc., / Translated from the French of Alexander Dumas, / by Henri L. Williams, Jr. /, for Peterson's edition of Alexander Dumas' great works. / Philadelphia: T. B. Peterson & brothers; / 306 Chestnut Street. The verso of the title consists of the publishers' 'blurb', a shortened list of titles by Dumas published by Peterson, and the necessary "entered according to Act of Congress, in the year 1868, by T.B. Peterson & brothers". The book measures 23.3 x 14.3 cm., and is a reprint of the 1867 Williams edition with the same pagination.

I have also been able to trace another, but mutilated, copy of the work in an American private institutional library. Lacking its title-page, it has 266 pages printed in double columns, and measures 24 cm.; there is no epilogue. No advertisements remain to help identification, but on internal evidence it would appear virtually certain that it is a copy of the edition published in New York by George Munro (*c.* 1876) in his *Seaside Library.*

The edition published by Williams (and this, incidentally, is the only work by Dumas translated by Williams which he published himself) was in the New York Public Library. Their copy, however, no longer exists and it is by courtesy of that institution that I possess a microfilm copy of that particular printing of Williams' version. The Peterson & Brothers edition is still, fortunately, with the British Library. The Library of Congress in its Main and Official Catalogues does not locate any copies, and its National Union Catalogue refers only to the edition in the New York Public Library which is no longer extant. James Kelly's *American Catalogue of Books* lists simply, "'**The count of Moret**'. Translated by Williams. 8vo., paper, 75 cents, Peterson, 1869"; and Petersons' catalogue in the *Publishers' Trade List Annual,* 1873, even more simply, "'**The count of Moret**'. Price 75 cents".

To carry the American side of the story further, there appeared among the advertisements for *The Royalist Daughters* and *The Castle of Souday* (both comprising the Williams' version of Dumas' *Les Louves de Machecoul*) a work entitled and spelt equally **The Count of Morian (or Morion); or, Woman's revenge** which, it has been suggested, might have been an announcement for *The count of Moret.* Since both of these last titles were copyrighted by Dick and Fitzgerald of New York in 1862, some four years before *Le comte de Moret* appeared serially, there could obviously be grave doubts as to the authenticity. In fact, this work is by Frederick Soulié, and my copy, with the title "*The count of Morion [sic]; or woman's revenge.* Translated from the French . . . by Edward Magauran, esq.", was published in New York by Williams Brothers, 24 Ann-Street. Boston: 6 Water-Street, in 1847.

This is the stage at which it may be said that the book vanished, the only verifiable volume extant of a translated version being the copy held by the British Library.

But, to enliven matters, there was published **Short Stories by Alexandre Dumas,** Ten Volumes in One, New York, Walter J. Black co., n.d. [1927], 8vo., 8 unnumbered pages 'Table of contents', 3 unnumbered pages, 'Introduction' signed 'G.W.B.', (1)-1003 in double columns. In point of fact, these are not short stories. The book is made up of extracts from some of Dumas' well-known and less well-known works, and includes also extracts from some of the spurious titles credited to him. But among these extracts there are eleven genuinely taken from *Le comte de Moret,* as well as one entitled *The death of Richelieu* which appeared neither in *Les Nouvelles* nor in Williams' version, but which could have been included in the final pages of the original manuscript and for some reason was not published.

In 1936, in what would seem to be the unlikely city of Buenos Aires, there was published: *El conde de Moret; novela historica que abarca el periodo entre Les tros*

mosquetaros, y Veinte años despues. Buenos Aires: Talleres gráficos argentinos L.J. Rosso, 1936, 23½ cm., pp. 2 preliminary leaves, (7)-581, 1. Page (7) comprises a preface signed "Evaristo Etchecopar", in which he writes: "La presente versión pertenece al Correo de ultamar . . . revista del siglo pasado extinguida en 1885 . . . En ella apareció el Conde de Moret en 1865 y siguió publicándose periódicamente, hasta que la muerte de Dumas vino a dejarla trunca". Copies of this book are held in the Library of Congress and the New York Public Library, but, strangely, in neither the extensive Biblioteca Nacional nor the Biblioteca de Palacio in Madrid.

The book was printed from the text published in the *Correo de Ultramar* which, from its very name, would have circulated in South America. The Spanish version was apparently made at the time of the serial issue in *Les Nouvelles,* included the material in the copies missing from the Bibliothèque Nationale, and clarified the position regarding Williams' deliberate disregard of ten vital chapters, as well as the other gap in the run of chapters referred to earlier.

To the sounding of trumpets, in 1944 *Le Sphinx rouge* (announced as an unpublished romance by Dumas) burst upon an unsuspecting French public, and *France-Soir* gave a "Version ramassée, limitée aux épisodes essentiels". In fact, *Le Sphinx rouge* was Dumas' *Le comte de Moret,* and the manuscript that reached *France-Soir* comprised only three sections of the original four of the romance. It was written on Dumas' familiar blue paper and each section was paginated separately—the first comprising 117 leaves, the second 120, and the third 171. According to *France-Soir* Dumas had offered the manuscript to an admirer, Madame T . . . , née Falcon, sister of the singer Jenny Falcon, and married to a member of the Russian aristocracy whose name was never disclosed.

After the Revolution of 1917 Madame . . . 's family emigrated to France, and in 1944 the manuscript became the property of the director of *Les Éditions universelles* and was duly published as Alexandre Dumas, *Le Sphinx rouge (Roman historique).* Les Éditions universelles, Paris; on the verso of the title is: "Copyright . . . Paris, 1946", and the announcement that 150 numbered copies had been printed on "pur fil des Papeteries de France, . . . , constituant authentiquement l'édition originale". The format is 18½ x 11½ cm., with the pagination: (7)-9 'note liminaire', (3), (13)-752, and 3 pages' table of contents, with a frontispiece portrait of Dumas and, underneath, ten holograph lines signed "fin du 3ᵉ volume A Dumas". This edition was reprinted with the same format and pagination in 1947.

It was not long before the readers of the *Bibliothèque de Lectures de Paris* were offered Alexandre Dumas' *Le comte de Moret, Roman historique.* Illustrations de

Maurice Sauvayre S.E.P.E. Paris, n.d. [1948], 18½ x 12½ cm., 4 volumes bound in 2, pp. (5)-6 'Alexandre Dumas et **"Le comte de Moret"**' par Roger Giron, (7)-286, and (5)-268; there are no tables of contents. Each volume has a woodcut frontispiece, and five and four other woodcuts respectively in the text. Twenty-four copies were printed on "papier Marais-crèvecœur". The editorial note on the verso of the title-page of volume 1 contradicts itself when it states that the Bibliothèque Nationale possesses the only copy of the journal in which the romance appeared "en son entier" by then going on to state that unhappily there are a few gaps which have been filled in with, in italics " . . . simples résumés très concis du texte disparu", which may, of course, have been summaries taken from the retranslated Spanish version. M. Giron states that *Le comte de Moret* was dedicated to Dimitri Pavlovich Narischkine "en memoire de l'hospitalité royale" which had been given to Dumas when he was in Russia in the years following 1858.

The collation of *Le Sphinx rouge* and *Le comte de Moret,* which are divided respectively into 'parties' and 'volumes', shows that the former, in addition to variations in the text, has had interpolated, in the first division of the book, four new chapter headings, while the second divisions of both books do not vary in so far as the titles of chapters are concerned. Moreover, the third divisions of both books once again vary in several chapter headings, and *Le Sphinx rouge* finally stops short at Chapter XXI of the "troixième partie".

The fourth volume of *Le comte de Moret,* Chapter 1, is Chapter XLIII in Williams' version. Williams' next three chapter headings are mis-spelt, and after Chapter XLVI he reverts with his numbering to XLV, repeats XLVI, and then goes to XLVII. Chapters VII-XVIII are omitted, but three chapters are interpolated. With his own Chapter L, Williams continues with Chapter XIX from *Le comte de Moret;* Chapter XX is given a garbled title and, after Chapter XXII of the French text (the work finishes at Chapter XXIII), Williams includes in his version the other garbled material which he was unwise enough to subjoin, comprising two chapters and an epilogue.

Subsequently the *Les Éditions universelles* version published as *Le Sphinx rouge* was republished on three occasions. The first was as: *Le Sphinx rouge* / par / Alexandre Dumas / collection Marabout; verso of title " . . . éditée et imprimée par Gérard & co . . ." (Verviers) Belgique; n.d. [*c.* 1955], 18 x 11.3 cm., pp. 5-539, 4 pages of publishers' advertisements, blank, notes on the book and its author inside back cover, illustrated paper covers. The second as: Alexandre Dumas / *Le Sphinx rouge* / Éditions Galic / . . . / Paris; n.d. [1964], 20.7 x 13.2 cm., pp. (1), (11)-373, grey boards, and the third as: Alexandre Dumas / *Le Sphinx rouge* / Éditions Baudelaire / Livre club des Champs-Élysées / . . . / Paris, n.d. [1966], 20 x 13 cm., pp. (I)-VII introductory note on Dumas, (1)-530; preceding the title-page is a photograph copy of Daumier's cartoon of Dumas and a photograph of Dumas' monument in the Place Malesherbes, Paris; this has coloured boards. This last edition was reprinted in 1967 with the same format and pagination. None of these reprints includes the "note liminaire" published in the original *Les Éditions universelles* edition.

There can only remain the hope that the missing final leaves of the fourth part of Dumas' holograph manuscript may come to light. This is not as impossible as it may seem, for manuscripts of his works, in whole or in part, have the uncanny knack of appearing quite out of the blue from time to time, and not only in auctioneers' and specialist booksellers' catalogues. Should this happen, we shall then have the Count in Dumas' full romantic portrayal, and perhaps an English translation may be published, not only as a literary curiosity, but on its merits as one of his major romances.

II. *Pietro Tasca*

That apparently lost holograph manuscripts of Dumas do in fact reappear entirely unexpectedly may be further exemplified by one such that was offered to me at the beginning of the war through a Jewish émigré from Vienna.

It was no less than the complete manuscript of a play in five acts in prose, wholly written on some ninety loose sheets in Dumas' familiar, beautifully-flowing hand and on his famous blue paper.

The manuscript bore no title or list of characters. The lack of title was possibly due to the loss of the first sheet, on which it was Dumas' invariable custom to write his titles in a large, even script, together with an indication of the acts and tableaux. But there may have been another perfectly good reason, which will be explained later. That there was no list of characters is not unexpected; Dumas rarely, save in a few of his early dramas, troubled to supply this in detail, leaving it doubtless to reveal itself in the course of rehearsals and duly to be supplied by the publisher.

One or two notes were written on the manuscript, one signed by Charles Chincholle. From this it would appear that the manuscript was in Dumas' possession towards the end of his life, when he was very friendly with the young Chincholle who, besides writing an interesting booklet (*Alexandre Dumas Aujourd'hui*, avec photographies par Pierre Petit. Paris, D. Jouast, 1867), contributed to Dumas' journal *Dartagnan* and had brief introductions by Dumas to two of his books—*Dans l'ombre* (Paris, Librairie internationale A. Lacroix, Verbroeckhoven et Cᵉ, Éditeurs . . . même maison à Bruxelles, a Leipzig, et a Livourne, 1871) and *Le lendemain de l'amour* (Paris, Calmann-Lévy, 1880).

Lacking a title, the play came to me as *Pietro Tasca,* after its main male character. The action of the drama is centred around a miscarriage of justice in the Venice of the Doges towards the end of the fifteenth century. There are alternative versions of the epilogue, and it would seem likely that it may have been the draft of a play which was thrown aside for more urgent work, then forgotten, and finally lost. From the simple fact of a recorded miscarriage of justice, Dumas had woven a satisfying drama, as could be expected in any historical or, indeed, other play he wrote.

To return to what I have mentioned earlier about the lack of title and other information, the holograph manuscript of another play by Dumas, *Les âmes vaillantes,* has seemingly disappeared, and that title could very well be applicable to *Pietro Tasca.* Glinel, an eminent authority on Dumas, stated[15] that *Les âmes vaillantes* in 5 acts, had been written for the Théâtre Ambigu-Comique, and mentioned a letter from Dumas to Anténor Joly, the then manager of that theatre, dated 26 February 1852 (Collection Ernest Lemaître, Laon). But Noël Parfait, secretary and friend of Dumas during his exile in Brussels between December 1851 and January 1853, in a letter to Glinel dated 5 August 1892, stated that the manuscript of *Les âmes vaillantes* had unfortunately disappeared.

However, and this is where the interest quickens, Dumas, fils, in Paris in January 1872, had a visitor who called himself His Royal Highness Prince George Kastriota Scanderberg, King of Albania and Epirus, Hereditary Prince of Croia, and of all the Albanian Colonies, Duke of Saint-Pierre in Galatina, and patrician of Rome, Naples and Venice. He was accompanied by, as Grand Marshal of the Palace, a retired Neapolitan commissioner of police, and, as Captain of the Guard, a retired French police inspector. He told Dumas that he had met his father in Naples in 1862, where the two had become so friendly that Dumas, père, had given him the manuscript of an unpublished play of his entitled *Les âmes vaillantes.*

J. Lucas-Dubreton in his *La vie d'Alexandre Dumas père,*[16] in its English version *Alexandre Dumas the fourth musketeer,*[17] relates how, in October 1862, Dumas had received a letter from the Greco-Albanian Council in London asking him to do for Athens and Constantinople what he had done with Garibaldi for Palermo and Naples. The letter was signed by the Prince of Scanderberg. Two more letters came, addressed "My dear Marquis", and, according to Lucas-Dubreton, Dumas proved gullible enough at this stage to offer his yacht *Emma* to the 'Prince' for the transport of ammunition. Then, one fine day, the Chief of Police of Naples sent for Dumas and told him that the pseudo-Prince was a trickster and intriguer.

In his book *Dumas Father and Son,*[18] Francis Gribble states that Scanderberg's real name was Del Prato, and that he was the son of an Italian carpenter. In 1859 he had served a sentence of six months imprisonment for fraud. He had come to Paris fully expecting to be safe there, as he knew that the police archives had been burnt during the Commune. He had prospered from the sale of the insignia of a fictitious 'Order of the Commander of Christ'. When the police found out who he was and came to arrest him, they found that he had been warned in time and had disappeared safely into Spain.

I wrote to Francis Gribble asking him whether he could give me any information concerning the manuscript of *Les âmes vaillantes* about which Scanderberg had spoken to Dumas, fils. He replied that the information about the Scanderberg episode had been taken from an article published many years ago in *Le Temps,* but he could not remember the exact date; he added that there was certainly no information about that missing play. I have diligently searched the files of *Le Temps* from the 1870s onwards and cannot find any such article; one may have appeared earlier, but I doubt even this. It may be, of course, that Francis Gribble had been mistaken and was, in fact, referring to an article in some other journal, but, even so, in my research I have never found any reference to *Les âmes vaillantes* in any French periodical published in the 19th century.

Dumas, of course, washed his hands of the whole affair. But did he pass on the manuscript of *Les âmes vaillantes,* and could it have been *Pietro Tasca,* to 'Scanderberg'? The absence of the first sheet is in keeping, for 'Scanderberg' would be very likely to destroy this if he had proposed selling the manuscript; to leave it might have been dangerous if others knew of Dumas' gift and to whom it went.

And now for further proof that this is, indeed, an unknown play by Dumas, whether it be entitled *Les âmes vaillantes* or *Pietro Tasca.* The sheets of blue paper are certainly one indication of its authenticity. Moreover, the writing has all the characteristics and tricks of penmanship that belong to Dumas—he has numbered the sheets of each act separately (but not individual tableaux where there is more than one in each act); that is, each act begins afresh on page 1, the sequence being continued until its conclusion. This manner of pagination is frequently to be noted in his drama manuscripts.

Again, and not an uncommon thing with Dumas, in the haste of writing he has forgotten the exact chosen designation of one character and another, even making the change in the middle of an act, thus explaining why there is no list of characters; this could be an indication of temporary cessation of work or of a draft, and it may also be the result of the influence of the writing of romances concurrently with dramas, the former gaining by the variation of their designations. In the manuscript

there are many turns of expression which are constantly to be met with in his work. There is the noted peculiarity of one speaker repeating part, or even the whole, of another's words; this is an extremely characteristic tendency and one so easily made irritating, but which Dumas' genius not only carried off satisfactorily but also frequently turned to masterly effect.

Another common habit in this drama is to marshal phrases or expressions in twos, threes, and even fours. So, too, at the conclusion of act III, the Mask's words: "Adieu, if you speak the truth, au revoir if you lie" may be connected with not a few Dumas phrases, of which perhaps the most famous is the conclusion to *Le vicomte de Bragelonne:* "Athos, Porthos, au revoir; Aramis, adieu for ever".

Passing, then, from what may be regarded as proofs of Dumas' skilful mechanism, I come to the more literary indications. The characters are for the most part essentially of the type beloved by him, including a mysterious masked man (how fond Dumas was of masked executioners; two other examples are provided in **"The three musketeers"** and in the drama **Cromwell et Charles 1er,** Paris, Marchant, 1835), and a woman who must atone for her guilt in such a way that it will be condoned by the audience. There are any number of clever situations and arresting scenes such as he excelled in, and I will mention but one of a dozen—the powerful opening scene played in a dim light and with no word spoken.

From his first dramatic efforts Dumas made a point of including in his most moving and tragic pieces an occasional lighter touch. In this play there is the conversation between some women and a sacristan, and in the trial scene the naïve and kindly evidence given by the character Felice. Dumas was always careful not to overdo these breaks in the poignancy, unlike Hugo, who often carried them to lengths of farce.

What, then, is the manuscript's true history, and why was it that it never came to be printed or published? The key to the puzzle may be somewhere among Dumas' lesser articles or in an unpublished 'causerie'.

I hold the firm belief that any Dumas manuscript of rarity and importance such as this should belong to France, and so I passed it to the late Jacques Guignard, Conservateur en Chef of the Bibliothèque de l'Arsenal, and now, handsomely bound, it is in that library.

Notes

[1] *Théâtre complet de Alex. Dumas* (Paris, 1874), (1)-34.

[2] *Alexandre Dumas, 1802-1870. Sa Vie Intime. Ses Œuvres* (Paris, 1902), p. 107.

[3] *Les supercheries littéraires dévoillées* (Paris, 1847), p. 426.

[4] Op. cit., p. 20.

[5] (Paris, 1863), iv. chap. cviii, p. 267.

[6] *Revue Biblio-Iconographique,* 6e année (1899), 3e Série, pp. 10-11.

[7] Op. cit., p. 173.

[8] Paris, 1861, vol. 1.

[9] Op. cit., p. 15.

[10] Op. cit., 2e *[sic]* année (1899), 3e série, p. 515.

[11] Op. cit., 6e année (1899), 3e série, p. 7.

[12] Ibid., p. 15.

[13] *Alexandre Dumas Aujourd'hui* (Paris, 1867), p. 22.

[14] *Alexandre Dumas en Manches de Chemise* (Paris, 1884), p. 16.

[15] *Revue Biblio-Iconographique,* 6e année (1899), 3e série, p. 15.

[16] Paris, 1927, *Vie des hommes illustres,* No. 14, pp. 209-12.

[17] Translated from the French of J. Lucas-Dubreton by Maida Castelman Darnton (London, 1929), pp. 232-36.

[18] London, 1930, pp. 162-65.

Don MacLennan (essay date 1988)

SOURCE: "Metastasis; or Dumas, Joyce and the Dark Avenger," in *English Studies in Africa: A Journal of the Humanities* 31, No. 2, 1988, pp. 119-27.

[*In the following essay, MacLennan identifies evidence of* The Count of Monte Cristo's *influence on* A Portrait of the Artist as a Young Man *by James Joyce.*]

> The count bowed, and stepped back. "Do you refuse?" said Mercédès, in a tremulous voice. "Pray, excuse me, madame," replied Monte Cristo, "but I never eat Muscatel grapes."[1]

It is obvious that Joyce read and digested Dumas's novel **The Count of Monte Cristo,** and that he selected

Monte Cristo (Edmond Dantès) as an archetypal hero, a model on which the unheroic Stephen[2] initially models his personality and whom he unconsciously adopts as a catalyst for his ultimate rebellion. Both novels are about revenge: Dumas's lengthily, Joyce's concisely and anti-climactically, as nobody in the novel takes any real notice of the "fearful Jesuit".[3] Monte Cristo has no difficulty with primary action; Stephen is presented as finding primary action (sex, politics and sport) distasteful and not in keeping with his or the novel's aesthetics.

It is, of course, standard practice for writers to use, criticize, bounce off, or improve on earlier texts (especially if those texts are a trifle inferior) as Shakespeare did in *A Midsummer Night's Dream.* Jane Austen dumped *The Mysteries of Udolpho* into the scouring vats of her art; and J. M. Coetzee has used an eighteenth-century novel as the matrix of his deconstruction of it. The phenomenon of intertextuality is not new: it may even be subsumable under a general notion of translation, the art of re-creating a text from a text in another language or from another age. Such use of texts by writers is, perhaps, another way of stressing the suggestive power or *latah* [a Malay word meaning "infinite suggestiveness", according to Anthony Burgess, *Earthly Powers* (Harmondsworth, 1982), p. 236.] of tradition, where the present is what it is by virtue of the deep layers of what has already been written. This does not mean that all writers will plunder texts in the same way or for the same reasons.

There has been a great deal of research focusing on intertextuality in Joyce. The earliest was Stuart Gilbert's.[4] The first five chapters of his book are a veritable mine of suggestions about Joyce's sources. Z. R. Bowen's *Musical Allusions in the Works of James Joyce*[5] is crucial for a full understanding of musico-poetic resonances of Joyce's texts. M. Reynolds's *Joyce and Dante: The Shaping Imagination*[6] and W. H. Schutte's *Joyce and Shakespeare*[7] are seminal works of explication. And no serious reader of Joyce can afford to not read H. Kenner's *Dublin's Joyce*[8] and *Flaubert, Joyce and Beckett: The Stoic Comedians.*[9] Joyce did, after all, prophesy that he would keep scholars busy for centuries to come.

In Joyce's novel, the young Stephen admires heroes like Napoleon, and has read **The Count of Monte Cristo.** His heroes are of crucial importance to him in his childhood where he can actually be a kind of hero, as when he complains to the Rector about his unjust punishment by Father Dolan for breaking his glasses. Through his courage he proves the falsity of the Prefect's claim that he is a "lazy idle loafer" and becomes a true hero for the boys of his class.

Stephen has grown up surrounded by talk of heroes, especially Irish ones like Parnell, and it does not take much to see that the drift of Joyce's novel is a transformation of Stephen from being a boyish hero, through the temptation to be a hero of religion (like Loyola), to becoming a hero of art (like Byron). That Joyce evolved Stephen as a progression of shed roles is not in dispute. That implicit texts or scenarios are inextricable from the presentation and development of character is also not in dispute. The focus of this paper is rather on the proleptic scenarios of Joyce's novels that are to be found in Dumas's. It is not an original claim that Joyce was an habitual imitator and parodist, but a comparison of the two novels does show, strikingly, how Joyce culled some of the comestibles for his metastatic process and made them artistically significant.

Edmond Dantès, returning from an arduous sea voyage and on the point of marrying his beloved Mercédès, becomes a victim of an elaborate frame-up. He is arrested and taken off to the island prison of the Château d'If, where he remains for fourteen years. Most of these years are spent in solitary confinement, until the day he decides to tunnel his way out to freedom and finds himself in the cell of the Abbé Faria. In the Abbé he discovers a spiritual father: the Abbé is an aristocrat, fabulously wealthy, a scientist, a linguist, an incorrigible inventor ("old artificer"), and a wise and pious Christian imprisoned for his political opposition to the regime. He is far from mad, and educates Edmond, pouring his vast and universal knowledge into the young man. The Abbé is truly the Daedalus to Edmond's Icarus.

The parallel to *A Portrait* is immediately apparent. First of all, the aunt with the unusual name, Dante,[10] suggests that Stephen's lineage is connected with that of Edmond Dantès. Stephen arrives at consciousness after a blameless voyage in the amniotic sea, declares innocently that he is going to marry Eileen, and is immediately castigated and told to "apologise". His first contrary experiences in life are thus sexual repression and religious guilt: subsequently he never can disentangle mortal and venial sin. Stephen is incarcerated in the Château d'If of self and guilt. Catholic Ireland keeps his spirit bound. His freedom is curtailed, and for fourteen years, from going to school to leaving university, he is a prisoner in his body, Dublin, and Ireland ("the old sow that eats her farrow"—*P.*, p. 208), with no immediate prospect of escape. His life is centred on the conviction that he must get free, "fly by those nets" (*P.*, p. 207) and escape the "sentinels". Adumbrating the new aesthetic of *A Portrait* the dying Abbé says to Edmond,

> . . . philosophy, as I understand it, is reducible to no rules by which it can be learned; it is the amalgamation of all the sciences, the golden cloud which bears the soul to heaven. (*M.C.,* p. 144)

Stephen learns nothing of the rules of life, only how to argue Aristotle's aesthetics and Aquinas's theology. Like Edmond he lurches blindly on, "exhaust[s] all human resources; and then [he] turn[s] to God" (*M.C.,* p. 109). For years Stephen is bemused, if not seduced, by the image of the priesthood, and he too "turns to God" when his life becomes intolerably confused and guilt-ridden. However, his appointed task in the novel is to transcend religion and escape from its clutches as Edmond Dantès escapes from the Château d'If. This is an artistic if not a psychological paradox: that we should live by changing places with the dead.

During his captivity Edmond wishes to die, but when he meets the Abbé he experiences a sudden surge of optimism:

> . . . the sight of an old man clinging to life with so desperate a courage, gave a fresh turn to his ideas, and inspired him with new courage and energy. (*M.C.,* p. 126)

But in Joyce's novel there are no universal men like the Abbé, only fragmented and inadequate men, in itself evidence of "Irish paralysis".

Edmond is the child of the Abbé's captivity. Like the celibate priests who educate Stephen and cram him with knowledge, the Abbé is Edmond's spiritual father. He says to Edmond:

> My profession condemns me to celibacy. God has sent you to me to console, at one and the same time, the man who could not be a father and the prisoner who could not get free. (*M.C.,* p. 162)

The celibate priests, too, would have Stephen believe that he will be heir to the fabulous treasures of Heaven, as Edmond will be heir to the Abbé's immense treasures hidden in the cave on the island of Monte Cristo.

As Edmond escapes by changing places with his spiritual father, so Stephen escapes his predicament by assuming the role of the poet-priest of "the eternal imagination" and supplanting his biological father with a father of his own conception. Only then is Stephen ready for the Fall into Life, and his Fall recalls Edmond's as he is hurled in a shroud from the walls of the Château:

> Dantès felt himself flung into the air like a wounded bird, falling, falling, falling with a rapidity that made his blood curdle . . . it seemed to him as if the time were a century. At last, with a terrific dash, he entered the ice-cold water, and as he did so he uttered a shrill cry . . . (*M.C.,* p. 175)

This episode foreshadows the one where the young Stephen is nudged into the slimy ditch (*P.*, p. 21) and also the episode that culminates in the epiphany of the young men swimming: "Cripes, I'm drownded" (*P.*, p. 173). Stephen's fall into reality, his baptism in life, makes his need to escape Ireland more urgent, for the life he is enmeshed in proves to be a nightmare from which he is trying to awake.[11] Home, family and Ireland become irrelevant as he prepares to fly away to Paris, the city, incidentally, where Edmond completes his revenge.

A Portrait is the story of a young man in revolt against his father and all those things his father represents—family, religion and politics. As jejune hero he struggles painfully through from childhood to adolescence, but his final victory is Pyrrhic because he remains "a cold fish". Stephen is not a romantic hero, for a romantic hero is one who is capable of primary action, like Byron and Monte Cristo. Stephen is an imprisoned sensibility through which shadows, analogues and epiphanies pass to be recorded on his *tabula rasa*. The method of the novel is, therefore, a progressive series of revelations, and of accumulating motifs, echoes and analogues. The mind of the hero, the would-be artist, discovers order in and imposes order on the chaotic manifold of experience. But Stephen is not Monte Cristo, or Napoleon or Byron or Milton's Satan because he cannot act in the real world. His growth is merely a sloughing off of progressively outworn shrouds or disguises. And where

the novel increases in richness and resonance, Stephen himself becomes more of an absence.

Monte Cristo, then, proves more than a role: he is an informing archetype of an escaped prisoner, who returns dazzlingly to life. In *A Portrait* the reader alone has access to the novel's dazzling plunge into life, only to watch (as is the case in Dumas's novel) the hero himself quietly withdraws into obscurity.

When Monte Cristo entertains two of his acquaintances on his bark, he gives one of them, Franz, a spoonful of hashish to eat. Reality melts away and Franz flies off on the viewless wings of hallucination. Edmond, now known to all as the Count of Monte Cristo, says to him:

> Well, unfurl your wings and fly into superhuman regions; fear nothing, there is a watch over you; and if your wings, like those of Icarus, melt before the sun, we are here to receive you. (*M.C.,*p. 288)

This is how Dumas describes Franz's experience:

> His body seemed to acquire an airy lightness, his perception brightened in a remarkable manner, his senses seemed to redouble their power, the horizon continued to expand; but it was not that gloomy horizon . . . but a blue, transparent, unbounded horizon, with all the blue of the ocean, all the spangles of the sun . . . then, in the midst of the songs of his sailors,—songs so clear and sounding, that they would have made a divine harmony had their notes been taken down,—he saw the Isle of Monte Cristo . . . (*M.C.,*p. 288)

Franz's experience with hashish is compared by Dumas to a vision of Aladdin's cave, to "shadows of the magic lantern". It is this island cave that Joyce refers to specifically in the following paragraphs:

> His evenings were his own; and he pored over a ragged translation of **The Count of Monte Cristo.** The figure of that dark avenger stood forth in his mind for whatever he had heard or divined in childhood of the strange and terrible. At night he built up on the parlour table an image of the wonderful island cave out of transfers and paper flowers and coloured tissue paper and strips of the silver and golden paper in which chocolate is wrapped. When he had broken up this scenery, weary of its tinsel, there would come to his mind the bright picture of Marseilles, of sunny trellises and of Mercedes.

> Outside Blackrock, on the road that led to the mountains, stood a small whitewashed house in the garden of which grew many rose-bushes: and in this house, he told himself, another Mercedes lived. Both on the outward and on the homeward journey he measured distance by this landmark: and in his imagination he lived through a long train of adventures, marvellous as those in the

LE COMTE
DE

MONTE-CRISTO

PAR

M. ALEXANDRE DUMAS

TOME PREMIER

L.T.P

PARIS

LEGRAND, TROUSSEL ET POMEY, LIBRAIRES-ÉDITEURS

48, RUE MONSIEUR-LE-PRINCE, 48

Près le Luxembourg

book itself, towards the close of which there appeared an image of himself, grown older and sadder, standing in a moonlit garden with Mercedes who had so many years before slighted his love, and with a sadly proud gesture of refusal, saying:

—Madam, I never eat muscatel grapes. (*P.,*p. 64)

The description of Franz's state of sublime euphoria is suggestive of Stephen's own when he sees the Bird Girl standing in the water:

A girl stood before him in midstream, alone and still, gazing out to sea. She seemed like one whom magic had changed into the likeness of a strange and beautiful seabird. Her long slender bare legs were delicate as a crane's and pure save where an emerald trail of seaweed had fashioned itself as a sign upon the flesh. Her thighs, fuller and softhued as ivory, were bared almost to the hips, where the white fringes of her drawers were like feathering of soft white down. Her slateblue skirts were kilted boldly about her waist and dovetailed behind her. Her bosom was a bird's, soft and slight, slight and soft as the breast of some dark-plumaged dove. But her long fair hair was girlish: and girlish, and touched with the wonder of mortal beauty, her face. (*P.,*p. 175)

Also echoed in this passage is the mute passion of Valentine communicating with the stricken Noirtier, a rich analogue of the unspoken and longed for passion that the Bird Girl communicates to Stephen:

Valentine, by means of her love, her patience, and her devotion, had learned to read in Noirtier's look all the varied feelings which were passing in his mind. To this dumb language, which was so unintelligible to others, she answered by throwing her whole soul into the expression of the countenance, and in this manner were the conversations sustained between the blooming girl and the helpless invalid, whose body could scarcely be called a living one, but who, nevertheless, possessed a fund of knowledge and penetration, united with a will as powerful as ever, although clogged by a body rendered utterly incapable of obeying its impulses. Valentine had solved this strange problem, and was able easily to understand his thoughts, and to convey her own in return. (*M.C.,*p. 596)

Stephen has no female to respond to his deep need. Even the fictional Count has in his protection an exquisite and sensual Greek girl whom he rescued but with whom he has no sexual relations.

Franz wakes:

The vision had entirely fled, and as if the statues had been but shadows coming from their tomb during his dream they vanished at his waking . . . He found that he was in a grotto, went towards the opening, and through a kind of fanlight saw a blue

sea and an azure sky. The air and water were shining in the beams of the morning sun . . . (*M.C.,*p. 289)

This is echoed in *A Portrait.* Stephen is prisoner in his vile body as Edmond is prisoner in the Château d'If; his soul longs to be free, to move into the sun. Edmond's grotto is the cave of art, alluring and beautiful, a temporary refuge from the life of the world.

Earlier in the novel the Abbé warns Edmond with a piece of Platonic recall or prevision:

I see it in the depths of the inner cavern. (*M.C.,*p. 166)

Physical escape is not enough, is only a beginning. There must also be some guarantee that the hero has achieved inner harmony and purpose, otherwise he is simply lugging his burdens about with him. Joyce's interpretation of the Abbé's proleptic vision is that art, too, is a prison, just as the world is a prison.

There is no doubt in Dumas's novel about the real actions performed by Edmond, whereas in *A Portrait* Stephen is trapped in the chronic inaction of Ireland where there seem to be no debates worth having and no heroic actions to be performed.

Yet Stephen, like Monte Cristo, becomes "the dark avenger" (*P.,*p. 64), the "Avenging Angel" (*M.C.,*p. 354). He has his revenge on society by outwardly complying with everything it wants and yet going his own way; by transcending the national obsessions with sport, alcohol, sex, history, religion, kinetic art, and politics. Where Monte Cristo's friends sip Lacryma Christi, Ireland is drowned in a lacrymose Catholicism. Stephen would like to see himself as an incognito, secret agent of revenge, an elusive, intellectual scourge, an *enfant terrible.* But he takes his revenge on the whole of his society in "silence, exile and cunning", and becomes the artist, the "priest of the eternal imagination, transmuting the daily bread of experience into the radiant body of everliving life" (*P.,*p. 225). His revenge on life is to turn life into literature. Only his schoolfellows seem to realize just how much posturing is involved, for the paradox remains that even though he plans to escape Ireland and revenge himself on the "priest-ridden race", he remains an unemployed Irish Catholic artist-priest. In this painful charade Stephen has become the cold, bloodless antithesis of a romantic hero:

" . . . do you think the count is really what he appears to be?" "What does he appear to be?"

"I really do look upon him as one of Byron's heroes whom Misery has marked with a fatal brand; some Manfred, some Lara, some Werther, one of those wrecks, as it were, of some ancient family, who, disinherited of their patrimony, have achieved one by force of their adventurous genius which has placed them above the laws of society . . . he is a being returned from the other world." (*M.C.*, pp. 421-22)

In his flight from reality, Stephen is comforted by the idea of a secret purpose, by the belief that he is "born to serve" the world as an outsider, an artist, an agent of Providence. The cost of this is, once again, anticipated by Dumas:

> 'Listen,—I have always heard tell of Providence, and yet I have never seen him, nor anything that resembles him, or which can make me believe that he exists. I wish to be Providence myself, for I feel that the most beautiful, noblest, most sublime thing in the world, is to recompense and punish.' Satan bowed his head and groaned. 'You mistake,' he said; 'Providence does exist, only you have never seen him, because the child of God is as invisible as the parent. You have seen nothing that resembles him, because he works by secret springs and moves by hidden ways. All I can do for you is to make you one of the agents of that Providence.' The bargain was concluded. "I may sacrifice my soul, but what matters it?" added Monte Cristo. "If the thing were to do again, I would again do it." (*M.C.*, p. 496)

Dumas catches here Monte Cristo's sense of ennui as the awareness sets in that his plans for revenge are actually working out faultlessly, and that it is no longer exciting to be an agent of Providence because he is acting from habit rather than from inspiration or desire.

In *A Portrait,* Stephen grows up assailed from both within and without. From without the attack is familial and social. The inner pressure on Stephen is desire, and he vacillates between natural desire and unnatural suppression of that desire through self-discipline and Loyola's spiritual exercises. Desire pushes him into life and into art, and art finally lifts him beyond desire. Stephen, Joyce is careful to point out, is not fulfilled. Like Noirtier, Stephen is struggling against a sensory handicap. Dumas might well be describing here a French equivalent of "Irish paralysis":

> Noirtier was sitting in an arm-chair, which moved upon castors, in which he was wheeled into the room in the morning, and in the same way drawn out again at night. He was placed before a large glass, which reflected the whole apartment, and permitted him to see, without any attempt to move, which would have been impossible, all who entered the room, and everything which was going on around him. Noirtier, although almost as immovable and helpless as a corpse looked at the new-comers with a quick and intelligent expression, perceiving at once, by their ceremonious courtesy, that they were come on business of an unexpected and official character. Sight and hearing were the only senses

remaining, and they appeared left, like two solitary sparks, to animate the miserable body which seemed fit for nothing but the grave; it was only, however, by means of one of these senses that he could reveal the thoughts and feelings which still worked in his mind, and the look by which he gave expression to this inner life resembled one of those distant lights which are sometimes seen in perspective by the benighted traveller whilst crossing some cheerless desert, apprising him that there is still one human being who, like himself, is keeping watch amidst the silence and obscurity of night. (*M.C.*, p. 595)

There are other parallels between Dumas's and Joyce's novels, but to conclude let me refer to one more of the main parallels. Dumas's novel is about a protracted revenge for an original sin. Monte Cristo, finally confronting Mercédès after so many years, claims:

> "I, betrayed, sacrificed, buried, have risen from my tomb, by the Grace of God, to punish that man." (*M.C.*, p. 885)

But he weakens, will not revenge himself on Mercédès's son because he is still in love with Mercédès. His only course of action is to disappear sadly from the world, empty handed:

> "Death is about to return to the tomb, the phantom to retire in darkness." (*M.C.*, p. 887)

Betrayal, sacrifice, death, resurrection, ascension—the life of Christ is also, ironically, a model for both novels. Stephen might well have used the renunciatory words of the saddened Count after he has refused to revenge himself on Mercédès's son:

> "No, it is not existence, then, that I regret, but the ruin of my projects, so slowly carried out, so laboriously framed." (*M.C.*, p. 889)

Eileen is denied the young Stephen; the hooded girl on the steps of the tram eludes his grasp (*P.*, p. 71). Stephen cannot obtain the love of a woman. The artist is doomed to make the "proud gesture of refusal": "Pray, excuse me, madame, but I never eat Muscatel grapes."

Notes

[1] A. Dumas, *The Count of Monte Cristo* (first published in French in 1845) (London, 1968), p. 700. Further references to this work will be made in the text (*M.C.*).

[2] In *A Portrait of the Artist as a Young Man* (London, 1966). All references are to this edition and will be given in the text (*P.*).

[3] As Mulligan calls him in Chapter 1 of *Ulysses*.

[4] S. Gilbert, *James Joyce's "Ulysses"* (London, 1930).

[5] New York, 1975.

[6] Princeton, 1981.

[7] New Haven, 1957.

[8] Bloomington, 1956.

[9] Boston, 1963.

[10] Mrs Dante Riordan, who taught him geography.

[11] *Ulysses* (New York, 1934), p. 35.

A. Craig Bell (essay date 1988)

SOURCE: Foreword to *Fernande: The Story of a Courtesan,* by Alexandre Dumas, translated by A. Craig Bell, Robert Hale, 1988, pp. 5-8.

[*In the following essay, Bell provides a brief examination of the influences behind* Fernande, *Dumas's story of an upper-class prostitute.*]

To the reader who knows only the Dumas of the historical romances this naturalistic novel of contemporary Parisian society with a courtesan as its 'heroine' will come as a surprise, and he will almost certainly wonder as to the reasons for his writing it. A brief explanation, then.

In 1842 Dumas wrote his second[1], and one of his best, historical romances, namely *Le Chevalier d'Harmental* (better known in England as *The Conspirators*) after which, surprisingly, between that year and 1844 (year of the ever-famous *Les Trois Mousquetaires*) he wrote no less than seven novels of which three are historical romances, and negligible,[2] and four novels of contemporary life which are by no means negligible.[3] Of these latter, *Fernande* is by far the greatest. Written in 1843 it was occasioned by the publishers of a work to be given the title of *La Grande Ville* and planned as a study of Paris and its society, who approached Dumas with a request for a contribution dealing with the shadier aspects of them. The result was the atonishing article *Filles, Lorettes et Courtisanes,* undertaken as he tells us in the preface, 'reluctantly, and only because no one else dared.'

In the course of his researches into this class of women he discovered that a surprisingly large number had been led to take up their sordid way of life after having been seduced while young and inexperienced by older men, and in many cases had come from respectable and even aristocratic families. This fact led him to consider making just such a woman the centrepiece of a novel, and from this idea he created Fernande—a woman who had come from an aristocratic family, had

received a good education and showed talent in art and music. But seduced and betrayed by a comrade-in-arms of her dead father who had asked him to take his place and be her 'guardian', and left alone and unbefriended to live as best she could, in a kind of desperate revenge on herself and society for her degradation she makes herself a high-class courtesan. And this life of hectic factitious gaiety is led by her until she meets the young, rich, handsome Baron Maurice de Barthèle. Forestalling by a decade the similar situation and affair of Armand Duval and Marguerite Gautier in his son's *La Dame aux Camélias* (in the preface to his novel Dumas *fils* acknowledges his debt to his father's creation), Fernande falls deeply in love with him as he with her although he is married, becomes his mistress and for his sake puts her former way of life behind her. With what result the novel narrates. In Dumas's own words:

> Our story is not so much a narrative of events as a drama of analysis. It is a moral autopsy we are undertaking. And just as in the soundest body there is some organic lesion through which sooner or later death strikes, so the noblest hearts hide secret weaknesses which serve to remind us that man is a compound of noble sentiments and petty actions.

While the courtesan Fernande is the keystone of the narrative, the other characters are drawn with consummate skill—in particular Madame de Barthèle with her goodness of heart and unorganised mind; while the waspish Madame de Neuilly is delineated with the observation and acidity of Jane Austen or Trollope.

In fact, the novel is a revelation of a new facet of Dumas's genius; and that it is authentic Dumas and not by any other hand is manifest to anyone who has read his sixty-odd novels to any extent. Every page is stamped with his style. Furthermore there is a sure and certain imprint to be found in the discussion (typically French, this) over Madame de Barthèle's luncheon table on the state of contemporary art, music and literature in the course of which, replying to Madame de Neuilly's horror at her (Fernande's) confessed admiration of Shakespeare: 'That barbarian,' Fernande replies, 'That barbarian is the being who has created the most after God,' and goes on to tell her that all women should have a cult of gratitude to him for his creation of the most admirable types of their sex in Desdemona, Miranda and Ophelia.

Dumas was proud of his Shakespearian dictum, which became famous, and which he was to repeat in his *Mes Mémoires* (1852-55). To savour to the full the allusion and atmosphere the reader should know that until the visit to Paris in 1827 of the English Shakespearean company under Kemble, in the minds of the French theatre-minded public and critics the Bard was indeed regarded as the 'barbarian' of Voltaire. But to the young militant Romantics Shakespeare completed a literary revolution begun by Scott and Byron. Two more than the rest were moved and inspired by the English players' performances: one was Alexandre Dumas, the other Hector Berlioz. The latter was so far carried away and so desperately in love with the Irish actress Henrietta Smithson, that he was said to have declared, 'I will marry Juliet and write my greatest symphony on the play!'[4] Dumas wrote differently but equally ecstatically: 'Imagine a man blind from birth suddenly receiving the gift of sight and discovering a whole world of which he had no idea existed . . . I realised that Shakespeare's works contained as much variety as the works of all the other playwrights combined, and recognised that next to the Creator himself, he had created more than any other being. . . . '

Later he was quoted as saying, 'I owe every Englishman a debt of gratitude for Scott, Byron and Shakespeare.' English readers should surely be grateful to the French writer for those words.

Notes

[1] His first was *Acté,* set in the time of Nero.

[2] Viz. *Sylvandire, Ascanio* and *Cécile.*

[3] Viz. *Georges, Amaury, Gabriel Lambert* and *Fernande.*

[4] Five years later, in fact, Harriet was married to Berlioz.

Renee Winegarten (essay date 1991)

SOURCE: "Alexandre Dumas: Fact and Fiction," in *New Criterion,* Vol. 9, No. 9, May, 1991, pp. 32-9.

[*In the following essay, Winegarten assesses Dumas's career and writings from a late-twentieth-century perspective, taking into account the changing standards in the evaluation of the author's work.*]

If reading is a vice that goes unpunished, as the poet has it, then Alexandre Dumas *père* (1802-1870) offers one of the principal means of access to that form of depravity for devotees too numerous to mention. Throughout the world, how many have tasted for the first time the refined pleasures, the ecstasies and thrills of reading, in *The Three Musketeers* and its sequels, or *The Count of Monte-Cristo*? How many have ventured to own that it was Dumas senior who set their feet on the primrose path, not just of dalliance, but of extremely serious liaisons with other novelists in the loftiest realms of literature? André Malraux, visiting Cayenne in his role as minister of culture, remembered a novel he had read as a small boy, Dumas's *Georges,* the adventures of a half-French mulatto with a will of steel who led a revolt against the British in the Caribbean. Malraux remarked elsewhere that he

had passed when young from *The Three Musketeers* to Balzac, implying a kind of progress to higher things.

There, the word "judgment" is out. Malraux was far from alone in suggesting that Dumas was not a figure of the first order. It has long been customary to look askance at that prodigiously prolific writer: his early historical importance as a dramatist is readily admitted in manuals of literature, but his novels do not usually form part of the syllabus like those of Mérimée, Stendhal, or Balzac. All the same, Mérimée (who—like Dumas—also wrote historical fiction) said that he admired Dumas more than Sir Walter Scott, the doyen of historical novelists. Certainly, Dumas is greater fun: he does not linger over description or preachment, and he is very rarely tedious.

Can Dumas be mentioned in the same breath with Balzac (who started out by writing lurid adventure stories but moved on afterwards)? Certainly, Dumas did not think of himself as an "artist," sacrificing life to perfection in art in the manner of Flaubert. On the contrary, his contemporaries saw him as an elemental force, and he was intent on living life to the full. Claude Schopp, the noted authority on Dumas, rightly subtitles his biography of a man who was large in every sense, "the genius of life."[1] As for Dumas—surprising as it must seem nowadays— he considered himself to be a disciple of "the realist school" of Aeschylus and Shakespeare. He called himself a humanist and a popularizing novelist. "I am movement and life," he declared. Verve and vigor were certainly among his supreme qualities.

There may be a change in Dumas's post-humous fate, possibly because greater consideration is now being given to popular aspects of writing or culture in general, if not always with sensible results. Moreover, pressure is being exerted to eliminate so-called elitism or discrimination when discussing all forms of creativity. Perhaps certain elements in Dumas's work carry a charge that is in accord with current modes and moods, and especially with a taste for melodrama. (Has that taste ever been totally eliminated? Even great works, especially in the realm of opera, contain more than a modicum of melodrama.) It would appear that Dumas is actually enjoying a revival of sorts. In any case, he has always occupied a secret alcove in the hearts of lovers of pure narrative and narrative skills, and admirers of generosity of spirit.

Not so long ago, Dumas's play *Antony* (1831), which was a huge success in its own day, would have seemed unactable on the modern stage. Yet it was presented (in translation) in the spring of 1990 at the famous Citizens' Theatre, Glasgow, and was found to be worthwhile and highly enjoyable. It was, however, surely a serious mistake to move the setting from the 1830s to the 1880s. The current mania of stage directors for moving dramas and operas out of their historical context is often a token of laziness, conceit, or condescension toward the public. ***Antony*** encapsulates the spirit of the early 1830s. The reason why the play made so deep an impression in 1831 was because it depicted the passionate relationship between a man and a woman "realistically," that is, in contemporary speech, dress, and manners, without classical decorum or historical remoteness. The play's success also owed a great deal, as Dumas himself generously owned, to the talents of Marie Dorval and Pierre Bocage, who displayed a "natural" or unrhetorical style of acting that took Paris by storm and made their reputation as Romantic actors *par excellence.*

Antony, the doomed young Byronic hero or anti-hero, is illegitimate, and can discover nothing about his parentage. Thus, although he is superior in every way to the gilded youth of the age, he can have no place in good society. He rebels and rails against its conventions and prejudices. The damage done to his personality is manifest. What might be called the existential anguish caused by his non-status is exacerbated by his despair at the social impossibility of his union with Adèle, the woman he loves, who has been obliged to suppress her passion for him in a loveless marriage to the respectable Colonel d'Hervey.

The lovers meet again after the passage of years: Adèle now has a child; she reluctantly repulses Antony, and takes flight. At an inn on her route, whither he has pursued her, he takes her by force in a jealous frenzy. Their secret liaison becomes known in society, where only casual affairs (as distinct from grand passions) are commonplace. When the absent husband is at the door, Antony stabs Adèle as she herself wishes, in order to preserve her reputation. "She resisted me, I killed her!" cries Antony, throwing his dagger at the Colonel's feet. Curtain. Antony knows that he will be executed for her murder. The new theme of 1831 was middle-class adultery, regarded as an extremely serious matter, because it affected money and inheritance. Dumas was quite as much interested in money, or rather wealth, as Balzac, whom he regarded as his rival.

On the face of it, there would seem to be little in ***Antony*** to occupy a modern audience. The play was, as Dumas said, "a love scene in five acts." Nonetheless, Antony's revolt against social prejudice and society in general, his race to sexual gratification, the conflict in Adèle between being true to her passion and obedience to ideas of family, convention, and convenience—these have not altogether lost their force, as the welcome accorded to the Glasgow production made plain. Nor has Dumas's dramatic urgency, as he hurtles his prose drama along, despite the ill-timed tirade on the aim of modern theater being to reveal the human heart in all its nakedness.

When Dumas wrote the play he was in the throes of his passion for the writer Mélanie Waldor (married to a military man by whom she had a daughter). He gave his own retrospective sexual jealousy to Antony. All this, together with Dumas's curious ancestry (about which more will have to be said), made him declare that he was Antony minus the murder, as Mélanie was Adèle minus the flight. In a poem which he said was written two years before the play, and which he appended to it as a preface, Dumas cried, "Woe, woe to me, cast by heaven into this world a stranger to its laws!" Adèle, too, alludes to Antony as one who seemed a "stranger" or outsider in the world. This was over a hundred years before Camus's novel *L'Etranger.* The wild tones that can be heard in the poem and the play are to be found in Dumas's frenzied letters to Mélanie Waldor. What now often seems to be role-playing or excess was actually the way people liked to address each other in that era.

At one remove, another play of Dumas's has been holding the boards recently in Paris and London. This is ***Kean, ou désordre et génie*** (1836), in the version made in 1953 by Jean-Paul Sartre at the request of the late Pierre Brasseur. A bravura performer, Brasseur had become internationally famous for his portrayal of the great Romantic actor Frédéric Lemaître in everybody's favorite French film, *Les Enfants du paradis.* Originally, Lemaître himself had taken a version of ***Kean*** by two hack writers to show to Dumas, who put life into it and transformed it into a striking vehicle for the noted thespian. As for Sartre, he was partial to melodrama and sought to revive it. He said he greatly loved Dumas, judging him to be an excellent novelist and the author of some very good plays.

Sartre kept to Dumas's outline and retained many of his predecessor's potent lines, while bringing to the subject his own existentialist preoccupations. In Dumas, Kean is the dissipated English actor of genius (who had died only a few years before), the social outcast in revolt against society, and the abuser of privilege in the Romantic manner. In Sartre's version the great actor turns into the existential "bastard," or, as Sartre expressed it, "this man who becomes an actor to elude his resentment against society, and who carries with him a kind of revolutionary force." In Paris in 1987 the role was taken with great acclaim by the film star Jean-Paul Belmondo, like Brasseur a bravura performer, in a lavish production. In London in 1990, in translation, it was again a huge popular success as played by Derek Jacobi, a sensitive and versatile actor though not by nature a bravura one. Sartre's existentialist game with the actor's lack of a sense of identity, when united with Dumas's exhilarating melodramatic plot, can prove a mixture difficult to resist in the theater.

Dumas had actually seen Kean himself, the great Shakespearian, perform in Paris; he also admired Kemble and Macready. Ever since, as a youth of seventeen, Dumas had attended a provincial performance of *Hamlet* in the pallid adaptation by Jean-François

Ducis, he worshiped Shakespeare and was mad about the theater. He made his name as a dramatist with historical plays, including ***Henri III et sa cour*** (1829), with its reminiscences of Shakespeare, Schiller, and Sir Walter Scott, a play that heralded the triumph of the French Romantic movement before its acknowledged dramatic advent with Victor Hugo's *Hernani.*

It was only afterwards that Dumas turned to writing novels, usually with the aid of a succession of collaborators, who included the helpful Auguste Macquet (or Augustus Mac Keat, as he liked to be known) and even the poet Gérard de Nerval. The wits used to refer to the enterprise as if it were a commercial firm, the House of Dumas and Company. Both ***The Three Musketeers*** and ***The Count of Monte-Cristo,*** for instance, were the work of Dumas and Macquet, though it would be difficult to see in them the presence of different hands—always supposing that the breathless reader could manage to stop to look for them. The two writers were often to be found working twelve hours a day, with at least two novels on the stocks at the same time. Indeed, when Dumas stood as a candidate in the elections of 1848, he put himself forward as "a worker," listing the sizable number of his works in justification of the title. According to him, these amounted to four hundred volumes and thirty-five dramas in twenty years. However, the electors decided not to revise their own more common notion of what constituted a proletarian and did not adopt him.

Not content with his huge output in fiction, Dumas often turned his novels into plays. It was common practice: George Sand took the same course (although, as Dumas thought, to less effect). Dumas employed collaborators and regurgitated his works in different genres because he needed money—for his mother, his wife, his children, his friends, all and sundry, including the extremely long line of his mistresses—though "line" inaccurately suggests succession rather than simultaneity. These last included numerous actresses, the opera singer Caroline Ungher (famous as Bellini's Norma and Donizetti's Parisina) and, in his declining years, the American Jewish equestrian performer Adah Isaacs Menken. Temperamentally, Dumas enjoyed the siege, but he was inclined to grow bored shortly after the surrender.

He lived extravagantly when he had money, ruining himself in building a château or mansion in various styles, including Gothic, Renaissance, and Moorish, with an English garden. He called it Monte-Cristo. It had a harem for his mistresses, and a menagerie of over two hundred animals. No fewer than six hundred friends were invited to the housewarming in July 1848, and there was always open house for numerous parasites. Dumas was wildly generous, and often in debt. "I have never refused money to anyone except to my creditors," he said once. It was the lordly attitude he gave to his Kean. The Count of Monte-Cristo himself, with his

fabulous inexhaustible wealth and the immense power it gives him, is the wish-fulfillment of a writer who dreamed of riches. Dumas made money enough but it slipped through his fingers.

The list of Dumas's works is daunting. It seems unlikely that anyone could have read them all. Here are no slim volumes in the refined manner of a Jane Austen, but novels each consisting of eight or ten tomes. Dumas belongs with those who produced in such quantity that quality and reputation inevitably suffer. Yet Baudelaire (critic as well as poet), while regarding Dumas's facility or "fearful dysentery" with disfavor, could not refrain from lauding the novelist's prodigious imagination: "this man . . . seems to represent universal vitality," he wrote. The sheer energy involved is breathtaking. Dumas lived in an age when writers were "geniuses," larger than life, incredibly productive and energetic (Victor Hugo, Balzac, George Sand).

Besides being a playwright and novelist, Dumas was one of the founders of modern journalism, at a time when the cheap popular press was being launched in France. He wrote about anything and everything: drama criticism (often padded out with lengthy quotations), reminiscences (occasionally improved by invention), lively accounts of his travels (he would be an indefatigable traveler—to Italy, Germany, England, Spain, Russia, North Africa, and elsewhere). Dumas even wrote on gastronomy and fashion. He founded papers of his own like the charmingly named *Le Mousquetaire, Le d'Artagnan, Le Monte-Cristo,* none of which enjoyed a long life. Never one to hide his light under a bushel, Dumas also claimed to have invented the *roman-feuilleton,* the novel published in the popular press in installments. If he did not invent it, he was certainly one of its most admired and sought-after practitioners. His fiction has survived much more readily than that of Eugène Sue, the once popular author of *The Mysteries of Paris* and *The Wandering Jew.*

His ambitions were vast—quite as vast as those of Balzac, who aimed to capture an entire society in all its aspects in a series of novels. "My first wish has no limit," said Dumas. "My first aspiration is always for the impossible." (He once contemplated writing a novel that began with Jesus and ended with the last man!) In effect, what he sought to do was to re-create the whole of French history and make it live in drama and fiction. Many around the world have acquired their first notions of French history from Dumas, just as they have gained their idea of American history from the cinema.

In the early nineteenth century, historical inquiry was seen as resolutely modern. Dumas might treat documents or memoirs in a cavalier fashion, but they provided the starting point for imaginative re-creation and inventiveness. From the fourteenth century he took the subject of what is perhaps his most famous play, ***La***

Tour de Nesle (1832), about the secret scandalous goings-on of Queen Marguerite de Bourgogne. Concealed under a mask, she makes a habit of having each young lover murdered after a single night of pleasure and the body thrown in the Seine. It is a satisfyingly lurid melodrama of hidden and mistaken identities, passion, power, intrigue, and incest. The French cinema in its heyday could hardly miss an opportunity to film such a subject.

Dumas contributed to the revival of interest in the late sixteenth century with his novels about the last Valois kings and the Wars of Religion. He also stimulated curiosity about the early seventeenth century—an era with a romantic tinge of its own. Men and women were thought to live in those days a more energetic and exciting kind of life than was experienced in a bourgeois industrial era like his. It is difficult now to see the age of Louis XIII and Cardinal Richelieu, or the revolt of the nobles known as the Fronde, without something of Dumas coloring one's view.

For many, the period is forever associated with the three (or four) musketeers who fight in unquenchable friendship, all for one and one for all, in the struggle to outwit the dangerously clever Milady. *Les Trois Mousquetaires* (1844), based partly on the apocryphal memoirs of d'Artagnan, the impoverished Gascon who became Captain of the King's Guard, was surely in Edmond Rostand's mind when he charted the exploits of Cyrano, the (honorary) Gascon scholar-poet-dramatist, and the Gascon cadets, in *Cyrano de Bergerac* (1897). The fact that both d'Artagnan and Cyrano once lived and breathed cannot altogether remove the impression that they are more vivid on the page or the stage than they are in history.

Then there was an epoch-making event much closer to Dumas's own period: the Revolution of 1789. He must have heard a good deal about it from those who lived through the upheaval. His own father had risen rapidly from the ranks to become a general in the revolutionary armies. The Revolution dominated Dumas's imagination as a writer, just as it did the minds of many of his contemporaries, all seeking to grasp the causes and the significance of such a blood-stained phenomenon, to explain and sometimes even to justify its grislier manifestations. In 1845-46 Dumas published a strange novel, *Le Chevalier de Maison-Rouge,* based on the memoirs of the so-called Marquis de Rougeville, who had joined a secret society that made several vain attempts to rescue the imprisoned Queen Marie-Antoinette.

Some of the seemingly most far-fetched episodes in this novel had their models in actuality. For instance, the woman protagonist who offers to change clothes with the Queen, in order to facilitate her escape, recalls the generosity of an English lady who asked to take the Queen's place. A similar offer was made to the imprisoned Mme Roland who, like the Queen she hated, declined to accept the sacrifice. In the novel, the Chevalier de Maison-Rouge stabs himself under the guillotine at the moment when the Queen is executed, in a scene typical of frenetic Romantic excess and horror—and yet a man was actually found still alive under the scaffold when the Queen was guillotined. Like many of his contemporaries, Dumas was haunted by the guillotine and its victims. After this book he wrote a cycle of novels on the pre-revolutionary and revolutionary period: *Joseph Balsamo, Le Collier de la Reine, Ange Pitou, La Comtesse de Charny,* in an attempt to chart the decline and fall of the French monarchy. This cycle has recently been reprinted, doubtless to coincide with the bicentenary of the Revolution. Later in life, Dumas would return to the theme of the Revolution and its consequences.

Although the novelist had no great sympathy for the Bourbon dynasty, he did feel deeply for prisoners whatever their allegiance—not only the unfortunate Queen Marie-Antoinette, but also the earlier "Man in the Iron Mask" (supposedly the twin brother of Louis XIV) who spent a lifetime in prison. Most famously, perhaps, there is his own hero, the long-suffering Edmond Dantès, confined for years in the dungeons of the château d'If at Marseilles. Dantès's cruel fate and his later role as relentless avenger were drawn from an actual case of betrayal and wrongful imprisonment found in the police archives. Like the Count of Monte-Cristo, the original victim was a master of impenetrable disguise. He did not share with his fictional counterpart, though, the rare gift to be at home in many different countries and languages.

This fellow feeling with prisoners probably derived from the fact that the novelist's father, General Dumas, had been imprisoned in Naples under the Bourbons who ruled the Kingdom of the Two Sicilies. It happened when he was returning from Napoleon Bonaparte's Egyptian campaign, and he never fully recovered from the sickness he contracted in the Neapolitan prison. Indeed, he died in 1806 when Dumas was not yet four years old. In Egypt, General Dumas had made the grave mistake of expressing a different view from that of General Bonaparte, who saw to it that he was sent into retirement and deprived of the pension due to him.

While Dumas spoke of Napoleon as his father's "murderer," he could not help admiring the military genius who promoted French *gloire*. When, after Napoleon's downfall in 1815, the Bonapartists (in opposition under the Bourbon Restoration) adopted the Emperor's belated conversion to "liberalism," Dumas could be found among their number. Later, he would become a friend of Prince Napoleon (son of the Emperor's brother, Jérôme, former King of Westphalia), and would visit the island of Monte-Cristo with him. There is no way of following the political intricacies and intrigues that led to Edmond Danteès's long and terrible incarceration without some acquaintance with the effect of the rapidly changing regimes of the years 1814-15, or with the cynical and unscrupulous characters who (like Edmond's enemies) knew how to profit by those changes to rise to positions of power and wealth. Unjust imprisonment is not a theme that has become outdated.

Dumas's ancestry was more likely to make him another Antony or outsider than a figure of established society. He and Alexander Pushkin were (as far as I know) the only heirs of Byron to have Africans among their forebears. The mighty Russian creator of *Eugene Onegin* was at once proud of his African great-grandfather and unhappy at what he called his own "negroid ugliness." Dumas was sometimes teased in a thoughtless manner about his touch of the tarbrush (as it used to be called); sometimes he met with real animosity. One of Dumas's enemies, no doubt jealous of his popular success, wrote that his collaborators worked like "Negro laborers under the whip of a mulatto." There was a play on words here, for the word "nègres" is used in French to mean not only blacks but literary assistants. When the electors of 1848 made it clear that they did not want a "Negro," Dumas thought of standing as a candidate for election in the Antilles. The writer's long-dead grandmother, Cessette Dumas, had been a black slave of Saint-Domingue (Haiti), at that time in part a French colony. She bore several illegitimate children to Colonel Antoine-Alexandre Davy de La Pailleterie, a Norman reprobate of noble but modest rank with the courtesy title of Marquis, who had gone to the colony to seek his fortune.

Three of the children were sold into slavery to help finance the father's return to France with his son, Thomas-Alexandre, whom he acknowledged. With the Revolution and careers open to talent, Thomas-Alexandre enlisted under his mother's name of Dumas in the army of the Republic, distinguished himself by performing singular feats of strength and heroic valor, and was rapidly promoted. He was able to marry the daughter of the former majordomo to the Ducs d'Orléans, first princes of the blood royal, who possessed a château at Villers-Cotterets, the town where the future writer was born. It was under the protection of the Duc d'Orléans (later King Louis-Philippe) and in his offices in the handsome Palais-Royal that the young Dumas would begin his career in Paris as a copy clerk.

Notwithstanding his friendship with the ill-fated Duc de Chartres (elder son of the Duc d'Orléans), who was to die in a tragic accident, Dumas did not prove particularly loyal to the Orléans house, the younger branch of the Bourbon dynasty. When the Revolution of July 1830 broke out, sealing the fate of the elder branch, Dumas dashed off to Soissons, a town close to his birthplace, to obtain powder for the insurgents. He was not at all pleased when Louis-Philippe ascended the throne. As he wrote in his memoirs (which, despite numerous vol-

umes, only reach to February 1833), the young men of the people who made the Revolution of 1830, that "ardent youth of the heroic proletariat," as he called them, are soon cast aside, and "the parasites of power" rise at their expense to position and command. There was never any doubt where his sympathies lay.

During the Revolution of 1848, Dumas was to be found in the streets, marching with the students and workers. Although in the beginning he supported Louis Napoleon (the first Emperor's putative nephew), Dumas was opposed to his presidency. The coup d'état of December 2, 1851, which set the scene for the Second Empire a year later, led to his departure for Brussels. However, he was not there as a political exile like Victor Hugo and so many others (with whom he sympathized), but rather because he was bankrupt. The construction and furnishing of his mansion, together with his lavish entertaining there, had largely contributed to his financial plight. He would be prosecuted in 1855 for public expressions of sympathy with the political exiles, and he visited Victor Hugo on his "rock" in Guernsey (in 1857)—a gesture of friendship much appreciated by the poet in exile.

By 1860, after obtaining a large advance for the publication of his complete works, Dumas was again in funds. He acquired a schooner and set sail for Sicily to join Garibaldi and the Thousand, who by then had taken Palermo. (The writer had encountered the popular liberator before, in Turin.) Dumas offered to obtain arms for Garibaldi who, having captured Naples, made him a freeman of the city where his father had once been incarcerated. In addition, the grateful Garibaldi appointed Dumas director of the Naples museums. The tireless novelist founded a paper, *L'Independente;* he also published a French version of Garibaldi's memoirs, and an account of the expedition of the Thousand. G. M. Trevelyan, the distinguished historian of the Sicilian campaign, observed that this account was "not inaccurate on the whole." Trevelyan also thought that the value of Dumas's edition of Garibaldi's memoirs as a historical document was "underrated."

As a result of his exploits and services for Garibaldi, Dumas was invited to join an insurrection in Albania, and was offered the rank of general, but he declined. He was by then over sixty. Those malicious observers, the brothers Goncourt, meeting him some years later, remarked on his marvelous talent as a raconteur. They said that he had an "enormous ego, as large as himself" but, they added, he was "overflowing with kindliness and sparkling with wit."

It is no wonder that Dumas is a name to conjure with among Italian writers. In Umberto Eco's recent novel, *Foucault's Pendulum,* for instance, the three friends, Casaubon, Belbo, and Diotallevi, have something of the three musketeers about them, with (it has been suggested) the computer named Abulafia making a fourth. In his inexhaustible, learned, and often hilarious variations on the vast theme of secret societies, Eco does not fail to mention Dumas's novel *Le Collier de la Reine,* echoing its author's view that the famous scandal over Queen Marie-Antoinette's necklace was prompted by a masonic plot to discredit the monarchy.

At the head of Eco's Chapter 97 is an epigraph from Dumas's novel **Joseph Balsamo.** Balsamo was a doctor and charlatan known as the Count of Cagliostro, born in Palermo in 1743, devotee of occultism and freemasonry, and exiled for his part in the scandal over the Queen's necklace. Readers will find in that chapter a discussion about the relative merits of the popular serial novel or *roman-feuilleton* and high art. This debate echoes current critical preoccupations. Where the *roman-feuilleton* "seems to speak in jest, basically it makes us see the world as it is, or at least as it will be. Women are much more like Milady than Clélia Conti," suggests Belbo. (The French translation names the idealized passionate Italian heroine of Stendhal's *La Chartreuse de Parme,* whereas the English version offers Dickens's sentimental Little Nell, who belongs to a different tradition entirely.)

How seriously are we meant to take Belbo's defense of the *roman-feuilleton* of Eugène Sue and Alexandre Dumas? What credence should be given to his suggestion (after Dumas himself) that the novel of adventure and romance is fundamentally "realistic," or potentially so, if that is what he means? Are we supposed to agree to his proposition that the vengeful, resourceful, sexually independent Milady, who nearly outwits d'Artagnan (ever ready to fall "in love" at the sight of an attractive woman), is a more normal or recognizable representative of womanhood than a heroine like Clélia? Is Umberto Eco playing with current feminist criteria here?

There follows Belbo's satirical pastiche of Eugène Sue (with his belief in the malign powers of the Jesuits) and of Dumas and the historical adventure novel, with allusions to Joseph Balsamo/Cagliostro and to Jeanne de La Motte, who was branded for her part in the scandal of the royal necklace. All this is doubtless written tongue-in-cheek, or half in jest, as part of an intellectual game, designed—like the rest of the book—to stimulate the reader's wits, blur the frontiers of fact and fiction in the current style, and confound us all with the author's cleverness. Nonetheless, it may indicate a line that could lead to a certain revaluation of Dumas's writings, should anyone venture to pursue it, or believe it worthwhile to do so.

For the fact remains: Dumas was loved, and is still loved in a way that contemporaries of his like Vigny or Mérimée or Sue are not. He wanted to give pleasure and he succeeded. Imaginative and narrative

skills like his are not to be despised. Besides, we are not obliged to stay on the heights all the time.

Notes

[1] *Alexandre Dumas: Genius of Life,* by Claude Schopp, translated from the French by A. J. Koch; Franklin Watts, 506 pages.

Dorothy Trench-Bonett (essay date 1991)

SOURCE: Introduction to *Charles VII at the Homes of His Great Vassals,* by Alexandre Dumas, Père, translated by Dorothy Trench-Bonett, The Noble Press, Inc., 1991, pp. 1-42.

[*In the following excerpt, Trench-Bonett discusses Dumas's African ancestry and how it affected his social relations and his writing.*]

I. The Dumas Family: Three Generations of Blacks in France

Alexandre Dumas *père* (1802-70) was the grandson of a French nobleman—and of an African slave. Not much is known about Marie-Cessette Dumas, his grandmother, who would bequeath to three generations of famous Frenchman both her color and her family name. She died in 1772 in Haiti, which was the French colony then known as Sainte Domingue.[1] It is not known whether she was born on that West Indian island or in Africa (although the fact that she had a French surname probably means that she was creole), nor is it known from which African people her ancestors came. Many Haitians have their roots in Dahomey—*vaudun,* the religion still practiced there, was originally the Fon people's religion.[2] But Haiti, like the rest of the West Indies and the United States, took in blacks from all of the West African nations, and Marie-Cessette Dumas could have been descended from any of these. It is not known how she caught the eye of the young man calling himself Antoine Delisle, who had come to Haiti to make his fortune in the 1730s—a young man who was really Antoine-Alexandre, the future Marquis de la Pailleterie.[3] It was recorded, though, that he paid "an exorbitant price" for her, probably because she was, by European standards, a beauty.[4] Once this price was paid, of course, she had no choice about becoming his lover; she was his property. They lived together for more than twenty years, until she died. She bore him four children: Adolphe, Jeannette, Marie-Rose and Thomas-Alexandre.

In 1772, when Antoine-Alexandre decided to return to France to reclaim his estate in Normandy, he left three of his children behind. Like their mother, they were legally his property, and he arranged a fictitious sale of them to a friend "on whom he could rely to treat them well." Perhaps they still have descendants living in Haiti. Thomas-Alexandre, the youngest child, born in 1762, was the Marquis' favorite; he wanted to bring him back with him to his own country. So the nobleman brought his black son to Port-au-Prince, where he "sold him to a ship's captain in return for his own passage." But he asked the captain to keep the boy with him and "put him on a ship to France as soon as his father [the marquis] had sent the necessary money."[5] And so Thomas-Alexandre, the future General Dumas, arrived in Europe in 1776, listed in the records as the "slave Alexandre," property of a Lieutenant Roussel. He went to live with his father in the suburb of St. Germain-en-Laye, outside of Paris.[6]

So far, this is not an unusual story. The Marquis de la Pailleterie was not the first European who decided to go to the New World and rebuild his family fortunes with black slave labor. Nor was he the first white man to take a black concubine. This practice was widespread throughout the Americas. In the southern part of our country, public opinion was against it, and mulattoes were generally not acknowledged by their fathers, but this was not the case in other parts of the New World. In Brazil, the British West Indies, and the Spanish, Dutch and Portuguese American colonies, it was not uncommon for white men to acknowledge black children, free them, educate them and leave them property. Many Frenchmen brought their mixed sons (though not their daughters) back to France. There were so many *gens de couleur* (blacks with some European ancestry) in France on the eve of the French Revolution that the Chevalier de St. Georges, a black French nobleman, was able to form a regiment composed completely of men of color.[7] But, although free mixed black people had privileges in the French colonies and were often wealthy, prejudice against them was extreme. If they could, they preferred to live in France. They faced prejudice there, too, as we shall see, but it was not comparable to the situation in the islands, where a free man of color was "excluded from the naval and military departments, from the practice of law, medicine and divinity, and all public offices or places of trust," and could have his right arm cut off if he ever struck a white man.[8] "Colored" was a term used to mean anyone with African ancestry—even if the person had one African great-great-great-great-great-grandparent and 127 who were white.

Obviously, Thomas-Alexandre could compare life at the court of Louis XVI and Marie-Antoinette to what his position would have been back in Sainte Domingue and know he was privileged. Not only was he free, but he was the acknowledged heir to a marquisate. The Davy de la Pailleterie family dated back to the sixteenth century,[9] had registered proof of its nobility in 1710 and 1712, and owned a castle in Normandy, at Bielleville-en-Caux.[10] However, it seems that the handsome young man, who was a very dark-skinned mulatto (portraits of him show that he did not look mixed but resembled a pure-blooded black), was made to remember, often, that he was not really considered the equal of a white man. On one occasion, while at the theatre with a white female friend, the young black was insulted by a Frenchman, who first tried to get the woman to come away with him. He called Thomas-Alexandre a "lackey" and a "half-breed" when he objected, saying that if they were in the West Indies, the black "would be fettered hand and foot."[11] When Dumas *père* told this story in his memoirs, he said that his father took revenge for these insults,[12] but what actually seems to have happened is that the woman left the theatre and "Thomas-Alexandre returned to his box, trembling with rage."[13] I don't know whether the author revised the story himself or was told an incorrect version by his father, but Thomas-Alexandre probably wished that he could have "thrown his insulter bodily out of the stalls and subsequently wounded him in duel," as the story Dumas tells recounts.[14] Thomas-Alexandre got some satisfaction though, as the other whites who were with the rude Frenchman forced him to apologize to the black man.

Other things besides his race concerned Thomas-Alexandre. He was continually at odds with his father, the Marquis, who in his old age had turned out to be a miser. Thomas-Alexandre, "trained to no particular profession, with no friends to help him to a career, depended entirely on his father's good will."[15] It was an intolerable situation. When the Marquis married his housekeeper to save money, Thomas-Alexandre, whose position as heir was now in jeopardy, joined the army. The father flew into a rage because the son had enlisted as a simple soldier, and forbade him to use his aristocratic name when serving so low in the ranks. So Thomas-Alexandre took his mother's name, Dumas. The Marquis died a short time later, in 1786, but Thomas-Alexandre renounced the title as well as the Davy de la Pailleterie coat of arms, taking as his slogan *Deus dedit, Deus dabit,* meaning, "God gave, God will give."[16]

God *did* give. When the French Revolution began three years later in 1789, Thomas-Alexandre left the Queen's service (the regiment he had originally joined was the Queen's dragoons) and joined the Revolutionary Army. Most French blacks took the same side. Who had more reason than they did to long for changes? Who believed more than they did in liberty, equality, fraternity, and the rights of man? For a while it seemed as though some of the changes that they hoped for would take place: white revolutionaries, such as the Marquis de Lafayette and Robespierre, agreed that it was sheer hypocrisy to talk of equality and fraternity while black slavery continued in colonies that were the property of France. "You urge without ceasing the Rights of Man, but you believe in them so little . . . that you have sanctified slavery constitutionally," Robespierre charged during the debates about abolition in the Assemblée Nationale. "Perish the colonies if the price is to be your happiness, your glory, your liberty!"[17] Slavery was not abolished, and Robespierre's government soon fell; he was so willing to let those who did not agree with him perish that he was largely responsible for the Reign of Terror. But the times were much more liberal than they had been under the Old Regime, and this was good for blacks.

In former days, under the old system of patronage and privilege, Thomas-Alexandre would have remained in the low ranks of the army forever, but now he was treated as his abilities deserved, and he "had a remarkably swift series of promotions. In July 1793, he was named *général de brigade;* barely two months later, *général en chef* [commander-in-chief] of the army of the Western Pyrenées; three months after that, *général en chef* of the army of the Alps, fielded by the government of the Revolutionary Committee of Public Safety. The next year he was made commander of the Brest Coast, and then *général de division* on the Sambre-et-Meuse. Later he commanded all calvary in the Italian campaign, then was appointed head of a calvary division at Mantua."[18]

Not only was Dumas quickly promoted, but he also quickly became famous for the remarkable feats he performed, feats that would seem incredible if so many witnesses had not vouched for them. The most famous of these exploits was probably his single-handed defense of the Bridge of Brixen, at Clausen in Austria, against an entire enemy squadron. "As the bridge was narrow, only two or three men could confront him at a time and Dumas sabered everyone who approached him. He was wounded three times and his coat was pierced by seven balls, but he stopped the enemy charge."[19] The terrified Austrians nicknamed him "the black devil." The color of his skin was also remarked on during the French invasion of Egypt: "his brown color . . . resembling the Arabs, strongly impressed the garrison." Napoleon, who was in charge of the armies by then, noticing this, "sent for the mulatto general and ordered him to head the garrison vanguard intruding inland, so its members could see the skin of the very first general they had to deal with was not of an unfamiliar hue."[20]

The black general soon fell out with Napoleon, though. It had become obvious that Napoleon's ambitions did not match the ideal of a republic. Dumas was brave enough to tell his colleague that he did not approve of these ambitions. Thus, though the black man's exploits were just as extraordinary in Egypt as they had been elsewhere (his prowess in battle caused the Arabs to call him "the angel," after the exterminating angel of the Koran),[21] Napoleon soon was beginning to hint that Dumas was stupid. "Intelligence is not his strong point," the Corsican is supposed to have said to the senior medical officer of the French army about Dumas.[22] He began to refer to the general not by his name but as "the colored man."[23] When Dumas, on his way back to France from Egypt, was shipwrecked off Naples and

imprisoned by the anti-republican Bourbon government, Napoleon made no move to try to free him. It may be relevant to recall here that it was Napoleon who, by trickery, captured another black man who believed in equality, the great Haitian general Toussaint l'Ouverture, and let him die in prison in 1803.[24]

Thomas-Alexandre did not die in prison, even though he was poisoned there.[25] In 1801 he was allowed to return to France—crippled, half-paralyzed, tormented by ulcers—a broken man. He returned to his family in the small town of Villers-Cotterets, where in 1792 he had married a French girl. Her name was Marie-Louise, her maiden name was Labouret, and the couple already had an eight-year old daughter. Soon after they were married, the couple had another daughter, Aimée. On July 14, 1802, another child was born to them. Named after his father and grandfather, he was called Alexandre Dumas.

The new baby lived, at first, in luxurious surroundings. The Dumas household was renting a little castle, called Les Fosses and had a cook, a gardener, and a *garde;* the general had a valet, Hippolyte, who was, like himself, black.[26] These prosperous times, however, did not last long. The general's health had continued to fail ever since his imprisonment, and Napoleon, who was crowned emperor in 1804, refused to give him either the back pay that he was due or a pension. In the last months of his life, Dumas went to Paris to ask the emperor for justice, but his former colleague would not even see him. Other old friends, fearing Napoleon's displeasure, also let him down. In 1806, Thomas-Alexandre returned to Villers-Cotterets to die. On his deathbed he is said to have asked God why he, who had commanded three armies at the age of thirty-five, should die in bed at forty "like a coward," leaving his wife and his children.[27] When he died, his daughter, Aimée, was thirteen years old; Alexandre was only four. The character Haydée in his novel *The Count of Monte Cristo* is supposed to have been the same age as Alexandre was when her father died. She states in chapter 86 of that book that four is not too young to remember "events that have . . . supreme importance."[28]

It seems as though she speaks for Dumas here, for in his own life this was also the case. All his life he remembered the general, and his admiration of the heroic figure of his father amounted to hero worship. It showed in little things—like his father he had a West Indian accent (although born and brought up in France)[29]—and in big things—Dumas tried to emulate the general's military feats whenever possible, involving himself eagerly in the fighting whenever there were liberal uprisings in France. He kept his father's memory alive; telling his own children his memories of Thomas-Alexandre and contributing money to raise a statue of the general in Haiti at the request of a delegation from the homeland.[30] He wrote about the general continually. A large proportion of his three thousand-page memoirs (written in 1850) concern his father's rather than his own life. His father haunted his fiction as well. The general may be found in heroic figures like Dumas' three musketeers, who routinely do the impossible; they are clearly based on the man who could hold off an army single handedly and do chin-ups in the stables, lifting his horse off the ground with his powerful thighs.[31] The theme of ingratitude that runs through Dumas' work, showing that those who do great things are not always greatly rewarded, was certainly based, too, on what he saw in his father's life. "I adored my father," he wrote in *Mémoires,* "even today the remembrance of . . . [him,] . . . each curve of his body and each feature of his face, is as present for me as if I had lost him yesterday; so much so that today I love him still, I love him with a love as tender, as profound and as real as if he had watched over my youth and as if I had had the happiness to pass from youth to adolescence leaning on his powerful arm."[32] It is clear that any serious study of Dumas must take into account this great influence on his life.

Writing to his former comrade General Brune in 1802, Thomas-Alexandre described his daughter Aimée as having "little black fingers."[33] Her famous brother could not have been described in the same way. He wrote in his memoirs that his mother had been afraid that he would be born black. She had seen a puppet show version of Faust while she was pregnant, and had been terrified, thinking that her baby, like the devil depicted there, might be the color of coal, "with a scarlet tongue and tail," a "throwback."[34] She began to call her unborn son "Berlick," the name of that devil, while he was still in the womb; when she saw his dark, newborn face, she screamed and fainted.[35] Alexandre's dark color at birth, though, was due to his having half-strangled on his umbilical cord. When he was able to breathe, his complexion cleared and it could be seen that he was blond and fair-skinned.[36] He did not keep these looks, however. Had Mme. Dumas known a black woman who was a mother, she might have been told that it was not likely that he would. Most black children are not born with the complexion they keep for life; darkness comes gradually. Marie-Cessette's grandson would always have blue eyes. But his blond hair changed in color and took on a frizzy texture; and his skin also changed. Photographs of him as a man show someone who, though pale for a black person, could never have been mistaken for white. In the United States he would have been considered "yellow" (or "high yellow"), "light-skinned" but most definitely a Negro.

Dumas in the United States, in the nineteenth century . . . the idea is difficult to imagine. He considered doing a lecture tour here, towards the end of his life, when he was very famous, his novels well known and respected, but he questioned whether "we had sufficiently conquered our negrophobia" to be able to receive him "as he is accustomed to be received in France."[37] It was an intelligent question. The year was 1864; the Emancipation Proclamation had already been given, although it would not be enforced in the rebellious South for another year, and blacks there would not be granted all the legal rights whites had until the 1960s. Dumas never did make this tour, so we cannot tell how he actually would have been received. A very famous foreigner, although black, might have been treated with some minimum of respect. The author of *The Three Musketeers* probably would not have been chased through the streets with crowds threatening to lynch him and his publishers (although this did happen to one nineteenth-century black composer who dared have his works performed in public, incredible as it may seem). The fact that Dumas was foreign accounts for the fact that his works had been translated and published in the United States, although not those works that discussed the troubles of blacks. He knew nothing of the struggles that contemporary American blacks faced when they wanted to publish books other than slave narratives, struggles we can read about in the lives of William Wells Brown, Harriet E. Wilson, Martin R. Delaney, Frank J. Webb.

These pioneer African-American novelists were lucky to know how to read and write. It was illegal to teach blacks to read in many states, and it could be hazardous even where it was legal, as Bronson Alcott learned when his school in Massachusetts was forced to close because he admitted a little black girl in 1839.[38] Even in the twentieth century, the author Richard Wright has described the stratagems he was forced to adopt in order to use the public library, since blacks in the southern states where he lived were not eligible for library cards.[39] It is probable that Dumas would not have been a novelist if he had been born in America; it is certain that he would not have written the same sort of books. But, of course, he would not have been born here—at least not with the same parents. His father probably could not have married his mother: it was most unusual for a white woman in the United States in the nineteenth century to have relations with a black.[40] And the general himself was a phenomenon that could not have occurred in the United States. Although a mulatto here was more likely to be freed than a full-blooded black, most mulattoes remained in slavery. Careers in the military were not open even to free colored men. We had a segregated army until the Korean War, and black troops fought under white officers (when they were allowed to fight). There were no black American generals until very recent times.

It is dangerous, though, to concentrate too much on the ways in which France in the last century (and even this century) was more congenial than the United States for blacks. This gives rise to a fallacy that is still common, the sort of thinking that assumes that "better" means "perfect," leading generations of African-Americans to believe that France is a haven completely free of racism, that being black there has no effect on a person's life. This very strong myth (fed in our own century by the large number of eminent blacks who have been expatriates and formed a community in Paris[41]) is partly responsible, in Dumas' case, I think, for the obscurity in which his work on African concerns has been allowed to rest. We have seen already how his father had to combat racism in France all his life. That Dumas himself also struggled with it is a fact that is very well documented.

His mother was very well satisfied with him once it turned out that he was not "Berlick." Their loving relationship is carefully described in **Mémoires.** He was a beloved member of a loving family—white grandparents, cousins, uncles, and aunts all completely accepting him (and his sister); he also never lacked for friends. These friends, though, could make it clear at times that they remembered that he was a different color. "You Negroes are all the same; you love glass beads and toys," Charles Nodier is known to have said to the writer, when he chose to buy, and wear, a great deal of gold jewelry after his first financial success.[42] Nodier, an eminent man of letters, respected Dumas and was responsible for the younger man's having had that success in writing. He introduced him to the producer who put on Dumas' first popular "serious" play. He certainly did not wish to hurt Dumas' feelings.

But the black man had enemies and people who were jealous of him, who were less kind. "That coon," is what Honoré de Balzac openly used to call him.[43] (Balzac's own novels, so famous now, did not, in his own time, sell well.) The classic actress Mlle. Mars, who performed in many of Dumas' important plays, disliked Dumas because he belonged to the Romantic school of writers as well as for his color. "Open the windows," she used to demand after he left the room, pretending that she could distinguish an offensive Negro smell.[44] The poet Paul Verlaine labeled an older Dumas "Uncle Tom" in a triolet he wrote after photographs of Dumas appeared in 1866 that showed him in controversial poses with a white American actress from the South, Adah Isaacs Menken. Miss Mencken was called "Miss Adah" in the poem. The reference was to the little white girl, Eva, and the old black slave, Tom, in Harriet Beecher Stowe's then popular novel, *Uncle Tom's Cabin.*[45] Most of Paris got the joke. They also laughed when popular report had the writer's son saying, "My father is so vain that he is capable of mounting behind his own carriage, if only to make people think that he keeps a black servant."[46] The caricaturist Cham also knew that he would amuse when he depicted Dumas in the guise of an African cannibal, stirring a pot full of characters dressed in historical costumes (a reference to the writer's historical works).[47]

No one seriously thought Dumas was a cannibal, of course, but on at least one occasion the writer's color *did* arouse fear. During the July Revolution of 1830,

Lafayette (the same man who had fought in the Revolutionary War in the United States) sent Dumas, who took an active part in this uprising, with orders to get ammunition from a powder magazine for the use of the men on the barricades who were trying to overthrow the government of Charles X. (Lafayette, by the way, had been shocked when he returned to the United States a few years earlier and saw the position of the blacks there. He told Thomas Jefferson frankly that such conditions did not concur with the ideas of equality for which he, for one, had fought.)[48] Dumas went to Soissons where the Commandant who held the powder magazine did not want to give up the ammunition. The man's wife, Mme. de Linières, who had lived through the revolution in Haiti in the 1790s, came in, and when she saw Dumas, a black man with guns in his hands, she began screaming hysterically. "Give up, give up, it's the second revolution of the Negroes," she told her husband, demanding that he surrender.[49] Dumas got his ammunition; no one could calm the woman down without that. This incident has its amusing side, but Dumas did not laugh when he campaigned for public office in the Yonne *department* a decade later and was heckled as a "marquis" (a reference to the Davy de la Pailleterie title) and as a "nigger."[50] He could beat the voter who made these remarks (and did), but he did not win the election; though Victor Hugo, his colleague, friend, and rival, won a similar one. Perhaps he should run for office in the West Indies, he bitterly remarked, saying that the people there would accept him as "one of them," if he sent a lock of his kinky hair.[51]

Some would say, perhaps, that these events and remarks were isolated incidents in what was basically a life full of success and extraordinary adulation. The fact that Dumas was black, after all, did not stop him from becoming a famous playwright, ranked with Victor Hugo and Lamartine; he still cannot be ignored when discussing the history of the Romantic drama in France. Nor did it stop him from changing careers when the classic theatre became popular again, making himself into *the* most successful writer of serial novels in the great age of serial writing in France, so famous that editors could (and did) sell anything, written by him or not, at fantastic prices when it was signed with his name. Nor did it stop him from being so idolized by the public that after performances of his plays people fought to touch him, ripping his clothes to shreds for souvenirs, behavior that is matched in our time only by fans at rock concerts.[52] Being black did not stop him from associating, on equal terms, with the other great writers during that great age of literature in France. Hugo, Georges Sand, Alphonse Lamartine, Alfred-Victor de Vigny were all acquaintances, many were close friends; younger writers like the Goncourt brothers were honored just to meet him.[53] He was on intimate terms with French royalty, in spite of his known republican opinions, and enjoyed the patronage of the house of Orléans. He traveled all over Europe, went to

Russia, the Middle East, and North Africa—often as the honored guest of potentates and kings. There is a story someone told about going to a royal party in Spain, and seeing the king, queen, and princess left alone in a corner while the guests all gathered around one man: it was, of course, Dumas, famed for his wit and brilliant conversation.[54] Giuseppe Garibaldi called him "tu." He collected honors and military decorations. He became wealthy enough to indulge his fantasies, building the spectacular, ostentatious castle Monte Cristo, named after his famous novel, and buying a yacht, like the count in that book.

And then there were the love affairs. Even after he lost the considerable good looks he had as a youth and became grey, elderly, and fat, he continued to attract some of the most famous beauties of his time. His famous son, his namesake (he had four children by four different women, the last when he was a very old man), complained that most of the women he met just wanted to be introduced to his father. He once was heard to complain in public that the old man gave him his shoes to break in when they were new and his mistresses when he was tired of them.[55] Despite some disappointments (he never was admitted to the Académie Française, an honor he coveted), and despite the fact that he was so careless with money that he ended up poor after all the millions he made (he was cared for, in extreme old age, by his son Alexandre Dumas), Dumas led a fairy-tale life, the sort of life of which most people are only able to dream. Perhaps he was able to make the marvelous seem so real in many of his novels because it was real in his own life.

If it does seem like quibbling to say that, in spite of all this, the writer always felt like an outsider and was always aware of his skin color, I can only offer the excuse that it was certainly true. Some remarks he made suggest that he, at times, felt inferior because of it. He once said to the actress Marie Dorval, comparing himself to de Vigny, that the other writer was a "true nobleman," not "a mulatto like myself."[56] He also told one of his black servants (throughout his life, he employed many blacks), who was leaving to go into the army, that if he made good there "everyone will swear you are white."[57] This kind of thinking was hardly to be avoided considering the society in which he lived. After all, one of the first lessons he ever learned was that "Berlick" would not have been worthy of the love even of the woman who bore him.

It is not remarkable that Dumas had these thoughts sometimes. What *is* remarkable is that he never tried to hide or obscure his heritage; that he wrote about slavery and the injustices done to blacks when these were things that did not concern him personally or affect his life; that he tried to portray the blacks in his works as human beings, not stereotypes, when he had no models for this kind of thinking in the books he read and no

idea how to go about doing it; and that he interested himself in the freedom of blacks in foreign countries and tried to do what he could for them. He was interested in freedom and equality for everyone, of course. He put his life at risk on the barricades in France, for instance, and donated time and money to Garibaldi's cause in Italy. But most liberals in his time cared about those causes. It was stylish to do so. It was *not* stylish, however, to write after he visited Africa (Tangier) in 1846 that he "felt the Moroccan scorn and hatred for the European invader."[58] He swam completely against French public opinion when he took the side of the North against the South during the American Civil War, trying to find a newspaper "willing to open a subscription to help" the Union's sick and wounded. He could not. He then proposed to write a history of the first four years of Abraham Lincoln's presidency, to refute the idea, popular in England as well as in France, that "the North intends not so much the freedom of the blacks as the oppression of the whites."[59] This project also fell through. But he tried. He does not deserve to have it believed of him that he was untouched by and did not care about the concerns of his people, because it's convenient, in order to sell *The Three Musketeers,* to suppress his political side.

Dumas died on December 5, 1870. Paris was occupied by the Germans at that time, and his funeral was not well attended. But when he was reinterred after the troubles were over at Villers-Cotterets, his birthplace, the eulogies the great spoke over him were such as any man might envy. His real and most lasting eulogy, though, is the popularity of his books, which people have never ceased to read from his time until our own, all over the world. He was the greatest of the three great Dumas.

However, it was Alexandre Dumas *fils,* his son, who was thought to be the greatest of his illustrious family in his own time. For the whole of the last part of the nineteenth century after Hugo's death, he was indisputably the preeminent man of letters in France. He received honors that his father never dreamed of, including election to the prestigious Académie, becoming one of the "forty immortals." It is ironic that today he is considered a one-book author, and that that book, *La Dame aux Camélias* [*Camille*], is best known through Giuseppe Verdi's music as *La Traviata.*

Armand Duval, the hero of *Camille* (Verdi changed his name to Alfredo), has never, to my knowledge, been portrayed as black. Yet it was common knowledge that Dumas *fils* based his hero on himself and that the 1847 novel, and the later 1852 play, were very thinly disguised autobiography. It is amusing to compare the grave and respectable M. Duval, Armand's father, with the bohemian elder Dumas, but most of the other characters in the work are supposed to be exact portraits, especially Marguerite, based on the beautiful courtesan Marie Duplessis, who died shortly before the young man wrote the novel at age twenty-four. The story told in it was true to the point that Dumas reproduced, word for word, actual correspondence between himself and his lover.[60]

He does not seem to have had the imagination that his father had. Many of his other works were also based on his own experiences: *Diane de Lys,* for example, on another love affair; *Le Fils Naturel* [*The Illegitimate Son*], though more loosely, on his problematic relationship with his father. When he was not writing disguised autobiography, he wrote plays about the social problems of his time. They were very well done, and it is not surprising that his contemporaries ranked him so highly as an author. Yet, the social problems that he wrote about have largely disappeared (and even in his own time, only concerned a small, elite segment of the population), the wit he was famed for was based on topical references that mean nothing to us now, and to the reader of today his plays are not very interesting. He would probably be known only as the son of his father were it not for his book about Marguerite Gautier. The kind of youthful emotion he describes in *Camille* (which is not sentimental, like *La Traviata*) is still understandable even today, when there are no longer any courtesans and when people no longer sacrifice themselves for love.

Dumas *fils* never wrote anything dealing with the concerns of blacks; it seems not to have been one of the social problems that interested him. In his own life, the stigma of illegitimacy bothered him a great deal more than his being a person of color. He was not black in appearance, as photographs of him clearly show. Armand Duval is "a tall, pale young man with blond hair"; so was Dumas *fils*.[61] It seems, at first glance, that he lived as a white man. Although he wrote about questions that concerned the bourgeoisie, he was not middle class in later life but lived among the aristocracy, married a Russian princess, and was wealthy, eminent, and respected, as well as a member of the Académie. It is rather a shock to find among the opinions the *Mercure de France* collected about him after his death (opinions that were mostly adulatory) such remarks as Léon Bloy's "that mulatto . . . was a fool and a hypocrite," and Adrien Remacle's "this Frenchman, a little bit negro, born clever [*malin*], created a morality of facade and preface."[62] And then one finds that, during his life, he took pride in his black ancestry, although it no longer showed in face or feature, or in the color of his skin. At the height of his fame, in 1887, when Léon Ganderax wished to please Dumas *fils* and compliment him, he could find no way more sure of doing it than by referring to his African origins. Ganderax called the eminent man "an admirable Negro" and said that he had "the temperament of a Negro" combined with "the highest degree of sharp-edged reasoning." And he finished by saying that Dumas *fils* was a worthy grandson of Thomas-Alexandre Dumas, the General, "the hero of Brixen."[63]

II. Alexandre Dumas: Black Writer, French Writer

When Dumas *père* gave his son, who wanted to be a writer, too, a list of authors to read, he recommended Virgil, Horace, Homer, Sophocles, and Euripides in the original Latin and Greek. He also thought that the young man should read Shakespeare, Dante, Schiller, and the Bible—and learn Corneille by heart. The contemporaries, or near contemporaries, that he recommended were André-Marie de Chénier, Hugo and Lamartine.[64] This list differed somewhat from the list that he had been given, as a young man beginning to write literature, of authors that *he* should read. Besides the authors on the list quoted above, he had also been recommended to familiarize himself with Aeschylus and Aristophanes; Seneca, Terence, and Plautus; Molière, Racine, Voltaire. He had been told to read Goethe, Walter Scott, James Fenimore Cooper, Ronsard, Milton, Byron, Johann Uhland, and Mathurin Régnier, and to familiarize himself with the history of France, through the classic authors like Jean de Joinville, Jean Froissart, the Count of Saint-Simon, and Mme. de la Fayette Richelieu.[65] He gives this list in his *Memoirs* but does not say how many of these authors he actually read, except to say that he was powerfully influenced by Scott, Cooper, and Byron.

Dumas needed a list of authors to read because he had very little formal education. As the son of the disgraced General Dumas, growing up during the period when Napoleon was in power, Dumas was denied a scholarship to either a *lycée* or a military school and his mother had had no money to send him. She was the only widow of a Revolutionary general who did not receive a pension, and the family was always close to dire poverty, since a woman in those days really could not support herself. She managed to obtain lessons for Alexandre with Abbé Grégoire, the village priest, where he learned "a little Latin, a little grammar"[66] and developed a very beautiful, rapid handwriting, which later stood him in good stead. He learned dancing, fencing, and how to fire a pistol (not with the priest), but he could not, or would not, learn arithmetic beyond multiplication. This was very possibly the reason that he proved to be so bad at handling his financial affairs in later life. His mother arranged for him to take music lessons (his sister sang beautifully and she wanted him to have this advantage, too), but he had "the worst voice in the world."[67] His mother wanted him to become a priest and actually had the chance to send him to a seminary, but the young boy ran away from this opportunity, like Aramis in *The Three Musketeers*.[68] His mother tried other careers for him, but he wasn't successful at any of them, until a 1819 performance of *Hamlet* (not the original, but Jean-François Ducis' French translation) inspired him to begin to write for the theatre, a decision in which he was encouraged by his friend Adolphe de Leuven.[69]

One notices at once that there were no black authors in the list of books that Dumas read. Of course, he was not familiar with any. He grew up and basically lived all his life in a vacuum as far as contact with blacks was concerned, although there were blacks writing during his lifetime. Within a few generations after the slave ships first landed in the New World, the transplanted Africans, though they had come from an oral culture like Homer's, had taken up the European's pen and begun to write about their experiences—in spite of the fact that they were given little encouragement to do so. The true explosion of slave narratives occurred during the nineteenth century in the United States, but Gustavus Vassa (Olaudah Equiano) (1745-97) in England and others wrote about their experiences before Dumas was born. Phillis Wheatley (1753-84) and Jupiter Hammon (1720-1800) wrote poetry in the New World. Benjamin Banneker (1731-1806), famous for other reasons, also wrote verse. In spite of adverse conditions, as we saw in the previous chapter, blacks like George Moses Horton, James M. Whitfield, and Frances Watkins Harper in America would write novels and poems during Dumas' lifetime as well. The United States was not the only country where blacks were writing. Auguste Lacaussade, another black Frenchman, born in 1817, was honored by the Académie for his poems, received the Prix Bordin in 1852, and was elected to membership in the Legion d'honueur in 1860.[70] Maria F. dos Reis published a novel in Brazil in 1859. And in Russia, where the conditions were not adverse, a young man of mixed black and white aristocratic ancestry like Dumas, the Frenchman's almost exact contemporary, was trying, during Dumas' lifetime, to write about *his* black experience, about his ancestors and his feelings about his race. This was, of course, Alexander Pushkin, most notably in his unfinished novel, *The Negro of Peter the Great.*[71] Dumas would never read this book.[72] He never traveled to the United States or Brazil, and when he went to Russia in his later years, Pushkin (who was murdered when he was thirty-seven years old) was long dead. So when the French author tried to read about the obvious difference between himself and his friends, family, lovers, compatriots, when he tried to find out about people who looked like him, he was forced to dig for morsels in the only literature with which he had any familiarity: the "classics"—literature by whites.

That any work with black characters fascinated him from the beginning is obvious. *Hamlet* was the first of Shakespeare's works to which he was introduced and, as mentioned before, he liked it so much that it inspired him to begin to write. But *Othello* had an even greater effect on him. Describing his reactions to the play about the Moor of Venice (probably the most famous work in Western literature whose hero is black), he would later say that it struck him as if he had been "a man born blind to whom sight is then given" and said that the performance opened an "enchanted Eden . . . for me."[73]

His own first piece of theatrical writing (with Adolphe de Leuven as a collaborator) was *Pélérinage a Ermenonville [Pilgrimage to Ermenonville].* A half-verse, half-prose "pastiche of Demoustier" is how he later described it, in *Mémoires.*[74] He went on to do some work in the vaudeville theatre, because he needed money. Some of these plays survive, but the first *serious* work that he tried was a translation of Schiller's *Die Vershwörung des Fiesko zu Genua* [*The Conspiracy of Fiesco at Genoa*]. This play, written by Schiller in 1783, has a Moor, Muley Hassan, as one of the main characters. He is a villain, Fiesco's tool in his plots against the Doria family. Dumas, who did an adaptation of the play rather than an exact translation, felt that it was important that it be recognized that Hassan was black. In his memoirs, he expressed anger at other translators of the play (which was very popular during the Romantic period) who suppressed the character of the moor or made him white.[75] His translation, *Fiesques de Lavagna,* made in 1823, was never performed and never published. Dumas later claimed that he burnt the manuscript, but it still exists. The play had a great effect on him: it is mentioned in *Monte Cristo* and was one of the influences on the writing of *Charles VII chez ses grands vassaux.*

It was for *Charles VII* that Dumas first created a major, original character who was black. Yacoub, the slave who is the hero of this play, will be discussed at length in the next section. The play was written in 1831, after Dumas had managed to become famous, along with works that had nothing to do with anything of special concern to blacks: the great Romantic plays *Christine, Antony,* and *Henri III et sa cour* [*Henry III and His Court*]. Although these plays are largely unknown in the United States, they are what his reputation as a major writer rests on today in France. These plays dealt with Dumas' other interests: In *Henri III,* he first showed his talent for dramatizing the history of France. He would always care a great deal about the history of his country and was instrumental in bringing it to the attention of the common man. In *Antony,* he achieved the revolutionary feat of setting a story about a difficult subject (adultery) in contemporary times, with real people, a story that, although melodramatic, was also realistic. One critic said that "Dumas gave evidence of early naturalistic tendencies by assigning his hero's character to the unhappy circumstances of his childhood as a foundling," a kind of character development that was unique when he wrote the play.[76] Antony, a "rebel and a bastard,"[77] was the first of Dumas' many "outsider" heroes. The play *Christine,* about Queen Christina of Sweden and the murder of Monaldeschi, first takes up the theme of ingratitude that Dumas would use in many of his novels (including the Musketeer series), particularly the ingratitude of the great. These plays were all fantastically successful. *Henri III and His Court* was the first Romantic play ever to be performed (although Hugo's *Cromwell* was written first), and *Antony* made Dumas famous all over France. *Charles*

VII, though not a failure, did not have this kind of spectacular success. None of the other plays that Dumas wrote during the 1830s (his most prolific period of dramatic writing) dealt with themes of specific interest to blacks. The most important of the works he wrote during this period are *The Tower of Nesle* (1832), still his most often performed work, which is a reworking of a play by Frédèric Gaillardet dealing with sex, intrigue, and murder in high places in medieval Paris; *Kean, or Disorder and Genius,* written in 1836, based on the life of the British actor Edmund Kean, famous for both his thespian skill and his dissolute, drunken life; and *Mademoiselle de Belle-Isle* (1839), a comedy of manners, set in eighteenth-century France.

Dumas' interests as a writer were varied. At no time did he feel, as black authors in the United States today are often made to feel, that only certain subjects were suitable for him to write about because he was black. The literature of the world has been greatly enriched because of the breadth of Dumas' interests. He felt free not only to try out different subject matter but different genres as well. When there was a reaction in favor of the classic drama in the 1840s,[78] he began to try to write novels, although he had only written plays previously. Novels translate more easily than plays do, especially plays in verse, and it is as a novelist that Dumas is best known today outside of France. Works like *The Three Musketeers, The Count of Monte Cristo, The Black Tulip, The Queen's Necklace, Ange Pitou (Storming the Bastille), The Countess of Charny, Twenty Years After, Chicot the Jester (La Dame de Monsoreau), Le Vicomte de Bragelonne* (which includes *The Man in the Iron Mask*) need little introduction to the English-speaking reader. Dumas also wrote cookbooks and children's books and he continued to translate. His version of Hoffmann's *The Nutcracker and the Mouse King,* which he called *La Casse-Noisette,* not the original, is the basis of Tchaikovsky's well-known ballet. He was well regarded as a travel writer,[79] wrote his memoirs, and founded two newspapers at different times of his life. If he never felt limited in subject matter or genre because he was black, a certain sensibility that can be attributed to his identity as a person of color *does* pervade much of his work. It is found in two recurrent themes in his fiction, the theme of the "outsider" and the theme of revenge.

Perhaps it is best to consider these themes first as they are presented in *Georges* (1843), one of Dumas' forgotten novels, and one of his most important, as it is the author's only novel in which the hero is black. Georges Munier is a "half-caste," the son of a mulatto father (as Dumas was), who lived on the island of Mauritius (formerly called Ile-de-France) near Africa, east of Madagascar in the Indian Ocean. Dumas never visited there, but he learned about it from a friend, Felicien Malleville, who grew up there.[80] Georges' color makes him unacceptable to the white planter society to which he aspires to belong; he's an outsider, an outcast. When he is insulted by a white man in one of the novel's key scenes, he cannot challenge the person who has offended him to a duel because a black man cannot strike a white man on Mauritius (just as in Sainte-Domingue, in Thomas-Alexandre's time, blacks there are outside of the code of honor that "gentlemen" live by). Georges goes away to live in Paris and returns to his island years later—wealthy, erudite, cosmopolitan. Still not accepted by the whites, he takes revenge on them by forming a slave rebellion, joining with the blacks that many other mulattoes despise. He also gains the love of the woman who was betrothed to the white man who had formerly offended him.[81]

At the beginning of this century, Frances Miltoun characterized *Georges* as "an autobiographical novel." It could only have been written, she claimed, by someone who, because of race, caste, or religion saw himself unfairly outclassed by his contemporaries.[82] *Georges* is not autobiographical in the way that *Ange Pitou (Storming the Bastille)* is autobiographical: in the latter novel, Dumas made the hero a boy from Villers-Cotterets and put many of his own experiences into it, although he set it in the time of the Revolution. But *Georges* certainly deals with feelings that Dumas seems to have felt. Although he was considered a gentleman and fought several duels, he could not call someone to account every time his color was called to his attention, and he did not. He was known as a good-natured man, but he seems to have experienced hostile feelings nonetheless: the kind of feelings that caused him to suspend the man who insulted him in Yonne over a bridge until he took the insult back, the kind of feelings that explain the revision of the story about Thomas-Alexandre in the theatre so that the black man got revenge for the slight.

The Count of Monte Cristo is, of course, Dumas' great novel about vengeance—"probably the greatest revenge novel ever written" says one critic.[83] It is not about white and black relations, though Dumas put long, passionate speeches about freedom into the mouth of the white slave Haydee,[84] but the plot is so similar to the plot of *Georges* that a comparison of the two books would be worthwhile. In *Monte Cristo,* which is, astonishingly enough, based on a true life story,[85] Dumas seems to be questioning by the end of the book whether vengeance is ultimately worthwhile even for the greatest wrong. Edmond Dantès at first thinks himself the instrument of God, but he eventually wonders whether he has gone too far when the innocent and even those he wants to reward begin to be affected by the train of events he sets in motion as he seeks his revenge. In *Le Vicomte de Bragelonne,* one of the sequels to *The Three Musketeers,* Athos, the most thoughtful of the musketeers, asks the same question when Milady's son begins to hunt down the musketeers for the murder of his mother, an act they thought was a just act of vengeance when they committed it. The question is abstract here and does not seem to have anything to do with race relations, but in *Charles VII,* it is clearly a racial question when Yacoub seeks vengeance on the men who captured him and stole his freedom. It is worth noting, though, that even Yacoub hesitates over whether the kindnesses the Count has done him are not sufficient to atone for his wrongs; and the question seems to be one about which Dumas was ambivalent.

Dantès, Georges, Yacoub, Antony, and other of Dumas' characters who seek vengeance have another trait in common: they are all different from the people around them, as Dumas was different from the people among whom he lived in real life. In the beginning of the novel of which he is the hero, Dantès is happy and well-adjusted in his society—a handsome, young, soon-to-be-married sailor of nineteen who is successful at his job and about to receive a promotion. But when he is reborn as the Count of Monte Cristo, after his long imprisonment and equally long travels, he is so different from his fellows that some of them question, half-jokingly, whether he is even human. There is a long section in which they consider that he might be a vampire. And he is able to associate with people that he knew intimately in former days completely unrecognized. There's no touch of the supernatural about the young man from Gascony, D'Artagnan, but at the beginning of the novel about him, he's also on the outside. Worse than that, he's ridiculous. *The Three Musketeers* begins with a scene in which everyone in the whole town of Meung laughs at him and his horse as he rides into town; he literally causes a riot. He later makes himself ridiculous again to Porthos, Athos, and Aramis, the three men whom he most wishes to impress, and even after he is accepted by them, they continue to remind him periodically that he is a Gascon, with different mannerisms and a different accent. Ange Pitou, in *Storming the Bastille,* doesn't fit in at first because he is a country bumpkin from Dumas' home town of Villers-Coterrets; Marie Antoinette in the French Revolution novels is continually reminded that she is not French but Austrian; the man in the iron mask has been excluded since birth from his rightful place as the king's son and from all human society, even before he's forced to wear the cage on his face that marks him like Cain. It's very easy to make a long list of Dumas characters who are on the outside, a theme in his novels that would make an interesting study.

Much remains to be studied critically in Dumas' novels and plays. His work has never received the critical attention that it deserves. One of the most popular authors of all time, he has not been considered to rank with the most significant, especially not in this country. There are several reasons for this, I think. His very popularity is a mark against him. Writers whose works are enjoyable to read often have to struggle against the kind of critical prejudice that

assumes "significant" means "dull." The fact that Dumas is such a fine storyteller has been held against him. Most people also probably first read him when they are young (his books are most easily found in libraries in the "juvenile" section) and assume, when they are older, that there is nothing more to him than what they understood when they were fifteen years of age. Dumas' life was so colorful and flamboyant, too, that the critics who want to study him tend to get sidetracked in discussing his duels and mistresses rather than his work. I was able to find many biographies when researching this essay, but not many critical studies, especially not recent ones.

There are other problems, too. Dumas was certainly an overly prolific writer. As the author (sometimes with collaborators) of over seven hundred works, he was often repetitive, and sometimes wrote things that were just plain bad; it is difficult to sort through all his books and impossible to read all of them. And then there is the question of the collaborators. The question "Exactly how much of the works of Dumas did Dumas actually write?" has been asked ever since Jean-Baptiste Jacquot, writing under the pseudonym Eugene de Mirecourt, published the scurrilous pamphlet *Fabrique de Romans, Alexandre Dumas & Cie. [Alexander Dumas & Co., Novel Factory]*[86] That Mirecourt was discredited in a court of a law because of this pamphlet, condemned to fifteen days in prison, forced to make a retraction, and later was proved to be a plagiarist himself has not seemed to matter; the mud still sticks.[87] This has happened even though when Dumas is known to have used a collaborator (the most important of these was Auguste Maquet), evidence exists showing who wrote which part of the books. Maquet was responsible for parts of the Musketeer novels and of *Monte Cristo,* but a court ruled that he had not done enough work on any of these books to be listed as co-author. Maquet wrote novels on his own as well, but none of them is any good.[88]

Bad translators have done more harm to Dumas in the English-speaking world than Mirecourt and Maquet, unfortunately. That Aramis should be called a "stout" young man in the most readily available translation of *The Three Musketeers* is bad enough.[89] Dumas actually wrote only that he was young, (Dumas wrote nothing about his size), but Dumas' language very often is rendered carelessly and imprecisely, in the mistaken idea that only the story counts with him. This makes it impossible to do many kinds of critical studies of his work. His works have also frequently been abridged in the most careless way, so that one has no sense, when reading his works in English, of the careful way that he plotted them in French.

The Man in the Iron Mask is the worst example of poor cutting. This book actually does not exist in French, since the English work with this name is a compilation of excerpts from several works, chopped up and pasted back together. Although it is an exciting story, it is no longer a work of literature but simply hash.[90] The edition of the **Count of Monte Cristo** that is easiest to find today is not quite so bad, but it has also been mercilessly cut—only about a quarter of the work has actually been translated. From what is left (though it is translated competently enough), it is impossible to see why Dickens and others so admired the novel. The careful plotting, the point and counterpoint of the great themes of revenge, resurrection, man's right to play God, mercy, and marriage (not to speak of the slavery theme) are no longer there; nothing remains except a simple story line.

Georges is Dumas' only work with a black theme that has ever been translated into English—and this was not done until 1975, one hundred and twenty-two years after it was first published. I have not found any translations of **Fiesques,** and **Charles VII chez ses grands vassaux** has never, until now, been published in the United States.

Notes

[1] André Maurois, *Les Trois Dumas* (Paris: Librairie Hachette, 1957), p. 12 and F. W. Hemmings, *Alexandre Dumas: The King of Romance* (New York: Charles Scribner's Sons, 1979), p. 5.

[2] Roger Bastide, *African Civilizations in the New World,* trans. Peter Green, (New York: Harper and Row, 1971), pp. 138-45.

[3] C. L. Sulzberger, *Fathers and Children: How Famous Men Were Influenced by Their Fathers* (New York: Arbor House, 1987), p. 42 and Hemmings, *Alexandre Dumas,* p. 4.

[4] Hemmings, *Alexandre Dumas,* p. 4.

[5] Ibid., p. 5.

[6] Sulzberger, *Fathers and Children,* p. 42.

[7] Maurois, *Les Trois Dumas,* p. 14.

[8] C. L. R. James, *The Black Jacobins: Toussaint L'Ouverture and the San Domingo Revolution,* 2nd ed. (New York: Random House, 1963), p. 38.

[9] Hemmings, *Alexandre Dumas,* p. 1.

[10] Claude Schopp *Alexandre Dumas: Genius of Life,* trans. A. J. Koch (New York and Toronto: Franklin Watts, 1988), p. 15.

[11] Hemmings, *Alexandre Dumas,* pp. 6-7 and Maurois *Les Trois Dumas,* p. 12.

[12] The affair is well documented, both in Dumas *père's Mes Mémoires* and in a contemporary police report. See Hemmings, *Alexandre Dumas,* p. 213 n. 6.

[13] Ibid., p. 7

[14] Ibid., p. 213 n. 6.

[15] Ibid., p. 7.

[16] Sulzberger, *Fathers and Children,* p. 43.

[17] James, *The Black Jacobins,* p. 76.

[18] Sulzberger, *Fathers and Children,* p. 40.

[19] Maurois, *Les Trois Dumas,* p. 19.

[20] Sulzberger, *Fathers and Children,* p. 47.

[21] Maurois, *Les Trois Dumas,* p.22.

[22] Sulzberger, *Fathers and Children,* p. 41.

[23] Maurois, *Les Trois Dumas,* p. 23.

[24] James, *The Black Jacobins,* p. 365. Toussaint died in part because he was not given proper medical care, his doctor and surgeon having been dismissed on the pretext that they would be useless to him since "the constitution of Negroes . . [is] . . totally different from that of Europeans" (Ibid., p. 363).

[25] Maurois, *Les Trois Dumas,* p. 25.

[26] Ibid., p. 30.

[27] Dumas, *père, My Memoirs,* trans. and ed. A. Craig Bell (Chilton Book Company Division, 1961), p. 17.

[28] Dumas, *père, Le Comte de Monte Cristo,* 3 vols. (Livre de Poche, 1973), 3:192.

[29] Dumas, *père, The Road to Monte Cristo: A Condensation from the Memoirs of Alexandre Dumas,* trans. James Eckert Goodman (New York: Charles Scribner's Sons, 1956), p. 202. Dumas refers to his "faintly creole" accent.

[30] Arthur F. Davidson, *Alexandre Dumas: His Life and Works* (Westminster: Archibald Constable & Co., 1902), p. 201.

[31] Maurois, *Les Trois Dumas,* p. 13.

[32] Schopp, *Alexandre Dumas,* pp. 9-10, and Dumas, *père, My Memoirs,* p. 18.

[33] Dumas, *père, My Memoirs,* p. 14.

[34] Hemmings, *Alexandre Dumas,* p. 17.

[35] Dumas, *père, The Road to Monte Cristo,* p. 3.

[36] Dumas, *père, My Memoirs,* p. 29.

[37] Hemmings, *Alexandre Dumas,* pp. 204-5.

[38] Madelon Bedell, *The Alcotts: Biography of a Family,* (New York: Clarkson N. Potton, Inc., 1980), p. 149.

[39] Richard Wright, *Black Boy: A Record of Childhood and Youth* (New York: Harper and Row, 1989, original 1937), p. 267-68.

[40] It is fair to note, however, that it was not completely unknown, in the eighteenth and nineteenth centuries, for a white woman to give birth to a mulatto child. Lemuel B. Haynes (1753-1833), a well-known black preacher, was the son of a white woman and a slave (see *Black Writers of America: A Comprehensive Anthology,* ed. Richard Barksdale and Keneth Kinnamon, [MacMillan, 1972], p. 226). In Harriet E. Wilson's novel *Our Nig* (1859), which Henry Louis Gates, Jr., believes to be autobiographical (see *Figures in Black: Words, Signs, and the "Racial" Self* [New York and Oxford University Press, 1987], p. 126), the character Frado has a mother who is white, though she is black. Both the real man and the fictional little girl were deserted, however, by mothers who were unable to support a kind of social disapproval and ostracism that Mme. Dumas neither expected nor received. Her parents and family were flattered when Thomas-Alexandre sought her hand in marriage (he had been living in their house, billeted there by the army) and the only stipulation her father made was that the young black reach the rank of general before the wedding took place (see Maurois *Les Trois Dumas,* p. 13).

[41] Well-known black expatriates to France in our century include Josephine Baker, James Baldwin, Richard Wright, and recently, Barbara Chase-Riboud.

[42] Davidson, *Alexandre Dumas,* p. 45, and Maurois, *Les Trois Dumas,* p. 78.

[43] Hemmings, *Alexandre Dumas,* p. 135.

[44] Ibid., p. 54.

[45] Maurois, *Les Trois Dumas,* p. 401.

[46] Davidson, *Alexandre Dumas,* p. 45.

[47] Davidson reproduces this sketch on p. 288.

[48] John C. Miller, *The Wolf by the Ears: Thomas Jefferson and Slavery* (New York: MacMillan, 1977), pp. 273-74.

[49] Dumas, *père, The Road to Monte Cristo,* p. 202, and Schopp, *Alexandre Dumas,* p. 153.

[50] Maurois, *Les Trois Dumas,* p. 266, and Hemmings, *Alexandre Dumas,* p. 154.

[51] Maurois, *Les Trois Dumas,* p. 266.

[52] Dumas, *père, My Memoirs,* p. 207, and Schopp, *Alexandre Dumas,* p. 79.

[53] Sulzberger, *Fathers and Children,* p. 53.

[54] Hemmings, *Alexandre Dumas,* p. 143.

[55] Ibid., p. 139.

[56] Dumas, *père, My Memoirs,* p. 195.

[57] Hemmings, *Alexandre Dumas,* p. 148.

[58] Schopp, *Alexandre Dumas,* p. 323.

[59] Ibid., p. 475.

[60] The famous letter from the novel in which Armand breaks off with Marguerite, telling her, "I'm not rich enough to love you as I would like, or poor enough to be loved as you would like," is a word for word reproduction of one that Dumas *fils* wrote to Marie Duplessis on August 30, 1845 (see Maurois, *Les Trois Dumas,* p. 222). He began the novel after rereading her letters to him after her death.

[61] Dumas, Alexandre, *fils, La Dame aux Caméllias* (Paris: Gallimard, 1975), p. 42.

[62] Ibid., p. 349.

[63] Maurois, *Les Trois Dumas,* pp. 487-89.

[64] Schopp, *Alexandre Dumas,* p. 308.

[65] Dumas, *père, My Memoirs,* pp. 103-4.

[66] Maurois, *Les Trois Dumas,* p. 35.

[67] Ibid., p. 34.

[68] Dumas, *père, My Memoirs,* pp. 25-8.

[69] Dumas, *père, The Road to Monte Cristo,* p. 43.

[70] Lomax, Alan, and Raoul Abdul, ed., *3,000 Years of Black Poetry* (Greenwich, Conn.: Fawcett Publishing House, 1970), p. 87.

[71] See Dorothy Trench-Bonett, "Alexander Pushkin—Black Russian Poet," *The Black Scholar,* 20 no. 2,

March/April 1989, pp. 2-9. *The Negro of Peter the Great* can be found in Alexander Sergeyevitch Pushkin, *The Captain's Daughter and Other Great Stories,* trans. T. Keane (New York: Random House, 1936), pp. 209-310.

72 Although he translated one story by Pushkin as "La Boule de Neige," including "Le Chasse-Neige" (see Davidson's list of Dumas' works in *Alexandre Dumas*), after his trip to Russia, Dumas, who could neither speak or read Russian, used a crib for this translation. Russia was considered a barbarous, backwards, "Asiatic" country by Western Europeans in Dumas' time; they knew nothing of Russian literature, and Dumas probably considered the Pushkin story a curiosity. I am unable to find any evidence that he knew that Pushkin was also black, nor could I figure out which of Pushkin's works was translated under that title.

73 Schopp, *Alexandre Dumas,* p. 93.

74 Ibid., p. 45.

75 Dumas, *père, Mes Mémoires,* quoted in Parigot, *Alexandre Dumas,* p. 26.

76 Maurice Valency, *The Flower and the Castle: An Introduction to Modern Drama* (New York: MacMillan, 1963), pp. 75, 76.

77 Maurois, *Les Trois Dumas,* p. 89.

78 Valency, *The Flower and the Castle,* p. 50. In 1843, Francois Ponsard's Lucrece, a drama in the classic style, had an unexpected success, and no dramas were produced in the Romantic style after this until the brief revival with Rostand.

79 The Chilton Company Book Division (Peter Owen) has translated several of these travel guides into English under the titles *Travels in Switzerland, From Paris to Cadiz, Tangier to Tunis,* and *Adventures in Czarist Russia.*

80 Hemmings, *Alexandre Dumas,* p. 126.

81 Alexandre Dumas, *père, Georges,* (New York: Random House, 1975).

82 Frances Miltoun, *Dumas' Paris* (Boston: L. C. Page & Co, 1905), p. 47.

83 Hemmings, *Alexandre Dumas,* p. 125.

84 See, for example, Alexandre Dumas, *père, Monte Cristo,* Livrede Piche, 1973, (3 volumes), vol. 3, p. 196. Interestingly, in *Monte Cristo,* there is not only the white slave, Haydee, but also a black slave, Ali. Ali has had his tongue cut out, however; he is a mute. Did Dumas make him mute, I wonder, because of the

lack of success he had had until this point in trying to tell the stories of blacks?

85 Hemmings, *Alexandre Dumas,* pp. 126-27 and Maurois, *Les Trois Dumas,* pp. 246-51, both give synopses of the true story of Francois Picaud, used as a basis for *Monte Cristo,* and discuss the many changes Dumas made for his plot. Hemmings also provides an excellent critical study of Dumas' novel on pp. 127-30.

86 Hemmings, *Alexandre Dumas,* p. 137-38.

87 Maurois, *Les Trois Dumas,* pp. 205-6.

88 See ibid., pp. 202-8 for a frank discussion of Dumas, Maquet, and the question of plagiarism vs. collaboration.

89 *The Three Musketeers.*

90 See foreword to Alexandre Dumas, *père, The Man in the Iron Mask.* (Dodd Mead, 1944).

Bibliography

Bastide, Roger. *African Civilisations in the New World.* Trans. Peter Green. New York: Harper and Row, 1971.

Black Writers of America: A Comprehensive Anthology. ed. Richard Barksdale and Keneth Kinnamon. New York: Macmillan, 1972.

de Bury, Blaze. *Alexandre Dumas, Sa Vie, Son Temps, Son Oeuvre.* Paris: Ancienne Maison Michel Levy Freres, 1885.

Davidson, Arthur F. *Alexandre Dumas, His Life and Works.* Westminister: Archibald Constable & Co., 1902.

Dumas, Alexandre, *fils. La Dame aux Camellias.* Paris: Gallimard, 1975.

Dumas, Alexandre, *père. Charles VII chez ses grands vassaux, (Tragedie en cinq actes).* Paris: Charles Lemesle, 1831.

Dumas, Alexandre, *père. Le Comte de Monte Cristo.* 3 vols. Livre de Poche, 1973.

Dumas, Alexandre, *père. My Memoirs.* Trans. A. Craig Bell. Chilton Company Book Division, 1961.

Dumas, Alexandre, *père. The Road to Monte Cristo: A Condensation from the Memoirs of Alexandre Dumas.* Ed. Jules Ekert Goodman. New York: Charles Scribner's Sons, 1956.

Dumas, Alexandre, *père. Les Trois Mousquetaires.* G. F. Flammarion, 1984.

Dumas, Alexandre, *père. La Tulipe Noire.* Collection Nelson, Calmann-Levy.

Dumas, Alexandre, *père. Vingt Ans Apres.* 2 vols. G. F. Flammarion.

Gates, Henry Louis, Jr. *Figures in Black: Words, Signs and the "Racial" Self.* New York and Oxford: Oxford University Press, 1987.

Hemmings, F. W. J. *Alexandre Dumas: The King of Romance.* New York: Charles Scribner's Sons, 1979.

James, C. L. R. *The Black Jacobins: Toussaint L'Ouverture and the San Domingo Revolution.* 2nd ed. New York: Random House, 1963.

Maurois, André. *Les Trois Dumas.* Paris: Librairie Hachette, 1957.

Maurois, André. *Three Musketeers: A Study of the Dumas Family.* Translation of *Les Trois Dumas* by Gerald Hopkins. London: Jonathan Cape, 1957.

Miltoun, Frances. *Dumas' Paris.* Boston: L. C. Page & Co., 1905.

Miquel, Pierre. *Histoire de France.* Libraire Artheme Fayard, 1976.

Parigot, Hippolyte. *Alexandre Dumas, père.* Paris: Librairie Hachette, 1902.

Parigot, Hippolyte. *Le Drame d'Alexandre Dumas: Etude Dramatique, Sociale et Litteraire.* Paris: Calmann Levy, 1899.

Robertson, J. G. "Other Sturmer und Dranger: Schiller's Early Years." *A History of German Literature.* William Blackwood & Sons, Ltd., 1949. Pp. 326-38.

Schopp, Claude. *Alexandre Dumas: Genius of Life.* Trans. A. J. Koch. New York and Toronto: Franklin Watts, 1988.

Scott, Sir Walter, *Quentin Durward.* New York: Dodd, Mead & Co., 1923.

Shakespeare, William. *The Tragedy of Othello, The Moor of Venice.* Folger Library Edition. New York: Washington Square Press, 1957.

Sulzberger, C. L. *Fathers and Children: How Famous Leaders Were Influenced by Their Fathers.* New York: Arbor House, 1987. Pp. 39-57.

Valency, Maurice. *The Flower and the Castle: An Introduction to Modern Drama.* New York: Macmillan, 1963. Pp. 11-90.

Adrian Kiernander (essay date 1996)

SOURCE: "Paris Was Always Burning: (Drag) Queens and Kings in Two Early Plays by Alexandre Dumas *père,*" in *Essays in Theatre,* Vol. 14, No. 2, May, 1996, pp. 158-73.

[*In the following essay, Kiernander explores aspects of androgyny and sexual ambiguity in the plays* Christine *and* Henri III et sa cour.]

It is apt that the writings of Alexandre Dumas père, which deal so frequently with overwhelming obsession, should have provoked similar extraordinary obsessions in his readers. The result of one such obsession is a vast repository of Dumas material, the book collection alone consisting of over 2,500 titles (many of them multi-volume works), in the Auckland City Library, collected in the first half of this century by a passionate New Zealand bibliophile Frank Wild Reed. Reed corresponded avidly with similar Dumas fanatics around the world, and his own substantial collection was augmented by the legacy of one of his older co-devotees, R. S. Garnett, an Englishman who bequeathed to Reed his even larger collection which he had in part acquired from the French collector Glinel, who in turn had acquired material, including unpublished manuscripts, from the estate of Dumas.[1]

Included in the collection are four generally unknown essays by Dumas which form part of a volume called **Les Étoiles du monde,** dealing with the "great" women of history, each chapter accompanied by an engraving of its subject. The four chapters contributed by Dumas have a common theme of sexual perversity, dealing with the L/lesbian poet Sappho, the Roman Lucrece, Cleopatra, and the transvestite Joan of Arc—it was in fact on a charge of transvestism that Joan was burned. Almost perversely, the engraving accompanying the essay on Joan, rather than depicting her as a female-to-male cross dresser, shows her looking as feminine as possible under the circumstances, wearing a kind of cast-iron crinoline. There seems to be a marked desire here to avoid the question of transvestism.

On the other hand, in the section dealing with Sappho, Dumas's essay is completely open and apparently non-judgemental about Sappho's poetry and biography indicating a sexual attraction to other women, and there is nothing in the accompanying engraving which seems pejorative—in fact she looks strikingly similar to the depiction of the French national hero Joan, and the same model may have been used for both images. During the course of the essay Dumas cites standard French translations of Sappho's major surviving poem, and then offers his own version on the grounds that the others are "insufficiently lesbian."

It is not clear whether Dumas himself selected these subjects to write about or whether they were assigned to him by the editors of the volume, but their existence throws an interesting light on Dumas's first two serious plays to be staged under his own name, *Henri III et sa cour* and *Christine,* both historical dramas based on the lives of monarchs, Henry III of France and Queen Christina of Sweden. Both of these figures were popularly reputed to have orientations towards lovers of the same sex, and both had (and still have) the reputation of being habitual transvestites.

What was there in these two that attracted the young Alexandre Dumas? And is it important? Much recent queer theory would cast doubt on the value of that kind of biographical inquiry which attempts to discover homosexual aspects of the lives of the historical and famous, and I resist the temptation to speculate about the biography of a writer whose professional nickname, *père,* attests to his heterosexual productivity—except to note that Alexandre Dumas *fils* was born out of wedlock, which is only one of many instances of a defiantly and prodigiously unorthodox uncontrollability in the author's sexual history—exuberantly non-monogamous and largely non-uxorious (though, according to legend, highly procreative)—which might be read as having some proto-queer features, if queer is in part characterised by a lack of conventional control and restraint and an indulgence in (particularly sexual) fantasy.

Instead I would like to look at some queer features of the two transvestite scripts as texts and to speculate on possible approaches to putting *Henri III,* the more theatrically promising of the two from this point of view, onto the stage as queer theatre. *Christine* is particularly interesting as a parallel example from the same period of a script that deals with another monarch notorious for transvestism; however it is a weaker script which would be less likely to have theatrical potential at the end of the twentieth century, and so will be given slighter attention in this paper. My reasons for choosing queer theory include the fact that this is the only current theoretical methodology which focuses on the intersections and interferences between the diversionary uncontrollability of sexual fantasy/desire and the controlling teleology of social and political power.

Some versions of queer theory have sought to rethink and reject the traditional trope of the marginalisation of gay and lesbian people;[2] in addition there has been a strategic counter-hegemonic move to focus on the pervasiveness of a broadly defined queerness in human society. In a provocative gesture which has been frequently quoted, Michael Warner has pointed out that sexuality is shaped by representations and claims that "fantasy and other kinds of representation are inherently uncontrollable, queer by nature. This focus on messy representation allows queer theory, like non-academic queer activism, to be both antiassimilationist

and antiseparatist: you can't eliminate queerness, says queer theory, or screen it out. It's everywhere. There's no place to hide, hetero-scum!" (Warner 19) The aspects of queer theory which are most important for the purposes of this paper are the recognition of the pervasive nature of queerness, the celebration of its festive resistance to control, by self or other, which links it with Bakhtinian theories of the carnivalesque, and its opposition to traditionalist discourses which, at the extreme, valorise sex only when it is heterosexual, monogamous, post- and intramarital, procreative, and hierarchical.

. . . . .

The chronology of the writing and production of the two scripts is somewhat confused and needs brief explanation. A version of *Christine* was written first but, although it was initially accepted for performance at the Théâtre Français, its staging was postponed. Then Dumas's huge success with the subsequent *Henri III,* which was the first Romantic drama to be staged at the Théâtre Français, beating Hugo's now more famous *Hernani* by a full year, prompted him to revise and tighten *Christine,* which was subsequently performed at the Odéon. In both scripts the ambivalently depicted personalities and practices of the homosexual/transvestite monarchs lead to a crisis of patriarchal authority, identity, and representation in the societies they rule, perhaps inevitably precipitated when the position of Big Daddy, the validating symbol of traditional patriarchal authority (see Donkin and Clement), is occupied by the figure of a capricious woman or a sodomitical drag queen.

The problematising of patriarchy in these scripts fits neatly with the patterns of monarchical crisis in the late 1820s when Dumas wrote them, a period when a shaky, *ersatz* monarchy had been reimposed on the rubble of the Revolution and the Empire. The Restoration was marked by a re-imposition of patriarchal social values which had been partially thrown off during the period of the revolution; liberalised laws introduced in the early 1790s concerning divorce and homosexuality, which had been gradually weakened under Napoleon, were overturned as soon as Louis XVIII acceded to the throne (Copley 24).

In what looks like evidence of a widespread anxiety about the status of patriarchal values, the subject of the first-written play was common currency, one of three dramatisations of the life of Queen Christina to be staged in Paris almost simultaneously; Dumas claimed that he was spurred to write his drama when he was impressed, at the Paris salon, by a depiction by a woman sculptor of an incident from the life of the Swedish queen: the assassination, at Christina's orders, of her Italian lover Monaldeschi. This murder of a man at the instigation of a woman seems to have been the most interesting feature of the Christina legend in Paris in the 1820s. Within a year of the production of Dumas's two plays came the 1830 uprising which toppled the would-be autocrat Charles X. For a few days France was once again moving towards being a republic (partly aided by a typically histrionic exploit by Dumas himself) only to compromise at the last minute with the coronation of Louis-Philippe, the Citizen King.

Contemporary recollections of the first performance of *Henri III* reinforce that the play was perceived by some as an anti-patriarchal gesture: there were stories that the younger members of the audience performed a noisy dance around the theatre's bust of Racine (Dumas himself commented wryly on this legend, pointing out that it is impossible because the bust of Racine is set into a wall) chanting "Racine vanquished! Voltaire vanquished!" (The French word *"enfonce"* is interesting in this context, being derived from a verb meaning "to pierce" or "to penetrate.") The fathers of French theatre, at least, were clearly perceived as being under attack by the play.[3] But like its ambivalent protagonist, the play's unsettling politics and its slippery relation to contemporary events are neatly illustrated by the reactions of the critics, one Royalist newspaper finding the play supportive of the monarchy, others calling it "a flagrant conspiracy against the throne and the altar" and lamenting that "Royalty and religion are delivered up to the beasts of the amphitheatre" (Bassan and Chevalley 34).

Dumas himself was similarly ambivalent. By a coincidence he was a junior clerk in the service of the Duke of Orleans at the time and audaciously had pressured his employer, who would soon become King Louis-Philippe, into attending the opening performance of *Henri III.* This was a potentially dangerous gesture, as the play was widely interpreted as an allegory of the French political situation before the 1830 revolution, with Henri taken to represent Charles X and Orleans identified with Henri's lethal opponent de Guise. Even King Charles read the play in this way and interrogated Orleans on the subject.[4] But almost immediately after Orleans became Louis-Philippe, Dumas, instead of trying to benefit from a relatively close relationship with the new monarch, ostentatiously resigned from his employment. He later re-established a close relationship with members of the royal family but remained a republican, and after the revolution of 1848 stood unsuccessfully for the National Assembly, quoting from his writings from 1831 onward as evidence of his republicanism and drawing a clear link between his work as a writer and as a politician. But his nuanced attitude, distinguishing finely between institutions and persons, is summed up in a slogan which he launches in his own voice: "Death to the monarchy! and God save the King!" ("A ses concitoyens" 4).

There is no doubt that official attitudes, even as late as the reign of Napoleon III, regarded some of his work as subversive of monarchy and authority. A censorship report banning revivals of *La Tour de Nesle* draws attention to the abasement of royal persons in other plays and questions how to allow a play "whose main character is a Queen of France . . . who, after every night's debauch, has the body of the lover to whom she has given herself thrown into the Seine." Calling it a tissue of crimes and monstrosities, the report demands that it be read in the light of "respect for crowned heads and the impression that such scenes must leave in the mind of the masses" (*La Censure* 78; my translation).

. . . . .

Aspects of the life of Queen Christina are relatively well known to us from the film with Greta Garbo, and though the film makes no reference to lesbianism, it does famously focus on Christina's penchant for dressing as a man. In the play, which has a loose, episodic structure extending over several years and ranging widely across Europe, Christine plays havoc with the certitudes and stability of authority not only by being a woman, but by repeatedly relinquishing and then reclaiming the Swedish throne. Early in the play she abdicates so casually as to effectively mock and devalue the importance of political power.

Henri de Valois is less well known in the twentieth-century anglophone world, so some facts about his bizarre history, a combination of *Richard III* and *Ubu Roi,* enrich a reading of the script. The third son of Henri II and Catherine de Medici, he had two older brothers between him and the French crown, so it probably made sense for him to accept the kingdom of Poland when it was offered, even though his father and his eldest brother, François II, had both already died and his brother Charles IX was the French King. But only six months after Henri became King of Poland, Charles died and Henri inherited the French crown. Hearing the news in a letter from his mother, he left Cracow secretly at once, according to popular history (see for example Cook 112), escaping through a window of the royal palace to return to France and enraging his Polish ex-subjects by taking the crown jewels with him. Recent scholarship suggests that the accusations of homosexuality which were popularly levelled at Henri as part of an oppositional political campaign in France may not have any foundation in historical fact (see Le Roy Ladurie 235; Cameron); nevertheless homosexual appetites and transvestite behaviour seem to have continued in the nineteenth century to be part of what was popularly known about him through the sources which Dumas may have used such as l'Estoile's chronicles of the period of Henri III. Certainly in his own day his authority was troubled by a number of scurrilous pamphlets and caricatures representing him as a "hermaphrodite," which circulated widely. The commentary on the image labelled

"Les Hermaphrodites" reads: "I am neither male nor female, and if I am in my right mind, which of the two should I choose? But what does it matter which one looks like? It is better to have them both together—one thus receives double pleasure."[5]

One scurrilous publication which appeared in the year of Henri's death (qtd. in Cameron 82) reveals clearly the linked anxieties about the penetration of the male body and castration which underlie the attacks on Henri. In addition to accusations of wearing make-up and women's clothing, the pamphlet claims that

> he devised a fantasy in his mind that through artifice he could be transformed in his shape, and to better execute his diabolic wish he summoned all the most excellent surgeons, physicians and philosophers of his time and permitted them to cauterise his body and to make all the openings and wounds that they wished, in order that they might render him apt to conjoin himself with men: at whose persuasion they cut him up in several places and castrated him. But in the end he remained, by the permission of God, useless in terms of both sexes.

Henri's contemporary, Elizabeth I of England, was able to take advantage of the discrepancy between her "body politic" and her "body natural," astutely exploiting as a woman the available images (which were helpful in her dealings with the representatives of an otherwise anxious patriarchy) of virgin, seductress, and mother (Montrose); for Henri, who lost control of his self-fashioning, the popular image of his sodomitic "body natural" was too monstrous to be linked to that of the Kingdom of France. In addition, sodomy, which in England was conceptually linked with papist heresy, was in France used by Henri's conservative Catholic enemies, as Stephen Orgel has pointed out, as a codeword for Protestantism, a reference to his moderate treatment of the Huguenots.

But if in history Henri was interpellated into queerness as an act of political opposition, his character, as depicted in the play, can be read as a defiant challenge to that interpellation, Henri flaunting the term of abuse and converting it into a badge of victory in the same way that the word "queer" itself has recently been turned back and used to affirm what it was previously used to attack. Judith Butler celebrates the promise she sees when "the subject who is 'queered' into public discourse through homophobic interpellations of various kinds *takes up* or *cites* that very term as the discursive basis for an opposition" ("Critically Queer" 23). The character Henri's flagrant and deliberate abuse of the dignity of high office is a form of citation of the queerness which was attributed to him. It operates in part as a strategy to problematise and oppose the play's representatives of orthodoxy.

The negative aspects of Henri's life are recorded in Dumas's sources but are deployed by him in strangely ambivalent ways, needlessly focusing on the outrageous behaviour of the King (who is a relatively inconsequential figure in the development of the main plot, though one of the most memorable figures in the script) but indulging in the pleasure of his transgressions, acknowledging the intelligence of his game-playing, and allowing him to score an important political victory at a late and crucial moment in the sub-plot. This ambivalence carries into the early stage history of the play, in which the actor playing the role changed the interpretation from what was intended to be a pejorative picture of the King to something much more sympathetic. This went against Dumas's stated instructions, but in his preface to the published script the playwright concedes that he rapidly saw that the actor's changes were an improvement on his own original concept.

Throughout the play, despite the political problems of his reign, Henri flagrantly toys with power, playing capricious games, promoting his favourites on whims, acknowledging that the real power in the realm is his manipulative mother while at the same time showing enough political acumen that the throne is neither clearly his nor not his but suspended in a state of destabilising uncertainty.

Dumas's script takes up the story late in the reign. Henri is King of France but is represented in the early part of the script as an apparent weakling under the controlling influence of his mother and surrounded by his *mignons,* the fashionable young men mainly from the minor nobility who were his favourites and whose political and social ascendancy was much resented by the established aristocracy.

Henri never actually appears on stage in women's clothing but in one of his first speeches he reveals that for a costume ball scheduled for that evening he is planning to appear as an Amazon, a detail Dumas must have got from an actual event, a masquerade held during the reign of Charles IX in celebration of the marriage of Henri de Navarre (the future Henri IV) in which King Charles, together with Henri, who was then duc d'Anjou, and their youngest brother François Hercule, duc d'Alençon, appeared as Amazons armed with bows and bare-breasted (Le Roy Ladurie 231). Nor, incidentally, does Christine appear in drag in the other play. However if the visual image of the transvestite monarch is repressed in both plays, the repressed returns through the introduction of travesty roles. In **Henri** the otherwise unnecessary figure of a cheeky pageboy is foregrounded, played of course by a woman, and in **Christine** a major cross-dressing plot is developed, involving a female character who disguises herself as a boy to be able to travel round Europe in the company of the man she is in love with.

The fact that we never see Henri in full drag may be the result of discretion on Dumas's part, but it might alternatively be read as something more threatening. Marjorie Garber in *Vested Interests* discusses the figure of the cross dresser, when looked *at* rather than *through,* as epistemologically unsettling, a third term upsetting the binarism of masculine-feminine, neither male nor female but something else entirely which disturbs the neat categories of self and other, insider and outsider, identification and alienation. Dumas's Henri, by being openly transvestite but leaving his transvestism invisible, is particularly treacherous territory, a double-cross dresser, a transvestite who refuses to show his true colours, who is impossible to look directly at but famous and flagrant enough not to be looked through. He is a known drag queen disguised as a man/king who upsets the hierarchies based on binarism but whose invisibility puts him just out of reach of the surveillance and punishment to which the traditionalist forces, now uncomfortably on the outer, would like to subject him.

Structurally the main narrative of **Henri III,** to which the figure of Henri is only peripheral, is a tight and skilful historical Romantic melodrama dealing principally with the illicit love of one of Henri's favourites, Saint Mégrin, for Catherine, the wife of Henri's powerful adversary, the duc de Guise (whose nickname was *"le Balafré,"* or "Scarface"). De Guise is the play's main representative of traditional patriarchal forces, the script foregrounding his roles as husband and as leader of the ultra-conservative Catholic League which is in conspiracy against the King. Here the script plays with genres, and therefore patterns of audience alignment, in quite unexpected ways. Instead of putting the duc de Guise, who is also called Henri, into a favourable light as an alternative to the King's dissipation and his threat to patriarchy, it does its best to make him the real villain of the piece, borrowing from theatrical genres as old as Roman comedy, medieval poetry and the commedia dell'arte. The love triangle in which the script involves him places both him and his wife in the tradition of the marriage of January and May, in which illicit young love always triumphs and the impassioned cuckold is shown as a comic Pantalone.[6] De Guise in the script alienates audience sympathies further by his brutal treatment of his wife whom he, wrongly at that point, suspects of infidelity. In a horrific scene in act 3, which aroused the passions of the first-night audience and contributed to the play's enormous success, de Guise forces his wife to write a letter to Saint Mégrin which will lure the young suitor into a trap, first intimidating her by trying to make her drink what she believes to be a cup of poison, and then by sheer brute force, crushing her arm with his mailed fist until, as the stage directions and dialogue make plain, it is bruised visibly blue. De Guise's aim is twofold—first to avenge his honour as a man and husband, and subsequently to depose Henri from the throne, thus gaining fully for himself the power he had held in veiled form as Regent during the reign of Henri's eldest brother François II.

. . . . .

I want to explore the difference that the fact of Henri's reputation, highlighted by contrast with de Guise, makes to the script, and the opportunities this offers for the intervention of queer theory in the reading and staging of the play. In other words, what happens as a result of the choice of a shifting, ambivalent, and treacherous character like Henri III as the central figure, rather than some other less queer king fighting off attempts at deposition? It might be expected that the choice of the hyperbolically (and potentially comic) non-masculine Henri would tend to swing "normal" sympathies in the direction of de Guise, but the script appears to foreclose such a response because of that character's overdetermined masculine brutality.

I want to read the action of the script as focusing on a dangerous rather than comic crisis for the hegemonic forces represented by de Guise and the Catholic League. The presence of the non-masculine man has long been, as Eve Sedgwick has argued, a powerful threat for the heterosexist but homosocial organisation of patriarchy, a threat which is neatly located with the use of the adjective "homophobic." Henri's position carries that threat into what is perceived to be, in patriarchal terms, the centre of social and political organisation.

For a start, the effeminate and/or transvestite monarch undermines one of the foundational ideals of patriarchal organisation, the precise fit between the family governed by the omniscient and omnipotent masculine father and the state ruled by an omniscient and omnipotent masculine king. These images naturalise each other by the precision of their structural similarity, and when even one of the two is problematised the "natural" status of both is weakened. In this play both are jeopardised, by Henri's outrageous effeminacy as king and by de Guise's error, his misreading, as husband, of the relationship between his wife and Saint Mégrin.

Also interesting in this context is the close link between the queer and the carnivalesque, which is very apparent in this play. Many of the elements of Bakhtin's description of the carnival are in evidence here—the sense of occasional celebration; the world turned upside down; the grotesque body open to penetration; the social and sexual *mésalliances* between people of different rank, and the general disruption of traditional hierarchies; and specifically the masked ball to which Henri is planning to wear his Amazon costume. (In case any of the audience have missed the point, one of the mignons, the Vicomte de Joyeuse, is planning to come as Alcibiades.) The problem with this carnival, from the point of view of the nobility, is that its lord of misrule is also the King of France, and that it threatens to burst the confines of its allotted space and take over the whole year, the entire realm. Henri's throne room is permanently converted into a riotous playground for the favourites where, for example, Saint Mégrin can, with impunity, blow shotgun pellets through a peashooter at the highest ranking Duke in the kingdom. More significantly, when de Guise disdains to fight a duel with Saint Mégrin on account of the difference in their rank, Henri capriciously offers to create the young man a Duke on the same social level so a combat can take place. The seriousness of what is at stake in this carnivalesque clash is made evident by Henri's need to cancel the masked ball in favour of a council of state when political events overtake his plans. In terms of the social life of the court and the politics of the behind-the-scenes struggle (not to mention the theatricality of the play itself) this represents a serious sacrifice.

Henri's transvestism poses a further challenge to the patriarchal organisation de Guise represents. Any hegemonic system such as patriarchy depends for its success on naturalising the terms of its own ascendancy, and it will do this by insisting upon stable images of identity, and by a close control over representation. The king is the king, the nobility is the nobility, and privilege is accorded to those men, but not women, who naturally deserve it through position, rank, birth, sex and a rightful place in the scheme of things. Henri's transvestism is a powerful force undermining the certainties which such a process of naturalisation depends upon, revealing gender—one of the plinths of this construct of privilege—as a form of performance.

Judith Butler has made the point that gender performativity is too often simplified into a straightforward option or role adopted in a state of perfect freedom of choice by a subject who is in a position to choose. She draws attention to the fallacy that "gender is a construction that one puts on, as one puts on clothes in the morning, that there is a 'one' who is prior to this gender, a one who goes to the wardrobe of gender and decides with deliberation which gender it will be today. This is a voluntarist account of gender which presumes a subject, intact, prior to its gendering." But this is not to say that gender is not performance. She continues:

> Gender is performative insofar as it is the *effect* of a regulatory regime of gender differences in which genders are divided and hierarchised *under constraint.* Social constraints, taboos, prohibitions, threats of punishment operate in the ritualised repetition of norms, and this repetition constitutes the temporalised scene of gender construction and destabilization. There is no subject who precedes or enacts this repetition of norms. To the extent that this repetition creates an effect of gender uniformity, a stable effect of masculinity or femininity, it produces and destabilises the notion of the subject as well, for the subject only comes into intelligibility through the matrix of gender. ("Critically Queer" 21-22)

Butler's writing suggests why a figure like the duc de Guise is threatened by a transvestite monarch. Henri is in fact the one who demonstrates the greater courage and audacity, attributes traditionally associated with masculinity, through his willingness to take advantage of the very limited free-play in the apparatus of gender, to defy the constraints of the regulatory regime, to ignore and evade, as King and as persona, the "taboos, prohibitions and threats of punishment." But more dangerously still, Henri gives the game away. By his gender transgressions he draws attention to that one fact that de Guise cannot afford to acknowledge—that even as a real man de Guise is no more a self-present subject than the unreal man currently occupying the throne. And since neither of them can *naturally* occupy the place of God/King/Father, the most legitimate performer of the role may be the one who can best play (with) it. In this scenario Henri is the rightful King after all.

The exhilarating and inextricably chiasmatic confusion of marked and unmarked binary terms provokes a crisis in the symbolic which, as Butler points out, is to be "understood as a crisis over what constitutes the limits of intelligibility" and which will "register as a crisis in the name and in the morphological stability that the name is said to confer" (*Bodies* 138). In a play where several of the characters have a multiplicity of titles there is a paradoxical shortage of names: "Henri" serves equally for the King, the father of the King, and the man who would be king, while both King Henri's mother and Duke Henri's wife are called Catherine. With this crisis in reference, is it any wonder that de Guise the patriarch becomes confused and anxious about the integrity of his own name, body, and identity, which threaten to be invaded or absorbed into those of his arch-rival and alter-ego?

I would like finally to think about what kind of production might realise something of this reading of the script of **Henri III** on the stage, and unsurprisingly queer theory suggests a recourse to queer theatre. Both blatant and passing cross-dressing by the actors, and casting against and across sex, would be starting points. So would be moves to break up the forward drive of the very strong narrative with carnivalesque moments of celebration and indulgence in the spectacle of the moment. Splitting and blending of the characters, with the possibility of confusion between Henri de Valois and Henri de Guise. Music throughout—it is in any case a melodrama. The script allows for costuming which is, in both senses of the word, fabulous. Finding a way to make a space for the censored drag ball, putting it into the performance but under erasure as an imperfectly repressed fantasy, so showing (and not showing, because it too would be under erasure) the visible image of Henri for once in his unused Amazon outfit, which it would be a shame to waste. Emphasising the references to magic which run through the script—the play opens with an unrealised promise of necromancy. Taking seriously the figuratively byzantine and literally labyrinthine events—several of the characters get about through secret passages—, extending and exaggerating them so that the script's sense of space and chronology was threatened. An intensification to the maximum of the marital brutality of the duc de Guise, and of the transgressive effeminacy of Henri—as Butler says, "[t]he hyperbolic gesture is crucial to the exposure of the homophobic 'law' which can no longer control the terms of its own abjecting strategies" ("Critically Queer" 23). Above all, my ideal production would attempt to make serious and savage the clash between the two Henris and to highlight what is dangerously at stake in the King's transvestism, rather than treating him as a feeble-minded weakling, a pop-camp joke. Peggy Phelan points out in her essay on Jenny Livingstone's film about the black transvestite world of New York, *Paris Is Burning*—from which I have adapted the title of this paper—: "[G]ender and sexuality are games played for keeps and no one who steps too far outside traditionally assigned roles is ever home free" (109).

All this may be leaving Dumas far behind, but any anti-patriarchal project is hardly likely to be concerned about someone whose nickname is "the father." As a father figure his role in the project of this production might be that of the sacrificial victim, if as an author he were not always already dead. Nevertheless Dumas the republican, the translator of Sappho, the vanquisher of Racine and Voltaire, the playwright whose works were censored for their offences against the decency and dignity of royalty, reappears at my elbow intent on having the last word, suggesting a rethinking of the play's often-quoted final line. In the play's closing moments, in a strange, savage, and shocking twist to the comic genre of the passionate cuckold, the Pantalone de Guise has just trapped and assassinated the young lover of his wife. Immediately turning his thoughts to his long-term goal, the throne of France, he says, "Good! and now that we've finished with the valet, let's take care of the master." Here is a doubled narrative closure, an overdetermined example of a typical patriarchal structure implying ultimate certainty and the univocal voice of history, which wraps up not only this play but also any putative sequel. Both the play's action and structure seem to be on the side of de Guise.

But as Dumas and his audience schooled in French history knew well, the ending of the story is different. The historical de Guise certainly had Saint Mégrin murdered, but during his subsequent attempts on the throne he was in turn murdered by agents of the weakling Henri, his body multiply penetrated in precisely the way that his homophobia fears the most. One of Dumas's sources even recounts a graphic detail in which Henri, coming to view the assassinated Duke, gives the dead body a kick in the face (L'Estoile 103). In the play Dumas gives a different, even more powerfully overlayered double ending, in which two simultaneous readings of the same line, one literal and one ironic,

contradict each other, further destabilising the certainties of hegemonic patriarchy. Staging that would be a real challenge for a production.

Notes

[1] A study of this huge and still largely unexamined collection as it relates to the plays of Dumas is currently under way, and the opening sections of this paper result from this still preliminary investigation. I would like to express my thanks to the curator of the Auckland City Library Rare Books Room, Donald Kerr, who has been extremely helpful to me in my initial searches of the material and whose bibliographical study of the collection is the only serious scholarly attempt to date to deal with Reed's life's work.

[2] Henry Abelove touches on this issue in "From Thoreau to Queer Politics," and expanded on it in a conference paper given at the Australian National University Humanities Research Centre in 1993.

[3] Another, though apparently apocryphal, anti-patriarchal story which circulated about the opening night, and which was related by Dumas, was that "a cry of death had been uttered by a young fanatic called Aumary Duval, who demanded the heads of the members of the Academy— a parricide cry since the unfortunate man was the son of M. Aumary Duval, member of the Institute, and nephew of M. Alexandre Duval of the Académie Française" (Bassan and Chevalley 28).

[4] According to Dumas, the Duke of Orleans dismissed any parallel by claiming that his wife was not unfaithful and, ironically given the events of only a few months later, that he was not disloyal.

[5] Stephen Orgel in "Gendering the Crown" has recently pointed out a strange irony in the perception of the feminised monarch which bears directly on the image of Henri III: contrasting with the negative connotations in the depiction of Henri's "femininity" is "a transvestite portrait of [Henri's grandfather] François II done by the Fontainebleau artist Nicolo Bellin da Modena around 1545." The portrait is accompanied by a verse which explains that "though the King is a Mars in war, in peace he is a Minerva or Diana."

[6] It is noteworthy that, even though the historical de Guise was only relatively young at the time of the events of the play, in the first production at the Théâtre-Français the actor, Joanny, who played the role was judged a little too old (Bassan and Chevalley 31), which may have accentuated the discrepancy between the ages of the Duke and Duchess.

Works Cited

Abelove, Henry. "From Thoreau to Queer Politics." *The Yale Journal of Criticism* 6.2 (1993): 17-27.

Bassan, Fernande, and Sylvie Chevalley. *Alexandre Dumas père et la Comédie Française.* Paris: Lettres Modernes, Minard, 1972.

Butler, Judith. *Bodies That Matter: On the Discursive Limits of "Sex".* New York: Routledge, 1993.

————. "Critically Queer." *GLQ: A Journal of Gay and Lesbian Studies* 1.1 (1994): 17-32.

Cameron, Keith. *Henri III, a Maligned or Malignant King?: Aspects of the Satirical Iconography of Henri de Valois.* Exeter: U Exeter, 1978.

*La Censure sous Napoléon III: Rapports Inédits et in extenso (1852 à 1866), préface de *** [sic] et interview de Edmond de Goncourt.* Paris: Savine, 1892.

Cook, E. Thornton. *The Royal Line of France.* London: Murray, 1933.

Copley, Anthony. *Sexual Moralities in France, 1780-1980: New Ideas on the Family, Divorce, and Homosexuality: an Essay on Moral Change.* London: Routledge, 1989.

Donkin, Ellen, and Susan Clement, eds. *Upstaging Big Daddy: Directing Theater As If Gender and Race Matter.* Ann Arbor: U of Michigan P, 1993.

Doty, Alexander. *Making Things Perfectly Queer: Interpreting Mass Culture.* Minneapolis: U of Minnesota P, 1993.

Dumas, Alexandre. "A Ses Concitoyens de Seine-et-Oise, Alexandre Dumas, candidat à la représentation nationale." [Election manifesto]. Paris, 1848.

————. *Christine, ou Stockholm, Fontainebleau et Rome. Théâtre Complet de Alex. Dumas.* Vol 1. Paris: Calman-Lévy, n.d. 199-306.

————. "Cléopatre, Reine d'Egypte." *Les Étoiles du monde* 81-98.

————. *Les Étoiles du monde: galerie historique des femmes les plus célèbres de tous les temps et de tous les pays.* Paris: Garnier, 1858.

————. *Henri III et sa Cour. Théâtre Complet de Alex. Dumas.* Vol 1. Paris: Calman-Lévy, n.d. 117-98.

————. "Jeanne d'Arc." *Les Étoiles du monde* 115-38.

————. "Lucrèce." *Les Étoiles du monde* 219-34.

————. "Sappho." *Les Étoiles du monde* 287-300.

Garber, Marjorie. *Vested Interests: Cross-Dressing and Cultural Anxiety.* New York: Routledge, 1992.

Halleys-Dabot, Victor. *La Censure dramatique et le théâtre: histoire des vingt demières années, 1850-1870.* Paris: Dentu, 1871.

————. *Histoire de la censure théâtrale en France.* Paris: Dentu, 1862.

Kerr, Donald. "Frank Wild Reed, the Antipodean Alexandrian: A Study of a Book Collector." Master's thesis. Victoria U of Wellington, NZ, 1992.

Le Roy Ladurie, Emmanuel. *L'État Royal: de Louis XI à Henri IV, 1460-1610.* Paris: Hachette, 1987.

L'Estoile. *Journal des choses memorables advenues durant tout le règne de Henry III Roy de France & de Pologne.* n.d.

Montrose, Louis Adrian. "'Shaping Fantasies': Figurations of Gender and Power in Elizabethan Culture." *Representing the English Renaissance.* Ed. Stephen Greenblatt. Berkeley: U. of California P, 1988. 31-64.

Orgel, Stephen. "Gendering the Crown." Unpublished essay. n.d.

Phelan, Peggy. *Unmarked: The Politics of Performance.* London: Routledge, 1993.

Sedgwick, Eve Kosofsky. *Epistemology of the Closet.* Berkeley: U of California P, 1990.

Warner, Michael. "From Queer to Eternity." *Voice Literary Supplement* 106 (Jun. 1992): 18-19.

FURTHER READING

Biographies

Davidson, Arthur F. "The Great Novels." In *Alexandre Dumas (père): His Life and Works,* pp. 216-56. Philadelphia: J. B. Lippincott, 1902.

> Covers the period 1843-53, when Dumas produced his most significant works of fiction.

Hemmings, F. W. J. "The Novelist." In *The King of Romance: A Portrait of Alexandre Dumas,* pp. 114-30. London: Hamish Hamilton, 1979.

> Examines Dumas's career as a novelist, from his beginnings in the years of "*roman-feuilleton* mania" during the 1840s through his collaboration with Auguste Maquet and the writing of his most celebrated works.

Lang, Andrew. Introduction to *My Memoirs,* by Alexandre Dumas, translated by E. M. Waller, pp. xvii-xxxiv. London: Methuen and Co., 1907.

Expands on aspects of Dumas's early life covered in the *Memoir* and provides an overview of the author's later career.

Ross, Michael. *Alexandre Dumas.* London: David and Charles, 1981, 293p.

Offers an examination not only of Dumas's major works but also of critical junctures in his life, such as his transition from dramatist to novelist.

Spurr, Harry A. "His Writings." In *The Life and Writings of Alexandre Dumas (1802-1870),* pp. 183-270. New York: Frederick A. Stokes, 1902.

A detailed anecdotal account of Dumas's development as a historical novelist.

Criticism

Arni, Ora. "The Semiotics of Transactions: Mauss, Lacan and *The Three Musketeers.*" *Modern Language Notes* 100, No. 4 (September 1985): 728-57.

Examines the passage "from hand to hand" in *The Three Musketeers* and relates aspects of this to semiotic theories of displacement.

Cooper, Barbara T. "The Backward Glance of Parody: Author-Audience Complicity in a Comic Reduction of Dumas's *Henri III et sa cour.*" *Essays in Literature* 13, No. 2 (Fall 1986): 313-26.

Offers a detailed study of *Cricri et ses mitrons,* a parody of *Henri III et sa cour* by Carmouche and others.

George, Albert J. "The Major Romantics." In *Short Fiction in France 1800-1850,* pp. 135-65. Syracuse, N.Y.: Syracuse University Press, 1964.

Offers a study of Dumas's short fiction alongside works of other "Major Romantics" such as Victor Hugo and George Sand.

Girard, Marcel. Introduction to *The Three Musketeers,* by Alexandre Dumas, pp. v-xi. London: J. M. Dent, 1966.

Places Dumas's novel in its historical setting with a brief review of its factual bases. Short but detailed bibliography of Dumas's works is included.

Jones, Julie. "Vargas Llosa's Mangachería: The Pleasures of Community." *Revista de Estudios Hispanicos* 20, No. 1 (January 1986): 77-89.

Examines the influence of Dumas's musketeer novels, along with Victor Hugo's *Notre Dame de Paris,* on scenes in Mario Vargas Llosa's *La Casa Verde.*

Lang, Andrew. "To Alexandre Dumas." In *Letters to Dead Authors,* pp. 100-108. London: Longmans, Green, 1892.

An apostrophe to Dumas which presents his work as a tonic to a "generation suffering from mental and physical anaemia."

Luciani, Vincent. "The Genesis of *Lorenzino:* A Study of Dumas Père's Method of Composition." *Philological Quarterly* XXXV, No. 2 (April 1956): pp. 175-85.

Examines the historical antecedents of Dumas's 1842 drama *Lorenzino,* based on the real-life figure Lorenzo de Medici.

Moraud, Marcel. "The Evolution of the Romantic Drama in the Plays of Alexandre Dumas and Victor Hugo." *Rice Institute Pamphlet* XV, No. 2 (April 1928): 95-111.

The second of three addresses on "The French Historical Drama," this piece reviews Dumas's beginnings as a dramatist in juxtaposition to the early career of his contemporary and competitor, Victor Hugo.

Raitt, A. W. "Alexandre Dumas *père.*" In *Life and Letters in France: The Nineteenth Century,* pp. 36-42. London: Thomas Nelson, 1965.

Examines, within its historical setting, the dramatic breakthrough made by Dumas in *Antony.*

Shaw, Kurt. "French Connections: The *Three Musketeers* Motif in Andrei Bitov's *Pushkinskii dom.*" *Canadian Slavonic Papers* 37, Nos. 1-2 (March-June 1995): 187-99.

Examines references to Dumas and *The Three Musketeers* in a novel by Soviet writer Andrei Bitov.

Stowe, Richard S. "The d'Artagnan Trilogy" and "Other Fiction." In *Alexandre Dumas père,* pp. 66-84 and 127-34. Boston: Twayne, 1976.

An overview not only of *Les trois mousquetaires, Vingt ans après,* and *Le vicomte de Bragelonne* of "The d'Artagnan Trilogy," but of other works such as *Georges* and *Les Frères corses.*

Vincendeau, Ginette. "Unsettling Memories." *Sight and Sound* 5, No. 7 (July 1995): 30-2.

Reviews *La Reine Margot,* the parody *D'Artagnan's Daughter,* and other film adaptations of Dumas's work.

Wood, Allen G. "Of Kings, Queens and Musketeers." *Papers on French Seventeenth Century Literature* XXIV, No. 46 (1997): 162-71.

Evaluates the representation of historical events provided in *Les trois mousquetaires.*

Additional coverage of Dumas's life and works is contained in the following sources published by Gale Research: *Dictionary of Literary Biography,* **Vol. 119;** *DISCovering Authors;* **and** *World Literature Criticism, 1500 to the Present.*

Felicia Hemans

1793-1835

(Born Felicia Dorothea Browne) English poet and dramatist.

For additional information on Hemans's life and works, see *NCLC*, Volume 29.

INTRODUCTION

A prolific poet whose work appeared frequently on both sides of the Atlantic during her lifetime, Hemans was a true celebrity poet of the early nineteenth century. Although many of her male contemporaries—including William Wordsworth and George Gordon, Lord Byron—have remained much more prominent in literary history, Hemans was in her own time one of the most generally loved writers of the era. She built her reputation upon works that focused on themes dear to the hearts of nineteenth-century readers, including religious, patriotic, and domestic subjects, and mastered a style now typically characterized as sentimental. Hemans's standard genres included long narrative poems and verse dramas, as well as short lyric poems.

Biographical Information

Hemans was born into the family of a Liverpool merchant whose business collapsed the year she was born; consequently, the family relocated to the Welsh countryside, the natural beauty of which echoed years later in much of her poetry. At a time when only upper- and middle-class males enjoyed formal educations, Hemans was fortunate to have parents who believed in educating their daughters. Her mother, a well-educated woman herself, taught Hemans many subjects, and she became proficient in several languages, including German, French, Italian, Spanish, Portuguese, and Latin. Demonstrating a precocious talent for verse, Hemans published her first two volumes of poetry in 1808, when she was only fourteen. Although the books, *Poems* and *England and Spain,* attracted little critical attention, they showcased her wide reading and technical facility and established her as a poet of promise, especially one with a flair for natural description and historical narrative. These were followed in 1812 by *The Domestic Affections,* a collection of poems about family life. In the same year, she married Alfred Hemans, an older man who held a captaincy in the army. Despite the demands of a growing family— she bore five sons in less than eight years—Hemans continued to write. She became well-known and admired among English readers, especially with such

broadly popular works as *The Restoration of the Works of Art to Italy* (1816) and *Modern Greece* (1817).

For undocumented reasons, Hemans and her husband separated in 1819. Although Hemans never referred to her failed marriage, biographers speculate that her husband might not have been sympathetic to her literary pursuits, and some commentators have attributed the pathos in many of Hemans's poems after this date to her husband's abandonment of the family. The separation also had a material effect on her writing: she now had to support her family, which consisted of her mother and sister as well as her sons. She produced numerous volumes in the next decade, including *Tales, and Historic Scenes in Verse* (1819), *The Sceptic* (1820), *The Forest Sanctuary, and Other Poems* (1825), and the verse drama *The Siege of Valencia* (1823). She also became a frequent contributor to the periodicals that fed the popular demand for poetry. By 1826, her popular and critical reputation prompted a complete edition of her works in the United States, and her poems became widely imitated. In her last years, despite the onset of a debilitating illness that sapped her strength, Hemans continued to write. She died in Dublin in 1835.

Major Works

Although the period during which Hemans wrote tends to be remembered by the five male poets canonized by British Romanticism—Wordsworth, Samuel Taylor Coleridge, Byron, Percy Bysshe Shelley, and John Keats—the period itself was actually more various both in terms of the poets writing, the poetic styles they employed, and the matter that a very enthusiastic reading public wished to consume. Hemans represented certain aspects of this popular taste at least as consistently as any of her male contemporaries. Although characteristically Romantic subjects make up an important part of her work—especially a typically Wordsworthian love of nature—her primary focus and her style reflect the overlap of the preceding Neoclassical style with emerging Romantic concerns. The majority of Hemans's verse demonstrates an adherence to these earlier conventions in meter, rhyme, and diction. And although her treatment of nature and domesticity overlapped with Wordsworth's, Hemans often handled these and other topics—religion, patriotism, and history—with an outlook more apparently conventional than those of Byron or Shelley.

After the 1808 books introduced a young Hemans to readers, her next efforts demonstrated her growing skills on similarly martial, patriotic subjects. *The Domestic Affections* and *The Restoration of The Works of Art to Italy* both lambasted England's enemy, France, in the Napoleonic Wars and celebrated the integrity of England's cause. *Modern Greece* offered another take on the same theme, further ingratiating Hemans in the hearts of English readers. In the next few years, she shifted slightly from contemporary political verse to historical verse with political implications, presenting her work to the public in *Tales, and Historic Scenes,* a verse drama called *The Vespers of Palermo* (1823), and "Dartmoor" (1821), which won the poetry prize from the Royal Society of Literature. To some degree, however, Hemans became and remained best known for verse that cast an ideal image of the home, as well as woman's place in it, and similarly but less markedly for her religious pieces. *The Siege of Valencia* and *The Forest Sanctuary* both portray family tragedies in a combination of historical and imaginative narrative. In 1828 and 1830, Hemans published two of her most important collections, *Records of Woman* and *Songs of the Affections* respectively; each of these contain shorter monologues, lyrics, and narrative poems that reflect on domestic sentiment and the virtues of femininity. In the years before her death, Hemans turned more and more emphatically to religious topics, culminating in two collections published in 1833 and 1834: *Hymns for Childhood* and *Scenes and Hymns of Life.*

Critical Reception

During the nineteenth century, Hemans was much admired for what were termed the moral and feminine qualities of her works, and her verse influenced popular taste in poetry long after her death. More illustrious writers, including Byron, Wordsworth, and Sir Walter Scott, admired certain of her pieces, although their reactions—summarized by Scott's remarks that Hemans's poetry was "too poetical," bearing "too many flowers . . . too little fruit"—were less enthusiastic than those of the general public. Although her poetry remained greatly loved and admired through the Victorian era, which was largely sympathetic to her values and her evident sentimentality, Hemans fell from favor at the turn of the twentieth century. Critics in the following generations dismissed her as trivial and stylistically unsophisticated, although she continued as a minor mainstay in primary education and anthologies of English poetry. Attention, and appreciation, only returned in the 1970s when feminist scholars were unearthing and reassessing the many prolific, eighteenth- and nineteenth-century women writers who had been all but forgotten by academics. For several decades, literature scholars have found rich terrain for discussion in Hemans's work, discerning in it not just the superficial conventions of the nineteenth century, but also the underlying tensions and anxieties of a culture undergoing monumental changes.

PRINCIPAL WORKS

England and Spain (poetry) 1808
Poems (poetry) 1808
The Domestic Affections (poetry) 1812
The Restoration of the Works of Art to Italy (poetry) 1816
Modern Greece (poetry) 1817
Translations from Camoëns and Other Poets, with Original Poetry (translations and poetry) 1818
Tales, and Historic Scenes in Verse (poetry) 1819
The Sceptic (poetry) 1820
Stanzas to the Memory of the Late King (poetry) 1820
"Dartmoor" (poetry) 1821
The Siege of Valencia. The Last Constantine, with Other Poems (drama) 1823
The Vespers of Palermo (drama) 1823
The Forest Sanctuary, and Other Poems (poetry) 1825
Records of Woman, with Other Poems (poetry) 1828
Songs of the Affections, with Other Poems (poetry) 1830
Hymns for Childhood (poetry) 1833
National Lyrics and Songs for Music (poetry) 1834
Scenes and Hymns of Life, with Other Religious Poems (poetry) 1834
The Works of Mrs. Hemans, 7 vols. (poetry and verse dramas) 1839

CRITICISM

The Dublin Review (essay date 1836)

SOURCE: "Life and Writings of Mrs. Hemans," in *The Dublin Review,* Vol. 2, No. 3, December, 1836, pp. 245-75.

[*In the following excerpt, the author reviews Hemans's writings in the context of the then just-published Me-*

morials *collected by Henry Chorley, which the reviewer rejects as too trivializing of Hemans as a poet.*]

It is to the causes to which we have here adverted, rather, perhaps, than to any special inclination in the genius of the writers themselves, that we must attribute the particular form under which the great body of our recent poetry has appeared. In the absence of that encouragement, which gave birth to poetical ventures of greater length, amongst their predecessors, the modern aspirants to the honours of the muse have been content to support their titles by efforts of less pretension; and the public, which would have set its face against more imposing displays of the art, has been won to listen to snatches of song, which, while they charmed by their sweetness, made no great demand upon its time and attention. A larger proportion of the verse of the day has, in obedience to the necessities of the case, assumed the lyric shape, and insinuated itself into notice, in the pages of one or other of the periodical publications. Much even of the popularity of Mrs. Hemans was won in the pages of these fostering volumes; and it was the popularity so obtained which enabled her subsequently to dispense with their aid, and come before the world in her own unassisted strength.

To a review of the poetical character of Mrs. Hemans, we are led by more than one consideration. With the single exception of Joanna Baillie, she is, perhaps, the only poetess of the day, who has established a chance of being heard, beyond the narrow circle of her contemporary flatterers. She has a right, therefore, to our attention: and though we have no design to inquire into the causes of the numerous poetical failures, to which female genius has been subjected, we deem it right, if possible, to ascertain the precise nature of her qualifications, and to point out the peculiar merits, by which she has been recommended to the notice of her countrymen.

But, besides this, we are anxious to rescue the fame of Mrs. Hemans from the obloquy cast on it, by the unfortunate publication which stands the seventh, at the head of this article. It purports to furnish memorials of that gifted lady, and illustrations of her literary character. The title, however, is an entire misnomer:—the book is written solely for the illustration of Mr. Henry Chorley himself; and includes, amongst its other contributions to that object, an absolute sacrifice of the interests of the poetess, in whose service he would be thought to have enlisted. What may be the feelings of the surviving relatives of the deceased, at the publication of this book, we pretend not to know: but, for ourselves, we must acknowledge, that we have risen from its perusal with such a sense of indignation at its vain and gossiping details, that we can scarcely bring ourselves to speak of them in terms of ordinary patience. Why was the world to be told of a correspondence, which, to name its least objectionable characteristic, is little better than the tattle

of a pair of sentimental milliners? Could not Mr. Chorley's vanity be illustrated by a more harmless process, could not his admission to the literary coteries be effected at a less cost, than the depreciation which Mrs. Hemans has been doomed to suffer at his hands?

There were many incidents in the life of Mrs. Hemans, which contributed to make her lot other than fortunate: amongst them all, there was none, perhaps, which may be regarded as so peculiarly unhappy, as the kind of association into which she appears to have been thrown, during her residence in the neighbourhood of Liverpool. For all the other evils of her destiny, her gift of song, and the fame, which was its high reward, brought something like a compensation; while the grave itself, which has since closed over her, afforded her, at length, a final refuge from their power. But *this* evil was one, which struck at those very gifts, and that very fame, which were her comforters under all her sorrows:—nay, through the medium of the publication in question, it has even been made to survive herself, and follow her with its depreciating influence beyond the tomb!

Our own impression, on the perusal of these records, was, that the character of Mrs. Hemans' mind, as displayed in her writings, had been estimated too highly. We thought it impossible to reconcile the existence of such exalted powers with the evidence which was now placed before us; and we resolved, therefore, to satisfy our doubts, and decide the question, by a reperusal of her works. If the result has failed to remove the difficulty, suggested by Mr. Chorley's records, it has, at least, established the fair writer in the supremacy of her intellectual powers. We can now appeal in her behalf, from her biographer to herself: we can place, against the evidence of Mr. Chorley's book, the evidence of her own books; and can thus rescue the general memory of the illustrious dead from the shadow flung upon it by these foolish records of a few foolish years.

Felicia Dorothea Browne, was born in Liverpool, on the 25th of September 1794, according to Mr. Chorley, but, according to another of her biographers, in 1793. Her father was a merchant, at one time, of some eminence; and her mother, whose family name was Wagner, though a German by birth, was of Italian descent. It is upon the strength of this fact, that Mr. Chorley has chosen to favour us with some vague and apocryphal statements regarding the pedigree of this same Miss Wagner, whose ancestral tree is said to have borne, at some uncertain periods, no less than three Doges. We have no authority to contradict this statement: but we have had some personal means of making acquaintance with the circumstances of Mrs. Hemans' history, and we must acknowledge, that we now hear of her "high lineage" for the first time. Of course, however, it is serviceable to Mr. Chorley's peculiar view of his subject. He talks about the influence of what he calls the *force du sang;* he speaks of the probability of her poetical temperament having been derived from her Italian origin; and he concludes by referring us generally to a foreign descent, for "that remarkable instinct towards the beautiful, which rarely forms so prominent a feature in the character of one wholly English born." We have no doubt that this will form a text of great authority amongst the milliners' apprentices; and as little that any of our poetesses, who may hereafter be looking for immortality at the hands of Mr. Chorley, will take especial care to find a Venetian Doge, or at the very least, a Neapolitan Bandit, lurking somewhere or other amongst the branches of their family trees. What, however, appears to us to have been of far more consequence, both in itself, and in its influence on the mind of the future poetess, is, that her mother was a woman richly endowed with virtues and accomplishments; and that she applied them to the instruction of her daughter, under circumstances the most favourable to the development of her fine natural powers.

Some unfortunate speculations, during the precarious period of the French Revolution, having broken up the commercial fortunes of her father, he retired with his family, at an early period of his gifted daughter's life, into North Wales. Here, in "a solitary, old, and spacious mansion, lying close to the seashore, and in front shut in by a chain of rocky hills," we should have thought that, without travelling to Italy for the purpose, Mr. Chorley might have found the origin of "that strong tinge of romance which," according to him, "from infancy pervaded every thought, word, and aspiration of her daily life:"—and here too, under the care of that admirable mother, of whose high fitness for the task, Mrs. Hemans is not the only daughter that has furnished evidence, the powers of her intellect were unfolded, and the vigour of her fancy grew. There was nothing remarkable in her youth; although Mr. Chorley fills his narrative with those common-places of biography, by which, with a view to confer a spurious interest on those who need no such appliance, persons who achieve distinction in after-life, are subsequently discovered to have been very wonderful children. Thus, we are informed that Mrs. Hemans had, in youth, a very strong memory,—a circumstance by no means sufficiently remarkable in childhood, to erect her into a prodigy. Then, again, we are told that having early discovered a taste for poetry (no uncommon thing either), she used to climb into an apple-tree, for the purpose of reading Shakspeare! Finally, we have anecdotes of such value as the following:—"One gentleman, who took a kind and efficient interest in the publication of her earliest poems, talked so much, and so warmly, about her, that his sister used to say—'Brother, you must be in love with that girl!'—to which he would answer,—'If I were twenty years younger, I would marry her!'" And again, there is a small piece of the sentimental, executed by a lady, who must have been not only remarkably fine, but also remarkably foolish; and

who is reported to have said, in the hearing of the little Felicia,—"That child is not made for happiness, I know; *her colour comes and goes too fast*"!

All this is very sorry and very sickly stuff, not worth relating, if it were true, leading to no possible conclusion, and proving nothing but the frivolity of the mind that could occupy itself in its collection. Indeed, Mr. Chorley himself seems to have been aware of his own weakness. Like Dangle, in the *"Critic,"* he evidently labours under a suspicion that we may have "heard something like this before:" and accordingly, he endeavours to astonish us with an anecdote, which, at least, possesses the merit of being uncommon:—"The sea-shore," says the biographer, "was her Forest of Ardennes; and she loved its loneliness and freedom well: *it was a favorite freak of her's,* WHEN QUITE A CHILD, *to get up privately, after the careful attendants had fancied her safe in bed, and making her way down to the waterside, to indulge herself with a stolen bath!!"* Truly, *this* anecdote, if authenticated, would be original indeed!—though even then, we think, that, as an illustration of character, it would have had a better effect, if introduced amongst the childish memorials of some future admiral, or circumnavigator. As it is, however, we suspect that somebody has been mystifying our author.

The reader will scarcely wonder, if we pause, for a moment, to remark Mr. Chorley's statements, relative to the uncommon beauty of his heroine. Mrs. Hemans was never beautiful. We have the best authority for asserting, that she had, at no time, any beauty, beyond that of youth; and in later years she certainly was extremely plain. How Mr. Chorley can have been induced to venture upon this subject, we are at a loss to imagine. To the illustration of Mrs. Hemans' fame such statements must necessarily be useless: to the reputation of the writer himself they must be positively injurious. They must impeach his judgment as a critic, and cast suspicion on his fidelity as a biographer.—But to return to Mrs. Hemans.

That, which *was* remarkable in the progress of this lady's youth, manifested itself at a later period, than that to which our author has referred. Charmed, undoubtedly, at an early age, with the productions of the muse, her "prevailing love of poetry" (we quote from a sensible and well-written memoir prefixed to the published volume of her "Remains") "soon naturally turned to a cultivation of the art, in her own person; and a volume of verses, written by her, when she was not yet eleven years old, attracted, from that circumstance, as well as from its intrinsic merit, no inconsiderable share of public attention. This little volume was, in the course of the four succeeding years, followed by two others, which evinced powers gradually but steadily expanding, and which were received with increasing fervour by the admirers of poetry."

The fact, however, is, that these volumes were of little value, excepting for the indications which they contained, of immature powers, from whose ripenings much was to be expected. The fulfilment of the promise which they exhibited was, however, postponed by events, of which we know little; but which, nevertheless, exercised the most powerful influence over the future fortunes, as well as mind, of the poetess. Her marriage with Captain Hemans, of the 4th regiment, a gentleman of the most respectable connexions, took place in her nineteenth year; and was followed a few years afterwards, and shortly before the birth of a fifth son, by a separation, which proved to be final, as regards this world. Of the causes, which led to this unhappy result, nothing is certainly known. Those which are generally assigned, are inadequate to explain it; and we may, therefore, presume, that the true ones involved feelings, which the parties interested had no disposition to parade before the world. If Mr. Chorley possesses the means of enlightening the curious on this subject, we give him all credit for the good taste which has induced him to be silent; and could only wish that it had been equally effectual in leading him to still farther suppressions. Certain it is, however, that this breaking up of those fortunes, which, under almost any circumstances, form the happiest destiny of woman—this unnatural widowhood to which she was condemned, not only communicated its tone of regret to her spirit, and murmur to her song, but has more than once, we think, been distinctly pointed out in some of the more tender passages of her poetry. Thus, in those snatches of Corinne-like song, which we meet with in Properzia Rossi, it is impossible not to believe, that her own history and feelings are shadowed out. Rossi was a celebrated female sculptor and poet, of Bologna, who is said to have died of an unrequited attachment, after the completion of her last work, a *basso-relievo* of Ariadne.

> It comes,—the power
> Within me born, flows back; my fruitless dower
> That could not win me love. Yet once again
> I greet it proudly, with its rushing train
> Of glorious images: they throng—they press—
> A sudden joy lights up my loneliness,—
> I shall not perish, all!
>   The bright work grows
> Beneath my hand, unfolding, as a rose,
> Leaf after leaf to beauty; line by line,
> I fix my thought, heart, soul, to burn, to shine,
> Thro' the pale marble's veins. It grows—and now
> I give my own life's history to thy brow,
> Forsaken Ariadne! thou shalt wear
> My form, my lineaments; but oh! more fair,
> Touched into lovelier being by the glow
> Which in me dwells, as by the summer light
> All things are glorified. From thee my woe
> Shall yet look beautiful to meet his sight,
> When I am passed away. Thou art the mould
> Wherein I pour the fervent thoughts, the untold,
> The self-consuming! Speak to him of me,
> Thou, the deserted by the lonely sea,

> With the soft sadness of thine earnest eye,—
> Speak to him, lorn one! deeply, mournfully,
> Of all my love and grief! Oh! could I throw
> Into thy frame a voice,—a sweet, and low,
> And thrilling voice of song! when he came nigh,
> To send the passion of its melody
> Through his pierced bosom—on its tones to bear
> My life's deep feeling, as the southern air
> Wafts the faint myrtle's breath,—to rise, to swell,
> To sink away in accents of farewell,
> Winning but one, *one* gush of tears, whose flow
> Surely my parted spirit yet might know,
> If love be strong as death.
>   How fair thou art,
> Thou form whose life is of my burning heart!
> Yet all the vision that within me wrought
> I cannot make thee! Oh! I might have given
> Birth to creations of far nobler thought;
> I might have kindled with the fire of heaven
> Things not of such as die! But I have been
> Too much alone:—a heart whereon to lean,
> With all these deep affections, that o'erflow
> My aching soul, and find no shore below,—
> An eye to be my star,—a voice to bring
> Hope o'er my path, like sounds that breathe of
>   spring;—
> These are denied me—dreamt of still in vain;
> Therefore my brief aspirings from the chain
> Are ever but as some wild, fitful song,
> Rising triumphantly, to die ere long
> In dirge-like echoes.
>   Yet the world will see
> Little of this, my parting work, in thee.
> Thou shalt have fame!—Oh, mockery! give the
>   reed
> From storms a shelter,—give the drooping vine
> Something round which its tendrils may entwine,—
> Give the parched flower a rain-drop,—and the
>   meed
> Of love's kind words to woman! Worthless fame!
> That in *his* bosom wins not for my name
> The abiding-place it asked! Yet how my heart,
> In its own fairy world of song and art,
> Once beat for praise!

And again:—

> Where'er I move
> The shadow of this broken-hearted love
> Is on me and around. Too well *they* know
> Whose life is all within—too soon and well,
> When there the blight hath settled! But I go
> Under the silent wings of peace to dwell;
> From the slow wasting, from the lonely pain,
> The inward burning of those words— *"in vain"*—
> Seared on the heart, I go. 'Twill soon be past.
> Sunshine and song, and bright Italian heaven,
> And thou—oh! thou, on whom my spirit cast
> Unvalued wealth—who knowest not what was given

In that devotedness—the sad, and deep,
And unrepaid—farewell! If I could weep
Once, only once, belov'd one, on thy breast,
Pouring my heart forth ere I sink to rest!
But *that* were happiness; and unto me
Earth's gift is *fame*. Yet I was formed to be
So richly blest! With thee to watch the sky,
Speaking not—feeling but that thou wert nigh;
With thee to listen, while the tones of song
Swept, even as part of our sweet air, along,—
To listen silently;—with thee to gaze
On forms, the deified of olden days,
This had been joy enough; and, hour by hour,
From its glad well-springs drinking life and
     power,
How had my spirit soared, and made its fame
A glory for thy brow! Dreams—dreams!—the
     fire
Burns faint within me. Yet I leave my name,
As a deep thrill may linger on the lyre,
When its full cords are hushed—awhile to
     live,
And, one day, haply in thy heart revive
Sad thoughts of me:—I leave it with a sound,
A spell o'er memory, mournfully profound,
I leave it on my country's air to dwell,—
Say proudly yet—*"'twas hers, who loved me
     well!"*

After her separation from her husband, Mrs. Hemans continued to reside with her mother and sister, at a quiet and secluded spot, in the neighbourhood of St. Asaph. Here it was that her powers grew to their full stature, and her mind, busied in laying up its store of acquirements, prepared itself for those magnificent efforts, by which it was afterwards distinguished. It was in this neighbourhood that the expanding tone and compass of her minstrelsy first waylaid the attention of such spirits as Byron and Shelley: it was here that she won the friendship of Milman and Reginald Heber; and it is to this spot, therefore, that we would point for testimonials to her genius, which are worth all the unmeaning anecdotes that Mr. Chorley has given to the world.

The life of Mrs. Hemans, subsequently to the termination of its wedded years, seems to divide itself into three distinct and unequal portions; the first, the longest and by far the most important, includes the remainder of her residence in North Wales; the second embraces the period which she passed in the neighbourhood of Liverpool; and the third extends over that, during which she was restored to the association of her own family in Ireland. The rapid developement of her mind, during the earliest of these periods, is well supposed by Mr. Chorley to have been promoted by those peculiar circumstances of her position, which, "by placing her in a household as a member, and not as its head, excused her from many of those small cares of domestic life, which might have

fretted away her day-dreams, and by interruption, have made of less avail the search for knowledge to which she bent herself with such eagerness." During this period it was, that she poured forth in rapid succession, the largest and by far the most valuable body of her poetry, beginning with her prize poems of **"Wallace"** and **"Dartmoor,"** some not very able translations from Camoens and others, and **"The Restoration of the Works of Art to Italy;"** and including the **"Tales and Historic Scenes," "The Sceptic," "Modern Greece," "The Vespers of Palermo," "The Welsh Melodies," "The Siege of Valencia," "The Forest Sanctuary," "The Records of Woman,"** and above all, the best and greatest portion of those fine detached lyrics, which, having separately contributed to float her up to the height of her popularity, upon their swelling music, have since been collected under various titles, such as **"Lays of Many Lands," "Songs of the Affections,"** &c. Here then is the place to pause, and before we proceed to the less pleasing task of examining that portion of her history which forms the principal material of Mr. Chorley's volumes, to make some enquiry into the character of her genius, and its claims on the admiration of posterity.

From this enquiry, we will at once discharge the earliest of the poems which we have mentioned; because they are, as Mr. Chorley observes, the produce of the transition state of her mind; and, standing, as she does, for judgment, at the bar of posterity, she has a right to be tried by the best of her productions, and the fruits of her matured powers. "Her first works," he correctly remarks, "are purely classical, or purely romantic: they may be compared to antique groups of sculpture, or the mailed ornamental figures of the middle ages set in motion. As she advanced on her way, sadly learning, the while, the grave lessons which time and trial teach, her songs breathed more of reality, and less of romance; the too exclusive and feverish reverence for high intellectual or imaginative endowment, yielded to a calmness, and a cheerfulness, and a willingness, more and more, not merely to speculate upon, but to partake of, the beauty in our daily paths."

It has been remarked, we believe by Mrs. Jameson, that "the poetry of Mrs. Hemans could only have been written by a woman;"—and although this is undoubtedly true, yet it is not less certain, that there is something wanted in it, which might most confidently have been looked for from a woman's muse.

The prominent qualities of Mrs. Hemans' poetical writings, are, a versification whose varied melody has scarcely been surpassed, a splendour of general diction,—whose pomp has occasionally been employed to conceal a poverty of thought,—and a frequent grace and picturesqueness of particular expression, which enrich it with the continual and unexpected claim of a *curiosa felicitas*. These, with an unlimited command of glowing imagery, an unfailing taste in its appropriation, extreme elegance of thought, and a fine perception of the tenderness of others, have contributed to conceal, from many of her admirers, the somewhat inconsistent fact, that Mrs. Hemans is, herself, deficient in tenderness. Near as she appears to have sometimes approached to it, it is, nevertheless, true, that she has nowhere, or very rarely, stirred the fountain of tears; and it is as true, that, notwithstanding an air of mournful philosophy breathed over her poetry, she has seldom sounded the "deeper deeps" of the spirit. The thoughts, with which her muse is most conversant, lie near the surface of a poetical mind like hers. Her pictures of passion want vitality, and appear rather to be sketched from the traditions of the intellect, than drawn from the deep feelings of a woman's heart. Often as the ear is agreeably startled by graceful expression in her gem-like verse, yet it is scarcely ever surprised with any of those lines, which it at once tranfers to the heart, to be a part of its treasury for ever. The grace of simplicity is one, which she has rarely reached,—one which she seldom even aimed at till later in life, when it failed her. It was not of the nature of her genius; and its want, united with the other characteristics which we have mentioned, contributed, in no inconsiderable degree, to produce that monotony, whereby her poetry is so unpleasantly distinguished.

But there is another cause for this monotony, arising from a defect in her philosophy; and this, also, she tried to correct in later life, and with better success. It consists in her tendency to draw from every subject, which she selects for her muse, its gloomier moral. The futility and mortality of all things furnish her constant theme: her notions of the poetical, indeed, seem, for a long time, to have been limited to these objects. She could not select such a topic as that of Bruce's triumphant feelings, beside the long-sought springs of the Nile, save for the purpose of describing the revulsion that came over him, as he thought of the weary space which he had traversed to find these little fountains, and the long distance and many dangers, which still reared themselves between him and his home. She surrounds a subject with all its external pomps, and adorns it with a robe of gorgeous imagery, that she may afterwards pluck out the dark heart of its mystery, in mockery of its pride. All the beauty, that spring confers upon the natural world, is contrasted with all the desolation which it too often brings to the heart. This, it is true, is frequently done for a high moral object, and in a gush of song which makes it incumbent upon us to furnish some of our evidences of her genius, from this class of subjects. But our complaint is, that it runs through her poetry, as its prevailing moral characteristic. "Vanity of vanities!"—"all is vanity!"—makes the perpetually recurring burthen of her song. We will quote:—

THE REVELLERS.

RING, joyous chords! ring out again!
A swifter still, and a wilder strain!

They are here—the fair face and the careless
    heart,
And stars shall wane ere the mirthful part.
—But I met a dimly mournful glance,
In a sudden turn of the flying dance!
I heard the tone of a heavy sigh,
In a pause of the thrilling melody!
And it is not well that woe should breathe
On the bright spring-flowers of the festal wreath.
—Ye that to thought or to grief belong,
    Leave—leave the hall of song!

Ring, joyous chords!—but who art *thou*,
With the shadowy locks o'er thy pale young
    brow,
And the world of dreamy gloom that lies
In the misty depths of thy soft dark eyes?
—Thou hast loved, fair girl! thou hast loved
    too well!
Thou art mourning now o'er a broken spell;
Thou hast poured thy heart's rich treasures
    forth,
And art unrepaid for their priceless worth!
Mourn on; yet come thou not *here* the while,
It is but a pain to see thee smile!
There is not a tone in our songs for thee—
    Home, with thy sorrows, flee!

Ring, joyous chords! ring out again!
—But what dost *thou* with the revel's train?
A silvery voice through the soft air floats,
But thou hast no part in the gladdening
    notes;
There are bright young faces that pass thee by,
But they fix no glance of thy wandering eye!
Away! there's a void in thy yearning breast,
Thou weary man! wilt thou *here* find rest?
Away! for thy thoughts from the scene have
    fled,
And the love of *thy* spirit is with the dead!
Thou art but more lone midst the sounds of
    mirth—
    Back to thy silent hearth!

Ring, joyous chords! ring forth again!
A swifter still, and a wilder strain!
—But *thou*, though a reckless mien be thine,
And thy cup be crowned with the foaming wine,
By the fitful bursts of thy laughter loud,
By thine eye's quick flash through its troubled
    cloud,
I know thee! it is but the wakeful fear
Of a haunted bosom that brings thee here!
I know thee!—thou fearest the solemn night,
With her piercing stars, and her deep wind's
    might!
There's a tone in her voice which thou fain
    would'st shun,
For it asks what the secret soul hath done!

And thou—there's a dark weight on thine—
   away!
    —Back to thy home, and pray!

Ring, joyous chords! ring out, again!
A swifter still, and a wilder strain!
And bring fresh wreaths!—we will banish all
Save the free in heart from our festive hall!
On through the maze of the fleet dance, on!
—But where are the young and the lovely?—
   gone!
Where are the brows with the red rose crowned,
And the floating forms with the bright zone
   bound?
And the waving locks and the flying feet,
That still should be where the mirthful meet!
—They are gone—they are fled—they are
   parted all!
    —Alas! the forsaken hall!

We must give one more splendid example from this class of her poetry,—only premising, that the sadness of the earthly morals, which it embodies, being ultimately relieved by the final hope to which they are referred, renders it not the most appropriate example of the manner to which we have been excepting. There are many others, which would have suited our purpose better; but that which we have selected is one of the very finest lyrics which Mrs. Hemans has bequeathed to us; and it moreover gives us an opportunity of pointing out another cause of the monotony which marks this lady's poetry. That cause is found in a habit of repeating herself, against which she was not sufficiently careful to guard. When a particular train of thought pleased her, she was tempted to return to it, for the purpose of again saying, in a new form, that which had been well said before. The feelings, so finely expounded in the following burst of music, have echoes in at least two several poems, which she wrote at subsequent periods,—one called **"Breathings of Spring,"** and the other **"The Birds of Passage."** The following poem, likewise, furnishes an example of the manner in which some of Mrs. Hemans's finest lyrics are frequently deprived of much of their full harmony, by feeble lines, which fall upon the ear with the effect of discord, amid the rich swell of their music, and which a habit of revision might have replaced by more lofty ones.

THE VOICE OF SPRING.

I come—I come! ye have called me long,
I come o'er the mountains with light and
   song!
Ye may trace my step o'er the wakening
   earth,
By the winds that tell of the violet's birth,
By the primrose stars in the shadowy grass,
By the green leaves opening as I pass.

I have breathed on the south, and the
   chestnut flowers
By thousands have burst from the forest-
   bowers,
And the ancient graves and the fallen fanes
Are veiled with wreaths, on Italian plains;
—But it is not for me, in my hour of bloom,
To speak of the ruin or the tomb!

I have looked o'er the hills of the stormy
   north,
And the larch has hung all his tassels forth;
The fisher is out on the sunny sea,
And the rein-deer bounds o'er the pastures
   free,
And the pine has a fringe of softer green,
And the moss looks bright where my foot
   hath been.

I have sent through the wood-paths a glowing
   sigh,
And called out each voice of the deep-blue
   sky;
From the night-bird's lay through the starry
   time,
In the groves of the soft Hesperian clime,
To the swan's wild note, by the Iceland
   lakes,
When the dark fir-branch into verdure breaks.

From the streams and founts I have loosed
   the chain,
They are sweeping on to the silvery main,
They are flashing down from the mountain
   brows,
They are flinging spray o'er the forest-boughs,
They are bursting fresh from their sparry
   caves,
And the earth resounds with the joy of
   waves!

Come forth, O ye children of gladness, come!
Where the violets lie may be now your home,
Ye of the rose lip and dew-bright eye,
And the bounding footstep, to meet me fly!
With the lyre, and the wreath, and the joyous
   lay,
Come forth to the sun—I may not stay.

Away from the dwellings of care-worn men,
The waters are sparkling in grove and glen!
Away from the chamber and sullen hearth,
The young leaves are dancing in breezy mirth!
Their light stems thrill to the wild-wood
   strains,
And youth is abroad in my green domains.

But ye! ye are changed since ye met me last!
There is something bright from your features passed!

There is that come over your brow and eye,
Which speaks of a world where the flowers
   must die!
—Ye smile! but your smile hath a dimness,
   yet,—
Oh! what have ye looked on since last we
   met?

Ye are changed—ye are changed!—and I see
   not here,
All whom I saw in the vanished year;
There were graceful heads, with their ringlets
   bright,
Which tossed in the breeze with a play of light,
There were eyes in whose glistening laughter
   lay
No faint remembrance of dull decay!

There were steps that flew o'er the cowslip's
   head,
As if for a banquet all earth were spread;
There were voices that rang through the sapphire
   sky,
And had not a sound of mortality!
Are they gone?—is their mirth from the
   mountains passed?
—Ye have looked on death since ye met me
   last!

I know whence the shadow comes o'er you,
   now,
Ye have strewn the dust on the sunny brow!
Ye have given the lovely to earth's embrace,
She hath taken the fairest of beauty's race,
With their laughing eyes and their festal crown,
They are gone from amongst you in silence
   down!

They are gone from amongst you, the young
   and fair,
Ye have lost the gleam of their shining hair!
—But I know of a land where there falls no
   blight,
I shall find them there, with their eyes of light!
Where death 'midst the blooms of the morn
   may dwell.
I tarry no longer;—farewell—farewell!

The summer is coming, on soft winds borne,
Ye may press the grape, ye may bind the corn!
For me, I depart to a brighter shore,
Ye are marked by care, ye are mine no more.
I go where the loved who have left you dwell,
And the flowers are not Death's—fare ye well—
   farewell!

To the error in her philosophy, of which we have spoken, she seems first to have been awakened by the study of the poetry of Wordsworth—too late, indeed, to communi-

cate to the best of her works the impress of the new wisdom which was stirred within her, but not too late to chasten her spirit by its dictates. The writings of this poet, so full at once of "the still sad music of humanity," and of the sweet promises and cheerful hopes, which are breathed out of all things, came finally to "haunt her like a passion;" and, had she made an earlier acquaintance with them, might have had a very salutary effect on her own muse. Her fine lines, beginning—

There is a strain to read amongst the hills,

are a worthy tribute of her love and veneration.

There is another peculiarity in the poetry of Mrs. Hemans, at which we have already distantly glanced. We have spoken of her habit of repeating her own thoughts in *separate* poems, and the peculiarity, to which we must now advert, is that of doing the like in the *same* poem. She takes, for example, a single idea for the subject of an entire lyric; and, after developing it, in her first verse, reproduces it in each of the subsequent ones,—taking care, however, to present it with some variations of aspect, and to clothe it in a pomp of words and picturesqueness of illustration, which sometimes succeed in concealing the sameness running through the whole. The poems of this class are very numerous, and some of them, such as **"The Songs of our Fathers," "The Spells of Home,"** &c., are, notwithstanding the generally fine flow of their melody, amongst the weakest of their author's efforts. Others again, such as **"The Sunbeam," "The Lost Pleiad,"** &c. have their monotony awakened into sudden life and grace, by the closing application of some striking moral; while others open to us a scene of surpassing beauty, arising either from the series of pictures which they present, or from the accompaniment of a touching commentary running along the entire piece.

Of the former kind may be mentioned **"The Treasures of the Deep"**—**"The Stranger in Louisiana,"** and **"Bring Flowers;"**—amongst the latter, **"The Departed," "The Adopted Child,"** and **"The Bird's Release."** One of each we will quote, in justification of our remarks. The first is founded on a passage in an early traveller, which mentions a people on the banks of the Mississippi, who burst into tears at the sight of a stranger. "The reason of this is, that they fancy their deceased friends and relations to be only gone on a journey; and, being in constant expectation of their return, look for them vainly amongst these foreign travellers." "J'ai passé, moi-même," says Chateaubriand, in his 'Souvenirs d'Amérique,' "Chez une peuple de l'Indienne qui se prenait à pleurer à la vue d'un voyageur, parce qu'il lui rappelait des amis partis pour la *Contrée des Ames,* et depuis long-tems en voyage."— It will be seen that the charm of this poem consists in the *one* thought running through the whole, and the rich painting and fine melody of the separate verses.

THE STRANGER IN LOUISIANA.

We saw thee, O stranger, and wept!
We looked for the youth of the sunny glance,
Whose step was the fleetest in chace or dance!
The light of his eye was a joy to see,
The path of his arrows a storm to flee!
But there came a voice from a distant shore—
He was called—he is found 'mid his tribe no
    more!
He is not in his place when the night-fires burn,
But we look for him still—he will yet return!
—His brother sat, with a drooping brow,
In the gloom of the shadowing cypress bough,—
We roused him—we bade him no longer pine,
For we heard a step—but the step was thine!

We saw thee, O stranger, and wept!
We looked for the maid of the mournful song,
Mournful though sweet—she hath left us long!
We told her the youth of her love was gone,
And she went forth to seek him—she passed
    alone;
We hear not her voice when the woods are still,
From the bower where it sang, like a silvery rill,
The joy of her Sire with her smile is fled,
The winter is white on his lonely head;
He hath none by his side, when the wilds we
    track,
He hath none when we rest—yet she comes
    not back!
We looked for her eye on the feast to shine,
For her breezy step—but the step was thine!

We saw thee, O stranger, and wept!
We looked for the chief who hath left the spear
And the bow of his battles forgotten here!
We looked for the hunter whose bride's lament
On the wind of the forest at eve is sent:
We looked for the first-born, whose mother's
    cry
Sounds wild and shrill through the midnight
    sky!
—Where are they?—thou'rt seeking some
    distant coast—
Oh! ask of them, stranger!—send back the lost!
Tell them we mourn by the dark blue streams,
Tell them our lives but of them are dreams!
Tell how we sat in the gloom to pine,
And to watch for a step—but the step was
    thine!

The verses which we shall quote as an example of the other kind, to which we have alluded, in the class of poems containing but one idea, are among the most elegant and finished productions in the entire range of Mrs. Hemans's poetry, and contain but the solitary blemish of the first line in the fourth stanza. They are based upon a custom which the Indians of Bengal and the coast of Malabar have, of bringing cages, filled with birds, to the graves of their friends, over which they set the birds at liberty. It is called—

THE BIRD'S RELEASE.

Go forth, for *she* is gone!
With the golden light of her wavy hair;
She is gone to the fields of the viewless air;
    She hath left her dwelling lone!

Her voice hath passed away!
It hath passed away like a summer breeze,
When it leaves the hills for the far blue seas,
    Where we may not trace its way.

Go forth, and, like her, be free!
With thy radiant wing and thy glancing eye,
Thou hast all the range of the sunny sky,
    And what is our grief to thee?

Is it aught ev'n to her we mourn?
Doth she look on the tears by her kindred shed?
Doth she rest with the flowers o'er her gentle
    head;
    Or float on the light wind borne?

We know not—but she is gone!
Her step from the dance, her voice from the
    song,
And the smile of her eye from the festal
    throng;—
    She hath left her dwelling lone!

When the waves at sunset shine,
We may hear thy voice, amid thousands more,
In the scented woods of our glowing shore,
    But we shall not know 'tis thine!

Ev'n so with the loved one flown!
Her smile in the star-light may wander by,
Her breath may be near in the wind's low sigh,
    Around us—but all unknown.

Go forth, we have loosed thy chain!
We may deck thy cage with the richest flowers,
Which the bright day rears in our eastern
    bowers,
    But thou wilt not be lured again.

Ev'n thus may the summer pour
All fragrant things on the land's green breast,
And the glorious earth like a bride be drest,
    But it wins *her* back no more!

But the harp of Mrs. Hemans, even in its shorter strains, is not confined to the limits of these subjects. It embraces many varieties of tone and topic, and running through "all moods of the lyre," is "master of all." Indeed, on turning over the volumes which contain them, with a view to this article, we have found such an embarrassing multitude, which seem to have the character of undying lays, that we cannot feel any apprehension for her future fame, if it be only from the effect of these detached lyrics. How fine and solemn, and, for once, how appropriately simple, are the sentiments and the music of the following:

THE TRUMPET.

The trumpet's voice hath roused the land,
  Light up the beacon pyre!
A hundred hills have seen the brand,
  And waved the sign of fire.
A hundred banners to the breeze
  Their gorgeous folds have cast—
And hark!—was that the sound of seas?
  —A king to war went past!

The chief is arming in his hall,
  The peasant by his hearth;
The mourner hears the thrilling call,
  And rises from the earth.
The mother on her first-born son
  Looks with a boding eye—
They come not back, though all be won,
  Whose young hearts leap so high.

The bard hath ceased his song, and bound
  The falchion to his side;
E'en for the marriage-altar crowned,
  The lover quits his bride.
And all this haste, and change, and fear,
  By *earthly* clarion spread!
How will it be when kingdoms hear
  The blast that wakes the dead?

And what can exceed the deep, and religious, and hymnlike beauty of the following?—

INVOCATION,

(Written after the Death of a Sister-in-law.)

Answer me, burning stars of night!
  Where is the spirit gone,
That past the reach of human sight,
  E'en as a breeze hath flown?
—And the stars answered me—'We roll
  In light and power on high,
But of the never-dying soul
  Ask things that cannot die!'

Oh! many-toned and chainless wind!
  Thou art a wanderer free;
Tell me if *thou* its place canst find,
  Far over mount and sea?
—And the wind murmured in reply,

'The blue deep I have crost
And met its banks and billows high,
  But not what thou hast lost!'

Ye clouds that gorgeously repose
  Around the setting sun,
Answer! have ye a home for those
  Whose earthly race is run?
The bright clouds answered—'We depart,
  We vanish from the sky;
Ask what is deathless in thy heart
  For that which cannot die!'

Speak, then, thou voice of God within!
  Thou of the deep, low tone!
Answer me through life's restless din,
  Where is the spirit flown?
—And the voice answered—'Be thou still!
  Enough to know is given;
Clouds, winds, and stars *their* task fulfil,
  Thine is to trust in heaven!'

The human mind, whatever may be its occupations, will never be without echoes for poetry like this!

But there is one other class of these lyrics on which we must bestow a single word of notice, before we proceed to the examination of Mrs. Hemans' more elaborate poetry—we mean her chivalric and other ballads. That she should succeed in this style might have been safely predicated of her, by every one familiar with the pomp and gorgeousness of her diction, and the occasionally stately sweep of her melody,—so peculiarly appropriate both to the chivalric lay, and to the battle song. Accordingly, she has produced some spirit-stirring examples of ballad, of which we must endeavour to find room for a single example. The subject is thus related by Madame de Stael:—

"Ivan le terrible étant dejà devenu vieux, assiégeait Novogorod. Les Boyards, le voyant affoibli, lui démandèrent s'il ne voulait pas donner le commandement de l'assaut à son fils. Sa fureur fut si grande à cette proposition, que rien ne put l'appaiser; son fils se prosterna à ses pieds; il le repoussa, avec un coup d'une telle violence que, deux jours après, le malheureux en mourut. Le père, alors en désespoir, devint indifférent à la guerre comme au pouvoir, et ne survécut que peu de mois à son fils."

IVAN THE CZAR.

He sat in silence on the ground,
  The old and haughty Czar;
Lonely though princes girt him round,
  And leaders of the war:
He had cast his jeweled sabre,
  That many a field had won,
To the earth, beside his youthful dead,
  His fair and first-born son.

With a robe of ermine for its bed,
  Was laid that form of clay,
Where the light, a stormy sunset shed,
  Through the rich tent made its way;
And a sad and solemn beauty
  On the pallid face came down,
Which the lord of nations mutely watched,
  In the dust, with his renown.

Low tones, at last, of woe and fear,
  From his full bosom broke;—
A mournful thing it was to hear
  How, then, the proud man spoke!
The voice that through the combat
  Had shouted far and high,
Came forth in strange, dull, hollow tones,
  Burdened with agony.

'There is no crimson on thy cheek,
  And on thy lip no breath;
I call thee, and thou dost not speak—
  They tell me this is death!
And fearful things are whispering,
  That *I* the deed have done—
For the honour of thy father's name,
  Look up—look up my son!

'Well might I know death's hue and mien,
  But on *thine* aspect, boy!
What, till this moment, have I seen,
  Save pride and tameless joy?
Swiftest thou wert to battle,
  And bravest there of all—
How *could* I think a warrior's frame
  Thus like a flower should fall!

'I will not bear that still, cold look—
  Rise up, thou fierce and free!
Wake as the storm wakes! I will brook
  All, save this calm, from thee!
Lift brightly up, and proudly,
  Once more thy kindling eyes!
Hath my word lost its power on earth?
  I say to thee, arise!

'Didst thou not know I loved thee well?
  Thou didst not! and art gone,
In bitterness of soul, to dwell
  Where man must dwell alone.
Come back, young fiery spirit!
  If but one hour—to learn
The secrets of the folded heart
  That seemed to thee so stern.

'Thou wert the first—the first fair child
  That in mine arms I pressed;
Thou wert the bright one that hast smiled,
  Like summer, on my breast!
I reared thee as an eagle,

To the chase thy steps I led,
I bore thee on my battle-horse,—
  I look upon thee—dead!

'Lay down my warlike banners here,
  Never again to wave,
And bury my red sword and spear,
  Chiefs! in my first-born's grave!
And leave me!—I have conquered,
  I have *slain*—my work is done!
Whom have I slain?—ye answer not,—
  Thou, too, art mute, my son!'

And thus his wild lament was poured
  Through the dark, resounding night;
And the battle knew no more his sword,
  Nor the foaming steed his might.
He heard strange voices moaning,
  In every wind that sighed;
From the searching stars of heaven he shrank,
  Humbly the conqueror died!

The peculiarities which we have described as characterising the muse of Mrs. Hemans, were all of them unpropitious to her success in dramatic writing. Her genius was essentially undramatic. Her very limited acquaintance with the action of life (arising out of the circumstances of her position), her one-sided view of its morals, and the habit which she had fostered, of relying upon a picturesque and highly-coloured diction, to conceal her want of power over the springs of the affections, were so many reasons which should have pointed out the hopelessness for her of any attempt in that walk of literature. Her characters all speak that highly-enriched phraseology, which never was the language of the passions, and which, in fact, takes from them all air of reality. The illusions of the drama it was altogether beyond her power to create. It was, as Mr. Chorley states, at the instigation of Reginald Heber, that she first attempted composition in this form; and, by the aid of Mr. Milman, her **"Vespers of Palermo"** was, after many delays, produced at Covent Garden, in the winter of 1823. As might have been anticipated, it failed. Besides its numerous other faults, the chapters are full of exaggeration, the plot is badly constructed, and its parts hang loosely together. Notwithstanding many fine passages which it contains, it is, in every point of view, one of the least successful of its author's performances.

"The Siege of Valencia" is a poem, which likewise assumes the dramatic form; but, being submitted to no other of the dramatic tests, may be read and judged of, as if it had appeared in any other shape. It is one of the finest of Mrs. Hemans' poems, and that which first exhibits her in full possession of her perfected powers. There is in it a more sustained energy than she had hitherto reached, or ever reached again; and it abounds in passages of earnest and passionate beauty. The Monk's tale is told with startling power; and the stern and lofty resolve of the high-souled father, subduing the throbs of natural agony at the bidding of principle, brought into perpetual conflict with the passionate pleadings and eloquent gushings of the mother, sweeping away all considerations of conventional duty in the wild rush of their irresistible tide, presents contrasts such as are of the very highest resources of art, and creates an interest in the heart of the most engrossing kind. To do justice to Mrs. Hemans, we should quote from this poem; but our space forbids our making extracts from its pages; and we can find no short passage which, detached from the rest, would convey any thing like a fair impression of its merit.

The **"Forest Sanctuary,"** was, we believe, considered, by the poetess herself, as her best work; and, in some respects, we are disposed to give the confirmation of our judgment to that opinion. We think that, in this poem, she has not only touched the spring of one of the finest secrets of the heart, but has also gone deeper into its hiding places than on any other occasion. We waive all consideration of the subject of the poem. It has a controversial basis,—to which Mrs. Hemans was manifestly unequal, both from the constitution of her mind, and from her entire want of the necèssary acquaintance with the subject. Her letters, published by Mr. Chorley, prove that, in matters of controversial politics and religion, she was versed in the merest common-places of bigotry,—common-places which were traditional with her, and not a deduction from any reasonings of her own. "The poem," she says, "is intended to describe the mental conflicts, as well as outward sufferings, of a Spaniard, who, flying from the religious persecutions of his own country, in the 16th century, takes refuge with his child in a North American forest. The story is supposed to be related by himself, amidst the wilderness which has afforded him an asylum." We leave her in quiet possession of her story, which we need not trouble by any criticism. As might be expected, it presents, in its natural pictures—whether of the boundless forest, or a burial at sea—many fine passages, of that peculiar beauty with which the muse of Mrs. Hemans is most conversant. But the one specimen of a more subtle perception and refined sensibility than the poetess has any where else exhibited, we desire to quote for our readers; though we are apprehensive that its exquisite delicacy and *tenderness* may fail to be adequately conveyed, when it is separated from the pages describing that conflict of feelings which had preceded it. The stanzas in question aim at picturing that shadow, which falls between two hearts, when they have passed, by a change in one of them, into the influence of separate faiths—the sense of an obstacle, felt for the first time, to the full and entire intermingling of their wedded spirits:—

> Alas! for those that love and may not blend in
>   prayer.

The thought is one of great delicacy; and it is wrought out with a very fine pencil.

> I looked on Leonor, and if there seemed
>   A cloud of more than pensiveness to rise
> In the faint smiles that o'er her features
>   gleamed,
>   And the soft darkness of her serious eyes,
>   Misty with tender gloom, I called it nought
>   But the fond exile's pang, a lingering thought
> Of her own vale, with all its melodies
> And living light of streams. Her soul would rest
> Beneath your shades, I said, bowers of the
>   gorgeous west!
>
> Oh! could we live in visions! could we hold
>   Delusion faster, longer, to our breast,
>   When it shuts from us, with its mantle's fold,
>   That which we see not, and are therefore
>   blest!
>   But they, our loved and loving,—they to
>   whom
>   We have spread out our souls in joy and
>   gloom,—
>   *Their* looks and accents unto our's address'd
>   Have been a language of familiar tone,
> Too long, to breathe, at last, dark sayings and
>   unknown.
>
> I told my heart 'twas but the exile's woe
>   Which pressed on that sweet bosom;—I
>   deceived
>   My heart but half,—a whisper faint and low,
>   Haunting it ever, and at times believed,
>   Spoke of some deeper cause. How oft we
>   seem
>   Like those that dream, and *know* the while
>   they dream,
>   'Midst the soft falls of airy voices grieved,
>   And troubled, while bright phantoms round
>   them play,
> By a dim sense that all will float and fade
>   away!
>
> Yet, as if chasing joy, I wooed the breeze,
>   To speed me onward with the wings of morn.
>   —Oh, far amidst the solitary seas,
>   Which were not made for man, what man
>   hath borne,
>   Answering their moan with his!—what *thou*
>   didst bear,
>   My lost and loveliest! while that secret care
>   Grew terror, and thy gentle spirit, worn
>   By its dull brooding weight, gave way at last,
> Beholding me as one from hope for ever cast.
>
> For unto thee, as through all change, revealed
>   Mine inward being lay. In other eyes
>   I had to bow me yet, and make a shield,
>   To fence my burning bosom, of disguise,
>   By the still hope sustained ere long to win
>   Some sanctuary, whose green retreats within,

My thoughts, unfettered, to their source might
    rise,
Like songs and scents of morn; but thou didst
    look
Through all my soul,—and thine even unto
    fainting shook.

Fallen, fallen I seemed—yet oh! not less
    beloved,
Though from thy love was plucked the early
    pride,
And harshly by a gloomy faith reproved,
And seared with shame! though each young
    flower had died,
There was the root, strong, living, not the less
That all it yielded now was bitterness;
Yet still such love as quits not misery's side,
Nor drops from guilt its ivy-like embrace,
Nor turns away from death's its pale heroic face.

Yes! thou hadst followed me through fear
    and flight;
Thou wouldst have followed had my
    pathway led
Even to the scaffold; had the flashing light
Of the raised axe made strong men shrink
    with dread,
Thou, 'midst the hush of thousands, wouldst
    have been
With thy clasped hands beside me kneeling
    seen,
And meekly bowing to the shame thy head—
The shame!—oh! making beautiful to view
The might of human love!—fair thing! so
    bravely true!

There was thine agony—to love so well
Where fear made love life's chastener.
    Heretofore
Whate'er of earth's disquiet round thee fell,
Thy soul, o'erpassing its dim bounds, could
    soar
Away to sunshine, and thy clear eye speak
Most of the skies when grief most touched
    thy cheek.
Now, that far brightness faded, never more
Couldst thou lift heavenwards, for its hope, thy
    heart,
Since at heaven's gate it seemed that thou and I
    must part.

Alas! and life hath moments when a glance
(If thought to sudden watchfulness be
    stirred)—
A flush—a fading of the cheek, perchance,
A word—less, less—the *cadence* of a word—
Lets in our gaze the mind's dim veil beneath,
Thence to bring haply knowledge fraught
    with death!

—Even thus, what never from thy lip was
    heard
Broke on my soul:—I knew that, in thy sight,
I stood, howe'er beloved, a recreant from the
    light!

With **"The Siege of Valencia"** and **"The Forest Sanctuary,"** the conspicuous progress of Mrs. Hemans' mind was at an end; and the future shews us nothing but its decline.

The death of her mother, in 1827, and the marriage of her sister, in the following year, combined with the desire of obtaining opportunities of society for herself, and additional facilities for the education of her sons, induced Mrs. Hemans to leave Wales, and fix her residence at Wavertree, in the neighbourhood of Liverpool. Here, with the exception of occasional absences, during which she twice visited Scotland, and once made an excursion to the English lakes, she passed the three years whose records fill the principal portion of Mr. Chorley's volumes. Of these records we have already intimated our opinion. Exhibiting, as they do, great weaknesses in the character of this gifted woman, we certainly do not envy the taste, which has exposed them to the world. Through the whole correspondence, and its accompanying commentaries, there is exhibited by her a craving vanity, a restless and feverish anxiety for display, a desire to be always *en représentation,* and all this under the studious affectation of very much disliking the eminence, on which she would remind her correspondents that she stands. It was at Wavertree that she formed her acquaintance with Mr. Chorley's family; and we find her constantly walking over to his house, with some adulatory letter in her pocket, or some story of the way in which her reputation has discovered her retreat, in order that she may explain to its members how disagreeable a thing is fame. Nor is this all. These stories, and these disclaimers, are not unfrequently accompanied by remarks on others,—persons, to whom she acknowledges that she is bound by ties of gratitude, but persons, nevertheless, on whom she passes observations, unguarded, and, perhaps, unmeant, but calculated to produce the most unpleasant feelings both in this country and in America.—Was it right in Mr. Chorley to give such documents, and such anecdotes to the world?

Another reprehensible, and, with her, ungraceful, habit of mind, which Mrs. Hemans seems to have contracted during her residence at Wavertree, was exhibited in an assumption of girlishness—an affectation of being a romp, under cover of which she was perpetually endeavouring to be thought to say and do the silliest things in the world. Sir Walter Scott once administered a reproof to her on the subject, of which she seems to have been so little sensible, that she reports it as a very delightful joke to Mr. Chorley, while he, again, is so unconscious of its significance, that, in his turn, he reports it to the world! We happen to know, that she did herself great wrong by these habits, and created impressions very much the reverse of those which she intended to produce.— But it is time to escape from these painful frivolities. The poetical life of Mrs. Hemans, during her residence at Wavertree, was a blank; and we gladly, therefore, pass on to views more agreeable to that love which we entertain for her memory.

In the spring of 1831, Mrs. Hemans took leave of England for the last time, and established her abode in Dublin. Here, in the society of her friends, her mind instantly regained its tone, and her spirit rose up once more to the full height of its moral stature. Indeed, her previous visit to the Lakes seems to have led the way to this better frame of feeling, and, perhaps, as a consequence, to her determination (formed amid their solitudes) of quitting Liverpool. The step was a wise one. All the habits and sentiments which had characterised her residence there, seem to have been as completely lost sight of, from the moment she had left it, as if they had never been entertained: even her subsequent letters to the writer of these Memoirs, though very kind (as her nature was), exhibit a dignity and self-possession which, we think, must have astonished him. It was obvious that the separation was one of more than distance. Here, too, by degrees, under the influences of reflection, and amid the warnings of sickness, a still further "change came o'er the spirit of her dream," and her heart became solemnised, as she drew within the shadow of that last dwelling to which she was fast hastening. She had for some time formed the design of dedicating her muse to the service of the temple; but the resolution was formed when she had no longer the opportunity of connecting its execution with the exercise of her fullest powers; and indeed, looking at the reasons to which we have adverted in the course of this notice, we doubt whether her powers were ever equal to the successful performance of such a scheme. Her poetry was, as we have seen, too much the result of her peculiarities of thinking and writing, to flourish in separation from them.

Her **"Scenes and Hymns of Life,"** published during this last portion of her days, and the poems collected as her poetical remains since her death, are, for the most part, written in this new tone, and devoted to this better philosophy. But their merit, in other respects, is far below that of her previous productions. Her lyric of **"Despondency and Aspiration,"** which has been praised, is obscure and faulty, and her **"Sabbath Sonnet,"** the latest music of her lyre, and her song of **"The Swan,"** though touching as dictated from a death-bed, and sacred for the feelings amid which it must have been composed, and for the subjects with which it deals, must look to those reasons alone for the interest with which it will long continue to be read. She exercised her high gift of song, for the last time (and in the service of him who gave it) on the 26th day of April, 1835: and on the 16th day of the following month, passed calmly away, through the portals of a gentle sleep, into the shadow of the grave.

In the course of our remarks upon her various poems, our estimate of her genius, and our opinion of her chances with posterity, have, we think, been sufficiently expressed.

She wrote too rapidly, and too much, and her powers were impaired by the too long indulgence of those peculiarities, to which we have alluded. But it has been truly said of her, by a writer of her own sex, whom Mr. Chorley quotes, that "she never degraded the poet's art: if she did not as well, as, under more fortunate circumstances, she might have done, she never published anything that might not be said to make a necessary part of her poetic reputation." It is hard upon her, that Mr. Chorley should have done this for her!—We can have no doubt whatever that the music of her fine lyrics will float down the stream of time; and that her name will be a familiar word on our children's lips. It is by her detached pieces that she has the best chance of surviving,—though not by them alone that she deserves to survive. Her poetry has not, in other instances, taken the best forms for popularity: but the one will preserve the other, and the gifted will read them both. We only trust that her name and works will go down to posterity, uninjured by the silly records contained in Mr. Chorley's memorials.

Tricia Lootens (essay date 1994)

SOURCE: "Hemans and Home: Victorianism, Feminine 'Internal Enemies,' and the Domestication of National Identity," in *PMLA,* Vol. 109, No. 2, March, 1994, pp. 238-53.

[*In the essay below, Lootens investigates the patriotism in Hemans's verse and, through this, the contradictions and complexities that underlay Victorian ideology.*]

If any phrase still evokes Victorianism as conceived early in this century, surely the first line of Felicia Hemans's **"Casabianca"** does. "The boy stood on the burning deck" conjures up a familiar vision of unconscious ironies and lost innocence. Calling to mind drawing rooms where parents comfortably weep to the recitation of earnest or sullen children, the line revives the mockery, nostalgia, and anxiety with which early-twentieth-century critics approached Victorian writing. To quote "the burning deck" raises a smile; to suggest that Hemans's verse be studied seriously raises the specter of creeping Victorianism. Wendell V. Harris worries that unless we admit works such as **"Casabianca"** to be beyond the literary pale—the "real, if unstated, limits" of canonicity—we may be driven to "defend the sentimental description and inspirational storytelling that delighted our grandparents" (117). More dramatically, Virgil Nemoianu warns feminists that recuperation of "marginalized" women's literature could "backfire cruelly": what if the likes of Felicia Hemans were unleashed on unsuspecting classrooms (240)?[1] At points, the survival of critical literary study seems to depend on twentieth-century critics' power to relegate to the parlors of the past the complacent Victorian pleasures represented by Hemans and her patriotic verse.

That Hemans's verse should thus symbolize Victorianism, and particularly Victorian patriotic feeling, is both fitting and ironic. Perhaps no single poet's work better expresses the power of Victorian domestic patriotism, which sought to cast warriors as tender homebodies and children's playing fields as military training grounds. Enlightenment patriotism might tend to invoke liberty, whether defined by reason or constitutional monarchy, and Romantic patriotism might call on the organic unity of the folk nation.[2] But Victorian culture tells soldiers that they fight for home, and it often does so in the voice of Felicia Hemans. Hemans's verse is never simply Victorian, however; and where it is most Victorian, it is perhaps least simple.

The Burning Deck: Patriotic Passions and Instabilities

Few poetic careers can have been more thoroughly devoted to the construction of national identity than was that of Felicia Hemans. From her first mild critical success, *England and Spain; or, Valour and Patriotism,* to her dying dream of composing a great patriotic work, Hemans positioned herself as a national poet. Her fascination with patriotism and her "engrossing" if ambivalent "delight in military glory" (Chorley 1: 21-22) were central to her work and inseparable from her famous melancholy and her concern with defining womanhood.

Ironically, what led Hemans to anticipate (if not, indeed, partially to effect) the Victorians' assumption of an intrinsic connection between the values of domestic sanctity and of imperial domination may have been her attempts to reconcile Romantic concepts of organic national identity with earlier thought. For Hemans was deeply committed to a form of Enlightenment thinking that envisioned the glory of nationalism as international. Like William Hazlitt, she believed that "patriotism is . . . a law of our rational and moral nature," a "broad and firm basis" on which "collateral circumstances" such as "language, literature, manners, national customs" are merely a "superstructure" (Hazlitt 68). She thus won fame not only as a poet of English patriotism but also as the author of **"The Landing of the Pilgrim Fathers"** (*Poetical Works* 431-32), and she glorified the courage both of Crusaders and of their Arab opponents. She wrote bloodthirsty British victory and battle songs, but her martial verse also celebrated (carefully chosen) armies of Greeks, Germans, Moors, Norwegians, Spaniards, and Welsh, among others. However anglicized and homogenized, Hemans's protagonists are nothing if not diverse in "collateral circumstances."[3]

All the same, Hemans was steeped in Scott and Wordsworth; she dreamed of nations united not merely by reason but also by mythic folk identities inseparable from relations to the land. While Hazlitt envisioned patriotism that could not be "in a strict or exclusive sense, a natural or personal affection," Hemans's patriotism attempted to unite such an affection to "reason and reflection" (Hazlitt 67), thus

creating a stable, satisfying feminine position that inextricably connected nation and family.[4] By her own account, she failed in this endeavor. Like many Romantic poets, she never produced the unified, monumental work of which she dreamed; her great regret, she said on her deathbed, was that she had never created "some more noble and complete work . . . which might permanently take its place as the work of a British poetess" (Chorley 2: 213).

Even aside from conflicts between Enlightenment internationalism and what Marlon Ross calls "the romance of Wordsworthian organicism" ("Romancing" 65), Hemans's national project may have faced insuperable obstacles. As the daughter of an Irish father and a part-German, part-Italian mother and as a resident of Wales for most of her life, Hemans herself might well have wondered precisely what a "British poetess" was; and as a woman, she faced major challenges to her ambition of writing patriotic poetry altogether. By 1808, the year in which her first book, *Poems,* was published, Hemans was already aware of her quandary. "My whole heart and soul are interested for the gallant patriots" of the Peninsular War, she wrote an aunt, "and though females are forbidden to interfere in politics, yet as I have a dear, dear brother . . . on the scene of action, I may be allowed to feel some ardor . . ." (Chorley 1: 25).[5] Hemans's strategy seems transparent, and indeed throughout her career the poet was to "plac[e] her political interest behind the veil of domesticity and writ[e] political poems that take as their immediate concern the trails of feminine affection" (Ross, *Contours* 285). In the end, however, the domestic veil may have been as destabilizing as the political interests it sought to feminize.

In 1812 Felicia Dorothea Browne married a soldier, Alfred Hemans, and though the marriage failed, she retained her "ardor" for military subjects. If, as Norma Clarke asserts, Hemans's most successful work, **"Records of Woman,"** continually "return[s] to and rework[s] the central event in her life as a woman artist: her husband's desertion of her . . . and her continuing literary fame" (80), it may also be true that the book returns to and reworks central issues in her life as a female patriot, including ambivalence about the connections between domestic happiness and military glory. Given the continuing critical tendency to read women's intellectual commitments as the result of their romantic experiences, it might be tempting to attribute such ambivalence to Hemans's marriage. This explanation would be a mistake, however, for the unmarried Felicia Browne was fully conversant with the patriotic positions of her time and was already grappling with (or seeking to evade or mediate) conflicts within their constructions of femininity and of domestic values. In *Poems,* published when Hemans was fifteen, the dialogue **"The Spartan Mother and Her Son"** (13-14) casts war purely as a chance to win either honor or a "glorious grave / Crown'd with the patriot-honours of the brave." "My noble

Isadas," the Spartan mother says, "to me what pride, / Were thou to die—as thy brave father died!" The remainder of the volume seems consistent with this position: the tear called up by the hero's death in **"Sacred to the Memory of Lord Nelson,"** for example (55-56), is "sweet" and "enthusiastic." Nevertheless, as a note in ***"The Domestic Affections," and Other Poems*** points out (89), in the same year that ***Poems*** was published Hemans composed a work in which self-division with respect to patriotism is unmistakable: **"War and Peace: A Poem"** (***"Domestic Affections"*** 89-121).

The overall argument of **"War and Peace"** is irreproachably conventional: although war is evil, "if *ever* conscious right, / if *ever* justice arm'd [God] for the fight," it is in the battle between "Albion" and France, the "Typhon of the world" (115, 106). At points, Hemans's imagined victory song seems to usher in nothing less than the millennium:

> "Goddess of th' unconquer'd isles,
> "Freedom! triumph in our smiles!
> "Blooming youth, and wisdom hoary,
> "Bards of fame, and sons of glory;
> "Albion! pillar of the main!
> "Monarchs! nations! join the strain!
> "Swell to heav'n th' exulting voice;
> "Mortals, triumph! earth, rejoice!
>
> (119)

And yet, close to halfway through the poem, something happens. On one page, Hemans celebrates Sir John Moore's victory at Corunna, promising him "high on [his] native shore a Cenotaph sublime" (101); on the next, she introduces figures of mortal mourners, successors to her earlier personification of Britain as a "Queen of Isles" whose "sorrow" over lost heroes merely "paled the kindling cheek of pride" (97, 98). "Near the cold urn th' imploring mother stands! / Fix'd is her eye, her anguish cannot weep! / There all her hopes with joyful virtue sleep!" The mother will die of "soul-consuming grief" that "[m]ourns in no language, seeks for no relief" (102). So will the "fair lovely mourner o'er a Father's tomb," deprived of the chance to offer "filial sweetness" at the "hour of death." "Ah! who can tell the thousands doom'd to moan, / Condemn'd by war, to hopeless grief unknown!" "Thou, laureate Victor!" Hemans apostrophizes her country,

> when thy blazon'd shield,
> Wears the proud emblems of the conquer'd field;
> When trophies glitter on thy radiant car,
> And thronging myriads hail thee from afar;
>
> . . . . .
>
> *Then* could thine eyes each drooping mourner see,
> Behold each hopeless anguish, caus'd by thee;

> Hear, for each measure of the votive strain,
> The rending sigh that murmurs o'er the slain;
> See, for each banner fame and victory wave,
> Some sufferer bending o'er a soldier's grave;
> How would that scene, with grief and horror fraught,
> Chill the warm glow, and check th' exulting Thought!
>
> (104, 105)

This passage seems meant as a bridge: having chastened England's victory celebrations, Hemans proceeds to evoke Napoleon as "Ambition," exercising the "Power of the ruthless arm, the deathful spear, / Unmov'd, unpitying in [his] dread career" (106). Yet by characterizing England's exulting "laureate Victor" as blind to the human costs of war, Hemans implicitly connects his figure to that of Napoleon. The apparent bridge comes to seem more like the loop in a roller coaster: the passage turns the givens of military glory on their heads, offering a glimpse of the two armies as parallel in destruction.

In some senses, this near reversal is paradigmatic for Hemans's patriotic verse. Throughout her career, she ransacked extensive readings in literature, folklore, and world history for exemplary narratives in which the threatened or actual dissolution of family ties intersected with the exercise of feminine national heroism. The result was a kind of vital, fragmented, and self-subversive catalog of feminine patriotic subject positions—a body of work whose development often seems more centrifugal than linear and whose force seems to derive from its erratic course among and through contradictions, whether they are domestic and military values, Romantic and Enlightenment interpretations of patriotism, Christian pacifism and delight in military glory, or what John Lucas would call epic and pastoral modes of national poetry (4-7, 16-17).

What Victorian readers found in Hemans, then, was a fragmented, compelling, and complex range of patriotic positions, and the verses this audience favored—such as the silly, sinister, and explosive **"Casabianca"** (***Poetical Works*** 398)—were often among the most disturbing. Like much of Hemans's work, **"Casabianca"** commemorates an actual event. By setting the tactically unnecessary death of a child at the heart of Britain's victory in the Battle of the Nile, the poem suggests the powerful, unstable fusion of domestic and military values that helped render Hemans's poetry influential. For despite this poem's idealistic emphasis on filial loyalty and chivalric family honor, **"Casabianca"** never fully defuses the horror of the history it evokes.

Young Casabianca, begging his unconscious father for release from a courageous, suicidal, and perhaps pointless exercise of military honor, is both patriotic martyr and senseless victim. The poem's didactic high point is its final lines: " . . . The noblest thing that perished there, / Was that young faithful heart." The child embodies patriarchal family honor in the highest, most chivalric sense. Noble young Casabianca, "beautiful and bright," is "as born to rule the storm—/ A creature of heroic blood, / A proud, though childlike form." Indeed, the courageous child is father to the warlike man: while practical considerations of national political power or of personal ambition may taint the father's courage, the son brings to the battle only his "young faithful heart." His death thus upholds and extends the family—and the national—honor, by restoring military endeavor to its originary purity and innocence, its sources in the child's love of and blind faith in home and family. The more strategically useless such a willing death in battle, the more pure and poignant its symbolic significance. Surely young Casabianca's heirs rode in "The Charge of the Light Brigade."

The poem's emotional center lies elsewhere, however, in the desperate child's reiterated "Speak, Father!" and his question "Must I stay?" Here the fusion of familial and national loyalties works on a different level. The child's futile cry for his father evokes an experience of abandonment that is both primitive and deeply domestic. By terming Casabianca's heart the "noblest thing" lost, Hemans divides this domestic embodiment of familial agony from the rest of the battle's costs and uses it to challenge, if not discredit, the "nobility" of the battle's conscious, adult actors—and victors. The scene is a damning enactment of the brutal waste of war, of the deadly implications of patriarchal honor, and of the betrayal of familial ties by adults intent on that honor. For a few moments, Casabianca is the ultimate orphan of war, yet he is also in some sense its unwitting propagator, just as his father is his unwitting murderer.

From Spartan Mothers to Internal Enemies: Hemans's Patriotic Heroines

Within what Helen Cooper, Adrienne Munich, and Susan Squier term the "war narrative of the sexual trope, in which love figures as both sexual congress and sexual productivity" ("Arms" 9), twentieth-century criticism has tended to position Hemans's patriotic heroines somewhere between the Spartan mother and Tennyson's sweetly bloodthirsty Maud. Many of Hemans's verses bear an affinity to Maud's "passionate ballad gallant and gay" (1052); they offer ample evidence of the extent to which the phrase "arms and the woman" evokes activities that may be at once military, maternal, and erotic (Cooper, Munich, and Squier, "Arms" 9-10). While Hemans's verses deploy such a trope, however, they also point beyond it. In the poems most beloved by Victorians, the military struggle is often finished; what resonates is not a battle cry but the voice of a lone "sufferer bending over" a soldier's body or "grave" (**"War and Peace"**; *"Domestic Affections"* 105). This feminine patriotism still stands in primary relation to soldiers' bodies, but that relation, which need be neither maternal nor erotic, is mediated by death rather than birth. In reaching out toward the dead—

whether to hold, accuse, or mourn them—Hemans's heroines and speakers give the phrase "arms and the woman" new meaning.

In *Phenomenology of Spirit,* Hemans's contemporary G. W. F. Hegel explores the cultural connections between femininity and the military dead, in terms of classical tragedy and of nineteenth-century conceptions of the state's relations to domesticity. The power of "divine law" is governed by femininity, he asserts, and it is this law that rules burial. Alive, soldiers belong to the state; dead, they must be "wed" to the "lap of the earth," returned to "elementary, eternal individuality."[6] For Hegel, the central feminine national figure is Antigone. If considered in the context of nation, he asserts, her rebellion would take on a new significance for the relations between femininity and the power of the state:

> Taken in this form, [Antigone's action], which had been conceived as a simple movement of individualized pathos, discloses another aspect, and both the crime and the resulting destruction of the community disclose the actual form of their existence. Thus, human law in its general existence, the community, which in its effectivity altogether is masculinity and in its actual effectivity is the government, moves and maintains itself by wrenching into itself the special status of the household gods or the autonomous individuation into families, of which femininity is in charge, and by holding them in the continuity of its fluidity. Simultaneously, however, the family is its element altogether, and the individual consciousness is its general operative basis.[7]

To assert its communal, impersonal jurisdiction, the law governed by masculinity ("human law," in Hegel's terms) must forcibly absorb and subdue its own "element." Masculinity may not allow the "divine law" governed by femininity to exercise autonomous authority but dare not deny its power altogether.

> To the extent that the community retains its existence only through the disruption of familial happiness and through the dissolution of self-awareness within the general [awareness], [the community] engenders itself through what it oppresses and through what is at the same time essential to it—[and thus engenders] in femininity altogether its internal enemy.[8]

The "fluid" state contains feminine authority as if by chemical suspension, immersing and yet not dissolving it. As the representative of "divine law" and of the "law of weakness and darkness," femininity is both sacred and dangerous.[9] Like civil law in wartime, it must be remembered and revered, but for safety's sake it cannot be obeyed. Whereas martial law is theoretically an anomaly of national history, however, masculine law may represent history itself. In Hemans as in Hegel, masculine law has always already "suspended" feminine authority. Life is war: the weak, dark, divine law of femininity must await the peace of the millennium. Until then, femininity must remain the "eternal irony of the community," a site of resistance that is as symbolically indispensable as it is practically futile.[10]

At points in her work, Hemans seems allied with Hegel. These moments glorify, mourn, and accept the need of the state to engender itself by what it oppresses: they attempt to mobilize the "domestic affections" to the service of militaristic patriotism. At other points, however, often in confrontations with the real or imagined bodies of the dead, such attempts seem to falter. Hemans may collapse distinctions between the powers of domesticity and of war, creating chillingly ruthless heirs of the Spartan mother, or she may chart a deadly collision course between female figures and a state whose brutality is implicitly unveiled as senseless. Poems in which despair jostles with energetic expressions of straightforward militarism, of feminist sexual politics, and of pacifism raise the specters of feminine "internal enemies" who refuse either to continue fighting for "divine law" or to reconcile themselves to failure.

Nineteenth-century women poets' grappling with issues of national identity has yet to be fully explored, but the verses of Elizabeth Barrett Browning, Frances E. W. Harper, Alice Meynell, and Lydia Sigourney indicate that Hemans's mournful patriotism is central to a complex poetic tradition.[11] As Hemans's work demonstrates, the "complementary but more often contradictory awarenesses" of national identity and of gender are inseparable (Lucas 7). Hemans's work suggests that national awarenesses are paradoxical and inescapably gendered and that gender is shaped by its own contradictory awarenesses, including conceptions of national identity. Establishing feminine melancholy as something akin to a patriotic duty, Hemans's verse endows the "nightingale's burden" of nineteenth-century women's poetry with national meaning (Walker 21-27). Her heroines' Victorian heir is less Tennyson's joyous Maud than the lachrymose Amelia of William Makepeace Thackeray's *Vanity Fair*.[12]

Hemans's deeply international (if culturally homogenized) patriotic heroines can be efficiently, if somewhat arbitrarily, divided into three groups.[13] Each group derives in some sense from the "lofty" Spartan mother whose "heroic worth" Hemans's early poems repeatedly praise (*Modern Greece* 28), and each establishes a connection between femininity and patriotism only to undermine it. The most striking, given Hemans's Victorian reputation for decorous calm,[14] are the desperate protagonists of narrative poems that recount clear-cut actions resembling those in newly recovered folk ballads. These poems explore and exoticize feminine modes of what Lucas would call epic heroism: violent, revolutionary, disruptive—and, not incidentally, ambiguously related to patriarchal power.

As purely righteous as religious martyrs, figures such as the Suliote mother, the wife of Asdrubal, the bride of the Greek isle, or the widow of Crescentius commit murder, suicide, or both as an ultimate expression of duty (*"Forest"* 179-81; *Tales* 189-96; *"Records"* 21-34; *Tales* 1-49). Their deadly energy derives from the political disruption of merged domestic and national order. As Asdrubal's wife cries before stabbing her children, "[T]he arms that cannot save / Have been their cradle, and shall be their grave" (*Tales* 196). These women have no choice: for them, as Hemans writes in *Modern Greece,* "all [is] lost—all, save the power to die / The wild indignant death of savage liberty" (26). Yet the exhilaration with which they enact as well as avenge their families' dissolution often blurs the line between self-sacrifice and rage. The Suliote's leap is perhaps too much like that of Hemans's Sappho, for example (*Poetical Works* 532); Asdrubal's wife, for all her noble classical motives, looks suspiciously like the allegedly more primitive protagonist of **"Indian Woman's Death-Song"** (*"Records"* 104-08), who drowns herself and her child to escape "woman's weary lot" (107); and while the bride of the Greek isle, last seen on a burning deck, avenges the death of her compatriots and groom, she also brilliantly reenacts her earlier anguish at separation from her mother, who must watch the conflagration from shore (*"Records"* 32-34). Indeed, Hemans's evocation of suttee in this poem suggests that the bride may stand as a torch to marital misery, an embodiment of preemptive self-sacrifice.[15]

These are figures in extremis; they are heroines, but for Hemans they are also women whose sanity, and perhaps even humanity, is questionable. Asdrubal's wife, for example, is "frantic . . . frenzied," a "being more than earthly, in whose eye / There dwells a strange and fierce ascendancy":

> The dark profusion of her locks unbound,
> Waves like a warrior's floating plumage round;
> Flush'd is her cheek, inspired her haughty mien,
> She seems th' avenging goddess of the scene.
> (*Tales* 194)

The widow of Crescentius is scarcely more reassuring. A sinister answer to the cross-dressing "Cesario" of Shakespeare's *Twelfth Night,* she uses her minstrel disguise to serenade and then poison the man who is her country's enemy and husband's killer. "Oh! there are sorrows which impart / A sternness foreign to the heart," she warns:

> And rushing with an earthquake's power,
> That makes a desert in an hour;
> Rouse the dread passions in their course,
> As tempests wake the billows' force!

The widow is a Byronic figure:

> "He died, and I was changed—my soul,
> A lonely wanderer, spurn'd control.
> From peace, and light, and glory hurl'd,

> The outcast of a purer world,
> I saw each brighter hope o'erthrown,
> And lived for one dread task alone."
>
> (*Tales* 28, 29, 36)

Seeing himself bereft of "freedom to fight for at home," Byron went off to fight for the freedom of his "neighbors." For Hemans, in contrast, revolutionary nationalism remained either the neighbors' business or the subject of nostalgia or of fantasy.[16]

Closest to many Victorian critics' hearts was another group of heroines—women like Ximena of **"The Siege of Valencia: A Dramatic Poem"** or Frau Stauffacher, the title character of **"The Switzer's Wife"** (*"Records"* 37-43). Meek, devout, and Madonna-like, the Switzer's wife mediates between epic and pastoral modes. Armed by the "sweet memory of our pleasant hearth," her husband has "strength—if aught be strong on earth"; her (good) name is "armour" for his "heart" (42, 43). Hemans is closing her Byron here. Behind a series of such poems stands her admiration for Goethe's glorification of women who send their warriors off with prayers and tearful smiles and often then languish and fade alone. Through the Switzer's wife, Hemans also edges toward home, for as her letters and verses make clear, the poet felt a strong bond to the Swiss. She paralleled their mountain independence with that of the Welsh; she identified their famous *Heimweh* 'homesickness' with her own (Owen 172); and perhaps above all, she seems to have seen in Switzerland a small, safe model of the interconnecting traditions of national independence and individual liberty that she envisioned for "Albion."[17] Intellectually and structurally, the Switzer's wife is an intermediate figure between revolutionary and domestic heroines. Indeed, she may have helped to mediate not only between pastoral and epic poetry but also between conceptions of Britain as an isolated, independent folk entity and as an imperial power (Ross, "Romancing" 56-57). Certainly mid-century readers failed to register any difference between the Swiss woman's release of her husband to protect a family home and a British woman's sacrifice in sending her husband off to defend an empire. Never mind that Switzerland was the nonimperial country par excellence (despite the Swiss mercenaries in whom homesickness was first diagnosed [Hobsbawm 137]); never mind that Frau Stauffacher's prayerful surrender of domestic happiness springs from the same revolutionary grounds as the actions of Hemans's violent heroines. The Switzer's wife could be appropriated by Victorians as an honorary English national heroine—an association that gave domestic courage a touch of glory, even while annexing the moral force of the local freedom fighter to imperial ends.

Where Frau Stauffacher acts, other heroines of domestic patriotism endure. Their narratives often begin with the warrior gone and cast women's national loyalty as synonymous with more or less passive acquiescence to the suffering caused by separation through war. Often that suffering is fatal. Once the poet and soldier Körner lies in a "hero's tomb," for example, his "faithful-hearted" sister seeks only "[d]eath, death, to still the yearning for the dead" (**"Körner and His Sister"**; *"Records"* 246-49). "Thou hast thine oak, thy trophy:—" Hemans assures Körner, "what that she?—/ Her own blest place by thee!" In **"Troubadour Song,"** such fading takes on a more sinister aspect (*Poetical Works* 383). A warrior, having eluded "a thousand arrows," returns home to find that his beloved has died "as roses die": "There was death within the smiling home—/ How had death found her there?"

Here, too, however, Hemans's poems undercut one another. Just as the patriotic violence of Asdrubal's wife has its subversive counterpart in the Indian woman's killing of herself and her child, so the sacrifice of the Switzer's wife has an exotic counterpart in nonpatriotic submission: that of the heroine of **"The Hebrew Mother,"** who surrenders her son to be educated by the male authorities of her religion (*Poetical Works* 400-01). Like the Indian woman, the Hebrew mother appears in a context that stresses the sexual-political implications of her action rather than the patriotic ones.

Hemans also provides a deadly, if sympathetic, exoticized counterfigure to the Switzer's wife: a pious, dovelike Muslim woman whose eloquence and maternal passion lead to the senseless devastation of an idyllic city in India (**"The Indian City"**; *"Records"* 83-96). To be sure, this heroine's actions do not precisely parallel those of her more famous sister. Had she not left home in pilgrimage, the Indians would not have slaughtered her son; and had she not sought vengeance, the lost Indian city would have continued to stand. Still, this mother is a disturbing reminder that good women may support or even inspire bad wars.

Hemans's famous **"Woman on the Field of Battle"** features a member of the poet's final group of heroines (*"Songs"* 123-26). "Strangely, sadly fair," the protagonist lies beside a "banner and shiver'd crest," proof that "amidst the best / [Her] work was done."

> Why?—ask the true heart why
> Woman hath been
> Ever, where brave men die,
> Unshrinking seen?
>
> Unto this harvest ground
> Proud reapers came,—
> Some, for that stirring sound,
> A warrior's name;
>
> Some, for the stormy play
> And joy of strife;
> And some, to fling away
> A weary life;—

But thou, pale sleeper, thou,
  With the slight frame,
And the rich locks, whose glow
    Death cannot tame:

Only one thought, one power,
  Thee could have led,
So, through the tempest's hour,
    To lift thy head!

The power, of course, is love, which wrenched this figure, like young Casabianca, from domestic safety to death
in battle. Domestic affection justified not only military
ardor but also action: love won the heroine "a place" in
the "harvest" of the "haughty Dead," the "reapers" who
beat the Grim Reaper himself by grasping honor, sport,
or surcease from weariness. So far, this poem seems
merely to unite the virtues of Hemans's desperate and
domestic heroines. The final verse, however, strikes a
new and disquieting note. What drove the heroine to the
battle-field was love of a particular kind:

Only the true, the strong,
  The love, whose trust
Woman's deep soul too long
    Pours on the dust!

Instead of being mutually reinforcing, the sacrifices of
domesticity and of nationalism become mutually subversive. Is this a Christian scene? Certainly no pacific
afterlife arises to redeem the spilling of this figure's
blood or of her love. As both are poured out "on the
dust," apparently in vain, families and empires implicitly blend in an image of pagan ritual (self-)slaughter
"too long" retained.

This point leads to the heart of a nineteenth-century
critical controversy: does Hemans's overwhelming
melancholy cast doubt on her faith in redemption,
whether of soldiers' blood or of women's love (including love of poetry)?[18] Proponents of both sides might
well have turned to the third group of Hemans heroines for support. Faltering or failed Spartan mothers,
the protagonists of Hemans's dramas and of associated
works such as **"The Abencerrage"** (*Tales* 51-156) are
torn apart by conflicts between national loyalties (including adherence to patriotically defined family honor)
and bonds of familial or romantic love; the characters'
position as Hegelian internal enemies is agonized and
perhaps unstable.

At their most helpless, these heroines may be fully disoriented and victimized, like Moraima, in **"De Chatillon"**
(*Poetical Works* 611-37), who says in confusion, "Who
leads the foe? . . . I meant—I mean—my people" (618).
At their most aggressive, they may echo Elmina, in **"The
Siege of Valencia"** (*"Siege"* 91-247), who curses not
only the Moors, for holding her sons hostage, but also her
husband, for being willing to sacrifice the captives. She

tells him that she hopes he comes to sit alone "within [his]
vast, forsaken halls" and to learn too late that "dim phantoms from ancestral tombs, . . . all—all *glorious*"—can
never "people that cold void" left by the loss of living
children. Elmina's rebellion is explicitly feminine:

Oh, cold and hard of heart!
Thou shouldst be born for empire, since thy soul
Thus lightly from all human bonds can free
Its haughty flight!—Men! men! Too much is
  yours
Of vantage; ye, that with a sound, a breath,
A shadow, thus can fill the desolate space
Of rooted up affections, o'er whose void
Our yearning hearts must wither!—So it is,
Dominion must be won!

               (122, 112-13)

Though traitorous, Elmina's cry echoes throughout
Hemans's work, most often in the voice of an internal
enemy whose feminine pacifism resigns itself to war
on earth by hoping for a peaceable kingdom to come.[19]

In **"The Image in Lava,"** a particularly powerful example of Hemans's feminine antiwar writing (*"Records"*
307-10), the discovery at Herculaneum of the stone
imprint of a mother's breast inspires an overt competition between the powers of the state and of the home:

Temple and tower have moulder'd,
  Empires from earth have pass'd,—
And woman's heart hath left a trace
  Those glories to outlast!

And childhood's fragile image
  Thus fearfully enshrin'd,
Survives the proud memorials rear'd
  By conquerors of mankind.

What could have been a simple moral becomes increasingly complex as the brief poem progresses.
Hemans's Herculanean mother, whose form was set
as "a mournful seal" by "love and agony," may have
chosen death. "Perchance all vainly lavish'd / [Her]
other love had been"; she might have found it "far
better . . . to perish" than to risk losing the only
person she had left to love. Thus, what imprinted itself "upon the dust," outliving "the cities of renown /
Wherein the mighty trust," may be an expression of
isolation and deprivation as well as of maternal love.
Perhaps domestic affections have been no real alternative to the powers of empire, after all. Perhaps the
image in lava memorializes not only the triumph but
also the inadequacy of such love:

Immortal, oh! immortal
  Thou art, whose earthly glow
Hath given these ashes holiness—
  It must, it *must* be so!

It must be so, Hemans seems to imply, because it would be too terrible if it was not. **"The Illuminated City"** (*"Records"* 283-85), a poem much admired by Victorian critics, offers a more secular echo of Elmina's feminine suspicion of military glory. Drowned in the "music of victory," which shakes its streets "like a conqueror's car," Hemans's dazzling city is an emblem of the "proud mantle" obscuring both the dead on the battlefield and their mourners at home, "[t]he things thou shouldst gaze on, the sad and true."[20] In her intimate tone, the isolated, wandering speaker in **"The Illuminated City"** unmistakably resembles the Cassandra-like speaker of **"Second Sight"** (*"Songs"* 249-51). The confessional opening line of the poem, "A mournful gift is mine, O friends!" proposes that the ability to pierce the veil of military glory is less a skill than a curse. Just as the speaker hears

> the still small moan of Time,
> Through the ivy branches made,
> Where the palace, in its glory's prime,
> With the sunshine stands array'd

she sees the "blood-red future stain / On the warrior's gorgeous crest" and "the bier amidst the bridal train / When they come with roses drest." "Second Sight" juxtaposes the deaths of empires, soldiers, and brides in the visions of a speaker who must remain homeless, short of heaven.

Domesticating the Empire: The Powers of Patriotic Graves

Much of this catalog of heroines belongs to the Romantic Hemans, from whose complex, passionate body of patriotic verse were winnowed the works that mid-century admirers made "British classics," grown "deep into the national heart" (Archibald Alison, qtd. in Moulton 260). Collected and genteel, this Victorian verse constitutes the pastoral Hemans, the Hemans whose Englishness is both stable and exemplary. It also represents the imperial Hemans, whose poetry helped put to rest what Ross calls "a specter haunting Britain at the verge of the nineteenth century . . . on the threshold of Britain's modernization of itself as a nation-state": the question of how to consolidate the notion of Englishness as an organic, indigenous national identity while simultaneously justifying imperial expansion beyond British home territory ("Romancing" 56, 57). Paradoxically, Hemans's attempt to mediate between rationalist and organic notions of national identity may have given rise to one of the greatest sources of her power as a Victorian patriotic poet: her emphasis on reverence for patriots' graves.

On the battlefield, soldiers' corpses may mock or challenge Hemans's victory celebrations, but in the (symbolically) domestic settings of her heroes' graves, military honor and family loyalty meet in peace. No longer at odds, mothers and military authorities join in reverence for the dead and in obedience to "divine law." Here alone the martial law of earthly existence may be safely superseded.

Conceived both as metaphors and as concrete objects, the graves of what Hemans loved to call the "honored dead" could symbolize the general fact of loss and the specific battles of national heroes; these sites could render the rational and universal impulse of patriotism local and spiritual. Unambiguously marking the merging of a people and a place, they served as points at which patriots literally became one with the land. Even one's "rational and moral nature" (Hazlitt 67) might well demand specific attachment to a plot where "earth's most glorious dust, / Once fired with valour, wisdom, song, / Is laid in holy trust" (Hemans, **"The English Boy"**; *Poetical Works* 502-03). In focusing local reverence for the literal and symbolic remains of patriotic heroism, then, heroes' graves not only unified distinct national folk communities but also bound those communities to the rest of the world by evoking the universal love and sorrows of liberty.

Capable of uniting local loyalties with rationalist internationalism and of joining the state with its feminine internal enemy, graves in Hemans could also serve as the sources of national poetry. Lying on a mountain that is both the Welsh Parnassus and "the birth-place of phantoms," the first-person speaker of **"The Rock of Cader-Idris"** (*Selection* 12) risks madness to face the "deep presence" not merely of the embodied "powers of the wind and the ocean" but also of the "mighty of ages departed." Only after looking the dead in the eye does the speaker awaken, "as from the grave . . . to inherit / A flame all immortal, a voice and a power!" If there is a "sense" that "gives soul to" nature's beauty, investing a landscape with mythic power, Hemans suggests, that soul arises from human connections with the dead.

Is Hemans the poet on the Welsh rock? If memory and graves claim a land, as she often implied, she claimed Wales, the ground of her "childhood, [her] home, and [her] dead" (**"A Farewell to Wales"**; *Poetical Works* 474). Yet she was not born there, and she did not think of herself as Welsh. In fact, even as she celebrates the Welsh bards' national identity, constituting herself as their heir, Hemans colludes in the dispersion of that identity. To Mary Russell Mitford, for example, she describes the "Welsh character" as not "yet merged in the English" character (Chorley 1: 127)—rather as if any regional specificity were doomed; and even her nationalistic "Welsh melodies" implicitly assign a "brighter lot" to Wales during the period of England's predominance (**"The Mountain-Fires"**; *Selection* 54).

As Hemans's relation to Wales suggests, then, while her attempt to bind abstract nation, physical land, and human affection through graves may indeed resolve some of the issues raised by efforts to unite rationalist and organic visions of patriotism, it poses other problems. Does honoring of the national dead constitute identity? By tending a country's graves, metaphorically and actually, may one claim to be a true heir to its bards? And if the English love a land they have colonized—even honor the valor of those who fought against them in defense of that land—have they thereby assumed or appropriated the country's national identity? Perhaps the graves of the honorable dead help dissolve national identities into mythic forms that are endlessly capable of appropriation. If so, it is not strange that Hemans's conception of graves as sites for the establishment and maintenance of national identity should have found tremendous resonance within Victorian imperialist discourse. "We cannot be *habitually* attached to places we never saw, and people we never heard of . . . ," Hazlitt writes. "Are the opposite extremities of the globe our native place, because they are a part of that geographical and political denomination, our country? Does natural affection expand in circles of latitude and longitude?" (67). Hemans's poetry offers a clear answer to Hazlitt's skepticism, for if anything can create a habitual attachment to a place one has never seen, it is the grave of a loved one.

It is probably no accident that in 1823, some six years before Christopher North made his famous assertion that the sun never sets on the British empire, Felicia Hemans wrote that "wave may not foam, nor wild wind sweep, / Where rest not England's dead" (**"England's Dead"; *"Siege"* 308-10**). Nor should the similarity between the titles of two of her most popular patriotic poems, **"England's Dead"** and **"The Homes of England,"** come as a surprise. For just as domestic mourning makes the empire into a home, expanding affection in terms of latitude and longitude, until it reaches and symbolically appropriates the final resting place of the beloved and honored dead, so domestic love makes the home into an empire.

"The Homes of England" is Hemans's most famous work on this subject and one of her best-known pieces altogether (***"Records"* 169-71**). When the poem first appeared, in the April 1827 edition of *Blackwood's,* it had an epigraph from Joanna Baillie beginning, "A land of peace. . . ." In volume form, however, **"The Homes of England"** has a new epigraph, from *Marmion:* "Where's the coward that would not dare / To fight for such a land?" Sentimental, reactionary pastoral fantasy at its crudest, **"The Homes of England"** links "stately," "merry," and "cottage" dwellings within a harmonious national hierarchy whose unity of "hut and hall" seems as much defensive as organic. Hemans's verse constitutes domestic harmony, whether national or familial, as not only a form of defense but also an incentive for aggressive striving after glory, be it in the battlefield or the marketplace. Woman's empire is the hearth, as one of Hemans's great admirers notes (Preface, 1836, ix), and in an imperialist country, Hemans suggests, the hearth must be an imperialist site.

Hemans's engagement in the elaboration of such discourse is far from inadvertent. Though the word *imperialist* was not used to designate an advocate of imperialism until after Hemans died, by the time she was fifteen she had constructed an Albion whose world domination was moral, military, economic, and perhaps sexual. "Hail ALBION," she writes in *England and Spain,*

> hail, thou land of freedom's birth!
> Pride of the main, and Phoenix of the earth!
> Thou second Rome, where mercy, justice, dwell,
> Whose sons in wisdom as in arms excel!
> Thine are the dauntless bands, like Spartans
> brave
>
> . . . . .
>
> Hail, ALBION, hail! to thee has fate denied
> Peruvain mines and rich Hindostan's pride;
>
> . . . . .
>
> Yet fearless Commerce, pillar of thy throne,
> Makes all the wealth of foreign climes thy own;
>
> . . . . .
>
> Look down, look down, exalted Shades! and
> view
> Your ALBION still to freedom's banner true!
>
> . . . . .
>
> See her secure in pride of virtue tow'r,
> While prostrate nations kiss the rod of pow'r!
>
> (4-8)

Hemans's conception of the home as both separate empire and the prerequisite for empire was also early and explicit. By 1812, in **"The Domestic Affections"** (***"Domestic Affections"* 148-72**), she personified "domestic affections" as a female figure who "dwells, unruffled, in her bow'r of rest, / *Her* empire, home!" while "war's red lightnings desolate the ball, / And thrones and empires in destruction fall" (150). Here homesickness is already a soldier's essential ration. Domestic memories alone "cheer the soldier's breast / In hostile climes, with spells benign and blest," arming him to face the dangers of "victory's choral strain," as well as of the "ensanguin'd plain" and the "armour's bright flash" (154). The "spells of home" (a favorite Hemans phrase) thus both fuel victory and temper the callousness triumph can instill; they endow soldiers with the power to kill enemies and to sympathize with the mourners whose love, memories, and sorrow hold together the home empire and its extension in the graves of the beloved, honorable dead.[21]

By the end of the century, deployment of the dead as outrunners of empire had become self-conscious enough to be the source of cynical humor. In Anthony Hope's

The God in the Car (1895), for example, an investor reporting on the progress of his central African scheme comments, "Everything's going very well. They've killed a missionary." "[R]egrettable in itself," he says, the action is "the first step toward empire" (Brantlinger 182). Rudyard Kipling's verse testifies, however, that the dead retained much of their imperial force. "Never the lotus closes, never the wild-fowl wake," reads his popular "The English Flag,"

> But a soul goes out on the East Wind that
>   died for England's sake—
> Man or woman or suckling, mother or bride or
>   maid—
> Because on the bones of the English the English
>   flag is stayed.

(146)[22]

In its combination of the grisly and the celebratory, Kipling's verse outdoes even Hemans's. For her, in **"Casabianca,"** for instance, the connection between reverence for the courage of the dead and sanctification of the circumstances of their deaths remains only implicit; for him, critics of imperial actions are worse than hyenas, unearthing corpses they cannot eat ("Hyenas"). In other respects, however, Kipling is as far from Hemans as is his Kim from young Casabianca; indeed, Kipling's view of empire as what Daniel Bivona calls a "privileged realm of play" can be fiercely antidomestic (36). If Hemans has a patriotic heir, it is rather Rupert Brooke, whose speaker in "The Soldier" returns not merely to dust but to "a richer dust . . . a dust whom England bore," creating a "corner of a foreign field / That is for ever England."

Even before Brooke, however, the Victorian discourse of imperial domestication was crumbling, along with the title character of Thomas Hardy's "Drummer Hodge," who, no longer English in any sense, is laid to rest in an unmarked South African grave where "his homely Northern breast and brain / Grow to some Southern tree." Indeed, **"The Soldier"** may mark both the culmination and the beginning of the end of Hemans's vision of domesticating patriotic graves. Such glorifications were powerless against attacks from the likes of Siegfried Sassoon, whose "doomed, conscripted, unvictorious ones" rise to deride their memorial at Menin Gate as a "sepulchre of crime" ("On Passing"), and whose speaker in "Glory of Women" might be addressing admirers of **"Casabianca"** when he says accusingly, "You believe / That chivalry redeems the war's disgrace."

The number of new editions of Hemans's work dropped off suddenly with the end of the Victorian era (Reiman). It is only fair to Hemans, however (and perhaps to some of her Victorian admirers), to note that her role as a poet of imperial mourning is no more stable than any of her other patriotic positions. **"The Indian with His Dead Child,"** for example (**"Songs"** 48-51), acknowledges the violence and racism of imperialism, even the domesticating imperialism of the dead. Having sat "alone, amidst

[the] hearthfires" of white settlers, who are indifferent to his sick "child's decay," the speaker must raise his son from the "grave-sod . . . . defiled" by the colonists and carry him hundreds of miles to escape the "spoiler's dwellings."

A community that attempts to prevent its members from returning the dead to the "lap of the earth," to "elementary, eternal individuality," destroys itself, Hegel writes (*Phänomenologie* 258).[23] For all Hemans's piety, what her speakers sometimes suggest—though do not endorse—is a fear even greater than the thought that they are living in such a community. What if no philosophical or religious principle makes order of such destruction? What if the virtuous power of the internal enemy is not guaranteed? What if it is not enough?

In her tremendously popular **"The Graves of a Household"** (**"Records"** 299-301), Hemans evokes a vacant British family graveyard that is the mirror image and perhaps the inevitable corollary of the burial ground in Hardy's "Drummer Hodge." "Sever'd, far and wide, / By mount, and stream, and sea," the graves of the family's children are flung throughout the empire and perhaps beyond. These dead are explicitly linked neither to imperial glory nor to one another: geographically separated, they may have lost even their connection in the memory of a "fond mother." Perhaps the Resurrection will reunite them; certainly Hemans's Christian faith would insist on this. And yet the poem makes no promises. "Alas! for love," read its final lines, "if *thou* wert all, / And nought beyond, oh earth!" The true title of **"The Graves of a Household"** might be **"The Grave of a Family,"** for the poem signals the end not only of the possibility but of the memory of living domestic love. On the other side of Hemans's imperial appropriation through burial stands the dissolution of domestic identity, familial and national. And with this, one returns to **"Casabianca,"** for a final reminder of what is left at the end of that poem: fragments, a paradigm of chivalric self-sacrifice, and the story of a courageous child's futile call for release.

Notes

[1] For Nemoianu, Hemans's "obsolete ideologies" and unremitting noncanonical "conservatism" could thwart radical pedagogy and endanger more canonical writers' tradition of critical thinking (240, 246).

[2] On liberty and eighteenth-century patriotism, see Lucas 23-32, 39-48, Cunningham 57-62, and Colley. See Ross, "Romancing" 56-57, and Woodring on "English poetic nationalism" (Woodring 45).

[3] Jeffrey, for example, praises Hemans for omitting the "revolting or extravagant excesses" of countries and periods besides her own and for retaining "much of what is most interesting and peculiar" in their legends (35).

[4] When I refer to femininity, I mean a condition that is not biological but culturally constructed and historically contingent. In dominant nineteenth-century British and American writings on the subject, womanhood is only truly embodied by married or marriageable "Anglo-Saxon" gentlewomen—and not even by all of them.

[5] "Some" was an understatement. As her biographer Henry Chorley notes, Hemans's "mind wrought incessantly upon scenes of heroic enterprise and glory" (1: 21).

[6] "[D]ie Familie . . . vermählt den Verwandten dem Schosse der Erde, der elementarischen unvergänglichen Individualität" (*Phänomenologie* 245). This translation, like all the English versions of Hegel, is my own. For a translation of the context, see Hegel, *Phenomenology* 271.

[7] "In dieser Form genommen, erhält das was als einfache Bewegung des individualisirten Pathos vorgestellt wurde, ein anderes Aussehen, und das Verbrechen und die dadurch begründete Zerstörung des Gemeinwesens die eigentliche Form ihres Daseyns.—Das menschliche Gesetz also in seinem allgemeinen Daseyn, das Gemeinwesen, in seiner Bethätigung überhaupt die Männlichkeit, in seiner wirklichen Bethätigung, die Regierung ist, bewegt und erhält sich dadurch, das es die Absonderung der Penaten oder die selbständige Vereinzelung in Familien, welchen die Weiblichkeit vorsteht, in sich aufzehrt, und sie in der Continuität seiner Flüssigkeit aufgelösst erhält. Die Familie ist aber zugleich überhaupt sein Element, das einzelne Bewusstseyn allgemeiner bethätigender Grund" (*Phänomenologie* 258). See also Hegel, *Phenomenology* 287-88.

[8] "Indem das Gemeinwesen sich nur durch die Störung der Familienglückseligkeit und die Auflösung des Selbstbewusstseyns in das allgemeine, sein Bestehen gibt, erzeugt es sich an dem, was es unterdrückt und was ihm zugleich wesentlich ist, an der Weiblichkeit überhaupt seinen innern Feind" (*Phänomenologie* 258-59). See also Hegel, *Phenomenology* 288.

[9] Divine law is "das Gesetz der Schwäche und der Dunkelheit" (Hegel, *Phänomenologie* 257). See also Hegel, *Phenomenology* 286. "What Hegel defines as 'Divine Law,'" Solomon notes, derives from "the structure of bourgeois society at the turn of the nineteenth century" (542).

[10] Femininity is "die ewige Ironie des Gemeinwesens . . ." (Hegel, *Phänomenologie* 259; see also his *Phenomenology* 288). Cooper, Munich, and Squier write that classical epic also presents "the dualities of man/woman, war/peace" and in so doing "both establishes the conception of the war narrative informing Western literary tradition and allows a questioning of those dualities" ("Arms" 10). *Arms and the Woman* strongly suggests how such dualisms may still authorize war narratives' reliance on a domesticity whose feminine representatives accept responsibility for preserving familial bonds and for submitting to the military destruction of those bonds. Bound as it is to what Hegel calls divine law, femininity both ensures the continuity of pacifist ideals and accedes to or assists in the downgrading of pacifism to weak utopianism. Freeman asserts, for example, that contemporary feminist pacifists who attempt to shift full responsibility for war to men or masculinity may merely participate "in the framework that allows, indeed is indispensable to, the conflict in the first place." Femininity, even in its association with pacifism, remains "the secondary term that copulates with . . . and enables" masculinity (308).

[11] Browning, the former "poet laureate of Hope End," mockingly imagines herself laureate of England, "cursing the Czar in Pindarics very prettily" (*Letters* 171), but she echoes Hemans in taking the national (and international) duties of womanhood seriously. An African American, Harper speaks as an internal enemy in poems such as "Home, Sweet Home" or "Do Not Cheer . . . ," but her "Appeal to My Country-women" challenges that stance's racial and political limits (185-86, 197-98, 193-95). Meynell, whose patriotic poetry was inspired by World War I, also appropriates and alters mournful patriotism, though for reasons different from those of the other poets named. See Baym, "Reinventing," on Sigourney.

[12] In the hours before Waterloo, Mrs. O'Dowd, in *Vanity Fair,* appears as a comic Venus outfitting her Mars, while Becky Sharp evinces "quite a Spartan equanimity" (363, 365). Amelia, however, has no classical model. In spotless white, with a crimson sash bleeding down her breast, she embodies the new patriotic femininity of the Hegelian internal enemy: though she is useless to her husband for practical purposes, she embodies an innocent pain whose symbolic force is capable of driving him to remorse, to prayer—and to the battlefield (359-60, 371-72).

For a revealing (and hilarious) evocation of the mid-century association of Hemans with feminine patriotism and melancholy, see Thackeray, *Newcomes* 253-70.

[13] Such a division must remain rough. It creates no clear space, for example, for the title character of "The Sicilian Captive" (*"Records"* 172-79), who sings herself to death from homesickness, or for the shepherd-poet's sister, who leaves off pining at home to lead her people to battle ("The Shepherd-Poet of the Alps"; *Poetical Works* 485-87).

[14] See the unsigned preface to the 1836 edition of Hemans's *Poetical Works* for early praise of her calmness (Preface vi). The anonymous preface to the 1854 *Poetical Works* contains a good mid-century example (Preface 3-8).

[15] As Baym notes, nineteenth-century glorifications of feminine self-sacrifice could deny "that women are submissive by nature and assert . . . that submission is the means by which a woman can overcome or at least check her chief adversary, God" (*Woman's Fiction* 166). If destruction was inevitable, one could at least seize the sacrificial moment, positioning oneself as martyr rather than victim.

[16] Revealingly, Hemans's celebrations of Welsh (and Scottish) patriotism all concern the past actions of men. "Savage liberty" seems no longer required, especially of British women. See Lucas, esp. 4-5, 16-17, on historical distancing from epic virtues in English poetry as a whole.

[17] The significantly entitled "The Spells of Home" (*"Records"* 286-88), for example, more or less generically associates the "freeman" with "the mountain-battles of his land." Homesickness is a recurrent theme in Hemans's personal writing and verse. For a discussion of the "tautological turn by which the domestic encapsulates nostalgia for itself" (288), see Brown.

[18] "Felicia Hemans" 75; "Religious Character" 25-30. See also Browning's "Felicia Hemans," which attempts to refute Letitia E. Landon's "Stanzas." Landon, whose readings of Hemans's melancholy could be ambiguous ("Character" 428-32), offers her own bleak vision of life as war in "The Battle Field."

[19] See Ross's revealing discussion of conflicts between familial and state values in "The Siege of Valencia" (*Contours* 274-85).

[20] In *Vanity Fair,* Thackeray provides a famous Victorian version of this stance (381, 385).

[21] See Browning's opposing alignment of domestic and national virtues in the preface to *Poems before Congress.*

[22] "If blood be the price of admiralty," sing the English dead in another of Kipling's verses, "Lord God, we ha' bought it fair!" ("Song" 187).

[23] "Der Todte, dessen Recht gekränkt ist, weiss darum für seine Rache Werkzeuge zu finden. . . . Diese Mächte sind andere Gemeinwesen, . . . Sie machen sich feindlich auf, und zerstören das Gemeinwesen, das seine Krafft, die Pietät der Familie, entehrt und zerbrochen hat" (Hegel, *Phänomenologie* 258; see also his *Phenomenology* 287).

Works Cited

Baym, Nina. "Reinventing Lydia Sigourney." *Feminism and American Literary History.* New Brunswick: Rutgers UP, 1992. 151-66.

———. *Woman's Fiction: A Guide to Novels by and about Women in America, 1820-1870.* Ithaca: Cornell UP, 1978.

Bivcna, Daniel. *Desire and Contradiction: Imperial Visions and Domestic Debates in Victorian Literature.* Manchester, Eng.: Manchester UP, 1990.

Brantlinger, Patrick. *Rule of Darkness.* Ithaca: Cornell UP, 1988.

Brooke, Rupert. "The Soldier." *The Collected Poems of Rupert Brooke.* New York: Lane, 1915. 111.

Brown, Gillian. "Nuclear Domesticity: Sequence and Survival." Cooper, Munich, and Squier 283-302.

Browning, Elizabeth Barrett. *Complete Works.* Ed. Charlotte Porter and Helen A. Clarke. 6 vols. 1900. New York: AMS, 1973.

———. "Felicia Hemans." Browning, *Works* 2: 81-83.

———. *Letters of Elizabeth Barrett Browning.* Ed. Frederic G. Kenyon. Vol. 2. London: Smith, 1898. 2 vols.

———. Preface. *Poems before Congress.* 1860. Browning, *Works* 3: 314-16.

Byron, George Gordon. [Stanzas.] *The Complete Poetical Works.* Ed. Jerome J. McGann. Vol. 4. Oxford: Clarendon-Oxford UP, 1986. 290. 6 vols.

Chorley, Henry F. *Memorials of Mrs. Hemans.* New York: Saunders, 1836. 2 vols.

Clarke, Norma. *Ambitious Heights: Writing, Friendship, Love—The Jewsbury Sisters, Felicia Hemans, and Jane Welsh Carlyle,* New York: Routledge, 1990.

Colley, Linda. "Radical Patriotism in Eighteenth-Century England." Samuel 169-87.

Cooper, Helen M., Adrienne Auslander Munich, and Susan Merrill Squier. "Arms and the Woman: The Con[tra]ception of the War Text." Cooper, Munich, and Squier, *Arms* 9-24.

———, eds. *Arms and the Woman: War, Gender, and Literary Representation.* Chapel Hill: U of North Carolina P, 1989.

Cunningham, Hugh. "The Language of Patriotism." Samuel 57-89.

"Felicia Hemans." *Leisure Hour* 1 (1852): 72-76.

Freeman, Barbara. "Epitaphs and Epigraphs: 'The End(s) of Man.'" Cooper, Munich, and Squier, *Arms* 303-22.

Hardy, Thomas. "Drummer Hodge." *Collected Poems of Thomas Hardy*. New York: Macmillan, 1925. 83.

Harper, Frances E. W. *Complete Poems*. Ed. Maryemma Graham. New York: Oxford UP, 1988.

Harris, Wendell V. "Canonicity." *PMLA* 106 (1991): 110-21.

Hazlitt, William. "On Patriotism: A Fragment." *The Round Table: Characters of Shakespear's Plays*. New York: Dutton, 1969. 67-68.

Hegel, Georg Wilhelm Friedrich. *Phänomenologie des Geistes*. Ed. Wolfgang Bonsiepen and Reinhard Heede. Hamburg: Meiner, 1990. Vol. 9 of *Gesammelte Werke*.

———. *Phenomenology of Spirit*. Trans. A. V. Müler. Oxford: Oxford UP, 1977.

Hemans, Felicia Dorothea. *"The Domestic Affections," and Other Poems*. 1812. *"The Domestic Affections" [and] The Restoration of the Works of Art to Italy [and] Wallace's Invocation to Bruce [and] The Sceptic*. New York: Garland, 1978.

———. *England and Spain; or, Valour and Patriotism*. 1808. Hemans, *Poems [and] England*.

———. *"The Forest Sanctuary"; and Other Poems*. 1825. *The Vespers of Palermo [and] "The Forest Sanctuary."* New York: Garland, 1978.

———. "The Homes of England." *Blackwood's* Apr. 1827:392.

———. *Modern Greece: A Poem*. 1817. Hemans, *Poems [and] England*.

———. *Poems*. 1808. Hemans, *Poems [and] England*.

———. *Poems [and] England and Spain [and] Modern Greece*. New York: Garland, 1978.

———. *Poetical Works of Mrs. Hemans*. London: Warne, 1900.

———. *"Records of Woman": with Other Poems*. 1828. *"Records of Woman."* New York: Garland, 1978.

———. *A Selection of Welsh Melodies*. 1822. Hemans, *Tales and Historic Scenes*.

———. *"The Siege of Valencia: A Dramatic Poem."* 1823. *"The Siege of Valencia."* New York: Garland, 1978.

———. *"Songs of the Affections," with Other Poems*. 1830. *"Songs of the Affections."* New York: Garland, 1978.

———. *Tales and Historic Scenes [and] Stanzas to the Memory of the Late King [and] Dartmoor [and] Welsh Melodies*. New York: Garland, 1978.

———. *Tales, and Historic Scenes, in Verse*. 1819. Hemans, *Tales and Historic Scenes*.

Hobsbawm, E. J. *The Age of Revolution*. Cleveland: World, 1962.

[Jeffrey, Francis]. "Felicia Hemans." *Edinburgh Review* 50 (1829): 32-47.

Kipling, Rudyard. "The English Flag." Kipling, *Writings* 11: 143-47.

———. "The Hyenas." Kipling, *Writings* 27: 56-57.

———. "The Song of the Dead." Kipling, *Writings* 11: 184-87.

———. *The Writings in Prose and Verse*. 32 vols. New York: Scribner's, 1909.

Landon, Letitia Elizabeth. "The Battle Field." *Poetical Works*. Ed. William B. Scott. London: Routledge, n.d. 337.

———. "On the Character of Mrs. Hemans' Writings." *Colburn's New Monthly Magazine* Aug. 1835: 425-33.

———. "Stanzas on the Death of Mrs. Hemans." *Colburn's New Monthly Magazine* Oct. 1835: 286-88.

Lucas, John. *England and Englishness: Ideas of Nationhood in English Poetry, 1688-1900*. Iowa City: U of Iowa P, 1990.

Moulton, Charles Wells, ed. "Felicia Dorothea Hemans." *The Library of Literary Criticism*. Buffalo: Moulton, 1902.

Nemoianu, Virgil. "Literary Canons and Social Value Options." *The Hospitable Canon: Essays on Literary Play, Scholarly Choice, and Popular Pressures*. Ed. Virgil Namoianu and Robert Royal. Philadelphia: Benjamins, 1991. 215-47.

[Owen, Harriet Mary Browne Hughes]. *Memoir of the Life and Writings of Mrs. Hemans*. 1839. Philadelphia: Lea, 1842.

Preface. *Poetical Works*. By Felicia Hemans. Philadelphia: Grigg, 1836. iii-xii.

Preface. *The Poetical Works of Mrs. Felicia Hemans*. By Felicia Hemans. Boston: Phillips, 1854. 1-8.

Reiman, Donald H. Introduction. Hemans, *Poems [and] England* x-xi.

"Religious Character of the Poetry of Mrs. Hemans." *Christian Review* 5 (1840): 23-33.

Ross, Marlon B. *The Contours of Masculine Desire.* New York: Oxford, 1989.

———. "Romancing the Nation-State: The Poetics of Romantic Nationalism." *Macropolitics of Nineteenth-Century Literature.* Ed. Jonathan Arac and Harriet Ritvo. Philadelphia: U of Pennsylvania P, 1991. 56-85.

Samuel, Raphael, ed. *Patriotism: The Making and Unmaking of British National Identity.* Vol. 1. New York: Routledge, 1989. 3 vols.

Sassoon, Siegfried. "Glory of Women." *The War Poems of Siegfried Sassoon.* London: Faber, 1983. 100.

———. "On Passing the New Menin Gate." *The War Poems of Siegfried Sassoon.* London: Faber, 1983. 153.

Solomon, Robert C. *In the Spirit of Hegel.* New York: Oxford, 1983.

Tennyson, Alfred. "Maud." *Poems of Tennyson.* Ed. Christopher Ricks. London: Longmans, 1969. 1037-93.

Thackeray, William Makepeace. *The Newcomes.* Vol. 2. London: Bradbury, 1855. 2 vols.

———. *Vanity Fair.* New York: Oxford UP, 1987.

Walker, Cheryl. *The Nightingale's Burden: Women Poets and American Culture before 1900.* Bloomington: Indiana UP, 1982.

Woording, Carl. *Politics in English Romantic Poetry.* Cambridge: Harvard UP, 1970.

Susan J. Wolfson (essay date 1994)

SOURCE: "'Domestic Affections' and 'the spear of Minerva': Felicia Hemans and the Dilemma of Gender," in *Re-Visioning Romanticism: British Women Writers, 1776-1837,* edited by Carol Shiner Wilson and Joel Haefner, University of Pennsylvania Press, 1994, pp. 128-66.

[*In the following essay, Wolfson contends that contradictions in Hemans's poetry stemmed from the fundamental conflict between the ideals of her verse—domestic serenity and feminine status quo—and the facts of her life, which required her to carry out the more traditionally masculine work of supporting her family and building a public reputation.*]

I. Discriminations of Gender

Back in the days of schoolroom and parlor recitations, Hemans's **"Casabianca"** ("The boy stood on the burning deck") enjoyed a regular place; another poem, **"The Landing of the Pilgrim Fathers"** ("The breaking waves dashed high / On a stern and rockbound coast"), became a beloved hymn, and **"The Stately Homes of England,"** an anthology standard—their popularity affirming Hemans's place as "the undisputed representative poet of Victorian imperial and domestic ideology."[1] Hemans wrote more than these pieces, volumes in fact. She was one of the most widely read, widely published, and professionally successful poets of the nineteenth century.[2] Yet by its close, she was being written off as a pretty inspirationalist, remembered only by her cherished anthology pieces.[3] Where Wordsworth described the "Poet" as a man speaking to men, Hemans seemed to epitomize the "poetess" as a woman speaking to women—and not for all time, but merely for the passing moment of nineteenth-century sentimental culture. The best that Arthur Symons could manage in his comprehensive retrospect was a summary statement that "it is difficult to say of Mrs. Hemans that her poems are not womanly, and yet it would be more natural to say that they are feminine" (*Romantic Movement* 295).

If this shift from "womanly" to "feminine" seems as opaque as it is discriminating, it is a true register of the role played by Hemans's poetry for readers of her century: the idealizing of female gender roles with the aura, and authority, of "natural" foundation. This ideal was valued in no small part because it was coming to seem merely ideal, an inverse reflection, and reflex, of the contradictory forces of modern life. Although Virgil Nemoianu cites Hemans as a reminder that the "whole field of [now] marginalized literature . . . is replete with acquiescence, formalized harmonies, and translations of obsolete ideologies" and "is *par excellence* the domain of conservatism" (*Hospitable Canon* 240), other readers find Hemans's poetry only tenuously conservative and far from replete. To Jerome McGann, it is consciously "haunted by death and insubstantiality" ("Literary History, Romanticism, and Felicia Hemans," this volume 220). Anne Mellor notes that the celebrations of "the enduring value of the domestic affections, the glory and beauty of maternal love, and the lasting commitment of a woman to her chosen mate" occupy a corpus of work "that constantly reminds us of the fragility of the very domestic ideology it endorses" (*Romanticism and Gender* 124), and Cora Kaplan has suggested that the gloss of "proper sentiments," "normative morality" and "the emerging stereotype of the pure, long-suffering female" are symbolic representations that mask anger turned inward (*Salt and Bitter and Good* 93-95).[4]

Under the power of their imaginary investments, nineteenth-century readers tended to isolate these anomalies as a peculiar "melancholy" and exclude them from its representations of Hemans as quintessentially "female," even a "feminine" ideal. So, too, with the actual, and in some ways "modern," circumstances of her life—her education, wide reading, and considerable help with domestic burdens. "We think the poetry of Mrs Hemans a fine exemplification of Female Poetry," stated Francis Jeffrey in an essay for *Edinburgh Review* (50: 34) later canonized by its reissue in the first edition of her collected works.[5] This social judgment is made to seem a guarantee of nature. Opening with a characteristic bluntness, "Women, we fear cannot do every thing; not even every thing they attempt," Jeffrey explains that they are "disqualified" not only by the "delicacy of their training and habits," but "still more" by the "disabling delicacy which pervades their conceptions and feelings; and . . . they are excluded by their actual inexperience of the realities they might wish to describe"—among these, "the true nature of the agents and impulses that give movement and direction to the stronger currents of ordinary life." Hemans's poetry proves that women's "proper and natural business is the practical regulation of private life, in all its bearings, affections, and concerns" (32).

Half a century later, W. M. Rossetii deploys these genderings with less gallantry. If Hemans's sensibility is "feminine in an intense degree," the weakness of her poetry is that it is "not only 'feminine' . . . but also 'female'": "besides exhibiting the fineness and charm of womanhood, it has the monotone of mere sex" ("Prefatory Notice" 24). Elizabeth Barrett wearied at this monotone, hearing in it not so much "mere sex" as the class and gender formation of being "too ladylike." "I admire her genius—love her memory—respect her piety & high moral tone," she writes to their mutual friend, Mary Russell Mitford, the "but" looming: "But she always does seem to me a lady rather than a woman, & so, much rather than a poetess. . . . She is polished all over to one smoothness & one level, & is monotonous in her best qualities" (23 November 1842; *Letters to Mitford* 1: 88). While Jeffrey is not so disparaging, it is still in a differentiated and diminished realm—distinct from the writing of "the stronger sex" (*Edinburgh* 50: 33)—that he frames his admiration for Hemans's poetry: "It is infinitely sweet, elegant, and tender—touching, perhaps, and contemplative, rather than vehement and overpowering; and not only finished throughout with an exquisite delicacy, and even serenity of execution, but informed with a purity and loftiness of feeling, and a certain sober and humble tone of indulgence and piety" (34). He means to praise "female genius" (34), even "to encourage women to write for publication" (33), but with a propriety of gender. So he concludes urging Hemans to respect that "tenderness and loftiness of feeling, and an ethereal purity of sentiment, which could only emanate from the soul of a woman" and to stick with "occasional verses" rather than "venture again on any thing so long" and awkward as *The Forest Sanctuary* (47)—an epic romance that Hemans herself regarded "as her finest work" (Rossetti, "Prefatory Notice" 17).

As baldly prescriptive as Jeffrey's remarks are, not only for Hemans but for women writers in general, he is tuned to the haunt and mainly "female" region of Hemans's song—home, religion, patriotism, the affections. Although, as we shall see, her poetry often destabilizes, darkens, or even contests the social structures of these values, for nineteenth-century readers the articulation of the value system was enough to contain, even efface any disturbances. Hemans's "delicacy of feeling," crooned the *Quarterly Review* in 1820, is "the fair and valued boast of our countrywomen"—all that is best in "an English lady" (24: 131); "she never ceases to be strictly *feminine* in the whole current of her thought and feeling," chimed *Edinburgh Monthly Review* in the same year; her subjects evince "the delicacy which belongs to the sex, and the tenderness and enthusiasm which form its finest characteristic" (3: 374). "Not because we consider her the best, but because we consider her by far the most feminine writer of the age," George Gilfillan says, he has made her the "first specimen" in his 1847 series in *Tait's Edinburgh Magazine* on "Female Authors": "All the woman in her shines. You could not . . . open a page of her writing without feeling this is written by a lady. Her inspiration always pauses at the feminine point" (NS 14: 360).

Hemans's cultural work in defining the "feminine" locus for ideals of gender, class, and nation is stressed in the first "memorial," by her friend and biographer, Henry Chorley. Referring to Anna Jameson's "rightly" saying that Hemans's poems "could not have been written by a man," he gives his own encomium to their "essentially womanly" character: "Their love is without selfishness—their passion pure from sensual coarseness—their high heroism . . . unsullied by any base alloy of ambition. In their religion, too, she is essentially womanly—fervent, trustful, unquestioning, 'hoping on, hoping ever'—in spite of a painfully acute consciousness of the peculiar trials of her sex" (*Memorials* 1: 138). For elaboration, he cites Maria Jane Jewsbury, a writer who became Hemans's friend: if "other women might be more commanding, more versatile, more acute," no one was "so exquisitely feminine" as she (1: 187).[6] Comparison to Jewsbury herself helps Hemans's sister, Harriett Hughes, to make the same point:

> it was scarcely possible to imagine two individual natures more strikingly contrasted—the one so intensely feminine, so susceptible and imaginative, so devoted to the tender and the beautiful; the other endowed with masculine energies, with a spirit that seemed born for ascendency, with strong powers of reasoning, fathomless profundity of thought. (*Memoir* 158)

Lydia Sigourney's preface to this edition sums up the tenor of this discourse: "critics and casual readers have united in pronouncing her poetry to be essentially feminine. The whole sweet circle of the domestic affections,—

the hallowed ministries of woman, at the cradle, the hearth-stone, and the death-bed, were its chosen themes . . . the disinterested, self-sacrificing virtues of her sex" ("Essay," Hughes xv). In an age of recoil from polemics for women's rights, Hemans was summoned to idealize the "essentially feminine" as essentially "domestic" and "self-sacrificing."[7] The conservative advice of arbiters such as Mrs. Sandford that "domestic life is the chief source of [woman's] influence," her "sphere," and the foundation of her happiness (*Woman* 2-5) was echoed by Hemans in many of the letters that Chorley printed: "There is *no* enjoyment to compare with the happiness of gladdening hearth and home for others," she writes to Mitford (another prolific woman of letters); "it is woman's own true sphere" (*Memorials* 1: 224).

The reiteration of these values was crucial to Hemans's reception, especially as a professional writer.[8] The *Quarterly,* with a dig at modern women of letters, pointedly praised Hemans as "a woman in whom talent and learning have not produced the ill effects so often attributed to them; her faculties seem to sit meekly on her. . . . she is always pure in thought and expression, cheerful, affectionate, and pious. . . . we have not found a line which a delicate woman might blush to have written" (24: 130-31).[9] Gilfillan valued her for giving "the life at once of a woman and a poetess" ("Female Authors" 360), and it mattered that Chorley (also with respect for the gendering of "poetess"[10]) could not only conclude his *Memorials* declaring that "the woman and the poetess were in her too inseparably united to admit of their being considered apart from each other" (2: 355) but also show Hemans measuring other poets by their domestic affections—for instance, Wordsworth:

> This author is the true *Poet of Home,* and of all the lofty feelings which have their root in the soil of home affections. (1: 174, her emphasis)

> his gentle and affectionate playfulness in the intercourse with all the members of his family, would of itself sufficiently refute Moore's theory in the Life of Byron, with regard to the unfitness of genius for domestic happiness. (2: 115)

As far as Chorley was concerned, Hemans had brought feminizing refinements to the national literature: she clothes "the Spirit of romance and chivalry . . . in a female form" and infuses it with deeper affections; in her "female hands," the "homely domestic ballad" is purged of "the grossness, which, of old, stained its strength," while her letters show a "mind in all its *womanliness*" (*Memorials* 1: 137-39). Jeffrey went further, praising Hemans for the happy Englishing of world literature. Taking her themes "from the legends of different nations and the most opposite states of society," Hemans

> retain[s] much of what is interesting and peculiar in each of them, without adopting, along with it, any of the revolting

or extravagant excesses which may characterise the taste or manners of the people or the age from which it has been derived. She has thus transfused into her German or Scandinavian legends the imaginative and daring tone of the originals, without the mystical exaggerations of the one, or the painful fierceness and coarseness of the other—she has preserved the clearness and elegance of the French, without their coldness or affectation—and the tenderness and simplicity of the early Italians, without their diffuseness or languor. (*Edinburgh Review* 50: 35)

Hemans's able broadcasting of English standards explains why even the *Quarterly,* for all its cautions about the ill effects of learning in women, could praise her intellect: "Mrs. Hemans . . . is not merely a clever woman, but a woman of very general reading, and of a mind improved by reflection and study" (24: 130).

The *Quarterly*'s admiration on this last point, however, is also a reminder of the atypical material circumstances that produced Hemans as a writer—ones that complicate iconic definitions of the "feminine." With the devotion of her mother and a large domestic library, she became a voracious reader and a precocious student, and quickly developed into a writer, indeed, a capably publishing poet at fourteen. But she was also a romantic. In her teens, she fell in love with Captain Alfred Hemans and married him in 1812, the year of her nineteenth birthday. She had produced two volumes of poems by then, and by 1818 she produced two more to favorable reviews, as well as five sons. Just before the birth of their last, the Captain left for Italy. The reasons are unclear; the explanation was ill health—in any event, she never saw him again.[11] This failed marriage turned out to be productive for her writing—perhaps motivating its compensatory sentimentalities but also a practical advantage. Deciding to support herself and her sons with her writing, Hemans returned to her mother's household in Wales. This situation relieved many of the conflicts usually besetting women writers: with no wifely obligation or husband to obey, with sisters, mother, and brothers to help with the boys and run the home, Hemans had freedom to read, study, write, and publish. The other advantage was ideological, the identification of her as a poetess not only *of* home, but *at* home—a daughter under "the maternal wing" (an image for both Sigourney and Hughes [*Memoir* xi, 52]). At home, Hemans's professional life was immunized against the stigma of "unfeminine" independence.[12] Thus Rossetti, despite his reservations about the real talents of this "admired and popular poetess," warmly describes her in her domestic sphere, a "loving daughter" and an "affectionate, tender, and vigilant mother" ("Notice" 15).

But even so blessed, it is revealing that Hemans, as a writer, has another view of home, one that attenuates its symbolic representation. In 1822, she laments,

> I am actually in the melancholy situation of Lord Byron's 'scorpion girt by fire'—'Her circle narrowing as she

goes,' for I have been pursued by the household troops through every room successively, and begin to think of establishing my *métier* in the cellar; . . . [in] talk of tranquillity and a quiet home, I stare about in wonder, having almost lost the recollection of such things, and the hope that they may probably be regained. . . . when I make my escape about "fall of eve" to some of the green, quiet hay-fields by which we are surrounded, and look back at the house . . . I can hardly conceive how so gentle-looking a dwelling can contrive to send forth such an incessant clatter of obstreperous sound through its honeysuckle-fringed window. (Hughes, *Memoir* 83-84)

Her tone is humorously aggrieved, but her allusion to *The Giaour* (423-38) hints at a torment. Moreover, the need to making a living by writing was always tuned to writing what would make a living. In poor health near the end of her life, she writes to a friend,

> It has ever been one of my regrets that the constant necessity of providing sums of money to meet the exigencies of the boys' education, has obliged me to waste my mind in what I consider mere desultory effusions. . . . My wish ever was to concentrate all my mental energy in the production of some more noble and complete work; something of pure and holy excellence (if there be not too much presumption in the thought), which might permanently take its place as the work of a British poetess. (Hughes, *Memoir* 300)

The restraints that Jeffrey would impose on Hemans's epic ambitions would be realized not so much by proprieties of gender as by material necessity.

The shadow-text in Hemans's story is the "constant necessity" of most women's lives, domestic labor. Sensing this anomaly without identifying it, Chorley wavers in assessing what he calls her "peculiar circumstances," which "by placing her in a household, as a member and not as its head, excused her from many of those small cares of domestic life."[13] Such cares, he realizes, might have compromised her development as a writer: she "might have . . . fretted away her day-dreams, and, by interruption, have made of less avail the search for knowledge to which she bent herself with such eagerness." But they also might have tempered the extreme "feminine" tone of her work, imparting some "masculine health and stamen, at the expense of some of its romance and music" (*Memorials* 1: 43); Hemans seemed too apt a demonstration of how "one of the gentler sex, shielded as she is by her position in society," can become "too exclusive in her devotions" (1: 24). On the verge of analyzing discrepancies in the "feminine" ideal, what Chorley can recognize is one impressive effect: the "often deeply melancholy" cast of Hemans's iconically feminine poetry, its tendency to dwell even "a little too exclusively upon the farewells and regrets of life—upon the finer natures broken in pieces by contact with [the] world" (1: 43-44). The other story he knows is Jewsbury's. Early "seized" with "the ambition of writing a book, being praised publicly, and associating with authors," and having just begun to publish at age eighteen, she found herself after the death

of her mother inheriting the management of the household and responsibility for her five younger siblings. Her daily life "became so painfully, laboriously domestic, that it was an absolute duty to crush intellectual tastes. I not only did not know a single author, but I did not know a single person of superior mind,—I did not even know how wretchedly deficient my own cultivation was . . . I could neither read nor write legitimately till the day was over" (Jewsbury, quoted in *Memorials* 1: 165-66).[14]

That Hemans's days were otherwise was crucial to the production of writing that, paradoxically, sustained famous commonplaces of female and domestic virtue.

II. Hemans in the Scales

Chorley's admiration of Hemans and Jewsbury is an unusual sympathy. In the introduction to *Memorials* he presents the dominant attitude, in Jewsbury's voice: if men "still secretly dread and dislike female talent, it is not for the reason generally supposed—because it may tend to obscure their own regal honours; but because it interferes with [men's] implanted and imbibed ideas of domestic life and womanly duty." While Chorley is sure that this "prejudice . . . is fading rapidly away" with "the increase of female authorship" (1: 8), the source of Jewsbury's sentences, *The History of an Enthusiast,* is less certain.

Its heroine is Julia, a young woman who, restless in her "dull, dreary and most virtuous domestic life," reads, dreams, and longs for the "more brilliant sphere" of a fame won by "mental efforts" (*History* 69): "I feel the hope of it, even now, the spirit of my spirit, the breath of my being, the life-blood of my life" (47). She gains this fame as a writer and a London celebrity; but glamor fades into ennui, which she assesses years onward in a letter to her happily married sister. The terms are gender-laden:

> Ah, what is genius to woman, but a splendid misfortune! What is fame to woman, but a dazzling degradation! She is exposed to the pitiless gaze of admiration; but little respect, and no love, blends with it. . . . However much as an individual she may have gained in name, and rank, and fortune, she has suffered as a woman; in the history of letters she may be associated with man, but her own sweet life is lost. (112-13)

The lament is double-edged, however, for in reporting the depletions and negations that beset a female genius, it also expresses frustration at this economy. Representing Julia's internalization of its measures, Jewsbury puts them in a critical perspective, showing their power of seeming unalterable, essential, as enduring as nature itself:

> This is her fate, these are her feelings, if her character predominantly possess the excellence of her sex. If it

be otherwise, if that which should be womanly in her is worldly, if she be not so gentle as vain, at heart a creature of ambition rather than of affection, she will be less unhappy; but, alas, she will also be less worthy of happiness! . . . A *man* may erect himself from such a state of despondency; throwing all his energies into some great work, something that shall beget for him "perpetual benediction;" he may live for, and with posterity. But a woman's mind—what is it?—a woman—what can she do?—her head is, after all, only another heart; she reveals her feelings through the medium of her imagination; she tells her dreams and dies. *Her* wreath is not of laurels but of roses, and withers ere it has been worn an hour! (113-15)

In the reflection that Jewsbury writes for Julia, the social fate of "her sex" appears as a guarantee of nature, an inborn tyranny of heart over head. The allusions to Wordsworth's macro-myths of despair—the "despondency" famously "corrected" in *The Excursion* and the amelioration of loss signaled by the phrase quoted from the "Immorality" Ode—are linked by Julia to gender-specific redemptions. Man may enjoy the "perpetual benediction" of mental energy and the fame it may beget. Women's accolades are of a different nature, epitomized for Julia by the wreath: hers is not the poet's laurels but a woman's roses, a headier but transient beauty.

What also begs notice, however, is the italicized language of gender. This double work of Jewsbury's text—its rhetoric of recognition shaded by complaint and protest—carries over into another key scene, a visit from Cecil Percy, whom Julia hoped would be her suitor but who always viewed her ambitions as not "feminine" (100). Not having seen her for six years, he is shocked to find "a sickly verdure, an unnatural bloom, . . . unsound at the core, withered at the root . . . with energies that only kindled their own funeral pile" (118). To him, fame has blighted both her femininity and, in consequence, men's admiration. "I should not like a lioness for a wife," he declares (120), and Jewsbury's narrator paraphrases his recoil: "She who is brilliant in mind, and gifted with the perilous gift of genius, may receive the homage of saloons, may be courted as a companion, and worshipped as a goddess; but for his help-meet, man chooses far otherwise" (127). Then come the sentences that Chorley, resisting their "prejudice," quotes in *Memorials:*

> Man does not secretly dread and dislike high intellect in woman, for the mean reason generally supposed—because it may tend to obscure his own regal honors; but because it interferes with his implanted and imbibed ideas of domestic life and womanly duty. (127)

This is a voice of social judgment that frames rather than simply reports Cecil's prim voice, and in its vibrant irritation at male prejudice Chorley hears a trenchant critique.[15] The phrase, "implanted and imbibed ideas," defines the socioculture that men take as naturally given. Jewsbury in turn discredits the orthodox Cecil. Julia may lose him to a proper English girl, but he never quite escapes the character of a passionless twit, and Jewsbury ends her *History* not with her enthusiast exposed as vain and vacant nor recuperated to domestic happiness, but recovering some of her original spirit. Deciding to leave England as a "second Mary Wolstonecroft [*sic*]" (143) to travel in Europe on her own, Julia draws inspiration from a poem of male rapture, "Ode to the West Wind," whose voice she speaks as her own: "O lift me as a wave, a leaf, a cloud; / I fall upon the thorns of life—I bleed; / A heavy weight of hours has chained and bowed / One too like thee, tameless, and swift, and proud" (160). Although Jewsbury leaves Julia's precise future left untold, what she does expose is the frustration of England in the 1830s to such a woman, and her *History* boldly severs her enthusiast from the constraints of a domestic script.

The regard of Hemans by English men of letters, accolades notwithstanding, has a good dose of Cecil Percy. Wordsworth admits that he "could say much very much in praise of Mrs Hemans" (August 1830; *Letters, Later Years* 2: 311), but he was inclined to regard her success as a clever commercial accomplishment only. "Mrs. Hemans," he writes in the headnote to some tender memorial verses, "was unfortunate as a Poetess in being obliged . . . to write for money, and that so frequently and so much, that she was compelled . . . to write as expeditiously as possible" (*Poetical Works* 4: 461).[16] In his letter, he noted a "draw-back" in this resourcefulness, which he tunes to the genderings of his headnote ("as a Poetess," "as a woman"): "Her conversation, like that of many literary Ladies, is too elaborate and studied—and perhaps the simplicity of her character is impaired by the homage which has been paid her—both for her accomplishments and her Genius" he laments (*Letters, Later Years* 2: 311), though he seemed to have no such worries about the effect of homage paid to his own account.

His difficulty was how to weigh accomplishment and genius in "a woman" whose "education had been [so] unfortunate" as to leave her "totally ignorant of housewifery," as his headnote puts it: this "spoilt child of the world . . . could as easily have managed the spear of Minerva as her needle." His droll distress about Hemans's refusal of "her" needle, the usual instrument of women's "work," may seem to contain as a comedy at her expense his unease with her intellectual power, projected as a spear-bearing deity of wisdom. But even the warrior Minerva had a domestic role as the proud Olympian weaver for the gods.[17] And in Wordsworth's household at least, women's needles not only clothed his family but also stitched his manuscripts.[18] Hemans thus poses a double affront—to notions of proper female labor and to the system of men's dependence on it for their own work. And so he means to remediate. "It was from observing these deficiencies," the headnote continues, "that, one day while she was under my roof, I purposely directed her attention to household economy, and told her I had purchased Scales, which I intended to present to a young lady as a wedding present; pointed out their utility (for her especial benefit). . . . Mrs. Hemans, not in the least suspecting my drift, reported this . . . to a friend . . . as a proof of my simplicity."

Hemans's own report of this scene is amusingly tuned to the ideological contest: the palpable simplicity of Wordsworth's design to point a wayward poetess into a proper female sphere of attention and her deftly polite resistance to his obvious "drift" by recourse to a wittily blinkered aestheticizing of his object of instruction:

> Imagine, . . . a bridal present made by Mr. Wordsworth, to a young lady in whom he is much interested—a poet's daughter, too! You will be thinking of a broach in the shape of a lyre, or a butterfly-shaped aigrette, or a forget-me-not ring, or some such "small gear"—nothing of the sort, but a good, handsome, substantial, useful-looking pair of scales, to hang up in her store-room! "For you must be aware, my dear Mrs. Hemans," said he to me very gravely, "how necessary it is occasionally for every lady to see things weighed herself." *"Poveretta me!"* I looked as *good as I could,* and, happily for me, the poetic eyes are not very clear-sighted, so that I believe no suspicion derogatory to my notability of character, has yet flashed upon the mighty master's mind: indeed I told him that I looked upon scales as particularly graceful things, and had great thoughts of having my picture taken with a pair in my hand. (Chorley, *Memorials* 2: 141-42)

Troping her alienation from Wordsworth's agenda in the voice of an Italianate lament, Hemans answers his discomfort with the pointed instrument that he finds unfeminine, the pen. While her published **"To Wordsworth"** praises his "gift of soul or eye" (*Records* 232-33), this private report is one of sharpest satires of his vision ever written.

Hemans's tipping the scales against Wordsworth is loaded with the imbalance that women writers imposed on customary male perspectives: not only were they suspected of domestic delinquency, but they made their own claims to authority and competed in the marketplace—often, like Hemans, with notable success. Wordsworth was not alone in wishing her to put down her pen and take up her needle. This was also the point of Byron's nasty puns of gender. To their mutual publisher, John Murray, he tags her "Mrs. Heman," "your feminine *He-Man*," "Mrs. Hewoman's" (*Letters and Journals* 7: 183; 158). The gendered joking is defensively sharpened by Hemans's commercial prowess, an achievement that seemed not only to disdain the female sphere but to challenge the men's: "I do not despise Mrs. Heman—but if [she] knit blue stockings instead of wearing them it would be better," Byron liberally declared (7: 182).

But if Byron and Wordsworth reflect the pressures to which Hemans was subject from without, she was pres-

sured from within by the asymmetry between her fame as the poet of the domestic affections and the depletions of these affections in her actual life—and the inability of her fame to compensate. This pressure reached a crisis when her mother died in 1827, for this was also the end of her status as child, and it felt like her own death: "I have lost the faithful, watchful, patient love, which for years had been devoted to me and mine; and I feel that the void it has left behind, must cause me to bear 'a yearning heart within me to the grave;' . . . I now feel wearied and worn, and longing, as she did, for rest" (Hughes 120). Rossetti rightly suspects that the "affections of daughter and mother were more dominant and vivid in [her] than conjugal love" ("Notice" 14). Hemans was temporarily cushioned by remaining in the family home, now managed by her brother and sister. But when this household was "scattered" by the former's relocation to Ireland and the latter's marriage, the house ceased to be a home. For "the first time in my life, [I am] holding the reins of government, independent, managing a household myself," she tells Mitford, adding, "I never liked anything less than *'ce triste empire de soi-même'*" (10 November 1828; Hughes 170).

In ***Records of Woman,*** published in 1828, Hemans included **"Madeline: A Domestic Tale"** (144-49), a fantasy of restoration that sets this sorrow into a cultural register. Madeline's wedding is also a painful parting from her mother, but this figurative death of her life as daughter is revoked by the sudden death of her husband. In one respect, this catastrophe is a symbol to woman of "the part / Which life will teach—to suffer and be still" (147), but it is also a narrative pivot that reverses and ameliorates this lesson, turning the lovelorn wife back into a beloved daughter. Lost in the death-in-life of widowhood, Madeline is rescued by her mother, whom she begs, in the poem's last couplet, to rematriate her to home: "Take back thy wanderer from this fatal shore, / Peace shall be ours beneath our vines once more" (149). This voice echoes many such regressive Romantic longings—ones heard in Shelley, Wordsworth, and Keats, whose texts often involve images of maternal nurture. But Hemans's conception is a more specific fantasy of the actual maternal home, and Madeline's yearning for the "true and perfect love" (149) of its care evokes a gender-specific paradise lost. The counterexample in ***Records*** is **"The Lady of the Castle"** (194-99) who runs off to become a king's mistress. She can be spoken of only with shock of gender: "how shall woman tell / Of woman's shame, and not with tears?—She fell! / That mother left that child!" (195). The consequences are radical: in "grief and shame," her husband seeks his death in foreign wars, and her daughter grows up a "blighted spirit" (196). Years later she returns, pale and impoverished, to seek her daughter, who does not recognize her, and instinctively shrinks back. This rejection is fatal to the failed mother, the implied moral judgment on her irrevocable betrayal of home.

Yet these exempla notwithstanding, the sum of Hemans's career—*The Domestic Affections* (1812), *Tales, and Historic Scenes* (1819), *Records of Woman* (1828), and *Songs of the Affections* (1830)—present a diverse, often divided array of female characters and social perspectives. There are women defined by domestic relations (Wife, Bride, Mother, Widow) or subsumed under the sign itself ("A Domestic Tale," "The Domestic Affections"). This sphere is often evoked as a cultural ideal, with its values gendered as feminine: supervised by women, home is a refuge from the world, a place of spiritual and emotional restoration, or even foundation of patriotic love. Yet in other poems Hemans wonders about these relations or pauses over the seemingly inescapable social fate of women to suffer and endure. Sometimes she uses a language of strength and power to infuse women's lives with heroic intensity; but at other times she strains this intensity with records of women in whom affection turns desperate, pathological, and life-destroying. And at still other times she presents women who rupture the domestic sphere with energies that not only betray and destroy its most fundamental codes but also challenge the deepest logic of the masculine world and its politics. These are women who, driven by spiritual honor and domestic

RECORDS OF WOMAN:

WITH OTHER POEMS.

BY

FELICIA HEMANS.

————Mightier far
Than strength of nerve or sinew, or the sway
Of magic potent over sun and star,
Is love, though oft to agony distrest,
And though his favourite seat be feeble woman's breast.
WORDSWORTH.

Das ist das Loos des Schönen auf der Erde!
SCHILLER.

THE SECOND EDITION.

WILLIAM BLACKWOOD, EDINBURGH:
AND T. CADELL, LONDON.
MDCCCXXVIII.

fidelity, defy male authority and avenge its treachery with violence, and whose protests may even take their children's lives with their own.

Hemans was more the recorder than the deliberate critic of these divided representations, whose deepest shadows, as we shall see, fall on her accounts of famous women, especially artists. "Fame can only afford *reflected* delight to a woman," she murmurs to Mitford (23 March 1828; Chorley, *Memorials* 1: 159); "How hollow sounds the voice of fame to an orphan!" (10 Nov.; 1: 234). Yet this reading of "woman" by her own sorrow does not dispel her dissatisfaction with the hollow images of women in other poets. She was quite frank about admiring Joanna Baillie, to whom she dedicated *Records,* for representing women who, in their "gentle fortitude, and deep self-devoting affection," are "perfectly different from the pretty *'unidea'd* girls,' who seem to form the *beau ideal* of our whole sex in the works of some modern poets" (ibid 1: 96). A critique of the "beau ideal" stirs remarkably in one of her earliest poems, **"The Domestic Affections"** (*Domestic Affections* 148-72), in the way that its processes of argument intermittently expose discrepancies of domestic experience and domestic ideal. It begins with standard polarities. Life in the world is prey to perpetual "storms of discord," "war's red lightnings," the desolation of thrones, the destruction of empires, and "rude tumultuous cares." The value of home is thus not just intrinsic—

> Hail sacred home! where soft affection's hand,
> With flow'rs of Eden twines her magic band,
> Where pure and bright, the social ardors rise,
> Concentrating all their holiest energies!
>
> (151)

—but accrues by what it contrasts and excludes:

> Nurs'd on the lap of solitude and shade,
> The violet smiles, embosom'd in the glade;
> There sheds her spirit on the lonely gale,
> Gem of seclusion! treasure of the vale!
> Thus, far retir'd from life's tumultuous road,
> Domestic bliss has fix'd her calm abode,
> Where hallow'd innocence and sweet repose
> May strew her shadowy path with many a rose.
>
> (149)

Hemans emphatically transfers terms of worldly power into the domestic sphere: "*Her* empire, home!—her throne, affection's breast!" (150).

These celebrations are stretched over some problematic terms, however. As Hemans describes home's "mental peace, o'er ev'ry prospect bright" (150), she also speaks of its shades and shadows, solitude, seclusion, and loneliness, and so fixed a withdrawal from "life's tumutuous road" (149) that the calm abode comes to seem a withdrawal from life itself. In this aspect, what is projected as a refuge from the world turns out to be very worldly, a reflexive ideal premised on female restriction. The only feminine presences in the world are phantasmic nurturers of masculine "Genius": "Fame" ("ev'ry life-pulse vibrates to her voice") and "Freedom" ("her throne of fire!"). Hemans's argument means to bind this feminine pulse and fire to the domestic hearth: with an instructive analogy, she tells us that "th'aspiring eagle" soon and always "descend[s] from his height sublime, / Day's burning fount, and light's empyreal clime . . . speeds to joys more calmly blest, / 'Midst the dear inmates of his lonely nest" (157-58). Yet the syntax marking this descent seems more than a little reluctant, and the word *lonely* in the destination is sufficiently jarring to shade the primary sense of its "inmates" from "cohabitants" into "fellow prisoners." The application of this image to "Genius" further strains the argument, for once again, an equivocal syntax crosses the design to celebrate the "softer pleasures of the social heart" at home:

> Thus Genius, mounting on his bright career,
> Thro' the wide regions of the mental sphere;
> And proudly waving, in his gifted hand,
> O'er Fancy's worlds, Invention's plastic wand;
> Fearless and firm, with lightning-eye surveys
> The clearest heav'n of intellectual rays!
> Yet, on his course tho' loftiest hopes attend,
> And kindling raptures aid him to ascend;
> (While in his mind, with high-born grandeur fraught,
> Dilate the noblest energies of thought;)
> Still, from the bliss, ethereal and refin'd,
> Which crowns the soarings of triumphant mind,
> At length he flies, to that serene retreat,
> Where calm and pure, the mild affections meet;
> Embosom'd there, to feel and to impart,
> The softer pleasures of the social heart!
>
> (157-58)

"At length" indeed: with the dilating grammar of *yet, while, still,* the rapturous phase before the syntactic pivot on *retreat* so temporizes that the retreat comes to seem a relinquishment and a reluctant fall. Writing to her aunt of her admiration for the "noble Spaniards" in the Peninsular campaign of 1808 (in which her brother and Captain Hemans served), young Felicia Browne gushes, "my whole heart and soul are interested for the gallant patriots," but not without realizing the social prohibition, that "females are forbidden to interfere in politics" (Chorley, *Memorials* 1: 31).

Not only do such prohibitions erode the poem's high claims for female domestic seclusion, but Hemans's elaborations darken the material rewards of home for women. The idealized map is one where there's no place like home for the "exhausted," "oppress'd," "wearied pilgrim" of life:

> Bower of repose! when torn from all we love,
> Thro' toil we struggle, or thro' distance rove;

> To *thee* we turn, still faithful, from afar,
> Thee, our bright vista! thee, our magnet star!
>
> (152)

Hemans's emphatic apostrophe "To *thee*" absorbs the host of apposite, ungendered first-person plurals that involve women as well as men in the trope of exile. By the end of the poem, however, she is concentrating on a gendered inequality of lived experience. With her domestic affection devoted to healing others, a woman must accept her own depletion. Home-bound and "whisp'ring peace" to world-battered men, she must "fondly struggl[e] to suppress *her own*" cares, and "conceal, with duteous art, / Her own deep sorrows in her inmost heart" (164, her italics). When Hemans protests, again with plaintive italics, "But who may charm *her* sleepless pang to rest, / Or draw the thorn that rankles in her breast?" (167), the only answer that she can propose is the "Faith" that transcends the phantom Eden of the earthly home to evoke an "Eden, freed from every thorn" (168), namely, the Eden of Heaven. The ideal of home, strained by what it must suppress and exclude, must finally be projected for women "Beyond the sphere of anguish, death, or time" (171)—beyond, that is, the sphere of their social and historical existence.

The language that portrays the "Elysian clime" of the world beyond (171) gains an even more subversive critical force in **"The Domestic Affections"** in the way it turns out to reflect the sphere of male genius *in* the world. "Genius mounting on *his* bright career, / Thro' the wide regions of the mental sphere" (157) is refigured in the anticipation of woman's death as the moment of *her* "mounting to [the] skies, / . . . releas'd . . . // . . . on exulting flight, / Thro' glory's boundless realms, and worlds of living light!" (168, my italics). Here are "triumphant" smiles and "radiant prospects" where her "mind's bright eye, with renovated fire, / Shall beam on glories—never to expire" (170-71). While "never" projects a transcendence of all worldly limits, it is significant that Hemans casts this scenario in the terms she used to figure earthly glory for men. Only in heaven, it seems, may women devote their affections, "Sublim'd, ennobled" (in the poem's last words), to something other than "assuaging woe" (172).

It is a sign of Felicia Browne's precocious genius that, in attempting to celebrate the domestic affections as a universal foundation of bliss, she winds up exposing a socially specific scheme so inwrought with suppression and denial for women as to evoke a longing for death as their only release. This mournful lesson haunts the scene of instruction in one of Hemans's most anthologized poems in the nineteenth century, **"Evening Prayer, at a Girls' School."**[19] Contemplating this ritual in a perspective evocative of Gray's on the boys of Eton college, its speaker superimposes the melancholy woman's life that she knows awaits:

> in those flute-like voices, mingling low,
> Is woman's tenderness—how soon her woe!

Her lot is on you—silent tears to weep
  And patient smiles to wear through suffering's
    hour
And sumless riches, from affection's deep,
  To pour on broken reeds—a wasted shower!
And to make idols, and to find them clay,
And to bewail that worship. Therefore pray!

(479)

The poem descends into the bitterness of a rueful female (if not feminist) solidarity:

Her lot is on you—to be found untired,
  Watching the stars out by the bed of pain,
With a pale cheek, and yet a brow inspired,
  And a true heart of hope, though hope be
    vain;
Meekly to bear with wrong, to cheer decay,
And oh! to love through all things. Therefore
    pray!

(479)

The scene of the girls' innocent prayer evolves into a prefigurative image of their only consolation for, and heroic resignation to, all that "Earth will forsake" (479), render vain, and commit to wrong and decay in their lives as women.

These bleak apprehensions inform stories about women such as "young Bianca," literally killed by domestic affection—or rather, disaffection (**"The Maremma,"** *Tales;* rpt. *Poetical Works* [Gall and Inglis] 125-30). Brought with her child by a jealous husband to Maremma to die a slow death by its infamous pollutions, Bianca is betrayed by both nature and domesticity. Here, nature, hailed in **"The Domestic Affections"** as the type and ally of home values, conspires in the husband's treachery: we are no sooner told of "Italian skies" where "Nature lavishes her warmest hues" than cautioned to "trust not her smile, her balmy breath . . . her charms but the pomp of Death!" The rhyme is a potent pairing; Nature, a false mother, leagues with Death, a treacherous husband who "woos . . . to slumber and to die." Both "charm with seductive wiles": "Where shall we turn, O Nature! if in *thee* / Danger is masked in beauty—death in smiles?" (126). Nature's deceit, personified both in Circe and in the loving husband who conceals "Deep in his soul" the "workings of each darker feeling" ("vengeance, hate remorse") (128), critically contests the naturalized ideals of **"The Domestic Affections."** Wife and son are utterly and fatally vulnerable to a man's "fancied guilt," with the story of their "Affliction" evolving a sensational contrast to **"Affection"** (127): the lesson that "It is our task to suffer—and our fate / To learn that mighty lesson soon or late" (130).

III. Domestic Fates

Hemans's ironies of domestic idealism culminate in ***Records of Woman.*** Even as she exoticizes these "Records"

into other cultures and eras (signaling these with historically-researched headnotes), "of Woman" proposes an essential that extends to the social understanding of her English readers. "For is not woman's [patient love] in all climes, the same?" cries Elmina in ***The Siege of Valencia*** (*Poetical Works* [Warne] 154). ***Records*** looks two ways, at the cultures it constructs and at Hemans's own. Although Hemans does not reflect critically on such displacements, this double orientation has a critical force in its common and recurring story: the failure of domestic ideals, in whatever cultural variety, to sustain and fulfill women's lives. What Rossetti disparages as a "monotone of mere sex" sounds in this volume as a reading of the fate of mere sex.

One sign of this fate is the constraint of female heroism to the demands of the affection. On the title-page of ***Records*** (iii) is a prescriptive epigraph from Wordsworth's "Laodamia" (86-90), the widow's protest to her husband's shade:

——Mightier far
Than strength of nerve or sinew, or the sway
Of magic potent over sun and star,
Is love, though oft to agony distrest,
And though his favourite seat be feeble woman's
    breast.

Thus the "strength" of Gertrude, the subject of a record subtitled **"Fidelity Till Death,"** sustains her husband in his torture unto death by his enemies with "high words . . . From woman's breaking heart" (***Records*** 58). **"The Switzer's Wife"** takes its epigraph from Jewsbury's "Arria" (*Phantasmagoria* 2: 122), about the heroically suicidal devotion of a Roman matron to her husband and the Roman ideology of honor. Hemans's **"Wife"** discovers her "power" in fidelity to the domestic and civic relations by which she is named and identified:

. . . she, that ever thro' her home had mov'd
  With the meek thoughtfulness and quiet smile
Of woman, calmly loving and belov'd,
  And timid in her happiness the while,
Stood brightly forth, and stedfastly, that hour,
Her clear glance kindling into sudden power.

Ay, pale she stood, but with an eye of light,
  And took her fair child to her holy breast,
And lifted her soft voice, that gathered might
  As it found language:—"Are we thus
    oppressed
Then must we rise upon our mountain-sod,
A man must arm, and woman call on God!"

(***Records*** 41)

When Werner (who *is* named) exclaims, "Worthy art thou . . . / / My bride, my wife, the mother of my child! / Now shall thy name be armour to my heart," the possessives reflect her roles of service and subordination, heroized by their "armour" to his action (43). What remains undisturbed in this crisis and its female epiphany is the norm of separate spheres and its gendered system of obligations.

An essay on noble and virtuous instances of "The Female Character" published in *Fraser's Magazine* in 1833 reflects the cultural investment in this conservatism. Telling readers that "the exalted heroism of a woman's soul may be excited by love, religion, patriotism, parental affection, gratitude, pity"—the standard inspirations—it also reminds them that even "these qualities are only evinced on extraordinary occasions. . . . it is only in situations requiring the exercise of the most powerful exertions that a female can divest herself of the retiring gentleness of her nature" (594-95). It is as an impulse of "nature," then, that we are to regard "instances of female heroism, of devoted attachment, and of endurance of suffering," especially for "love of offspring." Hemans, who is warmly praised in this essay, represents this last imperative in the maternal devotion of **"Pauline,"** taking it to a fatal extension as she perishes in the fire from which she would save her child. Her "strength" is organic to a mother's "deep love":

> there is no power
> To stay the mother from that rolling grave,
> Tho' fast on high the fiery volumes tower,
>
> . . . . .
>
> Mighty is anguish, with affection twined!
>
> (***Records*** 120)

Mighty affection is also the fate of "Imelda," who, finding her lover murdered by her brother (their fathers are enemies), determines to die with him:

> . . . love is strong. There came
> Strength upon woman's fragile heart and frame,
> There came swift courage! On the dewy ground
> She knelt, with all her dark hair floating round,
> Like a long silken stole; she knelt and press'd
> Her lips of glowing life to Azzo's breast,
> Drawing the poison forth.
>
> (***Records*** 67)

Even with the heroic analogue of Juliet's suicide for Romeo, the result is the same for her as it is for passive Bianca: women's affections succumb to the poison of men's undomestic passions. So, too, for the political prisoner in the first poem in ***Records,*** **"Arabella Stuart"** (3-20), who gambles with "male attire" (3) to escape to her lover. A series of mishaps returns her to prison, where her fortitude is voiced as an emergence in gender—"Feeling still my woman's spirit strong, / . . . / I bear, I strive, I bow not" (7); "my woman's heart / Shall wake a spirit and a power to bless, / Ev'n in this hour's o'er-shadowing fearfulness" (19). These "natural" resources, infusing affection with faith, feed a heroism only unto death; ultimately the re-

sources that are "woman's" cannot define an alternative or resistance to the power structures of men's politics.

"The Bride of the Greek Isle" (***Records*** 21-34) so emphatically constrains its daring heroine to this fate that it verges on social allegory. The issue of gender is keyed by epigraphs from Byron's *Sardanapalus* (21), which involve stark social divisions in the heroics they voice. The first is the Greek slave Myrrha's pledge to die with her lover, the defeated king: "Fear!—I'm a Greek, and how should I fear death? / A slave, and wherefore should I dread my freedom?" (1. 2. 479-80). The second is his pledge, "I will not live degraded" (1. 2. 629). Myrrha speaks from a social situation, slavery, by which a man and king would be "degraded" but from which her death may be idealized as freedom. While Hemans's Greek girl, "Eudora," is not a slave, her name identifies her as a commodity, a "good gift," blazoned and bejeweled, to be passed from father to husband ("She turns to her lover, she leaves her sire" [26]) and entailing in this passage into goods her own paradise lost: "Will earth give love like *yours* again? / Sweet mother!" (25). Hemans does not focus a critical perspective on this gendered economy, but she does tense its representation, both by displaying its operation and by hinting at a mysterious surplus, a potential resistance in the bride: "the glance of her dark resplendent eye" seems "[f]or the aspect of woman at times too high" (28).

This tension is released by a derailment of the patriarchal marriage plot, as pirates murder the groom and abduct the bride (the poem's title is potently ironic misnomer). Shifting her genre from romance to heroic melodrama, Hemans signals the emergent possibilities by staging a new female blazon in the record of the "mother's gaze" (22) that Eudora lamented to lose:

> lo! a brand
> Blazing up high in her lifted hand!
> And her veil flung back, and her free dark hair
> Sway'd by the flames as they rock and flare;
> And her fragile form to its loftiest height
> Dilated, as if by the spirit's might,
> And her eye with an eagle-gladness fraught,—
> Oh! could this work be of woman wrought?
> Yes, 'twas her deed!—by that haughty smile
> It was her's!—She hath kindled her funeral pile!
>
> (32-33)

As if kindled by the glances of Eudora's resplendent eye, the fire dilates her meek femininity into heroic female art, a "work . . . of woman wrought." The retaliatory blaze is a self-transformation, too, of the bride from the gift of man to man to an independent, eagle-glad energy. Eudora's bound, bejeweled and braided hair and veiled face are released into the cultural iconography of female revolutionary heroism—an elaboration exceeding the aspect mere revenge. To write "Man may not fetter, nor ocean tame / The might and wrath of the rushing flame!" (32)

is to convey not just Eudora's wrath but her self-wrought liberation from the fetters of men.

But if this exclamation congratulates a symbolic escape from commodification of one kind or another—marriage or slavery—Hemans's hesitation about the implied social allegory keeps such freedom a purchase by death, even restricting its transcendence with a simile that recuperates this heroism as a marriage of the suttee: "Proudly she stands, like an Indian bride / On the pyre" (33)—in effect, the pyre to which Myrrha commits herself as she compounds her fate with that of the man she calls both husband and master.[20] And Hemans's narrative further depletes Eudora's blaze with impotence: "The slave and his master alike" escape the ship, while the bride (like young Casabianca) "stands on the [burning] deck alone" (32), in a futile, if impressive heroism.

This self-consuming heroism also haunts the overtly political emergence of female passion in **"The Indian City"** (*Records* 83-96). When Maimuna's son is murdered for having wandered onto Brahmin sacred grounds, she first "bow[s] down mutely o'er her dead" (89), then, in an epiphany of power, vows revenge:

> She rose
> Like a prophetess from dark repose!
> And proudly flung from her face the veil,
> And shook the hair from her forehead pale,
> And 'midst her wondering handmaids stood,
> With the sudden glance of a dauntless mood.
> Ay, lifting up to the midnight sky
> A brow in its regal passion high,
> With a close and rigid grasp she press'd
> The blood-stain'd robe to her heaving breast,
> And said—"Not yet—not yet I weep,
> Not yet my spirit shall sink or sleep,
> Not till yon city, in ruins rent,
> Be piled for its victim's monument.
>
> (90-91)

The kindling gaze, the unveiled face, and unbound hair are Hemans's codes for the eruption of female power from cultural norms—for the rebellion of passion and pride against passivity and meekness. Here, the result is "Moslem war" (91):

> —Oh! deep is a wounded heart, and strong
> A voice that cries against mighty wrong;
> And full of death, as a hot wind's blight,
> Doth the ire of a crush'd affection light.
>
> (91-92)

Yet despite the epigraphic alignment of Maimuna with the anguish of Childe Harold (97), the poem always marks her as female. Her strength is not military but muse-like, of voice and body:

> Maimuna from realm to realm had pass'd,
> And her tale had rung like a trumpet's blast.

> . . . words from her pale lips pour'd,
> Each one a spell to unsheath the sword.
>
> . . . . .
>
> . . . her voice had kindled that lightning flame.
>
> (92-93)

Hemans does not regender this warrior woman (cf. Semiramis, the "Man-Queen" of *Sardanapalus*) but projects her into a heightened female power:

> She came in the might of a queenly foe,
> Banner, and javelin, and bended bow;
> But a deeper power on her forehead sate—
> *There* sought the warrior his star of fate;
> Her eye's wild flash through the tented line
> Was hailed as a spirit and a sign,
> And the faintest tone from her lip was caught,
> As a Sybil's breath of prophetic thought.
>
> (93)

And such power, though it shows what Jewsbury praised as Hemans's ability to "combine power and beauty" (*Athenæum* 171: 104), retains the inscription of a female fate: it achieves only a "Vain, bitter glory!" The bereft mother turns sickening "from her sad renown, / As a king in death might reject his crown" (93), and soon makes good on the analogy by dying herself. The domestic sphere is symbolically restored and her triumph contained by her burial with her son in the ruins of the city she destroyed—a tale summed in the poem's last line as "the work of one deep heart wrung!" (96).

These depletions bind the affectionate patriotism of heroines such as **"Woman on the Field of Battle"** (*Songs of the Affections* 123-26). No sooner are we told that she is there by the "power" of "love" than Hemans exposes its futility. In the poem's last words, it is a "love, whose trust / Woman's deep soul too long / Pours on the dust!" (126).[21] While "too long" seems a call for revaluation, Hemans's sense of a gendered fate is reflected in the way her starkest tales of women's revenge require the socially derealized genre of macabre romance and theatrically pathological characters. **"The Widow of Crescentius"** (*Tales* 1-49) is an example. Stephania, made thus by the treachery of Otho III of Germany, is introduced in images that mirror blazing Eudora: her "rich flow of raven hair / Streams wildly on the morning air" (11), and her "wild and high expression" is "fraught / With glances of impassion'd thought," a "fire within" (13). Like Maimuna, she is impelled into affairs of state by love, but her revenge is more sensational for its perversion of female codes. Acting with the impulse of a bride whose heart was "vainly form'd to prove / The pure devotedness of love" (20), she insinuates herself into Otho's court as a minstrel boy. Hemans then plays out a patent perversion of domestic affections and its codes of gender. Stephania-as-Guido "breathes . . . a strain / Of power to lull all earthly pain" (27), but in an aspect that exudes a dark Byronic passion, legible not only in iconography but even in diction:

> oft his features and his air
> A shade of troubled mystery wear,
> A glance of hurried wildness, fraught
> With some unfathomable thought.
> Whate'er that thought, still, unexpress'd,
> Dwells the sad secret in his breast;
> The pride his haughty brow reveals,
> All other passion well conceals.
>
>   (29-30)

Her actual revenge is a poison, an inversion of (female) nurture; and Hemans dwells on the effects in loving detail, launching her narrative with a wickedly tuned sonnet paragraph that begins thus:

> Away, vain dream!—on Otho's brow,
> Still darker lower the shadows now;
> Changed are his features, now o'erspread
> With the cold paleness of the dead;
> Now crimson'd with a hectic dye,
> The burning flush of agony!
> His lip is quivering, and his breast
> Heaves with convulsive pangs oppress'd;
> Now his dim eye seems fix'd and glazed,
> And now to heaven in anguish raised . . .
>
>   (33-34)

In a gloat of almost sixty lines, Hemans's poetry savors the poisoner's delight:

> And on the sufferer's mien awhile
> Gazing with stern vindictive smile,
> A feverish glow of triumph dyed
> His burning cheek, while thus he cried:
> "Yes! these are death pangs!—on the brow
> Is set the seal of vengeance now!"
>
>   (34-35)

She was clearly inspired. But Stephania's triumph is a fatal purchase. The tale ends with her imminent execution and closes in a perspective that effaces her heroism in the pace of men's history: "o'er thy dark and lowly bed / The sons of future days shall tread, / The pangs, the conflicts, of thy lot, / By them unknown, by thee forgot" (39)—an echo of the rueful reverence Pope wrote for Eloisa: "How happy is the blameless Vestal's lot! / The world forgetting, by the world forgot" (*Eloisa to Abelard* 207-8).

In other poems Hemans compounds women's self-sacrifice with infanticide—an act forced by a husband's betrayal or the threat of an invading army, or both—and presents this stark transgression of domestic codes as a radically domestic affection.[22] The singer of **"Indian Woman's Death-Song"** (*Records* 102-8) stands in a canoe rushing toward a cataract, "Proudly, and dauntlessly, and all alone, / Save that a babe [a girl] lay sleeping at her breast." This is a fatal heroism profoundly allied to affection:

> upon her Indian brow
> Sat a strange gladness, and her dark hair wav'd
> As if triumphantly. She press'd her child,
> In its bright slumber, to her beating heart,
> And lifted her sweet voice, that rose awhile
> Above the sound of waters, high and clear,
> Wafting a wild proud strain, her song of death.
>
>   (104-5)

Her song is a heroic Byronic anthem: "Roll swiftly to the Spirit's land, thou mighty stream and free! / Father of ancient waters, roll! and bear our lives with thee! . . . // Father of waves! roll on!" (105-6). But it is also inflected by the specific plight of a woman "driven to despair by her husband's desertion of her for another wife" (so reports the headnote [103]): the father waters thus seem only partly formula, for the name evokes the patriarchy by which this woman has been betrayed. This is the deepest resonance:

> And thou, my babe! tho' born, like me, for
>   woman's weary lot,
> Smile!—to that wasting of the heart, my own! I
>   leave thee not.
>
>   . . . . .
>
> Thy mother bears thee far, young Fawn! from
>   sorrow and decay.
>
> She bears thee to the glorious bowers where
>   none are heard to weep.
>
>   (107-8)

In a poem for which one of the epigraphs is "Let not my child be a girl, for very sad is the life of a woman" (104), the Indian woman's death-song claims the paternal river for deliverance to a world where the pangs of betrayal are no more.

By making the husband a political traitor in **"The Wife of Asdrubal"** (*Tales* 189-96), Hemans allies infanticide with national retaliation as well as desperate affection. In exchange for his life, Asdrubal, governor of Carthage, has secretly ceded the city to the invading Roman general. His family and betrayed countrymen hold out in the citadel, torching it when defeat is inevitable. As the flames spread, they retreat to the roof, from which Asdrubal's wife berates him, stabs their sons before his eyes, and throws their bodies from the roof. Infanticide merely accelerates the inevitable, and the mother's charge is against the craven father who "in bondage safe, [shall] yet in them expire" (196). That Carthage itself is feminine politicizes the passion of its "regal" wife as an emblem of cultural destiny. Her "wild courage" signifies a national defiance and radical self-determination in the face of defeat:

> But mark! from you fair temple's loftiest height
> What towering form bursts wildly on the sight,
> All regal in magnificent attire,
> And sternly beauteous in terrific ire?
>
> (194)

Yet Hemans can represent the politicized mother only by displacing her into the supernatural and a discourse of extreme sensationalism:

> She might be deem'd a Pythia in the hour
> Of dread communion and delirious power;
> A being more than earthly, in whose eye
> There dwells a strange and fierce ascendency.
>
> . . . . .
>
> a wild courage sits triumphant there,
> The stormy grandeur of a proud despair;
> A daring spirit, in its woes elate,
> Mightier than death, untameable by fate.
> The dark profusion of her locks unbound,
> Waves like a warrior's floating plumage round;
> Flush'd is her cheek, inspired her haughty mien,
> She seems th' avenging goddess of the scene.
>
> (194)

The comparison of her unbound locks to a warrior's plumage is a transvestic signal of a crisis in gender, one with domestic as well as political consequences:

> Are those *her* infants, that with suppliant-cry
> Cling round her, shrinking as the flame draws
>   nigh,
> Clasp with their feeble hands her gorgeous vest,
> And fain would rush for shelter to her breast?
> Is that a mother's glance, where stern disdain,
> And passion awfully vindictive, reign?
>
> (194-95)

In the spectacle of a mother whose "towering form" has become less (or more) than maternal, domestic affection turns fatal, political, and sensational all at once. "Think'st thou I love them not?" the Wife taunts Asdrubal; "'Tis mine with these to suffer and to die. / Behold their fate!—the arms that cannot save / Have been their cradle, and shall be their grave" (196). The poem closes with a lurid scene of the promised act:

> Bright in her hand the lifted dagger gleams,
> Swift from her children's hearts the life-blood
>   streams;
> With frantic laugh she clasps them to the breast;
> Whose woes and passions soon shall be at rest;

> Lifts one appealing, frenzied glance on high,
> Then deep midst rolling flames is lost to mortal
>   eye.
>
> (196)

Here the extremity of politicized rage is localized in one vengeful "Wife," but in **"The Suliote Mother"** (in *Lays of Many Lands* [1825]; rpt. *Poetical Works* [Warne] 321), Hemans makes it a pervasive social fate. She based this poem on a famous anecdote about Suli women who, seeing the Turkish army advance on their mountain fasthold and with their men already lost to a failed defense, hurled themselves with their children into a chasm to avoid rape and enslavement. No domestic betrayal compels this fatal heroic. The opening image is of the iconic mother standing "upon the loftiest peak, / Amidst the clear blue sky, / A bitter smile was on her cheek, / And a dark flash in her eye"—a flash fulfilled with the suicide chant, "Freedom, young Suliote! for thee and me!" In a world of men at war, the only sure "Freedom" in the domestic world, Hemans suggests, is death.

IV. Women and Fame

In *Literary Women,* Jane Williams cited *History of an Enthusiast* as an exemplum of "a selfish woman of genius, full of worldly ambition" (385), and in her obituary, "Mrs. Fletcher, Late Miss Jewsbury," Mrs. Ellis summoned the passage I quote on p. 135 ("Ah, what is genius to a woman, but a splendid misfortune! What is fame to woman, but a dazzling degradation!") to moralize about Jewsbury herself (39; cf. *History* 112-13). But if, as we have seen, both Jewsbury and her Julia are less precisely contained, Hemans was more susceptible to the instruction. Her assertive women take no joy in their power, and their heroism emerges only inversely to domestic happiness, or to life itself. Cleopatra in **"The Last Banquet of Antony and Cleopatra"** (*Tales* 157-69), is addressed only in the aspect of a momentary glory, a heroism on the eve of defeat:

> In all thy sovereignty of charms array'd,
>   To meet the storm with still unconquer'd
>   pride.
> Imperial being! e'en though many a stain
>   Of error be upon thee, there is power
> In thy commanding nature, which shall reign
>   O'er the stern genius of misfortune's hour
> And the dark beauty of thy troubled eye
> E'en now is all illumed with wild sublimity.
>
> (164)

Storm, stain, error, trouble, misfortune, balance the scale of power, pride, and charms.

In all her epithets, moreover—"echantress-queen!" "Proud siren of the Nile!" "Daughter of Afric!" (164-65), the missing term is "woman," its absence a sign of hollow glory. It is significant that the story of another woman of national fame, **"Joan of Arc, in Rheims"**

(*Records* 109-15), receives its epigraph from the first stanza of Hemans's **"Woman and Fame,"** a verse that rejects Fame's "charmed cup" to conclude, "Away! to me—a woman—bring / Sweet waters from affection's spring" (110). Staging this poem at the dauphin's coronation and its honors for Joan's "victorious power," Hemans interposes a domestic plot: when Joan recognizes her father and brothers in attendance, "She saw the pomp no more" (114)—a dissolve that Hemans tropes as a revelation of essential womanhood amid the glory of male politics. The evocation of home and family "Winning her back to nature," Joan "unbound / The helm of many battles from her head" (115)—the reverse of the Hemans women whose unbound hair signals their emergence from customary restraints.[23] The verb "Winning" designates the real victory, and its dative, "to nature," essentializes the motive force, summed in the moral apostrophe of the poem's close: "too much of fame / Had shed its radiance on thy peasant-name," Hemans writes, reminding readers that fate gives the "crown of glory unto woman's brow" only in sacrifice of "gifts beyond all price"—namely, the paradise (lost) of home with all its "loves" (115). When Chorley assures his readers that Hemans "wears under all her robes of triumph, the pitying heart of a woman" (*Memorials* 1: 27), it is not just wishful male fantasy, but her deep allegory. "How I look back upon the comparative peace and repose of Bronwylfa and Rhyllon," she wrote of her childhood homes at the height of her fame; "How have these things passed away from me, and how much more was I formed for their quiet happiness, than for the weary part of *femme célèbre* which I am now enacting!" (Hughes, *Memoir* 189). This elegy for her paradise lost is sharpened by a sense of unreality in present celebrity: a weary, stale, and flat, however, profitable, glamor, its alienation from domestic norms signaled by the ironic intonation of the French term.

The conflict between this cultural stricture on what is feminine (not *femme*) and Heman's celebrity on both sides of the Atlantic is most acute in her self-mirroring stories of female artists. As **"The Sicilian Captive"** (*Records* 172-79) sings mournfully of her lost home, the chief force of her art is its fatal effect on her: "She had pour'd out her soul with her song's last tone; / The lyre was broken, the minstrel gone!" (179). One of the deepest impressions on Hemans's imagination was produced by Gibson's "statue of Sappho, representing her at the moment she receives the tidings of Phaon's desertion. . . . There is a sort of *willowy* drooping in the figure which seems to express a weight of unutterable sadness, and one sinking arm holds the lyre so carelessly, that you almost fancy it will drop while you gaze. Altogether, it seems to speak piercingly and sorrowfully of the nothingness of fame, at least to woman" (Chorley, *Memorials* 2: 172-73).[24] This is a common story for Hemans: the lovelorn female poet loses her voice, then her instrument, and then, implicitly, her life. The poet silenced by sorrow is what "seems to speak" so

forcefully to Hemans, the sign that woman and fame can never reach a happy coincidence. When she herself writes a voice for Sappho, it is **"The Last Song of Sappho"** (*Poetical Works* [Warne 591]) at this moment of "desolate grace . . . penetrated with the feeling of utter abandonment" (headnote), just before her suicidal leap into the sea. In the song's last words, the fatal sea is the only recipient of her desire: "*Alone* I come—oh! give me peace, dark sea!" Her leap bears none of the political resistance of the Suli mother nor even the protest against "woman's weary lot" of the desperate Indian woman. Her voice is that of personal pain alone.

The calculus of heart and art is the transparent allegory of **"Properzia Rossi"** (*Records* 45-54), the monologue of a famous artist who, dying of unrequited love, embodies her desire in one last work of art. In this melancholy, fame is hollow, a "Worthless fame! / That in *his* bosom wins not for my name / Th'abiding place it asked" (52). Hemans's epigraph keynotes Rossi's desperate sense of the incommensurability of woman's desires and the artist's work:

> ——Tell me no more, no more
> Of my soul's lofty gifts! Are they not vain
> To quench its haunting thirst for happiness?
> Have I not love'd, and striven, and fail'd to bind
> One true heart unto me, whereon my own
> Might find a resting-place, a home for all
> Its burden of affections? I depart,
> Unknown, tho' Fame goes with me; I must leave
> The earth unknown. Yet it may be that death
> Shall give my name a power to win such tears
> As would have made life precious.
>
> (47)

The division of self between public "Fame" and a solitary "I," a common trope, is specified in Rossi's voice as a conflict of artist and woman. Her last gambit is to reconcile the two by making her art serve her desire, as a proxy to her beloved:

> For thee alone, for thee!
> May this last work, this farewell triumph be,
> Thou, lov'd so vainly! I would leave enshrined
> Something immortal of my heart and mind,
> That yet may speak to thee when I am gone,
> Shaking thine inmost bosom with a tone
> Of lost affection;—something that may prove
> What she hath been, whose melancholy love
> On thee was lavish'd.
>
> (48)

Artistic creation bears the frustrated impulses of heart and nature. Hemans keeps Rossi always aware of the substitution, always expressing her inspiration in the language of what she lacks:

> It comes,—the power
> Within me born, flows back; my fruitless dower

That could not win me love. Yet once again
I greet it proudly, with its rushing train
Of glorious images:—they throng—they press—
A sudden joy lights up my loneliness,—

(49)

The statement of normal "loneliness" blights the momentary rush of glory, and the rhyme of "power" and "fruitless dower" spells the dominant economy. Rossi's only and final hope is not for her art, but (in another recurring rhyme pair) to collapse her "fame" into a "name" that may move the Knight to sad thoughts and a final recognition: *"'Twas her's who lov'd me well!"* (54).

Records closes with the most overtly self-referential of these allegories of female fame, **"The Grave of a Poetess"** (160-63). It is striking that Hemans identifies its subject, Mary Tighe, only in a footnote as "the author of Psyche" and that her poem says little of the poetry, beyond eulogizing the "light of song" shrined in "woman's mind" (160-61). This effacement of Tighe is not so much judgmental as self-reflective: "her poetry has always touched me greatly from a similarity which I imagine I discover between her destiny and my own," Hemans remarked (Chorley, *Memorials* 2: 212). Her effort is to cherish Tighe's delivery from the transient beauties and inevitable pains of life on "moral ground," the repeated themes she reads in her poetry ("Thou has left sorrow in thy song"), and to imagine her redemption: "Now peace the woman's heart hath found, / And joy the poet's eye" (163).[25] In this divorce of "poet" from "woman," Hemans sides with what she takes to be the inevitable determinations of "woman's heart." Visiting Tighe's tomb three years later, she "env[ied] the repose of her who slept there" (*Memorials* 2: 211).

The epitome of this story is **"Woman and Fame"** (*Poetical Works* [Warne] 523), which Hemans heads with the final lines of her **"Corinne at the Capitol"** (ibid 503). But **"Corinne"** itself has an aesthetic effect that resists the moralism of its final lines. Its title is also that of Book II of de Staël's wildly popular novel, *Corinne, ou l'Italie,* where, for the first time, we see the artist Corinne performing in all genius and glory.[26] De Staël elaborates the whole triumph, even transcribing "Corinne's Improvisation at the Capitol" and concluding in a female apotheosis: "No longer a fearful woman, she was an inspired priestess, joyously devoting herself to the cult of genius" (32). As if conceding the prestige of this episode with female readers, Hemans conveys it through a seemingly enthusiastic woman's gaze:

Thou hast gained the summit now!
Music hails thee from below;—
Music, whose rich notes might stir
Ashes of the sepulchre;
Shaking with victorious notes
All the bright air as it floats.
Well may woman's heart beat high
Unto that proud harmony!

(523)

But her "well may" indicates a caution, and in her last stanza Hemans shifts this voice into a tone of severe correction implicitly keyed to the melancholy conclusion of de Staël's novel, with Corinne abandoned and fatally despondent:

Radiant daughter of the sun!
Now thy living wreath is won.
Crown'd of Rome!—Oh! art thou not
Happy in that glorious lot?—
Happy—happier far than thou,
With the laurel on thy brow,
She that makes the humblest hearth
Lovely but to one on earth!

(523)

In this summation, Corinne's crowd-pleasing at the Capitol is no match in happiness for serving "one" at home.[27] It was the sad conclusion of *Corinne,* far more than its energetic opening, that most profoundly impressed Hemans: "its close . . . has a power over me which is quite indescribable; some passages seem to give me back my own thoughts and feelings, my whole inner being" (Chorley, *Memorials* 1: 304). Fame, she insists in "Woman and Fame" itself, is no compensation for a life deprived of "affection" and the "record of one happy hour": "Thou has a voice, whose thrilling tone / Can bid each life-pulse beat . . . / . . . But mine, let mine—a woman's breast, / By words of home-born love be blessed" (523).

Yet this argument for "home-born love" does not mute the "thrilling tone" and "life-pulse beat" of the female artist to which **"Corinne"** gives over most of its stanzas. In her repeated rehearsals of this ideological dilemma, Hemans never entirely resolves this inconsistency. She continues to indulge the creative energies she means to discredit, even calling into question the controlling assumptions about the greater satisfactions of domestic bliss. This ambivalence keeps the margins, if not the center, of her writing unsettled. She had an uneasy interest in writing the "tale of an enchantress, who, to win and secure the love of a mortal, sacrifices one of her supernatural gifts of power after another" but "is repaid by satiety—neglect—desertion" rather than enduring domestic bliss. The "injurious influence" of contemplating this narrative, Chorley reports, "compelled [Hemans] to abandon" this project (*Memorials* 2: 4-5). But its latent debate about the sacrifice of talent for love returns in Hemans's subtly strained headnote for "Properzia Rossi," a text that first sets forth the pathos of Rossi's celebrity, then obliquely hints at the misguided focus of her affections:

Properzia Rossi, a celebrated female sculptor of Bologna, possessed also of talents for poetry and music, died in consequence of an unrequited attachment.—A painting by Ducis, represents her showing her last work, a bassorelievo of Ariadne, to a Roman Knight, the object of her affection, who regards it with indifference. (**Records** 45)

The first sentence gives the orthodox economy, but through Ducis, Hemans entertains a discrepant intuition: if Rossi's pathos is the failure of her poignant self-representation in Ariadne to move the Knight, Ducis's point may be the ultimate meagerness of the object of her affection that is exposed by the Knight's indifference to her talents. In one moment of Rossi's lament, Hemans concentrates on the joy of what *is* in Rossi's possession—the uncontaminated, independent gratifications of artistic creation and its emotional intensities:

> The bright work grows
> Beneath my hand, unfolding, as a rose,
> Leaf after leaf, to beauty; line by line,
> I fix my thought, heart, soul, to burn, to shine,
> Thro' the pale marble's veins. It grows—and now
> I give my own life's history to thy brow,
> Forsaken Ariadne! thou shalt wear
> My form, my lineaments; but oh! more fair,
> Touch'd into lovelier being by the glow
>   Which in me dwells, as by the summer-light
> All things are glorified.
>
>   (49)

This language of creative "power" is proto-critical in the way it appropriates one of the images in masculine poetics for female beauty, the rose, to convey the unfolding of a woman's art. A more specific investment for Hemans is reflected in the way that some of her terms for Rossi's sculpting—the work of the hand, the unfolding of leaf after leaf, the expression of self in form, in line after line—also apply to poetic work, a sign both of Rossi's "talents for poetry" (45) and her own sympathy with them.

The contradictions between these moments of gratification and the normative terms for women's self-esteem were experienced by Hemans and her contemporaries as a necessary restraint on an undeniable energy—but not without critical insight. When she learned of Jewsbury's death by cholera in India (where her husband was a chaplain of the East India Company), Hemans found a curious consolation in imagining her escape from a worse fate for one "so gifted" with unrealized talents:

> How much deeper power seemed to lie *coiled up,* as it were, in the recesses of her mind, than was ever manifested to the world in her writings . . . the full and finished harmony never drawn forth! Yet I would rather, a thousand times, that she should have perished thus, in the path of her chosen duties, than have seen her become the merely brilliant creature of London literary life, living upon those poor *succès de société,* which I think utterly ruinous to all that is lofty, and

holy, and delicate in the nature of a highly-endowed woman. (28 June 1834, her italics; qtd. in Chorley 2: 312-13; cf. 314-15)

Williams's *Literary Women* quotes these sentences as a caution (378-79), but Hemans's two italicized phrases tell a more complicated story. The patent excess of "a thousand times" not only does not suppress her admiration of the power that she senses coiled up in Jewsbury's mind; it exposes a compelling attraction. The alternative for the fatal "path of her chosen duties" is, in this coil of energy, no mere fame as a *succès de société,* but something Hemans could not, in the blinds of her cultural moment, yet imagine for such a "highly-endowed" woman. What Hemans's own writings stage and restage is a restless debate between domestic affections and the spear of Minerva. It is this unresolved dilemma of gender—of sentimentality versus ambition, of capitulation versus critical pressure—that constitutes the deeper power, and the most potent legacy, of Felicia Hemans's "feminine" poetics.

Notes

[1] The phrase is from Norma Clarke's *Ambitious Heights* (45). The latest (6th) edition of *The Norton Anthology of English Literature* (Abrams) represents Hemans with these two pieces and another favorite, "England's Dead," whose sentimental-imperial refrain is that wherever you go in this world, "*There* slumber England's dead!"

[2] Between 1808 and 1834, Hemans produced nineteen volumes (see Peter Trinder's list in *Mrs Hemans* 67-68), along with several periodical publications.

[3] In our century, Alan Hill is not alone in describing her as a "popular versifier" (*Letters of Dorothy Wordsworth,* 175, n. 1). Even Jennifer Breen's recent anthology, *Women Romantic Poets, 1785-1832,* which means to remedy the "long-neglected achievements" of this group (back jacket), is scanting of Hemans. Its introduction mentions her only in passing (xii), and the Notes dismiss her work as "generally . . . chauvinistic, sentimental, and derivative," reporting Wordsworth's lack of favor, despite her intense admiration of his work (160). She is represented meagerly by two of her least interesting poems—a short dirge of conventional pieties on the death of a child; and a set of reverential verses "To Wordsworth" (147-48).

[4] See Mellor's excellent discussion, *Romanticism and Gender* 124-43. Thanks to Tricia Lootens for calling my attention to Nemoianu's remark.

[5] This is the Cadell-Blackwood edition organized by Hemans's sister, Harriett Hughes.

[6] Chorley is quoting from Jewsbury's portrait of Egeria in *The History of a Nonchalant* (*The Three Histories* 193), popularly thought to have been drawn after Hemans. Rossetti's "Prefatory Notice" quotes lavishly

from it for a summary description of Hemans's character (22-23).

[7] For the durable view of Hemans's complicity in the cultural project of idealizing women's role in hearth and home, see Clarke, *Ambitious Heights* 55 et passim. Cora Kaplan's headnote in *Salt and Bitter and Good* (93-95) makes a similar point, but reads this complicity as strained.

[8] For informative discussions of the cultural stigma on publishing women writers, as well as of the wrenching conflicts felt by women such as Hemans and Jewsbury who internalized these codes, see Clarke's first two chapters in *Ambitious Heights,* "Contrary to Custom" and "The Pride of Literature," and Mary Poovey, *The Proper Lady and the Woman Writer.*

[9] As Clarke observes, praise of Hemans serves as "a stick to beat other women writers" (*Ambitious Heights* 33). A blunt example is Gilfillan's declaration that "not a little of [the] charm" of "Mrs. Hemans's poems . . . springs from their unstudied and extempore character . . . in fine keeping with the sex of the writer. You are saved the ludicrous image of double-dyed Blue, in papers and morning wrapper, sweating at some stupendous treatise or tragedy from morn to noon, and from noon to dewy eve" ("Female Authors" 360). The labors of the woman writer earn a mock-heroic allusion to the fall of the Satanically confederate architect, Mulciber: "he fell / From Heav'n, . . . from Morn / To Noon he fell, from Noon to dewy Eve" (*Paradise Lost* 1: 742-43).

[10] The term itself was not only diminutive and feminizing, but also discriminating. Rossetti's "Notice," having already suggested "the deficiency which she, merely as a woman, was almost certain to evince" (16), uses its final sentences to accord "Mrs. Hemans . . . a very honorable rank among poetesses" while reserving "he" for the gender of "the poet" (24). But even this domestication as a "poetess," Hemans herself concedes with ironic amusement, strains social propriety: she imagines that in the view of "ladies," she has to contend with "the ideas . . . they entertain of that altogether foreign monster, a *Poetess*" (Chorley, *Memorials* 2: 280, her emphasis).

[11] Her sister's *Memoir* insists that the failure of her marriage was painful (Hughes 56), while Chorley suggests that it was "literary pursuits" that "rendered it advisable for [Hemans] not to leave England" (*Memorials* 1: 42). For a discussion of the embarrassment this separation posed to early biographers, see Marlon Ross, *Contours of Masculine Desire* 252. Rossetti spends a full page of his "Notice" (14) speculating about the state of the marriage, the real "motive" of Captain Hemans's departure, and whether Hemans's fame had anything to do with the permanence of their separation.

[12] The depth and durability of this cultural judgment is reflected in Mrs. Sandford's *Woman, in Her Social and Domestic Character* (1832): "There is, indeed, something unfeminine in independence," she cautions; "It is contrary to nature and therefore it offends" (14). Refuting Wollstonecraft's antonymy of weakness and attractiveness, she disdains "a woman . . . acting the amazon. A really sensible woman feels her dependence. . . . her weaknes[s] is an attraction, not a blemish" (14). In "this respect," she adds, "Women . . . are something like children; the more they show their need of support, the more engaging they are" (15). Gilfillan makes the same point by complimenting Hemans, and women in general, "in Wordsworth's language": they lie in "Abraham's bosom all the year, / And God is with them, when they know it not" ("Female Authors" 362). The last line he misremembers, or perhaps deliberately recasts, from the sonnet, "It is a Beauteous Evening," in which, addressing the "Dear Child! dear girl!" walking with him on the beach, Wordsworth wrote "God being with thee when *we* knew it not" (my italics). Gilfillan converts Wordsworth's contemplation of the gap between unknowing adult and blessed child into a contrast of gender, opposing adult men to ignorant, childlike women. But if, as Norma Clarke remarks, Hemans's domestic shelter evoked "the cultural construction of the feminine as essentially childlike" (48), Wordsworth too could be implicated, for his work at home as a writer was greatly enabled by the labor of the (female) adults of his household.

[13] Sigourney's "Essay on the Genius of Mrs. Hemans" is an exception in calling attention to her atypical circumstances, noting "her freedom, for many years, from those cares which usually absorb a wife and mother, . . . her prolonged residence under the maternal wing," her "shelter[ing] from the burden of those cares which sometimes press out the life of song"; "the weight of domestic duty fell not heavily upon her, until time had settled the equilibrium of her powers, and poetic composition had become an inwrought habit of her existence" (Hughes, *Memoir* xi-xii).

[14] See also Dorothy Wordsworth's sympathy with Jewsbury's lot (*Letters, Later Years* 1: 434-35); though she had similar responsibilities, she at least had the advantage of sharing them with another adult woman (William's wife). Arbiters of conduct such as Mrs. Ellis converted Jewsbury's frustration into an emblem of proper priorities: though "there burned within her soul the unquenchable fire of a genius too powerful to be extinguished by the many cares of her arduous life, so fearful was she of being absorbed by any selfish pursuit, that she made it a point of conscience never to take up a book, until all her little charge had retired to rest for the night" ("Mrs. Fletcher, Late Miss Jewsbury" 34). For a pioneering study of Jewsbury's brief career, and of the importance of her interactions with Hemans and the Wordsworths, see Clarke's *Ambitious Heights.*

[15] Clarke's otherwise incisive reading of this tale as an allegory of Jewsbury's conflicts over her own literary fame (*Ambitious Heights* 83-86) mistakes these sen-

tences as Cecil's (84); Jewsbury presents them as a paraphrase of his reasoning. Chorley is more alert to the ironic distance and edginess of these sentences.

[16] In the penultimate stanza of the verses in question ("Extempore Effusion upon the Death of James Hogg"), Wordsworth cites Hemans not for her art, but for her "Holy Spirit, / Sweet as the spring, as ocean deep" (37-38; *Poetical Works* [ed. de Selincourt and Darbishire] 4: 276-78). Of the five writers mourned (also Hogg, Coleridge, Lamb, Crabbe), that only she is unnamed reports the breach of modesty posed by female fame. Wordsworth's stanza was sufficiently noteworthy, however, to become part of the lore on Hemans; Gilfillan closes his essay with it ("Female Authors" 363).

[17] I thank Carol Shiner Wilson for pointing this out to me.

[18] Hence Dorothy Wordsworth's journal: "still at work at the Pedlar, altering and refitting"; "I stitched up the Pedlar" (13-14 February and 7 March 1802; *Grasmere Journal* 90 and 98).

[19] This poem was first published in the 1826 *Forget Me Not* (Leighton, *Victorian Women Poets* 10-11), one of the popular gift-book annuals marketed chiefly to female readers. My text follows *Poetical Works* (Gall and Inglis) 478-79.

[20] Hemans's conversion of her Greek bride into "an Indian bride" not only evokes Myrrha but also the marital symbolism of the actual suttee. A poem she would have known, Jewsbury's "Song of the Hindoo Women, while accompanying a widow to the funeral pile of her husband," has an epigraph from "Forbes' Oriental Memoirs" reporting how this "living victim" comes to the funeral pile "dressed in her bridal jewels, surrounded by relations, priests, and musicians" (*Phantasmagoria* 2: 131).

[21] Lootens's "Hemans and Home" offers a fine discussion of the role of Hemans's poetry in formulating for Victorians, through an "erratic course among and through mutual contradictions," the links of domesticity to patriotism (241). Mellor's *Romanticism and Gender* provides a sharp reading of how Hemans exposes the futility and fatality of domestic affection when it is tested by the public realm (135-42).

[22] Kathleen Hickock remarks that of nineteenth-century English writers, only Hemans gave maternal infanticide "much notice" (*Representations of Women* 26).

[23] In emphasizing the way Joan's armor fails to hide the woman within but merely masks an essentially feminine self, Hemans evokes the cultural anxiety aroused by Joan's cross-dressing: she was tried as much for transvestism as for heresy (Marjorie Garber, *Vested Interests* 215-17).

[24] This heterosexual, and ultimately suicidal Sappho is the figure of Grillparzer's *Sappho,* published in 1819 in German; an Italian translation, which Byron thought "superb and sublime" (*Letters and Journals* 8: 25), appeared the same year. It is likely that Hemans, who read both German and Italian, knew Grillparzer's tale, as well as Pope's translation of Ovid's 15th epistle, "Sappho to Phaon" (1707).

[25] In a letter that she wrote about Tighe (which Clarke quotes in full), Hemans reveals the cultural allegorizing of Tighe's death as caution for ambitious women: "I heard much of her unhappiness was caused by her own excessive love of admiration and desire to shine in society, which quite withdrew her from Hearth and Home and all their holy enjoyments, and that her mother, standing by her deathbed passionately exclaimed [in the sort of voice that Jewsbury gives Cecil Percy]—'My Mary, my Mary, the pride of literature has destroyed you'" (Clarke, *Ambitious Heights* 50-51). Tighe is judged not only by anonymous diagnoses of an unhealthy desire to shine outside the hearth and home, but also, emphatically, by the guardians of the latter: her mother and Hemans, the culturally celebrated poet of hearth and home.

[26] *Corinne* was published in France in 1807 and quickly translated into English; it was immensely popular, especially with women, seeing forty editions in the nineteenth century. As "*the* book of the woman of genius," Ellen Moers remarks, its myth operated "as both inspiration and warning" (*Literary Women* 262).

[27] Leighton provides a superb reading of this poem's ambivalence in relation to the energetic celebration of de Staël's chapter (30-34).

Works Cited

Primary Works

Abrams, M. H. et al., eds. *The Norton Anthology of English Literature.* 5th ed. New York: Norton, 1986.

Breen, Jennifer, ed. *Women Romantic Poets, 1785-1832.* London: Dent Everyman, 1992.

Byron, George Gordon, Lord. *Byron's Letters and Journals.* Ed. Leslie A. Marchand. 12 vols. Cambridge, MA: Harvard University Press, 1973-82.

Chorley, Henry F. *Memorials of Mrs. Hemans. With Illustrations of Her Literary Character from Her Private Correspondence.* 2 vols. London: Saunders and Otley, 1836.

De Staël, Germaine. *Corinne, or Italy.* 1807. Tr. and ed. Avriel H. Goldberger. New Brunswick, NJ: Rutgers University Press, 1987.

Edinburgh Monthly Review 3 (1820): 373-83. Review of Hemans's *The Skeptic.*

Gilfillan, George. "Female Authors. No. 1—Mrs. Hemans." *Tait's Edinburgh Magazine* NS 14 (1847): 359-63.

Hemans, Felicia [Felicia Dorothea Browne]. *The Domestic Affections, and Other Poems*. London: T. Cadwell and W. Davies, 1812.

———. *The Poetical Works of Mrs. Felicia Hemans*. London: Gall and Inglis, 1876.

———. *The Poetical Works of Mrs. Felicia Hemans*. London: Frederick Warne, n.d.

———. *Records of Woman: With Other Poems*. Edinburgh: Blackwood, 1828; London: T. Cadell, 1828.

———. *Songs of the Affections, with Other Poems*. Edinburgh: Blackwood, 1830; London: T. Cadwell, 1830.

———. *Tales, and Historic Scenes, in Verse*. London: John Murray, 1819.

———. *Works*. Ed. Mrs. Sigourney. 3 vols. New York: C. S. Francis, 1849-52.

———. *The Works of Mrs Hemans; With a Memoir of Her Life, by Her Sister*. 7 vols. Edinburgh: Blackwood & Sons, 1839; London: T. Cadell, 1839; Philadelphia: Lea and Blanchard, 1839.

[Hughes, Harriett Mary (Browne)]. *Memoir of the Life and Writings of Felicia Hemans: By Her Sister; with an Essay on her Genius: By Mrs. Sigourney*. Philadelphia: Lea and Blanchard, 1839; New York: C. S. Francis, 1845.

[Jeffrey, Francis]. Review of *Records of Woman* (2nd ed.) and *The Forest Sanctuary* (2nd ed.). *Edinburgh Review* 50 (Oct. 1829): 32-47. In *Contributions to the Edinburgh Review by Francis Jeffrey*. Boston: Phillips, Sampson, 1854. 473-78.

[Jewsbury, Maria Jane.] "Original Papers. Literary Sketches No. 1. Felicia Hemans." *The Athenaeum* 171 (5 Feb. 1831): 104-5.

———. *The Three Histories: The History of an Enthusiast. The History of a Nonchalant. The History of a Realist*. 1830; Boston: Perkins & Marvin, 1831.

———. *Phantasmagoria; or Sketches of Life and Literature*. 2 vols. London: Hurst, Robinson, 1825.

Quarterly Review 24 (Oct. 1820): 130-39. Art. V. Review of several volumes by Hemans.

Rossetti, W[illiam] M[ichael]. "Prefatory Notice." *The Poetical Works of Mrs. Hemans*. Philadelphia: J. B. Lippincott, 1881. 11-24.

Sandford, Mrs. John. *Woman, in Her Social and Domestic Character*. 2nd. ed. London: Longman, Rees, Orme, Brown, Green & Longman, 1832.

Sigourney, Mrs. [Lydia H.]. "Essay on the Genius of Mrs. Hemans." Harriett Hughes vii-xxiii.

Williams, Jane. *The Literary Women of England*. London: Saunders, Otley, 1861.

Wordsworth, Dorothy. Grasmere Journal. In *Journals of Dorothy Wordsworth*. 2nd ed. Ed. Mary Moorman. Oxford: Oxford University Press, 1971.

———. *Letters of Dorothy Wordsworth, A Selection*. Ed. Alan G. Hill. Oxford: Clarendon Press, 1985.

[Wordsworth, William]. *The Poetical Works of William Wordsworth*. Ed. Ernest de Selincourt. 2nd ed. rev. Helen Darbishire. 5 vols. Oxford: Clarendon, 1952-59. Cited as *WPW*.

[Wordsworth, William and Dorothy Wordsworth]. *Letters: The Later Years, 1821-1853*. Ed. Rev. Alan G. Hill. Oxford: Clarendon Press, 1978-88.

Secondary Works

Clarke, Norma. *Ambitious Heights: Writing, Friendship, Love—The Jewsbury Sisters, Felicia Hemans, and Jane Welsh Carlyle*. London: Routledge, 1990.

Garber, Marjorie. *Vested Interests: Cross-Dressing and Cultural Anxiety*. New York: Routledge, 1992.

Hickock, Kathleen. *Representations of Women: Nineteenth-Century British Women's Poetry*. Westport, CT: Greenwood Press, 1984.

Kaplan, Cora. *Salt and Bitter and Good: Three Centuries of English and American Women Poets*. New York: Paddington, 1973.

Leighton, Angela. *Victorian Women Poets: Writing Against the Heart*. New York and London: Wheatsheaf/Harvester, 1992.

Lootens, Tricia. "Hemans and Home: Victorianism, Feminine 'Internal Enemies,' and the Domestication of National Identity." *PMLA* 109 (1994): 238-53.

Mellor, Anne K. *English Romantic Irony*. Cambridge, MA: Harvard University Press, 1980.

———. *Romanticism and Gender*. New York: Routledge, 1992.

Moers, Ellen. *Literary Women*. 1963. New York: Anchor/Doubleday, 1977.

Nemoianu, Virgil. "Literary Canons and Social Value Options." In *The Hospitable Canon: Essays on Literary Play, Scholarly Choice, and Popular Pressures.* Ed. Virgil Nemoianu and Robert Royal. Philadelphia and Amsterdam: John Benjamins, 1991. 215-47.

Poovey, Mary. *The Proper Lady and the Woman Writer: Ideology as Style in the Works of Mary Wollstonecraft, Mary Shelley, and Jane Austen.* Chicago: University of Chicago Press, 1984.

Ross, Marlon. *The Contours of Masculine Desire: Romanticism and the Rise of Women's Poetry.* New York: Oxford University Press, 1989.

Symons, Arthur. *The Romantic Movement in English Poetry.* New York: Dutton, 1909.

Trinder, Peter W. *Mrs. Hemans.* Aberystwyth: University of Wales Press, 1984.

Anthony John Harding (essay date 1995)

SOURCE: "Felicia Hemans and the Effacement of Women," in *Romantic Women Writers: Voices and Countervoices,* edited by Paula R. Feldman and Theresa M. Kelley, University Press of New England, 1995, pp. 138-49.

[*In the following essay, Harding traces a strain of violence and melancholy through several of Hemans's works; he concludes that this element suggests her "recognition that women's reality is an imposed reality."*]

> *The sentiments are so affectionate and innocent— the characters of the subordinate agents . . . are clothed in the light of such a mild and gentle mind— the pictures of domestic manners are of the most simple and attaching character: the pathos is irresistible and deep.—Percy Bysshe Shelley*

Affection, innocence, domesticity, pathos—the passage quoted in the epigraph above could almost be from a contemporary assessment of Felicia Hemans's **Records of Woman,** but it was actually written about *Frankenstein.* Percy Bysshe Shelley seems to be reassuring himself and us that Mary Shelley's novel is not, after all, wholly outside the bounds of women's discourse, despite its lurid subject matter and unwomanly preoccupation with violence and death.[1] It is one of those moments when the force of social expectation as it affects the reception of women's writing, even writing of a distinctly new and disturbing kind, becomes tellingly apparent.

Yet the shocking juxtaposition of domestic affection and death that made *Frankenstein* seem so disturbingly "unwomanly"

is also present in Felicia Hemans's work.[2] Death, in her poems, is not so much the enemy of domestic affection as the necessary dark backdrop against which the affections show their true brightness. At times, death virtually becomes a kind of guarantee of the significance of a life, particularly of a woman's life. The very pervasiveness of this ethos in Hemans's work, an ethos in which a woman's life is more worthy of memorializing the more it is played out against the backdrop of another's death and most especially if it finds its *own* highest realization in death, exposes to the modern reader the power of social expectation, of the social construction of gender.

In Hemans's poetry, domestic affection, or what Kurt Heinzelman has referred to as "the cult of domesticity," is so often not a counterbalance to violence and death nor a refuge from them, as it seemed to be for Percy Bysshe Shelley in his reading of *Frankenstein,* but a value that inexorably demands violence and death as its perfect tribute. Heinzelman's definition of the "cult of domesticity" is worth quoting at length:

> [T]he belief that the household is the site of value not merely or even primarily because of what it produces in the economic sense but because it provides the place where the individual personality may grow and the occasion to discover in that growth a way of integrating self and society, family and polis. . . . The cult of domesticity was a replacement for or sublimation of the family as a viable, self-sustaining economic entity; it thus depended upon a division of female and male labor in which commodity production came to be seen as the masculine activity while female economic activity was regarded as reproductive, whether literally in the case of childbearing or metaphorically in the form of service-based employment such as nanny, maid, governess, or indeed houseworker in general.[3]

In glorifying the ethic of female self-sacrifice and linking it in many poems (particularly later in her career) with the heroic deaths of women as sacrifices to the domestic ideal, Hemans delivers a new version of the Romantic hunger for transcendence, a version that purports to compensate women for their unpaid labor and the relative obscurity of their lives as nurturers and caregivers. Read "against the grain," however, Hemans's texts reveal the terrible price of the "cult of domesticity."

For rarely in Hemans does a woman's life earn significance on its own account. Its significance more often derives from its relationship to the transcendent, to the afterlife—that is, to what is *absent from it.* Death, not life, is the veil that must not be lifted. That Hemans does not set out to challenge received values (as Mary Shelley does, in some respects at least) makes her work all the more interesting, for she gives full expression to the seductiveness for women of this ethic of self-sacrifice. Yet whatever Hemans's intentions may have been, her poems expose the destructive potential of the prevailing metaphysic just as relentlessly as *Frankenstein* does.

Records of Woman, the title of Hemans's 1828 collection, seems promising enough to the reader hunting for forgotten literature by Romantic women writers. This should be, it seems, a treasure trove of women's experience, a sort of verse rival for Matilda Betham's *Biographical Dictionary of the Celebrated Women of Every Age and Country* (1804). So often, however, the tone in which these poems document women's life experiences disappoints us. It cannot be their sentimentality, for sentiment is exactly the point in so many of the poems; and in any case it is not right to permit Fielding, Sterne, and Dickens their sentimentality but object to it in Hemans. Rather, it is the total absorption of Hemans's women by values that appear to us patently hostile to women's individual identity and destructive of any intrinsic significance their lives may have.

In **"Madeline: A Domestic Tale,"** a young Frenchwoman leaves her mother to sail for America with her new husband. The parting of mother and daughter is described in language that is almost biblical in intensity. In an odd reversal of the prodigal son story in Luke 15 the daughter, at parting, "fell upon her mother's neck, and wept" (*Records of Woman,* 146). In America, the husband dies, and the daughter contracts a fever that threatens her life until, in a skillfully managed surreal moment fusing fevered dream with actuality, she gradually realizes that her mother is there to save her and take her home. The fact that the mother's appearance at her daughter's sickbed is described in such a way as to appear miraculous and that the moment when her daughter recognizes her is described as one of "true and perfect love" (149) indicates that motherhood is here given all of the sanctity of the strictest religion. Wordsworth never represented the power of mother-daughter bonding so convincingly, but the mother in Hemans's poem is idealized rather than individualized; she is never given a name, even though the story is as much hers as it is Madeline's. Indeed, the poem seems to suggest—contrary to its own ostensible moral—that women's personal lives and identities stand to be doubly obliterated, for if tragedy and death do not obliterate them, time eventually will: "we trace / The map of our own paths, and long ere years / With their dull steps the brilliant lines efface, / On sweeps the storm, and blots them out with tears" (147). The whole point of this "domestic tale" is that individuality is sacrificed to the mother-daughter relationship, and the poem permits no doubting of the primacy of that relationship, any more than, say, a George Herbert poem permits the reader to doubt the existence of God. To lament the effacement of individuals' lives by time and tragedy and then to contribute to that very effacement by having a character become all *mother* and nothing else seems to us not only inconsistent but a condoning and compounding of the socially sanctioned oppression of women. It seems to confirm the opinion of a recent writer that our culture "idealizes motherhood but holds real mothers in contempt" (Griffin 41).[4]

Dorothy Mermin has identified this problem accurately in a recent essay: "[W]hen women write, what is conventional or figurative in men's writing can seem awkwardly real . . . women's renunciations of worldly ambition go smoothly with the grain of social expectation, not interestingly against it: rather than making a real choice, they seem to be accepting their inevitable lot."[5] There is much truth in this, yet for me Mermin too easily abandons the cause and risks consigning writers like Hemans, especially, to the limbo of the once popular but now unreadable. Why should what is "awkwardly real" be automatically less interesting than what is "conventional or figurative," even though it may embarrass us or demand of us a different kind of reading? And may there not actually be considerable interest for a modern reader in what appears to "go smoothly with the grain of social expectation"?

The poem **"A Spirit's Return,"** in *Songs of the Affections* (1830), provides an instructive instance of what Mermin calls the "awkwardly real" and the way it can be read *against* the grain of social expectation. The speaker is a woman whose life on earth holds no value or interest for her, whose every hope is set on a transcendent world until she falls in love, and then her absorption in the man's identity is total. The poem makes it abundantly clear that she accepts the man's perceptions as definitive of reality: "There was no music but his voice to hear, / No joy but such as with *his* step drew near; / Light was but where he look'd—life where he moved . . ." (7). The man dies, and by the sheer power of love she calls up his spirit to reassure her that the relationship can continue beyond the grave. This ghost is no Lorenzo with sepulchral voice. The ghostly lover's speech is harmonious and angelic, but the narrator is filled with "the sick feeling that in *his* far sphere / *My* love could be as nothing!" (13). Her love, or rather her total absorption in his construction of reality, has left her with no existence of her own on this side of the grave. Her love and therefore her identity can be validated only in death. All of the significance that might belong to her as a person is, as it were, postponed or transferred to the afterlife. Romantic love and more especially the complete dependence of romantic love on the metaphysic of transcendence denies the woman in **"A Spirit's Return"** any positive status or significance in *this* world. The difference between this poem and Shelley's "Adonais," which ends on a similar note of passionate yearning for another world, is that in Shelley's poem the speaker's surrendering of earthly hope strikes us as tragic, the renunciation of the world as an act of intrinsic public and individual significance, but the woman's does not seem tragic because from the very beginning she had no identity that was not purely defined in absence.

Such absorption and obliteration of woman's existence in a destiny that is presumed to be of greater significance is equally apparent in other poems from the 1830 collection about heterosexual love (**"The Vaudois' Wife," "Thekla at Her Lover's Grave," "The Image in the Heart"**) and in poems on motherhood (**"The Charmed Picture"** and

"The Tomb of Madame Langhans"). In these poems it is death alone that validates the woman's significance, either because her lover has died and so ensured that his love for her, and hers for him, cannot change or because the woman has died and in the act of dying is identified with one or another noble cause. The female archetype that dominates *Songs of the Affections* is clearly the Mater Dolorosa. At the tomb of Madame Langhans, who has died in childbirth, the speaker feels "[a] solemn joy" and "a sense / Of triumph, blent with nature's gush of weeping, / As, kindling up the silent stone, I see / The glorious vision, caught by faith, of thee" (*Songs of the Affections,* 90). One of the few poems in the volume that is even moderately positive about *life* is **"The Fountain of Oblivion,"** in which the speaker, longing to drink a forgetful draught from the fountain, changes her mind at the last moment but only because she decides that memories of the past are all she has on which to form an idea of the afterlife and those who are now enjoying it: "'Tis from the past we shadow forth the land / Where smiles, long lost, again shall light our way . . ." (137). It is for the sake of the dead that she must remember her own past life.

Susan Wolfson has suggested that an element of therapeutic fantasy can be seen in some of Hemans's later poems, which "repeatedly fantasize escape . . . by destroying adult domesticity before it can even begin." Wolfson cites as one example **"The Bride of the Greek Isle,"** in which Eudora, a proud young Greek, is carried off by pirates on her wedding day. She avenges her abduction and the murder of her fiancé by setting fire to the pirates' ship, turning it into her own funeral pyre. As Wolfson points out, it is not simply that Eudora, though a woman, consummates a heroic act of vengeance; it is that "the deeper plot projects a release from marriage and from enslavement alike" (unpublished ms., 7-8). Whether or not the story is fantasized escape from domesticity on Hemans's part, however, **"The Bride of the Greek Isle"** clearly also belongs in the category of poems that seem to validate violent death as the epitome of womanly self-sacrifice.

This unforgiving ethic, granting significance to woman's life only when it is sacrificed to the equally depersonalized idealizations of heterosexual love and of motherhood, has its clearest expression in an odd and little-noticed poem among the "Miscellaneous Pieces" in *Records of Woman.* **"The Image in Lava,"** as Hemans explains in a note appended to the poem, is about "the impression of a woman's form, with an infant clasped to the bosom, found at the uncovering of Herculaneum" (307). Neither the woman nor her baby has a name. Excavation of a group of small houses, the homes of ordinary citizens, in the ancient Campanian city of Herculaneum, destroyed by the eruption of Vesuvius in A.D. 79, had begun in 1823. (Work was interrupted by the attempted revolution but resumed after the restoration of the king of Naples in 1824.) To judge by the frequency of reports in the *Times* of London, there was considerable interest in England in both the Pompeii and Herculaneum sites. At Herculaneum, before 1823, only a royal villa had been excavated, in the early eighteenth century under the patronage of King Charles III of Naples.[6]

Hemans could therefore represent the recently discovered "woman's form" as that of an anonymous *bourgeoise,* her sole known relationship being that of mother to the infant she clasps: "Haply of that fond bosom, / On ashes here impressed, / Thou wert the only treasure, child! / Whereon a hope might rest" (308). The eruption of Vesuvius has reduced this woman's existence to an appealing simplicity, effacing everything about her but her role as mother. Unlike, say, Joan of Arc or Properzia Rossi the sculptor, whose lives are celebrated elsewhere in the collection, this woman warrants memorializing not because of any special characteristics that belong to her as an individual but just because she was a nursing mother. Though an ordinary and anonymous citizen, she has achieved significance by becoming (unwillingly) a permanent symbol of a privileged social value. At the same time, the poem claims special significance for this "trace" of woman's existence, because, thanks to the instantaneous immortality bestowed by the volcanic eruption, it has outlasted the empire under which she lived. Empires decay, but this symbol of motherhood endures:

> Temple and tower have moulder'd,
>   Empires from earth have pass'd,—
> And woman's heart hath left a trace
>   Those glories to outlast!
>
>   (307)

The poem, then, does propose a scheme of value that explicitly counters the military conquest and statecraft we normally associate with the Roman Empire. "Domestic affection" is triumphantly validated, resurrected; the nineteenth-century allocation of a separate realm and discourse to women based on the division of life into public and domestic duties is found to be reflected back to Hemans's time from a Roman household of the first century A.D.[7]

Yet the modern reader is unlikely to feel that this positive celebration of a "trace" left by women's experience can compensate for the obliteration of the woman's own self. The poem neatly illustrates the problems faced by those wishing to retrieve the neglected voices of women of the Romantic period, particularly the voices of those who, like Hemans, recorded woman's experience without challenging the social paradigms by which that experience was defined. The woman's existence is recorded but at the cost of the complete obliteration of her actual identity and the reduction of her social being to one relationship and one function: motherhood.

It is possible to envisage an alternative and more positive feminist interpretation of Hemans's work, one emphasizing her resistance to patriarchal notions of identity and her affirmation of women's own sense of themselves. Rather than stressing the obliteration of women's identity by a patriarchal ideology, this approach would see in Hemans a subversion of male modes of self-definition, of "temple and tower," by a kind of volcanic eruption in which the dissolution of personal identity is the triumph of a deeper female knowledge. **"The Image in Lava"** would then qualify as a kind of "writing in white ink" (in Hélène Cixous's famous phrase), writing that does not confront male self-definition directly but inscribes a wholly other kind of signifying process, where boundaries of self and symbols dissolve and only joyous play remains.[8] Such an approach could also appeal to the feminist psychoanalysts who argue that women's lack of a rigid sense of self—their supposedly "more flexible or permeable ego boundaries"[9]—constitutes a strength; that it is only *misrepresented* as a weakness in patriarchal culture, that woman's ability to put her nurturing and caregiving role ahead of the requirements of a rigid self-definition is an entirely positive trait, and that it is in fact the *male* who is weak, since he is perpetually vulnerable to fear of whatever seems to threaten his sense of himself, whether it be emotion, death, or merely a more successful male rival.

The dangers of this approach are perhaps sufficiently obvious. Whatever the secret attraction of the loss of self, dissolution, and absorption into the irresistible powers of earth, the lava-flow of nonbeing—especially compared to the alternative, the absurdly vulnerable temples and towers of patriarchal religion and militarism—Hemans's poem historically epitomizes the way in which the temptations of self-sacrifice were exploited to persuade women that motherhood and self-denial guaranteed them significant lives—but only in the transcendent hereafter. Second, the characterization of women as somehow naturally having weak ego boundaries essentializes woman's nature, as a value system independent of and unaffected by the social order and its cult of domesticity. It is perhaps more instructive—more revealing of the nature of Hemans's resistance to effacement—to look for pressure points, those points where we can see momentarily emerging a concept of gender and gender roles different from the conventional one. If we wish to trace a literature of resistance hiding somewhere in the seemingly collaborationist work of the poet who wrote **"The Stately Homes of England,"**[10] we might look at those poems—and there are some—in which an overt transgression of gender boundaries takes place.

One such transgression of gender boundaries occurs in *The Forest Sanctuary.* The narrator, a Spaniard who has fled to North America to escape religious persecution, recalls watching his dearest boyhood friend, Alvar, being marched to the stake to be burned as a heretic. With Alvar are his two beautiful sisters, Theresa and Inez, whom the Inquisition has found equally guilty; they are to be burned in the same auto-da-fé. As might be

expected, Hemans gives full play to the pathos of the sisters' plight, first describing them as "flowers" whose beauty has suffered from their long imprisonment. However, the description of Theresa introduces a new note, that of tragic heroism. What is remarkable about this passage is that several images and concepts that the male Romantics consistently claimed as masculine—"energy," "fire," "prophecy," a "kindled eye"—are here invoked to characterize the dignified courage shown by the woman as she defies the power of the church:

> It seem'd as if her breast
> Had hoarded energies, till then suppress'd
> Almost with pain, and bursting from control,
> And finding first that hour their pathway free:
> —Could a rose brave the storm, such might her emblem be!
>
> For the soft gloom whose shadow still had hung
> On her fair brow, beneath its garlands worn,
> Was fled; and fire, like prophecy's had sprung
> Clear to her kindled eye.
>
> (20-21)

What is especially striking about this description, too, is that Hemans explicitly connects Theresa's brave and impassioned stance with the more conventionally "feminine" resources of affection and relationship, which are emphatically contrasted with the Byronic emotions a man might have felt in such a situation—scorn, pride, and "sense of wrong":

> It might be scorn—
> Pride—sense of wrong . . .
>   yet not *thus* upborne
> She mov'd. . . .
> And yet, alas! to see the strength which clings
> Round woman in such hours!—a mournful sight,
> Though lovely!—an o'erflowing of the springs,
> The full springs of affection, deep as bright!
>
> (21)

In other words, Theresa's ability to face martyrdom with resolute dignity is ascribed to a specifically female kind of strength, even while the images that describe her defiance are drawn from the predominantly masculine vocabulary of energy and prophecy ("masculine" in the male Romantics' scheme of things). This emphasis on the woman's courage in the face of death is balanced on the other side of the gender divide by the way the male narrator expresses profound paternal tenderness toward his young son, whom he has brought with him into exile to protect him from the violence of the Inquisition (7, 49). If *The Forest Sanctuary* shows a woman as capable of showing courage equivalent to any man's though arising from different, specifically female, sources, it also shows a man capable of tenderness like a woman's, though, again, based on a different, specifically male role. It has to be admitted, however, that both Theresa and the narrator are portrayed as exhibiting these unconventional qualities only under exceptionally dire conditions and that (as in **"The Bride of the Greek Isle"**) the woman's heroism is still a heroism of self-sacrifice and is in some sense for the sake of a male value system.

Another instance of the images of fire and prophecy being reappropriated for the female poet occurs in **"The Rock of Cader Idris"** (one of the "Welsh Melodies"). The poem is based on an old Welsh tradition that a bard who spends a night on the summit of Cader Idris will have the gift of poetic inspiration when he wakes, unless he is unlucky enough to die or go mad instead. The speaker, who has obviously survived this grueling initiation, claims the masculine Romantic attributes of "immortal flame," "voice," and "power." Although the poem is clearly spoken in the persona of the male bard, there is a sense in which (as in Blake's *Milton*) the precursor's voice is appropriated by the neophyte, in this case female: "I awoke to inherit / A flame all immortal, a voice, and a power!" (*Poetical Works,* 253).

As in many of Hemans's poems about a male literary tradition, though, the rearticulation of the bardic voice conceals something more traditionally feminine, a scene of reading. It is through *texts* that the tradition of Cader Idris descends to Hemans. Such a scene occurs also in **"Tasso and His Sister"** (a poem based on a couple of sentences in Germaine de Staël's *Corinne*) in a quite literal way. Tasso's sister is depicted reading aloud, to her children, Tasso's poetry—the deeds of Tancred and Godfrey. In the sixth stanza of the poem, Tasso himself suddenly stands before her, dressed as a poor pilgrim. His health, his reason, everything but his poetic gift has been destroyed by his long imprisonment. In several senses this is an epiphanic moment for Hemans's readers. The mother, surrounded by her attentive, wondering children, reads the text of her brother the poet ("words of power" they are called in the second stanza), and the sentiments that the poet appropriated for his text are realized once more, in the reader and her hearers. As if in proof of the power of this woman's reading, the poet himself materializes before them. The woman's reappropriation of the brother-poet's sentiments, her creative re-reading of his text, not only arouses wonder in the children who hear it but in a literal sense reunites the family that had long been divided by the tyrannical power of the state. This in itself suggests the special way in which Hemans's work may occasionally verge on a kind of literature of resistance. Tasso—for the male Romantics, an icon of the solitary poet's courageous resistance to arbitrary power—is almost literally resurrected by the force of a *woman's reading* but not (this time) as a solitary bard or Byronic hero but as member of a family. Poetry's "words of power" are placed at the service of family, not the mere exaltation of the solitary gifted male; and the exhausted,

half-mad Tasso, worn out by his struggle against tyranny, seems a timely image of the male Romantic cult of genius, now at the end of its tether, yielding to a different, more humanizing and socializing conception of the place of poetry and the conditions of its production.

Mellor comments on Hemans that "having accepted her culture's hegemonic inscription of the woman within the domestic sphere, Hemans's poetry subtly and painfully explored the ways in which that construction of gender finally collapses upon itself, bringing nothing but suffering, and the void of nothingness, to both women and men" (*Romanticism and Gender,* 142). I do not dispute that it does that, nor even that it is more truly characteristic of her poetry to do that, but I want to suggest here that it might sometimes have been received as achieving something more positive: the affirmation of a different way of valuing women's powers and of a correspondingly different poetic.

However, no alert reader can ignore the ways in which Hemans's poetry can be seen to collaborate with the existing social order, even to justify it, while her subtext reveals quite starkly the terrible price this social order exacts of women. One embarrassing fact to be faced—embarrassing at least for those feminists who consider the recuperation of previously ignored or marginalized texts to be an important part of the feminist project—is that Hemans, while marginal to the Romantic canon of today, was not exactly marginal in her time. Hemans was destined to be read as not a margin but a center, the embodiment of that hearth and home that would send forth Englishmen to subdue the world and to which the lucky ones would return, at least in thought, to remind themselves of why they were fighting or contracting malaria and typhoid in foreign parts. And yet, of course, this center was not a center of power, in the normal sense of the word. Political and economic power lay elsewhere and, moreover, needed what Hemans came to symbolize, a focal point around which loyal sentiment could gather. Judith Lowder Newton has argued convincingly that the increasing emphasis between 1800 and 1840 on the importance of women's "influence" was actually an attempt to assure middle-class women that "they *did* have work, power, and status after all"; their work was to "mitigate the harshness of an industrial capitalist world."[11] This division of labor is clear in an 1850 *Westminster Review* article, "Woman's Mission":

> [T]o warm, to cherish into purer life the motive that shall lead to the heroic act—this is her genius, her madness, her song flowing out, she knows not how, going she knows not whither, but returning never again. The woman . . . differs from man then in this—in possessing a greater capacity— a greater genius to influence. She influences through no direct exercise of power, but because she must. Influence breathes from her, and informs every thing and creature around, and we are only conscious of it by its results.[12]

But crediting women with power through influence effectively devalued all of their other capacities and denied women self-definition: a woman was to be identified by her services to others (Newton, *Women,* 4).

"The Image in Lava," "Tasso and His Sister," *The Forest Sanctuary,* and other such works cannot be put forward as "feminist" poems; but perhaps they belong in a feminist canon. **"The Image in Lava,"** like **"Madeline: A Domestic Tale"** and other poems in *Records of Woman,* precisely reveals the social construction of gender at the same time that it confidently affirms the triumph of the "female" traits of love and parental affection over the imperial male order, symbolized by the "temple," "tower," and "cities" now moldering in dust. This is not to say that Hemans's work can now survive only as somehow typical of contemporary social attitudes, the sort of thing that might be cited as "background" to the study of Mary Wollstonecraft or Emily Brontë. Her poems would not hold the interest they do if they did nothing other than "go smoothly with the grain of social expectation." The strong sentiments in these poems are conveyed through an always competent and sometimes brilliant lyric and narrative art. To us, Hemans's women may seem to be singing in their chains, but they do sing—and the very attractiveness, the quasi-religious discipline, of the ethic of self-sacrifice that pervades *Records of Woman* and *Songs of the Affections* contributes largely to the aesthetic value of her work. But it is an aesthetic value that we are bound to experience differently. As Jan Mukařovskỳ lucidly puts it,

> The work of art itself is not a constant. Every shift in time, space or social surroundings alters the existing artistic tradition through whose prism the art work is observed, and as a result of such shifts that aesthetic object also changes which in the awareness of a particular collective corresponds to a material artifact—an artistic product. . . . It is natural that with these shifts of the aesthetic object, aesthetic value also changes rather frequently.[13]

The pathos of Hemans's **"The Image in Lava"** is not only in the event that it records, the death of a woman whose life ended abruptly and tragically in A.D. 79, but in the fact that the poem itself is a trace left by Hemans's own effacement by a discourse that compelled her to comprehend woman principally on the terms established by the needs of the bourgeois family, which she sees impressed on the volcanic mud of Vesuvius. Like the embarrassing fact of Anne Killigrew's smallpox, meticulously recorded by John Dryden in his poem of praise to her (Mermin, "Women Becoming Poets," 353-54), Felicia Hemans's effacement may strike us now as having to do less with a strictly personal tragedy than with the recognition that women's reality is an imposed reality. We can recognize in the obscure woman of Herculaneum and her "dark fate" an image emblematic of Hemans's own situation and her own literary fate.

Notes

[1] Percy Bysshe Shelley, "On Frankenstein," in *Complete Works,* ed. R. Ingpen and W. Peck, 10 vols. (London and New York: Julian Editions, 1926-30), 6 (1929): 263-64.

[2] The works of Hemans cited herein are *The Poetical Works,* ed. William Michael Rossetti (London: Ward, Lock and Co., n.d.); *The Forest Sanctuary; and Other Poems* (1825; reprint, with *The Vespers of Palermo,* New York: Garland, 1978); *Records of Woman: With Other Poems* (1828; reprint, New York: Garland, 1978); and *Songs of the Affections, With Other Poems* (1830; reprint, New York: Garland, 1978).

[3] Kurt Heinzelman, "The Cult of Domesticity: Dorothy and William Wordsworth at Grasmere," in *Romanticism and Feminism,* ed. Anne K. Mellor (Bloomington: Indiana University Press, 1988), 53.

[4] Gail Griffin, "Alma Mater," in *Profession 90* (New York: Modern Language Association, 1990).

[5] Dorothy Mermin, "Women Becoming Poets: Katherine Philips, Aphra Behn, Anne Finch," *ELH* 57 (1990): 349.

[6] See August Mau, *Pompeii: Its Life and Art,* trans. Francis W. Kelsey (1902; reprint, New Rochelle, N.Y.: Caratzas, 1982), 26; and Michael Grant, *Cities of Vesuvius: Pompeii and Herculaneum* (London: Weidenfeld and Nicolson, 1971), 31-32. Reports appeared frequently in the *Times* (London) between 1821 (when the discovery at Pompeii of tradesmen's shops, barracks, a Temple of Justice, and an amphitheater was reported) and 1827 (the visit of the king and queen of Naples to Pompeii; see the *Times* [London], 5 February 1821, p. 3, and 4 July 1827, p. 2). Even though modern excavation in the Pompeii area began at Herculaneum in 1709, little was found there initially, and in the 1740s interest turned to Pompeii, which seemed to offer more to interest the archaeologist. The medium in which the woman's form was preserved must have been warm volcanic mud, rather than lava, strictly speaking (see Grant, *Cities,* 31). Neither Mau nor Grant mentions a woman with an infant being discovered at Herculaneum in the 1820s, however, and I have been unable to identify the precise source of Hemans's information.

[7] I have in mind here a remark of David Punter's: "in the eighteenth century . . . it became a crime against the social code for any woman to admit her real feelings or to confess to passion, and the main purpose of the education of 'ladies of condition' becomes this suppression of feeling and passion. Under these circumstances, one could say that male and female discourse developed increasingly into separate languages, insulated from each other by the different interests of the sexes in relation to the maintenance of the social order" (*The Literature of Terror: A History of Gothic Fictions from 1765 to the Present Day* [London: Longman, 1980], 95).

[8] I am grateful to Harriet Linkin for suggesting that I explore this alternative approach to Hemans and for point-

ing out the possible relevance of Cixous to the question of identity and its limitations as the site of feminist value.

[9] Nancy Chodorow, *The Reproduction of Mothering: Psychoanalysis and the Sociology of Gender* (Berkeley: University of California Press, 1978), 168-169.

[10] This poem, Anne K. Mellor points out, "endorses Burke's conservative political model of good government as the preservation of 'our little platoon,' of a nuclear English family controlled by the authority of 'canonized forefathers'" (*Romanticism and Gender* [New York: Routledge, 1993], 126).

[11] Judith Lowder Newton, *Women, Power, and Subversion: Social Strategies in British Fiction, 1778-1860* (Athens: University of Georgia Press, 1981), 19.

[12] *Westminster Review* 52 (1849-1850) no. 103 (January 1850): 354-55.

[13] Jan Mukařovský, *Aesthetic Function, Norm and Value as Social Facts,* trans. with notes by Mark E. Suino (Ann Arbor: University of Michigan, 1970), 60-61.

FURTHER READING

Biographies

Hughes, Harriet. *The Works of Mrs. Hemans with a Memoir of her Life,* Vol. 1. Edinburgh: William Blackwood and Sons, 1857, 352p.
    Biography of Hemans by her sister.

Ritchie, Lady. "Felicia Felix." In *Blackstick Papers,* pp. 16-30. New York: G. P. Putnam's Sons, Knickerbocker Press, 1908.
    Biographical portrait of Hemans including quotations and correspondence from literary friends.

Criticism

Review of *Modern Greece,* by Felicia Hemans. *Blackwood's Edinburgh Magazine* I, No. V (August 1817): 515-18.
    Favorable critical notice of *Modern Greece.*

Blain, Virginia. "'Thou with Earth's Music Answerest the Sky': Felicia Hemans, Mary Ann Browne, and the Myth of Poetic Sisterhood." *Women's Writing: The Elizabethan to Victorian Period* 2, No. 3 (1995): 251-69.
    Uses the false assumption that Hemans was the biological sister of poet Mary Ann Browne to illustrate certain nineteenth-century notions of sisterhood and

how these notions shaped the public's perception of women's poetry.

Chorley, Henry F. *Memorials of Mrs. Hemans, with Illustrations of Her Literary Character from Her Private Correspondence.* 2 vols. Philadelphia: Carey, Lea & Blanchard, 1836, 272p.
    Account of Hemans's literary development including excerpts from her letters.

Clarke, Norma. *Ambitious Heights: Writing, Friendship, Love—The Jewsbury Sisters, Felicia Hemans, and Jane Welsh Carlyle.* London: Routledge, 1990, 245p.
    Studies "the incompatibility of literary ambition and wifely duty" through the relationships between Carlyle, the Jewsbury sisters, and Hemans.

"Mrs. Hemans and the Picturesque School." *Fraser's Magazine for Town and Country* XXI, No. CXXII (February 1840): 127-46.
    Biographical and critical essay that also relates Hemans's powers of picturesque description to those of Homer, Virgil, Thomas Gray, and others.

McGann, Jerome J. "Literary History, Romanticism, and Felicia Hemans." In *Re-Visioning Romanticism: British Women Writers, 1776-1837,* edited by Carol Shiner Wilson and Joel Haefner, pp. 210-27. Philadelphia: University of Pennsylvania Press, 1994.
    A roundtable discussion among three scholars of Romanticism assessing Hemans's position in the canon of British Romantic poetry.

Park, L. J. Review of *The Forest Sanctuary and Other Poems,* by Felicia Hemans. *The Christian Examiner and Theological Review* III, No. V (September and October 1826): 403-18.
    Praises Hemans's *The Forest Sanctuary.*

Ross, Marlon B. *The Contours of Masculine Desire: Romanticism and the Rise of Women's Poetry.* Oxford: Oxford University Press, 1989, 344p.
    Studies Hemans as well as other women poets of her generation against the notions of Romanticism built around primary male poets in order to re-examine Romantic ideology and its buried gender dynamics.

Tuckerman, H. T. "Essay." In *Poems by Felicia Hemans with an Essay on her Genius,* edited by Rufus W. Griswold, pp. v-xvi. New York: Leavitt & Allen, n.d.
    Evaluative essay on Hemans's poetry in which the critic praises her "earnestness of soul" and her "pure, lofty, and earnest sentiment."

Additional coverage of Hemans's life and career is contained in the following source published by Gale Research: *Dictionary of Literary Biography,* Vol. 96.

Jules Vallès

1832-1885

(Born Louis-Jules Vallez; also wrote under the pseudonyms Asvell, Jean Max, Jean La Rue, and Jacques Vingtras) French novelist and journalist.

INTRODUCTION

The premiere historian of the Paris Commune uprising of 1871, Vallès was assured a controversial place in history when the Commune's experiment with anarchy became a model and inspiration for such theorists and revolutionaries as Karl Marx, Friedrich Engels, and Vladimir Lenin. Vallès drew upon his development as a militant journalist and insurrectionist, his difficult childhood, and his reluctantly pursued classical education to write his most widely read work, the largely autobiographic trilogy *Jacques Vingtras* (1879-1886). Important as an historical document, *Jacques Vingtras* also remains relevant as a critique of educational practices and of the isolating effects of capitalism and modern bourgeois institutions. Although linguistic playfulness and spontaneity distinguishes Vallès's writing from that of his contemporaries and successors, including Emile Zola, Victor Hugo, and Charles Baudelaire, the militant populism of his works exposed him to persecution, which eventually forced him into literary obscurity. It was not until the mid-twentieth century that scholars began to look past Vallès's political radicalism and to appreciate his qualities as a literary historian and prose stylist.

Biographical Information

Vallès was born Louis-Jules Vallez in the village of Puy-en-Velay, Auvergne, France, on June 11, 1832. Vallès's last name was spelled incorrectly on his birth certificate, but he maintained the error in his adult life to distance himself from his schoolteacher father, Jean-Louis Vallez. Vallès's father descended from and married into a farming family, and pursued a career as a teacher in order to obtain social status. Although Vallès's father remained on the lowest rung of the social ladder in the teaching profession, this occupation afforded Vallès the chance to obtain a classical education, and he excelled in Greek, Latin, and rhetoric. Vallès also became increasingly interested in socialist and revolutionary politics, especially in the wake of the 1848 uprising of students, artisans, and unemployed workers in Paris. He increasingly rejected the values and wishes of his father, particularly his father's insistence that he pass the *baccalauréate* examinations and enter into an academic career of his own.

As Vallès became more politically active, reportedly organizing resistance to Napoleon III's coup d'état in 1851, his father responded by putting him in an asylum in December 1851. Vallès, mobilizing his political contacts, was released from the asylum in March 1852; he then passed the *baccalauréate* and left for Paris, where he found his degree useless and his financial prospects dim. Vallès participated in the bohemian life of the Left Bank in Paris, attempting law school, tutoring at a boardinghouse, and performing secretarial work for Gustave Planche. During this period, Vallès wrote jingles, dictionary entries, pamphlets, tour guides, and newspaper articles. After his father's death in 1857, Vallès earned his living by contributing to or managing various liberal daily newspapers. That same year, Vallès anonymously published the novel *L'Argent*. This work represents the author as a man of letters turned stockbroker but deals with this transformation with such irony and sarcasm that Vallès's true opinions about the world of finance are readily apparent.

The death of Henri Murger in 1861 was a critical point in Vallès's life. Murger had written *Scènes de la vie de bohèmie*—a work sympathetic to the plight of the bohemians—but Vallès considered Murger's work unsuccessful in representing the hardships and pain of bohemian life. After Murger's death, Vallès made it his goal to provide a true picture of the life of the bohemians and his own generation. The first publication of this program was an article entitled "Les Réfractaires," published in *Figaro* in 1861. This article and various others written between 1857 and 1865 were collected in a fictional work entitled *Les Réfractaires* (1865). Almost contemporaneous with this work was the Romantic novella *Jean Delbenne* (1865). Reactionary articles written in 1865 and 1866 appeared in the fictional work entitled *La Rue* (1866), which described the urban battleground of Paris where the poor and marginal mixed with the more fortunate. Vallès increased his reactionary literary output in the following years by establishing seven short-lived newspapers: *La Rue* in 1867, *Journal de Sainte-Pélagie* in 1869 (January), *Peuple* in 1869 (February), *Réfractaire* in 1869 (May), *Corsaire* in 1869 (November), *Cri du Peuple* in 1871 (February), and *Drapeau* in 1871 (March).

When Prussia invaded France in 1870, Vallès was a leader of a revolutionary republican party that was defeated in the elections for a new government to negogiate peace. The new, monarchistic government took steps to remove the reactionaries from Paris, and the revolutionary movement fought back, forced the leaders of the official government to flee, and established the Paris Commune. Vallès served on the Commune's education commission and presided over its last meeting on May 21, 1871, when the official French government finally defeated the Communards. Vallès fled to London in exile in October 1871. There he wrote a play entitled *La Commune de Paris* (1872) and began the trilogy that would relate the social circumstances of his generation leading up to the Paris Commune. The first volume of this trilogy was entitled *Jacques Vintras I* (later called *Jacques Vingtras: L'Enfant*). Published through intermediaries, it appeared first in serial form in a Parisian paper in 1878 and then in book form in 1879, with each version being published under a different pen name. After amnesty for the Communards was proclaimed in 1880, Vallès returned to Paris and released additional works that had been written in exile but had not been published: *Jacques Vingtras: Le Bachelier* (1881) and a collection of portraits of London life entitled *La Rue à Londres* (1884). During this period, Vallès began his close relationship with Caroline Rémy, known as Sèverine, who served not only as his nurse and secretary in his years of ill health but also as editor, assuring that his works were finished, polished, and published. Vallès died in Paris on February 14, 1885. Sèverine collected, edited, and published the serialized version of Vallès's third and last Jacques Vingtras novel, *Jacques Vingtras: L'Insurgé: 1871* (1886).

Major Works

Vallès most significant literary achievement is his semi-autobiographical trilogy *Jacques Vingtras: L'Enfant, Jacques Vingtras: Le Bachelier,* and *Jacques Vingtras: L'Insurgé: 1871.* Tracing the development of an insurrectionist, the three novels chronicle the life of their eponymous protagonist from childhood (in *L'Enfant*) through institutional education and young adulthood (*Le Bachelier*) to his eventual realization as an insurrectionist in the Paris Commune (*L'Insurgé*). The books faithfully report the conditions of students, workers, and others who would join the movement of the Communards. The first two novels in particular offer powerful condemnations of bourgeois practices of child-rearing and education. Closely mirroring Vallès's own life, the last novel depicts the rise of Vingtras's career as a journalist, his involvement with the Paris Commune, and his hope for the future after escaping the fall of the Commune. More autobiographical writing appears in Vallès's documentation of his experiences in *La Rue à Londres*, written in London after the fall of the Commune. This work reveals Vallès's great love and appreciation for his native Paris (although his comparisons between Paris and London are sometimes misinformed), and is also marked by the same attention to sensory detail that distinguishes the *Jacques Vingtras* trilogy.

Critical Reception

Vallès's radical politics overshadowed his literary talents until well into the twentieth century. Upon Vallès's death, influential critic Ferdinand Brunetière began Vallès's obituary reluctantly, remarking, "I shall speak of a disagreeable man." Recent critics, however, have worked toward a "recuperation of Vallesian poetics." Robin Orr Bodkin (1992), for example, argues that lifting Vallès from his undeserved obscurity will demonstrate "how his contribution points directly to the textual innovations of Nathalie Sarraute, Céline, Raymond Queneau, and Samuel Becket among others, if not to postmodern textual presentation in general." Nonetheless, most critics have considered his most important contribution to be his documentation of events surrounding the Paris Commune. Gerhard Fischer (1981) calls Vallès's mostly unknown drama *La Commune de Paris* "an outstanding documentary work [which] directly describes the struggles and sufferings of the people of Paris." Moreover, to some critics, Vallès's depiction of the hopes and disappointments of the working classes offers a model for modern power relations. Charles Stivale (1992) suggests that Vallès's careful narration of the forces at play during a critical political moment reveals a foundation for hope, and "forcefully introduces the possibility of resistance and the necessity of history."

PRINCIPAL WORKS

Le Cri du Peuple [editor] (journalism) 1848-1871
L'Argent [published anonymously] (novel) 1857
Jean Delbenne [published anonymously] (novella) 1865
Les Réfractaires (novel) 1865
La Rue (novel) 1866
La Commune de Paris (play) 1872
Jacques Vingtras [under the name Jean La Rue] (novel) 1879; published as *Jacques Vingtras: L'Enfant,* 1881
Jacques Vingtras: Le Bachelier (novel) 1881
La Rue à Londres (essays) 1884
Jacques Vingtras: L'Insurgé: 1871 (novel) 1886

CRITICISM

Victor Brombert (essay date 1961)

SOURCE: "Vallès and the Pathos of Rebellion," in his *The Intellectual Hero: Studies in the French Novel, 1880-1955,* J. B. Lippincott Co., 1961, pp. 43-51.

[*In the following excerpt, Brombert contends that despite Vallès's often misunderstood humor, his works viscerally communicate the tragic circumstances of Leftist intellectuals who were not accepted by existing institutions or by the revolutionary workers they wished to support.*]

Jules Vallès' disheveled exuberance was not confined to literature. Son of a provincial schoolteacher who sent him to Paris to prepare for the Ecole Normale, he despised diplomas, preferred the more hot-blooded bohemian life, launched into revolutionary activities, gained experience in street fights and in the editorial rooms of militant papers, participated in the 1870 Commune, got a taste of jails and exile, and played until the end the dangerous game of revolt for revolt's sake. His colorful life, however, and even his role as founder of the revolutionary *Cri du Peuple,* might well be forgotten today were it not for the vigorous, succulent pages of his largely autobiographic *Jacques Vingtras* (1879-1886).

This trilogy, written with prankish zest, has not always been taken seriously. The linguistic verve suggests, from the first paragraph on, that the tone will remain truculent throughout. Metaphorical tours de force, onomatopoeic effects, scathing understatements, the abundant use of colloquialisms—all are part of Vallès' comic inventiveness. Indeed, the first volume, *L'Enfant,* appears primarily as a humorous though occasionally bitter series of childhood reminiscences written by a man who is eager and able to recapture the precise reactions of a young boy. *L'Enfant* is appropriately dedicated to all those who died of boredom in school, who were made to cry at home, who were "tyrannized by their teachers and thrashed by their parents."

The bare, raw, freshly whipped buttocks displayed in the opening pages are a concrete image of the petty misfortunes of young Jacques Vingtras. His childhood is not exactly happy. His parents, particularly his mother, seem to delight in punishing him or in forcing him to do what most thwarts him. Yet comic passages abound. The absurd home-made outfit his stingy mother forces him to wear; her grotesque demonstration of a peasant dance at an official party; pathetically amusing scenes at home or in school—in pages such as these, laughter seems to function as a belated vengeance.

For it soon becomes clear that Vallès' comic verve goes hand in hand with the theme of revolt. Vingtras' parents symbolize the petty bureaucratic aspirations of the lower middle class. His father, as well as the greedy director of the pension Legnagna, are part of a moral climate against which the boy and later the adolescent instinctively rebel. The shocking bitterness with which he evokes his mother (a cudgel, he says, could have replaced her!) must be set against the larger implications of his critique. The child feels drawn to every excess. The prison he has visited seems to him less atrocious than his school and he compares unfavorably the sad and smelly classrooms with the corner tavern filled with laughter and good cheer. The brawny adolescent watches with envy the apparently carefree movements of peasants at work. Vingtras' revolt is in fact the revolt of a *déclassé's* son.

It is indeed primarily against the teaching profession that Vallès directs his caustic verve. Vingtras' father thus appears as the pitiful caricature of the exploited, humiliated, regimented intellectual whose sole ambition is to maintain his precarious security, ever threatened by students and superiors. Despised, often hated by his students who persecute him through organized class disorders (the traditional *chahut*), he is in turn forced to scare them in order to have peace and to obtain the much needed private lessons. The slightest scandal could compromise his career. Since he is not even an *agrégé,* he is made to feel hierarchical differences with particular brutality.

There is, however, something besides pity in these pages. Vallès does not really succeed in hiding the bitterness with which he contemplates a cowardly father who, in order to hold on to a job, had his politically compromised son (still a minor) committed to an insane asylum. And yet this caricature is by no means limited to his father. Vallès is one of the many French writers who, in the wake of Balzac's *Louis Lambert,* have evoked their days of suffering at school: the cruelty of fellow students, the obstinate struggle between the boys and their teachers, the sordid hygienic conditions, the arbitrariness of a regime based on physical punishments and privations, the instruction in solitude imparted in this social microcosm, but also the dreams of friendship and emancipation that such a regime fosters. (Vallès himself had suffered and rebelled at the pension Lemeignan, the lycée Bonaparte in Paris and the lycée of Nantes.) Much of the first volume of *Jacques Vingtras* is thus devoted to a bemused, wistful, but also malicious portrayal of pedantic types: the professor who proves the existence of God by displacing beans and matchsticks on a table; the young *agrégé* of philosophy with the obsessive mania for being first everywhere; the Principal who sets greater store by a tidy and obedient servant than by a competent teacher. Very soon, however, the caricature becomes vengeful. It is with undisguised hate that Vallès describes the thick lower lip of one professor, Turpin, who persecutes fellowship students for the simple reason that they are poor. It is with equally undisguised indignation that he tells of the false official report whereby the Principal succeeds in having a defenseless teacher removed.

Examples of pettiness and flagrant injustice stud these pages. But neither the cowardice of the father nor the arbitrariness of despotic schoolmasters can account entirely for the virulence of the caricature. The reactions provoked by reminiscences may be spontaneous, but they are also quite evidently part of a more far-reaching critique of the entire intellectual proletariat. If the young boy seems to prefer rural occupations to those of the classroom, if in his mind he sets the prison and the tavern above the sordid corridors of his school, it is not merely out of an adolescent yearning for a supposedly carefree life. If he repeatedly (and always unfavorably) compares his father to his peasant uncles and cousins, it is because he feels that their healthy allegiance to manual work, far from degrading them, has preserved their dignity. His father, on the other hand, in his very ambition to emancipate himself, in his eagerness to gain elusive "honors" by means of diplomas, has chosen the humiliating path of the *déclassé.*

The personal reproach is, however, less important here than a sense of vicarious shame for a father who has been the victim of a social phenomenon. All around him Jacques Vingtras observes the symptoms of this new social disease. On the very morning he is to take important State examinations, he sees under a bridge a destitute figure busy washing a handkerchief in the river. The figure seems familiar: he recognizes a teacher dismissed some years ago. What had been his crime? Perhaps he had played a prank on the Principal, or written an article that provoked official ire. Who cares! The point is that this former teacher, washing handkerchiefs in the muddy river water, suddenly comes to symbolize his father's whole world: unintelligent headmasters, cruel students, cowardly inspectors, intriguing colleagues—and, most of all, the eternally humiliated and persecuted teacher.

Vingtras' sense of shame thus comprises an entire social class—indeed, the very class that Barrès will soon denounce in *Les Déracinés* and Bourget in *L'Etape:* the unhappy, uprooted and socially unstable *"prolétariat des bacheliers."* At his father's deathbed, Jacques Vingtras once more deplores the willful uprooting that has made him, in his own eyes, less than a complete human being. But it is significant that the sense of shame ceases to be vicarious: Jacques Vingtras himself feels caught up in a professional career, tied to a social reality. Caricature, at first an expression of adolescent revolt, then an instrument of comedy and social critique, finally merges with a sense of personal suffering. The violent accusations he hurls at his father cannot hide the fact that it is a personal drama in which Jacques Vingtras is caught:

> Why did I set foot in this profession! O father! Why did you commit the crime of not letting me become a worker! . . .
>
> What right did you have to condemn me to this cowardly career!

Not only has vicarious shame been translated into a personal shame, but the comic perspective has made way for a serious, dramatic treatment. The somewhat external critique of a social group becomes a deeply felt experience of loneliness and frustration. But above all—and it is here that Vallès' entire approach is ambiguous—the object of the caricature turns out to be the narrator himself, accuser and accused in one, the half-pathetic, half-heroic, socially determined figure of

an intellectual in conflict with society and himself. For Vingtras is the prisoner of his education no less than of a social reality. It is against this double imprisonment that he attempts to rebel, but rebellion is useless: whether he likes it or not, he is condemned to the intellectual's alienation, and this awareness of captivity only increases his shame.

Part of Vingtras' unhappiness is of course nothing more than a healthy discontent which can be traced to immediate material causes. Although he does derive some satisfaction from his activities (the excitement of delivering a shocking lecture, the pride of publishing a book, of founding a review, of writing articles for which he is sent to prison), the nasty truth is that no diploma and no amount of classical knowledge can feed his plebeian appetite. *Le Bachelier,* the second volume of the trilogy, is dedicated to "those who, nourished on Greek and Latin, died of hunger." It cannot be said that Vingtras does not try. His attempts, however, only amount to a long series of mortifications and minor catastrophes. As tutor in a boarding school, he spends his time wiping children's noses, cannot obtain his pay, and is falsely accused of assaulting the virtue of the headmaster's wife. He then gives private lessons, but that too leaves his stomach grumbling. As his stomach continues to protest, he becomes less and less proud. "I offered myself dirt cheap." But no school wants him, and he has to turn to other occupations: private secretary to a rich Austrian who treats him like a manservant; drama critic with instructions to interlard his column with advertisements for a coat factory; contributor to a charlatanic dictionary for which he concocts alleged quotations from Bossuet and Charron—these are only a few samples of what Vingtras considers an inescapable prostitution. When at long last he seems settled for a while in a semi-honorable position—at the *Mairie,* he verifies the sex of children brought in for birth certificates—he loses even that job when the scandal of his revolutionary lecture on Balzac becomes known.

Far more disturbing, however, than this sequence of minor calamities and the material hardships they entail, is the feeling that he is ensnared in a rootless social class which has all the claims and none of the rights of an authentic proletariat. Jacques Vingtras knows he is the victim of his background: a plebeian, who has betrayed his origins; heir to a bourgeois "humanist" culture, but at the same time irrevocably cut off from all bourgeois comforts and hostile to bourgeois ethics. He is in fact the typical representative of a social group which rapidly was expanding during the last decades of the nineteenth century—a group with which even an increasingly bureaucratized and bureaucracy-conscious France could not quite cope. No wonder Vingtras attempts to escape his depressing social fatum. But everything seems to conspire to maintain him in his social confinement. He wants to be an ordinary worker. But what has he learned to do with his hands? When he tries, his fellow workers make fun of him, convinced that he is a common criminal hiding from the police. He enters a commercial firm, but considered "too educated" he is dismissed after one month. He visits a printing shop, dreams of becoming a printer or a typographer, proposes himself as apprentice, but is told by the owner that it is too late, that he should have come at the age of twelve, that no one cares for *déclassés* who abandon school for the workshop!

Déclassé—that is indeed the key word here. Even the extreme Left suspects the "workers of the intellect." Though masking his self-pity behind the biting, exuberant style, Vallès does not succeed in disguising his sadness. Any contact with the proletariat—his brothers in suffering—is denied Vingtras. Nothing perhaps reveals more movingly his yearning for brotherhood than his joyful surprise when invited by the old rag-picker Gros: "He does me the honor of inviting me from time to time to a family dinner; and I am so happy to feel that I, the *déclassé,* am esteemed and loved by this professional rag-picker." There is little doubt: much of Vingtras' revolutionary zest, many of his insurgent activities, can be explained by this need to find and to affirm his solidarity.

One could, of course, point to a great deal of exaggeration in Vallès' trilogy. There is too unremitting an effort to attain hearty comic effects, too much metaphoric verve. The adolescent mood is somewhat artificially maintained. And after all, the lot of the *"bachelier"* was really not quite so hopeless as Vallès would have us believe. Yet in spite of aesthetic flaws and overstatements, it cannot be denied that at the root of this work there is a tragic sentiment, if not a tragic vision, which most often takes the form of rebellion.

To be sure, the myth of revolt at first appears as a manifestation of childish exuberance. The books on the French Revolution which the schoolboy discovers on his arrival in Paris impress him because they make Roman history seem pale by comparison. The discovery is an early revenge against his stuffy, despotic teachers. And there is still a great dose of puerility in the organization of the *Comité des Jeunes* which binds together a group of eighteen-year-old boys who, in a fake revolutionary atmosphere, exalt each other with fiery speeches that sound like imitative exercises. But in the last volume, significantly entitled *L'Insurgé,* the myth of the Revolution becomes more serious, the game is over: rebellion against family and school, and revolt against his own social condition, now take the form, for Vingtras, of direct participation in revolutionary activities. These pages, written much less as fiction than as a lyrical document of events witnessed, sing the heroic hours of La Villette, the street fighting, the glorious days of the Commune. In *L'Insurgé,* the theme of Revolt converges on political action, the myth of the Revolution bursts forth triumphantly. It is still with

a sense of adolescent joy that Vingtras heralds the Commune, as though its only purpose were to offer ebullient young men an opportunity for excitement:

> Arise! It's the Revolution. So there it is, the moment longed for ever since the father's first cruel gesture, the first slap in the face by the teacher, ever since the first breadless day, the first homeless night—there it is, the revenge against school, misery, against the December *coup d'état.*

It is significant that the political reason should come last, that the real justification of his militant enthusiasm is exclusively emotional. Here, however, there is a grave danger of misinterpreting the Vallèsian attitude by confining it to childlike effervescence. Paul Bourget's article, written on the occasion of Vallès' death, is a fair example of this sort of interpretation[1] Perceptively, Bourget attempts to explain Vallès by means of a shrewd stylistic analysis which brings out the childlike imagination of the author (his fondness for direct, concrete suggestions, for onomatopoeic effects) and his inability to formulate an abstract idea. Vallès thus appears as the opposite of the philosophic or scientific mind that sees all things in terms of formulas. "The gift of intellectual metamorphosis was denied him because of the very energy of his immediate animal sensations," writes Bourget, in an obvious effort to convince the reader that Vallès' taste for revolution was merely the unreasoned, destructive revolt of a child.

Clearly Vallès' yearning for a revolution was not an intellectual one. He found Marx's ideas cloudy. Ideologies interested him little indeed. Marcel Cachin, who wrote a preface to *L'Insurgé,*[2] voiced a typical Marxist point of view when reproaching Vallès with having been an isolated rebel, lacking the guidance of a specific political doctrine and unaware of the value of political discipline. But what neither a Bourget nor a Cachin were willing to recognize is that Vallès, in spite of his apparent dynamics of pure rebellion, is really not at all out to destroy, but to preserve, or rather to recapture something infinitely precious for him. ("All that which, in his case, looks like hatred, is only another form of love," writes Louis Guilloux.[3]) His quest may be above all emotional—yet it cannot be reduced to mere petulance: it is the deep yearning to be with others, to suffer for and with others. It is this yearning for some form of solidarity which explains in part his fascination with the destitute:

> *Je suis l'ami du pauvre hère*
> *Qui, dans l'ombre, a faim, froid, sommeil.*[4]

It also explains the particular excitement with which his hero receives letters from admirers after the publication of his book, and his deep joy as he becomes aware that his journalistic battles have endeared him to the workers. Finally, it is this very yearning to belong or join with the underprivileged that explains his militant attitudes.

The irony of the situation is that even in the midst of the virile fraternity of a revolution, Jacques Vingtras remains a stranger, a fleetingly accepted pariah. Alone in his pacifism, alone in his antimilitarism, he remains alone even under shell fire and in the midst of brave deeds. Attached, in spite of himself, to bourgeois values and to a bourgeois culture he would be happy to repudiate, Vingtras remains conscious throughout of his status as "*bachelier.*" The ministers of the Commune, his comrades, cannot understand what he means when he speaks of freedom of the press. Is he not forced to admit that revolutions are best organized and fought by those who, like Deputy Mayor Grêlier, display an utter contempt for the laws of grammar? He admires these leaders, these self-appointed ministers, who dictate revolutionary manifestoes studded with barbarisms, and who, while fighting tyranny, also organize a thorough insurrection against French syntax.[5]

But there is more than facile humor in this situation. Vallès is indeed broaching here one of the significant tragic themes of our day: the unhappy marriage between the Leftist intellectual and the revolutionary parties. Others, coming after him, have undoubtedly explored this subject with more self-consciousness, or greater depth and artistry. In Vallès' work the theme frequently remains only half formulated or marred by a touching naïveté. But although Vallès' treatment may at times be out of focus (historically, also, the subject was a little premature), it is undeniable that there is pathos in this tension between the *déclassé* intellectual's yearning for dignity through common action and the proletarian's suspicion of such a free choice. Caricature has given way to the old conflict between thought and action. If the already graying "schoolboy" shakes his fist at his lycée, it is because he feels that it did not teach him what he most needed to know, that the culture which he now carries like a burden has betrayed him. There is bitter irony in the fact that Vingtras is ordered by the Commune to organize the military defense of the university quarter. For this university, he feels, has failed to teach him what he most needed to learn: how to be a man among men.

Notes

[1] "Jules Vallès," in *Portraits d'écrivains et notes d'esthétique,* Etudes et Portraits, I, pp. 139-155.

[2] Les Editeurs Français Réunis, 1950.

[3] "A propos de Jules Vallès," *Nouvelle Revue Française,* October 1, 1930, p. 441.

[4] "I am the friend of the poor wretch/who, in the dark, is hungry, cold and sleepy." Quoted by Henri Avenel, *Histoire de la presse française depuis 1789 jusqu'à nos jours,* pp. 546-547.

[5] How wrong Maupassant was in suggesting that Vallès felt discouraged and *disgusted* by the stupidity of his comrades-in-arms! ("Va t'asseoir," *Le Gaulois,* September 8, 1881.)

Barbara P. Edmonds (essay date 1967)

SOURCE: "In Search of Jules Vallès," in *The French Review: Journal of the American Association of Teachers of French,* Vol. 40, 1967, pp. 636-42.

[*In the following essay, Edmonds considers the autobiographical aspects of Vallès's* Jacques Vingtras *trilogy and emphasizes Vallès's contribution to the development of French political literature written to support the working class.*]

Jules Vallès's colorful life (1832-1885) was marked by a bohemian existence, militant politics including participation in the Commune, imprisonment, and exile. In spite of destitution and failing health, he founded two leading newspapers of the day: *La Rue,* in 1867, with the cooperation of Zola; and *Le Cri du Peuple,* in 1871. During the twenty-year span of his literary productivity, he contributed articles to over thirty periodicals and wrote several novels and treatises. Although he received recognition as a journalist contributing to such newspapers as *Le Figaro,* his greatest literary achievement was ***Jacques Vingtras.*** This autobiographical trilogy appeared under three separate titles: ***L'Enfant*** (1879), first published as a serial under the pseudonym of La Chaussade; ***Le Bachelier*** (1881); and the posthumous ***L'Insurgé*** (1886). What captivates the reader is not so much the seething bitterness that characterizes his style, but the exceptional sensibility, the lyricism, and the sardonic humor with which Vallès evokes his wretched childhood, his years of penury, and his final revolt against the era he describes so accurately.

To have created so imposing a character as Vingtras from one's autobiography is no doubt a masterful accomplishment; yet for the most part literary critics have ignored Vallès, and history has maligned him by an uncanny silence. Lagarde and Michard mention him only in passing. Bédier and Hazard have consecrated two matter-of-fact lines to him, and Lanson alludes to him only briefly in connection with Michelet. Of course, Vallès never sought fame in his lifetime: "Je ne crois pas au Panthéon, je ne rêve pas le titre de grand homme, je ne tiens pas à être immortel après ma mort—je tiendrais seulement à vivre de mon vivant!" he said in ***L'Insurge***[1] Few critics, with the exception of Gaston Gille, have endeavored to correct the legend which has characterized him as a fanatic, an anarchist, and a nihilist. Vallès was none of these, as his work attests.[2]

Jules Vallès presents the figure of a rebel. His whole life was a protest against the despotism of family, school, and society. ***Jacques Vingtras*** is a kind of

Odyssey, but one with a modern theme—the theme of revolt. Like a Wagnerian leitmotiv, the theme of revolt dominates the work. It recurs with greater force in each volume, reaching a dramatic crescendo in *L'Insurgé.* It is precisely this theme which marks Vallès as a precursor of the twentieth-century French novel. In our time there have been many angry men in revolt, and many surpassed Vallès. Some, notably Gide, have even picked up Vallès's banner. It was Gide who said, "Familles, je vous hais!" when he preached a new gospel in *Les Nourritures terrestres.* Like Vallès he felt that the family and bourgeois traditionalism stifled one's authenticity. Gide's disciple, Roger Martin du Gard, created a second Jacques Vingtras in his rebellious Jacques Thibault.

Some protests have been violent in nature, such as Céline's *Voyage au bout de la nuit* which advocated breaking all barriers and showed a real compassion for the victims of society. Others have been more sophisticated, such as Camus's *L'Homme révolté.* But when in the nineteenth century Vallès cried out in anger against the abuses of his childhood, his useless classical education and the injustice of society, he was a solitary voice.

Jacques Vingtras is a turning point in the evolution of the French novel. What perhaps distinguishes Vallès most from his contemporaries and places him in the avant-garde of the nineteenth century is his commitment to a cause and to the militant literature it inspired. Vallès was the first French novelist to create from his autobiography a novel so openly militant and so historically accurate. In telling the story of his life against a backdrop of political woe which beset his generation, he made his pen an arm of revolution. Although Flaubert's *Education sentimentale* has much in common with *Jacques Vingtras,* Flaubert himself was far from being *engagé.* He depicted the June Days and political clubs with exceptional reality, but he was primarily interested in drawing the moral decadence of the generation reaching maturity in the wake of the upheaval of 1848. Thus *Jacques Vingtras* can be considered to have opened the way for the twentieth century concept of *littérature engagée.*

The theme of revolt in *Jacques Vingtras* undergoes a distinct evolution beginning with Vallès's miserable childhood and ending with his resistance on the barricades of the Commune. Vallès was in exile in England after the demise of the Commune in 1871 when he began to write the gripping story of his life. He was determined not simply to write his memoirs but to create a social novel which would have an awakening impact on mankind. In a letter from London in August 1876 to his lifelong friend Arnould, Vallès explained his aim in writing *L'Enfant,* the first volume of the trilogy:

> J'ai beaucoup souffert étant jeune et j'ai voulu que le problème de l'éducation et de la famille se dressât au milieu des larmes de l'enfant et des rires de l'humoriste. . . . Je tremble qu'on ne saigne mon Histoire d'un enfant, et c'est encore ce qui a arrêté ma main, noyé mon courage, en plus de la chaleur infâme de l'enfant souffrant. Mon bouquin est hardi comme tout, sous une forme gaie—on voit les dents sous le rire, et il y a des pères qui voudront me tuer. C'est un sujet—à traiter même en pièces—la famille![3]

> Mon livre peut devenir le point de départ d'une campagne en faveur des petits êtres ridiculisés ou meurtris! C'est là le but![4]

The book was a tremendous success. Of course Vallès was not the first to treat the plight of the mistreated child. One thinks immediately of Dickens in England and in France of Daudet's *Petit Chose* published in 1868 and *Jack* published in 1875. Vallès is reputed to have admired *Jack* but to have been disappointed when *Petit Chose* appeared. He wrote to Daudet, "Je trouvai *Petit Chose* indigne de vous. Vous écriviez un conte plutôt qu'une vie d'enfant."[5] Beginning with Jean-Jacques Rousseau and continuing throughout the nineteenth century there was increased interest in the child. The trend was manifested in nearly all the French Romantic poets, especially Victor Hugo. In 1863 Hugo published *Les Misérables* in which he depicted the child as the helpless victim of a social scheme which he adjudged wrong. From 1870 on the child became a primary literary theme. Each year saw the publication of a work dealing with the child by such writers as Alphonse Daudet, Anatole France, and Pierre Loti. This trend was not a literary novelty averred Victor Toursch. It was due to the evolution of society in the second half of the nineteenth century and to realistic and naturalistic writers devoted to a scrupulous observance of society.[6] But Vallès's trilogy was the first to break with sentimental romanticism. It was the first to tell the story of the unhappy, misunderstood child from the viewpoint of the child and to treat the theme in a vein of brutal realism and stinging satire.

The second volume of the trilogy, *Le Bachelier,* continues Vallès's lamentable saga of revolt. The dedication reads: "A ceux qui nourris de grec et de latin sont morts de faim." It traces the transformation of revolt against education into revolt against society. *Le Bachelier* deals mainly with Vallès's feverish struggle to earn a living as he prostituted his intelligence for a crust of bread. Long before he had become the clarion of the workers' plight, Vallès had pledged himself to the cause of the intellectual proletariat, the *bacheliers* whose heritage was *la misère en redingote.* In *Le Bachelier* and in *Les Réfractaires* Vallès has depicted a host of young men who were victims of their education. Many preferred to suffer in penury than to accept the place society offered them. Both novels show the boredom, frustration, and destitution of so many young men of that era who would have done better to have learned a trade than to have cudgeled their brains with Latin verse.[7] Vallès has drawn an inimitable portrait of *la vie de bohême* characterized by fierce realism and compelling pathos, but relieved from time to time by a humorous note. Vallès summed up the whole problem when he described one of these victims dying of hunger:

> S'il savait faire quelque chose, un étalage, une addition, la vente, mesurer du drap, pincer le tissu . . . Il ne sait rien, le pauvre diable, qu'un peu de latin et de grec, qu'il vendra sous forme de leçons. Où les trouver? Les souliers crèvent, le pantalon sourit, le linge manque. . . . [8]

Vallès was among the first to blame society for this outrage and to foresee in it a potential danger. What dire warnings he issued to the bourgeoisie to bury their prejudices, or one day the army of *déclassés* would take their revenge:

> Les voyez-vous foncer sur nous, pâles, muets, amaigris, battre la charge avec les os de leurs martyrs sur le tambour des révoltés, et agitant comme un étendard qu bout d'un glaive, la chemise teinte du sang du dernier de leurs suicidés?
>
> (*Les Réfractaires,* p. 99).

What appeared to be the prating of a visionary turned out to be a prophetic message when the *redingotes* fought side by side on the barricades with the *blouses* in 1871. *Le Bachelier* ends on a very restive note which provides the transition to part three: "Mais tu nous le paieras, société bête qui affame les instruits et les courageux, quand ils ne veulent pas être tes laquais! . . . Je forgerai l'outil, mais j'aiguiserai l'arme qui un jour t'ensanglantera!"[9]

Vallès the writer and Vallès the combattant are one and the same. It is impossible to separate the writer from the political cause to which he devoted his life. He said of himself, "Je lutte, je souffre, j'aime, je hais, donc je suis. J'avais trouvé ça, moi, sans avoir lu Descartes!"[10] The third volume of the trilogy, justly called *L'Insurgé,* is a stirring but disconnected chronicle of Vallès's stand against society from 1866 to 1871. His first public act was to cast his lot with the poor in 1869 when he ran unsuccessfully against Jules Simon under the label of "Candidat de la misère." Following the capitulation and armistice of January 1871 Vallès joined the disparate group of revolutionaries who seized power in Paris under the name of the Commune. Vallès not only became the poet and spokesman of the revolution in his militant newspaper *Le Cri du Peuple* but also fought on the barricades. *L'Insurgé* is a veritable document of historical realism as it depicts the sanguine events of the final days of the Commune. In *L'Insurgé* Vallès explained what the Commune meant to him:

> La voilà donc la minute espérée et attendue depuis la première cruauté du père, depuis la première gifle du cuistre, depuis le premier jour passé sans pain, depuis la première nuit passée sans logis—voilà la revanche du collège, de la misère et de décembre!
>
> (p. 174).

It seems that all his suffering, anger, and resentment found their expression in the Commune.

It is important to note that Vallès's role was never fanatical. He was never a member of the Communist party, nor did he ever ally himself with any doctrine whether political, or literary. Always a pacifist and an anti-militarist, he was destined to be an unheeded Cassandra even when France was plunged into war. On July 19, 1870, he was nearly killed in the Place du Palais Bourbon by a handful of war-mongers who objected to his blatant opposition to the war. The crowd milling about was carefree and gay as if in the midst of a celebration. "A Berlin! A Berlin!" they chanted. Needless to say, Vallès was terribly disillusioned by the general folly:

> Elle me fait horreur, notre Marseillaise de maintenant! Elle est devenue un cantique d'Etat. Elle n'entraîne point des volontaires, elle mène des troupeaux. Ce n'est pas le tocsin sonné par le véritable enthousiasme. C'est le tintement de la cloche au cou des bestiaux.
>
> . . . . .
>
> Rien ne dénote l'émotion et la crainte qui doivent tordre les cœurs quand on annonce que la Patrie va tirer l'épée. . . .
>
> (*L'Insurgé,* p. 111).

No one listened to Vallès. He was even arrested as a traitor for having cried out prophetically: "Et moi, je sens, à l'hésitation de mon cœur, que la défaite est en croupe sur les chevaux des cavaliers . . ." (*L'Insurgé,* p. 113).

From the records of the sessions held by the Commune and the articles of *Le Cri du Peuple* one is convinced of Vallès's restrained and moderating role. He always tried to placate the dissident factions and to deter the radicals who were setting fire to Paris and slaying hostages for pure vengeance. In a sense his newspaper articles are a continuation of *Jacques Vingtras* only more succinct since they deal with history in the making. *Le Cri du Peuple* is a moving document which mirrors the revolutionary verve of the times and throws light on the ignominious drama of the Commune. Although many of the articles are filled with names long forgotten and events of little interest to the modern reader, all of them are marked by zest, emotion, and stylistic genius.

Nevertheless, it is essential to read his articles to complete the picture of Vallès as a social theorist. It is obvious that throughout the trilogy he realized the need for a social program, only his arguments were basically instinctive and emotional. In *L'Insurgé* he lamented the lack of a positive plan for the amelioration of social conditions:

Tu as crevé de faim, Vingtras, et tu as presque chômé pendant quinze ans. Tu as dû alors, pendant les moments durs, tu as dû songer au remède contre la famine, et ruminer les articles frais d'un code de justice humaine! Qu'apportes-tu de nouveau, du fond de ta jeunesse affreuse? . . . Réfléchir! Etudier! Quand? . . . Allez donc peser les théories sociales quand il tombe de ces grêlons de fer dans le plateau de la balance!

(p. 187).

Later during his years of exile he was even more acutely aware of the pressing need for a social program. In a letter to his friend Arnould, dated September 6, 1877, he wrote:

En dehors de notre camaraderie sure et forte, il y a de l'amour des idées de justice et de liberté. De liberté! Tu as trouvé ta voie. Creuse ce sillon, pioche, pioche. Il faut un programme social—tant qu'il n'y en aura pas un, on s'égarera et on mourra dans l'ombre des idées à l'éclair des défaites.

(Le Proscrit, p. 155).

All his life Vallès fought on the side of the poor and the downtrodden. "J'aime ceux qui souffrent, cela est dans ma nature, je le sens," he wrote in *Le Bachelier* (p. 75). He consecrated his life to the people. He became their champion, their hope, and their spokesman. In the editorial of the first issue of *Le Cri du Peuple,* February 22, 1871, he set down his goal:

Ici les gens de toute opinion trouveront leur place à leur rang de détresse et de peine, au prorata de leurs souffrances. C'est la fédération de tous ceux qui sont de part l'organisation capitaliste, exploités et estropiés, jetés dans le malheur et le mal.

As Vallès saw it, the workers were wallowing in a morass from which there seemed to be little escape. What Vallès wanted most was to restore to the workers their lost dignity, much the same as Kyo in *La Condition humaine* who found his moment of truth in fighting for human dignity—a recurring theme in twentieth century literature. Vallès was not the only one to defend the workers during this period. In 1877 Zola published *L'Assommoir* in which he made some of the same points as Vallès. Yet he failed to do in *L'Assommoir* what Vallès did successfully in *Jacques Vingtras,* i.e., depict himself as a *redingotier* defending the working man. Later Zola succeeded in *Germinal* (1885) as he documented the daily existence of the proletariat.

In his final years Vallès continued his role as social picador in *Le Cri du Peuple,* resuscitated in 1883 after the amnesty. He was already ill with diabetes and bowed by a life of hardship. He never completed his account of the Commune. Séverine, a devoted friend, assembled the third volume, *L'Insurgé,* according to a pre-arranged plan. It was published in 1886 a year after his death. When Vallès died, he was peaceful in the thought that by his life and by his writings he had helped in some way to illuminate the tortuous path of social progress.

Notes

[1] Jules Vallès, *L'Insurgé* (Paris: Editeurs Français Réunis, 1950), p. 21. Subsequent references to this work will be indicated in parentheses immediately following the quoted lines.

[2] For an excellent biographical and critical study consult Gaston Gille, *Jules Vallès* (Paris: Jouve et Cie, 1941), 2 vols. My thanks to Dr. Melvin Zimmerman of the University of Maryland for his advice and assistance with my article.

[3] Vallès's correspondence with Arnould has been published collectively under the title *Le Proscrit* (Paris: Editeurs Français Réunis, 1950), p. 89.

[4] *Ibid.,* p. 230; May 29, 1879.

[5] Gille, I, 324.

[6] Victor Toursch, *L'Enfant français à la fin du XIX siècle d'après ses principauz romanciers* (Paris: Presses Modernes, 1939), p. iv.

[7] For an interesting discussion of this social and moral problem which plagued France in the last decade of the nineteenth century see Victor Brombert, "From Pathos to Rebellion," *The Intellectual Hero* (Philadelphia and New York: J. B. Lippincott Co., 1960).

[8] Jules Vallès, *Les Réfractaires* (Paris: Editeurs Français Réunis, 1955), p. 31.

[9] Jules Vallès, *Le Bachelier* (Paris: Editeurs Français Réunis, 1955), p. 445.

[10] Cited in Léon Hirsch, *Jules Vallès, l'insurgé* (Paris: Editions du Méridien, 1948). p. 14.

W. D. Redfern (essay date 1976)

SOURCE: "Vallès and the Existential Pun," in *Mosaic,* Vol. IX, No. 3, Spring, 1976, pp. 27-39.

[In the following essay, Redfern examines Vallès's use of wordplay, proposing that for Vallès the pun demonstrates both the power and the inadequacy of words. Moreover, Redfern suggests, Vallès's linguistic playfulness lends a sense of freedom and vitality to his work.]

Adām (man) was created out of *adamāh* (earth); and we know about Peter. In the beginning was the pun, in this case a simply divine pun. Cultural historians tell us that play with words (insult-competitions, lying tournaments, *joutes de jactance*) is one of the most beloved practices of human beings the world over and throughout recorded time. Why, then, has it become commonplace to apologise for punning?

In both journalism and novel-writing, Vallès brought his inborn love of playing with language to bear on often serious matters. He put play to work; he made play work. Huizinga says in *Homo Ludens:* "You can deny, if you like, nearly all abstractions: justice, beauty, truth, goodness, mind, God. You can deny seriousness, but not play."[1] This article on wordplay is a rough draft. In three senses: it is a first shot; it may taste like academic moonshine; but, in intention, it lets some fresh air in.

The fact that Vallès has only recently begun to receive the kind of attention he deserves stems mainly from three factors: his connexions with journalism, which disqualify him in some eyes from serious interest; his involvement in the Paris Commune, which, for some people, almost debars him from the status of human being; and the difficulty of pigeonholing him (though, as Valéry said, nobody gets drunk on the labels of wine-bottles). Vallès is a limbo writer, in this respect at least rather like Steinbeck in America.

In present day journalism, the emphasis on "house-style," on "re-writing," militates against militancy, or even individualism. In Vallès' own day, the Goncourts, forever warning of cultural take-over bids, were saying in 1867: "Ce temps c'est le commencement de l'écrasement du livre par le journal, de l'homme de lettres par le journaliste de lettres." The authoritarian nature of the Second Empire's press laws provoked by reaction in much of the press irony and allusiveness. Not that Vallès, who had a genius for gaffes and for blatancy, was all that keen on "cette guerre d'allusions voilées." He saw himself, in the polemical life of his day, more as a filibuster than as a smuggler.

Historians of the nineteenth-century press point to the prevalence of wordplay in the Second Empire period (e.g. Louis Veuillot's description of self-prostituting newspapers as "des feuilles de joie"). Journalism can indeed be seen, like the pun itself, as an in-between phenomenon, an intermediate zone between speech (especially political speech) and literature. Similarly, Vallès himself often seems stranded between the classical rhetoric dunned into him at school and the free-wheeling prose he spasmodically achieved. His way out of this tight corner was derision, deflation. He carried over into his fictional writings the telegraphic structures of journalistic prose: the use of shock-tactics (headlines, isolated and emphasised phrases), the punchy short sentences, the bloating of often minor details, the urge to make drama out of the humdrum, best summed up by the expression *faire tableau.*

Just as Flaubert, whose passion for puns was, according to Sartre, no mean training-ground for literary creation, maintained that "l'ironie n'enlève rien au pathétique: elle l'outre, au contraire," so Vallès believed that "le calembour n'empêche pas les convictions." As his Jacques Vingtras says of himself and his young fellow-rebels that they were not demagogues all the time: "On est un peu *farce* aussi; et après le tocsin de quatre-vingt-treize, c'est le carillon de nos dix-huit ans que nous sonnons à toute volée!" Before getting involved in matters of definition ("Naming the parts does not show us what makes a gun go off"),[2] I want to stress the very strong element in Vallès' work of wordplay simply as verbal pantomime, acting the goat. **Le Bachelier,** for instance, is full of students' larks, ritual games, verbal jousts. Everywhere, almost by reflex-action, Vallès knocks *l'esprit de sérieux.* (After being deserted by a woman, Jacques says: "Je suis resté sept nuits à m'arracher les cheveux; heureusement j'en ai beaucoup." In this hostility to gravity, words in Vallès often seem to take on a comic life of their own, performing somersaults, and sometimes coming a cropper, for Vallès, obsessed as he was with the phenomenon of accident-proneness, never even hopes for perfection. He is that rare bird, a militant with an unkillable sense of humour, directed at his own follies as well as at those of other people.

In *The Merchant of Venice,* Lorenzo exclaims: "How every fool can play upon the word!" Like other forms of language often looked down upon—slang, obscenities, incorrect grammar or pronunciation—wordplay frequently gets a bad press. The genealogy of the word *pun* is dubious, which is perhaps fitting for this stylistic offspring which some consider illegitimate (e.g. Lanson: "Le calembour est la forme la plus basse du sentiment des sonorités verbales: voilà pourquoi il lui arrive de rapprocher les grands artistes et les grands imbéciles"). The word *punster* usually denotes a pretty low form of life, like other words with the same ending: poetaster, monster, Westminster. Dr. Johnson thought that puns, or "quibbles," were not quite manly. For Hugo, the pun is "the guano of the wingèd mind." It is unclear whether Hugo was here pooh-poohing a bodily function or eulogising a fertiliser. (Beckett described his own work as a matter of fundamental sounds.)[3] This century many writers, like their Metaphysical ancestors, have used the pun (which Claude-Edmonde Magny calls "cette rime dévergondée" and Jean Ricardou a paroxystic form of rhyme, which likewise clinches a point) to create a kind of bifocal vision or squint, a deliberate ambivalence. Arthur Koestler points out that "association by sound-affinity—punning—is one of the notorious games of the underground, manifested in dreams, in the punning mania of children, and in mental disorders."[4] And indeed reiterated wordplay can veer close to idiocy. Most people have surely experienced the phenomenon whereby under stress the mind catches wildly at jingling words, in a desperate attempt to forestall or to lower the tension. Everyone puns, then, if only unconsciously. The pun has no doubt been partly reinstated nowadays, but it scarcely possesses as yet its *lettres de noblesse* (and as such it is a suitable vehicle for the rogue socialist Vallès).

People often apologise for committing puns which, traditionally, make listeners squirm, wince or grimace (as we also do of course when we witness a physical collision, a painful conjunction, about to take place). We talk of "atrocious" or "excruciating" puns. (Cf. the ambition expressed by Raymond Queneau: "Elever le calembour à la hauteur d'un supplice.")[5] It sounds as if punsters, those linguistic torturers, go in for *Schadenfreude*. And all teachers know the links between sadism and pedagogy: the urge to teach others a lesson. Punning is the art of overlaying and therefore of stressing and driving home: a didactic and a rhetorical device. It is characterised by incision. It is a cutting edge. Clearly, however, without the active participation of the listener or reader, the pun falls flat, for the *point* has to be taken (one suggested derivation is from the Italian word *punto*). Puns can be biting, or toothless. Large-scale punning can lead either to trivialisation or to the weird monumentalisation represented by *Finnegans Wake*. The pun can be the stock-in-trade of the low comedian, or of the most sophisticated humourist. It is a democratic trope, common property.

Moreover, it finds common ground between previously dissimilar objects or ideas. As such it is an acoustic metaphor. Like metaphors, it incites us to think on more than one level simultaneously (or at least with only a slight lag: the time needed to *twig* it). Double-think couched in double-talk. Both puns and metaphors in this way offer an escape from purely linear meaning. Durkheim called this a logical scandal. We might add, less pompously, that it is language on holiday. It can make us broaden our minds or double our attention. John Gross terms these two operations *fission* and *fusion*.

It could be that the sometimes guilty pleasure we derive from wordplay is due to a kind of pun itself: the idea that twists on words are connected in some way with ethical twisting or perversion. As a result, the punster simultaneously begs for a pat on the back and dreads a punch on the nose. Hence the defiance in his apologetic stance, the mixture of warding off and brazen summoning. As for the receiver (who like the receiver, or fence, of stolen goods, is in a fishy position), often he utters nervous laughter, uncertain whether or not to go for the obscene or dangerous meaning, and afraid of being thought dense or prudish. If he laughs,

he becomes an accomplice in the assault on a taboo. If a common response, then, to a pun is a sickly grin, the deliverer, for his part, often either leers or enunciates slowly, idiot-fashion, to underline the intended meaning.

A fertile terrain for wordplay is that provided by idioms, proverbial sayings, slogans, clichés, all of which congealed forms of language can be twisted or forced into new contexts, so as to rejuvenate them by giving them a maximum meaning (e.g. playing on the literal and the metaphorical senses of the same word. Vallès describes thus a youthful gathering: "Les oiseaux qui battent la vitre, nos coeurs qui battent la campagne," or "on taille un jambonneau et une bavette"). Zeugmas like these have been termed by Philippe Sollers "semantic kidnapping" and by Jean Ricardou "semantic cohabitation." This recycling is a highly useful act of linguistic ecology. The pun saves space and labour and conserves energy: it is a device of economy.

Wordplay is not a privilege of adults alone for, as Koestler points out, puns, like rhyme or assonance, are deeply rooted "in primitive and infantile forms of thought and utterance, in which sound and meaning are magically interwoven."[6] Indeed, we have only to listen to young children to acknowledge that they play with words, in the process of mastering them. They fondle and fool around with words; they dislocate and reassemble them, like their toys. A psychological study of children's humour argues that playing with proper names is an important prelude. The next stage of the process is a progression from playing with other people's meanings to presenting double-meanings oneself. "The change of another person's meaning has the underlying implication: You are not what you think you are. Similarly the transformation of one's own meaning suggests: I am not what you think I am. This also has initially an unsettling effect." The author goes on to use the Freudian concept of the "joke-façade," "which gets the sexual or hostile theme past inner and outer censorship."[7] This alternation between concealing and revealing ("Now you see it, now you don't") is clearly a major part of jokes. The other characteristic is the love of bringing together the high and the low (as in the advertisement for a certain toilet-paper which claimed it was "Tops for bottoms"). A further view of children's wordplay occurs in Molly Mahood's book on Shakespeare, where she supports "Freud's contention that punning releases a desire to talk nonsense which was suppressed in the nursery." Perhaps the Victorians were ashamed of puns because they had received an ultra-rational education from the English Rousseauists who tried to "inculcate the principles of Reason and Morality" at a tender age. Puns let us be unprincipled about both reason and morality.[8] I would myself say that the dislike, the fear sometimes, of wordplay tells us a lot, as do attitudes towards the human body, about the puritanical response to language of many people. Bodies and play go together (as do bodies and pain, suffering and play).

Perhaps most of all, wordplay, like other kinds of play, acts as a releasing agent. If not always born of freedom, wordplay can beget or betoken freedom (though we should note Lessing's sober reminder: "Not all are free who mock their chains")[9] If we think of the words *jeu* and *jouer,* we see that the several meanings: to play, to act, to gamble, to be slack, all contain the basic idea of room for manoeuvre, the possibility of modification. The key movement of puns is pivotal. The second meaning of a word or phrase rotates around the first one, or branches off from it. Puns are switch-words, like pointsmen at a junction. Koestler talks of "the displacement of attention, shift of emphasis, from a dominant to a previously neglected aspect of the whole, showing it in a new light."[10] He sees this as central to the whole process of creation. A pun says "Eureka!" ("You don't smella so good yourself," as Chico Marx replied).

Wordplay suddenly unmasks the hidden resources of language, and thus of the human spirit, its dynamic potential. It is a latent resource of language that can be tapped, and some temperaments simply will not resist wanting to mine and exploit this rich ore. It is a bonus. In case all this seems to favour mere self-indulgence, it is clear that a punster always works within limits. He cannot invent puns which are not already potential in his language. He merely unearths (dusts off sometimes) these hidden treasures. In one way an uncovering, in another the pun is a cover-up job, for the punster can usually take refuge, like the ironist, behind the pretence that he did not intend the other meaning of the *double-entendre,* just as the ironist can protest that he was speaking literally. It seems likely that wordplay suits temperaments which are neither preponderantly direct nor esoteric; its realm is that of the sly, the oblique, the tease.

L'Enfant

Puns, then, are often thought of as assaults on the listeners' sensibility. They can arise from a response to experience which, in Vallès' case, was frequently painful. He describes himself as "grinçant des dents quand des souvenirs d'humiliation [lui] grattaient la chair sur les os." By reaction, he twists words about, hoping to promote *le rire,* but usually *le rire, jaune.* In his articles on Dickens, whom he valued very highly, he stressed the importance of *contrast:* "La comédie de la souffrance, . . . c'est de l'antithèse que l'originalité jaillit." Vallès' mania for comparing—Then and Now, Here and There (e.g. town and country), Them and Us—springs from his instinct to think analogically rather than logically, from his admitted soft spot for nostalgia, and from his egalitarian impulse to contrast

the lot in life of different social classes. Forced comparisons are part of his general strategy of attack.

Now, literary exiles are often fond of puns (Nabokov, Beckett, Ionesco), perhaps because men can never take altogether seriously a language acquired second; because they then see the language from the outside: its mechanisms, its inertia; and because an exile, having two homes and languages, has a binary perspective. Even before his enforced transfer to England after the Commune, Vallès was always something of a resident alien within his homeland. His young hero, Jacques, feels estranged from his fellows, in *L'Enfant,* by reason of the outrageous clothes his mother foists on him: "Il m'est donné, au sein même de ma ville natale, à douze ans, de connaître, isolé dans ce pantalon, les douleurs sourdes de l'exil." One of the most recurrent uses of comic hyperbole in Vallès' work centres on the series of sartorial farces his hero endures, for he suffers greatly from the conjunction of his proud self and grotesque clothes. The grotesque is often said to be a way of seeing life as tragi-comic, in an unresolved tension or oscillation. Thus Jacques' mother often accuses him of being a monster (of ingratitude). Vallès'

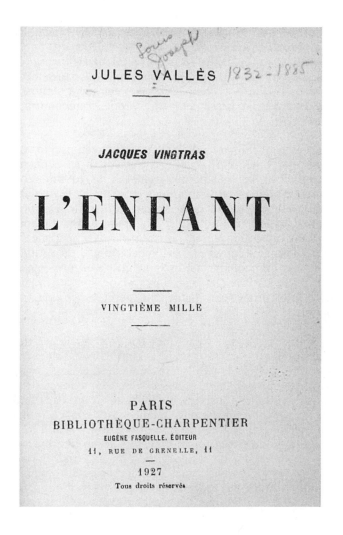

JULES VALLÈS

JACQUES VINGTRAS

L'ENFANT

VINGTIÈME MILLE

PARIS
BIBLIOTHÈQUE-CHARPENTIER
EUGÈNE FASQUELLE, ÉDITEUR
11, RUE DE GRENELLE, 11
1927
Tous droits réservés

descriptions turn Jacques at times into a *monstre,* a fairground freak. His makeshift apparel is always an obstacle to unaffected living, just as the periodic changes of abode by his family land him frequently in the street half buried beneath goods and chattels. With the most deathly serious intentions, his parents and he are forever providing onlookers with a free vaudeville knockabout routine. These clumsy displays occur at home, too, as when, in a scene of loaded tension after a row, Jacques accidentally breaks a glass picture-frame. He displaces the tension in a typical pun: "Je suis bien content tout de même d'avoir dérangé ce silence, *cassé la glace.*"

Mother and son, always at war, at least have one thing in common: a compulsion to exaggerate. Whether she is nagging, beating Jacques, or making him ludicrous clothes, she always goes too far, piles it on thick. If wordplay can be a device of economy, it can also be an excuse for expenditure. (And Vallès, with his interest in budgets, the price we have to pay for what we want, scans both sides of the balance-sheet.) Strangely, Vallès is both short-winded and prolix. Perhaps the prolixity comes from neurotic over-emphasis. He underlines his puns by italicising them—the equivalent of the music-hall comic's wink to the audience. As the French has it, *il abat son jeu.* It may well be, of course, a narrowly Anglo-Saxon objection to talk of exaggeration, or pretentiousness. Aristotle, for one, held that hyperbole was also a form of metaphor, presumably because it also enhances the object to which it is applied. It is possible that much of the inflation at work in Vallès' trilogy springs simply from his above-average epidermic sensitivity. He often talks of sights, smells, noises as *irritating* his senses (and he cherishes them for that very reason). His inflating propensity is counterbalanced, anyway, by constant deflationary tactics. When a fatuous schoolteacher eulogises Racine, saying: "Il ne reste plus qu'à fermer les autres livres," Jacques' practical response is to mutter: "Je ne demande pas mieux." When the teacher goes on: "Et à s'avouer impuissant." Jacques chimes in with: "C'est son affaire." This kind of knowing literal-mindedness is also a variety of punning, as when Jacques is concocting for material gain Greek and Latin verses with mechanical expertise: "La *qualité* n'est rien, c'est la *quantité* qui est tout." Another variety is the twisted idiom. After a duel in which Jacques is surprised to find himself emotionless, despite having been wounded in the thigh, he comments: "Ça ne me faisait pas plus qu'un cautère sur une jambe de bois." To describe a wound, he uses a term normally employed to denote a remedy, albeit a useless one. It is a picturesque way of dramatising a non-event.

On the whole, the rather smaller amount of wordplay in *L'Enfant,* in comparison with *Le Bachelier,* is perhaps explained by Vallès' effort to present the tale through the eyes (and skin) of the brutalised child, though at times he intrudes the grown man's indignation. There is not much space for joyful word-use in such a killjoy home, where lessons, verbal or physical, are repeatedly dinned into the boy. All the same, whenever Jacques does escape his pedantic schoolmaster father to play with a cobbler's children, he notes that these phonetically slap happy kids "parlaient avec des velours et des cuirs . . . C'est le métier qui veut ça." As Jacques himself is unfailingly drawn towards improper liaisons of various kinds, his remark is more envious than critical. Whenever he gets a minute on his own, he instinctively *plays* with experience (e.g. the scene where he describes looking at his grandmother's colourful curtains with his head between his legs). Vallès loves upturning received impressions and, like his reversed hero here, often achieves an apoplectic vision of things.

In *Le Bachelier,* setting out for Paris on a stage-coach, Jacques progresses rapidly from hoping that he is free at last from teachers and parents to wondering whether that other sort of policeman will be on the coach. When he spots a gendarme next to the driver, he swiftly minimises his own fears by ridiculing the man's uniform, with its leather straps "couleur d'omelette, des épaulettes en fromage." Keyed up by his own daring, Jacques then recalls in a rapidly escalating paroxysm an incident from *L'Enfant,* where a whole village violently resisted an attack by the gendarmerie. Deliriously, he maintains it is honourable to be executed for such behaviour, whereas it is thought ignominious to resist a father's aggression by knocking him aside. The circle, rather tortuously, is closed, from father back to father. The telescoped emotions of this sequence depend on a heavy load of past fears and apprehensions of what the future has in store. Play, here, has taken the anxious form of proliferating associations of tense images.

Le Bachelier

In *Le Bachelier,* Jacques, who at one point in his picaresque existence makes both ends meet by collecting puns for a publisher of cheapjack anthologies, tastes the mixed blessings of independence. Significantly, the dedication of this volume is composed of a play on words about Greek and Latin *roots,* and the impossibility of living off paper qualifications in them. Two levels are juxtaposed and will remain so throughout: learning and feeding, mental and physical nourishment or malnutrition. Vallès, who was more bolshy than Bolshevik, spent his life caught in the crossfire between conservative Right and authoritarian Left. Not surprisingly, he makes his young hero an in-between. Jacques' position is permanently suspended, mid-way. Just as the pun straddles two ideas with one sound, so Jacques hovers between cowardice and courage, adolescence and manhood, bourgeois students and manual workers. His dodgy financial state is typified by his "bridging-meal," half lunch and half dinner. Even while hating his parents, he feels bonded to them because they too are trapped in a nether region: their lifestyle is a bastard mixture of upstart peasant and ill-adapted petit bourgeois. Son and parents are displaced beings. Small wonder, then, that Jacques sees life as if it were an excruciating pun, a criss-cross he has to bear, with a grin.

But poverty breeds invention. Jacques' artifice of self-preservation relies on dodges like waving his tasteless crust of bread in the odour of frying fish from a neighbour's flat. In this state of deprivation, exaggeration runs riot (and Jacques as an embryonic militant is always on the look-out for riots which he can whip up). There is a marvellous section of sustained hyperbole concerning a minuscule garret, a room so tiny that even the fleas are crowded out. This swelling of the minimal is more than a passing joke; it has a real point, for the maladroit individualist Jacques can himself never *fit in* anywhere. Vallès' humour underlines more often than it undermines the true painfulness of Jacques' experiences. In addition, it often serves as self-protection: "Je couvrirai éternellement mes émotions intimes du masque de l'insouciance et de la perruque de l'ironie." Whistling in the dark to boost his morale. For instance, some young rebels, as they stand under bucketing rain, are asked whether they are fit for action (*trempés*). The wry answer can only be: yes.

The wordplay also acts as a release from a life of constant restriction: "J'ai toujours étouffé dans des habits trop étroits et faits pour d'autres, ou dans des traditions qui me révoltaient ou m'accablaient." Characteristically, he mingles ideological and sartorial oppression in a kind of running pun. When jumping stiffly downstairs feet together, in agonising discomfort, because so many sharp pins hold his begged and borrowed suit together, he can still make a joke about *la raideur anglaise* (which he attributes elsewhere to the British having swallowed whole the flagpole of the Union Jack). His very clothes, like puns, condense two meanings: his gigantic greatcoat is both a present encumbrance and a cherished relic from home.

Just as wardrobe fiasco dogs all his attempts at advancement, so his stylistic demon is the classical rhetoric drummed into him at school ("Ma tête avec ce qu'il y a dedans: thèmes, versions, discours, empilés comme du linge sale dans un panier!"). From readings in sober histories of French nineteenth century education, it is clear that Vallès was, in essentials, hardly exaggerating in this area of scholarly indoctrination. Jacques' head is a rag-bag of examination quotes, of miscellaneous and largely unusable culture. But he sports with his classical impedimenta, making it serve the purposes of comedy, of retaliation, and occasionally even of winning him a short-lived livelihood. Not that he

unfailingly makes capital out of his defects. A recurrent ambivalence in *Le Bachelier* is whether Jacques is in control of his hyperbole, or whether at times he stupidly allows himself to get bogged down in drawn-out petty details (e.g. a couple of pages on the fiddling business of coping with a decrepit hat, whose unpredictable movements on his head keep wrecking his concentration). On the other side, Jacques' readiness to go the whole hog with his wordplay, to risk extensions, to avoid apologising for them, can pay off with some excellent results (e.g. a few pages where his friend Matoussaint gets a job writing the biography of a philanthropist who used to distribute soup to the poor: "Sa famille veut élever une statue, elle a pensé qu'un livre, où seraient les anas de sa bonté, aiderait à consolider la gloire du défunt, que sa renommée tiendrait là-dedans comme une cuiller dans une soupe d'auvergnat, et c'est Matoussaint qui a été chargé de tremper le bol. Il s'en acquitte, consciencieusement, écumant les bonnes actions, les traits de charité qui surnagent dans la vie du défunt, comme des yeux sur un bouillon"). Matoussaint is paid in kind with copious soup, and grows portly: "Il est entré dans le pot du bonhomme" (a play on the theatrical term: "entrer dans la peau du bonhomme"). The climax of the episode is Matoussaint's unspecified pollution of the family soup—an ending which deflates the already mock-heroic pretensions of the prolonged wordplay.

Jacques is fully capable of self-mockery, too, as in this mixed metaphor, or Irish bull: "Ainsi finissent souvent ceux qui brûlent leurs vaisseaux devant le foyer paternel pour se lancer sur l'océan de la vie d'orages! Que j'en ai vu trébucher, parce qu'ils avaient voulu sauter à pieds joints par-dessus leur coeur." Vallès often jams on certain phrases, like a needle stuck in a faulty groove. His fondness for wordplay reveals a mind addicted to repetition more than to true concentration. He is a stylistic recidivist. A further example of his tactic of piling it on thick: Jacques is invited by the unscrupulous editor of a sentimental magazine to compose a pathetic tale about a hydrocephalous child, and is promised that, if it promotes sales, he could become "une grosse tête de la maison." We talk of "thumping" puns, and *to pun* also means to hammer home. *Le Canard enchaîné,* which appropriately honours Vallès amongst its favourite forebears, also practises this tactic of "le calembour-massue" (or "le calembourrage de crâne").

L'Insurgé

As *L'Insurgé* builds up steam, the jottings of events grow too hectic to allow for wordplay on the scale of the more leisurely *Le Bachelier.* Of course, ideologically opposed critics tend to see Jacques Vingtras' whole involvement in the Paris Commune as just playing-about (e.g. Bernard de Fallois' view that the Commune was to Jacques, as to Vallès, merely a classroom *chahut* on a larger scale).[11] It is true that in *L'Insurgé* Jacques refers to himself as "un écolier aux moustaches grisonnantes." But if it is a game, the rules keep changing at a frenzied pace, and the insurgents gradually find themselves enmeshed in another kind of deadly game, the *Kriegspiel* conducted by Bismarck and the Versailles Government. Jacques does not, for all that, conclude that "le jeu ne vaut pas la chandelle," for even in defeat he is immensely grateful for the experience he has lived through. And, even in its gravest moments, *L'Insurgé* rarely misses a chance for a usually pointed piece of wordplay. For example, when the patriotic crowd, which just before had been clamouring for bloodshed on a national scale, sees Jacques in the process of having a nosebleed, it sheers away and reprimands him for frightening babies—who are, incidentally, sitting in their prams all strapped up like *zouaves*. Vallès cultivated such excruciating juxtapositions because he felt they might appeal to the common reader ("Le peuple aime la grimace burlesque et hardie"). In his hands, this sometimes takes the form of an inverted preciosity which attempts to turn the tables for *different* sentimental reasons on a stock image or idea. After stating that doves are usually associated with voluptuousness, he takes pride in describing a scruffy dove which visits a poverty-stricken neighbour, pecking on her squalid windowpane for a few scraps of rancid bread.

His taste for the concrete leads him repeatedly to join the moral and the physical, as when an editor congratulates the starving Jacques on a hard-hitting article he has just submitted: "Cristi! vous avez de l'estomac." Jacques ponders: "Beaucoup trop! Je m'en suis aperçu souvent: les jours de jeûne surtout." Though inordinately fond of figurative speech himself, he frequently punctures the verbal balloons of others, especially if they are inflated for unthinking ideological purposes. When Jacques hears a demagogue spouting slogans about their ancestors in the 1789 Revolution ("Nos pères, ces géants"), he reacts by pointing out that his own grandfather was nicknamed "Short-arse" in his village. This capacity for undeceivedness helps him to spot that Gambetta has a very convenient illness whenever a crisis blows up: "Cette ficelle (this alibi) ne me va pas, je devine le pantin au bout." Lastly, in these desperate circumstances, Jacques often uses wordplay as a stoical joke, a Parthian shot, a radical cheek, as in gallows-humour. Waiting to be liquidated by Government troops, Jacques and some surviving Communards decide to spend their probably last moments getting drunk: "On peut bien boire le coup de l'étrier, avant de recevoir le coup du lapin." He is never averse to administering such self-corrections. As Vallès said elsewhere: "Nous paraissons des gamins souvent, à crier ainsi contre le vent, et à envoyer des chiquenaudes au nez des avalanches." Throughout the trilogy, life is seen as a series of only partly resolved contradictions. Jacques is forever on the brink of throwing in the towel, yet finding somewhere the will to come back for more.

Of the Trilogy, it is *Le Bachelier* which contains most wordplay. Perhaps this is only to be expected. Adolescence is supposed to be the age of sowing your wild oats. The young child was too severely hemmed in by his gaoler-parents, and the grown man too caught up in frantic public events for them to have as much time as the suspended *bachelier* for verbal antics.

If the pun is a crucial point at which two levels coincide, most, if not all, of Vallès' wordplay hits its target (e.g. a teacher bids farewell to Jacques on the eve of his *career*. Jacques instantly and in panic thinks back to another *bachelier* he has heard of, who, unable to find work, committed suicide by leaping into a stone-quarry (*carrière*); or the account of a teacher's effort to cram Latin into Jacques: "C'était comme un cautère sur une tête de bois," where the ideas of wasted energy and block-headed obstinacy are conjoined in a variation on a set expression). Even when prolix, Vallès is generally a pointed writer: "La blague ayant toujours sa cible sérieuse" (I am reminded of Balzac's reference to "des mots à double entente ou à double détente"). Although it might appear at times as if Vallès were only a linguistic playboy, in fact both he and his hero are extremely sensitive to the weight and import of words. Jacques frequently claims that his father's verbal onslaughts pained him more than did the physical beatings. Besides, in a heavily censored society like that of Vallès, the uses of literacy acquire even more urgent importance.

It is useless denying that on occasion Vallès' sensitivity lacks taste, proportion and control. Vallès, whose life-story is a string of near-misses (either triumphant or catastrophic), culminating in a considerably impaired survival, is an *approximate* writer, a man of lunges, who often loses on the roundabouts what he gains on the swings, and who often therefore flails about in some confusion. His ideas are sometimes commonplace, not to say corny (though, as Camus once said: "On appelle vérités premières celles qu'on découvre après toutes les autres"). We might, snobbishly, call this the "popular" side of his temperament. He is "un homme du peuple" (like all of us) in that he relies too much on instincts which are under-informed and half-baked. Vallès himself recognised that his style, like his head, was a ragbag: "J'ai fait mon style de pièces et de morceaux que l'on dirait ramassés, à coups de crochet, dans des coins malpropres et navrants." Similarly, the style of his public harangues he describes as composed of "quatre ou cinq effets criards comme des images d'Épinal." There is indeed a clear sentimental streak in Vallès, a love of the painfully obvious, instantly recognizable symbol or collocation ("Je ne voyais pas éclore mon avenir, mais je voyais pourrir mes fleurs"). He loves opposing primary colours: white/red, red/black. Wordplay can easily mince over into conceit, can be likewise far-fetched (e.g. describing a restaurant which has reneged on its former clientele of revolutionary paupers: "Cette maison, où l'on cassait la *coquille* aux préjugés, a pris pour emblème: A la renommée des *escargots*"). It could however be argued that his common melodramatising tendency derives from his very nerve, his relish in his own effects. The repetitions and emphases are usually more wilful than careless, and are designed either to demolish a hated idea by reiterated exposure, or to enhance it by heroic expansion. When he jams on certain expressions, as though afflicted by a stammer or hiccups, it is either because he is choking with barely contained anger or excitement, or simply because he is intoxicated by the exuberance of his own verbosity. Some of his harangues are undoubtedly pickled. He was the most metaphorical of men, yet his aim was plain speaking. Not that direct appeals rule out figurative speech, Christ knows. Besides his stress on verbalisation, on striking rhetorical postures, is tempered by recognition of those situations where words are either too much or not enough (e.g. in family crises), and by a great love of *physical* expenditure: e.g. boxing, in the old French style, *savate*. His hero fluctuates between the twin poles described by the terms *crâner* and *caner:* brazening it out and caving in. "Il me fallait toucher ou essayer de toucher le danger, avoir une cible à atteindre et des coups à redouter." This tit-for-tat is part of what Vallès meant by *la vie d'échange,* though this term also included less aggressive, more companionable and loving elements.

Like a boxer, a fairground barker or a music-hall comedian, Vallès' delivery is staccato. He tries to buttonhole, to pin down the listener or bystander. In his *Beyond the Pleasure Principle,* Freud links the compulsive repetition practised by children with the desire for mastery. He also notes that "as a child passes over from the passivity of the experience to the activity of the game, he hands on the disagreeable experience to one of his playmates and in this way revenges himself on a substitute." He compares this operation, in turn, with artistic play.[12] I stressed earlier Vallès' pedagogic urge to teach his readers a lesson, as a compensation perhaps for all the mind-stuffing he suffered as a child. Such a tactic of displacement, and the disconcerting shifts of emphasis, the lurching, sidestepping progress of his narratives, again recall the manoeuvres of *savate.* But the pun is brain as well as flesh: sleight of mind, cerebral legerdemain (James Joyce called *Finnegans Wake* "the hoax that jokes bilked"). The pun is essentially an anti-pariparxis. It is sure-footed even when straddling different sounds and concepts. Perhaps, just as we talk of controlled skids, we should speak of controlled slips of the pen or tongue.

The critic Claude Roy had in mind Sainte-Beuve and Renan when, infected no doubt by Vallès' punning mania, he compared the alacrity of Vallès' language with the rather pot-bellied gait of those contemporaries: "Le style Second Empire est prodigieusement rond: ronds d'huile, ronds de jambe, ronrons."[13] Another critic,

Albalat, surely hits the mark when he notes that "le style de Vallès vous prend parce qu'il saute aux yeux," and that it has "une sincérité sensationnelle" (i.e. it is a faithful rendering of what his nerve-ends registered). I am reminded of Montaigne's recipe: "Un parler succulent et hardi, tel sur le papier qu'à la bouche, non point tant délicat et peigné comme véhément et brusque." Wordplay, for Vallès, was a matter of internally coherent necessity. As Sartre said, "Une technique romanesque renvoie toujours à la métaphysique du romancier," though I suspect that whenever he heard the word *metaphysics,* Vallès always reached for his revolver.

Vallès was almost alone amongst writers of his day in sympathising with and joining in the Commune. He had none of that racialist fear of the common man which disfigures to no small degree the work of Flaubert or the Goncourts. The new intellectual proletariat represented by Vallès was, besides, as distasteful to Establishment writers as were the working-classes themselves. The Goncourts, who failed to see the importance of irreverence for social and personal hygiene, often wrote like shrill Bowdlers: "La *Blague* du XIXe siècle, cette grande démolisseuse . . . l'empoisonneuse de foi (possibly a pun itself, given the French un-Promethean obsession with livers), la tueuse de respect; la Blague avec son souffle canaille et sa risée salissante jetée à tout ce qui est honneur, amour, famille, le drapeau." *L'écriture artiste* was quite alien to Vallès, that fan of *savate,* and arguably the best middleweight in French literature.

We have taken over from the French the word *aplomb.* I often wish we would borrow its opposite, *de guinguois,* as it would fit the awkward customer Vallès to a T. "I like the deguinguois of this man." In the nineteenth century, he stands out like an honest sore thumb. Where the language of others is often pedestrian, his is jaywalker. I believe it is his very readiness to play with words, to take risks with different registers, often by flinging them together pellmell, that gives his work that self-igniting vitality, that bitty and variable lifelikeness which, to me, it so palpably possesses.

Finally, why defend wordplay? Play is indefensible. It simply is. Perhaps nothing else simply is quite so exquisitely and wholeheartedly as play. I offer no defence, therefore, for championing, and at times trying to emulate, one playboy of the Western word.

Notes

[1] London, 1949, p. 3. The footnotes in this essay are selective, to avoid needless detail. References to Vallès' works are mainly to the trilogy of Jacques Vingtras, available now in several different editions.

[2] Molly Mahood, *Shakespeare's Wordplay* (London, 1957), p. 19.

³ Quoted in John Fletcher, *The Novels of Samuel Beckett* (London, 1964), p. 227.

⁴ *The Act of Creation* (London, 1964), p. 314.

⁵ *Les Oeuvres complètes de Sally Mara* (Paris, 1962), p. 349.

⁶ *op. cit.,* p. 315.

⁷ Martha Wolfenstein, *Children's Humor* (Glencoe, 1954), pp. 79, 81, 159.

⁸ *op. cit.,* p. 30.

⁹ *Nathan der Weise,* IV, 4.

¹⁰ *op. cit.,* p. 77.

¹¹ "La Malchance de Vallès," *La Revue de Paris,* January 1955, pp. 112-18.

¹² London, 1955, p. 17.

¹³ *Le Commerce des classiques* (Paris, 1953), p. 252.

I. H. Birchall (essay date 1981)

SOURCE: "Jules Vallès: Education and the Novel," in *Gedenkschrift for Victor Poznanski,* edited by C. A. M. Noble, Peter Lang, 1981, pp. 129-46.

[*In the following essay, Birchall considers Vallès's trilogy* Jacques Vingtras *in relation to the German literary tradition of the* bildungsroman, *or educational novel. Birchall suggests that Vallès reworks the traditional* bildungsroman *by yoking together individual growth and social tranformation.*]

Novels, wrote Dr. Johnson, 'are written chiefly for the young, the ignorant, and the idle, to whom they serve as lectures of conduct and introductions into life.'¹ The connection between education and the novel can be traced back over more than two centuries. The emergence of the novel as a major literary *genre,* and the development of modern educational theory are contemporaneous processes in European thought, and can be located in common sources: the problematic relation of individual and society, and the greater weight given to environment in the formation of the individual human being. Rousseau's *Emile,* a founding text of educational thought, is written as a novel.

It is in German literature that the notion of an educational novel, the so-called *Bildungsroman,* receives its fullest development. The most notable examples are Goethe's *Wilhelm Meisters Lehrjahre* and *Wilhelm Meisters Wanderjahre,* where the educational process is seen as leading to a mature renunciation and acceptance of reality; the latter volume is subtitled *Die Entsagenden.*

In the nineteenth century there are innumerable examples of novels where the educational process is a key structuring element. It will suffice to mention a few names directly connected with the subject of this essay: Dickens *(David Copperfield, Hard Times, Nicholas Nickleby),* Flaubert *(L'Education Sentimentale, Bouvard et Pécuchet),* Daudet *(Jack, Le Petit Chose).*

In his highly influential work *Die Theorie des Romans* (1916), Georg Lukács argues that the novel of education is one of the fundamental types of the novel form; and moreover he sees it as often merging with another of the fundamental types, the Romantic novel of disillusion.

The work of Jules Vallès, and in particular his major fictional work, the **Jacques Vingtras** trilogy (1879-1886) stands in a problematic relation to this tradition. Education, from the point of view both of the maturation of an individual child and of the role of educational institutions in society, are recurrent and essential themes in his work. But nothing could be more alien to the *communard* Vallès than the Goethean ideal of renunciation. The **Vingtras** trilogy is, in a sense, a *Bildungsroman,* but one in which not only the transformation of an individual, but also the radical transformation of society, is posed as a central problem. This essay will seek to make some tentative observations about Vallès' use of the novel form, and to look for some explanations in his political evolution.

For Vallès, the novel form is linked to individualism. But for Vallès, individualism is posed in an essentially combative manner. In an article written in 1864, many years before he began work on the trilogy, he asserted:

> Et dans le domaine du livre, quelle place le roman a tenue, et quelle place il est destiné à tenir! On a beau crier, beau faire, signer la paix, la guerre, suivre des drapeaux ou pousser des chars; à côté de la vie publique, il y a la vie du coeur, l'homme derrière le citoyen, la personne au sein de la foule. Qui donc peindra cette existence du soir, si je puis dire, ces hasards et ces mystères? C'est au roman qu'il appartient de poursuivre cette étude de la vie intérieure, des dessous du monde et des secrets de l'âme. Il est, par ce temps d'enrégimentation féroce, comme un asile où l'homme s'est réfugié. Les coteries et les partis, la littérature militante et la politique retiennent dans des casernes ou dans des camps des citoyens, des fidèles ou des soldats: seul ou presque seul, le roman ouvre à l'individu un théâtre et un champ de bataille.²

In short, revolt is an essential constituent of the novel. Vallès has no undue respect for conventional literary

taste, and he deals harshly with those of his contemporaries whom he believes to have suppressed the factor of revolt. Daudet's *Le Petit Chose,* for example, sentimentalises childhood in a way that Vallès cannot accept: it is 'indigne' of its author, 'un conte plutôt qu'une vie d'enfant'.[3] Dickens, however, is highly acceptable, albeit that some standard Dickensian themes are given a peculiarly *vallésien* reading:

> Mais il n'est pas besoin, Dieu merci! d'avoir passé par là et d'avoir eu son coeur brisé dans sa poitrine d'enfant, pour être attendri au spectacle de David malheureux, de Smike martyr! Et ils ne sont pas les seuls que Dickens nous présente, humiliés, affamés, battus! Tout le long de l'oeuvre, on voit de pauvres créatures qui grandissent sous le vent de la misère et de la souffrance . . . Ah! maudits soient ces bourreaux lâches qui font venir des rides sur des fronts de dix ans! Maudits soient les pères comme Murdstone et Dieu veuille, pour l'honneur des fils qu'il n'y ait pas de mères comme madame Clennam![4]

To understand the treatment of the theme of education in Vallès' novels, it is necessary to say something of the role of education in nineteenth-century French society. Under both Louis-Philippe and the Second Empire, the educational system was a political battle-ground. In *L'Idiot de la Famille,* Sartre has given a vivid account of the struggle in the schools in the years after 1830, the resort to strike and occupation by the pupils. Yet the rebellious school-students were abandoned by their parents, who had made the revolution in 1830, but did not want to see their children carry on the revolution in permanence:

> La Contre-Révolution: ce qui a frappé de stupeur les mutins de mars, c'est l'accueil qu'ils ont reçu dans leurs familles: ils croyaient se battre pour elles, ils apprennent qu'ils les trahissaient. Les pères indignes se vantent d'être à l'origine du licenciement; sermons, courroux, larmes de mère, sanctions, rien n'est épargné aux enfants durant ces sombres vacances; ils ont tenté d'expliquer leur problème: peut-on tolérer une religion d'Etat au collège? et les géniteurs ont fait la sourde oreille: discipline d'abord, pas de liberté sans un ordre rigoureux et consenti. C'étaient les mêmes pourtant qui, deux ans plus tôt, lisaient du Voltaire à leurs fils et leur chuchotaient en souriant: écrasez l'infâme. Les mêmes qui professaient que la vertu majeure du libéral doit être la tolérance religieuse. Les jeunes garçons n'en croient pas leurs oreilles: les pères ont-ils changé? ou sont-ce les fils qui ont mal compris leur enseignement?[5]

Under Louis-Philippe, when Vallès was at school, there was revolt and creeping conservatism; under the Second Empire, when Vallès began to develop as a writer, there was open repression in the schools. As in so many repressive regimes since, the educational apparatus was used as a means of suppressing dissent and establishing the hegemony of the ruling élite. As a recent historian has put it:

> Désormais, le ministre de l'Instruction publique nomme tous les membres de l'Université depuis les professeurs de faculté jusqu'aux instituteurs, et les révoque sans qu'ils puissent se faire entendre, comme auparavant, par le Conseil supérieur, ce qui permet au ministre Fortoul d'exclure des esprits indociles, tels Victor Cousin, Emile Deschanel, Bersot, Michelet, Quinet, Jules Simon. Les membres du Conseil supérieur ne sont plus désignés par les grands corps sociaux, mais par le chef de l'Etat. Les professeurs de faculté sont astreints à indiquer d'avance le plan de leurs cours. Le port de la barbe, de réputation républicaine, leur est interdit ainsi qu'à leurs collégues des autres enseignements officiels.[6]

The official ideology of the Second Empire was resolutely anti-intellectual. Louis Bonaparte himself boasted that he was not 'de la famille des idéologues'.[7] As a journalistic contemporary of Vallès, Philibert Audebrand, put it: 'Le Second Empire, né dans les ténèbres d'une nuit de décembre, avait en horreur les vingt-quatre lettres de l'alphabet.'[8]

In *Le Bachelier* we get a picture of what the repression meant at the grassroots. Jacques Vingtras seeks a job in *l'enseignement libre* because he is not prepared to swear loyalty to the Empire. A little later he is offered a position which he turns down, because it would mean taking the job away from a well-known republican teacher who had refused to take the oath.[9] For Vallès 'education' as state institution is synonymous with repression; revolt in the school must therefore lead to revolt against society as a whole.

But such revolt had to find its mediations, its concrete expression—no easy task under the Second Empire. When the young Jacques Vingtras wants to express his revolt against school and family, he writes four words (in capital letters): 'JE VEUX ETRE OUVRIER'.[10] But, as he finds out, things are not so simple in a highly stratified society. His education has precisely unfitted him to be a worker. When he tries to get a job in a printshop, he is told:

> Par ce temps de révolution, nous n'aimons pas les déclassés qui sautent du collège dans l'atelier. Ils gâtent les autres.[11]

Eventually he is advised by a grey-haired old worker:

> Ne vous acharnez pas à vouloir devenir ouvrier! 'Commençant si tard, vous ne serez jamais qu'une mazette, et à cause même de votre éducation, vous seriez malheureux. Si révolté que vous vous croyiez, vous sentez encore trop le collège pour vous plaire avec les ignorants de l'atelier; vous ne leur plairiez

pas non plus! vous n'avez pas été gamin de Paris, et vous auriez des airs de monsieur. En tout cas, je vous le dis: au bout de la vie en blouse, c'est la vie en guenilles . . . Tous les ouvriers finissent à la charité, celle du gouvernement ou celle de leurs fils . . .[12]

Nor is Jacques' attempt to unite politically with the working-class any more successful. When he and his student friends attempt to arouse resistance to the *coup d'état* of December 1851, they receive a sharp rebuff from a worker who remembers all too well how the Republicans betrayed the revolution in June 1848: 'Jeune bourgeois! Est-ce votre père ou votre oncle qui nous a fusillés et déportés en Juin?'[13]

And so Vallès finds himself, during the Second Empire, confined to the intermediate strata of society, those who are too well-educated to join the workers, but unwilling or unable to join the ruling élite. Vallès chronicles these strata in his first book, *Les Réfractaires* (1865), a gallery of portraits of the educated outcasts of Second Empire society. Who were the *réfractaires?*

Poètes crottés, professeurs dégommés, inventeurs toqués, sculpteurs sans ciseau, peintres sans toile, violonistes sans âme, ils se rencontrent fatalement, un jour, une nuit, à certaines heures, dans certains coins, sur la marge de la vie sérieuse; ils se sentent, se reconnaissent et s'associent: ils organisent la résistance, ils collaborent contre la faim.

The Second Empire was an age of social mobility—in both directions. As Pierre Pillu has pointed out, at the very time when Zola's Rougons were rising into the upper échelons of Imperial society, Vallès' *réfractaires* were sinking into the gutters of Paris.[15] At a slightly higher level, many *normaliens* under the Second Empire entered the insecure profession of journalism rather than climb the ladder up the educational system.

Yet Vallès is not without hope for alliance between workers and *réfractaires.* His story *Le Bachelier Géant* tells of a young man who abandons academic ambition to join a circus. Yet when he mocks his academic spectators, he wins the applause of the workers (*les blouses,* for in Second Empire society class was still defined by dress).

Devant le public, je posais, et, de mon théâtre qui montait en fuyant, il m'arrivait de faire une chaire de langues, d'où j'embarrassais les pions sales et les professeurs bêtes; les blouses applaudissaient, et, sur chaque champ de foire, j'avais mon mois de popularité.[16]

More significantly, he shows how, in the period shortly before the Commune, political organisations, notably the Blanquist *sections,* provided a bridge to link *déclassé*

intellectuals and workers. In July 1870 Vingtras meets a young man who had been a pupil of his at the *lycée* in Caen. He inquires as to his fortunes:

J'ai crevé la faim! . . . Une fois mon bachot en poche, j'ai voulu faire mon droit. Mon père a pu me payer trois inscriptions: pas davantage! C'est un petit notaire de campagne que je croyais à peu près riche et qui m'a avoué en pleurant qu'il était pauvre, bien pauvre . . . Confiant dans ma réputation de fort en thème, j'ai couru les bahuts . . . Ah! Bien, oui! Ceux qui ont fait leurs classes à Paris ont encore des relations, sont protégés par leurs anciens maitres; mais le fort en thème de province, qui rêve d'exercer entre Montrouge et Montmartre, celui-là ferait mieux de se flanquer à l'eau, sans hésiter! . . . J'ai eu plus de courage . . . Je me suis fait ouvrier, ouvrier graveur. Je n'ai jamais été bien habile, mais je suis parvenu, avec mon burin maladroit, à gagner à peu près ma vie . . . Que de fois j'ai songé à vous, à ce que vous nous disiez de l'éducation universitaire! Je croyais que vous plaisantiez, dans ce temps-là! Oh! si je vous avais écouté! . . . Mais ce n'est pas tout ça! Je ne suis pas venu pour larmoyer mon histoire. Depuis trois ans, j'appartiens à une section blanquiste. *Les sections vont marcher!*[17]

But it was in the Commune itself that the barriers between workers and intellectuals could, for all too short a time, begin to break down. The Commune itself was a living embodiment of the unity of workers and intellectuals. Of the 81 *communards* elected on 26 March and 16 April, thirty-three were manual workers, and about thirty intellectuals, including 14 writers and journalists, and four teachers.[18] A writer like Vallès could now speak to an authentic mass audience; his paper, *Le Cri du Peuple,* had a circulation, between March and May 1871, variously estimated at 50,000 and 100,000.[19] The children of Paris, too, discovered the reality of revolt. After the Commune, 651 children of under sixteen years of age were charged with participation in the insurrection; the youngest was only seven years old.[20] For once, the dreams of Vallès' *Enfant* had become reality.

The Commune, then, represents the consummation of Vallès' revolt, the point at which the conflict between individual and society finds a solution which is both collective and revolutionary. Small wonder that, in 1884, just before his death, Vallès could look back on his career as a writer and see his greatest achievement as being collaboration in the poster proclaiming the Commune:

Et malgré le temps écoulé, après la défaite, après l'exil, je place au-dessus de toutes mes joies d'écrivain l'honneur d'avoir été collaborateur de cette affiche de cinquante lignes qui annonçait le grand drame social.[21]

What, exactly, is Vallès' critique of contemporary education? *Le Bachelier* is dedicated 'A Ceux qui nourris de grec et de latin sont morts de faim.'[22] This leads us into one essential theme in Vallès' critique, namely, that education is useless because it does not prepare the student to earn his living. In particular, the study of the classics is seen as irrelevant and futile:

> A une époque où nous nous fourrions encore les doigts dans le nez, on nous a affublés d'une tunique et d'un képi, trop larges, en cas d'hydrocéphalie ou de croissance, et l'on nous a enfermés dans des endroits qui s'appellent collèges sous la monarchie, et lycées après les révolutions. Là, au lieu de nous apprendre à parler français et à gagner notre vie, on nous a fait éplucher des racines grecques, conjuguer des verbes romains. Cela a duré un an, puis encore un an, puis encore un autre.

> C'était toujours "le vieil Homère" ou le "mélodieux Virgile"; on est sorti à dix-neuf ans ne sachant rien, rien, rien, obligé de commencer son éducation et de se faire, pour manger, répétiteur de gymnastique ou de baccalauréat, ou bien encore professeur ou journaliste.[23]

Les Réfractaires is full of stories of young men who failed to fulfil the promise their education held out. Thus he describes a bedraggled tramp, soaked by walking round in the rain:

> C'est horrible, n'est-ce pas? ce noyé a fait ses classes, *il a eu tous les prix au collège,* on a dépensé vingt mille francs pour l'instruire, il a été reçu *bachau* avec des blanches à Clermont, où l'on disait dans la salle qu'il serait ministre.[24]

Now, of course, such criticism is completely valid; French schools were full of bored children learning about the classics in a sterile and mechanical fashion, while unemployed *bacheliers* walked the streets looking for jobs and food. Nonetheless, the critique has its limits. To blame the education system simply for not preparing people for jobs, for not adapting them to the 'real world', is to take the 'real world' as given. To change the syllabus so that education becomes 'relevant' is in itself no guarantee of human emancipation, but rather a reform designed to bolster up the existing social order. There are some signs that Vallès, who called the Suez Canal an 'audacieuse et sublime entreprise' may sometimes be guilty of technocratic illusions.[25]

But this is not the dominant note in Vallès' critique of contemporary education. Time and time again he comes back to the theme of freedom; the educational system is to be condemned because it represses the freedom of the child. Aged only just sixteen, a *lycéen* in Nantes, Valles was caught up in the Revolution of 1848; as a member of the 'Club de la jeunesse républicaine de Bretagne et de Vendée', he moved a resolution calling for the aboliton of the *baccaulauréat* and demanding 'la liberté absolue de l'enfance.'[26]

A recurrent image to describe school in Vallès' writing is that of prison. 'Il est aussi difficile au sortir du collège d'être entier et personnel qu'il est difficile de sortir enthousiaste ou naif du bagne'.[27] 'Le collège.—Il donnait, comme tous les collèges, comme toutes les prisons, sur une rue obscure.'[28] Vallès never lost his sympathy for revolutionary methods in the struggle against scholastic repression. In 1882, only three years before his death, he wrote an article enthusiastically hailing school riots in Southern France:

> Révolte à Montpellier et à Toulouse!

> Allez-y, mes enfants!

> Cela ne sert à rien, mais pendant le boucan on ne travaille pas, et ce sera autant de temps de gagné.

> Faisons le compte:

> Huit jours pour mijoter la conspiration; trois jours de bastringue; huit jours de fièvre et de paresse après l'apaisement de l'émeute: voilà bien près de trois bonnes semaines perdues pour les études classiques.

> . . . Pas de ça, potachon! Il faut faire la grève des langues mortes, entends-tu!

> Oh! s'il se trouvait une classe tout entière qui refusât le latin et le grec, comme il y en a qui refusent de *balancer Jules* au régiment!

> Voir ça et mourir![29]

The images that Vallès chooses here, strike and mutiny, show how, by this time, the demand for educational change is inextricably linked to his awareness of the need for total social transformation.

This is not, however, the end of the story. For the whole question of the role of education in the process of social transformation is one that is central to the development of socialist thought in the nineteenth century. If we try to locate Vallès in relation to this development, we may gain some insight into the place of education in his general socialist perspective.

The main components of the problem are present in the work of the early Marx. Marx and Engels had argued that there is a necessary and logical development from the materialist idea that human beings are moulded by their environment, to the recognition of the necessity for socialist transformation:

> If man draws all his knowledge, sensation, etc., from the world of the senses and the experience gained in it, the empirical world must be arranged so that in it man experiences and gets used to what is really human and that he becomes aware of himself as

man. If correctly understood interest is the principle of all morals, man's private interest must be made to coincide with the interest of humanity. If man is unfree in the materialist sense, i.e., is free not through the negative power to avoid this or that, but through the positive power to assert his true individuality, crime must not be punished in the individual, but the anti-social source of crime must be destroyed, and each man must be given social scope for the vital manifestation of his being. If man is shaped by his surroundings, his surroundings must be made human. If man is social by nature, he will develop his true nature only in society, and the power of his nature must be measured not by the power of separate individuals but by the power of society.[30]

This important passage lays stress on the continuity between materialism and socialism; it shows the importance of 'education'—in the broadest sense of the term, the way in which society moulds the individual—in effecting a transformation of society and the human way of life, but if taken on its own, it contains a dangerous strand of elitism—it is sufficient for some unspecified individuals to change the educational process on behalf of everyone else. Marx was very much alive to this danger, which he perceived in many of the dominant schools of European socialism in the 1840s. Hence his insistence in *The Theses on Feuerbach:*

> The materialist doctrine that men are products of circumstances and upbringing, and that, therefore, changed men are products of other circumstances and changed upbringing, forgets that it is men that change circumstances and that the educator himself needs educating. Hence, this doctrine necessarily arrives at dividing society into two parts, of which one is superior to society (in Robert Owen, for example).

> The coincidence of the changing of circumstances and of human activity can be conceived and rationally understood only as revolutionizing practice.[31]

Marx's strictures against Owen could be equally directed against most of the socialist thinkers in France in the period up to the Commune. On the one hand were the Utopians, the followers of Fourier and others, who saw the socialist transformation in terms of persuading humanity to accept a brilliant and imaginative blueprint drawn up in advance. On the other hand, the followers of Blanqui—described by Vallès as resembling 'un éduqueur de mômes'[32]—who looked to the liberating action of a small group of determined and heroic individuals.

Vallès was not a Marxist. He distrusted theory and never involved himself deeply in economic or philosophical analysis, but it is striking that, in one of the very few references he makes to Marxism, he seizes precisely on the activist element referred to above, and shows a striking grasp of the notion of reification:

> Sais-tu que c'est beau, cette définition du Capital; travail mort qui comme un vampire suce et dévore le travail vivant! Et que cette idée de la marchandise, travail cristallisé, solidification de la peine, mérite qu'on y pense.[33]

At some points in his career Vallès himself comes very close to a Utopian position, arguing, for example, in 1864, that moulding ideas through literature is more important than direct political action.[34]

One issue to which Vallès is very acutely sensitive is the question of tradition. He is, of course, deeply hostile to the traditions of established society. But he is also aware that tradition can be a fatal impediment to the revolutionary cause; that the revolutionaries try to act out preconceived schemes taken from the past, rather than recognising every revolution as an act of invention and originality:

> Il ne faut pas, par exemple, que les révolutionnaires d'aujourd'hui copient les grands révolutionnaires d'hier. Tous les hommes de 93, cordeliers, jacobins, fédéralistes ou unitaires, ont dépensé un courage de héros et une énergie de géants à réaliser dans le monde un idéal rêvé sur les bancs du collège. Ils sont tombés victimes de leur erreur. N'en soyons point à notre tour les dupes![35]

It is noteworthy that Vallès sees the dreams of 'les bancs du collège' as so pernicious. It is also striking how close he came to the position put by Marx in *The Eighteenth Brumaire of Louis Bonaparte:*

> The tradition of the dead generations weighs like a nightmare on the minds of the living. And, just when they appear to be engaged in the revolutionary transformation of themselves and their material surroundings, in the creation of something which does not yet exist, precisely in such epochs of revolutionary crisis they timidly conjure up the spirits of the past to help them; they borrow their names, slogans and costumes so as to stage the new world-historical scene in this venerable disguise and borrowed language . . . The social revolution of the nineteenth century can only create its poetry from the future, not from the past.[36]

The lessons of the Commune showed the validity of this view. On the one hand one can point to the thoroughly conservative role played in the Commune by the old generation of 1848—Louis Blanc, Ledru-Rollin, etc.—who thought their experience and prestige made them the educators of the new generation, but in fact failed to understand what was profoundly original about the Commune. On the other hand one can see how the ideas of the 'workers' state' and the 'dictatorship of the proletariat' were elaborated in practice by the workers of Paris before being formulated by Marx, whose leadership consisted in learning from the masses rather than seeking to lecture to them.

The actual educational achievements of the Commune were slender, because of shortage of time and the urgency of other tasks. Vallès served on the 'Commission de l'enseignement', but the fruits of its labours were few. However, mention should be made of the '**Manifeste du Comité central des 20 arrondissements**' which Vallès helped to draft.[37] This contains the paragraph:

> Propagation de l'enseignement laïque intégral, professionnel, conciliant la liberté de conscience, les intérêts, les droits de l'enfant avec la liberté et les droits du père de famille.

If 1789 was the year of 'Les droits de l'Homme', then 1871 became the year of 'Les droits de l'enfant', and no small part of the credit lies with Vallès. Later, in *l'Enfant,* Vallès projected the slogan back to his childhood. 'J'irai à Paris . . . Je défendrai les DROITS DE L'ENFANT, comme d'autres les DROITS DE L'HOMME'.[38]

After this brief examination of Vallès' political and educational ideas, we can come back to the *Jacques Vingtras* trilogy, and try to suggest some of the factors that give the novels their extraordinary force.

First of all, a key structural aspect of the trilogy is the transition from individual to collective. Vallès had originally intended to write two separate works; an autobiographical novel about childhood, and a social novel dealing with 1848 and 1871. The happy decision to make the two into one means that instead of two probably mediocre works we got one masterpiece. For it is precisely the interplay of individual and collective, and the ultimate revelation of collective solutions to individual problems that gives the work its force. In *L'Enfant* the issues are posed on the level of the single family; yet Jacques is presented as so resolutely normal that it becomes clear that it is the world and not Jacques that must be changed.[39]

In *Le Bachelier* we see Jacques as a *déclassé,* increasingly aware of the inadequacy of individual solutions:

> Puis j'ai lu des livres, j'ai réfléchi, et le ne crois plus aussi fort que jadis à l'efficacité du régicide.
>
> C'est le mal social qu'il faudrait tuer.[40]

Le Bachelier ends with apparent surrender and failure:

> Vous vous rappelez Vingtras, celui qui ne parlait que de rosser les professeurs, et qui voulait brûler les collèges? . . .

—Oui.

—Eh bien! il s'est fait *pion.*

Sacré lâche![41]

But the defeat serves only to highlight the victory—albeit all too temporary—in *L'Insurgé* when Vingtras ceases to be the 'hero' in any sense of the term, and the collective becomes the true subject.

Secondly, the trilogy is uncompromisingly realist. It should be noted that, unlike other republicans such as Floquet and Ranc, Vallès greatly admired Zola's *L'Assommoir* for its vigorous and unsentimentalised account of working-class life.[42]

One respect in which Valles not only follows Zola, but goes beyond him, is the use of popular language. Slang, onomatopoeia, freshly coined words, all serve to make the work more alive and more concrete. There is no space here to develop the theme in detail; it will suffice to cite one passage from *L'Enfant,* where linguistic detail lies at the heart of the conflict-ridden relations between Jacques' parents. Class, education, the family—all are crystallised into a question of vocabulary:

> Mon père—Antoine—n'a plus voulu aller dans le monde avec ma mère.
>
> La soirée de la bourée lui a complètement tourné la tête, elle s'est grisée avec son succès; restant dans la veine trouvée, s'entêtant à suivre ce filon, elle parle *charabia* tout le temps, elle appelle les gens *mouchu* et *monchieu.*
>
> Mon père à la fin lui interdit formellement l'auvergnat.
>
> Elle répond avec amertume:
>
> Ah! c'est bien de la peine d'avoir reçu de l'éducation pour être jaloux d'une femme qui n'a pour elle que son *esprit naturel!* Mon pauvre ami, avec ta latinasserie et ta grécaillerie, tu en es réduit à défendre à ta femme, qui est de la campagne, de *t'éclipser!*
>
> Les querelles s'enveniment.
>
> Tu sais, Antoine, je t'ai fait assez de sacrifices, n'en demande pas trop! Tu as voulu que je ne dise plus *estatue,* je l'ai fait. Tu as voulu que je ne dise plus *ormoire,* je ne l'ai plus dit, mais ne me pousse pas à bout, vois-tu, ou je recommence.
>
> Elle continue:
>
> Et d'abord ma mère disait estatue . . . elle était aussi respectable que la tienne, sache-le bien![43]

Thirdly, *Jacques Vingtras* makes no concessions to complacency or aestheticism. For Vallès, practice is always the test. He concludes a polemic with Paul Alexis on the political role of literature by saying:

> Mais je vous laisse. Oh vient de sonner à ma porte. C'est la petite d'un fédéré, une fillette de douze ans, infirme, et que sa grand-mère a amenée à l'ancien commandant du 191e. Je ne vais pas compter les pois de sa robe ou les mailles de son fichu—je vais tâcher de la faire entrer à l'hospice.[44]

Hence the structure of *Jacques Vingtras* is very unlike that of most nineteenth-century novels. Nothing could be further removed from the Flaubertian ideal of the author being hidden behind his creation. Vallès is always present within his work, never willing to allow the conventions of fiction to have precedence over the need to convey ideas and experiences. The closed structure of the classic realist novel is abandoned; there is in effect no plot; the unity is provided by character and by history. Whereas most nineteenth century novelists-set their narratives safely in the completed remoteness of the past tense, Vallès prefers the present.

Marie-Claire Bancquart has made an excellent analysis of the structural devices used in Valles' narrative technique:

> Le roman est reconnu comme problématique. Ainsi est-il à la fois doté d'une continuité et d'une overture incessantes: la *Trilogie* prend place dans le mouvement de modification de la technique romanesque si marqué à la fin du XIXe siècle. Conjointement à la structure, le langage est modifié. Ce n'est plus une armature rhétorique qui fonde sa continuité: exclamatives, phrases nominales, infinitives, indépendantes donnent une liberté au discours. Mais celui-ci est lié par l'usage des "blancs" dans le roman. Héritage peut-être du "blanc" journalistique, qui, dans certains articles littéraires de l'époque (par exemple les nouvelles de Maupassant), crée l'impression de la durée, le "blanc" vallésien est, paradoxalement en apparence, le garant de la continuité narrative: c'est qu'il existe deux sortes de silence, le silence amorphe qui établit un hiatus, et le silence de relation qui prolonge et qui annonce. Silence musical en somme; c'est celui de Vallès dans la *Trilogie,* ce qui explique que le "blanc" ne soit pas seulement utilisé pour marquer le passage d'un épisode à un autre, mais, à l'intérieur des épisodes, pour créer la dimension du récitant à l'intérieur du récit. L'usage si fréquent et si personnel que fait Vallès du tiret s'interprète de la même manière: le tiret est une pause moins longue que le "blanc", qui permet de faire entendre, à l'intérieur même de la phrase, une respiration qui n'est comparable à aucune autre: celle de l'écrivain.[45]

In the light of this analysis, it is not fanciful to suggest that the difference between Vallès' episodic narrative and those of his realist contemporaries is very closely akin to Brecht's distinction of epic and dramatic forms in the theatre.

We can also note something rather akin to a Brechtian *Verfremdungseffekt,* in that, especially in *L'Insurgé,* Vallès seems to weary of the pretence that he is writing fiction. The pseudonyms used in earlier volumes vanish, and real historical characters—like Varlin—appear. Vingtras' newspaper, like Vallès', is called *Le Cri du Peuple.*[46] As the individual enters the dimension of history, the boundaries between fact and fiction, between novel and history, finally evaporate.

To sum up. It is my contention that the *Jacques Vingtras* trilogy is a great novel because it asks questions that are still alive. Transformation of the syllabus or transformation of the world: the choice is before us.

References

NB: For the trilogy, I have given references to the most accessible edition, the three volumes *L'Enfant, Le Bachelier, L'Insurgé* in the Livre de Poche edition (Paris 1963-64). Since a variety of compilations of Vallès' journalistic work exist, I have given references to the original source rather than to any secondary collection in which they may appear. However, no work on Vallès could fail to be indebted to the monumental labours of Roger Bellet in compiling and editing the scattered writings of Vallès. I have drawn notably on his edition of Vallès' *Oeuvres* in the Bibliothèque de la Pléiade; on his thesis *Jules Vallès Journaliste 1857-1885* (Université de Lille, 1976); and on his compilation *Jules Vallès: Littérature et Révolution* (Editeurs Français Réunis, Paris, 1969).

Notes

[1] *The Rambler,* Vol. I, No. 4 (31 March 1750)

[2] *Le Progrès de Lyon,* 14 February 1864.

[3] *La Rue,* 21 December 1879.

[4] *Le Courrier du Dimanche,* 1 October 1865.

[5] J.-P. Sartre, *L'Idiot de la Famille,* Gallimard, Paris, 1971, II, p. 1337.

[6] A. Dansette, *Du 2 Décembre au 4 Septembre,* Hachette, Paris, 1972, p. 22.

[7] Speech of 9 October, 1852, cited Dansette, *op. cit.,* p. 447.

[8] Cited R. Bellet, *Presse et Journalisme sous le Second Empire,* Arm and Colin, Paris, 1967, p. 5.

[9] *Le Bachelier,* pp. 235, 241.

[10] *L'Enfant,* p. 415.

[11] *Le Bachelier,* p. 52.

[12] *ibid,* p. 53.

[13] *ibid.,* p. 145.

[14] J. Vallès, *Oeuvres I, 1857-70,* Gallimard, Paris, 1975, p. 170.

[15] P. Pillu, 'Vallès et Zola', *Europe 468-469,* April-May 1968, p. 329.

[16] *Oeuvres I,* p. 282.

[17] *L'Insurgé,* pp. 214-15.

[18] M. Winock & J.-P. Azéma, *Les Communards,* Editions du Seuil, Paris, 1964, p. 74.

[19] A. Dupuy, *1870-1871, La Guerre, La Commune et la Presse,* Armand Colin, Paris, 1959, p. 106.

[20] Winock & Azéma, *op. cit.,* p. 155.

[21] *Le Cri du Peuple,* 7 January 1884.

[22] *Le Bachelier,* p. 7.

[23] *L'Evénement,* 17 February 1866.

[24] *Oeuvres I,* p. 144.

[25] *La Rue,* 2 September 1867.

[26] R. Bellet, *Jules Vallès Journaliste 1857-1885,* Université de Lille, 1976, I, p. 216.

[27] *Courrier Français,* 20 May 1866.

[28] *L'Enfant,* p. 41.

[29] *Gil-Blas,* 28 March 1882.

[30] K. Marx & F. Engels, *The Holy Family,* Foreign Languages Publishing House, Moscow, 1956, p. 176.

[31] K. Marx & F. Engels, *Selected Works,* Foreign Languages Publishing House, Moscow, 1958, II, pp. 403-4.

[32] *L'Insurgé,* p. 241.

[33] Letter to Arnould, 18 April 1878.

[34] *Le Progrès de Lyon,* 14 November 1864.

[35] *Le Progrès de Lyon,* 6 September 1864.

[36] K. Marx, *Surveys from Exile,* Penguin, London, 1973, pp. 146-9.

[37] Published in *Le Cri du Peuple,* 27 March 1871.

[38] *L'Enfant,* p. 422.

[39] Cf. M.-C. Bancquart, *Jules Vallès,* Seghers, Paris, 1971, pp. 23-4.

[40] *Le Bachelier,* p. 286.

[41] ibid., p. 445.

[42] Cf. letter to Zola of 11 June 1879.

[43] *L'Enfant,* p. 294.

[44] *Le Cri du Peuple,* 14 November, 1883.

[45] M.-C. Bancquart, *op. cit.,* p. 75.

[46] *L'Insurgé,* pp. 320, 322.

Gerhard Fischer (essay date 1981)

SOURCE: "Jules Vallès, *La Commune de Paris* (1872)," in his *The Paris Commune on the Stage: Vallès, Grieg, Brecht, Adamov,* European University Studies, Series 1: German Language and Literature, Vol. 422, Peter Lang, 1981, pp. 36-52.

[*In the following excerpt, Fischer demonstrates the value of Vallès's play* La Commune de Paris *as a detailed and personal history of the Paris Commune of 1871, arguing that although the plot and characterizations are unrealistic, the drama vividly portrays the social and political conflicts surrounding the event.*]

La Commune de Paris, subtitled by its author a "grand drame historique,"[1] is an extraordinarily long play, designed indeed on an impressive scale. The text of the book edition covers 341 pages, not counting the title pages preceding numerous textual divisions. The five acts of the play are subdivided into eleven tableaux, or scenic units, each requiring a new stage setting and each in turn consisting of many scenes. Vallès has meticulously entitled every act and tableau. The list of dramatic divisions and titles is as follows:

Act   I: Prologue

1. tableau: Le Peuple Vaincu

Act II: La Fin de l'Empire

    2. tableau: Un Prince Assassin

Act III: Le Siège de Paris

    3. tableau: Le Quatre Septembre

    4. tableau: Le Bombardement

Act IV: La Commune

    5. tableau: Le 18 Mars

    6. tableau: La Trahison

    7. tableau: La Préfecture de Police

    8. tableau: Le Fort d'Issy

    9. tableau: La Croix Rouge

Act V: La Reaction

    10. tableau: Satory

    11. tableau: La Cour Martiale et l'Evasion

The divisions into acts and tableaux correspond exactly with chronological caesurae.

Of the four plays under discussion, *La Commune de Paris* is the most comprehensive historically. It covers a period of twenty-four years, from June 1848 to June 1871. The drama begins with the end of the revolution of 1848, the last scene of Act I showing the deportation of the defeated insurgents after the last barricade has fallen in the Rue Saint-Antoine. The way is thus prepared for Napoleon III and his second Empire, and the next act demonstrates the policies of repression and restoration which follow in the wake of the lost revolution. This tableau takes place twenty-three years later; the end of the empire is already in sight. The scene is a ball house in the workers' quarter of La Villette which serves as a meeting place for a revolutionary club, and the political rally under the topic "The Organization of Labor and its Relations to Capital and Property"[2] is connected with the assassination of a young revolutionary journalist named Victor Noir by Pierre Bonaparte, a cousin of the Emperor, on January 10, 1870.[3] The third tableau plays in front of the City Hall, on September 4 and deals with the proclamation of the republic and the installation of the Provisionary Government of National Defence. Tableau IV (Act III) demonstrates the effects of the siege: women are waiting in line in front of a bakery to buy their rations of 300 grams of bread. The time is now January 5, and the rumour spreads that the Prussians have begun to bombard Paris. Dramatic proof of this news is offered when a shell hits a house and explodes on stage.

The following five tableaux of Act IV deal with the Commune proper. Tableau V is set on Place Pigalle at Montmartre and describes the eventful day of March 18: the abortive attempt of the government to steal the cannons of the National Guard, the fraternization of the regular troops with the people of Paris, the flight of the government and the difficulties of the surprised leaders of the National Guard who all of a sudden have to form a government. The next tableau which takes place on April 4 after the installation of the Council of the Commune evolves around the military problem, the scene is now a battlefield on the plateau of Châtillon near the street to Versailles. Due to treason, a sortie of the Communards in the direction of Versailles is repulsed, and the general of the Commune, Duval, is executed on the spot together with two of his officers although they had been promised that their lives would be spared. Tableau 7 shows the police headquarters under the Commune; here Vallès attempts to explain some of the daily work of the delegates of the Commune. The last two scenes of Act IV are again reserved for the military development. Tableau 8 enacts the fight around the fort of Issy, evacuated by the Commune troops on May 12.[4] The next scene at the intersection of Croix Rouge refers thematically back to the prologue: the Communards build barricades, offer heroic resistance against the invading troops and are finally defeated. On May 22 the end of the fight is at hand. Scene of the last act, consisting of tableaux X and XI, is the prison camp of Satory after the Bloody Week of May. A court martial pronounces its judgements; death or deportation is the rule.

Vallès' play thus covers a wide range of locations and extends over a period of a quarter of a century. The dramatic unity as well as the chronological continuity within this panoramic view is maintained primarily by the characters of the drama. There is a great number of actors, thirty-four identified by name plus many extras representing soldiers, workers, men, women and children of Paris. Although no clear protagonists emerge out of this multitude—like in the other plays about the Commune the revolutionary citizens appear much as a collective hero—some characters have leading parts and become representatives of the main social and political movements. One of the principal characters of *La Commune de Paris* is a worker named Pierre Beaudouin, whom Marie-Claire Bancquart and Lucien Scheler call "l'ouvrier le plus ouvrier"[5] in all the works of Vallès. He is a blacksmith and a factory worker.

At the beginning of the play, we meet Beaudouin, aged 28, as one of the leaders of the revolution of 1848. He has to witness the execution of his brother Louis, wrongly accused by the government troops of being a sniper, while Pierre Beaudouin himself is arrested. In Act II Beaudouin is 48. We gather that he has returned from deportation to the penal colony of New Caledonia after the general amnesty of 1856, and he now appears as the step-father of his niece Jeanne, the daughter of his late brother and a beautiful young woman. Like her uncle, Jeanne is a worker, brave and endowed with the same revolutionary spirit. During the siege and the time of the Commune, Beaudouin is a member of the Central Committee and proves to be an able and energetic captain of the National Guard charged with the defense of the fort of Issy (tableau VIII). He fights until the bitter end and is finally, after the defeat of the Commune, condemned to death. *La Commune de Paris* is thus also the life-story of a worker, seen before the background of Parisian history in which this man participated and which he helped to shape. Vallès himself has indicated that his hero is modelled on the historic figure of Jean Malézieux,[6] one of the veteran fighters of the Commune who participated already in the revolts of 1830 and 1834. Unlike Beaudouin in the play, Malézieux was again deported to New Caledonia after May 1871 and, after his return ten years later at the age of 76, he was unable to find work and to adjust to the new life and committed suicide.[7]

The main opponent of Beaudouin and the representative of the antirevolutionary forces is George Bonnal, a professional officer and reactionary bourgeois. Bonnal begins his career in 1848 as a young lieutenant who is responsible for the execution of Louis Beaudouin, participates as a colonel of the general staff in the attempted government coup of March 18, 1871, and in the civil war against the Commune of Paris. Finally he presides at the court martial of Satory and signs the death sentence of Pierre Beaudouin. The third principal figure of the play is Jacques Bryas, a bourgeois intellectual and left wing journalist. A friend of Beaudouin, Bryas is a revolutionary newcomer, as it were, who joins the *dramatis personae* only in Act II. He collaborates very briefly with the government of September 4, but realizes very soon the counterrevolutionary nature of this regime and henceforth becomes an ardent supporter of the Commune. Imprisoned together with Beaudouin in Satory, he manages to escape under circumstances which will be explained later in a different context. Vallès' work is to a large extent autobiographical, and it is not difficult to see in Jacques Bryas some of the traits of the communard and editor of *Le Cri du Peuple,* Jules Vallès.[8]

Other important characters of the play are Hélène de Vernay, a rich young widow and sister of Bonnal, and Adèle Chauvelot, daughter of an insurgent of 1848 who has decided that the good life of a fashionable bourgeois is more attractive than the poverty of her father and his circle of friends. But this life requires capital and so Adèle has become a *lorette:* "Je vis de ma beauté comme un bourgeois de ses rentes,"[9] as she puts it.

There is also her unsuccessful suitor Racatel, "sorte de déclassé,"[10] who turns traitor and spy for Versailles during the Commune. Among the many communards at least three may be mentioned: Kermadeux, a sergeant from Brittany who fraternizes with the National Guards and who pays for his devotion to the Commune with his life; Matouillet, a philosopher who discovers his military talents defending the capital against Versailles; and Sir Halifax, a British physician and philanthropist who donates his money and time to the Commune and organizes an ambulance service. Sir Halifax is again modelled after a historic figure,[11] but all other characters are fictitious.

The action of *La Commune de Paris* follows closely the historical developments as described above. The author's attention is specifically focused on the involvement of his three major characters in the individual events which make up the total of this revolutionary period. But the public aspect, so to speak, is only part of the play's dramatic matter. Interwoven in the historical framework is a net of private relations of love, aversion and jealousy which at times not only tend to take precedent over the political and historical developments but which are also constructed in such a melodramatic, unrealistic fashion that they threaten to destroy the seriousness of the whole drama. This "ridicule intrigue amoureuse surajoutée à l'histoire," as Marie-Claire Bancquart drastically puts it,[12] ties the main characters together in a circle of mutual or onesided affections, disregarding the most blatant social and ideological differences. Jeanne Beaudouin loves Jacques Bryas and is loved by him; however, the two are at first rather shy and unsure of their mutual feelings and find each other only late in the course of the play. Bryas is also loved by Madame de Vernay, but he has broken with her; she knows about his devotion to Jeanne and is violently jealous; yet she has to admit to herself the beauty and purity of her younger rival. Finally, Jeanne is loved by Vernay's brother, Bonnal: the reactionary colonel in love with the revolutionary girl of the people. We also have to remember that Bonnal is the one who had ordered Jeanne's father shot twenty years ago, and that her stepfather and uncle has identified him for her. Clearly there is enough conflict and complication for the most sensational melodrama.

These characters meet each other throughout the play, "par un hasard aussi opportun que surprenant,"[13] as the editors of *La Commune de Paris* remark. These very emotionally charged dramatic confrontations are written with all the conventions of French classical theatre, including soliloquies, asides and a polished rhetorical style. Tableau V may serve as an example of Vallès' dramatic imagination. Colonel Bonnal has been taken prisoner on March 18 by Bryas who is in command of Place Pigalle after the attack of the government troops has failed. Bryas soliloquizes:

Impossible de garder cet homme! . . . Après avoir si brusquement rompu avec sa soeur, elle prendrait cela pour un acte de rancune et de vengeance . . . Ce serait affreux! . . . Cependant, c'est un otage important . . . je ne puis prendre sur moi de le mettre en liberté . . . Je vais parler à Beaudouin . . . il décidera! (Se reprenant.) Et encore non . . . Beaudouin peut encore moins que moi décider du sort du colonel . . . Ne l'ai-je pas entendu, le 4 septembre, reprocher à Bonnal d'avoir, en juin 1848, fait fusiller Louis Beaudouin, le père de Jeanne, son frère à lui? . . . (Avec angoisse.) Que faire?[14]

The inner conflict between Bryas' political convictions, his duties as an officer of the National Guard and his personal feelings of honour is further sharpened when a little later Hélène de Vernay appears on the scene. She is accompanied, to complicate matters even more, by Bryas' mother who disapproves strongly of her son's revolutionary activities and who also demands that he should release Bonnal and immediately break with his friends. The discussion between the three is overheard by Jeanne who listens rather anxiously because she fears that Bryas might still be in love with Madame de Vernay.

> Mme DE VERNAY (avec indignation à Bryas). — Et vous allez rester avec ces assassins? [i.e., the insurgent National Guards.]

> BRYAS. — Oui! (S'animant.) Les assassins, Madame, sont au sein des gouvernements qui poussent le peuple à la révolter pour se donner le plaisir de le décimer et le mater, au nom de la répression. (A ce moment, on voit Jeanne qui, inquiète, à la vue des deux dames, descend, du fond de la scène, vers le groupe qui ne la voit pas venir.)

> Mme DE VERNAY. — Vous restez avec eux, soit! (Froissée.) Alors, tout est fini entre nous . . .

> BRYAS (froidement). — Madame, de mon côté . . . (Jeanne les ecoute depuis un instant) tout est fini depuis longtemps et j'ai souvent maudit le jour où nous sommes connus.

> Mme BRYAS (désespérée et éclatant). — Mon fils! . . .

> BRYAS. — Ma mère, laissez-moi. (Avec autorité.) Je le veux! . . . (A Madame de Vernay.) Seulement, afin que vous ne soyez pas convaincue que je suis de ceux qui fusillent, je rends la liberté à votre frère, un fusilleur de Juin! . . . (D'un mouvement brusque, il tourne le dos au groupe et aperçoit Jeanne, avec émotion.) Jeanne! elle a tout entendu! . . .

> JEANNE (émue). — Oui, j'ai tout entendu (avec élan) et je sais qu'enfin vous ne l'aimez plus. . . . [15]

This rather hopeless quadrangular relationship is only resolved in the very last scene of the play. Madame de Vernay sacrifices her love to the well-being of her lover and her rival, consenting to marry the unattractive lawyer Dubray-Flochin under the condition that he helps her arrange the flight of Jeanne and Bryas from the prison of Satory where the two are kept prisoners. With the tacit approval of her brother, Hélène de Vernay and Dubray-Flochin visit the young lovers and change clothes with them. Jeanne and Bryas, however, accept only after Pierre Beaudouin, also imprisoned, has intervened and advised them to choose freedom, "dans l'intérêt de la Révolution."[16]

The quoted passages are characteristic of the way Vallès has constructed his play. The plot remains dramatically as well as psychologically incredible, and the characters hardly surpass a uniform, stereotyped image which includes purity of feeling and intention, a certain tragic self-interpretation combined with, as a matter of course, the ever-present readiness for self-sacrifice. To be sure, these weaknesses can partly be explained by the fact that Vallès writes in the style and tradition of nineteenth century, prenaturalistic melodrama which is hardly suited to accommodate a topic like the Paris Commune. Vallès' dependence on contemporary but now obsolete theatrical conventions can be seen also in his declamatory language. As Marie-Claire Bancquart rightly observes: "Les personnages parlent, sur les barricades comme dans l'intimité, avocats ou artisans, un langage ampoulé, 'à effet,' qui rejoint cette fois le pire pastiche de l'Antiquité."[17] Besides the trite and implausible main plot there are a number of other formal weaknesses, such as a few sub-plots and dramatic episodes at the periphery of the central action, which make *La Commune de Paris* an extremely opaque and (because of its sheer length and number of characters and locations) a technically almost impossible play.[18] It is doubtless for these dramatic deficiencies that Vallès' play has never been performed and was published only a century after its composition.

One thought has to be added, however. The unrealistic, private plot line interwoven with the story of the Commune is not only a formal problem because of its theatrical faults regarding construction, characterization, etc., it also causes a conceptual failure related to the content of the play. The relationship between dramatic structure and subject matter is characterized by a disproportion: on one hand the grand historic scale of the revolution with its profound socio-political changes and unparalleled violence of bourgeois repression, on the other hand the awkward story of four love relations at cross-purposes, doubtlessly intended to be serious and tragic but lastly only pathetic. Furthermore, because of its great emotional impact, this type of plot which the author has chosen continually tends to reduce the historical conflict to the private level of the individual. Purely personal problems are brought into sharp conflict and appear even more pressing because of the background of the dramatic historical action. The characters hardly perceive of the extraordinary political conflict but always refer it to their own private circumstances which invariably take precedence, thus obscuring not only the historical events themselves but also the individual's involvement in them. The historical events, in other words, appear as catalyzing forces to bring about or to accentuate and sharpen personal conflicts, socio-political developments appear as stimuli to moral crises and personal problems of individual characters.[19]

We touch here, of course, on a fundamental issue inherent in every historical play and one which we will encounter again in the course of this study. The objective of the playwright of historical dramas is to put on stage social, military and political facts and events while at the same time to create dramatic characters who not merely function as personified mouthpieces or puppets of historical developments but who are fully rounded persons with their very own individual qualities and private preoccupations. Vallès has not solved this problem. The great historical conflict between a revolutionary Paris and a reactionary Versailles is reduced and personalized in the triangular confrontation between Jeanne, Bryas and Bonnal. The author's failure to achieve a satisfactory synthesis of historical and private drama and the disturbing melodramatic triteness of his story mar *La Commune de Paris.*

The plot treatment in *La Commune de Paris* constitutes one other disadvantage. In order to develop his rather extended and complicated intrigue, Vallès has to allow much space just to account for the various turns in the story of his four leading characters. As a result, the reader learns much about the private conflicts and pseudo-tragic involvements of the play's heroes, but comparatively little about the Commune. How exactly is the Paris Commune described in this play? We have noted already that Vallès has given quite a circumstantial consideration of the historical antecedent and the causes leading to the revolution of 1871. The Commune proper is dealt with in the play in act IV which is about as long as a normal play. Of the five tableaux of this act, three deal entirely with the military situation, the war between Paris and Versailles. The battle scenes of *La Commune de Paris* are rather stereotyped. The Versaillese are brutal, summarily executing their prisoners, and the Communards are brave, heroic, generous, defeated only because of spies and traitors. Thus in tableau VI, the Commune troops under General Duval suffer defeat because the plans of attack had been sold to Bonnal by the arch-opportunist Racatel.

The conflict is not only personalized as usual in this play, but Vallès' description is also historically false. We know that the sortie led by Duval failed because it was almost spontaneous, badly organized and executed by inexperienced officers and troops.[20] If there was treason it was inconsequential. A similar scene is repeated in tableau VIII. Here a spy and traitor delivers the fort of Issy into the hands of Versailles, again commanded by Bonnal, although it is later recaptured through the bravery of Beaudouin, Bryas and their troops. We have to note, however, that Vallès does not exclusively engage in this black-and-white characterization. He mentions also the lack of responsible leadership and discipline among the Communards as one of the reasons of their defeat. In tableau IX Bryas says at the barricade, when it is clear that the battle is lost:

> Tout est perdu, Jeanne! . . . la Garde nationale énervée par le Siège, et deux mois de luttes stériles, est indécise . . . mal commandée, elle est surtout indisciplinée. On n'en obtient pas ce que l'on pouvait en attendre . . .[21]

But this is an isolated statement. What is dramatized, i.e., enacted scenically, are the various acts of treachery, spying, and conspiracy against the Commune.

Otherwise, Vallès spends a great deal of time on discussions about strategy. The author clearly takes position against the Jacobin traditionalists who advocate to abandon the fortified positions around Paris and to return to the city in order to organize a defensive combat in the streets, each quarter for itself. At Issy one such group of traditionalists, who receive their inspirations mainly from the revolutionary tactics of 1830 and 1848, leave the fort, thus for once scenically demonstrating the ideological split within the Commune. In tableau IX the question of strategy centers around the barricades and their effectiveness. Again Vallès demonstrates that the reliance of the Communards on traditional models of revolutionary warfare leads to their defeat: "La barricade, utile jadis, est une erreur aujourd'hui . . . Elle étonnait autrefois la troupe, l'arretait . . . Aujourd'hui, le premier Saint-Cyrien venu s'en empare avec quelques hommes!"[22] The new tactic of the government troops consists in occupying the houses on street corners and to fire from the windows of the upper floors at the insurgents who find themselves trapped behind the barricades without cover. Against the protest of some leaders, like Bryas, the National Guards finally resort to setting houses on fire as a last resort to keep the Versaillese enemy from advancing.

Of the other two tableaux of act IV, one deals with the revolution of March 18, i.e., the historical event immediately preceding and leading to the Commune, and only one tableau (VII, La Préfecture de Police) treats the political work of the Commune. The location of this act is an office in the police headquarters headed by a delegate of the Commune who, however, does not appear himself. Racatel in his mission as spy for Versailles is waiting to see the police commissioner to gather some information. He first learns from an employee about the reduction in crime; the secret police is almost out of work.

> Ignorez-vous donc, mon cher, que, depuis la Commune, on n'entend plus parler de vols, d'à ttaques de nuit, d'assassinats? C'est à croire vraiment que la police d'autrefois les favorisait pour se rendre nécessaire, ou bien que tous les voleurs et bandits ont pris parti pour Versailles.[23]

This point, which has also been confirmed and emphasized by Marx,[24] is then ironically contrasted with the reports in the papers of Versailles on the alleged daily pillages, orgies and debaucheries in the Paris of the Commune. Vallès simplifies again by having Racatel read one such article full of lies and inflammatory defamations which he himself has written, without forgetting, of course, to show the pangs of conscience Racatel feels about his less than honorable role. This is only one more example of Vallès' dramatic technique throughout the play: a historical condition gives way to a personal moral conflict, based on the character of a dramatic figure, which then takes precedence and thus deflects attention from the greater political issue.

Elsewhere in the tableau, mention is made of the night work of bakers without reference to the later decision of the Commune about this problem; the police officers hear accusations against a National Guard officer who has supposedly kept the pay of his soldiers for himself, and against general Dombrowski, temporarily military leader of the Commune and suspected of treason. While all this is only mentioned and hinted at, the question of the Bank of France is dealt with at some length. Racatel, partly from serious and honest concern about the revolution which he has betrayed and partly as an *agent provocateur,* suggests to the chief of police that he take the bank in order to use it as a basis for negotiations with the Prussians, to guarantee the financial obligations of the Commune and as a deterrent against Versailles. However, the police commissioner refuses, just as Bryas does later for fear of being accused of theft.[25] Unfortunately, the rest of the tableau is exclusively concerned again with developing the personal plot relations. Bryas is suspected of treason, mainly because of his relations to Madame de Vernay and because of the efforts of his mother to make him quit the Commune. All the characters involved meet miraculously once more and after a long, complicated story about Bryas' whereabouts, he is finally cleared of all suspicions. Accompanied by the usual outbreaks of passion and heroic suffering and sacrifice, the plot deteriorates into sheer melodrama.

This then is all we learn about the political work and organization of the Commune. There is not a word about social and economic measures, not a word about the political and administrative structure. In one passage, Vallès mentions the division within the Council of the Commune:

> Elle se querelle avec tout le monde, elle veut tout conduire, et elle ne sait pas se conduire elle-même . . . Majorité par ici . . . Minorité par là . . . les uns tirent à hue, les autres à dia . . . [26]

But again the information is not developed; it remains unclear what these different factions within the council represented or how this division affected the work of the Commune. This extraordinary lack of information about objective facts, decrees and tendencies relating to the Commune is astonishing, to say the least, and not only because Vallès himself participated in the events and knew first-hand about what he was writing. We can understand the detailed treatment of the military developments because it is here that the Commune ultimately failed and the question of the civil war had to appear to the Communards as the most pressing and lastly decisive problem. But why this scarcity of information on the socio-political aspects of this revolution which for later generations are the most important and noteworthy?

One immediately obvious reason is the apologetic purpose of the play, the desire of the author to ask his compatriots for understanding and sympathy with the deported or exiled insurgents,[27] hence his insistence throughout the play on the honesty and the patriotism of the communards, hence his emphasis on the military necessity of their actions, particularly the setting of fires which had destroyed so many buildings in Paris and which had become an embittered argument for the condemnation of Vallès and his comrades. He doubtlessly wished to help sway public opinion to a mood of fairness and forgiveness in order to heal the wounds of the terrible civil war, and he hoped to prepare the way for an amnesty similar to that of 1856 which allowed the proscript of 1848 to return to France.[28] We have to remember that *La Commune de Paris* was written right after the defeat of the revolution, at a period of hate and repression during which everything that reminded of the Commune was hysterically denounced, at a time when communards were still being sentenced to prison or deportation.

But the primary reason for Vallès' failure to adequately describe and dramatize the political and economic realities of the Commune is, I contend, historical and political consciousness on the part of the author. Vallès was a *déclassé,* a leftist intellectual and radical journalist whose revolt was a protest against his own bourgeois past combined with an emotional and romantic attachment to the proletariat, as Victor Brombert has demonstrated[29]—not the result of a conscious scientific political and economic analysis. Thus Vallès lacks the ultimate understanding or even appreciation of some of the revolutionary measures he helped to realize, especially those of an organizational and economic nature. His preoccupation with abstract idealistic matter, such as his demand for complete freedom of the press at a moment of highest danger and crisis for the Commune, is only one other confirmation of this evaluation. A second factor is Vallès' traditionalist concept of the Commune as a free and autonomous political entity which constitutes the ultimate goal of the revolution. Vallès thus pays little attention to the socioeconomic basis of such an independent city of Paris; for him the political nature of the capital is the only question that matters. This idea emerges also in *La Commune de Paris,* namely when Bryas, like his fellow revolutionaries of the Central Committee, is surprisingly confronted with the necessity to form a government and to develop a political program after the flight of the Provisional Government on March 18:

> Paris libre! c'est une idée! . . . Voilà un programme tout trouvé!. . . . Fédération républicaine des grandes villes! . . . [30]

In his journal *Le Cri du Peuple* of March 21, 1871, we find the same thought. Here Vallès demands that "Paris doit donc se déclarer Ville Libre, commune affrachie, cité républicaine, se gouvernant elle-même et réalisant dans la mesure du possible la théorie du gouvernement direct appliqué dans la République Helvétique.[31] Vallès' understanding of the Commune is thus clearly inspired by historical bourgeois models, here the Swiss system of participatory democracy. He completely ignores the proletarian, antibourgeois character of the revolution for which he fought. Elsewhere he even cites the example of the free cities of the medieval Hanseatic League as a prototype of the French Communes.[32]

The concept of federalism, e.g., the federation of the communes of France, is of course part of the pre-socialist theories of Proudhon who had a great influence on Vallès. Proudhon envisioned the political and economic emancipation of the proletariat through workers' cooperatives, established on the basis of his theory of a just exchange between labor and capital which was to be arranged through the intermediary supervision of so-called exchange banks. In this utopian socialism[33] might lie also the reason for Vallès' ambivalent attitude and his uneasiness with regard to the seizure of the National Bank of France which emerges in *La Commune de Paris:* he neither clearly criticizes Bryas nor approves of his refusal to touch the bank. Vallès has himself admitted his indebtedness to Proudhon: "C'est lui, l'auteur des *Confessions,* qui a jeté la lumière dans mon esprit et m'a montré le néant de ces gloires authoritaires et jacobines."[34] Interesting here is the criticism of the later-day Jacobins and their fixation on the

traditional revolutionary precepts of 1789, such as the dictatorship of a Committee of Public Safety which appears also in his play.[35] The irony is only that Vallès is also and at the same time a traditionalist; his "socialisme romantique et global qu'il a hérité de 1848," as Marie-Claire Bancquart puts it,[36] is shaped after a revolutionary model based on the socio-economic conditions of artisans and the progressive liberal bourgeoisie which had only little relevance to the problems of the industrial proletariat of the Paris of 1871.

Vallès, or his alter ego Bryas, is in many ways ideologically representative of the Proudhonist members within the minority group of the Commune Council and, inasmuch as these revolutionaries did not consciously understand the importance and radical newness of some of the measure of the Commune, it is perhaps only natural that these developments are not represented in Vallès' dramatization. The greatest irony, however, seems that the author has created an industrial worker, Pierre Beaudouin, as his principal character who clearly is more consciously revolutionary and farseeing than his comrades, as demonstrated for instance in his comments about the out-dated tactics of Parisian barricade and street war or his decision to seize the bank, albeit too late. Unfortunately, Vallès has not given this character the opportunity to express more of his ideas, particularly as far as political and economic questions are concerned. Here ends, I contend, the understanding of Jules Vallès of the interpretation of the revolution with which he so totally identified.

After all this criticism of *La Commune de Paris* and its author, what remains to be said about the play? It is not entirely bad, and in parts it is even admirable. Of great documentary value as a dramatic eye-witness report and impressive in the scope with which it demonstrates the revolutionary continuity of 19th-century French history, the drama is rather less satisfactory as theater. The best scenes of *La Commune de Paris,* from a dramatic-technical point of view, are those which re-create the life of Paris and of the people of the city during these difficult times. One such scene is the one in Tableau IV during the siege in which a group of hungry and freezing Parisians are waiting in line in front of a bakery to receive their daily ration of 300 grams of bread only to find out much later that there is no bread at all. A little later in the same scene the people start cutting the trees which line the boulevards in order to use them for firewood, or for the same reason break down the fence around the large, empty house of a bourgeois who is waiting out the siege in Italy while they are being scolded by a bourgeois politician who lectures to them about the sacredness of private property. The best part of the play in my opinion is the treatment of the actual revolution on March 18 in Tableau V where Vallès succeeds fully in dramatizing the electric atmosphere of tension during the confrontation between the regular troops and the National Guards, the fraternization of the soldiers and the exuberant but at the same time anxious joy of the people at their victory. In these scenes Vallès achieves an atmosphere of realism full of precise details of observation and characterization which gives the play a convincing dramatic immediacy and vitality that is not too far away from the great social drama of his naturalist successors. Here the problem of the presentation of historical matter is also solved satisfactorily, in these scenes the great social and historical conflicts emerge much more clearly and more naturally, as it were, than in the contrived confrontation between a reactionary officer Bonnal and a revolutionary journalist Bryas. *La Commune de Paris* is not an analytical drama which attempts to interpret the course of history. Written immediately after the Commune, by an author who is intellectually and emotionally still clearly under the powerful influence of this experience, Vallès' drama is an outstanding documentary work, at its best when it directly describes the struggles and sufferings of the people of Paris, their dedication and their hopes to achieve a better life for themselves through their own revolutionary action.

Notes

1 Jules Vallès, *La Commune de Paris* (Paris: Les Editeurs Français Réunis, 1970), p. 25.

2 Page 74.

3 Vallès dates the scene January 12, but obviously confuses the date of the assassination with that of Noir's funeral which took place on that day. The funeral, incidentally, gave rise to a huge demonstration against the Empire, and Vallès has rightly chosen this important date and event to demonstrate "la fin de l'Empire." Cf. the comment by Frank Jellinek, *The Paris Commune of 1871*, p. 49.

4 Cf. the editor's note on this date, Vallès, *La Commune de Paris*, p. 242.

5 Page 16 (Preface).

6 Page 25. See also Vallès portrait of Malézieux in his *L'Insurgé*, ed. Lucien Scheler (Paris: Les Editeurs Français Réunis, 1950), p. 317.

7 See biographic note in *La Commune de 1871*, p. 435.

8 In fact Marie-Claire Bancquart suggests, and I agree, that the characterization of Bryas is a "transposition malheureuse" of the figure of the author. It fails partly because it lacks the immediacy and literary freshness of an autobiographic report which is elsewhere Vallès' primary quality.

9 Vallès, *La Commune de Paris*, p. 65.

10 Page. 25.

11 Cf. editor's note, *La Commune de Paris*, pp. 209-10.

12 Pages 77-78.

13 Page 11.

14 Pages 176-177.

15 Pages 191-192. A similarly contrived meeting takes place in tableau IX where the situation appears almost exactly reversed: Bryas is taken prisoner by Bonnal. See pages 292-295.

16 Page 376.

17 Marie-Claire Bancquart, *Jules Vallès* (Paris: Editions Pierre Seghers, 1971), p. 77.

18 Cf. Vallès, *La Commune de Paris*, p. 11.

19 Page 148.

20 Cf. Frank Jellinek, *The Paris Commune of 1871*, pp. 191-192, and Bruhat, *La Commune de 1871*, pp. 240-241.

21 Vallès, *La Commune de Paris*, p. 268.

22 Page 266.

23 Page 211.

24 Cf. Marx, *Der Bürgerkrieg in Frankreich*, p. 86.

25 Cf. Vallès, *La Commune de Paris*, pp. 269-70. At the end of the play we learn that Beaudouin, who certainly is the most consciously revolutionary character, has signed an order to seize the bank but by then it was too late already, according to Vallès.

26 Page 244.

27 The editors of the play call *La Commune de Paris* "[une] oeuvre apologétique," p. 8. Cf. also pp. 14-15 of Preface.

28 Amnesty was granted, however, only in 1880.

29 Victor Brombert, "Vallès and the Pathos of Rebellion," in *The Intellectual Hero: Studies in the French Novel, 1880-1955* (Philadelphia: J. B. Lippincott, 1961), pp. 43-51. Cf. especially p. 46 and 49.

30 Vallès, *La Commune de Paris*, p. 182.

31 Vallès, *Le Cri du Peuple*, ed. Lucien Scheler (Paris: Les Editeurs Français Réunis, 1953), p. 96.

[32] Pages 99-100.

[33] Marx's criticism of Proudhon is developed at length in *The Poverty of Philosophy* (*Das Elend der Philosophie*, Berlin: Verlag Marxistische Blätter, 1970). Cf. also Engels' critique in his preface to *Der Bürgerkrieg in Frankreich*, pp. 16-18, with his concluding sentence "Die Kommune [war] das Grab der Proudhonschen Schule des Sozialismus."

[34] From an article on Proudhon in *La Rue*, quoted in *Jules Vallès*, p. 109. See also Marie-Claire Bancquart's comment on Vallès' Proudhonistic convictions, *Jules Vallès*, p. 34.

[35] Cf. Vallès, *La Commune de Paris*, pp. 244-45.

[36] Bancquart, *Jules Vallès*, p. 81.

Works Cited

Bancquart, Marie-Claire. *Jules Vallès*. Paris: Editions Pierre Seghers, 1971.

Brombert, Victor. "Vallès and the Pathos of Rebellion." *The Intellectual Hero: Studies in the French Novel, 1880-1955*. Philadelphia and New York: J. B. Lippincott, 1961.

Jellinek, Frank. *The Paris Commune of 1871*. New York: Grosset and Dunlap, 1965.

Marx, Karl. *Der Bürgerkrieg in Frankreich*. Berlin: Dietz Verlag, 1963.

Marx, Karl. *Das Elend der Philosophie*. Berlin: Verlag Marxistische Blätter, 1970.

Vallès, Jules. *La Commune de Paris: Pièce en 5 actes et 11 tableaux*, préface et notes de Marie-Claire Bancquart et Lucien Scheler. Paris: Les Editeurs Français Réunis, 1970.

Vallès, Jules. *Le Cri du Peuple*, ed. Lucien Scheler. Paris: Les Editeurs Français Réunis, 1953.

Vallès, Jules. *L'Insurgé*, ed. Lucien Scheler. Paris: Les Editeurs Français Réunis, 1950.

Caryl Lloyd (essay date 1985)

SOURCE: "The Politics of Privacy in the Works of Jules Vallès," in *The French Review: Journal of the American Association of Teachers of French*, Vol. 58, No. 6, May, 1985, pp. 835-42.

[*In the following essay, Lloyd focuses on the depiction of space in the* Jacques Vingtras *trilogy, arguing that Vallès's negative portrayal of private spaces underscores the loneliness and isolation of bourgeois life. Vallès's contrasting views of public and private spaces, Lloyd contends, reveal a sophisticated understanding of the evolution of modern institutions.*]

The nineteenth century was an age of humanitarian reform of those institutions designed to house the alienated. It was also a period marked by the development of democratic institutions. The former is based on a philosophy of exclusion of unequals, the latter on inclusion of those considered to be the same before the law. The relationship between these two social trends, as paradox or logical consequence, can be fruitfully studied in the works of Jules Vallès, a participant in two of the major revolutions of the nineteenth century and, briefly, a resident of both asylum and prison.

Jules Vallès, the son of a poor schoolteacher, was educated in mid-nineteenth century France in institutions characterized by slavish respect for classical antiquity and belief in the pedagogical principles of corporal punishment, imitation of exemplary texts, and student passivity. The author quickly found his calling as perennial outsider in the Paris of 1848. During that revolution be led his school-fellows in protest against the rigid educational system and, in particular, against the tyranny of the bacclaureate exam. Later, as both journalist and activist, he attacked the government of Napoleon III whom he considered a usurper and a despot. He ran as a revolutionary socialist in the legislative elections of 1869 and participated in the insurrection leading to the establishment of the Commune in 1871. He was exiled until 1880. Vallès's best known work is an autobiographical trilogy depicting the life of Jacques Vingtras from his oppressive childhood, through student days in Paris, to the triumphs and defeat of the Commune. Entitled *L'Enfant, Le Bachelier,* and *L'Insurgé,* these three novels constitute a unique literature of revolt.[1]

Throughout the trilogy, the protagonist is acutely sensitive to the spaces he inhabits. The house that shelters his unhappy family is on a narrow and filthy street leading to a prison which the child considers more joyful than the family hearth. The association of house and prison, hardly a startling one in an age whose favorite satirical target was the complacent bourgeois, becomes increasingly significant as Jacques matures. He sees the dreary, cramped spaces as the reflection of a parental philosophy based on restriction and deformation of instincts. When he pricks his finger on a rose outside the house his mother snaps, "Ça t'apprendra" (*Enfant,* p. 48). Jacques is routinely beaten for the smallest infraction of family rules or simply for his own good. Although Jacques's father can claim membership in the petty bourgeoisie, both he and Jacques's mother are not far removed from their peasant origins and long to launch their son upward into the bourgeoisie. Their exclusion of the outside world is based not only on a fear of distraction, but of contamination from the lower classes.

Philippe Ariès, tracing the evolution of the family from the Middle Ages, notes that by the late eighteenth century:

> la bourgeoisie n'a plus supporté la pression de la multitude, ni le contact avec le peuple. Elle a fait secession: elle s'est retirée de la vaste société polymorphe pour s'organiser à part, en milieu homogène parmi ses familles closes, dans des logements prévus pour l'intimité, dans des quartiers neufs, gardés de toute contamination populaire.[2]

The family, increasingly isolated in its sameness, perpetuates a philosophy of self-confinement on its children. Vingtras's family, struggling up the social ladder, away from its peasant origins, was anxious to assimilate this particular bourgeois value.

Vallès's tableaux of mid-century France depict an aspect of the family which is part of a more general movement toward isolation. The "self-segregation of the middle class," historian Christopher Lasch has suggested, "had its counterpart in the forcible segregation of criminals and of deviants of all types, including finally even children who in this period came to be thought of as a special class of persons requiring special 'asylums' of their own."[3]

Indeed, in Vallès's work the child moves from the self-segregated family to the equally restrictive boarding school. For schools are also prisons overlooking somber streets. Throughout the trilogy, as Roger Bellet has noted, the prison image is dominant:

> Collège-prison du Puy, collège-prison de Saint-Etienne, collège-prison de Nantes; trois prisons similaires en trois espaces éloignées, trois prisons enfermant une enfance. Prisons qu'on appelle, dit quelque part Vallès, collèges sous les rois et lycées sous les régimes impériaux: mais les murs restent.[4]

It is not only an anxious parent or the stone walls of a boarding school but the absolute authority of the past which erects barriers between the child and life. A frustrated Jacques will find himself unable to view the present except through the prism of Greek and Roman models.

When attempting to write articles which would inspire the masses to revolt, Jacques is inhibited by his classical education. He cannot express his own ideas without using phrases and examples learned from an ancient text. He comments on his plight with characteristic irony. "On ne peut pas écrire pour les journaux républicains sans connaître à fond son Plutarque" (*Bachelier,* p. 121). His education seals him off from

the workers who find his hands too smooth and his language replete with literary references.

When Jacques escapes to the freedom of bohemian life in Paris, he inhabits a series of cell-like rooms which initially allow him to express his own independence and, at the same time, his membership in the freedom-loving bohemia of Parisian cafés and garrets: "Je suis chez moi!" (*Bachelier,* p. 121). In the last novel a defeated Jacques even finds refuge working in the hated lycée where he is able to experience "la tranquillité de l'asile" (*Insurgé,* p. 16). Later still, during the turmoil of the Commune, he flees to his room, barricading himself against the violence and confusion of the insurrection. During a stay in prison he insists, "Cette solitude ne m'effraie pas . . . Cette captivité n'est point pour moi la servitude: c'est la liberté. En cette atmosphère de calme et d'isolement, je m'appartiens tout entier" (*Insurgé,* p. 87).

Yet even in his first celebration of privacy there is a comic reminder of the limits of even freely chosen enclosures. In a moment of exuberance, Jacques jerks his head forward, smashing the glass of a window that was much closer than it seemed. In his days of student poverty he moves to smaller and smaller rooms until, in one abode, he is obliged to stoop not only to enter the room but to remain inside. Stretching out on the bed means curling his fingers and bending his knees. A long-legged friend forced to share the small space must sleep with either his head out the window or his feet in the hallway. When Jacques and his friends discuss politics they knock over furniture, their enthusiasm claiming more space than is allowed in a living room. The solitude of a warm room can be only a temporary refuge for, removed from social conflict, Jacques's spirit seems to fall asleep: "Mon esprit, à moi, s'endort loin du combat et loin du bruit; le souvenir du passé ne vibre plus dans mon cœur que comme peut vibrer, à l'oreille d'un fugitif, le roulement de tambour qui s'éloigne et qui meurt" (*Insurgé,* p. 17). During his brief respite from the insurrection, Jacques admits that closing himself in his room has the effect of walling in his thoughts: "J'ai fermé ma fenêtre, et mon cerveau s'est muré également—les idées ne venaient plus" (*Insurgé,* p. 227).

For Gaston Bachelard, "C'est souvent par la concentration même dans l'espace intime le plus réduit que la dialectique du dedans et du dehors prend toute sa force."[5] Jacques uses an organic image to express the same thought. The future self is a fetus kicking against the womb of the present self:" je sens mon cœur battre là-dedans à grands coups, et j'ai souvent comparé ces battements d'alors au saut que fait, dans un ventre de femme, l'enfant qui va naître" (*Bachelier,* p. 25). As if to strengthen the enclosure metaphor, Vingtras has his "child" come to life in front of the coffin of Henri Murger: "C'était mon livre, le fils de ma souffrance, qui avait donné signe de vie devant le cercueil du bohème enseveli en grande pompe" (*Insurgé,* p. 31).

For Jacques's generation Henri Murger (author of *Scènes de la vie bohème*) was the pied piper of bohemianism. He celebrated poverty and promoted the politics of individual differences. Vallès considered Murger's nonconformism (and its goal of self-expression) as a dangerously anti-social idea. Jacques's book is a bitter attack on a bohemianism which the protagonist saw as not significantly different from the bourgeois complacency it rejects. The coffin and the book it inspired are images of a deeply held belief: that concentration in intimate space does not foster either self-realization or social revolution.

Jacques's anger at Murger's cheerful poverty derives from his own experience of real poverty. He scorns those dark rooms where starving artists sought truth in splendid isolation from the people. He moves from the romance of personal alienation to an active role with those for whom alienation is an objective state, based on class differences. Fredric Jameson has described succinctly the end point of both bourgeois privacy and romantic alienation as "the privatization of contemporary life."[6] That privatization opens a wider and wider gap between the public and private sphere, privileging the latter in a sheltered status outside of history. Jacques's political instincts, born in the restrictive environment of bourgeois institutions, yet in opposition to bohemian individual freedom, are refined as he becomes a true outsider.

Public spaces are nearly adequate for Vallès-Vingtras and are certainly preferable to private ones.[7] During one of the many meetings prior to formation of the Commune, public space becomes a political ideal from which individual oratory and the authority of the podium are banned:

> La voix ne sonnera point ici comme dans les salles de bal, faites pour les coups de grosse caisse ou les coups de gueule—il n'y a pas l'acoustique des tempêtes oratoires. Le parleur n'aura point le piédestal de la tribune, du haut de laquelle on laisse tomber son geste et son regard . . . chacun causera de son banc, debout, dans la demi-lune de sa travée. (*Insurgé,* p. 249)

But it is the street, finally, more than public hall or café, where Jacques finds both the poetry and the politics of the people. When he arrives in Paris the young provincial is overwhelmed by the streets and the challenge he feels there: "Sur ce boulevard, la foule se renouvelait sans cesse; c'était le sang de Paris qui courait au cœur et j'étais perdu dans ce tourbillon comme un enfant de quartre ans abandonné sur une place" (*Bachelier,* p. 36). Horses fly through the streets, their nostrils flaring; the narrow alleys

teem with both life and refuse. Later those same streets become the battleground for all the city's outsiders:

> De tous côtés, par petits groupes, ou en bataillon comme nous, Paris monte vers Neuilly . . . Ce sont les morceaux d'armée qui se cherchent, des lambeaux de République qui se sont recollés dans le sang du mort. C'est la bête que Prudhomme appelle l'hydre de l'anarchie. (*Insurgé,* p. 134)

What before was urban chaos becomes, with the Commune, confrontation between the bourgeois and the masses, "an ordered modernism of mass movement."[8]

During the uprising, Jacques rushes from the streets where the people spontaneously express their will to the rooms where representatives fight to give shape to that impetus. He is able to publish the outlawed journal, *Le Cri du Peuple,* just as Vallès did during the same period. As his articles give courage to those fighting Jacques experiences a sense of fusion with the people and a certainty about his role: "Il me semble qu'il n'est plus à moi, ce cœur qu'ont échorché tant de laides blessures, et que c'est l'âme même de la foule qui maintenant emplit et gonfle ma poitrine" (*Insurgé,* p. 238). That fusion is not merely the attempt of a radical intellectual to shed his personal sense of alienation, but an acknowledgment of the importance of organization in revolutionary movements. It is not surprising that when Vallès was forced to publish under a pseudonym he would choose Jean La Rue, for Vallès saw himself as one who gave the streets their voice.[9]

Vallès's ideas about inside and outside as they relate to a definition of deviance are given analytical expression in *Le Tableau de Paris,*[10] a work written after his return from exile in England. It shows an understanding of modern institutions and their relationship to the paradox of bourgeois privacy. Vallès's student days in Paris coincided with the tenure of Baron Haussmann as Prefect of the Seine and the transformation of Paris into a city of broad vistas and boulevards. One imagines a Vallès acutely aware of a modern city because of the nine years' absence, and all the more suspicious of the Third Republic's promises.

Le Tableau presents the familiar celebration of street life, but of streets that only echo the class struggles of recent decades, and where opposition to social inequality is mute. In his discovery of a post-revolutionary city, the author witnesses an even more sinister change when he visits those institutions where the new society's outsiders are kept in isolation. His perspective, always one of sympathy for the oppressed, might seem in this case a romantic call for return to a more integrated time, to pre-revolutionary care for the alienated, to a rejection of humanitarian reform. It would be wrong, however, to accept such a simplification of Vallès's thought and to ignore its relationship to those concepts germinating in the trilogy. Vallès's treatment of modern institutions shows the insight of a serious social critic and the commitment of a revolutionary writer to remain alert to the changing face of social oppression. He offers at the same time a necessary caution to the uncritical progressives, those he calls "les humanitaires."

In the asylums, Vallès finds pathetic victims of a social order that confines women to less and less fulfilling roles in the increasingly isolated family. He finds irony in the fact that the word for muff, "manchon," is also the one used to describe the straight jacket. Indeed, in the women's section of the asylum, he observes refugees from society's restrictive roles: women who have refused to "take up the broom," one who claims a doctor made love to her and thereby deformed her body, a victim of Bovaryism, another whose husband drove her mad to be free of her, and finally one, perhaps more direct than the others, who says simply, "Je suis un homme!" (*Tableau,* p. 40). These are women for whom madness is an escape from the terrors of private domestic life and its sexual expectations; women who refuse to conform must be excluded until they accept.

In one of the book's longest sections Vallès visits Mazas, a penal institution which also isolates non-conformists. The author himself had served time in Mazas after his implication in the conspiracy against the Emperor. On this visit, Vallès contrasts Mazas to the Bastille of the Ancien Régime with its windowless, damp cells. The modern institution, in contrast, has white walls, shiny floors, and no trace of the instruments of torture that characterized the older institution. Light flows in through windows, thanks to humanitarian reformers. Where earlier the prisoner was spared the scrutiny of his jailers, the new prisoner becomes an object of therapeutic manipulation, deprived of the dignity of his solitary despair: "Le système nouveau met l'homme et son âme à nu. La clarté que lui ont envoyée, par les lucarnes, les humanitaires, devient l'ennemi de sa dignité et la complice des mouchards" (*Tableau,* p. 122). The initial meeting between prisoner and keepers reveals an entirely new concept of individual deviance. The prisoner is met by a cold, polite bureaucrat who asks for the following information: name, age, height, weight, religion, scars, eye color, and length of right foot. He is photographed and by that act the sun itself becomes an accomplice in the objectification of the man—a soldier, to use Vallès's metaphor, in society's army: "On a enbrigadé la science, enregimenté la photographie, mis le soleil au service de la Préfecture" (*Tableau,* p. 160). Prisoners acquire numbers in lieu of names as the modern institution reveals its dehumanizing face. While it is true that humanitarian reforms have changed the old system's "contaminating" grouping in a single enclosure of old, young, male, female, debtors, criminals, and lunatics (Lasch, p. 9), those same reforms are leading inexorably to a less obviously beneficial trend: the

categorization of individuals in "total institutions" and the resulting fragmentation of social life.[11] Social problems removed from the larger social text can be controlled but never solved.

The prisoner, in his false privacy, isolated from the social whole, yet subject to its definition, experiences not the plenitude of his otherness but the void of his being:

> Pendant un temps, la pensée trouve un aliment dans le passé, et, sur la page aveuglante et immaculée de la muraille, les souvenirs rôdent comme des mouches . . . Voilà qu'un vilain matin, on a épuisé cette source de consolation, et qu'on est devant ce qu'on a de vie morale comme devant un trou creux, d'où l'on n'arrachera rien et où l'on n'a rien à jeter . . . Jamais il ne s'est échappé d'une cellule une œuvre féconde. La vie n'y entre pas, la vie n'en sortira pas. On subit la nécessité de l'échange dans le monde des idées comme dans le monde des faits. (*Tableau,* p. 125)

For Michel Foucault, in his history of asylums, the reformers are responsible for this paradox which is that of all modern institutions:

> Libéré des chaînes qui faisaient d'elle un pur objet regardé, la folie perd, de manière paradoxale, l'essentiel de sa liberté, qui est celle de l'exaltation solitaire; elle devient responsable de ce qu'elle sait de sa vérité; elle s'emprisonne dans son regard indéfiniment renvoyé à elle-même; elle est enchaînee finalement à l'humiliation d'être objet pour soi. La prise de conscience est liée maintenant à la honte d'être identique à cet autre, d'être compromis en lui, et de s'être déjà méprisé avant d'avoir pu se reconnaître et se connaître.[12]

Vallès's prisoner in his forced privacy is faced with the void which is both the socially defined absence of normalcy and the fate of one removed from society. Humanizing deviance frees the outsider from purely external constraints, from chains, but defines him as "an empty vessel waiting to be filled with moral responsibility" (Lasch, p. 11). With Vallès's description of the inmate-outsider's plight, we come full circle to a vision of bourgeois loneliness and modern isolation.

Jules Vallès took great pains to distinguish his literary purpose from that of certain of his contemporaries. He despised the religiosity of Baudelaire's satanism and scorned the idiosyncratic bohemianism of his public and private life. He is a merciless critic of those authors he once admired once they stray from what he sees as literature's higher political purpose. Both Daudet and Zola are scorned for abandoning the people. Vallès also engaged in a bitter polemic with Paul Alexis, a voice for the Naturalists who, prior to the Dreyfus affair, maintained that writers and their works must not concern themselves with politics.[13] For most critics Vallès's significant contribution to social revolution and to literature is contained in his depiction of political conflict in mid-century France and through the Commune period. I would like to suggest that it is as much Vallès's perception of evolving modern institutions and of alienation as his presentation of specific historical struggles that deserve our attention.

Bachelard cautions us to resist "l'intuition géometrique" when considering the poetics of inside and outside space (*Poétique de l'espace,* p. 204). His caution is also useful for a study of the politics of space where, as we have seen, the privatization of life does not lead to the expression of an essential self nor to the discovery of inside and outside as distinct, mutually defining spaces. Privacy reveals its paradox as both concentration of emptiness and vulnerability to definition from the outside. Vallès's originality lies in his early perception of the failure of bourgeois privatization, a failure reflected in the self-segregated family and the concurrent growth of modern institutions: institutions that separate the criminal from the citizen, the mad from the sane, but also the poor from the rich, and finally, the bourgeois from himself.

Notes

[1] Vallès's works are cited in the following editions: *L'Enfant,* ed. Emilien Carassus (Paris: Garnier-Flammarion, 1969); *Le Bachelier,* ed. Emilien Carassus (Paris: Garnier-Flammarion, 1970); *L'Insurgé* (Paris: Les Editeurs Français Réunis, 1950).

[2] Philippe Ariès, *L'Enfant et la vie familiale sous l'Ancien Régime* (Paris: Editions du Seuil, 1973), pp. 466-67. Ariès, in this influential study, relates the evolution of family relations to the emergence of social classes. The organization of the household, with its "zone de vie privée toujours plus étendu," p. 451, becomes the organization of the city with distinct working class and bourgeois neighborhoods.

[3] Christopher Lasch, *The World of Nations* (New York: Vintage Books, 1974), p. 14. This book contains two useful essays which both synthesize relevant works on the evolution of institutions and offer an insightful framework in which to situate them: "Origins of the Asylum," and "Educational Structure and Cultural Fragmentation." For Lasch the evolution of modern segregated institutions has led to an impoverishment of family and other organic social relations and to the removal of social problems from the kind of scrutiny that could lead to their resolution.

[4] Roger Bellet, "L'Image de l'école chez Jules Vallès," *Revue des Sciences Humaines,* LXVI (April-June, 1979), p. 39.

[5] Gaston Bachelard, *La Poétique de l'espace* (Paris: Presses Universitaires de France, 1974), p. 205.

[6] Fredric Jameson, *The Political Unconscious* (Ithaca: Cornell University Press, 1981), p. 20.

[7] Jean-François Tétu, in his presentation, "Aspects de l'idéologie de la révolte chez Jules Vallès," *Colloque Jules Vallès* (Lyon: Presses Universitaires de Lyon, 1975) brings precision to the discussion of Vallès's political values by showing the movement from private enclosures in the first two novels of the trilogy to public spaces in *L'Insurgé,* the final novel: "De *l'Enfant* pas un lieu unique, mais trois centres topographiques entre lesquels Vingtras est ecartelé; la maison, l'école et la campagne; dans *le Bachelier,* ces trois lieux disparaissent, l'univers se ferme et se concentre entre les murs d'une chambre sordide ou d'une crémerie douteuse. *L'Insurgé* s'ouvre brutalement sur deux lieux très différents qui sont deux lieux d'action: la rue, pour les manifestations et l'émeute, et les bureaux d'un journal ou de la politique. Il y a, avec *l'Insurgé,* une brusque sortie hors de l'enfermement des deux premiers livres . . ." (p. 101).

[8] Marshall Berman, *All That Is Solid Melts into Air* (New York: Simon and Schuster, 1982), p. 164. In chapter three, "Baudelaire: Modernism in the Streets," Berman analyzes the poet's vision of the Paris recreated by Georges Eugene Haussmann. He describes the way in which, for Baudelaire, the modern city's "multitude of solitudes" come together in a purposeful, collective movement: "For a little while the chaotic modernism of solitary brusque moves gives way to an ordered modernism of mass movement," p. 164. Although he was no admirer of Baudelaire, Vallès shared his view of the new city's paradoxes.

[9] In her study, "Jules Vallès et le peuple," *Romantisme,* IX (1975), Marie-Claire Banquart analyzes Vallès's relationship to "le peuple." She sees his love of the streets as espousal of the outsider's cause: "Etre dehors, dans la rue; être en dehors, chez les monstres," p. 117.

[10] Jules Vallès, *Le Tableau de Paris* (Paris: Gallimard, 1932).

[11] In the chapter "On the Characteristics of Total Institutions," Erving Goffman develops a functional definition and theory: *Asylums* (Chicago: Aldine Publishing Co., 1962). For Goffman prisons, asylums, concentration camps, orphanages, convents, and all closed societies are places "of residence and work where a large number of like-situated individuals, cut off from the wider society for an appreciable period of time, together lead an enclosed, formally administered round of life," p. xiii. Goffman opened a fruitful field of inquiry by showing that these institutions (with their categorization of "like-situated individuals," their reliance on formal administration and discipline, and their paradoxical creation of a permeable surface separating inside and

outside spaces) have helped create the modern fragmented society characterized by "the management of men," p. 13.

[12] Michel Foucault, *Histoire de la folie à l'âge classique* (Paris: Gallimard, 1972), p. 519.

[13] See especially the following articles selected from a vast journalistic *œuvre* by Roger Bellet in *Littérature et révolution* (Paris: Les Editeurs Français Réunis, 1969): "Les Victimes du Livre," "Politique et littérature," "Charles Baudelaire," and "La Révolution."

Caryl Lloyd (essay date 1987)

SOURCE: "The Politics of Irony and Alienation: A Study of Jules Vallès' *Le Bachelier*," in *Romance Quarterly*, Vol. 34, No. 1, February, 1987, pp. 27-33.

[*In the following essay, Lloyd applies Karl Marx's notion of alienation to illuminate the character Jacques Vingtras's troubled relationship to both work and workers, emphasizing Vallès's use of irony as a textual representation of alienation.*]

> As in all previous history, whoever emerges as victor still participates in that triumph in which today's rulers march over the prostrate bodies of their victims. As is customary, the spoils are born aloft in that triumphal parade. These are generally called the cultural heritage. . . . They owe their existence, not merely to the toil of the great creators who have produced them, but equally to the anonymous forced labor of the latters' contemporaries. There has never been a document of culture which was not at one and the same time a document of barbarism.[1]

Fredric Jameson in his recent work on the political unconscious evokes Walter Benjamin's formulation not only as a caution to those critics who strive to find progressive forces in all cultural artifacts but as a reminder to Marxian critics, like himself, that the "will to domination" is the source of art's symbolic power.[2] That Jules Vallès' *Le Bachelier* is appealing to critics of existing political systems and at the same time remains relatively unknown to the general public[3] is perhaps explained by the political unconscious of its audience. *Le Bachelier,* set in 1848-1857, was first serialized in 1879 in *Le Cri du Peuple,* a socialist journal. It is the middle novel of a trilogy of revolt beginning with *L'Enfant* and ending with *L'Insurgé.* While it is probably known to some in the academic field, the work is certainly not foremost in bourgeois literature's triumphal parade. Perhaps it is too simple to say that that is because Vallès' side lost, but in one sense I think that may be true.

This paper does not assume that some novels are political either by intention or chance, while others contain eternal verities untouched by historical reality. As Jameson points out pertinently: "The convenient working distinction between cultural texts that are social and political and those that are not becomes something worse than an error: namely, a symptom and a reinforcement of the reification and privatization of contemporary life. . . . Such a distinction . . . between history or society and the 'individual' . . . maims our existence as individual subjects and paralyzes our thinking about time and change just as surely as it alienates us from our speech itself."[4]

The politics of *Le Bachelier* are more evident only in the sense that the novel presents the struggle of an individual to achieve a clear critical perspective on social reality without becoming mired in the romance of personal alienation. The protagonist, Jacques Vingtras, situates his struggle not only in interaction with political and social groups but in attempts to shake off the linguistic malaise alluded to by Jameson. Jacques's quest, in one sense, is for non-ironic speech.

Throughout the novel the author's intentional irony functions as a powerful tool in his critique, in his "tearing away the veil of mystification that surrounds the moment of truth present in every theory,"[5] in every social system's mythology. This function is replaced, by the novel's end, when the character makes a discovery about the social world and a simultaneous choice for political involvement in that world, an involvement which saves the character from a view of alienation as subjective response. He will found the concept in the social reality of the working poor and will thereby live out the deeper ironies of his culture. By rejoining and thereby defining social class Jacques accomplishes two things: he identifies opposition to the Second Empire as class struggle, and he gives a political definition of irony. Irony becomes the intellectual worker's alienation.

In a curious study of Karl Marx's romantic poetry, Leonard Wessell maintains that for Marx the proletariat becomes a bearer of the Promethean imperative, that the opposition between the "ought" and "is" is driven to its absolute limit when man's physical-economic being is threatened with negation. Summarizing Marx he states, "The proletariat is the union of particularity and universality, is and ought, existence and essence in an absolute state of opposition," and, Wessell concludes, with Marx, "The proletariat as the heart of philosophy simultaneously gains a theoretical, critical or ironic head."[6] Jacques, by joining the workers and retreating from intentional verbal irony, reclaims alienation and irony as levers "for the empirical study of the world and its transformation."[7] The identification with the collective good and simultaneously the rejection of an individual ironic perspective make *Le Bachelier* a significantly revolutionary work. A closer look at Marx's concept of work and alienation, and especially of the pitfalls awaiting those who use the terms casually, may clarify how this assertion about Vallès' novel is so.

For Marx alienation is a term which needs to be used with precision. It is an aberrant form of objectification, the latter being neither negative nor positive. Alienation, moreover, arises from specific social conditions: conditions under which man's objectification of his natural powers, through work, takes on forms which bring his essence as a human being into conflict with his existence.[8] For Marx, "the alienation of the worker in his product means that his labour becomes an object, an external existence, . . . that it exists outside him, independently, as something alien to him. . . . If the product of labour does not belong to the worker, if it confronts him as an alien power, this can only be because it belongs to some other man than the worker. If the worker's activity is a torment to him, to another it must be delight and his life's joy. Not the gods, not nature, but only man himself can be this alien power over man."[9]

Alienation, then, used by many to connote the subjective responses to a variety of ill-fitting circumstances, had quite specific denotations for Marx: namely, the separation of man's thinking process from his own work, from the product of his labor. Alienation signifies the distance between the worker's product, his creation, and his own creative being.

Historian Harry Braverman, commenting on tendencies in modern thought which identify alienation and class with subjective response rather than social function, complains that for conventional social scientists, "[c]lass does not really exist outside its subjective manifestations. Class, 'status,' 'stratification,' and even that favorite hobby horse of recent years which has been taken from Marx without the least understanding of its significance, 'alienation'—all of these are for bourgeois social science artifacts of consciousness and can be studied only as they manifest themselves in the minds . . . of the population."[10]

Before proceeding further and, I hope, closing the gap between Marx's concept of alienation and *Le Bachelier,* let me briefly situate the novel and its author in their times. The character in this autobiographical work is a young provincial whose desire is to find an authentic context for his political ideals in that period of French history when once again the republic was betrayed and a strong ruler enthroned. The coup d'état of December 2, 1851, ended a brief moment when republican hopes flourished in France. With the rise to power of Louis Napoleon, nephew of the first Napoleon, France entered the second half of the century with a contrast that ironists Victor Hugo and Karl Marx could not resist underlining. For Hugo, of course, the Second Empire was that of Napoleon le Petit, and for then-journalist Karl Marx,

covering events for an English journal, the new French emperor illustrated the Hegelian principle that "all facts and personages of great importance in world history occur, as it were, twice," adding his well-known conclusion, "the first time as tragedy, the second as farce."[11] In a society which mocks the revolutionary spirit of 1789 and 1848, Jacques is estranged from the social-economic order and the linguistic banality that characterizes and upholds it.

He is the son of a schoolteacher and has completed his baccalaureate degree: a *bachelier* at a time when only four thousand Frenchmen hold that distinction.[12] Yet he yearns for the republican community of sufferers, of the oppressed. "J'aime ceux qui souffrent, cela est le fond de ma nature, je le sens—et malgré ma brutalité et ma paresse, je me souviens, je pense, et ma tête travaille. Je lis les livres de misère."[13] "Ma tête travaille" is Jacques's statement of his aspirations and failure. He is a bourgeois intellectual, one who reads about suffering. Several times he attempts to join workers in action, but he is usually taken for a stool pigeon or agent provocateur. When he takes to the streets with his romantic bohemian fellows, Jacques finds himself scorned, much as did some demonstrators in May of 1968, as "des fils de papa," bourgeois boys playing at politics. During the demonstration of December 3, 1851, the "redingotes," symbol of bourgeois attire, take up arms and urge the workers to join them on the barricades. The workers cry out, "Jeune bourgeois! Est-ce votre père ou votre oncle qui nous a fusillés et déportés en juin?" (*Le Bachelier,* p. 147). Jacques hears them but does not yet understand their message: class is not a matter of feeling and rhetoric but of economics.

The author's life was also spent in opposition to the political and social status quo. In 1848, Jules Vallès, then a sixteen-year-old student, was inspired by the February days, a popular uprising against the monarchy of Louis Philippe, to draft revolutionary motions against the baccalaureate exam and academic discipline in general. He demonstrated against the closing of historian Jules Michelet's university course and after the coup d'état tried to organized resistance to the usurper. His father, unimpressed by his son's political zeal, had him committed to a mental institution. Upon his release Vallès was implicated in the Opéra-Comique conspiracy against the emperor, was imprisoned, wrote radical articles, and was arrested for treason; he was a "candidate of the poor," a revolutionary socialist, in the 1869 legislative elections; he was active in the events of 1870-71, the Paris uprising and Commune, and maintained his political opposition until death in 1885.

It is not surprising, given the author's political history, that his novel opens with a bitter dedication: "A ceux qui nourris de grec et de latin sont morts de faim, je dédie ce livre" (p. 21). The words frame the novel in situational irony: that of a nation which educates an elite and then isolates it from the country's economic life. Behind the classical feast fed to generations of *bacheliers* lies the economic reality of mid-century France: the impoverishment and starvation of the educated young. The ironic content of the dedication alerts us at the outset that the author intends to aid victims of the Second Empire. The reader is alerted to the fact that ironic contrasts are political acts based on republican values and that ironic distance is an essential tool of social criticism.

The dedication also implies that the meals of Homer, Cicero, and Aristotle were perhaps less nourishing than anyone had been led to believe. The first page finds Jacques mulling over words, looking through them to the economic reality they veil. "J'ai de l'éducation. 'Vous voilà armé pour le lutte,' a fait mon professeur en me disant adieu. 'Qui triomphe au collège entre en vainqueur dans la carrière'" (p. 23). The word "carrière" carries an untranslatable pun since it means both career and stone quarry. Jacques, musing on the word, discovers its ironic uses in the story of a successful student which ends when the man, out of work and penniless, throws himself headfirst into a stone quarry. Jacques'

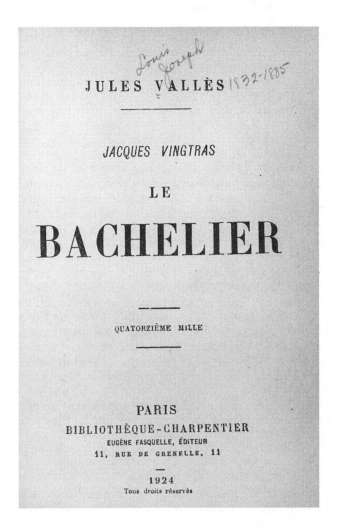

JULES VALLÈS *Louis Joseph* 1932-1885

JACQUES VINGTRAS

LE

BACHELIER

QUATORZIÈME MILLE

PARIS
BIBLIOTHÈQUE-CHARPENTIER
EUGÈNE FASQUELLE, ÉDITEUR
11, RUE DE GRENELLE. 11

1924
Tous droits réservés

judicious comment, "Ce n'est pas dans cette carrière qu'il faut entrer; je ne pense pas; il ne faut pas y entrer la tête la première, en tout cas," (p. 23) confirms our suspicions that words are offered with a narrator's warning, as Hannah Arendt has noted for our own time: that authority itself is threatened when a common language no longer exists.[14] If a career means an opening onto life's road, giving direction through work to one's whole being, and that career leads to a rocky death, then Vallès is surely offering a grim paradox and warning that bourgeois homilies are not only empty but dangerous.

Whenever Jacques attempts to write or speak he chokes on the words he uses—on the platitudes that he has learned. With his republican sympathies Jacques feels drawn to political action but finds, as his natural allies, not workers but other educated bourgeois. They form clubs and they attend the ironic lectures of Michelet. Jacques finds himself alternately enthralled and dismayed by the great man's rhetoric: " . . . quand il parlait, il avait des jets de flamme, qui me passaient comme une chaleur de brasier, dur le front. Il m'envoyait de la lumière comme un miroir vous envoie du soleil à la face. Mais souvent, bien souvent, il tisonnait trop et voulait faire trop d'étincelles: cela soulevait un nuage de cendres" (p. 85).

Jacques attempts to rally his small band against injustice but finds himself, like Michelet, a prisoner of flashy speech and of his own ironic distance from his words, in this case conveyed through an insistent repetition of words until their opposite meaning overcomes them: "Citoyens! Je sais à quoi m'engage l'honneur que vous m'imposez. Le président du Comité des Jeunes doit mourir et marcher à votre tête—ensuite être digne de vous, digne, digne . . . J'ai l'air de sonner les cloches. Digne, digne" (p. 137). Later, when a cuckoo clock marks the hour, Jacques can find no better words to incorporate than the idiotic sounds of the bird, as meaningful, finally, as his own foolish imitation of heroic speech and his relentless ironic undercutting of his own rhetoric: "Hou! Hou! Je m'empare de ce hou, hou-là! Hou! hou! L'oiseau de nuit dit 'hou, hou!' mais nous verrons bien ce que dira l'alouette gauloise, celle de nos pères (toujours nos pères!) quand elle partira vers le ciel en effleurant de son aile, la tête, peut-être fracassée déjà, du Comité des Jeunes" (p. 137). Similarly, when the Youth Committee decides to found a review, Jacques struggles to write a moving article on the theme of revolutionary tombs. He is unable to find an authentic idiom: "Je répétais toujours la même chose, et toujours en appelant les morts: 'Sortez, venez, rentrez, entendez-vous! O toi, ô vous!' Et j'avais mis du latin et cherché en cachette dans les discours de 93 . . . Sparte, Rome Athènes . . . On ne peut pas écrire pour les journaux républicains sans connaître à fond son Plutarque . . . Ce serait une impolitesse à faire aux hommes de 93 que de ne pas dire qu'ils ressemblent

aux grands hommes de nos livres de classe" (p. 121). The critic Emilien Carassus notes that Jacques suffers from "une indigestion littéraire."[15]

Bourgeois society has effectively contained the very thoughts with which Jacques would transform his world. Words fetter him to the past and provoke his own ironic asides. The idea of the republic to which both schools and politicians pay lip service is safely abstracted to a distant past. Ironic speech is inevitable when the language that shores up a bourgeois mythology of democracy confronts the reality of the anti-republican forces of order.

A dominant symbol of Jacques's malaise as an educated member of that society is the coat he must wear, a rather hideous jacket given him by his mother to assure his class fidelity: "Ma mère a dit souvent que rien ne faisait mieux qu'un pardessus sur le bras d'un homme, que ça complétait une toilette, que les paysans, eux n'avaient pas de pardessus, ni les ouvriers, ni aucune personne du commun" (p. 39). When he carries the big-buttoned yellow coat over his arms Jacques is approached by clothes merchants, interested in his jaundiced possession: "Ils prennent les basques, tâtent les boutons, comme des médecins qui soignent une variole, et s'en vont . . . Ils secouent la tête tristement, comme si ce drap était une peau malade et que je fusse un homme perdu" (p. 39). A few pages later the coat becomes a thief when a bureaucrat sees it lurking behind the door and throws it down the stairs. When Jacques finally sells the coat for food he confesses feeling like an indigent master selling a faithful slave. Implicit in the comic symbolism is the realization that goods acquire value only when they become commodities and that humans too may be nothing more than saleable goods. Jacques's tender feelings about his coat, which had, after all, sheltered and kept him company during his travels, provide an ironic contrast with the brutal treatment he and other unemployed workers suffer at the hands of those with money.

Jacques was nonetheless only half reluctant to part with his coat because he wanted to look like a worker—to wear overalls, the worker's "blouse." His naive project, a solution to his problem of vestiary malaise, reveals a belief which he soon abandoned: namely, that one can shed his past and his economic class by donning the proper apparel and attitudes, that class is a matter of consciousness.

An aging worker, broken and starving, convinces the boy that he would always be seen as a fomenter among the workers and therefore would not be hired, furthermore that those who had grown up in poverty would view his speech and manner suspiciously and that the life of a worker was one of misery and exploitation: "Avez-vous donc besoin d'être ouvrier pour courir vous faire tuer à une barricade, si la vie vous pèse! . . .

Allons! prenez votre parti de la redingote pauvre, et faites ce que l'on fait, quand on a eu les bras passés par force dans les manches de cet habit-là. Vous pourrez tomber de fatigue et de misère comme les pions ou les professeurs dont vous parlez! Si vous tombez, bonsoir! Si vous résistez, vous resterez debout au milieu des redingotes comme un défenseur de la blouse. Jeune homme, il y a là une place à prendre!" (pp. 58-59).

With these words Jacques abandons his escapist plans and accepts his fate. He will begin his true career as an intellectual worker. His successive employments would bring rueful smiles to the faces of unemployed graduate students. He delivers children to school, wipes their noses, is denied a teaching position because he refuses to sign a loyalty oath, teaches the alphabet but is fired when his over-educated nose shows repugnance for the smelly children. Ultimately he loses even his private lessons because of his political activity. It is at that point that Jacques moves closer to understanding the nature of work, and of irony, by trying to sell words.

Jacques will successively write for an overcoat trade journal, a boot and shoe magazine, he will free-lance satirical verse for those who wish to "cracher sur un ennemi," he sells anagrams and stories, condescends to write business letters which are so replete with classical allusions that he is quickly dismissed. Starving, Jacques approaches the grammarians and lexicographers, those who farm out their words as piece work. The laborers in this word-producing industry are a pitiful lot: "Ils sont une bande qui vivent sur ce dictionnaire, qui y vivent comme des naufragés sur un radeau en se disputant le vin et le biscuit—les yeux feroces, la folie de la faim au coeur. . . . Un contremaître à mine basse est chargé de distribuer l'ouvrage. La plupart se tiennent vis-à-vis de lui dans l'attitude des sauvages devant les idoles et lèchent ses bottes ressemelées" (p. 334). Jacques asks if he might have some crumbs, some of the more difficult or repugnant words: "J'ai demandé s'il ne restait pas quelques bribes pour moi; les mots difficiles, répugnants . . ." (p. 335). Later he invents quotations, attributing them to famous men of letters from France's past; these he sells to authors of grammars as illustrations of grammatical principles. His inventions provoke heated discussions among scholars and change the way certain authors will be judged by history. Complaining of the tedium of work for which he is paid by the line, by the number of words produced, Jacques explains his clever solution: "Quand j'ai à ajouter un example, je l'invente tout bonnement, et je mets entre parenthèses (Fléchier) (Bossuet) (Massillon) ou quelque autre grand prédicateur, de n'importe où, Cambrai, Meaux, Pontoise" (p. 337). Jacques's crocodile scruples only briefly trouble him: "C'est malhonnête, je trouble la source des littératures! . . . je change le génie de la langue . . . elle en souffrira peut-être un siècle . . . mais qui y a vu et qui y verra quelque

chose?" (pp. 336-37). In this final stage in the development of his class consciousness Jacques realizes that words are commodities dependent upon the starvation and humiliation of the mass of workers. Producing words, the creation of the culture's heritage, is comically reduced to piecework, the forerunner of the industrial assembly-line process. In its meaningless repetitiousness, in its fragmentation of the work process, and particularly in its separation of the worker's wholeness as a thinking being from the thing produced, the satire stands as an indictment of work in the Second Empire and as a comment on the relationship of culture to economics. The latter point is made most forcefully when Jacques finally writes his non-ironic masterpiece, the one by which he hopes to transform his world. The work derives, he says, from "le fond de mon coeur" (p. 319), and in it he claims: "J'ai peint les dégoûts et les douleurs d'un étudiant de jadis enterré dans l'insignifiance d'aujourd'hui. J'ai parlé de la politique et de la misère" (p. 319). The work is praised by diehard republicans and revolutionaries but none will publish it. It is rejected not only by the establishment's newspapers but by the surviving, and seriously compromised, republican reviews. The character, at this point, abandons working with words, just as he had given up wearing worker's garb. His alienation when he worked was precisely the separation, in Marx's sense of the term, of his creation from his creativity. Jacques realizes that he could only write non-ironically under a different political regime. In this way, then, irony, the distance between what ought to be and can be said, is the exact reflection of Jacques's economic alienation.

Near suicide, Jacques Vingtras gives in: he takes a loyalty oath to the regime and becomes a "pion" in a boarding school, the position which, in his eyes, is closest to that of a true worker yet is consonant with the social class to which he belongs. His capitulation, however, is far from defeat. It holds the promise of a future action: "Je vais mentir à tous mes serments d'insoumis! N'importe! il me faut l'outil qui fait le pain. . . . Mais tu nous le paieras, société bête! qui affame les instruits et les courageux quand ils ne veulent pas être tes laquais! . . . Je forgerai l'outil, mais j'aiguiserai l'arme qui un jour t'ensanglantera! Je vais manger à ta gamelle pour être fort: je vais m'exercer pour te tuer. . . . Derrière moi, il y aura peut-être un drapeau, avec des milliers de rebelles, et si le vieil ouvrier n'est pas mort, il sera content! Je serai devenu ce qu'il voulait; le commandant des redingotes rangées en bataille à côtés des blouses . . . (pp. 444-45).

The personal capitulation represents the distance Jacques has taken from alienation as the problem of personal awareness, from alienation as "an artifact of consciousness." His struggle will henceforth be the collective struggle. Early in the novel Jacques had confessed: "Je couvrirai éternellement mes émotions intimes du masque de l'insouciance et de la perruque de l'ironie . . ." (p.

26). This statement must finally be seen not as the confession of a defensive provincial but as part of the author's intentions for his character. The novel does not end in self-revelation but with the protagonist's abandonment of an obsession with personal authenticity, with the need for singularity. Jacques chooses instead self-realization through collective identification. He eschews personal theatrics: suicide, duels, the romance of poverty and bohemianism, and the politics of heroic gesture.

Functioning initially as a critique of bourgeois hypocrisy and false revolutionaries, irony is simply donned as the only apparel acceptable to Vingtras. He will choose to express the distance between what ought to be and what is, not in words but in action. His position on the proletarian rungs of the bourgeois economic ladder is seen by him as the only means of storing and perfecting rage for a better time, a time when collective speech will be possible, when irony disappears and words lead to action.

The evolution of this nineteenth-century hero runs counter to that of his contemporary and twentieth-century fellows. From an acute and immobilizing individual sensitivity Jacques rediscovers the group in a conscious reabsorption into the collective condition. Not a submission to *ananke,* nor an individual's challenge to a great city, and certainly not an acceptance of the tender indifference of the world, Jacques's undoubtedly unpopular choice to merge with the oppressed and prepare a united response to injustice, through class conflict, is the author's most significant political statement.

Notes

[1] Walter Benjamin, "Theses on the Philosophy of History," quoted in Fredric Jameson, *The Political Unconscious: Narrative as a Socially Symbolic Art* (Cornell University Press, 1981), p. 281.

[2] Jameson, p. 299.

[3] Although the third novel in Vallès' trilogy, *L'Insurgé,* was translated into English in 1974, both *L'Enfant,* and *Le Bachelier* remain untranslated. A recent revival of interest, including the 1970 publication of *Jules Vallès: Oeuvres complètes* (ed. Lucien Scheler and Marie Blancquart, Editions du Livre Club Diderot) notwithstanding, it is probably still accurate to observe as did Maurice Nadeau in a 1950 article entitled "Jules Vallès, écrivain moderne" (*Mercure de France,* 310, no. 1045, Sept. 1950, pp. 119-22) that Vallès remains a remarkably modern but unknown author. Nathan Kranowski is unequivocal in attributing that obscurity to the author's radical politics: "Why has he remained so little known if he is acknowledged to be an exceptionally fine stylist? The reason is not really hard to determine: It is his social

and political radicalism, which dominated his life and was viewed with such a mixture of fear and hostility that when he died in 1885, most people breathed a sigh of relief, and buried his works along with his bones" ("The Undeserved Obscurity of Jules Vallès," *Romance Notes,* 1973, no. 14, pp. 502-03).

[4] Jameson, p. 20.

[5] Karl Marx, *Early Writings,* ed. Quintin Hoare (New York: Vintage Books, 1975), p. 430.

[6] Leonard P. Wessel, Jr., *Karl Marx, Romantic Irony and the Proletariet* (Louisiana State University Press, 1979), p. 198.

[7] Alfred Schmidt, *The Concept of Nature in Marx,* trans. Ben Fowkes (London: New Left Books, 1971), pp. 129, 228.

[8] See discussion by Quintin Hoare in the glossary to Karl Marx, *Early Writings,* p. 429.

[9] *The Marx-Engels Reader,* ed. Robert C. Tucker (New York: W. W. Norton, 1978), pp. 71-78.

[10] Harry Braverman, *Labor and the Monopoly Capital: The Degradation of Work in the Twentieth Century* (New York: Monthly Review Press, 1979), pp. 27-28.

[11] Karl Marx, *The Eighteenth Brumaire of Louis Bonaparte* (New York: International Publishers, 1963), p. 15.

[12] Jules Vallès, *Le Bachelier,* ed. Emilien Carassus (Paris: Garnier-Flammarion, 1970), "Preface," p. 27.

[13] Jules Vallès, *Le Bachelier,* préface de Maurice Tournier (Paris: Gallimard, 1974), p. 74. All references to *Le Bachelier* are from this edition.

[14] Hannah Arendt, *Between Past and Future* (New York: Viking Press, 1956), pp. 91-141.

[15] *Le Bachelier* (Garnier-Flammarion), "Preface," p. 30.

Gretchen van Slyke (essay date 1987)

SOURCE: "Militancy in the Making: The Example of *Le Bachelier,*" in *Stanford French Review*, Vol. XI, No. 3, Fall, 1987, pp. 331-44.

[*In the following essay, van Slyke discusses* Le Bachelier *as an example of militant autobiography, using such an approach to demonstrate how the novel brings both author and reader into the text.*]

In proposing to study Vallès's *Le bachelier* as an example of what I call militant autobiography, my aim

is not to dispute the justly deserved reputation of this work. I do, however, wish to examine the paradoxical means by which *Le bachelier* has achieved that recognition. Why I say "paradoxical" will, I hope, become clear in the course of these reflections upon militant autobiography.

First off, one must ask whether *Le bachelier* may be considered a legitimate example of autobiography. This work does not conform to the autobiographical pact, as defined by Philippe Lejeune; that is, in *Le bachelier* Vallès does not assure the readers that he is faithfully recounting his life-story in his own name. In presenting the sketch of the Trilogy to Hector Malot, Vallès claimed that the work would be "Mon histoire, mon Dieu—ou presque mon histoire."[1] Furthermore, as Lejeune has remarked, the ambiguity of the pact which this work proposes to its readers is sustained by the suggestive yet equivocal relationship between the author's name, Jules Vallès, and the narrator/protagonist's name, Jacques Vingtras. They share initials, but there are both continuity and discontinuity between the *je* who signs the *dédicaces* of the volumes and the *je* who narrates the story.[2] The last volume of the Trilogy, *L'insurgé,* which recounts the events of the Commune and names the names of many historical figures, tends to impose a referential reading, despite the fact that Vingtras is an invented name. Moreover, as Lejeune has noted, Vallès did on occasion use the name Vingtras to present his own *mémoires* in journalistic pieces.[3] In spite of all these problems, Lejeune concludes that autobiography, particularly as it was understood and practiced at the time of Vallès, cannot be defined strictly in terms of the autobiographical pact. The readers' horizon of expectations, by which the effect produced by the text comes to be imagined as its cause, also enters into play. Thus, Lejeune opens up the notion of autobiography to include personal narratives which respect the autobiographical pact as well as those narratives which, by their tone, subject-matter, perspective and voice, create an effect so intimate that the readers must suppose that they are reading a novelistic transposition of personal experience.[4]

The second question, which will lead us to consider the specific conditions of militant autobiography, is much less obvious than the first. In my previous work on autobiography,[5] I have argued that the textual presence of the narratee is indispensable in this genre. Whereas the narratee may be seemingly insignificant and almost imperceptible in fictional narratives—I am thinking of the *narrataire degré zéro* posited by Gerald Prince[6]—this is not the case in autobiography. In the first place, the narrators of autobiographies are much more than mere elements of the narrative framework. If they did not intend to communicate something to someone, they would stick to the more private musings of a diary. Likewise, the narratees, insofar as they are a textual inscription of the interlocutors whom the narrator wishes to engage, occupy the receivers' place in this act of communication. But the narratees in autobiography are still more than imagined, inscribed models of the work's readers. They represent the eyes of the readers who will focus on the author/narrator and determine the meaning of the life which unfolds before them. Not only do the narratees condition what the narrator says and how that is said, but it is their inquisitive gaze which calls the narrator into existence. As soon as we want to represent ourselves for others, we have to attempt to see ourselves through their eyes. Since we have no choice but to describe ourselves as the other, there can be no such thing as auto-description. Therefore, without a narratee, the genre of autobiography cannot exist. Autobiography is in fact possible only as auto-hetero-biography insofar as the narratee (hetero) comes to occupy a position between the writing subject (auto) and the written object (biography).

Not only is the narratee a highly visible component of the autobiographical act, but examination of the interaction between the narrator and the narratee—of the contract which binds this couple—allows us to discern two distinct types of autobiography.

In the first type, which Rousseau's *Confessions* have probably made most familiar to us, the contract between the narrator and the narratee can best be summed up as that of a defendant vis-à-vis a judge. At least initially, this narrator occupies a position of inferiority in relation to the narratee; but while recounting the misadventures of the hapless protagonist, the narrator will do all that is possible in order to minimize the narratee's superiority. The narrator's ambivalence toward the narratee results in a highly ambiguous relationship between the two. Throughout the autobiographical trial, the defendant will furtively attempt to obtain the judge's absolution or, better yet, suspension of judgment or, best of all, complicity. In order to call forth the narratee's identification, this narrator presents the protagonist as a highly individualized and altogether extraordinary being who is obviously in need of special consideration. Thus, the public defense takes on the air of a private, even privileged confession on the part of misunderstood genius. Conceived in the image of the narrator's perceived relation to society, the interaction between narrator and narratee also appears as the means of modifying that relation. In this particular case, the desired modification would affect primarily the narrator, entirely to his own benefit.

The second type of autobiography, which I shall call didactic, continues, with various aims, the long tradition inaugurated by the *Confessions* of Saint Augustine. Because the narratees initially appear in a position of inferiority in relation to the narrator who undertakes to convince them of some general truth—religious, intellectual, or political—these two groups enter into a student/teacher contract. This narrator claims authority as a problem-solver; having been at one time subject to great perplexity and distress, he has discovered the means to steer through it. At the same time, the narratees are presumed to be still in critical straits. Thus, the narrator proposes that the narratees retrace the protagonist's itinerary and learn from that example. Just as the narrator and the protagonist come inevitably to coincide at the end of such retrospective undertakings, so too are the narratees invited to rise up and join them. Because there is, according to the narrator, little or nothing idiosyncratic in the cause of the distress once felt by the protagonist and supposedly still felt by the narratees, it is analyzed in universal terms and attributed to general causes. Likewise, the narrator, who leaves aside that which cannot be assimilated to his didactic aim, tends to dismiss his own particularities; for he claims the right to speak to and for a broadly defined group. Diametrically opposed to the first type of autobiography in its means and ends, didactic autobiography intends to modify the relationship between the narrator and the narratees, entirely to the benefit of the latter.

Le bachelier then appears to be a great paradox in the annals of didactic political autobiography, which I have been referring to here as militant autobiography. Among the conditions which characterize the didactic vein of autobiography, *Le bachelier* fulfills only one, and only partially. Unlike the extraordinary confessor Jean-Jacques—and I note in passing that Vingtras in *Le bachelier* insists on calling Rousseau a "pisse-froid"[7]—this narrator portrays himself as a representative social type. The grim life of the child and the young man is viewed as a product of the ideological pressures brought to bear upon the family unit insofar as *le bachelier*'s father, a peasant turned *bachelier* and teacher, takes his place in the series parent-professor-gendarme-State (25) and earthly father-Heavenly Father-Church (66-67). But far from putting the father in a position of power and autonomy, his place in these series is seen to result in alienation, displaced violence and untimely death:

> Sous ces yeux clos à jamais, dans ce creux du larmier où il n'y aura plus de pleurs, que de douleurs cachées! Je sens le coup de pouce des bourreaux en toges qui humiliaient et menaçaient. Pauvre universitaire! Un proviseur ou un principal tenait dans sa main de cuistre le pain, presque l'honneur de la famille.
>
> Je comprends qu'il ait eu des colères, qui retombèrent sur moi . . . Je me plains d'avoir souffert! Non, c'est lui qui a été la victime et l'histie!
>
> Cet homme, qui est là étendu, a juste quarante-huit ans! Il n'a pas reçu une balle dans le crâne, il n'a pas été écrasé par un camion . . . Il meurt d'avoir eu le coeur écrasé entre les pages des livres de classe; il meurt d'avoir cru à ces bêtises de l'autre monde. (437-38)

Consequently, the revolt of Vingtras against his father, which is not portrayed as reducible to problems in their interpersonal relation, comes to represent just one aspect of his general revolt against the bourgeois social order which prevailed in mid-nineteenth-century France.

But once we have noted the presence of a narrator who presents his fortunes as emblematic of social and ideological conflict, the analysis of *Le bachelier* as militant autobiography begins to founder. Traditionally all autobiography, apologetic as well as didactic, creates and maintains an explicit distinction between the narrator who speaks from a defined endpoint of development and the protagonist who is studied in the course of development. Moreover, this distinction is essential to didactic autobiography. Framing, attesting, commenting, judging, the narrator dominates the incompletely realized protagonist and, from the privileged vantage-point of the autobiography's end, makes quasi-teleological sense out of what only appeared to be the senseless vagaries of experience. From this position of authority, the narrator addresses the narratees, thereby assuring the dialogic dimension and the communicative function of the work. Thus, the narrator, the protagonist, and the narratees draw together to form a triad whose function is first to determine a life's meaning, then to transmit that meaning.

This hermeneutic triad, however, cannot readily be discerned in *Le bachelier.* How is this so? Philippe Lejeune's analysis of narrative technique in *L'enfant,* which also applies to *Le bachelier,* pinpoints the problem. In these works, it is difficult—if not impossible—to distinguish the voice of the narrator from that of the protagonist. Even Lejeune, who steadfastly maintains his distinction on the theoretical level, admits to seemingly insuperable problems while actually reading the text. In *Le bachelier,* Vingtras recounts his life over discrete and discontinuous moments from a point in time which seems to be nearly contemporaneous with the events recounted. Were it not for its division into chapters, this work could be mistaken for occasional jottings in a diary. In addition to the eclipse of the retrospective narrator, the generalized use of the historical present and of direct free style also tends to rub out the distinction between the narrator and the protagonist. Thus, there is nowhere in evidence that position of authority from which the autobiographical narrator, at the term of his development, confers meaning upon the life of the protagonist, in the process of development. Furthermore, this narrator, who suppresses any reference to his circumstances at the time of narrating, also refrains from invoking his narratees. By neither addressing nor referring to narratees, he apparently nullifies the communicative potential of this work. For all these reasons, militant didacticism seems to dissolve into the musings of monologue.

Lejeune's study of Vallès's narrative technique is masterful, but it overlooks the temporal dimension of this autobiography or, more specifically, the ways in which Vingtras develops through experience. Bearing in mind Lejeune's remarks insofar as they apply to *Le bachelier,* I shall attempt here to restore this narrative's temporal dimension, so important because it gradually explores and creates the elements necessary to insure the communicative potential of militant autobiography. By this I mean that the narrator and his narratees ultimately emerge from the voice of the protagonist. In order to grasp the narrator and the narratees in their process of formation, I shall study the development of the protagonist—both as a subject in society and as a subject in language[8]—in his struggle against alienation. Through this perspective, the narrative technique of *Le bachelier* can be seen to re-enact, in seemingly spontaneous fashion, the production of the hermeneutic triad, without which militant autobiography cannot exist.

On his departure for Paris, Vingtras enjoys a heady sense of autonomy:

> Je suis maître de mes gestes, maître de ma parole et de mon silence. Je sors enfin du berceau où mes braves gens de parents m'ont tenu emmailloté dix-sept ans, tout en me relevant pour me fouetter de temps en temps. (24)

Images of birth or rebirth abound to signify this long-awaited liberation from parents and professors. But such enjoyment is brief; for Vingtras, with tears of rage and humiliation smarting in his eyes, soon rediscovers alienation in the forms of poverty and dependence:

> Il me semble que je suis un de ces pauvres qui tendent la main vers une écuelle, aux portes des villages. (28)

His alienation, like that of his father, is represented as a result of their being fundamentally *déclassés* by their education. In order to avoid his sorry father's fate, Vingtras longs to join the ranks of the workers of Paris. If he were to become an apprentice-printer, he would be able to earn his bread and to pursue social revolution at the same time.[9] But this project turns out to be impossible. The head of the print-shop refuses Vingtras not only because he is too old to become an apprentice, but because his education makes him a bad risk:

> Par ce temps de révolution, nous n'aimons pas les déclassés qui sautent du collège dans l'atelier. Ils gâtent les autres. Puis cela indique un caractère mal fait, ou qu'on a déjà commis des fautes . . . croyez-moi, restez dans le milieu où vous avez vécu et faites comme tout le monde. (57)

Similar sentiments, but for very different reasons, are echoed by a sympathetic old worker:

Commençant si tard, vous ne serez jamais qu'une mazette, et à cause même de votre éducation, vous seriez malheureux. Si révolté vous vous croyiez, vous sentez encore trop le collège pour vous plaire avec les ignorants de l'atelier; vous ne leur plairiez pas non plus! (58)

But the old man, who proves to be an astute analyst, points out to Vingtras a way of making this place of alienation into a fulcrum for social action, of turning the *bachot* into an instrument of worker emancipation:

Avez-vous donc besoin d'être ouvrier pour courir vous faire tuer à une barricade, si la vie vous pèse! . . . Allons! prenez votre parti de la redingote pauvre, et faites ce que l'on fait, quand on a eu les bras passés par force dans les manches de cet habitlà. Vous pourrez tomber de fatigue et de misère comme les pions ou les professeurs dont vous parlez! Si vous tombez, bonsoir! Si vous résistez, vous resterez debout au milieu des redingotes comme un défenseur de la blouse. Jeune homme, il y a là une place à prendre! (58-59)

For a brief moment, the narrator's voice emerges from that of the protagonist in order to declare that these words, taken to heart, decided the rest of Vingtras's life:

C'est lui qui a décidé de ma vie.

C'est ce vieillard me montrant d'abord le pain de l'ouvrier sûr au début, mais remassé dans la charité au bout du chemin, puis accusant ma jeunesse d'être égoïste et lâche vis-à-vis de la faim; c'est lui qui me fit jeter au vent mon rêve d'un métier. Je rentrai parmi les bacheliers pauvres. (59)

Yet the rest of the narration, and at this point it has only begun, shows that it takes Vingtras several years to act effectively on the old worker's advice. Throughout the Second Republic, Vingtras devotes his energies to a group of young republicans. Despite his political ideals, he continues to occupy an alienated place. He perceives his role in that group as *livresque,* modeled on that of Porthos in Dumas's *Les trois mousquetaires* or of Baptiste in Murger's *Vie de bohème* (67). Unfortunately, at least in the opinion of Vingtras, this group's insistence on a certain *orthodoxie révolutionnaire* involves generalized rôle-playing, meaning compulsory adoration of Rousseau, Michelet, and Béranger and imitation of *les hommes de 93.* When the *coup d'état* of December 1851 shows that this group, as well as the entire *Montagne,* have utterly failed to gain the adhesion of the workers and thereby to counteract the revolutionary designs of Napoleon the Third, Vingtras dismisses them all as "Révolutionnaires de quatre sous!" who prefer high-faluting rhetoric and self-agrandizing drama to productive action (140).

The advent of the Second Empire inaugurates a new and even fiercer cycle of repression and alienation. News of Vingtras's *folies* on the barricades of Paris puts his father's teaching job in danger:

La peur courbe toutes les têtes, la peur des fonctionnaires nouveaux et des bonapartistes terrorisants! Ils promènent la faux dans les collèges, et jettent sur le pavé quiconque a couleur républicaine. (154)

Summoned to return to Nantes or to face arrest as a minor flouting paternal authority, he returns home to the same grim environment which impelled his first flight to the capital. Because of the "milieu d'espionnage et de terreur que Décembre a créé" (198), Paris, to which he returns several months later, appears no less grim: "Malheureux! Il n'y a plus qu'à se tapir comme une bête dans un trou, ou bien à sortir pour lécher la botte du vainqueur!" (201). Isolated, demoralized, vacillating between dreams of regicide and temptations of compromise, Vingtras leads a hand-to-mouth existence in which the hand bears to the mouth only various crumbs and fish-heads. The downward spiral of his job history—*pion au sifflet,* latin teacher for young ladies, shoemaker, writer for *saltimbanques,* journalist, publicity agent, society columnist, *demandeur de Nymphe* in public baths, dictionary collaborator,[10] calligrapher, book-keeper, shopclerk—only confirms his further experience of alienation. Throughout all this, Vingtras is back at ground zero in relation to the advice given him by the old worker. Far from seeking to take his place as *un défenseur des blouses au milieu des redingotes,* he continues to be haunted by the regressive fantasy of stripping off his education and working with his hands.

Ultimately faced with the poor-house, the morgue or the insance asylum, Vingtras reaches the nadir of demoralization. At this point, he accepts his mother's advice to become a *pion* and prepare his *doctorat.* At first sight, this decision signifies only surrender to the enemy: the son stepping into his father's shoes. But Vingtras is determined that it will not be so. He has finally accepted what the old worker told him years ago, that he is and will always be a *bachelier.* Out of this resignation is born the resolution to move into that place among the revolutionaries of the future which the old worker had pointed out as his proper station. In his last apostrophe to society, Vingtras declaims his *morale provisoire:*

Je vais manger à ta gamelle pour être fort: je vais m'exercer pour te tuer—puis j'avancerai sur toi . . . et je te casserai les pattes . . .

Derrière moi, il y aura peut-être un drapeau, avec des milliers de rebelles, et si le vieil ouvrier n'est pas mort, il sera content! Je serai devenu ce qu'il voulait: le commandant des redingotes rangées en bataille à côté des blouses . . . (444-45)

In his struggle against alienation, the development of Vingtras as a subject in language parallels his development as a subject in society. Contributing to his sense of autonomy on that first departure for Paris is Vingtras's certainty of mastering his tongue: he claims to be "maître de ma parole et de mon silence" (24). But it is naive to believe that language is merely a medium of self-expression. Over the last several decades, language has come to be viewed as a powerful means of inscribing the subject—as an alienated signifier—in a predetermined place within the vast interlocking networks of family and society. Once Vingtras has arrived in Paris, the illusion of linguistic autonomy vanishes. Because of the inadequation between words and experience, he encounters events which he cannot put down on paper. Worse yet, given his lack of conformity to linguistic and ideological codes in regard not only to his family but also his republican entourage, there are many things which he dares not say. Hounded into silence by these circumstances, Vingtras painfully rediscovers his linguistic alienation:

> J'ai besoin d'être seul; j'ai besoin d'entendre ce que je pense, au lieu de brailler et d'écouter brailler, comme je fais depuis huit jours. Je vis pour les autres depuis que je suis là; il ne me reste, le soir, qu'un murmure dans les oreilles . . . (51)

In his search for more adequate expression, Vingtras bears in mind the positive model of the editor of *La Voix du Peuple:*

> Ce style de Proudhon jette des flammes, autant que le soleil dans les vitres, et il me semble que je vois à travers les lignes flamboyer une baïonnette. (77)

But like Proudhon throughout the Second Republic, Vingtras encounters the problem of red pedantry:

> Il m'arrive souvent, le soir quand je suis seul, de me demander aussi si je n'ai pas quitté une cuistrerie pour une autre, et si après les classiques de l'Université, il n'y a pas les classiques de la révolution—avec des proviseurs rouges, et un bachot jacobin!
>
> Par moments, j'ai peur de n'être qu'un égoïste comme le vicil ouvrier m'appela quand je lui parlai d'être apprenti. Je voudrais dans les discours des républicains trouver des phrases qui correspondissent à mes colères . . .
>
> Quand don brûlera-t-on le Code et les collèges?
>
> Ils ne m'écoutent pas, me blaquent et m'accusent d'insulter les saints de la République. (126-27)

In an attempt to overcome the isolation and humiliation to which he is subject in the republican entourage, the voice of the protagonist launches desperate appeals to more sympathetic interlocuteurs who, inscribed as mere figures of desire, can only be called proto-narratees:

> Seul, seul de mon opinion! . . .
>
> Au secours, donc, les fils de pauvres! ceux dont les pères ont été fauchés par la Réquisition! Au secours, les descendants des sans-culottes! Au secours, tous ceux dont les mères ont maudit l'ogre de Corse! ceux qui étouffent dans les greniers, ceux dont les Lisettes ont faim! Au secours! . . .
>
> J'en suis pour mon ridicule et ma rage, et l'on est arrivé à traiter mon indignation de manie. (131)

But the linguistic alienation from which Vingtras suffers is not merely a result of his conformist comrades. On rereading the draft of an article one morning, Vingtras discovers, and to his great dismay, that he is incapable of respecting the republican codes of discourse. Having been commissioned to write about a martyr of the revolution, Vingtras goes to the hallowed burial place. But instead of giving all his attention to the republican's grave which, he says, "réclamait, au nom de la tradition, toute l'eau de mes yeux" (122), he weeps over a little girl who is burying her doll close to her mother's grave. Unable to assimilate this unsophisticated expression of subjectivity with the austere set-phrases of political hagiography, Vingtras condemns his simplicity as a shameful secret:

> J'emporterai ce secret avec moi dans la tombe.— Mais, je le sens bien, je n'ai rien dans la tête, rien que MES idées . . .
>
> Rien que MES idées A MOI, c'est terrible! Des idées comme en auraient un paysan, une bonne femme, un marchand de vin, un garçon de café! (122)

For Vingtras, this regrettable nonconformity is only a sign of incorrigible incompetence; and he disavows writing as a career.

After the *coup d'état* in December 1851, Vingtras reconsiders writing. Because of the republican's failure in the political arena, Vingtras has freed himself from their tyrannical eloquence: "Le *fla fla* des phrases, que signifie-t-il à côté du *clic clac* des sabres?" (140). Given the repression and increased isolation which bear down upon him in the imperial régime, the desire to break out of silence corresponds to the need to recover some sense of solidarity. Once again, Vingtras invokes some protonarratees who, in this ambiance of defeat, appear as no more than shadowy conjecture:

> Trouverai-je quelque part, dans un coin, parmi les redingotes, sinon parmi les vestes ou les blouses, quelqu'un à qui je puisse conter mon supplice, qui

soit capable de comprendre ce que je souffre, qui ait dans le coeur un peu de ma foi républicaine, de mon angoisse de vaincu! (164)

Out of this desire for socialist *camaraderie* comes the project of a militant book which would transpose political action, stymied in the Paris of Napoleon the Third, into polemical force:

Allons, Vingtras, en route pour la vie de pauvreté et de travail! Tu ne peux charger ton fusil! Prépare un beau livre! (207)

But then Vingtras, who foresees the problems the imperial censors would create for the publication of such a book, discovers within himself another form of censorship that affects the book's composition: that of the alienating codes of discourse that he has unknowingly internalized during those long years spent in school, codes which prevent him from forging language into a tool adequate to his purposes:

Après mon retour de Nantes, sous le coup du dégoût, j'ai renforcé en moi-même ma douleur, j'ai essayé de la noyer dans l'idée d'un livre qui attendrait cinq ans, dix ans pour passer au jour sa gueule comme un canon. Ah! bien oui! Je me suis heurté contre les stupidités de la *bachellerie* qui m'a laissé la tête gonflée de grec et le ventre presque toujours vide en face d'un monde qui me rit au nez. Avant d'écrire un livre comme on charge une pièce, il faut avoir jeté au vent le bagage qui gêne et mon écouvillon est gras de toute la graisse du collège, il faut un autre outil que ca au pointeur. Mon livre est dans mon coeur et point sur le papier. (284-85)

In despair, Vingtras rejects his half-baked book for an assassination plot against the emperor. That plot, in which he only half-heartedly believes, fails. After he gets out of prison, he returns to journalism. Having finally managed to expel the *gymnases antiques, jeunes Grecs* and *robes prétextes* (318) from his writing, Vingtras writes an article about youth, politics, and poverty which, in his judgment, shows no trace of that alienating school rhetoric: "Je retrouve le fond de mon coeur à travers ces ratures et dans ces explosions de phrases . . ." (319). But this vehemence, under the watchful eyes of the imperial censors, guarantees not success, but notoriety and prison. The publication of such pieces would result, moreover, in a dismissal of *le père Vingtras.* Jacques's dilemma is clear: "Ce que je fais de personnel est dangereux, ce que je fais sur le patron des autres est bête!" (320). After having overcome his own alienation in language, Vingtras is merely a more likely target of political censorship.

Only in the final pages of **Le bachelier** do the narrator and his narratees rise up out of the depths of the protagonist's sense of defeat. When demoralization gives way to the bitter joy of a "récapitulation

douloureuse" (440) and then to rage, the autobiographical project is born in Vingtras:

Ce n'est pas vrai: un bachelier ne peut pas faire n'importe quoi, pour manger! Ce n'est pas vrai!

Si quelqu'un vient me dire cela face à face, je lui dirai: TU MENS! et je le souffletererai de mes souvenirs! . . .

On ne trouve pas à vivre en vendant son temps, pour un mois, une journée ou une heure, en offrant sa fatigue, en tendant ses reins, en disant: "Payez au moins mon geste d'animal, ma sueur de sang!"

Je veux l'écrire en grosses lettres et le crier tout haut. (441-42)

At this point, Vingtras summons forth the narratee, who has finally achieved a clearly defined form:

Pauvre diable, qu'on nomme bachelier, entends-tu bien? si tes parents n'ont pas travaillé ou volé assez pour pouvoir te nourrir jusqu'à trente ans comme un cochon à l'engrais, si tu n'as pas pour vingt ans de son dans l'auge, tu es destiné à une vie de misère et de honte! (442)

This narratee closely resembles Vingtras; but the *bachelier*'s attempts to communicate with him are not a pretext for solipsistic ramblings. They, of course, resemble each other, for both are portrayed as representative social types. Having addressed the narratee in the second person, Vingtras now addresses himself in the second person. Not only does this step mark the emerging distinction between the protagonist and the narrator,[11] but it clearly delineates the narrator's didactic function in this autobiography:

Tu peux au moins, le long du ruisseau, sur le chemin de ton supplice, parler à ceux qu'on veut y traîner après toi!

Montre ta tête ravagée, avance ta poitrine creuse, exhibe ton coeur pourri ou saignant devant les enfants qui passent!

Fais-leur peur comme le Dante, quand il revenait de l'enfer!

Crie-leur de se défendre et de se cramponner des ongles et des dents et d'appeler aux secours, quand le père imbécile voudra les prendre pour les mener là où l'on fait ses *humanités.* (442)

Although the hermeneutic triad of protagonist, narrator, and narratee is now in place, what is now so clearly lacking in this militant autobiography is the positive message. Unlike Dante who came back from

Hell, Vingtras is still in the depths of this social inferno. Only after Vingtras rejects the option of suicide and decides to pursue his doctorate does he assume a combative stance and realign himself and those for whom he speaks against society:

> Je veux vivre.— . . . avec des *grades,* j'y arriverai: bachelier, on crève—docteur, on peut avoir son écuelle chez les marchands de soupe.
>
> Je vais mentir à tous mes serments d'insoumis! N'importe! il me faut l'outil qui fait le pain.
>
> Mais tu nous le paieras, société bête! qui affame les instruits et les courageux quand ils ne veulent pas être tes laquais! Va! tu ne perdras rien pour attendre!
>
> Je forgerai l'outil, mais j'aiguiserai l'arme qui un jour t'ensanglantera! (444)

Thus, out of language which had long enforced his alienation, Vingtras is at last determined to forge a tool of social emancipation which will fulfill the expectations of the old worker: "Je serai devenu ce qu'il voulait: le commandement des redingotes rangées en bataille à côté des blouses . . ." (445).

This end is therefore a beginning for the militant autobiographer. In the place where Vingtras is initially inscribed as a subject in society and in language, there is only a figure of alienation. But throughout his painful apprenticeship of limited autonomy in a hostile political order, Vingtras moves slowly toward that new "place à prendre" which the old worker pointed out to him. And once in that place, the protagonist assumes the form of the narrator, draws the shape of his narratees, and anticipates fulfillment of his militant project.

Notes

[1] Quoted by Philippe Lejeune, "Techniques de narration dans le récit d'enfance," *Colloque Jules Vallès* (Lyon: Presses Universitaires de Lyon, 1975) 52.

[2] See Marie-Claire Bancquart, *Jules Vallès* (Seghers, 1971) 28.

[3] Lejeune 70.

[4] Lejeune 53-54.

[5] "Le narrataire et l'autobiographie," *Francofonia* 2 (Spring 1982) 19-33.

[6] "Introduction à l'étude du narrataire," *Poétique* 14 (1973) 178-96.

[7] Jules Vallès, *Le bachelier* (Folio, 1974) 75-76. All further references to *Le bachelier* will be taken from this edition.

[8] In contrast to terms such as "self," which imply an essential, autonomous sense of identity, I have chosen to use the Lacanian term "subject" because it insists upon the relational nature of identity, produced and inscribed as a place within the interlocking networks of family and society.

[9] In nineteenth-century France, the *ouvriers typographes* were at the forefront of the workers' movement. Moreover, many prominent socialists of the July Monarchy, Proudhon and Leroux, for example, started out as printer's assistants.

[10] During the Second Empire, dictionary work was one of the last resorts for republicans who refused to *prêter serment* to Napoleon the Third, thereby making themselves unemployable in the public sector. Vallès describes dictionary collaborators as if they were occupants of the *radeau de la Méduse:* "Ils sont une bande qui vivent sur ce dictionnaire, qui y vivent comme des naufragés sur un radeau—en se disputant le vin et le biscuit—les yeux féroces, la folie et la faim au coeur. C'est épouvantable, ce spectacle!" (334).

[11] This distinction is firmly established on the last page of *Le bachelier,* narrated in the third person:

> Les talons noirs et les républicains sont mêlés.
>
> On se presse autour d'un vieux bohème qui vient de recevoir une nouvelle.
>
> "Vous vous rappelez Vingtras, celui qui ne parlait que de rosser les professeurs, et qui voulait brûler les collèges? . . .
>
> —Oui.
>
> —Eh bien! il s'est *pion.*
>
> —Sacré lâche!"

Walter Redfern (essay date 1992)

SOURCE: "*L'Enfant,*" in his *Feet First: Jules Vallès,* University of Glasgow French and German Publications, 1992, pp. 89-116.

[*In the following excerpt, Redfern examines the first book of Vallès's* Vingtras *trilogy,* L'Enfant, *focusing on Vallès's use of sensory detail and his keen perception of the joys and injustices of childhood and education.*]

In *Foucault's Pendulum,* Umberto Eco writes: 'The literature of memory: he knew himself that it was the last refuge of scoundrels'. Sometimes, no doubt, but for Vallès the past was the true homeland. The only convincing fiction he could write (and he applied the same

criterion to other writers) was born when he could master his facts. If home is 'the place where, when you have to go there, / They have to take you in',[1] it is also starting blocks. By the standards of ordinary success, Vallès, who never called his three novels a trilogy, was a late developer.

His fiction is heavily autobiographical, but not umbilicist. Just as simplicity cannot be swotted up, nor a sophisticate easily go native, so a grown man cannot rebecome his earlier self. He has, ineluctably, hindsight, and can hardly spurn the benefits of experience. All he can sanely aim for is to locate what is left of the child in the adult and use this to enrich his vision. Pedantic forms of keeping faith with an earlier self are self-denying and counterproductive. His old friend, Arthur Ranc, said in 1905: 'Il n'y a pas, à ma connaissance, de faussetés dans les volumes *Vingtras,* tout au plus quelques exagérations sans importance'.[2] The fact remains that Vallès took considerable liberties with the chronology of his life and omitted some significant experiences. Autobiographical fiction is a kind of double vision, which notoriously blurs, distorts, overlays. Vallès had to tackle the problem of getting X from A to B and onwards. Is it a smooth trajectory, or a zigzag (two steps forward, one step back)? If one of his profoundest desires was to avoid repeating his parents, being a chip off the old blockheads, then his retelling of his experience must refuse to imprison his hero. A kind of freedom, if not that indeterminacy so seductive to recent theorists, must be engineered.

Throughout the trilogy [*Jacques Vingtras*] life is lived and seen as a series of only partly resolved contradictions. Jacques Vingtras is frequently on the brink of throwing in the sponge, but then finding the will to come back for more. In each volume, life is a combat zone, with truces, parleys, assaults, cave-ins, harangues, wounds and deaths. It is an *exchange.* As he was permanently in opposition, Vallès thinks oppositionally. In the trilogy, he gets his own back: avenges himself, and reclaims his past.

A good deal of its material had been already aired, indirectly or proudly, in journalistic pieces, well before its actual composition. The trilogy reselects and reorders all this scattered material, and more. The two major first runs are *Lettre de Junius* (1861) and *Le Testament d'un blagueur.* In the first draft, the trio is an aunt, uncle and child—an obvious displacement, and a masking. Yet the aunt prepares for the mother, with her vetoes on coddling, the awful clothes and endless rules of etiquette she imposes on the child. The uncle is a cold fish. In an early version of the 'Victimes du livre' theme, he is spoilt by his 'Roman' idea of parental duty: 'Le pater familias antique, l'oncle familias moderne' (I, 133). We should note, however, that Vallès is more conventionally respectful here than in *L'Enfant.* Even so, in an anticipation of Nizan's

outcry—'J'avais vingt ans. Je ne laisserai personne dire que c'est le plus bel âge de la vie'.[3]—Vallès claims also to counter a received idea: 'Attaquer [. . .] une vieille phrase qui court le monde, à savoir: que l'enfance est le plus bel âge de la vie' (p. 129). *Lettre de Junius* is more cut-and-dried in its presentation of family conflict, and lacks the complexity and the brio of *L'Enfant.*

Le Testament d'un blagueur edges nearer to *L'Enfant,* though as a whole it is unsatisfactory, since the mystery of the hero's suicide is never elucidated. Nor is there much evidence of his supposed countervailing capacity for *la blague.* In this version, the parents are unremittingly cruel, and the mother is far more religious, breeding fear of hell-fire in the child. Although Vallès occasionally strikes the exact sardonic note ('On m'a envoyé à Paris en qualité de *bête à concours.* J'aurais pu venir par le train des bestiaux'—I, 1121), the derisive disgust more often sails unproductively over the top. On his education, he says:

> Je vais mâcher et remâcher, broyer, digérer, sécréter l'hexamètre, toute la saison. On ramassera mon fumier, et l'on recueillera mes rejets comme ceux d'un empoisonné: je les ravalerai par un trou de ma mémoire et le jour du grand concours, un matin de juillet, je recracherai le tout sur le papier, comme un nègre *rend, derrière* un buisson, le diamant qu'il a volé! (p. 1122).

This last simile forms part of a very contorted set of images of ingurgitation and regurgitation, already classic, of course, in student mythology. This testament contains a good many people, places and events that will reappear in *L'Enfant* (Mlle. Balandreau, la Polonie, clothes as imprisonment, the desire to be an artisan, and the complaints against classical education). But they seem more like beefing than indictment. Perhaps Vallès needed to get away from the scene of the crimes against the person before he could organise his fiction. Bellet remarks that this text was recited, at dinners, before it was written down, or rather dictated to a secretary (p. 1737). An over-genial, captive audience was the last thing he needed to test his authenticity.

One of the commoner uses of the novel since its inception has been the educational: educating the hero or heroine and, in the process, enlightening the reader—the novel of growing up, being schooled (by family, school and society). This option involves not only the largely linear narrative that most storytelling requires but also an instantly recognisable experience. We have all been children; few of us have hunted whales or built a cathedral spire. Was it English understatement that made Vallès write to his faithful friend, Malot, from England: 'Des mémoires de moi seraient presque intéressants' (*Corr. M.,* p. 60)? He was actually talking of his larger-scale project, but the attitude—voiding himself into his work—is constant: 'Je mettrai sans doute

là-dedans tout ce que j'ai, j'y logerai ce qui est *moi,* je me dépenserai jusqu'au bout, et quand ce sera fini, il se peut bien que je n'aie plus rien dans le ventre' (p. 146). More specifically on *L'Enfant* itself, he declares: 'La politique ne sera qu'incidente et viendra tard. Ce que je veux faire c'est un bouquin intime, d'émotion naïve, de passion jeune—que tout le monde pourra lire' (p. 98). He admits predecessors, for instance Alphonse Daudet's *Jack,* but feels sure he will create something fresh: 'Mon roman [. . .] est très vert, très ironique, original en diable il me semble' (p. 101). Its alternative, sardonic, title could be: *Les Plus Belles Années de la vie.* He had a clear sight of what he was creating: 'J'ai voulu faire un livre de sensations, presque de pensées, primesautier, coupé—avec une leçon terrible au bout malgré les ironies voulues, les grossièretés de parti pris' (p. 110). Although all the quotations above might strike a reader as typical of that song and dance, that *boniment,* that so fascinated Vallès when practised by *saltimbanques,* I believe Vallès had to talk through his project with his friend Malot, since, otherwise, he would have been talking largely to himself. He needed, here as elsewhere, 'la vie d'échange'.

The material and psychological conditions of the gestation of *L'Enfant* were harsh and dramatic: exile, censorship in France, considerable debts, self-doubts, and oscillations of ambition. Would he attempt a vast sociohistorical fresco, or stick to autobiographical fiction? He was not made for the invention of a purely imaginary world, and English society remained largely alien to him. Writing *L'Enfant,* Vallès could hear a crying, suffering child in the next apartment. He sent the contraband manuscript, disguised as padding for a doll, in a sardine-box resembling a small coffin, soon after the death of his love-child born of a liaison with a teacher. This sequence is over-determined; anyone can make a meal of it, though the loaded package was in fact a practical solution to escape the eyes of authority. Thus Philippe Bonnefis can comment: 'La finition est un problème d'obstétrique et non de simple rhétorique'.[4] For himself, Vallès explained: 'Je crois que je ne devrais pas dicter la colère. [. . .] C'est le lecteur qui, je l'espère, criera ce que je n'ai pas crié' (*Corr. A.,* p. 250). He appeals, then, to a free reader, but is not averse from jogging each of us in the ribs.

As well as the displacement effected in *Lettre de Junius* (and still, on occasion, in *L'Enfant*), there is that of pseudonyms. Despite his intense egopetality ('egocentricity' does not fit), Vallès often used pseudonyms out of a kind of *pudeur,* a desire to give aesthetic distance to real-life models, and, of course, at several crises in his life, a desire to survive by disguise. He felt an aversion not only from Baudelaire but from 'le coeur mis à nu' (see *Corr. M.,* p. 60). The disguises are often transparent. He wants to be caught, like the child playing hide-and-seek. In *Lettre de Junius,* repeating the tactic of *L'Argent,* he confesses: 'Je suis un inconnu qui a voulu forcer l'attention, me faire un nom en cachant le mien' (I, 129). It resembles the *roman à clef,* where readers' guesses at true identities are encouraged. Several of the pseudonyms he used while writing the trilogy in exile are connected either with his family history (Pascal—mother's maiden name) or provincial roots (La Chaussade, Colomb). They are giveaway, like *armes parlantes* in heraldry, to those who have minds to twig. Instinctively, he wants to stand up and be counted, to come clean. Vingtras itself may have been the name of a French doctor in London, or coincidentally that of a French occultist condemned by the Pope in 1843, and certainly an assonantal partner to Vallès.

L'Enfant

They fuck you up, your mum and dad.
They may not mean to, but they do.
They fill you with the faults they had
And add some extra, just for you.
(PHILIP LARKIN: 'This Be the Verse')

Vous ne réussirez pas à me dénaturer
(DIDEROT: Supplément au Voyage de Bougainville)

As Sartre, and common experience, tell us, society is first mediated, transfused, to us via our families. It was inevitable that Vallès should begin at the beginning, where we are all made, unmade, or make ourselves. Just as Nizan wanted to smash the iconic view of youth as the best years of our lives, so Vallès worked to dispel the foggy myth of idyllic childhood. *L'Enfant* tells of child-abuse. It cuts very close to the bone, and is a crucial first stage to Vallès's wider indictment of all forms of victimisation. It is no joke, and very funny. Its hero, Jacques, gags (jokes/retches) against parental gags (vetoes).

The basic opposition within *L'Enfant* is between home as prison, punitive and restrictive, and various efforts to escape. In a typical instance of pointed hyperbole, Jacques finds the local jail gayer in atmosphere than home or school. In addition, of course, he is attracted to *irréguliers* (especially one inmate who had killed a gendarme). It is clearly a kind of inverted snobbery, of reversed values, but it serves to underline how anti-natural the parental home is, totally lacking in laughter, light, common-or-garden flowers. The novel begins in ordinariness, semi-anonymity: 'Voilà le petit Chose qu'on fouette' (p. 141): thingamabob, which, like *chose,* embraces indiscriminately objects and people. Though not an exhibitionist mooner like Rousseau, Jacques offers us his belaboured rump as an image of a brutalised, not loveless but misloved, childhood. From the start, his parents, especially his mother, seek to impose a severe system of demands and sanctions, and their son in response seeks ways of circumventing it. A kindly neighbour, Mlle. Balandreau, offers to stand in as beater, but merely slaps her hands to simulate the punishment, and dresses his previous wounds. The system seeks also to inflict guilt, as when the father cuts his hand while carving a rough toy for the child. While knowing he is an innocent culprit, Jacques admits his guilt in a childish mixture of injured innocence and assumed culpability. 'Ma mère a bien fait de me battre' (p. 143). He makes prodigious efforts to justify her irrational logic:

> Elle se sacrifiait, elle étouffait ses faiblesses, elle tordait le cou au premier mouvement pour se livrer au second. Au lieu de m'embrasser, elle me pinçait;—vous croyez que cela ne lui coûtait pas!—Il lui arriva même de se casser les ongles. Elle me battait pour mon bien, voyez-vous. Sa main hésita plus d'une fois; elle dut prendre son pied. (p. 202)

This is Romantic irony: the second part of the last sentence militates against the spirit of the first half. As such, it is a mock defence. Vallès records her beatings as virtuoso performances; she is a one-woman-band with her son as the instruments. It sounds like Ravel's *Bolero,* a mechanised set of variations on a process: 'Elle m'a travaillé dans tous les sens, pincé, balafré, tamponné, bourré, souffleté, frotté, cardé et tanné' (p. 258). In fact, when she leaves off beating him at one period, he feels lost: 'Ce chômage m'inquiète' (p. 259). In such ways does the abnormal become the norm. He worries that his hide will go soft. He even stretches his understanding of her behaviour to include the pleasure she takes: 'Ma mère est contente quand elle me donne une gifle—cela l'émoustille, c'est le pétillement du hoche-queue, le plongeon du canard' (p. 197). This sounds almost approving. What is going on?

First of all: why should a child be any less illogical than grown-ups? Jacques is governed by a perverse but dogged logic: the effort to find good, or a less gratuitous evil, in parents to all appearances monstrous. This is a clear sign of a split consciousness. The child, wanting to be loved or at least to be allowed to live more naturally, assumes the logic of his opponents, whilst retaining an instinctive sense that this is not the way for people to live together. To understand is not to forgive all, but it is to mitigate resentment and to fellow-feel. Vallès here goes against the grain, though more down-to-earthly than Huysmans's Des Esseintes. In literary terms, the reminder that there is generally more to most people than meets the cursory or jaundiced eye is surely one of the prime functions of a good novel: a learning, or relearning, experience for the reader as for the protagonist. So, Vallès makes the boy apparently internalise his mother's force-feeding. The product is a strange kind of irony (not unlike free indirect speech, which can be similarly ambivalent), since surely the child cannot be so totally on his tormentor's side. Vallès allows for the well-attested fact that battered children very often do blame themselves for their suffering, and protect their parents by all kinds of subterfuges. Jacques joins in the conspiracy that puts him in the wrong. His semi-conscious wish is to find a rationale for irrationality. Besides, he even enjoys his mother's tyranny to the extent that it recognises him as a rebel, which flatters his ego. Even so, she brainwashes him so unrelentingly that it takes all his instinctual resources not to believe with her that 'il ne faut pas gâter les enfants'. *Gâter* = ruin / treat. He withstands the former, and holds out for the latter as a right. In all this, he works hard to understand the enemy: an invaluable lesson that he will go on adding to in adult life. Miming the enemy, taking her/him off, is a prime way of resisting and indeed of striking back.

The mother is energised by the fairly universal doctrine that 'Mother knows best'. As she has no outside work, she can focus on her only child the burning rays of her Spartan solicitude. Vallès presents Jacques's childhood as a rigorous training scheme in stoical endurance. Children, in the mother's view, must not be spoilt, pandered to, nor allowed to exercise freewill. Only Jacques's mother-wit saves him from his genitrix. And yet, unwittingly, she teaches her son craftiness, the art of survival: *per absurdum ad astra!* Everything she stridently disapproves of, he values. She steels him to rebel. One of the many ironic contradictions of her programme of upbringing is that, destining him for conformity, she thinks she is doing the opposite. When she stops him licking some windfall sweets, she adds sententiously: 'On commence par lécher le ventre des bonbons, on finit par lécher . . . ' (p. 182). She drifts off into euphemism, as befits her pseudo-*petit-bourgeois* 'gentility'. She wants not only to chastise her son's flesh, but chasten language. Her vetoes include rationing rare pleasures. The child wants freedom, not parole. Of sweets he says: 'Je les aime quand j'en ai trop' (p. 183). With perfect naturalness he loathes seeing pleasures corrupted by ethics. She never sees that kindness (and she does have sporadic onsets of humanity, when she drops her guard and lapses into simplicity) would have disciplined him far more effectively than severity ever has.

All she retains of whatever religious velleities once animated her are the twin tenets of crime and punishment. The forgiving God is terribly absent from her scheme of beliefs. She has a near-total lack of commiseration, not only for Jacques but for any unfortunates. It is not that she has no feelings, for she puts real passion, misapplied, into her regime. She often talks of her son in the third person, distancing and impersonalising him. Obsessed with him, she discounts and belittles him. At least, however, the child knows where he is with such a rigid person: she is consistent, not random. Yet it can only be sadism, a refinement of the lust to damage, that makes her, at one point, decide against a beating, for her son is largely inured to that, and opt for the worst sanction a sociable child can suffer: being deprived of his friends. (It is also part of her scheme to detach him from plebeian contacts). This act Jacques cannot justify: it is true, wicked cruelty. This swivelling between presenting the mother as comprehensible or as alien adds complexity to a figure who could have become an automaton and nothing else.

A conditioning programme, Pavlovian in its rigour, forces Jacques over five years to eat what he most loathes: onion hash.[5] The very day that he can stomach it without looking queasy, his mother takes it off the menu, for it was self-denial that she has been drumming into him. The progression goes from (those terrible French infinitives of legislation) 'ne pas s'écouter' to 'se forcer.' It is a regime in every sense. Life is not about pleasure. The mother labours constantly towards edification. 'Tu as pour mère une Romaine, Jacques!' (p. 280), as the hero ruefully notes. She works by aversion therapy. What he does like to eat, e.g. *gigot,* she gives him an overbellyful of, so much, he relates, that he nearly ended up baaing (p. 219). The father, for once, teaches a far gentler and more durable lesson about respect for bread (p. 162). On the other hand, the mother's would-be genteel strictures about table-manners cause Jacques, when visiting, to respond hypocritically to offers of tasty food. Such conditioning goes some way towards setting up a divided nature, training versus impulse, with falsity as the end-product. When he lets her down, it is usually because she has hoisted him to a false and unsuitable height.

The mother adds etiquette (outward behaviour) to self-denial (inward constraint). She embarks Jacques on deportment lessons, in her overall plan to make 'un Monsieur' out of him, but, after months of practice, by a kind of saving gracelessness, Jacques reaches only the level of a theatrical bumpkin. Trying hard to slide his feet in the approved manner, he disembowels the headmaster's carpet with a nail protruding from his shoe. Scenes such as these are knockabout farce, silent comedies. Father and son, bending at the same moment to pick up an umbrella, bang their heads together. Even rare family kisses are mistimed, misplaced. The presentation of flowers to his father on his name-day involves a lengthy period of rehearsal and anticipatory dread, before the inevitable fiasco. A kind of unconscious pun places his laboriously hand-written card in the *table de nuit:* the accompaniment to the *pot de géranium* next to the jerry. Jacques has to clamber up to the high parental bed to present his gift, helped by the father hoisting him by the seat of his pants. The whole charm and ceremonial nature of the occasion is turned literally arseways round. Jacques spills the pot, soils the bed, and is booted out of the bedroom (pp. 185-7). With the most deadly serious intentions, the family trio, when changing abode, create traffic jams with their piled-up belongings, their always excess baggage. It is an unwilled number, a vaudeville routine, and there are repeat performances. Vallès milks such joke situations for all, at times even more, than they are worth. In his own life, reports present

Vallès as an expert at clanging gaffes. So often, after a reasonably successful run in a job, he was fired for putting his foot in it. Yet this kind of failure is the most endearing part of Vallès, for it often rescues him from compromise.

Sartorial fiasco forced on the boy expands the attack on the parents, but also subjects the young hero to much mockery. This deflates him while inflating the description of grotesque clothes, ludicrous to behold, and constricting or abrasive to wear. Though his mother frequently accuses him of being a monster of ingratitude, the hideous clothes she foists on him turn him into *un monstre,* a freak. The habit makes the monkey. Once, the boy is dressed so weirdly that a traveller takes him for *une curiosité du pays,* and gallops up to inspect him. His mother's clothes reify him: 'J'ai l'air d'un poêle' (p. 166). They make him the odd one out. In exile, Vallès writes: 'Et il m'est donné, au sein même de ma ville natale, à douze ans, de connaître, isolé dans ce pantalon, les douleurs sourdes de l'exil' (*ibid.*). They distance, imprison; they are killjoys. They remove him so far from normality that on occasions his own mother, the perpetrator, can hardly recognise him, were it not for the stigmata on his bottom. The irony is that she wants to show him off, but is foolish enough to imagine that such hotchpotch accoutrement, such patchwork quilts, will do anything but make a spectacle of him. Vallès often mentions breeches splitting, and the dangers of unmeant exhibitionism, but, given looser bags, Jacques resembles 'un canard dont le derrière pousse' (p. 295). As clothes, for Vallès, are always political badges, Jacques is concerned that some of his make him look like a Legitimist. Vallès connects clothes and ideas, education. In both cases, Jacques is made to inherit the rags and tatters of the past, reach-me-downs, just as he eats the left-overs of school meals. His makeshift apparel is forever a hindrance to unaffected existence.

Economy rules his destiny. 'Jusqu'ici je n'ai rien eu qui fût à moi, pas même ma peau' (p. 222). Although the mother trails bribes to egg him on to win prizes at school, she renegues. Via her control of family finances, she is the power behind the throne, or rather the rickety *chaire,* but she is unaware of the low esteem in which teachers like her husband are universally held. As Carassus says: 'Jacques ne peut rien dépenser, ne peut même pas se dépenser; il lui faut tout économiser: les habits, le gigot, les forces aussi. [. . .] Il lui faut mener une vie de caisse d'épargne. Seules gifles et fessées sont distribuées à profusion.[6] The *tirelire,* savings to 'buy a man' to avoid military service, symbolises the future that never coincides with the present. Saving postpones; Jacques wants to enjoy life now.

As well as ubiquitous brainwashing, there are ritual ablutions. Historians of hygiene tell us that washing, at any social level, was at that time in France a rare event, seen as unhealthy if overdone. Jacques's mother seems ahead of her time in her ruthless persecution of dirt. She scrubs him with floor-soap weekly. Vallès's allusion to the Galatea legend (his allusions of this type are often hit-or-miss) is more of a joke than an invitation to depth (or even epidermis) psychology:

> Ma mère me jetait des seaux d'eau, en me poursuivant comme Galatée, et je devais comme Galatée––fuir pour être attrapé, mon beau Jacques! Je me vois encore dans le miroir de l'armoire, pudique dans mon impudeur, courant sur le carreau qu'on lavait du même coup, nu comme un amour, cul-de-lampe léger, ange du décrotté! Il me manquait un citron entre les dents, et du persil dans les narines, comme aux têtes de veau. J'avais leur reflet bleuâtre, fade et mollasse mais j'étais propre, par exemple. (pp. 219-20)

The classical reference is flanked, and its implications altered, by the culinary reminder: the boy is a hunk of meat. While there is undoubtedly a narcissistic element of self-delight, there seems no valid reason to import Oedipal overtones into this fresh scene of coarse refurbishment. As well as assaulting his nasal passages to 'clarify' them, the mother also brainwashes him with her pedantic saws; and seeks to launder his language via euphemisms: whitewash, or eyewash. When it comes to involving Jacques in housework, as usual she overdoes her instructions. In response, he piles it on thick (or takes off too much surface); 'il force la dose'. In this as in so many other ways, he and his mother form a kind of Jewish double act, exaggerating reciprocally, upping the ante.

Blatantly, Jacques is the *souffre-douleur*, emotional drudge, whipping boy, scapegoat, and safety valve. He is, therefore, useful. He is also a source of entertainment—the stooge, sidekick, or fall guy of the family show, 'comme l'ahuri des pantomimes, comme *l'innocent des escamoteurs*' (p. 198). In whatever role, he is the cynosure, *le point de mire*.[7] He acts as a buffer state 'entre le discours de [sa] mère et l'effroi de [son] père' (*ibid.*). He is either the apex of a triangle whose base angles gang up on him, or the white ribbon in a tug-of-war. Never does he enjoy the pair of them as parents. He functions as a crumbly mortar just holding together this grouplet threatened by collapse.

We have, then, to consider the trio, the unholy, holey trinity. Though irregularly capable of kindness, the father falls into the old teacher-parent's trap of avoiding favouritism by favouring victimisation. Here as elsewhere, the child is father to the man, for Jacques is glad to help out his father in their double bind. Vallès always looks for the desperate bonus of every situation, and here the son's acceptance of scapegoat status stops him being regarded by classmates as guilty by association. In the midst of humiliation, Jacques takes pride in being a tough, uncomplaining loser. As with the mother,

he tries to adopt the logic of his father's motives: 'C'est moi qui ai tort. Je le déshonore avec mes goûts vulgaires, mes instincts d'apprenti, mes manies d'ouvrier' (p. 246).

The traffic of suffering is not all one-way. Jacques witnesses the progress of his father's affair with the frankly sensual Mme. Brignolin. He is not jealous or ashamed; he simply feels a gooseberry. The father's infidelity is an attempt for once to assert some individuality, to yield to pleasing temptations. Mme. Brignolin loves dancing, even draws the normally anti-hedonistic Mme. Vingtras into it, who looks a sight next to the vivacious other woman. Jacques feels pity for his mother, the pitiless one, when her husband betrays her. When the drama breaks, 'il parle à ma mère d'une voix blanche, qui soupire ou siffle; on sent qu'il cherche à paraître bon et qu'il souffre; il lui montre une politesse qui fait mal et une tendresse fausse qui fait pitié. Il a le coeur ulcéré, je le vois' (p. 267). Even a young child is capable of registering such strains. It is a fishy, hurtful situation, caught exactly and poignantly by Vallès. 'Il a passé un courant de vieillesse sur ma vie, il a neigé sur moi. Je sens qu'il est tombé du malheur sur nos têtes' (p. 265). Jacques has been schooled by his parents to eschew spontaneity, and so he has to bottle up his torn feelings. The father now becomes savage in his beatings, though Jacques still tries to read his reasons: 'Il voyait tout à travers le dégoût ou la fureur!' (p. 268). He lies to Jacques, which hurts more than any leathering, by making out that his son has got him into trouble with the inspector, when it was his own adultery that had earned an official rebuke. Like his son, M. Vingtras has had unwilling choices made for him as a child, and all his adult life he has had to submit to the humiliating imposition of lowly work and status. As with the mother, an element of posturing enters into the relationship with his son: 'Il s'épuise à la fin, à force de vouloir paraître amer' (*ibid.*). Despite the grating non-coincidence between two sensibilities, father and son do enjoy a rare truce (e.g. or the boat to Nantes), a windfall of camaraderie.[8] The sleeping mother cannot abort their drinking together. Indeed, whenever the father shows signs of relenting, Jacques feels a soft spot for him. All in all, he is more of an accomplice, conniving at his wife's ill-treatment of their son, a collaborationist poltroon. He is not an ogre, but a moral pigmy, which makes it that much harder for his son to rise up in rebellion against him. All he can teach his son is essentially negative: what he must not do or be. And what he positively wants his son to do—to follow in his footsteps—the son rejects violently.

In spite of her longings to conform to a petit-bourgeois model, the mother remains something of an irregular. She puts on genteel airs when all around her is plebeian or peasant, but in middle-class circles she betrays her peasant origins. Like Jacques, she is ill-adapted; she does not fit in anywhere. This is displayed marvellously, excruciatingly, on a school social occasion when she charmlessly tries to re-seduce her straying mate. On the dance floor, she achieves clodhopping, strident gaiety—brave, provocative, blundering—when she executes her peasant stomp and erupts into raucous folk ditties. It is a grotesque performance. Despite having worked so long to overcome them, she has regressed to her origins. Though mortally embarrassed—less, however, than the onlookers—her son cannot help admiring her self-destructive courage. For once in her dowdy life, she lets her hair down and loosens the strait corsets of her pinched existence. Her son might well agree with her that the *bourrée* is as good as a fandango, for he too values peasant exoticism over the more foreign variety. Unlike him, however, she has little or no sense of the ridiculous, whereas he has it in the highest degree.

The father is ashamed of her public disgrace. He forbids her to use words from Auvergnat dialect, thus hoisting her by her own petard, for she tried to raise her son above his station, and now her husband attempts to jack her up. (A national programme promoting French to the detriment of local languages operated through the nineteenth century). In response, she puts their child in an impossible position by obliging him to spy on his father's goings. The marriage is palpably coming apart at the seams. Her own probably impoverished sex-life makes her enviously caustic towards more candidly erotic women.

Throughout *L'Enfant,* in contrast or counterpoint, are happier families, significantly supported by manual work (artisans or peasants). What young Jacques values on his stolen visits is their enjoyment of work and their noisy, disputational fun, so different from the grey grimness of his own home: 'C'est cordial, bavard, bon enfant: tout ça travaille, mais en jacassant; tout ça se dispute, mais en s'aimant' (p. 200). When the mother's away, the unmouselike Jacques can play. In these families, children are allowed to be kids. When Jacques escapes domestic pedantry to play with the cobbler's children, he notes that these phonetically slaphappy kids 'parlaient avec des velours et des cuirs;—c'est le métier qui veut ça' (pp. 201-202)—a perfectly pointed pun. As Jacques himself is unfailingly drawn towards improper liaisons, his remark is more matey than snobbishly censorious. Dimly aware of the tradition of anarchist shoemakers, Jacques would like to be a cobbler 'pour chanter et taper tout le jour' (p. 202). He is 'presque de la famille' (p. 200). One of the major reasons why *L'Enfant* is so vivacious a book is that its child-centre is a fully-fledged, if at times almost skinned-alive, member of a family unit (however ill-cemented), as he is of a larger family and local community. Hence the gossipy tone, the sense of shared experience, of mutual aid or malevolence. Street battles furnish Jacques's first encounter with barricades, tactics, defence and attack. No longer an only child, he learns the ethos of gangs and peer groups.

Annual holidays with relatives on the land clear his lungs and open his eyes, indeed all his senses. 'C'est le temps des vacances qui est le temps fécond pour l'enfant. Il a des heures à lui pour voir avec ses yeux et non avec les bésicles du maître' (II, 747). Tramping through fields, rolling in the hay, he immerses himself 'dans la vie familière, grasse, plantureuse et saine' (p. 190). His love of country life embraces hard work in the fields, for even in his utopia he includes industriousness: 'Les pays où l'on souffre, où l'on travaille, mais où l'on est libre' (p. 214). Always he compares with home. His father, who scorns peasants as clodhoppers, has to bow and scrape to superiors far more than they; he is worse off, in terms of self-respect, than a hired hand. Vallès undoubtedly, in *L'Enfant,* theatricalises and mythologises peasants, while keeping them solidly attached to the soil. Jacques loves the pell-mell meals linking family and farm workers. In contrast with the laughterless home, 'ils rient comme de gros bébés' and, untroubled by etiquette, wipe their noses with their fingers (p. 176). They carry nature with them, on them, in them. Their coarse, weather-beaten skins have areas of tender whiteness, 'comme un dos de brebis tondue ou de cochon jeune' (p. 117). Amongst them, the townee Jacques is 'un animal de luxe' (*ibid.*). The child loves sinking himself in furrows or grass, uttering bird-calls or rolling about like animal young. His killjoy mother tells him to take his Latin grammar with him, for she mistrusts vacancy. For his part, Jacques needs these oases in his generally bleak young life: these moments of stillness, pure existence, usually out of doors. He needs moments of peace, as well as brusque outbursts of violent exertion, solitude as well as crowds. In this whole area of truces, Vallès reveals his faith in alternation, his general sense of life as swings and roundabouts. This attitude injects hope into despair, but reminds hope that it is menaced.

As well as a cobbler, Jacques would want to be a farmhand. This does not represent thraldom but liberation: the possibility to unbutton himself, sprawl, expand. (Vallès omits the constraints and multiple hardships of peasant life, but Jacques sees it only on holiday, and the idealisation is passionate, not milksop). More widely, he is impressed by peasant hostility to the forces of law and order trying to enforce senseless regulations. Peasant fêtes (such as *le reinage*) are also mythologised, as the folknames given to participants hint, but what matters is the celebration of explosive pleasure—buttons popping, wine flowing. Even an intervillage punch-up is accepted as natural, an overspill of energy. Work, *fête,* fighting (or in Western film terms the range, the hoe-down and the barroom brawl). In contrast, when the family moves to Nantes, Jacques dislikes the local peasants: 'Ils ne sentent pas l'herbe, mais la vase. [. . .] Je leur trouve l'air dévot, dur et faux, à ces fils de la Vendée, à ces hommes de Bretagne' (p. 294). Political preference here biasses him against counter-revolutionary peasants.

Jacques finds welcome otherness not only away from the family, but also within it, when he visits relatives.

His deaf and dumb aunt Mélie engrosses him with her frenetic body-language, yet begets an interchange: 'Ses yeux, son front, ses lèvres, ses mains, ses pieds, ses nerfs, ses muscles, sa chair, sa peau, tout chez elle remue, jase, interroge, répond; elle vous harcéle de questions, elle demande des répliques. [. . .] Il faut se donner tout entier' (p. 148). Vallès energises, ventriloquises all he touches. Even the lacemaker's frames of his pious aunt Agnès are talkative. Though her looks repel him, he gazes steadfastly: 'Sa tête rappelle, par le haut, [. . .] une pomme de terre brûlée et, par le bas, une pomme de terre germée' (p. 149). Although he finds her affection suffocating, he extracts a consolation from her bed curtains which amuse him, especially if he looks at them with head between knees. Then he perceives fanciful creatures; he is literally seeing things. His artisan uncle Joseph has a lively body, so unlike the rigid corpse of the teaching profession. Another uncle, a *curé*, keeps no surveillance on Jacques. The mountain air clears the boy's head, and he enjoys the icy pleasures of fishing in streams. He meets other priests, whom he mistrusts when they betray anti-Protestant prejudice belied by his sighting of one in the flesh, who strikes him as an ordinary mortal. Jacques learns to unlearn on these escapes from school. His time with this uncle is a sequence of magic days followed by dreamless sleep, 'étourdi de parfums, écrasé de bonheur' (p. 242).

But he has to go back to school. This novel swings between the quick and the dead. Throughout *L'Enfant,* its *indécrottable* hero resists, with only partial success, the enforced psittacism of upbringing and schooling. He is by turns, or concurrently, *fort en thème, bête à pensums* and *bête à concours*. His education is principally a training in imitation: 'Mettez-vous à la place de Thémistocle' (p. 319). How can I, wonders Jacques, impersonate Mucius Scævola without the benefit of a charred wrist? Writing Latin verses as an exercise (mental callisthenics), Jacques parrots a pastiche of a poem about parrots: psittacism squared. Such reliance on the readymade leads inevitably to plagiarism. He first practises by forging indulgence-notes for a fellow pupil who owns books coveted by Jacques. Books lead him into crime: a nice twist on 'victimes du livre'. Yet he is a counterfeiter of some scruples, as he will not fake his father's signature in order to obtain some frogs. Vallès parodies confessional literature *à la* Jean-Jacques: 'Il m'est pénible de faire cette confession, mais je le dois à l'honneur de ma famille, au respect de la vérité, à la Banque de France, à moi-même' (p. 214). Of course, this self-indictment is ironic, since anything getting a child off school punishment is fair game to Vallès. By a twist of fate, Jacques, chastised for non-crimes, gets off scot-free for real ones, however venial. As when he refused earlier to see convicts as villains, 'je n'ai jamais eu le teint si frais, l'air si ouvert, que pendant cette période de faussariat' (p. 215—this is also a prophetic skit on Lombrosian deterministic theories of criminal physiognomy).

More gravely, Jacques plagiarises his schoolwork; he will press any material into service. In a splendid pun, as he cobbles up spondees and dactyls, he declares: 'La *qualité* n'est rien, c'est la *quantité* qui est tout' (p. 320). Hating Robespierre, Vallès could never create a sea-green, incorruptible hero. When Jacques confesses to a teacher that his successful *copie* has been a medley, he hears this frank justification of the system: 'Relevez-vous, mon enfant! Avoir ramassé ces épluchures et fait vos compositions avec? Vous n'êtes au collège que pour cela, pour mâcher et remâcher ce qui a été mâché par d'autres' (p. 321). Forgetting this lesson, later in Paris, 'je mets *du mien* dans mes devoirs. 'Il ne faut pas mattre du vôtre, je vous dis: il faut imiter les Anciens' (p. 336). The nearest Jacques ever gets to his cherished craft of shoemaking is 'le retapage et le ressemelage' of pre-existent materials (and, preparing his *agrégation,* his father is also a mosaicist, reassembling bits and pieces). All the time, however, Jacques keeps his eye and other senses on true values; reality, the present, win hands down: 'Je me moque de la Grèce et de l'Italie, du Tibre et de l'Eurotas. J'aime mieux le ruisseau de Farreyrolles, la bouse des vaches, le crottin des chevaux, et ramasser des pissenlits pour faire de la salade' (p. 321). His choice of contrasting things is wilfully elemental; he does not want to inhale the fumes of what he thinks of as academic shit.

Nowhere more sharply does Jacques see the deficiencies of his education than in mathematics. As we saw in the previous chapter concerning gymnastics, it was the abstract nature of the teaching that appalled him. In *Souvenirs d'un étudiant pauvre,* the hero complains: 'Les cuistres, eux, obligeaient mon esprit à suivre des explications *dans l'espace:* les gens du Grand Conseil de l'Université ne voulant pas matérialiser la science', and later: 'Au lycée, on en est encore à ce que j'appellerai bondieusarderie de la mathématique, à l'étude sans base visible et sans arêtes tranchées' (*SEP,* p. 67). Elsewhere he confesses to that literary disdain for numeracy which enrages scientists (I, 479). A variant of *Le Bachelier* widens the complaint to theoretical study itself: 'La théorie, qu'est-ce que c'est que ça! [. . .] Je n'ai que quatorze ans! Je voudrais savoir comment on fait, voilà tout! Je n'ai pas besoin de savoir pourquoi c'est comme ça?' (II, 1674). I should stress that Vallès's hostility to education as practised in his time is not that of *un cancre* but of a generally quite-achieving *bête à concours*. He changes his tune when he receives some far more valuable tuition from an Italian exile—a real Roman, not a textbook figment. This ex-mason uses fragments of plaster as visual and tactile aids in geometry lessons that at last mean something to the boy: *leçons de choses* in the proper sense.

A *leçon de choses (per absurdum)* is provided by the philosophy teacher, Beliben, who proves the existence of God by arranging beans on a table. Jacques counters this pedant with a kind of peasant dumb insolence. Of an academician who had devised two ethical systems instead of one, Vallès comments drily: 'A bondance de bien ne nuit pas' (p. 343): store is no sore. Vallès was fond of linking scurrilously philosophy and constipation,[9] though it is more than a joke, for Bergougnard's 'constipation' turns him into a puellicidal father. It is surely the adult Vallès who jibs and gibes so pointedly against finalism: 'Au lieu de pousser tant de haricots dans les coins, pourquoi M. Beliben ne dirait-il pas: "Voyez si Dieu est fin et s'il est bon! que lui a-t-il fallu pour raccommoder l'époux et l'épouse qui se fâchaient? Il a pris le derrière d'un enfant, du petit Vingtras, et en a fait le siège du raccommodement" ' (p. 199). Eschatology and scatology linked: the final issue of things.

Not surprisingly, Vallès describes a prizegiving ceremony in circus terms: the platform of notables as a line-up of performers, the uniformed officials like equestrians. The description switches rapidly from camels to elephants to seals. A man in an elephant-coloured suit gives Jacques his prize: 'Je croyais qu'il allait dire "Papa" et replonger dans son baquet' (p. 170). Little Jacques himself is a learned freak, a *bachelier nain*. If humour, belittlement are forms of retaliation and escape, books (hated when prescribed) are another. In detention late at night, Jacques finds a copy of *Robinson Crusoe*—the archetypal tale of self-reliant survival in your own preserve—and is totally absorbed in it till darkness blots out the words. 'Je peuple l'espace vide de mes pensées' (p. 211). It is a lifebuoy of a book, and a consoling comrade. Jacques is not its victim, but its devotee. It encourages him to plan a real escape from his prison-home: he will run away to sea. Having previously wished to be a peasant or an artisan, he now would settle for being a Negro, as he imagines Negro mothers love their children. The escape proves abortive, and Jacques has an early experience of being let down by fellow rebels. When he welcomes his father's thrashings because they harden his skin for the tough maritime life, it is not clear how much this is loaded irony, how much a defensive tactic of making virtue out of necessity, or how much exuberant hyperbole. When the family moves to Nantes, Jacques entertains great expectations of high seas and long-haul ships which are rapidly disappointed. Even in escapism, he is conscious of plagiarism, the takeover of ideas and phrases from books. When he dreams of stowing away, he is indeed a stowaway on the flights of others' imaginations, though he injects also his own drive.

In Paris, he finds his fellow pupils even more obsessed with competitive examinations and prizes than in the provinces. He sticks out like a sore thumb. He finds again that clichés rule; he must imitate the *tours heureux* of great writers, the rhetoric of trite images (Boileau: 'Boire un verre de vin qui rit dans la fougère'), and of

periphrases—the rifle as 'une arme qui vomit la mort' (p. 344). On his way to a *concours,* Jacques notices a wretch washing his handkerchief in the river with a book beside him: undoubtedly an impoverished *bachelier.* It is a traumatising insight into his own likely fate, a dire warning to all swots. Jacques fails the *concours,* and, back in Nantes, his *baccalauréat,* which, to him, is solely a matter of contacts, string-pulling, toeing the line and parroting (but he had listened to the wrong bird—p. 375).

This dashing of his father's high hopes and the severe strain on the family caused by the father's liaison poison the home atmosphere. The father grows more 'Roman' than ever, and he quotes to his son the Roman law concerning a father's right, if dishonoured, to kill his son. (This may well be a stand in for the real-life event of having his son locked up in an asylum, which is a kind of execution). Even within the *Code Napoléon,* the father has the right to threaten him with the police. As for the mother, when she visits Jacques in Paris, she is seemingly more mellowed, though naturally he remains on a war-footing. When she remarks that he is the image of her, he instantly counters, in his own mind, with a refusal to acknowledge. Swivelling back to her old ways, she accuses him: 'Ah! tu n'es pas le fils de ta mère' (p. 351). Jacques wonders briefly: 'Suis-je un enfant du hasard?' (*ibid.*). Now, rather than executing a crypto-Freudian song and dance about the several references, in *L'Enfant,* to the mother's not recognising her son in various contexts and get-ups, I take these incidents as black metajokes about the topos of the foundling, the aristocratic bye-blow, so common in literature. Jacques would certainly prefer other and better parents, and indeed seeks out substitute ones, but he can never kid himself that his real genitors do not exist. When it comes to the crunch, mother and son do not fail to identify each other. She has, after all, marked him for life. It is possible to have a tight and fraught relationship with a mother without incest or sado-masochism explaining anything of value.

In Paris, Jacques accuses her, in his head; the mother-wit which has supported him all his childhood is largely *esprit de l'escalier.* Most of the time the mother has been unanswerable; eventually the years of pent-up grievances explode, and he shocks her into a partial admission of her wrongs against him. She has been both magnet and Moloch, in either case a strong polarisation. She is a martyrant, a blend that is unpronounceable, and almost unspeakable. Like many a mother, she makes a great show of self-sacrifice, twisting or inventing facts to fit the myth of herself as the self-abnegatory pelican. Is she a monster? She surely has robotic tendencies, but machines can surprise us. She oscillates, belittling Jacques while wanting him to walk tall. Her variability is that of life itself, socking you when you least expect it. This is a valuable, if dolorous, lesson for the apprentice Jacques. In a beautifully ambivalent phrase, Jacques admits that he can do nothing 'sans exaspérer son amour' (p. 259). Yet she is rarely maternally protective, just spoilsport. (A friend said, picturesquely, of Vallès's mother: 'Elle n'a pas plus d'instinct maternel qu'une tortue n'a de moustaches'[10]). At least she does not seem to have culled her system from books, but from a mish-mash of folk, *petit-bourgeois* wisdom, proverbs, bromidioms, a kind of collective unconscious—though it is she who assembles and cooks the ingredients. 'Behind the laughter is the nagging suspicion that Jacques might have had a somewhat brighter childhood had he been placed, at an early age, in the capable hands of a well-meaning female gorilla'.[11] Vallès bites the breast that (might have) fed him (Jacques is in fact unsure whether he was farmed out to a wet nurse. He was certainly brought up *by hand!*). Very French, very un-English is the 'religion de la famille' invoked by the Goncourts.[12] No doubt it derives from a confusion of mother and motherland, so that it comes to seem unpatriotic to attack your mother. Though psychoanalytical readings would have Vallès hankering to return to the womb, and though he is keenly aware of how much he missed out on as a child, Jacques, on the contrary, strives mightily to slice the umbilical cord choking him. The last chapter of *L'Enfant* is entitled 'Délivrance'.

The family seems damned and doomed. In a fight, where the father rains nearly murderous blows on his son, Jacques at last resists, having formed the clear question in his head: why should parents have such unjust rights over their children? (In the 1880s, Vallès was to propose a league for the protection of children's rights). And yet, after this confrontation, Jacques physically defends his father against the irate parents of a pupil he slapped in class by fighting a duel against the oldest son of the family. This testimony of loyalty at last drags honesty out of M. Vingtras. Gradually, he moves from the impersonal *on* to the first person. 'Ce professorat a fait de moi une vieille bête qui a besoin d'avoir l'air méchant, et qui le devient, à force de faire le croquemitaine et les yeux creux . . . Ça vous tanne le coeur . . . On est cruel . . . J'ai été cruel' (p. 387). Jacques overhears his parents' shame-faced mutual confession, which the father fears making face to face, lest it harm his authority. He is as pedantic domestically as at school: 'Je lui parlerai toujours comme à un écolier' (p. 387). He asks his wife to act as go-between, and to tell the boy that his father is, against most of the weight of evidence, fond of him. He is a pathetic case of professional deformation, a distortion imposed on him but abetted by a deeply flawed, diminished but very recognisable humanity. Brupbacher expresses this astutely: 'Au prix de mille avanies, il s'est, si l'on ose dire, haussé à plat ventre de sa condition de fils de paysans pauvres au rang de pseudo-professeur'.[13] Jacques also discovers that, at the time of the duel, the father was on the verge of having his son locked up, as allowed by the law of the land. In a letter to his friend Arnould while writing *L'Enfant,* Vallès declares: 'Je hais l'État avant tout. C'est même l'Etat qui fait les pères féroces en sanctifiant l'autorité, en mettant audessus de la tête d'enfants comme des têtes d'insurgés un droit providentiel, une religion indiscutée, le respect de père en fils du respect de la loi' (*Corr. A.,* p. 143). Inculcated respect prevents real respect.

Does the child stand in, here, for the citizen? Vallès suggests that we citizens are in the position of children: spoken for, talked down to, kept in our place, which is to be seen and not heard. For Vallès, rebelliousness, like charity, begins at home. He was indelibly scarred, and vigorously spurred, by his childhood experience. When Jacques nerves himself to confront and resist at last his tyrannical parents, he is well on the way to political militancy. He starts reading about the French Revolution, though the images he evokes are those of peasant uprisings and artisan revolts, not crowds of city workers. These readings vault Jacques from dead languages to a living world. 'Être libre? je ne sais pas ce que c'est, mais je sais ce que c'est d'être victime, je le sais, tout jeune que je suis' (p. 364). He gets his first sight and smell of journalism, linking the ink of printing with the blood of revolution in that primary, passionate imagery so characteristic of Vallès. He sees his first political cafés and clubs: 'La blouse et la redingote s'asseyaient à la même table et l'on trinquait' (p. 366). Overall, though, Vallès saves his hero's proper political baptism for *Le Bachelier.* In *L'Enfant,* he is on the way. Vallès gives *L'Enfant* a deliberately bathetic ending: the mother more interested in the trousers lacerated in the duel than in the fight to defend family honour. For his part, Jacques will cherish his duelling scar, as he curiously values the marks of his mother's whippings. They identify him, what he is and where he comes from. His parents' attempts to denature, or re-nature, him make him prize the natural above all. Truly, if perversely, they have made him what he is. Throughout, Jacques's true education, acquired against scholastic or familial indoctrination, takes the form of a contest between common-sense and fakery or unnatural absurdity, in which pretensions are cut down to size. Likewise, his psychological growing up entails the transfer from superstitious fears of the unknown to authentic fears of the known: the world of oppression. It involves a loss of innocence, but even more a loss of naivety.

L'Enfant makes as much space for the parents' woes as for their son's. They are in a false position: *déplacés, déclassés, dépaysés, dépaysannés:* rootless, stranded between different traditions into none of which can they integrate themselves. They are 'ces paysans mal parvenus'.[14] Like their son, they are in-betweens; hence his occasional indulgence and fellow-feeling. *L'Enfant* describes the difficult-to-express but commonly-felt phenomenon of love despite, love against the grain, so that criticisms of Vallès as parenticidal are misplaced. The family trio is, severally and collectively, accident-prone. No project ever properly works out for them. Not, then, a facile matter of Me versus Them, but, more resonantly, of the three of us in a collective soup. This, at least, is the rough-and-ready balance sheet by the end of the novel, though, in details, on the way there, the scales bang up and down violently. To deny them out-of-hand, as many children would be tempted to do, would seem to their son like denying himself. It is over-nice rhetorical balancing when Léon Daudet speaks of 'Jacques Vingtras, qui ne blasphéma la famille que par besoin ardent de tendresse familiale'.[15] Feelings do not come as neatly on tap as that. Jacques's revolt is not, as Brombert claims, conservative. If he were an emotional tory, he would want the past reborn as it was, or as he invented it in rose-tinted retrospect. He wanted it better than it was. His nostalgia is prospective. He does not blame 'Society' entirely for the parents' delinquency. Not an anti-Rousseauist for nothing, he knows how romantically futile it is to blame the 'System'. Their individual, and dual, responsibility is made very clear. The mother is mean-hearted, the father a coward. Like all of us when pushed, Vallès is an essentialist. In terms of fictional fact, Jacques is not starved, battered systematically, kept locked in for long periods. He is treated harshly, cruelly, but, all told, it is doubtful whether, even today, his parents would be found guilty, in law, of criminal ill-treatment.

Is his family the exception or the rule? If it is exceptional, that implies idiosyncrasy, and he must cherish it, like all eccentricities. While he enjoys oases of joy with other families, he also witnesses there more murderous sadism than in his own. When Bergougnard, an old schoolmate of the father and ex-philosophy teacher, meets him again, he tells him that he, M. Vingtras, embodies 'l'Imagination folle', whereas Bergougnard is 'la Raison froide'. Pompously put, this has a grain of truth, for the father's other side visibly struggles to emerge in his extramarital affair. As Vallès comments in a pointed wordplay, 'il dit cela presque en grinçant des dents, comme s'il écrasait un dilemme et en mâchait les cornes' (p. 313). Indeed his coming brutality is a kind of aphrodisiac, like rhinoceros horn. The lead-in to his awful attack on his little daughter is comic, though with grating, sinister undertones. He has been brought in to tutor Jacques. He lectures on child chastisement from Greco-Roman classics—the authority; he beats to prove who is boss. The story gets blacker as we home in on this household where Bergougnard's philosophising is put into practice. 'La maison du sage. Tout d'un coup ses fils apparaissent à la fenêtre en se tordant comme des singes et en rugissant comme des chacals' (p. 315). Some of his children are sadistic, too, trapped in a production-line of brutality. Jacques hates young Bonaventure for his cruelty to animals, and envisages with equanimity crushing the tormentor to death. His violence thickens the emotional stew, as Bergougnard systematically beats Louisette, 'qui demandait pardon,

en joignant ses menottes, en tombant à genoux, se roulant de terreur devant son père qui la frappait encore . . . toujours. 'Mal, mal! Papa, papa!' (p. 316). Terror and madness coexist. The narrator remembers the screams of an octogenarian madwoman he once heard, hallucinating that she was being murdered. Thus 'la Raison froide' beats sense out of a young head. Jacques again feels vengeful: guillotine the man, or bury him alive. Oscar Wilde could not have been so facilely cynical about this almost unreadable scene of horror and pathos. You start off racking your brains, and you end up braining your child.

We can of course select out the sentimentally loaded words: *mignonne, ange, menotte,* but they do not soften the power of this scene. Sentimentality, besides, is one of those terms that resemble a peasant's bedsock: into it may be accommodated gold currency, or just smelly feet. In Vallès's case, it can be a matter of over-persuasiveness, bludgeoning the reader, rather than of that under-conviction which produces spurious writing. Coincidences, for example, are generally in *L'Enfant* exploited as a joke, one of life's capers, as when Jacques ends up unwittingly eating the rabbit which he earlier won at a fair, carried painfully inside his shirt like the legendary Spartan fox, and eventually let escape. One scene, however, veers close to the naked sentimentality for which Dickens is notorious: the death and disposal of a cherished dog, 'un être qui m'avait aimé, qui me léchait les mains quand elles étaient bleues et gonflées, et regardait, d'un œil où je croyais voir des larmes, son jeune maître qui essuyait les siennes' (p. 275). The parents' callousness in ordering the corpse to be thrown on the midden was sufficiently eloquent without the author rubbing our noses in the wet mess like tyro puppies. One further instance of sentimentality, involving untruthfulness to facts, comes when, reading about the poor people who participated in the French Revolution, Jacques says: 'Et je n'aimais que ces gens-là, parce que, seuls, les pauvres avaient été bons pour moi, quand j'étais petit' (p. 363). Like the slack tolerance of Camus's *La Peste* towards the end, this is sentimental because patently untrue to the previous facts of the text, in which several better-off people treated him kindly and some poor people refused him help. Even so, a couple of sentimental episodes do not scupper a book so vigorous overall as *L'Enfant.* Besides, Jacques's occasional sentimentality is varied by his pleasure in watching force-fed turkeys turn blue. A child can house both extremes. Vallès does not merit the strictures placed on Dickens by Carey: 'Such plastic children bring tears to grown-up eyes, because they represent an innocence which the grown-up wrongly imagines he once possessed himself'.[16] However much he grieved for himself, Vallès never forgot to embrace other children's sufferings, like those of Ricard, a bed-wetter, shamed by having his dank sheets put on public display each day. Mme. Vingtras is mean; the novel that she dominates is generous.

Whatever his sufferings, much of *L'Enfant* celebrates a highly sensuous and sensual child's sensations, for the most part intensely (if often unorthodoxly) pleasurable. Forbidden to play riskily on swings or trapezium with other kids, Jacques wonders roguishly whether he is more fragile. Has he been restuck together like a broken salad bowl? Perhaps his bum is heavier than his head, but he cannot weigh it separately to find out the answer. In a pertinent image, he jumps around the equipment 'comme un petit chien après un morceau de sucre placé trop haut' (p. 164). As with his aunt's curtains, he wants, like any child, to be upside down, to see the *mundus inversus,* which is precisely what Vallès himself is doing in this novel: adopting the posture of the child, giving us the child's slant. Jacques feels animal urges: to graze, to gambol; but he longs not only for such natural expansiveness, but also for man-about-town suavity, such as tipping a bootblack.

L'Enfant runs the whole gamut of the five senses. Taste (often imagined, given his Spartan diet). As regards religion, Jacques cannot help not taking prayers seriously, and the family attend midnight mass mainly because it is free entertainment, which the boy's imagination transforms into a pagan orgy. Passing pork butchers' shops laden with Christmas fare, Jacques experiences hallucinations of pork meat, obsessively, through the ritual:

> Le cordon de cire au bout de la perche de l'allumeur, le ruban rose, qui sert à faire des signets dans les livres, et jusqu'à la mèche d'un vicaire, qui tirebouchonne [. . .], la flamme même des cierges, la fumée qui monte en se tortillant des trous des encensoirs sont autant de petites queues de cochon que j'ai envie de tirer, de pincer ou de dénouer; que je visse par la pensée à un derrière de petit porc gras, rose et grognon, et qui me fait oublier la résurrection du Christ, le bon Dieu, Père, Fils, Vierge et Cie (p. 188).

Even sharp, irritating sensations of touch are welcome, as in 'le foin, où l'on s'enfouissait, jusqu'aux yeux, d'où l'on sortait hérissé et suant, avec des brins qui vous étaient restés dans le cou, le dos, les jambes, et vous piquaient comme des épingles' (p. 147). Jacques can find delight in the unlikeliest places, for instance a stray, impish sunbeam shining on a mountain of chamber-pots in a dormitory, 'pour y faire des siennes, s'y mirer, coqueter, danser, le mutin, et il s'en donnait à coeur joie' (p. 170). French has the evocative term *lèche-vitrines* for window-shopping, and Jacques gazes at objects behind glass so hungrily (boots, for example) that they appear to come alive (p. 172). Some descriptions are exquisitely precise, as in this of peasant knife-handles: 'Des manches de corne, avec de petits clous à cercle jaune, on dirait les yeux d'or des grenouilles' (p. 176). Is this the eye of a child or an adult poet? Cocteau said: 'Tous les enfants de neuf ans ont du génie, sauf Minou Drouet'.[17]

Jacques, like Juvenal with money, accepts all smells, whatever their provenance. Of a tannery, he notes, 'cette odeur montante, moutardeuse, verte—si l'on peut dire verte,—comme les cuirs qui faisandent dans l'humidité ou qui font sécher leur sueur au soleil' (p. 173). He speaks of 'mon nez reconnaissant' (*ibid.*): recognising / grateful. Vallès orchestrates sounds, as in this concert for three hungry stomachs: 'J'entends les boyaux de mon père qui grognent comme un tonnerre sous une voûte: les miens hurlent;—c'est un échange de borborygmes; ma mère ne peut empêcher, elle aussi, des glouglous et des bâillements' (p. 279). Jacques opens up all his senses ('j'ouvre des yeux énormes; j'écarte les narines et je dresse les oreilles' (p. 286)), and what he takes in 'double mes sens' (p. 237). At times, the descriptions blend all the senses into synaesthesia, as in this evocation of New Year presents, the bright spot of his grey year: 'Ces tons crus et ces goûts fins, [. . .] ces gloutonneries de l'œil, ces gourmandises de la langue, [. . .] ce libertinage du nez et cette audace du tympan, ce brin de folie, ce petit coup de fièvre' (p. 183).

Vallès is as perceptively evocative, as lyrical, about urban scenes as about nature. For instance, a market, crammed with uproar, movement and pungent smells, an open-air Noah's Ark running amok: 'Il y a des engueulades qui rougissent les yeux, bleuissent les joues, crispent les poings, cassent les oeufs, renversent les éventaires, dépoitraillent les matrones, et me remplissent d'une joie pure' (pp. 190-91). Some descriptions become apoplectic, as in this contrast of country fields and town allotments, where he notices that 'quelques feuilles jaunâtres, desséchées pendaient avec des teintes d'oreilles de poitrinaires. [. . .] Des melons qui ont l'air de boulets chauffés à blanc; des choux rouges, violets—on dirait des apoplexies' (p. 173). Even when pejorative in intent, Vallès's descriptions are excited, dynamic. Reading itself can transfer the living world into Jacques's sensibility. A fictional fishing-expedition: 'Un grand filet fuit au soleil, les gouttes d'eau roulent comme des perles, les poissons frétillent dans les mailles, deux pêcheurs sont dans l'eau jusqu'à la ceinture, c'est le frisson de la rivière' (p. 160). A hyperreal text. Not to be outdone, here is nature herself: 'La rivière en bas—qui s'étire comme un serpent sous les arbres, bornée d'une bande de sable jeune, plus fin que de la crème, et piqué de cailloux qui flambent comme des diamants' (p. 156). Few French writers (so many take French leave of their senses when they write) achieve this physical density, this uncerebral joy in sensations. I think of Giono, and again when I turn to sexuality.

From an early age Jacques is jealous of men getting the older women he fancies. Above all, he loves, and desires half-consciously, his superb country cousin Apollonie, and her 'blocs de beurre fermes et blancs comme les moules de chair qu'elle a sur sa poitrine. On s'arrache le beurre de la Polonie' (p. 154)—a double entendre: people would give anything for her butter / breasts. She teases him, caressing and tickling him; she smells of raspberries. From the rear she reminds of a pony which he does not quite know that he wants to mount. He makes do, very satisfyingly, by riding behind her, gripping hard as she rides bare-arsed. The whole scene is bathed in frank sensuality:

> Je sens la tiédeur de sa peau, je presse le doux de sa chair. Il me semble que cette chair se raffermit sous mes doigts qui s'appuient, et tout à l'heure, quand elle m'a regardé en tournant la tête, les lèvres ouvertes et le cou rengorgé, le sang m'est monté au crâne, a grillé mes cheveux. (p. 156)

Women and horses are linked again in the delectable shape of the circus equestrienne, Paola: 'Elle tord ses reins, elle cambre sa hanche, fait des poses; sa poitrine saute dans son corsage, et mon cœur bat la mesure sous mon gilet' (p. 192). He is a would-be peeping Jacques, and the passion becomes farcical when he is so absorbed in stalking her that he trips over a serving maid and grabs whatever is to hand, 'à pleine chair, je ne sais où; elle a cru que c'était le singe ou la trompe égarée de l'éléphant' (p. 193). In an impoverished childhood, copious flesh is cherished. In the Gnostic tradition, the 'pneumatic' are the elect. Jacques is grateful for big mercies, as in a scene on a coach: 'La grosse femme a une poitrine comme un ballon, avec une échancrure dans la robe qui laisse voir un V de chair blanche, douce à l'œil et qui semble croquante comme une cuisse de noix' (p. 194).

Mme. Devinol plays the classical French role of the older woman who breaks in the pubescent. When she takes his arm, he pumps up his biceps to near bursting point. Vallès does not omit the less glorious aspects of courtship—Jacques shaving prematurely: 'Je racle et je racle, et je fais sortir de ma peau une espèce de jus verdâtre, comme si on battait un vieux bas' (p. 331). Mme. Devinol grows more pressingly forward, and offers truffles (a reputed erotic stimulant hardly necessary when his own tuber is swelling). Stripping off in an inn after getting wet in the rain, their budding coitus is interrupted by intruders: Jacques can never conceal his identity; his telltale hat has been identified. As Vallès plays between youth and adult, in these sexual matters, the text grows equivocal, if seldom coy.

Puns are *équivoques,* supremely. They can be unmeant, as when Jacques's trouser leg rides up and his mother shouts out 'Jacques, baisse ta culotte' at the prize ceremony (p. 169). Or simple, as when Jacques lets the camel ('qui a bon dos') be blamed for his indiscretions at the circus (p. 194). They can be excruciating, and deeply serious, as in a heavily charged scene of family dispute. Jacques breaks a picture frame: 'Je suis bien content tout de même d'avoir dérangé ce silence, *cassé*

la glace, et ma famille en arrache les morceaux' (p. 198). The sentence swivels between literal, metaphorical and back to literal again. It is a serious pun because it leads into an extended section suggesting that the son's pain helps to heal the parents' rift. Other puns can be laboured. Jacques approaches the much beaten Ricard about running away: 'Je tâte Ricard; quand je dis je tâte, je parle au figuré: il me défend de le tâter (il a trop mal aux côtés)' (p. 250). This is pedantic, clumsy. Others are snappier. The cuckolded chemist, M. Brignolin, 'est toujours dans les *cornues*' (p. 258). Vallès even puns, in a variant, in his mock family escutcheon: 'Nous sommes une noblesse d'écurie. Du côté de mon père, on élevait les cochons, dans ma lignée maternelle on gardait les vaches. Nous portons pied de cochon sur queue de vache, avec tête de veau dans le fond de l'écusson' (II, 1711). (In slang, *tête de veau* = dumb cluck, *queue-de-vache* = mousy-coloured, *pied de cochon* = dirty trick. As 'un cochon' is a *remplaçant* for military service, his father did 'élever des cochons' after a fashion).

Puns often twist meanings in new directions. After the rhetorical question 'Qui remplace une mère?', Jacques answers: 'Mon Dieu! une trique remplacerait assez bien la mienne!' (p. 212). 'Triste comme un bonnet de nuit'. Mme. Brignolin says sadly to M. Vingtras. This usually occurs as 'une histoire triste comme un bonnet de nuit', a dull-as-ditchwater story. Here the sense is melancholy: the father is a sorry specimen (p. 254). A common form of twisting is exaggeration, comic hyperbole. A hat brushed against the pile makes Jacques look as if his hair were standing on end. 'Il a vu le diable, murmuraient les béates en se signant' (p. 168). A rare bout of affection from the mother has this result: 'Elle me donna un baiser à ressort qui me rejeta contre le mur où mon crâne enfonça un clou' (p. 273). This is probably a twist on the stock idea of knocking the nails of ideas into blockheads. The family threesome all exaggerate. The mother *charrie* in her upbringing (and downcasting) of Jacques; the father *renchérit* on the need to kowtow to superiors, *il force la note;* Jacques matches, mimes them; and Vallès often goes over the top in narrating all of this. We should ponder, nonetheless, the Jewish saying: 'Crooked parents can produce straight children'.[18]

All in all, Vallès handles so confidently the resources of rhetoric that we could talk of the mother, for instance, as a composite rhetorical figure: a living paradox, an oxymoron, a mixed metaphor, a chiasmus, a pun—all of these figures suggesting tugs and tensions, layered meanings. In the hated school, Vallès learned his lessons well, even though French pedagogy was back-to-front, *adverso pectore,* as Jacques notes (p. 320).

As for the structure of *L'Enfant,* the narration often suggests that something has only recently happened: 'Je m'étais piqué à une rose l'autre soir' (p. 144). Reflecting on his forgeries, Jacques wonders whether he might end up in prison: 'Et qui dit que je n'irai pas?' (p. 216). Vallès is here looking forward from a refound past to a future presented as still unfinished. The time-scheme of this novel is evidently slippery. An associative mind links, or more often juxtaposes, fragments; a patchwork quilt is being assembled. Let us consider a section, 'La Petite Ville' of Chapter Four.

The Porte de Pannesac is in the lower town of Le Puy. Jacques rejects his father's reverence for Roman monuments, but is fascinated by the grain trade centred on this area, which also houses the local baking trade and, as a sideline, hunting equipment, including fishing-rods. The text evokes the vivid sensations of fishing, and calls to his mind his reading of Captain Cook's travels among Pacific island fishermen. There follows a section on smells, good and bad (e.g. fish-glue), and a grocer's shop, packed with strong odours, including saltcod. Back on the street, Jacques's life is endangered by grain waggons driven by flour-covered men who remind him of Italian mascarades.

In contrast, in the upper town lies the teacher-training college, which keeps the figure of M. Vingtras in mind. Jacques, playing circumspectly to order with the director's son, wonders why other parents appear so unconcerned about their children's safety in playgrounds. The chapter ends on a note mingling quietude (after the uproar) and frustration. Jacques sitting on a bench like a little old man, both enjoying the stillness and dying to leap around like a young animal. The whole section comes no full circle, and follows no linear progress, but the associations of idea, sentiment or sensation give it a vital interconnectiveness, with swift shifts of mood that have their own inner logic. Even when, elsewhere, a situation seems about to develop in an orderly way, the narration often sidesteps or backtracks. Such shifts reflect Vallès's sense of the randomness of daily life. The journalistic experience explains much: the often feverish pace, the arresting headlines, followed by often jerky explication. The use of the graphic present promotes the illusion that much is just now happening; it aids immediacy.

Jacques acts as eye- and ear-witness, not always understanding what he sees or hears, though the hindsighted Vallès intimates that the boy has adequate inklings. Generally, the hindsight is disguised, as though by dark glasses. Jacques receives fragmentary hints (oranges, sign of gay living; he hears his parents arguing over 'elles', and only later understands his father's infidelity). Vallès knows how to spin out suspense, and to mimic the patchy business of twigging. Though narrated in the first person, the speaker frequently records an objectification of his self which derives from the gaze or attitudes of others: parents, teachers, bystanders. The impersonal idiom 'comme il faut' is at the core of his

mother's programme: this third person who does not exist, this god at the apex of a triangle whose base-angles are Me and Other People. This source of authority is located no place, hovering, like the 'petit bonhomme' struck to the classroom ceiling in mockery of God. The choice of the first person, in contrast, is self-affirming.

Vallès narrates through the vigilant eyes (and skin) of a brutalised child, to which is superimposed on occasion the grown man's more lucid indignation. Lejeune assumes he is doing Vallès a favour by enlisting him, on account of the superimposition of different voices which produces 'un texte vacillant', in the ranks of 'modern' autobiography.[19] For me, the often switchback narration is more agelessly a matter of an adult reliving a childhood and putting himself imaginatively into the adult shoes of the mother and father. There are alternances with the text—the parents taking it in turn to be inhuman/human. However disconnected *L'Enfant* often seems, the process of learning (and unlearning, de-indoctrination) that is at its heart is mainly a matter of making the right connexions. The child who enjoys seeing turkeys asphyxiating at the start is resolutely against all forms of enforced suffering by the end.

After bracketing *L'Enfant* with Darien's *Bas les cœurs!* and Céline's *Mort à crédit* as three great 'livres d'enfance', Campagnoli and Hersant make it clear that such books use the child as an operator: 'L'enfant n'est pas l'object d'un discours paternaliste, mais sujet d'un discours subversil'. The usual tradition, they argue, which passes from Fénelon through Hugo to Jules Renard, begets 'un jeune adulte, un *juvenis senex*'. Even if the child is in practical terms impotent, his powerlessness increases clear-sightedness, and in contrast we see the childishness of many adults.[20] In a wider view, Coveney states:

> If the central problem of the [nineteenth-century] artist was in fact one of adjustment, one can see the possibilities for identification between the artist and the consciousness of the child whose difficulty and chief source of pain often lie in adjustment and accommodation to environment. In childhood lay the perfect image of insecurity and isolation, of fear and bewilderment, of vulnerability and potential violation.[21]

This thoughtful comment leaves out the toughness, the powers of the child to resist onslaught, which are plentifully embodied in *L'Enfant.* Though some lines of Wordsworth might be transferable to Vallès's way of looking ('Shades of the prison-house begin to close / Upon the growing Boy', or 'As if his whole vocation / Were endless imitation'), no heaven lies around Jacques's infancy, and the child as visionary is hardly Vallès's *tasse de tilleul.*[22]

The *Bildungsroman* records a process of growing up, apprenticeship, acculturation and initiation. In *L'Enfant,* however, Vallès offers little clear sense of what his hero is heading towards, though a strong idea of what he is kicking against. In this respect, *L'Enfant* is open-ended. In ways very different from Sartre's Hugo in *Les Mains sales,* Jacques is 'non récupérable', incorrigible, *indécrottable.* He lives by trial and error; he is sorely tried and he errs frequently. At times, no doubt, the emotion in this novel, like the boy's backside, is raw, but if convincing recall depends on preserving into maturity the emotions and sensations of the child, then we have to take the raw with the cooked. Despite his above-average suffering, Jacques comes across as a normal child.

Zola, who had a lengthy if guarded relationship with Vallès, judged *L'Enfant* 'un livre vrai, un livre fait des documents humains les plus exacts, et les plus poignants. Voici dix ans qu'une œuvre ne m'avait remué à ce point'. Less keen on its exclamatory interventionism and the 'bouffonnerie inutile' of some pages, and writing after the Commune, for which he felt little sympathy, Zola ends with: 'Comment un homme du talent de M. Jules Vallès a-t-il pu gâter sa vie en se fourvoyant dans la politique. Jamais je ne lui pardonnerai'.[23] Politics is fit only for failures. Alphonse Daudet said of Vallès: 'Il avait l'embouchure, le vocable, le cri: rien à mettre dedans'.[24] Sounding brass, where Daudet was a tinkling cymbal. Given his fey facetiousness, his anaemic, weak-willed characters, his inability to capture the child's voice, his biologically snobbish Petit Chose and his unconvincing Jack, Daudet was in no position to pass judgment.

Jules Renard is altogether more interesting. His *Poil de carotte* has often been thought of as plagiarising *L'Enfant* (Léon Daudet and Barrès used to call Renard 'Poil de Vallès').[25] Renard's copy of *L'Enfant* was heavily scored with blue-pencil marks, though this could imply censorship as much as casing the joint. In his diary, Renard admitted: 'Pour être original, il suffit d'imiter les auteurs qui ne sont plus à la mode.[26] Even more revealingly, he states: 'J'ai été élevé par une bibliothèque'.[27] Not something Vallès could have accused himself or his parents of, for, though strongly affected by childhood reading—both models to reject or to endorse (Plutarch / Defoe), he is less bookified than many French writers, *livré aux livres* (even these words seem akin). Any touches of sadism in *L'Enfant* are wholly different in kind from those on show in *Poil de carotte,* where the whole family stands alien to the reader, and where the young hero stonily tortures and massacres little animals at great length. The mother's *méchanceté* is given, unexplained: an essence. Guichard contrasts the two writers in this way:

> Constamment, Vallès se laisse emporter par sa verve, et donne le coup de pouce à la vérité, avec sa jovialité brutale, alors que Renard pince les lèvres, parce qu'il scrre les dents. Vallès s'épanche alors que

Renard se retient, se contrôle. L'un délaie quand l'autre décante. L'un ajoute quand l'autre biffe. L'un 'en remet' quand l'autre en enlève. Vallès est un 'débondé' quand Renard est un 'constipé'.[28]

Where does the balance fall in this Gallic symmetry? Speaking in his own name on this issue, Renard says:

> J'ai lu très jeune *L'Enfant* de Jules Vallès. On m'a souvent dit plus tard que *Poil de carotte* était une imitation de *L'Enfant.* C'est inexact de fait; mais vous pensez bien que ce reproche m'honorait, car je considère *L'Enfant* comme un livre de premier ordre, un de ceux que tout écrivain français doit lire le plus tôt possible, un livre de direction. [. . .] C'est d'ailleurs surtout l'humour de Vallès qui m'a frappé. Je restais, étant sans doute trop jeune, plus insensible à l'amertume, aux plaintes sociales, un peu trop développées à mon doût, de Jules Vallès.[29]

This indeed rather tight-lipped, constipated hommage is as near as Renard ever gets to generosity towards another writer 'Chaque fois que le mot "Jules" n'est pas suivi du mot "Renard", j'ai du chagrin'.[30] Truly, he was like 'une araignée au centre de mon moi'.[31]

Vallès is generous. The epigraph to *L'Enfant* is 'à tous ceux qui crèverent d'ennui au collège ou qu'on fit pleurer dans la famille, qui, pendant leur enfance, furent tyrannisés par leurs maîtres ou rossés par leurs parents' (p. 139). *Le Bachelier* shows Jacques Vingtras widening out further from the initial base of *L'Enfant.*

Abbreviations

Full details of these works are given in the Bibliography. The frequent references to volumes I and II of Roger Bellet's Pléiade edition of the (Œuvres are given thus: (I, 935), followed by (p. 937), etc., for ones to the same volume following *closely* after in the English text until there is a change of cited source. It has not been reiterated between brackets that all page references to *L'Enfant, Le Bachelier,* and *L'Insurgé* are to Pléiade volume II.

Corr. A: Correspondance avec Arnould

Corr. M: Correspondance avec Malot

SEP: Souvenirs d'un étudiant pauvre

Notes

[1] Frost, R., 'The Death of the Hired Man', *North of Boston* (1914).

[2] Gille, p. 607.

[3] Nizan, P.: *Aden Arabie* (Maspero, 1960 [1931]), p. 65.

[4] Bonnefis, P.: *Vallès: du bon usage de la lame et de l'aiguille* (Lausanne: L'Age d'homme, 1982), p. 30.

[5] Before a projected dinner, Paul Alexis reminded Zola: 'Vous savez: pour le communard "ni oignon, ni ail, ni ciboule, ni ciboulette" '. In Bakker (ed.), *Naturalisme pas mort* (Toronto U.P., 1971), p. 182.

[6] Carassus, preface to *L'Enfant* (Garnier-Flammarion, 1968), pp. 23-4.

[7] 'Cynosure': dog's tail. Cf. the famous cartoon of Vallès as a mutt, on the cover of this book.

[8] The father 'était chien' (= stingy, nasty); the son 'avait du chien' (= spunky, sexy).

[9] Cf. Pléiade II, pp. 1565-6: 'M. Taine est un constipé [. . .], assis sur les "origines" de la France, n'accouchant de rien'.

[10] Frantz Jourdain, quoted in Choury, M. (ed.), *Les Poètes de la Commune* (Seghers, 1970), p. 221.

[11] Rollin, R. H., *The Comic Spirit in the Trilogy of Jules Vallès* (Ph.D., Bryn Mawr University, 1976), p. 265.

[12] Goncourt, *Journal,* III, 28.

[13] Brupbacher, *Socialisme et liberté,* p. 331.

[14] *Ibid.,* p. 330.

[15] Daudet, L., 'Jules Vallès', *Action française,* 14 février 1935.

[16] Carey, *The Violent Effigy,* p. 136.

[17] Cocteau, J., quoted in Barthes, R., *Mythologies* (Seuil, 1957), p. 154.

[18] Rosten, L. (ed.), *Treasury of Jewish Quotations* (New York: Bantam, 1977), p. 131.

[19] Lejeune, P., *Je est un autre* (Seuil, 1980), pp. 14-15; 28.

[20] Campagnoli, R. and Hersant, Y., 'Discours historique et discours romanesque', in *Ricerche sulla Comune* (Milan: Centro Grafico S, 1974), pp. 83-4.

[21] Coveney, P., *The Image of Childhood* (Baltimore: Penguin, 1967), pp. 31-2.

[22] Wordsworth, W., 'Intimations of Immortality', *Poems* (Penguin, 1982), I, pp. 525; 527.

[23] Zola, É., 'Jacques Vingtras', *œuvres complètes* (Tchou, 'Cercle du livre précieux', 1969), XII, pp. 589-593 (p. 592).

[24] Daudet, A., quoted in Daudet, L., *Flammes* (Grasset, 1930), p. 171.

[25] Daudet, L., 'Jules Vallès', p. 1. *Poil* here suggests both work-shyness and the hair of the dog that bit you.

[26] Renard, *Journal,* II, 510.

[27] *Ibid.,* p. 457.

[28] Guichard, L., *Jules Renard* (Gallimard, 1961), p. 88.

[29] Renard, *Lettres inédites* (Gallimard, 1957), p. 237.

[30] Renard, *Journal,* III, 816.

[31] Renard, *Journal,* II, 541.

Select Bibliography

Vallès: Editions

Bellet, R. (ed.) *Jules Vallès: Œuvres*. Gallimard (Pléiade), 1975, 1990, 2 vols.

Gille, G. (ed.) *L'Œuvre de Jules Vallès*. Le Club Français du Livre, 1968.

Scheler, L. & Bancquart, M.-C. *Jules Vallès, Œuvres complètes*. Livre Club Diderot, 1969-1970, 4 vols.

Scheler, L. (dir.) *Les Œuvres complètes de Jules Vallès*. Éditeurs français réunis, 1950-1972, 15 vols, as follows:

Le Proscrit: Correspondance avec Arthur Arnould, ed. L. Scheler.

Correspondance avec Hector Malot, ed. M.-C. Bancquart.

Souvenirs d'un étudiant pauvre; Le Candidat des pauvres; Lettre à Jules Mirès, eds. M.-C. Bancquart, L. Scheler.

Editions of the Trilogy

Garnier-Flammarion ed. É. Carassus, 1968-70.

Walter Redfern (essay date 1992)

SOURCE: "Exile and Return: *La Rue à Londres,*" in his *Feet First: Jules Vallès,* University of Glasgow French and German Publications, 1992, pp. 145-72.

[*In the following excerpt, Redfern discusses Vallès's exile in London, from about 1872 to1880, focusing on Vallès's contrasting views of Paris and London and the background for Vallès's book* La Rue à Londres. *Redfern also describes Vallès's efforts to work in Paris following his return from London and the defeat of the Paris Commune, particularly his work on the newspaper* Le Cri du peuple.]

Exile

Long before he was forced into it, Vallès hankered for a chosen exile, an expatriation (or 'exmatriation').[1] Eight years before his first trip to England in 1865, he observed some Englishmen in Paris: 'L'Anglais garde, dans son faux col trop raide et son coatchman [*sic*] trop large, un air étrange et distingué. Il est muet, il a caché sa langue au fond de sa valise; s'il ose parfois s'en servir, s'il parle, on ne comprend point son langage' (I, 63). An unpromising introduction: stiffness, reserve, incomprehensibility, otherness, and yet an imposing idiosyncrasy. When he actually set off for England, the unwitting dramatic irony as regards the future is intense: Je n'ai point le douloureux honneur de partir proscrit, rien ne m'oblige au rôle d'exilé' (p. 771). And again at the end: 'Après trois semaines de séjour à Londres, je m'aperçus que pour pouvoir parler de l'Angleterre, il fallait y passer dix ans.—Je regardais et je ne voyais pas; j'écoutais et n'entendais pas: je n'aime à parler que de ce que j'ai entendu et vu. Je me moquai de moi-même et repassai la mer' (p. 793). This honest admission of his limitations is typical. On the more positive side, he was already grateful for the haven offered here to (post-1851) *proscrits;* and impressed by policemen sorting out a brawl: 'Au lieu d'être violents parce qu'ils représentent l'État, ils étaient indulgents parce qu'ils étaient la loi' (p. 1559). He salutes the beneficial effects of self-control; 'Dans la rue comme au parlement, le *self governement* [*sic*] s'exerce et l'individualisme est en campagne' (p. 1566). When the trip became an exile, from late 1871, or early 1872 onwards to 1880, these mixed reactions to things and people English had ample time to develop in complexity.

He was sentenced to death *in absentia:* the ultimate sanction for taking French leave. Although he experienced England in many ways as a prison, a far from magnificent hulk, and has kept under surveillance like other political refugees, in fact his freedom of movement was constrained only by his financial state. This was adequate at the outset, by reason of receipts from *Le Cri du peuple* and a windfall inheritance, of which, despite legal tangles, he managed to get part; but for the bulk of his time in London he was severely strapped for cash. As he knew and partly gloried, his style was too blatantly telltale for his journalism to appear under pseudonyms in Paris papers. When this subsequently became more feasible, he badgered his friend Malot unmercifully (as he had already in the early 1860s) about loans, contracts, approaches to editors and publishers. Frequently using images of safety valves in his correspondence, Vallès occasionally apologised: 'Pardonnez ce qu'il y a d'égoiste dans ces exhalaisons à outrance' (*Corr. M.,* p. 187). When another friend, Arnould, rebuked him for his one-sided view of friend-

ship, Vallès, cut to the quick, responded speciously (*Corr. A.,* p. 285). His main defence was that he underwent, in effect, an eight-year fit of *le spleen,* the exile's blues. Even his affair with a Belgian schoolteacher, who bore him a daughter whom he loved deeply, ended tragically when the baby died after nine months on the fateful date of 2 December.

He enjoyed little comradeship or agreement with the other Communards in exile, finding, as always, the Marxists too aridly theoretical, and the Blanquists obsessed with armed insurrection. Indeed, Vallès seemed to be veering towards venture capitalism. He nursed various fruitless projects: a wine business, porcelain painting, a non-political weekly aimed at a comfortably-off English readership and bringing news of cultural life in Paris. This might in turn spin off a luxury art shop. Together with other exiles, he founded the short-lived French Athenaeum, a meeting place for lectures and language tuition. The even briefer-lived ***The Coming P*** (the title, suggesting a damp squib, shows Vallès's shaky grasp of English. The full 'People' would hardly have been incriminating, anyway) displays Vallès's energetic efforts to get into print (he tried as far afield as Russia, via Zola).[2] From about 1876, his correspondence talks repeatedly of a novel, a kind of *Vingtras IV,* for which he mooted various titles: *Les Réfractaires de Londres, Les Mystères de Londres, Les Misères de Londres, Londres infâme.* Much of the material for this project was used instead for ***La Rue à Londres.*** He started work on ***L'Enfant*** in 1876. He mentions reading few books in these years (though he kept up to date with the Paris press). Swotting up some books on banking and commerce, he commented: 'C'est lourd comme le plomb, ces livres sur l'or' (*Corr. M.,* p. 262). His trips away from London were to Belgium and Switzerland and, within Britain, to Brighton, Kent and Jersey; he did not venture to the industrial Midlands, North, Scotland or Wales.

As for psychological exile, Wittlin, on the basis of the Spanish *destierro* (deprivation of homeland) coined *destiempo:* 'The exile lives in two different times simultaneously, in the present and in the past. This life in the past is sometimes more intense [. . .] and tyrannises his entire psychology. [. . .] An exile, as it were professionally, moves backwards.[3] Home thoughts from foreign parts are normal, and the Irish Bull tells us that the exile is not at home when he is abroad. In some ways, Vallès in London thinking of Paris resembles Vallès in Paris recalling his provincial childhood. 'L'exil', he recognised, 'est une province. On n'y voit pas plus loin que le bout de sa manie!' In this perspective, even Paris becomes parochial: 'Sans autre parisiennerie que celle de la Commune racontée, reracontée, jugée, re-jugée—parisiennerie effroyablement provinciale!' (*Corr. M.,* pp. 81; 223). Exile reinstated the climate of childhood (and thus helped the writing of ***L'Enfant***): Vallès complains frequently of being left out in the cold, starved of warmth, contact and news. He is like a lover, or a desperate child, waiting for the postman in high anxiety and deeply frustrated when there is nothing for him. He refuses to understand why he does not get responses by return of post to his pleas, questions and demands. He sums up his state in these terms in a letter to a Paris editor: 'Vous avez la goutte, moi j'ai l'exil. Je ne veux pas vous arracher des larmes, je ne pose pas au martyr, je ne me drape pas, je m'embête. C'est embêtant, le manque de patrie!' (quoted II, p. xxxiv). Yet he learned to know in his bones that his exile changed his writing for the far better, that, in this area, it paid off handsomely. 'Il est à constater que le brouillard de Londres n'a jamais endolori le talent ni voilé la flamme dans les têtes françaises. Au contraire, il a trempé des styles, comme l'eau boueuse du Furens trempe les armes' (*TP,* p. 259).

La Rue à Londres

Vallès's documentary groundwork for *La Rue à Londres,* finally published in 1884 after a dozen or so years of fits and starts, was essentially the reading of French visitors to these shores: Flora Tristan, Ledru-Rollin, Louis Blanc, Alphonse Esquiros, Taine and Louis Enault (with wood engravings by Gustave Doré) (see II, 1983). *La Rue à Londres,* similarly, had drawings and etchings, by Auguste Lançon, an ex-*fedéré*. Possibly needing to boost his own morale, Vallès boasted to Malot in 1876: 'Ce serait le premier livre impartial sur l'Angleterre. Tous ont menti jusqu'ici depuis Esquiros jusqu'à Taine. Mettons qu'ils se sont trompés' (*Corr. M.,* p. 129). *La Rue à Londres* is not impartial; it is passionately wrong-headed, with moments of insight. In its admission of defeat (the English are beyond summary, if not beyond judgment), its rueful acknowledgment of the complexity of the subject, it is closer to interesting fiction than to a sociological survey feigning accuracy.

Much of the text is mnemonic. Afraid of losing Paris for good in fact or in memory, Vallès recites its characteristics, in opposition to those of London. Just as mother and son bounced off each other originally, Vallès always needs to play off polarities in this way, favouring now one, now the other, in a cross-Channel shuttle. He starts with *la rue,* his favourite space, in both cities. The streets of Paris win hands down: light, gay, not overcrowded and gloomy like their London counterparts. Here, there is little conversation, that 'vie d'échange' that Vallès needs like oxygen. He cannot tell the English apart, for they are like interchangeable mechanisms: 'Ils vont, ils viennent comme des *pistons* de machines, ils passent comme des courroies se mêlent, comme des trains se croisent' (II, 1135). Thus running together the Industrial Revolution and individual Londoners, Vallès gives fair notice of what will be his regular tactic of overstatement, of demonological (and, much more rarely, angelical) procedure. London 'n'a

pas pour deux liards de fantaisie' (p. 1137). Exiled, he rosifies Paris, polarising even public drunkenness in both cities: 'C'est la soulaison noire, point l'ivresse rose' (p. 1139). He was especially disgusted by female drunks, vomiting on the cobblestones (*ibid.*). He wilfully underestimates French alcoholism, accusing Zola of slandering *le peuple* in *L'Assommoir* (p. 1309). Shuttling, however, he notes that London streets are less military than Parisian ones: fewer soldiers, and they stroll unarmed (p. 1139).

Disoriented, he misses landmarks. 'Rien ne s'accuse en traits nets et logiques' (p. 1140). He sounds here like the quintessential neo-Cartesian Frenchman he never was. Though he accuses England of compartmentalisation, this is in fact what he misses: in London the poor and the rich live cheek by jowl (p. 1148). He offers a stereotyped French notion of English antisystematic thinking: 'L'esprit anglais ne sait pas classer ni déduire, voilà pourquoi mes voisins de la bibliothèque anglaise, tout en bûchant plus qu'on ne bûche chez nous, ne feront pas sortir du sol des idées nettes et claires. Leurs pensées flottent dans le brouillard, comme leur soleil s'y noie' (p. 1303). Amid all such diametrically opposed patterns, however, his eyes are open to a phenomenon still observable today: 'Une cité où les sergents de ville ont l'air poli et où les gentlemen ont l'air féroce' (p. 1140).

We have to wonder how many English homes Vallès penetrated, and in those he did how often he was slighted by long waits in the halls. (We must also wonder how many middle or upper-class homes Vallès was familiar with in Paris). Against the common British sense of French homes as impregnable bastions, Vallès presents English homes shut up against the world outside: 'Pays hostile, race murée!' (p. 1142). Vallès kicks against the cliché of 'le confortable anglais' (though I for one find little physical ease in French furniture): 'L'Angleterre est le pays du mal-vivre, du mal-loger, du mal-manger, du mal-s'asseoir, et du mal-dormir' (p. 1206). In these areas, Vallès misses concierges, a *table de nuit* for the jerry, and sauces on food (pp. 1207; 1211; 1213). Churches are no more welcoming than homes. Protestant temples are lugubrious, have less garish colour and smell than French Catholic ones; reformed religion offers an 'implacable tristesse' (p. 1144), and infiltrates everywhere Like Stendhal before him, Vallès was appalled at the British veto on breaking the Sabbath. The English Sunday lasts all week: 'La platitude du jour sacré' (p. 1194). Vallès almost renegues on his godlessness: 'La simplicité crue du protestantisme m'effraie plus que la grâce enivrante et enflammée du catholicisme, but luckily he pulls himself up short: 'L'encens et les bouquets font presque oublier Dieu dans les chapelles embaumées de France' (p. 1196). A few pages after the largely black-and-white opening, Vallès admits the complexity of the subject, and his own perplexity: 'Quelle ville! . . . toute pleine de contradictions énormes, amas de confusions!' (p. 1146).

The biggest contradiction is the coexisting grandeur and misery of London. Whereas the poor in Paris 'ont la pudeur de leur misère', the English paupers flaunt theirs, using the doorstep as a sofa (pp. 1146; 1148). 'On ne connaît point la blouse à Londres' (p. 1140). As ever, Vallès looks for badges of membership, identity tags, forgetting that the *blouse* concealed a host of different political persuasions. English workers prefer 'avoir l'air d'un commis, d'un clerc, d'un monsieur', as they buy reach-me-downs cast off by their social betters (p. 1283). Clothing unmaketh the man. In Petticoat Lane, he gives this sartorial ideology a rest, and reverts to his lifelong anxiety about arse-out breeks: 'N'es-tu pas las aussi de montrer ton derrière, pincé par le vent, et qui a la chair de poule? [. . .] Pour un shilling seulement, si tu ne tiens qu'à être pudique, tu auras une culotte à pont' (= full-fall trousers—p. 1279). He prefers, however, French skill in making-do and mending, wifely husbanding of resources (p. 1149).

While profoundly anxious about the fate of children in the gin-soaked slums, Vallès recognises that children are freer, allowed to be children more than in France (pp. 1150; 1215). Their parents, remaining standing to drink in pubs, are thus prevented from the real get-together for the exchange of ideas that large French café tables offer (p. 1170). It has been pointed out by Tholoniat that, in concentrating on the squalid public bars, Vallès neglected the back-room meeting-places of dissident groups.[4] He sees the *isoloir,* and not the snug. Perhaps his visceral need for drinking in company, compotation, was hindered by the level of his English and his disrelish for draught beer. All the time, and naturally, he holds it against England, his unnatural second home, for not being France. He remains, however, open to new experiences. Lacking small-group discussions, he enjoys open-air mass meetings (e.g. Hyde Park Corner). Even if there are no political slogans or graffiti on the walls, no revolutionary historical markers, even if the English 'n'ont point senti le tremblement social' (pp. 1140-41), Vallès is moved by large numbers freely speaking their minds in public, just as he admires elements of British justice such as *habeas corpus* (p. 1146).

He spends a lot of time on leisure activities, presumably believing that you can tell a great deal about a people by examining its pleasures. Theatre, dances and music halls are all dismissed as inferior in London. Vallès dislikes the auctioneer-style hammer of the master of ceremonies, which affords an attack on automated pleasures, piston-like movements of artistes: 'l'éternelle marche *à la soldat!*' (p. 1165). All the same, while finding English stage-movements gross, he still admires 'ces friands de l'énergie, ces gourmands de vigueur' (p. 1167). The cross-dressing, the drag routines, so central to the English tradition obviously troubled him. One area that delighted him was music-hall satire, mocking Crown and Government. He voices a bitter complaint

against all the spying on and censoring of free-tongued pleasure in France: 'Gabelous de la morale, gardes-chiourmes du goût' (p. 1162).

Vallès admitted to Séverine (and the phrases are delectably double-layered): 'La *Femme anglaise* ne m'a jamais enthousiasmé', and ('J'ai attaqué la femme anglaise, que j'ai coupée en deux' (*Corr. S.,* pp. 151; 73). While admitting eventually that pleasure with women is obtainable in London and its up-market tarts less blasé than French *horizontales,* Vallès misses *demi-mondaines* (in-betweens like himself) (p. 1271). He misses flirtatiousness, the come-on, the clear confidence that the girl or woman is the cynosure of male gazes. In England, women go off rapidly: 'On avait une gazelle hier, on a une girafe demain' (p. 1136). In contrast, 'la femme de trente ans, comme nous l'aimons, grasse et blanche, ou souple et dorée, appétissante comme un fruit mûr, irritante comme une odeur sauvage, on ne la frôle point, on ne la sent pas sur le pavé de Londres' (*ibid.*). English girls can be delectable (if boyish) up to a certain age, but then their blatant pursuit of marriage partners withers them. Perversely, he states that the very availability of English girls, the absence of social obstacles as in France, kills passion (p. 1261). On a more practical level, though finding breach of promise cases rather ludicrous, and though paternity payments derive from a mercantile logic, he finds them more humane than French practice. Reverting to male chauvinist wolfishness, he misses the ocular whistles of Latin men: 'C'est le seul pays d'Europe où j'aie vu circuler les gens sans regarder les passantes' (p. 1263). He obviously enjoys the chat decorating such lust, for he says of Englishmen: 'S'ils s'y mettaient, ils les examineraient comme des chevaux, tandis que le boule-vardier sait fleurir de politesse et ouater de discrétion son audace de suiveur, son grappin d'abordage' (*ibid.*). The aggressive last metaphor gives away the violence beneath the violets. In all his discussion of women on both sides of the Channel, Vallès keeps sliding betwen classes, so that he blurs the whole issue. Parisiennes are more hard-headed and more romantic; Englishwomen go in for *far-niente* (which class?) (p. 1265); they are also do-gooding campaigners, which transmutes them into a third sex, neither female nor male (p. 1272).

As for sport, (within 'le dur sport de la vie' (p. 1285)), while having some reservations, Vallès is full of praise. Derby Day is a *mundus inversus:* 'L'Angleterre s'y montre la tête en bas, les pieds en l'air (p. 1284). In this land of compartments, this is a free-for-all, promiscuity: 'Cette inondation de la foule, cette éruption de volcan, dans ce pays de cellules sociales et de mutisme pénitentiaire' (p. 1285). By this stage of his account, Vallès has wearied of being a registering eye: 'On veut être à la fois acteur et observateur dans la pièce' (*ibid.*). He revels in the jovial matiness of the omnibus ride (une kermesse entre quatre planches'—p. 1286)). Then, by a cinematic double-take, he realises he has conned himself. The joviality has blinded him to the have-nots, the beggars. Vallès feels anger at the insulting charity thrown to them: cruel scenes of mendicants made to beg like dogs or to jig about (p. 1290). As in theatres, however, vigour plays off against coarseness. 'Nulle part', he writes of the mass return home, 'jamais, il n'y eut ce pêle-mêle, cet encombrement, cette verve sauvage, cette fureur de casse-cou' (p. 1292). In this way, throughout *La Rue à Londres,* the rush to moralise has to take on board the extra-moral.

Fascinatedly appalled at bareknuckle boxing, he still believes that sporting prowess (strange how England was once reputed for it) helps to explain British world dominance: 'C'est à ces moeurs du *ring* et du *turf* que l'Angleterre doit d'être le champion de la résistance dans le champ clos du monde' (p. 1299). Picking up his previous attacks on the under-emphasis on physical education in France, he praises English schools (public schools, designed to produce élites—but Vallès focusses on the formation of self-reliance): 'Au lieu d'être élevés comme des métaphysiciens ou des poètes, les adolescents sont dressés comme des fils d'hercules ou de maîtres de natation' (p. 1294). In contrast, in Soho, he notes the degenerate scum of French expatriate society (p. 1196). Critical of many English forms of pleasure, he unreservedly lauds (after Dickens) the English Christmas: the presents, the fun, the good cheer and drink (for once), and the reading of popular romances and ghost-stories (pp. 1215-16). He appears to mistranslate Boxing Day as an occasion for drunken punch-ups in the streets (p. 1220). He enjoys pantomime, despite the cross-dressing, for there the (earthly) 'gods' rule the roost (p. 1221).

For all the emphasis on garish colours and ubiquitous advertising, Vallès never loses sight of the reverse picture. The sections on workhouses record his visits to these organised, measured infernos, with their highly programmed dispensing of charity. He is too streetwise not to realise the ambivalence of the whole workhouse phenomenon: it can abuse regulars, and be abused in turn by spongers and shirkers. Here again religion interferes. Some women there catch 'la névrose de la religion, ce qui est l'avortement des âmes' (p. 1246). In the world of actual work, at London docks, the visitor marvels in horror at the huge scale of operations generated to service the maritime colossus of the nineteenth century, the runaway growth of mechanisation. He notes the indigo warehouses where the workers salivate blue, the massive stores—a carceral cornucopia (pp. 1227-8). He tries unavailingly to anthropomorphise forbidding buildings: 'On voudrait leur voir un front, des yeux, des lèvres, [. . .] des fentes larges par où rirait un peu de lumière—des rides ou des cicatrices, au besoin! Non! c'est comme une colossale bedaine de pierre, ronde, unie, à la peau brune et tendre' (p. 1232). He remains open to the call of the open sea, ships off to the ends of the earth: 'Cela écorche et éblouit les yeux, cela aussi

recule le paysage et ouvre à l'affamé un horizon profond' (p. 1233). But the stevedores who have to stay, performing repetitive, uncreative tasks of loading and unloading, lack all rebelliousness; they are 'ces fakirs du chômage' (p. 1232). Human labour comes cheap: 'A quel prix est payée la balistique humaine?' (p. 1233). In keeping with their context, 'leur vie fait eau de toutes parts' (p. 1231). He watches the recruiting sergeants, and notes, by a bitter twist on 'cochons vendus', poor wretches paying to get into the army. As for the underclass of hooligans with their violent horseplay, Vallès feels a mixture of fear and distaste:

> C'est une race terrible, allez, et je ne voudrais pas que ma patrie devînt leur ennemie—ni leur amie. [. . .] Musulmans sans soleil, ces fils de la Grande Bretagne! Ils ont la résignation muette des Orientaux, sous leur ciel de fer. Ils sont fiers d'être Anglais, c'est assez—et ils se consolent de n'avoir pas de chemise en regardant flotter un lambeau de drapeau. (pp. 1276-7)

Have things changed so much today?

'Qu'on le sache bien, l'Anglais a la haine instinctive, aveugle, de ce qui est français' (p. 1205). This is probably truer than we want to think. Periodically, Vallès reverts to the initial polarisation, and can then slump into cliché: 'Ainsi nous sont-ils hostiles de toute la force de leur tristesse et de leur patriotisme religieux et glacial. C'est le brouillard furieux qui en veut au soleil; c'est le rire blême qui en veut au rire clair; c'est le duel de la bière et du vin!' (p. 1205). He makes the standard charges: we are non-enthusiasts, whereas the French need to 'penser tout haut' (p. 1260). And yet he recognises a futile quality in his own country's humour, in comparison with English phlegm: 'Nous paraissons des gamins souvent, à crier ainsi contre le vent, et à envoyer des chiquenaudes au nez des avalanches' (*ibid.*). The Englishman practises not only 'le rire jaune', but also 'vit jaune' (*Corr, A.,* p. 201).

At one point, Vallès spends two whole paragraphs, inflating the problems of getting back into the crowd at a procession to a symbol of the impenetrability of English society. So doing he points to the crux of the exile's dilemma: 'On ne pénètre pas dans un milieu où l'on n'a pas racine' (p. 1275). Like the crowd in the Commune, England remains unreadable. Like the Thames: 'Cette eau ne reflète rien, elle est comme le visage des Anglais' (p. 1153). An abyss of twenty miles lies between Calais and Dover (p. 1325). For all that, Vallès remembers to express his authentic gratitude for lessons in freedoms, and especially for the transnational haven of the British Museum Library, far better stocked on French history than the Bibliothèque Nationale: 'J'ai pu vivre en pleine terre nationale pendant neuf ans d'exil' (p. 1306).

Hyperbole is the commonest mode of *La Rue à Londres.* 'Par esprit de patriotisme, parce qu'ils ont le Derby et la mer, ils ont tous des têtes de cheval ou de poisson' (p. 1135). The reader, even non-English, is tempted to respond: 'What! All of them? Why do rabid individualists so often generalise manically?' Lugubrious conceits occur frequently, as in this Thames-side scene: 'On voit se balancer dans l'air des sacs mous qui oscillent au bout des poulies avec des pesanteurs et des gigotements de pendus. On pend ici; c'est laid et sourd, cela plaît bien' (p. 1155). Perhaps he prefers the sharp clunk of the guillotine.

It is a patchwork text, 'cousu de pièces découpées, rapportées, accolées' (Bellet, II, 1982). Vallès was fully conscious of this himself, as he makes clear in his instructions to his secretary, Séverine: 'Cela aura *l'enlevé* d'un croquis, le je-ne-sais-quoi saisissant des observations collées chaudes mais sans suite sur le papier. A vous d'étayer et de dresser cela comme on pare un plat fait de morceaux' (***Corr. S.,*** p. 90). Tholoniat detects a dominance of the colour yellow in these fragmented descriptions:

> L'Anglais vit jaune, il rit jaune dans sa barbe de même couleur; le brouillard est couleur merde d'oie; la Tamise, les murs, les écriteaux ont des reflets jaunâtres. L'énergie du couple rouge-noir atteint son entropie avec les couleurs seulement définies par le terne, le pâle et le blafard.[5]

In a generally overheated article, trying to enlist Vallès into German Expressionism, Blanc accurately observes: 'Vallès gauchit les perspectives, tourmente les lignes, noircit le tableau. La *vision* remplace la vue.'[6]

As Bellet puts it pungently, but for once with inadequate nuance, apart from political freedom, Vallès relished virtually nothing about England, for whose life he felt an aversion as visceral as that which, as a child, he had felt for onions (II, p. xii). Any English person hailing from outside London would exclaim how unfair it is to judge all England via the capital, which many natives find every bit as alien and hateful as do many foreigners. Critics underplay the shuttle or seesaw tactic of *La Rue à Londres,* which at different points seems to have been written (as indeed it was) from opposite sides of the Channel, so that Vallès refers at times to England as 'là-bas'. Two principal critical approaches predominate. The documentary (Tholoniat): Vallès's account is lacunary, inaccurate and biassed; and the aesthetic (Blanc): never mind the lesser contact with observable reality, what internally coherent picture does Vallès create? On the issue of his non-visits to provincial cities, where, Vallès recognised, working-class militancy would have been more obvious, Tholoniat suggests that the experience of the Commune—the provinces refusing to emulate Paris—might have blinkered him. Vallès, besides, was reluctant to admit that other

forms of worker organisation—trade unions, provident societies—offered more gradualist forms of activism than he was yet ready to value.[7] To his credit, he did not exaggerate the scale of poverty in London, but, like Taine, did little to analyse its causes, only its consequences. Cardboard cities are not recent inventions. Tholoniat points out that the number of skilled and well-paid workers was much higher than that of exploited semi-skilled or un-skilled workers: 'Ce manque d'homogénéité de la classe ouvrière—et non la résignation—peut expliquer son apparent manque de combativite.'[8] My own estimation is that the facts Vallès incorporates are generally accurate, but that he omitted—more through ignorance than perverseness—crucial areas. What is unforgettable about *La Rue à Londres* is the sense of a man mortally afraid of but fighting back against *étouffement:* asphyxiation, silencing, anonymity: a forgotten man lost in the crowd.

'Unlike the London residents of other origin, the French Londoner [. . .] remains above all a Frenchman, and retains all the feelings, characteristics, and customs of his race'.[9] Of course, Vallès did not realise how French he was until he had to live in England. Yet, while undoubtedly as quintessentially French as Montaigne or Diderot, he seems 'Anglo-Saxon' in many ways, and even before he set foot here. His love of sport and of country fresh air; his fondness for eccentrics, all those who march to different drummers; his empirical bent which made him suspect all systems, Marxist, Jacobin or Proudhonist; his awareness of overlap and contamination between all would be clear divisions of thought and behaviour; his passion for exploiting, by wordplay and coinage, the often underused potential of his native tongue; his support of and identification with the underdog, the plucky loser ('Il faut toujours applaudir aux révoltés, surtout quand ils sont vaincus'—I, 343). Though he spent a long time in England, he did not get far with assimilating the language, but in attitudes he comes partway to meet the anti-extremist. Playing the shuttle too, I would repeat that Vallès is very un-French in his near-immunity to intellectual incest, yet very French in his belief that cultural devaluation might seriously shake society, and very un-French again in his unworldly-wise capacity for surprise. 'Suis-je devenu Anglais en détestant John Bull? Ai-je perdu le flair et le tact français? Je ne crois pas. J'ai gagné comme tous les camarades, au contraire, le dédain des ficelles, et le désir de netteté en affaires. 'Oui: non'. Ah! l'on gagne cela en Angleterre!' (***Corr. M.,*** p. 264).

At a low ebb when trying to get another *La Rue* off the ground in 1879, he writes to Parisian correspondents:

> J'en suis á me réjouir d'être resté dans un exil rigoureux, dans une Angleterre où les placards éclatent comme des pétards, oà il y a des manifestations de 100,000 hommes. Vous m'ôtez le courage. Nous sommes plus gais et plus Parisiens à Londres que la moitié des

Parisiens que j'ai revus. [. . .] Vous parlez de mon normandisme d'aujourd'hui. Eh bien, mon cher, appelez ça anglaisisme et vous aurez trouvé le mot. Je ne ferai rien, rien, rien avec quelqu'un sans traité à l'anglaise, sûr, indéniable, débattu, délini, et convenant à tous les deux.[10]

The blatant hypocrisy, the up-front reserve of the English ('perfidious Albion') have given way in Vallès's mind to this reliability. Vallès clearly plays one side off against the other, depending on circumstances. He was too French for the English and too English for the French. *A cheval,* again: in mid-Channel.

Return and Le Cri du peuple

His problems with this *La Rue,* which lasted only one month, demonstrate how little Vallès was cut out for working by proxies, or doing anything from a distance. He came alive only in the scrum—the least Olympian, the least *point de vue de Sirius* (Beuve-Méry) of French journalists. He could not, as he hoped, address the sons of his political enemies without joining them in the fray back in Paris, which had been largely quiescent during his exile, after the Commune. Would his return reveal him as an anachronism?

Edmond de Goncourt aimed to freeze Vallès in a stereotype: 'L'amer que Vallès a en lui, il le soigne, il le caresse, il le dorlote, il le travaille, il le porte en ville, pour le tenir toujours en haleine, comprenant fort bien que s'il venait à le perdre, il serait un ténor dépossédé de son *ut*'.[11] It is true, and understandable, that on his return Vallès made frequent references backward, trying to reknot broken threads. As usual, he came clean. Turning down in 1881 offers of two Paris candidacies, he stresses that he fights lost battles: 'J'aime mieux être le porte-parole du passé [. . .] C'est un rôle qui vaut bien l'autre—je serai le député des vaincus. [. . .] Je veux être l'historien de la grande foule anonyme qui se révolta et fut écrasée en 1871' (II, pp. 717-18). Although he accepted that workers value their dearly-won suffrage, he seemed to feel a near-anarchist disdain about using his own vote. His mistrust of professional politicians remained intact. 'Nous ne sommes pas des politiciens, nous sommes les soldats et les peintres de l'idée sociale', manning 'notre barricade sans fusils' (pp. 395; 397). The Palais-Bourbon, in his eyes, was fundamentally unserious, a theatre or even trestles, 'l'asile des phrasassiers' (*Cri du peuple,* 30 mai 1884).

It is not surprising that he steered clear as much as possible of any adherence to constituted parties or doctrines: anarchism or collectivism. 'Je ne vais pas m'enfermer dans un bivouac, quand j'ai devant moi tout le champe de bataille révolutionnaire'. Don't fence me in. As before, he stresses that it is the will, the intentions, that matter in political action, and not class

provenance. Here the habit does not designate the monk. In a twist on the idiom 'montrer patte blanche', he says no one needs to 'montrer main noire'; it did not matter in the Commune (II, pp. 440; 444). As Bellet comments, 'la vieille terreur vallésienne du clos, du circonscrit, du fermé, du muré, de la grille et de la chapelle, trouve sa correspondance idéologique et politique dans le refus de choisir une "école" socialiste au lieu d'une autre' (*JVJR,* p. 450).

As for Marxism, Vallès makes no mention of the First International until around 1870, and generally betrays little sense of class in the normal sense. In the 1870s surfaced a tendency, for French leftwingers, especially those in exile in London, to amalgamate Marx and Bismarck (perhaps a phonic coincidence, the second being almost the first twice over) on the grounds of pan-Germanist ambitions. In his letters to Arnould, Vallès asked him to boil down *Das Kapital,* 'si difficile à lire!' He heads straight for Marx's powerful metaphors: 'Saistu que c'est beau, cette définition du Capital: travail mort qui comme un vampire suce et dévore le travail vivant! [. . .] Et que cette idée de la marchandise, travail cristallisé, solidification de la peine, mérite qu'on y pense' (***Corr. A.,*** p. 219). While he had little grasp of the more abstract concepts of economics, he did retain a fascination with the Stock Market and the world of banking (*JVJR,* p. 451). As we saw in Chapter Two, Vallès coincides, all the same, with Marx in his hostility to historical plagiarism.

> The social revolution of the nineteenth century can only create its poetry from the future, not from the past. It cannot begin its own work until it has sloughed off all its superstitious regard for the past. [. . .] In order to arrive at its own content, the revolution of the nineteenth century must let the dead bury the dead.[12]

In harking back to the Commune, Vallès was hardly even dreaming of seeing it replicated. It was the spirit, and the justice of the Communards' cause, that must be kept alive, and pursued by other means. Though he defended Kropotkin, Vallès wrote against terrorism: 'L'assassinat politique isolé ne porte pas' (II, 1425). As in the previous two decades, he placed more trust and hope in the free exchange of ideas, 'le terrain de rendez-vous' (the word used less in the amatory sense than in that of a duelling-space) represented by his second *Cri du peuple.* He wanted to coalesce, or help to make coexist, the mutually exclusive and reciprocally destructive forces of the left. Such an effort at neutrality was very necessary for the times and the situation in France.

Readers' letters were invited, thus hoping to convert the French press from its traditional tribune stance into more of a dialogue, 'une tribune ouverte'. Generous space was given to popular *feuilletons* in order to increase circulation by making the paper more reader-friendly. Similarly, small emblems were placed at the head of each column to flag its contents at a glance: a bell (for parliamentary affairs), a trowel (for workers' meetings), or an eye (for police news). As an editor and journalist, Vallès always worked for the eye-catching, but not cony-catching. *Le Cri du peuple* campaigned against colonial expeditions to Tonkin ('La vivisection humaine va commencer'—II, 1093), for teachers, for reforms in the judicial system (especially the abolition of the death penalty). In Vallès's ideal republic, every citizen would do a stint as a constable (*Cri du peuple,* 5 avril 1884). He always stressed the 'social question' over politics (i.e. ideology, which he left largely to Guesde in the pages of the paper), though he never resolved the question of how you could separate the two.

In a campaign for children's rights, Vallès stresses that he wants prevention of cruelty, not revenge against brutal parents (II, 1369). One of his last articles protests the brainwashing of children by didactic plays disguised as fantasies. Children's dreams are essential, but not at the cost of abolishing reality. This is presumably why *Robinson Crusoe,* which combines exoticism and hard work, is so central to Vallès's canon. Why not awaken children to the exciting new world of science and industry, as in Jules Verne's work? (pp. 1422-4). On the question of progress, he can seem backward-turned, as when he criticises capitalist enterprises for taking over rubbish-collection in Paris, thus depriving hundreds of *chiffonniers* of a livelihood. He neglects the improvement in sanitation. Yet even here he has a point. Such *biffins* supplied other service industries (including restaurants) with recyclable materials. Greens might find these practices easier to stomach than others. Vallès is as well-informed on the daily budgets of *biffins* as he was earlier of those of *saltimbanques* (pp. 1105-1107).

Again and again, he returned to the primordial things: work, roof, bread, blood, tears, sweat. To his old category of society's *forçats,* he added the large numbers trapped and alienated in soulless factory-work. He came to see strikes as the only effective weapon available to workers. One of his last public appearances was at a solidarity meeting for the miners of Anzin in 1884, when desperately ill with the diabetes which would kill him in a few months. That the government was nervous about the popular appeal and influence of *Le Cri du peuple* is indicated by the Ballerich affair, when two policemen broke in and started shooting at the editorial staff. When one of the two was killed by self-defending fire, Vallès's apartment and even his sick-bed were violently searched. Perrot sums up the political standpoint of *Le Cri du peuple* in these terms: 'Un socialisme sans doctrine, protestataire et humanitaire, nostalgique et messianique, généreux et confus, perpétuellement résurgent dans la tradition française: un socialisme style flamboyant'.[13]

Vallès's helpmeet after his return to France was Séverine. She used her husband's money to launch *Le Cri du peuple* in 1883. Their deep relationship, intimate but seemingly non-carnal, is encapsulated in her cry on Vallès's death: 'C'était mon père . . . C'était mon enfant!' Her frankly warm-hearted encomium makes a nicely sexist division of his influence on her: 'Il me donna un cœur de citoyenne et un cerveau de citoyen'.[14] When she eventually left *Le Cri du peuple* in 1888, after disagreements with Vallès's successors over its increasingly sectarian slant, she frequented, in a very Vallèsian phrase, 'l'école buissonnière de la Révolution'.[15] She and Vallès enjoyed an exceptional osmosis; she assimilated his ways of thinking and expressing himself, and he trusted her judgment implicitly. His utter reliance on her puts a more benign slant on his perennial anxiety over plagiarism. As a cleric commented, she was a splended mixture of a *pétroleuse* (in words, not deeds) and a *sœur de charité.*[16] Fittingly, in the same way that Vallès escaped 'la Semaine sanglante' in an ambulance, so the director of that service, Dr. Sémerie, introduced Vallès to Séverine and her doctor husband in Brussels. She would nurse his remaining years, when his lifelong taste for heavy peasant food did little to help his diabetes. She brought him comfort and stability, after a life of much insecurity and frequent deprivation. She played a major part in running the paper and in preparing *L'Insurgé* and *La Rue à Londres* for publication. She protected Vallès when alive and after his death. In *La Rue à Londres,* he makes a moving dedication to Séverine: 'Vous avez fait à ma vie cadeau d'un peu de votre grâce et de votre jeunesse, vous avez fait à mon œuvre l'offrande du meilleur de votre esprit et de votre cœur' (II, 1133).

Committed Literature

The idea of committed literature pulls together Vallès's two lifelong concerns: politics and literature. There, above all, he is in his characteristic position: *à cheval.* This straddle is archetypically that of the committed writer (of the left), reneguing on his generally middle-class or *petit-bourgeois* origins, yet rarely, if ever, integrated into and adopted by the working-classes. He is thus often stranded in no man's land, caught in the crossfire. This situation can be alternately or simultaneously exhilarating and anguishing. Of course, all of us live less dramatically in a murky middle ground between metaphor and concrete reality, the spirit and the letter. Tension reputedly energises. Vallès was not *un écrivain de chapelle,* and so was largely unforgivable to any side in the French literary church.

Mi-figue, mi-raisin, in his first book, *L'Argent,* Vallès was proclaiming the need to live with your times. At no point did he adopt the posture of the intellectual fakir. Indeed, so convinced was he always of the necessity to have convictions, that he was ready to salute those of his political opponents, for instance Barbey d'Aurevilly:

'Je hais la politique autoritaire et dévote de M. Barbey d'Aurevilly. [. . .] Mais il est resté *lui,* avec toutes les vertus de ses vices' (I, pp. 349; 348). There is a strong element of the willy-nilly in all this ('en dehors de toute volonté de l'écrivain' (II, 1340)); the writer has to respond to historical reality, which is much bigger than any individual. 'Tout se tient. La littérature change de tour quand la politique change de face' (I, 400). Vallès always persisted, however, in distinguishing the social from the political: 'J'aime mieux, après tout, la littérature qui refait les moeurs que la politique qui fait les lois' (p. 435). These terms suggest that he places far more weight on how society regulates itself (with some guidance from the likes of Vallès) than on abstract theories of how it ought to be organised. As Bellet comments: 'Il a le sentiment, aigu et profond, de la rencontre inéluctable des mouvements artistiques et sociaux, quelles que soient les différences de leurs rythmes propres et même si, souvent, le rythme des mouvements artistiques et littéraires, plus rapide, devance tous les autres' (p. 1418). That is, the writer is not only in step; he may be prancing ahead. Whatever he does, he must never fear, as Nietzsche urged, 'to trespass upon actuality.'[17]

Not all agree. Tocqueville spoke of the crisscross contamination of politics and literature, each aping the other, so that politicians often talk like books, and authors think they can set their countries to rights.[18] The grassroots American novelist James Farrell puts his spoke in: 'Literary men have the habit of rushing into the periphery of politics, and they contribute to political struggle—not knowledge, not practical experience, not theoretical analyses, but rhetoric. Rhetoric is the one commodity in politics of which there has never been a scarcity'. It is possible that, when Socrates spoke of 'the unexamined life', he had in mind much political discourse, and much literature that marches in too tight a step with it. We are all so hardened to jargon, cliché and double talk (in electioneering, party manifestoes and press conferences) that we sometimes fail to appreciate the much richer and denser ambiguities of good literature. Many, besides, want fiction to be more obviously up-front than it can or should be; they want it akin to pamphleteering, political correctness. Against such persuasions, a committed writer like Vallès demonstrates how resistance to ideology (mind-bending), even that of your ostensible allies, is every bit as important as endorsement of it. 'Commitment', besides, is not a good translation of the Sartrian *engagement.* It has legal, forensic overtones, and misses the input of *gage* (promise, wager). Commitment sounds like that which is imposed on you; *engagement* what you will yourself to choose (as in 'engaged to be married').

Most Naturalists were essentially 'down there on a visit': slumming. They were exploiting a seam, less like miners than like investors. They rarely sided with the oppressed creatures they described. Even though Vallès,

in the 1860s, termed the Goncourts' style 'tourmenté, prétentieux, *scudérique',* and described their stance as 'le coin d'un cénacle, mais ce n'est pas la vie', he was generous enough to conclude: 'Ce n'est pas senti, mais comme c'est observé!' (I, pp. 350-53). He did not practise 'l'onanisme rétinien' of which they boasted.[19] Zola did not relish Vallès's calling him 'un rouge en littérature, un communard de la plume' (II, 120). It is fairly comical to watch each bank of the divide tugging the communal blanket to one side in these ways, Vallès claiming that Daudet, the Goncourts and Zola were revolutionary despite themselves, a prophetic twist on the Soviet notion of 'objective guilt'; and the Naturalists trying to water down Vallès's firebrand writings. Gradually, however, Vallès's rough logic made him openly hostile. Naturalists were 'maniaques de la constatation, mouleurs de michés, point mouleurs de vrais mâles!' (a pun on *michés* and *godemichés:* brothel clients and dildoes). They waste their talents on lubricious tales, instead of speaking up for real suffering (pp. 1100-1101). Despite seeming to be censorious about subject matter here, it was the pretence of political neutrality that Vallès really could not stomach.

Many of these matters came to a head when Vallès engaged in a polemic with a spokesman for the Zola school of Naturalists, Paul Alexis, who hoped for the advent of a press 'où [. . .] la politique, n'occupant plus que la place qu'elle occupera alors dans la vie des peuples, sera reléguée entre le Sport et les Annonces, piteusement'.[20] He was reacting no doubt to earlier charges addressed to him by Vallès: 'L'homme qui dit n'avoir pas d'opinions politiques en a une. Il est le collaborateur et le complice de tous ceux qui ont mis la main sur le pouvoir' (II, 812). Vallès scoops Sartre here. The only alternative to *engagement* is parasitism: 'Ou insurgé ou courtisan: il n'y a pas à sortir de là'. Vallès goes on to compare would be abstentionists with the 'platonic' (i.e. non-participatory) clients in brothels (*ibid.*).

Already in the 1860s, Vallès had mocked one such illustrious abdicator, Baudelaire, whom he presumably could not forgive for reneguing on his young man's fling with revolution in 1848 (*'Le 2 DÉCEMBRE m'a physiquement dépolitiqué'*).[21] Like Sartre, Vallès homes in on the posturing man and neglects the writer. He is totally wrong, as a result, in judging that Baudelaire's fame will be short-lived. For Vallès, Baudelaire is the perfect mugwump, on the fence, or on both sides of it at once. He hedged his bets on the religious issue. No doubt, too, Vallès's harsh attack on Baudelaire, whom he knew from bohemian cafés, is part of his general attack on the unquestioning cult of genius, the *monstre sacré.* The crucial criticism is that of bad faith: 'Il n'avait pas la santé d'un débauché et avait dans son enfer une petite porte masquée par où l'on pouvait remonter au ciel' (I, 973). In other words, in all his pacts with Satan, Baudelaire always inserted an escape clause. 'Il y avait en lui du prêtre, de la vieille femme et du cabotin. C'était surtout un cabotin' (p. 971). It is ironical that he accuses Baudelaire of being a ham actor, when this was the regular complaint about Vallès's public persona. He misses the point of the dandiacal, wilful mystification.

Another *preuve par l'absurde* of the value of *engagement* is the sad André Gill. Vallès felt strong sympathy for this excellent caricaturist when he went insane and was locked up. While he could forgive, he never could forget, and Gill's earlier contribution to the cause of contestation had not been followed through; indeed in the Commune Gill had been a turncoat. For Vallès, true commitment preserves sanity, a view which runs absolutely counter to the common twentieth-century dismissal of all political passion as neurotic (II, 721). Before he lost his reason, however, Gill struck home with these remarks about Vallès's stance: 'On a eu dans sa vie une heure pendant laquelle on s'est trouvé particulièrement beau, on s'est *gobé;* dans la glace on s'est trouvé des airs de héros ou de martyr. [. . .] Héros et martyrs! Vous en riiez autrefois. [. . .] Ne soyez pas une vieille barbe, l'Homère entêté d'une épopée ratée.[22] Vallès's problem was a common one: even when you are right, it is hard to avoid appearing self-righteous. Vallès recognised that courage is not on tap to everyone, but inciters must possess some, otherwise they have double standards: calling for blood, then running away (see II, 116). Surely Vallès makes the lily-livered reader at least temporarily ashamed, when he talks of 'ces gens qui se sont fait de leur impuissance un piédestal, et parlent du haut de leur impuissance comme Démosthène du haut de la tribune' (I, 954). Vallès's work is a reminder, writing against the self-induced amnesia both readers and writers so facilely fall into. 'Forgetfulness, especially of classes and class conflict, is a common theme of bourgeois culture, a theme which can be related to the concept of art as a transcendent form of activity'.[23] While never approaching the later notion of 'socialist realism', Vallès's views are certainly close to what has been called 'critical realism', already present in Vallès's lecture on Balzac and later acknowledged as a significant category by Engels: 'Est-ce que les socialistes socialisants ont écrit contre la famille, la vertu et l'or des pages plus cruelles que Dumas fils, Flaubert, de Goncourt, Zola?' (II, 1340). Vallès detects the ideological dimension, the would-be manipulation, even of children's literature: 'Tous [. . .] montraient le doigt de Dieu, partout où il y avait un trou où le fourrer' (p. 744). The Jesuits always knew that you have to catch them young.

Even when denied for ideological reasons, the urge to political partisanship is ubiquitous in a cultural tradition like the French given to embattled polemic.

You have to take sides, make your bed and lie on it. None of this entails crude propaganda. As Engels said of *Tendenz-Literatur:* 'I believe that there is no compulsion for the writer to put into the reader's hands the future historical resolution of the social conflicts which he is depicting'.[24] The just society can be talked about, if at all, only in the optative mood. *L'Insurgé* in its practice concurs with this theory. Does this view concede that written attacks can only ever be paper tigers, that political novels can never pack any political clout? Significantly, it is a writer most removed from the fray, Mallarmé, who makes the wildest claim: 'La vraie bombe c'est le livre.[25] This statement is pathetic in the truest sense, but a Symbolist poet supporting anarchist explosions would tend to take metaphors for actualities, and experimental writing for a revolutionary deed (a pathos still to be found in some deconstructionist criticism). Vallès knew full well that the pen is never mightier than the sword, but he believed that it may on occasion give added impetus to the sword-arm. Above all, Vallès never suspects or seeks impunity: a price has always to be paid for any decisions acted upon.

I have mentioned Sartre (a self-confessed 'victime du livre' if ever there was one) before in connexion with Vallès. *Les Mots* unmercifully probes the posture of writer-as-saviour. It is regrettable that, by a strabismic oversight, Sartre missed a powerful trick when he all but omitted Vallès as a vigorous forebear (with real claws) of *littérature engagée*. In *Qu'est-ce que la littérature?* he mentions only, in contrast with seventeenth-century social satire, 'la grande satire de Beaumarchais, de P.-L. Courier, de J. Vallès, de Céline'.[26] At least he puts Vallès in suitable company. He and Vallès share a similar revulsion for Baudelaire's *cabotinage*. Both see the writer as a free consciousness addressing a free reader linked by a relationship of trust (a leap in the dark). When Vallès turned down the offer of a seat in the Académie Goncourt, and indeed denounced the whole project, he recalls, all due allowances made, Sartre's refusal of the Nobel Prize. Neither of these committed writers wanted to be rewarded with a *prix de sagesse* for being literary good boys.

Shortly before Vallès's death, Edmond de Goncourt recorded an anecdote that I would prefer not to be apocryphal: 'Robert Caze, parlant de la maladie de la pose chez Vallès, raconte qu'il l'a vu manger une choucroute dans une brasserie du Quartier Latin, avec un tablier de franc-maçon, dont il s'essuyait les lèvres.[27] If true, it would demonstrate his durably iconoclastic attitude to congealed rituals. I wonder what he would have made of his own funeral in 1885: a suitably mixed event, a rehearsal for Hugo's even more massive funeral three months later: very large crowds, scuffles and punch-ups, some German socialists provoking cries of 'Down with Germany'—ironical in that Vallès was never keen on Marx or Germany.

. . . . .

Abbreviations

Corr. A: *Correspondance avec Arnould*

Corr. M: *Correspondance avec Malot*

Corr. S: *Correspondance avec Séverine*

TP: *Le Tableau de Paris*

JVJR: Roger Bellet: *Jules Vallès, journalisme et révolution*

AJV: *Les Amis de Jules Vallès*

Notes

[1] Rogozinski, D., 'Franchise autobiographique', *AJV*, 1 (1984), 66.

[2] One of his few comments on this was: 'Je sais un peu l'anglais' (*Corr. A.*, p. 79). He mentions very few English acquaintances, and these usually spoke French.

[3] Dr. J. Wittlin, cited in Tabori, P., *The Anatomy of Exile* (Harrap, 1972), p. 32.

[4] Tholoniat, R., 'Vallès et Flora Tristan face à l'Angleterre victorienne', *L'Information historique,* XLV, 1 (1983), 35.

[5] Tholoniat, 'Jules Vallès imagier londonien', *AJV,* 7 (1989), 61.

[6] Blanc, J.-N., 'Une ville écrite: l'expressionisme dans *La Rue à Londres',* *AJV,* 10 (1990), 53.

[7] Tholoniat, 'Gavroche et Joë. L'Enfant et l'Insurgé. Deux mythes personnels de Jules Vallès face à la réalité anglaise', *AJV,* 1 (1984), 87-8.

[8] Tholoniat, 'La Pauvreté à Londres à travers *Notes sur l'Angleterre* de Taine et *La Rue à Londres* de Vallès', *Confluents,* 1 (1976), 92.

[9] Villars, P., 'French London', in Sims, G.R. (ed.), *Living London* (Cassell, 1901), II, 134.

[10] Callet, A., 'Lettres d'exil', *La Revue du Palais* (février 1918), pp. 397-8.

[11] Goncourt, *Journal,* III, 104.

[12] Marx, *The Eighteenth Brumaire of Louis Bonaparte,* p. 149.

[13] Perrot, M., foreword to Feller, H., 'Physionomie d'un quotidien: *Le Cri du peuple* (1883-9)', *Le Mouvement social,* 53 (1965), 68.

[14] Séverine, *Choix de papiers,* pp. 22-3.

[15] Quoted in Le Garrec, E., *Séverine* (Seuil, 1982), p. 306.

[16] Quoted in Gille, G., *Jules Vallès,* p. 520.

[17] Nietzsche, F., *The Genealogy of Morals* (New York: Doubleday, 1956), p. 235.

[18] Tocqueville, A. de, *L'Ancien Régime et la Révolution* (Gallimard, 1967), pp. 240-41.

[19] See Bellet's excellent article: 'Les Goncourt et Jules Vallès: une rencontre', *Francofonia,* 19 (1990), 130.

[20] Alexis, P., *Le Matin,* 17 août 1884. Alexis, however, wrote regularly for *Le Cri du peuple,* often under the pseudonym of Trublot. See also his curious story, 'Jean Vingtrin' (*AJV,* 2 [1985], pp. 49 ff.), where a writer switches off from the cacophonous gunfire of the Commune to concentrate, unperturbed, on his civilisation-saving life work.

[21] Baudelaire, *Correspondance générale* (Conard, 1947), I, 152.

[22] Delfau, p. 104.

[23] Rifkin, A., 'Cultural Movement and the Paris Commune', *Art History,* II, 2 (1979), 207.

[24] Engels, F., *Über Kunst und Literatur* (Berlin, 1949), p. 143.

[25] Mallarmé, quoted in Mauclair, C., *Servitude et grandeur littéraires* (Ollendorff, 1922), p. 116.

[26] Sartre, *Situations II* (Gallimard, 1948), p. 140.

[27] Goncourt, *Journal,* III, 446.

Select Bibliography

Vallès: Editions

Correspondance avec Hector Malot, ed. M.-C. Bancquart.
La Rue, ed. P. Pillu.

Le Tableau de Paris, eds. M.-C. Bancquart, L. Scheler.

Vallès—Séverine: Correspondance, ed. L. Scheler.

Books, Theses, Chapters, Articles

Bellet, R. *Jules Vallès, Journalisme et Révolution.* Tusson: Du Lérot, 1987-1989, 2 vols.

Delfau, G. *Jules Vallès: L'Exil à Londres.* Bordas, 1971.

Gille, G. *Jules Vallès, 1832-1885: ses révoltes, sa maîtrise, son prestige.* Flammarion, 1941, 2 vols.

Charles J. Stivale (essay date 1992)

SOURCE: *"Le Plissement* and *La fêlure:* The Paris Commune in Vallès's *L'Insurgé* and Zola's *La Débâcle,"* in *Modernity and Revolution in Late Nineteenth-Century France,* edited by Barbara T. Cooper and Mary Donaldson-Evans, University of Delaware Press, 1992, pp. 143-54.

[*In the following excerpt, Stivale contrasts Vallès's and Emile Zola's representation of the Paris Commune of 1871, arguing that Vallès's emphasis on identifying and naming historical agents in his narration of class conflict makes possible the recognition and resistance of seemingly natural sources of power.*]

In his provocative analysis of Zola's *La Bête humaine* in *The Logic of Sense,* Gilles Deleuze develops the bipolar oscillation which occurs in Zola's work between the *la petite hérédité des instincts* ("small heredity of instincts") and the *la grande hérédité* ("grand heredity"), both of *la fêlure* ("the fissure") and of the *l'Instinct de mort* ("death Instinct").[1] According to this model, the instincts alone seem to drive the subject's actions in the case of Jacques Lantier's love for Séverine which apparently palliates the effects of the hereditary *fêlure.* But, at the same time, says Deleuze, *la fêlure* "is actualized in each body in relation to the instincts which open a way for it, sometimes mending it a little, sometimes widening it, up to the final shattering" (*LS* pp. 325; 378). Thus, in yielding to the silent "death Instinct" by killing Séverine, Jacques returns to the death from which their love had originally sprung, then finally succumbs himself to the "death Instinct" embodied by the "epic symbol" of the train (*LS* p. 332; 385). It is tempting to extend this bipolar model to other novels by Zola as does Deleuze briefly for *Thérèse Raquin, L'Assommoir,* and *Nana,* and in this essay, I propose to examine Zola's presentation of the Paris Commune in *La Débâcle* in light of *la fêlure,*[2] and then to consider a different depiction of this event, from Vallès's **L'Insurgé,** with an alternate model of analysis, what Deleuze calls *le plissement* ("folding") in his recent study entitled *Foucault.*[3]

With the term *plissement,* Deleuze designates a mode of comprehending the process of subjectivation, or assemblage of the subject, from two perspectives. Conceived not only in terms of the concurrent dimensions of knowledge, power, and thought, this process also posits the imbrication of "inside" and "outside"—"the inside *of* the outside," says Deleuze, insofar as "the outside is not a fixed limit but a moving matter animated by peristaltic movements, folds and foldings that together make up an inside" (*F* pp. 96-97; 103-104). Deleuze explains how, in Foucault's work, the dualism on the level of

knowledge, i.e., between the visual and the articulable, exists as a form of exteriority and dispersion, two multiplicities that "open up onto a third: a multiplicity of relations between forces, a multiplicity of diffusion which no longer splits into two and is free of any dualizable form" (*F* pp. 83-84; 90). It is the interior/exterior functioning of the dimensions of knowledge, power, and thought that the mode of *le plissement* brings into perspective, and by juxtaposing the Commune episodes in *La Débâcle* and **L'Insurgé,** I wish to examine two distinct ways in which the fictional subject is constituted through contrasting modes of textualizing history.

As David Baguley has shown in his study of focalization in the *le récit de guerre* ("the war tale"),[4] the final chapters of *La Débâcle* stand in sharp opposition to the sections that precede them; that is, until their escape from the prison camp following the defeat at Sedan, the focal protagonists, Jean Macquart and Maurice Levasseur, are united in their participation in the hereditary paroxysms of the final days of the decrepit Second Empire. Subsequently, however, *la fêlure* operates an abrupt bifurcation with their disunion into different narrative and psychosocial directions. In the terms of Deleuze's analysis in *The Logic of Sense,* the "small heredity" functions in Jean Macquart throughout the novel, generally, as he leads his platoon in the struggle within the military institution of the State apparatus. More specifically, he creates a lasting bond with the previously dissolute Maurice and thereby guides him through an ordeal in which the "grand heredity of *la fêlure*" is displaced temporarily from Maurice's unstable character and is textualized historically in the crumbling Second Empire and embodied in the decaying personage of Napoléon III. But, the bifurcation of Maurice's near disappearance for several chapters into Paris, while Jean recuperates at Remilly, results in a shift in the hereditary matrix: the "small heredity of instincts" emerges, on one hand, with Jean's will to reenlist in the military apparatus and blind allegiance to the apparently "healing" force which the Versailles government comes to embody and enact. On the other hand, the "small heredity" directs Maurice's alienation from the military apparatus and his *détraquement* ("breakdown") in Paris progressively towards the "death Instinct" of the "grand heredity" as he is swept, as it were, into the historical undertow of the increasingly deranged oppositional forces which conquer and then defend the city throughout the Commune.

In order to resolve this conflict of the "small heredity" in its search for an object, Zola must resort to the device of the two chance encounters of Jean and Maurice in the streets of Paris. The first one culminates in a decisive schism:

Tous deux restèrent quelques secondes face à face, [Maurice] dans l'exaspération du coup de démence

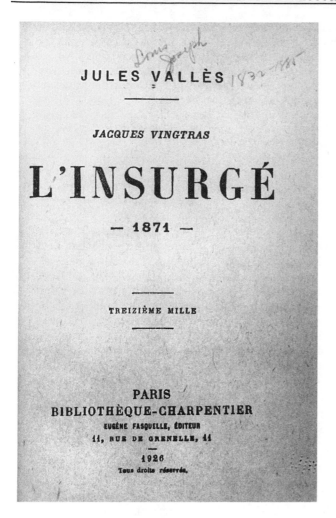

JULES VALLÈS

JACQUES VINGTRAS

L'INSURGÉ

— 1871 —

TREIZIÈME MILLE

PARIS
BIBLIOTHÈQUE-CHARPENTIER
EUGÈNE FASQUELLE, ÉDITEUR
11, RUE DE GRENELLE, 11
—
1926
Tous droits réservés.

qui emportait Paris entier, ce mal venu de loin, des ferments mauvais du dernier règne, [Jean] fort de son bon sens et de son ignorance, sain encore d'avoir poussé à part, dans la terre du travail et de l'épargne. (D. p. 871)

("They both remained staring at each other for several seconds, [Maurice] in the exasperation of the mad impulse that was overwhelming all of Paris, the sickness brought from afar, the bad ferment of the previous reign, [Jean] fortified by his good sense and his ignorance, still healthy from having grown up elsewhere, in the land of toil and thrift.")

But this incompatibility, not so much ideological, suggests Sandy Petrey, as "the contrast . . . between two states of health,"[5] fails to dislodge them from their mutually fraternal embrace:

Tous les deux étaient frères pourtant, un lien solide les attachait, et ce fut un acharnement, lorsque, soudain, une bousculade qui se produisit, les sépara. (D p. 871)

("However, both of them were brothers, a solid bond held them together, and it was a desperate moment when, suddenly, a commotion which arose separated them.")

This dislocation of fraternity and the slide toward *la fêlure* occur only through a second chance encounter, prepared by and within the historical momentum of the "grand heredity" during *la Semaine sanglante* (the "Bloody Week," May 21-28, 1871). Maurice passes through successive states dominated by *ce rêve fou* ("this mad dream") of Paris's destruction (*D*. pp. 876), by the emotional and physical *ivresse* ("inebriation") on the barricades (*D* pp. 877-882), then by "a doubt" (*D* p. 881) and *une nausée* ("a sickness") (*D* p. 882) produced when he recognizes a former soldier from Sedan, the opportunistic Chouteau, now a fellow *communard* setting the city ablaze. These reflections before the conflagration and destruction of Paris lead Maurice to the edge of *la fêlure* and the "death Instinct" with his conclusion delivered via the indirect mode: "If he had made a mistake, at least let him pay for his error with his own blood!" (*D* p. 881).[6] However, the *communards'* opposition also sweeps Jean, despite his often-mentioned "good peasant sense," into the same maelstrom of the "grand heredity":

Le récit des abominations de la Commune . . . le jetaient hors de lui, blessant son respect de la propriété et son besoin d'ordre. . . . Les incendies étaient venus l'affoler. . . . Et lui dont les exécutions sommaires, la veille, avaient serré le coeur, ne s'appartenait plus, farouche, les yeux hors de la tête, tapant, hurlant. (D p. 883)

("The story of the Commune's abominations . . . drove him beyond himself, wounding his respect for property and his need for order. . . . The fires came to madden him,. . . . And although the summary executions the previous evening had wrenched his heart, he could no longer control himself, now savage, his eyes bulging, striking, screaming.")

The collision of instinct with its object and the dislocation of fraternity are prepared, as Deleuze suggests, "in relations between temperaments which are always stretched out over" *la fêlure* (*LS* pp. 323; 375) in the fatal encounter that Naomi Schor calls their "dysphoric reunion".[7]

Ce fut sous la poussée furieuse du destin, [Jean] courut, il cloua l'homme sur la barricade, d'un coup de baïonnette. Maurice n'avait pas eu le temps de se retourner. Il jeta un cri, il releva la tête. . . . "Oh! Jean, mon vieux Jean, est-ce toi?" (D p. 883)

("It was under a furious thrust of fate that [Jean] ran, impaling the man on the barricade with a stab of his bayonet. Maurice did not have the time to turn around. He let out a cry, lifted his head. . . . 'Oh! Jean, my friend Jean, is it you?'")

Throughout the episodes preceding and following Sedan, Maurice has served for Jean as "the Same," that is, a brother-in-arms and would-be brother-in-law, given the growing relationship between Jean and Maurice's sister, Henriette.[8] But, in the paroxysm of the Commune and of the "death Instinct," this "Same" becomes "the Other," Maurice as *ce lettré* ("this educated man") transformed into "an instinctive being" (*D* p. 860) possessed by "a blind need for vengeance and destruction" (*D* p. 868). Just as Jacques must kill Séverine in *La Bête humaine,* Deleuze suggests, "in order for the small heredity to link up with the grand, and for all the instincts to enter" *la fêlure* (*LS* pp. 329; 381), Jean must also kill Maurice. But this death coincides with a transformed model of *la fêlure* as presented in the dénouement, for Maurice's individual "breakdown," his commitment to the final gasp of the Second Empire's "death Instinct" through the Commune, yields to Jean's cataclysmic vision of the necessity for national healing, rebirth and return to order which Zola depicts in the final lines:

> *Le champ ravagé était en friche, la maison brûlée était parterre; et Jean, le plus humble et le plus douloureux, s'en alla, marchant à l'avenir, à la grande et rude besogne de toute une France à refaire.* (*D* p. 912)

> ("The ravaged field lay fallow, the burned house was flattened; and Jean, the most humble and afflicted man, moved on, walking toward the future, toward the great and difficult task of remaking all of France.")

While the depiction of historical events in *La Débâcle* is eventually supplanted by Zola's mythology of *la fêlure,* Vallès quite effectively depicts another mode of existence in revolt, Jacques Vingtras's life in the process of *plissement* ("folding"). This process, which Deleuze links in Foucault's work to the theme of the double, consists of "an interiorization of the outside," a redoubling of the Other, a repetition of the Different: "It is never the other who is a double in the doubling process, it is a self that lives in me as the double of the other: I do not encounter myself on the outside, I find the other in me" (*F* pp. 98; 105). This operation which, says Deleuze, "resembles exactly the invagination of a tissue in embryology, or the act of doubling in sewing" (*F* pp. 98; 105), recalls the incessant struggle between Jacques Vingtras and his mother in *L'Enfant,* which Philippe Bonnefis has discussed by studying Madame Vingtras's efforts on behalf of Jacques—to wash him, to feed him, to control his comportment, and most notably, to dress him—and thereby to "divide herself or to double herself in him: (*"se dédouble[r] ou se redouble[r] en lui"*).[9]

Furthermore, the context of Greek life to which Deleuze refers in his reflection on Foucault's *L'Usage des plaisirs* is entirely appropriate regarding Jacques Vingtras, whose father endorses fully the "classic" regime of strengthening through suffering to which a colleague, the professor Bergougnard, submits his children:

> *Il rossait les siens au nom de Sparte et de Rome— Sparte les jours de gifles, et Rome les jours de fessées.* (*E* p. 246)[10]

> ("He would whip his children in the name of Sparta and Rome, Sparta on the days of slapping and Rome on the days of spanking.")

For Deleuze emphasizes the importance of what Foucault calls a "'relation to oneself' that consciously derives from one's relations with others" and a "'self-constitution' that consciously derives from the moral code as a rule for knowledge" (*F* pp. 100; 107). In the Trilogy, these constitutive relations emerge at the end of *L'Enfant* and struggle for independence in the period preceding and following 1848 in *Le Bachelier.* "It is as if," says Deleuze, "the relations of the outside folded back to create a doubling, allow a relation to oneself to emerge, and constitute an inside which is hollowed out and develops its own unique dimension" (*F* pp. 100; 107), that is, "a dimension of subjectivity derived from power and knowledge, without being dependent on them" (*F* pp. 101; 109). For Jacques Vingtras, this process of resistance is an assemblage of words, images, concepts, and propositions in which the subject constitutes the locus of a continuous life experimentation that escapes the line of death (in *Le Bachelier*), first during the events of 1848, then in the years of difficult economic survival under the Second Empire. Prepared by these bitter experiences and by his growing commitment to oppositional journalism and writing (in the first half of *L'Insurgé*), Vingtras faces the Commune as a subject traversed by the pressures and the constitution of *le plissement,* situated by history as it positions both the subject-group of the *bacheliers* transformed into insurgents, and their struggle with subjugation, i.e., with the "unfolding," by conflicting forces of power from outside and within the group (*F* pp. 103; 110).[11] Yet, Vingtras maintains a "relation to himself" by exerting a force of resistance, "the outside" as "opening on to a future: nothing ends, since nothing has begun, but everything is transformed" (*F* pp. 89; 95).

This process of subjectivation is textualized, on a molar level, by the various subject positions which Vingtras assumes during the conflictual *plissement* of the Commune depicted in *L'Insurgé*'s second half. Having been forced into hiding in February, 1871, following his condemnation for participating in the 31 October 1870 attempted coup, Vingtras can return to activity with his credibility doubly reinforced. Not only was he also condemned for signing *l'Affiche rouge* in January, thereby openly opposing the so-called "Government of National Defense," but as editor of *Le Cri du peuple,* he is empowered to proclaim the political import of the Communal insurrection, presented through Vallès's own editorial of March 28, 1871, reprinted in chapter XXVI and attributed to Jacques Vingtras:

> '*Quoiqu'il arrive, dussions-nous être de nouveau vaincus et mourir demain, notre génération est consolée! Nous sommes payés de vingt ans de défaites et d'angoisses. . . . Et toi, marmot, qui joues aux billes derrière la barricade, viens que je t'embrasse aussi! . . . Nous avons saigné et pleuré pour toi. Tu recueilleras notre héritage. Fils des désespérés, tu seras un homme libre.*' (*I* p. 253)

("Whatever happens, even if we must be defeated again and die tomorrow, our generation is consoled! We are paid back for twenty years of defeats and agony. . . . And you, kid, playing marbles behind the barricade, come let me hug you too! . . . We have bled and cried for you. You will reap our heritage. Son of desperate men, you will be a free man.")

Vingtras affirms his insurgent activity further as popular delegate from the *XVe arrondissement* to the Commune's "Central Committee"; as mediator throughout the Commune in internal struggles between *communards* of differing radical stripes; and as committed partisan during *la Semaine sanglante;* then outlaw from the Versailles government in his flight into exile. But this triumphant political stance is nonetheless tempered by Vingtras's continuing "self-constitution" (i.e., the articulation of an alternate moral code) and by his concomitant "relation to oneself" of resistance. This dual process of subjectivation can be seen in the numerous moments of reflection in which Vingtras humbly recognizes his own limits in the various subject positions, and even the very limits of the insurrectional possibilities, but also maintains a firm commitment to his chosen path.

Furthermore, this process of subjectivation is textualized on a molecular level, in terms of the mediating role fulfilled by Jacques Vingtras as "author function," for example, in the system of nomination developed throughout *L'Insurgé.*[12] While toponyms abound in Zola's meticulous description of the events during and following Sedan, he barely mentions the historical agents of the Commune at all, limiting his references to four *communards* responsible for the military defense (*D* pp. 876, 879), and privileging instead the proponents of the Versailles government. At one point, in fact, the narrator reveals himself behind Maurice's ruminations:

> A la vérité *après les élections, les noms des membres de la Commune l'avaient un peu surpris par l'extraordinaire mélange de modérés, de*

> *révolutionnaires, de socialistes de toutes sectes, à qui la grande oeuvre se trouvait confiée.* (*D* p. 874)

(*"In truth,"* the narrator insists, "after the elections, the names of the members of the Commune had surprised him somewhat by the extraordinary mix of moderates, revolutionaries, socialists of all stripes, to whom the great task was confided,") (my emphasis).

This appeal to *la vérité* ("truth") indicates the author's commitment to depicting only a particular form of justice, and the next sentence is barely credible as issuing from Maurice's focalization, given his limited revolutionary experience in Paris since his arrival in November: "He knew several of these men, he judged them to be quite mediocre" (*D* p. 874).

Zola generally refers to the crowd of *communards* as collective agent with the metonymical toponym, "Paris," and this would seem to correspond to what Naomi Schor has identified as the "double crowd structure" in *La Débâcle,* the collective agent of "macroconflict" constituting the locus of "the central microconflict of the novel, the one opposing Jean to Maurice."[13] In *L'Insurgé,* by contrast, the only agent to maintain a fictional name is Vingtras, from whose perspective the actual participants in the historical events are presented in detail, frankly criticized or exalted, but all put into an active, dispersed play of agents in diverse subject positions.[14] Situated within this nominative *plissement,* the fictional name "Jacques Vingtras" does not function as simple title or form of ridicule as in *L'Enfant* and *Le Bachelier.* In *L'Insurgé,* this name also coincides with a multiplicity of subject positions, for example, as a form of self-address, as formula of reproach and of praise, and as the locus of oscillation regarding the strength of commitment to the Commune. A crucial example occurs during the street fighting of *la Semaine sanglante,* in chapter XXXII, entitled *Les Incendies* ("The Fires"). Beseeched by "a dairymaid who had extended me credit" to oppose the strategy of conflagration, Vingtras pauses "in a tête-à-tête with myself for a moment." But rather than slide into a suicidal abyss as does Maurice at the sight of Chouteau, thereby refusing any subjectivation in his flight toward the "death Instinct," Vingtras returns to the fray, proclaiming, "It's all thought out! I'm staying with those who are shooting—and who will be shot!" (*I* p. 304). Thus, when called upon by fellow *communards* "to put your name there, Vingtras!," that is, to set fire to a bakery, Vingtras responds, "'There it is!—and burn down another shack, if needs be!'" (*I* p. 308). In other words, in finally assuming actively the name of the father, Vingtras eschews any compromise with the State apparatus and its bourgeois system of nomination. Rather, he inscribes it actively in the struggle against the system which supported the paternal teaching as well as career-in-teaching, and thereby affirms his "relation to himself" through the "becoming insurgent" and consequent flight from Paris, without resorting to the ultimate mysticism, i.e., the "good peasant sense" of Jean Macquart.

To conclude, I wish to return to *La Débâcle* in order to contrast its dénouement with *L'Insurgé*'s: in both novels, we find *une dernière vision euphorisante* ("a final 'euphorizing' vision"), to use David Baguley's description, but the effect of these images is quite the opposite. As Baguley suggests, Jean's vision "comes to empty out the social and political conflicts in order to assimilate history into nature, for already the order of nature (Jean) has abolished the (dis)order of history."[15] Maurice's death followed by Jean's vision not only eliminates the threshold of focalization for the Commune chapters, but also the vehicle of the novel's historic consciousness—"not only the end of history," says Baguley, "but the debacle of History itself."[16] I would argue further that Zola uses the Commune as an alibi for expounding the salutary political myth with which the cycle of *Les Rougon-Macquart* effectively ends.[17] This moralizing dénouement does not merely reproduce the tendentious ambivalence which characterized Zola's own political writing on the Commune[18] and thus a rather problematic process of subjectivation within history. This strategy also yields a narrative *plissement* of the forces of rupture (Maurice) with those of the natural order (Jean), between which no naming can occur and no locus of subjectivation is textualized other than the gaping abyss in which history and justice can no longer supplant *la fêlure*.[19]

In contrast, the narrative progression in *L'Insurgé* develops the process of *plissement* quite differently. The process of nomination articulates the dispersed field of historical agents, thus avoiding the injustice of their occulation behind a mythic appeal to collective salvation. Furthermore, the protagonist and "author function," Jacques Vingtras, is himself constituted as the locus of knowledge, power, and thought, on the "fold" of history and experience, a process of subjectivation and "becoming insurgé" as marginalized and minor. This "author function" is constantly engaged in an assemblage of conflicts between the subjugated, oppressed group and the enunciative, experimental subject group, always threatened with suppression (as the chapters of Vingtras's flight amply demonstrate), yet always ready for more expressive becomings, even in exile, as revealed in the final chapter, *L'Evasion* ("The Escape"):

> *Bien d'autres enfants ont été battus comme*
> *moi, bien d'autres bacheliers ont eu*
> *faim, qui sont arrivés au cimetière sans avoir*
> *leur jeunesse vengée.*
> *Toi, tu as rassemblé tes misères et tes*
> *peines, et tu as amené ton peloton de*
> *recrues à cette révolte qui fut la grande*
> *fédération des douleurs.*
> *De quoi te plains-tu? . . .*
>
> *(I* p. 341)

("Many other children were beaten like me, many other *bacheliers* were hungry, arriving at the cemetery without having had their youth avenged./ You, you have brought together your misery and pain, and you have led your platoon of recruits to this revolt which was the great federation of suffering./ What do you have to complain about?")

But, in contrast to Maurice's embrace of the abyss and to Jean's "extraordinary sensation" of "a dawn" which would bring from "a fury of fate, a cluster of disasters," from "the rubble and the dead in all quarters, . . . an entire world to reconstruct!" (*D* p. 911), Vingtras escapes toward a renewed political commitment:

> *Je viens de passer un ruisseau qui est la*
> *frontière.*
> *Ils ne m'auront pas! Et je pourrai être avec*
> *le peuple encore, si le peuple est*
> *rejeté dans la rue et acculé dans la bataille.*
>
> *(I* p. 341)

("I just passed a stream that is the border./ They won't capture me! And I will again be with the people, if the people are thrown into the street and cornered in battle.")

Then, rather than arriving at a mystical vision of "the rejuvenation of eternal nature, of eternal humanity" (*D* p. 912), Vingtras's final vision presents the metaphor of a different "euphoric" horizon, one of bloody struggle for oppressed subject groups, both past and future:

> *Je regarde le ciel du côté où je sens Paris.*
> *Il est d'un bleu cru, avec des nuées rouges.*
> *On dirait une grande blouse*
> *inondée de sang.*
>
> *(I* pp. 340-41)

("I am looking at the sky in the direction that I sense Paris./ It's a harsh blue, with red clouds. One would say a great tunic soaked in blood.")

With Jean Macquart's final vision, "this great and difficult task of remaking all of France," Zola does not simply perpetuate the naturalist rejection of politics in the ahistorical devalorization of any cause that would upset the forces of order and "eternal nature." He also denies textually the existence of those historical agents at odds with order and nature, and in so doing, elaborates a revision better suited to a xenophobic ideological practice rarely associated with the author of *J'Accuse*. In contrast, Vallès's efforts to name and thereby articulate an assemblage of subject positions in history reveal the double play of "the inside of the outside," folding the historical "moving matter" into the difficult struggle of a continuous "self-constitution." While this process is certainly limited in the particular desperation arising from the repression of the Commune, what remains unlimited, nonetheless, is the potential for becomings, for the inevitable reconstitution of the subject's "relation to itself" in the *plissement* whose process is concomitant with those of knowledge and power, but situated on the fold of thought which forcefully introduces the possibility of resistance and the necessity of history.

Notes

[1] Gilles Deleuze, *The Logic of Sense,* trans. Mark Lester with Charles J. Stivale, ed. Constantin V. Boundas (New York: Columbia University Press, 1990), originally published as *Logique du sens* (Paris: Minuit, 1969), abbreviated *LS* in the text (the first page number refers to the translation, the second to the French original).

[2] Emile Zola, *La Débâcle* in *Les Rougon-Macquart,* Vol. 5 (Paris: Gallimard, Pléiade, 1960), abbreviated D in the text (all translations my own).

[3] Gilles Deleuze, *Foucault,* trans. Sean Hand (Minneapolis: University of Minnesota Press, 1988), originally published as *Foucault* (Paris: Minuit, 1986), abbreviated F in the text (the first page number refers to the translation, the second to the French original).

[4] David Baguley, "Le Récit de guerre: narration et focalisation dans 'La Débâcle'," *Littérature* 50 (1983): 82-90.

[5] Sandy Petrey, "La République de *La Débâcle,*" *Les Cahiers naturalistes* 54 (1980): 93 (my translation).

[6] On the "indirect mode," see Vaheed K. Ramazani, *The Free Indirect Mode. Flaubert and the Poetics of Irony* (Charlottesville, VA: University Press of Virginia, 1988), 43-50.

[7] Naomi Schor, *Zola's Crowds* (Baltimore & London: The Johns Hopkins University Press, 1978), 116.

[8] Naomi Schor argues that the introduction of Henriette, "Maurice's fraternal twin (and surrogate mother-protector)," is the necessary "expedient to interrupt the natural course of events," i.e., Zola's rendering explicit the homosexual male bond between Jean and Maurice which progresses toward an impossible consummation. That the relationship between Jean and Henriette itself is never consummated "not only averts a homosexual marriage by proxy, but attests to the profound class divisions which, according to Zola, produced the Commune and its bloody repression." *Ibid.,* 117-118.

[9] Philippe Bonnefis, *Vallès: Du bon usage de la lame et de l'aiguille* (Lausanne: L'Age d'Homme, 1982), 95 (my translation).

[10] Jules Vallès, *L'Enfant* (Paris: Editeurs français réunis, 1964), abbreviated E in the text; *Le Bachelier* (Paris:

Editeurs français réunis, 1955); *L'Insurgé* (Paris: Editeurs français réunis, 1973), abbreviated *I* in the text (all translations are my own).

[11] On "subjugated groups" and "subject groups," see also Gilles Deleuze and Félix Guattari, *Anti-Oedipus,* trans. Robert Hurley, Mark Seem and Helen R. Lane (New York: Viking, 1977; reprint, Minneapolis: University of Minnesota Press, 1983), 348-50; originally published as *L'Anti-Œdipe, Capitalisme et schizophrénie* I (Paris: Minuit, 1972; 1975), 416-19.

[12] The term "author function" *(fonction-auteur)* is proposed by Michel Foucault in "What is an Author?," *Language, Counter-Memory, Practice,* trans. Donald F. Bouchard and Sherry Simon (Ithaca: Cornell University Press, 1977), 113-38, originally published as "Qu'est-ce qu'un auteur?," *Bulletin de la société française de philosophie,* 63.3 (1969): 75-95. For a development of the role of the "author-function" and of the molar and molecular stratification in the Jacques Vingtras Trilogy, see Charles J. Stivale, *Oeuvre de sentiment, oeuvre de combat: La trilogie de Jules Vallès* (Lyon: Presses universitaires de Lyon, 1988).

[13] Schor, *Zola's Crowds,* 114.

[14] On the onomastic play in the Trilogy, see Charles J. Stivale, "La Signature de Jules Vallès dans la trilogie de *Jacques Vingtras:* Entre autobiographie et fiction," *French Literature Series* XII (1985): 108-11.

[15] Baguley, "Récit de guerre," 90 (my translation).

[16] *Ibid.*

[17] Regarding this "ending," see David Gross, "Emile Zola as Political Reporter in 1871: What He Said and What He Had to Say," *Literature and History* 7 (1978): 34-47; and David Baguley, "Formes et significations: sur le dénouement de *La Débâcle,*" *Cahiers de l'U.E.R. Froissart* 5 (1980): 65-72.

[18] Zola's writings on and during the Commune have been studied at some length; see, for example, Pierre Cogny, "Le Discours de Zola sur la Commune: Étude d'un problème de réception," *Les Cahiers naturalistes* 54 (1980): 17-24; Henri Mitterand, *Zola journaliste de l'affaire Manet à l'affaire Dreyfus* (Paris: Armand Colin, 1962), 133-56; Roger Ripoll, "Zola et les Communards," *Europe* 468-69 (1968): 16-26; Rodolphe Walter, "Zola et la Commune: un exil volontaire," *Les Cahiers naturalistes* 43 (1972): 25-37; Henry H. Weinberg, "Zola and the Paris Commune: The *La Cloche* Chronicles," *Nineteenth-Century French Studies* 8.1-2 (1979-1980): 79-86.

[19] On "justice" and "naming," see Jean-François Lyotard, *Instructions païennes* (Paris: Galilée, 1977), 16-35; and

Le différend (Paris: Minuit, 1983), 56-92, trans. as *The Differend. Phrases in Dispute,* trans. Georges Van Den Abbeele (Minneapolis: University of Minnesota Press, 1988), 32-58.

FURTHER READING

Criticism

Bodkin, Robin Orr. "The Creative Askesis of Jules Vallès." In *Repression and Expression: Literary and Social Coding in Nineteenth-Century France*, edited by Carrol F. Coates, pp. 111-34. New York: Peter Lang, 1996.

> Connects Vallès to French poets Charles Baudelaire and Arthur Rimbaud in the early development of modernist poetics, specifically a poetics of resistance.

Bruce, Donald. "Discourse Analysis in Cultural Theory: 'Une Discipline Transversale.'" *Canadian Review of Comparative Literature* 22, No. 1 (March 1995): 63-92.

> Considers the example of *Le Bachelier* to discuss the usefulness of discourse analysis in understanding the historical specificity of literary texts and other works of art.

Bruce, Donald, and Terry Butler. "Towards the Discourse of the Commune: Characteristic Phenomena in Jules Vallès's *Jacques Vingtras*." *Texte et Informatique* 13-14 (1993): 219-49.

> Uses computer-aided analysis to discover the characteristics (including neologisms, narrative rupture, and wordplay) of Vallès's texts about the Paris Commune uprising of 1871.

Kranowski, Nathan. "The Undeserved Obscurity of Jules Vallès." *Romance Notes* XIV, No. 3 (Spring 1973): 501-7.

> Maintains that Vallès's radicalism relegated him to second tier in the official canon of great French writers, which includes Victor Hugo and Emile Zola.

Thomas, Jean-Jacques. "Revolutionary Signs and Discourse." In *Modernity and Revolution in Late Nineteenth-Century France,* edited by Barbara T. Cooper and Mary Donaldson-Evans, pp. 129-42. Newark: University of Delaware Press, 1992.

> Compares the semiotics of Victor Hugo, Emile Zola, and Vallès to argue that Vallès remained always an author of the people.

Additional coverage of Vallès's life and career is contained in the following source published by Gale Research: *Dictionary of Literary Biography,* Vol. 123.

Nineteenth-Century
Literature Criticism

Cumulative Indexes
Volumes 1-71

How to Use This Index

The main references

> **Calvino, Italo**
> 1923–1985 .... CLC 5, 8, 11, 22, 33, 39,
> 73; SSC 3

list all author entries in the following Gale Literary Criticism series:

BLC = *Black Literature Criticism*
CLC = *Contemporary Literary Criticism*
CLR = *Children's Literature Review*
CMLC = *Classical and Medieval Literature Criticism*
DA = *DISCovering Authors*
DAB = *DISCovering Authors: British*
DAC = *DISCovering Authors: Canadian*
DAM = *DISCovering Authors: Modules*
      DRAM: *Dramatists Module*; *MST*: *Most-Studied Authors Module*;
      MULT: *Multicultural Authors Module*; *NOV*: *Novelists Module*;
      POET: *Poets Module*; *POP*: *Popular Fiction and Genre Authors Module*
DC = *Drama Criticism*
HLC = *Hispanic Literature Criticism*
LC = *Literature Criticism from 1400 to 1800*
NCLC = *Nineteenth-Century Literature Criticism*
PC = *Poetry Criticism*
SSC = *Short Story Criticism*
TCLC = *Twentieth-Century Literary Criticism*
WLC = *World Literature Criticism, 1500 to the Present*

The cross-references

> See also CANR 23; CA 85-88;
>   obituary CA116

list all author entries in the following Gale biographical and literary sources:

AAYA = *Authors & Artists for Young Adults*
AITN = *Authors in the News*
BEST = *Bestsellers*
BW = *Black Writers*
CA = *Contemporary Authors*
CAAS = *Contemporary Authors Autobiography Series*
CABS = *Contemporary Authors Bibliographical Series*
CANR = *Contemporary Authors New Revision Series*
CAP = *Contemporary Authors Permanent Series*
CDALB = *Concise Dictionary of American Literary Biography*
CDBLB = *Concise Dictionary of British Literary Biography*
DLB = *Dictionary of Literary Biography*
DLBD = *Dictionary of Literary Biography Documentary Series*
DLBY = *Dictionary of Literary Biography Yearbook*
HW = *Hispanic Writers*
JRDA = *Junior DISCovering Authors*
MAICYA = *Major Authors and Illustrators for Children and Young Adults*
MTCW = *Major 20th-Century Writers*
NNAL = *Native North American Literature*
SAAS = *Something about the Author Autobiography Series*
SATA = *Something about the Author*
YABC = *Yesterday's Authors of Books for Children*

Literary Criticism Series
Cumulative Author Index

1; DA; DAB; DAC; DAM MST, MULT, POET, POP; WLCS
See also AAYA 7, 20; BW 2; CA 65-68; CANR 19, 42, 65; DLB 38; MTCW; SATA 49

Anna Comnena 1083-1153 **CMLC 25**

Annensky, Innokenty (Fyodorovich) 1856-1909 **TCLC 14**
See also CA 110; 155

Annunzio, Gabriele d'
See D'Annunzio, Gabriele

Anodos
See Coleridge, Mary E(lizabeth)

Anon, Charles Robert
See Pessoa, Fernando (Antonio Nogueira)

Anouilh, Jean (Marie Lucien Pierre) 1910-1987 **CLC 1, 3, 8, 13, 40, 50; DAM DRAM; DC 8**
See also CA 17-20R; 123; CANR 32; MTCW

Anthony, Florence
See Ai

Anthony, John
See Ciardi, John (Anthony)

Anthony, Peter
See Shaffer, Anthony (Joshua); Shaffer, Peter (Levin)

Anthony, Piers 1934- **CLC 35; DAM POP**
See also AAYA 11; CA 21-24R; CANR 28, 56; DLB 8; MTCW; SAAS 22; SATA 84

Antoine, Marc
See Proust, (Valentin-Louis-George-Eugene-) Marcel

Antoninus, Brother
See Everson, William (Oliver)

Antonioni, Michelangelo 1912- **CLC 20**
See also CA 73-76; CANR 45

Antschel, Paul 1920-1970
See Celan, Paul
See also CA 85-88; CANR 33, 61; MTCW

Anwar, Chairil 1922-1949 **TCLC 22**
See also CA 121

Apollinaire, Guillaume 1880-1918 **TCLC 3, 8, 51; DAM POET; PC 7**
See also Kostrowitzki, Wilhelm Apollinaris de
See also CA 152

Appelfeld, Aharon 1932- **CLC 23, 47**
See also CA 112; 133

Apple, Max (Isaac) 1941- **CLC 9, 33**
See also CA 81-84; CANR 19, 54; DLB 130

Appleman, Philip (Dean) 1926- **CLC 51**
See also CA 13-16R; CAAS 18; CANR 6, 29, 56

Appleton, Lawrence
See Lovecraft, H(oward) P(hillips)

Apteryx
See Eliot, T(homas) S(tearns)

Apuleius, (Lucius Madaurensis) 125(?)-175(?) **CMLC 1**

Aquin, Hubert 1929-1977 **CLC 15**
See also CA 105; DLB 53

Aragon, Louis 1897-1982 **CLC 3, 22; DAM NOV, POET**
See also CA 69-72; 108; CANR 28; DLB 72; MTCW

Arany, Janos 1817-1882 **NCLC 34**

Arbuthnot, John 1667-1735 **LC 1**
See also DLB 101

Archer, Herbert Winslow
See Mencken, H(enry) L(ouis)

Archer, Jeffrey (Howard) 1940- **CLC 28; DAM POP**
See also AAYA 16; BEST 89:3; CA 77-80; CANR 22, 52; INT CANR-22

Archer, Jules 1915- **CLC 12**
See also CA 9-12R; CANR 6, 69; SAAS 5; SATA 4, 85

Archer, Lee
See Ellison, Harlan (Jay)

Arden, John 1930- **CLC 6, 13, 15; DAM DRAM**
See also CA 13-16R; CAAS 4; CANR 31, 65, 67; DLB 13; MTCW

Arenas, Reinaldo 1943-1990 **CLC 41; DAM MULT; HLC**
See also CA 124; 128; 133; DLB 145; HW

Arendt, Hannah 1906-1975 **CLC 66, 98**
See also CA 17-20R; 61-64; CANR 26, 60; MTCW

Aretino, Pietro 1492-1556 **LC 12**

Arghezi, Tudor **CLC 80**
See also Theodorescu, Ion N.

Arguedas, Jose Maria 1911-1969 **CLC 10, 18**
See also CA 89-92; DLB 113; HW

Argueta, Manlio 1936- **CLC 31**
See also CA 131; DLB 145; HW

Ariosto, Ludovico 1474-1533 **LC 6**

Aristides
See Epstein, Joseph

Aristophanes 450B.C.-385B.C. **CMLC 4; DA; DAB; DAC; DAM DRAM, MST; DC 2; WLCS**
See also DLB 176

Arlt, Roberto (Godofredo Christophersen) 1900-1942 **TCLC 29; DAM MULT; HLC**
See also CA 123; 131; CANR 67; HW

Armah, Ayi Kwei 1939- **CLC 5, 33; BLC 1; DAM MULT, POET**
See also BW 1; CA 61-64; CANR 21, 64; DLB 117; MTCW

Armatrading, Joan 1950- **CLC 17**
See also CA 114

Arnette, Robert
See Silverberg, Robert

Arnim, Achim von (Ludwig Joachim von Arnim) 1781-1831 **NCLC 5; SSC 29**
See also DLB 90

Arnim, Bettina von 1785-1859 **NCLC 38**
See also DLB 90

Arnold, Matthew 1822-1888 **NCLC 6, 29; DA; DAB; DAC; DAM MST, POET; PC 5; WLC**
See also CDBLB 1832-1890; DLB 32, 57

Arnold, Thomas 1795-1842 **NCLC 18**
See also DLB 55

Arnow, Harriette (Louisa) Simpson 1908-1986 **CLC 2, 7, 18**
See also CA 9-12R; 118; CANR 14; DLB 6; MTCW; SATA 42; SATA-Obit 47

Arp, Hans
See Arp, Jean

Arp, Jean 1887-1966 **CLC 5**
See also CA 81-84; 25-28R; CANR 42

Arrabal
See Arrabal, Fernando

Arrabal, Fernando 1932- **CLC 2, 9, 18, 58**
See also CA 9-12R; CANR 15

Arrick, Fran **CLC 30**
See also Gaberman, Judie Angell

Artaud, Antonin (Marie Joseph) 1896-1948 **TCLC 3, 36; DAM DRAM**
See also CA 104; 149

Arthur, Ruth M(abel) 1905-1979 **CLC 12**
See also CA 9-12R; 85-88; CANR 4; SATA 7, 26

Artsybashev, Mikhail (Petrovich) 1878-1927 **TCLC 31**

Arundel, Honor (Morfydd) 1919-1973 **CLC 17**
See also CA 21-22; 41-44R; CAP 2; CLR 35; SATA 4; SATA-Obit 24

Arzner, Dorothy 1897-1979 **CLC 98**

Asch, Sholem 1880-1957 **TCLC 3**
See also CA 105

Ash, Shalom
See Asch, Sholem

Ashbery, John (Lawrence) 1927- **CLC 2, 3, 4, 6, 9, 13, 15, 25, 41, 77; DAM POET**
See also CA 5-8R; CANR 9, 37, 66; DLB 5, 165; DLBY 81; INT CANR-9; MTCW

Ashdown, Clifford
See Freeman, R(ichard) Austin

Ashe, Gordon
See Creasey, John

Ashton-Warner, Sylvia (Constance) 1908-1984 **CLC 19**
See also CA 69-72; 112; CANR 29; MTCW

Asimov, Isaac 1920-1992 **CLC 1, 3, 9, 19, 26, 76, 92; DAM POP**
See also AAYA 13; BEST 90:2; CA 1-4R; 137; CANR 2, 19, 36, 60; CLR 12; DLB 8; DLBY 92; INT CANR-19; JRDA; MAICYA; MTCW; SATA 1, 26, 74

Assis, Joaquim Maria Machado de
See Machado de Assis, Joaquim Maria

Astley, Thea (Beatrice May) 1925- **CLC 41**
See also CA 65-68; CANR 11, 43

Aston, James
See White, T(erence) H(anbury)

Asturias, Miguel Angel 1899-1974 **CLC 3, 8, 13; DAM MULT, NOV; HLC**
See also CA 25-28; 49-52; CANR 32; CAP 2; DLB 113; HW; MTCW

Atares, Carlos Saura
See Saura (Atares), Carlos

Atheling, William
See Pound, Ezra (Weston Loomis)

Atheling, William, Jr.
See Blish, James (Benjamin)

Atherton, Gertrude (Franklin Horn) 1857-1948 **TCLC 2**
See also CA 104; 155; DLB 9, 78, 186

Atherton, Lucius
See Masters, Edgar Lee

Atkins, Jack
See Harris, Mark

Atkinson, Kate **CLC 99**
See also CA 166

Attaway, William (Alexander) 1911-1986 **CLC 92; BLC 1; DAM MULT**
See also BW 2; CA 143; DLB 76

Atticus
See Fleming, Ian (Lancaster); Wilson, (Thomas) Woodrow

Atwood, Margaret (Eleanor) 1939- **CLC 2, 3, 4, 8, 13, 15, 25, 44, 84; DA; DAB; DAC; DAM MST, NOV, POET; PC 8; SSC 2; WLC**
See also AAYA 12; BEST 89:2; CA 49-52; CANR 3, 24, 33, 59; DLB 53; INT CANR-24; MTCW; SATA 50

Aubigny, Pierre d'
See Mencken, H(enry) L(ouis)

Aubin, Penelope 1685-1731(?) **LC 9**
See also DLB 39

Auchincloss, Louis (Stanton) 1917- **CLC 4, 6, 9, 18, 45; DAM NOV; SSC 22**
See also CA 1-4R; CANR 6, 29, 55; DLB 2; DLBY 80; INT CANR-29; MTCW

Auden, W(ystan) H(ugh) 1907-1973 **CLC 1, 2, 3, 4, 6, 9, 11, 14, 43; DA; DAB; DAC; DAM DRAM, MST, POET; PC 1; WLC**
See also AAYA 18; CA 9-12R; 45-48; CANR

20; MTCW

Barker, Harley Granville
See Granville-Barker, Harley
See also DLB 10

Barker, Howard 1946- **CLC 37**
See also CA 102; DLB 13

Barker, Pat(ricia) 1943- **CLC 32, 94**
See also CA 117; 122; CANR 50; INT 122

Barlow, Joel 1754-1812 **NCLC 23**
See also DLB 37

Barnard, Mary (Ethel) 1909- **CLC 48**
See also CA 21-22; CAP 2

Barnes, Djuna 1892-1982 **CLC 3, 4, 8, 11, 29; SSC 3**
See also CA 9-12R; 107; CANR 16, 55; DLB 4, 9, 45; MTCW

Barnes, Julian (Patrick) 1946- **CLC 42; DAB**
See also CA 102; CANR 19, 54; DLB 194; DLBY 93

Barnes, Peter 1931- **CLC 5, 56**
See also CA 65-68; CAAS 12; CANR 33, 34, 64; DLB 13; MTCW

Baroja (y Nessi), Pio 1872-1956 **TCLC 8; HLC**
See also CA 104

Baron, David
See Pinter, Harold

Baron Corvo
See Rolfe, Frederick (William Serafino Austin Lewis Mary)

Barondess, Sue K(aufman) 1926-1977 **CLC 8**
See also Kaufman, Sue
See also CA 1-4R; 69-72; CANR 1

Baron de Teive
See Pessoa, Fernando (Antonio Nogueira)

Barres, (Auguste-) Maurice 1862-1923 **TCLC 47**
See also CA 164; DLB 123

Barreto, Afonso Henrique de Lima
See Lima Barreto, Afonso Henrique de

Barrett, (Roger) Syd 1946- **CLC 35**

Barrett, William (Christopher) 1913-1992 **CLC 27**
See also CA 13-16R; 139; CANR 11, 67; INT CANR-11

Barrie, J(ames) M(atthew) 1860-1937 **TCLC 2; DAB; DAM DRAM**
See also CA 104; 136; CDBLB 1890-1914; CLR 16; DLB 10, 141, 156; MAICYA; YABC 1

Barrington, Michael
See Moorcock, Michael (John)

Barrol, Grady
See Bograd, Larry

Barry, Mike
See Malzberg, Barry N(athaniel)

Barry, Philip 1896-1949 **TCLC 11**
See also CA 109; DLB 7

Bart, Andre Schwarz
See Schwarz-Bart, Andre

Barth, John (Simmons) 1930- **CLC 1, 2, 3, 5, 7, 9, 10, 14, 27, 51, 89; DAM NOV; SSC 10**
See also AITN 1, 2; CA 1-4R; CABS 1; CANR 5, 23, 49, 64; DLB 2; MTCW

Barthelme, Donald 1931-1989 **CLC 1, 2, 3, 5, 6, 8, 13, 23, 46, 59; DAM NOV; SSC 2**
See also CA 21-24R; 129; CANR 20, 58; DLB 2; DLBY 80, 89; MTCW; SATA 7; SATA-Obit 62

Barthelme, Frederick 1943- **CLC 36**
See also CA 114; 122; DLBY 85; INT 122

Barthes, Roland (Gerard) 1915-1980 **CLC 24, 83**
See also CA 130; 97-100; CANR 66; MTCW

Barzun, Jacques (Martin) 1907- **CLC 51**
See also CA 61-64; CANR 22

Bashevis, Isaac
See Singer, Isaac Bashevis

Bashkirtseff, Marie 1859-1884 **NCLC 27**

Basho
See Matsuo Basho

Bass, Kingsley B., Jr.
See Bullins, Ed

Bass, Rick 1958- **CLC 79**
See also CA 126; CANR 53

Bassani, Giorgio 1916- **CLC 9**
See also CA 65-68; CANR 33; DLB 128, 177; MTCW

Bastos, Augusto (Antonio) Roa
See Roa Bastos, Augusto (Antonio)

Bataille, Georges 1897-1962 **CLC 29**
See also CA 101; 89-92

Bates, H(erbert) E(rnest) 1905-1974 **CLC 46; DAB; DAM POP; SSC 10**
See also CA 93-96; 45-48; CANR 34; DLB 162, 191; MTCW

Bauchart
See Camus, Albert

Baudelaire, Charles 1821-1867 **NCLC 6, 29, 55; DA; DAB; DAC; DAM MST, POET; PC 1; SSC 18; WLC**

Baudrillard, Jean 1929- **CLC 60**

Baum, L(yman) Frank 1856-1919 **TCLC 7**
See also CA 108; 133; CLR 15; DLB 22; JRDA; MAICYA; MTCW; SATA 18

Baum, Louis F.
See Baum, L(yman) Frank

Baumbach, Jonathan 1933- **CLC 6, 23**
See also CA 13-16R; CAAS 5; CANR 12, 66; DLBY 80; INT CANR-12; MTCW

Bausch, Richard (Carl) 1945- **CLC 51**
See also CA 101; CAAS 14; CANR 43, 61; DLB 130

Baxter, Charles (Morley) 1947- **CLC 45, 78; DAM POP**
See also CA 57-60; CANR 40, 64; DLB 130

Baxter, George Owen
See Faust, Frederick (Schiller)

Baxter, James K(eir) 1926-1972 **CLC 14**
See also CA 77-80

Baxter, John
See Hunt, E(verette) Howard, (Jr.)

Bayer, Sylvia
See Glassco, John

Baynton, Barbara 1857-1929 **TCLC 57**

Beagle, Peter S(oyer) 1939- **CLC 7, 104**
See also CA 9-12R; CANR 4, 51; DLBY 80; INT CANR-4; SATA 60

Bean, Normal
See Burroughs, Edgar Rice

Beard, Charles A(ustin) 1874-1948 **TCLC 15**
See also CA 115; DLB 17; SATA 18

Beardsley, Aubrey 1872-1898 **NCLC 6**

Beattie, Ann 1947- **CLC 8, 13, 18, 40, 63; DAM NOV, POP; SSC 11**
See also BEST 90:2; CA 81-84; CANR 53; DLBY 82; MTCW

Beattie, James 1735-1803 **NCLC 25**
See also DLB 109

Beauchamp, Kathleen Mansfield 1888-1923
See Mansfield, Katherine
See also CA 104; 134; DA; DAC; DAM MST

Beaumarchais, Pierre-Augustin Caron de 1732-1799 **DC 4**
See also DAM DRAM

Beaumont, Francis 1584(?)-1616 **LC 33; DC 6**
See also CDBLB Before 1660; DLB 58, 121

Beauvoir, Simone (Lucie Ernestine Marie Bertrand) de 1908-1986 **CLC 1, 2, 4, 8, 14, 31, 44, 50, 71; DA; DAB; DAC; DAM MST, NOV; WLC**
See also CA 9-12R; 118; CANR 28, 61; DLB 72; DLBY 86; MTCW

Becker, Carl (Lotus) 1873-1945 **TCLC 63**
See also CA 157; DLB 17

Becker, Jurek 1937-1997 **CLC 7, 19**
See also CA 85-88; 157; CANR 60; DLB 75

Becker, Walter 1950- **CLC 26**

Beckett, Samuel (Barclay) 1906-1989 **CLC 1, 2, 3, 4, 6, 9, 10, 11, 14, 18, 29, 57, 59, 83; DA; DAB; DAC; DAM DRAM, MST, NOV; SSC 16; WLC**
See also CA 5-8R; 130; CANR 33, 61; CDBLB 1945-1960; DLB 13, 15; DLBY 90; MTCW

Beckford, William 1760-1844 **NCLC 16**
See also DLB 39

Beckman, Gunnel 1910- **CLC 26**
See also CA 33-36R; CANR 15; CLR 25; MAICYA; SAAS 9; SATA 6

Becque, Henri 1837-1899 **NCLC 3**
See also DLB 192

Beddoes, Thomas Lovell 1803-1849 **NCLC 3**
See also DLB 96

Bede c. 673-735 **CMLC 20**
See also DLB 146

Bedford, Donald F.
See Fearing, Kenneth (Flexner)

Beecher, Catharine Esther 1800-1878 **NCLC 30**
See also DLB 1

Beecher, John 1904-1980 **CLC 6**
See also AITN 1; CA 5-8R; 105; CANR 8

Beer, Johann 1655-1700 **LC 5**
See also DLB 168

Beer, Patricia 1924- **CLC 58**
See also CA 61-64; CANR 13, 46; DLB 40

Beerbohm, Max
See Beerbohm, (Henry) Max(imilian)

Beerbohm, (Henry) Max(imilian) 1872-1956 **TCLC 1, 24**
See also CA 104; 154; DLB 34, 100

Beer-Hofmann, Richard 1866-1945 **TCLC 60**
See also CA 160; DLB 81

Begiebing, Robert J(ohn) 1946- **CLC 70**
See also CA 122; CANR 40

Behan, Brendan 1923-1964 **CLC 1, 8, 11, 15, 79; DAM DRAM**
See also CA 73-76; CANR 33; CDBLB 1945-1960; DLB 13; MTCW

Behn, Aphra 1640(?)-1689 **LC 1, 30; DA; DAB; DAC; DAM DRAM, MST, NOV, POET; DC 4; PC 13; WLC**
See also DLB 39, 80, 131

Behrman, S(amuel) N(athaniel) 1893-1973 **CLC 40**
See also CA 13-16; 45-48; CAP 1; DLB 7, 44

Belasco, David 1853-1931 **TCLC 3**
See also CA 104; DLB 7

Belcheva, Elisaveta 1893- **CLC 10**
See also Bagryana, Elisaveta

Beldone, Phil "Cheech"
See Ellison, Harlan (Jay)

Beleno
See Azuela, Mariano

Belinski, Vissarion Grigoryevich 1811-1848 **NCLC 5**
See also DLB 198

Belitt, Ben 1911- **CLC 22**
See also CA 13-16R; CAAS 4; CANR 7; DLB 5

43; DAB; DAM MST, POET
See also CA 9-12R; 112; CANR 33, 56; CDBLB
1945-1960; DLB 20; DLBY 84; MTCW
Bettelheim, Bruno 1903-1990 **CLC 79**
See also CA 81-84; 131; CANR 23, 61; MTCW
Betti, Ugo 1892-1953 **TCLC 5**
See also CA 104; 155
Betts, Doris (Waugh) 1932- **CLC 3, 6, 28**
See also CA 13-16R; CANR 9, 66; DLBY 82;
INT CANR-9
Bevan, Alistair
See Roberts, Keith (John Kingston)
Bey, Pilaff
See Douglas, (George) Norman
Bialik, Chaim Nachman 1873-1934 **TCLC 25**
Bickerstaff, Isaac
See Swift, Jonathan
Bidart, Frank 1939- **CLC 33**
See also CA 140
Bienek, Horst 1930- **CLC 7, 11**
See also CA 73-76; DLB 75
Bierce, Ambrose (Gwinett) 1842-1914(?)
**TCLC 1, 7, 44; DA; DAC; DAM MST; SSC
9; WLC**
See also CA 104; 139; CDALB 1865-1917;
DLB 11, 12, 23, 71, 74, 186
Biggers, Earl Derr 1884-1933 **TCLC 65**
See also CA 108; 153
Billings, Josh
See Shaw, Henry Wheeler
Billington, (Lady) Rachel (Mary) 1942- **C L C
43**
See also AITN 2; CA 33-36R; CANR 44
Binyon, T(imothy) J(ohn) 1936- **CLC 34**
See also CA 111; CANR 28
Bioy Casares, Adolfo 1914-1984 **CLC 4, 8, 13,
88; DAM MULT; HLC; SSC 17**
See also CA 29-32R; CANR 19, 43, 66; DLB
113; HW; MTCW
Bird, Cordwainer
See Ellison, Harlan (Jay)
Bird, Robert Montgomery 1806-1854 **NCLC 1**
Birney, (Alfred) Earle 1904-1995 **CLC 1, 4, 6,
11; DAC; DAM MST, POET**
See also CA 1-4R; CANR 5, 20; DLB 88;
MTCW
Bishop, Elizabeth 1911-1979 **CLC 1, 4, 9, 13,
15, 32; DA; DAC; DAM MST, POET; PC
3**
See also CA 5-8R; 89-92; CABS 2; CANR 26,
61; CDALB 1968-1988; DLB 5, 169;
MTCW; SATA-Obit 24
Bishop, John 1935- **CLC 10**
See also CA 105
Bissett, Bill 1939- **CLC 18; PC 14**
See also CA 69-72; CAAS 19; CANR 15; DLB
53; MTCW
Bitov, Andrei (Georgievich) 1937- **CLC 57**
See also CA 142
Biyidi, Alexandre 1932-
See Beti, Mongo
See also BW 1; CA 114; 124; MTCW
Bjarme, Brynjolf
See Ibsen, Henrik (Johan)
Bjoernson, Bjoernstjerne (Martinius) 1832-
1910 **TCLC 7, 37**
See also CA 104
Black, Robert
See Holdstock, Robert P.
Blackburn, Paul 1926-1971 **CLC 9, 43**
See also CA 81-84; 33-36R; CANR 34; DLB
16; DLBY 81
Black Elk 1863-1950 **TCLC 33; DAM MULT**

See also CA 144; NNAL
Black Hobart
See Sanders, (James) Ed(ward)
Blacklin, Malcolm
See Chambers, Aidan
Blackmore, R(ichard) D(oddridge) 1825-1900
TCLC 27
See also CA 120; DLB 18
Blackmur, R(ichard) P(almer) 1904-1965
CLC 2, 24
See also CA 11-12; 25-28R; CAP 1; DLB 63
Black Tarantula
See Acker, Kathy
Blackwood, Algernon (Henry) 1869-1951
TCLC 5
See also CA 105; 150; DLB 153, 156, 178
Blackwood, Caroline 1931-1996 **CLC 6, 9, 100**
See also CA 85-88; 151; CANR 32, 61, 65; DLB
14; MTCW
Blade, Alexander
See Hamilton, Edmond; Silverberg, Robert
Blaga, Lucian 1895-1961 **CLC 75**
See also CA 157
Blair, Eric (Arthur) 1903-1950
See Orwell, George
See also CA 104; 132; DA; DAB; DAC; DAM
MST, NOV; MTCW; SATA 29
Blais, Marie-Claire 1939- **CLC 2, 4, 6, 13, 22;
DAC; DAM MST**
See also CA 21-24R; CAAS 4; CANR 38; DLB
53; MTCW
Blaise, Clark 1940- **CLC 29**
See also AITN 2; CA 53-56; CAAS 3; CANR
5, 66; DLB 53
Blake, Fairley
See De Voto, Bernard (Augustine)
Blake, Nicholas
See Day Lewis, C(ecil)
See also DLB 77
Blake, William 1757-1827 **NCLC 13, 37, 57;
DA; DAB; DAC; DAM MST, POET; PC
12; WLC**
See also CDBLB 1789-1832; DLB 93, 163;
MAICYA; SATA 30
Blasco Ibanez, Vicente 1867-1928 **TCLC 12;
DAM NOV**
See also CA 110; 131; HW; MTCW
Blatty, William Peter 1928- **CLC 2; DAM POP**
See also CA 5-8R; CANR 9
Bleeck, Oliver
See Thomas, Ross (Elmore)
Blessing, Lee 1949- **CLC 54**
Blish, James (Benjamin) 1921-1975 **CLC 14**
See also CA 1-4R; 57-60; CANR 3; DLB 8;
MTCW; SATA 66
Bliss, Reginald
See Wells, H(erbert) G(eorge)
Blixen, Karen (Christentze Dinesen) 1885-1962
See Dinesen, Isak
See also CA 25-28; CANR 22, 50; CAP 2;
MTCW; SATA 44
Bloch, Robert (Albert) 1917-1994 **CLC 33**
See also CA 5-8R; 146; CAAS 20; CANR 5;
DLB 44; INT CANR-5; SATA 12; SATA-Obit
82
Blok, Alexander (Alexandrovich) 1880-1921
TCLC 5; PC 21
See also CA 104
Blom, Jan
See Breytenbach, Breyten
Bloom, Harold 1930- **CLC 24, 103**
See also CA 13-16R; CANR 39; DLB 67
Bloomfield, Aurelius

See Bourne, Randolph S(illiman)
Blount, Roy (Alton), Jr. 1941- **CLC 38**
See also CA 53-56; CANR 10, 28, 61; INT
CANR-28; MTCW
Bloy, Leon 1846-1917 **TCLC 22**
See also CA 121; DLB 123
Blume, Judy (Sussman) 1938- **CLC 12, 30;
DAM NOV, POP**
See also AAYA 3; CA 29-32R; CANR 13, 37,
66; CLR 2, 15; DLB 52; JRDA; MAICYA;
MTCW; SATA 2, 31, 79
Blunden, Edmund (Charles) 1896-1974 **C L C
2, 56**
See also CA 17-18; 45-48; CANR 54; CAP 2;
DLB 20, 100, 155; MTCW
Bly, Robert (Elwood) 1926- **CLC 1, 2, 5, 10, 15,
38; DAM POET**
See also CA 5-8R; CANR 41; DLB 5; MTCW
Boas, Franz 1858-1942 **TCLC 56**
See also CA 115
Bobette
See Simenon, Georges (Jacques Christian)
Boccaccio, Giovanni 1313-1375 **CMLC 13;
SSC 10**
Bochco, Steven 1943- **CLC 35**
See also AAYA 11; CA 124; 138
Bodel, Jean 1167(?)-1210 **CMLC 28**
Bodenheim, Maxwell 1892-1954 **TCLC 44**
See also CA 110; DLB 9, 45
Bodker, Cecil 1927- **CLC 21**
See also CA 73-76; CANR 13, 44; CLR 23;
MAICYA; SATA 14
Boell, Heinrich (Theodor) 1917-1985 **CLC 2,
3, 6, 9, 11, 15, 27, 32, 72; DA; DAB; DAC;
DAM MST, NOV; SSC 23; WLC**
See also CA 21-24R; 116; CANR 24; DLB 69;
DLBY 85; MTCW
Boerne, Alfred
See Doeblin, Alfred
Boethius 480(?)-524(?) **CMLC 15**
See also DLB 115
Bogan, Louise 1897-1970 **CLC 4, 39, 46, 93;
DAM POET; PC 12**
See also CA 73-76; 25-28R; CANR 33; DLB
45, 169; MTCW
Bogarde, Dirk **CLC 19**
See also Van Den Bogarde, Derek Jules Gaspard
Ulric Niven
See also DLB 14
Bogosian, Eric 1953- **CLC 45**
See also CA 138
Bograd, Larry 1953- **CLC 35**
See also CA 93-96; CANR 57; SAAS 21; SATA
33, 89
Boiardo, Matteo Maria 1441-1494 **LC 6**
Boileau-Despreaux, Nicolas 1636-1711 **LC 3**
Bojer, Johan 1872-1959 **TCLC 64**
Boland, Eavan (Aisling) 1944- **CLC 40, 67,
113; DAM POET**
See also CA 143; CANR 61; DLB 40
Boll, Heinrich
See Boell, Heinrich (Theodor)
Bolt, Lee
See Faust, Frederick (Schiller)
Bolt, Robert (Oxton) 1924-1995 **CLC 14; DAM
DRAM**
See also CA 17-20R; 147; CANR 35, 67; DLB
13; MTCW
Bombet, Louis-Alexandre-Cesar
See Stendhal
Bomkauf
See Kaufman, Bob (Garnell)
Bonaventura **NCLC 35**

See also DLB 90

Bond, Edward 1934- **CLC 4, 6, 13, 23; DAM DRAM**
See also CA 25-28R; CANR 38, 67; DLB 13; MTCW

Bonham, Frank 1914-1989 **CLC 12**
See also AAYA 1; CA 9-12R; CANR 4, 36; JRDA; MAICYA; SAAS 3; SATA 1, 49; SATA-Obit 62

Bonnefoy, Yves 1923- **CLC 9, 15, 58; DAM MST, POET**
See also CA 85-88; CANR 33; MTCW

Bontemps, Arna(ud Wendell) 1902-1973 **C L C 1, 18; BLC 1; DAM MULT, NOV, POET**
See also BW 1; CA 1-4R; 41-44R; CANR 4, 35; CLR 6; DLB 48, 51; JRDA; MAICYA; MTCW; SATA 2, 44; SATA-Obit 24

Booth, Martin 1944- **CLC 13**
See also CA 93-96; CAAS 2

Booth, Philip 1925- **CLC 23**
See also CA 5-8R; CANR 5; DLBY 82

Booth, Wayne C(layson) 1921- **CLC 24**
See also CA 1-4R; CAAS 5; CANR 3, 43; DLB 67

Borchert, Wolfgang 1921-1947 **TCLC 5**
See also CA 104; DLB 69, 124

Borel, Petrus 1809-1859 **NCLC 41**

Borges, Jorge Luis 1899-1986 CLC 1, 2, 3, 4, 6, 8, 9, 10, 13, 19, 44, 48, 83; DA; DAB; DAC; DAM MST, MULT; HLC; PC 22; SSC 4; WLC
See also AAYA 19; CA 21-24R; CANR 19, 33; DLB 113; DLBY 86; HW; MTCW

Borowski, Tadeusz 1922-1951 **TCLC 9**
See also CA 106; 154

Borrow, George (Henry) 1803-1881 NCLC 9
See also DLB 21, 55, 166

Bosman, Herman Charles 1905-1951 T C L C 49
See also Malan, Herman
See also CA 160

Bosschere, Jean de 1878(?)-1953 **TCLC 19**
See also CA 115

Boswell, James 1740-1795 **LC 4; DA; DAB; DAC; DAM MST; WLC**
See also CDBLB 1660-1789; DLB 104, 142

Bottoms, David 1949- **CLC 53**
See also CA 105; CANR 22; DLB 120; DLBY 83

Boucicault, Dion 1820-1890 **NCLC 41**

Boucolon, Maryse 1937(?)-
See Conde, Maryse
See also CA 110; CANR 30, 53

Bourget, Paul (Charles Joseph) 1852-1935 **TCLC 12**
See also CA 107; DLB 123

Bourjaily, Vance (Nye) 1922- **CLC 8, 62**
See also CA 1-4R; CAAS 1; CANR 2; DLB 2, 143

Bourne, Randolph S(illiman) 1886-1918 **TCLC 16**
See also CA 117; 155; DLB 63

Bova, Ben(jamin William) 1932- **CLC 45**
See also AAYA 16; CA 5-8R; CAAS 18; CANR 11, 56; CLR 3; DLBY 81; INT CANR-11; MAICYA; MTCW; SATA 6, 68

Bowen, Elizabeth (Dorothea Cole) 1899-1973 **CLC 1, 3, 6, 11, 15, 22; DAM NOV; SSC 3, 28**
See also CA 17-18; 41-44R; CANR 35; CAP 2; CDBLB 1945-1960; DLB 15, 162; MTCW

Bowering, George 1935- **CLC 15, 47**
See also CA 21-24R; CAAS 16; CANR 10; DLB 53

Bowering, Marilyn R(uthe) 1949- **CLC 32**
See also CA 101; CANR 49

Bowers, Edgar 1924- **CLC 9**
See also CA 5-8R; CANR 24; DLB 5

Bowie, David **CLC 17**
See also Jones, David Robert

Bowles, Jane (Sydney) 1917-1973 CLC 3, 68
See also CA 19-20; 41-44R; CAP 2

Bowles, Paul (Frederick) 1910-1986 CLC 1, 2, 19, 53; SSC 3
See also CA 1-4R; CAAS 1; CANR 1, 19, 50; DLB 5, 6; MTCW

Box, Edgar
See Vidal, Gore

Boyd, Nancy
See Millay, Edna St. Vincent

Boyd, William 1952- **CLC 28, 53, 70**
See also CA 114; 120; CANR 51

Boyle, Kay 1902-1992 CLC 1, 5, 19, 58; SSC 5
See also CA 13-16R; 140; CAAS 1; CANR 29, 61; DLB 4, 9, 48, 86; DLBY 93; MTCW

Boyle, Mark
See Kienzle, William X(avier)

Boyle, Patrick 1905-1982 **CLC 19**
See also CA 127

Boyle, T. C. 1948-
See Boyle, T(homas) Coraghessan

Boyle, T(homas) Coraghessan 1948- CLC 36, 55, 90; DAM POP; SSC 16
See also BEST 90:4; CA 120; CANR 44; DLBY 86

Boz
See Dickens, Charles (John Huffam)

Brackenridge, Hugh Henry 1748-1816 N C L C 7
See also DLB 11, 37

Bradbury, Edward P.
See Moorcock, Michael (John)

Bradbury, Malcolm (Stanley) 1932- CLC 32, 61; DAM NOV
See also CA 1-4R; CANR 1, 33; DLB 14; MTCW

Bradbury, Ray (Douglas) 1920- CLC 1, 3, 10, 15, 42, 98; DA; DAB; DAC; DAM MST, NOV, POP; SSC 29; WLC
See also AAYA 15; AITN 1, 2; CA 1-4R; CANR 2, 30; CDALB 1968-1988; DLB 2, 8; MTCW; SATA 11, 64

Bradford, Gamaliel 1863-1932 **TCLC 36**
See also CA 160; DLB 17

Bradley, David (Henry, Jr.) 1950- **CLC 23; BLC 1; DAM MULT**
See also BW 1; CA 104; CANR 26; DLB 33

Bradley, John Ed(mund, Jr.) 1958- **CLC 55**
See also CA 139

Bradley, Marion Zimmer 1930- CLC 30; DAM POP
See also AAYA 9; CA 57-60; CAAS 10; CANR 7, 31, 51; DLB 8; MTCW; SATA 90

Bradstreet, Anne 1612(?)-1672 LC 4, 30; DA; DAC; DAM MST, POET; PC 10
See also CDALB 1640-1865; DLB 24

Brady, Joan 1939- **CLC 86**
See also CA 141

Bragg, Melvyn 1939- **CLC 10**
See also BEST 89:3; CA 57-60; CANR 10, 48; DLB 14

Braine, John (Gerard) 1922-1986 CLC 1, 3, 41
See also CA 1-4R; 120; CANR 1, 33; CDBLB 1945-1960; DLB 15; DLBY 86; MTCW

Bramah, Ernest 1868-1942 **TCLC 72**
See also CA 156; DLB 70

Brammer, William 1930(?)-1978 **CLC 31**
See also CA 77-80

Brancati, Vitaliano 1907-1954 **TCLC 12**
See also CA 109

Brancato, Robin F(idler) 1936- **CLC 35**
See also AAYA 9; CA 69-72; CANR 11, 45; CLR 32; JRDA; SAAS 9; SATA 97

Brand, Max
See Faust, Frederick (Schiller)

Brand, Millen 1906-1980 **CLC 7**
See also CA 21-24R; 97-100

Branden, Barbara **CLC 44**
See also CA 148

Brandes, Georg (Morris Cohen) 1842-1927 **TCLC 10**
See also CA 105

Brandys, Kazimierz 1916- **CLC 62**

Branley, Franklyn M(ansfield) 1915- CLC 21
See also CA 33-36R; CANR 14, 39; CLR 13; MAICYA; SAAS 16; SATA 4, 68

Brathwaite, Edward Kamau 1930- **CLC 11; BLCS; DAM POET**
See also BW 2; CA 25-28R; CANR 11, 26, 47; DLB 125

Brautigan, Richard (Gary) 1935-1984 CLC 1, 3, 5, 9, 12, 34, 42; DAM NOV
See also CA 53-56; 113; CANR 34; DLB 2, 5; DLBY 80, 84; MTCW; SATA 56

Brave Bird, Mary 1953-
See Crow Dog, Mary (Ellen)
See also NNAL

Braverman, Kate 1950- **CLC 67**
See also CA 89-92

Brecht, (Eugen) Bertolt (Friedrich) 1898-1956 **TCLC 1, 6, 13, 35; DA; DAB; DAC; DAM DRAM, MST; DC 3; WLC**
See also CA 104; 133; CANR 62; DLB 56, 124; MTCW

Brecht, Eugen Berthold Friedrich
See Brecht, (Eugen) Bertolt (Friedrich)

Bremer, Fredrika 1801-1865 **NCLC 11**

Brennan, Christopher John 1870-1932 T C L C 17
See also CA 117

Brennan, Maeve 1917- **CLC 5**
See also CA 81-84

Brent, Linda
See Jacobs, Harriet A(nn)

Brentano, Clemens (Maria) 1778-1842 N C L C 1
See also DLB 90

Brent of Bin Bin
See Franklin, (Stella Maria Sarah) Miles (Lampe)

Brenton, Howard 1942- **CLC 31**
See also CA 69-72; CANR 33, 67; DLB 13; MTCW

Breslin, James 1930-1996
See Breslin, Jimmy
See also CA 73-76; CANR 31; DAM NOV; MTCW

Breslin, Jimmy **CLC 4, 43**
See also Breslin, James
See also AITN 1; DLB 185

Bresson, Robert 1901- **CLC 16**
See also CA 110; CANR 49

Breton, Andre 1896-1966 CLC 2, 9, 15, 54; PC 15
See also CA 19-20; 25-28R; CANR 40, 60; CAP 2; DLB 65; MTCW

Breytenbach, Breyten 1939(?)- **CLC 23, 37; DAM POET**
See also CA 113; 129; CANR 61

Bridgers, Sue Ellen 1942-   **CLC 26**
See also AAYA 8; CA 65-68; CANR 11, 36;
CLR 18; DLB 52; JRDA; MAICYA; SAAS
1; SATA 22, 90

Bridges, Robert (Seymour) 1844-1930 **T C L C
1; DAM POET**
See also CA 104; 152; CDBLB 1890-1914;
DLB 19, 98

Bridie, James   **TCLC 3**
See also Mavor, Osborne Henry
See also DLB 10

Brin, David 1950-   **CLC 34**
See also AAYA 21; CA 102; CANR 24; INT
CANR-24; SATA 65

Brink, Andre (Philippus) 1935- **CLC 18, 36,
106**
See also CA 104; CANR 39, 62; INT 103;
MTCW

Brinsmead, H(esba) F(ay) 1922-   **CLC 21**
See also CA 21-24R; CANR 10; CLR 47;
MAICYA; SAAS 5; SATA 18, 78

Brittain, Vera (Mary) 1893(?)-1970 **CLC 23**
See also CA 13-16; 25-28R; CANR 58; CAP 1;
DLB 191; MTCW

Broch, Hermann 1886-1951   **TCLC 20**
See also CA 117; DLB 85, 124

Brock, Rose
See Hansen, Joseph

Brodkey, Harold (Roy) 1930-1996   **CLC 56**
See also CA 111; 151; DLB 130

Brodsky, Iosif Alexandrovich 1940-1996
See Brodsky, Joseph
See also AITN 1; CA 41-44R; 151; CANR 37;
DAM POET; MTCW

Brodsky, Joseph 1940-1996 **CLC 4, 6, 13, 36,
100; PC 9**
See also Brodsky, Iosif Alexandrovich

Brodsky, Michael (Mark) 1948-   **CLC 19**
See also CA 102; CANR 18, 41, 58

Bromell, Henry 1947-   **CLC 5**
See also CA 53-56; CANR 9

Bromfield, Louis (Brucker) 1896-1956 **T C L C
11**
See also CA 107; 155; DLB 4, 9, 86

Broner, E(sther) M(asserman) 1930- **CLC 19**
See also CA 17-20R; CANR 8, 25; DLB 28

Bronk, William 1918-   **CLC 10**
See also CA 89-92; CANR 23; DLB 165

Bronstein, Lev Davidovich
See Trotsky, Leon

Bronte, Anne 1820-1849   **NCLC 4, 71**
See also DLB 21, 199

Bronte, Charlotte 1816-1855 **NCLC 3, 8, 33,
58; DA; DAB; DAC; DAM MST, NOV;
WLC**
See also AAYA 17; CDBLB 1832-1890; DLB
21, 159, 199

Bronte, Emily (Jane) 1818-1848 **NCLC 16, 35;
DA; DAB; DAC; DAM MST, NOV, POET;
PC 8; WLC**
See also AAYA 17; CDBLB 1832-1890; DLB
21, 32, 199

Brooke, Frances 1724-1789   **LC 6**
See also DLB 39, 99

Brooke, Henry 1703(?)-1783   **LC 1**
See also DLB 39

Brooke, Rupert (Chawner) 1887-1915 **T C L C
2, 7; DA; DAB; DAC; DAM MST, POET;
WLC**
See also CA 104; 132; CANR 61; CDBLB
1914-1945; DLB 19; MTCW

Brooke-Haven, P.
See Wodehouse, P(elham) G(renville)

Brooke-Rose, Christine 1926(?)-   **CLC 40**
See also CA 13-16R; CANR 58; DLB 14

Brookner, Anita 1928- **CLC 32, 34, 51; DAB;
DAM POP**
See also CA 114; 120; CANR 37, 56; DLB 194;
DLBY 87; MTCW

Brooks, Cleanth 1906-1994 **CLC 24, 86, 110**
See also CA 17-20R; 145; CANR 33, 35; DLB
63; DLBY 94; INT CANR-35; MTCW

Brooks, George
See Baum, L(yman) Frank

Brooks, Gwendolyn 1917- **CLC 1, 2, 4, 5, 15,
49; BLC 1; DA; DAC; DAM MST, MULT,
POET; PC 7; WLC**
See also AAYA 20; AITN 1; BW 2; CA 1-4R;
CANR 1, 27, 52; CDALB 1941-1968; CLR
27; DLB 5, 76, 165; MTCW; SATA 6

Brooks, Mel   **CLC 12**
See also Kaminsky, Melvin
See also AAYA 13; DLB 26

Brooks, Peter 1938-   **CLC 34**
See also CA 45-48; CANR 1

Brooks, Van Wyck 1886-1963   **CLC 29**
See also CA 1-4R; CANR 6; DLB 45, 63, 103

Brophy, Brigid (Antonia) 1929-1995 **CLC 6,
11, 29, 105**
See also CA 5-8R; 149; CAAS 4; CANR 25,
53; DLB 14; MTCW

Brosman, Catharine Savage 1934-   **CLC 9**
See also CA 61-64; CANR 21, 46

Brother Antoninus
See Everson, William (Oliver)

The Brothers Quay
See Quay, Stephen; Quay, Timothy

Broughton, T(homas) Alan 1936-   **CLC 19**
See also CA 45-48; CANR 2, 23, 48

Broumas, Olga 1949-   **CLC 10, 73**
See also CA 85-88; CANR 20, 69

Brown, Alan 1950-   **CLC 99**
See also CA 156

Brown, Charles Brockden 1771-1810 **N C L C
22**
See also CDALB 1640-1865; DLB 37, 59, 73

Brown, Christy 1932-1981   **CLC 63**
See also CA 105; 104; DLB 14

Brown, Claude 1937- **CLC 30; BLC 1; DAM
MULT**
See also AAYA 7; BW 1; CA 73-76

Brown, Dee (Alexander) 1908- **CLC 18, 47;
DAM POP**
See also CA 13-16R; CAAS 6; CANR 11, 45,
60; DLBY 80; MTCW; SATA 5

Brown, George
See Wertmueller, Lina

Brown, George Douglas 1869-1902 **TCLC 28**
See also CA 162

Brown, George Mackay 1921-1996 **CLC 5, 48,
100**
See also CA 21-24R; 151; CAAS 6; CANR 12,
37, 67; DLB 14, 27, 139; MTCW; SATA 35

Brown, (William) Larry 1951-   **CLC 73**
See also CA 130; 134; INT 133

Brown, Moses
See Barrett, William (Christopher)

Brown, Rita Mae 1944- **CLC 18, 43, 79; DAM
NOV, POP**
See also CA 45-48; CANR 2, 11, 35, 62; INT
CANR-11; MTCW

Brown, Roderick (Langmere) Haig-
See Haig-Brown, Roderick (Langmere)

Brown, Rosellen 1939-   **CLC 32**
See also CA 77-80; CAAS 10; CANR 14, 44

Brown, Sterling Allen 1901-1989 **CLC 1, 23,**
59; BLC 1; DAM MULT, POET
See also BW 1; CA 85-88; 127; CANR 26; DLB
48, 51, 63; MTCW

Brown, Will
See Ainsworth, William Harrison

Brown, William Wells 1813-1884   **NCLC 2;
BLC 1; DAM MULT; DC 1**
See also DLB 3, 50

Browne, (Clyde) Jackson 1948(?)-   **CLC 21**
See also CA 120

Browning, Elizabeth Barrett 1806-1861
**NCLC 1, 16, 61, 66; DA; DAB; DAC; DAM
MST, POET; PC 6; WLC**
See also CDBLB 1832-1890; DLB 32, 199

Browning, Robert 1812-1889 **NCLC 19; DA;
DAB; DAC; DAM MST, POET; PC 2;
WLCS**
See also CDBLB 1832-1890; DLB 32, 163;
YABC 1

Browning, Tod 1882-1962   **CLC 16**
See also CA 141; 117

Brownson, Orestes (Augustus) 1803-1876
NCLC 50

Brownson, Orestes Augustus 1803-1876
NCLC 50
See also DLB 1, 59, 73

Bruccoli, Matthew J(oseph) 1931-   **CLC 34**
See also CA 9-12R; CANR 7; DLB 103

Bruce, Lenny   **CLC 21**
See also Schneider, Leonard Alfred

Bruin, John
See Brutus, Dennis

Brulard, Henri
See Stendhal

Brulls, Christian
See Simenon, Georges (Jacques Christian)

Brunner, John (Kilian Houston) 1934-1995
CLC 8, 10; DAM POP
See also CA 1-4R; 149; CAAS 8; CANR 2, 37;
MTCW

Bruno, Giordano 1548-1600   **LC 27**

Brutus, Dennis 1924- **CLC 43; BLC 1; DAM
MULT, POET**
See also BW 2; CA 49-52; CAAS 14; CANR 2,
27, 42; DLB 117

Bryan, C(ourtlandt) D(ixon) B(arnes) 1936-
CLC 29
See also CA 73-76; CANR 13, 68; DLB 185;
INT CANR-13

Bryan, Michael
See Moore, Brian

Bryant, William Cullen 1794-1878 **NCLC 6,
46; DA; DAB; DAC; DAM MST, POET;
PC 20**
See also CDALB 1640-1865; DLB 3, 43, 59,
189

Bryusov, Valery Yakovlevich 1873-1924
TCLC 10
See also CA 107; 155

Buchan, John 1875-1940   **TCLC 41; DAB;
DAM POP**
See also CA 108; 145; DLB 34, 70, 156; YABC
2

Buchanan, George 1506-1582   **LC 4**
See also DLB 152

Buchheim, Lothar-Guenther 1918-   **CLC 6**
See also CA 85-88

Buchner, (Karl) Georg 1813-1837 **NCLC 26**

Buchwald, Art(hur) 1925-   **CLC 33**
See also AITN 1; CA 5-8R; CANR 21, 67;
MTCW; SATA 10

Buck, Pearl S(ydenstricker) 1892-1973 **CLC 7,
11, 18; DA; DAB; DAC; DAM MST, NOV**

See also AITN 1; CA 1-4R; 41-44R; CANR 1,
34; DLB 9, 102; MTCW; SATA 1, 25

Buckler, Ernest 1908-1984   **CLC 13; DAC;**
DAM MST
See also CA 11-12; 114; CAP 1; DLB 68; SATA
47

Buckley, Vincent (Thomas) 1925-1988**CLC 57**
See also CA 101

Buckley, William F(rank), Jr. 1925-**CLC 7, 18,**
37; DAM POP
See also AITN 1; CA 1-4R; CANR 1, 24, 53;
DLB 137; DLBY 80; INT CANR-24; MTCW

Buechner, (Carl) Frederick 1926-**CLC 2, 4, 6,**
9; DAM NOV
See also CA 13-16R; CANR 11, 39, 64; DLBY
80; INT CANR-11; MTCW

Buell, John (Edward) 1927-   **CLC 10**
See also CA 1-4R; DLB 53

Buero Vallejo, Antonio 1916-   **CLC 15, 46**
See also CA 106; CANR 24, 49; HW; MTCW

Bufalino, Gesualdo 1920(?)-   **CLC 74**
See also DLB 196

Bugayev, Boris Nikolayevich 1880-1934
TCLC 7; PC 11
See also Bely, Andrey
See also CA 104; 165

Bukowski, Charles 1920-1994**CLC 2, 5, 9, 41,**
82, 108; DAM NOV, POET; PC 18
See also CA 17-20R; 144; CANR 40, 62; DLB
5, 130, 169; MTCW

Bulgakov, Mikhail (Afanas'evich) 1891-1940
TCLC 2, 16; DAM DRAM, NOV; SSC 18
See also CA 105; 152

Bulgya, Alexander Alexandrovich 1901-1956
TCLC 53
See also Fadeyev, Alexander
See also CA 117

Bullins, Ed 1935-   **CLC 1, 5, 7; BLC 1; DAM**
DRAM, MULT; DC 6
See also BW 2; CA 49-52; CAAS 16; CANR
24, 46; DLB 7, 38; MTCW

Bulwer-Lytton, Edward (George Earle Lytton)
1803-1873   **NCLC 1, 45**
See also DLB 21

Bunin, Ivan Alexeyevich 1870-1953 **TCLC 6;**
SSC 5
See also CA 104

Bunting, Basil 1900-1985   **CLC 10, 39, 47;**
DAM POET
See also CA 53-56; 115; CANR 7; DLB 20

Bunuel, Luis 1900-1983   **CLC 16, 80; DAM**
MULT; HLC
See also CA 101; 110; CANR 32; HW

Bunyan, John 1628-1688   **LC 4; DA; DAB;**
DAC; DAM MST; WLC
See also CDBLB 1660-1789; DLB 39

Burckhardt, Jacob (Christoph) 1818-1897
NCLC 49

Burford, Eleanor
See Hibbert, Eleanor Alice Burford

Burgess, AnthonyCLC 1, 2, 4, 5, 8, 10, 13, 15,
22, 40, 62, 81, 94; DAB
See also Wilson, John (Anthony) Burgess
See also AAYA 25; AITN 1; CDBLB 1960 to
Present; DLB 14, 194

Burke, Edmund 1729(?)-1797 **LC 7, 36; DA;**
DAB; DAC; DAM MST; WLC
See also DLB 104

Burke, Kenneth (Duva) 1897-1993 **CLC 2, 24**
See also CA 5-8R; 143; CANR 39; DLB 45,
63; MTCW

Burke, Leda
See Garnett, David

Burke, Ralph
See Silverberg, Robert

Burke, Thomas 1886-1945   **TCLC 63**
See also CA 113; 155; DLB 197

Burney, Fanny 1752-1840   **NCLC 12, 54**
See also DLB 39

Burns, Robert 1759-1796   **PC 6**
See also CDBLB 1789-1832; DA; DAB; DAC;
DAM MST, POET; DLB 109; WLC

Burns, Tex
See L'Amour, Louis (Dearborn)

Burnshaw, Stanley 1906-   **CLC 3, 13, 44**
See also CA 9-12R; DLB 48; DLBY 97

Burr, Anne 1937-   **CLC 6**
See also CA 25-28R

Burroughs, Edgar Rice 1875-1950 **TCLC 2,**
32; DAM NOV
See also AAYA 11; CA 104; 132; DLB 8;
MTCW; SATA 41

Burroughs, William S(eward) 1914-1997**CLC**
1, 2, 5, 15, 22, 42, 75, 109; DA; DAB; DAC;
DAM MST, NOV, POP; WLC
See also AITN 2; CA 9-12R; 160; CANR 20,
52; DLB 2, 8, 16, 152; DLBY 81, 97; MTCW

Burton, Richard F. 1821-1890   **NCLC 42**
See also DLB 55, 184

Busch, Frederick 1941-   **CLC 7, 10, 18, 47**
See also CA 33-36R; CAAS 1; CANR 45; DLB
6

Bush, Ronald 1946-   **CLC 34**
See also CA 136

Bustos, F(rancisco)
See Borges, Jorge Luis

Bustos Domecq, H(onorio)
See Bioy Casares, Adolfo; Borges, Jorge Luis

Butler, Octavia E(stelle) 1947-**CLC 38; BLCS;**
DAM MULT, POP
See also AAYA 18; BW 2; CA 73-76; CANR
12, 24, 38; DLB 33; MTCW; SATA 84

Butler, Robert Olen (Jr.) 1945-**CLC 81; DAM**
POP
See also CA 112; CANR 66; DLB 173; INT 112

Butler, Samuel 1612-1680   **LC 16, 43**
See also DLB 101, 126

Butler, Samuel 1835-1902   **TCLC 1, 33; DA;**
DAB; DAC; DAM MST, NOV; WLC
See also CA 143; CDBLB 1890-1914; DLB 18,
57, 174

Butler, Walter C.
See Faust, Frederick (Schiller)

Butor, Michel (Marie Francois) 1926-**CLC 1,**
3, 8, 11, 15
See also CA 9-12R; CANR 33, 66; DLB 83;
MTCW

Butts, Mary 1892(?)-1937   **TCLC 77**
See also CA 148

Buzo, Alexander (John) 1944-   **CLC 61**
See also CA 97-100; CANR 17, 39, 69

Buzzati, Dino 1906-1972   **CLC 36**
See also CA 160; 33-36R; DLB 177

Byars, Betsy (Cromer) 1928-   **CLC 35**
See also AAYA 19; CA 33-36R; CANR 18, 36,
57; CLR 1, 16; DLB 52; INT CANR-18;
JRDA; MAICYA; MTCW; SAAS 1; SATA
4, 46, 80

Byatt, A(ntonia) S(usan Drabble) 1936- **C L C**
19, 65; DAM NOV, POP
See also CA 13-16R; CANR 13, 33, 50; DLB
14, 194; MTCW

Byrne, David 1952-   **CLC 26**
See also CA 127

Byrne, John Keyes 1926-
See Leonard, Hugh

See also CA 102; INT 102

Byron, George Gordon (Noel) 1788-1824
NCLC 2, 12; DA; DAB; DAC; DAM MST,
POET; PC 16; WLC
See also CDBLB 1789-1832; DLB 96, 110

Byron, Robert 1905-1941   **TCLC 67**
See also CA 160; DLB 195

C. 3. 3.
See Wilde, Oscar (Fingal O'Flahertie Wills)

Caballero, Fernan 1796-1877   **NCLC 10**

Cabell, Branch
See Cabell, James Branch

Cabell, James Branch 1879-1958   **TCLC 6**
See also CA 105; 152; DLB 9, 78

Cable, George Washington 1844-1925 **T C L C**
4; SSC 4
See also CA 104; 155; DLB 12, 74; DLBD 13

Cabral de Melo Neto, Joao 1920-   **CLC 76;**
DAM MULT
See also CA 151

Cabrera Infante, G(uillermo) 1929-**CLC 5, 25,**
45; DAM MULT; HLC
See also CA 85-88; CANR 29, 65; DLB 113;
HW; MTCW

Cade, Toni
See Bambara, Toni Cade

Cadmus and Harmonia
See Buchan, John

Caedmon fl. 658-680   **CMLC 7**
See also DLB 146

Caeiro, Alberto
See Pessoa, Fernando (Antonio Nogueira)

Cage, John (Milton, Jr.) 1912-   **CLC 41**
See also CA 13-16R; CANR 9; DLB 193; INT
CANR-9

Cahan, Abraham 1860-1951   **TCLC 71**
See also CA 108; 154; DLB 9, 25, 28

Cain, G.
See Cabrera Infante, G(uillermo)

Cain, Guillermo
See Cabrera Infante, G(uillermo)

Cain, James M(allahan) 1892-1977**CLC 3, 11,**
28
See also AITN 1; CA 17-20R; 73-76; CANR 8,
34, 61; MTCW

Caine, Mark
See Raphael, Frederic (Michael)

Calasso, Roberto 1941-   **CLC 81**
See also CA 143

Calderon de la Barca, Pedro 1600-1681   **L C**
23; DC 3

Caldwell, Erskine (Preston) 1903-1987**CLC 1,**
8, 14, 50, 60; DAM NOV; SSC 19
See also AITN 1; CA 1-4R; 121; CAAS 1;
CANR 2, 33; DLB 9, 86; MTCW

Caldwell, (Janet Miriam) Taylor (Holland)
1900-1985**CLC 2, 28, 39; DAM NOV, POP**
See also CA 5-8R; 116; CANR 5

Calhoun, John Caldwell 1782-1850**NCLC 15**
See also DLB 3

Calisher, Hortense 1911-**CLC 2, 4, 8, 38; DAM**
NOV; SSC 15
See also CA 1-4R; CANR 1, 22, 67; DLB 2;
INT CANR-22; MTCW

Callaghan, Morley Edward 1903-1990**CLC 3,**
14, 41, 65; DAC; DAM MST
See also CA 9-12R; 132; CANR 33; DLB 68;
MTCW

Callimachus c. 305B.C.-c. 240B.C. **CMLC 18**
See also DLB 176

Calvin, John 1509-1564   **LC 37**

Calvino, Italo 1923-1985**CLC 5, 8, 11, 22, 33,**
39, 73; DAM NOV; SSC 3

See also CA 85-88; 116; CANR 23, 61; DLB 196; MTCW

Cameron, Carey 1952- **CLC 59**
See also CA 135

Cameron, Peter 1959- **CLC 44**
See also CA 125; CANR 50

Campana, Dino 1885-1932 **TCLC 20**
See also CA 117; DLB 114

Campanella, Tommaso 1568-1639 **LC 32**

Campbell, John W(ood, Jr.) 1910-1971 **C L C 32**
See also CA 21-22; 29-32R; CANR 34; CAP 2; DLB 8; MTCW

Campbell, Joseph 1904-1987 **CLC 69**
See also AAYA 3; BEST 89:2; CA 1-4R; 124; CANR 3, 28, 61; MTCW

Campbell, Maria 1940- **CLC 85; DAC**
See also CA 102; CANR 54; NNAL

Campbell, (John) Ramsey 1946-**CLC 42; SSC 19**
See also CA 57-60; CANR 7; INT CANR-7

Campbell, (Ignatius) Roy (Dunnachie) 1901-1957 **TCLC 5**
See also CA 104; 155; DLB 20

Campbell, Thomas 1777-1844 **NCLC 19**
See also DLB 93; 144

Campbell, Wilfred **TCLC 9**
See also Campbell, William

Campbell, William 1858(?)-1918
See Campbell, Wilfred
See also CA 106; DLB 92

Campion, Jane **CLC 95**
See also CA 138

Campos, Alvaro de
See Pessoa, Fernando (Antonio Nogueira)

Camus, Albert 1913-1960**CLC 1, 2, 4, 9, 11, 14, 32, 63, 69; DA; DAB; DAC; DAM DRAM, MST, NOV; DC 2; SSC 9; WLC**
See also CA 89-92; DLB 72; MTCW

Canby, Vincent 1924- **CLC 13**
See also CA 81-84

Cancale
See Desnos, Robert

Canetti, Elias 1905-1994**CLC 3, 14, 25, 75, 86**
See also CA 21-24R; 146; CANR 23, 61; DLB 85, 124; MTCW

Canin, Ethan 1960- **CLC 55**
See also CA 131; 135

Cannon, Curt
See Hunter, Evan

Cao, Lan 1961- **CLC 109**
See also CA 165

Cape, Judith
See Page, P(atricia) K(athleen)

Capek, Karel 1890-1938 **TCLC 6, 37; DA; DAB; DAC; DAM DRAM, MST, NOV; DC 1; WLC**
See also CA 104; 140

Capote, Truman 1924-1984**CLC 1, 3, 8, 13, 19, 34, 38, 58; DA; DAB; DAC; DAM MST, NOV, POP; SSC 2; WLC**
See also CA 5-8R; 113; CANR 18, 62; CDALB 1941-1968; DLB 2, 185; DLBY 80, 84; MTCW; SATA 91

Capra, Frank 1897-1991 **CLC 16**
See also CA 61-64; 135

Caputo, Philip 1941- **CLC 32**
See also CA 73-76; CANR 40

Caragiale, Ion Luca 1852-1912 **TCLC 76**
See also CA 157

Card, Orson Scott 1951-**CLC 44, 47, 50; DAM POP**
See also AAYA 11; CA 102; CANR 27, 47; INT

CANR-27; MTCW; SATA 83

Cardenal, Ernesto 1925- **CLC 31; DAM MULT, POET; HLC; PC 22**
See also CA 49-52; CANR 2, 32, 66; HW; MTCW

Cardozo, Benjamin N(athan) 1870-1938 **TCLC 65**
See also CA 117; 164

Carducci, Giosue (Alessandro Giuseppe) 1835-1907 **TCLC 32**
See also CA 163

Carew, Thomas 1595(?)-1640 **LC 13**
See also DLB 126

Carey, Ernestine Gilbreth 1908- **CLC 17**
See also CA 5-8R; SATA 2

Carey, Peter 1943- **CLC 40, 55, 96**
See also CA 123; 127; CANR 53; INT 127; MTCW; SATA 94

Carleton, William 1794-1869 **NCLC 3**
See also DLB 159

Carlisle, Henry (Coffin) 1926- **CLC 33**
See also CA 13-16R; CANR 15

Carlsen, Chris
See Holdstock, Robert P.

Carlson, Ron(ald F.) 1947- **CLC 54**
See also CA 105; CANR 27

Carlyle, Thomas 1795-1881 **NCLC 70; DA; DAB; DAC; DAM MST**
See also CDBLB 1789-1832; DLB 55; 144

Carman, (William) Bliss 1861-1929 **TCLC 7; DAC**
See also CA 104; 152; DLB 92

Carnegie, Dale 1888-1955 **TCLC 53**

Carossa, Hans 1878-1956 **TCLC 48**
See also DLB 66

Carpenter, Don(ald Richard) 1931-1995**C L C 41**
See also CA 45-48; 149; CANR 1

Carpentier (y Valmont), Alejo 1904-1980**CLC 8, 11, 38, 110; DAM MULT; HLC**
See also CA 65-68; 97-100; CANR 11; DLB 113; HW

Carr, Caleb 1955(?)- **CLC 86**
See also CA 147

Carr, Emily 1871-1945 **TCLC 32**
See also CA 159; DLB 68

Carr, John Dickson 1906-1977 **CLC 3**
See also Fairbairn, Roger
See also CA 49-52; 69-72; CANR 3, 33, 60; MTCW

Carr, Philippa
See Hibbert, Eleanor Alice Burford

Carr, Virginia Spencer 1929- **CLC 34**
See also CA 61-64; DLB 111

Carrere, Emmanuel 1957- **CLC 89**

Carrier, Roch 1937-**CLC 13, 78; DAC; DAM MST**
See also CA 130; CANR 61; DLB 53

Carroll, James P. 1943(?)- **CLC 38**
See also CA 81-84

Carroll, Jim 1951- **CLC 35**
See also AAYA 17; CA 45-48; CANR 42

Carroll, Lewis **NCLC 2, 53; PC 18; WLC**
See also Dodgson, Charles Lutwidge
See also CDBLB 1832-1890; CLR 2, 18; DLB 18, 163, 178; JRDA

Carroll, Paul Vincent 1900-1968 **CLC 10**
See also CA 9-12R; 25-28R; DLB 10

Carruth, Hayden 1921- **CLC 4, 7, 10, 18, 84; PC 10**
See also CA 9-12R; CANR 4, 38, 59; DLB 5, 165; INT CANR-4; MTCW; SATA 47

Carson, Rachel Louise 1907-1964 **CLC 71;**

DAM POP
See also CA 77-80; CANR 35; MTCW; SATA 23

Carter, Angela (Olive) 1940-1992 **CLC 5, 41, 76; SSC 13**
See also CA 53-56; 136; CANR 12, 36, 61; DLB 14; MTCW; SATA 66; SATA-Obit 70

Carter, Nick
See Smith, Martin Cruz

Carver, Raymond 1938-1988 **CLC 22, 36, 53, 55; DAM NOV; SSC 8**
See also CA 33-36R; 126; CANR 17, 34, 61; DLB 130; DLBY 84, 88; MTCW

Cary, Elizabeth, Lady Falkland 1585-1639 **LC 30**

Cary, (Arthur) Joyce (Lunel) 1888-1957 **TCLC 1, 29**
See also CA 104; 164; CDBLB 1914-1945; DLB 15, 100

Casanova de Seingalt, Giovanni Jacopo 1725-1798 **LC 13**

Casares, Adolfo Bioy
See Bioy Casares, Adolfo

Casely-Hayford, J(oseph) E(phraim) 1866-1930 **TCLC 24; BLC 1; DAM MULT**
See also BW 2; CA 123; 152

Casey, John (Dudley) 1939- **CLC 59**
See also BEST 90:2; CA 69-72; CANR 23

Casey, Michael 1947- **CLC 2**
See also CA 65-68; DLB 5

Casey, Patrick
See Thurman, Wallace (Henry)

Casey, Warren (Peter) 1935-1988 **CLC 12**
See also CA 101; 127; INT 101

Casona, Alejandro **CLC 49**
See also Alvarez, Alejandro Rodriguez

Cassavetes, John 1929-1989 **CLC 20**
See also CA 85-88; 127

Cassian, Nina 1924- **PC 17**

Cassill, R(onald) V(erlin) 1919- **CLC 4, 23**
See also CA 9-12R; CAAS 1; CANR 7, 45; DLB 6

Cassirer, Ernst 1874-1945 **TCLC 61**
See also CA 157

Cassity, (Allen) Turner 1929- **CLC 6, 42**
See also CA 17-20R; CAAS 8; CANR 11; DLB 105

Castaneda, Carlos 1931(?)- **CLC 12**
See also CA 25-28R; CANR 32, 66; HW; MTCW

Castedo, Elena 1937- **CLC 65**
See also CA 132

Castedo-Ellerman, Elena
See Castedo, Elena

Castellanos, Rosario 1925-1974**CLC 66; DAM MULT; HLC**
See also CA 131; 53-56; CANR 58; DLB 113; HW

Castelvetro, Lodovico 1505-1571 **LC 12**

Castiglione, Baldassare 1478-1529 **LC 12**

Castle, Robert
See Hamilton, Edmond

Castro, Guillen de 1569-1631 **LC 19**

Castro, Rosalia de 1837-1885**NCLC 3; DAM MULT**

Cather, Willa
See Cather, Willa Sibert

Cather, Willa Sibert 1873-1947 **TCLC 1, 11, 31; DA; DAB; DAC; DAM MST, NOV; SSC 2; WLC**
See also AAYA 24; CA 104; 128; CDALB 1865-1917; DLB 9, 54, 78; DLBD 1; MTCW; SATA 30

See also CA 113; 153; DLB 70

Childress, Alice 1920-1994**CLC 12, 15, 86, 96; BLC 1; DAM DRAM, MULT, NOV; DC 4**
See also AAYA 8; BW 2; CA 45-48; 146; CANR 3, 27, 50; CLR 14; DLB 7, 38; JRDA; MAICYA; MTCW; SATA 7, 48, 81

Chin, Frank (Chew, Jr.) 1940-   **DC 7**
See also CA 33-36R; DAM MULT

Chislett, (Margaret) Anne 1943-   **CLC 34**
See also CA 151

Chitty, Thomas Willes 1926-   **CLC 11**
See also Hinde, Thomas
See also CA 5-8R

Chivers, Thomas Holley 1809-1858**NCLC 49**
See also DLB 3

Chomette, Rene Lucien 1898-1981
See Clair, Rene
See also CA 103

Chopin, Kate **TCLC 5, 14; DA; DAB; SSC 8; WLCS**
See also Chopin, Katherine
See also CDALB 1865-1917; DLB 12, 78

Chopin, Katherine 1851-1904
See Chopin, Kate
See also CA 104; 122; DAC; DAM MST, NOV

Chretien de Troyes c. 12th cent. -   **CMLC 10**

Christie
See Ichikawa, Kon

Christie, Agatha (Mary Clarissa) 1890-1976
CLC 1, 6, 8, 12, 39, 48, 110; DAB; DAC; DAM NOV
See also AAYA 9; AITN 1, 2; CA 17-20R; 61-64; CANR 10, 37; CDBLB 1914-1945; DLB 13, 77; MTCW; SATA 36

Christie, (Ann) Philippa
See Pearce, Philippa
See also CA 5-8R; CANR 4

Christine de Pizan 1365(?)-1431(?)   **LC 9**

Chubb, Elmer
See Masters, Edgar Lee

Chulkov, Mikhail Dmitrievich 1743-1792**LC 2**
See also DLB 150

Churchill, Caryl 1938-   **CLC 31, 55; DC 5**
See also CA 102; CANR 22, 46; DLB 13; MTCW

Churchill, Charles 1731-1764   **LC 3**
See also DLB 109

Chute, Carolyn 1947-   **CLC 39**
See also CA 123

Ciardi, John (Anthony) 1916-1986 **CLC 10, 40, 44; DAM POET**
See also CA 5-8R; 118; CAAS 2; CANR 5, 33; CLR 19; DLB 5; DLBY 86; INT CANR-5; MAICYA; MTCW; SAAS 26; SATA 1, 65; SATA-Obit 46

Cicero, Marcus Tullius 106B.C.-43B.C.
CMLC 3

Cimino, Michael 1943-   **CLC 16**
See also CA 105

Cioran, E(mil) M. 1911-1995   **CLC 64**
See also CA 25-28R; 149

Cisneros, Sandra 1954-**CLC 69; DAM MULT; HLC**
See also AAYA 9; CA 131; CANR 64; DLB 122, 152; HW

Cixous, Helene 1937-   **CLC 92**
See also CA 126; CANR 55; DLB 83; MTCW

Clair, Rene   **CLC 20**
See also Chomette, Rene Lucien

Clampitt, Amy 1920-1994   **CLC 32; PC 19**
See also CA 110; 146; CANR 29; DLB 105

Clancy, Thomas L., Jr. 1947-
See Clancy, Tom

See also CA 125; 131; CANR 62; INT 131; MTCW

Clancy, Tom   **CLC 45, 112; DAM NOV, POP**
See also Clancy, Thomas L., Jr.
See also AAYA 9; BEST 89:1, 90:1

Clare, John 1793-1864 **NCLC 9; DAB; DAM POET**
See also DLB 55, 96

Clarin
See Alas (y Urena), Leopoldo (Enrique Garcia)

Clark, Al C.
See Goines, Donald

Clark, (Robert) Brian 1932-   **CLC 29**
See also CA 41-44R; CANR 67

Clark, Curt
See Westlake, Donald E(dwin)

Clark, Eleanor 1913-1996   **CLC 5, 19**
See also CA 9-12R; 151; CANR 41; DLB 6

Clark, J. P.
See Clark, John Pepper
See also DLB 117

Clark, John Pepper 1935-   **CLC 38; BLC 1; DAM DRAM, MULT; DC 5**
See also Clark, J. P.
See also BW 1; CA 65-68; CANR 16

Clark, M. R.
See Clark, Mavis Thorpe

Clark, Mavis Thorpe 1909-   **CLC 12**
See also CA 57-60; CANR 8, 37; CLR 30; MAICYA; SAAS 5; SATA 8, 74

Clark, Walter Van Tilburg 1909-1971**CLC 28**
See also CA 9-12R; 33-36R; CANR 63; DLB 9; SATA 8

Clarke, Arthur C(harles) 1917-**CLC 1, 4, 13, 18, 35; DAM POP; SSC 3**
See also AAYA 4; CA 1-4R; CANR 2, 28, 55; JRDA; MAICYA; MTCW; SATA 13, 70

Clarke, Austin 1896-1974   **CLC 6, 9; DAM POET**
See also CA 29-32; 49-52; CAP 2; DLB 10, 20

Clarke, Austin C(hesterfield) 1934-**CLC 8, 53; BLC 1; DAC; DAM MULT**
See also BW 1; CA 25-28R; CAAS 16; CANR 14, 32, 68; DLB 53, 125

Clarke, Gillian 1937-   **CLC 61**
See also CA 106; DLB 40

Clarke, Marcus (Andrew Hislop) 1846-1881
NCLC 19

Clarke, Shirley 1925-   **CLC 16**

Clash, The
See Headon, (Nicky) Topper; Jones, Mick; Simonon, Paul; Strummer, Joe

Claudel, Paul (Louis Charles Marie) 1868-1955
TCLC 2, 10
See also CA 104; 165; DLB 192

Clavell, James (duMaresq) 1925-1994**CLC 6, 25, 87; DAM NOV, POP**
See also CA 25-28R; 146; CANR 26, 48; MTCW

Cleaver, (Leroy) Eldridge 1935-**CLC 30; BLC 1; DAM MULT**
See also BW 1; CA 21-24R; CANR 16

Cleese, John (Marwood) 1939-   **CLC 21**
See also Monty Python
See also CA 112; 116; CANR 35; MTCW

Cleishbotham, Jebediah
See Scott, Walter

Cleland, John 1710-1789   **LC 2**
See also DLB 39

Clemens, Samuel Langhorne 1835-1910
See Twain, Mark
See also CA 104; 135; CDALB 1865-1917; DA; DAB; DAC; DAM MST, NOV; DLB 11, 12,

23, 64, 74, 186, 189; JRDA; MAICYA; YABC 2

Cleophil
See Congreve, William

Clerihew, E.
See Bentley, E(dmund) C(lerihew)

Clerk, N. W.
See Lewis, C(live) S(taples)

Cliff, Jimmy   **CLC 21**
See also Chambers, James

Clifton, (Thelma) Lucille 1936- **CLC 19, 66; BLC 1; DAM MULT, POET; PC 17**
See also BW 2; CA 49-52; CANR 2, 24, 42; CLR 5; DLB 5, 41; MAICYA; MTCW; SATA 20, 69

Clinton, Dirk
See Silverberg, Robert

Clough, Arthur Hugh 1819-1861   **NCLC 27**
See also DLB 32

Clutha, Janet Paterson Frame 1924-
See Frame, Janet
See also CA 1-4R; CANR 2, 36; MTCW

Clyne, Terence
See Blatty, William Peter

Cobalt, Martin
See Mayne, William (James Carter)

Cobb, Irvin S. 1876-1944   **TCLC 77**
See also DLB 11, 25, 86

Cobbett, William 1763-1835   **NCLC 49**
See also DLB 43, 107, 158

Coburn, D(onald) L(ee) 1938-   **CLC 10**
See also CA 89-92

Cocteau, Jean (Maurice Eugene Clement) 1889-1963**CLC 1, 8, 15, 16, 43; DA; DAB; DAC; DAM DRAM, MST, NOV; WLC**
See also CA 25-28; CANR 40; CAP 2; DLB 65; MTCW

Codrescu, Andrei 1946-**CLC 46; DAM POET**
See also CA 33-36R; CAAS 19; CANR 13, 34, 53

Coe, Max
See Bourne, Randolph S(illiman)

Coe, Tucker
See Westlake, Donald E(dwin)

Coen, Ethan 1958-   **CLC 108**
See also CA 126

Coen, Joel 1955-   **CLC 108**
See also CA 126

The Coen Brothers
See Coen, Ethan; Coen, Joel

Coetzee, J(ohn) M(ichael) 1940- **CLC 23, 33, 66; DAM NOV**
See also CA 77-80; CANR 41, 54; MTCW

Coffey, Brian
See Koontz, Dean R(ay)

Cohan, George M(ichael) 1878-1942**TCLC 60**
See also CA 157

Cohen, Arthur A(llen) 1928-1986 **CLC 7, 31**
See also CA 1-4R; 120; CANR 1, 17, 42; DLB 28

Cohen, Leonard (Norman) 1934- **CLC 3, 38; DAC; DAM MST**
See also CA 21-24R; CANR 14, 69; DLB 53; MTCW

Cohen, Matt 1942-   **CLC 19; DAC**
See also CA 61-64; CAAS 18; CANR 40; DLB 53

Cohen-Solal, Annie 19(?)-   **CLC 50**

Colegate, Isabel 1931-   **CLC 36**
See also CA 17-20R; CANR 8, 22; DLB 14; INT CANR-22; MTCW

Coleman, Emmett
See Reed, Ishmael

See also CA 37-40R; CAAS 17, CANR 14, 32, 64; DLB 105

Dagerman, Stig (Halvard) 1923-1954 **TCLC 17**
See also CA 117; 155

Dahl, Roald 1916-1990 **CLC 1, 6, 18, 79; DAB; DAC; DAM MST, NOV, POP**
See also AAYA 15; CA 1-4R; 133; CANR 6, 32, 37, 62; CLR 1, 7, 41; DLB 139; JRDA; MAICYA; MTCW; SATA 1, 26, 73; SATA-Obit 65

Dahlberg, Edward 1900-1977 **CLC 1, 7, 14**
See also CA 9-12R; 69-72; CANR 31, 62; DLB 48; MTCW

Daitch, Susan 1954- **CLC 103**
See also CA 161

Dale, Colin **TCLC 18**
See also Lawrence, T(homas) E(dward)

Dale, George E.
See Asimov, Isaac

Daly, Elizabeth 1878-1967 **CLC 52**
See also CA 23-24; 25-28R; CANR 60; CAP 2

Daly, Maureen 1921- **CLC 17**
See also AAYA 5; CANR 37; JRDA; MAICYA; SAAS 1; SATA 2

Damas, Leon-Gontran 1912-1978 **CLC 84**
See also BW 1; CA 125; 73-76

Dana, Richard Henry Sr. 1787-1879 **NCLC 53**

Daniel, Samuel 1562(?)-1619 **LC 24**
See also DLB 62

Daniels, Brett
See Adler, Renata

Dannay, Frederic 1905-1982 **CLC 11; DAM POP**
See also Queen, Ellery
See also CA 1-4R; 107; CANR 1, 39; DLB 137; MTCW

D'Annunzio, Gabriele 1863-1938 **TCLC 6, 40**
See also CA 104; 155

Danois, N. le
See Gourmont, Remy (-Marie-Charles) de

Dante 1265-1321 **CMLC 3, 18; DA; DAB; DAC; DAM MST, POET; PC 21; WLCS**

d'Antibes, Germain
See Simenon, Georges (Jacques Christian)

Danticat, Edwidge 1969- **CLC 94**
See also CA 152

Danvers, Dennis 1947- **CLC 70**

Danziger, Paula 1944- **CLC 21**
See also AAYA 4; CA 112; 115; CANR 37; CLR 20; JRDA; MAICYA; SATA 36, 63; SATA-Brief 30

Dario, Ruben 1867-1916 **TCLC 4; DAM MULT; HLC; PC 15**
See also CA 131; HW; MTCW

Darley, George 1795-1846 **NCLC 2**
See also DLB 96

Darwin, Charles 1809-1882 **NCLC 57**
See also DLB 57, 166

Daryush, Elizabeth 1887-1977 **CLC 6, 19**
See also CA 49-52; CANR 3; DLB 20

Dashwood, Edmee Elizabeth Monica de la Pasture 1890-1943
See Delafield, E. M.
See also CA 119; 154

Daudet, (Louis Marie) Alphonse 1840-1897 **NCLC 1**
See also DLB 123

Daumal, Rene 1908-1944 **TCLC 14**
See also CA 114

Davenport, Guy (Mattison, Jr.) 1927- **CLC 6, 14, 38; SSC 16**
See also CA 33-36R; CANR 23; DLB 130

Davidson, Avram 1923-
See Queen, Ellery
See also CA 101; CANR 26; DLB 8

Davidson, Donald (Grady) 1893-1968 **CLC 2, 13, 19**
See also CA 5-8R; 25-28R; CANR 4; DLB 45

Davidson, Hugh
See Hamilton, Edmond

Davidson, John 1857-1909 **TCLC 24**
See also CA 118; DLB 19

Davidson, Sara 1943- **CLC 9**
See also CA 81-84; CANR 44, 68; DLB 185

Davie, Donald (Alfred) 1922-1995 **CLC 5, 8, 10, 31**
See also CA 1-4R; 149; CAAS 3; CANR 1, 44; DLB 27; MTCW

Davies, Ray(mond Douglas) 1944- **CLC 21**
See also CA 116; 146

Davies, Rhys 1901-1978 **CLC 23**
See also CA 9-12R; 81-84; CANR 4; DLB 139, 191

Davies, (William) Robertson 1913-1995 **CLC 2, 7, 13, 25, 42, 75, 91; DA; DAB; DAC; DAM MST, NOV, POP; WLC**
See also BEST 89:2; CA 33-36R; 150; CANR 17, 42; DLB 68; INT CANR-17; MTCW

Davies, W(illiam) H(enry) 1871-1940 **TCLC 5**
See also CA 104; DLB 19, 174

Davies, Walter C.
See Kornbluth, C(yril) M.

Davis, Angela (Yvonne) 1944- **CLC 77; DAM MULT**
See also BW 2; CA 57-60; CANR 10

Davis, B. Lynch
See Bioy Casares, Adolfo; Borges, Jorge Luis

Davis, Harold Lenoir 1896-1960 **CLC 49**
See also CA 89-92; DLB 9

Davis, Rebecca (Blaine) Harding 1831-1910 **TCLC 6**
See also CA 104; DLB 74

Davis, Richard Harding 1864-1916 **TCLC 24**
See also CA 114; DLB 12, 23, 78, 79, 189; DLBD 13

Davison, Frank Dalby 1893-1970 **CLC 15**
See also CA 116

Davison, Lawrence H.
See Lawrence, D(avid) H(erbert Richards)

Davison, Peter (Hubert) 1928- **CLC 28**
See also CA 9-12R; CAAS 4; CANR 3, 43; DLB 5

Davys, Mary 1674-1732 **LC 1**
See also DLB 39

Dawson, Fielding 1930- **CLC 6**
See also CA 85-88; DLB 130

Dawson, Peter
See Faust, Frederick (Schiller)

Day, Clarence (Shepard, Jr.) 1874-1935 **TCLC 25**
See also CA 108; DLB 11

Day, Thomas 1748-1789 **LC 1**
See also DLB 39; YABC 1

Day Lewis, C(ecil) 1904-1972 **CLC 1, 6, 10; DAM POET; PC 11**
See also Blake, Nicholas
See also CA 13-16; 33-36R; CANR 34; CAP 1; DLB 15, 20; MTCW

Dazai Osamu 1909-1948 **TCLC 11**
See also Tsushima, Shuji
See also CA 164; DLB 182

de Andrade, Carlos Drummond
See Drummond de Andrade, Carlos

Deane, Norman
See Creasey, John

de Beauvoir, Simone (Lucie Ernestine Marie Bertrand)
See Beauvoir, Simone (Lucie Ernestine Marie Bertrand) de

de Beer, P.
See Bosman, Herman Charles

de Brissac, Malcolm
See Dickinson, Peter (Malcolm)

de Chardin, Pierre Teilhard
See Teilhard de Chardin, (Marie Joseph) Pierre

Dee, John 1527-1608 **LC 20**

Deer, Sandra 1940- **CLC 45**

De Ferrari, Gabriella 1941- **CLC 65**
See also CA 146

Defoe, Daniel 1660(?)-1731 **LC 1; DA; DAB; DAC; DAM MST, NOV; WLC**
See also CDBLB 1660-1789; DLB 39, 95, 101; JRDA; MAICYA; SATA 22

de Gourmont, Remy(-Marie-Charles)
See Gourmont, Remy (-Marie-Charles) de

de Hartog, Jan 1914- **CLC 19**
See also CA 1-4R; CANR 1

de Hostos, E. M.
See Hostos (y Bonilla), Eugenio Maria de

de Hostos, Eugenio M.
See Hostos (y Bonilla), Eugenio Maria de

Deighton, Len **CLC 4, 7, 22, 46**
See also Deighton, Leonard Cyril
See also AAYA 6; BEST 89:2; CDBLB 1960 to Present; DLB 87

Deighton, Leonard Cyril 1929-
See Deighton, Len
See also CA 9-12R; CANR 19, 33, 68; DAM NOV, POP; MTCW

Dekker, Thomas 1572(?)-1632 **LC 22; DAM DRAM**
See also CDBLB Before 1660; DLB 62, 172

Delafield, E. M. 1890-1943 **TCLC 61**
See also Dashwood, Edmee Elizabeth Monica de la Pasture
See also DLB 34

de la Mare, Walter (John) 1873-1956 **TCLC 4, 53; DAB; DAC; DAM MST, POET; SSC 14; WLC**
See also CA 163; CDBLB 1914-1945; CLR 23; DLB 162; SATA 16

Delaney, Franey
See O'Hara, John (Henry)

Delaney, Shelagh 1939- **CLC 29; DAM DRAM**
See also CA 17-20R; CANR 30, 67; CDBLB 1960 to Present; DLB 13; MTCW

Delany, Mary (Granville Pendarves) 1700-1788 **LC 12**

Delany, Samuel R(ay, Jr.) 1942- **CLC 8, 14, 38; BLC 1; DAM MULT**
See also AAYA 24; BW 2; CA 81-84; CANR 27, 43; DLB 8, 33; MTCW

De La Ramee, (Marie) Louise 1839-1908
See Ouida
See also SATA 20

de la Roche, Mazo 1879-1961 **CLC 14**
See also CA 85-88; CANR 30; DLB 68; SATA 64

De La Salle, Innocent
See Hartmann, Sadakichi

Delbanco, Nicholas (Franklin) 1942- **CLC 6, 13**
See also CA 17-20R; CAAS 2; CANR 29, 55; DLB 6

del Castillo, Michel 1933- **CLC 38**
See also CA 109

Deledda, Grazia (Cosima) 1875(?)-1936 **TCLC 23**

Dugan, Alan 1923-   **CLC 2, 6**
See also CA 81-84; DLB 5

du Gard, Roger Martin
See Martin du Gard, Roger

Duhamel, Georges 1884-1966   **CLC 8**
See also CA 81-84; 25-28R; CANR 35; DLB
65; MTCW

Dujardin, Edouard (Emile Louis) 1861-1949
TCLC 13
See also CA 109; DLB 123

Dulles, John Foster 1888-1959   **TCLC 72**
See also CA 115; 149

Dumas, Alexandre (Davy de la Pailleterie)
1802-1870 **NCLC 11, 71; DA; DAB; DAC;**
DAM MST, NOV; WLC
See also DLB 119, 192; SATA 18

Dumas (fils), Alexandre 1824-1895 **NCLC 9;**
DC 1
See also AAYA 22; DLB 192

Dumas, Claudine
See Malzberg, Barry N(athaniel)

Dumas, Henry L. 1934-1968   **CLC 6, 62**
See also BW 1; CA 85-88; DLB 41

du Maurier, Daphne 1907-1989 **CLC 6, 11, 59;**
DAB; DAC; DAM MST, POP; SSC 18
See also CA 5-8R; 128; CANR 6, 55; DLB 191;
MTCW; SATA 27; SATA-Obit 60

Dunbar, Paul Laurence 1872-1906 **TCLC 2,**
12; BLC 1; DA; DAC; DAM MST, MULT,
POET; PC 5; SSC 8; WLC
See also BW 1; CA 104; 124; CDALB 1865-
1917; DLB 50, 54, 78; SATA 34

Dunbar, William 1460(?)-1530(?)   **LC 20**
See also DLB 132, 146

Duncan, Dora Angela
See Duncan, Isadora

Duncan, Isadora 1877(?)-1927   **TCLC 68**
See also CA 118; 149

Duncan, Lois 1934-   **CLC 26**
See also AAYA 4; CA 1-4R; CANR 2, 23, 36;
CLR 29; JRDA; MAICYA; SAAS 2; SATA
1, 36, 75

Duncan, Robert (Edward) 1919-1988 **CLC 1,**
2, 4, 7, 15, 41, 55; DAM POET; PC 2
See also CA 9-12R; 124; CANR 28, 62; DLB
5, 16, 193; MTCW

Duncan, Sara Jeannette 1861-1922 **TCLC 60**
See also CA 157; DLB 92

Dunlap, William 1766-1839   **NCLC 2**
See also DLB 30, 37, 59

Dunn, Douglas (Eaglesham) 1942- **CLC 6, 40**
See also CA 45-48; CANR 2, 33; DLB 40;
MTCW

Dunn, Katherine (Karen) 1945-   **CLC 71**
See also CA 33-36R

Dunn, Stephen 1939-   **CLC 36**
See also CA 33-36R; CANR 12, 48, 53; DLB
105

Dunne, Finley Peter 1867-1936   **TCLC 28**
See also CA 108; DLB 11, 23

Dunne, John Gregory 1932-   **CLC 28**
See also CA 25-28R; CANR 14, 50; DLBY 80

Dunsany, Edward John Moreton Drax Plunkett
1878-1957
See Dunsany, Lord
See also CA 104; 148; DLB 10

Dunsany, Lord   **TCLC 2, 59**
See also Dunsany, Edward John Moreton Drax
Plunkett
See also DLB 77, 153, 156

du Perry, Jean
See Simenon, Georges (Jacques Christian)

Durang, Christopher (Ferdinand) 1949- **C L C**
27, 38
See also CA 105; CANR 50

Duras, Marguerite 1914-1996 **CLC 3, 6, 11, 20,**
34, 40, 68, 100
See also CA 25-28R; 151; CANR 50; DLB 83;
MTCW

Durban, (Rosa) Pam 1947-   **CLC 39**
See also CA 123

Durcan, Paul 1944- **CLC 43, 70; DAM POET**
See also CA 134

Durkheim, Emile 1858-1917   **TCLC 55**

Durrell, Lawrence (George) 1912-1990 **C L C**
1, 4, 6, 8, 13, 27, 41; DAM NOV
See also CA 9-12R; 132; CANR 40; CDBLB
1945-1960; DLB 15, 27; DLBY 90; MTCW

Durrenmatt, Friedrich
See Duerrenmatt, Friedrich

Dutt, Toru 1856-1877   **NCLC 29**

Dwight, Timothy 1752-1817   **NCLC 13**
See also DLB 37

Dworkin, Andrea 1946-   **CLC 43**
See also CA 77-80; CAAS 21; CANR 16, 39;
INT CANR-16; MTCW

Dwyer, Deanna
See Koontz, Dean R(ay)

Dwyer, K. R.
See Koontz, Dean R(ay)

Dye, Richard
See De Voto, Bernard (Augustine)

Dylan, Bob 1941-   **CLC 3, 4, 6, 12, 77**
See also CA 41-44R; DLB 16

Eagleton, Terence (Francis) 1943-
See Eagleton, Terry
See also CA 57-60; CANR 7, 23, 68; MTCW

Eagleton, Terry   **CLC 63**
See also Eagleton, Terence (Francis)

Early, Jack
See Scoppettone, Sandra

East, Michael
See West, Morris L(anglo)

Eastaway, Edward
See Thomas, (Philip) Edward

Eastlake, William (Derry) 1917-1997 **CLC 8**
See also CA 5-8R; 158; CAAS 1; CANR 5, 63;
DLB 6; INT CANR-5

Eastman, Charles A(lexander) 1858-1939
TCLC 55; DAM MULT
See also DLB 175; NNAL; YABC 1

Eberhart, Richard (Ghormley) 1904- **CLC 3,**
11, 19, 56; DAM POET
See also CA 1-4R; CANR 2; CDALB 1941-
1968; DLB 48; MTCW

Eberstadt, Fernanda 1960-   **CLC 39**
See also CA 136; CANR 69

Echegaray (y Eizaguirre), Jose (Maria Waldo)
1832-1916   **TCLC 4**
See also CA 104; CANR 32; HW; MTCW

Echeverria, (Jose) Esteban (Antonino) 1805-
1851   **NCLC 18**

Echo
See Proust, (Valentin-Louis-George-Eugene-)
Marcel

Eckert, Allan W. 1931-   **CLC 17**
See also AAYA 18; CA 13-16R; CANR 14, 45;
INT CANR-14; SAAS 21; SATA 29, 91;
SATA-Brief 27

Eckhart, Meister 1260(?)-1328(?)   **CMLC 9**
See also DLB 115

Eckmar, F. R.
See de Hartog, Jan

Eco, Umberto 1932- **CLC 28, 60; DAM NOV,**
POP
See also BEST 90:1; CA 77-80; CANR 12, 33,

Eddison, E(ric) R(ucker) 1882-1945 **TCLC 15**
See also CA 109; 156

Eddy, Mary (Morse) Baker 1821-1910 **T C L C**
71
See also CA 113

Edel, (Joseph) Leon 1907-1997   **CLC 29, 34**
See also CA 1-4R; 161; CANR 1, 22; DLB 103;
INT CANR-22

Eden, Emily 1797-1869   **NCLC 10**

Edgar, David 1948-   **CLC 42; DAM DRAM**
See also CA 57-60; CANR 12, 61; DLB 13;
MTCW

Edgerton, Clyde (Carlyle) 1944-   **CLC 39**
See also AAYA 17; CA 118; 134; CANR 64;
INT 134

Edgeworth, Maria 1768-1849   **NCLC 1, 51**
See also DLB 116, 159, 163; SATA 21

Edmonds, Paul
See Kuttner, Henry

Edmonds, Walter D(umaux) 1903-   **CLC 35**
See also CA 5-8R; CANR 2; DLB 9; MAICYA;
SAAS 4; SATA 1, 27

Edmondson, Wallace
See Ellison, Harlan (Jay)

Edson, Russell   **CLC 13**
See also CA 33-36R

Edwards, Bronwen Elizabeth
See Rose, Wendy

Edwards, G(erald) B(asil) 1899-1976 **CLC 25**
See also CA 110

Edwards, Gus 1939-   **CLC 43**
See also CA 108; INT 108

Edwards, Jonathan 1703-1758   **LC 7; DA;**
DAC; DAM MST
See also DLB 24

Efron, Marina Ivanovna Tsvetaeva
See Tsvetaeva (Efron), Marina (Ivanovna)

Ehle, John (Marsden, Jr.) 1925-   **CLC 27**
See also CA 9-12R

Ehrenbourg, Ilya (Grigoryevich)
See Ehrenburg, Ilya (Grigoryevich)

Ehrenburg, Ilya (Grigoryevich) 1891-1967
CLC 18, 34, 62
See also CA 102; 25-28R

Ehrenburg, Ilyo (Grigoryevich)
See Ehrenburg, Ilya (Grigoryevich)

Ehrenreich, Barbara 1941-   **CLC 110**
See also BEST 90:4; CA 73-76; CANR 16, 37,
62; MTCW

Eich, Guenter 1907-1972   **CLC 15**
See also CA 111; 93-96; DLB 69, 124

Eichendorff, Joseph Freiherr von 1788-1857
NCLC 8
See also DLB 90

Eigner, Larry   **CLC 9**
See also Eigner, Laurence (Joel)
See also CAAS 23; DLB 5

Eigner, Laurence (Joel) 1927-1996
See Eigner, Larry
See also CA 9-12R; 151; CANR 6; DLB 193

Einstein, Albert 1879-1955   **TCLC 65**
See also CA 121; 133; MTCW

Eiseley, Loren Corey 1907-1977   **CLC 7**
See also AAYA 5; CA 1-4R; 73-76; CANR 6

Eisenstadt, Jill 1963-   **CLC 50**
See also CA 140

Eisenstein, Sergei (Mikhailovich) 1898-1948
TCLC 57
See also CA 114; 149

Eisner, Simon
See Kornbluth, C(yril) M.

Ekeloef, (Bengt) Gunnar 1907-1968 **CLC 27;**

DAM POET
See also CA 123; 25-28R

Ekelof, (Bengt) Gunnar
See Ekeloef, (Bengt) Gunnar

Ekelund, Vilhelm 1880-1949 **TCLC 75**

Ekwensi, C. O. D.
See Ekwensi, Cyprian (Odiatu Duaka)

Ekwensi, Cyprian (Odiatu Duaka) 1921-**CLC 4; BLC 1; DAM MULT**
See also BW 2; CA 29-32R; CANR 18, 42; DLB 117; MTCW; SATA 66

Elaine **TCLC 18**
See also Leverson, Ada

El Crummo
See Crumb, R(obert)

Elder, Lonne III 1931-1996 **DC 8**
See also BLC 1; BW 1; CA 81-84; 152; CANR 25; DAM MULT; DLB 7, 38, 44

Elia
See Lamb, Charles

Eliade, Mircea 1907-1986 **CLC 19**
See also CA 65-68; 119; CANR 30, 62; MTCW

Eliot, A. D.
See Jewett, (Theodora) Sarah Orne

Eliot, Alice
See Jewett, (Theodora) Sarah Orne

Eliot, Dan
See Silverberg, Robert

Eliot, George 1819-1880 **NCLC 4, 13, 23, 41, 49; DA; DAB; DAC; DAM MST, NOV; PC 20; WLC**
See also CDBLB 1832-1890; DLB 21, 35, 55

Eliot, John 1604-1690 **LC 5**
See also DLB 24

Eliot, T(homas) S(tearns) 1888-1965**CLC 1, 2, 3, 6, 9, 10, 13, 15, 24, 34, 41, 55, 57, 113; DA; DAB; DAC; DAM DRAM, MST, POET; PC 5; WLC**
See also CA 5-8R; 25-28R; CANR 41; CDALB 1929-1941; DLB 7, 10, 45, 63; DLBY 88; MTCW

Elizabeth 1866-1941 **TCLC 41**

Elkin, Stanley L(awrence) 1930-1995 **CLC 4, 6, 9, 14, 27, 51, 91; DAM NOV, POP; SSC 12**
See also CA 9-12R; 148; CANR 8, 46; DLB 2, 28; DLBY 80; INT CANR-8; MTCW

Elledge, Scott **CLC 34**

Elliot, Don
See Silverberg, Robert

Elliott, Don
See Silverberg, Robert

Elliott, George P(aul) 1918-1980 **CLC 2**
See also CA 1-4R; 97-100; CANR 2

Elliott, Janice 1931- **CLC 47**
See also CA 13-16R; CANR 8, 29; DLB 14

Elliott, Sumner Locke 1917-1991 **CLC 38**
See also CA 5-8R; 134; CANR 2, 21

Elliott, William
See Bradbury, Ray (Douglas)

Ellis, A. E. **CLC 7**

Ellis, Alice Thomas **CLC 40**
See also Haycraft, Anna
See also DLB 194

Ellis, Bret Easton 1964- **CLC 39, 71; DAM POP**
See also AAYA 2; CA 118; 123; CANR 51; INT 123

Ellis, (Henry) Havelock 1859-1939 **TCLC 14**
See also CA 109; DLB 190

Ellis, Landon
See Ellison, Harlan (Jay)

Ellis, Trey 1962- **CLC 55**

See also CA 146

Ellison, Harlan (Jay) 1934- **CLC 1, 13, 42; DAM POP; SSC 14**
See also CA 5-8R; CANR 5, 46; DLB 8; INT CANR-5; MTCW

Ellison, Ralph (Waldo) 1914-1994 **CLC 1, 3, 11, 54, 86; BLC 1; DA; DAB; DAC; DAM MST, MULT, NOV; SSC 26; WLC**
See also AAYA 19; BW 1; CA 9-12R; 145; CANR 24, 53; CDALB 1941-1968; DLB 2, 76; DLBY 94; MTCW

Ellmann, Lucy (Elizabeth) 1956- **CLC 61**
See also CA 128

Ellmann, Richard (David) 1918-1987**CLC 50**
See also BEST 89:2; CA 1-4R; 122; CANR 2, 28, 61; DLB 103; DLBY 87; MTCW

Elman, Richard (Martin) 1934-1997 **CLC 19**
See also CA 17-20R; 163; CAAS 3; CANR 47

Elron
See Hubbard, L(afayette) Ron(ald)

Eluard, Paul **TCLC 7, 41**
See also Grindel, Eugene

Elyot, Sir Thomas 1490(?)-1546 **LC 11**

Elytis, Odysseus 1911-1996 **CLC 15, 49, 100; DAM POET; PC 21**
See also CA 102; 151; MTCW

Emecheta, (Florence Onye) Buchi 1944-**CLC 14, 48; BLC 2; DAM MULT**
See also BW 2; CA 81-84; CANR 27; DLB 117; MTCW; SATA 66

Emerson, Mary Moody 1774-1863 **NCLC 66**

Emerson, Ralph Waldo 1803-1882 **NCLC 1, 38; DA; DAB; DAC; DAM MST, POET; PC 18; WLC**
See also CDALB 1640-1865; DLB 1, 59, 73

Eminescu, Mihail 1850-1889 **NCLC 33**

Empson, William 1906-1984**CLC 3, 8, 19, 33, 34**
See also CA 17-20R; 112; CANR 31, 61; DLB 20; MTCW

Enchi, Fumiko (Ueda) 1905-1986 **CLC 31**
See also CA 129; 121

Ende, Michael (Andreas Helmuth) 1929-1995 **CLC 31**
See also CA 118; 124; 149; CANR 36; CLR 14; DLB 75; MAICYA; SATA 61; SATA-Brief 42; SATA-Obit 86

Endo, Shusaku 1923-1996 **CLC 7, 14, 19, 54, 99; DAM NOV**
See also CA 29-32R; 153; CANR 21, 54; DLB 182; MTCW

Engel, Marian 1933-1985 **CLC 36**
See also CA 25-28R; CANR 12; DLB 53; INT CANR-12

Engelhardt, Frederick
See Hubbard, L(afayette) Ron(ald)

Enright, D(ennis) J(oseph) 1920-**CLC 4, 8, 31**
See also CA 1-4R; CANR 1, 42; DLB 27; SATA 25

Enzensberger, Hans Magnus 1929- **CLC 43**
See also CA 116; 119

Ephron, Nora 1941- **CLC 17, 31**
See also AITN 2; CA 65-68; CANR 12, 39

Epicurus 341B.C.-270B.C. **CMLC 21**
See also DLB 176

Epsilon
See Betjeman, John

Epstein, Daniel Mark 1948- **CLC 7**
See also CA 49-52; CANR 2, 53

Epstein, Jacob 1956- **CLC 19**
See also CA 114

Epstein, Joseph 1937- **CLC 39**
See also CA 112; 119; CANR 50, 65

Epstein, Leslie 1938- **CLC 27**
See also CA 73-76; CAAS 12; CANR 23, 69

Equiano, Olaudah 1745(?)-1797 **LC 16; BLC 2; DAM MULT**
See also DLB 37, 50

ER **TCLC 33**
See also CA 160; DLB 85

Erasmus, Desiderius 1469(?)-1536 **LC 16**

Erdman, Paul E(mil) 1932- **CLC 25**
See also AITN 1; CA 61-64; CANR 13, 43

Erdrich, Louise 1954- **CLC 39, 54; DAM MULT, NOV, POP**
See also AAYA 10; BEST 89:1; CA 114; CANR 41, 62; DLB 152, 175; MTCW; NNAL; SATA 94

Erenburg, Ilya (Grigoryevich)
See Ehrenburg, Ilya (Grigoryevich)

Erickson, Stephen Michael 1950-
See Erickson, Steve
See also CA 129

Erickson, Steve 1950- **CLC 64**
See also Erickson, Stephen Michael
See also CANR 60, 68

Ericson, Walter
See Fast, Howard (Melvin)

Eriksson, Buntel
See Bergman, (Ernst) Ingmar

Ernaux, Annie 1940- **CLC 88**
See also CA 147

Eschenbach, Wolfram von
See Wolfram von Eschenbach

Eseki, Bruno
See Mphahlele, Ezekiel

Esenin, Sergei (Alexandrovich) 1895-1925 **TCLC 4**
See also CA 104

Eshleman, Clayton 1935- **CLC 7**
See also CA 33-36R; CAAS 6; DLB 5

Espriella, Don Manuel Alvarez
See Southey, Robert

Espriu, Salvador 1913-1985 **CLC 9**
See also CA 154; 115; DLB 134

Espronceda, Jose de 1808-1842 **NCLC 39**

Esse, James
See Stephens, James

Esterbrook, Tom
See Hubbard, L(afayette) Ron(ald)

Estleman, Loren D. 1952-**CLC 48; DAM NOV, POP**
See also CA 85-88; CANR 27; INT CANR-27; MTCW

Euclid 306B.C.-283B.C. **CMLC 25**

Eugenides, Jeffrey 1960(?)- **CLC 81**
See also CA 144

Euripides c. 485B.C.-406B.C.**CMLC 23; DA; DAB; DAC; DAM DRAM, MST; DC 4; WLCS**
See also DLB 176

Evan, Evin
See Faust, Frederick (Schiller)

Evans, Evan
See Faust, Frederick (Schiller)

Evans, Marian
See Eliot, George

Evans, Mary Ann
See Eliot, George

Evarts, Esther
See Benson, Sally

Everett, Percival L. 1956- **CLC 57**
See also BW 2; CA 129

Everson, R(onald) G(ilmour) 1903- **CLC 27**
See also CA 17-20R; DLB 88

Everson, William (Oliver) 1912-1994 **CLC 1,**

Firbank, Louis 1942-
See Reed, Lou
See also CA 117

Firbank, (Arthur Annesley) Ronald 1886-1926
TCLC 1
See also CA 104; DLB 36

Fisher, M(ary) F(rances) K(ennedy) 1908-1992
CLC 76, 87
See also CA 77-80; 138; CANR 44

Fisher, Roy 1930-   CLC 25
See also CA 81-84; CAAS 10; CANR 16; DLB 40

Fisher, Rudolph 1897-1934TCLC 11; BLC 2;
DAM MULT; SSC 25
See also BW 1; CA 107; 124; DLB 51, 102

Fisher, Vardis (Alvero) 1895-1968   CLC 7
See also CA 5-8R; 25-28R; CANR 68; DLB 9

Fiske, Tarleton
See Bloch, Robert (Albert)

Fitch, Clarke
See Sinclair, Upton (Beall)

Fitch, John IV
See Cormier, Robert (Edmund)

Fitzgerald, Captain Hugh
See Baum, L(yman) Frank

FitzGerald, Edward 1809-1883   NCLC 9
See also DLB 32

Fitzgerald, F(rancis) Scott (Key) 1896-1940
TCLC 1, 6, 14, 28, 55; DA; DAB; DAC;
DAM MST, NOV; SSC 6, 31; WLC
See also AAYA 24; AITN 1; CA 110; 123;
CDALB 1917-1929; DLB 4, 9, 86; DLBD 1,
15, 16; DLBY 81, 96; MTCW

Fitzgerald, Penelope 1916-   CLC 19, 51, 61
See also CA 85-88; CAAS 10; CANR 56; DLB
14, 194

Fitzgerald, Robert (Stuart) 1910-1985CLC 39
See also CA 1-4R; 114; CANR 1; DLBY 80

FitzGerald, Robert D(avid) 1902-1987CLC 19
See also CA 17-20R

Fitzgerald, Zelda (Sayre) 1900-1948TCLC 52
See also CA 117; 126; DLBY 84

Flanagan, Thomas (James Bonner) 1923-
CLC 25, 52
See also CA 108; CANR 55; DLBY 80; INT
108; MTCW

Flaubert, Gustave 1821-1880NCLC 2, 10, 19,
62, 66; DA; DAB; DAC; DAM MST, NOV;
SSC 11; WLC
See also DLB 119

Flecker, Herman Elroy
See Flecker, (Herman) James Elroy

Flecker, (Herman) James Elroy 1884-1915
TCLC 43
See also CA 109; 150; DLB 10, 19

Fleming, Ian (Lancaster) 1908-1964 CLC 3,
30; DAM POP
See also CA 5-8R; CANR 59; CDBLB 1945-
1960; DLB 87; MTCW; SATA 9

Fleming, Thomas (James) 1927-   CLC 37
See also CA 5-8R; CANR 10; INT CANR-10;
SATA 8

Fletcher, John 1579-1625   LC 33; DC 6
See also CDBLB Before 1660; DLB 58

Fletcher, John Gould 1886-1950   TCLC 35
See also CA 107; DLB 4, 45

Fleur, Paul
See Pohl, Frederik

Flooglebuckle, Al
See Spiegelman, Art

Flying Officer X
See Bates, H(erbert) E(rnest)

Fo, Dario 1926-   CLC 32, 109; DAM DRAM

See also CA 116; 128; CANR 68; DLBY 97;
MTCW

Fogarty, Jonathan Titulescu Esq.
See Farrell, James T(homas)

Folke, Will
See Bloch, Robert (Albert)

Follett, Ken(neth Martin) 1949-   CLC 18;
DAM NOV, POP
See also AAYA 6; BEST 89:4; CA 81-84; CANR
13, 33, 54; DLB 87; DLBY 81; INT CANR-
33; MTCW

Fontane, Theodor 1819-1898   NCLC 26
See also DLB 129

Foote, Horton 1916-CLC 51, 91; DAM DRAM
See also CA 73-76; CANR 34, 51; DLB 26; INT
CANR-34

Foote, Shelby 1916-CLC 75; DAM NOV, POP
See also CA 5-8R; CANR 3, 45; DLB 2, 17

Forbes, Esther 1891-1967   CLC 12
See also AAYA 17; CA 13-14; 25-28R; CAP 1;
CLR 27; DLB 22; JRDA; MAICYA; SATA 2

Forche, Carolyn (Louise) 1950- CLC 25, 83,
86; DAM POET; PC 10
See also CA 109; 117; CANR 50; DLB 5, 193;
INT 117

Ford, Elbur
See Hibbert, Eleanor Alice Burford

Ford, Ford Madox 1873-1939TCLC 1, 15, 39,
57; DAM NOV
See also CA 104; 132; CDBLB 1914-1945;
DLB 162; MTCW

Ford, Henry 1863-1947   TCLC 73
See also CA 115; 148

Ford, John 1586-(?)   DC 8
See also CDBLB Before 1660; DAM DRAM;
DLB 58

Ford, John 1895-1973   CLC 16
See also CA 45-48

Ford, Richard 1944-   CLC 46, 99
See also CA 69-72; CANR 11, 47

Ford, Webster
See Masters, Edgar Lee

Foreman, Richard 1937-   CLC 50
See also CA 65-68; CANR 32, 63

Forester, C(ecil) S(cott) 1899-1966   CLC 35
See also CA 73-76; 25-28R; DLB 191; SATA
13

Forez
See Mauriac, Francois (Charles)

Forman, James Douglas 1932-   CLC 21
See also AAYA 17; CA 9-12R; CANR 4, 19,
42; JRDA; MAICYA; SATA 8, 70

Fornes, Maria Irene 1930-   CLC 39, 61
See also CA 25-28R; CANR 28; DLB 7; HW;
INT CANR-28; MTCW

Forrest, Leon (Richard) 1937-1997   CLC 4;
BLCS
See also BW 2; CA 89-92; 162; CAAS 7; CANR
25, 52; DLB 33

Forster, E(dward) M(organ) 1879-1970 C L C
1, 2, 3, 4, 9, 10, 13, 15, 22, 45, 77; DA; DAB;
DAC; DAM MST, NOV; SSC 27; WLC
See also AAYA 2; CA 13-14; 25-28R; CANR
45; CAP 1; CDBLB 1914-1945; DLB 34, 98,
162, 178, 195; DLBD 10; MTCW; SATA 57

Forster, John 1812-1876   NCLC 11
See also DLB 144, 184

Forsyth, Frederick 1938-CLC 2, 5, 36; DAM
NOV, POP
See also BEST 89:4; CA 85-88; CANR 38, 62;
DLB 87; MTCW

Forten, Charlotte L.   TCLC 16; BLC 2
See also Grimke, Charlotte L(ottie) Forten

See also DLB 50

Foscolo, Ugo 1778-1827   NCLC 8

Fosse, Bob   CLC 20
See also Fosse, Robert Louis

Fosse, Robert Louis 1927-1987
See Fosse, Bob
See also CA 110; 123

Foster, Stephen Collins 1826-1864 NCLC 26

Foucault, Michel 1926-1984   CLC 31, 34, 69
See also CA 105; 113; CANR 34; MTCW

Fouque, Friedrich (Heinrich Karl) de la Motte
1777-1843   NCLC 2
See also DLB 90

Fourier, Charles 1772-1837   NCLC 51

Fournier, Henri Alban 1886-1914
See Alain-Fournier
See also CA 104

Fournier, Pierre 1916-   CLC 11
See also Gascar, Pierre
See also CA 89-92; CANR 16, 40

Fowles, John 1926-CLC 1, 2, 3, 4, 6, 9, 10, 15,
33, 87; DAB; DAC; DAM MST
See also CA 5-8R; CANR 25; CDBLB 1960 to
Present; DLB 14, 139; MTCW; SATA 22

Fox, Paula 1923-   CLC 2, 8
See also AAYA 3; CA 73-76; CANR 20, 36,
62; CLR 1, 44; DLB 52; JRDA; MAICYA;
MTCW; SATA 17, 60

Fox, William Price (Jr.) 1926-   CLC 22
See also CA 17-20R; CAAS 19; CANR 11; DLB
2; DLBY 81

Foxe, John 1516(?)-1587   LC 14
See also DLB 132

Frame, Janet 1924-CLC 2, 3, 6, 22, 66, 96; SSC
29
See also Clutha, Janet Paterson Frame

France, Anatole   TCLC 9
See also Thibault, Jacques Anatole Francois
See also DLB 123

Francis, Claude 19(?)-   CLC 50

Francis, Dick 1920-CLC 2, 22, 42, 102; DAM
POP
See also AAYA 5, 21; BEST 89:3; CA 5-8R;
CANR 9, 42, 68; CDBLB 1960 to Present;
DLB 87; INT CANR-9; MTCW

Francis, Robert (Churchill) 1901-1987 C L C
15
See also CA 1-4R; 123; CANR 1

Frank, Anne(lies Marie) 1929-1945TCLC 17;
DA; DAB; DAC; DAM MST; WLC
See also AAYA 12; CA 113; 133; CANR 68;
MTCW; SATA 87; SATA-Brief 42

Frank, Elizabeth 1945-   CLC 39
See also CA 121; 126; INT 126

Frankl, Viktor E(mil) 1905-1997   CLC 93
See also CA 65-68; 161

Franklin, Benjamin
See Hasek, Jaroslav (Matej Frantisek)

Franklin, Benjamin 1706-1790   LC 25; DA;
DAB; DAC; DAM MST; WLCS
See also CDALB 1640-1865; DLB 24, 43, 73

Franklin, (Stella Maria Sarah) Miles (Lampe)
1879-1954   TCLC 7
See also CA 104; 164

Fraser, (Lady) Antonia (Pakenham) 1932-
CLC 32, 107
See also CA 85-88; CANR 44, 65; MTCW;
SATA-Brief 32

Fraser, George MacDonald 1925-   CLC 7
See also CA 45-48; CANR 2, 48

Fraser, Sylvia 1935-   CLC 64
See also CA 45-48; CANR 1, 16, 60

Frayn, Michael 1933-CLC 3, 7, 31, 47; DAM

DRAM, NOV
See also CA 5-8R; CANR 30, 69; DLB 13, 14, 194; MTCW

Fraze, Candida (Merrill) 1945-   **CLC 50**
See also CA 126

Frazer, J(ames) G(eorge) 1854-1941**TCLC 32**
See also CA 118

Frazer, Robert Caine
See Creasey, John

Frazer, Sir James George
See Frazer, J(ames) G(eorge)

Frazier, Charles 1950-   **CLC 109**
See also CA 161

Frazier, Ian 1951-   **CLC 46**
See also CA 130; CANR 54

Frederic, Harold 1856-1898   **NCLC 10**
See also DLB 12, 23; DLBD 13

Frederick, John
See Faust, Frederick (Schiller)

Frederick the Great 1712-1786   **LC 14**

Fredro, Aleksander 1793-1876   **NCLC 8**

Freeling, Nicolas 1927-   **CLC 38**
See also CA 49-52; CAAS 12; CANR 1, 17, 50; DLB 87

Freeman, Douglas Southall 1886-1953 **T C L C 11**
See also CA 109; DLB 17

Freeman, Judith 1946-   **CLC 55**
See also CA 148

Freeman, Mary Eleanor Wilkins 1852-1930
TCLC 9; SSC 1
See also CA 106; DLB 12, 78

Freeman, R(ichard) Austin 1862-1943 **T C L C 21**
See also CA 113; DLB 70

French, Albert 1943-   **CLC 86**

French, Marilyn 1929-**CLC 10, 18, 60; DAM DRAM, NOV, POP**
See also CA 69-72; CANR 3, 31; INT CANR-31; MTCW

French, Paul
See Asimov, Isaac

Freneau, Philip Morin 1752-1832   **NCLC 1**
See also DLB 37, 43

Freud, Sigmund 1856-1939   **TCLC 52**
See also CA 115; 133; CANR 69; MTCW

Friedan, Betty (Naomi) 1921-   **CLC 74**
See also CA 65-68; CANR 18, 45; MTCW

Friedlander, Saul 1932-   **CLC 90**
See also CA 117; 130

Friedman, B(ernard) H(arper) 1926- **CLC 7**
See also CA 1-4R; CANR 3, 48

Friedman, Bruce Jay 1930-   **CLC 3, 5, 56**
See also CA 9-12R; CANR 25, 52; DLB 2, 28; INT CANR-25

Friel, Brian 1929-   **CLC 5, 42, 59; DC 8**
See also CA 21-24R; CANR 33, 69; DLB 13; MTCW

Friis-Baastad, Babbis Ellinor 1921-1970**CLC 12**
See also CA 17-20R; 134; SATA 7

Frisch, Max (Rudolf) 1911-1991**CLC 3, 9, 14, 18, 32, 44; DAM DRAM, NOV**
See also CA 85-88; 134; CANR 32; DLB 69, 124; MTCW

Fromentin, Eugene (Samuel Auguste) 1820-1876   **NCLC 10**
See also DLB 123

Frost, Frederick
See Faust, Frederick (Schiller)

Frost, Robert (Lee) 1874-1963**CLC 1, 3, 4, 9, 10, 13, 15, 26, 34, 44; DA; DAB; DAC; DAM MST, POET; PC 1; WLC**

See also AAYA 21; CA 89-92; CANR 33; CDALB 1917-1929; DLB 54; DLBD 7; MTCW; SATA 14

Froude, James Anthony 1818-1894 **NCLC 43**
See also DLB 18, 57, 144

Froy, Herald
See Waterhouse, Keith (Spencer)

Fry, Christopher 1907- **CLC 2, 10, 14; DAM DRAM**
See also CA 17-20R; CAAS 23; CANR 9, 30; DLB 13; MTCW; SATA 66

Frye, (Herman) Northrop 1912-1991**CLC 24, 70**
See also CA 5-8R; 133; CANR 8, 37; DLB 67, 68; MTCW

Fuchs, Daniel 1909-1993   **CLC 8, 22**
See also CA 81-84; 142; CAAS 5; CANR 40; DLB 9, 26, 28; DLBY 93

Fuchs, Daniel 1934-   **CLC 34**
See also CA 37-40R; CANR 14, 48

Fuentes, Carlos 1928-**CLC 3, 8, 10, 13, 22, 41, 60, 113; DA; DAB; DAC; DAM MST, MULT, NOV; HLC; SSC 24; WLC**
See also AAYA 4; AITN 2; CA 69-72; CANR 10, 32, 68; DLB 113; HW; MTCW

Fuentes, Gregorio Lopez y
See Lopez y Fuentes, Gregorio

Fugard, (Harold) Athol 1932-**CLC 5, 9, 14, 25, 40, 80; DAM DRAM; DC 3**
See also AAYA 17; CA 85-88; CANR 32, 54; MTCW

Fugard, Sheila 1932-   **CLC 48**
See also CA 125

Fuller, Charles (H., Jr.) 1939-**CLC 25; BLC 2; DAM DRAM, MULT; DC 1**
See also BW 2; CA 108; 112; DLB 38; INT 112; MTCW

Fuller, John (Leopold) 1937-   **CLC 62**
See also CA 21-24R; CANR 9, 44; DLB 40

Fuller, Margaret   **NCLC 5, 50**
See also Ossoli, Sarah Margaret (Fuller marchesa d')

Fuller, Roy (Broadbent) 1912-1991**CLC 4, 28**
See also CA 5-8R; 135; CAAS 10; CANR 53; DLB 15, 20; SATA 87

Fulton, Alice 1952-   **CLC 52**
See also CA 116; CANR 57; DLB 193

Furphy, Joseph 1843-1912   **TCLC 25**
See also CA 163

Fussell, Paul 1924-   **CLC 74**
See also BEST 90:1; CA 17-20R; CANR 8, 21, 35, 69; INT CANR-21; MTCW

Futabatei, Shimei 1864-1909   **TCLC 44**
See also CA 162; DLB 180

Futrelle, Jacques 1875-1912   **TCLC 19**
See also CA 113; 155

Gaboriau, Emile 1835-1873   **NCLC 14**

Gadda, Carlo Emilio 1893-1973   **CLC 11**
See also CA 89-92; DLB 177

Gaddis, William 1922- **CLC 1, 3, 6, 8, 10, 19, 43, 86**
See also CA 17-20R; CANR 21, 48; DLB 2; MTCW

Gage, Walter
See Inge, William (Motter)

Gaines, Ernest J(ames) 1933- **CLC 3, 11, 18, 86; BLC 2; DAM MULT**
See also AAYA 18; AITN 1; BW 2; CA 9-12R; CANR 6, 24, 42; CDALB 1968-1988; DLB 2, 33, 152; DLBY 80; MTCW; SATA 86

Gaitskill, Mary 1954-   **CLC 69**
See also CA 128; CANR 61

Galdos, Benito Perez
See Perez Galdos, Benito

Gale, Zona 1874-1938**TCLC 7; DAM DRAM**
See also CA 105; 153; DLB 9, 78

Galeano, Eduardo (Hughes) 1940-   **CLC 72**
See also CA 29-32R; CANR 13, 32; HW

Galiano, Juan Valera y Alcala
See Valera y Alcala-Galiano, Juan

Gallagher, Tess 1943-   **CLC 18, 63; DAM POET; PC 9**
See also CA 106; DLB 120

Gallant, Mavis 1922-   **CLC 7, 18, 38; DAC; DAM MST; SSC 5**
See also CA 69-72; CANR 29, 69; DLB 53; MTCW

Gallant, Roy A(rthur) 1924-   **CLC 17**
See also CA 5-8R; CANR 4, 29, 54; CLR 30; MAICYA; SATA 4, 68

Gallico, Paul (William) 1897-1976   **CLC 2**
See also AITN 1; CA 5-8R; 69-72; CANR 23; DLB 9, 171; MAICYA; SATA 13

Gallo, Max Louis 1932-   **CLC 95**
See also CA 85-88

Gallois, Lucien
See Desnos, Robert

Gallup, Ralph
See Whitemore, Hugh (John)

Galsworthy, John 1867-1933**TCLC 1, 45; DA; DAB; DAC; DAM DRAM, MST, NOV; SSC 22; WLC 2**
See also CA 104; 141; CDBLB 1890-1914; DLB 10, 34, 98, 162; DLBD 16

Galt, John 1779-1839   **NCLC 1**
See also DLB 99, 116, 159

Galvin, James 1951-   **CLC 38**
See also CA 108; CANR 26

Gamboa, Federico 1864-1939   **TCLC 36**

Gandhi, M. K.
See Gandhi, Mohandas Karamchand

Gandhi, Mahatma
See Gandhi, Mohandas Karamchand

Gandhi, Mohandas Karamchand 1869-1948
TCLC 59; DAM MULT
See also CA 121; 132; MTCW

Gann, Ernest Kellogg 1910-1991   **CLC 23**
See also AITN 1; CA 1-4R; 136; CANR 1

Garcia, Cristina 1958-   **CLC 76**
See also CA 141

Garcia Lorca, Federico 1898-1936**TCLC 1, 7, 49; DA; DAB; DAC; DAM DRAM, MST, MULT, POET; DC 2; HLC; PC 3; WLC**
See also CA 104; 131; DLB 108; HW; MTCW

Garcia Marquez, Gabriel (Jose) 1928-**CLC 2, 3, 8, 10, 15, 27, 47, 55, 68; DA; DAB; DAC; DAM MST, MULT, NOV, POP; HLC; SSC 8; WLC**
See also AAYA 3; BEST 89:1, 90:4; CA 33-36R; CANR 10, 28, 50; DLB 113; HW; MTCW

Gard, Janice
See Latham, Jean Lee

Gard, Roger Martin du
See Martin du Gard, Roger

Gardam, Jane 1928-   **CLC 43**
See also CA 49-52; CANR 2, 18, 33, 54; CLR 12; DLB 14, 161; MAICYA; MTCW; SAAS 9; SATA 39, 76; SATA-Brief 28

Gardner, Herb(ert) 1934-   **CLC 44**
See also CA 149

Gardner, John (Champlin), Jr. 1933-1982
CLC 2, 3, 5, 7, 8, 10, 18, 28, 34; DAM NOV, POP; SSC 7
See also AITN 1; CA 65-68; 107; CANR 33; DLB 2; DLBY 82; MTCW; SATA 40; SATA-

Obit 31

Gardner, John (Edmund) 1926-**CLC 30; DAM POP**
See also CA 103; CANR 15, 69; MTCW

Gardner, Miriam
See Bradley, Marion Zimmer

Gardner, Noel
See Kuttner, Henry

Gardons, S. S.
See Snodgrass, W(illiam) D(e Witt)

Garfield, Leon 1921-1996 **CLC 12**
See also AAYA 8; CA 17-20R; 152; CANR 38, 41; CLR 21; DLB 161; JRDA; MAICYA; SATA 1, 32, 76; SATA-Obit 90

Garland, (Hannibal) Hamlin 1860-1940 **TCLC 3; SSC 18**
See also CA 104; DLB 12, 71, 78, 186

Garneau, (Hector de) Saint-Denys 1912-1943 **TCLC 13**
See also CA 111; DLB 88

Garner, Alan 1934-**CLC 17; DAB; DAM POP**
See also AAYA 18; CA 73-76; CANR 15, 64; CLR 20; DLB 161; MAICYA; MTCW; SATA 18, 69

Garner, Hugh 1913-1979 **CLC 13**
See also CA 69-72; CANR 31; DLB 68

Garnett, David 1892-1981 **CLC 3**
See also CA 5-8R; 103; CANR 17; DLB 34

Garos, Stephanie
See Katz, Steve

Garrett, George (Palmer) 1929-**CLC 3, 11, 51; SSC 30**
See also CA 1-4R; CAAS 5; CANR 1, 42, 67; DLB 2, 5, 130, 152; DLBY 83

Garrick, David 1717-1779 **LC 15; DAM DRAM**
See also DLB 84

Garrigue, Jean 1914-1972 **CLC 2, 8**
See also CA 5-8R; 37-40R; CANR 20

Garrison, Frederick
See Sinclair, Upton (Beall)

Garth, Will
See Hamilton, Edmond; Kuttner, Henry

Garvey, Marcus (Moziah, Jr.) 1887-1940 **TCLC 41; BLC 2; DAM MULT**
See also BW 1; CA 120; 124

Gary, Romain **CLC 25**
See Kacew, Romain
See also DLB 83

Gascar, Pierre **CLC 11**
See also Fournier, Pierre

Gascoyne, David (Emery) 1916- **CLC 45**
See also CA 65-68; CANR 10, 28, 54; DLB 20; MTCW

Gaskell, Elizabeth Cleghorn 1810-1865**NCLC 70; DAB; DAM MST; SSC 25**
See also CDBLB 1832-1890; DLB 21, 144, 159

Gass, William H(oward) 1924-**CLC 1, 2, 8, 11, 15, 39; SSC 12**
See also CA 17-20R; CANR 30; DLB 2; MTCW

Gasset, Jose Ortega y
See Ortega y Gasset, Jose

Gates, Henry Louis, Jr. 1950-**CLC 65; BLCS; DAM MULT**
See also BW 2; CA 109; CANR 25, 53; DLB 67

Gautier, Theophile 1811-1872 **NCLC 1, 59; DAM POET; PC 18; SSC 20**
See also DLB 119

Gawsworth, John
See Bates, H(erbert) E(rnest)

Gay, Oliver
See Gogarty, Oliver St. John

Gaye, Marvin (Penze) 1939-1984 **CLC 26**
See also CA 112

Gebler, Carlo (Ernest) 1954- **CLC 39**
See also CA 119; 133

Gee, Maggie (Mary) 1948- **CLC 57**
See also CA 130

Gee, Maurice (Gough) 1931- **CLC 29**
See also CA 97-100; CANR 67; SATA 46

Gelbart, Larry (Simon) 1923- **CLC 21, 61**
See also CA 73-76; CANR 45

Gelber, Jack 1932- **CLC 1, 6, 14, 79**
See also CA 1-4R; CANR 2; DLB 7

Gellhorn, Martha (Ellis) 1908-1998 **CLC 14, 60**
See also CA 77-80; 164; CANR 44; DLBY 82

Genet, Jean 1910-1986**CLC 1, 2, 5, 10, 14, 44, 46; DAM DRAM**
See also CA 13-16R; CANR 18; DLB 72; DLBY 86; MTCW

Gent, Peter 1942- **CLC 29**
See also AITN 1; CA 89-92; DLBY 82

Gentlewoman in New England, A
See Bradstreet, Anne

Gentlewoman in Those Parts, A
See Bradstreet, Anne

George, Jean Craighead 1919- **CLC 35**
See also AAYA 8; CA 5-8R; CANR 25; CLR 1; DLB 52; JRDA; MAICYA; SATA 2, 68

George, Stefan (Anton) 1868-1933**TCLC 2, 14**
See also CA 104

Georges, Georges Martin
See Simenon, Georges (Jacques Christian)

Gerhardi, William Alexander
See Gerhardie, William Alexander

Gerhardie, William Alexander 1895-1977 **CLC 5**
See also CA 25-28R; 73-76; CANR 18; DLB 36

Gerstler, Amy 1956- **CLC 70**
See also CA 146

Gertler, T. **CLC 34**
See also CA 116; 121; INT 121

Ghalib **NCLC 39**
See also Ghalib, Hsadullah Khan

Ghalib, Hsadullah Khan 1797-1869
See Ghalib
See also DAM POET

Ghelderode, Michel de 1898-1962 **CLC 6, 11; DAM DRAM**
See also CA 85-88; CANR 40

Ghiselin, Brewster 1903- **CLC 23**
See also CA 13-16R; CAAS 10; CANR 13

Ghose, Aurabinda 1872-1950 **TCLC 63**
See also CA 163

Ghose, Zulfikar 1935- **CLC 42**
See also CA 65-68; CANR 67

Ghosh, Amitav 1956- **CLC 44**
See also CA 147

Giacosa, Giuseppe 1847-1906 **TCLC 7**
See also CA 104

Gibb, Lee
See Waterhouse, Keith (Spencer)

Gibbon, Lewis Grassic **TCLC 4**
See also Mitchell, James Leslie

Gibbons, Kaye 1960-**CLC 50, 88; DAM POP**
See also CA 151

Gibran, Kahlil 1883-1931 **TCLC 1, 9; DAM POET, POP; PC 9**
See also CA 104; 150

Gibran, Khalil
See Gibran, Kahlil

Gibson, William 1914- **CLC 23; DA; DAB; DAC; DAM DRAM, MST**

See also CA 9-12R; CANR 9, 42; DLB 7; SATA 66

Gibson, William (Ford) 1948- **CLC 39, 63; DAM POP**
See also AAYA 12; CA 126; 133; CANR 52

Gide, Andre (Paul Guillaume) 1869-1951 **TCLC 5, 12, 36; DA; DAB; DAC; DAM MST, NOV; SSC 13; WLC**
See also CA 104; 124; DLB 65; MTCW

Gifford, Barry (Colby) 1946- **CLC 34**
See also CA 65-68; CANR 9, 30, 40

Gilbert, Frank
See De Voto, Bernard (Augustine)

Gilbert, W(illiam) S(chwenck) 1836-1911 **TCLC 3; DAM DRAM, POET**
See also CA 104; SATA 36

Gilbreth, Frank B., Jr. 1911- **CLC 17**
See also CA 9-12R; SATA 2

Gilchrist, Ellen 1935-**CLC 34, 48; DAM POP; SSC 14**
See also CA 113; 116; CANR 41, 61; DLB 130; MTCW

Giles, Molly 1942- **CLC 39**
See also CA 126

Gill, Patrick
See Creasey, John

Gilliam, Terry (Vance) 1940- **CLC 21**
See also Monty Python
See also AAYA 19; CA 108; 113; CANR 35; INT 113

Gillian, Jerry
See Gilliam, Terry (Vance)

Gilliatt, Penelope (Ann Douglass) 1932-1993 **CLC 2, 10, 13, 53**
See also AITN 2; CA 13-16R; 141; CANR 49; DLB 14

Gilman, Charlotte (Anna) Perkins (Stetson) 1860-1935 **TCLC 9, 37; SSC 13**
See also CA 106; 150

Gilmour, David 1949- **CLC 35**
See also CA 138, 147

Gilpin, William 1724-1804 **NCLC 30**

Gilray, J. D.
See Mencken, H(enry) L(ouis)

Gilroy, Frank D(aniel) 1925- **CLC 2**
See also CA 81-84; CANR 32, 64; DLB 7

Gilstrap, John 1957(?)- **CLC 99**
See also CA 160

Ginsberg, Allen 1926-1997**CLC 1, 2, 3, 4, 6, 13, 36, 69, 109; DA; DAB; DAC; DAM MST, POET; PC 4; WLC 3**
See also AITN 1; CA 1-4R; 157; CANR 2, 41, 63; CDALB 1941-1968; DLB 5, 16, 169; MTCW

Ginzburg, Natalia 1916-1991**CLC 5, 11, 54, 70**
See also CA 85-88; 135; CANR 33; DLB 177; MTCW

Giono, Jean 1895-1970 **CLC 4, 11**
See also CA 45-48; 29-32R; CANR 2, 35; DLB 72; MTCW

Giovanni, Nikki 1943-**CLC 2, 4, 19, 64; BLC 2; DA; DAB; DAC; DAM MST, MULT, POET; PC 19; WLCS**
See also AAYA 22; AITN 1; BW 2; CA 29-32R; CAAS 6; CANR 18, 41, 60; CLR 6; DLB 5, 41; INT CANR-18; MAICYA; MTCW; SATA 24

Giovene, Andrea 1904- **CLC 7**
See also CA 85-88

Gippius, Zinaida (Nikolayevna) 1869-1945
See Hippius, Zinaida
See also CA 106

Giraudoux, (Hippolyte) Jean 1882-1944

TCLC 2, 7; DAM DRAM
See also CA 104; DLB 65

Gironella, Jose Maria 1917-　　CLC 11
See also CA 101

Gissing, George (Robert) 1857-1903TCLC 3,
24, 47
See also CA 105; DLB 18, 135, 184

Giurlani, Aldo
See Palazzeschi, Aldo

Gladkov, Fyodor (Vasilyevich) 1883-1958
TCLC 27

Glanville, Brian (Lester) 1931-　　CLC 6
See also CA 5-8R; CAAS 9; CANR 3; DLB 15,
139; SATA 42

Glasgow, Ellen (Anderson Gholson) 1873-1945
TCLC 2, 7
See also CA 104; 164; DLB 9, 12

Glaspell, Susan 1882(?)-1948　　TCLC 55
See also CA 110; 154; DLB 7, 9, 78; YABC 2

Glassco, John 1909-1981　　CLC 9
See also CA 13-16R; 102; CANR 15; DLB 68

Glasscock, Amnesia
See Steinbeck, John (Ernst)

Glasser, Ronald J. 1940(?)-　　CLC 37

Glassman, Joyce
See Johnson, Joyce

Glendinning, Victoria 1937-　　CLC 50
See also CA 120; 127; CANR 59; DLB 155

Glissant, Edouard 1928-　　CLC 10, 68; DAM
MULT
See also CA 153

Gloag, Julian 1930-　　CLC 40
See also AITN 1; CA 65-68; CANR 10

Glowacki, Aleksander
See Prus, Boleslaw

Gluck, Louise (Elisabeth) 1943-CLC 7, 22, 44,
81; DAM POET; PC 16
See also CA 33-36R; CANR 40, 69; DLB 5

Glyn, Elinor 1864-1943　　TCLC 72
See also DLB 153

Gobineau, Joseph Arthur (Comte) de 1816-
1882　　NCLC 17
See also DLB 123

Godard, Jean-Luc 1930-　　CLC 20
See also CA 93-96

Godden, (Margaret) Rumer 1907-　CLC 53
See also AAYA 6; CA 5-8R; CANR 4, 27, 36,
55; CLR 20; DLB 161; MAICYA; SAAS 12;
SATA 3, 36

Godoy Alcayaga, Lucila 1889-1957
See Mistral, Gabriela
See also BW 2; CA 104; 131; DAM MULT;
HW; MTCW

Godwin, Gail (Kathleen) 1937- CLC 5, 8, 22,
31, 69; DAM POP
See also CA 29-32R; CANR 15, 43, 69; DLB
6; INT CANR-15; MTCW

Godwin, William 1756-1836　　NCLC 14
See also CDBLB 1789-1832; DLB 39, 104, 142,
158, 163

Goebbels, Josef
See Goebbels, (Paul) Joseph

Goebbels, (Paul) Joseph 1897-1945 TCLC 68
See also CA 115; 148

Goebbels, Joseph Paul
See Goebbels, (Paul) Joseph

Goethe, Johann Wolfgang von 1749-1832
NCLC 4, 22, 34; DA; DAB; DAC; DAM
DRAM, MST, POET; PC 5; WLC 3
See also DLB 94

Gogarty, Oliver St. John 1878-1957TCLC 15
See also CA 109; 150; DLB 15, 19

Gogol, Nikolai (Vasilyevich) 1809-1852NCLC

5, 15, 31; DA; DAB; DAC; DAM DRAM,
MST; DC 1; SSC 4, 29; WLC
See also DLB 198

Goines, Donald 1937(?)-1974CLC 80; BLC 2;
DAM MULT, POP
See also AITN 1; BW 1; CA 124; 114; DLB 33

Gold, Herbert 1924-　　CLC 4, 7, 14, 42
See also CA 9-12R; CANR 17, 45; DLB 2;
DLBY 81

Goldbarth, Albert 1948-　　CLC 5, 38
See also CA 53-56; CANR 6, 40; DLB 120

Goldberg, Anatol 1910-1982　　CLC 34
See also CA 131; 117

Goldemberg, Isaac 1945-　　CLC 52
See also CA 69-72; CAAS 12; CANR 11, 32;
HW

Golding, William (Gerald) 1911-1993CLC 1,
2, 3, 8, 10, 17, 27, 58, 81; DA; DAB; DAC;
DAM MST, NOV; WLC
See also AAYA 5; CA 5-8R; 141; CANR 13,
33, 54; CDBLB 1945-1960; DLB 15, 100;
MTCW

Goldman, Emma 1869-1940　　TCLC 13
See also CA 110; 150

Goldman, Francisco 1954-　　CLC 76
See also CA 162

Goldman, William (W.) 1931-　CLC 1, 48
See also CA 9-12R; CANR 29, 69; DLB 44

Goldmann, Lucien 1913-1970　　CLC 24
See also CA 25-28; CAP 2

Goldoni, Carlo 1707-1793LC 4; DAM DRAM

Goldsberry, Steven 1949-　　CLC 34
See also CA 131

Goldsmith, Oliver 1728-1774LC 2; DA; DAB;
DAC; DAM DRAM, MST, NOV, POET;
DC 8; WLC
See also CDBLB 1660-1789; DLB 39, 89, 104,
109, 142; SATA 26

Goldsmith, Peter
See Priestley, J(ohn) B(oynton)

Gombrowicz, Witold 1904-1969CLC 4, 7, 11,
49; DAM DRAM
See also CA 19-20; 25-28R; CAP 2

Gomez de la Serna, Ramon 1888-1963CLC 9
See also CA 153; 116; HW

Goncharov, Ivan Alexandrovich 1812-1891
NCLC 1, 63

Goncourt, Edmond (Louis Antoine Huot) de
1822-1896　　NCLC 7
See also DLB 123

Goncourt, Jules (Alfred Huot) de 1830-1870
NCLC 7
See also DLB 123

Gontier, Fernande 19(?)-　　CLC 50

Gonzalez Martinez, Enrique 1871-1952
TCLC 72
See also CA 166; HW

Goodman, Paul 1911-1972　　CLC 1, 2, 4, 7
See also CA 19-20; 37-40R; CANR 34; CAP 2;
DLB 130; MTCW

Gordimer, Nadine 1923-CLC 3, 5, 7, 10, 18, 33,
51, 70; DA; DAB; DAC; DAM MST, NOV;
SSC 17; WLCS
See also CA 5-8R; CANR 3, 28, 56; INT CANR-
28; MTCW

Gordon, Adam Lindsay 1833-1870 NCLC 21

Gordon, Caroline 1895-1981CLC 6, 13, 29, 83;
SSC 15
See also CA 11-12; 103; CANR 36; CAP 1;
DLB 4, 9, 102; DLBY 81; MTCW

Gordon, Charles William 1860-1937
See Connor, Ralph
See also CA 109

Gordon, Mary (Catherine) 1949- CLC 13, 22
See also CA 102; CANR 44; DLB 6; DLBY
81; INT 102; MTCW

Gordon, N. J.
See Bosman, Herman Charles

Gordon, Sol 1923-　　CLC 26
See also CA 53-56; CANR 4; SATA 11

Gordone, Charles 1925-1995CLC 1, 4; DAM
DRAM; DC 8
See also BW 1; CA 93-96; 150; CANR 55; DLB
7; INT 93-96; MTCW

Gore, Catherine 1800-1861　　NCLC 65
See also DLB 116

Gorenko, Anna Andreevna
See Akhmatova, Anna

Gorky, Maxim 1868-1936TCLC 8; DAB; SSC
28; WLC
See also Peshkov, Alexei Maximovich

Goryan, Sirak
See Saroyan, William

Gosse, Edmund (William) 1849-1928TCLC 28
See also CA 117; DLB 57, 144, 184

Gotlieb, Phyllis Fay (Bloom) 1926- CLC 18
See also CA 13-16R; CANR 7; DLB 88

Gottesman, S. D.
See Kornbluth, C(yril) M.; Pohl, Frederik

Gottfried von Strassburg fl. c. 1210- CMLC
10
See also DLB 138

Gould, Lois　　CLC 4, 10
See also CA 77-80; CANR 29; MTCW

Gourmont, Remy (-Marie-Charles) de 1858-
1915　　TCLC 17
See also CA 109; 150

Govier, Katherine 1948-　　CLC 51
See also CA 101; CANR 18, 40

Goyen, (Charles) William 1915-1983CLC 5, 8,
14, 40
See also AITN 2; CA 5-8R; 110; CANR 6; DLB
2; DLBY 83; INT CANR-6

Goytisolo, Juan 1931-　CLC 5, 10, 23; DAM
MULT; HLC
See also CA 85-88; CANR 32, 61; HW; MTCW

Gozzano, Guido 1883-1916　　PC 10
See also CA 154; DLB 114

Gozzi, (Conte) Carlo 1720-1806　NCLC 23

Grabbe, Christian Dietrich 1801-1836N C L C
2
See also DLB 133

Grace, Patricia 1937-　　CLC 56

Gracian y Morales, Baltasar 1601-1658LC 15

Gracq, Julien　　CLC 11, 48
See also Poirier, Louis
See also DLB 83

Grade, Chaim 1910-1982　　CLC 10
See also CA 93-96; 107

Graduate of Oxford, A
See Ruskin, John

Grafton, Garth
See Duncan, Sara Jeannette

Graham, John
See Phillips, David Graham

Graham, Jorie 1951-　　CLC 48
See also CA 111; CANR 63; DLB 120

Graham, R(obert) B(ontine) Cunninghame
See Cunninghame Graham, R(obert) B(ontine)
See also DLB 98, 135, 174

Graham, Robert
See Haldeman, Joe (William)

Graham, Tom
See Lewis, (Harry) Sinclair

Graham, W(illiam) S(ydney) 1918-1986 C L C
29

See also CA 127; 111; CANR 56; DAM MULT;
HW

Guild, Nicholas M. 1944- **CLC 33**
See also CA 93-96

Guillemin, Jacques
See Sartre, Jean-Paul

Guillen, Jorge 1893-1984 **CLC 11; DAM MULT, POET**
See also CA 89-92; 112; DLB 108; HW

Guillen, Nicolas (Cristobal) 1902-1989 **C L C 48, 79; BLC 2; DAM MST, MULT, POET; HLC**
See also BW 2; CA 116; 125; 129; HW

Guillevic, (Eugene) 1907- **CLC 33**
See also CA 93-96

Guillois
See Desnos, Robert

Guillois, Valentin
See Desnos, Robert

Guiney, Louise Imogen 1861-1920 **TCLC 41**
See also CA 160; DLB 54

Guiraldes, Ricardo (Guillermo) 1886-1927 **TCLC 39**
See also CA 131; HW; MTCW

Gumilev, Nikolai (Stepanovich) 1886-1921 **TCLC 60**
See also CA 165

Gunesekera, Romesh 1954- **CLC 91**
See also CA 159

Gunn, Bill **CLC 5**
See also Gunn, William Harrison
See also DLB 38

Gunn, Thom(son William) 1929- **CLC 3, 6, 18, 32, 81; DAM POET**
See also CA 17-20R; CANR 9, 33; CDBLB 1960 to Present; DLB 27; INT CANR-33; MTCW

Gunn, William Harrison 1934(?)-1989
See Gunn, Bill
See also AITN 1; BW 1; CA 13-16R; 128; CANR 12, 25

Gunnars, Kristjana 1948- **CLC 69**
See also CA 113; DLB 60

Gurdjieff, G(eorgei) I(vanovich) 1877(?)-1949 **TCLC 71**
See also CA 157

Gurganus, Allan 1947- **CLC 70; DAM POP**
See also BEST 90:1; CA 135

Gurney, A(lbert) R(amsdell), Jr. 1930- **C L C 32, 50, 54; DAM DRAM**
See also CA 77-80; CANR 32, 64

Gurney, Ivor (Bertie) 1890-1937 **TCLC 33**

Gurney, Peter
See Gurney, A(lbert) R(amsdell), Jr.

Guro, Elena 1877-1913 **TCLC 56**

Gustafson, James M(oody) 1925- **CLC 100**
See also CA 25-28R; CANR 37

Gustafson, Ralph (Barker) 1909- **CLC 36**
See also CA 21-24R; CANR 8, 45; DLB 88

Gut, Gom
See Simenon, Georges (Jacques Christian)

Guterson, David 1956- **CLC 91**
See also CA 132

Guthrie, A(lfred) B(ertram), Jr. 1901-1991 **CLC 23**
See also CA 57-60; 134; CANR 24; DLB 6; SATA 62; SATA-Obit 67

Guthrie, Isobel
See Grieve, C(hristopher) M(urray)

Guthrie, Woodrow Wilson 1912-1967
See Guthrie, Woody
See also CA 113; 93-96

Guthrie, Woody **CLC 35**

See also Guthrie, Woodrow Wilson

Guy, Rosa (Cuthbert) 1928- **CLC 26**
See also AAYA 4; BW 2; CA 17-20R; CANR 14, 34; CLR 13; DLB 33; JRDA; MAICYA; SATA 14, 62

Gwendolyn
See Bennett, (Enoch) Arnold

H. D. **CLC 3, 8, 14, 31, 34, 73; PC 5**
See also Doolittle, Hilda

H. de V.
See Buchan, John

Haavikko, Paavo Juhani 1931- **CLC 18, 34**
See also CA 106

Habbema, Koos
See Heijermans, Herman

Habermas, Juergen 1929- **CLC 104**
See also CA 109

Habermas, Jurgen
See Habermas, Juergen

Hacker, Marilyn 1942- **CLC 5, 9, 23, 72, 91; DAM POET**
See also CA 77-80; CANR 68; DLB 120

Haeckel, Ernst Heinrich (Philipp August) 1834-1919 **TCLC 80**
See also CA 157

Haggard, H(enry) Rider 1856-1925 **TCLC 11**
See also CA 108; 148; DLB 70, 156, 174, 178; SATA 16

Hagiosy, L.
See Larbaud, Valery (Nicolas)

Hagiwara Sakutaro 1886-1942 **TCLC 60; PC 18**

Haig, Fenil
See Ford, Ford Madox

Haig-Brown, Roderick (Langmere) 1908-1976 **CLC 21**
See also CA 5-8R; 69-72; CANR 4, 38; CLR 31; DLB 88; MAICYA; SATA 12

Hailey, Arthur 1920- **CLC 5; DAM NOV, POP**
See also AITN 2; BEST 90:3; CA 1-4R; CANR 2, 36; DLB 88; DLBY 82; MTCW

Hailey, Elizabeth Forsythe 1938- **CLC 40**
See also CA 93-96; CAAS 1; CANR 15, 48; INT CANR-15

Haines, John (Meade) 1924- **CLC 58**
See also CA 17-20R; CANR 13, 34; DLB 5

Hakluyt, Richard 1552-1616 **LC 31**

Haldeman, Joe (William) 1943- **CLC 61**
See also CA 53-56; CAAS 25; CANR 6; DLB 8; INT CANR-6

Haley, Alex(ander Murray Palmer) 1921-1992 **CLC 8, 12, 76; BLC 2; DA; DAB; DAC; DAM MST, MULT, POP**
See also BW 2; CA 77-80; 136; CANR 61; DLB 38; MTCW

Haliburton, Thomas Chandler 1796-1865 **NCLC 15**
See also DLB 11, 99

Hall, Donald (Andrew, Jr.) 1928- **CLC 1, 13, 37, 59; DAM POET**
See also CA 5-8R; CAAS 7; CANR 2, 44, 64; DLB 5; SATA 23, 97

Hall, Frederic Sauser
See Sauser-Hall, Frederic

Hall, James
See Kuttner, Henry

Hall, James Norman 1887-1951 **TCLC 23**
See also CA 123; SATA 21

Hall, (Marguerite) Radclyffe 1886-1943 **TCLC 12**
See also CA 110; 150

Hall, Rodney 1935- **CLC 51**
See also CA 109; CANR 69

Halleck, Fitz-Greene 1790-1867 **NCLC 47**
See also DLB 3

Halliday, Michael
See Creasey, John

Halpern, Daniel 1945- **CLC 14**
See also CA 33-36R

Hamburger, Michael (Peter Leopold) 1924- **CLC 5, 14**
See also CA 5-8R; CAAS 4; CANR 2, 47; DLB 27

Hamill, Pete 1935- **CLC 10**
See also CA 25-28R; CANR 18

Hamilton, Alexander 1755(?)-1804 **NCLC 49**
See also DLB 37

Hamilton, Clive
See Lewis, C(live) S(taples)

Hamilton, Edmond 1904-1977 **CLC 1**
See also CA 1-4R; CANR 3; DLB 8

Hamilton, Eugene (Jacob) Lee
See Lee-Hamilton, Eugene (Jacob)

Hamilton, Franklin
See Silverberg, Robert

Hamilton, Gail
See Corcoran, Barbara

Hamilton, Mollie
See Kaye, M(ary) M(argaret)

Hamilton, (Anthony Walter) Patrick 1904-1962 **CLC 51**
See also CA 113; DLB 10

Hamilton, Virginia 1936- **CLC 26; DAM MULT**
See also AAYA 2, 21; BW 2; CA 25-28R; CANR 20, 37; CLR 1, 11, 40; DLB 33, 52; INT CANR-20; JRDA; MAICYA; MTCW; SATA 4, 56, 79

Hammett, (Samuel) Dashiell 1894-1961 **C L C 3, 5, 10, 19, 47; SSC 17**
See also AITN 1; CA 81-84; CANR 42; CDALB 1929-1941; DLBD 6; DLBY 96; MTCW

Hammon, Jupiter 1711(?)-1800(?) **NCLC 5; BLC 2; DAM MULT, POET; PC 16**
See also DLB 31, 50

Hammond, Keith
See Kuttner, Henry

Hamner, Earl (Henry), Jr. 1923- **CLC 12**
See also AITN 2; CA 73-76; DLB 6

Hampton, Christopher (James) 1946- **CLC 4**
See also CA 25-28R; DLB 13; MTCW

Hamsun, Knut **TCLC 2, 14, 49**
See also Pedersen, Knut

Handke, Peter 1942- **CLC 5, 8, 10, 15, 38; DAM DRAM, NOV**
See also CA 77-80; CANR 33; DLB 85, 124; MTCW

Hanley, James 1901-1985 **CLC 3, 5, 8, 13**
See also CA 73-76; 117; CANR 36; DLB 191; MTCW

Hannah, Barry 1942- **CLC 23, 38, 90**
See also CA 108; 110; CANR 43, 68; DLB 6; INT 110; MTCW

Hannon, Ezra
See Hunter, Evan

Hansberry, Lorraine (Vivian) 1930-1965 **CLC 17, 62; BLC 2; DA; DAB; DAC; DAM DRAM, MST, MULT; DC 2**
See also AAYA 25; BW 1; CA 109; 25-28R; CABS 3; CANR 58; CDALB 1941-1968; DLB 7, 38; MTCW

Hansen, Joseph 1923- **CLC 38**
See also CA 29-32R; CAAS 17; CANR 16, 44, 66; INT CANR-16

Hansen, Martin A. 1909-1955 **TCLC 32**

Hanson, Kenneth O(stlin) 1922- **CLC 13**

See also CA 53-56; CANR 7

Hardwick, Elizabeth 1916-　**CLC 13; DAM NOV**
See also CA 5-8R; CANR 3, 32; DLB 6; MTCW

Hardy, Thomas 1840-1928**TCLC 4, 10, 18, 32, 48, 53, 72; DA; DAB; DAC; DAM MST, NOV, POET; PC 8; SSC 2; WLC**
See also CA 104; 123; CDBLB 1890-1914; DLB 18, 19, 135; MTCW

Hare, David 1947-　**CLC 29, 58**
See also CA 97-100; CANR 39; DLB 13; MTCW

Harewood, John
See Van Druten, John (William)

Harford, Henry
See Hudson, W(illiam) H(enry)

Hargrave, Leonie
See Disch, Thomas M(ichael)

Harjo, Joy 1951-　**CLC 83; DAM MULT**
See also CA 114; CANR 35, 67; DLB 120, 175; NNAL

Harlan, Louis R(udolph) 1922-　**CLC 34**
See also CA 21-24R; CANR 25, 55

Harling, Robert 1951(?)-　**CLC 53**
See also CA 147

Harmon, William (Ruth) 1938-　**CLC 38**
See also CA 33-36R; CANR 14, 32, 35; SATA 65

Harper, F. E. W.
See Harper, Frances Ellen Watkins

Harper, Frances E. W.
See Harper, Frances Ellen Watkins

Harper, Frances E. Watkins
See Harper, Frances Ellen Watkins

Harper, Frances Ellen
See Harper, Frances Ellen Watkins

Harper, Frances Ellen Watkins 1825-1911
TCLC 14; BLC 2; DAM MULT, POET; PC 21
See also BW 1; CA 111; 125; DLB 50

Harper, Michael S(teven) 1938-　**CLC 7, 22**
See also BW 1; CA 33-36R; CANR 24; DLB 41

Harper, Mrs. F. E. W.
See Harper, Frances Ellen Watkins

Harris, Christie (Lucy) Irwin 1907-　**CLC 12**
See also CA 5-8R; CANR 6; CLR 47; DLB 88; JRDA; MAICYA; SAAS 10; SATA 6, 74

Harris, Frank 1856-1931　**TCLC 24**
See also CA 109; 150; DLB 156, 197

Harris, George Washington 1814-1869**NCLC 23**
See also DLB 3, 11

Harris, Joel Chandler 1848-1908　**TCLC 2; SSC 19**
See also CA 104; 137; CLR 49; DLB 11, 23, 42, 78, 91; MAICYA; YABC 1

Harris, John (Wyndham Parkes Lucas) Beynon 1903-1969
See Wyndham, John
See also CA 102; 89-92

Harris, MacDonald　**CLC 9**
See also Heiney, Donald (William)

Harris, Mark 1922-　**CLC 19**
See also CA 5-8R; CAAS 3; CANR 2, 55; DLB 2; DLBY 80

Harris, (Theodore) Wilson 1921-　**CLC 25**
See also BW 2; CA 65-68; CAAS 16; CANR 11, 27, 69; DLB 117; MTCW

Harrison, Elizabeth Cavanna 1909-
See Cavanna, Betty
See also CA 9-12R; CANR 6, 27

Harrison, Harry (Max) 1925-　**CLC 42**

See also CA 1-4R; CANR 5, 21; DLB 8; SATA 4

Harrison, James (Thomas) 1937-**CLC 6, 14, 33, 66; SSC 19**
See also CA 13-16R; CANR 8, 51; DLBY 82; INT CANR-8

Harrison, Jim
See Harrison, James (Thomas)

Harrison, Kathryn 1961-　**CLC 70**
See also CA 144; CANR 68

Harrison, Tony 1937-　**CLC 43**
See also CA 65-68; CANR 44; DLB 40; MTCW

Harriss, Will(ard Irvin) 1922-　**CLC 34**
See also CA 111

Harson, Sley
See Ellison, Harlan (Jay)

Hart, Ellis
See Ellison, Harlan (Jay)

Hart, Josephine 1942(?)-**CLC 70; DAM POP**
See also CA 138

Hart, Moss 1904-1961**CLC 66; DAM DRAM**
See also CA 109; 89-92; DLB 7

Harte, (Francis) Bret(t) 1836(?)-1902**TCLC 1, 25; DA; DAC; DAM MST; SSC 8; WLC**
See also CA 104; 140; CDALB 1865-1917; DLB 12, 64, 74, 79, 186; SATA 26

Hartley, L(eslie) P(oles) 1895-1972**CLC 2, 22**
See also CA 45-48; 37-40R; CANR 33; DLB 15, 139; MTCW

Hartman, Geoffrey H. 1929-　**CLC 27**
See also CA 117; 125; DLB 67

Hartmann, Sadakichi 1867-1944　**TCLC 73**
See also CA 157; DLB 54

Hartmann von Aue c. 1160-c. 1205**CMLC 15**
See also DLB 138

Hartmann von Aue 1170-1210　**CMLC 15**

Haruf, Kent 1943-　**CLC 34**
See also CA 149

Harwood, Ronald 1934-　**CLC 32; DAM DRAM, MST**
See also CA 1-4R; CANR 4, 55; DLB 13

Hasegawa Tatsunosuke
See Futabatei, Shimei

Hasek, Jaroslav (Matej Frantisek) 1883-1923
TCLC 4
See also CA 104; 129; MTCW

Hass, Robert 1941-　**CLC 18, 39, 99; PC 16**
See also CA 111; CANR 30, 50; DLB 105; SATA 94

Hastings, Hudson
See Kuttner, Henry

Hastings, Selina　**CLC 44**

Hathorne, John 1641-1717　**LC 38**

Hatteras, Amelia
See Mencken, H(enry) L(ouis)

Hatteras, Owen　**TCLC 18**
See also Mencken, H(enry) L(ouis); Nathan, George Jean

Hauptmann, Gerhart (Johann Robert) 1862-1946　**TCLC 4; DAM DRAM**
See also CA 104; 153; DLB 66, 118

Havel, Vaclav 1936-　**CLC 25, 58, 65; DAM DRAM; DC 6**
See also CA 104; CANR 36, 63; MTCW

Haviaras, Stratis　**CLC 33**
See also Chaviaras, Strates

Hawes, Stephen 1475(?)-1523(?)　**LC 17**
See also DLB 132

Hawkes, John (Clendennin Burne, Jr.) 1925-**CLC 1, 2, 3, 4, 7, 9, 14, 15, 27, 49**
See also CA 1-4R; CANR 2, 47, 64; DLB 2, 7; DLBY 80; MTCW

Hawking, S. W.

See Hawking, Stephen W(illiam)

Hawking, Stephen W(illiam) 1942-　**CLC 63, 105**
See also AAYA 13; BEST 89:1; CA 126; 129; CANR 48

Hawthorne, Julian 1846-1934　**TCLC 25**
See also CA 165

Hawthorne, Nathaniel 1804-1864　**NCLC 39; DA; DAB; DAC; DAM MST, NOV; SSC 3, 29; WLC**
See also AAYA 18; CDALB 1640-1865; DLB 1, 74; YABC 2

Haxton, Josephine Ayres 1921-
See Douglas, Ellen
See also CA 115; CANR 41

Hayaseca y Eizaguirre, Jorge
See Echegaray (y Eizaguirre), Jose (Maria Waldo)

Hayashi, Fumiko 1904-1951　**TCLC 27**
See also CA 161; DLB 180

Haycraft, Anna
See Ellis, Alice Thomas
See also CA 122

Hayden, Robert E(arl) 1913-1980　**CLC 5, 9, 14, 37; BLC 2; DA; DAC; DAM MST, MULT, POET; PC 6**
See also BW 1; CA 69-72; 97-100; CABS 2; CANR 24; CDALB 1941-1968; DLB 5, 76; MTCW; SATA 19; SATA-Obit 26

Hayford, J(oseph) E(phraim) Casely
See Casely-Hayford, J(oseph) E(phraim)

Hayman, Ronald 1932-　**CLC 44**
See also CA 25-28R; CANR 18, 50; DLB 155

Haywood, Eliza 1693(?)-1756　**LC 44**
See also DLB 39

Haywood, Eliza (Fowler) 1693(?)-1756**LC 1, 44**

Hazlitt, William 1778-1830　**NCLC 29**
See also DLB 110, 158

Hazzard, Shirley 1931-　**CLC 18**
See also CA 9-12R; CANR 4; DLBY 82; MTCW

Head, Bessie 1937-1986**CLC 25, 67; BLC 2; DAM MULT**
See also BW 2; CA 29-32R; 119; CANR 25; DLB 117; MTCW

Headon, (Nicky) Topper 1956(?)-　**CLC 30**

Heaney, Seamus (Justin) 1939-**CLC 5, 7, 14, 25, 37, 74, 91; DAB; DAM POET; PC 18; WLCS**
See also CA 85-88; CANR 25, 48; CDBLB 1960 to Present; DLB 40; DLBY 95; MTCW

Hearn, (Patricio) Lafcadio (Tessima Carlos) 1850-1904　**TCLC 9**
See also CA 105; 166; DLB 12, 78

Hearne, Vicki 1946-　**CLC 56**
See also CA 139

Hearon, Shelby 1931-　**CLC 63**
See also AITN 2; CA 25-28R; CANR 18, 48

Heat-Moon, William Least　**CLC 29**
See also Trogdon, William (Lewis)
See also AAYA 9

Hebbel, Friedrich 1813-1863**NCLC 43; DAM DRAM**
See also DLB 129

Hebert, Anne 1916-**CLC 4, 13, 29; DAC; DAM MST, POET**
See also CA 85-88; CANR 69; DLB 68; MTCW

Hecht, Anthony (Evan) 1923-　**CLC 8, 13, 19; DAM POET**
See also CA 9-12R; CANR 6; DLB 5, 169

Hecht, Ben 1894-1964　**CLC 8**
See also CA 85-88; DLB 7, 9, 25, 26, 28, 86

Hedayat, Sadeq 1903-1951　　　　**TCLC 21**
See also CA 120
Hegel, Georg Wilhelm Friedrich 1770-1831
　　NCLC 46
See also DLB 90
Heidegger, Martin 1889-1976　　　　**CLC 24**
See also CA 81-84; 65-68; CANR 34; MTCW
Heidenstam, (Carl Gustaf) Verner von 1859-
　　1940　　　　**TCLC 5**
See also CA 104
Heifner, Jack 1946-　　　　**CLC 11**
See also CA 105; CANR 47
Heijermans, Herman 1864-1924　　**TCLC 24**
See also CA 123
Heilbrun, Carolyn G(old) 1926-　　**CLC 25**
See also CA 45-48; CANR 1, 28, 58
Heine, Heinrich 1797-1856　　　**NCLC 4, 54**
See also DLB 90
Heinemann, Larry (Curtiss) 1944-　**CLC 50**
See also CA 110; CAAS 21; CANR 31; DLBD
　　9; INT CANR-31
Heiney, Donald (William) 1921-1993
See Harris, MacDonald
See also CA 1-4R; 142; CANR 3, 58
Heinlein, Robert A(nson) 1907-1988**CLC 1, 3,**
　　8, 14, 26, 55; DAM POP
See also AAYA 17; CA 1-4R; 125; CANR 1,
　　20, 53; DLB 8; JRDA; MAICYA; MTCW;
　　SATA 9, 69; SATA-Obit 56
Helforth, John
See Doolittle, Hilda
Hellenhofferu, Vojtech Kapristian z
See Hasek, Jaroslav (Matej Frantisek)
Heller, Joseph 1923-**CLC 1, 3, 5, 8, 11, 36, 63;**
　　DA; DAB; DAC; DAM MST, NOV, POP;
　　WLC
See also AAYA 24; AITN 1; CA 5-8R; CABS
　　1; CANR 8, 42, 66; DLB 2, 28; DLBY 80;
　　INT CANR-8; MTCW
Hellman, Lillian (Florence) 1906-1984**CLC 2,**
　　4, 8, 14, 18, 34, 44, 52; DAM DRAM; DC 1
See also AITN 1, 2; CA 13-16R; 112; CANR
　　33; DLB 7; DLBY 84; MTCW
Helprin, Mark 1947-**CLC 7, 10, 22, 32; DAM**
　　NOV, POP
See also CA 81-84; CANR 47, 64; DLBY 85;
　　MTCW
Helvetius, Claude-Adrien 1715-1771　**LC 26**
Helyar, Jane Penelope Josephine 1933-
See Poole, Josephine
See also CA 21-24R; CANR 10, 26; SATA 82
Hemans, Felicia 1793-1835　　　**NCLC 29, 71**
See also DLB 96
Hemingway, Ernest (Miller) 1899-1961 **C L C**
　　1, 3, 6, 8, 10, 13, 19, 30, 34, 39, 41, 44, 50,
　　61, 80; DA; DAB; DAC; DAM MST, NOV;
　　SSC 25; WLC
See also AAYA 19; CA 77-80; CANR 34;
　　CDALB 1917-1929; DLB 4, 9, 102; DLBD
　　1, 15, 16; DLBY 81, 87, 96; MTCW
Hempel, Amy 1951-　　　　**CLC 39**
See also CA 118; 137
Henderson, F. C.
See Mencken, H(enry) L(ouis)
Henderson, Sylvia
See Ashton-Warner, Sylvia (Constance)
Henderson, Zenna (Chlarson) 1917-1983**S S C**
　　29
See also CA 1-4R; 133; CANR 1; DLB 8; SATA
　　5
Henley, Beth　　　　**CLC 23; DC 6**
See also Henley, Elizabeth Becker
See also CABS 3; DLBY 86

Henley, Elizabeth Becker 1952-
See Henley, Beth
See also CA 107; CANR 32; DAM DRAM,
　　MST; MTCW
Henley, William Ernest 1849-1903　　**TCLC 8**
See also CA 105; DLB 19
Hennissart, Martha
See Lathen, Emma
See also CA 85-88; CANR 64
Henry, O.　　　　**TCLC 1, 19; SSC 5; WLC**
See also Porter, William Sydney
Henry, Patrick 1736-1799　　　　**LC 25**
Henryson, Robert 1430(?)-1506(?)　**LC 20**
See also DLB 146
Henry VIII 1491-1547　　　　**LC 10**
Henschke, Alfred
See Klabund
Hentoff, Nat(han Irving) 1925-　　**CLC 26**
See also AAYA 4; CA 1-4R; CAAS 6; CANR
　　5, 25; CLR 1; INT CANR-25; JRDA;
　　MAICYA; SATA 42, 69; SATA-Brief 27
Heppenstall, (John) Rayner 1911-1981　**C L C**
　　10
See also CA 1-4R; 103; CANR 29
Heraclitus c. 540B.C.-c. 450B.C.　　**CMLC 22**
See also DLB 176
Herbert, Frank (Patrick) 1920-1986 **CLC 12,**
　　23, 35, 44, 85; DAM POP
See also AAYA 21; CA 53-56; 118; CANR 5,
　　43; DLB 8; INT CANR-5; MTCW; SATA 9,
　　37; SATA-Obit 47
Herbert, George 1593-1633　　　**LC 24; DAB;**
　　DAM POET; PC 4
See also CDBLB Before 1660; DLB 126
Herbert, Zbigniew 1924-　　　**CLC 9, 43; DAM**
　　POET
See also CA 89-92; CANR 36; MTCW
Herbst, Josephine (Frey) 1897-1969 **CLC 34**
See also CA 5-8R; 25-28R; DLB 9
Hergesheimer, Joseph 1880-1954　　**TCLC 11**
See also CA 109; DLB 102, 9
Herlihy, James Leo 1927-1993　　　**CLC 6**
See also CA 1-4R; 143; CANR 2
Hermogenes fl. c. 175-　　　　**CMLC 6**
Hernandez, Jose 1834-1886　　　**NCLC 17**
Herodotus c. 484B.C.-429B.C.　　**CMLC 17**
See also DLB 176
Herrick, Robert 1591-1674**LC 13; DA; DAB;**
　　DAC; DAM MST, POP; PC 9
See also DLB 126
Herring, Guilles
See Somerville, Edith
Herriot, James 1916-1995**CLC 12; DAM POP**
See also Wight, James Alfred
See also AAYA 1; CA 148; CANR 40; SATA
　　86
Herrmann, Dorothy 1941-　　　　**CLC 44**
See also CA 107
Herrmann, Taffy
See Herrmann, Dorothy
Hersey, John (Richard) 1914-1993**CLC 1, 2, 7,**
　　9, 40, 81, 97; DAM POP
See also CA 17-20R; 140; CANR 33; DLB 6,
　　185; MTCW; SATA 25; SATA-Obit 76
Herzen, Aleksandr Ivanovich 1812-1870
　　NCLC 10, 61
Herzl, Theodor 1860-1904　　　　**TCLC 36**
Herzog, Werner 1942-　　　　**CLC 16**
See also CA 89-92
Hesiod c. 8th cent. B.C.-　　　　**CMLC 5**
See also DLB 176
Hesse, Hermann 1877-1962**CLC 1, 2, 3, 6, 11,**
　　17, 25, 69; DA; DAB; DAC; DAM MST,

NOV; SSC 9; WLC
See also CA 17-18; CAP 2; DLB 66; MTCW;
　　SATA 50
Hewes, Cady
See De Voto, Bernard (Augustine)
Heyen, William 1940-　　　　**CLC 13, 18**
See also CA 33-36R; CAAS 9; DLB 5
Heyerdahl, Thor 1914-　　　　**CLC 26**
See also CA 5-8R; CANR 5, 22, 66; MTCW;
　　SATA 2, 52
Heym, Georg (Theodor Franz Arthur) 1887-
　　1912　　　　**TCLC 9**
See also CA 106
Heym, Stefan 1913-　　　　**CLC 41**
See also CA 9-12R; CANR 4; DLB 69
Heyse, Paul (Johann Ludwig von) 1830-1914
　　TCLC 8
See also CA 104; DLB 129
Heyward, (Edwin) DuBose 1885-1940 **T C L C**
　　59
See also CA 108; 157; DLB 7, 9, 45; SATA 21
Hibbert, Eleanor Alice Burford 1906-1993
　　CLC 7; DAM POP
See also BEST 90:4; CA 17-20R; 140; CANR
　　9, 28, 59; SATA 2; SATA-Obit 74
Hichens, Robert (Smythe) 1864-1950 **T C L C**
　　64
See also CA 162; DLB 153
Higgins, George V(incent) 1939-**CLC 4, 7, 10,**
　　18
See also CA 77-80; CAAS 5; CANR 17, 51;
　　DLB 2; DLBY 81; INT CANR-17; MTCW
Higginson, Thomas Wentworth 1823-1911
　　TCLC 36
See also CA 162; DLB 1, 64
Highet, Helen
See MacInnes, Helen (Clark)
Highsmith, (Mary) Patricia 1921-1995**CLC 2,**
　　4, 14, 42, 102; DAM NOV, POP
See also CA 1-4R; 147; CANR 1, 20, 48, 62;
　　MTCW
Highwater, Jamake (Mamake) 1942(?)- **C L C**
　　12
See also AAYA 7; CA 65-68; CAAS 7; CANR
　　10, 34; CLR 17; DLB 52; DLBY 85; JRDA;
　　MAICYA; SATA 32, 69; SATA-Brief 30
Highway, Tomson 1951-**CLC 92; DAC; DAM**
　　MULT
See also CA 151; NNAL
Higuchi, Ichiyo 1872-1896　　　**NCLC 49**
Hijuelos, Oscar 1951- **CLC 65; DAM MULT,**
　　POP; HLC
See also AAYA 25; BEST 90:1; CA 123; CANR
　　50; DLB 145; HW
Hikmet, Nazim 1902(?)-1963　　　**CLC 40**
See also CA 141; 93-96
Hildegard von Bingen 1098-1179 **CMLC 20**
See also DLB 148
Hildesheimer, Wolfgang 1916-1991　**CLC 49**
See also CA 101; 135; DLB 69, 124
Hill, Geoffrey (William) 1932- **CLC 5, 8, 18,**
　　45; DAM POET
See also CA 81-84; CANR 21; CDBLB 1960
　　to Present; DLB 40; MTCW
Hill, George Roy 1921-　　　　**CLC 26**
See also CA 110; 122
Hill, John
See Koontz, Dean R(ay)
Hill, Susan (Elizabeth) 1942-　　**CLC 4, 113;**
　　DAB; DAM MST, NOV
See also CA 33-36R; CANR 29, 69; DLB 14,
　　139; MTCW
Hillerman, Tony 1925- **CLC 62; DAM POP**

See Hostos (y Bonilla), Eugenio Maria de
Hostos, Eugenio Maria
  See Hostos (y Bonilla), Eugenio Maria de
Hostos (y Bonilla), Eugenio Maria de 1839-1903
    TCLC 24
  See also CA 123; 131; HW
Houdini
  See Lovecraft, H(oward) P(hillips)
Hougan, Carolyn 1943-   **CLC 34**
  See also CA 139
Household, Geoffrey (Edward West) 1900-1988
    CLC 11
  See also CA 77-80; 126; CANR 58; DLB 87;
    SATA 14; SATA-Obit 59
Housman, A(lfred) E(dward) 1859-1936
    TCLC 1, 10; DA; DAB; DAC; DAM MST,
    POET; PC 2; WLCS
  See also CA 104; 125; DLB 19; MTCW
Housman, Laurence 1865-1959   **TCLC 7**
  See also CA 106; 155; DLB 10; SATA 25
Howard, Elizabeth Jane 1923-   **CLC 7, 29**
  See also CA 5-8R; CANR 8, 62
Howard, Maureen 1930-   **CLC 5, 14, 46**
  See also CA 53-56; CANR 31; DLBY 83; INT
    CANR-31; MTCW
Howard, Richard 1929-   **CLC 7, 10, 47**
  See also AITN 1; CA 85-88; CANR 25; DLB 5;
    INT CANR-25
Howard, Robert E(rvin) 1906-1936 **TCLC 8**
  See also CA 105; 157
Howard, Warren F.
  See Pohl, Frederik
Howe, Fanny 1940-   **CLC 47**
  See also CA 117; CAAS 27; SATA-Brief 52
Howe, Irving 1920-1993   **CLC 85**
  See also CA 9-12R; 141; CANR 21, 50; DLB
    67; MTCW
Howe, Julia Ward 1819-1910   **TCLC 21**
  See also CA 117; DLB 1, 189
Howe, Susan 1937-   **CLC 72**
  See also CA 160; DLB 120
Howe, Tina 1937-   **CLC 48**
  See also CA 109
Howell, James 1594(?)-1666   **LC 13**
  See also DLB 151
Howells, W. D.
  See Howells, William Dean
Howells, William D.
  See Howells, William Dean
Howells, William Dean 1837-1920 **TCLC 7, 17,**
    41
  See also CA 104; 134; CDALB 1865-1917;
    DLB 12, 64, 74, 79, 189
Howes, Barbara 1914-1996   **CLC 15**
  See also CA 9-12R; 151; CAAS 3; CANR 53;
    SATA 5
Hrabal, Bohumil 1914-1997   **CLC 13, 67**
  See also CA 106; 156; CAAS 12; CANR 57
Hsun, Lu
  See Lu Hsun
Hubbard, L(afayette) Ron(ald) 1911-1986
    CLC 43; DAM POP
  See also CA 77-80; 118; CANR 52
Huch, Ricarda (Octavia) 1864-1947 **TCLC 13**
  See also CA 111; DLB 66
Huddle, David 1942-   **CLC 49**
  See also CA 57-60; CAAS 20; DLB 130
Hudson, Jeffrey
  See Crichton, (John) Michael
Hudson, W(illiam) H(enry) 1841-1922 **TCLC**
    29
  See also CA 115; DLB 98, 153, 174; SATA 35
Hueffer, Ford Madox

See Ford, Ford Madox
Hughart, Barry 1934-   **CLC 39**
  See also CA 137
Hughes, Colin
  See Creasey, John
Hughes, David (John) 1930-   **CLC 48**
  See also CA 116; 129; DLB 14
Hughes, Edward James
  See Hughes, Ted
  See also DAM MST, POET
Hughes, (James) Langston 1902-1967 **CLC 1,**
    5, 10, 15, 35, 44, 108; BLC 2; DA; DAB;
    DAC; DAM DRAM, MST, MULT, POET;
    DC 3; PC 1; SSC 6; WLC
  See also AAYA 12; BW 1; CA 1-4R; 25-28R;
    CANR 1, 34; CDALB 1929-1941; CLR 17;
    DLB 4, 7, 48, 51, 86; JRDA; MAICYA;
    MTCW; SATA 4, 33
Hughes, Richard (Arthur Warren) 1900-1976
    CLC 1, 11; DAM NOV
  See also CA 5-8R; 65-68; CANR 4; DLB 15,
    161; MTCW; SATA 8; SATA-Obit 25
Hughes, Ted 1930- **CLC 2, 4, 9, 14, 37; DAB;**
    DAC; PC 7
  See also Hughes, Edward James
  See also CA 1-4R; CANR 1, 33, 66; CLR 3;
    DLB 40, 161; MAICYA; MTCW; SATA 49;
    SATA-Brief 27
Hugo, Richard F(ranklin) 1923-1982 **CLC 6,**
    18, 32; DAM POET
  See also CA 49-52; 108; CANR 3; DLB 5
Hugo, Victor (Marie) 1802-1885 **NCLC 3, 10,**
    21; DA; DAB; DAC; DAM DRAM, MST,
    NOV, POET; PC 17; WLC
  See also DLB 119, 192; SATA 47
Huidobro, Vicente
  See Huidobro Fernandez, Vicente Garcia
Huidobro Fernandez, Vicente Garcia 1893-
    1948   **TCLC 31**
  See also CA 131; HW
Hulme, Keri 1947-   **CLC 39**
  See also CA 125; CANR 69; INT 125
Hulme, T(homas) E(rnest) 1883-1917 **TCLC**
    21
  See also CA 117; DLB 19
Hume, David 1711-1776   **LC 7**
  See also DLB 104
Humphrey, William 1924-1997   **CLC 45**
  See also CA 77-80; 160; CANR 68; DLB 6
Humphreys, Emyr Owen 1919-   **CLC 47**
  See also CA 5-8R; CANR 3, 24; DLB 15
Humphreys, Josephine 1945-   **CLC 34, 57**
  See also CA 121; 127; INT 127
Huneker, James Gibbons 1857-1921 **TCLC 65**
  See also DLB 71
Hungerford, Pixie
  See Brinsmead, H(esba) F(ay)
Hunt, E(verette) Howard, (Jr.) 1918- **CLC 3**
  See also AITN 1; CA 45-48; CANR 2, 47
Hunt, Kyle
  See Creasey, John
Hunt, (James Henry) Leigh 1784-1859 **NCLC**
    70; DAM POET
  See also DLB 96, 110, 144
Hunt, (James Henry) Leigh 1784-1859 **NCLC**
    1; DAM POET
Hunt, Marsha 1946-   **CLC 70**
  See also BW 2; CA 143
Hunt, Violet 1866(?)-1942   **TCLC 53**
  See also DLB 162, 197
Hunter, E. Waldo
  See Sturgeon, Theodore (Hamilton)
Hunter, Evan 1926- **CLC 11, 31; DAM POP**

  See also CA 5-8R; CANR 5, 38, 62; DLBY 82;
    INT CANR-5; MTCW; SATA 25
Hunter, Kristin (Eggleston) 1931-   **CLC 35**
  See also AITN 1; BW 1; CA 13-16R; CANR
    13; CLR 3; DLB 33; INT CANR-13;
    MAICYA; SAAS 10; SATA 12
Hunter, Mollie 1922-   **CLC 21**
  See also McIlwraith, Maureen Mollie Hunter
  See also AAYA 13; CANR 37; CLR 25; DLB
    161; JRDA; MAICYA; SAAS 7; SATA 54
Hunter, Robert (?)-1734   **LC 7**
Hurston, Zora Neale 1903-1960 **CLC 7, 30, 61;**
    BLC 2; DA; DAC; DAM MST, MULT,
    NOV; SSC 4; WLCS
  See also AAYA 15; BW 1; CA 85-88; CANR
    61; DLB 51, 86; MTCW
Huston, John (Marcellus) 1906-1987 **CLC 20**
  See also CA 73-76; 123; CANR 34; DLB 26
Hustvedt, Siri 1955-   **CLC 76**
  See also CA 137
Hutten, Ulrich von 1488-1523   **LC 16**
  See also DLB 179
Huxley, Aldous (Leonard) 1894-1963 **CLC 1,**
    3, 4, 5, 8, 11, 18, 35, 79; DA; DAB; DAC;
    DAM MST, NOV; WLC
  See also AAYA 11; CA 85-88; CANR 44;
    CDBLB 1914-1945; DLB 36, 100, 162, 195;
    MTCW; SATA 63
Huxley, T(homas) H(enry) 1825-1895 **NCLC**
    67
  See also DLB 57
Huysmans, Joris-Karl 1848-1907 **TCLC 7, 69**
  See also CA 104; 165; DLB 123
Hwang, David Henry 1957- **CLC 55; DAM**
    DRAM; DC 4
  See also CA 127; 132; INT 132
Hyde, Anthony 1946-   **CLC 42**
  See also CA 136
Hyde, Margaret O(ldroyd) 1917-   **CLC 21**
  See also CA 1-4R; CANR 1, 36; CLR 23; JRDA;
    MAICYA; SAAS 8; SATA 1, 42, 76
Hynes, James 1956(?)-   **CLC 65**
  See also CA 164
Ian, Janis 1951-   **CLC 21**
  See also CA 105
Ibanez, Vicente Blasco
  See Blasco Ibanez, Vicente
Ibarguengoitia, Jorge 1928-1983   **CLC 37**
  See also CA 124; 113; HW
Ibsen, Henrik (Johan) 1828-1906 **TCLC 2, 8,**
    16, 37, 52; DA; DAB; DAC; DAM DRAM,
    MST; DC 2; WLC
  See also CA 104; 141
Ibuse, Masuji 1898-1993   **CLC 22**
  See also CA 127; 141; DLB 180
Ichikawa, Kon 1915-   **CLC 20**
  See also CA 121
Idle, Eric 1943-   **CLC 21**
  See also Monty Python
  See also CA 116; CANR 35
Ignatow, David 1914-1997   **CLC 4, 7, 14, 40**
  See also CA 9-12R; 162; CAAS 3; CANR 31,
    57; DLB 5
Ihimaera, Witi 1944-   **CLC 46**
  See also CA 77-80
Ilf, Ilya   **TCLC 21**
  See also Fainzilberg, Ilya Arnoldovich
Illyes, Gyula 1902-1983   **PC 16**
  See also CA 114; 109
Immermann, Karl (Lebrecht) 1796-1840
    NCLC 4, 49
  See also DLB 133
Inchbald, Elizabeth 1753-1821   **NCLC 62**

See also DLB 39, 89
Inclan, Ramon (Maria) del Valle
See Valle-Inclan, Ramon (Maria) del
Infante, G(uillermo) Cabrera
See Cabrera Infante, G(uillermo)
Ingalls, Rachel (Holmes) 1940- **CLC 42**
See also CA 123; 127
Ingamells, Rex 1913-1955 **TCLC 35**
Inge, William (Motter) 1913-1973 **CLC 1, 8, 19; DAM DRAM**
See also CA 9-12R; CDALB 1941-1968; DLB 7; MTCW
Ingelow, Jean 1820-1897 **NCLC 39**
See also DLB 35, 163; SATA 33
Ingram, Willis J.
See Harris, Mark
Innaurato, Albert (F.) 1948(?)- **CLC 21, 60**
See also CA 115; 122; INT 122
Innes, Michael
See Stewart, J(ohn) I(nnes) M(ackintosh)
Innis, Harold Adams 1894-1952 **TCLC 77**
See also DLB 88
Ionesco, Eugene 1909-1994CLC 1, 4, 6, 9, 11, 15, 41, 86; DA; DAB; DAC; DAM DRAM, MST; WLC
See also CA 9-12R; 144; CANR 55; MTCW; SATA 7; SATA-Obit 79
Iqbal, Muhammad 1873-1938 **TCLC 28**
Ireland, Patrick
See O'Doherty, Brian
Iron, Ralph
See Schreiner, Olive (Emilie Albertina)
Irving, John (Winslow) 1942-CLC 13, 23, 38, 112; DAM NOV, POP
See also AAYA 8; BEST 89:3; CA 25-28R; CANR 28; DLB 6; DLBY 82; MTCW
Irving, Washington 1783-1859 **NCLC 2, 19; DA; DAB; DAM MST; SSC 2; WLC**
See also CDALB 1640-1865; DLB 3, 11, 30, 59, 73, 74, 186; YABC 2
Irwin, P. K.
See Page, P(atricia) K(athleen)
Isaacs, Jorge Ricardo 1837-1895 **NCLC 70**
Isaacs, Susan 1943- **CLC 32; DAM POP**
See also BEST 89:1; CA 89-92; CANR 20, 41, 65; INT CANR-20; MTCW
Isherwood, Christopher (William Bradshaw) 1904-1986 **CLC 1, 9, 11, 14, 44; DAM DRAM, NOV**
See also CA 13-16R; 117; CANR 35; DLB 15, 195; DLBY 86; MTCW
Ishiguro, Kazuo 1954- **CLC 27, 56, 59, 110; DAM NOV**
See also BEST 90:2; CA 120; CANR 49; DLB 194; MTCW
Ishikawa, Hakuhin
See Ishikawa, Takuboku
Ishikawa, Takuboku 1886(?)-1912 **TCLC 15; DAM POET; PC 10**
See also CA 113; 153
Iskander, Fazil 1929- **CLC 47**
See also CA 102
Isler, Alan (David) 1934- **CLC 91**
See also CA 156
Ivan IV 1530-1584 **LC 17**
Ivanov, Vyacheslav Ivanovich 1866-1949 **TCLC 33**
See also CA 122
Ivask, Ivar Vidrik 1927-1992 **CLC 14**
See also CA 37-40R; 139; CANR 24
Ives, Morgan
See Bradley, Marion Zimmer
J. R. S.

See Gogarty, Oliver St. John
Jabran, Kahlil
See Gibran, Kahlil
Jabran, Khalil
See Gibran, Kahlil
Jackson, Daniel
See Wingrove, David (John)
Jackson, Jesse 1908-1983 **CLC 12**
See also BW 1; CA 25-28R; 109; CANR 27; CLR 28; MAICYA; SATA 2, 29; SATA-Obit 48
Jackson, Laura (Riding) 1901-1991
See Riding, Laura
See also CA 65-68; 135; CANR 28; DLB 48
Jackson, Sam
See Trumbo, Dalton
Jackson, Sara
See Wingrove, David (John)
Jackson, Shirley 1919-1965 **CLC 11, 60, 87; DA; DAC; DAM MST; SSC 9; WLC**
See also AAYA 9; CA 1-4R; 25-28R; CANR 4, 52; CDALB 1941-1968; DLB 6; SATA 2
Jacob, (Cyprien-)Max 1876-1944 **TCLC 6**
See also CA 104
Jacobs, Harriet A(nn) 1813(?)-1897NCLC 67
Jacobs, Jim 1942- **CLC 12**
See also CA 97-100; INT 97-100
Jacobs, W(illiam) W(ymark) 1863-1943 **TCLC 22**
See also CA 121; DLB 135
Jacobsen, Jens Peter 1847-1885 **NCLC 34**
Jacobsen, Josephine 1908- **CLC 48, 102**
See also CA 33-36R; CAAS 18; CANR 23, 48
Jacobson, Dan 1929- **CLC 4, 14**
See also CA 1-4R; CANR 2, 25, 66; DLB 14; MTCW
Jacqueline
See Carpentier (y Valmont), Alejo
Jagger, Mick 1944- **CLC 17**
Jahiz, Al- c. 776-869 **CMLC 25**
Jahiz, al- c. 780-c. 869 **CMLC 25**
Jakes, John (William) 1932- **CLC 29; DAM NOV, POP**
See also BEST 89:4; CA 57-60; CANR 10, 43, 66; DLBY 83; INT CANR-10; MTCW; SATA 62
James, Andrew
See Kirkup, James
James, C(yril) L(ionel) R(obert) 1901-1989 **CLC 33; BLCS**
See also BW 2; CA 117; 125; 128; CANR 62; DLB 125; MTCW
James, Daniel (Lewis) 1911-1988
See Santiago, Danny
See also CA 125
James, Dynely
See Mayne, William (James Carter)
James, Henry Sr. 1811-1882 **NCLC 53**
James, Henry 1843-1916 **TCLC 2, 11, 24, 40, 47, 64; DA; DAB; DAC; DAM MST, NOV; SSC 8; WLC**
See also CA 104; 132; CDALB 1865-1917; DLB 12, 71, 74, 189; DLBD 13; MTCW
James, M. R.
See James, Montague (Rhodes)
See also DLB 156
James, Montague (Rhodes) 1862-1936 **T C L C 6; SSC 16**
See also CA 104
James, P. D. **CLC 18, 46**
See also White, Phyllis Dorothy James
See also BEST 90:2; CDBLB 1960 to Present; DLB 87

James, Phillip
See Moorcock, Michael (John)
James, William 1842-1910 **TCLC 15, 32**
See also CA 109
James I 1394-1437 **LC 20**
Jameson, Anna 1794-1860 **NCLC 43**
See also DLB 99, 166
Jami, Nur al-Din 'Abd al-Rahman 1414-1492 **LC 9**
Jammes, Francis 1868-1938 **TCLC 75**
Jandl, Ernst 1925- **CLC 34**
Janowitz, Tama 1957- **CLC 43; DAM POP**
See also CA 106; CANR 52
Japrisot, Sebastien 1931- **CLC 90**
Jarrell, Randall 1914-1965CLC 1, 2, 6, 9, 13, 49; DAM POET
See also CA 5-8R; 25-28R; CABS 2; CANR 6, 34; CDALB 1941-1968; CLR 6; DLB 48, 52; MAICYA; MTCW; SATA 7
Jarry, Alfred 1873-1907 **TCLC 2, 14; DAM DRAM; SSC 20**
See also CA 104; 153; DLB 192
Jarvis, E. K.
See Bloch, Robert (Albert); Ellison, Harlan (Jay); Silverberg, Robert
Jeake, Samuel, Jr.
See Aiken, Conrad (Potter)
Jean Paul 1763-1825 **NCLC 7**
Jefferies, (John) Richard 1848-1887NCLC 47
See also DLB 98, 141; SATA 16
Jeffers, (John) Robinson 1887-1962CLC 2, 3, 11, 15, 54; DA; DAC; DAM MST, POET; PC 17; WLC
See also CA 85-88; CANR 35; CDALB 1917-1929; DLB 45; MTCW
Jefferson, Janet
See Mencken, H(enry) L(ouis)
Jefferson, Thomas 1743-1826 **NCLC 11**
See also CDALB 1640-1865; DLB 31
Jeffrey, Francis 1773-1850 **NCLC 33**
See also DLB 107
Jelakowitch, Ivan
See Heijermans, Herman
Jellicoe, (Patricia) Ann 1927- **CLC 27**
See also CA 85-88; DLB 13
Jen, Gish **CLC 70**
See also Jen, Lillian
Jen, Lillian 1956(?)-
See Jen, Gish
See also CA 135
Jenkins, (John) Robin 1912- **CLC 52**
See also CA 1-4R; CANR 1; DLB 14
Jennings, Elizabeth (Joan) 1926- **CLC 5, 14**
See also CA 61-64; CAAS 5; CANR 8, 39, 66; DLB 27; MTCW; SATA 66
Jennings, Waylon 1937- **CLC 21**
Jensen, Johannes V. 1873-1950 **TCLC 41**
Jensen, Laura (Linnea) 1948- **CLC 37**
See also CA 103
Jerome, Jerome K(lapka) 1859-1927TCLC 23
See also CA 119; DLB 10, 34, 135
Jerrold, Douglas William 1803-1857NCLC 2
See also DLB 158, 159
Jewett, (Theodora) Sarah Orne 1849-1909 **TCLC 1, 22; SSC 6**
See also CA 108; 127; DLB 12, 74; SATA 15
Jewsbury, Geraldine (Endsor) 1812-1880 **NCLC 22**
See also DLB 21
Jhabvala, Ruth Prawer 1927-CLC 4, 8, 29, 94; DAB; DAM NOV
See also CA 1-4R; CANR 2, 29, 51; DLB 139, 194; INT CANR-29; MTCW

Kienzle, William X(avier) 1928- **CLC 25; DAM POP**
See also CA 93-96; CAAS 1; CANR 9, 31, 59; INT CANR-31; MTCW

Kierkegaard, Soren 1813-1855 **NCLC 34**

Killens, John Oliver 1916-1987 **CLC 10**
See also BW 2; CA 77-80; 123; CAAS 2; CANR 26; DLB 33

Killigrew, Anne 1660-1685 **LC 4**
See also DLB 131

Kim
See Simenon, Georges (Jacques Christian)

Kincaid, Jamaica 1949- **CLC 43, 68; BLC 2; DAM MULT, NOV**
See also AAYA 13; BW 2; CA 125; CANR 47, 59; DLB 157

King, Francis (Henry) 1923-**CLC 8, 53; DAM NOV**
See also CA 1-4R; CANR 1, 33; DLB 15, 139; MTCW

King, Kennedy
See Brown, George Douglas

King, Martin Luther, Jr. 1929-1968 **CLC 83; BLC 2; DA; DAB; DAC; DAM MST, MULT; WLCS**
See also BW 2; CA 25-28; CANR 27, 44; CAP 2; MTCW; SATA 14

King, Stephen (Edwin) 1947-**CLC 12, 26, 37, 61, 113; DAM NOV, POP; SSC 17**
See also AAYA 1, 17; BEST 90:1; CA 61-64; CANR 1, 30, 52; DLB 143; DLBY 80; JRDA; MTCW; SATA 9, 55

King, Steve
See King, Stephen (Edwin)

King, Thomas 1943- **CLC 89; DAC; DAM MULT**
See also CA 144; DLB 175; NNAL; SATA 96

Kingman, Lee **CLC 17**
See also Natti, (Mary) Lee
See also SAAS 3; SATA 1, 67

Kingsley, Charles 1819-1875 **NCLC 35**
See also DLB 21, 32, 163, 190; YABC 2

Kingsley, Sidney 1906-1995 **CLC 44**
See also CA 85-88; 147; DLB 7

Kingsolver, Barbara 1955-**CLC 55, 81; DAM POP**
See also AAYA 15; CA 129; 134; CANR 60; INT 134

Kingston, Maxine (Ting Ting) Hong 1940-
CLC 12, 19, 58; DAM MULT, NOV; WLCS
See also AAYA 8; CA 69-72; CANR 13, 38; DLB 173; DLBY 80; INT CANR-13; MTCW; SATA 53

Kinnell, Galway 1927- **CLC 1, 2, 3, 5, 13, 29**
See also CA 9-12R; CANR 10, 34, 66; DLB 5; DLBY 87; INT CANR-34; MTCW

Kinsella, Thomas 1928- **CLC 4, 19**
See also CA 17-20R; CANR 15; DLB 27; MTCW

Kinsella, W(illiam) P(atrick) 1935- **CLC 27, 43; DAC; DAM NOV, POP**
See also AAYA 7; CA 97-100; CAAS 7; CANR 21, 35, 66; INT CANR-21; MTCW

Kipling, (Joseph) Rudyard 1865-1936 **TCLC 8, 17; DA; DAB; DAC; DAM MST, POET; PC 3; SSC 5; WLC**
See also CA 105; 120; CANR 33; CDBLB 1890-1914; CLR 39; DLB 19, 34, 141, 156; MAICYA; MTCW; YABC 2

Kirkup, James 1918- **CLC 1**
See also CA 1-4R; CAAS 4; CANR 2; DLB 27; SATA 12

Kirkwood, James 1930(?)-1989 **CLC 9**
See also AITN 2; CA 1-4R; 128; CANR 6, 40

Kirshner, Sidney
See Kingsley, Sidney

Kis, Danilo 1935-1989 **CLC 57**
See also CA 109; 118; 129; CANR 61; DLB 181; MTCW

Kivi, Aleksis 1834-1872 **NCLC 30**

Kizer, Carolyn (Ashley) 1925-**CLC 15, 39, 80; DAM POET**
See also CA 65-68; CAAS 5; CANR 24; DLB 5, 169

Klabund 1890-1928 **TCLC 44**
See also CA 162; DLB 66

Klappert, Peter 1942- **CLC 57**
See also CA 33-36R; DLB 5

Klein, A(braham) M(oses) 1909-1972**CLC 19; DAB; DAC; DAM MST**
See also CA 101; 37-40R; DLB 68

Klein, Norma 1938-1989 **CLC 30**
See also AAYA 2; CA 41-44R; 128; CANR 15, 37; CLR 2, 19; INT CANR-15; JRDA; MAICYA; SAAS 1; SATA 7, 57

Klein, T(heodore) E(ibon) D(onald) 1947-
CLC 34
See also CA 119; CANR 44

Kleist, Heinrich von 1777-1811 **NCLC 2, 37; DAM DRAM; SSC 22**
See also DLB 90

Klima, Ivan 1931- **CLC 56; DAM NOV**
See also CA 25-28R; CANR 17, 50

Klimentov, Andrei Platonovich 1899-1951
See Platonov, Andrei
See also CA 108

Klinger, Friedrich Maximilian von 1752-1831
NCLC 1
See also DLB 94

Klingsor the Magician
See Hartmann, Sadakichi

Klopstock, Friedrich Gottlieb 1724-1803
NCLC 11
See also DLB 97

Knapp, Caroline 1959- **CLC 99**
See also CA 154

Knebel, Fletcher 1911-1993 **CLC 14**
See also AITN 1; CA 1-4R; 140; CAAS 3; CANR 1, 36; SATA 36; SATA-Obit 75

Knickerbocker, Diedrich
See Irving, Washington

Knight, Etheridge 1931-1991**CLC 40; BLC 2; DAM POET; PC 14**
See also BW 1; CA 21-24R; 133; CANR 23; DLB 41

Knight, Sarah Kemble 1666-1727 **LC 7**
See also DLB 24, 200

Knister, Raymond 1899-1932 **TCLC 56**
See also DLB 68

Knowles, John 1926- **CLC 1, 4, 10, 26; DA; DAC; DAM MST, NOV**
See also AAYA 10; CA 17-20R; CANR 40; CDALB 1968-1988; DLB 6; MTCW; SATA 8, 89

Knox, Calvin M.
See Silverberg, Robert

Knox, John c. 1505-1572 **LC 37**
See also DLB 132

Knye, Cassandra
See Disch, Thomas M(ichael)

Koch, C(hristopher) J(ohn) 1932- **CLC 42**
See also CA 127

Koch, Christopher
See Koch, C(hristopher) J(ohn)

Koch, Kenneth 1925- **CLC 5, 8, 44; DAM POET**
See also CA 1-4R; CANR 6, 36, 57; DLB 5; INT CANR-36; SATA 65

Kochanowski, Jan 1530-1584 **LC 10**

Kock, Charles Paul de 1794-1871 **NCLC 16**

Koda Shigeyuki 1867-1947
See Rohan, Koda
See also CA 121

Koestler, Arthur 1905-1983**CLC 1, 3, 6, 8, 15, 33**
See also CA 1-4R; 109; CANR 1, 33; CDBLB 1945-1960; DLBY 83; MTCW

Kogawa, Joy Nozomi 1935- **CLC 78; DAC; DAM MST, MULT**
See also CA 101; CANR 19, 62

Kohout, Pavel 1928- **CLC 13**
See also CA 45-48; CANR 3

Koizumi, Yakumo
See Hearn, (Patricio) Lafcadio (Tessima Carlos)

Kolmar, Gertrud 1894-1943 **TCLC 40**

Komunyakaa, Yusef 1947-**CLC 86, 94; BLCS**
See also CA 147; DLB 120

Konrad, George
See Konrad, Gyoergy

Konrad, Gyoergy 1933- **CLC 4, 10, 73**
See also CA 85-88

Konwicki, Tadeusz 1926- **CLC 8, 28, 54**
See also CA 101; CAAS 9; CANR 39, 59; MTCW

Koontz, Dean R(ay) 1945- **CLC 78; DAM NOV, POP**
See also AAYA 9; BEST 89:3, 90:2; CA 108; CANR 19, 36, 52; MTCW; SATA 92

Kopit, Arthur (Lee) 1937-**CLC 1, 18, 33; DAM DRAM**
See also AITN 1; CA 81-84; CABS 3; DLB 7; MTCW

Kops, Bernard 1926- **CLC 4**
See also CA 5-8R; DLB 13

Kornbluth, C(yril) M. 1923-1958 **TCLC 8**
See also CA 105; 160; DLB 8

Korolenko, V. G.
See Korolenko, Vladimir Galaktionovich

Korolenko, Vladimir
See Korolenko, Vladimir Galaktionovich

Korolenko, Vladimir G.
See Korolenko, Vladimir Galaktionovich

Korolenko, Vladimir Galaktionovich 1853-1921 **TCLC 22**
See also CA 121

Korzybski, Alfred (Habdank Skarbek) 1879-1950 **TCLC 61**
See also CA 123; 160

Kosinski, Jerzy (Nikodem) 1933-1991**CLC 1, 2, 3, 6, 10, 15, 53, 70; DAM NOV**
See also CA 17-20R; 134; CANR 9, 46; DLB 2; DLBY 82; MTCW

Kostelanetz, Richard (Cory) 1940- **CLC 28**
See also CA 13-16R; CAAS 8; CANR 38

Kostrowitzki, Wilhelm Apollinaris de 1880-1918
See Apollinaire, Guillaume
See also CA 104

Kotlowitz, Robert 1924- **CLC 4**
See also CA 33-36R; CANR 36

Kotzebue, August (Friedrich Ferdinand) von 1761-1819 **NCLC 25**
See also DLB 94

Kotzwinkle, William 1938- **CLC 5, 14, 35**
See also CA 45-48; CANR 3, 44; CLR 6; DLB 173; MAICYA; SATA 24, 70

Kowna, Stancy
See Szymborska, Wislawa

See Leimbach, Marti
See also CA 130

Leimbach, Marti   **CLC 65**
See also Leimbach, Martha

Leino, Eino   **TCLC 24**
See also Loennbohm, Armas Eino Leopold

Leiris, Michel (Julien) 1901-1990   **CLC 61**
See also CA 119; 128; 132

Leithauser, Brad 1953-   **CLC 27**
See also CA 107; CANR 27; DLB 120

Lelchuk, Alan 1938-   **CLC 5**
See also CA 45-48; CAAS 20; CANR 1

Lem, Stanislaw 1921-   **CLC 8, 15, 40**
See also CA 105; CAAS 1; CANR 32; MTCW

Lemann, Nancy 1956-   **CLC 39**
See also CA 118; 136

Lemonnier, (Antoine Louis) Camille 1844-1913
TCLC 22
See also CA 121

Lenau, Nikolaus 1802-1850   **NCLC 16**

L'Engle, Madeleine (Camp Franklin) 1918-
CLC 12; DAM POP
See also AAYA 1; AITN 2; CA 1-4R; CANR 3,
21, 39, 66; CLR 1, 14; DLB 52; JRDA;
MAICYA; MTCW; SAAS 15; SATA 1, 27,
75

Lengyel, Jozsef 1896-1975   **CLC 7**
See also CA 85-88; 57-60

Lenin 1870-1924
See Lenin, V. I.
See also CA 121

Lenin, V. I.   **TCLC 67**
See also Lenin

Lennon, John (Ono) 1940-1980   **CLC 12, 35**
See also CA 102

Lennox, Charlotte Ramsay 1729(?)-1804
NCLC 23
See also DLB 39

Lentricchia, Frank (Jr.) 1940-   **CLC 34**
See also CA 25-28R; CANR 19

Lenz, Siegfried 1926-   **CLC 27**
See also CA 89-92; DLB 75

Leonard, Elmore (John, Jr.) 1925-**CLC 28, 34,
71; DAM POP**
See also AAYA 22; AITN 1; BEST 89:1, 90:4;
CA 81-84; CANR 12, 28, 53; DLB 173; INT
CANR-28; MTCW

Leonard, Hugh   **CLC 19**
See also Byrne, John Keyes
See also DLB 13

Leonov, Leonid (Maximovich) 1899-1994
CLC 92; DAM NOV
See also CA 129; MTCW

Leopardi, (Conte) Giacomo 1798-1837**NCLC
22**

Le Reveler
See Artaud, Antonin (Marie Joseph)

Lerman, Eleanor 1952-   **CLC 9**
See also CA 85-88; CANR 69

Lerman, Rhoda 1936-   **CLC 56**
See also CA 49-52

Lermontov, Mikhail Yuryevich 1814-1841
NCLC 47; PC 18

Leroux, Gaston 1868-1927   **TCLC 25**
See also CA 108; 136; CANR 69; SATA 65

Lesage, Alain-Rene 1668-1747   **LC 28**

Leskov, Nikolai (Semyonovich) 1831-1895
NCLC 25

Lessing, Doris (May) 1919-**CLC 1, 2, 3, 6, 10,
15, 22, 40, 94; DA; DAB; DAC; DAM MST,
NOV; SSC 6; WLCS**
See also CA 9-12R; CAAS 14; CANR 33, 54;
CDBLB 1960 to Present; DLB 15, 139;

DLBY 85, MTCW

Lessing, Gotthold Ephraim 1729-1781   **LC 8**
See also DLB 97

Lester, Richard 1932-   **CLC 20**

Lever, Charles (James) 1806-1872 **NCLC 23**
See also DLB 21

Leverson, Ada 1865(?)-1936(?)   **TCLC 18**
See also Elaine
See also CA 117; DLB 153

Levertov, Denise 1923-1997 **CLC 1, 2, 3, 5, 8,
15, 28, 66; DAM POET; PC 11**
See also CA 1-4R; 163; CAAS 19; CANR 3,
29, 50; DLB 5, 165; INT CANR-29; MTCW

Levi, Jonathan   **CLC 76**

Levi, Peter (Chad Tigar) 1931-   **CLC 41**
See also CA 5-8R; CANR 34; DLB 40

Levi, Primo 1919-1987   **CLC 37, 50; SSC 12**
See also CA 13-16R; 122; CANR 12, 33, 61;
DLB 177; MTCW

Levin, Ira 1929-   **CLC 3, 6; DAM POP**
See also CA 21-24R; CANR 17, 44; MTCW;
SATA 66

Levin, Meyer 1905-1981   **CLC 7; DAM POP**
See also AITN 1; CA 9-12R; 104; CANR 15;
DLB 9, 28; DLBY 81; SATA 21; SATA-Obit
27

Levine, Norman 1924-   **CLC 54**
See also CA 73-76; CAAS 23; CANR 14; DLB
88

Levine, Philip 1928-   **CLC 2, 4, 5, 9, 14, 33;
DAM POET; PC 22**
See also CA 9-12R; CANR 9, 37, 52; DLB 5

Levinson, Deirdre 1931-   **CLC 49**
See also CA 73-76

Levi-Strauss, Claude 1908-   **CLC 38**
See also CA 1-4R; CANR 6, 32, 57; MTCW

Levitin, Sonia (Wolff) 1934-   **CLC 17**
See also AAYA 13; CA 29-32R; CANR 14, 32;
JRDA; MAICYA; SAAS 2; SATA 4, 68

Levon, O. U.
See Kesey, Ken (Elton)

Levy, Amy 1861-1889   **NCLC 59**
See also DLB 156

Lewes, George Henry 1817-1878   **NCLC 25**
See also DLB 55, 144

Lewis, Alun 1915-1944   **TCLC 3**
See also CA 104; DLB 20, 162

Lewis, C. Day
See Day Lewis, C(ecil)

Lewis, C(live) S(taples) 1898-1963**CLC 1, 3, 6,
14, 27; DA; DAB; DAC; DAM MST, NOV,
POP; WLC**
See also AAYA 3; CA 81-84; CANR 33;
CDBLB 1945-1960; CLR 3, 27; DLB 15,
100, 160; JRDA; MAICYA; MTCW; SATA
13

Lewis, Janet 1899-   **CLC 41**
See also Winters, Janet Lewis
See also CA 9-12R; CANR 29, 63; CAP 1;
DLBY 87

Lewis, Matthew Gregory 1775-1818**NCLC 11,
62**
See also DLB 39, 158, 178

Lewis, (Harry) Sinclair 1885-1951   **TCLC 4,
13, 23, 39; DA; DAB; DAC; DAM MST,
NOV; WLC**
See also CA 104; 133; CDALB 1917-1929;
DLB 9, 102; DLBD 1; MTCW

Lewis, (Percy) Wyndham 1882(?)-1957**TCLC
2, 9**
See also CA 104; 157; DLB 15

Lewisohn, Ludwig 1883-1955   **TCLC 19**
See also CA 107; DLB 4, 9, 28, 102

Lewton, Val 1904-1951   **TCLC 76**

Leyner, Mark 1956-   **CLC 92**
See also CA 110; CANR 28, 53

Lezama Lima, Jose 1910-1976**CLC 4, 10, 101;
DAM MULT**
See also CA 77-80; DLB 113; HW

L'Heureux, John (Clarke) 1934-   **CLC 52**
See also CA 13-16R; CANR 23, 45

Liddell, C. H.
See Kuttner, Henry

Lie, Jonas (Lauritz Idemil) 1833-1908(?)
TCLC 5
See also CA 115

Lieber, Joel 1937-1971   **CLC 6**
See also CA 73-76; 29-32R

Lieber, Stanley Martin
See Lee, Stan

Lieberman, Laurence (James) 1935- **CLC 4,
36**
See also CA 17-20R; CANR 8, 36

Lieh Tzu fl. 7th cent. B.C.-5th cent. B.C.
CMLC 27

Lieksman, Anders
See Haavikko, Paavo Juhani

Li Fei-kan 1904-
See Pa Chin
See also CA 105

Lifton, Robert Jay 1926-   **CLC 67**
See also CA 17-20R; CANR 27; INT CANR-
27; SATA 66

Lightfoot, Gordon 1938-   **CLC 26**
See also CA 109

Lightman, Alan P(aige) 1948-   **CLC 81**
See also CA 141; CANR 63

Ligotti, Thomas (Robert) 1953-**CLC 44; SSC
16**
See also CA 123; CANR 49

Li Ho 791-817   **PC 13**

Liliencron, (Friedrich Adolf Axel) Detlev von
1844-1909   **TCLC 18**
See also CA 117

Lilly, William 1602-1681   **LC 27**

Lima, Jose Lezama
See Lezama Lima, Jose

Lima Barreto, Afonso Henrique de 1881-1922
TCLC 23
See also CA 117

Limonov, Edward 1944-   **CLC 67**
See also CA 137

Lin, Frank
See Atherton, Gertrude (Franklin Horn)

Lincoln, Abraham 1809-1865   **NCLC 18**

Lind, Jakov   **CLC 1, 2, 4, 27, 82**
See also Landwirth, Heinz
See also CAAS 4

Lindbergh, Anne (Spencer) Morrow 1906-
CLC 82; DAM NOV
See also CA 17-20R; CANR 16; MTCW; SATA
33

Lindsay, David 1878-1945   **TCLC 15**
See also CA 113

Lindsay, (Nicholas) Vachel 1879-1931 **TCLC
17; DA; DAC; DAM MST, POET; WLC**
See also CA 114; 135; CDALB 1865-1917;
DLB 54; SATA 40

Linke-Poot
See Doeblin, Alfred

Linney, Romulus 1930-   **CLC 51**
See also CA 1-4R; CANR 40, 44

Linton, Eliza Lynn 1822-1898   **NCLC 41**
See also DLB 18

Li Po 701-763   **CMLC 2**

Lipsius, Justus 1547-1606   **LC 16**

Mallet-Joris, Francoise 1930-   **CLC 11**
  See also CA 65-68; CANR 17; DLB 83
Malley, Ern
  See McAuley, James Phillip
Mallowan, Agatha Christie
  See Christie, Agatha (Mary Clarissa)
Maloff, Saul 1922-   **CLC 5**
  See also CA 33-36R
Malone, Louis
  See MacNeice, (Frederick) Louis
Malone, Michael (Christopher) 1942-**CLC 43**
  See also CA 77-80; CANR 14, 32, 57
Malory, (Sir) Thomas 1410(?)-1471(?) **LC 11;**
  DA; DAB; DAC; DAM MST; WLCS
  See also CDBLB Before 1660; DLB 146; SATA
  59; SATA-Brief 33
Malouf, (George Joseph) David 1934-**CLC 28,**
  86
  See also CA 124; CANR 50
Malraux, (Georges-)Andre 1901-1976**CLC 1,**
  4, 9, 13, 15, 57; DAM NOV
  See also CA 21-22; 69-72; CANR 34, 58; CAP
  2; DLB 72; MTCW
Malzberg, Barry N(athaniel) 1939-   **CLC 7**
  See also CA 61-64; CAAS 4; CANR 16; DLB 8
Mamet, David (Alan) 1947-**CLC 9, 15, 34, 46,**
  91; DAM DRAM; DC 4
  See also AAYA 3; CA 81-84; CABS 3; CANR
  15, 41, 67; DLB 7; MTCW
Mamoulian, Rouben (Zachary) 1897-1987
  CLC 16
  See also CA 25-28R; 124
Mandelstam, Osip (Emilievich) 1891(?)-1938(?)
  TCLC 2, 6; PC 14
  See also CA 104; 150
Mander, (Mary) Jane 1877-1949   **TCLC 31**
  See also CA 162
Mandeville, John fl. 1350-   **CMLC 19**
  See also DLB 146
Mandiargues, Andre Pieyre de   **CLC 41**
  See also Pieyre de Mandiargues, Andre
  See also DLB 83
Mandrake, Ethel Belle
  See Thurman, Wallace (Henry)
Mangan, James Clarence 1803-1849**NCLC 27**
Maniere, J.-E.
  See Giraudoux, (Hippolyte) Jean
Manley, (Mary) Delariviere 1672(?)-1724 **L C**
  1
  See also DLB 39, 80
Mann, Abel
  See Creasey, John
Mann, Emily 1952-   **DC 7**
  See also CA 130; CANR 55
Mann, (Luiz) Heinrich 1871-1950   **TCLC 9**
  See also CA 106; 164; DLB 66
Mann, (Paul) Thomas 1875-1955 **TCLC 2, 8,**
  14, 21, 35, 44, 60; DA; DAB; DAC; DAM
  MST, NOV; SSC 5; WLC
  See also CA 104; 128; DLB 66; MTCW
Mannheim, Karl 1893-1947   **TCLC 65**
Manning, David
  See Faust, Frederick (Schiller)
Manning, Frederic 1887(?)-1935   **TCLC 25**
  See also CA 124
Manning, Olivia 1915-1980   **CLC 5, 19**
  See also CA 5-8R; 101; CANR 29; MTCW
Mano, D. Keith 1942-   **CLC 2, 10**
  See also CA 25-28R; CAAS 6; CANR 26, 57;
  DLB 6
Mansfield, KatherineTCLC 2, 8, 39; DAB; SSC
  9, 23; WLC
  See also Beauchamp, Kathleen Mansfield

  See also DLB 162
Manso, Peter 1940-   **CLC 39**
  See also CA 29-32R; CANR 44
Mantecon, Juan Jimenez
  See Jimenez (Mantecon), Juan Ramon
Manton, Peter
  See Creasey, John
Man Without a Spleen, A
  See Chekhov, Anton (Pavlovich)
Manzoni, Alessandro 1785-1873   **NCLC 29**
Mapu, Abraham (ben Jekutiel) 1808-1867
  NCLC 18
Mara, Sally
  See Queneau, Raymond
Marat, Jean Paul 1743-1793   **LC 10**
Marcel, Gabriel Honore 1889-1973 **CLC 15**
  See also CA 102; 45-48; MTCW
Marchbanks, Samuel
  See Davies, (William) Robertson
Marchi, Giacomo
  See Bassani, Giorgio
Margulies, Donald   **CLC 76**
Marie de France c. 12th cent. - **CMLC 8; PC**
  22
Marie de l'Incarnation 1599-1672   **LC 10**
Marier, Captain Victor
  See Griffith, D(avid Lewelyn) W(ark)
Mariner, Scott
  See Pohl, Frederik
Marinetti, Filippo Tommaso 1876-1944**TCLC**
  10
  See also CA 107; DLB 114
Marivaux, Pierre Carlet de Chamblain de 1688-
  1763   **LC 4; DC 7**
Markandaya, Kamala   **CLC 8, 38**
  See also Taylor, Kamala (Purnaiya)
Markfield, Wallace 1926-   **CLC 8**
  See also CA 69-72; CAAS 3; DLB 2, 28
Markham, Edwin 1852-1940   **TCLC 47**
  See also CA 160; DLB 54, 186
Markham, Robert
  See Amis, Kingsley (William)
Marks, J
  See Highwater, Jamake (Mamake)
Marks-Highwater, J
  See Highwater, Jamake (Mamake)
Markson, David M(errill) 1927-   **CLC 67**
  See also CA 49-52; CANR 1
Marley, Bob   **CLC 17**
  See also Marley, Robert Nesta
Marley, Robert Nesta 1945-1981
  See Marley, Bob
  See also CA 107; 103
Marlowe, Christopher 1564-1593**LC 22; DA;**
  DAB; DAC; DAM DRAM, MST; DC 1;
  WLC
  See also CDBLB Before 1660; DLB 62
Marlowe, Stephen 1928-
  See Queen, Ellery
  See also CA 13-16R; CANR 6, 55
Marmontel, Jean-Francois 1723-1799   **LC 2**
Marquand, John P(hillips) 1893-1960**CLC 2,**
  10
  See also CA 85-88; DLB 9, 102
Marques, Rene 1919-1979   **CLC 96; DAM**
  MULT; HLC
  See also CA 97-100; 85-88; DLB 113; HW
Marquez, Gabriel (Jose) Garcia
  See Garcia Marquez, Gabriel (Jose)
Marquis, Don(ald Robert Perry) 1878-1937
  TCLC 7
  See also CA 104; 166; DLB 11, 25
Marric, J. J.

  See Creasey, John
Marryat, Frederick 1792-1848   **NCLC 3**
  See also DLB 21, 163
Marsden, James
  See Creasey, John
Marsh, (Edith) Ngaio 1899-1982   **CLC 7, 53;**
  DAM POP
  See also CA 9-12R; CANR 6, 58; DLB 77;
  MTCW
Marshall, Garry 1934-   **CLC 17**
  See also AAYA 3; CA 111; SATA 60
Marshall, Paule 1929-   **CLC 27, 72; BLC 3;**
  DAM MULT; SSC 3
  See also BW 2; CA 77-80; CANR 25; DLB 157;
  MTCW
Marsten, Richard
  See Hunter, Evan
Marston, John 1576-1634**LC 33; DAM DRAM**
  See also DLB 58, 172
Martha, Henry
  See Harris, Mark
Marti, Jose 1853-1895**NCLC 63; DAM MULT;**
  HLC
Martial c. 40-c. 104   **PC 10**
Martin, Ken
  See Hubbard, L(afayette) Ron(ald)
Martin, Richard
  See Creasey, John
Martin, Steve 1945-   **CLC 30**
  See also CA 97-100; CANR 30; MTCW
Martin, Valerie 1948-   **CLC 89**
  See also BEST 90:2; CA 85-88; CANR 49
Martin, Violet Florence 1862-1915 **TCLC 51**
Martin, Webber
  See Silverberg, Robert
Martindale, Patrick Victor
  See White, Patrick (Victor Martindale)
Martin du Gard, Roger 1881-1958 **TCLC 24**
  See also CA 118; DLB 65
Martineau, Harriet 1802-1876   **NCLC 26**
  See also DLB 21, 55, 159, 163, 166, 190; YABC
  2
Martines, Julia
  See O'Faolain, Julia
Martinez, Enrique Gonzalez
  See Gonzalez Martinez, Enrique
Martinez, Jacinto Benavente y
  See Benavente (y Martinez), Jacinto
Martinez Ruiz, Jose 1873-1967
  See Azorin; Ruiz, Jose Martinez
  See also CA 93-96; HW
Martinez Sierra, Gregorio 1881-1947**TCLC 6**
  See also CA 115
Martinez Sierra, Maria (de la O'LeJarraga)
  1874-1974   **TCLC 6**
  See also CA 115
Martinsen, Martin
  See Follett, Ken(neth Martin)
Martinson, Harry (Edmund) 1904-1978 **C L C**
  14
  See also CA 77-80; CANR 34
Marut, Ret
  See Traven, B.
Marut, Robert
  See Traven, B.
Marvell, Andrew 1621-1678   **LC 4, 43; DA;**
  DAB; DAC; DAM MST, POET; PC 10;
  WLC
  See also CDBLB 1660-1789; DLB 131
Marx, Karl (Heinrich) 1818-1883   **NCLC 17**
  See also DLB 129
Masaoka Shiki   **TCLC 18**
  See also Masaoka Tsunenori

Moreas, Jean   TCLC 18
See also Papadiamantopoulos, Johannes

Morgan, Berry 1919-   CLC 6
See also CA 49-52; DLB 6

Morgan, Claire
See Highsmith, (Mary) Patricia

Morgan, Edwin (George) 1920-   CLC 31
See also CA 5-8R; CANR 3, 43; DLB 27

Morgan, (George) Frederick 1922-   CLC 23
See also CA 17-20R; CANR 21

Morgan, Harriet
See Mencken, H(enry) L(ouis)

Morgan, Jane
See Cooper, James Fenimore

Morgan, Janet 1945-   CLC 39
See also CA 65-68

Morgan, Lady 1776(?)-1859   NCLC 29
See also DLB 116, 158

Morgan, Robin (Evonne) 1941-   CLC 2
See also CA 69-72; CANR 29, 68; MTCW;
SATA 80

Morgan, Scott
See Kuttner, Henry

Morgan, Seth 1949(?)-1990   CLC 65
See also CA 132

Morgenstern, Christian 1871-1914 TCLC 8
See also CA 105

Morgenstern, S.
See Goldman, William (W.)

Moricz, Zsigmond 1879-1942   TCLC 33
See also CA 165

Morike, Eduard (Friedrich) 1804-1875NCLC
10
See also DLB 133

Moritz, Karl Philipp 1756-1793   LC 2
See also DLB 94

Morland, Peter Henry
See Faust, Frederick (Schiller)

Morren, Theophil
See Hofmannsthal, Hugo von

Morris, Bill 1952-   CLC 76

Morris, Julian
See West, Morris L(anglo)

Morris, Steveland Judkins 1950(?)-
See Wonder, Stevie
See also CA 111

Morris, William 1834-1896   NCLC 4
See also CDBLB 1832-1890; DLB 18, 35, 57,
156, 178, 184

Morris, Wright 1910-   CLC 1, 3, 7, 18, 37
See also CA 9-12R; CANR 21; DLB 2; DLBY
81; MTCW

Morrison, Arthur 1863-1945   TCLC 72
See also CA 120; 157; DLB 70, 135, 197

Morrison, Chloe Anthony Wofford
See Morrison, Toni

Morrison, James Douglas 1943-1971
See Morrison, Jim
See also CA 73-76; CANR 40

Morrison, Jim   CLC 17
See also Morrison, James Douglas

Morrison, Toni 1931-CLC 4, 10, 22, 55, 81, 87;
BLC 3; DA; DAB; DAC; DAM MST,
MULT, NOV, POP
See also AAYA 1, 22; BW 2; CA 29-32R;
CANR 27, 42, 67; CDALB 1968-1988; DLB
6, 33, 143; DLBY 81; MTCW; SATA 57

Morrison, Van 1945-   CLC 21
See also CA 116

Morrissy, Mary 1958-   CLC 99

Mortimer, John (Clifford) 1923-CLC 28, 43;
DAM DRAM, POP
See also CA 13-16R; CANR 21, 69; CDBLB

1960 to Present; DLB 13; INT CANR-21;
MTCW

Mortimer, Penelope (Ruth) 1918-   CLC 5
See also CA 57-60; CANR 45

Morton, Anthony
See Creasey, John

Mosca, Gaetano 1858-1941   TCLC 75

Mosher, Howard Frank 1943-   CLC 62
See also CA 139; CANR 65

Mosley, Nicholas 1923-   CLC 43, 70
See also CA 69-72; CANR 41, 60; DLB 14

Mosley, Walter 1952- CLC 97; BLCS; DAM
MULT, POP
See also AAYA 17; BW 2; CA 142; CANR 57

Moss, Howard 1922-1987 CLC 7, 14, 45, 50;
DAM POET
See also CA 1-4R; 123; CANR 1, 44; DLB 5

Mossgiel, Rab
See Burns, Robert

Motion, Andrew (Peter) 1952-   CLC 47
See also CA 146; DLB 40

Motley, Willard (Francis) 1909-1965 CLC 18
See also BW 1; CA 117; 106; DLB 76, 143

Motoori, Norinaga 1730-1801   NCLC 45

Mott, Michael (Charles Alston) 1930-CLC 15,
34
See also CA 5-8R; CAAS 7; CANR 7, 29

Mountain Wolf Woman 1884-1960   CLC 92
See also CA 144; NNAL

Moure, Erin 1955-   CLC 88
See also CA 113; DLB 60

Mowat, Farley (McGill) 1921-CLC 26; DAC;
DAM MST
See also AAYA 1; CA 1-4R; CANR 4, 24, 42,
68; CLR 20; DLB 68; INT CANAR-24;
JRDA; MAICYA; MTCW; SATA 3, 55

Moyers, Bill 1934-   CLC 74
See also AITN 2; CA 61-64; CANR 31, 52

Mphahlele, Es'kia
See Mphahlele, Ezekiel
See also DLB 125

Mphahlele, Ezekiel 1919-1983 CLC 25; BLC
3; DAM MULT
See also Mphahlele, Es'kia
See also BW 2; CA 81-84; CANR 26

Mqhayi, S(amuel) E(dward) K(rune Loliwe)
1875-1945TCLC 25; BLC 3; DAM MULT
See also CA 153

Mrozek, Slawomir 1930-   CLC 3, 13
See also CA 13-16R; CAAS 10; CANR 29;
MTCW

Mrs. Belloc-Lowndes
See Lowndes, Marie Adelaide (Belloc)

Mtwa, Percy (?)-   CLC 47

Mueller, Lisel 1924-   CLC 13, 51
See also CA 93-96; DLB 105

Muir, Edwin 1887-1959   TCLC 2
See also CA 104; DLB 20, 100, 191

Muir, John 1838-1914   TCLC 28
See also CA 165; DLB 186

Mujica Lainez, Manuel 1910-1984 CLC 31
See also Lainez, Manuel Mujica
See also CA 81-84; 112; CANR 32; HW

Mukherjee, Bharati 1940-CLC 53; DAM NOV
See also BEST 89:2; CA 107; CANR 45; DLB
60; MTCW

Muldoon, Paul 1951-CLC 32, 72; DAM POET
See also CA 113; 129; CANR 52; DLB 40; INT
129

Mulisch, Harry 1927-   CLC 42
See also CA 9-12R; CANR 6, 26, 56

Mull, Martin 1943-   CLC 17
See also CA 105

Mulock, Dinah Maria
See Craik, Dinah Maria (Mulock)

Munford, Robert 1737(?)-1783   LC 5
See also DLB 31

Mungo, Raymond 1946-   CLC 72
See also CA 49-52; CANR 2

Munro, Alice 1931-   CLC 6, 10, 19, 50, 95;
DAC; DAM MST, NOV; SSC 3; WLCS
See also AITN 2; CA 33-36R; CANR 33, 53;
DLB 53; MTCW; SATA 29

Munro, H(ector) H(ugh) 1870-1916
See Saki
See also CA 104; 130; CDBLB 1890-1914; DA;
DAB; DAC; DAM MST, NOV; DLB 34, 162;
MTCW; WLC

Murasaki, Lady   CMLC 1

Murdoch, (Jean) Iris 1919-CLC 1, 2, 3, 4, 6, 8,
11, 15, 22, 31, 51; DAB; DAC; DAM MST,
NOV
See also CA 13-16R; CANR 8, 43, 68; CDBLB
1960 to Present; DLB 14, 194; INT CANR-
8; MTCW

Murfree, Mary Noailles 1850-1922   SSC 22
See also CA 122; DLB 12, 74

Murnau, Friedrich Wilhelm
See Plumpe, Friedrich Wilhelm

Murphy, Richard 1927-   CLC 41
See also CA 29-32R; DLB 40

Murphy, Sylvia 1937-   CLC 34
See also CA 121

Murphy, Thomas (Bernard) 1935- CLC 51
See also CA 101

Murray, Albert L. 1916-   CLC 73
See also BW 2; CA 49-52; CANR 26, 52; DLB
38

Murray, Judith Sargent 1751-1820 NCLC 63
See also DLB 37, 200

Murray, Les(lie) A(llan) 1938-CLC 40; DAM
POET
See also CA 21-24R; CANR 11, 27, 56

Murry, J. Middleton
See Murry, John Middleton

Murry, John Middleton 1889-1957 TCLC 16
See also CA 118; DLB 149

Musgrave, Susan 1951-   CLC 13, 54
See also CA 69-72; CANR 45

Musil, Robert (Edler von) 1880-1942 TCLC
12, 68; SSC 18
See also CA 109; CANR 55; DLB 81, 124

Muske, Carol 1945-   CLC 90
See also Muske-Dukes, Carol (Anne)

Muske-Dukes, Carol (Anne) 1945-
See Muske, Carol
See also CA 65-68; CANR 32

Musset, (Louis Charles) Alfred de 1810-1857
NCLC 7
See also DLB 192

My Brother's Brother
See Chekhov, Anton (Pavlovich)

Myers, L(eopold) H(amilton) 1881-1944
TCLC 59
See also CA 157; DLB 15

Myers, Walter Dean 1937- CLC 35; BLC 3;
DAM MULT, NOV
See also AAYA 4, 23; BW 2; CA 33-36R;
CANR 20, 42, 67; CLR 4, 16, 35; DLB 33;
INT CANR-20; JRDA; MAICYA; SAAS 2;
SATA 41, 71; SATA-Brief 27

Myers, Walter M.
See Myers, Walter Dean

Myles, Symon
See Follett, Ken(neth Martin)

Nabokov, Vladimir (Vladimirovich) 1899-1977

See also CA 104; 153

Pirsig, Robert M(aynard) 1928-**CLC 4, 6, 73; DAM POP**
See also CA 53-56; CANR 42; MTCW; SATA 39

Pisarev, Dmitry Ivanovich 1840-1868 **NCLC 25**

Pix, Mary (Griffith) 1666-1709 **LC 8**
See also DLB 80

Pixerecourt, (Rene Charles) Guilbert de 1773-1844 **NCLC 39**
See also DLB 192

Plaatje, Sol(omon) T(shekisho) 1876-1932 **TCLC 73; BLCS**
See also BW 2; CA 141

Plaidy, Jean
See Hibbert, Eleanor Alice Burford

Planche, James Robinson 1796-1880**NCLC 42**

Plant, Robert 1948- **CLC 12**

Plante, David (Robert) 1940- **CLC 7, 23, 38; DAM NOV**
See also CA 37-40R; CANR 12, 36, 58; DLBY 83; INT CANR-12; MTCW

Plath, Sylvia 1932-1963 **CLC 1, 2, 3, 5, 9, 11, 14, 17, 50, 51, 62, 111; DA; DAB; DAC; DAM MST, POET; PC 1; WLC**
See also AAYA 13; CA 19-20; CANR 34; CAP 2; CDALB 1941-1968; DLB 5, 6, 152; MTCW; SATA 96

Plato 428(?)B.C.-348(?)B.C. **CMLC 8; DA; DAB; DAC; DAM MST; WLCS**
See also DLB 176

Platonov, Andrei **TCLC 14**
See also Klimentov, Andrei Platonovich

Platt, Kin 1911- **CLC 26**
See also AAYA 11; CA 17-20R; CANR 11; JRDA; SAAS 17; SATA 21, 86

Plautus c. 251B.C.-184B.C. **CMLC 24; DC 6**

Plick et Plock
See Simenon, Georges (Jacques Christian)

Plimpton, George (Ames) 1927- **CLC 36**
See also AITN 1; CA 21-24R; CANR 32; DLB 185; MTCW; SATA 10

Pliny the Elder c. 23-79 **CMLC 23**

Plomer, William Charles Franklin 1903-1973 **CLC 4, 8**
See also CA 21-22; CANR 34; CAP 2; DLB 20, 162, 191; MTCW; SATA 24

Plowman, Piers
See Kavanagh, Patrick (Joseph)

Plum, J.
See Wodehouse, P(elham) G(renville)

Plumly, Stanley (Ross) 1939- **CLC 33**
See also CA 108; 110; DLB 5, 193; INT 110

Plumpe, Friedrich Wilhelm 1888-1931**TCLC 53**
See also CA 112

Po Chu-i 772-846 **CMLC 24**

Poe, Edgar Allan 1809-1849 **NCLC 1, 16, 55; DA; DAB; DAC; DAM MST, POET; PC 1; SSC 1, 22; WLC**
See also AAYA 14; CDALB 1640-1865; DLB 3, 59, 73, 74; SATA 23

Poet of Titchfield Street, The
See Pound, Ezra (Weston Loomis)

Pohl, Frederik 1919- **CLC 18; SSC 25**
See also AAYA 24; CA 61-64; CAAS 1; CANR 11, 37; DLB 8; INT CANR-11; MTCW; SATA 24

Poirier, Louis 1910-
See Gracq, Julien
See also CA 122; 126

Poitier, Sidney 1927- **CLC 26**

See also BW 1; CA 117

Polanski, Roman 1933- **CLC 16**
See also CA 77-80

Poliakoff, Stephen 1952- **CLC 38**
See also CA 106; DLB 13

Police, The
See Copeland, Stewart (Armstrong); Summers, Andrew James; Sumner, Gordon Matthew

Polidori, John William 1795-1821 **NCLC 51**
See also DLB 116

Pollitt, Katha 1949- **CLC 28**
See also CA 120; 122; CANR 66; MTCW

Pollock, (Mary) Sharon 1936-**CLC 50; DAC; DAM DRAM, MST**
See also CA 141; DLB 60

Polo, Marco 1254-1324 **CMLC 15**

Polonsky, Abraham (Lincoln) 1910- **CLC 92**
See also CA 104; DLB 26; INT 104

Polybius c. 200B.C.-c. 118B.C. **CMLC 17**
See also DLB 176

Pomerance, Bernard 1940- **CLC 13; DAM DRAM**
See also CA 101; CANR 49

Ponge, Francis (Jean Gaston Alfred) 1899-1988 **CLC 6, 18; DAM POET**
See also CA 85-88; 126; CANR 40

Pontoppidan, Henrik 1857-1943 **TCLC 29**

Poole, Josephine **CLC 17**
See also Helyar, Jane Penelope Josephine
See also SAAS 2; SATA 5

Popa, Vasko 1922-1991 **CLC 19**
See also CA 112; 148; DLB 181

Pope, Alexander 1688-1744 **LC 3; DA; DAB; DAC; DAM MST, POET; WLC**
See also CDBLB 1660-1789; DLB 95, 101

Porter, Connie (Rose) 1959(?)- **CLC 70**
See also BW 2; CA 142; SATA 81

Porter, Gene(va Grace) Stratton 1863(?)-1924 **TCLC 21**
See also CA 112

Porter, Katherine Anne 1890-1980**CLC 1, 3, 7, 10, 13, 15, 27, 101; DA; DAB; DAC; DAM MST, NOV; SSC 4, 31**
See also AITN 2; CA 1-4R; 101; CANR 1, 65; DLB 4, 9, 102; DLBD 12; DLBY 80; MTCW; SATA 39; SATA-Obit 23

Porter, Peter (Neville Frederick) 1929-**CLC 5, 13, 33**
See also CA 85-88; DLB 40

Porter, William Sydney 1862-1910
See Henry, O.
See also CA 104; 131; CDALB 1865-1917; DA; DAB; DAC; DAM MST; DLB 12, 78, 79; MTCW; YABC 2

Portillo (y Pacheco), Jose Lopez
See Lopez Portillo (y Pacheco), Jose

Post, Melville Davisson 1869-1930 **TCLC 39**
See also CA 110

Potok, Chaim 1929- **CLC 2, 7, 14, 26, 112; DAM NOV**
See also AAYA 15; AITN 1, 2; CA 17-20R; CANR 19, 35, 64; DLB 28, 152; INT CANR-19; MTCW; SATA 33

Potter, (Helen) Beatrix 1866-1943
See Webb, (Martha) Beatrice (Potter)
See also MAICYA

Potter, Dennis (Christopher George) 1935-1994 **CLC 58, 86**
See also CA 107; 145; CANR 33, 61; MTCW

Pound, Ezra (Weston Loomis) 1885-1972**CLC 1, 2, 3, 4, 5, 7, 10, 13, 18, 34, 48, 50, 112; DA; DAB; DAC; DAM MST, POET; PC 4; WLC**

See also CA 5-8R; 37-40R; CANR 40; CDALB 1917-1929; DLB 4, 45, 63; DLBD 15; MTCW

Povod, Reinaldo 1959-1994 **CLC 44**
See also CA 136; 146

Powell, Adam Clayton, Jr. 1908-1972**CLC 89; BLC 3; DAM MULT**
See also BW 1; CA 102; 33-36R

Powell, Anthony (Dymoke) 1905-**CLC 1, 3, 7, 9, 10, 31**
See also CA 1-4R; CANR 1, 32, 62; CDBLB 1945-1960; DLB 15; MTCW

Powell, Dawn 1897-1965 **CLC 66**
See also CA 5-8R; DLBY 97

Powell, Padgett 1952- **CLC 34**
See also CA 126; CANR 63

Power, Susan 1961- **CLC 91**

Powers, J(ames) F(arl) 1917-**CLC 1, 4, 8, 57; SSC 4**
See also CA 1-4R; CANR 2, 61; DLB 130; MTCW

Powers, John J(ames) 1945-
See Powers, John R.
See also CA 69-72

Powers, John R. **CLC 66**
See also Powers, John J(ames)

Powers, Richard (S.) 1957- **CLC 93**
See also CA 148

Pownall, David 1938- **CLC 10**
See also CA 89-92; CAAS 18; CANR 49; DLB 14

Powys, John Cowper 1872-1963**CLC 7, 9, 15, 46**
See also CA 85-88; DLB 15; MTCW

Powys, T(heodore) F(rancis) 1875-1953 **TCLC 9**
See also CA 106; DLB 36, 162

Prado (Calvo), Pedro 1886-1952 **TCLC 75**
See also CA 131; HW

Prager, Emily 1952- **CLC 56**

Pratt, E(dwin) J(ohn) 1883(?)-1964 **CLC 19; DAC; DAM POET**
See also CA 141; 93-96; DLB 92

Premchand **TCLC 21**
See also Srivastava, Dhanpat Rai

Preussler, Otfried 1923- **CLC 17**
See also CA 77-80; SATA 24

Prevert, Jacques (Henri Marie) 1900-1977 **CLC 15**
See also CA 77-80; 69-72; CANR 29, 61; MTCW; SATA-Obit 30

Prevost, Abbe (Antoine Francois) 1697-1763 **LC 1**

Price, (Edward) Reynolds 1933-**CLC 3, 6, 13, 43, 50, 63; DAM NOV; SSC 22**
See also CA 1-4R; CANR 1, 37, 57; DLB 2; INT CANR-37

Price, Richard 1949- **CLC 6, 12**
See also CA 49-52; CANR 3; DLBY 81

Prichard, Katharine Susannah 1883-1969 **CLC 46**
See also CA 11-12; CANR 33; CAP 1; MTCW; SATA 66

Priestley, J(ohn) B(oynton) 1894-1984**CLC 2, 5, 9, 34; DAM DRAM, NOV**
See also CA 9-12R; 113; CANR 33; CDBLB 1914-1945; DLB 10, 34, 77, 100, 139; DLBY 84; MTCW

Prince 1958(?)- **CLC 35**

Prince, F(rank) T(empleton) 1912- **CLC 22**
See also CA 101; CANR 43; DLB 20

Prince Kropotkin
See Kropotkin, Peter (Aleksieevich)

Prior, Matthew 1664-1721   LC 4
    See also DLB 95
Prishvin, Mikhail 1873-1954   TCLC 75
Pritchard, William H(arrison) 1932- CLC 34
    See also CA 65-68; CANR 23; DLB 111
Pritchett, V(ictor) S(awdon) 1900-1997 C L C
    5, 13, 15, 41; DAM NOV; SSC 14
    See also CA 61-64; 157; CANR 31, 63; DLB
    15, 139; MTCW
Private 19022
    See Manning, Frederic
Probst, Mark 1925-   CLC 59
    See also CA 130
Prokosch, Frederic 1908-1989   CLC 4, 48
    See also CA 73-76; 128; DLB 48
Prophet, The
    See Dreiser, Theodore (Herman Albert)
Prose, Francine 1947-   CLC 45
    See also CA 109; 112; CANR 46
Proudhon
    See Cunha, Euclides (Rodrigues Pimenta) da
Proulx, Annie
    See Proulx, E(dna) Annie
Proulx, E(dna) Annie 1935-   CLC 81; DAM
    POP
    See also CA 145; CANR 65
Proust, (Valentin-Louis-George-Eugene-)
    Marcel 1871-1922 TCLC 7, 13, 33; DA;
    DAB; DAC; DAM MST, NOV; WLC
    See also CA 104; 120; DLB 65; MTCW
Prowler, Harley
    See Masters, Edgar Lee
Prus, Boleslaw 1845-1912   TCLC 48
Pryor, Richard (Franklin Lenox Thomas) 1940-
    CLC 26
    See also CA 122
Przybyszewski, Stanislaw 1868-1927TCLC 36
    See also CA 160; DLB 66
Pteleon
    See Grieve, C(hristopher) M(urray)
    See also DAM POET
Puckett, Lute
    See Masters, Edgar Lee
Puig, Manuel 1932-1990CLC 3, 5, 10, 28, 65;
    DAM MULT; HLC
    See also CA 45-48; CANR 2, 32, 63; DLB 113;
    HW; MTCW
Pulitzer, Joseph 1847-1911   TCLC 76
    See also CA 114; DLB 23
Purdy, A(lfred) W(ellington) 1918-CLC 3, 6,
    14, 50; DAC; DAM MST, POET
    See also CA 81-84; CAAS 17; CANR 42, 66;
    DLB 88
Purdy, James (Amos) 1923- CLC 2, 4, 10, 28,
    52
    See also CA 33-36R; CAAS 1; CANR 19, 51;
    DLB 2; INT CANR-19; MTCW
Pure, Simon
    See Swinnerton, Frank Arthur
Pushkin, Alexander (Sergeyevich) 1799-1837
    NCLC 3, 27; DA; DAB; DAC; DAM
    DRAM, MST, POET; PC 10; SSC 27;
    WLC
    See also SATA 61
P'u Sung-ling 1640-1715   LC 3; SSC 31
Putnam, Arthur Lee
    See Alger, Horatio, Jr.
Puzo, Mario 1920-CLC 1, 2, 6, 36, 107; DAM
    NOV, POP
    See also CA 65-68; CANR 4, 42, 65; DLB 6;
    MTCW
Pygge, Edward
    See Barnes, Julian (Patrick)

Pyle, Ernest Taylor 1900-1945
    See Pyle, Ernie
    See also CA 115; 160
Pyle, Ernie 1900-1945   TCLC 75
    See also Pyle, Ernest Taylor
    See also DLB 29
Pym, Barbara (Mary Crampton) 1913-1980
    CLC 13, 19, 37, 111
    See also CA 13-14; 97-100; CANR 13, 34; CAP
    1; DLB 14; DLBY 87; MTCW
Pynchon, Thomas (Ruggles, Jr.) 1937-CLC 2,
    3, 6, 9, 11, 18, 33, 62, 72; DA; DAB; DAC;
    DAM MST, NOV, POP; SSC 14; WLC
    See also BEST 90:2; CA 17-20R; CANR 22,
    46; DLB 2, 173; MTCW
Pythagoras c. 570B.C.-c. 500B.C. CMLC 22
    See also DLB 176
Q
    See Quiller-Couch, SirArthur (Thomas)
Qian Zhongshu
    See Ch'ien Chung-shu
Qroll
    See Dagerman, Stig (Halvard)
Quarrington, Paul (Lewis) 1953-   CLC 65
    See also CA 129; CANR 62
Quasimodo, Salvatore 1901-1968   CLC 10
    See also CA 13-16; 25-28R; CAP 1; DLB 114;
    MTCW
Quay, Stephen 1947-   CLC 95
Quay, Timothy 1947-   CLC 95
Queen, Ellery   CLC 3, 11
    See also Dannay, Frederic; Davidson, Avram;
    Lee, Manfred B(ennington); Marlowe,
    Stephen; Sturgeon, Theodore (Hamilton);
    Vance, John Holbrook
Queen, Ellery, Jr.
    See Dannay, Frederic; Lee, Manfred
    B(ennington)
Queneau, Raymond 1903-1976 CLC 2, 5, 10,
    42
    See also CA 77-80; 69-72; CANR 32; DLB 72;
    MTCW
Quevedo, Francisco de 1580-1645   LC 23
Quiller-Couch, SirArthur (Thomas) 1863-1944
    TCLC 53
    See also CA 118; 166; DLB 135, 153, 190
Quin, Ann (Marie) 1936-1973   CLC 6
    See also CA 9-12R; 45-48; DLB 14
Quinn, Martin
    See Smith, Martin Cruz
Quinn, Peter 1947-   CLC 91
Quinn, Simon
    See Smith, Martin Cruz
Quiroga, Horacio (Sylvestre) 1878-1937
    TCLC 20; DAM MULT; HLC
    See also CA 117; 131; HW; MTCW
Quoirez, Francoise 1935-   CLC 9
    See also Sagan, Francoise
    See also CA 49-52; CANR 6, 39; MTCW
Raabe, Wilhelm 1831-1910   TCLC 45
    See also DLB 129
Rabe, David (William) 1940-   CLC 4, 8, 33;
    DAM DRAM
    See also CA 85-88; CABS 3; CANR 59; DLB 7
Rabelais, Francois 1483-1553LC 5; DA; DAB;
    DAC; DAM MST; WLC
Rabinovitch, Sholem 1859-1916
    See Aleichem, Sholom
    See also CA 104
Rachilde 1860-1953   TCLC 67
    See also DLB 123, 192
Racine, Jean 1639-1699   LC 28; DAB; DAM
    MST

Radcliffe, Ann (Ward) 1764-1823NCLC 6, 55
    See also DLB 39, 178
Radiguet, Raymond 1903-1923   TCLC 29
    See also CA 162; DLB 65
Radnoti, Miklos 1909-1944   TCLC 16
    See also CA 118
Rado, James 1939-   CLC 17
    See also CA 105
Radvanyi, Netty 1900-1983
    See Seghers, Anna
    See also CA 85-88; 110
Rae, Ben
    See Griffiths, Trevor
Raeburn, John (Hay) 1941-   CLC 34
    See also CA 57-60
Ragni, Gerome 1942-1991   CLC 17
    See also CA 105; 134
Rahv, Philip 1908-1973   CLC 24
    See also Greenberg, Ivan
    See also DLB 137
Raimund, Ferdinand Jakob 1790-1836NCLC
    69
    See also DLB 90
Raine, Craig 1944-   CLC 32, 103
    See also CA 108; CANR 29, 51; DLB 40
Raine, Kathleen (Jessie) 1908-   CLC 7, 45
    See also CA 85-88; CANR 46; DLB 20; MTCW
Rainis, Janis 1865-1929   TCLC 29
Rakosi, Carl 1903-   CLC 47
    See also Rawley, Callman
    See also CAAS 5; DLB 193
Raleigh, Richard
    See Lovecraft, H(oward) P(hillips)
Raleigh, Sir Walter 1554(?)-1618   LC 31, 39
    See also CDBLB Before 1660; DLB 172
Rallentando, H. P.
    See Sayers, Dorothy L(eigh)
Ramal, Walter
    See de la Mare, Walter (John)
Ramon, Juan
    See Jimenez (Mantecon), Juan Ramon
Ramos, Graciliano 1892-1953   TCLC 32
Rampersad, Arnold 1941-   CLC 44
    See also BW 2; CA 127; 133; DLB 111; INT
    133
Rampling, Anne
    See Rice, Anne
Ramsay, Allan 1684(?)-1758   LC 29
    See also DLB 95
Ramuz, Charles-Ferdinand 1878-1947TCLC
    33
    See also CA 165
Rand, Ayn 1905-1982 CLC 3, 30, 44, 79; DA;
    DAC; DAM MST, NOV, POP; WLC
    See also AAYA 10; CA 13-16R; 105; CANR
    27; MTCW
Randall, Dudley (Felker) 1914-CLC 1; BLC 3;
    DAM MULT
    See also BW 1; CA 25-28R; CANR 23; DLB
    41
Randall, Robert
    See Silverberg, Robert
Ranger, Ken
    See Creasey, John
Ransom, John Crowe 1888-1974 CLC 2, 4, 5,
    11, 24; DAM POET
    See also CA 5-8R; 49-52; CANR 6, 34; DLB
    45, 63; MTCW
Rao, Raja 1909-   CLC 25, 56; DAM NOV
    See also CA 73-76; CANR 51; MTCW
Raphael, Frederic (Michael) 1931-CLC 2, 14
    See also CA 1-4R; CANR 1; DLB 14
Ratcliffe, James P.

See Mencken, H(enry) L(ouis)
Rathbone, Julian 1935-   **CLC 41**
  See also CA 101; CANR 34
Rattigan, Terence (Mervyn) 1911-1977**CLC 7;**
  DAM DRAM
  See also CA 85-88; 73-76; CDBLB 1945-1960;
  DLB 13; MTCW
Ratushinskaya, Irina 1954-   **CLC 54**
  See also CA 129; CANR 68
Raven, Simon (Arthur Noel) 1927- **CLC 14**
  See also CA 81-84
Ravenna, Michael
  See Welty, Eudora
Rawley, Callman 1903-
  See Rakosi, Carl
  See also CA 21-24R; CANR 12, 32
Rawlings, Marjorie Kinnan 1896-1953**TCLC 4**
  See also AAYA 20; CA 104; 137; DLB 9, 22,
  102; JRDA; MAICYA; YABC 1
Ray, Satyajit 1921-1992   **CLC 16, 76; DAM MULT**
  See also CA 114; 137
Read, Herbert Edward 1893-1968   **CLC 4**
  See also CA 85-88; 25-28R; DLB 20, 149
Read, Piers Paul 1941-   **CLC 4, 10, 25**
  See also CA 21-24R; CANR 38; DLB 14; SATA 21
Reade, Charles 1814-1884   **NCLC 2**
  See also DLB 21
Reade, Hamish
  See Gray, Simon (James Holliday)
Reading, Peter 1946-   **CLC 47**
  See also CA 103; CANR 46; DLB 40
Reaney, James 1926-   **CLC 13; DAC; DAM MST**
  See also CA 41-44R; CAAS 15; CANR 42; DLB
  68; SATA 43
Rebreanu, Liviu 1885-1944   **TCLC 28**
  See also CA 165
Rechy, John (Francisco) 1934- **CLC 1, 7, 14, 18, 107; DAM MULT; HLC**
  See also CA 5-8R; CAAS 4; CANR 6, 32, 64;
  DLB 122; DLBY 82; HW; INT CANR-6
Redcam, Tom 1870-1933   **TCLC 25**
Reddin, Keith   **CLC 67**
Redgrove, Peter (William) 1932-   **CLC 6, 41**
  See also CA 1-4R; CANR 3, 39; DLB 40
Redmon, Anne   **CLC 22**
  See also Nightingale, Anne Redmon
  See also DLBY 86
Reed, Eliot
  See Ambler, Eric
Reed, Ishmael 1938-**CLC 2, 3, 5, 6, 13, 32, 60; BLC 3; DAM MULT**
  See also BW 2; CA 21-24R; CANR 25, 48; DLB
  2, 5, 33, 169; DLBD 8; MTCW
Reed, John (Silas) 1887-1920   **TCLC 9**
  See also CA 106
Reed, Lou   **CLC 21**
  See also Firbank, Louis
Reeve, Clara 1729-1807   **NCLC 19**
  See also DLB 39
Reich, Wilhelm 1897-1957   **TCLC 57**
Reid, Christopher (John) 1949-   **CLC 33**
  See also CA 140; DLB 40
Reid, Desmond
  See Moorcock, Michael (John)
Reid Banks, Lynne 1929-
  See Banks, Lynne Reid
  See also CA 1-4R; CANR 6, 22, 38; CLR 24;
  JRDA; MAICYA; SATA 22, 75
Reilly, William K.

See Creasey, John
Reiner, Max
  See Caldwell, (Janet Miriam) Taylor (Holland)
Reis, Ricardo
  See Pessoa, Fernando (Antonio Nogueira)
Remarque, Erich Maria 1898-1970 **CLC 21; DA; DAB; DAC; DAM MST, NOV**
  See also CA 77-80; 29-32R; DLB 56; MTCW
Remizov, A.
  See Remizov, Aleksei (Mikhailovich)
Remizov, A. M.
  See Remizov, Aleksei (Mikhailovich)
Remizov, Aleksei (Mikhailovich) 1877-1957
  TCLC 27
  See also CA 125; 133
Renan, Joseph Ernest 1823-1892   **NCLC 26**
Renard, Jules 1864-1910   **TCLC 17**
  See also CA 117
Renault, Mary   **CLC 3, 11, 17**
  See also Challans, Mary
  See also DLBY 83
Rendell, Ruth (Barbara) 1930- **CLC 28, 48; DAM POP**
  See also Vine, Barbara
  See also CA 109; CANR 32, 52; DLB 87; INT
  CANR-32; MTCW
Renoir, Jean 1894-1979   **CLC 20**
  See also CA 129; 85-88
Resnais, Alain 1922-   **CLC 16**
Reverdy, Pierre 1889-1960   **CLC 53**
  See also CA 97-100; 89-92
Rexroth, Kenneth 1905-1982 **CLC 1, 2, 6, 11, 22, 49, 112; DAM POET; PC 20**
  See also CA 5-8R; 107; CANR 14, 34, 63;
  CDALB 1941-1968; DLB 16, 48, 165;
  DLBY 82; INT CANR-14; MTCW
Reyes, Alfonso 1889-1959   **TCLC 33**
  See also CA 131; HW
Reyes y Basoalto, Ricardo Eliecer Neftali
  See Neruda, Pablo
Reymont, Wladyslaw (Stanislaw) 1868(?)-1925
  TCLC 5
  See also CA 104
Reynolds, Jonathan 1942-   **CLC 6, 38**
  See also CA 65-68; CANR 28
Reynolds, Joshua 1723-1792   **LC 15**
  See also DLB 104
Reynolds, Michael Shane 1937-   **CLC 44**
  See also CA 65-68; CANR 9
Reznikoff, Charles 1894-1976   **CLC 9**
  See also CA 33-36; 61-64; CAP 2; DLB 28, 45
Rezzori (d'Arezzo), Gregor von 1914-**CLC 25**
  See also CA 122; 136
Rhine, Richard
  See Silverstein, Alvin
Rhodes, Eugene Manlove 1869-1934**TCLC 53**
Rhodius, Apollonius c. 3rd cent. B.C.- **CMLC 28**
  See also DLB 176
R'hoone
  See Balzac, Honore de
Rhys, Jean 1890(?)-1979 **CLC 2, 4, 6, 14, 19, 51; DAM NOV; SSC 21**
  See also CA 25-28R; 85-88; CANR 35, 62;
  CDBLB 1945-1960; DLB 36, 117, 162;
  MTCW
Ribeiro, Darcy 1922-1997   **CLC 34**
  See also CA 33-36R; 156
Ribeiro, Joao Ubaldo (Osorio Pimentel) 1941-
  CLC 10, 67
  See also CA 81-84
Ribman, Ronald (Burt) 1932-   **CLC 7**
  See also CA 21-24R; CANR 46

Ricci, Nino 1959-   **CLC 70**
  See also CA 137
Rice, Anne 1941-   **CLC 41; DAM POP**
  See also AAYA 9; BEST 89:2; CA 65-68; CANR
  12, 36, 53
Rice, Elmer (Leopold) 1892-1967 **CLC 7, 49; DAM DRAM**
  See also CA 21-22; 25-28R; CAP 2; DLB 4, 7;
  MTCW
Rice, Tim(othy Miles Bindon) 1944- **CLC 21**
  See also CA 103; CANR 46
Rich, Adrienne (Cecile) 1929-**CLC 3, 6, 7, 11, 18, 36, 73, 76; DAM POET; PC 5**
  See also CA 9-12R; CANR 20, 53; DLB 5, 67;
  MTCW
Rich, Barbara
  See Graves, Robert (von Ranke)
Rich, Robert
  See Trumbo, Dalton
Richard, Keith   **CLC 17**
  See also Richards, Keith
Richards, David Adams 1950- **CLC 59; DAC**
  See also CA 93-96; CANR 60; DLB 53
Richards, I(vor) A(rmstrong) 1893-1979**CLC 14, 24**
  See also CA 41-44R; 89-92; CANR 34; DLB
  27
Richards, Keith 1943-
  See Richard, Keith
  See also CA 107
Richardson, Anne
  See Roiphe, Anne (Richardson)
Richardson, Dorothy Miller 1873-1957**TCLC 3**
  See also CA 104; DLB 36
Richardson, Ethel Florence (Lindesay) 1870-1946
  See Richardson, Henry Handel
  See also CA 105
Richardson, Henry Handel   **TCLC 4**
  See also Richardson, Ethel Florence (Lindesay)
  See also DLB 197
Richardson, John 1796-1852**NCLC 55; DAC**
  See also DLB 99
Richardson, Samuel 1689-1761**LC 1, 44; DA; DAB; DAC; DAM MST, NOV; WLC**
  See also CDBLB 1660-1789; DLB 39
Richler, Mordecai 1931-**CLC 3, 5, 9, 13, 18, 46, 70; DAC; DAM MST, NOV**
  See also AITN 1; CA 65-68; CANR 31, 62; CLR
  17; DLB 53; MAICYA; MTCW; SATA 44,
  98; SATA-Brief 27
Richter, Conrad (Michael) 1890-1968**CLC 30**
  See also AAYA 21; CA 5-8R; 25-28R; CANR
  23; DLB 9; MTCW; SATA 3
Ricostranza, Tom
  See Ellis, Trey
Riddell, Charlotte 1832-1906   **TCLC 40**
  See also CA 165; DLB 156
Riding, Laura   **CLC 3, 7**
  See also Jackson, Laura (Riding)
Riefenstahl, Berta Helene Amalia 1902-
  See Riefenstahl, Leni
  See also CA 108
Riefenstahl, Leni   **CLC 16**
  See also Riefenstahl, Berta Helene Amalia
Riffe, Ernest
  See Bergman, (Ernst) Ingmar
Riggs, (Rolla) Lynn 1899-1954 **TCLC 56; DAM MULT**
  See also CA 144; DLB 175; NNAL
Riis, Jacob A(ugust) 1849-1914   **TCLC 80**
  See also CA 113; DLB 23

NCLC 16

Samarakis, Antonis 1919-   CLC 5
    See also CA 25-28R; CAAS 16; CANR 36

Sanchez, Florencio 1875-1910   TCLC 37
    See also CA 153; HW

Sanchez, Luis Rafael 1936-   CLC 23
    See also CA 128; DLB 145; HW

Sanchez, Sonia 1934- CLC 5; BLC 3; DAM
    MULT; PC 9
    See also BW 2; CA 33-36R; CANR 24, 49; CLR
    18; DLB 41; DLBD 8; MAICYA; MTCW;
    SATA 22

Sand, George 1804-1876NCLC 2, 42, 57; DA;
    DAB; DAC; DAM MST, NOV; WLC
    See also DLB 119, 192

Sandburg, Carl (August) 1878-1967CLC 1, 4,
    10, 15, 35; DA; DAB; DAC; DAM MST,
    POET; PC 2; WLC
    See also AAYA 24; CA 5-8R; 25-28R; CANR
    35; CDALB 1865-1917; DLB 17, 54;
    MAICYA; MTCW; SATA 8

Sandburg, Charles
    See Sandburg, Carl (August)

Sandburg, Charles A.
    See Sandburg, Carl (August)

Sanders, (James) Ed(ward) 1939-   CLC 53
    See also CA 13-16R; CAAS 21; CANR 13, 44;
    DLB 16

Sanders, Lawrence 1920-1998CLC 41; DAM
    POP
    See also BEST 89:4; CA 81-84; 165; CANR
    33, 62; MTCW

Sanders, Noah
    See Blount, Roy (Alton), Jr.

Sanders, Winston P.
    See Anderson, Poul (William)

Sandoz, Mari(e Susette) 1896-1966   CLC 28
    See also CA 1-4R; 25-28R; CANR 17, 64; DLB
    9; MTCW; SATA 5

Saner, Reg(inald Anthony) 1931-   CLC 9
    See also CA 65-68

Sannazaro, Jacopo 1456(?)-1530   LC 8

Sansom, William 1912-1976 CLC 2, 6; DAM
    NOV; SSC 21
    See also CA 5-8R; 65-68; CANR 42; DLB 139;
    MTCW

Santayana, George 1863-1952   TCLC 40
    See also CA 115; DLB 54, 71; DLBD 13

Santiago, Danny   CLC 33
    See also James, Daniel (Lewis)
    See also DLB 122

Santmyer, Helen Hoover 1895-1986 CLC 33
    See also CA 1-4R; 118; CANR 15, 33; DLBY
    84; MTCW

Santoka, Taneda 1882-1940   TCLC 72

Santos, Bienvenido N(uqui) 1911-1996 C L C
    22; DAM MULT
    See also CA 101; 151; CANR 19, 46

Sapper   TCLC 44
    See also McNeile, Herman Cyril

Sapphire 1950-   CLC 99

Sappho fl. 6th cent. B.C.-   CMLC 3; DAM
    POET; PC 5
    See also DLB 176

Sarduy, Severo 1937-1993   CLC 6, 97
    See also CA 89-92; 142; CANR 58; DLB 113;
    HW

Sargeson, Frank 1903-1982   CLC 31
    See also CA 25-28R; 106; CANR 38

Sarmiento, Felix Ruben Garcia
    See Dario, Ruben

Saroyan, William 1908-1981CLC 1, 8, 10, 29,
    34, 56; DA; DAB; DAC; DAM DRAM,
    MST, NOV; SSC 21; WLC
    See also CA 5-8R; 103; CANR 30; DLB 7, 9,
    86; DLBY 81; MTCW; SATA 23; SATA-Obit
    24

Sarraute, Nathalie 1900-CLC 1, 2, 4, 8, 10, 31,
    80
    See also CA 9-12R; CANR 23, 66; DLB 83;
    MTCW

Sarton, (Eleanor) May 1912-1995CLC 4, 14,
    49, 91; DAM POET
    See also CA 1-4R; 149; CANR 1, 34, 55; DLB
    48; DLBY 81; INT CANR-34; MTCW;
    SATA 36; SATA-Obit 86

Sartre, Jean-Paul 1905-1980CLC 1, 4, 7, 9, 13,
    18, 24, 44, 50, 52; DA; DAB; DAC; DAM
    DRAM, MST, NOV; DC 3; WLC
    See also CA 9-12R; 97-100; CANR 21; DLB
    72; MTCW

Sassoon, Siegfried (Lorraine) 1886-1967C L C
    36; DAB; DAM MST, NOV, POET; PC 12
    See also CA 104; 25-28R; CANR 36; DLB 20,
    191; MTCW

Satterfield, Charles
    See Pohl, Frederik

Saul, John (W. III) 1942-CLC 46; DAM NOV,
    POP
    See also AAYA 10; BEST 90:4; CA 81-84;
    CANR 16, 40; SATA 98

Saunders, Caleb
    See Heinlein, Robert A(nson)

Saura (Atares), Carlos 1932-   CLC 20
    See also CA 114; 131; HW

Sauser-Hall, Frederic 1887-1961   CLC 18
    See also Cendrars, Blaise
    See also CA 102; 93-96; CANR 36, 62; MTCW

Saussure, Ferdinand de 1857-1913   TCLC 49

Savage, Catharine
    See Brosman, Catharine Savage

Savage, Thomas 1915-   CLC 40
    See also CA 126; 132; CAAS 15; INT 132

Savan, Glenn 19(?)-   CLC 50

Sayers, Dorothy L(eigh) 1893-1957 TCLC 2,
    15; DAM POP
    See also CA 104; 119; CANR 60; CDBLB 1914-
    1945; DLB 10, 36, 77, 100; MTCW

Sayers, Valerie 1952-   CLC 50
    See also CA 134; CANR 61

Sayles, John (Thomas) 1950-   CLC 7, 10, 14
    See also CA 57-60; CANR 41; DLB 44

Scammell, Michael 1935-   CLC 34
    See also CA 156

Scannell, Vernon 1922-   CLC 49
    See also CA 5-8R; CANR 8, 24, 57; DLB 27;
    SATA 59

Scarlett, Susan
    See Streatfeild, (Mary) Noel

Schaeffer, Susan Fromberg 1941- CLC 6, 11,
    22
    See also CA 49-52; CANR 18, 65; DLB 28;
    MTCW; SATA 22

Schary, Jill
    See Robinson, Jill

Schell, Jonathan 1943-   CLC 35
    See also CA 73-76; CANR 12

Schelling, Friedrich Wilhelm Joseph von 1775-
    1854   NCLC 30
    See also DLB 90

Schendel, Arthur van 1874-1946   TCLC 56

Scherer, Jean-Marie Maurice 1920-
    See Rohmer, Eric
    See also CA 110

Schevill, James (Erwin) 1920-   CLC 7
    See also CA 5-8R; CAAS 12

Schiller, Friedrich 1759-1805   NCLC 39, 69;
    DAM DRAM
    See also DLB 94

Schisgal, Murray (Joseph) 1926-   CLC 6
    See also CA 21-24R; CANR 48

Schlee, Ann 1934-   CLC 35
    See also CA 101; CANR 29; SATA 44; SATA-
    Brief 36

Schlegel, August Wilhelm von 1767-1845
    NCLC 15
    See also DLB 94

Schlegel, Friedrich 1772-1829   NCLC 45
    See also DLB 90

Schlegel, Johann Elias (von) 1719(?)-1749L C
    5

Schlesinger, Arthur M(eier), Jr. 1917-CLC 84
    See also AITN 1; CA 1-4R; CANR 1, 28, 58;
    DLB 17; INT CANR-28; MTCW; SATA 61

Schmidt, Arno (Otto) 1914-1979   CLC 56
    See also CA 128; 109; DLB 69

Schmitz, Aron Hector 1861-1928
    See Svevo, Italo
    See also CA 104; 122; MTCW

Schnackenberg, Gjertrud 1953-   CLC 40
    See also CA 116; DLB 120

Schneider, Leonard Alfred 1925-1966
    See Bruce, Lenny
    See also CA 89-92

Schnitzler, Arthur 1862-1931TCLC 4; SSC 15
    See also CA 104; DLB 81, 118

Schoenberg, Arnold 1874-1951   TCLC 75
    See also CA 109

Schonberg, Arnold
    See Schoenberg, Arnold

Schopenhauer, Arthur 1788-1860   NCLC 51
    See also DLB 90

Schor, Sandra (M.) 1932(?)-1990   CLC 65
    See also CA 132

Schorer, Mark 1908-1977   CLC 9
    See also CA 5-8R; 73-76; CANR 7; DLB 103

Schrader, Paul (Joseph) 1946-   CLC 26
    See also CA 37-40R; CANR 41; DLB 44

Schreiner, Olive (Emilie Albertina) 1855-1920
    TCLC 9
    See also CA 105; 154; DLB 18, 156, 190

Schulberg, Budd (Wilson) 1914-   CLC 7, 48
    See also CA 25-28R; CANR 19; DLB 6, 26,
    28; DLBY 81

Schulz, Bruno 1892-1942TCLC 5, 51; SSC 13
    See also CA 115; 123

Schulz, Charles M(onroe) 1922-   CLC 12
    See also CA 9-12R; CANR 6; INT CANR-6;
    SATA 10

Schumacher, E(rnst) F(riedrich) 1911-1977
    CLC 80
    See also CA 81-84; 73-76; CANR 34

Schuyler, James Marcus 1923-1991CLC 5, 23;
    DAM POET
    See also CA 101; 134; DLB 5, 169; INT 101

Schwartz, Delmore (David) 1913-1966CLC 2,
    4, 10, 45, 87; PC 8
    See also CA 17-18; 25-28R; CANR 35; CAP 2;
    DLB 28, 48; MTCW

Schwartz, Ernst
    See Ozu, Yasujiro

Schwartz, John Burnham 1965-   CLC 59
    See also CA 132

Schwartz, Lynne Sharon 1939-   CLC 31
    See also CA 103; CANR 44

Schwartz, Muriel A.
    See Eliot, T(homas) S(tearns)

Schwarz-Bart, Andre 1928-   CLC 2, 4
    See also CA 89-92

Sheldon, Alice Hastings Bradley 1915(?)-1987
 See Tiptree, James, Jr.
  See also CA 108; 122; CANR 34; INT 108;
  MTCW
Sheldon, John
 See Bloch, Robert (Albert)
Shelley, Mary Wollstonecraft (Godwin) 1797-
  1851NCLC 14, 59; DA; DAB; DAC; DAM
  MST, NOV; WLC
   See also AAYA 20; CDBLB 1789-1832; DLB
   110, 116, 159, 178; SATA 29
Shelley, Percy Bysshe 1792-1822   NCLC 18;
  DA; DAB; DAC; DAM MST, POET; PC
  14; WLC
   See also CDBLB 1789-1832; DLB 96, 110, 158
Shepard, Jim 1956-   **CLC 36**
 See also CA 137; CANR 59; SATA 90
Shepard, Lucius 1947-   **CLC 34**
 See also CA 128; 141
Shepard, Sam 1943- **CLC 4, 6, 17, 34, 41, 44;**
  DAM DRAM; DC 5
   See also AAYA 1; CA 69-72; CABS 3; CANR
   22; DLB 7; MTCW
Shepherd, Michael
 See Ludlum, Robert
Sherburne, Zoa (Morin) 1912-   **CLC 30**
 See also CA 13; CA 1-4R; CANR 3, 37;
  MAICYA; SAAS 18; SATA 3
Sheridan, Frances 1724-1766   **LC 7**
 See also DLB 39, 84
Sheridan, Richard Brinsley 1751-1816**N C L C**
  5; DA; DAB; DAC; DAM DRAM, MST;
  DC 1; WLC
   See also CDBLB 1660-1789; DLB 89
Sherman, Jonathan Marc   **CLC 55**
Sherman, Martin 1941(?)-   **CLC 19**
 See also CA 116; 123
Sherwin, Judith Johnson 1936-   **CLC 7, 15**
 See also CA 25-28R; CANR 34
Sherwood, Frances 1940-   **CLC 81**
 See also CA 146
Sherwood, Robert E(mmet) 1896-1955**T C L C**
  3; DAM DRAM
   See also CA 104; 153; DLB 7, 26
Shestov, Lev 1866-1938   **TCLC 56**
Shevchenko, Taras 1814-1861   **NCLC 54**
Shiel, M(atthew) P(hipps) 1865-1947**TCLC 8**
 See also Holmes, Gordon
 See also CA 106; 160; DLB 153
Shields, Carol 1935-   **CLC 91, 113; DAC**
 See also CA 81-84; CANR 51
Shields, David 1956-   **CLC 97**
 See also CA 124; CANR 48
Shiga, Naoya 1883-1971   **CLC 33; SSC 23**
 See also CA 101; 33-36R; DLB 180
Shilts, Randy 1951-1994   **CLC 85**
 See also AAYA 19; CA 115; 127; 144; CANR
  45; INT 127
Shimazaki, Haruki 1872-1943
 See Shimazaki Toson
 See also CA 105; 134
Shimazaki Toson 1872-1943   **TCLC 5**
 See also Shimazaki, Haruki
 See also DLB 180
Sholokhov, Mikhail (Aleksandrovich) 1905-
  1984   **CLC 7, 15**
   See also CA 101; 112; MTCW; SATA-Obit 36
Shone, Patric
 See Hanley, James
Shreve, Susan Richards 1939-   **CLC 23**
 See also CA 49-52; CAAS 5; CANR 5, 38, 69;
  MAICYA; SATA 46, 95; SATA-Brief 41
Shue, Larry 1946-1985**CLC 52; DAM DRAM**

 See also CA 145; 117
Shu-Jen, Chou 1881-1936
 See Lu Hsun
 See also CA 104
Shulman, Alix Kates 1932-   **CLC 2, 10**
 See also CA 29-32R; CANR 43; SATA 7
Shuster, Joe 1914-   **CLC 21**
Shute, Nevil   **CLC 30**
 See also Norway, Nevil Shute
Shuttle, Penelope (Diane) 1947-   **CLC 7**
 See also CA 93-96; CANR 39; DLB 14, 40
Sidney, Mary 1561-1621   **LC 19, 39**
Sidney, Sir Philip 1554-1586 **LC 19, 39; DA;**
  DAB; DAC; DAM MST, POET
   See also CDBLB Before 1660; DLB 167
Siegel, Jerome 1914-1996   **CLC 21**
 See also CA 116; 151
Siegel, Jerry
 See Siegel, Jerome
Sienkiewicz, Henryk (Adam Alexander Pius)
  1846-1916   **TCLC 3**
   See also CA 104; 134
Sierra, Gregorio Martinez
 See Martinez Sierra, Gregorio
Sierra, Maria (de la O'LeJarraga) Martinez
 See Martinez Sierra, Maria (de la O'LeJarraga)
Sigal, Clancy 1926-   **CLC 7**
 See also CA 1-4R
Sigourney, Lydia Howard (Huntley) 1791-1865
  NCLC 21
   See also DLB 1, 42, 73
Siguenza y Gongora, Carlos de 1645-1700**L C**
  8
Sigurjonsson, Johann 1880-1919   **TCLC 27**
Sikelianos, Angelos 1884-1951   **TCLC 39**
Silkin, Jon 1930-   **CLC 2, 6, 43**
 See also CA 5-8R; CAAS 5; DLB 27
Silko, Leslie (Marmon) 1948-**CLC 23, 74; DA;**
  DAC; DAM MST, MULT, POP; WLCS
   See also AAYA 14; CA 115; 122; CANR 45,
   65; DLB 143, 175; NNAL
Sillanpaa, Frans Eemil 1888-1964   **CLC 19**
 See also CA 129; 93-96; MTCW
Sillitoe, Alan 1928-   **CLC 1, 3, 6, 10, 19, 57**
 See also AITN 1; CA 9-12R; CAAS 2; CANR
  8, 26, 55; CDBLB 1960 to Present; DLB 14,
  139; MTCW; SATA 61
Silone, Ignazio 1900-1978   **CLC 4**
 See also CA 25-28; 81-84; CANR 34; CAP 2;
  MTCW
Silver, Joan Micklin 1935-   **CLC 20**
 See also CA 114; 121; INT 121
Silver, Nicholas
 See Faust, Frederick (Schiller)
Silverberg, Robert 1935- **CLC 7; DAM POP**
 See also AAYA 24; CA 1-4R; CAAS 3; CANR
  1, 20, 36; DLB 8; INT CANR-20; MAICYA;
  MTCW; SATA 13, 91
Silverstein, Alvin 1933-   **CLC 17**
 See also CA 49-52; CANR 2; CLR 25; JRDA;
  MAICYA; SATA 8, 69
Silverstein, Virginia B(arbara Opshelor) 1937-
  CLC 17
   See also CA 49-52; CANR 2; CLR 25; JRDA;
   MAICYA; SATA 8, 69
Sim, Georges
 See Simenon, Georges (Jacques Christian)
Simak, Clifford D(onald) 1904-1988**CLC 1, 55**
 See also CA 1-4R; 125; CANR 1, 35; DLB 8;
  MTCW; SATA-Obit 56
Simenon, Georges (Jacques Christian) 1903-
  1989   **CLC 1, 2, 3, 8, 18, 47; DAM POP**
   See also CA 85-88; 129; CANR 35; DLB 72;

 DLBY 89; MTCW
Simic, Charles 1938-   **CLC 6, 9, 22, 49, 68;**
  DAM POET
   See also CA 29-32R; CAAS 4; CANR 12, 33,
   52, 61; DLB 105
Simmel, Georg 1858-1918   **TCLC 64**
 See also CA 157
Simmons, Charles (Paul) 1924-   **CLC 57**
 See also CA 89-92; INT 89-92
Simmons, Dan 1948-   **CLC 44; DAM POP**
 See also AAYA 16; CA 138; CANR 53
Simmons, James (Stewart Alexander) 1933-
  CLC 43
   See also CA 105; CAAS 21; DLB 40
Simms, William Gilmore 1806-1870 **NCLC 3**
 See also DLB 3, 30, 59, 73
Simon, Carly 1945-   **CLC 26**
 See also CA 105
Simon, Claude 1913-1984 **CLC 4, 9, 15, 39;**
  DAM NOV
   See also CA 89-92; CANR 33; DLB 83; MTCW
Simon, (Marvin) Neil 1927-**CLC 6, 11, 31, 39,**
  70; DAM DRAM
   See also AITN 1; CA 21-24R; CANR 26, 54;
   DLB 7; MTCW
Simon, Paul (Frederick) 1941(?)-   **CLC 17**
 See also CA 116; 153
Simonon, Paul 1956(?)-   **CLC 30**
Simpson, Harriette
 See Arnow, Harriette (Louisa) Simpson
Simpson, Louis (Aston Marantz) 1923-**CLC 4,**
  7, 9, 32; DAM POET
   See also CA 1-4R; CAAS 4; CANR 1, 61; DLB
   5; MTCW
Simpson, Mona (Elizabeth) 1957-   **CLC 44**
 See also CA 122; 135; CANR 68
Simpson, N(orman) F(rederick) 1919-**CLC 29**
 See also CA 13-16R; DLB 13
Sinclair, Andrew (Annandale) 1935- **CLC 2,**
  14
   See also CA 9-12R; CAAS 5; CANR 14, 38;
   DLB 14; MTCW
Sinclair, Emil
 See Hesse, Hermann
Sinclair, Iain 1943-   **CLC 76**
 See also CA 132
Sinclair, Iain MacGregor
 See Sinclair, Iain
Sinclair, Irene
 See Griffith, D(avid Lewelyn) W(ark)
Sinclair, Mary Amelia St. Clair 1865(?)-1946
 See Sinclair, May
 See also CA 104
Sinclair, May 1863-1946   **TCLC 3, 11**
 See also Sinclair, Mary Amelia St. Clair
 See also CA 166; DLB 36, 135
Sinclair, Roy
 See Griffith, D(avid Lewelyn) W(ark)
Sinclair, Upton (Beall) 1878-1968 **CLC 1, 11,**
  15, 63; DA; DAB; DAC; DAM MST, NOV;
  WLC
   See also CA 5-8R; 25-28R; CANR 7; CDALB
   1929-1941; DLB 9; INT CANR-7; MTCW;
   SATA 9
Singer, Isaac
 See Singer, Isaac Bashevis
Singer, Isaac Bashevis 1904-1991**CLC 1, 3, 6,**
  9, 11, 15, 23, 38, 69, 111; DA; DAB; DAC;
  DAM MST, NOV; SSC 3; WLC
   See also AITN 1, 2; CA 1-4R; 134; CANR 1,
   39; CDALB 1941-1968; CLR 1; DLB 6, 28,
   52; DLBY 91; JRDA; MAICYA; MTCW;
   SATA 3, 27; SATA-Obit 68

Southworth, Emma Dorothy Eliza Nevitte 1819-1899   NCLC 26
Souza, Ernest
    See Scott, Evelyn
Soyinka, Wole 1934-CLC 3, 5, 14, 36, 44; BLC 3; DA; DAB; DAC; DAM DRAM, MST, MULT; DC 2; WLC
    See also BW 2; CA 13-16R; CANR 27, 39; DLB 125; MTCW
Spackman, W(illiam) M(ode) 1905-1990C L C 46
    See also CA 81-84; 132
Spacks, Barry (Bernard) 1931-   CLC 14
    See also CA 154; CANR 33; DLB 105
Spanidou, Irini 1946-   CLC 44
Spark, Muriel (Sarah) 1918-CLC 2, 3, 5, 8, 13, 18, 40, 94; DAB; DAC; DAM MST, NOV; SSC 10
    See also CA 5-8R; CANR 12, 36; CDBLB 1945-1960; DLB 15, 139; INT CANR-12; MTCW
Spaulding, Douglas
    See Bradbury, Ray (Douglas)
Spaulding, Leonard
    See Bradbury, Ray (Douglas)
Spence, J. A. D.
    See Eliot, T(homas) S(tearns)
Spencer, Elizabeth 1921-   CLC 22
    See also CA 13-16R; CANR 32, 65; DLB 6; MTCW; SATA 14
Spencer, Leonard G.
    See Silverberg, Robert
Spencer, Scott 1945-   CLC 30
    See also CA 113; CANR 51; DLBY 86
Spender, Stephen (Harold) 1909-1995CLC 1, 2, 5, 10, 41, 91; DAM POET
    See also CA 9-12R; 149; CANR 31, 54; CDBLB 1945-1960; DLB 20; MTCW
Spengler, Oswald (Arnold Gottfried) 1880-1936 TCLC 25
    See also CA 118
Spenser, Edmund 1552(?)-1599LC 5, 39; DA; DAB; DAC; DAM MST, POET; PC 8; WLC
    See also CDBLB Before 1660; DLB 167
Spicer, Jack 1925-1965 CLC 8, 18, 72; DAM POET
    See also CA 85-88; DLB 5, 16, 193
Spiegelman, Art 1948-   CLC 76
    See also AAYA 10; CA 125; CANR 41, 55
Spielberg, Peter 1929-   CLC 6
    See also CA 5-8R; CANR 4, 48; DLBY 81
Spielberg, Steven 1947-   CLC 20
    See also AAYA 8, 24; CA 77-80; CANR 32; SATA 32
Spillane, Frank Morrison 1918-
    See Spillane, Mickey
    See also CA 25-28R; CANR 28, 63; MTCW; SATA 66
Spillane, Mickey   CLC 3, 13
    See also Spillane, Frank Morrison
Spinoza, Benedictus de 1632-1677   LC 9
Spinrad, Norman (Richard) 1940-   CLC 46
    See also CA 37-40R; CAAS 19; CANR 20; DLB 8; INT CANR-20
Spitteler, Carl (Friedrich Georg) 1845-1924 TCLC 12
    See also CA 109; DLB 129
Spivack, Kathleen (Romola Drucker) 1938- CLC 6
    See also CA 49-52
Spoto, Donald 1941-   CLC 39
    See also CA 65-68; CANR 11, 57
Springsteen, Bruce (F.) 1949-   CLC 17

    See also CA 111
Spurling, Hilary 1940-   CLC 34
    See also CA 104; CANR 25, 52
Spyker, John Howland
    See Elman, Richard (Martin)
Squires, (James) Radcliffe 1917-1993CLC 51
    See also CA 1-4R; 140; CANR 6, 21
Srivastava, Dhanpat Rai 1880(?)-1936
    See Premchand
    See also CA 118
Stacy, Donald
    See Pohl, Frederik
Stael, Germaine de 1766-1817
    See Stael-Holstein, Anne Louise Germaine Necker Baronn
    See also DLB 119
Stael-Holstein, Anne Louise Germaine Necker Baronn 1766-1817   NCLC 3
    See also Stael, Germaine de
    See also DLB 192
Stafford, Jean 1915-1979CLC 4, 7, 19, 68; SSC 26
    See also CA 1-4R; 85-88; CANR 3, 65; DLB 2, 173; MTCW; SATA-Obit 22
Stafford, William (Edgar) 1914-1993 CLC 4, 7, 29; DAM POET
    See also CA 5-8R; 142; CAAS 3; CANR 5, 22; DLB 5; INT CANR-22
Stagnelius, Eric Johan 1793-1823 NCLC 61
Staines, Trevor
    See Brunner, John (Kilian Houston)
Stairs, Gordon
    See Austin, Mary (Hunter)
Stannard, Martin 1947-   CLC 44
    See also CA 142; DLB 155
Stanton, Elizabeth Cady 1815-1902TCLC 73
    See also DLB 79
Stanton, Maura 1946-   CLC 9
    See also CA 89-92; CANR 15; DLB 120
Stanton, Schuyler
    See Baum, L(yman) Frank
Stapledon, (William) Olaf 1886-1950 T C L C 22
    See also CA 111; 162; DLB 15
Starbuck, George (Edwin) 1931-1996CLC 53; DAM POET
    See also CA 21-24R; 153; CANR 23
Stark, Richard
    See Westlake, Donald E(dwin)
Staunton, Schuyler
    See Baum, L(yman) Frank
Stead, Christina (Ellen) 1902-1983 CLC 2, 5, 8, 32, 80
    See also CA 13-16R; 109; CANR 33, 40; MTCW
Stead, William Thomas 1849-1912 TCLC 48
Steele, Richard 1672-1729   LC 18
    See also CDBLB 1660-1789; DLB 84, 101
Steele, Timothy (Reid) 1948-   CLC 45
    See also CA 93-96; CANR 16, 50; DLB 120
Steffens, (Joseph) Lincoln 1866-1936 T C L C 20
    See also CA 117
Stegner, Wallace (Earle) 1909-1993CLC 9, 49, 81; DAM NOV; SSC 27
    See also AITN 1; BEST 90:3; CA 1-4R; 141; CAAS 9; CANR 1, 21, 46; DLB 9; DLBY 93; MTCW
Stein, Gertrude 1874-1946TCLC 1, 6, 28, 48; DA; DAB; DAC; DAM MST, NOV, POET; PC 18; WLC
    See also CA 104; 132; CDALB 1917-1929; DLB 4, 54, 86; DLBD 15; MTCW

Steinbeck, John (Ernst) 1902-1968CLC 1, 5, 9, 13, 21, 34, 45, 75; DA; DAB; DAC; DAM DRAM, MST, NOV; SSC 11; WLC
    See also AAYA 12; CA 1-4R; 25-28R; CANR 1, 35; CDALB 1929-1941; DLB 7, 9; DLBD 2; MTCW; SATA 9
Steinem, Gloria 1934-   CLC 63
    See also CA 53-56; CANR 28, 51; MTCW
Steiner, George 1929-   CLC 24; DAM NOV
    See also CA 73-76; CANR 31, 67; DLB 67; MTCW; SATA 62
Steiner, K. Leslie
    See Delany, Samuel R(ay, Jr.)
Steiner, Rudolf 1861-1925   TCLC 13
    See also CA 107
Stendhal 1783-1842NCLC 23, 46; DA; DAB; DAC; DAM MST, NOV; SSC 27; WLC
    See also DLB 119
Stephen, Adeline Virginia
    See Woolf, (Adeline) Virginia
Stephen, SirLeslie 1832-1904   TCLC 23
    See also CA 123; DLB 57, 144, 190
Stephen, Sir Leslie
    See Stephen, SirLeslie
Stephen, Virginia
    See Woolf, (Adeline) Virginia
Stephens, James 1882(?)-1950   TCLC 4
    See also CA 104; DLB 19, 153, 162
Stephens, Reed
    See Donaldson, Stephen R.
Steptoe, Lydia
    See Barnes, Djuna
Sterchi, Beat 1949-   CLC 65
Sterling, Brett
    See Bradbury, Ray (Douglas); Hamilton, Edmond
Sterling, Bruce 1954-   CLC 72
    See also CA 119; CANR 44
Sterling, George 1869-1926   TCLC 20
    See also CA 117; 165; DLB 54
Stern, Gerald 1925-   CLC 40, 100
    See also CA 81-84; CANR 28; DLB 105
Stern, Richard (Gustave) 1928-   CLC 4, 39
    See also CA 1-4R; CANR 1, 25, 52; DLBY 87; INT CANR-25
Sternberg, Josef von 1894-1969   CLC 20
    See also CA 81-84
Sterne, Laurence 1713-1768LC 2; DA; DAB; DAC; DAM MST, NOV; WLC
    See also CDBLB 1660-1789; DLB 39
Sternheim, (William Adolf) Carl 1878-1942 TCLC 8
    See also CA 105; DLB 56, 118
Stevens, Mark 1951-   CLC 34
    See also CA 122
Stevens, Wallace 1879-1955 TCLC 3, 12, 45; DA; DAB; DAC; DAM MST, POET; PC 6; WLC
    See also CA 104; 124; CDALB 1929-1941; DLB 54; MTCW
Stevenson, Anne (Katharine) 1933-CLC 7, 33
    See also CA 17-20R; CAAS 9; CANR 9, 33; DLB 40; MTCW
Stevenson, Robert Louis (Balfour) 1850-1894 NCLC 5, 14, 63; DA; DAB; DAC; DAM MST, NOV; SSC 11; WLC
    See also AAYA 24; CDBLB 1890-1914; CLR 10, 11; DLB 18, 57, 141, 156, 174; DLBD 13; JRDA; MAICYA; YABC 2
Stewart, J(ohn) I(nnes) M(ackintosh) 1906-1994   CLC 7, 14, 32
    See also CA 85-88; 147; CAAS 3; CANR 47; MTCW

See King, Stephen (Edwin)

Sylvia
　See Ashton-Warner, Sylvia (Constance)

Symmes, Robert Edward
　See Duncan, Robert (Edward)

Symonds, John Addington 1840-1893 **N C L C 34**
　See also DLB 57, 144

Symons, Arthur 1865-1945　　　　**TCLC 11**
　See also CA 107; DLB 19, 57, 149

Symons, Julian (Gustave) 1912-1994 **CLC 2, 14, 32**
　See also CA 49-52; 147; CAAS 3; CANR 3, 33, 59; DLB 87, 155; DLBY 92; MTCW

Synge, (Edmund) J(ohn) M(illington) 1871-1909 **TCLC 6, 37; DAM DRAM; DC 2**
　See also CA 104; 141; CDBLB 1890-1914; DLB 10, 19

Syruc, J.
　See Milosz, Czeslaw

Szirtes, George 1948-　　　　　**CLC 46**
　See also CA 109; CANR 27, 61

Szymborska, Wislawa 1923-　　　**CLC 99**
　See also CA 154; DLBY 96

T. O., Nik
　See Annensky, Innokenty (Fyodorovich)

Tabori, George 1914-　　　　　**CLC 19**
　See also CA 49-52; CANR 4, 69

Tagore, Rabindranath 1861-1941 **TCLC 3, 53; DAM DRAM, POET; PC 8**
　See also CA 104; 120; MTCW

Taine, Hippolyte Adolphe 1828-1893 **N C L C 15**

Talese, Gay 1932-　　　　　　**CLC 37**
　See also AITN 1; CA 1-4R; CANR 9, 58; DLB 185; INT CANR-9; MTCW

Tallent, Elizabeth (Ann) 1954-　　**CLC 45**
　See also CA 117; DLB 130

Tally, Ted 1952-　　　　　　　**CLC 42**
　See also CA 120; 124; INT 124

Tamayo y Baus, Manuel 1829-1898 **NCLC 1**

Tammsaare, A(nton) H(ansen) 1878-1940 **TCLC 27**
　See also CA 164

Tam'si, Tchicaya U
　See Tchicaya, Gerald Felix

Tan, Amy (Ruth) 1952- **CLC 59; DAM MULT, NOV, POP**
　See also AAYA 9; BEST 89:3; CA 136; CANR 54; DLB 173; SATA 75

Tandem, Felix
　See Spitteler, Carl (Friedrich Georg)

Tanizaki, Jun'ichiro 1886-1965 **CLC 8, 14, 28; SSC 21**
　See also CA 93-96; 25-28R; DLB 180

Tanner, William
　See Amis, Kingsley (William)

Tao Lao
　See Storni, Alfonsina

Tarassoff, Lev
　See Troyat, Henri

Tarbell, Ida M(inerva) 1857-1944 **TCLC 40**
　See also CA 122; DLB 47

Tarkington, (Newton) Booth 1869-1946 **TCLC 9**
　See also CA 110; 143; DLB 9, 102; SATA 17

Tarkovsky, Andrei (Arsenyevich) 1932-1986 **CLC 75**
　See also CA 127

Tartt, Donna 1964(?)-　　　　　**CLC 76**
　See also CA 142

Tasso, Torquato 1544-1595　　　　**LC 5**

Tate, (John Orley) Allen 1899-1979 **CLC 2, 4, 6, 9, 11, 14, 24**
　See also CA 5-8R; 85-88; CANR 32; DLB 4, 45, 63; MTCW

Tate, Ellalice
　See Hibbert, Eleanor Alice Burford

Tate, James (Vincent) 1943-　**CLC 2, 6, 25**
　See also CA 21-24R; CANR 29, 57; DLB 5, 169

Tavel, Ronald 1940-　　　　　**CLC 6**
　See also CA 21-24R; CANR 33

Taylor, C(ecil) P(hilip) 1929-1981　**CLC 27**
　See also CA 25-28R; 105; CANR 47

Taylor, Edward 1642(?)-1729　　**LC 11; DA; DAB; DAC; DAM MST, POET**
　See also DLB 24

Taylor, Eleanor Ross 1920-　　　**CLC 5**
　See also CA 81-84

Taylor, Elizabeth 1912-1975　**CLC 2, 4, 29**
　See also CA 13-16R; CANR 9; DLB 139; MTCW; SATA 13

Taylor, Frederick Winslow 1856-1915 **T C L C 76**

Taylor, Henry (Splawn) 1942-　　**CLC 44**
　See also CA 33-36R; CAAS 7; CANR 31; DLB 5

Taylor, Kamala (Purnaiya) 1924-
　See Markandaya, Kamala
　See also CA 77-80

Taylor, Mildred D.　　　　　　**CLC 21**
　See also AAYA 10; BW 1; CA 85-88; CANR 25; CLR 9; DLB 52; JRDA; MAICYA; SAAS 5; SATA 15, 70

Taylor, Peter (Hillsman) 1917-1994 **CLC 1, 4, 18, 37, 44, 50, 71; SSC 10**
　See also CA 13-16R; 147; CANR 9, 50; DLBY 81, 94; INT CANR-9; MTCW

Taylor, Robert Lewis 1912-　　　**CLC 14**
　See also CA 1-4R; CANR 3, 64; SATA 10

Tchekhov, Anton
　See Chekhov, Anton (Pavlovich)

Tchicaya, Gerald Felix 1931-1988　**CLC 101**
　See also CA 129; 125

Tchicaya U Tam'si
　See Tchicaya, Gerald Felix

Teasdale, Sara 1884-1933　　　　**TCLC 4**
　See also CA 104; 163; DLB 45; SATA 32

Tegner, Esaias 1782-1846　　　　**NCLC 2**

Teilhard de Chardin, (Marie Joseph) Pierre 1881-1955　　　　　　**TCLC 9**
　See also CA 105

Temple, Ann
　See Mortimer, Penelope (Ruth)

Tennant, Emma (Christina) 1937- **CLC 13, 52**
　See also CA 65-68; CAAS 9; CANR 10, 38, 59; DLB 14

Tenneshaw, S. M.
　See Silverberg, Robert

Tennyson, Alfred 1809-1892　**NCLC 30, 65; DA; DAB; DAC; DAM MST, POET; PC 6; WLC**
　See also CDBLB 1832-1890; DLB 32

Teran, Lisa St. Aubin de　　　　**CLC 36**
　See also St. Aubin de Teran, Lisa

Terence 195(?)B.C.-159B.C. **CMLC 14; DC 7**

Teresa de Jesus, St. 1515-1582　　**LC 18**

Terkel, Louis 1912-
　See Terkel, Studs
　See also CA 57-60; CANR 18, 45, 67; MTCW

Terkel, Studs　　　　　　　　**CLC 38**
　See also Terkel, Louis
　See also AITN 1

Terry, C. V.
　See Slaughter, Frank G(ill)

Terry, Megan 1932-　　　　　**CLC 19**
　See also CA 77-80; CABS 3; CANR 43; DLB 7

Tertz, Abram
　See Sinyavsky, Andrei (Donatevich)

Tesich, Steve 1943(?)-1996　　**CLC 40, 69**
　See also CA 105; 152; DLBY 83

Teternikov, Fyodor Kuzmich 1863-1927
　See Sologub, Fyodor
　See also CA 104

Tevis, Walter 1928-1984　　　　**CLC 42**
　See also CA 113

Tey, Josephine　　　　　　　**TCLC 14**
　See also Mackintosh, Elizabeth
　See also DLB 77

Thackeray, William Makepeace 1811-1863 **NCLC 5, 14, 22, 43; DA; DAB; DAC; DAM MST, NOV; WLC**
　See also CDBLB 1832-1890; DLB 21, 55, 159, 163; SATA 23

Thakura, Ravindranatha
　See Tagore, Rabindranath

Tharoor, Shashi 1956-　　　　**CLC 70**
　See also CA 141

Thelwell, Michael Miles 1939-　　**CLC 22**
　See also BW 2; CA 101

Theobald, Lewis, Jr.
　See Lovecraft, H(oward) P(hillips)

Theodorescu, Ion N. 1880-1967
　See Arghezi, Tudor
　See also CA 116

Theriault, Yves 1915-1983　　**CLC 79; DAC; DAM MST**
　See also CA 102; DLB 88

Theroux, Alexander (Louis) 1939- **CLC 2, 25**
　See also CA 85-88; CANR 20, 63

Theroux, Paul (Edward) 1941- **CLC 5, 8, 11, 15, 28, 46; DAM POP**
　See also BEST 89:4; CA 33-36R; CANR 20, 45; DLB 2; MTCW; SATA 44

Thesen, Sharon 1946-　　　　**CLC 56**
　See also CA 163

Thevenin, Denis
　See Duhamel, Georges

Thibault, Jacques Anatole Francois 1844-1924
　See France, Anatole
　See also CA 106; 127; DAM NOV; MTCW

Thiele, Colin (Milton) 1920-　　**CLC 17**
　See also CA 29-32R; CANR 12, 28, 53; CLR 27; MAICYA; SAAS 2; SATA 14, 72

Thomas, Audrey (Callahan) 1935- **CLC 7, 13, 37, 107; SSC 20**
　See also AITN 2; CA 21-24R; CAAS 19; CANR 36, 58; DLB 60; MTCW

Thomas, D(onald) M(ichael) 1935- **CLC 13, 22, 31**
　See also CA 61-64; CAAS 11; CANR 17, 45; CDBLB 1960 to Present; DLB 40; INT CANR-17; MTCW

Thomas, Dylan (Marlais) 1914-1953 **TCLC 1, 8, 45; DA; DAB; DAC; DAM DRAM, MST, POET; PC 2; SSC 3; WLC**
　See also CA 104; 120; CANR 65; CDBLB 1945-1960; DLB 13, 20, 139; MTCW; SATA 60

Thomas, (Philip) Edward 1878-1917 **T C L C 10; DAM POET**
　See also CA 106; 153; DLB 19

Thomas, Joyce Carol 1938-　　　**CLC 35**
　See also AAYA 12; BW 2; CA 113; 116; CANR 48; CLR 19; DLB 33; INT 116; JRDA; MAICYA; MTCW; SAAS 7; SATA 40, 78

Thomas, Lewis 1913-1993　　　**CLC 35**
　See also CA 85-88; 143; CANR 38, 60; MTCW

Thomas, Paul
  See Mann, (Paul) Thomas
Thomas, Piri 1928-   **CLC 17**
  See also CA 73-76; HW
Thomas, R(onald) S(tuart) 1913- **CLC 6, 13,**
  48; DAB; DAM POET
    See also CA 89-92; CAAS 4; CANR 30;
    CDBLB 1960 to Present; DLB 27; MTCW
Thomas, Ross (Elmore) 1926-1995 **CLC 39**
  See also CA 33-36R; 150; CANR 22, 63
Thompson, Francis Clegg
  See Mencken, H(enry) L(ouis)
Thompson, Francis Joseph 1859-1907**TCLC 4**
  See also CA 104; CDBLB 1890-1914; DLB 19
Thompson, Hunter S(tockton) 1939- **CLC 9,**
  17, 40, 104; DAM POP
    See also BEST 89:1; CA 17-20R; CANR 23,
    46; DLB 185; MTCW
Thompson, James Myers
  See Thompson, Jim (Myers)
Thompson, Jim (Myers) 1906-1977(?)**CLC 69**
  See also CA 140
Thompson, Judith   **CLC 39**
Thomson, James 1700-1748   **LC 16, 29, 40;**
  DAM POET
  See also DLB 95
Thomson, James 1834-1882 **NCLC 18; DAM**
  POET
  See also DLB 35
Thoreau, Henry David 1817-1862**NCLC 7, 21,**
  61; DA; DAB; DAC; DAM MST; WLC
  See also CDALB 1640-1865; DLB 1
Thornton, Hall
  See Silverberg, Robert
Thucydides c. 455B.C.-399B.C.   **CMLC 17**
  See also DLB 176
Thurber, James (Grover) 1894-1961 **CLC 5,**
  11, 25; DA; DAB; DAC; DAM DRAM,
  MST, NOV; SSC 1
    See also CA 73-76; CANR 17, 39; CDALB
    1929-1941; DLB 4, 11, 22, 102; MAICYA;
    MTCW; SATA 13
Thurman, Wallace (Henry) 1902-1934**T C L C**
  6; BLC 3; DAM MULT
  See also BW 1; CA 104; 124; DLB 51
Ticheburn, Cheviot
  See Ainsworth, William Harrison
Tieck, (Johann) Ludwig 1773-1853 **NCLC 5,**
  46; SSC 31
  See also DLB 90
Tiger, Derry
  See Ellison, Harlan (Jay)
Tilghman, Christopher 1948(?)-   **CLC 65**
  See also CA 159
Tillinghast, Richard (Williford) 1940-**CLC 29**
  See also CA 29-32R; CAAS 23; CANR 26, 51
Timrod, Henry 1828-1867   **NCLC 25**
  See also DLB 3
Tindall, Gillian (Elizabeth) 1938-   **CLC 7**
  See also CA 21-24R; CANR 11, 65
Tiptree, James, Jr.   **CLC 48, 50**
  See also Sheldon, Alice Hastings Bradley
  See also DLB 8
Titmarsh, Michael Angelo
  See Thackeray, William Makepeace
Tocqueville, Alexis (Charles Henri Maurice
  Clerel Comte) 1805-1859 **NCLC 7, 63**
Tolkien, J(ohn) R(onald) R(euel) 1892-1973
  CLC 1, 2, 3, 8, 12, 38; DA; DAB; DAC;
  DAM MST, NOV, POP; WLC
    See also AAYA 10; AITN 1; CA 17-18; 45-48;
    CANR 36; CAP 2; CDBLB 1914-1945; DLB
    15, 160; JRDA; MAICYA; MTCW; SATA 2,

  32; SATA-Obit 24
Toller, Ernst 1893-1939   **TCLC 10**
  See also CA 107; DLB 124
Tolson, M. B.
  See Tolson, Melvin B(eaunorus)
Tolson, Melvin B(eaunorus) 1898(?)-1966
  CLC 36, 105; BLC 3; DAM MULT, POET
    See also BW 1; CA 124; 89-92; DLB 48, 76
Tolstoi, Aleksei Nikolaevich
  See Tolstoy, Alexey Nikolaevich
Tolstoy, Alexey Nikolaevich 1882-1945**T C L C**
  18
  See also CA 107; 158
Tolstoy, Count Leo
  See Tolstoy, Leo (Nikolaevich)
Tolstoy, Leo (Nikolaevich) 1828-1910**TCLC 4,**
  11, 17, 28, 44, 79; DA; DAB; DAC; DAM
  MST, NOV; SSC 9, 30; WLC
    See also CA 104; 123; SATA 26
Tomasi di Lampedusa, Giuseppe 1896-1957
  See Lampedusa, Giuseppe (Tomasi) di
  See also CA 111
Tomlin, Lily   **CLC 17**
  See also Tomlin, Mary Jean
Tomlin, Mary Jean 1939(?)-
  See Tomlin, Lily
  See also CA 117
Tomlinson, (Alfred) Charles 1927-**CLC 2, 4, 6,**
  13, 45; DAM POET; PC 17
    See also CA 5-8R; CANR 33; DLB 40
Tomlinson, H(enry) M(ajor) 1873-1958**TCLC**
  71
  See also CA 118; 161; DLB 36, 100, 195
Tonson, Jacob
  See Bennett, (Enoch) Arnold
Toole, John Kennedy 1937-1969 **CLC 19, 64**
  See also CA 104; DLBY 81
Toomer, Jean 1894-1967**CLC 1, 4, 13, 22; BLC**
  3; DAM MULT; PC 7; SSC 1; WLCS
    See also BW 1; CA 85-88; CDALB 1917-1929;
    DLB 45, 51; MTCW
Torley, Luke
  See Blish, James (Benjamin)
Tornimparte, Alessandra
  See Ginzburg, Natalia
Torre, Raoul della
  See Mencken, H(enry) L(ouis)
Torrey, E(dwin) Fuller 1937-   **CLC 34**
  See also CA 119
Torsvan, Ben Traven
  See Traven, B.
Torsvan, Benno Traven
  See Traven, B.
Torsvan, Berick Traven
  See Traven, B.
Torsvan, Berwick Traven
  See Traven, B.
Torsvan, Bruno Traven
  See Traven, B.
Torsvan, Traven
  See Traven, B.
Tournier, Michel (Edouard) 1924-**CLC 6, 23,**
  36, 95
    See also CA 49-52; CANR 3, 36; DLB 83;
    MTCW; SATA 23
Tournimparte, Alessandra
  See Ginzburg, Natalia
Towers, Ivar
  See Kornbluth, C(yril) M.
Towne, Robert (Burton) 1936(?)-   **CLC 87**
  See also CA 108; DLB 44
Townsend, Sue   **CLC 61**
  See also Townsend, Susan Elaine

  See also SATA 55, 93; SATA-Brief 48
Townsend, Susan Elaine 1946-
  See Townsend, Sue
    See also CA 119; 127; CANR 65; DAB; DAC;
    DAM MST
Townshend, Peter (Dennis Blandford) 1945-
  CLC 17, 42
  See also CA 107
Tozzi, Federigo 1883-1920   **TCLC 31**
  See also CA 160
Traill, Catharine Parr 1802-1899 **NCLC 31**
  See also DLB 99
Trakl, Georg 1887-1914   **TCLC 5; PC 20**
  See also CA 104; 165
Transtroemer, Tomas (Goesta) 1931-**CLC 52,**
  65; DAM POET
    See also CA 117; 129; CAAS 17
Transtromer, Tomas Gosta
  See Transtroemer, Tomas (Goesta)
Traven, B. (?)-1969   **CLC 8, 11**
    See also CA 19-20; 25-28R; CAP 2; DLB 9,
    56; MTCW
Treitel, Jonathan 1959-   **CLC 70**
Tremain, Rose 1943-   **CLC 42**
  See also CA 97-100; CANR 44; DLB 14
Tremblay, Michel 1942- **CLC 29, 102; DAC;**
  DAM MST
  See also CA 116; 128; DLB 60; MTCW
Trevanian   **CLC 29**
  See also Whitaker, Rod(ney)
Trevor, Glen
  See Hilton, James
Trevor, William 1928- **CLC 7, 9, 14, 25, 71;**
  SSC 21
    See also Cox, William Trevor
    See also DLB 14, 139
Trifonov, Yuri (Valentinovich) 1925-1981
  CLC 45
  See also CA 126; 103; MTCW
Trilling, Lionel 1905-1975   **CLC 9, 11, 24**
    See also CA 9-12R; 61-64; CANR 10; DLB 28,
    63; INT CANR-10; MTCW
Trimball, W. H.
  See Mencken, H(enry) L(ouis)
Tristan
  See Gomez de la Serna, Ramon
Tristram
  See Housman, A(lfred) E(dward)
Trogdon, William (Lewis) 1939-
  See Heat-Moon, William Least
    See also CA 115; 119; CANR 47; INT 119
Trollope, Anthony 1815-1882**NCLC 6, 33; DA;**
  DAB; DAC; DAM MST, NOV; SSC 28;
  WLC
    See also CDBLB 1832-1890; DLB 21, 57, 159;
    SATA 22
Trollope, Frances 1779-1863   **NCLC 30**
  See also DLB 21, 166
Trotsky, Leon 1879-1940   **TCLC 22**
  See also CA 118
Trotter (Cockburn), Catharine 1679-1749**L C**
  8
  See also DLB 84
Trout, Kilgore
  See Farmer, Philip Jose
Trow, George W. S. 1943-   **CLC 52**
  See also CA 126
Troyat, Henri 1911-   **CLC 23**
  See also CA 45-48; CANR 2, 33, 67; MTCW
Trudeau, G(arretson) B(eekman) 1948-
  See Trudeau, Garry B.
    See also CA 81-84; CANR 31; SATA 35
Trudeau, Garry B.   **CLC 12**

See also Trudeau, G(arretson) B(eekman)
See also AAYA 10; AITN 2
Truffaut, Francois 1932-1984   **CLC 20, 101**
See also CA 81-84; 113; CANR 34
Trumbo, Dalton 1905-1976   **CLC 19**
See also CA 21-24R; 69-72; CANR 10; DLB 26
Trumbull, John 1750-1831   **NCLC 30**
See also DLB 31
Trundlett, Helen B.
See Eliot, T(homas) S(tearns)
Tryon, Thomas 1926-1991   **CLC 3, 11; DAM POP**
See also AITN 1; CA 29-32R; 135; CANR 32; MTCW
Tryon, Tom
See Tryon, Thomas
Ts'ao Hsueh-ch'in 1715(?)-1763   **LC 1**
Tsushima, Shuji 1909-1948
See Dazai Osamu
See also CA 107
Tsvetaeva (Efron), Marina (Ivanovna) 1892-1941   **TCLC 7, 35; PC 14**
See also CA 104; 128; MTCW
Tuck, Lily 1938-   **CLC 70**
See also CA 139
Tu Fu 712-770   **PC 9**
See also DAM MULT
Tunis, John R(oberts) 1889-1975   **CLC 12**
See also CA 61-64; CANR 62; DLB 22, 171; JRDA; MAICYA; SATA 37; SATA-Brief 30
Tuohy, Frank   **CLC 37**
See also Tuohy, John Francis
See also DLB 14, 139
Tuohy, John Francis 1925-
See Tuohy, Frank
See also CA 5-8R; CANR 3, 47
Turco, Lewis (Putnam) 1934-   **CLC 11, 63**
See also CA 13-16R; CAAS 22; CANR 24, 51; DLBY 84
Turgenev, Ivan 1818-1883   **NCLC 21; DA; DAB; DAC; DAM MST, NOV; DC 7; SSC 7; WLC**
Turgot, Anne-Robert-Jacques 1727-1781   **L C 26**
Turner, Frederick 1943-   **CLC 48**
See also CA 73-76; CAAS 10; CANR 12, 30, 56; DLB 40
Tutu, Desmond M(pilo) 1931-**CLC 80; BLC 3; DAM MULT**
See also BW 1; CA 125; CANR 67
Tutuola, Amos 1920-1997**CLC 5, 14, 29; BLC 3; DAM MULT**
See also BW 2; CA 9-12R; 159; CANR 27, 66; DLB 125; MTCW
Twain, MarkTCLC 6, 12, 19, 36, 48, 59; SSC 6, 26; WLC**
See also Clemens, Samuel Langhorne
See also AAYA 20; DLB 11, 12, 23, 64, 74
Tyler, Anne 1941- **CLC 7, 11, 18, 28, 44, 59, 103; DAM NOV, POP**
See also AAYA 18; BEST 89:1; CA 9-12R; CANR 11, 33, 53; DLB 6, 143; DLBY 82; MTCW; SATA 7, 90
Tyler, Royall 1757-1826   **NCLC 3**
See also DLB 37
Tynan, Katharine 1861-1931   **TCLC 3**
See also CA 104; DLB 153
Tyutchev, Fyodor 1803-1873   **NCLC 34**
Tzara, Tristan 1896-1963   **CLC 47; DAM POET**
See also CA 153; 89-92
Uhry, Alfred 1936-   **CLC 55; DAM DRAM,**

POP
See also CA 127; 133; INT 133
Ulf, Haerved
See Strindberg, (Johan) August
Ulf, Harved
See Strindberg, (Johan) August
Ulibarri, Sabine R(eyes) 1919-**CLC 83; DAM MULT**
See also CA 131; DLB 82; HW
Unamuno (y Jugo), Miguel de 1864-1936   **TCLC 2, 9; DAM MULT, NOV; HLC; SSC 11**
See also CA 104; 131; DLB 108; HW; MTCW
Undercliffe, Errol
See Campbell, (John) Ramsey
Underwood, Miles
See Glassco, John
Undset, Sigrid 1882-1949**TCLC 3; DA; DAB; DAC; DAM MST, NOV; WLC**
See also CA 104; 129; MTCW
Ungaretti, Giuseppe 1888-1970**CLC 7, 11, 15**
See also CA 19-20; 25-28R; CAP 2; DLB 114
Unger, Douglas 1952-   **CLC 34**
See also CA 130
Unsworth, Barry (Forster) 1930-   **CLC 76**
See also CA 25-28R; CANR 30, 54; DLB 194
Updike, John (Hoyer) 1932-**CLC 1, 2, 3, 5, 7, 9, 13, 15, 23, 34, 43, 70; DA; DAB; DAC; DAM MST, NOV, POET, POP; SSC 13, 27; WLC**
See also CA 1-4R; CABS 1; CANR 4, 33, 51; CDALB 1968-1988; DLB 2, 5, 143; DLBD 3; DLBY 80, 82, 97; MTCW
Upshaw, Margaret Mitchell
See Mitchell, Margaret (Munnerlyn)
Upton, Mark
See Sanders, Lawrence
Urdang, Constance (Henriette) 1922-**CLC 47**
See also CA 21-24R; CANR 9, 24
Uriel, Henry
See Faust, Frederick (Schiller)
Uris, Leon (Marcus) 1924- **CLC 7, 32; DAM NOV, POP**
See also AITN 1, 2; BEST 89:2; CA 1-4R; CANR 1, 40, 65; MTCW; SATA 49
Urmuz
See Codrescu, Andrei
Urquhart, Jane 1949-   **CLC 90; DAC**
See also CA 113; CANR 32, 68
Ustinov, Peter (Alexander) 1921-   **CLC 1**
See also AITN 1; CA 13-16R; CANR 25, 51; DLB 13
U Tam'si, Gerald Felix Tchicaya
See Tchicaya, Gerald Felix
U Tam'si, Tchicaya
See Tchicaya, Gerald Felix
Vachss, Andrew (Henry) 1942-   **CLC 106**
See also CA 118; CANR 44
Vachss, Andrew H.
See Vachss, Andrew (Henry)
Vaculik, Ludvik 1926-   **CLC 7**
See also CA 53-56
Vaihinger, Hans 1852-1933   **TCLC 71**
See also CA 116; 166
Valdez, Luis (Miguel) 1940-   **CLC 84; DAM MULT; HLC**
See also CA 101; CANR 32; DLB 122; HW
Valenzuela, Luisa 1938- **CLC 31, 104; DAM MULT; SSC 14**
See also CA 101; CANR 32, 65; DLB 113; HW
Valera y Alcala-Galiano, Juan 1824-1905   **TCLC 10**
See also CA 106

Valery, (Ambroise) Paul (Toussaint Jules) 1871-1945   **TCLC 4, 15; DAM POET; PC 9**
See also CA 104; 122; MTCW
Valle-Inclan, Ramon (Maria) del 1866-1936   **TCLC 5; DAM MULT; HLC**
See also CA 106; 153; DLB 134
Vallejo, Antonio Buero
See Buero Vallejo, Antonio
Vallejo, Cesar (Abraham) 1892-1938**TCLC 3, 56; DAM MULT; HLC**
See also CA 105; 153; HW
Vallès, Jules 1832-1885   **NCLC 71**
See also DLB 123
Vallette, Marguerite Eymery
See Rachilde
Valle Y Pena, Ramon del
See Valle-Inclan, Ramon (Maria) del
Van Ash, Cay 1918-   **CLC 34**
Vanbrugh, Sir John 1664-1726 **LC 21; DAM DRAM**
See also DLB 80
Van Campen, Karl
See Campbell, John W(ood, Jr.)
Vance, Gerald
See Silverberg, Robert
Vance, Jack   **CLC 35**
See also Kuttner, Henry; Vance, John Holbrook
See also DLB 8
Vance, John Holbrook 1916-
See Queen, Ellery; Vance, Jack
See also CA 29-32R; CANR 17, 65; MTCW
Van Den Bogarde, Derek Jules Gaspard Ulric Niven 1921-
See Bogarde, Dirk
See also CA 77-80
Vandenburgh, Jane   **CLC 59**
Vanderhaeghe, Guy 1951-   **CLC 41**
See also CA 113
van der Post, Laurens (Jan) 1906-1996**CLC 5**
See also CA 5-8R; 155; CANR 35
van de Wetering, Janwillem 1931-   **CLC 47**
See also CA 49-52; CANR 4, 62
Van Dine, S. S.   **TCLC 23**
See also Wright, Willard Huntington
Van Doren, Carl (Clinton) 1885-1950 **T C L C 18**
See also CA 111
Van Doren, Mark 1894-1972   **CLC 6, 10**
See also CA 1-4R; 37-40R; CANR 3; DLB 45; MTCW
Van Druten, John (William) 1901-1957**TCLC 2**
See also CA 104; 161; DLB 10
Van Duyn, Mona (Jane) 1921- **CLC 3, 7, 63; DAM POET**
See also CA 9-12R; CANR 7, 38, 60; DLB 5
Van Dyne, Edith
See Baum, L(yman) Frank
van Itallie, Jean-Claude 1936-   **CLC 3**
See also CA 45-48; CAAS 2; CANR 1, 48; DLB 7
van Ostaijen, Paul 1896-1928   **TCLC 33**
See also CA 163
Van Peebles, Melvin 1932- **CLC 2, 20; DAM MULT**
See also BW 2; CA 85-88; CANR 27, 67
Vansittart, Peter 1920-   **CLC 42**
See also CA 1-4R; CANR 3, 49
Van Vechten, Carl 1880-1964   **CLC 33**
See also CA 89-92; DLB 4, 9, 51
Van Vogt, A(lfred) E(lton) 1912-   **CLC 1**
See also CA 21-24R; CANR 28; DLB 8; SATA 14

Walker, George F. 1947-   **CLC 44, 61; DAB; DAC; DAM MST**
See also CA 103; CANR 21, 43, 59; DLB 60

Walker, Joseph A. 1935-   **CLC 19; DAM DRAM, MST**
See also BW 1; CA 89-92; CANR 26; DLB 38

Walker, Margaret (Abigail) 1915- **CLC 1, 6; BLC; DAM MULT; PC 20**
See also BW 2; CA 73-76; CANR 26, 54; DLB 76, 152; MTCW

Walker, Ted   **CLC 13**
See also Walker, Edward Joseph
See also DLB 40

Wallace, David Foster 1962-   **CLC 50**
See also CA 132; CANR 59

Wallace, Dexter
See Masters, Edgar Lee

Wallace, (Richard Horatio) Edgar 1875-1932 **TCLC 57**
Scc also CA 115; DLB 70

Wallace, Irving 1916-1990 **CLC 7, 13; DAM NOV, POP**
See also AITN 1; CA 1-4R; 132; CAAS 1; CANR 1, 27; INT CANR-27; MTCW

Wallant, Edward Lewis 1926-1962 **CLC 5, 10**
See also CA 1-4R; CANR 22; DLB 2, 28, 143; MTCW

Walley, Byron
See Card, Orson Scott

Walpole, Horace 1717-1797   **LC 2**
See also DLB 39, 104

Walpole, Hugh (Seymour) 1884-1941 **TCLC 5**
See also CA 104; 165; DLB 34

Walser, Martin 1927-   **CLC 27**
See also CA 57-60; CANR 8, 46; DLB 75, 124

Walser, Robert 1878-1956 **TCLC 18; SSC 20**
See also CA 118; 165; DLB 66

Walsh, Jill Paton   **CLC 35**
See also Paton Walsh, Gillian
See also AAYA 11; CLR 2; DLB 161; SAAS 3

Walter, Villiam Christian
See Andersen, Hans Christian

Wambaugh, Joseph (Aloysius, Jr.) 1937- **CLC 3, 18; DAM NOV, POP**
See also AITN 1; BEST 89:3; CA 33-36R; CANR 42, 65; DLB 6; DLBY 83; MTCW

Wang Wei 699(?)-761(?)   **PC 18**

Ward, Arthur Henry Sarsfield 1883-1959
See Rohmer, Sax
See also CA 108

Ward, Douglas Turner 1930-   **CLC 19**
See also BW 1; CA 81-84; CANR 27; DLB 7, 38

Ward, Mary Augusta
See Ward, Mrs. Humphry

Ward, Mrs. Humphry 1851-1920   **TCLC 55**
See also DLB 18

Ward, Peter
See Faust, Frederick (Schiller)

Warhol, Andy 1928(?)-1987   **CLC 20**
See also AAYA 12; BEST 89:4; CA 89-92; 121; CANR 34

Warner, Francis (Robert le Plastrier) 1937- **CLC 14**
See also CA 53-56; CANR 11

Warner, Marina 1946-   **CLC 59**
See also CA 65-68; CANR 21, 55; DLB 194

Warner, Rex (Ernest) 1905-1986 **CLC 45**
See also CA 89-92; 119; DLB 15

Warner, Susan (Bogert) 1819-1885 **NCLC 31**
See also DLB 3, 42

Warner, Sylvia (Constance) Ashton
See Ashton-Warner, Sylvia (Constance)

Warner, Sylvia Townsend 1893-1978 **CLC 7, 19; SSC 23**
See also CA 61-64; 77-80; CANR 16, 60; DLB 34, 139; MTCW

Warren, Mercy Otis 1728-1814   **NCLC 13**
See also DLB 31, 200

Warren, Robert Penn 1905-1989 **CLC 1, 4, 6, 8, 10, 13, 18, 39, 53, 59; DA; DAB; DAC; DAM MST, NOV, POET; SSC 4; WLC**
See also AITN 1; CA 13-16R; 129; CANR 10, 47; CDALB 1968-1988; DLB 2, 48, 152; DLBY 80, 89; INT CANR-10; MTCW; SATA 46; SATA-Obit 63

Warshofsky, Isaac
See Singer, Isaac Bashevis

Warton, Thomas 1728-1790   **LC 15; DAM POET**
See also DLB 104, 109

Waruk, Kona
See Harris, (Theodore) Wilson

Warung, Price 1855-1911   **TCLC 45**

Warwick, Jarvis
See Garner, Hugh

Washington, Alex
See Harris, Mark

Washington, Booker T(aliaferro) 1856-1915 **TCLC 10; BLC 3; DAM MULT**
See also BW 1; CA 114; 125; SATA 28

Washington, George 1732-1799   **LC 25**
See also DLB 31

Wassermann, (Karl) Jakob 1873-1934 **TCLC 6**
See also CA 104; DLB 66

Wasserstein, Wendy 1950-   **CLC 32, 59, 90; DAM DRAM; DC 4**
See also CA 121; 129; CABS 3; CANR 53; INT 129; SATA 94

Waterhouse, Keith (Spencer) 1929- **CLC 47**
See also CA 5-8R; CANR 38, 67; DLB 13, 15; MTCW

Waters, Frank (Joseph) 1902-1995   **CLC 88**
See also CA 5-8R; 149; CAAS 13; CANR 3, 18, 63; DLBY 86

Waters, Roger 1944-   **CLC 35**

Watkins, Frances Ellen
See Harper, Frances Ellen Watkins

Watkins, Gerrold
See Malzberg, Barry N(athaniel)

Watkins, Gloria 1955(?)-
See hooks, bell
See also BW 2; CA 143

Watkins, Paul 1964-   **CLC 55**
See also CA 132; CANR 62

Watkins, Vernon Phillips 1906-1967 **CLC 43**
See also CA 9-10; 25-28R; CAP 1; DLB 20

Watson, Irving S.
See Mencken, H(enry) L(ouis)

Watson, John H.
See Farmer, Philip Jose

Watson, Richard F.
See Silverberg, Robert

Waugh, Auberon (Alexander) 1939-   **CLC 7**
See also CA 45-48; CANR 6, 22; DLB 14, 194

Waugh, Evelyn (Arthur St. John) 1903-1966 **CLC 1, 3, 8, 13, 19, 27, 44, 107; DA; DAB; DAC; DAM MST, NOV, POP; WLC**
See also CA 85-88; 25-28R; CANR 22; CDBLB 1914-1945; DLB 15, 162, 195; MTCW

Waugh, Harriet 1944-   **CLC 6**
See also CA 85-88; CANR 22

Ways, C. R.
See Blount, Roy (Alton), Jr.

Waystaff, Simon
See Swift, Jonathan

Webb, (Martha) Beatrice (Potter) 1858-1943 **TCLC 22**
See also Potter, (Helen) Beatrix
See also CA 117

Webb, Charles (Richard) 1939-   **CLC 7**
See also CA 25-28R

Webb, James H(enry), Jr. 1946-   **CLC 22**
See also CA 81-84

Webb, Mary (Gladys Meredith) 1881-1927 **TCLC 24**
See also CA 123; DLB 34

Webb, Mrs. Sidney
See Webb, (Martha) Beatrice (Potter)

Webb, Phyllis 1927-   **CLC 18**
See also CA 104; CANR 23; DLB 53

Webb, Sidney (James) 1859-1947 **TCLC 22**
See also CA 117; 163; DLB 190

Webber, Andrew Lloyd   **CLC 21**
See also Lloyd Webber, Andrew

Weber, Lenora Mattingly 1895-1971 **CLC 12**
See also CA 19-20; 29-32R; CAP 1; SATA 2; SATA-Obit 26

Weber, Max 1864-1920   **TCLC 69**
See also CA 109

Webster, John 1579(?)-1634(?)   **LC 33; DA; DAB; DAC; DAM DRAM, MST; DC 2; WLC**
See also CDBLB Before 1660; DLB 58

Webster, Noah 1758-1843   **NCLC 30**

Wedekind, (Benjamin) Frank(lin) 1864-1918 **TCLC 7; DAM DRAM**
See also CA 104; 153; DLB 118

Weidman, Jerome 1913-   **CLC 7**
See also AITN 2; CA 1-4R; CANR 1; DLB 28

Weil, Simone (Adolphe) 1909-1943 **TCLC 23**
See also CA 117; 159

Weinstein, Nathan
See West, Nathanael

Weinstein, Nathan von Wallenstein
See West, Nathanael

Weir, Peter (Lindsay) 1944-   **CLC 20**
See also CA 113; 123

Weiss, Peter (Ulrich) 1916-1982 **CLC 3, 15, 51; DAM DRAM**
See also CA 45-48; 106; CANR 3; DLB 69, 124

Weiss, Theodore (Russell) 1916- **CLC 3, 8, 14**
See also CA 9-12R; CAAS 2; CANR 46; DLB 5

Welch, (Maurice) Denton 1915-1948 **TCLC 22**
See also CA 121; 148

Welch, James 1940-   **CLC 6, 14, 52; DAM MULT, POP**
See also CA 85-88; CANR 42, 66; DLB 175; NNAL

Weldon, Fay 1931- **CLC 6, 9, 11, 19, 36, 59; DAM POP**
See also CA 21-24R; CANR 16, 46, 63; CDBLB 1960 to Present; DLB 14, 194; INT CANR-16; MTCW

Wellek, Rene 1903-1995   **CLC 28**
See also CA 5-8R; 150; CAAS 7; CANR 8; DLB 63; INT CANR-8

Weller, Michael 1942-   **CLC 10, 53**
See also CA 85-88

Weller, Paul 1958-   **CLC 26**

Wellershoff, Dieter 1925-   **CLC 46**
See also CA 89-92; CANR 16, 37

Welles, (George) Orson 1915-1985 **CLC 20, 80**
See also CA 93-96; 117

Wellman, John McDowell 1945-
See Wellman, Mac
See also CA 166

Wilkins, Mary
See Freeman, Mary Eleanor Wilkins
Willard, Nancy 1936-   **CLC 7, 37**
See also CA 89-92; CANR 10, 39, 68; CLR 5; DLB 5, 52; MAICYA; MTCW; SATA 37, 71; SATA-Brief 30
Williams, C(harles) K(enneth) 1936-**CLC 33, 56; DAM POET**
See also CA 37-40R; CAAS 26; CANR 57; DLB 5
Williams, Charles
See Collier, James L(incoln)
Williams, Charles (Walter Stansby) 1886-1945 **TCLC 1, 11**
See also CA 104; 163; DLB 100, 153
Williams, (George) Emlyn 1905-1987**CLC 15; DAM DRAM**
See also CA 104; 123; CANR 36; DLB 10, 77; MTCW
Williams, Hugo 1942-   **CLC 42**
See also CA 17-20R; CANR 45; DLB 40
Williams, J. Walker
See Wodehouse, P(elham) G(renville)
Williams, John A(lfred) 1925-**CLC 5, 13; BLC 3; DAM MULT**
See also BW 2; CA 53-56; CAAS 3; CANR 6, 26, 51; DLB 2, 33; INT CANR-6
Williams, Jonathan (Chamberlain) 1929-**CLC 13**
See also CA 9-12R; CAAS 12; CANR 8; DLB 5
Williams, Joy 1944-   **CLC 31**
See also CA 41-44R; CANR 22, 48
Williams, Norman 1952-   **CLC 39**
See also CA 118
Williams, Sherley Anne 1944-**CLC 89; BLC 3; DAM MULT, POET**
See also BW 2; CA 73-76; CANR 25; DLB 41; INT CANR-25; SATA 78
Williams, Shirley
See Williams, Sherley Anne
Williams, Tennessee 1911-1983**CLC 1, 2, 5, 7, 8, 11, 15, 19, 30, 39, 45, 71, 111; DA; DAB; DAC; DAM DRAM, MST; DC 4; WLC**
See also AITN 1, 2; CA 5-8R; 108; CABS 3; CANR 31; CDALB 1941-1968; DLB 7; DLBD 4; DLBY 83; MTCW
Williams, Thomas (Alonzo) 1926-1990**CLC 14**
See also CA 1-4R; 132; CANR 2
Williams, William C.
See Williams, William Carlos
Williams, William Carlos 1883-1963**CLC 1, 2, 5, 9, 13, 22, 42, 67; DA; DAB; DAC; DAM MST, POET; PC 7; SSC 31**
See also CA 89-92; CANR 34; CDALB 1917-1929; DLB 4, 16, 54, 86; MTCW
Williamson, David (Keith) 1942-   **CLC 56**
See also CA 103; CANR 41
Williamson, Ellen Douglas 1905-1984
See Douglas, Ellen
See also CA 17-20R; 114; CANR 39
Williamson, Jack   **CLC 29**
See also Williamson, John Stewart
See also CAAS 8; DLB 8
Williamson, John Stewart 1908-
See Williamson, Jack
See also CA 17-20R; CANR 23
Willie, Frederick
See Lovecraft, H(oward) P(hillips)
Willingham, Calder (Baynard, Jr.) 1922-1995 **CLC 5, 51**
See also CA 5-8R; 147; CANR 3; DLB 2, 44; MTCW

Willis, Charles
See Clarke, Arthur C(harles)
Willy
See Colette, (Sidonie-Gabrielle)
Willy, Colette
See Colette, (Sidonie-Gabrielle)
Wilson, A(ndrew) N(orman) 1950-   **CLC 33**
See also CA 112; 122; DLB 14, 155, 194
Wilson, Angus (Frank Johnstone) 1913-1991 **CLC 2, 3, 5, 25, 34; SSC 21**
See also CA 5-8R; 134; CANR 21; DLB 15, 139, 155; MTCW
Wilson, August 1945-**CLC 39, 50, 63; BLC 3; DA; DAB; DAC; DAM DRAM, MST, MULT; DC 2; WLCS**
See also AAYA 16; BW 2; CA 115; 122; CANR 42, 54; MTCW
Wilson, Brian 1942-   **CLC 12**
Wilson, Colin 1931-   **CLC 3, 14**
See also CA 1-4R; CAAS 5; CANR 1, 22, 33; DLB 14, 194; MTCW
Wilson, Dirk
See Pohl, Frederik
Wilson, Edmund 1895-1972**CLC 1, 2, 3, 8, 24**
See also CA 1-4R; 37-40R; CANR 1, 46; DLB 63; MTCW
Wilson, Ethel Davis (Bryant) 1888(?)-1980 **CLC 13; DAC; DAM POET**
See also CA 102; DLB 68; MTCW
Wilson, John 1785-1854   **NCLC 5**
Wilson, John (Anthony) Burgess 1917-1993
See Burgess, Anthony
See also CA 1-4R; 143; CANR 2, 46; DAC; DAM NOV; MTCW
Wilson, Lanford 1937-   **CLC 7, 14, 36; DAM DRAM**
See also CA 17-20R; CABS 3; CANR 45; DLB 7
Wilson, Robert M. 1944-   **CLC 7, 9**
See also CA 49-52; CANR 2, 41; MTCW
Wilson, Robert McLiam 1964-   **CLC 59**
See also CA 132
Wilson, Sloan 1920-   **CLC 32**
See also CA 1-4R; CANR 1, 44
Wilson, Snoo 1948-   **CLC 33**
See also CA 69-72
Wilson, William S(mith) 1932-   **CLC 49**
See also CA 81-84
Wilson, (Thomas) Woodrow 1856-1924**TCLC 79**
See also CA 166; DLB 47
Winchilsea, Anne (Kingsmill) Finch Counte 1661-1720
See Finch, Anne
Windham, Basil
See Wodehouse, P(elham) G(renville)
Wingrove, David (John) 1954-   **CLC 68**
See also CA 133
Wintergreen, Jane
See Duncan, Sara Jeannette
Winters, Janet Lewis   **CLC 41**
See Lewis, Janet
See also DLBY 87
Winters, (Arthur) Yvor 1900-1968 **CLC 4, 8, 32**
See also CA 11-12; 25-28R; CAP 1; DLB 48; MTCW
Winterson, Jeanette 1959-**CLC 64; DAM POP**
See also CA 136; CANR 58
Winthrop, John 1588-1649   **LC 31**
See also DLB 24, 30
Wiseman, Frederick 1930-   **CLC 20**
See also CA 159

Wister, Owen 1860-1938   **TCLC 21**
See also CA 108; 162; DLB 9, 78, 186; SATA 62
Witkacy
See Witkiewicz, Stanislaw Ignacy
Witkiewicz, Stanislaw Ignacy 1885-1939 **TCLC 8**
See also CA 105; 162
Wittgenstein, Ludwig (Josef Johann) 1889-1951 **TCLC 59**
See also CA 113; 164
Wittig, Monique 1935(?)-   **CLC 22**
See also CA 116; 135; DLB 83
Wittlin, Jozef 1896-1976   **CLC 25**
See also CA 49-52; 65-68; CANR 3
Wodehouse, P(elham) G(renville) 1881-1975 **CLC 1, 2, 5, 10, 22; DAB; DAC; DAM NOV; SSC 2**
See also AITN 2; CA 45-48; 57-60; CANR 3, 33; CDBLB 1914-1945; DLB 34, 162; MTCW; SATA 22
Woiwode, L.
See Woiwode, Larry (Alfred)
Woiwode, Larry (Alfred) 1941-   **CLC 6, 10**
See also CA 73-76; CANR 16; DLB 6; INT CANR-16
Wojciechowska, Maia (Teresa) 1927-**CLC 26**
See also AAYA 8; CA 9-12R; CANR 4, 41; CLR 1; JRDA; MAICYA; SAAS 1; SATA 1, 28, 83
Wolf, Christa 1929-   **CLC 14, 29, 58**
See also CA 85-88; CANR 45; DLB 75; MTCW
Wolfe, Gene (Rodman) 1931- **CLC 25; DAM POP**
See also CA 57-60; CAAS 9; CANR 6, 32, 60; DLB 8
Wolfe, George C. 1954-   **CLC 49; BLCS**
See also CA 149
Wolfe, Thomas (Clayton) 1900-1938**TCLC 4, 13, 29, 61; DA; DAB; DAC; DAM MST, NOV; WLC**
See also CA 104; 132; CDALB 1929-1941; DLB 9, 102; DLBD 2, 16; DLBY 85, 97; MTCW
Wolfe, Thomas Kennerly, Jr. 1931-
See Wolfe, Tom
See also CA 13-16R; CANR 9, 33; DAM POP; DLB 185; INT CANR-9; MTCW
Wolfe, Tom   **CLC 1, 2, 9, 15, 35, 51**
See also Wolfe, Thomas Kennerly, Jr.
See also AAYA 8; AITN 2; BEST 89:1; DLB 152
Wolff, Geoffrey (Ansell) 1937-   **CLC 41**
See also CA 29-32R; CANR 29, 43
Wolff, Sonia
See Levitin, Sonia (Wolff)
Wolff, Tobias (Jonathan Ansell) 1945-   **C L C 39, 64**
See also AAYA 16; BEST 90:2; CA 114; 117; CAAS 22; CANR 54; DLB 130; INT 117
Wolfram von Eschenbach c. 1170-c. 1220 **CMLC 5**
See also DLB 138
Wolitzer, Hilma 1930-   **CLC 17**
See also CA 65-68; CANR 18, 40; INT CANR-18; SATA 31
Wollstonecraft, Mary 1759-1797   **LC 5**
See also CDBLB 1789-1832; DLB 39, 104, 158
Wonder, Stevie   **CLC 12**
See also Morris, Steveland Judkins
Wong, Jade Snow 1922-   **CLC 17**
See also CA 109
Woodberry, George Edward 1855-1930

See also CA 161
Zorrilla y Moral, Jose 1817-1893   **NCLC 6**
Zoshchenko, Mikhail (Mikhailovich) 1895-1958
      TCLC 15; SSC 15
   See also CA 115; 160
Zuckmayer, Carl 1896-1977   **CLC 18**
   See also CA 69-72; DLB 56, 124
Zuk, Georges
   See Skelton, Robin
Zukofsky, Louis 1904-1978**CLC 1, 2, 4, 7, 11,
   18; DAM POET; PC 11**
   See also CA 9-12R; 77-80; CANR 39; DLB 5,
   165; MTCW
Zweig, Paul 1935-1984   **CLC 34, 42**
   See also CA 85-88; 113
Zweig, Stefan 1881-1942   **TCLC 17**
   See also CA 112; DLB 81, 118
Zwingli, Huldreich 1484-1531   **LC 37**
   See also DLB 179

Literary Criticism Series
Cumulative Topic Index

This index lists all topic entries in Gale's *Classical and Medieval Literature Criticism, Contemporary Literary Criticism, Literature Criticism from 1400 to 1800, Nineteenth-Century Literature Criticism,* and *Twentieth-Century Literary Criticism.*

Topic Index

Yellow Journalism NCLC 36: 383-456
   overviews, 384-96
   major figures, 396-413

Young Playwrights Festival
   1988—CLC 55: 376-81
   1989—CLC 59: 398-403
   1990—CLC 65: 444-8

Topic Index

NCLC Cumulative Nationality Index

Nationality Index

Title Index

ISBN 0-7876-1246-4

90000

9 780787 612467